How to Use the Maps in *World History, 4th Edition*

Here are some basic map concepts that will help you to get the most out of the maps in this textbook.

- Always look at the scale, which allows you to determine the distance in miles or kilometers between locations on the map.

- Examine the legend carefully. It explains the colors and symbols used on the map.

- Note the locations of mountains, rivers, oceans, and other geographic features, and consider how these would affect such human activities as agriculture, commerce, travel, and warfare.

- Read the map caption thoroughly. It provides important information, sometimes not covered in the text itself, and poses a thought question to encourage you to think beyond the mere appearance of the map and make connections across chapters, regions, and concepts.

- Several "spot maps" appear in each chapter, to allow you to view in detail smaller areas that may not be apparent in larger maps. For example, a spot map in Chapter 12 lets you zoom in on Charlemagne's Empire.

- Many of the text's maps also carry a globe icon alongside the title, which indicates that the map appears in interactive form on the text's website: http://www.wadsworth.com/history_d/special_features/ext/duiker_maps/index.htm

D1223700

GREENLAND
(DEN.)

RUSSIA   ALASKA
          (U.S.)

CANADA

UNITED
STATES

ATLANTIC

OCEAN

BAHAMAS   W
MEXICO   CUBA   (M
                    DOMINICAN REP.
HAWAII   HAITI   PUERTO RICO
(U.S.)   ST. KITTS
                    BELIZE   VIRGIN ISLANDS   ANTIGUA
          GUATEMALA HONDURAS   ST. LUCIA   DOMINICA
          EL SALVADOR NICARAGUA   ST. VINCENT   BARBADOS   GAM
                                              GRENADA   GUINEA-BISS
PACIFIC   COSTA RICA   TRINIDAD & TOBAGO
                    PANAMA   VENEZUELA   GUYANA   SIER
                                        SURINAME
                    COLOMBIA   FR. GUYANA

              ECUADOR

              PERU   BRAZIL   ATL

OCEAN

          KIRIBATI
NAURU
SOLOMON   TUVALU   TOKELAU
ISLANDS   WEST.   AM.
          SAMOA   SAMOA
VANUATU FIJI   BOLIVIA
                    COOK   PARAGUAY
     TONGA   NIUE   IS.
          (N.Z.) (N.Z.)   FRENCH
               POLYNESIA
NEW
CALEDONIA   URUGUAY
                    PITCAIRN
                    (U.K.)

                                   CHILE
                                   ARGENTINA

NEW
ZEALAND

                         FALKLAND IS.
                         (U.K.)

www.wadsworth.com

wadsworth.com is the World Wide Web site for Wadsworth and is your direct source to dozens of online resources.

At *wadsworth.com* you can find out about supplements, demonstration software, and student resources. You can also send e-mail to many of our authors and preview new publications and exciting new technologies.

wadsworth.com
Changing the way the world learns®

VOLUME II: SINCE 1400

WORLD HISTORY

4TH EDITION

WILLIAM J. DUIKER
THE PENNSYLVANIA STATE UNIVERSITY

JACKSON J. SPIELVOGEL
THE PENNSYLVANIA STATE UNIVERSITY

THOMSON

WADSWORTH

Australia • Canada • Mexico • Singapore • Spain
United Kingdom • United States

THOMSON

WADSWORTH

Publisher: Clark Baxter
Development Editor: Sue Gleason
Assistant Editor: Julie Yardley
Editorial Assistant: Eno Sarris
Technology Project Manager: Jennifer Ellis
Marketing Manager: Caroline Croley
Marketing Assistant: Mary Ho
Advertising Project Manager: Tami Strang
Project Manager, Editorial Production: Ray Crawford
Print/Media Buyer: Jessica Reed
Permissions Editor: Elizabeth Zuber
Copy Editor: Bruce Emmer
Art Editor: Dovetail Publishing Services, Image Quest

Production Service: Dovetail Publishing Services
Text Designer: Diane Beasley
Photo Researcher: Image Quest
Map Illustrator: Maps.com
Cover Designer: Lisa Devenish
Cover Image: Unloading goods from Portuguese ship, from *Arrival of Portuguese in Japan,* folding screen, Namban (1594–1618) Japanese (detail). The Art Archive/Museo Nacional de Soares dos Reis Proto, Portugal/Dagli Orti
Cover Printer: Phoenix Color Corp
Compositor: New England Typographic Service
Printer: R.R. Donnelley & Sons—Willard
Photo credits begin on page 904

For more information about our products, contact us at:
Thomson Learning Academic Resource Center
1-800-423-0563
For permission to use material from this text, contact us by:
Phone: 1-800-730-2214   **Fax:** 1-800-730-2215
Web: http://www.thomsonrights.com

Library of Congress Control Number: 2003107415

Student Edition with InfoTrac College Edition:
ISBN 0-534-60365-3
Student Edition without InfoTrac College Edition:
ISBN 0-534-60386-6

Instructor's Edition: ISBN 0-534-60388-2

Wadsworth Group/Thomson Learning
10 Davis Drive
Belmont, CA 94002-3098
USA

Asia
Thomson Learning
5 Shenton Way #01-01
UIC Building
Singapore 068808

Australia/New Zealand
Thomson Learning
102 Dodds Street
Southbank, Victoria 3006
Australia

Canada
Nelson
1120 Birchmount Road
Toronto, Ontario M1K 5G4
Canada

Europe/Middle East/Africa
Thomson Learning
High Holborn House
50/51 Bedford Row
London WC1R 4LR
United Kingdom

Latin America
Thomson Learning
Seneca, 53
Colonia Polanco
11560 Mexico D.F.
Mexico

Spain/Portugal
Paraninfo
Calle/Magallanes, 25
28015 Madrid, Spain

ABOUT THE AUTHORS

WILLIAM J. DUIKER is liberal arts professor emeritus of East Asian studies at The Pennsylvania State University. A former U.S. diplomat with service in Taiwan, South Vietnam, and Washington, D.C., he received his doctorate in Far Eastern history from Georgetown University in 1968, where his dissertation dealt with the Chinese educator and reformer Cai Yuanpei. At Penn State, he has written widely on the history of Vietnam and modern China, including the widely acclaimed *The Communist Road to Power in Vietnam* (revised edition, Westview Press, 1996), which was selected for a Choice Outstanding Academic Book Award in 1982–1983 and 1996–1997. Other recent books are *China and Vietnam: The Roots of Conflict* (Berkeley, 1987), *Sacred War: Nationalism and Revolution in a Divided Vietnam* (McGraw-Hill, 1995), and *Ho Chi Minh* (Hyperion, 2000). While his research specialization is in the field of nationalism and Asian revolutions, his intellectual interests are considerably more diverse. He has traveled widely and has taught courses on the History of Communism and non-Western civilizations at Penn State, where he was awarded a Faculty Scholar Medal for Outstanding Achievement in the spring of 1996.

To Yvonne,
for adding sparkle to this book, and to my life
W.J.D.

JACKSON J. SPIELVOGEL is associate professor emeritus of history at The Pennsylvania State University. He received his Ph.D. from The Ohio State University, where he specialized in Reformation history under Harold J. Grimm. His articles and reviews have appeared in such journals as *Moreana*, *Journal of General Education*, *Catholic Historical Review*, *Archiv für Reformationsgeschichte*, and *American Historical Review*. He has also contributed chapters or articles to *The Social History of the Reformation*, *The Holy Roman Empire: A Dictionary Handbook*, *Simon Wiesenthal Center Annual of Holocaust Studies*, and *Utopian Studies*. His work has been supported by fellowships from the Fullbright Foundation and the Foundation for Reformation Research. At Penn State, he helped inaugurate the Western civilization courses as well as a popular course on Nazi Germany. His book *Hitler and Nazi Germany* was published in 1987 (fourth edition, 2001). He is the author of *Western Civilization*, published in 1991 (fifth edition, 2003). Professor Spielvogel has won five major university-wide teaching awards. During the year 1988–1989, he held the Penn State Teaching Fellowship, the university's most prestigious teaching award. In 1996, he won the Dean Arthur Ray Warnock Award for Outstanding Faculty Member, and in 2000, received the Schreyer Honors College Excellence in Teaching Award.

To Diane,
whose love and support made it all possible
J.J.S

BRIEF CONTENTS

Detailed Contents

Part III   THE EMERGENCE OF NEW WORLD PATTERNS (1400–1800)   350

Part IV MODERN PATTERNS OF WORLD HISTORY (1800–1945)   508

Part V TOWARD A GLOBAL CIVILIZATION? THE WORLD SINCE 1945 720

Chapter 29

Toward the Pacific Century? 848

Reflection: Toward a Global Civilization? The World Since 1945 880

DOCUMENT CREDITS

CHRONOLOGIES

MAPS

PREFACE

For several million years after primates first appeared on the surface of the earth, human beings lived in small communities, seeking to survive by hunting, fishing, and foraging in a frequently hostile environment. Then suddenly, in the space of a few thousand years, there was an abrupt change of direction as human beings in a few widely scattered areas of the globe began to master the art of cultivating food crops. As food production increased, the population in those areas rose correspondingly, and people began to congregate in larger communities. Governments were formed to provide protection and other needed services to the local population. Cities appeared and became the focal point of cultural and religious development. Historians refer to this process as the beginnings of civilization.

For generations, historians in Europe and the United States have pointed to the rise of such civilizations as marking the origins of the modern world. Courses on Western civilization conventionally begin with a chapter or two on the emergence of advanced societies in Egypt and Mesopotamia and then proceed to ancient Greece and the Roman Empire. From Greece and Rome, the road leads directly to the rise of modern civilization in the West.

There is nothing inherently wrong with this approach. Important aspects of our world today can indeed be traced back to these early civilizations, and all human beings the world over owe a considerable debt to their achievements. But all too often this interpretation has been used to imply that the course of civilization has been linear in nature, leading directly from the emergence of agricultural societies in ancient Mesopotamia to the rise of advanced industrial societies in Europe and North America. Until recently, most courses on world history taught in the United States routinely focused almost exclusively on the rise of the West, with only a passing glance at other parts of the world, such as Africa, India, and East Asia. The contributions made by those societies to the culture and technology of our own time were often passed over in silence.

Several reasons have been advanced to justify this approach. Some have argued that students simply are not interested in what is unfamiliar to them. Others have said that it is more important that young minds understand the roots of their own heritage than that of peoples elsewhere in the world. In many cases, however, the motivation for this Eurocentric approach has been the belief that since the time of Socrates and Aristotle Western civilization has been the sole driving force in the evolution of human society.

Such an interpretation, however, represents a serious distortion of the process. During most of the course of human history, the most advanced civilizations have been not in the West, but in East Asia or the Middle East. A relatively brief period of European dominance culminated with the era of imperialism in the late nineteenth century, when the political, military, and economic power of the advanced nations of the West spanned the globe. During recent generations, however, that dominance has gradually eroded, partly as the result of changes taking place within Western societies and partly because new centers of development are emerging elsewhere on the globe—notably in East Asia, where the growing economic strength of Japan and many of its neighbors has led to the now familiar prediction that the twenty-first century will be known as the Pacific Century.

World history, then, is not simply a chronicle of the rise of the West to global dominance, nor is it a celebration of the superiority of the civilization of Europe and the United States over other parts of the world. The history of the world has been a complex process in which many branches of the human community have taken an active part, and the dominance of any one area of the world has been a temporary rather than a permanent phenomenon. It will be our purpose in this book to present a balanced picture of this story, with all respect for the richness and diversity of the tapestry of the human experience. Due attention must be paid to the rise of the West, of course, since that has been the most dominant aspect of world history in recent centuries. But the contributions made by other peoples must be given adequate consideration as well, not only in the period prior to 1500 when the major centers of civilization were located in Asia, but also in our own day, where a multipolar picture of development is clearly beginning to emerge.

Anyone who wishes to teach or write about world history must decide whether to present the topic as an integrated whole or as a collection of different cultures. The world that we live in today, of course, is in many respects an interdependent one in terms of economics as well as culture and communications, a reality that is often expressed by the phrase "global village." The convergence of peoples across the surface of the earth into an integrated world system began in early times and intensified after the rise of capitalism in the early modern era. In growing recognition of this trend, historians trained in global history, as well as instructors in the growing number of world history courses, have now begun to speak and write of a "global approach" that turns attention away from the study of individual civilizations and focuses instead on the "big picture" or, as the world historian Fernand Braudel termed it, interpreting world history as a river with no banks.

On the whole, this development is to be welcomed as a means of bringing the common elements of the evolution of human society to our attention. But there is a problem involved in this approach. For the vast majority of their time on earth, human beings have lived in partial or virtually total isolation from each other. Differences in climate, location, and geographical features have created human societies very different from each other in culture and historical experience. Only in relatively recent times—the commonly accepted date has long been the beginning of the age of European exploration at the end of the fifteenth century, but some would now push it back to the era of the Mongol empire or even further—have cultural interchanges begun to create a common "world system," in which events taking place in one part of the world are rapidly transmitted throughout the globe, often with momentous consequences. In recent generations, of course, the process of global interdependence has been proceeding even more rapidly. Nevertheless, even now the process is by no means complete, as ethnic and regional differences continue to exist and to shape the course of world history. The tenacity of these differences and sensitivities is reflected not only in the rise of internecine conflicts in such divergent areas as Africa, India, and Eastern Europe, but also in the emergence in recent years of such regional organizations as the Organization of African Unity, the Association for the Southeast Asian Nations, and the European Economic Community. Political leaders in various parts of the world speak routinely of "Arab unity," the "African road to socialism," and the "Confucian path to economic development."

The second problem is a practical one. College students today are all too often not well informed about the distinctive character of civilizations such as China and India and, without sufficient exposure to the historical evolution of such societies, will assume all too readily that the peoples in these countries have had historical experiences similar to ours and will respond to various stimuli in a similar fashion to those living in Western Europe or the United States. If it is a mistake to ignore those forces that link us together, it is equally a mistake to underestimate those factors that continue to divide us and to differentiate us into a world of diverse peoples.

Our response to this challenge has been to adopt a global approach to world history while at the same time attempting to do justice to the distinctive character and development of individual civilizations and regions of the world. The presentation of individual cultures will be especially important in Parts I and II, which cover a time when it is generally agreed that the process of global integration was not yet far advanced. Later chapters will begin to adopt a more comparative and thematic approach, in deference to the greater number of connections that have been established among the world's peoples since the fifteenth and sixteenth centuries. Part V will consist of a series of chapters that will center on individual regions of the world while at the same time focusing on common problems related to the Cold War and the rise of global problems such as overproduction and environmental pollution. Moreover, sections entitled "Reflection" at the close of the five major parts of the book will attempt to link events together in a broad comparative and global framework.

We have sought balance in another way as well. Many textbooks tend to simplify the content of history courses by emphasizing an intellectual or political perspective or, most recently, a social perspective, often at the expense of sufficient details in a chronological framework. This approach is confusing to students whose high school social studies programs have often neglected a systematic study of world history. We have attempted to write a well-balanced work in which political, economic, social, religious, intellectual, cultural, and military history have been integrated into a chronologically ordered synthesis.

To enliven the past and let readers see for themselves the materials that historians use to create their pictures of the past, we have included primary sources (boxed documents) in each chapter that are keyed to the discussion in the text. The documents include examples of the religious, artistic, intellectual, social, economic, and political aspects of life in different societies and reveal in a vivid fashion what civilization meant to the individual men and women who shaped it by their actions.

Each chapter has a lengthy introduction and conclusion to help maintain the continuity of the narrative and to provide a synthesis of important themes. Anecdotes in the chapter introductions convey more dramatically the major theme or themes of each chapter. Timelines at the end of each chapter enable students to see the major developments of an era at a glance and within crosscultural categories, while the more detailed chronologies reinforce the events discussed in the text. An annotated bibliography at the end of each chapter reviews the most recent literature on each period and also gives references to some of the older, "classic" works in each field.

Extensive maps and illustrations serve to deepen the reader's understanding of the text. New to the fourth edition are map captions, designed to enrich students' awareness of the importance of geography to history, and a large number of spot maps, which enable students to see at a glance the region or subject being discussed in the text. The maps have also been revised where needed. To facilitate understanding of cultural movements, illustrations of artistic works discussed in the text are placed next to the discussions. Chapter outlines and focus questions, including analytical questions, at the beginning of each chapter help students with an overview and guide them to the main subjects of each chapter. A glossary of important terms and a pronunciation guide are included to enrich an understanding of the text.

After reexamining the entire book and analyzing the comments and reviews of many colleagues who have found the book to be a useful instrument for introducing their students to world history, we have also made a number of other changes for the fourth edition. In the first place, we have continued our effort to reduce the size of the book without affecting the quality of the material contained therein. As part of this effort, we have reorganized the material of five European chapters into three new chapters. These are Chapter 12, "The Making of Europe in the Middle Ages"; Chapter 13, "Renewal, Reform, and State Building in Europe"; and Chapter 17, "Europe on the Eve of a New World Order." Moreover, Chapters 31 and 32 have been synthesized into a new Chapter 29, "Toward the Pacific Century?" We have also tried to delete excess words while retaining all essential material as well as the narrative thrust of previous editions.

Second, we have sought to strengthen the global framework of the book, but not at the expense of reducing the attention assigned to individual regions of the world. The essays entitled "Reflection" that appear at the end of each of the five parts have been shortened slightly to accommodate the advice of many of our reviewers and to enable us to more concisely draw comparisons and contrasts across geographical, cultural, and chronological lines. Each Reflection section contains two boxed essays, each highlighted with an illustration, to single out issues of particular importance to that period of history. Moreover, additional comparative material has also been added to each chapter to help students be aware of similar developments globally. Among other things, this material includes new comparative sections, such as "Comparison of the Roman and Han Empires" in Chapter 5 and "Europe, China, and Scientific Revolutions" in Chapter 13, as well as comparative illustrations. We hope that these techniques will assist instructors who wish to encourage their students to adopt a comparative approach to their understanding of the human experience.

Third, this new edition contains additional information on the role of women in world history. In conformity with our own convictions, as well as what we believe to be recent practice in the field, we have tried where possible to introduce such material at the appropriate point in the text, rather than to set aside separate sections devoted exclusively to women's issues.

Finally, a number of new illustrations, boxed documents, and maps have been added, and the bibliographies have been revised to take account of newly published material. The chronologies and maps have been fine-tuned as well, to help the reader locate in time and space the multitude of indi-

viduals and place names that appear in the book. To keep up with the ever-growing body of historical scholarship, new or revised material has been added throughout the book on many topics, including early civilizations around the world; the Aryans in India; the Zhou dynasty in China; Sparta; Alexander and the Mauryan Empire in India; Roman trade with China; comparison of Roman and Han Chinese empires; the first Americans; the Maya; first civilizations in South America; Islam; early civilizations in Africa; the spread of Buddhism; the Song dynasty in China; the Mongols; early Japan; the African slave trade; the Ottoman Empire; the Mughals; Ming China; Tokugawa Japan; the impact of Western expansion on indigenous peoples; the impact of the discovery of the Pacific Islands in the eighteenth century; the defeat of Napoleon; slave revolt in Haiti; how industrialized nations limited industrialization in their colonies; Latin America; Canada; the impact of World War I on Africa, East Asia, and the Pacific; the Russian Revolution; and the Asian theater of World War II. In addition, all of the chapters in Part V have been updated to bring our treatment of contemporary events up to the present.

Because courses in world history at American and Canadian colleges and universities follow different chronological divisions, a one-volume comprehensive edition, a two-volume edition of this text, and a volume covering events to 1400 are being made available to fit the needs of instructors. Teaching and learning ancillaries include:

Instructor's Manual with Test Bank   Prepared by Eugene Larson, Los Angeles, Pierce College. Contains Chapter Outlines, Class Lecture/Discussion Topics, Thought/Discussion Questions for Primary Sources (Boxed Documents), Possible Student Projects, and Examination Questions (Essay, Identification, and Multiple Choice).

ExamView®   Create, deliver, and customize tests and study guides (both print and online) in minutes with this easy-to-use assessment and tutorial system. *ExamView*® offers both a Quick Test Wizard and an Online Test Wizard that guide you step-by-step through the process of creating tests, while its unique "WYSIWYG" capability allows you to see the test you are creating on the screen exactly as it will print or display online. You can build tests of up to 250 questions using up to 12 question types. Using *ExamView*®'s complete word processing capabilities, you can enter an unlimited number of new questions or edit existing questions.

Map Acetates and Commentary for World History   Includes more than 100 four-color map images from the text and other sources. Map commentary for each map is prepared by James Harrison, Siena College. Three-hole punched and shrinkwrapped.

History Video Library   Includes Film For Humanities (these are available to qualified adoptions), CNN videos, and Grade Improvement: Taking Charge of Your Learning.

Multimedia Manager for World History: A Microsoft Power Point Link Tool.   An advanced PowerPoint presentation tool containing text-specific lecture outlines, figures, and images. In addition, it provides the flexibility to customize each presentation by editing what we have provided or by adding your own collection of slides, videos, and animations. All of the map acetates and selected photos have been incorporated into each lecture. The extensive map commentaries for each map are available through the "Comments" feature of PowerPoint.

Sights and Sounds of History   Prepared by David Redles, Cuyahoga Community College. Short, focused video clips, photos, artwork, animations, music, and dramatic readings are used to bring life to historical topics and events which are most difficult for students to appreciate from a textbook alone. For example, students will experience the grandeur of Versailles and the defeat felt by a German soldier at Stalingrad. The video segments, each averaging 4 minutes long, make excellent lecture launchers. Available on Laserdisk or VHS video.

Study Guide   Prepared by Dianna Rhyan Kardulias, Columbus State Community College. Contains Chapter Outlines, Terms and Persons to Know, Mapwork, Datework, Primary Sourcework, Artwork, Identifying Important Concepts Behind the Conclusion, and new Multiple Choice questions and Web Resources. Available in two volumes.

Map Exercise Workbook   Prepared by Cynthia Kosso, Northern Arizona University. Has been thoroughly revised and improved. Contains over 20 maps and exercises, which ask students to identify important cities and countries. Also includes critical thinking questions for each unit. Available in two volumes.

World History MapTutor   This new mapping CD-ROM allows students to learn by manipulating maps through "locate and label" exercises, animations, and critical thinking exercises.

Migrations in Modern World History 1500–2000 CD-ROM An interactive multimedia curriculum on CD-ROM by Patrick Manning and the World History Center. Includes over 400 primary source documents; analytical questions to help the student develop his/her own interpretations of history; timelines; and additional suggested resources, including books, films, and web sites.

CNN Video for Western Civilization and World History   Twelve two- to five-minute CNN segments are easy to integrate into classroom discussions or as lecture launchers. Topics range from India's caste system to Pearl Harbor.

Document Exercise Workbooks   Prepared by Donna Van Raaphorst, Cuyahoga Community College. Contains a collection of exercises based around primary source documents pertaining to world history.

Journey of Civilizations CD ROM for Windows   Prepared by David Redles, Cuyahoga Community College. This CD takes students on 18 interactive journeys through history. Enhanced with QuickTime movies, animations, sound clips, maps, and more, the journeys allow students engage in history as active participants rather than as readers of past events.

Magellan World History Atlas   Available to bundle with any history text; contains 44 historical four-color maps, including the conflict in Afghanistan, 2001, and States of the World, 2001.

Internet Guide for History, Third Edition   Prepared by John Soares. Provides newly revised and up-to-date Internet exercises by topic. Available at

http://history.wadsworth.com.

Kishlansky, Sources in World History, Second and Third Editions This reader is a collection of documents designed to supplement any world history text. Available in two volumes.

Web Tutor™   This content-rich, Web-based teaching and learning tool helps students succeed by taking the course beyond classroom boundaries to an anywhere, anytime environment. *Web Tutor*™ offers real-time access to a full array of study tools, including flashcards (with audio), practice quizzes, online tutorials, and Web links. Web Tutor also provides rich communication tools, including a course calendar, asynchronous discussion, "real-time" chat, and an integrated e-mail system. Available for Blackboard and WebCT.

InfoTrac® College Edition   An online university that lets students explore and use full-length articles from more than 900 periodicals for four months. When students log on with their personal ID, they will immediately see how easy it is to search. Students can print out the articles, which date back as far as four years.

Historic Times: The Wadsworth History Resource Center

http://history.wadsworth.com/

Features a career section, forum, and links to museums, historical documents, and other fascinating sites. From the Resource Center you can access the book-specific web site, which contains the following: chapter by chapter tutorial quizzing, *InfoTrac®* activities, Internet activities, interactive maps and timelines, glossary, and hyperlinks for the student, and an online instructor's manual and downloadable PowerPoint files for the Instructor.

ACKNOWLEDGMENTS

oth authors gratefully acknowledge that without the generosity of many others, this project could not have been completed. William Duiker would like to thank Kumkum Chatterjee and On-cho Ng for their helpful comments about unfamiliar issues related to the history of India and premodern China. His long-time colleague Cyril Griffith, now deceased, was a cherished friend and a constant source of information about modern Africa. Art Goldschmidt has been of invaluable assistance in reading several chapters of the manuscript, as well as in unraveling many of the mysteries of Middle Eastern civilization. Finally, he remains profoundly grateful to his wife, Yvonne V. Duiker, Ph.D. She has not only given her usual measure of love and support when this appeared to be an insuperable task, but she has also contributed her own time and expertise to enrich the sections on art and literature, thereby adding life and sparkle to this, as well as the earlier editions of the book. To her, and to his daughters Laura and Claire, he will be forever thankful for bringing joy to his life.

Jackson Spielvogel would like to thank Art Goldschmidt, David Redles, and Christine Colin for their time and ideas and, above all, his family for their support. The gifts of love, laughter, and patience from his daughters, Jennifer and Kathryn, his sons, Eric and Christian, and his daughters-in-law, Liz and Laurie, were invaluable. Diane, his wife and best friend, provided him with editorial assistance, wise counsel, and the loving support that made a project of this magnitude possible.

Thanks to Wadsworth's comprehensive review process, many historians were asked to evaluate our manuscript. We are grateful to the following for the innumerable suggestions that have greatly improved our work:

Najia Aarim
SUNY College at Fredonia
Henry Maurice Abramson
Florida Atlantic University
Charles F. Ames, Jr.
Salem State College
Nancy Anderson
Loyola University
Gloria M. Aronson
Normandale College
Charlotte Beahan
Murray State University
Doris Bergen
University of Vermont
Martin Berger
Youngstown State University
Deborah Biffton
University of Wisconsin-LaCrosse
Charmarie Blaisdell
Northeastern University
Patricia J. Bradley
Auburn University at Montgomery
Dewey Browder
Austin Peay State University
Antonio Calabria
University of Texas at San Antonio
Alice-Catherine Carls
University of Tennessee-Martin
Yuan Ling Chao
Middle Tennessee State University

Mark W. Chavalas
University of Wisconsin
Hugh Clark
Ursinus College
Joan Coffey
Sam Houston State University
John Davis
Radford University
Ross Dunn
San Diego State University
Lane Earn
University of Wisconsin-Oshkosh
Roxanne Easley
Central Washington University
C. T. Evans
Northern Virginia Community College
Edward L. Farmer
University of Minnesota
William W. Farris
University of Tennessee
Ronald Fritze
Lamar University
Joe Fuhrmann
Murray State University
Robert Gerlich
Loyola University
Marc J. Gilbert
North Georgia College
William J. Gilmore-Lehne
Richard Stockton College of New Jersey

Richard M. Golden
University of North Texas
Joseph M. Gowaskie
Rider College
Jonathan Grant
Florida State University
Don Gustafson
Augsburg College
Deanna Haney
Lansing Community College
Ed Haynes
Winthrop College
Linda Kerr
University of Alberta at Edmonton
Zoltan Kramar
Central Washington University
Douglas Lea
Kutztown University
David Leinweber
Emory University
Thomas T. Lewis
Mount Senario College
Craig A. Lockard
University of Wisconsin-Green Bay
George Longenecker
Norwich University
Robert Luczak
Vincennes University
Patrick Manning
Northeastern University

Dolores Nason McBroome
Humboldt State University

John McDonald
Northern Essex Community College

Andrea McElderry
University of Louisville

Jeff McEwen
*Chattanooga State Technical
Community College*

David L. McMullen
*University of North Carolina at
Charlotte*

John A. Mears
Southern Methodist University

Marc A. Meyer
Berry College

Stephen S. Michot
*Mississippi County Community
College*

John Ashby Morton
Benedict College

William H. Mulligan
Murray State University

Henry A. Myers
James Madison University

Marian P. Nelson
University of Nebraska at Omaha

Sandy Norman
Florida Atlantic University

Patrick M. O'Neill
Broome Community College

Norman G. Raiford
Greenville Technical College

Jane Rausch
University of Massachusetts-Amherst

Dianna K. Rhyan
Columbus State Community College

Merle Rife
Indiana University of Pennsylvania

Patrice C. Ross
Columbus State Community College

John Rossi
LaSalle University

Eric C. Rust
Baylor University

Jane Samson
University of Alberta

Keith Sandiford
University of Manitoba

Elizabeth Sarkinnen
Mt. Hood Community College

Bill Schell
Murray State University

Robert M. Seltzer
Hunter College

David Shriver
Cuyahoga Community College

Amos E. Simpson
University of Southwestern Louisiana

Wendy Singer
Kenyon College

Marvin Slind
Washington State University

Paul Smith
Washington State University

John Snetsinger
*California Polytechnic State
University*

George Stow
LaSalle University

Patrick Tabor
Chemeketa Community College

Tom Taylor
Seattle University

John G. Tuthill
University of Guam

Joanne Van Horn
Fairmont State College

Pat Weber
University of Texas-El Paso

Douglas L. Wheeler
University of New Hampshire

David L. White
Appalachian State University

Elmira B. Wicker
Southern University-Baton Rouge

Glee Wilson
Kent State University

Harry Zee
Cumberland County College

The authors are truly grateful to the people who have helped us to produce this book. We especially want to thank Clark Baxter, whose faith in our ability to do this project was inspiring. Sue Gleason thoughtfully guided the overall development of the fourth edition, and Julie Yardley orchestrated the preparation of outstanding teaching and learning ancillaries. Bruce Emmer and Pat Lewis were, as usual, outstanding copy editors. Sarah Evertson provided valuable assistance in obtaining permissions for the illustrations. We are grateful to the staff of New England Typographic Service for providing their array of typesetting and page layout abilities. Jon Peck, of Dovetail Publishing Services, was as cooperative and cheerful as he was competent in matters of production management.

A Note to Students about Languages and the Dating of Time

One of the most difficult challenges in studying world history is coming to grips with the multitude of names, words, and phrases in unfamiliar languages. Unfortunately, this problem has no easy solution. We have tried to alleviate the difficulty, where possible, by providing an English-language translation of foreign words or phrases, a glossary, and a pronunciation guide. The issue is especially complicated in the case of Chinese, since two separate systems are commonly used to transliterate the spoken Chinese language into the Roman alphabet. The Wade-Giles system, invented in the nineteenth century, was the most frequently used until recent years, when the pinyin system was adopted by the People's Republic of China as its own official form of transliteration. We have opted to use the latter, since it appears to be gaining acceptance in the United States, but the initial use of a Chinese word is accompanied by its Wade-Giles equivalent in parentheses for the benefit of those who may encounter the term in their outside reading.

In our examination of world history, we need also to be aware of the dating of time. In recording the past, historians try to determine the exact time when events occurred. World War II in Europe, for example, began on September 1, 1939, when Adolf Hitler sent German troops into Poland, and ended on May 7, 1945, when Germany surrendered. By using dates, historians can place events in order and try to determine the development of patterns over periods of time.

If someone asked you when you were born, you would reply with a number, such as 1984. In the United States, we would all accept that number without question, because it is part of the dating system followed in the Western world (Europe and the Western Hemisphere). In this system, events are dated by counting backward or forward from the birth of Christ (assumed to be the year 1). An event that took place 400 years before the birth of Christ would most commonly be dated 400 B.C. (before Christ). Dates after the birth of Christ are labeled as A.D. These letters stand for the Latin words *anno domini*, which mean "in the year of the Lord" (or the year of the birth of Christ). Thus an event that took place 250 years after

the birth of Christ is written A.D. 250, or in the year of the Lord 250. It can also be written as 250, just as you would not give your birth year as A.D. 1984, but simply 1984.

Some historians now prefer to use the abbreviations B.C.E. ("before the common era") and C.E. ("common era") instead of B.C. and A.D. This is especially true of world historians who prefer to use symbols that are not so Western or Christian oriented. The dates, of course, remain the same. Thus, 1950 B.C.E. and 1950 B.C. would be the same year, as would A.D. 40 and 40 C.E. In keeping with the current usage by many world historians, this book will use the terms B.C.E. and C.E.

Historians also make use of other terms to refer to time. A decade is 10 years; a century is 100 years; and a millennium is 1,000 years. The phrase fourth century B.C.E. refers to the fourth period of 100 years counting backward from 1, the assumed date of the birth of Christ. Since the first century B.C.E. would be the years 100 B.C.E. to 1 B.C.E., the fourth century B.C.E. would be the years 400 B.C.E. to 301 B.C.E. We could say, then, that an event in 350 B.C.E. took place in the fourth century B.C.E.

The phrase fourth century C.E. refers to the fourth period of 100 years after the birth of Christ. Since the first period of 100 years would be the years 1 to 100, the fourth period or fourth century would be the years 301 to 400. We could say, then, for example, that an event in 350 took place in the fourth century. Likewise, the first millennium B.C.E. refers to the years 1000 B.C.E. to 1 B.C.E.; the second millennium C.E. refers to the years 1001 to 2000.

The dating of events can also vary from people to people. Most people in the Western world use the Western calendar, also known as the Gregorian calendar after Pope Gregory XIII who refined it in 1582. The Hebrew calendar, on the other hand, uses a different system in which the year one is the equivalent of the Western year 3760 B.C.E., considered by Jews to be the date of the creation of the world. Thus, the Western year 2003 will be the year 5763 on the Jewish calendar. The Islamic calendar begins year 1 on the day Muhammad fled Mecca, which is the year 622 on the Western calendar.

THEMES FOR UNDERSTANDING WORLD HISTORY

*I*n examining the past, historians often organize their material on the basis of themes that enable them to ask and try to answer basic questions about the past. The following ten themes are especially important.

1. *Political systems*. The study of politics seeks to answer certain basic questions that historians have about the structure of a society: How were people governed? What was the relationship between the ruler and the ruled? What people or groups of people (the political elites) held political power? What actions did people take to change their form of government? Historians also examine the causes and results of wars in order to understand the impact of war on human development.

2. *The role of ideas*. Ideas have great power to move people to action. For example, in the twentieth century, the idea of nationalism, which is based on a belief in loyalty to one's nation, helped produce two great conflicts—World War I and World War II. Together these wars cost the lives of more than fifty million people. The spread of ideas from one society to another has also played an important role in world history. From the earliest times, trade has especially served to bring different civilizations into contact with one another, and the transmission of religious and cultural ideas soon followed.

3. *Economics and history*. A society depends for its existence on certain basic needs. How did it grow its food? How did it make its goods? How did it provide the services people needed? How did individual people and governments use their limited resources? Did they spend more money on hospitals or military forces? By answering these questions, historians examine the different economic systems that have played a role in history.

4. *Social life and gender issues*. From a study of social life, we learn about the different social classes that make up a society. But we also examine how people dressed and found shelter, how and what they ate, and what they did for fun. The nature of family life and how knowledge was passed from one generation to another through education are also part of the social life of a society. So, too, are gender issues: What different roles did men and women play in their societies? How and why were those roles different?

5. *The importance of culture*. We cannot understand a society without looking at its culture, or the common ideas, beliefs, and patterns of behavior that are passed on from one generation to another. Culture includes both high culture and popular culture. High culture consists of the writings of a society's thinkers and the works of its artists. A society's popular culture is the world of ideas and experiences of ordinary people. Today the media have embraced the term *popular culture* to describe the most current trends and fashionable styles.

6. *Religion in history*. Throughout history, people have sought to find a deeper meaning to human life. How have the world's great religions, such as Hinduism, Buddhism, Judaism, Christianity, and Islam, influenced people's lives? How have these religions spread to create new patterns of culture?

7. *The role of individuals*. In discussing the role of politics, ideas, economics, social life, cultural developments, and religion, we have dealt with groups of people and forces that often seem beyond the control of any one person. But mentioning the names of Cleopatra, Queen Elizabeth I, Napoleon, and Hitler reminds us of the role of individuals in history. Decisive actions by powerful individuals have indeed played a crucial role in the course of history.

8. *The impact of science and technology*. For thousands of years, people around the world have made scientific discoveries and technological innovations that have changed our world. From the creation of stone tools that made farming easier to the advanced computers that guide our airplanes, science and technology have altered how humans have related to their world.

9. *The environment and history*. Throughout history, peoples and societies have been affected by the physical world in which they live. Climatic changes alone have been an important factor in human history. Peoples and societies, in turn, have also made an impact on their world. Human activities have affected the physical environment and even endangered the very existence of entire societies and species.

10. *The migration of peoples*. One characteristic of world history is an almost constant migration of peoples. Vast numbers of peoples abandoned their homelands and sought to live elsewhere. Sometimes the migration was peaceful. More often than not, however, the migration meant invasion and violent conflict.

Part III

THE EMERGENCE OF NEW WORLD PATTERNS

(1400–1800)

Beginning in the fifteenth century, a new force entered the world scene in the form of a revived Europe. The period of history known as the early modern era (1400–1800) was marked in Europe by an explosion of scientific knowledge and the appearance of a new secular ideology that emphasized the power of human beings to dominate nature and improve their material surroundings. After the breakdown of Christian unity in the Reformation era, Europeans engaged in a vigorous period of state building that resulted in the creation of independent monarchies in western and central Europe, which formed the basis for a new European state system.

The rise of early modern Europe had an immediate as well as a long-term impact on the rest of the world. The first stage began with the discovery of the Americas by Christopher Columbus in 1492 and the equally important voyages of Vasco da Gama and Ferdinand Magellan into the Indian and Pacific Oceans. These voyages and those that followed in this so-called Age of Discovery or Age of Exploration not only injected European sea power into new areas of the world but also vastly extended the maritime trade network until for the first time it literally encircled the globe. Some historians have characterized this period as the beginning of an era of European dominance.

Significant as it was, however, the emergence of Europe as a major player on the world stage was by no means the only important feature of this period. An excessive emphasis on the expanding European civilization tends to overlook the fact that other areas of the world were realizing impressive achievements of their own. Two great new Islamic empires founded by the Ottomans in Turkey and the Safavids in Persia, arose in the Middle East, while a third, that of the Mughals, unified the Indian subcontinent for the first time in nearly two thousand years. Islam was now firmly established in Africa south of the Sahara and in Asia as far east as the Indonesian archipelago.

In most of Asia, the European revival had only minimal effects. Portuguese merchants reached the coast of China in the early sixteenth century and landed on the islands of Japan a generation later. Merchants and missionaries from various European countries were active in both countries by the end of the century. But the ruling authorities in China and Japan, like their counterparts in the mainland states in Southeast Asia, became increasingly wary of the impact of Europeans' activities on their own societies, and by the eighteenth century, the Western presence in the region had markedly declined.

The first thrust of European expansion, then, significantly changed the face of the world, but it did not firmly establish European dominance. China remained, in the eyes of many, the most advanced and most sophisticated civilization on earth, and its achievements were imitated by its neighbors and admired by philosophers in far-off Europe. The era of Muslim dominance over the seas had come to an end, but Islam was still a force to be reckoned with. The bulk of Africa remained essentially outside the purview of European influence.

© Giraudon/Art Resource, NY

Chapter 13

RENEWAL, REFORM, AND STATE BUILDING IN EUROPE

FOCUS QUESTIONS

- What were the main features of the Renaissance, and how did it differ from the Middle Ages?
- What were the main tenets of Lutheranism, Calvinism, and Anabaptism, and how did they differ from each other and from Catholicism?
- Why is the period between 1560 and 1650 in Europe called an age of crisis, and how did the turmoil contribute to the artistic and intellectual developments of the period?
- What was absolutism, and what were the main characteristics of the absolute monarchies that merged in France, Prussia, Austria, and Russia? Why did England follow a different path?
- ➤ What did Copernicus, Kepler, Galileo, and Newton contribute to a new vision of the universe, and how did their vision differ from the Ptolemaic conception of the universe? What was the significance of this new vision?

After the disintegrative patterns of the fourteenth century, Europe began a remarkable recovery that encompassed a revival of arts and letters in the fifteenth century, known as the Renaissance, and a religious renaissance in the sixteenth century, known as the Reformation. The religious division of Europe (Catholics versus Protestants) that was a result of the Reformation was instrumental in beginning a series of wars that dominated much of European history from 1560 to 1650 and exacerbated the economic and social crises that were besetting the region.

One of the responses to the crises of the seventeenth century was a search for order. The most general trend was an extension of monarchical power as a stabilizing force. This development, which historians have called absolutism or absolute monarchy, was most evident in France during the flamboyant reign of Louis XIV, regarded by some as the perfect embodiment of an absolute monarch. In his memoirs, the duc de Saint-Simon, who had firsthand experience of French court life, said that Louis was "the very figure of a hero, so imbued with a natural but most imposing majesty that it appeared even in his most insignificant gestures and movements." The king's natural grace gave him a special charm: "He was as dignified and majestic in his dressing gown as when dressed in robes of state, or on horseback at the head of his troops." He spoke well and learned quickly. He was naturally kind, and "he loved truth, justice, order, and reason." His life was orderly: "Nothing could be regulated with greater exactitude than were his days and hours." His self-control was impeccable: "He did not lose control of himself ten times in his whole life, and then only with inferior persons." But even absolute monarchs had faults, and Saint-Simon had the courage to point them out: "Louis XIV's vanity was without limit or restraint," which led to his "distaste for . . . all independence of character and sentiment in others," as well as his "mistakes of judgment in matters of importance."

The seventeenth century in Europe also witnessed the Scientific Revolution, which brought to Europeans a new way of viewing the universe and their place in it. In time, the Scientific Revolution would add to Europe's growing sense of power as changes in government, the economy, and the military enabled Europeans to move out into the global stage in a dramatic fashion. •

THE RENAISSANCE

People who lived in Italy between 1350 and 1550 or so believed that they had witnessed a rebirth of classical antiquity—the world of the Greeks and Romans. To them, this marked a new age, which historians later called the Renaissance (French for "rebirth") and viewed as a distinct period of European history, which began in Italy and then spread to the rest of Europe.

Renaissance Italy was largely an urban society. The city-states became the centers of Italian political, economic, and social life. Within this new urban society, a secular spirit emerged as increasing wealth created new possibilities for the enjoyment of worldly things.

The Renaissance was also an age of recovery from the disasters of the fourteenth century, including the Black Death, political disorder, and economic recession. In pursuing that recovery, Italian intellectuals became intensely interested in the glories of their own past, the Greco-Roman culture of antiquity.

A new view of human beings emerged as people in the Italian Renaissance began to emphasize individual ability. The fifteenth-century Florentine architect Leon Battista Alberti expressed the new philosophy succinctly: "Men can do all things if they will."[1] This high regard for human worth and for individual potentiality gave rise to a new social ideal of the well-rounded personality or "universal person" (*l'uomo universale*) who was capable of achievements in many areas of life.

Renaissance Society

After the severe economic reversals and social upheavals of the fourteenth century, the European economy gradually recovered as manufacturing and trade increased in volume. The Italians and especially the Venetians expanded their wealthy commercial empire, rivaled only by the increasingly powerful Hanseatic League, a commercial and military alliance of north German coastal towns. Not until the sixteenth century, when overseas discoveries gave new importance to the states facing the Atlantic, did the Italian city-states begin to suffer from the competitive advantages of the more powerful national territorial states.

In the Middle Ages, society was divided into three estates: the clergy, or first estate, whose preeminence was grounded in the belief that people should be guided to spiritual ends; the nobility, or second estate, whose privileges rested on the principle that nobles provided security and justice for society; and the peasants and inhabitants of the towns and cities, the third estate. Although this social order continued into the Renaissance, some changes also became evident.

THE NOBILITY

Throughout much of Europe, the landholding nobles faced declining real incomes during most of the fourteenth and fifteenth centuries. Many members of the old nobility survived, however, and new blood also infused its ranks. By 1500, the nobles, old and new, who constituted between 2 and 3 percent of the population in most countries, managed to dominate society, as they had done in the

Middle Ages, holding important political posts and serving as advisers to the king.

By 1500, certain ideals came to be expected of the noble, or aristocrat. These were best expressed in *The Book of the Courtier*, by the Italian Baldassare Castiglione (1478–1529). Castiglione described the three fundamental attributes of the perfect courtier. First, nobles are born, not made, and they should exhibit impeccable character, grace, and talents. Second, the perfect noble must participate in military and bodily exercises, because the principal profession of a courtier was arms; however, unlike the medieval knight, who was primarily concerned with military skill, the Renaissance noble must also seek a classical education and adorn his life with the arts. Third, the noble was expected to follow a certain standard of conduct. Nobles should not hide their accomplishments but show them with grace. The aim of the perfect noble was to serve his prince in an effective and honest way.

PEASANTS AND TOWNSPEOPLE

Except in the heavily urban areas of northern Italy and Flanders, peasants made up the overwhelming mass of the third estate—they constituted 85 to 90 percent of the total European population. Serfdom decreased as the manorial system continued its decline. Increasingly, the labor dues owed by a peasant to his lord were converted into rents paid in money. By 1500, especially in western Europe, more and more peasants were becoming legally free.

The remainder of the third estate were inhabitants of towns and cities, originally merchants and artisans. But by the fifteenth century, the Renaissance town or city had become more complex. At the top of urban society were the patricians, whose wealth from capitalistic enterprises in trade, industry, and banking enabled them to dominate their urban communities economically, socially, and politically. Below them were the petty burghers—the shopkeepers, artisans, guildmasters, and guildsmen—who were largely concerned with providing goods and services for local consumption. Below these two groups were the propertyless workers earning pitiful wages and the unemployed, living squalid and miserable lives. These poor city-dwellers constituted 30 to 40 percent of the urban population.

FAMILY AND MARRIAGE IN RENAISSANCE ITALY

The family bond was a source of great security in the urban world of Renaissance Italy. To maintain the family, parents carefully arranged marriages, often to strengthen business or family ties. Details were worked out well in advance, sometimes when children were only two or three, and reinforced by a legally binding marriage contract (see the box on p. 355). The important aspect of the contract was the size of the dowry, a sum of money presented by the wife's family to the husband upon marriage.

The father-husband was the center of the Italian family. He gave it his name, managed all finances (his wife had no share in his wealth), and made the crucial decisions that determined his children's lives. A father's authority over his children was absolute until he died or formally freed his children. In Renaissance Italy, children did not become adults on reaching a certain age; adulthood came only when the father went before a judge and formally emancipated them. The age of emancipation varied from early teens to late twenties.

The wife managed the household, a position that gave women a certain degree of autonomy in their daily lives. Most wives, however, also knew that their primary function was to bear children. Upper-class wives were frequently pregnant; Alessandra Strozzi of Florence, for example, who had been married at the age of sixteen, bore eight children in ten years. For women in the Renaissance, childbirth was a fearful occasion. Not only was it painful, but it could be deadly; possibly as many as one woman in ten died in childbirth.

The Intellectual Renaissance

The emergence and growth of individualism and secularism as characteristics of the Italian Renaissance are most noticeable in the intellectual and artistic realms. The most important literary movement associated with the Renaissance is humanism.

ITALIAN RENAISSANCE HUMANISM

Renaissance humanism was an intellectual movement based on the study of the classics, the literary works of Greece and Rome. Humanists studied the liberal arts—grammar, rhetoric, poetry, moral philosophy or ethics, and history—all based on the writings of ancient Greek and Roman authors. We call these subjects the humanities.

Petrarch (1304–1374), who has often been called the father of Italian Renaissance humanism, did more than any other individual in the fourteenth century to foster the development of Renaissance humanism. Petrarch sought to find forgotten Latin manuscripts and set in motion a ransacking of monastic libraries throughout Europe. He also began the humanist emphasis on the use of pure classical Latin. Humanists used the works of Cicero as a model for prose and those of Virgil for poetry. As Petrarch said, "Christ is my God; Cicero is the prince of the language."

In Florence, the humanist movement took a new direction at the beginning of the fifteenth century. Fourteenth-century humanists such as Petrarch had described the intellectual life as one of solitude. They rejected family and a life of action in the community. However, the humanists who worked as secretaries for the city council of Florence took a new interest in civic life. They came to believe that it was the duty of an intellectual to live an active life for one's state. Humanists came to believe that their study of

MARRIAGE NEGOTIATIONS

Marriages were so important in maintaining families in Renaissance Italy that much energy was put into arranging them. Parents made the choices for their children, for considerations that had little to do with the modern notion of love. This selection is taken from the letters of a Florentine matron of the illustrious Strozzi family to her son Filippo in Naples. The family's considerations were complicated by the fact that the son was in exile.

ALESSANDRA STROZZI TO HER SON FILIPPO IN NAPLES

[April 20, 1464] Concerning the matter of a wife [for Filippo], it appears to me that if Francesco di Messer Tanagli wishes to give his daughter, that it would be a fine marriage. . . . Now I will speak with Marco [Parenti, Alessandra's son-in-law], to see if there are other prospects that would be better, and if there are none, then we will learn if he wishes to give her [in marriage]. . . . Francesco Tanagli has a good reputation, and he has held office, not the highest, but still he has been in office. You may ask: "Why should he give her to someone in exile?" There are three reasons. First, there aren't many young men of good family who have both virtue and property. Secondly, she has only a small dowry, 1,000 florins, which is the dowry of an artisan [although not a small sum, either—senior officials in the government bureaucracy earned 300 florins a year]. . . . Third, I believe that he will give her away, because he has a large family and he will need help to settle them. . . .

[July 26, 1465] Francesco is a good friend of Marco and he trusts him. On S. Jacopo's day, he spoke to him discreetly and persuasively, saying that for several months he had heard that we were interested in the girl and . . . that when we had made up our minds, she will come to us willingly. [He said that] you were a worthy man, and that his family had always made good marriages, but that he had only a small dowry to give her, and so he would prefer to send her outside of Florence to someone of worth, rather than to give her to someone here, from among those who were available, with little money. . . . We have information that she is affable and competent. She is responsible for a large family (there are twelve children, six boys and six girls), and the mother is always pregnant and isn't very competent. . . .

[August 31, 1465] I have recently received some very favorable information [about the Tanagli girl] from two individuals. . . . They are in agreement that whoever gets her will be content. . . . Concerning her beauty, they told me what I had already seen, that she is attractive and well-proportioned. Her face is long, but I couldn't look directly into her face, since she appeared to be aware that I was examining her . . . and so she turned away from me like the wind. . . . She reads quite well . . . and she can dance and sing. . . .

So yesterday I sent for Marco and told him what I had learned. And we talked about the matter for a while, and decided that he should say something to the father and give him a little hope, but not so much that we couldn't withdraw, and find out from him the amount of the dowry. . . . May God help us to choose what will contribute to our tranquility and to the consolation of us all. . . .

[September 13, 1465] Marco came to me and said that he had met with Francesco Tanagli, who had spoken very coldly, so that I understand that he had changed his mind.

[Filippo Strozzi eventually married Fiametta di Donato Adimari in 1466.]

---

the humanities should be put to the service of the state. It is no accident that humanists served as secretaries in Italian city-states or at courts of princes or popes.

Also evident in the humanism of the first half of the fifteenth century was a growing interest in classical Greek civilization. One of the first Italian humanists to gain a thorough knowledge of Greek was Leonardo Bruni, who became an enthusiastic pupil of the Byzantine scholar Manuel Chrysoloras, who taught in Florence from 1396 to 1400.

THE IMPACT OF PRINTING

The Renaissance witnessed the development of printing, which made an immediate impact on European intellectual life and thought. Printing from hand-carved wooden blocks had been done in the West since the twelfth century and in China even before that. What was new in the fifteenth century in Europe was multiple printing with movable metal type. The development of printing from movable type was a gradual process that culminated some time between 1445 and 1450; Johannes Gutenberg of Mainz played an important role in bringing the process to completion. Gutenberg's Bible, completed in 1455 or 1456, was the first true book produced from movable type.

By 1500, there were more than a thousand printers in Europe, who collectively had published almost forty thousand titles (between eight and ten million copies). Probably 50 percent of these books were religious—Bibles and biblical commentaries, books of devotion, and sermons. Next in importance were the Latin and Greek classics, medieval grammars, legal handbooks, and works on philosophy.

The printing of books encouraged the development of scholarly research and the desire to attain knowledge. Printing also stimulated the development of an ever-expanding lay reading public, a development that had an enormous impact on European society. Printing allowed European civilization to compete for the first time with the civilization of China.

The Artistic Renaissance

Renaissance artists sought to imitate nature in their works of art. Their search for naturalism became an end in itself: to persuade onlookers of the reality of the object or event they were portraying. At the same time, the new artistic standards reflected the new attitude of mind in which human beings became the focus of attention, the "center and measure of all things," as one artist proclaimed.

The frescoes by Masaccio (1401–1428) in Florence have long been regarded as the first masterpieces of Early Renaissance art. With his use of monumental figures, a more realistic relationship between figures and landscape, and the visual representation of the laws of perspective, a new realistic style of painting was born. Onlookers became aware of a world of reality that appeared to be a continuation of their own.

This new Renaissance style was absorbed and modified by other Florentine painters in the fifteenth century. Especially important were two major developments. One emphasized the technical side of painting —understanding the laws of perspective and the geometrical organization of outdoor space and light. The second development was the investigation of movement and anatomical structure. The realistic portrayal of the human nude became one of the foremost preoccupations of Italian Renaissance art. By the end of the fifteenth century, Italian painters had created a new artistic environment. Many artists had mastered the new techniques for a scientific observation of the world around them and were now ready to move into new forms of creative expression. This marked the shift to the High Renaissance.

The High Renaissance was dominated by the work of three artistic giants, Leonardo da Vinci (1452–1519), Raphael (1483–1520), and Michelangelo (1475–1564). Leonardo carried on the fifteenth-century experimental tradition by studying everything and even dissecting human bodies in order to see how nature worked. But Leonardo stressed the need to advance beyond such realism and initiated the high Renaissance's preoccupation with the idealization of nature, an attempt to generalize from realistic portrayal to an ideal form.

At twenty-five, Raphael was already regarded as one of Italy's best painters. He was acclaimed for his numerous madonnas, in which he attempted to achieve an ideal of beauty far surpassing human standards. He is well known

LEONARDO DA VINCI, *THE LAST SUPPER*.   Leonardo da Vinci was the impetus behind the High Renaissance concern for the idealization of nature, moving from a realistic portrayal of the human figure to an idealized form. Evident in Leonardo's *Last Supper* is his effort to depict a person's character and inner nature through gesture and movement. Unfortunately, Leonardo used an experimental technique in this fresco, which soon led to its physical deterioration.

RAPHAEL, *SCHOOL OF ATHENS*.   Raphael arrived in Rome in 1508 and began to paint a series of frescoes commissioned by Pope Julius II for the papal apartments at the Vatican. In *School of Athens*, painted about 1510–1511, Raphael created an imaginary gathering of ancient philosophers. In the center stand Plato and Aristotle. At the left is Pythagoras, showing his system of proportions on a slate. At the right is Ptolemy, holding a celestial globe.

for his frescoes in the Vatican Palace; his *School of Athens* reveals a world of balance, harmony, and order—the underlying principles of the art of the classical world of Greece and Rome.

Michelangelo, an accomplished painter, sculptor, and architect, was fiercely driven by a desire to create, and he worked with great passion and energy on a remarkable number of projects. Michelangelo was influenced by Neoplatonism, especially evident in his figures on the ceiling of the Sistine Chapel. These muscular figures reveal an ideal type of human being with perfect proportions. In good Neoplatonic fashion, their beauty is meant to be

MICHELANGELO, *CREATION OF ADAM*.   In 1508, Pope Julius II recalled Michelangelo to Rome and commissioned him to decorate the ceiling of the Sistine Chapel. This colossal project was not completed until 1512. Michelangelo attempted to tell the story of the Fall of Man by depicting nine scenes from the biblical Book of Genesis. In this scene, the well-proportioned figure of Adam, meant by Michelangelo to be a reflection of divine beauty, awaits the divine spark.

a reflection of divine beauty; the more beautiful the body, the more God-like the figure.

THE NORTHERN ARTISTIC RENAISSANCE

In trying to provide an exact portrayal of their world, the artists of the north (especially the Low Countries) and Italy took different approaches. In Italy, the human form became the primary vehicle of expression as Italian artists sought to master the technical skills that allowed them to portray humans in realistic settings. The large wall spaces of Italian churches had given rise to the art of fresco painting, but in the north, the prevalence of Gothic cathedrals with their stained-glass windows resulted in more emphasis on illuminated manuscripts and wooden panel painting for altarpieces. The space available in these works was limited, and great care was put into depicting each object, leading northern painters to become masters at rendering details.

The most influential northern school of art in the fifteenth century was centered in Flanders. Jan van Eyck (c. 1380–1441) was among the first to use oil paint, a medium that enabled the artist to use a varied range of colors and create fine details. In *Giovanni Arnolfini and His Bride*, van Eyck's attention to detail is staggering. Nevertheless, van Eyck's comprehension of perspective was still uncertain. His work is indicative of northern Renaissance painters, who, in their effort to imitate nature, did so not by mastery of the laws of perspective and proportion but by empirical observation of visual reality and the accurate portrayal of details. By the end of the fifteenth century, however, artists from the north began to study in Italy and were more and more influenced by what artists were doing there.

The State in the Renaissance

In the second half of the fifteenth century, attempts were made to reestablish the centralized power of monarchical governments after the political disasters of the fourteenth century. Some historians called these states the "new monarchies," especially those of France, England, and Spain (see Map 13.1).

WESTERN EUROPE

The Hundred Years' War left France prostrate. But the war had also developed a degree of French national feeling toward a common enemy that the kings could use to reestablish monarchical power. The development of a French territorial state was greatly advanced by King Louis XI (1461–1483), known as the Spider because of his wily and devious ways. Louis strengthened the use of the *taille*—an annual direct tax usually on land or property— as a permanent tax imposed by royal authority, giving him

⇒ JAN VAN EYCK, *GIOVANNI ARNOLFINI AND HIS BRIDE.* Northern painters took great care in depicting each object and became masters at rendering details. This emphasis on a realistic portrayal is clearly evident in this oil painting, supposedly a portrait of Giovanni Arnolfini, an Italian merchant who had settled in Bruges, and his wife, Giovanna Cenami.

a sound, regular source of income, which created the foundations of a strong French monarchy.

The Hundred Years' War had also strongly affected the English. The cost of the war in its final years and the losses to the labor force strained the English economy. At the end of the war, England faced even greater turmoil when a civil war, known as the War of the Roses, erupted and aristocratic factions fought over the monarchy until 1485, when Henry Tudor established a new dynasty.

As the first Tudor king, Henry VII (1485–1509) worked to establish a strong monarchical government. Henry ended the private wars of the nobility by abolishing their private armies. He was also very thrifty. By not overburdening the nobility and the middle class with taxes, Henry won their favor, and they provided him much support.

Spain, too, experienced the growth of a strong national monarchy by the end of the fifteenth century. During the Middle Ages, several independent Christian kingdoms had emerged in the course of the long reconquest of the Iberian peninsula from the Muslims. Two of the strongest were Aragon and Castile. When Isabella of Castile (1474–1504) married Ferdinand of Aragon (1479–1516) in 1469, it was a major step toward unifying Spain. The two rulers worked to strengthen royal control of government.

MAP 13.1 Europe in the Fifteenth Century.   By the second half of the fifteenth century, states in western Europe, particularly France, Spain, and England, had begun the process of modern state building. With varying success, they reined in the power of the church and nobles, increased the ability to levy taxes, and established effective government bureaucracies. ➤ *What aspects of Europe's political boundaries help explain why France and the Holy Roman Empire were often at war with each other?*

Ferdinand and Isabella also pursued a policy of strict religious uniformity. Spain possessed two large religious minorities, the Jews and the Muslims, both of which had been largely tolerated in medieval Spain. Increased persecution in the fourteenth century, however, led most Spanish Jews to convert to Catholicism. In 1492, Ferdinand and Isabella took the drastic step of expelling all professed Jews from Spain. Muslims, too, were then "encouraged" to convert to Catholicism, and in 1502, Isabella issued a decree expelling all professed Muslims from her kingdom.

CENTRAL AND EASTERN EUROPE

Unlike France, England, and Spain, the Holy Roman Empire failed to develop a strong monarchical authority. The failure of the German emperors in the thirteenth cen-

tury ended any chance of centralized monarchical authority, and Germany became a land of hundreds of virtually independent states. After 1438, the position of Holy Roman emperor was held in the hands of the Habsburg dynasty. Having gradually acquired a number of possessions along the Danube, known collectively as Austria, the house of Habsburg had become one of the wealthiest landholders in the empire and by the mid-fifteenth century had begun to play an important role in European affairs.

In eastern Europe, rulers struggled to achieve the centralization of the territorial states. Religious differences troubled the area, as Roman Catholics, Eastern Orthodox Christians, and other groups, including the Mongols, confronted each other. In Poland, the nobles gained the upper hand and established the right to elect their kings, a policy that drastically weakened royal authority. In Hungary, King Matthias Corvinus (1458–1490) broke the power of the wealthy lords and created a well-organized central administration. After his death, his work was largely undone.

Since the thirteenth century, Russia had been under the domination of the Mongols. Gradually, the princes of Moscow rose to prominence by using their close relationship to the Mongol khans to increase their wealth and expand their possessions. During the reign of the great Prince Ivan III (1462–1505), a new Russian state was born. Ivan III annexed other Russian principalities and took advantage of dissension among the Mongols to throw off their yoke by 1480.

THE ITALIAN STATES

During the Middle Ages, Italy had failed to develop a centralized monarchical state. Papal opposition to the Hohenstaufens in the thirteenth century had virtually guaranteed that. Moreover, the kingdom of Naples in the south was dominated by the French house of Anjou,

Sicily was ruled by the Spanish house of Aragon, and the papacy remained in shaky control of much of central Italy as rulers of the Papal States. Lack of centralized authority had enabled numerous city-states in northern and central Italy to remain independent of any political authority. Three of them—Milan, Venice, and Florence—managed to become fairly well centralized territorial states (see Map 13.2).

Milan, located at the crossroads of the main trade routes from Italian coast cities to the Alpine passes, was one of the richest city-states in Italy. In the fourteenth century, members of the Visconti family established themselves as dukes of Milan and extended their power over all of Lombardy. After the death of the last Visconti ruler of Milan in 1447, a *condottiere* (leader of a mercenary band) named Francesco Sforza turned on his Milanese employers, conquered the city, and became its new duke. Both Visconti and Sforza rulers worked to create the institutions of a strongly centralized territorial state.

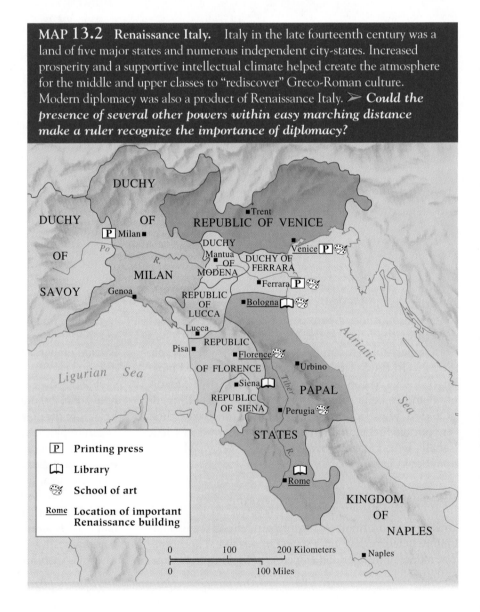

MAP 13.2 Renaissance Italy. Italy in the late fourteenth century was a land of five major states and numerous independent city-states. Increased prosperity and a supportive intellectual climate helped create the atmosphere for the middle and upper classes to "rediscover" Greco-Roman culture. Modern diplomacy was also a product of Renaissance Italy. ➢ *Could the presence of several other powers within easy marching distance make a ruler recognize the importance of diplomacy?*

[P] Printing press

[Library symbol] Library

[art palette symbol] School of art

<u>Rome</u> Location of important Renaissance building

The other major northern Italian state was the republic of Venice, which had grown rich from trade throughout the eastern Mediterranean and into northern Europe. A small oligarchy of merchant-aristocrats, who had become extremely wealthy through their commercial activities, ran the Venetian government on behalf of their own interests. Venice's commercial empire brought in enormous revenues and gave it the status of an international power. At the end of the fourteenth century, Venice embarked on the conquest of a territorial state in northern Italy to protect its overland trade routes.

The republic of Florence dominated the region of Tuscany. In the course of the fourteenth century, a small but wealthy merchant oligarchy established control of the Florentine government, led the Florentines in a series of successful wars against their neighbors, and established Florence as a major territorial state in northern Italy. In 1434, Cosimo de' Medici (1434–1464) took control of the ruling oligarchy. Although the wealthy Medici family maintained republican forms of government for appearance's sake, it ran the government from behind the scenes. Through lavish patronage and the careful courting of political allies, the Medici were successful in dominating the city at a time when Florence was the cultural center of Italy.

The growth of powerful monarchical states led to trouble for the Italians and brought an end to the independence of the Italian states. Attracted by the riches of Italy, the French king Charles VIII (1483–1498) led an army of thirty thousand men into Italy and occupied the kingdom of Naples. Other Italian states turned for help to the Spanish, who gladly complied. For the next thirty years, the French and Spanish competed to dominate Italy. The terrible sack of Rome in 1527 by the armies of the Spanish king Charles I brought a temporary end to the Italian wars. Thereafter, the Spaniards dominated Italy.

MACHIAVELLI AND THE NEW STATECRAFT

No one gave better expression to the Italians' preoccupation with political power than Niccolò Machiavelli (1469–1527), who wrote *The Prince* (1513), one of the most influential works on political power in the Western world. Machiavelli's major concerns in *The Prince* were the acquisition, maintenance, and expansion of political power as the means to restore and maintain order in his time. In the Middle Ages, many political theorists stressed the ethical side of a prince's activity—how a ruler ought to behave based on Christian moral principles. Machiavelli bluntly contradicted this approach: "For the gap between how people actually behave and how they ought to behave is so great that anyone who ignores everyday reality in order to live up to an ideal will soon discover he had been taught how to destroy himself, not how to preserve himself."[2] Machiavelli considered his approach far more realistic than that of his medieval forebears. Politi-

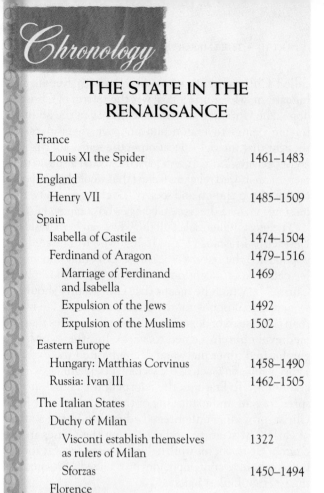

cal activity, therefore, could not be restricted by moral considerations. The prince acts on behalf of the state and for the sake of the state must be willing to let his conscience sleep. Machiavelli was among the first to abandon morality as the basis for the analysis of political activity.

THE REFORMATION OF THE SIXTEENTH CENTURY

The Protestant Reformation is the name given to the religious reform movement that divided the western church into Catholic and Protestant groups. Although Martin Luther began the Reformation in the early sixteenth century, several earlier developments had set the stage for religious change.

Prelude to Reformation

During the second half of the fifteenth century, the new classical learning of the Italian Renaissance spread to the European countries north of the Alps and spawned a movement called Christian humanism or Northern Renaissance humanism, whose major goal was the reform of Christendom. The Christian humanists believed in the ability of human beings to reason and improve themselves and thought that through education in the sources of classical, and especially Christian, antiquity, they could instill an inner piety or an inward religious feeling that would bring about a reform of the church and society. To change society, they must first change the human beings who compose it.

The most influential of all the Christian humanists was Desiderius Erasmus (1466–1536), who formulated and popularized the reform program of Christian humanism. He called his conception of religion "the philosophy of Christ," by which he meant that Christianity should be a guiding philosophy for the direction of daily life rather than the system of dogmatic beliefs and practices that the medieval church seemed to stress. In other words, he emphasized inner piety and deemphasized the external forms of religion (such as the sacraments, pilgrimages, fasts, and relics). To Erasmus, the reform of the church meant spreading an understanding of the philosophy of Jesus Christ, providing enlightened education in the sources of early Christianity, and criticizing the abuses in the church. No doubt his work helped prepare the way for the Reformation; as contemporaries proclaimed, "Erasmus laid the egg that Luther hatched."

Church and Religion on the Eve of the Reformation

Corruption in the Catholic church was another factor that encouraged people to want reform. Between 1450 and 1520, a series of popes—called the Renaissance popes—failed to meet the church's spiritual needs. The popes were supposed to be the spiritual leaders of the Catholic church but as leaders of the Papal States were all too often involved in worldly interests. Julius II (1503–1513), the fiery "warrior-pope," personally led armies against his enemies, much to the disgust of pious Christians, who viewed the pope as a spiritual leader. As one intellectual wrote, "How, O bishop standing in the room of the Apostles, dare you teach the people the things that pertain to war?" Many high church officials were also concerned with money and used their church offices as opportunities to advance their careers and their wealth, and many ordinary parish priests seemed ignorant of their spiritual duties.

While the leaders of the church were failing to meet their responsibilities, ordinary people were clamoring for meaningful religious expression and certainty of salvation. As a result, for some the process of salvation became almost mechanical. Collections of relics grew as more and more people sought certainty of salvation through veneration of these relics. Frederick the Wise, elector of Saxony and Martin Luther's prince, had amassed over five thousand relics to which were attached indulgences that could reduce one's time in purgatory by 1,443 years. (An indulgence is a remission, after death, of all or part of the punishment due to sin.)

Martin Luther and the Reformation in Germany

Martin Luther was a monk and a professor at the University of Wittenberg, where he lectured on the Bible. Probably sometime between 1513 and 1516, through his study of the Bible, he arrived at an answer to a problem—the assurance of salvation—that had disturbed him since his entry into the monastery.

Catholic doctrine had emphasized that both faith and good works were required of a Christian to achieve personal salvation. In Luther's eyes, human beings, weak and powerless in the sight of an almighty God, could never do enough good works to merit salvation. Through his study of the Bible, Luther came to believe that humans are not saved through their good works but through faith in the promises of God, made possible by the sacrifice of Jesus on the cross. This doctrine of salvation, or justification by grace through faith alone, became the primary doctrine of the Protestant Reformation. Because Luther had arrived at this doctrine from his study of the Bible, the Bible became for Luther as for all other Protestants the chief guide to religious truth.

Luther did not see himself as a rebel, but he was greatly upset by the widespread selling of indulgences. Especially offensive in his eyes was the monk Johann Tetzel, who hawked indulgences with the slogan: "As soon as the coin in the coffer [money box] rings, the soul from purgatory springs." Greatly angered, he issued in 1517 a stunning indictment of the abuses in the sale of indulgences, the Ninety-Five Theses (see the box on p. 363). Thousands of copies were printed and quickly spread to all parts of Germany.

By 1520, Luther had begun to move toward a more definite break with the Catholic church and called on the German princes to overthrow the papacy in Germany and establish a reformed German church. Through all his calls for change, Luther expounded more and more on his new doctrine of salvation. It is faith alone, he said, not good works, that justifies and brings salvation through Christ.

Unable to accept Luther's ideas, the church excommunicated him in January 1521. He had also been summoned in 1520 to appear before the imperial diet or Reichstag of the Holy Roman Empire, convened by the newly elected Emperor Charles V (1519–1556). Ordered to recant the heresies he had espoused, Luther refused and made the famous reply that became the battle cry of the Reformation:

> Unless I am convicted by Scripture and plain reason—I do not accept the authority of popes and councils, for they have contradicted each other—my conscience is captive to the Word of God. I cannot and I will not recant anything, for to go against conscience is neither right nor safe. Here I stand, I cannot do otherwise. God help me. Amen.[3]

LUTHER AND THE NINETY-FIVE THESES

To most historians, the publication of Luther's Ninety-Five Theses marks the beginning of the Reformation. To Luther, they were simply a response to what he considered to be the blatant abuses committed by sellers of indulgences. Although written in Latin, the theses were soon translated into German and disseminated widely across Germany. They made an immense impression on Germans already dissatisfied with the ecclesiastical and financial policies of the papacy.

MARTIN LUTHER, SELECTIONS FROM THE NINETY-FIVE THESES

5. The Pope has neither the will nor the power to remit any penalties beyond those he has imposed either at his own discretion or by canon law.

20. Therefore the Pope, by his plenary remission of all penalties, does not mean "all" in the absolute sense, but only those imposed by himself.

21. Hence those preachers of Indulgences are wrong when they say that a man is absolved and saved from every penalty by the Pope's Indulgences.

27. It is mere human talk to preach that the soul flies out [of purgatory] immediately [when] the money clinks in the collection box.

28. It is certainly possible that when the money clinks in the collection box greed and avarice can increase; but the intercession of the Church depends on the will of God alone.

50. Christians should be taught that, if the Pope knew the exactions of the preachers of Indulgences, he would rather have the basilica of St. Peter reduced to ashes than built with the skin, flesh, and bones of his sheep [the indulgences that so distressed Luther were being sold to raise money for the construction of the new St. Peter's Basilica in Rome].

81. This wanton preaching of pardons makes it difficult even for learned men to redeem respect due to the Pope from the slanders or at least the shrewd questionings of the laity.

82. For example: "Why does not the Pope empty purgatory for the sake of most holy love and the supreme need of souls? This would be the most righteous of reasons, if he can redeem innumerable souls for sordid money with which to build a basilica, the most trivial of reasons."

86. Again: "Since the Pope's wealth is larger than that of the crassest Crassi of our time, why does he not build this one basilica of St. Peter with his own money, rather than with that of the faithful poor?"

90. To suppress these most conscientious questionings of the laity by authority only, instead of refuting them by reason, is to expose the Church and the Pope to the ridicule of their enemies, and to make Christian people unhappy.

94. Christians should be exhorted to seek earnestly to follow Christ, their Head, through penalties, deaths, and hells.

95. And let them thus be more confident of entering heaven through many tribulations rather than through a false assurance of peace.

WOODCUT: LUTHER VERSUS THE POPE. In the 1520s, after Luther's return to Wittenberg, his teachings began to spread rapidly, ending ultimately in a reform movement supported by state authorities. Pamphlets containing picturesque woodcuts were important in the spread of Luther's ideas. In the woodcut shown here, the crucified Jesus attends Luther's service on the left, while on the right the pope is at a table selling indulgences.

Staatliche Museen Bildarchiv Preussischer Kulturbesitz, Kupferstichkabinett, Berlin (West), Photo: Jorg P. Anders

Members of the Reichstag were outraged and demanded that Luther be captured and delivered to the emperor. But Luther's ruler, Elector Frederick of Saxony, stepped in and protected him.

During the next few years, Luther's religious movement became a revolution. Luther was able to gain the support of many of the German rulers among the three hundred or so states that made up the Holy Roman Empire. These rulers quickly took control of the churches in their territories. The Lutheran churches in Germany (and later in Scandinavia) quickly became territorial or state churches in which the state supervised the affairs of the church. As part of the development of these state-dominated churches, Luther also instituted new religious services to replace the Catholic Mass. These focused on Bible reading, preaching of the word of God, and song.

Politics and Religion in the German Reformation

From its very beginning, the fate of Luther's movement was closely tied to political affairs. In 1519, Charles I, king of Spain and the grandson of Emperor Maximilian, was elected Holy Roman emperor as Charles V. Charles V ruled over an immense empire, consisting of Spain and its overseas possessions, the traditional Austrian Habsburg lands, Bohemia, Hungary, the Low Countries, and the kingdom of Naples in southern Italy. Politically, Charles wanted to maintain his enormous empire; religiously, he hoped to preserve the unity of his empire in the Catholic faith. However, a number of problems kept him preoccupied and cost him both his dream and his health.

The chief political concern of Charles V was his rivalry with the king of France, Francis I (1515–1547). Their conflict over disputed territories led to four wars that lasted more than twenty years. At the same time, Charles faced opposition from Pope Clement VII (1523–1534), who, guided by political considerations, joined the side of Francis I. The advance of the Ottoman Turks (see Chapter 15) into the eastern part of Charles's empire forced the emperor to divert forces there as well.

Finally, the internal political situation in the Holy Roman Empire was also not in Charles's favor. Germany was a land of several hundred territorial states. Although all owed loyalty to the emperor, in the Middle Ages these states had become quite independent of imperial authority. By the time Charles V was able to bring military forces to Germany in 1546, Lutheranism had become well established and the Lutheran princes were well organized. Unable to defeat them, Charles was forced to negotiate a truce. An end to religious warfare in Germany came in 1555 with the Peace of Augsburg. The division of Christianity was formally acknowledged; Lutheran states were to have the same legal rights as Catholic states. Although the German states were now free to choose between

Catholicism and Lutheranism, the peace settlement did not recognize the principle of religious toleration for individuals. The right of each German ruler to determine the religion of his subjects was accepted, but not the right of the subjects to choose their own religion.

The Spread of the Protestant Reformation

With the Peace of Augsburg, what had at first been merely feared was now certain: the ideal of Christian unity was forever lost. The rapid spread of new Protestant groups made this a certainty.

CALVIN AND CALVINISM

John Calvin (1509–1564) was educated in his native France but after his conversion to Protestantism was forced to flee for the safety of Switzerland. In 1536, he published the first edition of the *Institutes of the Christian Religion*, a masterful synthesis of Protestant thought that immediately secured Calvin's reputation as one of the new leaders of Protestantism.

On most important doctrines, Calvin stood very close to Luther. He adhered to the doctrine of justification by faith alone to explain how humans achieved salvation. But Calvin also placed much emphasis on the absolute sovereignty of God or the all-powerful nature of God—what Calvin called the "power, grace, and glory of God." One of the ideas derived from his emphasis on the absolute sovereignty of God—predestination—gave a unique cast to Calvin's teachings. This "eternal decree," as Calvin called it, meant that God had predestined some people to be saved (the elect) and others to be damned (the reprobate). According to Calvin, "He has once for all determined, both whom He would admit to salvation, and whom He would condemn to destruction."[4] Although Calvin stressed that there could be no absolute certainty of salvation, his followers did not always make this distinction. The practical psychological effect of predestination was to give later Calvinists an unshakable conviction that they were doing God's work on earth, making Calvinism a dynamic and activist faith.

In 1536, Calvin began working to reform the city of Geneva. He was able to fashion a tightly organized church order that employed both clergy and laymen in the service of the church. The Consistory, a special body for enforcing moral discipline, functioned as a court to oversee the moral life, daily behavior, and doctrinal orthodoxy of Genevans and to admonish and correct deviants. Citizens in Geneva were punished for such varied "crimes" as dancing, singing obscene songs, drunkenness, swearing, and playing cards.

Calvin's success in Geneva enabled the city to become a vibrant center of Protestantism. Following Calvin's lead, missionaries trained in Geneva were sent to all parts of Europe. Calvinism became established in France, the Netherlands, Scotland, and central and eastern Europe, and by the mid-sixteenth century, Calvin's Geneva stood as the fortress of the Reformation.

THE ENGLISH REFORMATION

The English Reformation was rooted in politics, not religion. King Henry VIII (1509–1547) had a strong desire to divorce his first wife, Catherine of Aragon, with whom the king had a daughter, Mary, but no male heir. He wanted to marry Anne Boleyn, with whom the king had fallen in love. Impatient with the pope's unwillingness to grant him an annulment of his marriage, Henry turned to England's own church courts. As archbishop of Canterbury and head of the highest church court in England, Thomas Cranmer ruled in May 1533 that the king's marriage to Catherine was "absolutely void." At the beginning of June, Anne was crowned queen, and three months later a child was born, a girl (the future queen Elizabeth I), much to the king's disappointment.

In 1534, at Henry's request, Parliament moved to finalize the break of the Church of England with Rome. The Act of Supremacy of 1534 declared that the king was "the only supreme head on earth of the Church of England," a position that gave him control of doctrine, clerical appointments, and discipline. Although Henry VIII had broken with the papacy, little change occurred in matters of doctrine, theology, and ceremony. Some of his supporters, including Archbishop Cranmer, sought a religious reformation as well as an administrative one, but Henry was unyielding. But he died in 1547 and was succeeded by his son, the underage and sickly Edward VI (1547–1553), and during Edward's reign, Cranmer and others inclined toward Protestant doctrines were able to move the Church of England (or Anglican church) in a more Protestant direction. New acts of Parliament gave the clergy the right to marry and created a new Protestant church service.

Edward VI was succeeded by Mary (1553–1558), a Catholic who attempted to return England to Catholicism. Her actions aroused much anger, however, especially when "bloody Mary" burned more than three hundred Protestant heretics. By the end of Mary's reign, England was more Protestant than it had been at the beginning.

THE ANABAPTISTS

The Anabaptists were the radical reformers of the Protestant Reformation. To Anabaptists, the true Christian church was a voluntary association of believers who had undergone spiritual rebirth and had then been baptized into the church. Anabaptists advocated adult rather than infant baptism. They also wanted to return to the practices and spirit of early Christianity and considered all

believers to be equal. Each church chose its own minister, who might be any member of the community since all Christians were considered priests (though women were often excluded).

Finally, unlike the Catholics and other Protestants, most Anabaptists believed in the complete separation of church and state. Government was to be excluded from the realm of religion and could not exercise political jurisdiction over real Christians. Anabaptists refused to hold political office or bear arms because many took the commandment "Thou shall not kill" literally. Their political beliefs as much as their religious beliefs caused the Anabaptists to be regarded as dangerous radicals who threatened the very fabric of sixteenth-century society. Indeed, the chief thing Protestants and Catholics could agree on was the need to persecute Anabaptists.

The Social Impact of the Protestant Reformation

The Protestants were especially important in developing a new view of the family. Because Protestantism had eliminated any idea of special holiness for celibacy and had abolished both monasticism and a celibate clergy, the family could be placed at the center of human life, and a new stress on "mutual love between man and wife" could be extolled.

But were doctrine and reality the same? Most often, reality reflected the traditional roles of husband as the ruler and wife as the obedient servant whose chief duty was to please her husband. Luther stated it clearly:

> The rule remains with the husband, and the wife is compelled to obey him by God's command. He rules the home and the state, wages war, defends his possessions, tills the soil, builds, plants, etc. The woman on the other hand is like a nail driven into the wall . . . so the wife should stay at home and look after the affairs of the household, as one who has been deprived of the ability of administering those affairs that are outside and that concern the state. She does not go beyond her most personal duties.[5]

Obedience to her husband was not a wife's only role; her other important duty was to bear children. To Calvin and Luther, this function of women was part of the divine plan, and for most Protestant women, family life was their only destiny (see the box on p. 366). Overall, the Protestant Reformation did not noticeably transform women's subordinate place in society.

The Catholic Reformation

By the mid-sixteenth century, Lutheranism had become established in Germany and Scandinavia and Calvinism in Switzerland, France, the Netherlands, and eastern Europe. In England, the split from Rome had resulted in

A PROTESTANT WOMAN

In the initial zeal of the Protestant Reformation, women were frequently allowed to play unusual roles. Catherine Zell of Germany (c. 1497–1562) first preached beside her husband in 1527. After the death of her two children, she devoted the rest of her life to helping her husband and their Anabaptist faith. This selection is taken from one of her letters to a young Lutheran minister who had criticized her activities.

CATHERINE ZELL TO LUDWIG RABUS OF MEMMINGEN

I, Catherine Zell, wife of the late lamented Mathew Zell, who served in Strasbourg, where I was born and reared and still live, wish you peace and enhancement in God's grace. . . .

From my earliest years I turned to the Lord, who taught and guided me, and I have at all times, in accordance with my understanding and His grace, embraced the interests of His church and earnestly sought Jesus. Even in youth this brought me the regard and affection of clergymen and others much concerned with the church, which is why the pious Mathew Zell wanted me as a companion in marriage; and I, in turn, to serve the glory of Christ, gave devotion and help to my husband, both in his ministry and in keeping his house. . . . Ever since I was ten years old I have been a student and a sort of church mother, much given to attending sermons. I have loved and frequented the company of learned men, and I conversed much with them, not about dancing, masquerades, and worldly pleasures but about the kingdom of God. . . .

Consider the poor Anabaptists, who are so furiously and ferociously persecuted. Must the authorities everywhere be incited against them, as the hunter drives his dog against wild animals? Against those who acknowledge Christ the Lord in very much the same way we do and over which we broke with the papacy? Just because they cannot agree with us on lesser things, is this any reason to persecute them and in them Christ, in whom they fervently believe and have often professed in misery, in prison, and under the torments of fire and water?

Governments may punish criminals, but they should not force and govern belief, which is a matter for the heart and conscience not for temporal authorities. . . . When the authorities pursue one, they soon bring forth tears, and towns and villages are emptied.

---

the creation of a national church. The situation in Europe did not look particularly favorable to the Roman Catholic church (see Map 13.3). However, the Catholic church also underwent a revitalization in the sixteenth century, giving it new strength. There were three chief pillars of the Catholic Reformation: the Jesuits, a reformed papacy, and the Council of Trent.

The Society of Jesus, known as the Jesuits, was founded by a Spanish nobleman, Ignatius of Loyola (1491–1556). Loyola gathered together a small group of individuals who were recognized as a religious order by the pope in 1540. The new order was grounded on the principles of absolute obedience to the papacy, a strict hierarchical order for the society, the use of education to achieve its goals, and a dedication to engage in "conflict for God." A special vow of absolute obedience to the pope made the Jesuits an important instrument for papal policy. Jesuit missionaries proved singularly successful in restoring Catholicism to parts of Germany and eastern Europe.

A reformed papacy was another important factor in the development of the Catholic Reformation. The involvement of Renaissance popes in dubious finances and Italian political and military affairs had created numerous sources of corruption. It took the jolt of the Protestant Reformation to bring about serious reform. Pope Paul III (1534–1549) perceived the need for change and took the audacious step of appointing a reform commission to ascertain the church's ills. The commission's report in 1537 blamed the church's problems on the corrupt policies of

IGNATIUS OF LOYOLA. The Jesuits became the most important new religious order of the Catholic Reformation. Shown here in a sixteenth-century painting by an unknown artist is Ignatius of Loyola, founder of the Society of Jesus. Loyola is seen kneeling before Pope Paul III, who officially recognized the Jesuits in 1540.

© Scala/Art Resource, NY

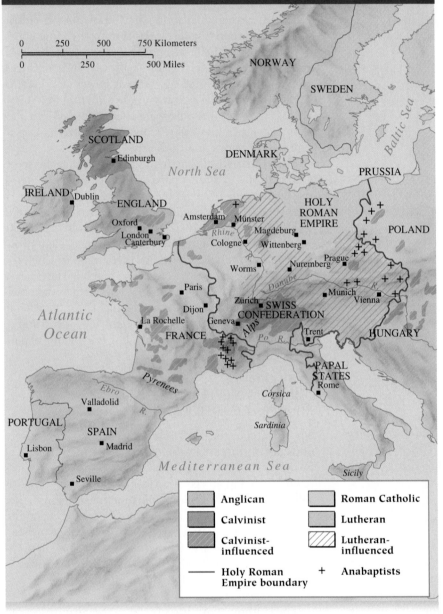

MAP 13.3 Catholics and Protestants in Europe by 1560.   The Reformation continued to evolve beyond the basic split of the Lutherans from the Catholics. Several Protestant sects broke away from the teachings of Martin Luther, each with a separate creed and different ways of worship. In England, Henry VIII broke with the Catholic church for political and dynastic reasons. ➤ *Which areas of Europe were solidly Catholic, which were solidly Lutheran, and which were neither?*

popes and cardinals. It was also Paul III who formally recognized the Jesuits and began the Council of Trent.

In March 1545, a group of high church officials met in the city of Trent on the border between Germany and Italy and initiated the Council of Trent, which met intermittently from 1545 to 1563 in three major sessions. The final decrees of the Council of Trent reaffirmed traditional Catholic teachings in opposition to Protestant beliefs.

Scripture and tradition were affirmed as equal authorities in religious matters; only the church could interpret Scripture. Both faith and good works were declared necessary for salvation. Belief in purgatory and in the use of indulgences was strengthened, although the selling of indulgences was prohibited.

After the Council of Trent, the Roman Catholic church possessed a clear body of doctrine and a unified

KEY EVENTS OF
THE REFORMATION ERA

Luther's Ninety-Five Theses	1517
Excommunication of Luther	1521
Act of Supremacy in England	1534
Pontificate of Paul III	1534–1549
John Calvin's *Institutes of the Christian Religion*	1536
Jesuits recognized as a religious order	1540
Council of Trent	1545–1563
Peace of Augsburg	1555

church under the acknowledged supremacy of the popes. The Roman Catholic church had become one Christian denomination among many. With a new spirit of confidence, the Catholic church entered a militant phase, as well prepared as the Calvinists to do battle for the Lord. An era of religious warfare was about to unfold.

EUROPE IN CRISIS: WAR, REVOLUTION, AND SOCIAL DISINTEGRATION, 1560–1650

Between 1560 and 1650, Europe experienced religious wars, revolutions and constitutional crises, economic and social disintegration, and a witchcraft craze. It was truly an age of crisis.

Politics and the Wars of Religion in the Sixteenth Century

By 1560, Calvinism and Catholicism had become militant religions dedicated to spreading the word of God as they interpreted it. Although their struggle for the minds and hearts of Europeans was at the heart of the religious wars of the sixteenth century, economic, social, and political forces also played an important role in these conflicts.

THE FRENCH WARS OF RELIGION (1562–1598)

Religion was central to the French civil wars of the sixteenth century. The growth of Calvinism had led to persecution by the French kings, but the latter did little to stop the spread of Calvinism. Huguenots (as the French Calvinists were called) constituted only about 7 percent of the population, but 40 to 50 percent of the French nobility became Huguenots, including the house of Bourbon, which stood next to the Valois in the royal line of succession. The conversion of so many nobles made the Huguenots a potentially dangerous political threat to monarchical power. Still, the Calvinist minority was greatly outnumbered by the Catholic majority, and the Valois monarchy was staunchly Catholic. At the same time, an extreme Catholic party, known as the ultra-Catholics, favored strict opposition to the Huguenots.

The religious issue was not the only factor that contributed to the French civil wars. Towns and provinces, which had long resisted the growing power of monarchical centralization, were only too willing to join a revolt against the monarchy. So were the nobles, and the fact that so many of them were Calvinists created an important base of opposition to the crown.

For thirty years, battles raged in France between Catholic and Calvinist parties. Finally, in 1589, Henry of Navarre, the political leader of the Huguenots and a member of the Bourbon dynasty, succeeded to the throne as Henry IV (1589–1610). Realizing, however, that he would never be accepted by Catholic France, Henry converted to Catholicism. With his coronation in 1594, the Wars of Religion had finally come to an end. The Edict of Nantes in 1598 solved the religious problem by acknowledging Catholicism as the official religion of France while guaranteeing the Huguenots the right to worship and to enjoy all political privileges, including the holding of public offices.

PHILIP II AND THE CAUSE OF MILITANT CATHOLICISM

The greatest advocate of militant Catholicism in the second half of the sixteenth century was King Philip II of Spain (1556–1598), the son and heir of Charles V. Philip's reign ushered in an age of Spanish greatness, both politically and culturally. Philip II had inherited from his father Spain, the Netherlands, and possessions in Italy and the New World. To strengthen his control, Philip insisted on strict conformity to Catholicism and strong, monarchical authority. Achieving the latter was not an easy task, because each of the lands of his empire had its own structure of government.

The Catholic faith was crucial to the Spanish people and their ruler. Driven by a heritage of crusading fervor, Spain saw itself as a nation of people chosen by God to save Catholic Christianity from the Protestant heretics. Philip II, the "most Catholic king," became the champion of Catholicism throughout Europe. Spain's leadership of a "holy league" against Turkish encroachments in the Mediterranean resulted in a stunning victory over the Turkish fleet in the Battle of Lepanto in 1571. But Philip's problems with the Netherlands and the English Queen Elizabeth led to his greatest misfortunes.

Philip's attempt to strengthen his control in the Spanish Netherlands, which consisted of seventeen provinces (modern Netherlands and Belgium), soon led to a revolt. The nobles, who stood to lose the most politically, strongly opposed Philip's efforts. Religion also became a major catalyst for rebellion when Philip attempted to crush Calvinism. Violence erupted in 1566, when Calvinists—especially nobles—began to destroy statues and stained-glass windows in Catholic churches. Philip responded by sending ten thousand veteran Spanish and Italian troops to crush the rebellion. But the revolt became organized, especially in the northern provinces, where the Dutch, under the leadership of William of Nassau, the prince of Orange, offered growing resistance. The struggle dragged on for decades until 1609, when a twelve-year truce ended the war, virtually recognizing the independence of the northern provinces. These seven northern provinces, which called themselves the United Provinces of the Netherlands, became the core of the modern Dutch state.

To most Europeans, Spain still seemed the greatest power of the age at the beginning of the seventeenth century, but the reality was quite different. The treasury was empty; Philip II went bankrupt in 1596 from excessive expenditures on war; and his successor did the same in 1607 by spending a fortune on his court. The armed forces were obsolescent, and the government was inefficient. Spain continued to play the role of a great power, but real power had shifted to England.

THE ENGLAND OF ELIZABETH

When Elizabeth Tudor, the daughter of Henry VIII and Anne Boleyn, ascended the throne in 1558, England was home to fewer than four million people. Yet during her reign, the small island kingdom became leader of the Protestant nations of Europe and laid the foundations for a world empire.

Intelligent, cautious, and self-confident, Elizabeth moved quickly to solve the difficult religious problem she inherited from her half-sister, Queen Mary. Elizabeth's religious policy was based on moderation and compromise. She repealed the Catholic laws of Mary's reign, and a new Act of Supremacy designated Elizabeth as "the only supreme governor" of both church and state. The Church of England under Elizabeth was basically Protestant, but it was of a moderate bent that kept most people satisfied.

Caution and moderation also dictated Elizabeth's foreign policy. Gradually, however, Elizabeth was drawn into conflict with Spain. Having resisted for years the idea of invading England as too impractical, Philip II of Spain was finally persuaded to do so by advisers who assured him that the people of England would rise against their queen when the Spaniards arrived. A successful invasion of England would mean the overthrow of heresy and the return of England to Catholicism. Philip ordered preparations for a fleet of warships, the Armada, to spearhead the invasion of England.

The Armada was a disaster. The Spanish fleet that finally set sail had neither the ships nor the manpower that Philip had planned to send. Battered by a number of encounters with the English, the Spanish fleet sailed back to Spain by a northward route around Scotland and Ireland, where it was further pounded by storms. Although the English and Spanish would continue their war for another sixteen years, the defeat of the Armada guaranteed for the time being that England would remain a Protestant country.

Economic and Social Crises: Witchcraft Mania

The period of European history from 1560 to 1650 witnessed severe economic and social crises as well as political upheaval. Economic contraction began to be evident in some parts of Europe by the 1620s. In the 1630s and 1640s, as imports of silver from the Americas declined, economic recession intensified, especially in the Mediterranean area. Once the industrial and financial center of Europe in the age of the Renaissance, Italy was now becoming an economic backwater.

Population trends of the sixteenth and seventeenth centuries also reveal Europe's worsening conditions. The population of Europe increased from 60 million in 1500 to 85 million by 1600, the first major recovery of European population since the devastation of the Black Death in the mid-fourteenth century. However, records also indicate a decline of the population by 1650, especially in central and southern Europe. Europe's longtime adversaries—war, famine and plague—continued to affect population levels. Europe's entry into another "little ice age" after the middle of the sixteenth century, when average temperatures fell, affected harvests and gave rise to famines. Europe's problems created social tensions, some of which became manifested in an obsession with witches.

Hysteria over witchcraft affected the lives of many Europeans in the sixteenth and seventeenth centuries. Neighbors accused neighbors of witchcraft, leading to widespread trials of witches. Perhaps more than 100,000 people were prosecuted throughout Europe on charges of witchcraft. As more and more people were brought to trial, the fear of witches, as well as the fear of being accused of witchcraft, escalated to frightening levels (see the box on p. 370).

Common people—usually those who were poor and without property—were more likely to be accused of witchcraft. Indeed, where lists are given, those mentioned most often are milkmaids, peasant women, and servant girls. In the witchcraft trials of the sixteenth and seventeenth centuries, more than 75 percent of the accused were women, most of them single or widowed and many over fifty years old.

That women should be the chief victims of witchcraft trials was hardly accidental. Nicholas Rémy, a witchcraft judge in France in the 1590s, found it "not unreasonable

A WITCHCRAFT TRIAL IN FRANCE

Persecutions for witchcraft reached their high point in the sixteenth and seventeenth centuries, when tens of thousands of people were brought to trial. In this excerpt from the minutes of a trial in France in 1652, we can see why the accused witch stood little chance of exonerating herself.

THE TRIAL OF SUZANNE GAUDRY

28 May, 1652. . . . Interrogation of Suzanne Gaudry, prisoner at the court of Rieux. . . . During interrogations on May 28 and May 29, the prisoner confessed to a number of activities involving the devil.

Deliberation of the Court—June 3, 1652

The undersigned advocates of the Court have seen these interrogations and answers. They say that the aforementioned Suzanne Gaudry confesses that she is a witch, that she had given herself to the devil, that she had renounced God, Lent, and baptism, that she has been marked on the shoulder, that she has cohabited with the devil and that she has been to the dances, confessing only to have cast a spell upon and caused to die a beast of Philippe Cornié. . . .

Third Interrogation, June 27

This prisoner being led into the chamber, she was examined to know if things were not as she had said and confessed at the beginning of her imprisonment.

—Answers no, and that what she has said was done so by force.

Pressed to say the truth, that otherwise she would be subjected to torture, having pointed out to her that her aunt was burned for this same subject.

—Answers that she is not a witch. . . .

She was placed in the hands of the officer in charge of torture, throwing herself on her knees, struggling to cry, uttering several exclamations, without being able, nevertheless, to shed a tear. Saying at every moment that she is not a witch.

The Torture

On this same day, being at the place of torture.

This prisoner, before being strapped down, was admonished to maintain herself in her first confessions and to renounce her lover.

—Says that she denies everything she has said, and that she has no lover. Feeling herself being strapped down, says that she is not a witch, while struggling to cry. . . and upon being asked why she confessed to being one, said that she was forced to say it.

Told that she was not forced, that on the contrary she declared herself to be a witch without any threat.

—Says that she confessed it and that she is not a witch, and being a little stretched [on the rack] screams ceaselessly that she is not a witch.

Asked if she did not confess that she had been a witch for twenty-six years.

—Says that she said it, that she retracts it, crying that she is not a witch.

Asked if she did not make Philippe Cornié's horse die, as she confessed.

—Answers no, crying Jesus-Maria, that she is not a witch.

The mark having been probed by the officer, in the presence of Doctor Bouchain, it was adjudged by the aforesaid doctor and officer truly to be the mark of the devil.

Being more tightly stretched upon the torture rack, urged to maintain her confessions.

—Said that it was true that she is a witch and that she would maintain what she had said.

Asked how long she has been in subjugation to the devil.

—Answers that it was twenty years ago that the devil appeared to her, being in her lodgings in the form of a man dressed in a little cowhide and black breeches. . . .

Verdict

July 9, 1652. In the light of the interrogations, answers, and investigations made into the charge against Suzanne Gaudry, . . . seeing by her own confessions that she is said to have made a pact with the devil, received the mark from him, . . . and that following this, she had renounced God, Lent, and baptism and had let herself be known carnally by him, in which she received satisfaction. Also, seeing that she is said to have been a part of nocturnal carols and dances.

For expiation of which the advice of the undersigned is that the office of Rieux can legitimately condemn the aforesaid Suzanne Gaudry to death, tying her to a gallows, and strangling her to death, then burning her body and burying it here in the environs of the woods.

that this scum of humanity, i.e., witches, should be drawn chiefly from the feminine sex." To another judge, it came as no surprise that witches would confess to sexual experiences with Satan: "The Devil uses them so, because he knows that women love carnal pleasures, and he means to bind them to his allegiance by such agreeable provocations."[6]

By the mid-seventeenth century, the witchcraft hysteria had begun to subside. As governments grew stronger, fewer magistrates were willing to accept the unsettling and divisive conditions generated by the trials of witches. Moreover, by the end of the seventeenth and beginning of the eighteenth centuries, more and more people were questioning altogether their old attitudes toward religion and found it especially contrary to reason to believe in the old view of a world haunted by evil spirits.

Seventeenth-Century Crises: Revolution and War

Although many Europeans responded to the upheavals of the second half of the sixteenth century with a desire for peace and order, the first fifty years of the seventeenth century continued to be a period of crisis. A series of rebellions and civil wars rocked the domestic stability of many European governments. A devastating war that affected much of Europe also added to the sense of crisis.

THE THIRTY YEARS' WAR (1618–1648)

The Thirty Years' War began in 1618 in the Germanic lands of the Holy Roman Empire as a struggle between Catholic forces, led by the Habsburg Holy Roman Emperors, and Protestant—primarily Calvinist—nobles in Bohemia who rebelled against Habsburg authority (see Map 13.4). What began as a struggle over religious issues soon became a wider conflict perpetuated by political motivations as both minor and major European powers—Denmark, Sweden, France, and Spain—entered the war. The competition for European leadership between the Bourbon dynasty of France and the Habsburg dynasties of Spain and the Holy Roman Empire was an especially important factor. Nevertheless, most of the battles were fought on German soil.

The war in Germany was officially ended in 1648 by the Peace of Westphalia, which proclaimed that all German states, including the Calvinist ones, were free to determine their own religion. The major contenders gained new territories, and France emerged as the dominant nation in Europe. The more than three hundred states that made up the Holy Roman Empire were recognized as independent states, and each was given the power to conduct its own foreign policy; this brought an end to the Holy Roman Empire as a political entity and ensured German disunity for another two hundred years. The Peace of Westphalia made it clear that political motives, not religious convictions, had become the guiding force in public affairs.

RESPONSE TO CRISIS: THE PRACTICE OF ABSOLUTISM

Many people responded to the crises of the seventeenth century by searching for order. An increase in monarchical power became an obvious means for achieving stability. The result was what historians have called absolutism or absolute monarchy. Absolutism meant that the sovereign power or ultimate authority in the state rested in the hands of a king who claimed to rule by divine right—the idea that kings received their power from God and were responsible to no one except God. Late sixteenth-century political theorists believed that sovereign power

consisted of the authority to make laws, tax, administer justice, control the state's administrative system, and determine foreign policy.

France Under Louis XIV

France during the reign of Louis XIV (1661–1715) has traditionally been regarded as the best example of the practice of absolute monarchy in the seventeenth century. French culture, language, and manners reached into all levels of European society. French diplomacy and wars overwhelmed the political affairs of western and central Europe. The court of Louis XIV seemed to be imitated everywhere in Europe.

One of the keys to Louis's power was his control of the central policy-making machinery of government because it was part of his own court and household. The royal court located at Versailles served three purposes simultaneously: it was the personal household of the king, the location of central governmental machinery, and the place where powerful subjects came to find favors and offices for themselves and their clients. The greatest danger to Louis's personal rule came from the very high nobles and princes of the blood (the royal princes), who considered it their natural role to assert the policy-making role of royal ministers. Louis eliminated this threat by removing them from the royal council, the chief administrative body of the king, and enticing them to his court, where he could keep them preoccupied with court life and out of politics. Instead of the high nobility and royal princes, Louis relied for his ministers on nobles who came from relatively new aristocratic families. His ministers were expected to be subservient; "I had no intention of sharing my authority with them," Louis said.

Louis's domination of his ministers and secretaries gave him control of the central policy-making machinery of government and thus authority over the traditional areas of monarchical power: the formulation of foreign policy, the making of war and peace, the assertion of the secular power

⟫⟫ **SUN KINGS, WEST AND EAST.**   At the end of the seventeenth century, two powerful rulers dominated the affairs of their regions and saw themselves as sun kings—the sources of light for their people. On the left, Louis XIV, who ruled France from 1643 to 1715, is seen in a portrait by Hyacinth Rigaud that captures the king's sense of royal dignity and grandeur. On the right, Kangxi, who ruled China from 1661 to 1722, is seen in a nineteenth-century portrait that shows the ruler seated in majesty on his imperial throne.

of crown against any religious authority, and the ability to levy taxes to fulfill these functions. However, Louis had considerably less success with the internal administration of the kingdom. The traditional groups and institutions of French society—the nobles, officials, town councils, guilds, and representative estates in some provinces—were simply too powerful for the king to have direct control over the lives of his subjects. As a result, the control of the central government over the provinces and the people was carried out largely by the careful bribery of the important people to see that the king's policies were executed.

The cost of building palaces, maintaining his court, and pursuing his wars made finances a crucial issue for Louis XIV. He was most fortunate in having the services of Jean-Baptiste Colbert (1619–1683) as controller general of finances. Colbert sought to increase the wealth and power of France by general adherence to mercantilism, a set of principles that dominated economic thought in the seventeenth century. According to the mercantilists, the prosperity of a nation depended on a plentiful supply of bullion (gold and silver). For this reason, it was desirable to achieve

a favorable balance of trade in which goods exported were of greater value than those imported, promoting an influx of gold and silver payments that would increase the quantity of bullion. Mercantilism focused on the role of the state, believing that state intervention in the economy was desirable for the sake of the national good.

Colbert was an avid practitioner of mercantilism. To decrease imports and increase exports, he granted subsidies to individuals who established new industries. To improve communications and the transportation of goods internally, he built roads and canals. To decrease imports directly, Colbert raised tariffs on foreign goods.

The increase in royal power that Louis pursued led the king to develop a professional army numbering 100,000 men in peacetime and 400,000 in time of war. To achieve the prestige and military glory befitting an absolute king as well as to ensure the domination of his Bourbon dynasty over European affairs, Louis waged four wars between 1667 and 1713. His ambitions roused much of Europe to form coalitions that were determined to prevent the certain destruction of the European balance of power by Bourbon

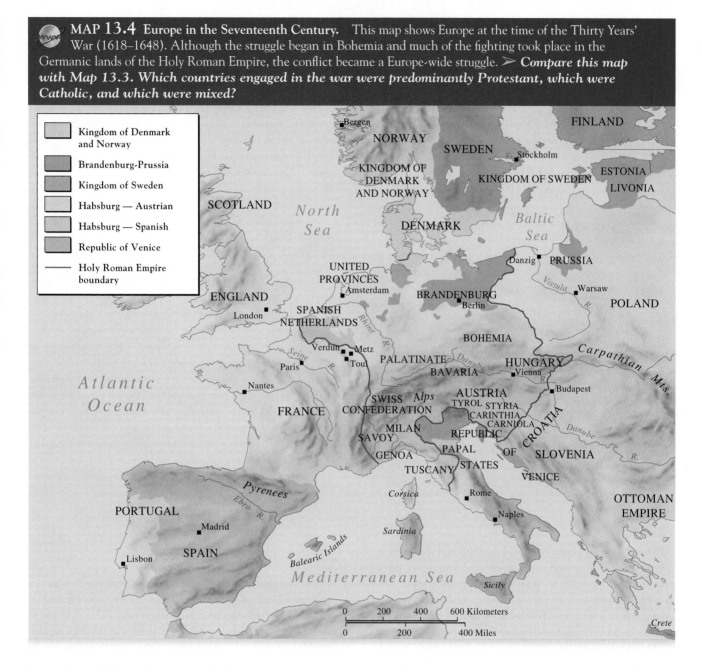

MAP 13.4 Europe in the Seventeenth Century.   This map shows Europe at the time of the Thirty Years' War (1618–1648). Although the struggle began in Bohemia and much of the fighting took place in the Germanic lands of the Holy Roman Empire, the conflict became a Europe-wide struggle. ➤ *Compare this map with Map 13.3. Which countries engaged in the war were predominantly Protestant, which were Catholic, and which were mixed?*

hegemony. Although Louis added some territory to France's northeastern frontier and established a member of his own Bourbon dynasty on the throne of Spain, he also left France impoverished and surrounded by enemies.

Absolutism in Central and Eastern Europe

During the seventeenth century, a development of great importance for the modern Western world took place with the appearance in central and eastern Europe of three new powers: Prussia, Austria, and Russia.

Frederick William the Great Elector (1640–1688) laid the foundation for the Prussian state. Realizing that the land he had inherited, known as Brandenburg-Prussia, was a small, open territory with no natural frontiers for defense, Frederick William built an army of forty thousand men, making it the fourth largest in Europe. To sustain the army, Frederick William established the General War Commissariat to levy taxes for the army and oversee its growth. The Commissariat soon evolved into an agency for civil government as well. The new bureaucratic machine became the elector's chief instrument to govern the state. Many of its officials were members of the Prussian landed aristocracy, the Junkers, who also served as officers in the all-important army.

In 1701, Frederick William's son Frederick officially gained the title of king. Elector Frederick III became King Frederick I, and Brandenburg-Prussia simply Prussia. In the eighteenth century, Prussia emerged as a great power in Europe.

PETER THE GREAT DEALS
WITH A REBELLION

During his first visit to the West, in 1697–1698, Peter received word that the Streltsy, an elite military unit stationed in Moscow, had revolted against his authority. Peter hurried home and crushed the revolt in a very savage fashion. This selection is taken from an Austrian account of how Peter dealt with the rebels.

PETER AND THE STRELTSY

How sharp was the pain, how great the indignation, to which the tsar's Majesty was mightily moved, when he knew of the rebellion of the Streltsy, betraying openly a mind panting for vengeance! He was still tarrying at Vienna, quite full of the desire of setting out for Italy; but, fervid as was his curiosity of rambling abroad, it was, nevertheless, speedily extinguished on the announcement of the troubles that had broken out in the bowels of his realm. Going immediately to Lefort . . . , he thus indignantly broke out: "Tell me, Francis, how I can reach Moscow by the shortest way, in a brief space, so that I may wreak vengeance on this great perfidy of my people, with punishments worthy of their abominable crime. Not one of them shall escape with impunity. Around my royal city, which, with their impious efforts, they planned to destroy, I will have gibbets and gallows set upon the walls and ramparts, and each and every one of them will I put to a direful death." Nor did he long delay the plan for his justly excited wrath; he took the quick post, as his

ambassador suggested, and in four weeks' time he had got over about three hundred miles without accident, and arrived the 4th of September, 1698—a monarch for the well disposed, but an avenger for the wicked.

His first anxiety after his arrival was about the rebellion—in what it consisted, what the insurgents meant, who dared to instigate such a crime. And as nobody could answer accurately upon all points, and some pleaded their own ignorance, others the obstinacy of the Streltsy, he began to have suspicions of everybody's loyalty. . . . No day, holy or profane, were the inquisitors idle; every day was deemed fit and lawful for torturing. There were as many scourges as there were accused, and every inquisitor was a butcher. . . . The whole month of October was spent in lacerating the backs of culprits with the knout and with flames; no day were those that were left alive exempt from scourging or scorching; or else they were broken upon the wheel, or driven to the gibbet, or slain with the ax. . . .

To prove to all people how holy and inviolable are those walls of the city which the Streltsy rashly meditated scaling in a sudden assault, beams were run out from all the embrasures in the walls near the gates, in each of which two rebels were hanged. This day beheld about two hundred and fifty die that death. There are few cities fortified with as many palisades as Moscow has given gibbets to her guardian Streltsy.

The Austrian Habsburgs had long played a significant role in European politics as Holy Roman emperors. By the end of the Thirty Years' War, the Habsburg hopes of creating an empire in Germany had been dashed. In the seventeenth century, the house of Austria created a new empire in eastern and southeastern Europe.

The nucleus of the new Austrian Empire remained the traditional Austrian hereditary possessions: Lower and Upper Austria, Carinthia, Carniola, Styria, and Tyrol. To these had been added the kingdom of Bohemia and parts of northwestern Hungary. After the defeat of the Turks in 1687 (see Chapter 15), Austria took control of all of Hungary, Transylvania, Croatia, and Slovenia, thus establishing the Austrian Empire in southeastern Europe. By the beginning of the eighteenth century, the house of Austria had assembled an empire of considerable size.

The Austrian monarchy, however, never became a highly centralized, absolutist state, primarily because it contained so many different national groups. The Austrian Empire remained a collection of territories held together by the Hapburg emperor, who was archduke of Austria, king of Bohemia, and king of Hungary. Each of these regions, however, had its own laws and political life.

FROM MOSCOW TO RUSSIA

A new Russian state had emerged in the fifteenth century under the leadership of the principality of Moscow and its grand dukes. In the sixteenth century, Ivan IV (1533–1584) became the first ruler to take the title of *tsar* (the Russian word for *Caesar*). Ivan expanded the territories of Russia eastward and crushed the power of the Russian nobility. He was known as Ivan the Terrible because of his ruthless deeds, among them stabbing his son to death in a heated argument. When Ivan's dynasty came to an end in 1598, it was followed by a period of anarchy that did not end until the Zemsky Sobor (national assembly) chose Michael Romanov as the new tsar, establishing a dynasty that lasted until 1917. One of its most prominent members was Peter the Great.

Peter the Great (1689–1725) was an unusual character. A towering, strong man at 6 feet 9 inches tall, Peter enjoyed a low kind of humor—belching contests and crude jokes—and vicious punishments, including floggings, impalings, and roastings (see the box above). Peter received a firsthand view of the West when he made a trip there in 1697–1698 and returned to Russia with a firm determination to westernize or Europeanize Russia. He was especially eager to borrow European technology in order to give him the army and navy he needed to make Russia a great power.

As could be expected, one of his first priorities was the reorganization of the army and the creation of a navy. Employing both Russians and Europeans as officers, he conscripted peasants for twenty-five-year stints of service to build a standing army of 210,000 men. Peter has also been given credit for forming the first Russian navy.

To impose the rule of the central government more effectively throughout the land, Peter divided Russia into provinces. Although he hoped to create a "police state," by which he meant a well-ordered community governed in accordance with law, few of his bureaucrats shared his concept of duty to the state. Peter hoped for a sense of civic duty, but his own forceful personality created an atmosphere of fear that prevented it.

The object of Peter's domestic reforms was to make Russia into a great state and military power. His primary goal was to "open a window to the west," meaning an ice-free port easily accessible to Europe. This could only be achieved on the Baltic, but at that time, the Baltic coast was controlled by Sweden, the most important power in northern Europe. A long and hard-fought war with Sweden won Peter the lands he sought. In 1703, Peter began the construction of a new city, Saint Petersburg, his window to the west and a symbol that Russia was looking westward to Europe. Under Peter, Russia became a great military power and, by his death in 1725, an important European state.

ENGLAND AND THE EMERGENCE OF CONSTITUTIONAL MONARCHY

Not all states were absolutist in the seventeenth century. One of the most prominent examples of resistance to absolute monarchy came in England, where king and Parliament struggled to determine the roles each should play in governing England.

Revolution and Civil War

With the death of Queen Elizabeth I in 1603, the Tudor dynasty became extinct, and the Stuart line of rulers was inaugurated with the accession to the throne of Elizabeth's cousin, King James VI of Scotland, who became James I (1603–1625) of England. James espoused the divine right of kings, a viewpoint that alienated Parliament, which had grown accustomed under the Tudors to act on the premise that monarch and Parliament together ruled England as a "balanced polity." Then, too, the Puritans—Protestants within the Anglican church who, inspired by Calvinist theology, wished to eliminate every trace of Roman Catholicism from the Church of England—were alienated by the king's strong defense of the Anglican church. Much of England's gentry, mostly well-to-do landowners, had become Puritans, and this Puritan gentry formed an important and substantial part of the House of Commons, the lower house of Parliament. It was not wise to alienate these men.

The conflict that had begun during the reign of James came to a head during the reign of his son Charles I (1625–1649). Charles also believed in divine-right monarchy, and religious differences also added to the hostility between Charles I and Parliament. The attempt of Charles to impose more ritual on the Anglican church struck the Puritans as a return to Catholic practices. When Charles tried to force the Puritans to accept his religious policies, thousands of them went off to the "howling wildernesses" of America.

Grievances mounted until England finally slipped into a civil war (1642–1648) won by the parliamentary forces, due largely to the New Model Army of Oliver Cromwell, the only real military genius of the war. The New Model Army was composed primarily of more extreme Puritans known as the Independents, who, in typical Calvinist fashion, believed they were doing battle for God. As Cromwell wrote in one of his military reports, "Sir, this is none other but the hand of God; and to Him alone belongs the glory." We might give some credit to Cromwell; his soldiers were well trained in the new military tactics of the seventeenth century.

Civil War in England

0   150   300 Kilometers

0   125   250 Miles

North Sea

SCOTLAND

Edinburgh

IRELAND

ENGLAND

Cambridge

Oxford   London

English Channel

☐ Area supporting Parliament, 1643

☐ Area supporting Royalists, 1643

After the execution of Charles I on January 30, 1649, Parliament abolished the monarchy and the House of Lords and proclaimed England a republic or commonwealth. But Cromwell and his army, unable to work effectively with Parliament, dispersed it by force and established a military dictatorship. After Cromwell's death in 1658, the army decided that military rule was no longer feasible and restored the monarchy in the person of Charles II, the son of Charles I.

Restoration and a Glorious Revolution

Charles was sympathetic to Catholicism, and Parliament's suspicions were aroused in 1672 when Charles took the audacious step of issuing the Declaration of Indulgence, which suspended the laws that Parliament had passed against Catholics and Puritans after the restoration of the monarchy. Parliament forced the king to suspend the declaration.

THE BILL OF RIGHTS

*I*n 1688, the English experienced yet another revolution, a bloodless one in which the Stuart king James II was replaced by Mary, James's daughter, and her husband, William of Orange. After William and Mary had assumed power, Parliament passed a Bill of Rights that specified the rights of Parliament and laid the foundation for a constitutional monarchy.

THE BILL OF RIGHTS

Whereas the said late King James II having abdicated the government, and the throne being thereby vacant, his Highness the prince of Orange (whom it hath pleased Almighty God to make the glorious instrument of delivering this kingdom from popery and arbitrary power) did (by the device of the lords spiritual and temporal, and diverse principal persons of the Commons) cause letters to be written to the lords spiritual and temporal, being Protestants, and other letters to the several counties, cities, universities, boroughs, and Cinque Ports, for the choosing of such persons to represent them, as were of right to be sent to parliament, to meet and sit at Westminster upon the two and twentieth day of January, in this year 1689, in order to such an establishment as that their religion, laws, and liberties might not again be in danger of being subverted; upon which letters elections have been accordingly made.

And thereupon the said lords spiritual and temporal and Commons, pursuant to their respective letters and elections, being now assembled in a full and free representation of this nation, taking into their most serious consideration the best means for attaining the ends aforesaid, do in the first place (as their ancestors in like case have usually done), for the vindication and assertion of their ancient rights and liberties, declare:

1. That the pretended power of suspending laws, or the execution of laws, by regal authority, without consent of parliament is illegal.

2. That the pretended power of dispensing with the laws, or the execution of law by regal authority, as it hath been assumed and exercised of late, is illegal.

3. That the commission for erecting the late court of commissioners for ecclesiastical causes, and all other commissions and courts of like nature, are illegal and pernicious.

4. That levying money for or to the use of the crown by pretense of prerogative, without grant of parliament, for longer time or in other manner than the same is or shall be granted, is illegal.

5. That it is the right of the subjects to petition the king, and all commitments and prosecutions for such petitioning are illegal.

6. That the raising or keeping a standing army within the kingdom in time of peace, unless it be with consent of parliament, is against law.

7. That the subjects which are Protestants may have arms for their defense suitable to their conditions, and as allowed by law.

8. That election of members of parliament ought to be free.

9. That the freedom of speech, and debates or proceedings in parliament, ought not to be impeached or questioned in any court or place out of parliament.

10. That excessive bail ought not to be required, nor excessive fines imposed, nor cruel and unusual punishments inflicted.

11. That jurors ought to be duly impaneled and returned, and jurors which pass upon men in trials for high treason ought to be freeholders.

12. That all grants and promises of fines and forfeitures of particular persons before conviction are illegal and void.

13. And that for redress of all grievances, and for the amending, strengthening, and preserving of the laws, parliament ought to be held frequently.

The accession of James II (1685–1688) to the crown virtually guaranteed a new constitutional crisis for England. An open and devout Catholic, his attempt to further Catholic interests made religion once more a primary cause of conflict between king and Parliament. James named Catholics to high positions in the government, army, navy, and universities. Parliamentary outcries against James's policies stopped short of rebellion because members knew that he was an old man and that his successors were his Protestant daughters Mary and Anne, born to his first wife. But on June 10, 1688, a son was born to James II's second wife, also a Catholic. Suddenly the specter of a Catholic hereditary monarchy loomed large. A group of prominent English noblemen invited the Dutch chief executive,

William of Orange, husband of James's daughter Mary, to invade England. William and Mary raised an army and invaded England while James, his wife, and their infant son fled to France. With little bloodshed, England had undergone its "Glorious Revolution."

In January 1689, Parliament offered the throne to William and Mary, who accepted it along with the provisions of a bill of rights (see the box above). The Bill of Rights affirmed Parliament's right to make laws and levy taxes. The rights of citizens to keep arms and have a jury trial were also confirmed. By deposing one king and establishing another, Parliament had destroyed the divine-right theory of kingship (William was, after all, king by grace of Parliament, not God) and asserted its right to participate

© Réunion des Musées Nationaux/Art Resource, NY

PETER PAUL RUBENS, *THE LANDING OF MARIE DE' MEDICI AT MARSEILLES.* Peter Paul Rubens played a key role in spreading the Baroque style from Italy to other parts of Europe. In *The Landing of Marie de' Medici at Marseilles*, Rubens made a dramatic use of light and color, bodies in motion, and luxurious nudes to heighten the emotional intensity of the scene. This was one of a cycle of twenty-one paintings dedicated to the queen mother of France.

in the government. Parliament did not have complete control of the government, but it now had the right to participate in affairs of state. Over the next century, it would gradually prove to be the real authority in the English system of constitutional monarchy.

EUROPEAN CULTURE

Art and intellectual activity experienced dramatic changes in the sixteenth and seventeenth centuries. Especially important in developing a new view of the world was the Scientific Revolution.

Art: The Baroque

The artistic movement known as the Baroque dominated the Western artistic world for a century and a half. The Baroque began in Italy in the last quarter of the sixteenth century and spread to the rest of Europe and Latin America. Baroque artists sought to harmonize the classical ideals of Renaissance art with the spiritual feelings of the sixteenth-century religious revival. In large part, Baroque art and architecture reflected the search for power that was characteristic of much of the seventeenth century. Baroque churches and palaces featured richly ornamented facades, sweeping stair-

cases, and an overall splendor meant to impress people. Kings and princes wanted not only their subjects but also other kings and princes to be in awe of their power.

Baroque painting was known for its use of dramatic effects to arouse the emotions, especially evident in the works of Peter Paul Rubens (1577–1640), a prolific artist and an important figure in the spread of the Baroque from Italy to other parts of Europe. In his artistic masterpieces, bodies in violent motion, heavily fleshed nudes, a dramatic use of light and shadow, and rich sensuous pigments converge to express intense emotions.

A Golden Age of Literature in England

In England, writing for the stage reached new heights between 1580 and 1640. The golden age of English literature is often called the Elizabethan Era because much of the English cultural flowering occurred during her reign. Of all the forms of Elizabethan literature, none expressed the energy and intellectual versatility of the era better than drama. And no dramatist is more famous or more accomplished than William Shakespeare (1564–1614).

WILLIAM SHAKESPEARE: IN PRAISE OF ENGLAND

William Shakespeare is one of the most famous play-wrights in the Western world. He was a universal genius, outclassing all others in his psychological insights, depth of characterization, imaginative skills, and versatility. His historical plays reflected the patriotic enthusiasm of the English in the Elizabethan Era, as this excerpt from Richard II illustrates.

WILLIAM SHAKESPEARE, RICHARD II

This royal throne of kings, this sceptered isle,
This earth of majesty, this seat of Mars,
This other Eden, demi-Paradise,
This fortress built by Nature for herself
Against infection and the hand of war,
This happy breed of men, this little world,
This precious stone set in the silver sea,
Which serves it in the office of a wall
Or as a moat defensive to a house
Against the envy of less happier lands—
This blessed plot, this earth, this realm, this England,

This nurse, this teeming womb of royal kings,
Feared by their breed and famous by their birth,
Renowned for their deeds as far from home,
For Christian service and true chivalry,
As is the sepulcher in stubborn Jewry [the Holy Sepulcher in Jerusalem]
Of the world's ransom, blessed Mary's Son—
This land of such dear souls, this dear dear land,
Dear for her reputation through the world,
Is now leased out, I die pronouncing it,
Like a tenement or pelting farm.
England, bound in with the triumphant sea,
Whose rocky shore beats back the envious siege
Of watery Neptune, is now bound in with shame,
With inky blots and rotten parchment bonds.
That England, that was wont to conquer others,
Hath made a shameful conquest of itself.
Ah, would the scandal vanish with my life,
How happy then were my ensuing death!

Shakespeare was a "complete man of the theater." Although best known for writing plays, he was also an actor and a shareholder in the chief acting company of the time, the Lord Chamberlain's Company, which played in various London theaters. Shakespeare is to this day hailed as a genius. A master of the English language, he imbued its words with power and majesty. And his technical proficiency was matched by incredible insight into human psychology. Whether writing tragedies or comedies, Shakespeare exhibited a remarkable understanding of the human condition (see the box above).

The Scientific Revolution

In the Middles Ages, many educated Europeans took an intense interest in the world around them. But these "natural philosophers," as medieval scientists were known, relied on a few ancient authorities, especially Aristotle, and preferred refined logical analysis to systematic observations of the natural world. A number of changes and advances in the fifteenth and sixteenth centuries may have played a major role in helping "natural philosophers" abandon their old views and develop new ones.

The Renaissance humanists mastered Greek and Latin and made available new works of Galen, Ptolemy, Archimedes, and Plato. These writings made it apparent that some ancient thinkers had disagreed with Aristotle and other accepted authorities of the Middle Ages.

Other developments also encouraged new ways of thinking. Technical problems, such as calculating the tonnage of ships accurately, served to stimulate scientific activity because they required careful observations and precise measurements. The invention of new instruments and machines, such as the telescope and the microscope, made fresh scientific discoveries possible. And the printing press played a crucial role in spreading innovative ideas quickly and easily.

The study of mathematics, which spurred the scientific achievements of the sixteenth and seventeenth centuries, was promoted in the Renaissance by the rediscovery of the works of ancient mathematicians. Copernicus, Kepler, Galileo, and Newton were all great mathematicians who believed that the secrets of nature would be revealed through the language of mathematics. The mention of these names also reminds us that the Scientific Revolution was largely the work of a few great intellectuals.

TOWARD A NEW HEAVEN: A REVOLUTION IN ASTRONOMY

The philosophers of the Middle Ages had used the ideas of Aristotle, Ptolemy (the greatest astronomer of antiquity, who lived in the second century C.E.), and Christianity to construct the Ptolemaic or geocentric conception of the universe. In this conception, the universe was seen as a series of concentric spheres with a fixed or

MEDIEVAL CONCEPTION OF THE UNIVERSE. As this sixteenth-century illustration shows, the medieval cosmological view placed the earth at the center of the universe, surrounded by a series of concentric spheres. The earth was imperfect and constantly changing, while the heavenly bodies that surrounded it were perfect and incorruptible. Beyond the tenth and final sphere was heaven, where God and all the saved souls were located.

THE COPERNICAN SYSTEM. The Copernican system was presented in *On the Revolutions of the Heavenly Spheres*, published shortly before Copernicus's death. As shown in this illustration from the first edition of the book, Copernicus maintained that the sun was the center of the universe while the planets, including the earth, revolved around it. Moreover, the earth rotated daily on its axis.

motionless earth at its center. Composed of material substance, the earth was imperfect and constantly changing. The spheres that surrounded the earth were made of a crystalline, transparent substance and moved in circular orbits around the earth. These heavenly bodies, pure orbs of light, were embedded in the moving, concentric spheres and in 1500 numbered ten. Working outward from the earth, the first eight spheres contained the moon, Mercury, Venus, the sun, Mars, Jupiter, Saturn, and the fixed stars. The ninth sphere imparted to the eighth sphere of the fixed stars its daily motion, while the tenth sphere was frequently described as the prime mover that moved itself and imparted motion to the other spheres. Beyond the tenth sphere was the Empyrean Heaven—the location of God and all the saved souls. God and the saved souls were at one end of the universe, then, and humans were at the center. They had power over the earth, but their real purpose was to achieve salvation.

Nicholas Copernicus (1473–1543), a native of Poland, was a mathematician who felt that Ptolemy's geocentric system failed to accord with the observed motions of the heavenly bodies and hoped that his heliocentric (sun-centered) conception would offer a more accurate explanation. Copernicus argued that the sun was motionless at the

center of the universe. The planets revolved around the sun in the order of Mercury, Venus, the earth, Mars, Jupiter, and Saturn. The moon, however, revolved around the earth. Moreover, what appeared to be the movement of the sun around the earth was really explained by the daily rotation of the earth on its axis and the journey of the earth around the sun each year. But Copernicus did not reject the idea that the heavenly spheres moved in circular orbits, and his system did not work considerably better than the Ptolemaic system.

The next step in destroying the geocentric conception and supporting the Copernican system was taken by Johannes Kepler (1571–1630). A brilliant German mathematician and astronomer, Kepler arrived at laws of planetary motion that confirmed Copernicus's heliocentric theory. In his first law, however, he contradicted Copernicus by showing that the orbits of the planets around the sun were not circular but elliptical, with the sun at one focus of the ellipse rather than at the center.

Kepler's work destroyed the basic structure of the Ptolemaic system. People could now think in new terms of the actual paths of planets revolving around the sun in elliptical orbits. But important questions remained unanswered. What were the planets made of? And how does

THE STARRY MESSENGER

The Italian Galileo Galilei was the first European to use a telescope to make systematic observations of the heavens. His observations, as reported in The Starry Messenger *in 1610, stunned European intellectuals by revealing that the celestial bodies were not perfect and immutable, as had been believed, but were apparently composed of materials similar to the earth. In this selection, Galileo describes how he devised a telescope and what he saw with it.*

GALILEO GALILEI, *THE STARRY MESSENGER*

About ten months ago a report reached my ears that a certain Fleming had constructed a spyglass by means of which visible objects, though very distant from the eye of the observer, were distinctly seen as if nearby. Of this truly remarkable effect several experiences were related, to which some persons gave credence while others denied them. A few days later the report was confirmed to me in a letter from a noble Frenchman at Paris, Jacques Badovere, which caused me to apply myself wholeheartedly to inquire into the means by which I might arrive at the invention of a similar instrument. This I did shortly afterwards, my basis being the theory of refraction. First I prepared a tube of lead, at the ends of which I fitted two glass lenses, both plane on one side while on the other side one was spherically convex and the other concave. Then placing my eye near the concave lens I perceived objects satisfactorily large and near, for they appeared three times closer and nine times larger than when seen with the naked eye alone. Next I constructed another one, more accurate, which represented objects as enlarged more than sixty times. Finally, sparing neither labor nor expense, I succeeded in constructing for myself so excellent an instrument that objects seen by means of it appeared nearly one thousand times larger and over thirty times closer than when regarded with our natural vision.

It would be superfluous to enumerate the number and importance of the advantages of such an instrument at sea as well as on land. But forsaking terrestrial observations, I turned to celestial ones, and first saw the moon from as near at hand as if it were scarcely two terrestrial radii. After that I observed often with wondering delight both the planets and the fixed stars, and since I saw these latter to be very crowded, I began to seek (and eventually found) a method by which I might measure their distances apart. . . .

Now let us review the observations made during the past two months, once more inviting the attention of all who are eager for true philosophy to the first steps of such important contemplations. Let us speak first of that surface of the moon which faces us. For greater clarity I distinguish two parts of this surface, a lighter and a darker; the lighter part seems to surround and to pervade the whole hemisphere, while the darker part discolors the moon's surface like a kind of cloud, and makes it appear covered with spots. . . . From observation of these spots repeated many times I have been led to the opinion and conviction that the surface of the moon is not smooth, uniform, and precisely spherical as a great number of philosophers believe it (and the other heavenly bodies) to be, but is uneven, rough, and full of cavities and prominences, being not unlike the face of the earth, relieved by chains of mountains and deep valleys.

---

one explain motion in the universe? An Italian scientist achieved the next important breakthrough to a new cosmology by answering the first question.

Galileo Galilei (1564–1642) taught mathematics and was the first European to make systematic observations of the heavens by means of a telescope, inaugurating a new age in astronomy. Galileo turned his telescope to the skies and made a remarkable series of discoveries: mountains on the moon, four moons revolving around Jupiter, and sunspots. Galileo's observations seemed to destroy yet another aspect of the traditional cosmology in that the universe seemed to be composed of material similar to that of earth rather than a perfect and unchanging substance.

Galileo's revelations, published in *The Starry Messenger* in 1610, made Europeans aware of a new picture of the universe (see the box above). But in the midst of his newfound acclaim, Galileo found himself under increasing suspicion by the authorities of the Catholic church. The Catholic church condemned Copernicanism and ordered Galileo to abandon the Copernican thesis. The church attacked the Copernican system because it threatened not only Scripture but also an entire conception of the universe. The heavens were no longer a spiritual world but a world of matter.

By the 1630s and 1640s, most astronomers had come to accept the new heliocentric conception of the universe. Nevertheless, the problem of explaining motion in the universe and tying together the ideas of Copernicus, Galileo, and Kepler had not yet been done. This would be the work of an Englishman who has long been considered the greatest genius of the Scientific Revolution.

Born in 1642, Isaac Newton attended Cambridge University, where he later accepted a chair in mathematics and wrote his major work, *Mathematical Principles of Natural Philosophy*, known simply as the *Principia* by the first word of its Latin title. In the first book of the *Principia*, Newton defined the three laws of motion that govern the planetary bodies, as well as objects on earth. Crucial to his whole argument was the universal law of gravitation, which explained why the planetary bodies did not go off in straight lines but continued in elliptical orbits about the sun. In mathematical terms, Newton explained that every object in the universe is attracted to every other object by a force called gravity.

Newton had demonstrated that one mathematically proven universal law could explain all motion in the universe. At the same time, the Newtonian synthesis created a new cosmology in which the universe was seen as one huge, regulated machine that operated according to natural laws in absolute time, space, and motion. Newton's world-machine concept dominated the modern worldview until the twentieth century, when Albert Einstein's concept of relativity created a new picture of the universe.

WOMEN IN THE ORIGINS OF MODERN SCIENCE

Women as well as men were involved in the Scientific Revolution. One of the most prominent female scientists of the seventeenth century, Margaret Cavendish (1623–1673), came from an aristocratic background. Cavendish was a participant in the crucial scientific debates of her time. She wrote a number of works on scientific matters, including *Observations upon Experimental Philosophy* and *Grounds of Natural Philosophy*. In these works, she was especially critical of the growing belief that humans through science were the masters of nature: "We have no power at all over natural causes and effects. . . . For man is but a small part, . . . his powers are but particular actions of Nature, and he cannot have a supreme and absolute power."[7]

In Germany, many of the women interested in science were astronomers. The most famous was Maria Winkelmann (1670–1720). She was educated by her father and uncle and received training in astronomy from a nearby self-taught astronomer. Her opportunity to be a practicing astronomer came when she married Gottfried Kirch, Germany's foremost astronomer. She became his assistant at the astronomical observatory operated in Berlin by the Academy of Science. She made some original contributions, including a hitherto undiscovered comet, as her husband related:

> Early in the morning (about 2:00 A.M.) the sky was clear and starry. Some nights before, I had observed a variable star, and my wife (as I slept) wanted to find and see it for herself. In so doing, she found a comet in the sky. At which time she woke me, and I found that it was indeed a comet. . . . I was surprised that I had not seen it the night before.[8]

When her husband died in 1710, Winkelmann applied for a position as assistant astronomer at the Berlin Academy, for which she was highly qualified. As a woman—with no university degree—she was denied the post by the academy's members, who feared that it would establish a precedent by hiring a woman ("mouths would gape").

Winkelmann's difficulties with the Berlin Academy reflect the obstacles women faced in being accepted in scientific work, which was considered a male preserve. All of these women scientists were exceptional women because a life devoted to any kind of scholarship was still viewed as at odds with the domestic duties women were expected to perform.

TOWARD NEW EARTH: DESCARTES AND RATIONALISM

The new conception of the universe contained in the cosmological revolution of the sixteenth and seventeenth centuries inevitably had an impact on the Western view of humankind. Nowhere is this more evident than in the work of the French philosopher René Descartes (1596–1650). The starting point for Descartes's new system was doubt. As Descartes explained at the beginning of his most famous work, *Discourse on Method*, written in 1637, he decided to set aside all that he had learned and begin again. One fact seemed to Descartes beyond doubt—his own existence:

> But I immediately became aware that while I was thus disposed to think that all was false, it was absolutely necessary that I who thus thought should be something; and noting that this truth *I think, therefore I am*, was so steadfast and so assured that the suppositions of the skeptics, to whatever extreme they might all be carried, could not avail to shake it, I concluded that I might without scruple accept it as being the first principle of the philosophy I was seeking.[9]

With this emphasis on the mind, Descartes asserted that he would accept only things that his reason said were true.

From his first postulate, Descartes deduced an additional principle, the separation of mind and matter. Descartes argued that since "the mind cannot be doubted but the body and material world can, the two must be radically different." From this came an absolute dualism between mind and matter, or what has also been called Cartesian dualism. Using mind or human reason and its best instrument, mathematics, humans can understand the material world because it is pure mechanism, a machine that is governed by its own physical laws because it was created by God—the great geometrician.

Descartes's separation of mind and matter allowed scientists to view matter as dead or inert, as something that was totally separate from themselves and could be investigated independently by reason. The split between mind and body led Westerners to equate their identity with mind and reason rather than with the whole organism. Descartes has rightly been called the father of modern rationalism.

THE SPREAD OF SCIENTIFIC KNOWLEDGE

In the course of the Scientific Revolution, attention was paid to the problem of establishing the proper means to examine and understand the physical realm. The result was the creation of a scientific method—a way to examine and understand nature—that was crucial to the evolution of science in the modern world. Curiously enough, it was an Englishman with few scientific credentials who developed a scientific method that became widely used. Francis Bacon (1561–1626), a lawyer, believed that a correct scientific method should be built on inductive principles, which means that scientists should proceed from the particular to the general. Carefully organized experiments and systematic, thorough observations would lead to correct general principles.

Bacon was clear about what he believed his scientific method could accomplish. He stated that "the true and lawful goal of the sciences is none other than this: that human life be endowed with new discoveries and power." He wanted science to contribute to the "mechanical arts" by creating devices that would benefit industry, agriculture, and trade. Bacon was prophetic when he said that "I am laboring to lay the foundation, not of any sect or doctrine, but of human utility and power." And how would this "human power" be used? To "conquer nature in action."[10] The control and domination of nature became a central proposition of modern science and the technology that accompanied it.

The spread of scientific ideas to a wide public was greatly aided by the new scientific societies. The English Royal Society evolved out of informal gatherings of scientists at London and Oxford in the 1640s. It received little government support, and its fellows simply co-opted new members. The French Royal Academy of Sciences, in contrast, received abundant state support and remained under government control. Both the English and French societies showed that science should proceed along the lines of a cooperative venture.

EUROPE, CHINA, AND SCIENTIFIC REVOLUTIONS

An interesting question that arises is why the Scientific Revolution occurred in Europe and not in China. In the Middle Ages, China had been the most technologically advanced civilization in the world. After 1500, that distinction passed to the West. Historians are not sure why.

LOUIS XIV AND COLBERT VISIT THE ACADEMY OF SCIENCES.   In the seventeenth century, individual scientists received royal and princely patronage, and a number of learned societies were established. In France, Louis XIV, urged on by his minister Colbert, gave formal recognition to the French Academy in 1666. In this painting by Henri Testelin, Louis XIV is shown seated, surrounded by Colbert and members of the French Royal Academy of Sciences.

Some have compared the sense of order in Chinese society to the competitive spirit existing in Europe. Others have emphasized China's ideological viewpoint that favored living in harmony with nature rather than trying to dominate it. One historian has even suggested that China's civil service system drew the "best and the brightest" into government service, to the detriment of other occupations.

CONCLUSION

In the next chapter, we will examine how the movement of Europeans outside of Europe began to change the shape of world history. But what had made this development possible? After all, the religious division of Europe had led to almost a hundred years of religious warfare complicated by serious political, economic, and social issues before Europeans finally admitted that they would have to accept different ways to worship God.

At the same time, the concept of a united Christendom, held as an ideal since the Middle Ages, had been irrevocably destroyed by the religious wars, enabling a system of nation-states to emerge in which power politics took on increasing significance. Within those states slowly emerged some of the machinery that made possible a growing centralization of power. In those states called absolutist, strong monarchs with the assistance of their aristocracies took the lead in providing the leadership for greater centralization. In all the major European states, a growing concern for power led to larger armies and greater conflict, stronger economies, and more powerful governments. From a global point of view, the political and economic power of Europeans was beginning to slowly outstrip that of other peoples.

The Scientific Revolution also represents a major turning point in modern civilization. With a new conception of the universe came a new conception of humankind. The work of Descartes and Bacon left Europeans with the separation of mind and matter and the belief that by using only reason they could understand and dominate the world of nature. Combined with the eighteenth-century Enlightenment (see Chapter 17) the Scientific Revolution gave the West an intellectual boost that contributed to the increased confidence of Western civilization. Europeans—with their strong governments, prosperous economies, and strengthened military forces—began to dominate other parts of the world, leading to a growing belief in the superiority of their civilization.

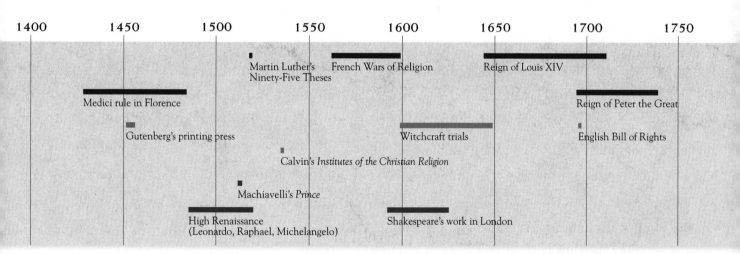

CHAPTER NOTES

1. Quoted in Jacob Burckhardt, *The Civilization of the Renaissance in Italy,* trans. S. G. C. Middlemore (London, 1960), p. 81.
2. Niccolò Machiavelli, *The Prince,* trans. David Wootton (Indianapolis, Ind., 1995), p. 48.
3. Quoted in Roland Bainton, *Here I Stand: A Life of Martin Luther* (New York, 1950), p. 144.
4. John Calvin, *Institutes of the Christian Religion,* trans. John Allen (Philadelphia, 1936), vol. 1, p. 228; vol. 2, p. 181.
5. Quoted in Bonnie S. Anderson and Judith P. Zinsser, *A History of Their Own: Women in Europe from Prehistory to the Present* (New York, 1988), vol. 1, p. 259.
6. Quoted in Joseph Klaits, *Servants of Satan: The Age of Witch Hunts* (Bloomington, Ind., 1985), p. 68.
7. Quoted in Londa Schiebinger, *The Mind Has No Sex? Women in the Origins of Modern Science* (Cambridge, Mass., 1989), pp. 52–53.

8. Ibid., p. 85.
9. René Descartes, *Philosophical Writing*, ed. and trans. Norman K. Smith (New York, 1958), pp. 118–119.

10. Francis Bacon, *The Great Instauration*, trans. Jerry Weinberger (Arlington Heights, Ill., 1989), pp. 2, 8, 2, 16, 21.

SUGGESTED READING

The classic study of the Italian Renaissance is J. Burckhardt, *The Civilization of the Renaissance in Italy* (London, 1960), first published in 1860. General works on the Renaissance in Europe include D. L. Jensen, *Renaissance Europe*, 2d ed. (Lexington, Mass., 1991); P. Burke, *The European Renaissance: Centres and Peripheries* (Oxford, 1998); J. R. Hale, *The Civilization of Europe in the Renaissance* (New York, 1994); and the classic work by M. P. Gilmore, *The World of Humanism, 1453–1517* (New York, 1962). For a good summary of recent literature on the Renaissance, see P. Burke, *The Renaissance* (New York, 1997). For beautifully illustrated introductions to the Renaissance, see G. Holmes, *Renaissance* (New York, 1996), and M. Aston, ed., *The Panorama of the Renaissance* (New York, 1996).

Numerous facets of social life in the Renaissance are examined in J. R. Hale, *Renaissance Europe: The Individual and Society* (London, 1971). On family and marriage, see D. Herlihy, *The Family in Renaissance Italy* (St. Louis, Mo., 1974), and the valuable C. Klapisch-Zuber, *Women, Family, and Ritual in Renaissance Italy* (Chicago, 1985). Women are examined in M. L. King, *Women of the Renaissance* (Chicago, 1991).

Brief introductions to Renaissance humanism can be found in D. Kelley, *Renaissance Humanism* (Boston, 1991), and C. G. Nauert Jr., *Humanism and the Culture of Renaissance Europe* (Cambridge, 1995). The impact of printing is exhaustively examined in E. Eisenstein, *The Printing Press as an Agent of Change*, 2 vols. (New York, 1978). Good surveys of Renaissance art include R. Turner, *Renaissance Florence: The Invention of a New Art* (New York, 1997); F. Hartt, *History of Italian Renaissance Art*, 4th ed. (Englewood Cliffs, N.J., 1994); and L. Murray, *The High Renaissance* (New York, 1967).

For a general work on the political development of Europe in the Renaissance, see J. H. Shennan, *The Origins of the Modern European State, 1450–1725* (London, 1974). On France, see D. Potter, *A History of France, 1460–1560* (London, 1995). Early Renaissance England is examined in J. R. Lander, *Crown and Nobility, 1450–1509* (London, 1976). Good coverage of Renaissance Spain can be found in J. N. Hillgarth, *The Spanish Kingdoms, 1250–1516*, vol. 2, *Castilian Hegemony, 1410–1516* (New York, 1978). The best overall study of the Italian states is L. Martines, *Power and Imagination: City-States in Renaissance Italy* (New York, 1979). Machiavelli's life can be examined in Q. Skinner, *Machiavelli* (Oxford, 1981).

Basic surveys of the Reformation period include H. J. Grimm, *The Reformation Era, 1500–1650*, 2d ed. (New York, 1973); D. L. Jensen, *Reformation Europe*, 2d ed. (Lexington, Mass., 1990); G. R. Elton, *Reformation Europe, 1517–1559* (Cleveland, Ohio, 1963); C. Lindberg, *The European Reformations* (Cambridge, Mass., 1996); and E. Cameron, *The European Reformation* (New York, 1991). Also see the interesting and useful book by S. Ozment, *Protestants: The Birth of a Revolution* (New York, 1992).

The classic account of Martin Luther's life is R. Bainton, *Here I Stand: A Life of Martin Luther* (New York, 1950). More recent works include J. M. Kittelson, *Luther the Reformer: The Story of the Man and His Career* (Minneapolis, Minn., 1986), and H. A. Oberman, *Luther: Man Between God and the Devil* (New York, 1992). The most comprehensive account of the various groups and individuals who are called Anabaptist is G. H. Williams, *The Radical Reformation*, 2d ed. (Kirksville, Mo., 1992). Two worthwhile surveys of the English Reformation are A. G. Dickens, *The English Reformation*, 2d ed. (New York, 1989), and G. R. Elton, *Reform and Reformation: England, 1509–1558* (Cambridge, Mass., 1977). On John Calvin, see A. McGrath, *A Life of John Calvin: A Study in the Shaping of Western Culture* (Cambridge, Mass., 1990), and W. J. Bouwsma, *John Calvin* (New York, 1988).

On the impact of the Reformation on the family, see J. F. Harrington, *Reordering Marriage and Society in Reformation Germany* (New York, 1995). A good introduction to the Catholic Reformation can be found in M. R. O'Connell, *The Counter-Reformation, 1559–1610* (New York, 1974).

On the French Wars of Religion, see M. P. Holt, *The French Wars of Religion, 1562–1629* (New York, 1995), and R. J. Knecht, *The French Wars of Religion, 1559–1598*, 2d ed. (New York, 1996). A good biography of Philip II is G. Parker, *Philip II*, 3d ed. (Chicago, 1995). Elizabeth's reign can be examined in C. Haigh, *Elizabeth I*, 2d ed. (New York, 1998). On the Thirty Years' War, see G. Parker, *The Thirty Years' War*, 2d ed. (London, 1997), and R. G. Asch, *The Thirty Years' War: The Holy Roman Empire and Europe, 1618–1648* (New York, 1997). A good general work on the period of the English Revolution is M. A. Kishlansky, *A Monarchy Transformed* (London, 1996).

Witchcraft hysteria can be examined in J. B. Russell, *A History of Witchcraft* (London, 1980), and B. P. Levack, *The Witch-Hunt in Early Modern Europe* (London, 1987).

For brief accounts of seventeenth-century French history, see R. Briggs, *Early Modern France, 1560–1715* (Oxford, 1977), and J. B. Collins, *The State in Early Modern France* (Cambridge, 1995). A solid and very readable biography of Louis XIV is J. B. Wolf, *Louis XIV* (New York, 1968). For a brief study, see P. R. Campbell, *Louis XIV, 1661–1715* (London, 1993). On the creation of an Austrian state, see R. J. W. Evans, *The Making of the Habsburg Monarchy, 1550–1700* (Oxford, 1979), and C. Ingrao, *The Habsburg Monarchy, 1618–1815* (Cambridge, 1994). F. L. Carsten, *The Origins of Prussia* (Oxford, 1954), remains an outstanding study of early Prussian history. Works on Peter the Great include M. S. Anderson, *Peter the Great*, 2d ed. (New York, 1995), and L. Hughes, *Russia in the Age of Peter the Great* (New Haven, Conn., 1998). On England, see W. A. Speck, *The Revolution of 1688* (Oxford, 1988).

For a general survey of Baroque culture, see J. S. Held, *Seventeenth and Eighteenth Century Art: Baroque Painting, Sculpture, Architecture* (New York, 1971). The literature on Shakespeare is enormous. For a biography, see A. L. Rowse, *The Life of Shakespeare* (New York, 1963).

Four general surveys of the Scientific Revolution are A. G. R. Smith, *Science and Society in the Sixteenth and Seventeenth Centuries* (London, 1972); J. R. Jacob, *The Scientific Revolution: Aspirations and* *Achievements, 1500–1700* (Atlantic Highlands, N.J., 1998); S. Shapin, *The Scientific Revolution* (Chicago, 1996); and J. Henry, *The Scientific Revolution and the Origins of Modern Science* (New York, 1997).

INFOTRAC COLLEGE EDITION

For additional reading, go to InfoTrac College Edition, your online research library at http://web1.infotrac-college.com

Enter the search term "Renaissance" using the Subject Guide.

Enter the search term "Reformation" using the Subject Guide.

Enter the search term "Machiavelli" using Keywords.

Enter the search terms "Martin and Luther not King" using Keywords.

Enter the search terms "Thirty Years' War" using Keywords.

Enter the search terms "Louis XIV" using Keywords.

New Encounters: The Creation of a World Market

Chapter Outline

- An Age of Exploration and Expansion
- Africa in Transition
- Southeast Asia in the Era of the Spice Trade
- Conclusion

Focus Questions

- Why did Europeans begin to embark on voyages of discovery and expansion at the end of the fifteenth century?
- How did Portugal and Spain acquire their overseas empires, and how did their empires differ?
- How and why did the Europeans expand into Africa, and what were the main consequences of their presence there?
- What were the main features of the African slave trade, and what effects did it have on Africa?
- ➤ What were the main characteristics of Southeast Asian civilization, and how was it affected by the coming of Islam and the Europeans?

*W*hen, in the spring of 1498, a local official asked the Portuguese explorer Vasco da Gama why he had come all the way to India from his homeland in Europe, he replied simply, "Christians and spices." Da Gama might have been more accurate if he had reversed the order of his objectives. As it turned out, God was probably much less important than gold and glory to Europeans like himself who participated in the Age of Exploration that was already under way. Still, da Gama's comments at Calicut were an accurate forecast of the future, for his voyage inaugurated an extended period of European expansion into Asia, led by merchant adventurers and missionaries, that lasted several hundred years and had effects that are still felt today. Eventually, it resulted in a Western takeover of existing trade routes in the Indian Ocean and the establishment of colonies throughout Asia, Africa, and Latin America. So complete did Western dominance seem that some historians assumed that the peoples of the non-Western world were mere passive recipients in this process, absorbing and assimilating the advanced knowledge of the West and offering nothing in return. Historians writing about the period after 1500 often talked metaphorically about the "impact of the West" and the "response" of non-Western peoples.

That image of impact and response, however, is not an entirely accurate description of what took place between the end of the fifteenth century and the end of the eighteenth. Although European rule was firmly established in Latin America and the island regions of Southeast Asia, traditional governments and institutions elsewhere remained largely intact and in some areas, notably South Asia and the Middle East, displayed considerable vitality. Moreover, although da Gama and his contemporaries are deservedly famous for their contribution to a new era of maritime commerce that circled the globe, they were not alone in extending the world trade network and transporting goods and ideas from one end of the earth to the other. Islam, too, was on the march, blazing new trails into Southeast Asia and across the Sahara to the civilizations that flourished along the banks of the Niger River. In this chapter, we turn our attention to the stunning expansion in the scope and volume of commercial and cultural contacts that took place in the generations preceding and following da Gama's historic voyage to India, as well as to the factors that brought about this expansion. •

AN AGE OF EXPLORATION AND EXPANSION

The voyage of Vasco da Gama has customarily been seen as a crucial step in the opening of trade routes to the East. In the sense that the voyage was a harbinger of future European participation in the spice trade, this view undoubtedly has merit. In fact, however, as has been pointed out in earlier chapters, the Indian Ocean had been a busy thoroughfare for centuries. The spice trade had been carried on by sea in the region since the days of the legendary Queen of Sheba, and Chinese junks had sailed to the area in search of cloves and nutmeg since the Tang dynasty. Then, during the early fifteenth century, Chinese fleets sailed into the Indian Ocean and all the way to the coast of East Africa in search of trade and alliances (see Chapter 16).

Islam and the Spice Trade

By the fourteenth century, a growing percentage of the spice trade was being transported in Muslim ships sailing from ports in India or the Middle East. Muslims, either Arabs or Indian converts, had taken part in the Indian Ocean trade for centuries, and by the thirteenth century, Islam had established a presence in seaports on the islands of Sumatra and Java and was gradually moving inland. In 1292, the Venetian traveler Marco Polo observed that Muslims were engaging in missionary activity in northern Sumatra: "This kingdom is so much frequented by the Saracen merchants that they have converted the natives to the Law of Mahomet—I mean the townspeople only, for the hill people live for all the world like beasts, and eat human flesh, as well as other kinds of flesh, clean or unclean."[1]

But the major impact of Islam came in the early fifteenth century with the rise of the new sultanate at Malacca, whose founder was a Muslim convert. With its strategic location astride the strait of the same name (see Map 14.1), Malacca "is a city that was made for commerce; . . . the trade and commerce between the different nations for a thousand leagues on every hand must come to Malacca,"[2] said a sixteenth-century Portuguese visitor. Within a few years, Malacca had surpassed the old Hindu state of Majapahit on the island of Java and become the leading power in the region.

Unfortunately for the Muslim traders who had come to Southeast Asia for the spice trade, others would also covet that trade. Although China's interest in the area would soon come to an end, the arrival of Vasco da Gama's fleet was a sure sign that others would soon follow. Southeast Asia was on the verge of a new era in which outside forces would compete aggressively to exploit the region's vast riches.

A New Player: Europe

For almost a millennium, Catholic Europe had been confined to one area. Its one major attempt to expand beyond those frontiers, the Crusades, had largely failed. Of course, Europe had never completely lost contact with the outside world: the goods of Asia and Africa made their way into medieval castles, the works of Muslim philosophers were read in medieval universities, and the Vikings in the ninth and tenth centuries had even explored the eastern fringes of North America. Nevertheless, Europe's contacts with non-European civilizations remained limited until the fifteenth century, when Europeans began to embark on a remarkable series of overseas journeys. What caused European seafarers to undertake such dangerous voyages to the ends of the earth?

Europeans had long been attracted to the East. In the Middle Ages, myths and legends of an exotic land of great riches and magic were widespread. Although Muslim

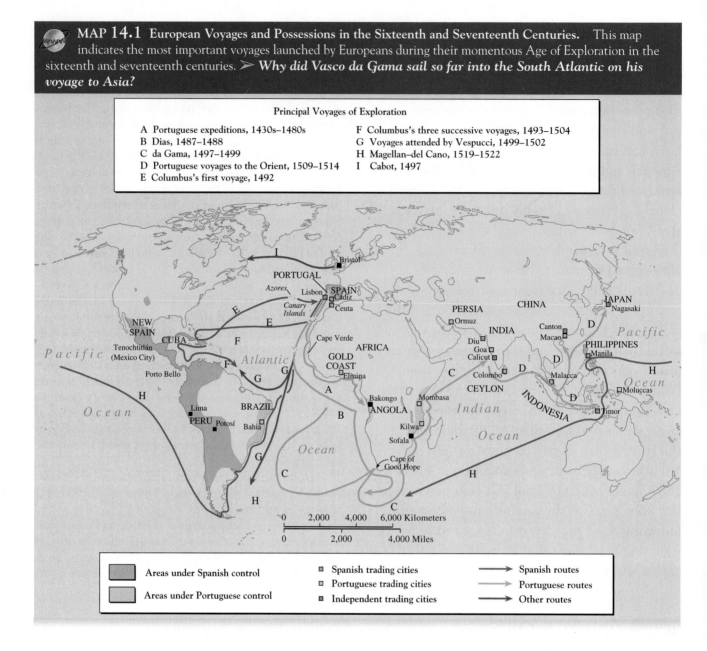

MAP 14.1 European Voyages and Possessions in the Sixteenth and Seventeenth Centuries. This map indicates the most important voyages launched by Europeans during their momentous Age of Exploration in the sixteenth and seventeenth centuries. ➤ *Why did Vasco da Gama sail so far into the South Atlantic on his voyage to Asia?*

Principal Voyages of Exploration

A Portuguese expeditions, 1430s–1480s
B Dias, 1487–1488
C da Gama, 1497–1499
D Portuguese voyages to the Orient, 1509–1514
E Columbus's first voyage, 1492
F Columbus's three successive voyages, 1493–1504
G Voyages attended by Vespucci, 1499–1502
H Magellan–del Cano, 1519–1522
I Cabot, 1497

control of Central Asia cut Europe off from the countries farther east, the Mongol conquests in the thirteenth century had reopened the doors. The most famous medieval travelers to the East were the Polos of Venice. In 1271, Nicolò and Maffeo, merchants from Venice, accompanied by Nicolò's son Marco, undertook the lengthy journey to the court of the great Mongol ruler Khubilai Khan (see Chapter 10). As one of the great Khan's ambassadors, Marco traveled to Japan as well and did not return to Italy until 1295. An account of his experiences, the *Travels*, proved to be the most informative of all the descriptions of Asia by medieval European travelers. Others, like the Franciscan friar John Plano Carpini, had preceded the Polos, but in the fourteenth century the conquests of the Ottoman Turks and then the breakup of the Mongol Empire reduced Western traffic to the East. With the clos-

ing of the overland routes, a number of people in Europe became interested in the possibility of reaching Asia by sea. Christopher Columbus had a copy of Marco Polo's *Travels* in his possession when he began to envision his epoch-making voyage across the Atlantic Ocean.

An economic motive thus looms large in Renaissance European expansion (see Chapter 13). The rise of capitalism in Europe was undoubtedly a powerful spur to the process. Merchants, adventurers, and government officials had high hopes of finding precious metals and expanding the areas of trade, especially for the spices of the East. Spices continued to be transported to Europe via Arab intermediaries but were outrageously expensive. Adventurous Europeans did not hesitate to express their desire to share in the wealth. As one Spanish conquistador explained, he and his kind went to the New World to "serve God and His Majesty, to give light to those who were in darkness, and to grow rich, as all men desire to do."[3]

This statement expresses another major reason for the overseas voyages—religious zeal. A crusading mentality was particularly strong in Portugal and Spain, where the Muslims had largely been driven out in the Middle Ages. Contemporaries of Prince Henry the Navigator of Portugal said that he was motivated by "his great desire to make increase in the faith of our Lord Jesus Christ and to bring him all the souls that should be saved." The naval academy established by the prince to promote overseas exploration was subsidized in part by a militantly anti-Muslim Christian brotherhood. Although most scholars believe that the religious motive was secondary to economic considerations, it would be foolish to overlook the genuine desire on the part of both explorers and conquistadors, let alone missionaries, to convert the heathen to Christianity. Hernán Cortés, the conqueror of Mexico, asked his Spanish rulers if it was not their duty to ensure that the native Mexicans "are introduced into and instructed in the holy Catholic faith."[4] Spiritual and secular affairs were closely intertwined in the sixteenth century. No doubt,

grandeur and glory as well as plain intellectual curiosity and a spirit of adventure also played some role in European expansion.

If "God, glory, and gold" were the primary motives, what made the voyages possible? First of all, the expansion of Europe was a state enterprise, tied to the growth of centralized monarchies during the Renaissance. By the second half of the fifteenth century, European monarchies had increased both their authority and their resources and were in a position to turn their energies beyond their borders. That meant the invasion of Italy for France, but for Portugal, a state not strong enough to pursue power in Europe, it meant going abroad. The Spanish scene was more complex, since the Spanish monarchy was strong enough by the sixteenth century to pursue power both on the Continent and beyond.

At the same time, by the end of the fifteenth century, European states had a level of knowledge and technology that enabled them to achieve a regular series of voyages beyond Europe. Although the highly schematic and symbolic medieval maps were of little help to sailors, the *portolani*, or detailed charts made by medieval navigators

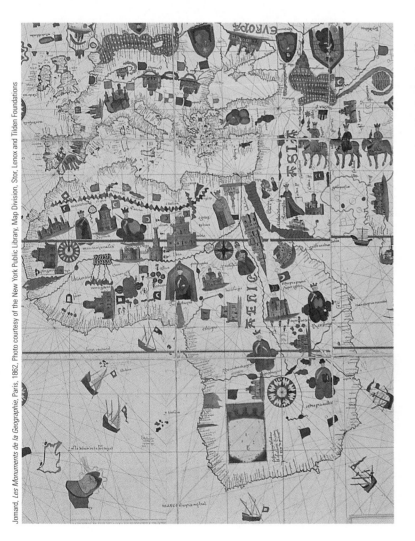

⇒ **A SIXTEENTH-CENTURY MAP OF AFRICA.** Advances in mapmaking also contributed to the European Age of Exploration. Here a section of a world map by the early-sixteenth-century Spanish cartographer Juan de la Cosa shows the continent of Africa. Note the drawing of the legendary Prester John, mentioned in Chapter 8, at the right, and the Portuguese caravels with their lateen sails in the South Atlantic Ocean.

and mathematicians in the thirteenth and fourteenth centuries, were more useful. With details on coastal contours, distances between ports, and compass readings, they proved of great value for voyages in European waters. But because the *portolani* were drawn on a flat scale and took no account of the curvature of the earth, they were of little use for longer overseas voyages. Only when seafarers began to venture beyond the coasts of Europe did they begin to accumulate information about the actual shape of the earth. By the end of the fifteenth century, cartography had developed to the point that Europeans possessed fairly accurate maps of the known world.

In addition, Europeans had developed remarkably seaworthy ships as well as new navigational techniques. European shipmakers had mastered the use of the stern-post rudder (an import from China) and had learned how to combine the use of lateen sails with a square rig. With these innovations, they could construct ships mobile enough to sail against the wind and engage in naval warfare and also large enough to mount heavy cannon and carry a substantial amount of goods over long distances. Previously, sailors had used a quadrant and their knowledge of the position of the polestar to ascertain their latitude. Below the equator, however, this technique was useless. Only with the assistance of new navigational aids such as the compass (a Chinese invention) and the astrolabe (an astronomical instrument used to measure the altitude of the sun and the stars above the horizon) were they able to explore the high seas with confidence.

A final spur to exploration was the growing knowledge of the wind patterns in the Atlantic Ocean (see Map 14.4 on p. 411). The first European fleets sailing southward along the coast of West Africa had found their efforts to return hindered by the strong winds that blew steadily from the north along the coast. By the late fifteenth cen-

➤ THE CARAVEL, WORKHORSE OF THE AGE OF EXPLORATION.   Prior to the fifteenth century, most European ships were either small craft with lateen sails used in the Mediterranean or slow, unwieldy square-rigged vessels operating in the North Atlantic. By the sixteenth century, European naval architects began to build ships that combined the maneuverability and speed offered by lateen sails (widely used by sailors in the Indian Ocean) with the carrying capacity and seaworthiness of the square-riggers. For a century, caravels were the feared "sea-raiders" of the oceans.

tury, however, sailors had learned to tack out into the ocean, where they were able to catch westerly winds in the vicinity of the Azores islands that brought them back to the coast of western Europe. Christopher Columbus used this technique in his voyages to the Americas, and others relied on their new knowledge of the winds to round the continent of Africa in search of the Spice Islands.

The Portuguese Maritime Empire

Portugal took the lead in exploration when it began exploring the coast of Africa under the sponsorship of Prince Henry the Navigator (1394–1460). Prince Henry's motives were a blend of seeking a Christian kingdom as an ally against the Muslims, acquiring new trade opportunities for Portugal, and extending Christianity. In 1419, he founded a school for navigators on the southwestern coast of Portugal. Shortly thereafter, Portuguese fleets began probing southward along the western coast of Africa in search of gold, which had for centuries been carried northward from south of the Atlas Mountains in central Morocco. In 1441, Portuguese ships reached the Senegal River, just north of Cape Verde, and brought home a cargo of black Africans, most of whom were sold as slaves to wealthy buyers elsewhere in Europe. Within a few years, an estimated thousand slaves were shipped annually from the area back to Lisbon. Inadvertently, the Portuguese had found a way to circumvent the traditional trans-Saharan slave route from Central Africa to the Mediterranean.

Continuing southward, in 1471 the Portuguese discovered a new source of gold along the southern coast of the hump of West Africa (an area that would henceforth be known to Europeans as the Gold Coast). A few years later, they established contact with the state of Bakongo, near the mouth of the Congo River in Central Africa, and with the inland state of Benin, north of the Gold Coast. To facilitate trade in gold, ivory, and slaves (some slaves were brought back to Lisbon and others were bartered to local merchants for gold), the Portuguese leased land from local rulers and built stone forts along the coast.

Hearing reports of a route to India around the southern tip of Africa, Portuguese sea captains continued their probing. In 1487, Bartolomeu Dias took advantage of westerly winds in the South Atlantic to round the Cape of Good Hope, but he feared a mutiny from his crew and returned home without continuing onward. Ten years later, a fleet under the command of Vasco da Gama rounded the cape and stopped at several ports controlled by Muslim merchants along the coast of East Africa, including Sofala, Kilwa, and Mombasa. Then, having located a Muslim navigator who was familiar with seafaring in the region, da Gama's fleet crossed the Arabian

Courtesy of William J. Duiker

➤ **MALINDI, GATEWAY TO ASIA**   The seaport of Malindi, located on the eastern coast of present-day Kenya, was Vasco da Gama's jumping-off point for his historic voyage to India. It was here that he located a navigator willing to guide his fleet eastward across the Indian Ocean. In later years, merchant vessels often stopped at the port en route to the Spice Islands. Shown here is the graveyard of a Christian church built by early Portuguese missionaries as they wended their way to Asia in search of souls to save. Reportedly the church was erected under the direction of Francis Xavier, later to achieve renown for his missionary efforts in China and Japan.

Sea and arrived off the port of Calicut on the southwestern coast of India, on May 18, 1498. The Portuguese crown had sponsored da Gama's voyage with the clear objective of destroying the Muslim monopoly over the spice trade, a monopoly that had been intensified by the Ottoman conquest of Constantinople in 1453 (see Chapter 15). Calicut was a major entrepôt on the long route from the Spice Islands to the Mediterranean Sea, but the ill-informed Europeans believed it was the source of the spices themselves. They had also heard there was a Christian community in the area, supposedly established by the apostle Thomas in the first century C.E.

On arriving in Calicut, da Gama announced to his surprised hosts that he had arrived in search of "Christians and spices." He did not find the first, but he did find the second. Although he lost two ships en route, da Gama's remaining vessels returned to Europe with their holds filled with ginger and cinnamon, a cargo that earned the investors a profit of several thousand percent.

During the next years, the Portuguese set out to gain control of the spice trade. In 1510, Admiral Afonso de Albuquerque established his headquarters at Goa, on the western coast of India south of present-day Bombay. From there the Portuguese raided Arab shippers, provoking the

THE PORTUGUESE CONQUEST
OF MALACCA

In 1511, a Portuguese fleet led by Afonso de Albuquerque attacked the Muslim sultanate at Malacca, on the west coast of the Malay peninsula. Occupation of the port gave the Portuguese control over the strategic Strait of Malacca and the route to the Spice Islands. In this passage, Albuquerque tells his men the reasons for the attack. Note that he sees control of Malacca as a way to reduce the power of the Muslim world. The relevance of economic wealth to military power continues to underlie conflicts among nations today. The Pacific War in the 1940s, for example, began as a result of a conflict over control of the rich resources of Southeast Asia.

THE COMMENTARIES OF THE GREAT AFONSO DE ALBUQUERQUE, SECOND VICEROY OF INDIA

Although there be many reasons which I could allege in favor of our taking this city and building a fortress therein to maintain possession of it, two only will I mention to you, on this occasion. . . .

The first is the great service which we shall perform to Our Lord in casting the Moors out of this country. . . . If we can only achieve the task before us, it will result in the Moors resigning India altogether to our rule, for the greater part of them—or perhaps all of them—live upon the trade of this country and are become great and rich, and lords of extensive treasures. . . . For when we were committing ourselves to the business of cruising in the Straits (of the Red Sea), where the King of Portugal had often ordered me to go (for it was there that His Highness considered we could cut down the commerce which the Moors of Cairo, of Mecca, and of Judah, carry on with these parts), Our Lord for his service thought right to lead us hither, for when Malacca is taken the places on the Straits must be shut up, and they will never more be able to introduce their spiceries into those places.

And the other reason is the additional service which we shall render to the King D. Manuel in taking this city, because it is the headquarters of all the spiceries and drugs which the Moors carry every year hence to the Straits without our being able to prevent them from so doing; but if we deprive them of this their ancient market there, there does not remain for them a single port, nor a single situation, so commodious in the whole of these parts, where they can carry on their trade in these things. . . . I hold it as very certain that if we take this trade of Malacca away out of their hands, Cairo and Mecca are entirely ruined, and to Venice will no spiceries be conveyed except that which her merchants go and buy in Portugal.

following comment from an Arab source: "[The Portuguese] took about seven vessels, killing those on board and making some prisoner. This was their first action, may God curse them."[5] In 1511, Albuquerque attacked Malacca itself.

For Albuquerque, control of Malacca would serve two purposes. It could help to destroy the Arab spice trade network by blocking passage through the Strait of Malacca, and it could also provide the Portuguese with a way station en route to the Spice Islands and other points east (see the box above). After a short but bloody battle, the Portuguese seized the city and put the local Arab population to the sword. They then proceeded to erect the normal accoutrements of the day—a fort, a factory (a common term at the time for a warehouse), and a church.

The Spice Islands

0 — 500 Kilometers
0 — 300 Miles

'Molucca Sea
Tidor — Halmahera
Pacific Ocean
Island of New Guinea
Ceram
Banda Sea — Banda Islands

From Malacca, the Portuguese launched expeditions farther east, to China and the Moluccas, then known as the Spice Islands. There they signed a treaty with a local sultan for the purchase and export of cloves to the European market. Within a few years, they had managed to seize control of the spice trade from Muslim traders and had garnered substantial profits for the Portuguese monarchy.

Why were the Portuguese so successful? Basically, their success was a matter of guns and seamanship. The first Portuguese fleet to arrive in Indian waters was relatively modest in size. It consisted of three ships and twenty guns, a force sufficient for self-defense and intimidation but not for serious military operations. Sixteenth-century Portuguese fleets were more heavily armed and were capable of inflicting severe defeats if necessary on local naval and land forces. The Portuguese by no means possessed a monopoly on the use of firearms and explosives, but they used the maneuverability of their light ships to maintain their distance while bombarding the enemy with their powerful cannons. Such tactics gave them a military superiority over lightly armed rivals that they were able to exploit until the arrival of other European forces several decades later.

⇒ **AN EARLY JEWISH COMMUNITY IN INDIA.** When Vasco de Gama arrived in the port city of Cochin, along the western coast of India, in 1498, he was surprised to discover the presence of a Jewish community that had been in the area since as early as the first century C.E. Jewish merchants from the Middle East had settled there to take part in the trading network that stretched westward from the Indian Ocean all the way to the Mediterranean Sea. Shown here is the entrance gate to the Jewish quarter in Cochin. Inside the gates are a number of commercial establishments and a synagogue that dates back to the fourteenth century.

Voyages to the "New World"

While the Portuguese were seeking access to the spice trade of the Indies by sailing eastward through the Indian Ocean, the Spanish attempted to reach the same destination by sailing westward across the Atlantic. Although the Spanish came to overseas discovery and exploration later than the Portuguese, their greater resources enabled them to establish a far grander overseas empire.

An important figure in the history of Spanish exploration was an Italian from Genoa, Christopher Columbus (1451–1506). Knowledgeable Europeans were aware that the world was round but had little understanding of its circumference or the extent of the continent of Asia. Convinced that the circumference of the earth was smaller than contemporaries believed and that Asia was larger, Columbus felt that Asia could be reached by sailing due west instead of eastward around Africa. After being rejected by the Portuguese, he persuaded Queen Isabella of Spain to finance his exploratory expedition, which reached the Americas in October 1492 and explored the coastline of Cuba and the northern shores of the neighboring island of Hispaniola. Columbus believed that he had reached Asia and in three subsequent voyages (1493, 1498, and 1502) sought in vain to find a route through the outer islands to the Asian mainland. In his four voyages, Columbus reached all the major islands of the Caribbean, which he called the Indies, as well as Honduras in Central America.

Although Columbus clung to his belief until his death, other explorers soon realized that he had discovered a new frontier altogether. State-sponsored explorers joined the

⇒ **COLUMBUS LANDS IN THE NEW WORLD.** In the log that he wrote during his first voyage to the Americas, Christopher Columbus noted that the peoples of the New World were intelligent and friendly, and relations between them and the Spanish were amicable at first. Later, however, the conquistadors began to mistreat the local people. Here is a somewhat imaginative painting of the first encounter from a European perspective. Note the upturned eyes on Columbus and several of his companions, suggesting that their motives were spiritual rather than material.

race to the New World. A Venetian seafarer, John Cabot, explored the New England coastline of the Americas under a license from King Henry VII of England. The continent of South America was discovered accidentally by the Portuguese sea captain Pedro Cabral in 1500. Amerigo Vespucci, a Florentine, accompanied several voyages and wrote a series of letters describing the geography of the New World. The publication of these letters led to the use of the name "America" (after Amerigo) for the new lands.

The newly discovered territories were referred to as the New World, even though they possessed flourishing civilizations populated by millions of people when the Europeans arrived. But the Americas were new to the Europeans, who quickly saw opportunities for conquest and exploitation. The Spanish, in particular, were interested because in 1494 the Treaty of Tordesillas had divided the newly discovered world into separate Portuguese and Spanish spheres of influence. Thereafter, the route east around the Cape of Good Hope was to be reserved for the Portuguese, while the route across the Atlantic (except for the eastern hump of South America) was assigned to Spain. The Spanish conquistadors were a hardy lot of mostly upper-class individuals motivated by a typical sixteenth-century blend of glory, greed, and religious crusading zeal. Although sanctioned by the Castilian crown, these groups were financed and outfitted privately, not by the government.

Their superior weapons, organizational skills, and determination brought the conquistadors incredible success. Beginning in 1519 with a small band of men, Hernán Cortés took three years to overthrow the mighty Aztec empire in central Mexico, led by the chieftain Moctezuma (see Chapter 6). By 1550, the Spanish had gained control of northern Mexico. Between 1531 and 1536, another expedition led by a hardened and somewhat corrupt soldier, Francisco Pizarro (1470–1541), took control of the

SPANISH ACTIVITIES IN THE AMERICAS

Christopher Columbus's first voyage to the Americas	1492
Last voyages of Columbus	1502–1504
Spanish conquest of Mexico	1519–1522
Francisco Pizarro's conquest of the Incas	1531–1536

Inca empire high in the Peruvian Andes. The Spanish conquests were undoubtedly facilitated by the previous arrival of European diseases, which had decimated the local population. Although it took another three decades before the western part of Latin America was brought under Spanish control (the Portuguese took over Brazil), already by 1535, the Spanish had created a system of colonial administration that made the New World an extension of the old—at least in European eyes.

Administration of the Spanish Empire in the New World

Spanish policy toward the inhabitants of the New World, whom the Europeans called Indians, was a combination of confusion, misguided paternalism, and cruel exploitation. Confusion arose over the nature of the Indians. Unsure whether these strange creatures were "full men" or not, Spanish doctors of law debated how to fit them into currently existing European legal patterns. While the conquistadors made decisions based on expediency and their own interests, Queen Isabella declared the Indi-

Courtesy of William J. Duiker

HAVANA, SPAIN'S LIFELINE TO THE NEW WORLD. After the conquest of Mexico by Hernán Cortés, trade between Spain and its new possession flourished. Spanish navigators soon discovered that the Bay of Havana, on the north shore of the island of Cuba, was an ideal stopping point for fleets en route to and from the New World, and a city sprang up along the banks of its harbor. To protect the population from the ravages of enemy fleets—notably the English—Spanish authorities erected a number of fortifications along the coast near the city. Shown here is El Moro castle, an early fortification located at the entrance to the bay. It has long served as a visual symbol of the city of Havana.

Las Casas and the Spanish Treatment of the American Natives

Bartolomé de Las Casas (1474–1566) was a Dominican monk who participated in the conquest of Cuba and received land and Indians in return for his efforts. But in 1514, he underwent a radical transformation that led him to believe that the Indians had been cruelly mistreated by his fellow Spaniards. He spent the remaining years of his life (he lived to the age of ninety-two) fighting for the Indians. This section is taken from his most influential work, Brevísima Relación de la Destrucción de las Indias, *known to English readers as* The Tears of the Indians. *This work was largely responsible for the legend of the Spanish as inherently "cruel and murderous fanatics." Many scholars today feel that Las Casas may have exaggerated his account to shock his contemporaries into action.*

BARTOLOMÉ DE LAS CASAS, *THE TEARS OF THE INDIANS*

There is nothing more detestable or more cruel than the tyranny which the Spaniards use toward the Indians for the getting of pearl. Surely the infernal torments cannot much exceed the anguish that they endure, by reason of that way of cruelty; for they put them under water some four or five ells deep, where they are forced without any liberty of respiration, to gather up the shells wherein the Pearls are; sometimes they come up again with nets full of shells to take breath, but if they stay any while to rest themselves, immediately comes a hangman row'd in a little boat, who as soon as he hath well beaten them, drags them again to their labor. Their food is nothing but filth, and the very same that contains the Pearl, with small portion of that bread which that Country affords; in the first whereof there is little nourishment; and as for the latter, it is made with great difficulty, besides that they have not enough of that neither for sustenance; they lie upon the ground in fetters, lest they should run away; and many times they are drown'd in this labor, and are never seen again till they swim upon the top of the waves; oftentimes they also are devoured by certain sea monsters, that are frequent in those seas. Consider whether this hard usage of the poor creatures be consistent with the precepts which God commands concerning charity to our neighbor, by those that cast them so undeservedly into the dangers of a cruel death, causing them to perish without any remorse or pity, or allowing them the benefit of the Sacraments, or the knowledge of Religion; it being impossible for them to live any time under the water; and this death is so much the more painful, by reason that by the coarctation of the breast, while the lungs strive to do their office, the vital parts are so afflicted that they die vomiting the blood out of their mouths. Their hair also, which is by nature black, is hereby changed and made of the same color with that of the sea Wolves; their bodies are also so besprinkled with the froth of the sea, that they appear rather like monsters than men.

---

ans to be subjects of Castile and instituted the *encomienda* system, which permitted the conquering Spaniards to collect tribute from the natives and use them as laborers. In return, the holders of an *encomienda* were supposed to protect the Indians and supervise their spiritual and material needs. In practice, this meant that the settlers were free to implement the system as they pleased. Three thousand miles from Spain, Spanish settlers largely ignored their government and brutally used the Indians to pursue their own economic interests. Indians were put to work on sugar plantations and in the lucrative gold and silver mines. Forced labor, starvation, and especially disease took a fearful toll of Indian lives. With little or no natural resistance to European diseases, the Indians of America were ravaged by smallpox, measles, and typhus brought by the explorers and the conquistadors. Although scholarly estimates of native populations vary drastically, a reasonable guess is that at least half of the natives died of European diseases. On Hispaniola alone, out of an initial population of 100,000 natives when Columbus arrived in 1493, only 300 Indians survived by 1570. In 1542, largely in response to the publications of Bartolomé de Las Casas, a Dominican monk who championed the Indians (see the box above), the government abolished the *encomienda* system and provided more protection for the natives.

A board of trade known as the *Casa de Contratactión* supervised all economic matters related to the New World, but the chief organ of colonial administration was the Council of the Indies. The council nominated colonial viceroys, oversaw their activities, and kept an eye on ecclesiastical affairs in the colonies. Spanish possessions in the New World were initially divided between New Spain (Mexico, Central America, and the Caribbean islands), with its center in Mexico City, and Peru (western South America), with its capital at Lima. Each area was governed by a viceroy who served as the king's chief civil and military officer and was aided by advisory groups called *audiencias*, which also functioned as supreme judicial bodies.

By papal agreement, the Catholic monarchs of Spain were given extensive rights over ecclesiastical affairs in the New World. They could nominate church officials, build churches, collect fees, and supervise the various religious orders that conducted missionary activities. Catholic

AN AZTEC'S LAMENT

*I*n an earlier chapter, we observed the Spanish conquest of Mexico from the point of view of the invaders. Here we present an Aztec account. Aztec memoirs of the battle were collected by the Spanish a few years after the seizure of Tenochtitlán and were later translated from the original Nahuatl into Spanish or other European languages. In this passage, an Aztec observer describes the enormous sense of sorrow he felt at the tragedy that had befallen his compatriots. Note that the writer concludes that the defeat was ordained by the "Giver of Life" because of his displeasure with the Aztec people.

FLOWERS AND SONGS OF SORROW

Nothing but flowers and songs of sorrow
are left in Mexico and Tlatelolco,
where once we saw warriors and wise men.

We know it is true
that we must perish,

for we are mortal men.
You, the Giver of Life,
you have ordained it.

We wander here and there
in our desolate poverty.
We are mortal men.
We have seen bloodshed and pain
where once we saw beauty and valor.

We are crushed to the ground;
we lie in ruins.
There is nothing but grief and suffering
in Mexico and Tlatelolco,
where once we saw beauty and valor.

Have you grown weary of your servants?
Are you angry with your servants,
O Giver of Life?

---

monks had remarkable success converting and baptizing hundreds of thousands of Indians in the early years of the conquest. Soon after the missionaries came the establishment of dioceses, parishes, schools, and hospitals—all the trappings of a European society.

The Impact of European Expansion

The arrival of the Europeans had an enormous impact on both the conquerors and the conquered. The native American civilizations, which (as we discussed in Chapter 6) had their own unique qualities and a degree of sophistication rarely appreciated by the conquerors, were virtually destroyed, while the native populations were ravaged by diseases introduced by the Europeans. Ancient social and political structures were ripped up and replaced by European institutions, religion, language, and culture (see the box above).

How does one evaluate the psychological impact of colonization on the colonizers? The relatively easy European success in dominating native peoples undoubtedly reinforced the conviction of Europeans in the inherent superiority of their civilization. The Scientific Revolution of the eighteenth century, to be followed by the era of imperialism a century later, then served to strengthen the Eurocentric perspective that has long pervaded Western civilization in its relationship with the rest of the world.

European expansion also affected the conquerors in the economic arena. Wherever they went in the Americas, Europeans sought gold and silver. One Aztec observer commented that the Spanish conquerors "longed and lusted for gold. Their bodies swelled with greed, and their hunger was ravenous; they hungered like pigs for that gold."[6] Rich silver deposits were found and exploited in Mexico and southern Peru (modern Bolivia). When the mines at Potosí in Peru were opened in 1545, the value of precious metals imported into Europe quadrupled. It has been estimated that between 1503 and 1650, some 16 million kilograms of silver and 185,000 kilograms of gold entered the port of Seville, fueling a price revolution that affected the Spanish economy.

But gold and silver were only two of the products sent to Europe from the New World. Into Seville flowed sugar, dyes, cotton, vanilla, and hides from livestock raised on the South American pampas. New agricultural products native to the Americas, such as potatoes, coffee, corn, manioc, and tobacco, were also imported. Because of its trading posts in Asia, Portugal soon challenged the Italian states as the chief entry point of the eastern trade in spices, jewels, silk, carpets, ivory, leather, and perfumes, although the Venetians clung tenaciously to a portion of the spice trade until they lost out to the Dutch in the seventeenth century. Economic historians believe that the increase in the volume and area of European trade and the rise in fluid capital due to this expansion were crucial factors in producing a new era of commercial capitalism that represented the first step toward the world economy that has characterized the modern era.

European expansion, which was in part a product of European rivalries, also deepened those rivalries and increased the tensions among European states. Bitter conflicts arose over the cargoes coming from the New World and Asia. Although the Spanish and Portuguese were first in the competition, by the end of the sixteenth

Courtesy of William J. Duiker

⇺ MANIOC, FOOD FOR THE MILLIONS.
One of the plants native to the Americas that European adventurers would take back to the Old World was manioc (also known as cassava or yuca). A tuber like the potato, manioc is a prolific crop that grows well in poor, dry soils, but it lacks the high nutrient value of grain crops such as wheat and rice and for that reason never became popular in Europe (except as the source of tapioca). It was introduced to Africa in the seventeenth century and eventually became a staple food for up to one-third of the population of the continent. Shown here (inset) is a manioc plant growing in east Africa.

century, new competitors were entering the scene and beginning to challenge the dominance of the Iberian powers. The first to arrive were the English and the Dutch.

Why did Europeans risk their lives to explore new lands far from friendly shores? For some, expansion abroad brought hopes for land, riches, and social advancement. One Spaniard commented in 1572 that many "poor young men" left Spain for Mexico, where they might hope to acquire landed estates and call themselves "gentlemen." Although some wives accompanied their husbands abroad, many ordinary European women found new opportunities for marriage in the New World because of the lack of white women. In the violence-prone world of early Spanish America, a number of women also found themselves rich after their husbands were killed unexpectedly. In one area of Central America, women owned about 25 percent of the landed estates by 1700.

New Rivals

Portugal's efforts to dominate the trade of the Indian Ocean were never totally successful. The Portuguese lacked both the numbers and the wealth to overcome local resistance and colonize the Asian regions. Moreover, their massive investments in ships and laborers for their empire (hundreds of ships and hundreds of thousands of workers in shipyards and overseas bases) proved very costly. Only half of the ships involved in the India trade survived for a second journey. Disease, shipwreck, and battles took a heavy toll of life. The empire was simply too large and Portugal too small to maintain it, and by the end of the century, the Portuguese were being severely challenged by rivals.

The Spanish had established themselves in Asia in the early 1520s, when Ferdinand Magellan, seeking a western route to the Spice Islands across the Pacific Ocean, had sailed around the southern tip of South America, crossed the Pacific, and landed on the island of Cebu in the Philippine Islands. Although Magellan and some forty of his crew were killed in a skirmish with the local population, one of the two remaining ships, now under the command of the Spanish navigator Sebastian del Cano, sailed on to Tidor, in the Moluccas, and thence around the world via the Cape of Good Hope. In the words of a contemporary historian, they arrived in Cádiz "with precious cargo and fifteen men surviving out of a fleet of five sail."[7]

As it turned out, the Spanish could not follow up on Magellan's accomplishment, and in 1529 they sold their rights in Tidor to the Portuguese. But Magellan's voyage was not a total loss. In the absence of concerted resistance from the local population, the Spanish managed to consolidate their control over the Philippines, which eventually became a major Spanish base in the carrying trade across the Pacific. Spanish galleons carried silk and other luxury goods to Acapulco in exchange for silver from the mines of Mexico.

The primary threat to the Portuguese toehold in Southeast Asia, however, came from the English and the Dutch, both of whom were now strongly influenced by mercantilist theory (see Chapter 13). In 1591, the first English expedition to the Indies through the Indian Ocean arrived in London with a cargo of pepper. Nine years later, a private joint-stock company, the East India Company, was founded to provide a stable source of capital for future voyages. In 1608, an English fleet landed at Surat, on the northwestern coast of India. Eventually, a commercial treaty was signed, and a permanent English representative was assigned to the Mughal imperial court. Trade with Southeast Asia soon followed.

The Dutch were quick to follow suit. Dutch sailors had managed to obtain Portuguese maps of the Indian coast, and the first Dutch fleet arrived in India in 1595. In 1602,

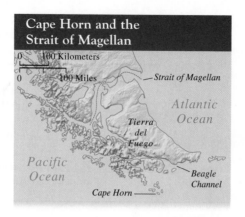

Cape Horn and the Strait of Magellan

the Dutch East India Company was established under government sponsorship and was soon actively competing with the English and the Portuguese in the region.

The Dutch, the French, and the English also began to make inroads on Spanish and Portuguese possessions in the Americas. War and steady pressure from their Dutch and English rivals eroded Portuguese trade in both the West and the East, although Portugal continued to profit from its large colonial empire in Brazil. A formal administration system had been instituted in Brazil in 1549, and Portuguese migrants had established massive plantations there to produce sugar for export to the Old World. The Spanish also maintained an enormous South American empire, but Spain's importance as a commercial power declined rapidly in the seventeenth century because of a drop in the output of the silver mines, the poverty of the Spanish monarchy, and the stifling hand of the Spanish aristocracy as well as the pressure of its English rival.

The Dutch formed their own Dutch West India Company in 1621 to compete with Spanish and Portuguese interests in the Americas. But although it made some inroads in Portuguese Brazil and the Caribbean, the company's profits were never large enough to compensate for the expenditures. Dutch settlements were also established on the North American continent. The main-

➤➤ PASSAGE TO THE UNKNOWN. During its historic first voyage around the world in the early sixteenth century, Ferdinand Magellan's fleet passed through this passage near the southern tip of South America. Now known as the Strait of Magellan, this narrow body of water between the mainland and the nearby island of Tierra del Fuego remains to sailors one of the most terrifying in the world, with 100-mile-per-hour winds gusting regularly through this passage between the Pacific and the Atlantic Oceans.

Courtesy of William J. Duiker

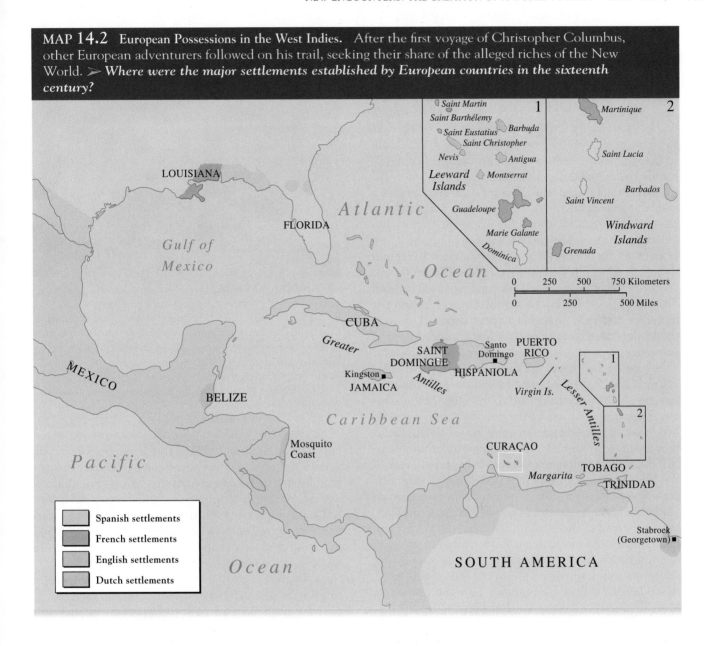

MAP 14.2 European Possessions in the West Indies. After the first voyage of Christopher Columbus, other European adventurers followed on his trail, seeking their share of the alleged riches of the New World. ➤ *Where were the major settlements established by European countries in the sixteenth century?*

land colony of New Netherlands stretched from the mouth of the Hudson River as far north as Albany, New York. In the meantime, French colonies appeared in the Lesser Antilles, and in Louisiana, at the mouth of the Mississippi River.

In the second half of the seventeenth century, however, rivalry and years of warfare with the English and the French (who had also become active in North America) brought the decline of the Dutch commercial empire in the New World. In 1664, the English seized the colony of New Netherlands and renamed it New York, and the Dutch West India Company soon went bankrupt. In 1663, Canada became the property of the French crown and was administered like a French province. But the French failed to provide adequate men or money, allowing their continental wars to take precedence over the conquest of the North American continent. By the early eighteenth cen-

tury, the French began to cede some of their American possessions to their English rival.

The English, meanwhile, had proceeded to create a colonial empire in the New World along the Atlantic seaboard of North America. The failure of the Virginia Company made it evident that colonizing American lands was not necessarily conducive to quick profits. But the desire to escape from religious oppression combined with economic interests did make successful colonization possible, as the Massachusetts Bay Company demonstrated. The Massachusetts colony had only four thousand settlers in its early years, but by 1660 their number had swelled to forty thousand. Although the English had established control over most of the eastern seaboard by the end of the seventeenth century, the North American colonies still remained of minor significance to the English economy.

AFRICA IN TRANSITION

Although the primary objective of the Portuguese in rounding the Cape of Good Hope was to find a sea route to the Spice Islands, they soon discovered that profits were to be made en route, along the eastern coast of Africa. In the early sixteenth century, a Portuguese fleet commanded by Francisco de Almeida seized a number of East African port cities, including Kilwa, Sofala, and Mombasa, and built forts along the coast in an effort to control the trade in the area. Above all, the Portuguese wanted to monopolize the trade in gold, which was mined by Bantu workers in the hills along the upper Zambezi River and then shipped to Sofala on the coast (see Chapter 8). For centuries, the gold trade had been monopolized by local Shona peoples at Zimbabwe. In the fifteenth century, it had come under the control of a Shona dynasty known as the Mwene Metapa. The Mwene Metapa had originally controlled the region south of the Zambezi River and may have been the builders of the impressive city known today as Great Zimbabwe, but sometime in the fifteenth century, they moved northeastward to the valley of the Zambezi. Here they encountered the arriving Portuguese, who had begun to move inland to gain access to the lucrative gold trade and had established ports on the Zambezi River. The Portuguese opened treaty relations with the Mwene Metapa, and Jesuit priests were eventually posted to the court in 1561. At first, the Mwene Metapa found the Europeans useful as an ally against local rivals, but by the end of the sixteenth century, the Portuguese had established a protectorate and forced the local ruler to grant title to large tracts of land to European officials and private individuals living in the area. Eventually, those lands would be integrated into the colony of Mozambique. The Portuguese, however, lacked the personnel, the capital, and the expertise to dominate local trade and in the late seventeenth century, a vassal of the Mwene Metapa succeeded in driving them from the plateau; his descendants maintained control of the area for the next two hundred years.

North of the Zambezi River, Bantu peoples were coming under pressure not only from the Portuguese but also from pastoralists migrating southward from the southern Sudan. The latter were frequently aggressive and began to occupy the rift valley and parts of the lake district that had previously been controlled by Bantu farmers. In some cases, the conflict between farmers and pastoralists was fairly clear-cut. In Rwanda and Burundi, immediately west of Lake Victoria, farming Hutu peoples (Bantu speakers) defended their hilltop communities against roving Tutsi pastoralists occupying the surrounding lowlands.

The first Europeans to settle in southern Africa were the Dutch. After an unsuccessful attempt to seize the Portuguese settlement on the island of Mozambique off the

FORT JESUS AT MOMBASA. Mombasa, a port city on the eastern coast of Africa, was a jumping-off point for the Portuguese as they explored the lands bordering on the Indian Ocean. Erected in the early sixteenth century atop a bluff overlooking the harbor, Fort Jesus remained an imposing symbol of European power until 1698, when the Portuguese were expelled by the Arabs. Castles built in this style are situated along the sea routes to the Spice Islands, but the European presence has now departed.

East African coast, in 1652 the Dutch set up a way station at the Cape of Good Hope to serve as a base for their fleets en route to the East Indies. At first, the new settlement was meant simply to provide food and other provisions to Dutch ships, but eventually it developed into a permanent colony. Dutch farmers, known as Boers and speaking a Dutch dialect that evolved into Afrikaans, began to settle in the sparsely occupied areas outside the city of Cape Town. The temperate climate and the absence of tropical diseases made the territory near the cape practically the only land south of the Sahara that the Europeans had found suitable for habitation.

West Africa had been penetrated from across the Sahara since ancient times, and contact undoubtedly increased after the establishment of Muslim control over the Mediterranean coastal regions. Muslim traders crossed the desert carrying Islamic values, political culture, and legal traditions along with their goods. The early stage of state formation had culminated with the kingdom of Mali, symbolized by the renowned Mansa Musa, whose pilgrimage to Mecca in the fourteenth century had left an indelible impression on observers.

After Mali's decline, it was succeeded by the kingdom of Songhai. Under King Askia Mohammed (1493–1528), the leader of a pro-Islamic faction who had seized power from members of the original founding family, the state increasingly relied on Islamic institutions and ideology to strengthen national unity and centralize authority (see the box on p. 401). Askia Mohammed himself embarked on a pilgrimage to Mecca and was recognized by

KING OF SONGHAI

*T*he Epic of Askia Mohammed *is an oral history passed down through generations of West Africans. It relates the heroic deeds of the famous monarch who led the kingdom of Songhai to the zenith of its power in the early sixteenth century. In the epic, the young hero, called Mamar Kassaye, becomes chieftain by killing his evil uncle Si (Sonni Ali Ber, who ruled Songhai from 1463 to 1492). Once in power, Mamar consolidated the expanding Songhai kingdom and ruled it until his death in 1528. He was revered for his piety, his patronage of scholarship at Timbuktu, and his celebrated pilgrimage to Mecca. The following passage describes his assumption of power and the means he used to convert his subjects to Islam.*

THE EPIC OF ASKIA MOHAMMED

His father gave him a white stallion, really white, really, really, really, really, really, really, really white like, like percale.
He gave him all the things necessary.
He gave him two lances.
He gave him a saber, which he wore.
He gave him a shield.
He bid him good-bye.

…

The horse gallops swiftly, swiftly, swiftly, swiftly, swiftly, swiftly he is approaching.
He comes into view suddenly, leaning forward on his mount.
Until, until, until, until, until, until, until he touches the prayer skin of his uncle, then he reins his horse there.

…

As he approaches the prayer skin of his uncle,
He reins his horse.
He unslung his lance, and pierced his uncle with it until the lance touched the prayer skin.

Until the spear went all the way to the prayer skin.

…

They took away the body, and Mamar came to sit down on the prayer skin of his uncle.
They prayed.
They took away the body to bury it.
That is how Mamar took the chieftaincy.

…

He ruled then, he ruled, he ruled, he ruled, he converted.
Throughout Mamar's reign, what he did was to convert people.
Any village that he hears is trying to resist,
That is not going to submit,
He gets up and destroys the village.
If the village accepts, he makes them pray.
If they resist, he conquers the village, he burns the village.
Mamar made them convert, Mamar made them convert, Mamar made them convert.
Until, until, until, until, until, until he got up and said he would go to Mecca.

…

They build a mosque before his arrival.
When he arrives, he and his people,
He teaches the villagers prayers from the Koran.
He makes them pray.
They—they learn how to pray.
After that, in the morning, he continues on.
Every village that follows his orders, that accepts his wishes,
He conquers them, he moves on.
Every village that refuses his demand,
He conquers it, he burns it, he moves on.
Until the day—Mamar did that until, until, until, until the day he arrived at the Red Sea.

---

the caliph of Cairo as the Muslim ruler of the Niger River valley. On his return from Mecca, he tried to revive Timbuktu as a major center of Islamic learning but had little success in converting his subjects. He did preside over a significant increase in trans-Saharan trade, which provided a steady source of income to Songhai and other kingdoms in the region. Despite the efforts of Askia Mohammed and his successors, centrifugal forces within Songhai eventually led to its breakup after his death.

The period of Songhai's decline was also a time of increased contact with Europeans. The English, the French, and the Dutch all became active in the West African trade in the mid-sixteenth century. The Dutch, in particular, encroached on the Portuguese spheres of influence. During the mid-seventeenth century, the Dutch seized a number of Portuguese forts along the West African coast while at the same time taking over the bulk of the Portuguese trade across the Indian Ocean.

The Slave Trade

The European exploration of the African coastline had little apparent significance for most peoples living in the interior of the continent, except for a few who engaged in direct or indirect trade with the foreigners. But for peoples living on or near the coast, the impact was often great indeed. As the trade in slaves increased during the sixteenth through the eighteenth centuries, thousands, and then millions, were removed from their homes and forcibly exported to plantations in the New World.

Traffic in slaves had existed for centuries before the arrival of Portuguese fleets along African shores. West African states like the kingdoms of Mali and Songhai routinely used slaves (mostly captured in battles with neighboring rivals) as agricultural laborers. In East Africa and the upper Nile valley, slavery had been practiced since ancient times and continued at a fairly steady level during the fifteenth century, with the major trade routes snaking across the Sahara and up the Nile River. The primary market for African slaves was the Middle East, where most were used as domestic servants. Slavery also existed in many European countries, where a few slaves from Africa or war captives from the regions north of the Black Sea were used for domestic purposes or as agricultural workers in the lands adjacent to the Mediterranean.

At first, the Portuguese simply replaced European slaves with African ones. During the second half of the fifteenth century, about a thousand slaves were taken to Portugal each year; the vast majority were apparently destined to serve as domestic servants for affluent families throughout Europe. But the discovery of the New World in the 1490s and the subsequent planting of sugarcane in South America and the islands of the Caribbean changed the situation. Cane sugar was native to Indonesia and had first been introduced to Europeans from the Middle East during the Crusades. By the fifteenth century, it was grown (often by slaves from Africa or the region of the Black Sea) in modest amounts on Cyprus, Sicily, and southern regions of the Iberian peninsula. But when the Ottoman Empire seized much of the eastern Mediterranean (see Chapter 15), the Europeans needed to seek out new areas suitable for cultivation. In 1490, the Portuguese established sugar plantations worked by African laborers at São Tomé, an island in the Bay of Biafra off the central coast of Africa. Demand increased as sugar gradually replaced honey as a sweetener, especially in northern Europe.

But the primary impetus to the sugar industry came from the colonization of the Americas. During the sixteenth century, plantations were established along the eastern coast of Brazil and on several islands in the Caribbean.

Because the cultivation of cane sugar is an arduous process demanding both skill and large quantities of labor, the new plantations required more workers than could be provided by the Indian population in the New World, many of whom had died of diseases imported from the Old World. Since the climate and soil of much of West Africa were not especially conducive to the cultivation of sugar, African slaves began to be shipped to Brazil and the Caribbean to work on the plantations. The first were sent from Portugal, but in 1518, a Spanish ship carried the first boatload of African slaves directly from Africa to the New World.

During the next two centuries, the trade in slaves increased by massive proportions (see Map 14.3). An estimated 275,000 enslaved Africans were exported to other countries during the sixteenth century, with 2,000 going annually to the Americas alone. During the next century, the total climbed to over a million and jumped to six million in the eighteenth century, when the trade spread from West and Central Africa to East Africa. Even during the nineteenth century, when Great Britain and a number of other European countries attempted to end the slave trade, nearly two million were exported. It has been estimated that altogether as many as ten million African slaves were transported to the Americas between the early sixteenth and the late nineteenth centuries. As many as two million were exported to other areas during the same period.

One reason for these astonishing numbers, of course, was the tragically high death rate. Though figures on the number of slaves who died on the journey are almost entirely speculative, a high proportion undoubtedly died on the voyage before arriving at their destination. We know that mortality rates for Europeans in the West Indies were ten to twenty times higher than in Europe,

✥▶ **A SLAVE SHIP.**   Beginning in the sixteenth century, European traders began to ship native Africans to the Americas to be used as slave labor on the plantations. During the first shipments, up to one-third of the human cargo died of disease. (Even among crew members, mortality rates were sometimes as high as one in four.) Later merchants became more efficient and reduced losses to about 10 percent. As this sketch shows, the victims were still crammed together in an inhumane manner.

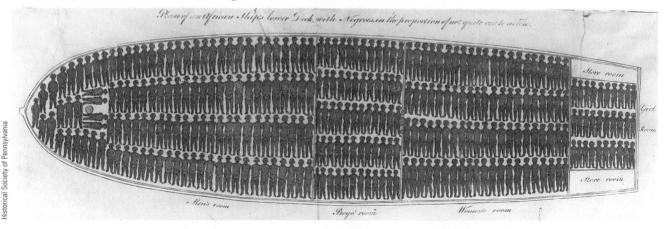

Historical Society of Pennsylvania

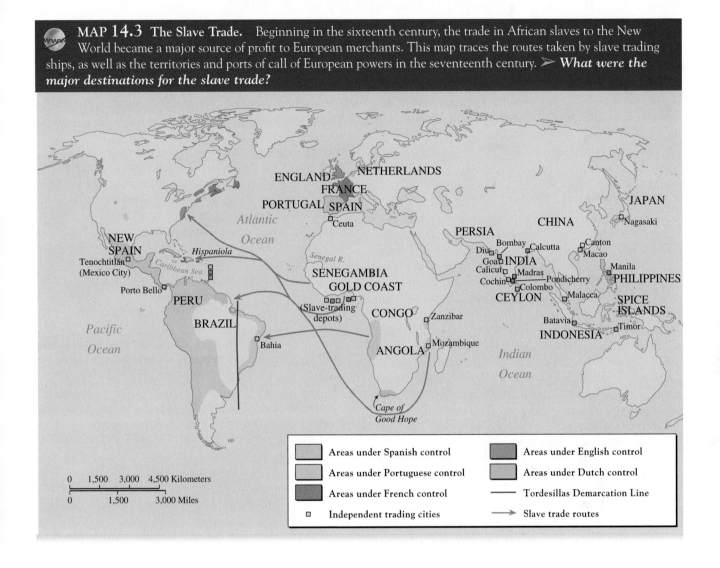

MAP 14.3 The Slave Trade.   Beginning in the sixteenth century, the trade in African slaves to the New World became a major source of profit to European merchants. This map traces the routes taken by slave trading ships, as well as the territories and ports of call of European powers in the seventeenth century. ➤ *What were the major destinations for the slave trade?*

and a European arriving in the West Indies had a life expectancy of five to ten years (in Africa, where yellow fever was prevalent, the average life expectancy for an arriving European was only about one year). Ironically, African slaves who survived the brutal voyage fared somewhat better than whites: death rates for newly arrived Europeans in the West Indies averaged more than 125 per 1,000 annually, but the figure for Africans was only about 30 per 1,000.

The reason for these staggering death rates was clearly more than maltreatment, although that was certainly a factor. As we have seen, the transmission of diseases from one continent to another brought high death rates among those lacking immunity. African slaves were somewhat less susceptible to European diseases than the American Indian populations. Indeed, they seem to have possessed a degree of immunity, perhaps because their ancestors had developed antibodies to "white people's diseases" owing to the trans-Saharan trade. The Africans would not have had immunity to native American diseases, however.

The mortality rates, of course, were higher for immigrants than for those born in the New World, who as children gradually developed at least a partial immunity to many of the more fatal diseases. Death rates for native-born slaves tended to be significantly lower than for recent arrivals, which raises the question of why the slave population did not begin to rise after the initial impact of settlement had worn off. The answer appears to be a matter of economics. In the first place, only half as many women were enslaved as men, birthrates for women living in slavery were low, and infant mortality was high. In the second place, as long as the price of slaves was low, many slave owners in the West Indies apparently believed that purchasing a new slave was less expensive than raising a child from birth to working age at adolescence. After the price of slaves began to rise during the eighteenth century, plantation owners started to devote more efforts to replenishing the supply of workers by natural means.

Slaves were obtained by traditional means. Before the coming of the Europeans in the fifteenth century, most

A Slave Market in Africa

Traffic in slaves had been carried on in Africa since the kingdom of the pharaohs in ancient Egypt. But the slave trade increased dramatically after the arrival of European ships off the coast of West Africa. The following passage by a Dutch observer describes a slave market in Africa and the conditions on the ships that carried the slaves to the New World. Note the difference in tone between this account and the far more critical views expressed in Chapter 22.

SLAVERY IN AFRICA: A FIRSTHAND REPORT

Not a few in our country fondly imagine that parents here sell their children, men their wives, and one brother the other. But those who think so deceive themselves, for this never happens on any other account but that of necessity, or some great crime; most of the slaves that are offered to us are prisoners of war, who are sold by the victors as their booty.

When these slaves come to Fida, they are put in prison all together; and when we treat concerning buying them, they are brought out into a large plain. There, by our surgeons, whose province it is, they are thoroughly examined, even to the smallest member, and that naked too, both men and women, without the least distinction or modesty. Those that are approved as good are set on one side; and the lame or faulty are set by as invalids. . . .

The invalids and the maimed being thrown out, . . . the remainder are numbered, and it is entered who delivered them. In the meanwhile, a burning iron, with the arms or name of the companies, lies in the fire, with which ours are marked on the breast. This is done that we may distinguish them from the slaves of the English, French, or others (which are also marked with their mark), and to prevent the Negroes exchanging them for worse, at which they have a good hand.

I doubt not but this trade seems very barbarous to you, but since it is followed by mere necessity, it must go on; but we take all possible care that they are not burned too hard, especially the women, who are more tender than the men.

When we have agreed with the owners of the slaves, they are returned to their prison. There from that time forward they are kept at our charge, costing us two pence a day a slave; which serves to subsist them, like our criminals, on bread and water. To save charges, we send them on board our ships at the very first opportunity, before which their masters strip them of all they have on their backs so that they come aboard stark naked, women as well as men. In this condition they are obliged to continue, if the master of the ship is not so charitable (which he commonly is) as to bestow something on them to cover their nakedness.

You would really wonder to see how these slaves live on board, for though their number sometimes amounts to six or seven hundred, yet by the careful management of our masters of ships, they are so regulated that it seems incredible. And in this particular our nation exceeds all other Europeans, for the French, Portuguese and English slave ships are always foul and stinking; on the contrary, ours are for the most part clean and neat.

The slaves are fed three times a day with indifferent good victuals, and much better than they eat in their own country. Their lodging place is divided into two parts, one of which is appointed for the men, the other for the women, each sex being kept apart. Here they lie as close together as it is possible for them to be crowded.

We are sometimes sufficiently plagued with a parcel of slaves which come from a far inland country who very innocently persuade one another that we buy them only to fatten and afterward eat them as a delicacy. When we are so unhappy as to be pestered with many of this sort, they resolve and agree together (and bring over the rest to their party) to run away from the ship, kill the Europeans, and set the vessel ashore, by which means they design to free themselves from being our food.

I have twice met with this misfortune; and the first time proved very unlucky to me, I not in the least suspecting it, but the uproar was quashed by the master of the ship and myself by causing the abettor to be shot through the head, after which all was quiet.

slaves in Africa were prisoners or war captives or had inherited their status. Many served as domestic servants or as wageless workers for the local ruler, and some were permitted to purchase their freedom under certain conditions. When Europeans first began to take part in the slave trade, they would normally purchase slaves from local African merchants at the infamous slave markets in exchange for gold, guns, or other European manufactured goods such as textiles or copper or iron utensils (see the box above). At first, local slave traders obtained their supply from immediately surrounding regions, but as demand increased, they had to move farther inland to locate their

victims. In a few cases, local rulers became concerned about the impact of the slave trade on the political and social well-being of their societies. In a letter to the king of Portugal in 1526, King Affonso of Congo (Bakongo) complained that "so great, Sire, is the corruption and licentiousness that our country is being completely depopulated."[8] As a general rule, however, local monarchs viewed the slave trade as a source of income, and many launched forays against defenseless villages in search of unsuspecting victims.

Historians once thought that Europeans controlled the terms of the slave trade and were able to obtain victims

THE PENETRATION OF AFRICA

Life of Prince Henry the Navigator	1394–1460
Portuguese ships reach the Senegal River	1441
Bartolomeu Dias sails around the tip of Africa	1487
First Portuguese sugar plantation at São Tomé	1490
First boatload of slaves to the Americas	1518
Dutch way station established at Cape of Good Hope	1652
Ashanti kingdom established in West Africa	1680
Portuguese expelled from Mombasa	1728

at bargain prices. Recently, however, it has become clear that African intermediaries—private merchants, local elites, and trading state monopolies—were very active in the process and were often able to dictate the price, volume, and availability of slaves to European purchasers. The majority of the slaves sold to European buyers were males; females, who were in great demand in Africa and on the trans-Saharan trade, tended to be reserved for those markets. The slave merchants were often paid in various types of imported goods, including East Asian textiles (highly desired for their bright colors and durability), furniture, and other manufactured products. Until the end of the seventeenth century, the Portuguese preferred gold to slaves and would sometimes pay for the gold by selling slaves to African kingdoms that were short of labor. In fact, not until the beginning of the eighteenth century did slaves surpass gold and ivory as the continent's leading exports.

The effects of the slave trade varied from area to area. It might be assumed that apart from the tragic effects on the lives of individual victims and their families, the practice would have led to the depopulation of vast areas of the continent. This did occur in some areas, notably in modern Angola, south of the Congo River basin, and in thinly populated areas in East Africa, but it was less true in West Africa. There high birthrates were often able to counterbalance the loss of able-bodied adults, and the introduction of new crops from the New World, such as maize, peanuts, and manioc, led to an increase in food production that made it possible to support a larger population. One of the many cruel ironies of history is that while the institution of slavery was a tragedy for many, it benefited others.

Still, there is no denying the reality that from a moral point of view, the slave trade represented a tragic loss

for millions of Africans, not only for the individual victims, but also for their families. One of the more poignant aspects of the trade is that as many as 20 percent of those sold to European slavers were children, a statistic that may be partly explained by the fact that many European countries had enacted regulations that permitted more children than adults to be transported aboard the ships.

How did Europeans justify cruelty of such epidemic proportions? In some cases, they rationalized that slave traders were only carrying on a tradition that had existed for centuries throughout the Mediterranean and African world. In others, they eased their consciences by noting that slaves brought from Africa would now be exposed to the Christian faith and would be able to replace American Indian workers, many of whom were considered too physically fragile for the heavy human labor involved in cutting sugarcane.

Political and Social Structures in a Changing Continent

Of course, the Western economic penetration of Africa had other dislocating effects. As in other parts of the non-Western world, the importation of manufactured goods from Europe undermined the foundations of local cottage industry and impoverished countless families. The demand for slaves and the introduction of firearms intensified political instability and civil strife. At the same time, the impact of the Europeans should not be exaggerated. Only in a few isolated areas, such as South Africa and Mozambique, were permanent European settlements established. Elsewhere, at the insistence of African rulers and merchants, European influence generally did not penetrate beyond the coastal regions.

Nevertheless, inland areas were often affected by events taking place elsewhere. In the western Sahara, for example, the diversion of trade routes toward the coast led to the weakening of the old Songhai trading empire and its eventual conquest by a vigorous new Moroccan dynasty in the late sixteenth century. Morocco had long hoped to expand its influence into the Sahara in order to seize control over the commerce in gold and salt, and in 1590 Moroccan forces defeated Songhai's army at Gao, on the Niger River, and then occupied the great caravan center of Timbuktu. Even after the departure of the invaders, Songhai was beyond recovery, and the next two centuries were marked by civil disorder among tribal groups and intense competition between Muslims in the cities and towns and adherents of traditional African religions in rural areas.

European influence had a more direct impact along the coast of West Africa, especially in the vicinity of European forts such as Dakar and Sierra Leone, but no European colonies were established there before 1800. Most of the numerous African states in the area from

Cape Verde to the delta of the Niger River were sufficiently strong to resist Western encroachments, and they often allied with each other to force European purchasers to respect their monopoly over trading operations. Some, like the powerful Ashanti kingdom, established in 1680 on the Gold Coast, profited substantially from the rise in seaborne commerce. Some states, particularly along the so-called Slave Coast, in what is now Dahomey and Togo, or in the densely populated Niger River delta, took an active part in the slave trade. The demands of slavery and the temptations of economic profit, however, also contributed to the increase in conflict among the states in the area.

This was especially true in the region of the Congo River, where Portuguese activities eventually led to the splintering of the Congo Empire and two centuries of rivalry and internal strife among the successor states in the area. A similar pattern developed in East Africa, where Portuguese activities led to the decline and eventual collapse of the Mwene Metapa. Northward along the coast, in present-day Kenya and Tanzania, African rulers, assisted by Arab forces from Oman and Muscat in the Arabian peninsula, expelled the Portuguese from Mombasa in 1728. Swahili culture now regained some of the dynamism it had possessed before the arrival of Vasco da Gama and his successors. But with much shipping now diverted southward to the route around the Cape of Good Hope, the commerce of the area never completely recovered and was increasingly dependent on the export of slaves and ivory obtained through contacts with African states in the interior.

SOUTHEAST ASIA IN THE ERA OF THE SPICE TRADE

In Southeast Asia, the encounter with the West that began with the arrival of Portuguese fleets in the Indian Ocean at the end of the fifteenth century eventually resulted in the breakdown of traditional societies and the advent of colonial rule. The process was a gradual one, however. By 1700, although the Dutch retained their hold on the islands, Europeans had generally abandoned the Southeast Asian mainland. As we will see in a later chapter, though, the mainland's reprieve was only temporary.

The Arrival of the West

As we have seen, the Spanish soon followed the Portuguese into Southeast Asia. By the seventeenth century, the Dutch, English, and French had begun to join the scramble for rights to the lucrative spice trade.

Chronology

THE SPICE TRADE

Vasco da Gama lands at Calicut in southwestern India	1498
Portuguese seize Malacca	1511
Portuguese ships land in southern China	1514
Magellan's voyage around the world	1519–1522
East India Company established	1600
Vereenigde Oost-Indische Compagnie (VOC) established	1602
English arrive at Surat in northwestern India	1608
Dutch fort established at Batavia	1619
Dutch seize Malacca from the Portuguese	1641
Burmese sack of Ayuthaya	1767
British seize Malacca from the Dutch	1795

Within a short time, the Dutch, through the aggressive and well-financed Dutch East India Company (Vereenigde Oost-Indische Compagnie, or VOC, which possessed ten times the capital of the English East India Company), had not only succeeded in elbowing their rivals out of the spice trade but had also begun to consolidate their political and military control over the area. On the island of Java, where they established a fort at Batavia (today's Jakarta) in 1619, the Dutch found that it was necessary to bring the inland regions under their control to protect their position. Rather than establishing a formal colony, however, they tried to rule as much as possible through the local landed aristocracy. On Java and the neighboring island of Sumatra, the VOC established pepper plantations, which soon became the source of massive profits for Dutch merchants in Amsterdam. Elsewhere they attempted to monopolize the clove trade by limiting cultivation of the crop to one island. By the end of the eighteenth century, the Dutch had succeeded in bringing almost the entire Indonesian archipelago under their control.

The arrival of the Europeans had somewhat less impact on mainland Southeast Asia, where cohesive monarchies in Burma, Thailand, and Vietnam resisted foreign encroachment. In addition, the coveted spices did not thrive on the mainland, so the Europeans' efforts there were far

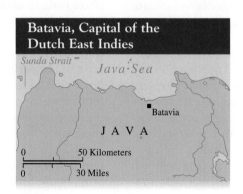

Batavia, Capital of the Dutch East Indies

Sunda Strait

Java Sea

JAVA

Batavia

0   50 Kilometers

0   30 Miles

⟫ **BATAVIA, CAPITAL OF THE DUTCH EAST INDIES.** After seizing control of the spice trade from European and Islamic rivals, the Dutch established their headquarters at Batavia, on the northern coast of Java, in 1619. Eventually, the canals shown in this photograph became breeding grounds for malaria-bearing mosquitos, forcing the Dutch to move a few miles to the south, the site of modern-day Jakarta.

The Art Archive, London

less determined than in the islands. The Portuguese did establish limited trade relations with several mainland states, including the Thai kingdom at Ayuthaya, Burma, Vietnam, and the remnants of the old Angkor kingdom in Cambodia. By the early seventeenth century, other nations had followed and had begun to compete actively for trade and missionary privileges. As was the case elsewhere, the Europeans soon became involved in local factional disputes as a means of obtaining political and economic advantages. In Burma, the English and the French supported rival groups in the internal struggles of the monarchy until a new dynasty emerged and threw the foreigners out. A similar process took place at Ayuthaya, where the French were forced to evacuate the area in the late seventeenth century.

In Vietnam, the arrival of Western merchants and missionaries coincided with a period of internal conflict among ruling groups in the country. After their arrival in the mid-seventeenth century, the European powers characteristically began to intervene in local politics, with the Portuguese and the Dutch supporting rival factions. By the end of the century, when it became clear that economic opportunities were limited, most European states abandoned their factories (trading stations) in the area. French missionaries attempted to remain, but

their efforts were hampered by the local authorities, who viewed the Catholic insistence that converts give their primary loyalty to the pope as a threat to the legal status and prestige of the Vietnamese emperor (see the box on p. 408).

State and Society in Precolonial Southeast Asia

Between 1400 and 1800, Southeast Asia experienced the last flowering of traditional culture before the advent of European rule in the nineteenth century. Although the coming of the Europeans had an immediate and direct impact in some areas, notably the Philippines and parts of the Malay world, in most areas Western influence was still relatively limited. Europeans occasionally dabbled in local politics and modified regional trade patterns, but they generally were not a decisive factor in the evolution of local political or social systems.

Nevertheless, Southeast Asian societies were changing in several subtle ways—in their trade patterns, their means of livelihood, and their religious beliefs. In some ways, these changes accentuated the differences between individual states in the region. Yet beneath these differences was an underlying commonality of life for most people.

AN EXCHANGE OF ROYAL CORRESPONDENCE

In 1681, King Louis XIV of France wrote a letter to the "king of Tonkin" (the Trinh family head, then acting as viceroy to the Vietnamese ruler) requesting permission for Christian missionaries to proselytize in Vietnam. The latter politely declined the request on the grounds that such activity was prohibited by ancient custom. In fact, Christian missionaries had been active in Vietnam for years, and their intervention in local politics had aroused the anger of the court in Hanoi.

A LETTER TO THE KING OF TONKIN FROM LOUIS XIV

Most high, most excellent, most mighty, and most magnanimous Prince, our very dear and good friend, may it please God to increase your greatness with a happy end!

We hear from our subjects who were in your Realm what protection you accorded them. We appreciate this all the more since we have for you all the esteem that one can have for a prince as illustrious through his military valor as he is commendable for the justice which he exercises in his Realm. We have even been informed that you have not been satisfied to extend this general protection to our subjects but, in particular, that you gave effective proofs of it to Messrs. Deydier and de Bourges. We would have wished that they might have been able to recognize all the favors they received from you by having presents worthy of you offered you; but since the war which we have had for several years, in which all of Europe had banded together against us, prevented our vessels from going to the Indies, at the present time, when we are at peace after having gained many victories and expanded our Realm through the conquest of several important places, we have immediately given orders to the Royal Company to establish itself in your kingdom as soon as possible, and have commanded Messrs. Deydier and de Bourges to remain with you in order to maintain a good relationship between our subjects and yours, also to warn us on occasions that might present themselves when we might be able to give you proofs of our esteem and of our wish to concur with your satisfaction as well as with your best interests.

By way of initial proof, we have given orders to have brought to you some presents which we believe might be agreeable to you. But the one thing in the world which we desire most, both for you and for your Realm, would be to obtain for your subjects who have already embraced the law of the only true God of heaven and earth, the freedom to profess it, since this law is the highest, the noblest, the most sacred, and especially the most suitable to have kings reign absolutely over the people.

We are even quite convinced that, if you knew the truths and the maxims which it teaches, you would give first of all to your subjects the glorious example of embracing it. We wish you this incomparable blessing together with a long and happy reign, and we pray God that it may please Him to augment your greatness with the happiest of endings.

Written at Saint-Germain-en-Laye, the 10th day of January, 1681,

Your very dear and good friend,
Louis

ANSWER FROM THE KING OF TONKIN TO LOUIS XIV

The King of Tonkin sends to the King of France a letter to express to him his best sentiments, saying that he was happy to learn that fidelity is a durable good of man and that justice is the most important of things. Consequently practicing of fidelity and justice cannot but yield good results. Indeed, though France and our Kingdom differ as to mountains, rivers, and boundaries, if fidelity and justice reign among our villages, our conduct will express all of our good feelings and contain precious gifts. Your communication, which comes from a country which is a thousand leagues away, and which proceeds from the heart as a testimony of your sincerity, merits repeated consideration and infinite praise. Politeness toward strangers is nothing unusual in our country. There is not a stranger who is not well received by us. How then could we refuse a man from France, which is the most celebrated among the kingdoms of the world and which for love of us wishes to frequent us and bring us merchandise? These feelings of fidelity and justice are truly worthy to be applauded. As regards your wish that we should cooperate in propagating your religion, we do not dare to permit it, for there is an ancient custom, introduced by edicts, which formally forbids it. Now, edicts are promulgated only to be carried out faithfully; without fidelity nothing is stable. How could we disdain a well-established custom to satisfy a private friendship? . . .

We beg you to understand well that this is our communication concerning our mutual acquaintance. This then is my letter. We send you herewith a modest gift, which we offer you with a glad heart.

This letter was written at the beginning of winter and on a beautiful day.

Despite the diversity of cultures and religious beliefs in the area, Southeast Asians were in most respects closer to each other than they were to peoples outside the region. For the most part, the states and peoples of Southeast Asia were still in control of their own destiny.

RELIGION AND KINGSHIP

During the early modern era, both Buddhism and Islam became well established in Southeast Asia, and Christianity began to attract some converts, especially in the Philippines. Buddhism was dominant in lowland areas on the mainland, from Burma to Vietnam. At first, Muslim influence was felt mainly on the Malay peninsula and along the northern coast of Java and Sumatra, where local merchants encountered their Muslim counterparts from foreign lands on a regular basis. At the same time, traditional religious beliefs continued to survive, especially in inland areas, where the local populations either ignored the new doctrines or integrated them into their traditional forms of spirit worship. Buddhists in rural Burma and Thailand, for example, might also believe in nature spirits. On Java and Sumatra, where Islam was slow to penetrate into the interior, the result was a division between devout Muslims in the cities and essentially animist peasants in the rural villages that persists to this day.

Both Buddhism and Islam brought other changes in their train—temple education for Buddhists and schools for Islamic scholars and new religious and moral restrictions on human behavior such as refraining from eating pork and drinking wine for Muslims (though some foreign Muslims complained that the latter rule was not always followed). Because Islam discouraged the traditional tattooing of the body, Muslim converts turned to the technique of decorating textiles called *batik*.

Buddhism and Islam also helped shape Southeast Asian political institutions. As the political systems began to mature, they evolved into four main types: Buddhist kings, Javanese kings, Islamic sultans, and Vietnamese emperors (for the case of Vietnam, which was strongly influenced by China, see Chapter 11). In each case, institutions and concepts imported from abroad were adapted to local circumstances.

The Buddhist style of kingship took shape between the eleventh and the fifteenth centuries, as Theravada Buddhism spread throughout the area. It became the predominant political system in the Buddhist states of mainland Southeast Asia—Burma, Ayuthaya, Laos, and Cambodia. Perhaps the dominant feature of the Buddhist model was the godlike character of the monarch, who was considered by virtue of his karma to be innately superior to other human beings and served as a link between human society and the cosmos. Court rituals stressed the sacred character of the monarch, and even the palace was modeled after the symbolic design of the Hindu universe. In its center was an architectural rendering of sacred Mount Meru, the legendary home of the gods.

The Javanese model was a blend of Buddhist and Islamic political traditions. Like their Buddhist counterparts, Javanese monarchs possessed a sacred quality and maintained the balance between the sacred and the material world, but as Islam penetrated the Indonesian islands in the fifteenth and sixteenth centuries, the monarchs began to lose their semidivine quality.

The Islamic model was found mainly on the Malay peninsula and along the coast of the Indonesian archipelago. In this pattern, the head of state was a sultan, who was viewed as a mortal, although he still possessed some magical qualities. The sultan served as a defender of the faith and staffed his bureaucracy mainly with aristocrats, but he also frequently relied on the Muslim community of scholars—the *ulama*—and was expected, at least in theory, to rule according to the *Shari'a* (see the box on p. 410).

ECONOMY AND SOCIETY

During the early period of European penetration, the economy of most Southeast Asian societies was based on agriculture, as it had been for thousands of years. Still, by the sixteenth century, commerce was beginning to affect daily life, especially in the cities that were beginning to proliferate along the coasts or on navigable rivers. In part, this was because agriculture itself was becoming more commercialized as cash crops like sugar and spices replaced subsistence farming in rice or other cereals in some areas.

Regional and interregional trade were already expanding before the coming of the Europeans. The central geographical location of Southeast Asia enabled it to become a focal point in a widespread trading network. Spices, of course, were the mainstay of the interregional trade, but Southeast Asia exchanged other products as well. The region exported tin (mined in Malaya since the tenth century), copper, gold, tropical fruits and other agricultural products, cloth, gems, and luxury goods in exchange for manufactured goods, ceramics, and high-quality textiles such as silk from China. Although on balance the region was an importer of manufactured goods, it produced some high-quality goods of its own. The ceramics of Vietnam and Thailand, though not made with the high-firing techniques used in China, were still of good quality. The Portuguese traveler Duarte Barbosa observed that the Javanese were skilled cabinetmakers, weapons manufacturers, shipbuilders, and locksmiths. The royal courts were both the main producers and the primary consumers of luxury goods, most of which were produced by highly skilled slaves in the employ of the court.

In general, Southeast Asians probably enjoyed a somewhat higher living standard than most of their contemporaries elsewhere in Asia. Although most of the population was poor by modern Western standards, hunger was not a widespread problem. Several factors help explain this relative prosperity. In the first place, most of Southeast Asia has been blessed by a salubrious climate. The uniformly high temperatures and the abundant rainfall enable

THE TIMELY END OF
SULTAN ZAINAL-'ABIDIN

*A*cheh, on the northern tip of the island of Sumatra, was one of the first areas in Southeast Asia to be converted to Islam. This passage from the History of Acheh *describes the cruel habits of Sultan Zainal-'Abidin, who ruled in the early seventeenth century. Note the understated way in which the author describes his deposition.*

HISTORY OF ACHEH

Then Sultan Seri'Alam was deposed and Sultan Zainal was installed.

The former had occupied the throne for one year before passing away. He passed away in the year 995 (A.H.) [1617 C.E.]. . . .

After the kingdom of Acheh Dar as-Salam and all its subject territories had been handed over to Sultan Zainal-'Abidin, he would always go out on to the arena and would have rutting elephants as well as ones which were not rutting charge each other, and as a result several people were gored to death by them, and the Bunga Setangkai palace was rammed and then collapsed in ruins together with its annexes. . . . He would order men to beat each other and to duel with staves and shields, and would order Achehnese champion fencers to compete with Indian ones, so that several of the Achehnese and Indian fencers were killed and some were wounded. . . .

If the Sultan were holding audience in a certain place all the chiefs were instructed to sit in homage in the hot sun or in the rain without distinction between the good or the evil. . . .

When the chiefs noticed these habits of the Sultan, and observed that they were growing worse day by day, they said to each other, "What should we do about our lord, for if his oppression of us is like this while he is still young, what will it be like when he is older? According to us, if he continues to be ruler everything will certainly fall in ruins about our ears." Then Sharif al-Muluk Maharaja Lela said, "If that is how it is, it would be best for us to depose our lord the Sultan."

After the chiefs had reached agreement on this matter, one evening the Sultan summoned persons to recite texts in praise of God, and the chiefs were summoned along with them. On that occasion they were reciting texts in the Friday annex. The Sultan was then put on an elephant and was taken to Makota 'Alam. When he arrived at Makota 'Alam [where he was put to death] . . . the Sultan had occupied the throne for two years when he passed away. He passed away in the year 997. In that same year Sultan 'Ala ad-Din Ri'ayat Shah Marhum Sayyid al-Mukkamil was installed.

---

as many as two or even three crops to be grown each year. Second, although the soil in some areas is poor, the alluvial deltas on the mainland are fertile, and the volcanoes of Indonesia periodically spew forth rich volcanic ash that renews the mineral resources of the soil of Sumatra and Java. Finally, with some exceptions, most of Southeast Asia was relatively thinly populated. According to one estimate, the population of the entire region in 1600 was about twenty million, or about 5.5 persons per square kilometer, well below levels elsewhere in Asia. Only in a few areas such as the Red River delta in northern Vietnam was overpopulation a serious problem.

Social institutions tended to be fairly homogeneous throughout Southeast Asia. Compared with China and India, there was little social stratification, and the nuclear family predominated. In general, women fared better in

➤ **THE JAPANESE BRIDGE AT HOI AN.** The Europeans were not the only people who sailed far from native shores in the pursuit of commercial profit during the Age of Exploration. Even prior to the arrival of the first Portuguese fleets in eastern Asia, merchants from within the region as well as from the Middle East had established a vigorous trading network stretching from Japan into the Indian Ocean. Among the active participants were the Japanese. Shown here is a bridge erected in the port city of Hoi An, along the coast of Vietnam south of present-day Da Nang. The bridge spanned a creek entering the harbor and separated the Japanese section of town from other neighborhoods inhabited by Chinese merchants or Europeans. Japanese merchants shipped a variety of tropical goods from the area, as well as local porcelain.

MAP 14.4 **The Pattern of World Trade from the Sixteenth to the Eighteenth Centuries.** This map shows the major products that were traded by European merchants throughout the world during the era of European exploration. Prevailing wind patterns in the oceans are shown on the map. ➤ *What were the primary sources of gold and silver, so sought after by Columbus and his successors?*

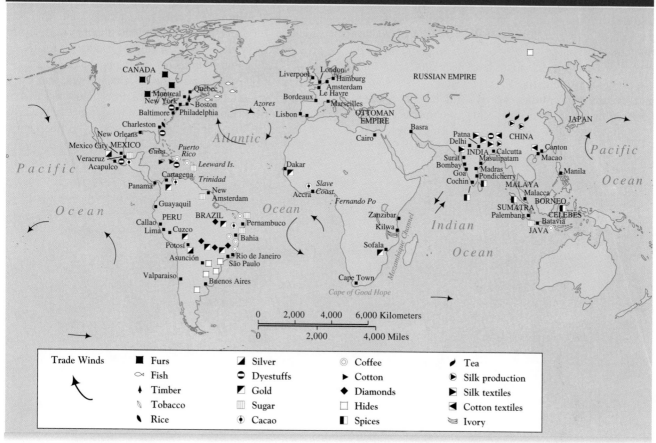

Trade Winds				
■ Furs	◩ Silver	◎ Coffee	◢ Tea	
∽ Fish	⬤ Dyestuffs	► Cotton	◖ Silk production	
⬥ Timber	◪ Gold	◆ Diamonds	◪ Silk textiles	
◺ Tobacco	▥ Sugar	☐ Hides	◤ Cotton textiles	
◣ Rice	◉ Cacao	■ Spices	〰 Ivory	

the region than anywhere else in Asia. Daughters often had the same inheritance rights as sons, and family property was held jointly between husband and wife. Wives were often permitted to divorce their husbands, and monogamy was the rule rather than the exception. In some cases, the family of the groom provided the dowry in marriage, and married couples often went to live in the wife's village. Although women were usually restricted to specialized work, such as making ceramics, weaving, or transplanting the rice seedlings into the main paddy fields, and rarely possessed legal rights equal to those of men, they enjoyed a comparatively high degree of freedom and status in most societies in the region and, as we saw in Chapter 9, were sometimes involved in commerce. In the Indonesian islands, for example, women apparently devised a simple fourteen-character alphabet based on the Indian script to record their business transactions. This written language was often passed on to their daughters, while their sons were trained to read sacred works in religious schools.

 # CONCLUSION

During the fifteenth century, Europeans burst onto the world scene. Beginning with the seemingly modest ventures of the Portuguese ships that sailed southward along the West African coast, the process accelerated with the epoch-making voyages of Christopher Columbus to the Americas and Vasco da Gama to the Indian Ocean in the 1490s. Soon a number of other European states had entered the scene, and by the end of the eighteenth century, they had created a global trade network dominated by Western ships and Western power that distributed foodstuffs, textile goods, spices, and precious minerals from one end of the globe to the other (see Map 14.4).

In less than three hundred years, the European Age of Exploration changed the face of the world. In some areas, such as the Americas and the Spice Islands, it led to the destruction of indigenous civilizations and the establishment of European colonies. In others, as in Africa, South Asia, and mainland Southeast Asia, it left native regimes intact but had a strong impact on local societies and regional trade patterns.

At the time, many European observers viewed the process in a favorable light. Not only did it expand world trade and foster the exchange of new crops and discoveries between the Old and the New Worlds (a process that will be discussed in the Reflection at the end of Part III), but it also introduced the message of Jesus Christ to "heathen peoples" around the globe. Most modern historians have been much more critical, concluding that European activities during the sixteenth and seventeenth centuries created a "tributary mode of production" based on European profits from unequal terms of trade that foreshadowed the exploitative relationship char-

acteristic of the later colonial period. Other scholars have questioned that contention, however, and argue that although Western commercial operations had a significant impact on global trade patterns, they did not—at least not before the eighteenth century—freeze out non-European participants. Muslim merchants, for example, were long able to evade European efforts to eliminate them from the spice trade, and the trans-Saharan caravan trade was relatively unaffected by European merchant shipping along the West African coast. In some cases, the European presence may even have encouraged new economic activity, as in the Indian subcontinent (see Chapter 16). If there was an "age of Western dominance," then, it did not take shape until much later.

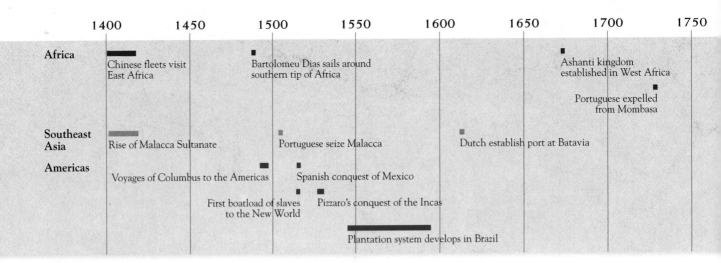

CHAPTER NOTES

1. Harry J. Benda and John A. Larkin, eds., *The World of Southeast Asia: Selected Historical Readings* (New York, 1967), p. 13.
2. J. H. Parry, *The European Reconnaissance: Selected Documents* (New York, 1968), p. 113, quoting from Armando Cortesão, *The Summa Oriental of Tomé Pires* (London, 1944), vol. 2, pp. 283–287.
3. Quoted in J. H. Parry, *The Age of Reconnaissance: Discovery, Exploration, and Settlement, 1450 to 1650* (New York, 1963), p. 33.
4. Quoted in Richard B. Reed, "The Expansion of Europe," in Richard DeMolen, ed., *The Meaning of the Renaissance and Reformation* (Boston, 1974), p. 308.
5. K. N. Chaudhuri, *Trade and Civilization in the Indian Ocean: An Economic History from the Rise of Islam to 1750* (Cambridge, 1985), p. 65.
6. Miguel Leon-Portilla, ed., *The Broken Spears: The Aztec Account of the Conquest of Mexico* (Boston, 1969), p. 51.
7. Quoted in Parry, *Age of Reconnaissance*, pp. 176–177.
8. Quoted in Basil Davidson, *Africa in History: Themes and Outlines* (London, 1968), p. 137.

SUGGESTED READING

Classic works on the period of European expansion include J. H. Parry, *The Age of Reconnaissance: Discovery, Exploration, and Settlement, 1450 to 1650* (New York, 1963); B. Penrose, *Travel and Discovery in the Renaissance, 1420–1620* (New York, 1962); and the brief work by J. H. Parry, *The Establishment of European Hegemony, 1415–1715* (New York, 1961). Also see K. M. Panikkar, *Asia and Western Dominance* (London, 1959), and H. Furber, *Rival Empires of Trade in the Orient, 1600–1800* (Minneapolis, Minn. 1976). For a more critical interpretation, see E. Wolf, *Europe and the People Without History* (Berkeley, Calif., 1982), and A. G. Frank, *World Accumulation, 1492–1789* (New York, 1978).

On the technological aspects, see C. M. Cipolla, *Guns, Sails, and Empires: Technological Innovation and the Early Phases of European Expansion, 1400–1700* (New York, 1965); F. Fernandez-Armesto, ed., *The Times Atlas of World Exploration* (New York, 1991); and R. C. Smith, *Vanguard of Empire: Ships of Exploration in the Age of Columbus* (Oxford, 1993); also see A. Pagden, *Lords of All the World: Ideologies of Empire in Spain, Britain, and France, c. 1500–c. 1800* (New Haven, Conn., 1995). For an overview on the impact of European expansion in the Indian Ocean, see K. N. Chaudhuri, *Trade and Civilization in the Indian Ocean: An Economic History from the Rise of Islam to 1750* (Cambridge, 1985). For a series of stimulating essays reflecting modern scholarship, see J. D. Tracy, *The Rise of Merchant Empires: Long-Distance Trade in the Early Modern World, 1350–1750* (Cambridge, 1990).

On European expansion in the Americas, see S. E. Morison, *The European Discovery of America: The Southern Voyages, 1492–1616* (New York, 1974). For a fundamental work on Spanish colonization, see J. H. Parry, *The Spanish Seaborne Empire* (New York, 1966). The most recent work on the conquistadors is H. Thomas, *Conquest: Montezuma, Cortés, and the Fall of Old Mexico* (New York, 1993). See also the richly illustrated H. Innes, *The Conquistadors* (New York, 1969). The human effects of the interaction of New and Old World cultures are examined thoughtfully in A. W. Crosby, *The Columbian Exchange: Biological and Cultural Consequences of 1492* (Westport, Conn., 1972).

On Portuguese expansion, the fundamental work is C. R. Boxer, *The Portuguese Seaborne Empire, 1415–1825* (New York, 1969). For a more recent interpretation, see W. B. Diffie and G. D. Winius, *Foundations of the Portuguese Empire, 1415–1580* (Minneapolis, Minn., 1979). On the Dutch, see J. I. Israel, *Dutch Primacy in World Trade, 1585–1740* (Oxford, 1989). The effects of European trade in Southeast Asia are discussed in A. Reid, *Southeast Asia in the Age of Commerce, 1450–1680* (New Haven, Conn., 1989).

On the African slave trade, the standard work is P. Curtin, *The African Slave Trade: A Census* (Madison, Wis., 1969). For more recent treatments, see P. Lovejoy, *Transformations in Slavery: A History of Slavery in Africa* (1983), and P. Manning, *Slavery and African Life* (Cambridge, 1990); H. Thomas, *The Slave Trade* (New York, 1997), provides a useful overview. Also see C. Palmer, *Human Cargoes: The British Slave Trade to Spanish America, 1700–1739* (Urbana, Ill., 1981), and K. F. Kiple, *The Caribbean Slave: A Biological History* (Cambridge, 1984).

For a brief introduction to women's experiences during the Age of Exploration and global trade, see S. Hughes and B. Hughes, *Women in World History*, vol. 2 (Armonk, N.Y., 1997). For a more theoretical discussion of violence and gender in the early modern period, consult R. Trexler, *Sex and Conquest: Gendered Violence, Political Order, and the European Conquest of the Americas* (Ithaca, N.Y., 1995). The native American female experience with the European encounter is presented in R. Gutierrez, *When Jesus Came the Corn Mothers Went Away: Marriage, Sexuality and Power in New Mexico, 1500–1846* (Stanford, Calif., 1991), and K. Anderson, *Chain Her by One Foot: The Subjugation of Women in Seventeenth Century New France* (London, 1991).

INFOTRAC COLLEGE EDITION

For additional reading, go to InfoTrac College Edition, your online research library at
http://web1.infotrac-college.com

Enter the search terms "Vasco da Gama" using Keywords.

Enter the search terms "Christopher Columbus" using the Subject Guide.

Enter the search term "mercantilism" using the Subject Guide.

Enter the search terms "Africa history" using Keywords.

Chapter 15

© Sonia Halliday Photographs

THE MUSLIM EMPIRES

FOCUS QUESTIONS
- Why are the Ottoman, Safavid, and Mughal Empires sometimes called "gunpowder empires," and how accurate is that characterization?
- What were the main characteristics of each of the Muslim empires, and in what ways were they similar?
- What contact did each of the Muslim empires have with Europeans, and how was each empire affected by that contact?
- What role did women play in each of the Muslim empires?
- ➤ How did each of the great Muslim empires come into existence, and why did they ultimately decline?

One of the primary objectives of European leaders in seeking a route to the Spice Islands was to lessen the political and economic power of Islam by reducing the Muslims' strong position in the global trade network. As we saw in Chapter 14, Portuguese fleets, followed by those of the Spanish, the English, and the Dutch, had some success in wresting control over the spice trade from Muslim shippers, although the latter were never totally driven out of the business. By the eighteenth century, the Indian Ocean had ceased to be an Arab preserve and had become, in some respects, a European lake.

Thus the European dream of controlling global trade markets had become a reality. But in the broader scheme of things, the goal of crippling the power of Islam was not entirely realized, for Europe's success had not been achieved by the collapse of its great rival. To the contrary, the Muslim world, which appeared to have entered a period of decline with the collapse of the Abbasid caliphate during the era of the Mongols, managed to revive in the shadow of Europe's Age of Exploration, a period that also saw the rise of three great Muslim empires. These powerful Muslim states—

of the Ottomans, the Safavids, and the Mughals—dominated the Middle East and the South Asia subcontinent and brought stability to a region that had been in turmoil for centuries.

This stability lasted for about two hundred years. By the end of the eighteenth century, much of India and the Middle East had come under severe European pressure and had returned to a state of anarchy, and the Ottoman Empire had entered a period of gradual decline. But that decline was due more to internal factors than to the challenge posed by a resurgent Europe. •

THE OTTOMAN EMPIRE

The Ottoman Turks were among the various Turkic-speaking peoples who had spread westward from Central Asia in the ninth, tenth, and eleventh centuries. The first to dominate were the Seljuk Turks, who initially attempted to revive the declining Abbasid caliphate in Baghdad. Later they established themselves in the Anatolian peninsula at the expense of the Byzantine Empire. Turks served as warriors or administrators, while the peasants who tilled the farmland were mainly Greek.

In the late thirteenth century, a new group of Turks under the tribal leader Osman (1280–1326) began to consolidate their power in the northwestern corner of the Anatolian peninsula. That land had been given to them by the Seljuk rulers as a reward for helping drive out the Mongols in the late thirteenth century. At first, the Osman Turks were relatively peaceful and engaged in pastoral pursuits, but as the Seljuk empire began to disintegrate in the early fourteenth century, they began to expand and founded the Osmanli (later to be known as Ottoman) dynasty.

A key advantage for the Ottomans was their location in the northwestern corner of the peninsula. From there they were able to expand westward and eventually control the Bosporus and the Dardanelles, between the Mediterranean and the Black Seas. The Byzantine Empire, of course, had controlled the area for centuries, serving as a buffer between the Muslim Middle East and the Latin West. The Byzantines, however, had been severely weakened by the sack of Constantinople in the Fourth Crusade (in 1204) and the Western occupation of much of the empire for the next half century. In 1345, Ottoman forces under their leader Orkhan I (1326–1360) crossed the Bosporus for the first time to support a usurper against the Byzantine emperor in Constantinople. Setting up their first European base at Gallipoli at the Mediterranean entrance to the Dardanelles, Turkish forces expanded gradually into the Balkans and allied with fractious Serbian and Bulgar forces against the Byzantines. In these unstable conditions, the Ottomans gradually established permanent settlements throughout the area, where Turkish beys (provincial governors in the Ottoman Empire; from the Turkish *beg,* "knight") drove out the previous landlords and collected taxes from the local Slavic peasants. The Ottoman leader now began to claim the title of sultan or sovereign of his domain.

In 1360, Orkhan was succeeded by his son Murad I, who consolidated Ottoman power in the Balkans, set up a capital at Edirne (modern Adrianople), and gradually reduced the Byzantine emperor to a vassal. Murad did not initially attempt to conquer Constantinople because his forces were composed mostly of the traditional Turkish cavalry and lacked the ability to breach the strong walls of the city. Instead, he began to build up a strong military administration based on the recruitment of Christians into an elite guard. Called Janissaries (from the Turkish *yeni cheri,* "new troops"), they were recruited from the local Christian population in the Balkans and then converted to Islam and trained as foot soldiers or administrators. One of the major advantages of the Janissaries was that they were directly subordinated to the sultanate and therefore owed their loyalty to the person of the sultan. Other military forces were organized by the beys and were thus loyal to their local tribal leaders.

The Janissary corps also represented a response to changes in warfare. As the knowledge of firearms spread in the late fourteenth century, the Turks began to master the new technology, including siege cannons and muskets. The traditional nomadic cavalry charge was now outmoded and was superseded by infantry forces armed with muskets. Thus the Janissaries provided a well-armed infantry who served both as an elite guard to protect the palace and as a means of extending Turkish control in the Balkans. With his new forces, Murad defeated the Serbs at the famous Battle of Kosovo in 1389 and ended Serbian hegemony in the area.

Under Murad's successor, Bayazid I (1389–1402), the Ottomans advanced northward, annexed Bulgaria, and slaughtered the flower of French cavalry at a major battle on the Danube. A defeat at the hands of the Mongol warrior Tamerlane (see Chapter 9) in 1402 proved to be only a temporary setback. When Mehmet II (1451–1481) succeeded to the throne, he was determined to capture Constantinople. Already in control of the Dardanelles, he ordered the construction of a major fortress on the Bosporus just north of the city, which put the Turks in a position to strangle the Byzantines.

The last Byzantine emperor desperately called for help from the Europeans, but only the Genoese came to his defense. With eighty thousand troops ranged against only seven thousand defenders, Mehmet laid siege to Constantinople in 1453. In their attack on the city, the Turks made use of massive cannons with 26-foot barrels that could launch stone balls weighing up to 1,200 pounds each. The Byzantines stretched heavy chains across the Golden Horn, the inlet that forms the city's harbor, to

THE FALL OF CONSTANTINOPLE

F̲ew events in the history of the Ottoman Empire are more dramatic than the conquest of Constantinople in 1453. In this excerpt, the conquest is described by Kritovoulos, a Greek who later served in the Ottoman administration. Although the author did not witness the conquest itself, he was apparently well informed about the event and provides us with a vivid description.

KRITOVOULOS, *LIFE OF MEHMED THE CONQUEROR*

So saying, he [the Sultan] led them himself. And they, with a shout on the run and with a fearsome yell, went on ahead of the Sultan, pressing on up to the palisade. After a long and bitter struggle they hurled back the Romans [Byzantines] from there and climbed by force up the palisade. They dashed some of their foe down into the ditch between the great wall and the palisade, which was deep and hard to get out of, and they killed them there. The rest they drove back to the gate.

He had opened this gate in the great wall, so as to go easily over to the palisade. Now there was a great struggle there and great slaughter among those stationed there, for they were attacked by the heavy infantry and not a few others in irregular formation, who had been attracted from many points by the shouting. There the Emperor Constantine [Constantine XIII Paleologus], with all who were with him, fell in gallant combat.

The heavy infantry were already streaming through the little gate into the City, and others had rushed in through the breach in the great wall. Then all the rest of the army, with a rush and a roar, poured in brilliantly and scattered all over the City. And the Sultan stood before the great wall, where the standard also was and the ensigns, and watched the proceedings. The day was already breaking. . . .

The soldiers fell on them [the citizens] with anger and great wrath. For one thing, they were actuated by the hardships of the siege. For another, some foolish people had hurled taunts and curses at them from the battlements all through the siege. Now, in general they killed so as to frighten all the City, and to terrorize and enslave all by the slaughter.

When they had had enough of murder, and the City was reduced to slavery, some of the troops turned to the mansions of the mighty, by bands and companies and divisions, for plunder and spoil. Others went to the robbing of churches, and others dispersed to the simple homes of the common people, stealing, robbing, plundering, killing, insulting, taking and enslaving men, women, and children, old and young, priests, monks—in short, every age and class. . . .

After this the Sultan entered the City and looked about to see its great size, its situation, its grandeur and beauty, its teeming population, its loveliness, and the costliness of its churches and public buildings and of the private houses and community houses and those of the officials. . . . When he saw what a large number had been killed, and the ruin of the buildings, and the wholesale ruin and destruction of the City, he was filled with compassion and repented not a little at the destruction and plundering. Tears fell from his eyes as he groaned deeply and passionately: "What a city we have given over to plunder and destruction." . . .

As for the great City of Constantine, raised to a great height of glory and dominion and wealth in its own times, overshadowing to an infinite degree all the cities around it, renowned for its glory, wealth, authority, power, and greatness, and all its other qualities, it thus came to its end.

---

prevent a naval attack from the north and prepared to make their final stand behind the 13-mile-long wall along the western edge of the city. But Mehmet's forces seized the tip of the peninsula north of the Golden Horn and then dragged their ships overland across the peninsula from the Bosporus and put them into the water behind the chains. Finally, the walls were breached; the Byzantine emperor died in the final battle (see the box above). Mehmet II, standing before the

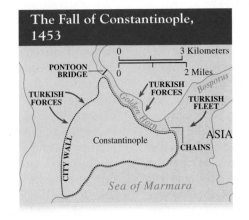

The Fall of Constantinople, 1453

palace of the emperor, paused to reflect on the passing nature of human glory. But it was not long before he and the Ottomans were again on the march.

Expansion of the Empire

With their new capital at Constantinople, renamed Istanbul, the Ottoman Turks were now a dominant force in the Balkans and the Anatolian peninsula. They now began to advance to the east against the Shi'ite kingdom of the Safavids in Persia (see "The Safavids" later in this chapter), which had been promoting rebellion among the Anatolian tribal population and disrupting Turkish trade through the Middle East. After defeating the Safavids at a major battle in 1514, Emperor Selim I (1512–1520) consolidated Turkish control over Mesopotamia and then turned his

MS Fr.9087,f.207, Bibliotheque Nationale, Paris; photo © Sonia Halliday Photographs

© Sonia Halliday Photographs

MEHMET II, CONQUEROR OF CONSTANTINOPLE.
Identified with the seizure of Constantinople from the Byzantine Empire in 1453, Mehmet II was one of the most illustrious Ottoman sultans. This Turkish miniature portrays Mehmet II with his handkerchief, a symbol of the supreme power of the Ottoman ruler. He is also smelling a rose, representing his cultural interests, especially as patron of the arts.

THE TURKISH CONQUEST OF CONSTANTINOPLE.
Mehmet II put a stranglehold on the Byzantine capital of Constantinople with a surprise attack by Turkish ships, which were dragged overland and placed in the water behind the enemy's defense lines. In addition, the Turks made use of massive cannons that could launch stone balls weighing up to 1,200 pounds each. The heavy bombardment of the city walls presaged the beginning of a new era of warfare in Europe. Notice the fanciful Gothic interpretation of the city in this contemporary French miniature of the siege of Constantinople.

attention to the Mamluks in Egypt, who had failed to support the Ottomans in their struggle against the Safavids. The Mamluks were defeated in Syria in 1516; Cairo fell a year later. Now controlling several of the holy cities of Islam, including Jerusalem, Mecca, and Medina, Selim declared himself to be the new caliph, or succes-

sor to Muhammad. During the next few years, Turkish armies and fleets advanced westward along the African coast, occupying Tripoli, Tunis, and Algeria and eventually penetrating almost to the Strait of Gibraltar (see Map 15.1). In their advance, the invaders had taken advantage of the progressive disintegration of the Nasrid dynasty in Morocco, which had been in decline for decades and had lost its last foothold on the European continent when Granada fell to the rising power of Spain in 1492.

The impact of Turkish rule on the peoples of North Africa was relatively light. Like their predecessors, the Turks were Muslims, and they preferred where possible to administer their conquered regions through local rulers. Central government direction was achieved through appointed *pashas* who collected taxes (and then paid a

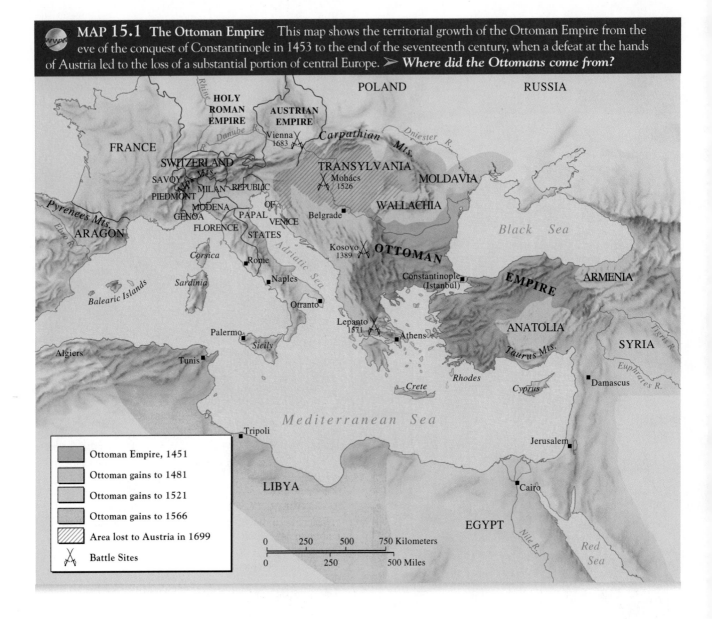

MAP 15.1 The Ottoman Empire This map shows the territorial growth of the Ottoman Empire from the eve of the conquest of Constantinople in 1453 to the end of the seventeenth century, when a defeat at the hands of Austria led to the loss of a substantial portion of central Europe. ➤ *Where did the Ottomans come from?*

fixed percentage as tribute to the central government), maintained law and order, and were directly responsible to Istanbul. The Turks ruled from coastal cities like Algiers, Tunis, and Tripoli and made no attempt to control the interior beyond maintaining the trade routes through the Sahara to the trading centers along the Niger River. Meanwhile, local pirates along the Barbary Coast—the northern coast of Africa from Egypt to the Atlantic Ocean—competed with their Christian rivals in raiding the shipping that passed through the Mediterranean.

By the seventeenth century, the links between the imperial court in Istanbul and its appointed representatives in the Turkish regencies in North Africa had begun to decline. Some of the pashas were dethroned by local elites, while others, such as the bey of Tunis, became hereditary rulers. Even Egypt, whose agricultural wealth and control over the route to the Red Sea made it the most important country in the area to the Turks, gradu-

ally became autonomous under a new official class of Janissaries. Many of them became wealthy landowners by exploiting their official function to collect tax revenues far in excess of what they had to remit to Istanbul. In the early eighteenth century, the Mamluks returned to power, although the Turkish government managed to retain some control by means of a viceroy appointed from Istanbul.

TURKISH EXPANSION IN EUROPE

After their conquest of Constantinople in 1453, the Ottoman Turks tried to complete their conquest of the Balkans, where they had been established since the fourteenth century. Although they were successful in taking the Romanian territory of Wallachia in 1476, the resistance of the Hungarians initially kept the Turks from advancing up the Danube valley. From 1480 to 1520, inter-

A PORTRAIT OF SULEYMAN THE MAGNIFICENT

*S*uleyman the Magnificent was perhaps the greatest of all Ottoman sultans. Like King Louis XIV of France and Emperor Kangxi of China, he presided over his domain at the peak of its military and cultural achievement. This description of him was written by Ghislain de Busbecq, the Habsburg ambassador to Constantinople. Busbecq observed Suleyman at first hand and, as this excerpt indicates, was highly impressed by the Turkish ruler.

GHISLAIN DE BUSBECQ, *THE TURKISH LETTERS*

The Sultan was seated on a rather low sofa, no more than a foot from the ground and spread with many costly coverlets and cushions embroidered with exquisite work. Near him were his bow and arrows. His expression, as I have said, is anything but smiling, and has a sternness which, though sad, is full of majesty. On our arrival we were introduced into his presence by his chamberlains, who held our arms—a practice which has always been observed since a Croatian sought an interview and murdered the Sultan Amurath in a revenge for the slaughter of his master, Marcus the Despot of Serbia. After going through the pretense of kissing his hand, we were led to the wall facing him backwards, so as not to turn our backs or any part of them toward him. He then listened to the recital of my message, but, as it did not correspond with his expectations (for the demands of my imperial master [the Habsburg emperor Ferdinand I] were full of dignity and independence, and, therefore, far from acceptable to one who thought that his slightest wishes ought to be obeyed) he assumed an expression of disdain, and merely answered "Giusel, Giusel," that is, "Well, Well." We were then dismissed to our lodging. . . .

You will probably wish me to describe the impression which Suleyman made upon me. He is beginning to feel the weight of years, but his dignity of demeanor and his general physical appearance are worthy of the ruler of so vast an empire. He has always been frugal and temperate, and was so even in his youth, when he might have erred without incurring blame in the eyes of the Turks. Even in his earlier years he did not indulge in wine or in those unnatural vices to which the Turks are often addicted. Even his bitterest critics can find nothing more serious to allege against him than his undue submission to his wife and its result in his somewhat precipitate action in putting Mustapha [his firstborn son, by another wife] to death, which is generally imputed to her employment of love potions and incantations. It is generally agreed that, ever since he promoted her to the rank of his lawful wife, he has possessed no concubines, although there is no law to prevent his doing so. He is a strict guardian of his religion and its ceremonies, being not less desirous of upholding his faith than of extending his dominions. For his age—he has almost reached his sixtieth year—he enjoys quite good health, though his bad complexion may be due to some hidden malady; and indeed it is generally believed that he has an incurable ulcer or gangrene on his leg. This defect of complexion he remedies by painting his face with a coating of red powder, when he wishes departing ambassadors to take with them a strong impression of his good health; for he fancies that it contributes to inspire greater fear in foreign potentates if they think that he is well and strong. I noticed a clear indication of this practice on the present occasion; for his appearance when he received me in the final audience was very different from that which he presented when he gave me an interview on my arrival.

---

nal problems and the need to consolidate their eastern frontiers kept the Turks from any further attacks on Europe.

Suleyman I the Magnificent (1520–1566; see the box above), however, brought the Turks back to Europe's attention. Advancing up the Danube, the Turks seized Belgrade in 1521 and won a major victory over the Hungarians at the Battle of Mohács on the Danube in 1526. Subsequently, the Turks overran most of Hungary, moved into Austria, and advanced as far as Vienna, where they were finally repulsed in 1529. At the same time, they extended their power into the western Mediterranean and threatened to turn it into a Turkish lake until a large Turkish fleet was destroyed by the Spanish at Lepanto in 1571. Despite the defeat, the Turks continued to hold nominal suzerainty over the southern shores of the Mediterranean.

Although Europeans frequently called for new Christian Crusades against the "infidel" Turks, the Ottoman Empire was by the beginning of the seventeenth century being treated like any other European power by European rulers seeking alliances and trade concessions. During the first half of the seventeenth century, the Ottoman Empire was a "sleeping giant." Involved in domestic bloodletting and heavily threatened by a challenge from Persia, the Ottomans were content with the status quo in eastern Europe. But under a new line of grand vezirs in the second half of the seventeenth century, the Ottoman Empire again took the offensive. By mid-1683, the Ottomans had marched through the Hungarian plain and laid siege to Vienna. Repulsed by a mixed army of Austrians, Poles, Bavarians, and Saxons, the Turks retreated and were pushed out of Hungary by a new European coalition. Although they

THE OTTOMAN EMPIRE

Reign of Osman I	1280–1326
Ottoman Turks first cross the Bosporus	1345
Murad I consolidates Turkish power in the Balkans	1360
Ottomans defeat Serbian Army at Kosovo	1389
Tamerlane defeats Ottoman army at Ankara	1402
Rule of Mehmet II (the Conqueror)	1451–1481
Turkish conquest of Constantinople	1453
Turks defeat Mamluks in Syria and seize Cairo	1516–1517
Reign of Suleyman I (the Magnificent)	1520–1566
Defeat of Hungarians at Battle of Mohács	1526
Defeat of Turks at Vienna	1529
Battle of Lepanto	1571

THE SIEGE OF VIENNA. After seizing the Byzantine capital of Constantinople in 1453, Turkish forces began advancing into southern Europe to extend the borders of the Ottoman Empire. By 1529, they had reached the gates of Vienna, capital of the Habsburg Empire, which they placed under siege. In this contemporary painting from the Topkapi Palace in Istanbul, Turkish forces across the Danube River have besieged the walled city, shown in the background. Despite the use of cannons, first introduced to the West by Ottoman forces during this campaign, the siege was unsuccessful.

retained the core of their empire, the Ottoman Turks would never again be a threat to Europe. Although the Turkish empire held together for the rest of the seventeenth and the eighteenth centuries, it would be faced with new challenges from the ever growing Austrian Empire in southeastern Europe and the new Russian giant to the north.

The Nature of Turkish Rule

Like other Muslim empires in Persia and India, the Ottoman political system was the result of the evolution of tribal institutions into a sedentary empire. At the apex of the Ottoman system was the sultan, who was the supreme authority in both a political and a military sense. The origins of this system can be traced back to the bey, who was only a tribal leader, a first among equals, who could claim loyalty from his chiefs so long as he could provide booty and grazing lands for his subordinates. Disputes were settled by tribal law, while Muslim laws were secondary. Tribal leaders collected taxes— or booty—from areas under their control and sent one-fifth on to the bey. Both administrative and military power were centralized under the bey, and the capital was wherever the bey and his administration happened to be.

But the rise of empire brought about changes and an adaptation to Byzantine traditions of rule. The status and prestige of the sultan now increased relative to the subordinate tribal leaders, and the position took on the trappings of imperial rule. Court rituals were inherited from the Byzantines and Persians, and a centralized administrative system was adopted that increasingly isolated the sultan in his palace. The position of the sultan was hereditary, with a son, although not necessarily the eldest, always succeeding the father. This practice led to chronic succession struggles upon the death of individual sultans, and the losers were often executed (strangled with a silk bowstring) or later imprisoned. Heirs to the throne were assigned as provincial governors to provide them with experience.

The heart of the sultan's power was in the Topkapi Palace in the center of Istanbul. Topkapi (meaning "cannon gate") was constructed in 1459 by Mehmet II and served as an administrative center as well as the private residence of the sultan and his family. Eventually, it had a staff of twenty thousand employees. The private domain of the sultan was called the harem ("sacred place"). Here he resided with his concubines. Normally, a sultan did not marry but chose several concubines as his favorites; they were accorded this status after they gave birth to sons. When a son became a sultan, his mother became known as the queen mother and served as adviser to the throne. This tradition, initiated by the influential wife of Suleyman the Magnificent, often resulted in considerable authority for the queen mother in the affairs of state.

Members of the harem, like the Janissaries, were often of slave origin and formed an elite element in Ottoman society. Since the enslavement of Muslims was forbidden, slaves were taken among non-Islamic peoples. Some concubines were prisoners selected for the position, while others were purchased or offered to the sultan as a gift. They were then trained and educated like the Janissaries in a system called *devshirme* ("collection"). *Devshirme* had originated in the practice of requiring local clan leaders to provide prisoners to the sultan as part of their tax obligation. Talented males were given special training for eventual placement in military or administrative positions, while their female counterparts were trained for service in the harem, with instruction in reading, the Koran, sewing and embroidery, and musical performance. They were ranked according to their status, and some were permitted to leave the harem to marry officials. If they were later divorced, they were sometimes allowed to return to the harem.

Unique to the Ottoman Empire from the fifteenth century onward was the exclusive use of slaves to reproduce its royal heirs. Contrary to myth, few of the women of the imperial harem were used for sexual purposes, as the majority were relatives of the sultan's extended family—sisters, daughters, widowed mothers, and in-laws, with their own personal slaves and entourage. Contemporary European observers compared the atmosphere in the Topkapi harem to a Christian nunnery, with its hierarchical organization, enforced chastity, and rule of silence.

Because of their proximity to the sultan, the women of the harem often wielded so much political power that the era has been called "the sultanate of women." Queen mothers administered the imperial household and engaged in diplomatic relations with other countries while controlling the marital alliances of their daughters with senior civilian and military officials or members of other royal families in the region. One princess was married seven separate times from the age of two after her previous husbands died either in battle or by execution.

The sultan ruled through an imperial council that met four days a week and was chaired by the chief minister known as the grand vezir (*wazir*, sometimes rendered in English as *vizier*). The sultan often attended behind a screen, whence he could privately indicate his desires to the grand vezir. The latter presided over the imperial bureaucracy. Like the palace guard, the bureaucrats were not an exclusive group but were chosen at least partly by merit from a palace school for training officials. Most officials were Muslims by birth, but some talented Janissaries became senior members of the bureaucracy, and almost all the later grand vezirs came from the *devshirme* system.

Local administration during the imperial period was a product of Turkish tribal tradition and was similar in some respects to fief-holding in Europe. The empire was divided into provinces and districts governed by officials who, like their tribal predecessors, combined both civil and military functions. They were assisted by bureaucrats trained in the palace school in Istanbul. Senior officials were assigned land in fief by the sultan and were then responsible for collecting taxes and supplying armies to the empire. These lands were then farmed out to the local cavalry elite called the *sipahis*, who exacted a tax from all peasants in their fiefdoms for their salary. These local officials were not hereditary aristocrats, but sons often inherited their fathers' landholdings, and the vast majority were descendants of the tribal beys who had served as a tribal elite during the preimperial period.

Religion and Society in the Ottoman World

Like most Turkic-speaking peoples in the Anatolian peninsula and throughout the Middle East, the Ottoman ruling elites were Sunni Muslims. Ottoman sultans had claimed the title of caliph ("defender of the faith") since the early sixteenth century and thus theoretically were responsible for guiding the flock and maintaining Islamic law, the *Shari'a*. In practice, the sultan assigned these duties to a supreme religious authority, who administered the law and maintained a system of schools for educating Muslims.

Islamic law and customs were applied to all Muslims in the empire. Like their rulers, most Turkic-speaking people were Sunni Muslims, but some communities were attracted to Sufism (see Chapter 7) or other heterodox doctrines. The government tolerated such activities so long as their practitioners remained loyal to the empire, but in the early sixteenth century, unrest among these groups—some of whom converted to the Shi'ite version of Islamic doctrine—outraged the conservative *ulama* and eventually led to war against the Safavids (see "The Safavids" later in this chapter).

Non-Muslims—mostly Orthodox Christians (Greeks and Slavs), Jews, and Armenian Christians—formed a significant minority within the empire, which treated them with relative tolerance. Non-Muslims were compelled to pay a head tax (because of their exemption from military service), and they were permitted to practice their religion or convert to Islam, although Muslims were prohibited from adopting another faith. Most of the population in European areas of the empire remained Christian, but in some places, such as the territory now called Bosnia, substantial numbers converted to Islam.

Each religious group within the empire was organized as an administrative unit called a *millet* ("nation" or "community"). Each group, including the Muslims themselves, had its own patriarch or grand rabbi who dealt as an intermediary with the government and administered the community according to its own laws. The leaders of the individual nations were responsible to the sultan and his officials for the behavior of the subjects under their care and collected taxes for transmission to the government. Each nation established its own system of justice, set its own educational policies, and provided welfare for the needy.

Technically, women in the Ottoman Empire were subject to the same restrictions that afflicted their counterparts in other Muslim societies, but their position was ameliorated to some degree by various factors. In the first place, non-Muslims were subject to the laws and customs of their own religions; thus Orthodox Christian, Jewish, and Armenian Christian women were spared some of the restrictions applied to their Muslim sisters. In the second place, Islamic laws as applied in the Ottoman Empire defined the legal position of women comparatively tolerantly. Women were permitted to own and inherit property, including their dowries. They could not be forced into marriage and in certain cases were permitted to seek a divorce. As we have seen, women often exercised considerable influence in the palace and in a few instances even served as senior officials, such as governors of provinces. The relatively tolerant attitude toward women in Ottoman-held territories has been ascribed by some to Turkish tribal traditions, which took a more egalitarian view of sex roles than the sedentary societies of the region did.

The Ottomans in Decline

The Ottoman Empire reached its zenith under Suleyman the Magnificent, often known as Suleyman Kanuni, or "the lawgiver," who launched the conquest of Hungary. But Suleyman also sowed the seeds of the empire's eventual decline. He executed his two most able sons on suspicion of factionalism and was succeeded by Selim II (the Sot, or "the drunken sultan"), the only surviving son.

By the seventeenth century, signs of internal rot had begun to appear, although the first loss of imperial territory did not occur until 1699, at the Battle of Carlowitz. Apparently, a number of factors were involved. In the first place, the administrative system inherited from the tribal period began to break down. Although the *devshirme* system of training officials continued to function, *devshirme* graduates were now permitted to marry and inherit property and to enroll their sons in the palace corps. Thus they were gradually transformed from a meritocratic administrative elite into a privileged and often degenerate hereditary caste. Local administrators were corrupted and taxes rose as the central bureaucracy lost its links with rural areas. The imperial treasury was depleted by constant wars, and transport and communications were neglected. Interest in science and technology, once a hallmark of the Arab empire, was in decline. In addition, the empire was increasingly beset by economic difficulties, caused by the diversion of trade routes away from the eastern Mediterranean and the price inflation brought about by the influx of cheap American silver.

Another sign of change within the empire was the increasing degree of material affluence and the impact of Western ideas and customs. Sophisticated officials and merchants began to mimic the habits and lifestyles of their European counterparts, dressing in the European fashion, purchasing Western furniture and art objects, and ignoring Muslim strictures against the consumption of alcohol and sexual activities outside marriage. During the sixteenth and early seventeenth centuries, coffee and tobacco were introduced into polite Ottoman society, and cafés for the consumption of both began to appear in the major cities (see the box on p. 423). One sultan in the early seventeenth century issued a decree prohibiting the consumption of both coffee and tobacco, arguing (correctly, no doubt) that many cafés were nests of antigovernment intrigue. He even began to wander incognito through the streets of Istanbul at night. Any of his subjects detected in immoral or illegal acts were summarily executed and their bodies left on the streets as an example to others.

There were also signs of a decline in competence within the ruling family. Whereas the first sultans reigned twenty-seven years on average, later ones averaged only thirteen years. The throne now went to the oldest surviving male, while his rivals were kept secluded in a latticed cage and thus had no governmental experience if they succeeded to rule. Later sultans also became less involved in government, and more power flowed to the office of the grand vezir (called the Sublime Porte) or to eunuchs and members of the harem. Palace intrigue increased as a result.

Ottoman Art

The Ottoman sultans were enthusiastic patrons of the arts and maintained large ateliers of artisans and artists, primarily at the Topkapi Palace in Istanbul but also in other important cities of the vast empire. The period from Mehmet II in the fifteenth century to the early eighteenth century witnessed the flourishing of pottery, rugs, silk and other textiles, jewelry, arms and armor, and calligraphy. All adorned the palaces of the new rulers, testifying to their opulence and exquisite taste. The artists came from all parts of the realm and beyond. Besides Turks, there were Persians, Greeks, Armenians, Hungarians, and Italians, all vying for the esteem and generous rewards of the sultans and fearing that losing favor might mean losing their heads! In the second half of the sixteenth century, Istan-

A TURKISH DISCOURSE ON COFFEE

Coffee was first introduced to Turkey from the Arabian peninsula in the mid-sixteenth century and allegedly came to Europe during the Turkish seige of Vienna in 1527. The following account was written by Katib Chelebi, a seventeenth-century Turkish author who, among other things, compiled an extensive encyclopedia and bibliography. Here, in The Balance of Truth, *he describes how coffee entered the empire and the problems it caused for public morality. (In the Muslim world, as in Europe and later in colonial America, the drinking of coffee was associated with coffeehouses, where rebellious elements often gathered to promote antigovernment activities.) Chelebi died in Istanbul in 1657, reportedly while drinking a cup of coffee.*

KATIB CHELEBI, *THE BALANCE OF TRUTH*

[Coffee] originated in Yemen and has spread, like tobacco, over the world. Certain sheikhs, who lived with their dervishes in the mountains of Yemen, used to crush and eat the berries . . . of a certain tree. Some would roast them and drink their water. Coffee is a cold dry food, suited to the ascetic life and sedative of lust. . . .

It came to Asia Minor by sea, about 1543, and met with a hostile reception, fetwas [decrees] being delivered against it. For they said, Apart from its being roasted, the fact that it is drunk in gatherings, passed from hand to hand, is suggestive of loose living. It is related of Abul-Suud Efendi that he had holes bored in the ships that brought it, plunging their cargoes of coffee into the sea. But these strictures and prohibitions availed nothing. . . . One coffeehouse was opened after another, and men would gather together, with great eagerness and enthusiasm, to drink. Drug addicts in particular, finding it a life-giving thing, which increased their pleasure, were willing to die for a cup.

Storytellers and musicians diverted the people from their employments, and working for one's living fell into disfavor. Moreover the people, from prince to beggar, amused themselves with knifing one another. Toward the end of 1633, the late Ghazi Gultan Murad, becoming aware of the situation, promulgated an edict, out of regard and compassion for the people, to this effect: Coffeehouses throughout the Guarded Domains shall be dismantled and not opened hereafter. Since then, the coffeehouses of the capital have been as desolate as the heart of the ignorant. . . . But in cities and towns outside Istanbul, they are opened just as before. As has been said above, such things do not admit of a perpetual ban.

---

bul alone listed over 150 craft guilds, ample proof of the artistic activity of the era.

By far the greatest contribution of the Ottoman Empire to world art was its architecture, especially the magnificent mosques of the second half of the sixteenth century. Traditionally, prayer halls in mosques were subdivided by numerous pillars that supported small individual domes, creating a private, forestlike atmosphere. The Turks, however, modeled their new mosques on the open floor plan of the Byzantine church of Santa Sophia (completed in 537), which had been turned into a mosque by Mehmet II, and began to push the pillars toward the outer wall to create a prayer hall with an uninterrupted central area under one large dome. With this plan, large numbers of believers could worship in unison in accordance with Muslim preference. By the mid-sixteenth century, the greatest of all Ottoman architects, Sinan, began erecting the first of his eighty-one mosques with an uncluttered prayer area. Each was topped by an imposing dome, and often, as at Edirne, the entire building was framed with four towering narrow minarets. By emphasizing its vertical lines, the minarets camouflaged the massive stone bulk of the structure and gave it a feeling of incredible lightness. These four graceful minarets would find new expression sixty years later in India's white marble Taj Mahal (see "Mughal Culture" later in this chapter).

The lightness of the exterior was reinforced in the mosque's interior by the soaring height of the dome and the numerous windows. Added to this were delicate plasterwork and tile decoration that transformed the mosque into a monumental oasis of spirituality, opulence, and power. Sinan's masterpieces, such as the Suleymaniye and the Blue Mosque of Istanbul, were always part of a large socioreligious compound that included a library, school, hospital, mausoleums, and even bazaars, all of equally magnificent construction.

Earlier, the thirteenth-century Seljuk Turks of Anatolia had created beautiful tile decorations with two-color mosaics. Now Ottoman artists invented a new glazed tile art with painted flowers and geometrical designs in brilliant blue, green, yellow, and their own secret "tomato red." Entire walls, both interior and exterior, were covered with the painted tiles, which adorned palaces as well as mosques. Produced at Iznik (the old Nicaea), the distinctive tiles and pottery were in great demand; the city's ateliers boasted more than three hundred artisans in the late sixteenth century.

The sixteenth century also witnessed the flourishing of textiles and rugs. The Byzantine emperor Justinian had introduced the cultivation of silkworms to the West in the sixth century, and the silk industry resurfaced under the Ottomans. Its capital was at Bursa, where factories produced silks for wall hangings, soft covers, and especially court costumes. Perhaps even more famous than Turkish silk are the rugs. But whereas silks were produced under the patronage of the sultans, rugs were a peasant industry. Each village boasted its own distinctive design and

 THE BLUE MOSQUE, ISTANBUL. The magnificent mosques built under the patronage of Suleyman the Magnificent are a great legacy of the Ottoman Empire and a fitting supplement to Santa Sophia (Hagia Sophia) Cathedral, built by the Byzantine emperor Justinian in the sixth century C.E. Towering under a central dome, these mosques seem to defy gravity, and, like European Gothic cathedrals, convey a sense of weightlessness. The Blue Mosque, so called for the blue tiles in its interior, is one of the most impressive and most graceful in Istanbul. A far cry from the seventh-century desert mosques constructed of palm trunks, the Ottoman mosques stand among the architectural wonders of the world.

color scheme for the rugs it produced. Common to all the rugs, however, was the use of the knot from the Gordes region—hence the term "Gordian knot."

THE SAFAVIDS

After the collapse of the empire of Tamerlane in the early fifteenth century, the area extending from Persia into Central Asia lapsed into anarchy. The Uzbeks, Turkic-speaking peoples from Central Asia, were the chief political and military force in the area. From their capital at Bokhara, they maintained a semblance of control over the highly fluid tribal alignments until the emergence of the Safavid dynasty in Persia at the beginning of the sixteenth century.

The Safavid dynasty was founded by Shah Ismail (1487–1524), the descendant of a sheikh called Safi al-Din (thus the name Safavid), who traced his origins to Ali, the fourth imam of the Muslim faith. In the early fourteenth century, Safi had been the leader of a community of Turkic-speaking tribespeople in Azerbaijan, near the Caspian Sea. Safi's community was only one of many Sufi mystical religious groups throughout the area. In time the doctrine spread among nomadic groups throughout the Middle East and was transformed into the more activist Shi'i heresy. Its adherents were known as "red heads" because of their distinctive red cap with twelve folds, meant to symbolize allegiance to the twelve imams of the Shi'i faith.

In 1501, Ismail's forces seized much of Iran and Iraq, and he called himself the shah of a new Persian state.

Baghdad was subdued in 1508 and the Uzbeks in Bokhara shortly thereafter. Ismail now sent Shi'ite preachers into Anatolia to proselytize and promote rebellion among Turkish tribal peoples in the Ottoman Empire. In retaliation, the Ottoman sultan, Selim I, advanced against the Safavids in Iran and won a major battle near Tabriz in 1514. But Selim could not maintain control of the area, and Ismail regained Tabriz a few years later.

The Ottomans returned to the attack in the 1580s and forced the new Safavid shah, Abbas I (1587–1629), to sign a punitive peace in which much territory was lost. The capital was subsequently moved from Tabriz in the northwest to Isfahan in the south. Still, it was under Shah Abbas that the Safavids reached the zenith of their glory. He established a system similar to the Janissaries in Turkey to train administrators to replace the traditional warrior elite. He also used the period of peace to strengthen his army, now armed with modern weapons, and in the early seventeenth century he attempted to regain the lost territories. Although he had some initial success, war resumed in the 1620s, and a lasting peace was not achieved until 1638 (see Map 15.2).

Abbas the Great had managed to strengthen the dynasty significantly, and for a time after his death in 1629, it remained stable and vigorous. But succession conflicts plagued the dynasty. Partly as a result, the power of the more militant Shi'ites began to increase at court and in Safavid society at large. The intellectual freedom that had characterized the empire at its height was curtailed under the pressure of religious orthodoxy, and Iranian women, who had enjoyed considerable freedom and influence during the early empire, were forced to withdraw into seclusion and behind the veil. Meanwhile, attempts to suppress the religious beliefs of minorities led to increased popular unrest. In the early eighteenth century, Afghan warriors took advantage of local revolts to seize the capital of Isfahan, forcing the remnants of the Safavid ruling family to retreat to Azerbaijan, their original homeland. The Ottomans seized territories along the western border. Eventually, order was restored by the military adventurer Nadir Shah Afshar, who launched an extended series of campaigns that restored the country's borders and even occupied the Mughal capital of Delhi (see "Twilight of the Mughals" later in this chapter). After his death, the Zand dynasty ruled until the end of the eighteenth century.

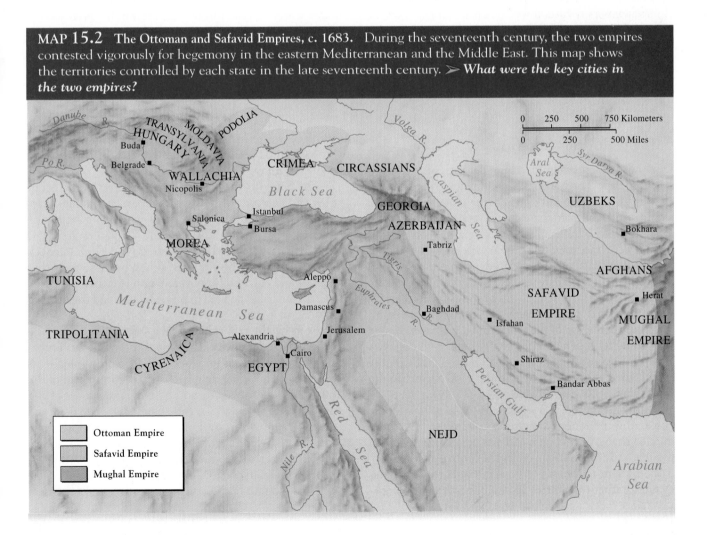

MAP 15.2   The Ottoman and Safavid Empires, c. 1683.   During the seventeenth century, the two empires contested vigorously for hegemony in the eastern Mediterranean and the Middle East. This map shows the territories controlled by each state in the late seventeenth century. ➤ *What were the key cities in the two empires?*

THE RELIGIOUS ZEAL OF
SHAH ABBAS THE GREAT

Shah Abbas I, probably the greatest of the Safavid rulers, expanded the borders of his empire into areas of the southern Caucasus inhabited by Christians and other non-Muslim peoples. After Persian control was assured, he instructed that the local population be urged to convert to Islam for its own protection and the glory of God. In this passage, his biographer, the Persian historian Eskander Beg Monshi, recounts the story of that effort.

THE CONVERSION OF A NUMBER OF CHRISTIANS TO ISLAM

This year the Shah decreed that those Armenians and other Christians who had been settled in [the southern Caucasus] and had been given agricultural land there should be invited to become Muslims. Life in this world is fraught with vicissitudes, and the Shah was concerned lest, in a period when the authority of the central government was weak, these Christians . . . might be subjected to attack by the neighboring Lor tribes (who are naturally given to causing injury and mischief), and their women and children carried off into captivity. In the areas in which these Christian groups resided, it was the Shah's purpose that the places of worship which they had built should become mosques, and the muezzin's call should be heard in them,

so that these Christians might assume the guise of Muslims, and their future status accordingly be assured. . . .

Some of the Christians, guided by God's grace, embraced Islam voluntarily; others found it difficult to abandon their Christian faith and felt revulsion at the idea. They were encouraged by their monks and priests to remain steadfast in their faith. After a little pressure had been applied to the monks and priests, however, they desisted, and these Christians saw no alternative but to embrace Islam, though they did so with reluctance. The women and children embraced Islam with great enthusiasm, vying with one another in their eagerness to abandon their Christian faith and declare their belief in the unity of God. Some five thousand people embraced Islam. As each group made the Muslim declaration of faith, it received instruction in the Koran and the principles of the religious law of Islam, and all bibles and other Christian devotional material were collected and taken away from the priests.

In the same way, all the Armenian Christians who had been moved to [the area] were also forcibly converted to Islam. . . . Most people embraced Islam with sincerity, but some felt an aversion to making the Muslim profession of faith. True knowledge lies with God! May God reward the Shah for his action with long life and prosperity!

Safavid Politics and Society

Like the Ottoman Empire, Iran under the Safavids was a mixed society. The Safavids had come to power with the support of nomadic Turkic-speaking tribal groups, and leading elements from those groups retained considerable influence within the empire. But the majority of the population were Iranian; most of them were farmers or townspeople, with attitudes inherited from the relatively sophisticated and urbanized culture of pre-Safavid Iran. Faced with the problem of integrating unruly Turkic-speaking tribal peoples with the sedentary Persian-speaking population of the urban areas, the Safavids used the Shi'ite faith as a unifying force (see the box above). The shah himself acquired an almost divine quality and claimed to be the spiritual leader of all Islam. Shi'ism was declared the state religion.

Although there was a landed aristocracy, aristocratic power and influence were firmly controlled by strong-minded shahs, who confiscated aristocratic estates when possible and brought them under the control of the crown. Appointment to senior positions in the bureaucracy was by merit rather than birth. To avoid encouraging compe-

tition between Turkish and non-Turkish elements, Shah Abbas I hired a number of foreigners from neighboring countries for positions in his government.

The Safavid shahs took a direct interest in the economy and actively engaged in commercial and manufacturing activities, although there was also a large and affluent urban bourgeoisie. Like the Ottoman sultan, one shah regularly traveled the city streets incognito to check on the honesty of his subjects. When he discovered that a baker and butcher were overcharging for their products, he had the baker cooked in his own oven and the butcher roasted on a spit.

At its height, Safavid Iran was a worthy successor to the great Persian empires of the past, although it was probably not as wealthy as its Mughal and Ottoman neighbors to the east and west. Hemmed in by the sea power of the Europeans to the south and by the land power of the Ottomans to the west, the early Safavids had no navy and were forced to divert overland trade with Europe through southern Russia to avoid an Ottoman blockade. In the early seventeenth century, the situation improved when Iranian forces, in cooperation with the English, seized the island of Hormuz from Portugal and established a new sea-

Chronology

THE SAFAVIDS

Ismail seizes Iran and Iraq and becomes shah of Persia	1501
Ismail conquers Baghdad and defeats Uzbeks	1508
Reign of Shah Abbas I	1587–1629
Truce achieved between Ottomans and Safavids	1638
Collapse of Safavid Empire	1723

port on the southern coast at Bandar Abbas. As a consequence, commercial ties with Europe began to increase.

Safavid Art and Literature

Persia witnessed an extraordinary flowering of the arts during the reign of Shah Abbas I. His new capital of Isfahan was a grandiose planned city with wide visual perspectives and a sense of order almost unique in the region. Shah Abbas ordered his architects to position his palaces, mosques, and bazaars around the Maydan-i-Shah, a massive rectangular polo ground. Much of the original city is still in good condition and remains the gem of modern Iran. The immense mosques are richly decorated with elaborate blue tiles. The palaces are delicate structures with unusual slender wooden columns. These architectural wonders of Isfahan epitomize the grandeur, delicacy, and color that defined the Safavid golden age. To adorn the splendid buildings, Safavid artisans created imaginative metalwork, tile decorations, and original and delicate glass vessels. The ceramics of the period, imitating Chinese prototypes of celadon or blue-and-white Ming design, largely ignored traditional Persian designs.

The greatest area of productivity, however, was in textiles. Silk weaving based on new techniques became a national industry. The silks depicted birds, animals, and flowers in a brilliant mass of color with silver and gold threads. Above all, carpet weaving flourished, stimulated by the great demand for Persian carpets in the West. Still highly prized all over the world, these seventeenth-century carpets reflect the grandeur and artistry of the Safavid dynasty.

The long tradition of Persian painting continued in the Safavid era but changed from paintings to line drawings

THE ROYAL ACADEMY OF ISFAHAN. Along with institutions such as libraries and hospitals, theological schools were often included in the mosque compound. One of the most sumptuous was the Royal Academy of Isfahan, built by the shah of Iran in the early eighteenth century. This view shows the large courtyard surrounded by arcades of student rooms, reminiscent of the arrangement of monks' cells in European cloisters.

ASCENSION OF THE PROPHET MUHAMMAD. During the sixteenth century, exquisite illuminated manuscripts were produced by book workshops at the Safavid court in Tabriz. Shown here is an illustration of Muhammad's ascension to Heaven, as described in the Koran. Muhammad is veiled, in accordance with the accepted practice of not showing his facial features. Riding a celestial creature with the face of a woman, he arrives in Jerusalem to join Abraham, Jesus, and other prophets in prayer at the site of the Temple of Solomon. From there he ascends to Heaven to meet Allah, thus making the Dome of the Rock one of the sacred sites of the Muslim religion. Then Muhammad returned to Mecca, where he died in the year 632 C.E.

and from landscape scenes to portraits, mostly of young ladies, boys, lovers, or dervishes. Although some Persian artists studied in Rome, Safavid art was little influenced by the West. Riza-i-Abassi, the most famous artist of this period, created exquisite works on simple naturalistic subjects, such as an ox plowing, hunters, or lovers. Soft colors, delicacy, and flowing movement were the dominant characteristics of the painting of this era.

THE GRANDEUR OF THE MUGHALS

In retrospect, the period from the sixteenth to the eighteenth centuries can be viewed both as a high point of traditional culture in India and as the first stage of perhaps its greatest challenge. The era began with the creation of one of the subcontinent's greatest empires—that of the Mughals. Mughal rulers, although foreigners and Muslims

like many of their immediate predecessors, nevertheless brought India to a peak of political power and cultural achievement. For the first time since the Mauryan dynasty, the entire subcontinent was united under a single government, with a common culture that inspired admiration and envy throughout the entire region.

The Mughal Empire reached its peak in the sixteenth century under the famed Emperor Akbar and maintained its vitality under a series of strong rulers for another century (see Map 15.3). Then the dynasty began to weaken, a process that was hastened by the increasingly insistent challenge of the foreigners arriving by sea. The Portuguese, who first arrived in 1498, were little more than an irritant. Two centuries later, however, Europeans began to seize control of regional trade routes and to meddle in the internal politics of the subcontinent. By the end of the eighteenth century, nothing remained of the empire but a shell.

But some historians see the seeds of decay less in the challenge from abroad than in internal weakness—in the very nature of the dynasty itself, which was always more a heterogeneous collection of semiautonomous political forces than a centralized empire in the style of neighboring China. At its height, the dynasty was fully capable of fending off the demands of the Europeans. But after two centuries of expansion and consolidation, it began to lose its vitality, and by the end of the eighteenth century, it had lapsed into a mere shadow of its former self. Into the vacuum left by its final decrepitude stepped the British, who used a combination of firepower and guile to consolidate their power over the subcontinent.

The Mughal Dynasty: A "Gunpowder Empire"?

When the Portuguese fleet led by Vasco da Gama arrived at the port of Calicut in the spring of 1498, the Indian subcontinent was still divided into a number of Hindu and Muslim kingdoms. But it was on the verge of a new era of unity that would be brought about by a foreign dynasty called the Mughals. Like so many recent rulers of northern India, the founders of the Mughal Empire were not natives of India but came from the mountainous region north of the Ganges River. The founder of the dynasty, known to history as Babur (1483–1530), had an illustrious pedigree. His father was descended from the great Asian conqueror Tamerlane, his mother from the Mongol conqueror Genghis Khan.

Babur had inherited a fragment of Tamerlane's empire in an upland valley of the Syr Darya River. Driven south by the rising power of the Uzbeks and then the Safavid dynasty in Persia, Babur and his warriors seized Kabul in 1504 and, thirteen years later, crossed the Khyber Pass to India.

Following a pattern that we have seen before, Babur began his rise to power by offering to help an ailing dynasty against its opponents. Although his own forces were far

THE MUGHAL CONQUEST OF NORTHERN INDIA

Babur, the founder of the great Mughal dynasty, began his career by allying with one Indian prince against another and then turned on his ally to put himself in power, a tactic that had been used by the Ottomans and the Mongols before him (see Chapter 10). In this excerpt from his memoirs, Babur describes his triumph over the powerful army of his Indian enemy, the Sultan Ibrâhim.

BABUR, MEMOIRS

They made one or two very poor charges on our right and left divisions. My troops making use of their bows, plied them with arrows, and drove them in upon their center. The troops on the right and the left of their center, being huddled together in one place, such confusion ensued, that the enemy, while totally unable to advance, found also no road by which they could flee. The sun had mounted spear-high when the onset of battle began, and the combat lasted till midday, when the enemy were completely broken and routed, and my friends victorious and exulting. By the grace and mercy of Almighty God, this arduous undertaking was rendered easy for me, and this mighty army, in the space of half a day, laid in the dust. Five or six thousand men were discovered lying slain, in one spot, near Ibrâhim. We reckoned that the number lying slain, in different parts of this field of battle, amounted to fifteen or sixteen thousand men. On reaching Agra, we found, from the accounts of the natives of Hindustân, that forty or fifty thousand men had fallen in this field. After routing the enemy, we continued the pursuit, slaughtering, and making them prisoners. . . .

It was now afternoon prayers when Tahir Taberi, the younger brother of Khalîfeh, having found Ibrâhim lying dead amidst a number of slain, cut off his head, and brought it in. . . .

In consideration of my confidence in Divine aid, the Most High God did not suffer the distress and hardships that I had undergone to be thrown away, but defeated my formidable enemy, and made me the conqueror of the noble country of Hindustân. This success I do not ascribe to my own strength, nor did this good fortune flow from my own efforts, but from the fountain of the favor and mercy of God.

---

smaller than those of his adversaries, he possessed advanced weapons, including artillery, and used them to great effect. His use of mobile cavalry was particularly successful against the massed forces, supplemented by mounted elephants, of his enemy. In 1526, with only twelve thousand troops against an enemy force nearly ten times that size, Babur captured Delhi and established his power in the plains of northern India (see the box above). Over the next several years, he continued his conquests in northern India, until his early death in 1530 at the age of forty-seven.

Babur's success was due in part to his vigor and his charismatic personality, which earned him the undying loyalty of his followers. His son and successor Humayun (1530–1556) was, in the words of one British historian, "intelligent but lazy." Whether or not this is a fair characterization, Humayun clearly lacked the will to consolidate his father's conquests and the personality to inspire personal loyalty among his subjects. In 1540, he was forced to flee to Persia, where he lived in exile for sixteen years. Finally, with the aid of the Safavid shah of Persia, he returned to India and reconquered Delhi in 1555 but died the following year in a household accident, reportedly from injuries suffered in a fall after smoking a pipeful of opium.

Humayun was succeeded by his son Akbar (1556–1605). Born while his father was living in exile, Akbar was only fourteen when he mounted the throne. Illiterate but highly intelligent and industrious, Akbar set out to extend his domain, then limited to Punjab and the upper Ganges River valley. "A monarch," he remarked, "should be ever intent on conquest, otherwise his neighbors rise in arms against him. The army should be exercised in warfare, lest from want of training they become self-indulgent."[1] By the end of his life, he had brought Mughal rule to most of the subcontinent, from the Himalaya Mountains to the Godavari River in central India and from Kashmir to the mouths of the Brahmaputra and the Ganges. In so doing, Akbar had created the greatest Indian empire since the Mauryan dynasty nearly two thousand years earlier. Some historians believe Akbar's success was due to the use of heavy artillery, which enabled his armies to besiege and subdue the traditional stone fortresses of his rivals. This "gunpowder empire" thesis has been challenged by the historian Douglas Streusand, who argues that the Mughals used "the carrot and the stick" to extend their authority relying not just on heavy artillery but also on other forms of siege warfare and the offer of negotiations. Whatever the case, the end result was an empire that appeared highly centralized from the outside but was actually a collection of semiautonomous principalities ruled by provincial elites and linked together by the overarching majesty of the Mughal emperor.

Akbar and Indo-Muslim Civilization

Although Akbar was probably the greatest of the conquering Mughal monarchs, like his famous predecessor Asoka, he is best known for the humane character of his

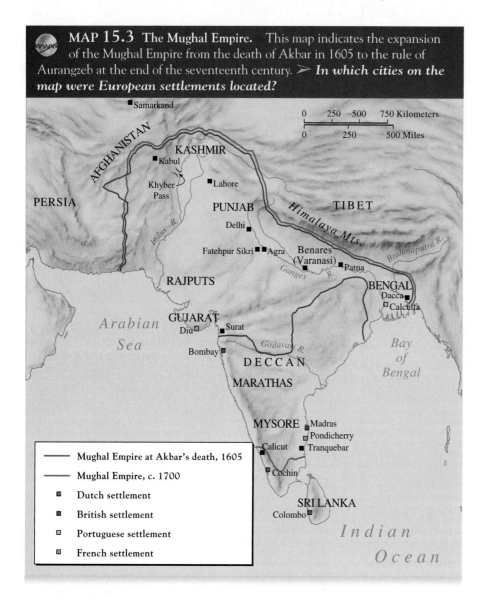

MAP 15.3 The Mughal Empire. This map indicates the expansion of the Mughal Empire from the death of Akbar in 1605 to the rule of Aurangzeb at the end of the seventeenth century. ➤ *In which cities on the map were European settlements located?*

Map legend:
- Mughal Empire at Akbar's death, 1605
- Mughal Empire, c. 1700
- Dutch settlement
- British settlement
- Portuguese settlement
- French settlement

rule. Above all, he accepted the diversity of Indian society and took steps to reconcile his Muslim and Hindu subjects.

Though raised an orthodox Muslim, Akbar had been exposed to other beliefs during his childhood and had little patience with the pedantic views of Muslim scholars at court. As emperor, he displayed a keen interest in other religions, not only tolerating Hindu practices in his own domains but also welcoming the expression of Christian views by his Jesuit advisers. Akbar put his policy of religious tolerance into practice by taking a Hindu princess as one of his wives, and the success of this marriage may well have had an effect on his religious convictions. He patronized classical Indian arts and architecture and abolished many of the restrictions faced by Hindus in a Muslim-dominated society.

During his later years, Akbar became steadily more hostile to Islam. To the dismay of many Muslims at court, he sponsored a new form of worship called the Divine Faith (*Din-i-Ilahi*), which combined characteristics of several religions with a central belief in the infallibility of all decisions reached by the emperor. Some historians have maintained that Akbar totally abandoned Islam and adopted a Persian model of imperial divinity. But others have pointed out that the emperor was claiming only divine guidance, not divine status, and suggest that the new ideology was designed to cement the loyalty of officials to the person of the monarch. Whatever the case, the new faith aroused deep hostility in Muslim circles and rapidly vanished after his death.

Akbar also extended his innovations to the empire's administration. Although the upper ranks of the government continued to be dominated by nonnative Muslims, a substantial proportion of lower-ranking officials were Hindus, and a few Hindus were appointed to positions of importance. At first, most officials were paid salaries, but later they were ordinarily assigned sections of agricultural

THE POWER BEHIND THE THRONE

During his reign as Mughal emperor, Jahangir (1605–1628) was addicted to alcohol and opium. Because of his weakened condition, his Persian wife Nur Jahan began to rule on his behalf. She also groomed his young son Khurram to rule as the future emperor Shah Jahan and arranged for him to marry her own niece Mumtaz Mahal, thereby cementing her influence over two successive Mughal rulers. During this period, Nur Jahan was the de facto ruler of India, exerting her influence in both internal and foreign affairs during an era of peace and prosperity. Although the extent of her influence was often criticized at court, her performance impressed many European observers, as these remarks by two English visitors attest.

NUR JAHAN, EMPRESS OF MUGHAL INDIA

If anyone with a request to make at Court obtains an audience or is allowed to speak, the King hears him indeed, but will give no definite answer of Yes or No, referring him promptly to Asaf Khan, who in the same way will dispose of no important matter without communicating with his sister, the Queen, and who regulates his attitude in such a way that the authority of neither of them may be diminished. Anyone then who obtains a favour must thank them for it, and not the King. . . .

Her abilities were uncommon; for she rendered herself absolute, in a government in which women are thought incapable of bearing any part. Their power, it is true, is sometimes exerted in the haram; but, like the virtues of the magnet, it is silent and unperceived. Nur Jahan stood forth in public; she broke through all restraint and custom, and acquired power by her own address, more than by the weakness of Jahangir. . . .

Her former and present supporters have been well rewarded, so that now most of the men who are near the King owe their promotion to her, and are consequently under . . . obligations to her. . . . Many misunderstandings result, for the King's orders or grants of appointments, etc., are not certainties, being of no value until they have been approved by the Queen.

---

land for their temporary use; they kept a portion of the taxes paid by the local peasants in lieu of a salary. These local officials, known as *zamindars*, were expected to forward the rest of the taxes from the lands under their control to the central government. *Zamindars* often recruited a number of military and civilian retainers and accumulated considerable power in their localities.

The same tolerance that marked Akbar's attitude toward religion and administration extended to the Mughal legal system. While Muslims were subject to the Islamic codes (the *Shari'a*), Hindu law (the *Dharmashastra*) applied to areas settled by Hindus, who after 1579 were no longer required to pay the hated *jizya*, or poll tax on non-Muslims. Punishments for crime were relatively mild, at least by the standards of the day, and justice was administered in a relatively impartial and efficient manner.

Overall, Akbar's reign was a time of peace and prosperity. Although all Indian peasants were required to pay about one-third of their annual harvest to the state through the *zamindars*, the system was applied fairly, and when drought struck in the 1590s, the taxes were reduced or even suspended altogether. Thanks to a long period of relative peace and political stability, commerce and manufacturing flourished. Foreign trade, in particular, thrived as Indian goods, notably textiles, tropical food products, spices, and precious stones, were exported in exchange for gold and silver. Tariffs on imports were low. Much of the foreign commerce was handled by Arab traders, since the Indians, like their Mughal rulers, did not care for travel by sea. Internal trade, however, was dominated by large merchant castes, who also were active in banking and handicrafts.

Twilight of the Mughals

Akbar died in 1605 and was succeeded by his son Jahangir (1605–1628). During the early years of his reign, Jahangir continued to strengthen central control over the vast empire. Eventually, however, his grip began to weaken (according to his memoirs, he "only wanted a bottle of wine and a piece of meat to make merry"), and the court fell under the influence of one of his wives, the Persian-born Nur Jahan (see the box above). The empress took advantage of her position to enrich her own family and arranged for her niece Mumtaz Mahal to marry her husband's third son and ultimate successor, Shah Jahan. When Shah Jahan succeeded to the throne in 1628, he quickly demonstrated the single-minded quality of his grandfather (albeit in a much more brutal manner), ordering the assassination of all of his rivals in order to secure his position.

During a reign of three decades, Shah Jahan maintained the system established by his predecessors while expanding the boundaries of the empire by successful campaigns in the Deccan Plateau and against Samarkand, north of the Hindu Kush. But Shah Jahan's rule was marred by his failure to deal with the growing domestic problems. He had inherited a nearly empty treasury because of Empress Nur Jahan's penchant for luxury and ambitious charity projects. Though the majority of his subjects lived in grinding poverty, Shah Jahan's frequent military campaigns and expensive building projects put a heavy strain on the imperial finances and compelled him to raise taxes. At the same time, the government did little to improve rural conditions. In a country where transport was primitive (it often took three months to travel the 600 miles between Patna, in the middle of the Ganges River valley, and Delhi) and drought conditions frequent, the dynasty made few efforts to increase agricultural efficiency or to improve the roads or the irrigation network. A Dutch merchant in Gujarat described conditions during a famine in the mid-seventeenth century:

> As the famine increased, men abandoned towns and villages and wandered helplessly. It was easy to recognize their condition: eyes sunk deep in head, lips pale and covered with slime, the skin hard, with the bones showing through, the belly nothing but a pouch hanging down empty, knuckles and kneecaps showing prominently. One would cry and howl for hunger, while another lay stretched on the ground dying in misery; wherever you went, you saw nothing but corpses.[2]

In 1648, Shah Jahan moved his capital from Agra to Delhi and built the famous Red Fort in his new capital city. But he is best known for the Taj Mahal in Agra, widely considered to be the most beautiful building in India, if not in the entire world. The story is a romantic one—that the Taj was built by the emperor in memory of his wife Mumtaz Mahal, who had died giving birth to her thirteenth child at the age of thirty-nine. But the story has a less attractive side: the expense of the building, which employed twenty thousand masons over twenty years, forced the government to raise agricultural taxes, further impoverishing many Indian peasants.

Succession struggles returned to haunt the dynasty in the mid-1650s when Shah Jahan's illness led to a struggle for power between his sons Dara Shikoh and Aurangzeb. Dara Shikoh was described by his contemporaries as progressive and humane, although possessed of a violent temper and a strong sense of mysticism. But he apparently lacked political acumen and was outmaneuvered by Aurangzeb (1658–1707), who had Dara Shikoh put to death and then imprisoned his father in the fort at Agra.

Aurangzeb is one of the most controversial individuals in the history of India. A man of high principle, he attempted to eliminate many of what he considered to be India's social evils, prohibiting the immolation of widows on their husband's funeral pyre (sati), the castration of eunuchs, and the exaction of illegal taxes. With less success, he tried to forbid gambling, drinking, and prostitution. But Aurangzeb, a devout and somewhat doctrinaire Muslim, also adopted a number of measures that reversed the policies of religious tolerance established by his predecessors. The building of new Hindu temples was prohibited and the Hindu poll tax was restored. Forced conversions to Islam were resumed, and non-Muslims were driven from the court. Aurangzeb's heavy-handed religious policies led to considerable domestic unrest and to a revival of Hindu fervor during the last years of his reign. A number of revolts also broke out against imperial authority.

During the eighteenth century, Mughal power was threatened from both within and without. Fueled by the growing power and autonomy of the local gentry and merchants, rebellious groups in provinces throughout the empire, from the Deccan to the Punjab, began to reassert local authority and reduce the power of the Mughal emperor to that of a "tinsel sovereign." Increasingly divided, India was vulnerable to attack from abroad. In 1739, Delhi was sacked by the Persians, who left it in ashes and carried off its splendid Peacock Throne.

A number of obvious reasons for the virtual collapse of the Mughal Empire can be identified, including the draining of the imperial treasury and the decline in competence of the Mughal rulers. But it should also be noted that even at its height under Akbar, the empire was a loosely knit collection of heterogeneous principalities held together by the authority of the throne, which tried to combine Persian concepts of kingship with the Indian tradition of decentralized power. Decline set in when centrifugal forces gradually began to predominate over centripetal ones.

Ironically, one element in this process was the very success of the system, which led to the rapid expansion of wealth and autonomous power at the local level. As local elites increased their wealth and influence, they became less willing to accept the authority and financial demands from Delhi. The reassertion of Muslim orthodoxy under Aurangzeb and his successors simply exacerbated the problem. This process was hastened by the growing European military and economic presence along the periphery of the empire.

The Impact of Western Power in India

As we have seen, the first Europeans to arrive were the Portuguese. Although they established a virtual monopoly over regional trade in the Indian Ocean, they did not aggressively seek to penetrate the interior of the subcontinent. The situation changed at the end of the sixteenth century, when the English and the Dutch entered the scene. Soon both powers were in active competition with Portugal, and with each other, for trading privileges in the region (see the box on p. 433).

Penetration of the new market was not easy. When the first English fleet arrived at Surat, a thriving port on the northwestern coast of India, in 1608, their request for trading privileges was rejected by Emperor Jahangir, at the suggestion of the Portuguese advisers already in residence at the imperial court. Needing lightweight Indian cloth to trade for spices in the East Indies, the English persisted, and in 1616, they were finally permitted to install their own ambassador at the imperial court in Agra. Three years later, the first English factory was established at Surat.

During the next several decades, the English presence in India steadily increased while Mughal power gradually waned. By mid-century, additional English factories had been established at Fort William (now the great city of Calcutta) on the Hoogly River near the Bay of Bengal and at Madras on the southeastern coast. From there English ships carried Indian-made cotton goods to the East Indies, where they were bartered for spices, which

THE USES OF THE COCONUT

The Portuguese traveler Duarte Barbosa was one of the most astute observers of the lands that he visited as an official of the Portuguese crown in the early sixteenth century. Here, in a section devoted to the lands of Malabar, on the southwestern coast of India, he writes of the many uses that the local population made of the coconut palm. Many peoples of Asia still use the coconut in similar ways in our own day.

DUARTE BARBOSA, *THE BOOK OF DUARTE BARBOSA*

This land, or rather the whole land of Malabar, is covered along the strand with palm trees as high as lofty cypresses, the trunk whereof is extremely clean and smooth, and on the top a crown of branches among which grows a great fruit which they call *cocos*, it is a fruit of which they make great profit, and whereof they load many cargoes yearly. They bear their fruit every year without fail, never either more or less. All the folk of Malabar have these palms, and by their means they are free from any dearth, even though other food be lacking, for they produce ten or twelve things all very needful for the service of man, by which they help and profit themselves greatly, and everything is produced in every month of the year.

In the first place they produce these cocos, a very sweet and grateful fruit when green; from them is drawn milk like that of almonds, and each one when green, has within it a pint of a fresh and pleasant water, better than that from a spring. When they are dry this same water thickens within them into a white fruit as large as an apple which also is very sweet and dainty. The coco itself after being dried is eaten, and from it they get much oil by pressing it, as we do. And from the shell which they have close to the kernel is made charcoal for the goldsmiths, who work with no other kind. And from the outer husk which throws out certain threads, they make all the cord which they use, a great article of trade in many parts. And from the sap of the tree itself they extract a *must*, from which they make wine, or properly speaking a strong water, and that in such abundance that many shops are laden with it, for export. From this same *must* they make very good vinegar, and also a sugar of extreme sweetness which is much sought after in India. From the leaf of the tree they make many things, in accordance with the size of the branch. They thatch the houses with them, for as I have said above, no house is roofed with tiles, save the temples or the palaces; all others are thatched with palm leaves. From the same tree they get timber for their houses and firewood as well, and all this in such abundance that ships take in cargoes thereof for export.

Other palm trees there are of a lower kind whence they get the leaves on which the Heathen write; it serves as paper. There are other very slender palms the trunks of which are of extreme height and smoothness; these bear a fruit as large as walnuts which they call Areca, which they eat with betel. Among them it is held in high esteem. It is very ugly and disagreeable in taste.

---

were shipped back to England. Tensions between local authorities and the English over the payment of taxes led to a short war in 1686. The English were briefly expelled, but after differences were patched up, Aurangzeb permitted them to return.

English success in India attracted rivals, including the Dutch and the French. The Dutch abandoned their interests to concentrate on the spice trade in the middle of the seventeenth century, but the French were more persistent and established factories of their own. For a brief period,

Courtesy of William J. Duiker

THE CHINESE NETS AT COCHIN. Cochin, one of the port cities visited by Vasco da Gama during his first visit to India in 1498, had long been a major stopover on the trade routes across the Indian Ocean. Nearly a century previously, it had been visited by Chinese fleets en route to Africa. These voyages, to be discussed in the next chapter, left their own legacy, as Indian fishers learned from Chinese sailors how to place large nets in the water of the harbor to catch fish. After the arrival of the Portuguese, much of the local population was converted to Christianity. Shown here are the "Chinese nets" of Cochin, which are still in use. A few yards away is the first Christian church erected in India. An old synagogue, which perhaps dates back to the pre-European era, is located a mile away.

THE MUGHAL ERA

Arrival of Vasco da Gama at Calicut	1498
Babur seizes Delhi	1526
Death of Babur	1530
Humayun recovers throne in Delhi	1555
Death of Humayun and accession of Akbar	1556
First Jesuit mission to Agra	1580
Death of Akbar and accession of Jahangir	1605
Arrival of English at Surat	1608
Reign of Emperor Shah Jahan	1628–1657
Foundation of English fort at Madras	1639
Aurangzeb succeeds to the throne	1658
Bombay ceded to England	1661
Death of Aurangzeb	1707
French capture Madras	1746
Battle of Plassey	1757

under the ambitious empire builder Joseph François Dupleix, the French competed successfully with the British. But the military genius of Sir Robert Clive, an aggressive British administrator and empire builder who eventually became the chief representative of the East India Company in the subcontinent, and the refusal of the French government to provide financial support for Dupleix's efforts eventually left the French with only their fort at Pondicherry and a handful of small territories on the southeastern coast.

In the meantime, Clive began to consolidate British control in Bengal, where the local ruler had attacked Fort William and imprisoned the local British population in the infamous Black Hole of Calcutta (an underground prison for holding the prisoners, many of whom died in captivity). In 1757, a small British force numbering about three thousand defeated a Mughal-led army over ten times that size in the Battle of Plassey. As part of the spoils of victory, the British East India Company exacted from the now-decrepit Mughal court the authority to collect taxes from extensive lands in the area surrounding Calcutta. Less than ten years later, British forces seized the reigning Mughal emperor in a skirmish at Buxar, and the British began to consolidate their economic and administrative control over Indian territory through the surrogate power of the now powerless Mughal court (see Map 15.4).

To officials of the East India Company, the expansion of their authority into the interior of the subcontinent probably seemed like a simple commercial decision, a move designed to seek guaranteed revenues to pay for the increasingly expensive military operations in India. To historians, it marks a major step in the gradual transfer of all of the Indian subcontinent to the British East India Company and later, in 1858, to the British crown. The process was more haphazard than deliberate. Under a new governor general, Warren Hastings, the British attempted to consolidate areas under their control and defeat such rivals as the rising Hindu Marathas, who exploited the decline of the Mughals to expand their own empire in Maharashtra.

The company's takeover of vast landholdings, notably in the eastern Indian states of Orissa and Bengal, may have been a windfall for enterprising British officials, but it was a disaster for the Indian economy. In the first place, it resulted in the transfer of capital from the local Indian aristocracy to company officials, most of whom sent their profits back to Britain. Second, it hastened the destruction of once healthy local industries, because British goods such as machine-made textiles were imported duty-free into India to compete against local products. Finally, British expansion hurt the peasants. As the British took over the administration of the land tax, they also applied British law, which allowed the lands of those unable to pay the tax to be confiscated. In the 1770s, a series of massive famines led to the death of an estimated one-third of the population in the areas under company administration. The British government attempted to resolve the problem by assigning tax lands to the local revenue collectors (*zamindars*) in the hope of transforming them into English-style rural gentry, but many collectors themselves fell into bankruptcy and sold their lands to absentee bankers while the now landless peasants remained in abject poverty. It was hardly an auspicious beginning to "civilized" British rule.

As a result of such problems, Britain's rise to power in India did not go unchallenged. Astute Indian commanders avoided pitched battles with the well-armed British troops but harassed and ambushed them in the manner of guerrillas in our time. Said Haidar Ali, one of Britain's primary rivals for control in southern India:

> You will in time understand my mode of warfare. Shall I risk my cavalry which cost a thousand rupees each horse, against your cannon ball which cost two pice? No! I will march your troops until their legs swell to the size of their bodies. You shall not have a blade of grass, nor a drop of water. I will hear of you every time your drum beats, but you shall not know where I am once a month. I will give your army battle, but it must be when I please, and not when you choose.[3]

Unfortunately for India, not all its commanders were as astute as Haidar Ali. In the last years of the eighteenth century, when the East India Company's authority came into the capable hands of Lord Cornwallis and his successor, Lord Mornington, the future marquess of Wellesley, the stage was set for the final consolidation of British rule over the subcontinent.

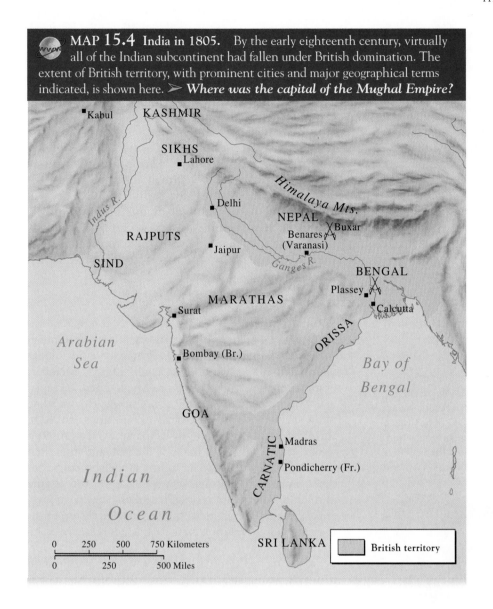

MAP 15.4 India in 1805. By the early eighteenth century, virtually all of the Indian subcontinent had fallen under British domination. The extent of British territory, with prominent cities and major geographical terms indicated, is shown here. ➤ *Where was the capital of the Mughal Empire?*

Society and Culture Under the Mughals

The Mughals were the last of the great traditional Indian dynasties. Like so many of their predecessors since the fall of the Guptas nearly a thousand years before, the Mughals were Muslims. But like the Ottoman Turks, the best Mughal rulers did not simply impose Islamic institutions and beliefs on a predominantly Hindu population; they combined Muslim with Hindu and even Persian concepts and cultural values in a unique social and cultural synthesis that still today seems to epitomize the greatness of Indian civilization.

DAILY LIFE

Whether Mughal rule had much effect on the lives of ordinary Indians seems somewhat problematic. The treatment of women is a good example. Women had tradi-

tionally played an active role in Mongol tribal society—many actually fought on the battlefield alongside the men—and Babur and his successors often relied on the women in their families for political advice. Women from aristocratic families were often awarded honorific titles, received salaries, and were permitted to own land and engage in business. Women at court sometimes received an education, and Emperor Akbar reportedly established a girls' school at Fatehpur Sikri to provide teachers for his own daughters. Aristocratic women often expressed their creative talents by writing poetry, painting, or playing music. Women of all castes were adept at spinning thread, either for their own use or to sell to weavers to augment the family income. Weaving was carried out in home production units by all the members of the subcaste weaving families. They sold simple cloth to local villages and fine cottons, silks, and wool to the Mughal court. By Akbar's rule, in fact, the textile manufacturing was of such high quality and so well established that India sold cloth to much of the world: Arabia, the coast of East Africa, Egypt, Southeast Asia, and Europe.

To a certain degree, these Mughal attitudes toward women may have had an impact on Indian society. Women were allowed to inherit land, and some even possessed *zamindar* rights. Women from mercantile castes sometimes took an active role in business activities. At the same time, however, as Muslims, the Mughals subjected women to certain restrictions under Islamic law. On the whole, these Mughal practices coincided with and even accentuated existing tendencies in Indian society. The Muslim practice of isolating women and preventing them from associating with men outside the home (*purdah*) was adopted by many upper-class Hindus as a means of enhancing their status or protecting their women from unwelcome advances by Muslims in positions of authority. In other ways, Hindu practices were unaffected. The custom of *sati* continued to be practiced despite efforts by the Mughals to abolish it,

⇒ **THE PALACE OF THE WINDS AT JAIPUR.**   Built by the maharaja of Jaipur in 1799, this imposing building, part of a palace complex, is today actually only a facade. Behind the intricate pink sandstone window screens, the women of the palace were able to observe city life while at the same time remaining invisible to prying eyes. The palace, like most of the buildings in the city of Jaipur, was constructed of sandstone, a product of the nearby desert of Rajasthan.

© SEF/Art Resource, NY

and child marriage (most women were betrothed before the age of ten) remained common. Women were still instructed to obey their husbands without question and to remain chaste.

For their part, Hindus sometimes attempted to defend themselves and their religious practices against the efforts of some Mughal monarchs to impose the Islamic religion and Islamic mores on the indigenous population. In some cases, despite official prohibitions, Hindu men forcibly married Muslim women and then converted them to the native faith, while converts to Islam normally lost all of their inheritance rights within the Indian family. Government orders to destroy Hindu temples were often ignored by local officials, sometimes as the result of bribery or intimidation. Sometimes Indian practices had an influence on the Mughal elites, as many Mughal chieftains married Indian women and adopted Indian forms of dress.

Long-term stability led to increasing commercialization and the spread of wealth to new groups within Indian society. The Mughal era saw the emergence of an affluent landed gentry and a prosperous merchant class. Members of prestigious castes from the pre-Mughal period reaped many of the benefits of the increasing wealth, but some of these changes transcended caste boundaries and led to the emergence of new groups who achieved status and wealth on the basis of economic achievement rather than traditional kinship ties. During the late eighteenth century, this economic prosperity was shaken by the decline of the Mughal Empire and the increasing European presence. But many prominent Indians reacted by establishing commercial relationships with the foreigners. For a time, that relationship often worked to the Indians' benefit. Later, as we shall see, they would have cause to regret the arrangement.

MUGHAL CULTURE

The era of the Mughals was one of synthesis in culture as well as in politics and religion. The Mughals combined Islamic themes with Persian and indigenous motifs to produce a unique style that enriched and embellished Indian art and culture. The Mughal emperors were zealous patrons of the arts and enticed painters, poets, and artisans from as far away as the Mediterranean. Apparently, the generosity of the Mughals made it difficult to refuse a trip to India. It was said that they would reward a poet with his weight in gold.

Undoubtedly, the Mughals' most visible achievement was in architecture. Here they integrated Persian and Indian styles in a new and sometimes breathtakingly beautiful form best symbolized by the Taj Mahal, built by the emperor Shah Jahan in the mid-seventeenth century. Although the human and economic cost of the Taj tarnishes the romantic legend of its construction, there is no denying the beauty of the building. It had evolved

Courtesy Carol C. Coffin

↠ **THE TAJ MAHAL.** The Taj Mahal was completed in 1653 by Emperor Shah Jahan as a tomb to glorify the memory of his beloved wife. Raised on a marble platform above the Jumna River, the Taj is dramatically framed by contrasting twin red sandstone mosques, magnificent gardens, and a long reflecting pool that mirrors and magnifies its beauty. The effect is one of monumental size, near blinding brilliance, and delicate lightness, a startling contrast to the heavier and more masculine Baroque style then popular in Europe.

from a style that originated several decades earlier with the tomb of Humayun, which was built by his widow in Agra in 1565 during the reign of Akbar.

Humayun's mausoleum had combined Persian and Islamic motifs in a square building finished in red sandstone and topped with a dome. The style was repeated in a number of other buildings erected throughout the empire, but the Taj brought the style to perfection. Working with a model created by his Persian architect, Shah Jahan raised the dome and replaced the red sandstone with brilliant white marble. The entire exterior and interior surface is decorated with cut-stone geometrical patterns, delicate black stone tracery, or intricate inlay of colored precious stones in floral and Koranic arabesques. The technique of creating dazzling floral mosaics of lapis lazuli, malachite, carnelian, turquoise, and mother of pearl may have been introduced by Italian artists at the Mughal court. Shah Jahan had intended to erect a similar building in black marble across the river for his own remains, but the plans were abandoned after he was deposed by his son Aurangzeb. Shah Jahan spent his last years imprisoned in a room in the Red Fort at Agra; from his windows, he could see the beautiful memorial to his beloved wife.

The Taj was by no means the only magnificent building erected during the Mughal era. Akbar, who, in the words of a contemporary, "dresses the work of his mind and heart in the garment of stone and clay," was the first of the great Mughal builders. His first palace at Agra, the Red Fort, was begun in 1565. A few years later, he ordered the construction of a new palace at Fatehpur Sikri, 26 miles west of Agra. The new palace was built in honor of a Sufi mystic who had correctly forecast the birth of a son to the emperor. In gratitude, Akbar decided to build a new capital city and palace on the site of the mystic's home

in the village of Sikri. Over a period of fifteen years, from 1571 to 1586, a magnificent new city in red sandstone was constructed. Although the city was abandoned before completion and now stands almost untouched, it is a popular destination for tourists and pilgrims.

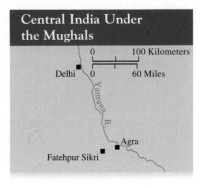

Central India Under the Mughals

The other major artistic achievement of the Mughal period was painting. Painting had never been one of the great attainments of Indian culture due in part to a technological difficulty. Paper was not introduced to India from Persia until the latter part of the fourteenth century, so traditionally painting had been done on palm leaves, which had severely hampered artistic creativity. By the fifteenth century, Indian painting had made the transition from palm leaf to paper, and the new medium eventually stimulated a burst of creativity, particularly in the genre of miniatures, or book illustrations.

As in so many other areas of endeavor, painting in Mughal India resulted from the blending of two cultures. While living in exile, Emperor Humayun had learned to admire Persian miniatures. On his return to India in 1555, he invited two Persian masters to live in his palace and introduce the technique to his adopted land. His successor, Akbar, appreciated the new style and popularized it with his patronage. He established a state workshop at Fatehpur Sikri for two hundred artists, mostly Hindus, who worked under the guidance of the Persian masters to create the Mughal school of painting.

FATEHPUR SIKRI.   In gratitude to a Sufi mystic who had correctly forecast the birth of his son, Akbar chose the mystic's village of Sikri as the site for his new palace and capital city. Completed at great speed in 1586, the splendid city, which was built of red sandstone and measured 2 miles long and a mile wide, was soon abandoned because of an inadequate water supply. Its elaborate palaces, mosque, reflecting pools and courtyards, harems, and impressive victory gate all symbolize the elegance and greatness of Akbar's reign.

The "Akbar style" combined Persian with Indian motifs, such as the use of extended space and the portrayal of physical human action, characteristics not usually seen in Persian art. Akbar also apparently encouraged the imitation of European art forms, including the portrayal of Christian subjects, the use of perspective, lifelike portraits, and the shading of colors in the Renaissance style. The depiction of the human figure in Mughal painting outraged orthodox Muslims at court, but Akbar argued that the painter, "in sketching anything that has life . . . must come to feel that he cannot bestow individuality upon his work, and is thus forced to think of God, the Giver of Life, and will thus increase in knowledge."[4]

Painting during Akbar's reign followed the trend toward realism and historical narrative that had originated in the Ottoman Empire. For example, Akbar had the illustrated *Book of Akbar* made to record his military exploits and court activities. Many of these paintings of Akbar's life portray him in action in his real world. After his death, his son and grandson continued the patronage of the arts.

The development of Indian literature was held back by the absence of printing, which was not introduced until the end of the Mughal era. Literary works were inscribed by calligraphers, and one historian has estimated that the library of Agra contained more than 24,000 volumes. Poetry, in particular, flourished under the Mughals, who established poet laureates at court. Poems were written in the Persian style and in the Persian language. In fact, Persian became the official language of the court until the sack of Delhi in 1739. At the time, the Indians' anger at their conquerors led them to adopt Urdu as the new language for the court and for poetry. By that time, Indian verse on the Persian model had already lost its original vitality and simplicity and had become more artificial in the manner of court literature everywhere.

Another aspect of the long Mughal reign was a Hindu revival of devotional literature, much of it dedicated to Krishna and Rama. The retelling of the Ramayana in the vernacular, beginning in the southern Tamil languages in the eleventh century and spreading slowly northward, culminated in the sixteenth-century Hindi version by the great poet Tulsidas (1532–1623). His *Ramcaritmanas* presents the devotional story with a deified Rama and Sita. Tulsidas's genius was in combining the conflicting cults of

⇴ THE CONSTRUCTION OF FATEHPUR SIKRI. In this contemporary Mughal painting, artisans are completing construction of the Elephant Gate at Akbar's new capital of Fatehpur Sikri. Since both the Ottoman Empire and Mughal India used Persian as their court language, they learned to appreciate the illuminated manuscript techniques produced by Safavid workshops in Persia and adapted them to their own cultural heritage. Emperor Akbar, the greatest Mughal ruler, enthusiastically embraced the art of bookmaking, peopling his royal workshops with more than one hundred artists. The illustrated manuscripts from Mughal India rival those of Safavid Persia in brilliance and imagination and provide fascinating historical details of military campaigns and court ceremonies, as well as scenes from daily life.

Vishnu and Siva into a unified and overwhelming love for the divine, which he expressed in some of the most moving of all Indian poetry. The *Ramcaritmanas* has eclipsed its two-thousand-year-old Sanskrit ancestor in popularity and even became the basis of an Indian television series in the late 1980s.

 # CONCLUSION

The three empires that we have discussed in this chapter exhibit a number of striking similarities. First of all, they were Muslim in their religious affiliation, although the Safavids were Shi'ite rather than Sunni, a distinction that often led to mutual tensions and conflict. More important, perhaps, they were all of nomadic origin, and the political and social institutions that they adopted carried the imprint of their preimperial past. Once they achieved imperial power, however, all three ruling dynasties displayed an impressive capacity to administer a large empire and brought a degree of stability to peoples who had all too often lived in conditions of internal division and war.

Another similarity is that the mastery of the techniques of modern warfare, including the use of firearms, played a central role in all three empires' ability to overcome their rivals and rise to regional hegemony. Some scholars have therefore labeled them "gunpowder empires" in the belief that technical prowess in the art of warfare was a key element in their success. Although that is undoubtedly true, we should not forget that other factors, such as dynamic leadership, political acumen, and the possession of an ardent following motivated by religious zeal, were equally if not more important in their drive to power and ability to retain it. Weapons by themselves do not an empire make.

The rise of these powerful Muslim states coincided with the opening period of European expansion at the end of the fifteenth century and the beginning of the sixteenth. The military and political talents of these empires helped protect much of the Muslim world from the resurgent forces of Christianity. To the contrary, the Ottoman Turks carried their empire into the heart of Christian Europe and briefly reached the gates of the great city of Vienna. By the end of the eighteenth century, however, the Safavid dynasty had imploded, and the powerful Mughal Empire was in a state of virtual collapse. Only the Ottoman Empire was still functioning. Yet it too had lost much of its early expansionistic vigor and was showing signs of internal decay.

The reasons for the decline of these empires have inspired considerable debate among historians. One factor was undoubtedly the expansion of European power into the Indian Ocean and the Middle East. But internal causes were probably more important in the long run. All three empires experienced growing factionalism within the ruling elite, incompetence within the palace, and the emergence of divisive forces in the empire at large—factors that have marked the passing of traditional empires since early times. Climatic change (the region was reportedly hotter and drier after the beginning of the seventeenth century) may have been a hidden reason. Paradoxically, one of the greatest strengths of these empires—their mastery of gunpowder—may have simultaneously been a serious weakness in that it allowed them to develop a complacent sense of security. With little incentive to turn their attention to new developments in science and technology, they were increasingly vulnerable to attack by the advanced nations of the West. The weakening of the gunpowder empires created a political vacuum into which the dynamic and competitive forces of European capitalism were quick to enter.

The gunpowder empires, however, were not the only states in the Old World that were able to resist the first outward thrust of European expansion. Farther to the east, the mature civilizations in China and Japan successfully faced a similar challenge from Western merchants and missionaries. Unlike their counterparts in South Asia and the Middle East, as the nineteenth century dawned, they continued to thrive.

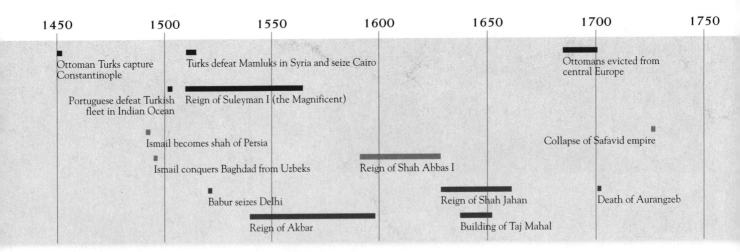

| 1450 | 1500 | 1550 | 1600 | 1650 | 1700 | 1750 |

Ottoman Turks capture Constantinople

Turks defeat Mamluks in Syria and seize Cairo

Ottomans evicted from central Europe

Portuguese defeat Turkish fleet in Indian Ocean

Reign of Suleyman I (the Magnificent)

Ismail becomes shah of Persia

Collapse of Safavid empire

Ismail conquers Baghdad from Uzbeks

Reign of Shah Abbas I

Babur seizes Delhi

Reign of Shah Jahan

Death of Aurangzeb

Reign of Akbar

Building of Taj Mahal

CHAPTER NOTES

1. Vincent A. Smith, *The Oxford History of India* (Oxford, 1967), p. 341.
2. Quoted in Michael Edwardes, *A History of India: From the Earliest Times to the Present Day* (London, 1961), p. 188.
3. Quoted in Edwardes, *History of India*, p. 220.
4. Quoted in Roy C. Craven, *Indian Art: A Concise History* (New York, 1976), p. 205.

SUGGESTED READING

The most complete general survey of the Ottoman Empire is S. J. Shaw, *History of the Ottoman Empire and Modern Turkey* (Cambridge, 1976). Shaw is difficult reading but informative on administrative matters. A more readable albeit less definitive account is Lord Kinross, *The Ottoman Centuries: The Rise and Fall of the Ottoman Empire* (New York, 1977), which is larded with human-interest stories. Also of interest is B. Lewis, *Istanbul and the Civilization of the Ottoman Empire* (Norman, Okla., 1963), written by a veteran Arabist.

For a dramatic account of the conquest of Constantinople in 1453, see S. Runciman, *The Fall of Constantinople, 1453* (Cambridge, 1965). The life of Mehmet II is chronicled in F. Babinger, *Mehmed the Conqueror and His Time*, trans. R. Manheim (Princeton, N.J., 1979). On Suleyman the Magnificent, see R. Merriman, *Suleiman the Magnificent, 1520–1566* (Cambridge, 1944). On the Safavids, see R. M. Savory, *Iran Under the Safavids* (Cambridge, 1980), and E. B. Monshi, *History of Shah Abbas the Great*, 2 vols. (Boulder, Colo., 1978).

For a concise introduction to Ottoman art, consult D. T. Rice, *Islamic Art* (London, 1975); E. J. Grube, *The World of Islam* (New York, 1967); and J. Bloom and S. Blair, *Islamic Arts* (London, 1997).

For an overview of the Mughal era, see S. Wolpert, *New History of India* (New York, 1989). A more dramatic account for the general reader is W. Hansen, *The Peacock Throne: The Drama of Mogul India* (New York, 1972).

There are a number of specialized works on various aspects of the period. For a treatment of the Mughal era in the context of Islamic rule in India, see S. M. Ikram, *Muslim Civilization in India* (New York, 1964). The concept of "gunpowder empires" is persuasively analyzed in D. E. Streusand, *The Formation of the Mughal Empire* (Delhi, 1989). Economic issues predominate in much recent scholarship. For example, S. Subrahmanyan, *The Political Economy of Commerce: Southern India, 1500–1650* (Cambridge, 1990), focuses on the interaction between internal and external trade in southern India during the early stages of the period. The Mughal Empire is analyzed in a broad Central Asian context in R. C. Foltz, *Mughal India and Central Asia* (Karachi, 1998). Finally, K. N. Chaudhuri, *Trade and Civilization in the Indian Ocean: An Economic History from the Rise of Islam to 1750* (Cambridge, 1985), views Indian commerce in the perspective of the regional trade network throughout the Indian Ocean.

Personal accounts of the period are numerous, although most are by European visitors. For some examples, see R. C. Temple, ed., *The Travels of Peter Mundy, in Europe and Asia, 1608–1667* (Cambridge, 1907–1936); J. B. Tavernier, *Travels in India* (London, 1925); T. Roe, *The Embassy of Sir Thomas Roe, 1615–1619* (London, 1926); and F. Bernier, *Travels in the Mogul Empire, 1656–1668* (London, 1968). For an inside look, see J. Leyden and W. Erskine, trans., *Memoirs of Zehir-ed-Din Muhammad Babur* (London, 1921).

Standard works on Mughal art and culture include A. L. Basham, *A Cultural History of India* (Oxford, 1975); R. C. Craven, *Indian Art: A Concise History* (New York, 1976); and M. C. Beach, *The Imperial Image* (Washington, D.C., 1981).

For treatments of all three Muslim empires in a comparative context, see J. J. Kissling et al., *The Last Great Muslim Empires* (Princeton, N.J., 1996), and M. G. S. Hodgson, *Rethinking World History: Essays on Europe, Islam, and World History* (Cambridge, 1993).

For an introduction to the women of the Ottoman Empire and those of the Mughal Empire, see S. Hughes and B. Hughes, *Women in World History*, vol. 2 (Armonk, N.Y., 1997). For a more detailed presentation of women in the imperial harem, consult L. P. Peirce, "Beyond Harem Walls: Ottoman Royal Women and the Exercise of Power," in *Gendered Domains: Rethinking Public and Private in Women's History*, ed. D. O. Helly and S. M. Reverby (Ithaca, N.Y., 1992), and L. P. Peirce, *The Imperial Harem: Women and Sovereignty in the Ottoman Empire* (Oxford, 1993). The fascinating story of the royal woman who played an important role behind the scenes is found in E. B. Findly, *Nur Jahan: Empress of Mughal India* (Oxford, 1993).

INFOTRAC COLLEGE EDITION

For additional reading, go to InfoTrac College Edition, your online research library at
http://web1.infotrac-college.com

Enter the search term "Islam" using the Subject Guide.

Enter the search terms "Ottoman Empire" using Keywords.

Enter the search term "Safavid" using Keywords.

Enter the search term "Mughal" using Keywords.

Chapter 16

THE EAST ASIAN WORLD

CHAPTER OUTLINE

- CHINA AT ITS APEX
- TOKUGAWA JAPAN
- KOREA: THE HERMIT KINGDOM
- CONCLUSION

FOCUS QUESTIONS

- Why were the Manchus so successful at establishing a foreign dynasty in China, and what were the main characteristics of their rule?
- How did China and Japan respond to the coming of the Europeans, and what impact did the Europeans have on these East Asian civilizations in the sixteenth through eighteenth centuries?
- How did the unification of Japan come about, and how did the Tokugawa rulers maintain that unity?
- How did the economy and society of Japan change during the Tokugawa era, and how did Japanese culture reflect those changes?
- ➤ How did the economy and society of China change during the Ming and Qing eras, and to what degree did these changes seem to be leading toward an industrial revolution on the Western model?

*I*n December 1717, the emperor Kangxi returned from a hunting trip north of the Great Wall and began to suffer from dizzy spells. Conscious of his approaching date with mortality—he was now nearly seventy years of age—the emperor called together his sons and leading government officials in the imperial palace and issued the following edict:

> *The rulers of the past all took reverence for Heaven's laws and reverence for their ancestors as the fundamental way in ruling the country. To be sincere in reverence for Heaven and ancestors entails the following: Be kind to men from afar and keep the able ones near, nourish the people, think of the profit of all as being the real profit and the mind of the whole country as being the real mind, be considerate to officials and act as the father to the people, protect the state before danger comes and govern well before there is any disturbance, be always diligent and always careful, and maintain the balance between leniency and strictness, between principle and expediency, so that long-range plans can be made for the country: That's all there is to it.*[1]

As a primer for political leadership, the emperor's edict reflects the genius of Confucian philosophy at its best and has a timeless quality that applies to our age as well as to the Golden Age of the Qing dynasty.

Kangxi reigned during one of the most glorious eras in the long history of China. Under the Ming (1369–1644) and the early Qing (1644–1911) dynasties, the empire expanded its borders to a degree not seen since the Han and the Tang. Chinese culture was the envy of its neighbors and earned the admiration of many European visitors, including Jesuit priests and Enlightenment philosophes.

On the surface, China appeared to be an unchanging society patterned after the Confucian vision of a "golden age" in the remote past. This indeed was the image presented by China's rulers, who referred constantly to tradition as a model for imperial institutions and cultural values. Although few observers could have been aware of it at the time, however, China was changing—and rather rapidly.

A similar process was under way in neighboring Japan. A vigorous new shogunate called the Tokugawa rose to power in the early seventeenth century and managed to revitalize the traditional system in a somewhat more centralized form that enabled it to survive for another 250 years. But major structural changes were taking place in Japanese society, and by the nineteenth century, tensions were growing as the gap between theory and reality widened.

One of the many factors involved in the quickening pace of change in both countries was contact with the West, which began with the arrival of Portuguese ships in Chinese and Japanese ports in the first half of the sixteenth century. The Ming and the Tokugawa initially opened their doors to European trade and missionary activity. Later, however, Chinese and Japanese rulers became concerned about the corrosive effects of Western ideas and practices and attempted to protect their traditional societies from external intrusion. But neither could forever resist the importunities of Western trading nations, and when the doors to the West were finally reopened in the mid-nineteenth century, both societies were ripe for radical change. •

CHINA AT ITS APEX

In 1514, a Portuguese fleet dropped anchor off the coast of China, just south of the Pearl River estuary and present-day Hong Kong. It was the first direct contact between the Chinese Empire and the West since the arrival of the Venetian adventurer Marco Polo two centuries earlier, and it opened an era that would eventually change the face of China and, indeed, all the world.

From the Ming to the Qing

Marco Polo had reported on the magnificence of China after visiting Beijing during the reign of Khubilai Khan, the great Mongol ruler. By the time the Portuguese fleet arrived off the coast of China, of course, the Mongol Empire had long since disappeared. It had gradually weakened after the death of Khubilai Khan and was finally overthrown in 1368 by a massive peasant rebellion under the leadership of Zhu Yuanzhang, who had declared himself the founding emperor of a new Ming (Bright) dynasty and assumed the reign title of Ming Hongwu (Ming Hung Wu, or Ming Martial Emperor). The Ming inaugurated a new era of greatness in Chinese history. Under a series of strong rulers, China extended its rule into Mongolia and Central Asia. The Ming even briefly reconquered Vietnam, which, after a thousand years of Chinese rule, had reclaimed its independence following the collapse of the Tang dynasty in the tenth century. Along the northern frontier, the Emperor Yongle (Yung Lo; 1402–1424) strengthened the Great Wall and pacified the nomadic tribespeople who had troubled China in previous centuries. A tributary relationship was established with the Yi dynasty in Korea.

The internal achievements of the Ming were equally impressive. When they replaced the Mongols in the fourteenth century, the Ming turned to traditional Confucian institutions as a means of ruling their vast empire. These included the six ministries at the apex of the bureaucracy, the use of the civil service examinations to select members of the bureaucracy, and the division of the empire into provinces, districts, and counties. As before, Chinese villages were relatively autonomous, and local councils of elders continued to be responsible for adjudicating disputes, initiating local construction and irrigation projects, mustering a militia, and assessing and collecting taxes.

The society that was governed by this vast hierarchy of officials was a far cry from the predominantly agrarian society that had been ruled by the Han. In the burgeoning

Courtesy of William J. Duiker

THE GREAT WALL OF CHINA Although the Great Wall is popularly believed to be over two thousand years old, the part of the wall that is most frequently visited by tourists was a reconstruction undertaken during the early Ming dynasty as a means of protection against invasion from the north. Part of that wall, which was built to protect the imperial capital of Beijing, is shown here.

cities near the coast and along the Yangtze River valley, factories and workshops were vastly increasing the variety and output of their manufactured goods. The population had doubled, and new crops had been introduced, greatly expanding the food output of the empire.

In 1405, in a splendid display of Chinese maritime might, Yongle sent a fleet of Chinese trading ships under the eunuch admiral Zhenghe (Cheng Ho) through the Strait of Malacca and out into the Indian Ocean; there they traveled as far west as the east coast of Africa, stop-

ping on the way at ports in South Asia. The size of the fleet was impressive: it included nearly 28,000 sailors on sixty-two ships, some of them junks larger by far than any other oceangoing vessels the world had yet seen. China seemed about to become a direct participant in the vast trade network that extended as far west as the Atlantic Ocean, thus culminating the process of opening China to the wider world that had begun with the Tang dynasty.

Why the expeditions were undertaken has been a matter of some debate. Some historians assume that economic profit was the main reason. Others point to Yongle's native curiosity and note that the voyage—and the six others that followed it—returned not only with goods but also with a plethora of information about the outside world as well as with some items unknown in China (the emperor was especially intrigued by the giraffes and placed them in the imperial zoo, where they were identified by soothsayers with the coming of good government). Others speculate that the emperor was seeking to ascertain the truth of rumors that his immediate predecessor, Emperor Jianwen or Chien Wen (1398–1402), had escaped to Southeast Asia to live in exile.

Whatever the case, the voyages resulted in a dramatic increase in Chinese knowledge about the world and the nature of ocean travel. It also brought massive profits for their sponsors, including individuals connected with Admiral Zhenghe at court. This aroused resentment among conservatives within the bureaucracy, some of whom viewed commercial activities with a characteristic measure of Confucian disdain. One commented that an end to the voyages would provide the Chinese people with a respite "so that they can devote themselves to husbandry [agriculture] and schooling."

Shortly after Yongle's death, the voyages were discontinued, never to be revived. An early European visitor reported that "no one sails the sea from north to south; it is prohibited by the king, in order that the country may not become known."[2] The decision had long-term consequences and in the eyes of many modern historians marks a turning inward of the Chinese state, away from commerce and toward a more traditional emphasis on agriculture, away from the exotic lands to the south and toward the heartland of the country in the Yellow River valley.

Ironically, the move toward the Yellow River had been initiated by Yongle himself when he had decided to move the Ming capital from Nanjing, in central China, where the ships were built and the voyages launched, back to Beijing, where official eyes were firmly focused on the threat from beyond the Great Wall to the north. As a means of reducing that threat, Yongle ordered the resettlement of thousands of families from the rich Yangtze valley. The emperor had presumably not intended to set forces in motion that would divert the country from its growing contacts with the external world. After all, he had been the driving force behind Zhenghe's voyages. But the end result was a shift in the balance of power from central China, where it had been since the southern Song dynasty, back to northern China, where it had originated and would remain for the rest of the Ming era. China would not look outward again for over four centuries.

FIRST CONTACTS WITH THE WEST

Despite the Ming's retreat from active participation in the maritime trade, when the Portuguese arrived in 1514, China was in command of a vast empire that stretched from the steppes of Central Asia to the China Sea, from the Gobi Desert to the tropical rain forests of Southeast Asia. From the lofty perspective of the imperial throne in Beijing, the Europeans could only have seemed like an unusually exotic form of barbarian to be placed within the familiar framework of the tributary system, the hierarchical arrangement in which rulers of all other countries were regarded as "younger brothers" of the Son of Heaven. Indeed, the bellicose and uncultured behavior of the Portuguese so outraged Chinese officials that they expelled the Europeans, but after further negotiations, the Portuguese were permitted to occupy the tiny territory of Macao, a foothold they would retain until the end of the twentieth century.

Initially, the arrival of the Europeans did not have much impact on Chinese society. Direct trade between Europe and China was limited, and Portuguese ships became involved in the regional trade network, carrying silk to Japan in return for Japanese silver. Eventually, the Spanish also began to participate, using the Philippines as an anchor in the galleon trade between China and the great silver mines in the Americas.

More influential than trade, perhaps, were the ideas introduced by Christian missionaries. Among the most active and the most effective were highly educated Jesuits, who were familiar with European philosophical and scientific developments. Recognizing the Chinese pride in their own culture, the Jesuits attempted to draw parallels between Christian and Confucian concepts (for example, they identified the Western concept of God with the Chinese character for Heaven) and to show the similarities between Christian morality and Confucian ethics. European inventions such as the clock, the prism, and various astronomical and musical instruments impressed Chinese officials, hitherto deeply imbued with a sense of the superiority of Chinese civilization, and helped Western ideas win acceptance at court. An elderly Chinese scholar expressed his wonder at the miracle of eyeglasses:

> White glass from across the Western Seas
> Is imported through Macao:
> Fashioned into lenses big as coins,
> They encompass the eyes in a double frame.
> I put them on—it suddenly becomes clear;
> I can see the very tips of things!
> And read fine print by the dim-lit window
> Just like in my youth.[3]

For their part, the missionaries were much impressed with many aspects of Chinese civilization, and reports of their experiences heightened European curiosity about this great society on the other side of the world (see the box on p. 446).

THE MING BROUGHT TO EARTH

During the late sixteenth century, the Ming began to decline as a series of weak rulers led to an era of corruption, concentration of land ownership, and ultimately peasant rebellions and tribal unrest along the northern frontier. The inflow of vast amounts of foreign silver led to an alarming increase in inflation. Then the arrival of the English and the Dutch disrupted the silver trade; silver imports plummeted, severely straining the Chinese economy by raising the value of the metal relative to that of copper. Crop yields declined due to harsh weather—linked to the "little ice age" of the early seventeenth century—and the resulting scarcity reduced the ability of the government to provide food in times of imminent starvation. High taxes, provoked in part by increased official corruption, led to peasant unrest and worker violence in urban areas. A folk song of the period, addressed to the "Lord of Heaven," complained,

> Old skymaster,
> You're getting on, your ears are deaf, your eyes are gone.
> Can't see people, can't hear words.
> Glory for those who kill and burn;
> For those who fast and read the scriptures,
> Starvation.
> Fall down, old master sky, how can you be so high?
> How can you be so high? Come down to earth.[4]

As always, internal problems were accompanied by unrest along the northern frontier. Following long precedent, the Ming had attempted to pacify the frontier tribes by forging alliances with them, arranging marriages between them and the local aristocracy, and granting trade privileges. One of the alliances was with the Manchus (also known as the Jurchen), the descendants of peoples who had briefly established a kingdom in northern China during the early thirteenth century. The Manchus, a mixed agricultural and hunting people, lived northeast of the Great Wall in the area known today as Manchuria.

At first the Manchus were satisfied with consolidating their territory and made little effort to extend their rule south of the Great Wall. But during the first decades of the seventeenth century, the problems of the Ming dynasty began to come to a head. A major epidemic devastated the population in many areas of the country. The suffering brought on by the epidemic helped spark a vast peasant revolt led by Li Zicheng (Li Tzu-ch'eng, 1604–1651). Li was a postal worker in central China who had been dismissed from his job as part of a cost-saving measure by the imperial court, now increasingly preoccupied by tribal

THE ART OF PRINTING

Europeans obtained much of their early information about China from the Jesuits who served at the Ming court in the sixteenth and seventeenth centuries. Clerics such as the Italian Matteo Ricci (1552–1610) found much to admire in Chinese civilization. Here Ricci expresses a keen interest in Chinese printing methods, which at that time were well in advance of the techniques used in the West.

MATTEO RICCI, *THE DIARY OF MATTHEW RICCI*

The art of printing was practiced in China at a date somewhat earlier than that assigned to the beginning of printing in Europe, which was about 1405. It is quite certain that the Chinese knew the art of printing at least five centuries ago, and some of them assert that printing was known to their people before the beginning of the Christian era, about 50 B.C. Their method of printing differs widely from that employed in Europe, and our method would be quite impracticable for them because of the exceedingly large number of Chinese characters and symbols. . . .

Their method of making printed books is quite ingenious. The text is written in ink, with a brush made of very fine hair, on a sheet of paper which is inverted and pasted on a wooden tablet. When the paper has become thoroughly dry, its surface is scraped off quickly and with great skill, until nothing but a fine tissue bearing the characters remains on the wooden tablet. Then, with a steel graver, the workman cuts away the surface following the outlines of the characters until these alone stand out in low relief. From such a block a skilled printer can make copies with incredible speed, turning out as many as fifteen hundred copies in a single day. . . . This scheme of engraving wooden blocks is well adapted for the large and complex nature of the Chinese characters, but I do not think it would lend itself very aptly to our European type, which could hardly be engraved upon wood because of its small dimensions.

Their method of printing has one decided advantage, namely, that once these tablets are made, they can be preserved and used for making changes in the text as often as one wishes. Additions and subtractions can also be made as the tablets can be readily patched. . . . We have derived great benefit from this method of Chinese printing, as we employ the domestic help in our homes to strike off copies of the books on religious and scientific subjects which we translate into Chinese from the languages in which they were written originally. In truth, the whole method is so simple that one is tempted to try it for himself after once having watched the process. The simplicity of Chinese printing is what accounts for the exceedingly large numbers of books in circulation here and the ridiculously low prices at which they are sold.

---

attacks along the frontier (see Map 16.1). In the 1630s, Li managed to extend the revolt throughout the country and finally occupied the capital of Beijing in 1644. The last Ming emperor committed suicide by hanging himself from a tree in the palace gardens.

But Li was unable to hold his conquest. The overthrow of the Ming dynasty presented a great temptation to the Manchus. With the assistance of many military commanders who had deserted from the Ming, they conquered Beijing on their own. Li Zicheng's army disintegrated, and the Manchus declared the creation of a new dynasty with the reign title of the Qing (Ch'ing, or Pure). Once again, China was under foreign rule.

The Greatness of the Qing

The accession of the Manchus to power in Beijing was not universally applauded. Their ruthless policies and insensitivity to Chinese customs soon provoked resistance. Some Ming loyalists fled to Southeast Asia, but others continued their resistance to the new rulers from inside the country. To make it easier to identify the rebels, the government ordered all Chinese to adopt Manchu dress and hairstyles. All Chinese males were to shave their foreheads and braid their hair into a queue; those who refused were to be executed. As a popular saying put it, "Lose your hair or lose your head."[5]

But the Manchus eventually proved to be more adept at adapting to Chinese conditions than their predecessors, the Mongols. Unlike the latter, who had tried to impose their own methods of ruling, the Manchus adopted the Chinese political system (although, as we shall see, they retained their distinct position within it) and were gradually accepted by most Chinese as the legitimate rulers of the country.

Like all of China's great dynasties, the Qing was blessed with a series of strong early rulers who pacified the country, rectified many of the most obvious social and economic inequities, and restored peace and prosperity. For the Ming dynasty, these strong emperors had been Hongwu and Yongle; under the Qing, they would be Kangxi (K'ang Hsi) and Qianlong (Ch'ien Lung). The two Qing monarchs ruled China for well over a century, from the middle of the seventeenth century to the end of the eighteenth, and were responsible for much of the greatness of Manchu China.

Kangxi (1661–1722) was arguably the greatest ruler in Chinese history. Ascending to the throne at the age of seven, he was blessed with diligence, political astuteness, and a strong character and began to take charge of Qing administration while still an adolescent. During the six decades of his reign, Kangxi not only stabilized impe-

MAP **16.1**   **China and Its Enemies During the Late Ming Era.**   During the seventeenth century, the Ming dynasty faced challenges on two fronts, from China's traditional adversaries—nomadic groups north of the Great Wall—and from new arrivals—European merchants—who had begun to press for trading privileges along the southern coast. ➤ *How do these threats differ from those faced by previous dynasties in China?*

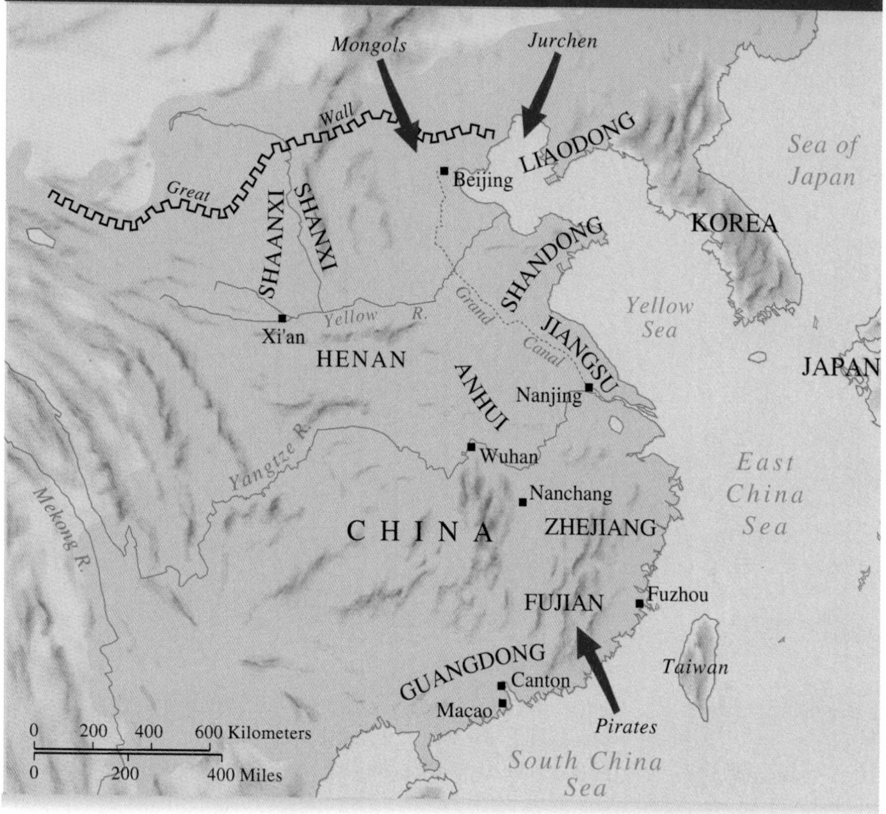

rial rule by pacifying the restive peoples along the northern and western frontiers but also managed to make the dynasty acceptable to the general population. As an active patron of arts and letters, he cultivated the support of scholars through a number of major projects.

During Kangxi's reign, the activities of the Western missionaries, Dominicans and Franciscans as well as Jesuits, reached their height. The emperor was quite tolerant of the Christians, and several Jesuit missionaries became influential at court. Several hundred court officials converted to Christianity, as did an estimated 300,000 ordinary Chinese. But the Christian effort was ultimately undermined by squabbling among the Western religious orders over the Jesuit policy of accommodating local beliefs and practices in order to facilitate conversion. The Jesuits had acquiesced to the emperor's insistence that traditional Confucian rituals such as ancestor worship were civil ceremonies and thus could be undertaken by Christian converts. Jealous Dominicans and Franciscans complained to the pope, who issued an edict ordering all missionaries and converts to conform to the official orthodoxy set forth in Europe. At first, Kangxi attempted to resolve the problem by appealing directly to the Vatican, but the pope was uncompromising. After Kangxi's death, his successor began to suppress Christian activities throughout China.

Kangxi's achievements were carried on by his successors, Yongzheng (Yung Cheng, 1722–1736) and Qianlong (1736–1795). Like Kangxi, Qianlong was known for his diligence, tolerance, and intellectual curiosity, and he too combined vigorous military action against the unruly tribes along the frontier with active efforts to promote economic prosperity, administrative efficiency, and scholarship and artistic excellence. The result was continued growth for the Manchu Empire throughout much of the eighteenth century.

QING POLITICS

One reason for the success of the Manchus was their ability to adapt to their new environment. They retained the Ming political system with relatively few changes. They also tried to establish their legitimacy as China's rightful rulers by stressing their devotion to the principles of Confucianism. Emperor Kangxi ostentatiously studied the sacred Confucian classics and issued a "sacred edict" that proclaimed

SIXTEEN CONFUCIAN COMMANDMENTS

Although the Qing dynasty was of foreign origin, its rulers found Confucian maxims convenient for maintaining the social order. In 1670, the great emperor Kangxi issued the Sacred Edict to popularize Confucian values among the common people. The edict was read publicly at periodic intervals in every village in the country and set the standard for behavior throughout the empire. Note the similarities and differences with the Japanese decree on p. 463 later in this chapter.

KANGXI'S SACRED EDICT

1. Esteem most highly filial piety and brotherly submission, in order to give due importance to the social relations.
2. Behave with generosity toward your kindred, in order to illustrate harmony and benignity.
3. Cultivate peace and concord in your neighborhoods, in order to prevent quarrels and litigations.
4. Recognize the importance of husbandry and the culture of the mulberry tree, in order to ensure a sufficiency of clothing and food.
5. Show that you prize moderation and economy, in order to prevent the lavish waste of your means.
6. Give weight to colleges and schools, in order to make correct the practice of the scholar.
7. Extirpate strange principles, in order to exalt the correct doctrine.
8. Lecture on the laws, in order to warn the ignorant and obstinate.
9. Elucidate propriety and yielding courtesy, in order to make manners and customs good.
10. Labor diligently at your proper callings, in order to stabilize the will of the people.
11. Instruct sons and younger brothers, in order to prevent them from doing what is wrong.
12. Put a stop to false accusations, in order to preserve the honest and good.
13. Warn against sheltering deserters, in order to avoid being involved in their punishment.
14. Fully remit your taxes, in order to avoid being pressed for payment.
15. Unite in hundreds and tithing, in order to put an end to thefts and robbery.
16. Remove enmity and anger, in order to show the importance due to the person and life.

---

to the entire empire the importance of the moral values established by the master (see the box above).

Still, the Manchus, like the Mongols, were ethnically, linguistically, and culturally distinct from their subject population. The Qing attempted to cope with this reality by adopting a two-pronged strategy. On the one hand, the Manchus, representing less than 2 percent of the entire population, were legally defined as distinct from everyone else in China. The Manchu nobles retained their aristocratic privileges, while their economic base was protected by extensive landholdings and revenues provided from the state treasury. Other Manchus were assigned farmland and organized into military units, called banners, which were stationed as separate units in various strategic positions throughout China. These "bannermen" were the primary fighting force of the empire. Ethnic Chinese were prohibited from settling in Manchuria and were still compelled to wear their hair in a queue as a sign of submission to the ruling dynasty.

But while the Qing attempted to protect their distinct identity within an alien society, they also recognized the need to bring ethnic Chinese into the top ranks of imperial administration. Their solution was to create a system, known as dyarchy, in which all important administrative positions were shared equally by Chinese and Manchus. Of the six members of the grand secretariat, three were Manchu and three were Chinese. Each of the six ministries had an equal number of Chinese and Manchu members, and Manchus and Chinese also shared responsibilities at the provincial level.

Below the provinces, Chinese were dominant. Although the system did not work perfectly, the Manchus' willingness to share power did win over the allegiance of many Chinese. Meanwhile, the Manchus themselves, despite official efforts to preserve their separate language and culture, were increasingly assimilated into Chinese civilization.

The new rulers also tinkered with the civil service examination system. In an effort to make it more equitable, quotas were established for each major ethnic group and each province to prevent the positions from being monopolized by candidates from certain provinces in central China that had traditionally produced large numbers of officials. In practice, however, the examination system probably became less equitable during the Manchu era because increasingly positions were assigned to candidates who had purchased their degree rather than competing through the system. Moreover, positions were becoming harder to obtain because their number did not rise fast enough to match the unprecedented increase in population under Qing rule.

CHINA ON THE EVE OF THE WESTERN ONSLAUGHT

In some ways, China was at the height of its power and glory in the mid-eighteenth century. But it was also under Qianlong that the first signs of the internal decay of the Manchu dynasty began to appear. The clues were familiar ones. Qing military campaigns along the frontier were expensive and placed heavy demands on the imperial treasury. As the emperor aged, he became less astute in selecting his subordinates and fell under the influence of corrupt elements at court, including the notorious Manchu official Heshen (Ho Shen). Funds officially destined for military or other official use were increasingly siphoned off to Heshen or his favorites, arousing resentment among military and civilian officials.

Corruption at the center led inevitably to unrest in rural areas, where higher taxes, bureaucratic venality, and rising pressure on the land because of the growing population had produced economic hardship. The heart of the unrest was in central China, where discontented peasants who had recently been settled on infertile land launched a revolt known as the White Lotus Rebellion (1796–1804). The revolt was eventually suppressed but at great expense.

Unfortunately for China, the decline of the Qing dynasty occurred just as China's modest relationship with the West was about to give way to a new era of military confrontation and increased pressure for trade. The first problems came in the north, where Russian traders seek-

ing skins and furs began to penetrate the region between Siberian Russia and Manchuria. Earlier the Ming dynasty had attempted to deal with the Russians by the traditional method of placing them in a tributary relationship and playing them off against other non-Chinese groups in the area. But the tsar refused to play by Chinese rules. His envoys to Beijing ignored the tribute system and refused to perform the kowtow (the ritual of prostration and knocking the head on the ground performed by foreign emissaries before the emperor), the classical symbol of fealty demanded of all foreign ambassadors to the Chinese court. Formal diplomatic relations were finally established in 1689, when the Treaty of Nerchinsk (negotiated with the aid of Jesuit missionaries resident at the Qing court) settled the boundary dispute and provided for regular trade between the two countries. Through such arrangements, the Manchus were able not only to pacify the northern frontier but also to extend their rule over Xinjiang and Tibet to the west and southwest (see Map 16.2). In the meantime, tributary relations were established with such

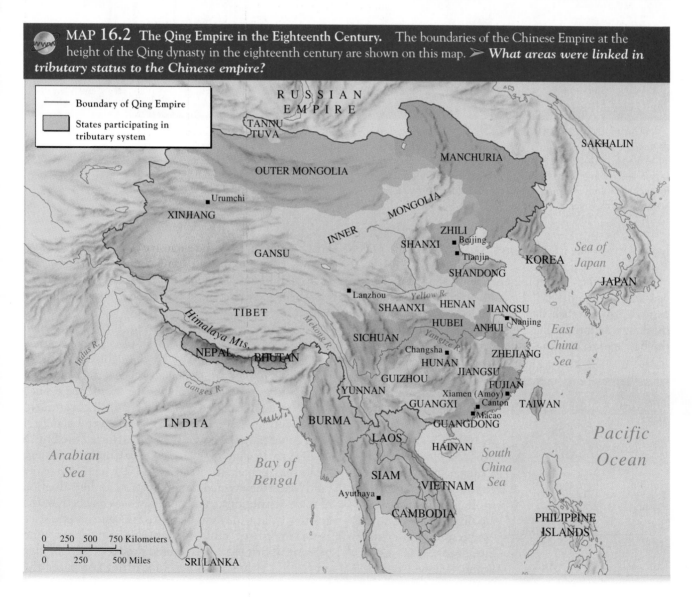

MAP 16.2 The Qing Empire in the Eighteenth Century. The boundaries of the Chinese Empire at the height of the Qing dynasty in the eighteenth century are shown on this map. ➤ *What areas were linked in tributary status to the Chinese empire?*

The Art Archive/Marine Museum Stockholm/Dagli Orti (A)

EUROPEAN WAREHOUSES AT CANTON. Aggravated by the growing presence of foreigners in the eighteenth century, the Chinese court severely restricted the movement of European traders in China. They were permitted to live only in a compound near Canton during the seven months of the trading season and could go into the city only three times a month. In this painting, the Dutch and British flags fly over the warehouses and residences of the foreign community, while Chinese sampans and junks sit anchored in the river.

neighboring countries as Korea, Burma, Vietnam, and Ayuthaya.

Dealing with the foreigners who arrived by sea was more difficult. By the end of the seventeenth century, the English had replaced the Portuguese as the dominant force in European trade. Operating through the East India Company, which served as both a trading unit and the administrator of English territories in Asia, the English established their first trading post at Canton in 1699. Over the next decades, trade with China, notably the export of tea and silk to England, increased rapidly. To limit contact between Chinese and Europeans, the Qing licensed Chinese trading firms at Canton to be the exclusive conduit for trade with the West. Eventually, the Qing confined the Europeans to a small island just outside the city walls and permitted them to reside there only from October through March.

For a while, the British tolerated this system, which brought considerable profit to the East India Company and its shareholders. But by the end of the eighteenth century, the British had begun to demand access to other cities along the Chinese coast and that the country be opened to British manufactured goods. The British government and traders alike were restive at the uneven balance of trade between the two countries, which forced the British to ship vast amounts of silver bullion to China in exchange for its silks, porcelains, and teas. In 1793, a mission under Lord Macartney visited Beijing to press for liberalization of trade restrictions. A compromise was reached on the kowtow (Macartney was permitted to bend on one knee as was the British custom), but Qianlong expressed no interest in British manufactured products (see the box on p. 451). An exasperated Macartney compared the

Canton in the Eighteenth Century

Canton

EUROPEAN FACTORIES *Pearl River*

THE TRIBUTE SYSTEM IN ACTION

In 1793, the British emissary Lord Macartney visited the Qing Empire to request the opening of formal diplomatic and trading relations between his country and China. Emperor Qianlong's reply, addressed to King George III of Britain, illustrates how the imperial court in Beijing viewed the world. King George could not have been pleased. The document provides a good example of the complacency with which the Celestial Empire viewed the world beyond its borders.

A DECREE OF EMPEROR QIANLONG

An Imperial Edict to the King of England: You, O King, are so inclined toward our civilization that you have sent a special envoy across the seas to bring to our Court your memorial of congratulations on the occasion of my birthday and to present your native products as an expression of your thoughtfulness. On perusing your memorial, so simply worded and sincerely conceived, I am impressed by your genuine respectfulness and friendliness and greatly pleased.

As to the request made in your memorial, O King, to send one of your nationals to stay at the Celestial Court to take care of your country's trade with China, this is not in harmony with the state system of our dynasty and will definitely not be permitted. Traditionally people of the European nations who wished to render some service under the Celestial Court have been permitted to come to the capital. But after their arrival they are obliged to wear Chinese court costumes, are placed in a certain residence, and are never allowed to return to their own countries. This is the established rule of the Celestial Dynasty with which presumably you, O King, are familiar. Now you, O King, wish to send one of your nationals to live in the capital, but he is not like the Europeans who come to Peking as Chinese employees, live there, and never return home again, nor can he be allowed to go and come and maintain any correspondence. This is indeed a useless undertaking.

Moreover the territory under the control of the Celestial Court is very large and wide. There are well-established regulations governing tributary envoys from the outer states to Peking [Beijing], giving them provisions (of food and traveling expenses) by our post-houses and limiting their going and coming. There has never been a precedent for letting them do whatever they like. Now if you, O King, wish to have a representative in Peking, his language will be unintelligible and his dress different from the regulations; there is no place to accommodate him. . . .

The Celestial Court has pacified and possessed the territory within the four seas. Its sole aim is to do its utmost to achieve good government and to manage political affairs, attaching no value to strange jewels and precious objects. The various articles presented by you, O King, this time are accepted by my special order to the office in charge of such functions in consideration of the offerings having come from a long distance with sincere good wishes. As a matter of fact, the virtue and prestige of the Celestial Dynasty having spread far and wide, the kings of the myriad nations come by land and sea with all sorts of precious things. Consequently there is nothing we lack, as your principal envoy and others have themselves observed. We have never set much store on strange or ingenious objects, nor do we need any more of your country's manufactures. . . .

Chinese Empire to "an old, crazy, first-rate man-of-war" that had once awed its neighbors "merely by her bulk and appearance" but was now destined under incompetent leadership to be "dashed to pieces on the shore."[6] With his contemptuous dismissal of the British request, the emperor had inadvertently sowed the seeds for a century of humiliation.

Changing China

During the Ming and Qing dynasties, China remained a predominantly agricultural society; nearly 85 percent of its people were farmers. But although most Chinese still lived in rural villages, the economy was undergoing a number of changes that have led some historians to suggest that China, under other circumstances, might have experienced an industrial revolution as in the West. In this view, the arrival of Western imperialism in the nineteenth century not only failed to stimulate economic change but may actually have hindered it.

THE POPULATION EXPLOSION

In the first place, the center of gravity was continuing to shift steadily from the north to the south. In the early centuries of Chinese civilization, the bulk of the population had been located along the Yellow River. Smaller settlements were located along the Yangtze and in the mountainous regions of the south, but the administrative and economic center of gravity was clearly in the north. By the Song period, however, that emphasis had already begun to shift drastically as a result of climatic changes, deforestation, and continuing pressure from nomads in the Gobi Desert. By the early Qing, the economic breadbasket of China was located along the Yangtze River or in the mountains to the south. One concrete indication of this shift occurred during the Ming dynasty, when Emperor Yongle ordered the renovation of the Grand Canal to facilitate the shipment of rice from the Yangtze delta to the food-starved north.

Moreover, the population was beginning to increase rapidly. For centuries, China's population had remained

Chronology

CHINA DURING THE EARLY MODERN ERA

Rise of Ming dynasty	1369
Voyages of Zhenghe	1405–1433
Portuguese arrive in southern China	1514
Matteo Ricci arrives in China	1601
Li Zicheng occupies Beijing	1644
Manchus seize China	1644
Reign of Kangxi	1661–1722
Treaty of Nerchinsk	1689
First English trading post at Canton	1699
Reign of Qianlong	1736–1795
Lord Macartney's mission to China	1793
White Lotus Rebellion	1796–1804

within a range of 50 to 100 million, rising in times of peace and prosperity and falling in periods of foreign invasion and internal anarchy. During the Ming and the early Qing, however, the population increased from an estimated 70 to 80 million in 1390 to over 300 million at the end of the eighteenth century. There were probably several reasons for this population increase: the relatively long period of peace and stability under the early Qing; the introduction of new crops from the Americas, including peanuts, sweet potatoes, and maize; and the planting of a new species of faster-growing rice from Southeast Asia.

Of course, this population increase meant much greater population pressure on the land, smaller farms, and a razor-thin margin of safety in case of climatic disaster. The imperial court attempted to deal with the problem through a variety of means, most notably by preventing the concentration of land in the hands of wealthy landowners. Nevertheless, by the eighteenth century, almost all the land that could be irrigated was already under cultivation, and the problems of rural hunger and landlessness became increasingly serious.

SEEDS OF INDUSTRIALIZATION

Another change that took place during the early modern period in China was the steady growth of manufacturing and commerce. Taking advantage of the long era of peace and prosperity, merchants and manufacturers began to expand their operations beyond their immediate provinces. Commercial networks began to operate on a regional and sometimes even a national basis, as trade in silk, metal and wood products, porcelain, cotton goods, and cash crops like cotton and tobacco developed rapidly.

Foreign trade also expanded as Chinese merchants set up extensive contacts with countries in Southeast Asia.

Although this rise in industrial and commercial activity resembles the changes occurring in western Europe, China and Europe differed in several key ways. In the first place, members of the bourgeoisie in China were not as independent as their European counterparts. In China, trade and manufacturing remained under the firm control of the state. In addition, political and social prejudices against commercial activity remained strong. Reflecting an ancient preference for agriculture over manufacturing and trade, the state levied heavy taxes on manufacturing and commerce while attempting to keep agricultural taxes low.

One of the consequences of these differences was a growing technological gap between China and Europe. The Chinese reaction to European clockmaking techniques provides an example. In the early seventeenth century, the Jesuit Matteo Ricci introduced advanced European clocks driven by weights or springs. The emperor was fascinated and found the clocks more reliable than Chinese methods of keeping time. Over the next decades, European timepieces became a popular novelty at court, but the Chinese expressed little curiosity about the technology involved, provoking one European to remark that playthings like cuckoo clocks "will be received here with much greater interest than scientific instruments or *objets d'art*."[7]

Daily Life in Qing China

Despite the changes in the economy, daily life in China under the Ming and early Qing dynasties continued to follow traditional patterns. As in earlier periods, Chinese society was organized around the family. As in earlier times, the ideal family unit in Qing China was the joint family, in which as many as three or even four generations lived under the same roof. When sons married, they brought their wives to live with them in the family homestead. Prosperous families would add a separate section to the house to accommodate the new family unit. Unmarried daughters would also remain in the house. Aging parents and grandparents remained under the same roof until they died and were cared for by younger members of the household. This ideal did not always correspond to reality, however, since many families did not possess sufficient land to support a large household. One historian has estimated that only about 40 percent of Chinese families actually lived in joint families.

The family continued to be important in early Qing times for much the same reasons as in earlier times. As a labor-intensive society based primarily on the cultivation of rice, China needed large families to help with the harvest and to provide security for parents too old to work in the fields. Sons were particularly prized, not only because they had strong backs but also because they would raise their own families under the parental roof. With few opportunities for employment outside the family, sons had little choice but to remain with their parents and help on the land. Within the family, the oldest male was king, and his wishes theoretically had to be obeyed by all family members. These values were reiterated in Emperor Kangxi's Sacred Edict, which listed filial piety and loyalty to the family as its first two maxims (see the box on p. 448).

For many Chinese, the effects of these values were most apparent in the choice of a marriage partner. Marriages were normally arranged for the benefit of the family, often by a go-between, and the groom and bride were usually not consulted. Frequently, they did not meet until the marriage ceremony. Under such conditions, love was clearly a secondary consideration. In fact, it was often viewed as detrimental, since it inevitably distracted the attention of the husband and wife from their primary responsibility to the larger family unit.

Although this emphasis on filial piety might seem to represent a blatant disregard for individual rights, the obligations were not all on the side of the children. The father was expected to provide support for his wife and children and, like the ruler, was supposed to treat those in his care with respect and compassion. All too often, however, the male head of the family was able to exact his privileges without performing his responsibilities in return.

Beyond the joint family was the clan. Sometimes called a lineage, a clan was an extended kinship unit consisting of dozens or even hundreds of joint and nuclear families linked together by a clan council of elders and a variety of other common social and religious functions. The clan served a number of useful purposes. Some clans possessed lands that could be rented out to poorer families, or richer families within the clan might provide land for the poor. Since there was no general state-supported educational system, sons of poor families might be invited to study in a school established in the home of a more prosperous relative. If the young man succeeded in becoming an official, he would be expected to provide favors and prestige for the clan as a whole.

Like joint families, clans were not universal, and millions of Chinese had none. The clans apparently originated in the great landed families of the Tang period and managed to survive despite periodic efforts by the imperial court to weaken and destroy them. In many cases, clan solidarity was weakened by intralineage conflicts or differing levels of status and economic achievement. Nevertheless, in the early modern period, they were still an influential force at the local level and were particularly prevalent in the south.

THE ROLE OF WOMEN

In traditional China, the role of women had always been inferior to that of men. A sixteenth-century Spanish visitor to South China observed that Chinese women were "very secluded and virtuous, and it was a very rare thing for us to see a woman in the cities and large towns, unless it was an old crone." Women were more visible, he said, in rural areas, where they frequently could be seen working in the fields.[8]

The concept of female inferiority had deep roots in Chinese history. This view was embodied in the belief that only a male would carry on sacred family rituals and that men alone had the talent to govern others. Only males could aspire to a career in government or scholarship. Within the family system, the wife was clearly subordinated to the husband. Legally, she could not divorce her husband or inherit property. The husband, however, could divorce his wife if she did not produce male heirs, or he could take a second wife as well as a concubine for his pleasure. A widow suffered especially, because she had to either raise her children on a single income or fight off her former husband's greedy relatives, who would coerce her to remarry since, according to the law, they would then inherit all of her previous property and her original dowry.

Female children were less desirable because of their limited physical strength and because their parents would be required to pay a dowry to the parents of their future husband. Female children normally did not receive an education, and in times of scarcity when food was in short supply, daughters might even be put to death.

Though women were clearly inferior to men in theory, this was not always the case in practice. Capable women often compensated for their legal inferiority by playing a strong role within the family. Women were often in charge of educating the children and handled the family budget. Some privileged women also received training in the Confucian classics, although their schooling was generally for a shorter time and less rigorous than that of their male counterparts. A few produced significant works of art and poetry (see the box on p. 454).

All in all, however, life for women in traditional China was undoubtedly difficult. In Chinese novels, women were treated as scullery maids or love objects. They were frequently under the domination of both their husband and their mother-in-law, and in some cases the bullying was so brutal that suicide seemed to be the only way out.

Cultural Developments

During the late Ming and the early Qing dynasties, traditional culture in China reached new heights of achievement. With the rise of a wealthy urban class, the demand for art, porcelain, textiles, and literature was at a premium.

THE RISE OF THE CHINESE NOVEL

During the Ming dynasty, a new form of literature arose that eventually evolved into the modern Chinese novel. Although considered less respectable than poetry and

A CHINESE WOMAN ARTIST

During the early Qing era, some women from gentry families became skilled painters, studying in the privacy of their homes, as they were not expected to practice their art in public. Some were taught by other family members or by distant relatives, who were referred to as the "teachers of the inner chambers." Often a shared interest in art created a strong bond between a married couple, as witnessed here in this son's account of his mother's artistic venture.

VIEW FROM THE JADE TERRACE

As a child she learned to read by asking the boys of her clan to pass along what they learned in school. Her strict mother initially frowned on such unfeminine conduct and forbade her to take time away from her needlework to practice with the brush. Undeterred, Chen Shu one day made a copy of a famous painting hanging on the wall of her father's study. For this she was beaten, but a god intervened by appearing to her mother in a dream and saying: "I have given your daughter a brush. Someday she will be famous. How can you forbid it?" This tale served to underscore the idea that Chen Shu was destined for great achievement and perhaps was used to explain her devotion to pursuits regarded by some as unnecessary, even undesirable, for women.

Chen Shu married into the Qian family . . . becoming the second wife of Qian Lunguang. Qian did not distinguish himself as an official, but he did earn a modest reputation as a calligrapher and poet. Shared artistic interests were a part of the couple's relationship, and Qian occasionally added poetic inscriptions to Chen's paintings. . . .

The Qian family associated with some of the leading scholars of the area and took pleasure in entertaining guests, evidently in a manner beyond the family's means. To defray the costs of these gatherings, Chen Shu pawned her clothing and sold her jewelry and paintings. . . .

The shape of Chen Shu's artistic career was determined by her primary roles as wife and mother. From the 1680s through the first decade of the seventeenth century, much of her time was devoted to caring for her four children . . . , parents-in-law, and mother. . . . Chen Shu undoubtedly continued to paint during these busy years, but her last three decades seem to have been her most productive; her surviving dated paintings were executed between 1700 and 1735.

In 1721 Qian Chenqun, her eldest son, . . . received an appointment to the Hanlin Academy. . . . When her son asked the [imperial] court's permission to visit her in 1735, she nobly insisted that he stay at his post and . . . set out to join him in the capital. . . . She was then seventy-five years old. . . . Late in the spring of the following year she died in Beijing. . . .

In the course of his successful career under the Qianlong emperor, Qian Chenqun frequently presented paintings by his mother to the throne. The emperor received Chen Shu's works with pleasure and wrote on many of them with his characteristic lack of restraint.

---

nonfiction prose, these groundbreaking works (often written anonymously or under pseudonyms) were enormously popular, especially among well-to-do urban dwellers.

Written in a colloquial style, the new fiction was characterized by a realism that resulted in vivid portraits of Chinese society. Many of the stories sympathized with society's downtrodden—often helpless maidens—and dealt with such crucial issues as love, money, marriage, and power. Adding to the realism were sexually explicit passages that depicted the private side of Chinese life. Readers delighted in sensuous tales that, no matter how pornographic, always professed a moral lesson; the villains were punished and the virtuous rewarded. During the more puritanical Qing era, a number of the more erotic works were censored or banned and found refuge in Japan, where several have recently been rediscovered by scholars.

Gold Vase Plum, known in English translation as *The Golden Lotus*, presents a cutting exposé of the decadent aspects of late Ming society. Considered by many the first realistic social novel—preceding its European counterparts by two centuries—*The Golden Lotus* depicts the depraved life of a wealthy landlord who cruelly manipulates those around him for sex, money, and power. In a rare exception in Chinese fiction, the villain is not punished for his evil ways; justice is served instead by the misfortunes that befall his descendants.

The Dream of the Red Chamber is generally considered China's most distinguished popular novel. Published in 1791, some 150 years after *The Golden Lotus*, it tells of the tragic love between two young people caught in the financial and moral disintegration of a powerful Chinese clan. The hero and the heroine, both sensitive and spoiled, represent the inevitable decline of the Chia family and come to an equally inevitable tragic end, she in death and he in an unhappy marriage to another.

THE ART OF THE MING AND THE QING

During the Ming and the early Qing, China produced its last outpouring of traditional artistic brilliance. Although most of the creative work was modeled on past examples, the art of this period is impressive for its technical perfection and breathtaking quantity.

In architecture, the most outstanding example is the Imperial City in Beijing. Building on the remnants of the palace of the Yuan dynasty, the Ming emperor Yongle

Courtesy of William J. Duiker

THE TEMPLE OF HEAVEN.   This temple, located in the capital city of Beijing, is one of the most important historical structures in China. Built in 1420 at the order of the Ming emperor Yongle, it served as the location for the emperor's annual ceremony appealing to Heaven for a good harvest. Yongle's temple burned to the ground in 1889 but was immediately rebuilt according to the original design.

ordered renovations when he returned the capital to Beijing in 1421. Succeeding emperors continued to add to the palace, but the basic design has not changed since the Ming era. Surrounded by high walls, the immense compound is divided into a maze of private apartments and offices and an imposing ceremonial quadrangle with a series of stately halls for imperial audiences and banquets. The grandiose scale, richly carved marble, spacious gardens, and graceful upturned roofs also contribute to the splendor of the "Forbidden City."

The decorative arts flourished in this period, especially the intricately carved lacquerware and the boldly shaped and colored cloisonné, a type of enamelwork in which colored areas are separated by thin metal bands. Silk production reached its zenith, and the best-quality silks were highly prized in Europe, where chinoiserie, as Chinese art of all kinds was called, was in vogue. Perhaps the most famous of all the achievements of the Ming era was its blue-and-white porcelain, still prized by collectors throughout the world. One variety caused such a sensation in the Netherlands that the Dutch began to manufacture their own blue-and-white porcelain at a new factory set up in Delft.

During the Qing dynasty, artists produced great quantities of paintings, mostly for home consumption. The wealthy city of Yangzhou on the Grand Canal emerged as an active artistic center. Inside the Forbidden City in Beijing, court painters worked alongside Jesuit artists and experimented with Western techniques. European art, however, did not greatly influence Chinese painting at this time; some dismissed it as mere "craftsmanship." Scholarly painters and the literati totally rejected foreign techniques

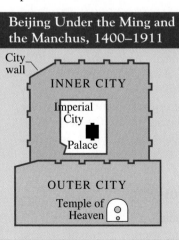

Beijing Under the Ming and the Manchus, 1400–1911

City wall

INNER CITY

Imperial City

Palace

OUTER CITY

Temple of Heaven

THE IMPERIAL CITY IN BEIJING.   During the fifteenth century, the Ming dynasty erected an immense imperial city on the remnants of the palace of Khubilai Khan in Beijing. Surrounded by $6\frac{1}{2}$ miles of walls, the enclosed compound is divided into a maze of private apartments and offices; it also includes an imposing ceremonial quadrangle with stately halls for imperial audiences and banquets. Because it was off-limits to commoners, the compound was known as the Forbidden City.

WORLD-CLASS CHINA WARE.   Ming porcelain was noted throughout the world for its delicate blue-and-white floral decorations. The blue coloring was produced with cobalt that had originally been brought from the Middle East along the Silk Road and was known in China as "Mohammedan blue." In the early seventeenth century, the first Ming ware arrived in the Netherlands, where it was called *kraak* because it had been loaded on two Portuguese carracks seized by the Dutch fleet. It took Dutch artisans over a century to learn how to produce a porcelain as fine as the examples brought from China.

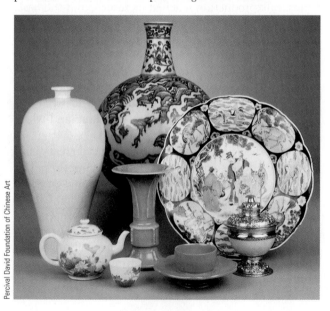

and became obsessed with traditional Chinese styles. As a result, Qing painting became progressively more repetitive and stale. Ironically, the Qing dynasty thus represents the apogee of traditional Chinese art and the beginning of its decline.

TOKUGAWA JAPAN

At the end of the fifteenth century, the traditional Japanese system was at a point of near anarchy. With the decline in the authority of the Ashikaga shogunate at Kyoto, clan rivalries had exploded into an era of warring states similar to the period of the same name in Zhou dynasty China. Even at the local level, power was frequently diffuse. The typical daimyo (great lord) domain had often become little more than a coalition of fief-holders held together by a loose allegiance to the manor lord. Prince Shotoku's dream of a united Japan appeared to be only a distant memory (see Chapter 11). In actuality, Japan was on the verge of an extended era of national unification and peace under the rule of its greatest shogunate—the Tokugawa.

The Three Great Unifiers

The process began in the mid-sixteenth century with the emergence of three very powerful political figures, Oda Nobunaga (1568–1582), Toyotomi Hideyoshi

(1582–1598), and Tokugawa Ieyasu (1598–1616). In 1568, Oda Nobunaga, the son of a samurai and a military commander under the Ashikaga shogunate, seized the imperial capital of Kyoto and placed the reigning shogun under his domination. During the next few years, the brutal and ambitious Nobunaga attempted to consolidate his rule throughout the central plains by defeating his rivals and suppressing the power of the Buddhist estates, but he was killed by one of his generals in 1582 before the process was complete. He was succeeded by Toyotomi Hideyoshi, a farmer's son who had worked his way up through the ranks to become a military commander. Originally lacking a family name of his own, he eventually adopted the name Toyotomi ("abundant provider") to embellish his reputation for improving the material standards of his domain. Hideyoshi located his capital at Osaka, where he built a castle to accommodate his headquarters, and gradually extended his power outward to the southern islands of Shikoku and Kyushu (see Map 16.3). By 1590, he had persuaded most of the daimyo on the Japanese islands to accept his authority and created a national currency. Then he invaded Korea in an abortive effort to export his rule to the Asian mainland.

Despite their efforts, however, neither Nobunaga nor Hideyoshi was able to eliminate the power of the local daimyo. Both were compelled to form alliances with some daimyo in order to destroy other more powerful rivals.

At the conclusion of his conquests in 1590, Toyotomi Hideyoshi could claim to be the supreme proprietor of all registered lands in areas under his authority. But he then reassigned those lands as fiefs to the local daimyo, who declared their allegiance to him. The daimyo in turn began to pacify the countryside, carrying out extensive "sword hunts" to disarm the population and attracting samurai to their service. The Japanese tradition of decentralized rule had not been overcome.

After Hideyoshi's death in 1598, Tokugawa Ieyasu, the powerful daimyo of Edo (modern Tokyo), moved to fill the vacuum. Neither Hideyoshi nor Oda Nobunaga had claimed the title of shogun, but Ieyasu named himself shogun in 1603, initiating the most powerful and long-lasting of all Japanese shogunates. The Tokugawa rulers completed the restoration of central authority begun by Nobunaga and Hideyoshi and remained in power until 1868, when a war dismantled the entire system. As a contemporary phrased it, "Oda pounds the national rice cake, Hideyoshi kneads it, and in the end Ieyasu sits down and eats it."[9]

Opening to the West

The unification of Japan took place almost simultaneously with the coming of the Europeans. Portuguese traders sailing in a Chinese junk that may have been

THE SIEGE OF OSAKA CASTLE.   After the death of Toyotomi Hideyoshi in 1598, titular authority in Japan passed on to his infant son, Hideyori, whose supporters located their headquarters at Osaka Castle in central Japan. In 1615, the powerful warlord Tokugawa Ieyasu seized the castle, as shown here, and scattered Hideyori's supporters. The family's control over Japan lasted nearly 250 years. Note the presence of firearms, introduced by the Europeans half a century earlier.

A PRESENT FOR LORD TOKITAKA

The Portuguese introduced firearms to Japan in the sixteenth century, and Japanese warriors were quick to explore the possibilities of these new weapons. In this passage, the daimyo of a small island off the southern tip of Japan receives an explanation of how to use the new weapons and is fascinated by the results. Note how Lord Tokitaka attempts to understand the procedures in terms of traditional Daoist beliefs.

THE JAPANESE DISCOVER FIREARMS

"There are two leaders among the traders, the one called Murashusa, and the other Christian Mota. In their hands they carried something two or three feet long, straight on the outside with a passage inside, and made of a heavy substance. The inner passage runs through it although it is closed at the end. At its side there is an aperture which is the passageway for fire. Its shape defies comparison with anything I know. To use it, fill it with powder and small lead pellets. Set up a small . . . target on a bank. Grip the object in your hand, compose your body, and closing one eye, apply fire to the aperture. Then the pellet hits the target squarely. The explosion is like lightning and the report like thunder. Bystanders must cover their ears. . . . This thing with one blow can smash a mountain of silver and a wall of iron. If one sought to do mischief in another man's domain and he was touched by it, he would lose his life instantly. Needless to say this is also true for the deer and stag that ravage the plants in the fields."

Lord Tokitaka saw it and thought it was the wonder of wonders. He did not know its name at first nor the details of its use. Then someone called it "iron-arms," although it was not known whether the Chinese called it so, or whether it was so called only on our island. Thus, one day, Tokitaka spoke to the two alien leaders through an interpreter: "Inca-pable though I am, I should like to learn about it." Whereupon, the chiefs answered, also through an interpreter: "If you wish to learn about it, we shall teach you its mysteries." Tokitaka then asked, "What is its secret?" The chief replied: "The secret is to put your mind aright and close one eye." Tokitaka said: "The ancient sages have often taught how to set one's mind aright, and I have learned something of it. If the mind is not set aright, there will be no logic for what we say or do. Thus, I understand what you say about setting our minds aright. However, will it not impair our vision for objects at a distance if we close an eye? Why should we close an eye?" To which the chiefs replied: "That is because concentration is important in everything. When one concentrates, a broad vision is not necessary. To close an eye is not to dim one's eyesight but rather to project one's concentration farther. You should know this." Delighted, Tokitaka said: "That corresponds to what Lao Tzu has said, 'Good sight means seeing what is very small.' "

That year the festival day of the Ninth Month fell on the day of the Metal and the Boar. Thus, one fine morning the weapon was filled with powder and lead pellets, a target was set up more than a hundred paces away, and fire was applied to the weapon. At first the people were astonished; then they became frightened. But in the end they all said in unison: "We should like to learn!" Disregarding the high price of the arms, Tokitaka purchased from the aliens two pieces of the firearms for his family treasure. As for the art of grinding, sifting, and mixing of the powder, Tokitaka let his retainer, Shinokawa Shoshiro, learn it. Tokitaka occupied himself, morning and night, and without rest in handling the arms. As a result, he was able to convert the misses of his early experiments into hits—a hundred hits in a hundred attempts.

---

blown off course by a typhoon had landed on the islands in 1543. Within a few years, Portuguese ships were stopping at Japanese ports on a regular basis to take part in the regional trade between Japan, China, and Southeast Asia. The first Jesuit missionary, Francis Xavier, arrived in 1549.

Initially, the visitors were welcomed. The curious Japanese (the Japanese were "very desirous of knowledge," said Francis Xavier) were fascinated by tobacco, clocks, spectacles, and other European goods, and local daimyo were interested in purchasing all types of European weapons and armaments (see the box above). Oda Nobunaga and Toyotomi Hideyoshi found the new firearms helpful in defeating their enemies and unifying the islands. The effect on Japanese military architecture was particularly striking as local lords began to erect castles on the European model. Many of these castles, such as Hideyoshi's castle at Osaka, still exist today.

The missionaries also had some success. Though confused by misleading translations of sacred concepts in both cultures (Francis Xavier was notoriously poor at learning foreign languages), they converted a number of local daimyo, some of whom may have been motivated in part by the desire for commercial profits. By the end of the sixteenth century, thousands of Japanese in the southernmost islands of Kyushu and Shikoku had become Christians. One converted daimyo ceded the superb natural harbor of the modern city of Nagasaki to the Society of Jesus, which proceeded to use the new settlement for both missionary and trading purposes. But papal claims to the loyalty of all Japanese Christians and the European habit of intervening in local politics soon began to arouse suspicion in official circles. Missionaries added to the problem by deliberately destroying local idols and shrines and turning some temples into Christian schools or churches.

TOYOTOMI HIDEYOSHI EXPELS THE MISSIONARIES

When Christian missionaries in sixteenth-century Japan began to interfere in local politics and criticize traditional religious practices, Toyotomi Hideyoshi issued an edict calling for their expulsion. In this letter to the Portuguese viceroy in Asia, Hideyoshi explains his decision. Note his conviction that Buddhists, Confucianists, and followers of Shinto all believe in the same God and his criticism of Christianity for rejecting all other faiths.

TOYOTOMI HIDEYOSHI, LETTER TO THE VICEROY OF THE INDIES

Ours is the land of the Gods, and God is mind. Everything in nature comes into existence because of mind. Without God there can be no spirituality. Without God there can be no way. God rules in times of prosperity as in times of decline. God is positive and negative and unfathomable. Thus, God is the root and source of all existence. This God is spoken of by Buddhism in India, Confucianism in China, and Shinto in Japan. To know Shinto is to know Buddhism as well as Confucianism.

As long as man lives in this world, Humanity will be a basic principle. Were it not for Humanity and Righteousness, the sovereign would not be a sovereign, nor a minis-ter of a state a minister. It is through the practice of Humanity and Righteousness that the foundations of our relationships between sovereign and minister, parent and child, and husband and wife are established. If you are interested in the profound philosophy of God and Buddha, request an explanation and it will be given to you. In your land one doctrine is taught to the exclusion of others, and you are not yet informed of the [Confucian] philosophy of Humanity and Righteousness. Thus there is no respect for God and Buddha and no distinction between sovereign and ministers. Through heresies you intend to destroy the righteous law. Hereafter, do not expound, in ignorance of right and wrong, unreasonable and wanton doctrines. A few years ago the so-called Fathers came to my country seeking to bewitch our men and women, both of the laity and clergy. At that time punishment was administered to them, and it will be repeated if they should return to our domain to propagate their faith. It will not matter what sect or denomination they represent—they shall be destroyed. It will then be too late to repent. If you entertain any desire of establishing amity with this land, the seas have been rid of the pirate menace, and merchants are permitted to come and go. Remember this.

Inevitably, the local authorities reacted. In 1587, Toyotomi Hideyoshi issued an edict prohibiting further Christian activities within his domains. Japan, he declared, was "the land of the Gods," and the destruction of shrines by the foreigners was "something unheard of in previous ages." To "corrupt and stir up the lower classes" to commit such sacrileges, he declared, was "outrageous."[10] The parties responsible (the Jesuits) were ordered to leave the country within twenty days. Hideyoshi was careful to distinguish missionary from trading activities, however, and merchants were permitted to continue their operations (see the box above).

The Jesuits protested the expulsion, and eventually Hideyoshi relented, permitting them to continue proselytizing so long as they were discreet. But he refused to repeal the edicts, and when the aggressive activities of newly arrived Spanish Franciscans aroused his ire, he ordered the execution of nine missionaries and a number of their Japanese converts. When the missionaries continued to interfere in local politics (some even tried to incite the daimyo in the southern islands against the shogunate government in Edo), Tokugawa Ieyasu completed the process by ordering the eviction of all missionaries in 1612. The persecution of Japanese Christians intensified, leading to an abortive revolt by Christian peasants on the island of Kyushu in 1637, which was bloodily suppressed.

At first, Japanese authorities hoped to maintain commercial relations with European countries even while suppressing the Western religion, but eventually they decided to prohibit foreign trade altogether and closed the two major foreign factories on the island of Hirado and at Nagasaki. The sole remaining opening to the West was at Deshima Island in Nagasaki harbor, where a small Dutch community was permitted to engage in limited trade with Japan (the Dutch, unlike the Portuguese and the Spanish, had not allowed missionary activities to interfere with their commercial interests). Dutch ships were permitted to dock at Nagasaki harbor only once a year and, after close inspection, were allowed to remain for two or three months. Conditions on the island of Deshima itself were quite confining: the Dutch physician Engelbert Kaempfer complained that the Dutch lived in "almost

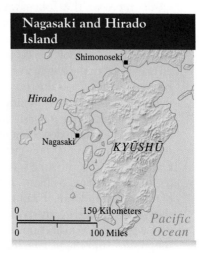

Nagasaki and Hirado Island

Shimonoseki

Hirado

Nagasaki

KYŪSHŪ

0   150 Kilometers
0   100 Miles

Pacific Ocean

Collection Musée Guimet, Paris. Photo © Michael Holford, London

THE PORTUGUESE ARRIVE AT NAGASAKI. Portuguese traders landed in Japan by accident in 1543. In a few years, they arrived regularly, taking part in a regional trade network between Japan, China, and Southeast Asia. In these panels done in black lacquer and gold leaf, we see a late-sixteenth-century Japanese interpretation of the first Portuguese landing at Nagasaki.

perpetual imprisonment."[11] Nor were the Japanese free to engage in foreign trade. A small amount of commerce took place with China, but Japanese subjects of the shogunate were forbidden to leave the country on penalty of death.

The Tokugawa "Great Peace"

Once in power, the Tokugawa attempted to strengthen the system that had governed Japan for over three hundred years. They followed precedent in ruling through the *bakufu*, composed now of a coalition of daimyo, and a council of elders. But the system was more centralized than it had been previously. Now the shogunate government played a dual role. It set national policy on behalf of the emperor in Kyoto while simultaneously governing the shogun's own domain, which included about one-quarter of the national territory as well as the three great cities of Edo, Kyoto, and Osaka. As before, the state was divided into separate territories, called domains (*han*), which were ruled by a total of about 250 individual daimyo lords. The daimyo were themselves divided into two types: the *fudai* (inside) daimyo, who were mostly small daimyo directly subordinate to the shogunate, and the *tozama* (outside) daimyo, who were larger and more independent lords usually more distant from the center of shogunate power in Edo.

In theory, the daimyo were essentially autonomous, since they were able to support themselves from taxes on their lands (the shogunate received its own revenues from its extensive landholdings). In actuality, the shogunate

was able to guarantee daimyo loyalties by compelling daimyo lords to maintain two residences, one in their own domains and the other at Edo, and to leave their families in Edo as hostages for the daimyo's good behavior. Keeping up two residences also placed the Japanese nobility in a difficult economic position. Some were able to defray the high costs by concentrating on cash crops such as sugar, fish, and forestry products, but most were rice producers, and their revenues remained roughly the same throughout the period. The daimyo were also able to protect their economic interests by depriving their samurai retainers of their proprietary rights over the land and transforming them into salaried officials. The fief thus became a stipend, and the personal relationship between the daimyo and his retainers gradually gave way to a bureaucratic authority.

The Tokugawa also tinkered with the social system by limiting the size of the samurai class and reclassifying samurai who supported themselves by tilling the land as commoners. In fact, with the long period of peace brought about by Tokugawa rule, the samurai gradually ceased to be a warrior class and were required to live in the castle towns. As a gesture to their glorious past, samurai were still permitted to wear their two swords, and a rigid separation was maintained between persons of samurai status and the nonaristocratic segment of the population. Jesuit missionary Francis Xavier observed that "on no account would a poverty-stricken gentleman marry with someone outside the gentry, even if he were given great sums to do so."[12]

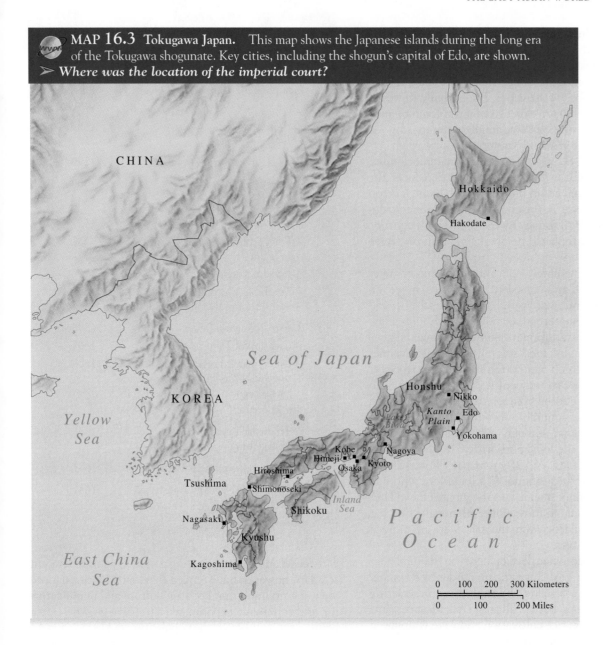

MAP 16.3 Tokugawa Japan. This map shows the Japanese islands during the long era of the Tokugawa shogunate. Key cities, including the shogun's capital of Edo, are shown. ➤ *Where was the location of the imperial court?*

SEEDS OF CAPITALISM

The long period of peace under the Tokugawa shogunate made possible a dramatic rise in commerce and manufacturing, especially in the growing cities of Edo, Kyoto, and Osaka. By the mid-eighteenth century, Edo, with a population of more than one million, was one of the largest cities in the world. The growth of trade and industry was stimulated by a rising standard of living—driven in part by technological advances in agriculture and an expansion of arable land—and the voracious appetites of the aristocrats for new products. The daimyo's need for income also contributed as many of them began to promote the sale of local goods from their domains, such as textiles, forestry products, sugar, and sake (fermented rice wine).

Most of this commercial expansion took place in the major cities and the castle towns, where the merchants and artisans lived along with the samurai, who were clustered in neighborhoods surrounding the daimyo's castle. Banking flourished and paper money became the normal medium of exchange in commercial transactions. Merchants formed guilds not only to control market conditions but also to facilitate government control and the collection of taxes. Under the benign if somewhat contemptuous supervision of Japan's noble rulers, a Japanese merchant class gradually began to emerge from the shadows to play a significant role in the life of the Japanese nation. Some historians view the Tokugawa era as the first stage in the rise of an indigenous form of capitalism.

Eventually, the increased pace of industrial activity spread beyond the cities into rural areas. As in Great Britain, cotton was a major factor. Cotton had been introduced to China during the Song dynasty and had spread to Korea and Japan shortly thereafter. Traditionally, however, cotton cloth had been too expensive for the common people, who instead wore clothing made of hemp. Imports increased during the sixteenth century, however, when cotton cloth began to be used for uniforms, matchlock fuses, and sails. Eventually, technological advances reduced the cost, and specialized communities for producing cotton cloth began to appear in the countryside and were gradually transformed into towns. By the eighteenth century, cotton had firmly replaced hemp as the cloth of choice for most Japanese.

Not everyone benefited from the economic changes of the seventeenth and eighteenth centuries, however, notably the samurai, who were barred by tradition and prejudice from commercial activities. Although some profited from their transformation into a managerial class on the daimyo domains, most still relied on their revenues from rice lands, which were often insufficient to cover their rising expenses; consequently, they fell heavily into debt. Others were released from servitude to their lord and became "masterless samurai." Occasionally, these unemployed warriors (known as *ronin*, or "wave men") revolted or plotted against the local authorities. In one episode, made famous in song and story as the "Forty-Seven Ronin," the masterless samurai of a local lord who had been forced to commit suicide by a shogunate official later assassinated the official in revenge. Although their act received wide popular acclaim, the *ronin* were later forced to take their own lives.

The effects of economic developments on the rural population during the Tokugawa era are harder to estimate. Some farm families benefited by exploiting the growing demand for cash crops. But not all prospered. Most peasants continued to rely on rice cultivation and were whipsawed between declining profits and rising costs and taxes (as daimyo expenses increased, land taxes often took up to 50 percent of the annual harvest). Many were forced to become tenants or to work as wage laborers on the farms of wealthy neighbors or in village industries. When rural conditions in some areas became desperate, peasant revolts erupted. According to one estimate, nearly seven thousand disturbances took place during the Tokugawa era. In general, though, the rural unrest was probably motivated less by a decline in the standard of living than by local factors and a new sense of peasant assertiveness. Peasant disturbances became a more or less routine means of protesting against rising taxes and official corruption or of demanding "benevolence" from the manor lord in times of climatic disaster.

Some Japanese historians, influenced by a Marxist view of history, have interpreted such evidence as an indication that the Tokugawa economic system was highly exploitative,

with feudal aristocrats oppressing powerless peasants. Recent scholars, however, have tended to adopt a more balanced view, maintaining that both agriculture and manufacturing and commerce experienced extensive growth. Some point out that although the population doubled in the seventeenth century, a relatively low rate for the time period, so did the amount of cultivable land, while agricultural technology made significant advances.

The relatively low rate of population growth probably meant that Japanese peasants were spared the kind of land hunger that many of their counterparts in China faced. Recent evidence indicates that the primary reasons for the relatively low rate of population growth were late marriage, abortion, and infanticide. As Honda Toshiaki, a late-eighteenth-century demographer, described:

Aware that if they have many children they will not have any property to leave them, [husbands and wives] confer and decide that rather than rear children who in later years will have great difficulty in making a decent living, it is better to take precautions before they are born and not add another mouth to feed. If they do have a child, they secretly destroy it, calling the process by the euphemism of "thinning out."[13]

KEEPING TO THE STRAIGHT AND NARROW IN TOKUGAWA JAPAN

Like the Qing dynasty in China, the Tokugawa shoguns attempted to keep their subjects in line with decrees that carefully prescribed all kinds of behavior. As this decree, which was circulated in all Japanese villages, shows, the bakufu sought to be the moral instructor as well as the guardian and protector of the Japanese people. Compare and contrast this decree with Emperor Kangxi's Sacred Edict in the box earlier in this chapter.

MAXIMS FOR PEASANT BEHAVIOR

1. Young people are forbidden to congregate in great numbers.
2. Entertainments unsuited to peasants, such as playing the samisen or reciting ballad dramas, are forbidden.
3. Staging sumo matches is forbidden for the next five years.
4. The edict on frugality issued by the *han* at the end of last year must be observed.
5. Social relations in the village must be conducted harmoniously.
6. If a person has to leave the village for business or pleasure, that person must return by ten at night.
7. Father and son are forbidden to stay overnight at another person's house. An exception is to be made if it is to nurse a sick person.
8. Corvée [obligatory labor] assigned by the *han* must be performed faithfully.
9. Children who practice filial piety must be rewarded.
10. One must never get drunk and cause trouble for others.
11. Peasants who farm especially diligently must be rewarded.
12. Peasants who neglect farm work and cultivate their paddies and upland fields in a slovenly and careless fashion must be punished.
13. The boundary lines of paddy and upland fields must not be changed arbitrarily.
14. Recognition must be accorded to peasants who contribute greatly to village political affairs.
15. Fights and quarrels are forbidden in the village.
16. The deteriorating customs and morals of the village must be rectified.
17. Peasants who are suffering from poverty must be identified and helped.
18. This village has a proud history compared to other villages, but in recent years bad times have come upon us. Everyone must rise at six in the morning, cut grass, and work hard to revitalize the village.
19. The punishments to be meted out to violators of the village code and gifts to be awarded the deserving are to be decided during the last assembly meeting of the year.

Life in the Village

The changes that took place during the Tokugawa era had a major impact on the lives of ordinary Japanese. In some respects, the result was an increase in the power of the central government at the village level. The shogunate increasingly relied on Confucian maxims advocating obedience and hierarchy to enhance its authority with the general population. Decrees from the *bakufu* instructed the peasants on all aspects of their lives, including their eating habits and their behavior (see the box above). At the same time, the increased power of the government led to more autonomy from the local daimyo for the peasants. Villages now had more control over their local affairs and were responsible to the central government as much as to the nearby manor lord, although land taxes were still paid to the daimyo.

At the same time, the Tokugawa era saw the emergence of the nuclear family (*ie*) as the basic unit in Japanese society. In previous times, Japanese peasants had few legal rights. Most were too poor to keep their conjugal family unit intact or to pass property on to their children. Many lived at the manorial residence or worked as servants in the households of more affluent villagers. Now, with farm income on the rise, the nuclear family took on the same form as in China, although without the joint family concept. The Japanese system of inheritance was based on primogeniture. Family property was passed on to the eldest son, although younger sons often received land from their parents to set up their own families after marriage.

Another result of the changes under the Tokugawa was that women were somewhat more restricted than they had been previously. The rights of females were especially restricted in the samurai class, where Confucian values were highly influential. Male heads of households had broad authority over property, marriage, and divorce; wives were expected to obey their husbands on pain of death. Males often took concubines or homosexual partners, while females were expected to remain chaste. The male offspring of samurai parents studied the Confucian classics in schools established by the daimyo, while females were reared at home, where only the fortunate might receive a rudimentary training in reading and writing Chinese characters. Some women, however, became accomplished poets and painters since, in aristocratic circles, female literacy was prized for enhancing the refinement, social graces, and moral virtue of the home. Under the Tokugawa, it was the obligation of the wife in elite families to reflect her husband's rank and status through a strict code of comportment and dress.

Women were similarly at a disadvantage among the common people. Marriages were arranged, and as in China, the new wife moved in with the family of her husband. A wife who did not meet the expectations of her spouse or his family was likely to be divorced. Still, gender relations were more egalitarian than among the nobility. Women were generally valued as childbearers and homemakers, and both sexes worked in the fields. Coeducational schools were established in villages and market towns, and about one-quarter of the students were female. Poor families, however, often put infant daughters to death or sold them into prostitution and the "floating world" of entertainment (see "The Literature of the New Middle Class" later in this chapter). During the late Tokugawa era, peasant women became more outspoken and active in social protests and in some cases played a major role in provoking demonstrations against government exactions or exploitative acts by landlords or merchants.

Such attitudes toward women operated within the context of the increasingly rigid stratification of Japanese society. Deeply conservative in their social policies, the Tokugawa rulers established strict legal distinctions between the four main classes in Japan (warriors, artisans, peasants, and merchants). Intermarriage between classes was forbidden in theory, although sometimes the prohibitions were ignored in practice. Below these classes were Japan's outcasts, the *eta*. Formerly, they were permitted to escape their status, at least in theory. The Tokugawa made their status hereditary and enacted severe discriminatory laws against them, regulating their place of residence, their dress, and even their hairstyles.

Tokugawa Culture

Under the Tokugawa, the tensions between the old society and the emerging new one were starkly reflected in the arena of culture. On the one hand, the classical culture, influenced by Confucian themes, Buddhist quietism, and the samurai warrior tradition, continued to flourish under the patronage of the shogunate. On the other, a vital new set of cultural values began to appear, especially in the cities. This innovative era witnessed the rise of popular literature written by and for the townspeople. With the development of woodblock printing in the early seventeenth century, literature became available to the common people, literacy levels rose, and lending libraries increased the accessibility of the printed word. In contrast to the previous mood of doom and gloom, the new prose was cheerful and even frivolous, its primary aim being to divert and amuse.

THE LITERATURE OF THE NEW MIDDLE CLASS

The best examples of this new urban fiction are the works of Saikaku (1642–1693), considered one of Japan's finest novelists. Saikaku's greatest novel, *Five Women Who Loved Love*, relates the amorous exploits of five women of the merchant class. Based partly on real-life experiences, it broke from the Confucian ethic of wifely fidelity to her husband and portrayed women who were willing to die for love—and all but one eventually did. Despite the tragic circumstances, the tone of the novel is upbeat and sometimes comic, and the author's wry comments prevent the reader from becoming emotionally involved with the heroines' misfortunes. In addition to heterosexual novels for the merchant class, Saikaku wrote of homosexual liaisons among the samurai.

In the theater, the rise of *Kabuki* threatened the long dominance of the *No* play, replacing the somewhat restrained and elegant thematic and stylistic approach of the classical drama with a new emphasis on violence, music, and dramatic gestures. Significantly, the new drama emerged not from the rarefied world of the court but from the new world of entertainment and amusement. Its very commercial success, however, led to difficulties with the government, which periodically attempted to restrict or even suppress it. Early *Kabuki* was often performed by prostitutes, and shogunate officials, fearing that such activities could have a corrupting effect on the nation's morals, prohibited women from appearing on the stage; at the same time, they attempted to create a new professional class of male actors to impersonate female characters on stage. The decree had a mixed effect, however, because it encouraged homosexual activities, which had been popular among the samurai and in Buddhist monasteries since medieval times. Yet the use of male actors also promoted a greater emphasis on physical activities such as acrobatics and swordplay and furthered the evolution of *Kabuki* into a mature dramatic art.

In contrast to the popular literature of the Tokugawa period, poetry persevered in its more serious tradition. Although linked verse, so popular in the fourteenth and fifteenth centuries, found a more lighthearted expression in the sixteenth century, the most exquisite poetry was produced in the seventeenth century by the greatest of all Japanese poets, Basho (1644–1694). He was concerned with the search for the meaning of existence and the poetic expression of his experience. Basho's genius lies in his sudden juxtaposition of a general or eternal condition with an immediate perception, an electrical spark that instantly reveals a moment of truth. With his love of Daoism and Zen Buddhism, Basho found answers to his quest for the meaning of life in nature, and his poems are grounded in seasonal imagery. The following are among his most famous poems:

The ancient pond
A frog leaps in
The sound of the water.

On the withered branch
A crow has alighted—
The end of autumn.

His last poem, dictated to a disciple only three days prior to his death, succinctly expressed his frustration with the unfinished business of life:

On a journey, ailing—
my dreams roam about
on a withered moor.

Like all great artists, Basho made his poems seem effortless and simple. He speaks directly to everyone, everywhere.

TOKUGAWA ART

Art also reflected the dynamism and changes in Japanese culture under the Tokugawa regime. The shogun's order that all daimyo and their families live every other year in Edo set off a burst of building as provincial rulers competed to erect the most magnificent mansion. Furthermore, the shoguns themselves constructed splendid castles adorned with sumptuous, almost ostentatious decor and furnishings. And the prosperity of the newly rising merchant class added fuel to the fire. Japanese paintings, architecture, textiles, and ceramics all flourished during this affluent era.

Court painters filled magnificent multipaneled screens with gold foil, which was also used to cover walls and even ceilings. This lavish use of gold foil mirrored the grandeur of the new Japanese rulers but also served a practical purpose: it reflected light in the dark castle rooms, where windows were kept small for defensive purposes. In contrast to the almost gaudy splendors of court painting, however, some Japanese artists of the late sixteenth century returned to the tradition of black ink wash. No longer copying the Chinese, these masterpieces expressed Japanese themes and techniques. In *Pine Forest* by Tohaku, a pair of six-panel screens depicting pine trees, 85 percent of the paper is left blank, suggesting mist and the quiet of an autumn dawn.

Although Japan was isolated from the Western world during much of the Tokugawa era, Japanese art was enriched by ideas from other cultures. Japanese pottery makers borrowed both techniques and designs from Korea to produce handsome ceramics. The passion for "Dutch learning" inspired Japanese to study Western medicine, astronomy, and languages and also led to experimentation with oil painting and Western ideas of perspective and the interplay of light and dark. Some painters depicted the "southern barbarians," with their strange ships and costumes, large noses, and plumed hats. Europeans desired Japanese lacquerware and metalwork, inlaid with ivory and mother-of-pearl, and especially the ceramics, which were now as highly prized as those of the Chinese.

Courtesy of William J. Duiker

⟫ **A JAPANESE CASTLE.**   In imitation of European castle architecture, the Japanese perfected a new type of fortress-palace in the early seventeenth century. Strategically placed high on a hilltop, constructed of heavy stone with tiny windows and fortified by numerous watchtowers and massive walls, these strongholds were impregnable to arrows and catapults. They served as a residence for the local daimyo, while the castle compound also housed his army and contained the seat of the local government. Himeji Castle, shown here, is one of the most beautiful in Japan.

Perhaps the most famous of all Japanese art of the Tokugawa era is the woodblock print. Genre painting, or representations of daily life, began in the sixteenth century and found its new mass-produced form in the eighteenth-century woodblock print. The now literate mercantile class was eager for illustrated texts of the amusing and bawdy tales that had circulated in oral tradition. At first, these prints were done in black and white, but later they included vibrant colors. The self-confidence of the age is dramatically captured in these prints, which represent a collective self-portrait of the late Tokugawa urban classes. Some prints depict entire city blocks filled with people, trades, and festivals, while others show the interiors of houses; thus they provide us with excellent visual documentation of the times. Others portray the "floating world" of the entertainment quarter, with scenes of carefree revelers enjoying the pleasures of life.

One of the most renowned of the numerous block-print artists was Utamaro (1754–1806), who painted erotic and sardonic women in everyday poses, such as walking down the street, cooking, or drying their bodies after a bath.

Hokusai (1760–1849) was famous for *Thirty-Six Views of Mount Fuji*, a new and bold interpretation of the Japanese landscape. Finally, Ando Hiroshige (1797–1858) developed the genre of the travelogue print in his *Fifty-Three Stations of the Tokaido Road*, which presented ordinary scenes of daily life, both in the country and in the cities, all enveloped in a lyrical, quiet mood.

Why did a new popular culture begin to appear in Tokugawa Japan while traditional values continued to prevail in neighboring China? One factor was the rapid growth of the cities as the main point of convergence for all the dynamic forces taking place in Japanese society. But other factors may have been at work as well. Despite the patent efforts of the Tokugawa rulers to promote traditional Confucian values, Confucian doctrine had historically occupied a relatively weak position in Japanese society. In China, the scholar-gentry class served as the traditional defenders and propagators of traditional orthodoxy, but the samurai, who were steeped in warrior values and had little exposure to Confucian learning, did not play a similar role in Japan. Tokugawa policies also contributed. Whereas the scholar-gentry class in Qing China continued to reside in the villages, serving as members of the local council or as instructors in local schools, the samurai class in Japan was deliberately isolated from the remainder of the population by government fiat and class privilege. The result was an ideological and cultural vacuum that would eventually be filled by the growing population of merchants and artisans in the major cities.

KOREA: THE HERMIT KINGDOM

While Japan was gradually moving away from its agrarian origins, the Yi dynasty in Korea was attempting to pattern its own society on the Chinese model. The dynasty had been founded by the military commander Yi Song Gye in the late fourteenth century and immediately set out to establish close political and cultural relations with the Ming dynasty. From their new capital at Seoul, located on the Han River in the center of the peninsula, the Yi rulers accepted a tributary relationship with their powerful neighbor and engaged in the wholesale adoption of Chinese institutions and values. As in China, the civil service examinations tested candidates on their knowledge of the Confucian classics, and success was viewed as an essential step toward upward mobility.

There were differences, however. As in Japan, the dynasty continued to restrict entry into the bureaucracy to members of the aristocratic class, known in Korea as the *yangban* (or "two groups," the civilian and military). At the same time, the peasantry remained in serflike conditions, working on government estates or on the manor holdings of the landed elite. A class of slaves (*chonmin*) labored on government plantations or served in certain

THE FLOATING WORLD OF EDO. In eighteenth-century Japan, the self-confidence of the newly affluent bourgeoisie expressed itself in the woodblock print. Many prints portrayed the "floating world," as the pleasure district in Edo was called. Seen here are courtesans, storytellers, jesters, and various other entertainers. Like their counterparts in Europe, city-dwellers in Japan were beginning to create a new popular culture distinct from the elite culture of the nobility as reflected by the growing popularity of *Kabuki* drama.

occupations, such as butchers and entertainers, considered beneath the dignity of other groups in the population.

Eventually, Korean society began to show signs of independence from Chinese orthodoxy. In the fifteenth century, a phonetic alphabet for writing the Korean spoken language (*hangul*) was devised. Although it was initially held in contempt by the elites and used primarily as a teaching device, eventually it became the medium for private correspondence and the publishing of fiction for a popular audience. At the same time, changes were taking place in the economy, where rising agricultural production contributed to a population increase and the appearance of a small urban industrial and commercial sector, and in society, where the long domination of the *yangban* class began to weaken. As their numbers increased and their power and influence declined, some *yangban* became merchants or even moved into the ranks of the peasantry, further blurring the distinction between the aristocratic class and the common people.

In general, Korean rulers tried to keep the country isolated from the outside world, but they were not always successful. The Japanese invasion under Toyotomi Hideyoshi in the late sixteenth century had a disastrous impact on Korean society. A Manchu force invaded northern Korea in the 1630s and eventually compelled the Yi dynasty to grant allegiance to the new imperial government in Beijing. Korea was relatively untouched by the arrival of European merchants and missionaries, although information about Christianity was brought to the peninsula by Koreans returning from tribute missions to China, and a small

 ONE OF THE FIFTY-THREE STATIONS ALONG THE TOKAIDO ROAD. This block print by the famous Japanese artist Hiroshige shows the movement of goods along the main trunk road stretching from Kyoto to Edo in mid-nineteenth-century Japan. With gentle humor, Hiroshige portrayed in a series of color paintings the customs of travelers passing through various post stations along the east coast road. These romantic and somewhat fanciful scenes, very popular at the time, evoke an idyllic past, filling today's viewer with nostalgia for the old Japan.

Catholic community was established there in the late eighteenth century.

CONCLUSION

When Christopher Columbus sailed from southern Spain in his three ships in August 1492, he was seeking a route to China and Japan. He did not find it, but others soon did. In 1514, Portuguese ships arrived on the coast of southern China. Thirty years later, a small contingent of Portuguese merchants became the first Europeans to set foot on the islands of Japan.

At first the new arrivals were welcomed, if only as curiosities. Eventually, several European nations estab-

SEOUL PALACE PAGODA. When the Yi dynasty came into power in the late fourteenth century, it established its capital at Seoul on the Han River. There it constructed a new palace. Korean public architecture was highly influenced by the Chinese classical model, as the multitiered pagoda on the palace grounds attests.

lished trade relations with China and Japan, and Christian missionaries of various religious orders were active in both countries and in Korea as well. But their success was short-lived. Europeans eventually began to be perceived as detrimental to law and order, and during the seventeenth century, the majority of the foreign merchants and missionaries were evicted from all three countries. From that time until the middle of the nineteenth century, China, Japan, and Korea were relatively little affected by events taking place beyond their borders.

That fact deluded many observers into the assumption that the societies of East Asia were essentially stagnant, characterized by agrarian institutions and values reminiscent of those of the feudal era in Europe. As we have seen, however, that picture is misleading, for all three countries were changing and by the early nineteenth century were quite different from what they had been three centuries earlier.

Ironically, these changes were especially marked in Tokugawa Japan, an allegedly "closed country," where traditional classes and institutions were under increasing strain, not only from the emergence of a new merchant class, but also from the centralizing tendencies of the powerful Tokugawa shogunate. Some historians have seen strong parallels between Tokugawa Japan and early modern Europe, which gave birth to centralized empires and a strong merchant class during the same period. The image of the monarchy is reflected in a song sung at the shrine of Toyotomi Hideyoshi in Kyoto:

> *Who's that*
> *Holding over four hundred provinces*
> *In the palm of his hand*
> *And entertaining at a tea-party?*
> *It's His Highness*
> *So mighty, so impressive!*[14]

By the beginning of the nineteenth century, then, powerful tensions, reflecting a growing gap between ideal and reality, were at work in both Chinese and Japanese society. Under these conditions, both countries were soon forced to face a new challenge from the aggressive power of an industrializing Europe.

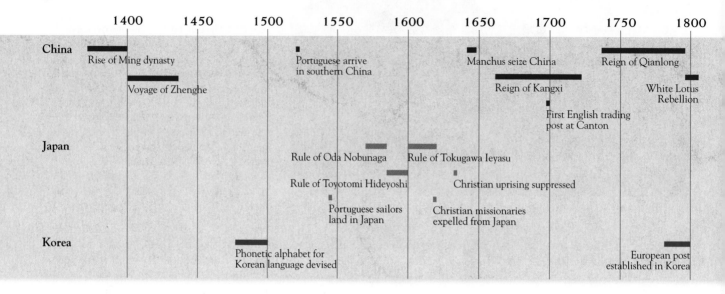

CHAPTER NOTES

1. From Jonathan D. Spence, *Emperor of China: Self-Portrait of K'ang Hsi* (New York, 1974), pp. 143–144.
2. Quoted in J. H. Parry, ed., *The European Reconnaissance: Selected Documents* (New York, 1968), p. 129.
3. Richard Strassberg, *The World of K'ang Shang-jen: A Man of Letters in Early Ch'ing China* (New York, 1983), p. 275.
4. Quoted in Frederick Wakeman Jr., *The Great Enterprise: The Manchu Reconstruction of Imperial Order in Seventeenth-Century China* (Berkeley, Calif., 1985), p. 16.
5. Lynn Struve, *The Southern Ming, 1644–1662* (New Haven, Conn., 1984), p. 61.
6. J. L. Cranmer-Byng, *An Embassy to China: Lord Macartney's Journal, 1793–1794* (London, 1912), p. 340.
7. Daniel J. Boorstin, *The Discoverers: A History of Man's Search to Know His World and Himself* (New York, 1983), p. 63.
8. C. R. Boxer, ed., *South China in the Sixteenth Century* (London, 1953), p. 265.
9. Chie Nakane and Sinzaburo Oishi, eds., *Tokugawa Japan* (Tokyo, 1990), p. 14.
10. Quoted in Jurgis Elisonas, "Christianity and the Daimyo," in John Whitney Hall, ed., *The Cambridge History of Japan*, vol. 4 (Cambridge, 1991), p. 360.
11. Engelbert Kaempfer, *The History of Japan: Together with a Description of the Kingdom of Siam, 1690–1692*, vol. 2 (Glasgow, 1906), pp. 173–174.
12. Parry, *European Reconnaissance*, p. 144.
13. Quoted in Donald Keene, *The Japanese Discovery of Europe, 1720–1830*, rev. ed. (Stanford, Calif., 1969), p. 114.
14. Quoted in Ryusaku Tsunda et al., *Sources of Japanese Tradition* (New York, 1964), p. 313.

SUGGESTED READING

For a general overview of this period in East Asian history, see volumes 8 and 9 of F. W. Mote and D. Twitchett, eds., *The Cambridge History of China* (Cambridge, 1976), and J. W. Hall, ed., *The Cambridge History of Japan*, vol. 4 (Cambridge, 1991).

For information on Chinese voyages into the Indian Ocean, see P. Snow, *The Star Raft: China's Encounter with Africa* (Ithaca, N.Y., 1988). Also see Ma Huan, *Ying-hai Sheng-lan: The Overall Survey of the Ocean's Shores* (Bagkok, 1996), an ocean survey by a fifteenth-century Chinese cataloger. Early documents on European activities can be found in J. H. Parry, *The European Reconnaissance: Selected Documents* (New York, 1968).

On the late Ming, see J. D. Spence, *The Search for Modern China* (New York, 1990), and L. Struve, *The Southern Ming, 1644–1662* (New Haven, Conn., 1984). On the rise of the Qing, see F. Wakeman Jr., *The Great Enterprise: The Manchu Reconstruction of Imperial Order in Seventeenth-Century China* (Berkeley, Calif., 1985). On Kangxi, see J. D. Spence, *Emperor of China: Self-Portrait of K'ang Hsi* (New York, 1974). Social issues are discussed in S. Naquin and E. Rawski, *Chinese Society in the Eighteenth Century* (New Haven, Conn., 1987). Also see J. D. Spence and J. Wills, eds., *From Ming to Ch'ing* (New Haven, Conn., 1979). For a very interesting account of Jesuit missionary experiences in China, see L. J. Gallagher, ed. and trans., *China in the Sixteenth Century: The Journals of Matthew Ricci, 1583–1616* (New York, 1953). For brief biographies of Ming-Qing luminaries such as Wang Yangming, Zheng Chenggong, and Emperor Qianlong, see J. E. Wills Jr., *Mountains of Fame: Portraits in Chinese History* (Princeton, N.J., 1994).

The best surveys of Chinese literature are Liu Wu-chi, *An Introduction to Chinese Literature* (Bloomington, Ind., 1966); S. Owen, *An Anthology of Chinese Literature: Beginnings to 1911* (New York, 1996);

and V. Mair, *The Columbia Anthology of Traditional Chinese Literature* (New York, 1994). For a concise and comprehensive introduction to the Chinese art of this period, see M. Sullivan, *The Arts of China*, 4th ed. (Berkeley, Calif., 1999); C. Clunas, *Art in China* (Oxford, 1997); and M. Tregear, *Chinese Art*, rev. ed. (London, 1997). For the best introduction to the painting of this era, see J. Cahill, *Chinese Painting* (New York, 1977), and Yang Xin et al., *Three Thousand Years of Chinese Paintings* (New Haven, Conn., 1997).

On Japan before the rise of the Tokugawa, see J. W. Hall et al., eds., *Japan Before Tokugawa: Political Consolidation and Economic Growth* (Princeton, N.J., 1981), and G. Elison and B. L. Smith, eds., *Warlords, Artists, and Commoners: Japan in the Sixteenth Century* (Honolulu, 1981). See also M. E. Berry, *Hideyoshi* (Cambridge, Mass., 1982), the first biography of this fascinating figure in Japanese history. On the first Christian activities, see G. Elison, *Deus Destroyed: The Image of Christianity in Early Modern Japan* (Cambridge, Mass., 1973), and C. R. Boxer, *The Christian Century in Japan, 1549–1650* (Berkeley, Calif., 1951). Buddhism is dealt with in N. McMullin, *Buddhism and the State in Sixteenth Century Japan* (Princeton, N.J., 1984).

On the Tokugawa era, see H. Bolitho, *Treasures Among Men: The Fudai Daimyo in Tokugawa Japan* (New Haven, Conn., 1974), and R. B. Toby, *State and Diplomacy in Early Modern Japan: Asia in the Development of the Tokugawa Bakufu* (Princeton, N.J., 1984). See also R. N. Bellah, *Tokugawa Religion: The Values of Pre-Industrial Japan* (New York, 1957), and C. I. Mulhern, ed., *Heroic with Grace: Legendary Women of Japan* (Armonk, N.Y., 1991). Three other worthwhile studies are S. Vlastos, *Peasant Protests and Uprisings in Tokugawa Japan* (Berkeley, Calif., 1986); H. Ooms, *Tokugawa Ideology: Early Constructs, 1570–1680* (Princeton, N.J., 1985); and C. Nakane, ed., *Tokugawa Japan: The Social and Economic Antecedents of Modern Japan* (Tokyo, 1990).

For a brief introduction to women in the Ming and Qing dynasties as well as the Tokugawa era, see S. Hughes and B. Hughes, *Women in World History*, vol. 2 (Armonk, N.Y., 1997). To witness Chinese village life in 1670, consult the classic J. D. Spence, *The Death of Woman Wang* (New York, 1978). For women's literacy in seventeenth-century China, see J. Handlin, "Lu K'un's New Audience: The Influence of Women's Literacy on Sixteenth-Century Thought," in *Women in Chinese Society*, eds. M. Wolf and R. Witke (Stanford, Calif., 1975), and D. Ko, *Teachers of the Inner Chambers: Women and Culture in Seventeenth Century China* (Stanford, Calif., 1994). Most valuable is the collection of articles edited by G. L. Bernstein, *Re-Creating Japanese Women, 1600–1945* (Berkeley, Calif., 1991).

Of specific interest to Japanese literature of the Tokugawa era are D. Keene, *World Within Walls: Japanese Literature of the Pre-Modern Era, 1600–1867* (New York, 1976). Of special value for the college student are D. Keene's *Anthology of Japanese Literature* (New York, 1955), *The Pleasures of Japanese Literature* (New York, 1988), and *Japanese Literature: An Introduction for Western Readers* (London, 1953). For an introduction to Basho's life, poems, and criticism, consult the stimulating *Basho and His Interpreters: Selected Hokku with Commentary* (Stanford, Calif., 1991), by M. Ueda.

For the most comprehensive and accessible overview of Japanese art, see P. Mason, *Japanese Art* (New York, 1993). For a concise introduction to Japanese art of the Tokugawa era, see J. Stanley-Baker, *Japanese Art* (London, 1984). For magnificent photographs and stimulating interpretation, consult D. Elisseeff and V. Elisseeff, *Art of Japan* (New York, 1985), and J. E. Kidder Jr., *The Art of Japan* (London, 1985).

⚲ INFOTRAC COLLEGE EDITION

For additional reading, go to InfoTrac College Edition, your online research library at
http://web1.infotrac-college.com

Enter the search terms "Ming China" using Keywords.

Enter the search terms "China history" using Keywords.

Enter the search terms "Japan history" using Keywords.

Enter the search term "Tokugawa" using Keywords.

Enter the search term "Qing" using Keywords.

Chapter 17

The West on the Eve of a New World Order

Chapter Outline

- The Enlightenment
- Economic Changes and the Social Order
- Changing Patterns of War: Global Confrontation
- Colonial Empires and Revolution in the Western Hemisphere
- Toward a New Political Order: Enlightened Absolutism
- The French Revolution
- The Age of Napoleon

Focus Questions

- Who were the leading figures of the Enlightenment, and what were their main contributions?
- What changes occurred in the European economy in the eighteenth century, and to what degree were these changes reflected in social patterns?
- How did Spain and Portugal administer their American colonies, and what were the main characteristics of Latin American society in the eighteenth century?
- What do historians mean by the term *enlightened absolutism*, and to what degree did eighteenth-century Prussia, Austria, and Russia exhibit its characteristics?
- What were the causes, the main events, and the results of the American Revolution and the French Revolution? Which aspects of the French Revolution did Napoleon preserve, and which did he destroy?
- ➤ In what ways were the American Revolution, the French Revolution, and the seventeenth-century English revolutions alike? In what ways were they different?

*H*istorians have often portrayed the eighteenth century as the final phase of Europe's old order, before the violent upheaval and reordering of society associated with the French Revolution. The old order—still largely agrarian, dominated by kings and landed aristocrats, and grounded in privileges for nobles, clergy, towns, and provinces—seemed to continue a basic pattern that had prevailed in Europe since medieval times. However, just as a new intellectual order based on rationalism and secularism was emerging in Europe, demographic, economic, social, and political patterns were beginning to change in ways that proclaimed the emergence of a modern new order.

A key factor in the emergence of the new world order was the French Revolution. On the morning of July 14, 1789, a Parisian mob of some eight thousand men and women in search of weapons streamed toward the Bastille, a royal armory filled with arms and ammunition. The Bastille was also a state prison, and although it held only seven prisoners at the time, in the eyes of these angry Parisians, it was a glaring symbol of the government's despotic policies. It was defended by the marquis de Launay and a small garrison of 114 men. The attack on the Bastille began in earnest in the early afternoon, and after three hours of fighting, de Launay and the garrison surrendered. Angered by the loss of ninety-eight protesters, the victors beat de Launay to death, cut off his head, and carried it aloft in triumph through the streets of Paris. When King Louis XVI was told the news of the fall of the Bastille by the duc de La Rochefoucauld-Liancourt, he exclaimed, "Why, this is a revolt." "No, Sire," replied the duke. "It is a revolution."

The French Revolution has been portrayed as a major turning point in European political and social history, as a time when the institutions of the old regime were destroyed and a new order was created based on individual rights, representative institutions, and a concept of loyalty to the nation rather than the monarch. The revolutionary upheavals of the era, especially in France, did create new liberal and national political ideals, summarized in the French revolutionary slogan, "Liberty, Equality, Fraternity," that transformed France and then spread to other European countries and the rest of the world. •

❧ THE ENLIGHTENMENT

The impetus for political and social change in the eighteenth century stemmed in part from the Enlightenment. The Enlightenment was a movement of intellectuals who were greatly impressed with the accomplishments of the Scientific Revolution. When they used the word *reason*—one of their favorite words—they were advocating the application of the scientific method to the understanding of all life. All institutions and all systems of thought were subject to the rational, scientific way of thinking if people would only free themselves from the shackles of past, worthless traditions, especially religious ones. If Isaac Newton could discover the natural laws regulating the world of nature, they too, by using reason, could find the laws that governed human society. This belief in turn led them to hope that they could make progress toward a better society than the one they had inherited. *Reason, natural law, hope, progress*—these were the buzzwords in the heady atmosphere of eighteenth-century Europe.

The Path to Enlightenment

The seventeenth century had witnessed a growing skepticism about religion and an increasing secularization of thought. Skepticism about both Christianity and European culture was nourished by the reports of world travelers. Traders, missionaries, and explorers began to publish books that gave accounts of many different cultures. The great geographical adventures of the eighteenth century, especially the discovery of the Pacific island of Tahiti and of New Zealand and Austrialia by James Cook, also aroused much enthusiasm in Europe. Cook's *Travels,* an account of his journey, became a best-seller.

For some European intellectuals, the existence of exotic peoples, such as the natives of Tahiti, presented an image of a "natural man" who was far happier than many Europeans. One such intellectual wrote:

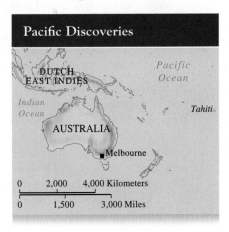

The life of savages is so simple, and our societies are such complicated machines! The Tahitian is close to the origin of the world, while the European is closer to its old age. . . . They understand nothing about our manners or our laws, and they are bound to see in them nothing but shackles disguised in a hundred different ways. Those shackles could only provoke the indignation and scorn of creatures in whom the most profound feeling is a love of liberty.[1]

The idea of the "noble savage" would play an important role in the political work of some eighteenth-century intellectuals.

The travel literature of the seventeenth and eighteenth centuries also led to the realization that there were highly developed civilizations with different customs in other parts of the world. China was especially singled out. One German university professor praised Confucian morality as superior to the intolerant attitudes of Christianity. Some European intellectuals began to evaluate their own civilization relative to others. What had seemed to be practices grounded in reason now appeared to be matters of custom.

NEWTON AND LOCKE

Major sources of inspiration for the Enlightenment were two Englishmen, Isaac Newton and John Locke. Newton contended that the world and everything in it worked like a giant machine. Enchanted by the grand design of this world-machine, the intellectuals of the Enlightenment were convinced that by following Newton's rules of reasoning, they could discover the natural laws that governed politics, economics, justice, and religion.

John Locke's theory of knowledge also made a great impact. In his *Essay Concerning Human Understanding*, written in 1690, Locke denied the existence of innate ideas and argued instead that every person was born with a *tabula rasa*, a blank mind:

> Let us then suppose the mind to be, as we say, white paper, void of all characters, without any ideas. How comes it to be furnished? Whence comes it by that vast store which the busy and boundless fancy of man has painted on it with an almost endless variety? Whence has it all the materials of reason and knowledge? To this I answer, in one word, from experience. . . . Our observation, employed either about external sensible objects or about the internal operations of our minds perceived and reflected on by ourselves, is that which supplies our understanding with all the materials of thinking.[2]

By denying innate ideas, Locke's philosophy implied that people were molded by their environment, by whatever they perceived through their senses from their surrounding world. By changing the environment and subjecting people to proper influences, they could be changed and a new society created. And how should the environment be changed? Newton had paved the way: reason enabled enlightened people to discover the natural laws to which all institutions should conform.

The Philosophes and Their Ideas

The intellectuals of the Enlightenment were known by the French term *philosophes*, although they were not all French and few were philosophers in the strict sense of the term. They were literary people, professors, journalists, economists, political scientists, and above all, social reformers. They came from both the nobility and the middle class, and a few even stemmed from lower-middle-class origins. Although it was a truly international and cosmopolitan movement, the Enlightenment also enhanced the dominant role being played by French culture; Paris was its recognized capital. Most of the leaders of the Enlightenment were French. The French philosophes, in turn, affected intellectuals elsewhere and created a movement that touched the entire Western world, including the British and Spanish colonies in America (see Map 17.1).

To the philosophes, the role of philosophy was not just to discuss the world but to change it. As one writer said, the philosophe "applies himself to the study of society with the purpose of making his kind better and happier." To the philosophes, reason was a scientific method, and it relied on an appeal to facts. A spirit of rational criticism was to be applied to everything, including religion and politics.

Spanning almost a century, the Enlightenment evolved with each succeeding generation, becoming more radical as new thinkers built on the contributions of their predecessors. A few individuals, however, dominated the landscape so completely that we can gain insight into the core ideas of the philosophes by focusing on the three French giants—Montesquieu, Voltaire, and Diderot.

MONTESQUIEU

Charles de Secondat, the baron de Montesquieu (1689–1755), came from the French nobility. His most famous work, *The Spirit of the Laws*, was published in 1748. In this comparative study of governments, Montesquieu attempted to apply the scientific method to the social and political arena to ascertain the "natural laws" governing the social and political relationships of human beings. Montesquieu distinguished three basic kinds of governments: republics, which are suitable for small states and based on citizen involvement; monarchy, appropriate for middle-sized states and grounded in the ruling class's adherence to law; and despotism, apt for large empires and relying on fear to inspire obedience. Montesquieu used England as an example of monarchy, and it was his analysis of England's constitution that led to his most lasting contribution to political thought—the importance of checks and balances achieved by means of a separation of powers. He believed that England's system, with its separate executive, legislative, and judicial powers that served to limit and control each other, provided the greatest freedom and security for a state. The translation of his work into English two years after publication ensured its being read by American political leaders, who eventually incorporated its principles into the U.S. Constitution.

VOLTAIRE

The greatest figure of the Enlightenment was François-Marie Arouet, known simply as Voltaire (1694–1778). Son of a prosperous middle-class family from Paris, he studied

THE ATTACK ON RELIGIOUS INTOLERANCE

Although Voltaire's ideas on religion were in no way original, his lucid prose, biting satire, and clever wit caused his works to be widely read and all the more influential. These two selections present different sides of Voltaire's attack on religious intolerance. The first is from his straightforward treatise The Ignorant Philosopher, *and the second is from his only real literary masterpiece, the novel* Candide, *where he uses humor to make the same fundamental point about religious intolerance.*

VOLTAIRE, *THE IGNORANT PHILOSOPHER*

The contagion of fanaticism then still subsists. . . . The author of the Treatise upon Toleration has not mentioned the shocking executions wherein so many unhappy victims perished in the valleys of Piedmont. He has passed over in silence the massacre of six hundred inhabitants of Valtelina, men, women, and children, who were murdered by the Catholics in the month of September, 1620. I will not say it was with the consent and assistance of the archbishop of Milan, Charles Borome, who was made a saint. Some passionate writers have averred this fact, which I am very far from believing; but I say, there is scarce any city or borough in Europe where blood has not been spilt for religious quarrels; I say, that the human species has been perceptibly diminished because women and girls were massacred as well as men; I say, that Europe would have had a third larger population if there had been no theological disputes. In fine, I say, that so far from forgetting these abominable times, we should frequently take a view of them, to inspire an eternal horror for them; and that it is for our age to make reparation by toleration, for this long collection of crimes, which has taken place through the want of toleration, during sixteen barbarous centuries.

Let it not then be said, that there are no traces left of that shocking fanaticism, of the want of toleration; they are still everywhere to be met with, even in those countries that are esteemed the most humane. The Lutheran and Calvinist preachers, were they masters, would, perhaps, be as little inclined to pity, as obdurate, as insolent as they upbraid their antagonists with being.

VOLTAIRE, *CANDIDE*

At last [Candide] approached a man who had just been addressing a big audience for a whole hour on the subject of charity. The orator peered at him and said:

"What is your business here? Do you support the Good Old Cause?"

"There is no effect without a cause," replied Candide modestly. "All things are necessarily connected and arranged for the best. It was my fate to be driven from Lady Cunégonde's presence and made to run the gauntlet, and now I have to beg my bread until I can earn it. Things could not have happened otherwise."

"Do you believe that the Pope is Antichrist, my friend?" said the minister.

"I have never heard anyone say so," replied Candide; "but whether he is or he isn't, I want some food."

"You don't deserve to eat," said the other. "Be off with you, you villain, you wretch! Don't come near me again or you'll suffer for it."

The minister's wife looked out of the window at that moment, and seeing a man who was not sure that the Pope was Antichrist, emptied over his head a chamber pot, which shows to what lengths ladies are driven by religious zeal.

---

law, although he achieved his first success as a playwright. Voltaire was a prolific author and wrote an almost endless stream of pamphlets, novels, plays, letters, philosophical essays, and histories. His writings brought him both fame and wealth.

Voltaire was especially well known for his criticism of traditional religion and his strong attachment to the ideal of religious toleration (see the box above). As he grew older, Voltaire became ever more strident in his denunciations. "Crush the infamous thing," he thundered repeatedly—the infamous thing being religious fanaticism, intolerance, and superstition.

Throughout his life, Voltaire championed not only religious tolerance but also deism, a religious outlook shared by most other philosophes. Deism was built on the Newtonian world-machine, which implied the existence of a mechanic (God) who had created the universe. To Voltaire and most other philosophes, the universe was like a clock, and God was the clockmaker who had created it, set it in motion, and allowed it to run according to its own natural laws.

DIDEROT

Denis Diderot (1713–1784) was the son of a skilled craftsman from eastern France who became a freelance writer so that he could be free to study and read in many subjects and languages. One of Diderot's favorite topics was Christianity, which he condemned as fanatical and unreasonable. As he

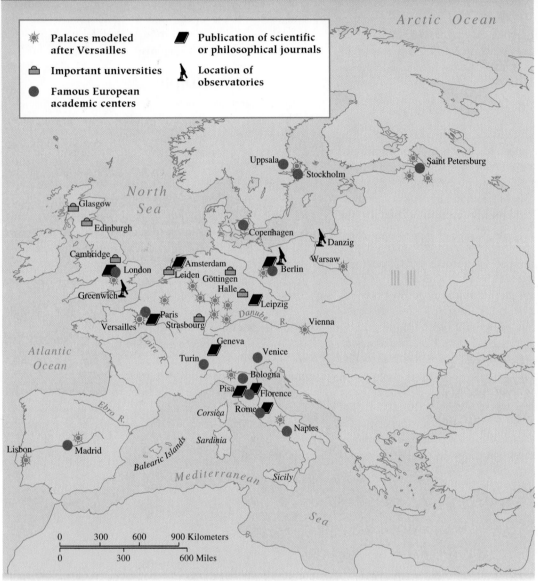

MAP 17.1 The Enlightenment in Europe. "Have the courage to use your own intelligence!" Immanuel Kant's words epitomize the role of the individual in using reason to understand all aspects of life—the natural world and the sphere of human nature, behavior, and institutions. ➢ *Which countries or regions were at the center of the Enlightenment, and what reasons could account for peripheral regions' being less involved?*

grew older, his literary attacks on Christianity grew more vicious. Of all religions, Christianity, he averred, was the worst, "the most absurd and the most atrocious in its dogma."

Diderot's most famous contribution to the Enlightenment was the *Encyclopedia, or Classified Dictionary of the Sciences, Arts, and Trades,* a twenty-eight-volume compendium of knowledge that he edited and referred to as the "great work of his life." Its purpose, according to Diderot, was to "change the general way of thinking." It did precisely that in becoming a major weapon of the philosophes' crusade against the old French society. The contributors included many philosophes who attacked religious intolerance and

advocated a program for social, legal, and political improvements that would lead to a society that was more cosmopolitan, more tolerant, more humane, and more reasonable. The *Encyclopedia* was sold to doctors, clergymen, teachers, lawyers, and even military officers, thus spreading the ideas of the Enlightenment.

TOWARD A NEW "SCIENCE OF MAN"

The Enlightenment belief that Newton's scientific methods could be used to discover the natural laws underlying all areas of human life led to the emergence in the eighteenth century of what the philosophes called a "science of man," or what we would call the social sciences. In a number of areas, such as economics, politics, and education, the philosophes arrived at natural laws that they believed governed human actions.

The Physiocrats and Adam Smith have been viewed as founders of the modern discipline of economics. The leader of the Physiocrats was François Quesnay (1694–1774), a highly successful French doctor. Quesnay and the Physiocrats claimed they would discover the natural economic laws that governed human society. Their major "natural law" of economics was that individuals should be left free to pursue their own economic self-interest. Through the actions of these individuals, all society would ultimately benefit. Consequently, they argued that the state should in no way interrupt the free play of natural economic forces by government regulations on the economy, but should leave it alone, a doctrine that subsequently became known as *laissez-faire* (French for "leave it alone").

The best statement of *laissez-faire* was made in 1776 by a Scottish philosopher, Adam Smith (1723–1790), in his famous work *The Wealth of Nations*. Like the Physiocrats, Smith believed that the state should not interfere in economic matters; indeed, he gave to government only three basic functions: it should protect society from invasion (army), defend its citizens from injustice (police), and keep up certain public works, such as roads and canals that private individuals could not afford.

THE LATER ENLIGHTENMENT

By the late 1760s, a new generation of philosophes who had grown up with the worldview of the Enlightenment began to move beyond their predecessors' beliefs. Most famous was Jean-Jacques Rousseau (1712–1778), whose political beliefs were presented in two major works. In his *Discourse on the Origins of the Inequality of Mankind*, Rousseau argued that people had adopted laws and governors in order to preserve their private property. In the process, they had become enslaved by government. What, then, should people do to regain their freedom? In his celebrated treatise *The Social Contract*, published in 1762, Rousseau found an answer in the concept of the social contract. In a social contract, an entire society agreed to be governed by its general will. Each individual might have a particular will contrary to the general will, but if the individual put his particular will (self-interest) above the general will, he should be forced to abide by the general will. "This means nothing less than that he will be forced to be free," said Rousseau, because the general will was not only political but also ethical; it represented what the entire community ought to do.

Another influential treatise by Rousseau was his novel *Émile*, one of the Enlightenment's most important works on education. Rousseau's fundamental concern was that education should foster, rather than restrict, children's natural instincts. Rousseau's own experiences had shown him the importance of the emotions. What he sought was a balance between heart and mind, between emotion and reason.

A LONDON COFFEEHOUSE. Coffeehouses had first appeared in the major cities of the Ottoman Empire in the sixteenth century, where they were often associated with antigovernment activity. Coffeehouses spread quickly throughout Europe by the beginning of the eighteenth century and became a means for spreading Enlightenment ideas. In addition to drinking coffee, patrons of coffeehouses could read magazines and newspapers, exchange ideas, play chess, smoke, and even engage in business transactions. In this scene from a London coffeehouse of 1705, well-attired gentlemen make bids on commodities. Bidding went on until pins, which had been placed in lit candles, fell to the table. Thus bidding stopped when patrons could "hear a pin drop."

THE RIGHTS OF WOMEN

*M*ary Wollstonecraft responded to an unhappy childhood in a large family by seeking to lead an independent life. Few occupations were available for middle-class women in her day, but she survived by working as a teacher, chaperone, and governess to aristocratic children. All the while, she wrote and developed her ideas on the rights of women. This excerpt was taken from her Vindication of the Rights of Woman, written in 1792. This work led to her reputation as the foremost British feminist thinker of the eighteenth century.

MARY WOLLSTONECRAFT, *VINDICATION OF THE RIGHTS OF WOMAN*

It is a melancholy truth—yet such is the blessed effect of civilization—the most respectable women are the most oppressed; and, unless they have understandings far superior to the common run of understandings, taking in both sexes, they must, from being treated like contemptible beings, become contemptible. How many women thus waste life away the prey of discontent, who might have practiced as physicians, regulated a farm, managed a shop, and stood erect, supported by their own industry, instead of hanging their heads surcharged with the dew of sensibility, that consumes the beauty to which it at first gave luster. . . .

Proud of their weakness, however, [women] must always be protected, guarded from care, and all the rough toils that dignify the mind. If this be the fiat of fate, if they will make themselves insignificant and contemptible, sweetly to waste "life away," let them not expect to be valued when their beauty fades, for it is the fate of the fairest flowers to be admired and pulled to pieces by the careless hand that plucked them. In how many ways do I wish, from the purest benevolence, to impress this truth on my sex; yet I fear that they will not listen to a truth that dear-bought experience has brought home to many an agitated bosom, nor willingly resign the privileges of rank and sex for the privileges of humanity, to which those have no claim who do not discharge its duties. . . .

Would men but generously snap our chains, and be content with rational fellowship instead of slavish obedience, they would find us more observant daughters, more affectionate sisters, more faithful wives, and more reasonable mothers—in a word, better citizens. We should then love them with true affection, because we should learn to respect ourselves; and the peace of mind of a worthy man would not be interrupted by the idle vanity of his wife.

But Rousseau did not necessarily practice what he preached. His own children were sent to orphanages, where many children died at a young age. Rousseau also viewed women as "naturally" different from men. In Rousseau's *Émile*, Sophie, Émile's intended wife, was educated for her role as wife and mother by learning obedience and the nurturing skills that would enable her to provide loving care for her husband and children. Not everyone in the eighteenth century, however, agreed with Rousseau.

THE "WOMAN QUESTION" IN THE ENLIGHTENMENT

For centuries, many male intellectuals had argued that the nature of women made them inferior to men and made male domination of women necessary and right. Female thinkers in the eighteenth century, however, provided suggestions for improving the conditions of women. The strongest statement for the rights of women was advanced by the English writer Mary Wollstonecraft (1759–1797), viewed by many as the founder of modern European feminism.

In her *Vindication of the Rights of Women*, written in 1792, Wollstonecraft pointed out two contradictions in the views of women held by such Enlightenment thinkers as Rousseau. To argue that women must obey men, she said, was contrary to the beliefs of the same individuals that a system based on the arbitrary power of monarchs over their subjects or slave owners over their slaves was wrong. The subjection of women to men was equally wrong. In addition, she argued that the Enlightenment was based on an ideal of reason innate in all human beings. If women have reason, then they too are entitled to the same rights that men have. Women, Wollstonecraft declared, should have equal rights with men in education and in economic and political life as well (see the box above).

Culture in an Enlightened Age

Although the Baroque style that had dominated the seventeenth century continued to be popular, by the 1730s, a new style affecting decoration and architecture known as Rococo had spread throughout Europe. Unlike the Baroque, which stressed power, grandeur, and movement, Rococo emphasized grace, charm, and gentle action. Rococo rejected strict geometrical patterns and had a fondness for curves; it liked to follow the wandering lines of natural objects, such as seashells and flowers. It made much use of interlaced designs colored in gold with delicate contours and graceful arcs. Highly secular, its lightness and charm spoke of the pursuit of pleasure, happiness, and love.

Some of Rococo's appeal is evident already in the work of Antoine Watteau (1684–1721), whose lyrical views of aristocratic life, refined, sensual, and civilized, with gen-

© Réunion des Musées Nationaux/Art Resource, NY

⟫ **ANTOINE WATTEAU, *THE PILGRIMAGE TO CYTHERA*.** Antoine Watteau was one of the most gifted painters in eighteenth-century France. His portrayal of aristocratic life reveals a world of elegance, wealth, and pleasure. In this painting, Watteau depicts a group of aristocratic pilgrims about to depart the island of Cythera, where they have paid homage to Venus, the goddess of love.

tlemen and ladies in elegant dress, revealed a world of upper-class pleasure and joy. Underneath that exterior, however, was an element of sadness as the artist revealed the fragility and transitory nature of pleasure, love, and life.

Another aspect of Rococo was that its decorative work could easily be paired with Baroque architecture. The palace at Versailles had made an enormous impact on Europe. "Keeping up with the Bourbons" became important as European rulers built grandiose palaces. While imitating Versailles in size, they were not so much modeled after the French classical style as they were after the seventeenth-century Italian Baroque, as modified by a series of brilliant German and Austrian sculptor-architects. This Baroque-Rococo architectural style typified eighteenth-century palaces and church buildings, and often the same architects designed both. This is evident in the work of one of the greatest architects of the eighteenth century, Balthasar Neumann (1687–1753). One of Neumann's masterpieces was the pilgrimage church of the Vierzehnheiligen (The Fourteen Saints) in southern Germany. Secular and spiritual merge in its lavish and fanciful ornamentation; light, bright colors; and elaborate, rich detail.

⟫ **VIERZEHNHEILIGEN, EXTERIOR VIEW.** Balthasar Neumann, one of the most prominent architects of the eighteenth century, used the Baroque-Rococo style of architecture to design some of the most beautiful buildings of the century. Pictured here is the exterior of his pilgrimage church of the Vierzehnheiligen (Fourteen Saints), located in southern Germany. Although as monumental in size as the Taj Mahal, completed in seventeenth-century India (see page 437), the Vierzehnheiligen possesses a sense of heaviness that differs considerably from the delicate lightness of the Indian architectural masterpiece.

MUSIC

The eighteenth century was unsurpassed in the history of European music. In the first half of the century, two composers—Handel and Bach—stand out as musical geniuses. Johann Sebastian Bach (1685–1750) came from a family of musicians. During his tenure as director of church music

Courtesy of James R. Spencer

at the church of Saint Thomas in Leipzig in 1723, Bach composed his Mass in B Minor, his St. Matthew's Passion, and the cantatas and motets that have established his reputation as one of the greatest composers of all time. For Bach, music was above all a means to worship God; his task in life, he said, was to make "well-ordered music in the honor of God."

George Frederick Handel (1685–1759) was, like Bach, born in Saxony in Germany and in the same year. Unlike Bach, however, he was profoundly secular in temperament. He began his career by writing operas in the Italian manner and thereafter remained faithful to the Italian Baroque style. Although he wrote much secular music, Handel is best known for his religious music. Handel's *Messiah* has been called "one of those rare works that appeal immediately to everyone, and yet is indisputably a masterpiece of the highest order."[3]

Bach and Handel perfected the Baroque musical style with its monumental and elaborate musical structures. Two geniuses of the second half of the eighteenth century—Haydn and Mozart—were innovators who wrote music known today as classical.

Franz Joseph Haydn (1732–1809) spent most of his adult life as musical director for the Esterhazy brothers, wealthy Hungarian princes. Haydn was incredibly prolific, composing 104 symphonies in addition to string quartets, concerti, songs, oratorios, and Masses. His visits to England in 1790 and 1794 introduced him to another world, where musicians wrote for public concerts rather than princely patrons. This "liberty," as he called it, induced him to write his two great oratorios, *The Creation* and *The Seasons*, both of which were dedicated to the common people.

Wolfgang Amadeus Mozart (1756–1791) was a child prodigy who gave his first harpsichord concert at six and wrote his first opera at twelve. He, too, sought a patron, but his discontent with the overly demanding archbishop of Salzburg forced him to move to Vienna, where his failure to achieve a permanent patron made his life miserable. Nevertheless, he wrote music prolifically and passionately: string quartets, sonatas, symphonies, concerti, and operas. *The Marriage of Figaro*, *The Magic Flute*, and *Don Giovanni* are three of the world's greatest operas. Mozart composed with an ease of melody and a blend of grace and precision that arguably no one has ever excelled.

HIGH CULTURE

Historians have grown accustomed to distinguishing between a civilization's high culture and its popular culture. High culture is the literary and artistic culture of the educated and wealthy ruling classes; popular culture is the written and unwritten culture of the masses, most of which has traditionally been passed down orally. By the eighteenth century, European high culture reflected the learned tastes of theologians, scientists, philosophers, intellectuals, poets, and dramatists, for all of whom Latin remained a truly international language.

Especially noticeable in the eighteenth century was an expansion of both the reading public and publishing. Whereas French publishers issued three hundred titles in 1750, about sixteen hundred were being published yearly in the 1780s. Although many of these titles were still geared for small groups of the educated elite, many were also directed to the new reading public of the middle classes, which included women and even urban artisans.

An important aspect of the growth of publishing and reading in the eighteenth century was the development of magazines for the general public. Great Britain saw 25 different periodicals published in 1700, 103 in 1760, 158 in 1780. Along with magazines came daily newspapers. The first was printed in London in 1702, but by 1780, thirty-seven other English towns had their own newspapers.

POPULAR CULTURE

The distinguishing characteristic of popular culture is its collective nature. Group activity was especially common in the festival, a broad name used to cover a variety of celebrations: community festivals in Catholic Europe that celebrated the feast day of the local patron saint; annual festivals, such as Christmas and Easter, that go back to medieval Christianity; and Carnival, which was celebrated in the Mediterranean world of Spain, Italy, and France as well as in Germany and Austria. All of these festivals shared common characteristics. They were special occasions on which people ate, drank, and celebrated to excess. In traditional societies, festival was a time of play, since much of the rest of the year consisted of unrelieved work. As the poet Thomas Gray in 1739 said of Carnival in Turin: "One half of the remaining part of the year is passed in remembering the last [Carnival], the other in expecting the future Carnival."[4]

Indeed, the ultimate festival was Carnival, which began after Christmas and lasted until the start of Lent, the forty-day period of fasting and purification leading up to Easter. Because during Lent people were expected to abstain from meat, sex, and most recreations, Carnival was a time of great indulgence when heavy consumption of food and drink were the norm. It was a time of intense sexual activity as well. Songs with double meanings that would ordinarily be considered offensive could be sung publicly at this time of year. A float of Florentine "keymakers," for example, sang this ditty to the ladies: "Our tools are fine, new and useful. We always carry them with us. They are good for anything. If you want to touch them, you can."

ECONOMIC CHANGES AND THE SOCIAL ORDER

The eighteenth century in Europe witnessed the beginning of economic changes that ultimately had a strong impact on the rest of the world.

New Economic Patterns

Europe's population began to grow around 1750 and continued to increase steadily. The total European population was probably around 120 million in 1700, 140 million in 1750, and 190 million in 1790. A falling death rate was perhaps the most important reason for this population growth. Of great significance in lowering death rates was the disappearance of bubonic plague, but so was diet. More plentiful food and better transportation of food supplies led to improved nutrition and relief from devastating famines.

More plentiful food was in part a result of improvements in agricultural practices and methods in the eighteenth century, especially in Britain, parts of France, and the Low Countries. Food production increased as more land was farmed, yields per acre increased, and climate improved. Also important to the increased yields was the cultivation of new vegetables, including two important American crops, the potato and maize (Indian corn). Both had been brought to Europe from the Americas in the sixteenth century.

In European industry in the eighteenth century, the most important product was textiles, most of which were still produced by master artisans in guild workshops. But a shift in textile production to the countryside was spreading to many rural areas of Europe by the "putting-out" or "domestic" system in which a merchant-capitalist entrepreneur bought the raw materials, mostly wool and flax, and "put them out" to rural workers who spun the raw material into yarn and then wove it into cloth on simple looms. Capitalist-entrepreneurs sold the finished product, made a profit, and used it to purchase materials to manufacture more. This system became known as the "cottage industry" because the spinners and weavers did their work on spinning wheels and looms in their own cottages.

In the eighteenth century, overseas trade boomed. Some historians speak of the emergence of a true global economy, pointing to the patterns of trade that interlocked Europe, Africa, the Far East, and the Americas (see Map 17.2). One such pattern involved the influx of gold and silver into Spain from its colonial American empire. Much of this gold and silver made its way to Britain, France, and the Netherlands in return for manufactured goods. British, Dutch, and French merchants in turn used their profits to buy tea, spices, silk and cotton goods from China and India

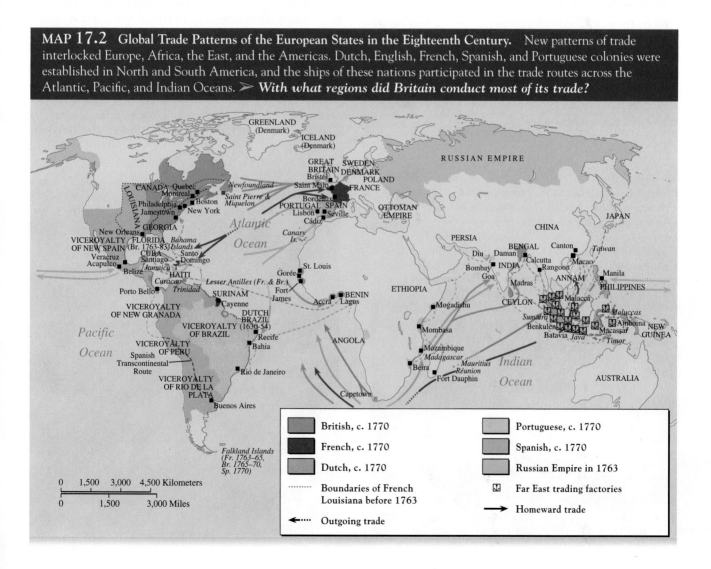

MAP 17.2 **Global Trade Patterns of the European States in the Eighteenth Century.** New patterns of trade interlocked Europe, Africa, the East, and the Americas. Dutch, English, French, Spanish, and Portuguese colonies were established in North and South America, and the ships of these nations participated in the trade routes across the Atlantic, Pacific, and Indian Oceans. ➤ *With what regions did Britain conduct most of its trade?*

to sell in Europe. Another important source of trading activity involved the plantations of the Western Hemisphere. The plantations were worked by African slaves and produced tobacco, cotton, coffee, and sugar, all products in demand by Europeans. In a third pattern of trade, British merchant ships carried British manufactured goods to Africa, where they were traded for a cargo of slaves, which were then shipped to Virginia and paid for by tobacco, which was in turn shipped back to Britain, where it was processed and then sold in Germany for cash.

Commercial capitalism created enormous prosperity for some European countries. By 1700, Spain, Portugal, and the Dutch Republic, which had earlier monopolized overseas trade, found themselves increasingly overshadowed by France and England, which built enormously profitable colonial empires in the course of the eighteenth century. After the French lost the Seven Years' War in 1763, Britain emerged as the world's strongest overseas trading nation, and London became the world's greatest port.

European Society in the Eighteenth Century

The pattern of Europe's social organization, first established in the Middle Ages, continued well into the eighteenth century. Society was still divided into the traditional "orders" or "estates" determined by heredity. Governments helped maintain these divisions. In Prussia, for example, a law of 1794 forbade marriage between noble males and middle-class females.

Because society was still mostly rural in the eighteenth century, the peasantry constituted the largest social group, about 85 percent of Europe's population. There were rather wide differences within this group, however, especially between free peasants and serfs. In eastern Germany, eastern Europe, and Russia, serfs remained tied to the lands of their noble landlords. In contrast, peasants in Britain, northern Italy, the Low Countries, Spain, most of France, and some areas of western Germany were largely free.

The nobles, who constituted only 2 to 3 percent of the European population, played a dominating role in society. Being born a noble automatically guaranteed a place at the top of the social order, with all its attendant special privileges and rights. Nobles, for example, were exempt from many forms of taxation. Since medieval times, landed aristocrats had functioned as military officers, and eighteenth-century nobles held most of the important offices in the administrative machinery of state and controlled much of the life of their local districts.

Townspeople were still a distinct minority of the total population except in the Dutch Republic, Britain, and parts of Italy. At the end of the eighteenth century, about one-sixth of the French population lived in towns of two thousand people or more. The biggest city in Europe was London, with a million inhabitants; Paris was a little more than half that size.

Many cities in western and even central Europe had a long tradition of patrician oligarchies that continued to control their communities by dominating town and city councils. Just below the patricians stood an upper crust of the middle classes: nonnoble officeholders, financiers and bankers, merchants, wealthy *rentiers* who lived off

➤ **THE ARISTOCRATIC WAY OF LIFE.** The eighteenth-century country house in Britain fulfilled the desire of aristocrats for both elegance and greater privacy. The painting below by Richard Wilson shows a typical English country house of the eighteenth century, surrounded by a simple and serene landscape. Thomas Gainsborough's *Conversation in the Park*, shown at right, captures the relaxed life of two aristocrats in the park of their country estate.

© Erich Lessing/Art Resource, NY

Collection of the Earl of Pembroke, Wilton House, Wilts., UK/Bridgeman Art Library

their investments, and important professionals, including lawyers. Another large urban group was the lower middle class, made up of master artisans, shopkeepers, and small traders. Below them were the laborers or working classes and a large group of unskilled workers who served as servants, maids, and cooks at pitifully low wages.

CHANGING PATTERNS OF WAR: GLOBAL CONFRONTATION

The philosophes condemned war as a foolish waste of life and resources in stupid quarrels of no value to humankind. Despite their words, the rivalry among states that led to costly struggles remained unchanged in the European world of the eighteenth century. Europe consisted of a number of self-governing, individual states that were chiefly guided by the self-interest of the ruler. And as Frederick the Great of Prussia said, "The fundamental rule of governments is the principle of extending their territories."

In 1740, a major conflict erupted over the succession to the Austrian throne. After the death of the Habsburg emperor Charles VI, King Frederick II of Prussia took advantage of the succession of a woman, Maria Theresa (1740–1780), to the throne of Austria by invading Austrian Silesia. The vulnerability of Maria Theresa encouraged France to enter the war against its traditional enemy Austria; in turn, Maria Theresa allied with Great Britain, which feared French domination of Continental affairs.

The War of the Austrian Succession (1740–1748) was fought in three areas of the world. In Europe, Prussia seized Silesia from Austria while France occupied the Austrian Netherlands. In Asia, France took Madras in India from the British, and in North America, the British captured the French fortress of Louisbourg at the entrance to the Saint Lawrence River. By 1748, all parties were exhausted and agreed to a peace treaty that guaranteed the return of all occupied territories to their original owners, with the exception of Silesia.

The Seven Years' War: A Global War

Maria Theresa refused to accept the loss of Silesia and prepared for its return by working diplomatically to separate Prussia from its chief ally, France. In 1756, Austria achieved a diplomatic revolution. French-Austrian rivalry had existed since the late sixteenth century. But two new rivalries now replaced the old one: the rivalry of Britain and France over colonial empires and the rivalry of Austria and Prussia over Silesia. France abandoned Prussia and allied with Austria. Russia, which saw Prussia as a major hindrance to Russian goals in central Europe, joined the new alliance. In turn, Great Britain allied with Prussia. These new alliances now led to another worldwide war.

Again there were three major areas of conflict: Europe, India, and North America (see Map 17.3). In Europe, the British and Prussians fought the Austrians, Russians, and French. With his superb army and military skill, Frederick the Great of Prussia was able for some time to defeat the Austrian, French, and Russian armies. Eventually, however, his forces were gradually worn down and faced utter defeat until a new Russian tsar, Peter III, withdrew Russian troops from the conflict. A stalemate ensued, ending the European conflict in 1763. All occupied territories were returned, and Austria officially recognized Prussia's permanent control of Silesia.

The struggle between Britain and France in the rest of the world had more decisive results. In India, the French had returned Madras to Britain after the War of the Austrian Succession, but the struggle continued. Ultimately, the British under Robert Clive won out, not because they had better forces but because they were more persistent. By the Treaty of Paris in 1763, the French withdrew and left India to the British.

➤ ROBERT CLIVE IN INDIA. Robert Clive was the leader of the army of the British East India Company. He had been commanded to fight the ruler of Bengal in order to gain trading privileges. To make his job easier, Clive arranged a meeting with Mir Jaffier, the commander of Bengal's army, in order to win him over to the British side. Although not present at the meeting, British artist Francis Hayman imaginatively re-created the scene in this 1760 painting.

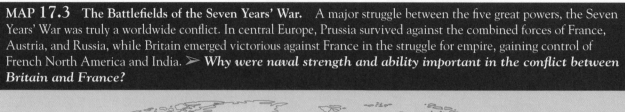

MAP 17.3 The Battlefields of the Seven Years' War.   A major struggle between the five great powers, the Seven Years' War was truly a worldwide conflict. In central Europe, Prussia survived against the combined forces of France, Austria, and Russia, while Britain emerged victorious against France in the struggle for empire, gaining control of French North America and India. ➤ *Why were naval strength and ability important in the conflict between Britain and France?*

By far the greatest conflicts of the Seven Years' War took place in North America. French North America (Canada and Louisiana) was thinly populated and run by the French government as a vast trading area. British North America had come to consist of thirteen colonies on the eastern coast of the present United States. They were thickly populated, containing about 1.5 million people by 1750, and were also prosperous.

British and French rivalry in North America led to two primary areas of contention. One consisted of the waterways of the Gulf of Saint Lawrence, protected by the fortress of Louisbourg and by forts near the Great Lakes and Lake Champlain that protected French Quebec and French traders. The other was the unsettled Ohio River valley. The French began to move down from Canada and up from Louisiana to establish forts in the Ohio River valley. To British settlers in the thirteen colonies, French activity threatened to cut off this vast area for their exploitation.

Despite initial French successes, British fortunes revived. The French had more troops in North America but less naval support. The defeat of French fleets in 1759 left the French unable to reinforce their garrisons. In 1759, British forces under General Wolfe defeated the French under General Montcalm on the Plains of Abraham, outside Quebec. The British went on to seize Montreal, the Great Lakes area, and the Ohio valley. The French were forced to make peace. By the Treaty of Paris, they ceded Canada and the lands east of the Mississippi to England. Their ally Spain transferred Spanish Florida to British control; in return, the French gave their Louisiana territory to the Spanish. By 1763, Great Britain had become the world's greatest colonial power.

COLONIAL EMPIRES AND REVOLUTION IN THE WESTERN HEMISPHERE

The colonial empires in the Western Hemisphere were an integral part of the European economy in the eighteenth century and became entangled in the conflicts of the European states. Nevertheless, the colonies of Latin America and British North America were developing along lines that sometimes differed significantly from those of Europe.

The Society of Latin America

In the sixteenth century, Portugal came to dominate Brazil while Spain established a colonial empire in the New World that included Central America, most of South America, and parts of North America. Within the lands of Central and South America, a new civilization arose that we have come to call Latin America (see Map 17.4).

Latin America was a multiracial society. Already by 1501, Spanish rulers allowed intermarriage between Europeans and native American Indians, whose offspring became known as *mestizos*. In addition, over a period of three centuries, possibly as many as eight million African slaves were brought to Spanish and Portuguese America to work the plantations. Mulattoes—the offspring of Africans and whites—joined mestizos and descendants of whites, Africans, and native Indians to produce a unique society in Latin America. Unlike Europe, and unlike British North America, which remained a largely white offshoot of Europe, Latin America developed a fairly well integrated multiracial society.

THE ECONOMIC FOUNDATIONS

Both the Portuguese and the Spanish sought to profit from their colonies in Latin America. One source of wealth came from the abundant supplies of gold and silver. The Spaniards were especially successful, finding supplies of gold in the Caribbean and New Granada (Colombia) and silver in Mexico and the viceroyalty of Peru. Most of the gold and silver was sent to Europe, and little remained in the New World to benefit the people whose labor had produced it.

Although the pursuit of gold and silver offered prospects of fantastic financial rewards, agriculture proved to be a more abiding and more rewarding source of prosperity for Latin America. A noticeable feature of Latin American agriculture was the dominant role of the large landowner. Both Spanish and Portuguese landowners created immense estates, which left the Indians either to work as peons—native peasants permanently dependent on the landowners—on their estates or as poor farmers on marginal lands. This system of large landowners and dependent peasants has remained one of the persistent features of Latin American society. By the eighteenth century, both Spanish

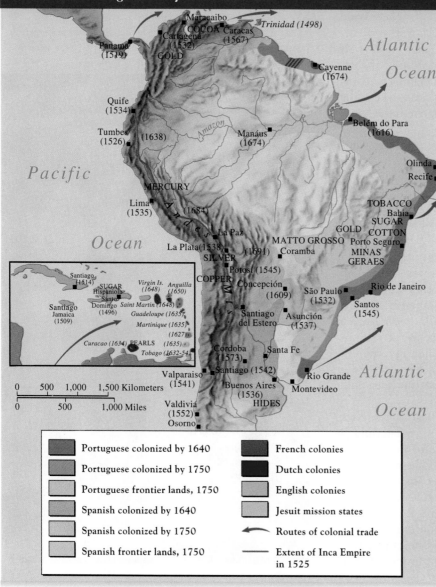

MAP 17.4 Latin America in the Eighteenth Century. In the eighteenth century, Latin America was largely the colonial preserve of the Spanish, although Portugal continued to dominate Brazil. The Latin American colonies supplied the Spanish and Portuguese with gold, silver, sugar, tobacco, cotton, and animal hides. ➤ *How do you explain the ability of Europeans to dominate such large areas of Latin America?*

Legend:
- Portuguese colonized by 1640
- Portuguese colonized by 1750
- Portuguese frontier lands, 1750
- Spanish colonized by 1640
- Spanish colonized by 1750
- Spanish frontier lands, 1750
- French colonies
- Dutch colonies
- English colonies
- Jesuit mission states
- Routes of colonial trade
- Extent of Inca Empire in 1525

and Portuguese landowners were producing primarily for sale abroad.

Trade was another avenue for the economic exploitation of the American colonies. Latin American colonies became sources of raw materials for Spain and Portugal as gold, silver, sugar, tobacco, diamonds, animal hides, and a number of other natural products made their way to Europe. In turn, the mother countries supplied their colonists with manufactured goods. Both Spain and Portugal closely regulated the trade of their American colonies to keep others out, but both the British and the French became too powerful to be excluded from this lucrative Latin American market.

THE STATE AND THE CHURCH IN COLONIAL LATIN AMERICA

Portuguese Brazil and Spanish America were colonial empires that lasted over three hundred years. The difficulties of communication and travel between the New World and Europe made the attempts of the Spanish and Portuguese monarchs to provide close regulation of their empires virtually impossible, which left colonial officials in Latin America with much autonomy in implementing imperial policies. However, the Iberians tried to keep the most important posts of colonial government in the hands of Europeans.

Beginning in the mid-sixteenth century, the Portuguese monarchy began to assert its control over Brazil by establishing the position of governor-general. The governor-general (later called a viceroy) developed a bureaucracy but had at best only loose control over the captains-general, who were responsible for governing the districts into which Brazil was divided.

To rule his American empire, the king of Spain appointed a viceroy, the first of which was established for New Spain (Mexico) in 1535. Another viceroy was appointed for Peru in 1543. In the eighteenth century, two additional viceroyalties—New Granada and La Plata—were added. Viceroyalties were in turn subdivided into smaller units. All of the major government positions were held by Spaniards. For creoles—American-born whites—the chief opportunity to hold a government post was in city councils.

From the beginning of their conquest of the New World, Spanish and Portuguese rulers were determined to Christianize the native peoples. This policy gave the Catholic church an important role to play in the New World—a role that added considerably to church power. Catholic missionaries fanned out to different parts of the Spanish Empire. To facilitate their efforts, missionaries brought Indians together into villages where the natives could be converted, taught trades, and encouraged to grow crops (see the box on p. 485). Their missions enabled missionaries to control the lives of the Indians and keep them docile.

The Catholic church constructed hospitals, orphanages, and schools, which instructed Indian students in the rudiments of reading, writing, and arithmetic. The church also provided outlets for women other than marriage. Nunneries were places of prayer and quiet contemplation, but women in religious orders, many of them of aristocratic background, often lived well and operated outside their establishments by running schools and hospitals. Indeed, one of these nuns, Sor Juana Inés de la Cruz (1651–1695), was one of seventeenth-century Latin America's best-known literary figures. She wrote poetry and prose and urged that women be educated.

SOR JUANA INÉS DE LA CRUZ. Nunneries in colonial Latin America gave women—especially upper-class women—some opportunity for intellectual activity. As a woman, Juana Inés de la Cruz was denied admission to the University of Mexico. Consequently, she entered a convent, where she wrote poetry and plays until her superiors forced her to focus on less worldly activities.

THE MISSION

In 1609, two Jesuit priests embarked on a missionary calling with the Guaraní Indians in eastern Paraguay. Eventually, the Jesuits established more than thirty missions in the region. Well organized and zealous, the Jesuits transformed their missions into profitable business activities. This description of a Jesuit mission in Paraguay was written by Félix de Azara, a Spanish soldier and scientist.

FÉLIX DE AZARA, DESCRIPTION AND HISTORY OF PARAGUAY AND RIO DE LA PLATA

Having spoken of the towns founded by the Jesuit fathers, and of the manner in which they were founded, I shall discuss the government which they established in them. . . . In each town resided two priests, a curate and a subcurate, who had certain assigned functions. The subcurate was charged with all the spiritual tasks, and the curate with every kind of temporal responsibility. . . .

The curate allowed no one to work for personal gain; he compelled everyone, without distinction of age or sex, to work for the community, and he himself saw to it that all were equally fed and dressed. For this purpose the curates placed in storehouses all the fruits of agriculture and the products of industry, selling in the Spanish towns their surplus of cotton, cloth, tobacco, vegetables, skins, and wood, transporting them in their own boats down the nearest rivers, and returning with implements and whatever else was required.

From the foregoing one may infer that the curate disposed of the surplus funds of the Indian towns, and that no Indian could aspire to own private property. This deprived them of any incentive to use reason or talent, since the most industrious, able, and worthy person had the same food, clothing, and pleasures as the most wicked, dull, and indolent. It also follows that although this form of government was well designed to enrich the communities it also caused the Indian to work at a languid pace, since the wealth of his community was of no concern to him.

It must be said that although the Jesuit fathers were supreme in all respects, they employed their authority with a mildness and a restraint that command admiration. They supplied everyone with abundant food and clothing. They compelled the men to work only half a day, and did not drive them to produce more. Even their labor was given a festive air, for they went in procession to the fields, to the sound of music . . . and the music did not cease until they had returned in the same way they had set out. They gave them many holidays, dances, and tournaments, dressing the actors and the members of the municipal councils in gold or silver tissue and the most costly European garments, but they permitted the women to act only as spectators.

They likewise forbade the women to sew; this occupation was restricted to the musicians, sacristans, and acolytes. But they made them spin cotton; and the cloth that the Indians wove, after satisfying their own needs, they sold together with the surplus cotton in the Spanish towns, as they did with the tobacco, vegetables, wood, and skins. The curate and his companion, or subcurate, had their own plain dwellings, and they never left them except to take the air in the great enclosed yard of their college. They never walked through the streets of the town or entered the house of any Indian or let themselves be seen by any woman—or indeed, by any man, except for those indispensable few through whom they issued their orders.

British North America

In the eighteenth century, Spanish power in the New World was increasingly challenged by the British. (The United Kingdom of Great Britain came into existence in 1707, when the governments of England and Scotland were united; the term *British* came into use to refer to both English and Scots.) In eighteenth-century Britain, the king or queen and Parliament shared power, with Parliament gradually gaining the upper hand. The monarch chose ministers who were responsible to the crown and who set policy and guided Parliament. Parliament had the power to make laws, levy taxes, pass budgets, and indirectly influence the monarch's ministers.

The eighteenth-century British Parliament was dominated by a landed aristocracy divided into two groups: the upper aristocracy or peers, who sat for life in the House of Lords, and the landed gentry, who were elected to the House of Commons. The two groups had much in common; both were landowners, and they frequently intermarried. The deputies to the House of Commons were chosen from the towns and counties not by popular vote but by holders of property.

In 1714, a new dynasty—the Hanoverians—was established when the last Stuart ruler, Queen Anne (1702–1714), died without an heir. The crown was offered to the nearest relatives, Protestant rulers of the German state of Hanover. Because the first Hanoverian king (George I) did not speak English and neither the first nor the second George had much familiarity with the British system, their chief ministers were allowed to handle Parliament. Robert Walpole served as prime minister from 1721 to 1742 and pursued a peaceful foreign policy. But growing trade and industry led to a growing middle class that favored expansion of trade and world empire. These people found a spokesman in William Pitt the Elder, who became prime minister in 1757 and expanded the British Empire by acquiring Canada and India in the Seven Years' War.

THE AMERICAN REVOLUTION

At the end of the Seven Years' War in 1763, Great Britain had become the world's greatest colonial power. In North America, Britain controlled Canada and the lands east of the Mississippi. After the Seven Years' War, British policymakers sought to obtain new revenues from the colonies to pay for British army expenses in defending the colonists. An attempt to levy new taxes by the Stamp Act of 1765 led to riots and the law's quick repeal.

The Americans and British had different conceptions of empire. The British envisioned a single empire with Parliament as the supreme authority throughout. The Americans, in contrast, had their own representative assemblies. They believed that neither king nor Parliament should interfere in their internal affairs and that no tax could be levied without the consent of their own assemblies.

Crisis followed crisis in the 1770s until 1776, when the colonists decided to declare their independence from the British Empire. On July 4, 1776, the Second Continental Congress approved a declaration of independence written by Thomas Jefferson. A stirring political document, the Declaration of Independence affirmed the Enlightenment's natural rights of "life, liberty, and the pursuit of happiness" and declared the colonies to be "free and independent states absolved from all allegiance to the British crown." The war for American independence had formally begun.

Of great importance to the colonies' cause was their support by foreign countries who were eager to gain revenge for earlier defeats at the hands of the British. French officers and soldiers served in the American Continental Army under George Washington as commander in chief. When the army of General Cornwallis was forced to surrender to a combined American and French army and French fleet under Washington at Yorktown in 1781, the British decided to call it quits. The Treaty of Paris, signed in 1783, recognized the independence of the American colonies and granted the Americans control of the territory from the Appalachians to the Mississippi River.

BIRTH OF A NEW NATION

The thirteen American colonies had gained their independence, but a fear of concentrated power and concern for their own interests caused them to have little enthusiasm for establishing a united nation with a strong central government, and so the Articles of Confederation, ratified in 1781, did not create one. A movement for a different form of national government soon arose. In the summer of 1787, fifty-five delegates attended a convention in Philadelphia to revise the Articles of Confederation.

The convention's delegates—wealthy, politically experienced, and well educated—rejected revision and decided instead to devise a new constitution.

The proposed United States Constitution established a central government distinct from and superior to governments of the individual states. The national government was given the power to levy taxes, raise a national army, regulate domestic and foreign trade, and create a national currency. The central or federal government was divided into three branches, each with some power to check the functioning of the others. A president would serve as the chief executive with the power to execute laws, veto the legislature's acts, supervise foreign affairs, and direct military forces. Legislative power was vested in the second branch of government, a bicameral legislature composed of the Senate, elected by the state legislatures, and the House of Representatives, elected directly by the people. A supreme court and other courts "as deemed necessary" by Congress provided the third branch of government. They would enforce the Constitution as the "supreme law of the land."

The Constitution was approved by the states—by a slim margin. Important to its success was a promise to add a bill of rights to the Constitution as the new government's first piece of business. Accordingly, in March 1789, the new Congress enacted the first ten amendments to the Constitution, ever since known as the Bill of Rights. These guaranteed freedom of religion, speech, press, petition, and assembly, as well as the right to bear arms, protection against unreasonable searches and arrests, trial by jury, due process of law, and protection of property rights. Many of these rights were derived from the natural rights philosophy of the eighteenth-century philosophes and the American colonists. Is it any wonder that many European intellectuals saw the American Revolution as the embodiment of the Enlightenment's political dreams?

TOWARD A NEW POLITICAL ORDER: ENLIGHTENED ABSOLUTISM

There is no doubt that Enlightenment thought had some impact on the political development of European states in the eighteenth century. The philosophes believed in natural rights, which were thought to be inalienable privileges that ought not to be withheld from any person. These natural rights included equality before the law, freedom of religious worship, freedom of speech and press, and the right to assemble, hold property, and pursue happiness.

But how were these natural rights to be established and preserved? Most philosophes believed that people needed to be ruled by an enlightened ruler. What, however, made rulers enlightened? They must allow religious toleration, freedom of speech and press, and the rights of private property. They must foster the arts, sciences, and education. Above all, they must obey the laws and enforce them fairly for all subjects. Only strong monarchs seemed capable of overcoming vested interests and effecting the reforms society needed. Reforms then should come from above (from absolute rulers) rather than from below (from the people).

Many historians once assumed that a new type of monarchy emerged in the later eighteenth century, which they called "enlightened despotism" or "enlightened absolutism." Monarchs such as Frederick II of Prussia, Catherine the Great of Russia, and Joseph II of Austria supposedly followed the advice of the philosophes and ruled by enlightened principles. Recently, however, scholars have questioned the usefulness of the concept of "enlightened absolutism." We can determine the extent to which it can be applied by examining the major "enlightened absolutists" of the later eighteenth century.

Prussia: The Army and the Bureaucracy

Two able Prussian kings in the eighteenth century, Frederick William I and Frederick II, made Prussia into a major European power in the eighteenth century. Frederick William I (1713–1740) strove to maintain a highly efficient bureaucracy of civil service workers. The bureaucracy had its own code in which the supreme values were obedience, honor, and service to the king as the highest duty.

Frederick William's other major concern was the army. By the end of his reign, he had nearly doubled the army's size from 45,000 to 83,000 men. Although tenth in physical size and thirteenth in population in Europe, Prussia had the fourth-largest army (after France, Russia, and Austria). The nobility or landed aristocracy known as Junkers, who owned large estates with many serfs, were the officers in the Prussian army. These officers, too, had a strong sense of service to the king or state. As Prussian nobles, they believed in duty, obedience, and sacrifice. The Prussian army, because of its size and excellent reputation, was the most important institution in the state.

Frederick II, known as Frederick the Great (1740–1786), was one of the best-educated and most cultured monarchs in the eighteenth century. He was well versed in Enlightenment thought and even invited Voltaire to live at his court for several years. A believer in the king as the "first servant of the state," Frederick the Great was a conscientious ruler who enlarged the Prussian army (to 200,000 men) and kept a strict watch over the bureaucracy.

For a time, Frederick seemed quite willing to make enlightened reforms. He abolished the use of torture except in treason and murder cases and also granted limited freedom of speech and press, as well as complete religious toleration. However, he kept Prussia's rigid social structure and serfdom intact and avoided any additional reforms.

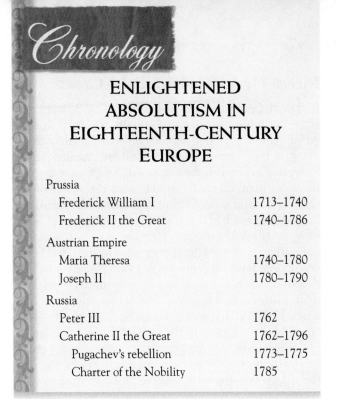

Chronology

ENLIGHTENED ABSOLUTISM IN EIGHTEENTH-CENTURY EUROPE

Prussia	
Frederick William I	1713–1740
Frederick II the Great	1740–1786
Austrian Empire	
Maria Theresa	1740–1780
Joseph II	1780–1790
Russia	
Peter III	1762
Catherine II the Great	1762–1796
Pugachev's rebellion	1773–1775
Charter of the Nobility	1785

The Austrian Empire of the Habsburgs

The Austrian Empire had become one of the great European states by the beginning of the eighteenth century. Yet it was difficult to rule because it was a sprawling empire composed of many different nationalities, languages, religions, and culture (see Map 17.5). Empress Maria Theresa (1740–1780) managed to make administrative reforms that helped centralize the Austrian Empire, but they were done for practical reasons—to strengthen the power of the Habsburg state—and were accompanied by an enlargement and modernization of the armed forces. Maria Theresa remained staunchly conservative and was not open to the wider reform calls of the philosophes. But her successor was.

Joseph II (1780–1790) was determined to make changes. He believed in the need to sweep away anything standing in the path of reason. As he said, "I have made Philosophy the lawmaker of my empire, her logical applications are going to transform Austria." Joseph's reform program was far-reaching. He abolished serfdom, abrogated the death penalty, and established the principle of equality of all before the law. Joseph produced drastic religious reforms as well, including complete religious toleration. Altogether, Joseph II issued six thousand decrees and eleven thousand laws in his effort to transform Austria.

Joseph's reform program proved overwhelming for Austria, however. He alienated the nobility by freeing the serfs and alienated the church by his attacks on the monastic establishment. Even the serfs were unhappy, unable to comprehend the drastic changes inherent in Joseph's policies. Joseph realized his failure when he wrote the epitaph for his own gravestone: "Here lies Joseph II, who was unfortunate in everything that he undertook." His successors undid many of his reforms.

Russia Under Catherine the Great

In Russia, Peter the Great was followed by six weak successors who were put in power and deposed by the palace guard. After a faction of nobles murdered the last of these, Peter III, his German widow emerged as autocrat of all the Russians. Catherine II the Great (1762–1796) was an intelligent woman who was familiar with the works of the philosophes and seemed to favor enlightened reforms. She invited the French philosophe Diderot to Russia and, when he arrived, urged him to speak frankly "as man to man." He did, outlining a far-reaching program of political and financial reform. But Catherine was skeptical about impractical theories, which, she said, "would have turned everything in my kingdom upside down." She did consider the idea of a new law code that would recognize the principle of the equality of all people in the eyes of the law. But in the end she did nothing, knowing that her success depended on the support of the Russian nobility. In 1785, she gave the nobles a charter that exempted them from taxes.

⇒ **CATHERINE THE GREAT.**   Autocrat of Russia, Catherine was an intelligent ruler who favored reform. She found it expedient, however, to retain much of the old system in order to keep the support of the landed nobility. This portrait by Dmitry Levitsky shows her in legislative regalia in the Temple of Justice in 1783.

Catherine's policy of favoring the landed nobility led to even worse conditions for the Russian peasants and a rebellion. Led by an illiterate Cossack, Emelyan Pugachev, the rebellion spread across southern Russia. But the rebellion soon faltered. Pugachev was captured, tortured, and executed. The rebellion collapsed completely, and Catherine responded by even greater measures against the peasantry.

Above all, Catherine proved a worthy successor to Peter the Great in her policies of territorial expansion westward into Poland and southward to the Black Sea. Russia spread southward by defeating the Turks. Russian expansion westward occurred at the expense of neighboring Poland. In three partitions of Poland, Russia gained about 50 percent of Polish territory.

Of the rulers we have discussed, only Joseph II sought truly radical changes based on Enlightenment ideas. Both Frederick II and Catherine II liked to talk about enlightened reforms, and they even attempted some. But the policies of neither seemed seriously affected by Enlightenment thought. Necessities of state and maintenance of the existing system took precedence over reform. Indeed, many historians maintain that Joseph, Frederick, and Catherine were all primarily guided by a concern for the power and well-being of their states. In the final analysis, heightened state power was used to create armies and wage wars to gain more power.

It would be foolish, however, to overlook the fact that the ability of enlightened rulers to make reforms was also limited by political and social realities. Everywhere in Europe, the hereditary aristocracy was still the most powerful class in society. Enlightened reforms were often limited to administrative and judicial measures that did not seriously undermine the powerful interests of the European nobility. As the chief beneficiaries of a system based on traditional rights and privileges for their class, they were not willing to support a political ideology that trumpeted the principle of equal rights for all. The first serious challenge to their supremacy would come in the French Revolution, an event that blew open the door to the modern world of politics.

THE FRENCH REVOLUTION

The year 1789 witnessed two far-reaching events, the beginning of a new United States of America under its revamped Constitution and the eruption of the French Revolution. Compared to the American Revolution a decade earlier, the French Revolution was more complex, more violent, and far more radical in its attempt to reconstruct both a new political and a new social order.

Background to the French Revolution

The root causes of the French Revolution must be sought in the condition of French society. Before the Revolution, France was a society grounded in privilege and

MAP 17.5   Europe in 1763.   By the middle of the eighteenth century, five major powers dominated Europe—Prussia, Austria, Russia, Britain, and France. Each sought to enhance its power both domestically, through a bureaucracy that collected taxes and ran the military, and internationally, by capturing territory or preventing other powers from capturing territory. ➤ *Given the distribution of Prussian and Habsburg holdings, in what areas of Europe were they most likely to compete for land and power?*

inequality. Its population of 27 million was divided, as it had been since the Middle Ages, into three orders or estates.

SOCIAL STRUCTURE OF THE OLD REGIME

The first estate consisted of the clergy and numbered about 130,000 people who owned approximately 10 percent of the land. Clergy were exempt from the *taille*, France's chief tax. Clergy were also radically divided: the higher clergy, stemming from aristocratic families, shared the interests of the nobility, while the parish priests were often poor and from the class of commoners.

The second estate was the nobility, composed of about 350,000 people who owned about 25 to 30 percent of the land. The nobility had continued to play an important and even crucial role in French society in the eighteenth century, holding many of the leading positions in the government, the military, the law courts, and the higher church offices. The nobles sought to expand their power at the expense of the monarchy and to maintain their control over positions in the military, church, and government. Moreover, the possession of privileges remained a hallmark of the nobility. Common to all nobles were tax exemptions, especially from the *taille*.

The third estate, or the commoners of society, constituted the overwhelming majority of the French population. They were divided by vast differences in occupation, level of education, and wealth. The peasants, who alone constituted 75 to 80 percent of the total population, were by far the largest segment of the third estate. They owned about 35 to 40 percent of the land, although their landholdings varied from area to area and over half had little or no land on which to survive. Serfdom no longer existed on any large scale in France, but French peasants still had obligations to their local landlords that they deeply resented. These "relics of feudalism," or aristocratic privileges, were obligations that survived from an earlier age and included the payment of fees for the use of village facilities, such as the flour mill, community oven, and winepress.

Another part of the third estate consisted of skilled craftspeople, shopkeepers, and other wage earners in the cities. In the eighteenth century, a rise in consumer prices greater than the increase in wages left these urban groups with a noticeable decline in purchasing power. Their daily struggle for survival led many of these people to play an important role in the Revolution, especially in Paris.

About 8 percent of the population, or 2.3 million people, constituted the bourgeoisie or middle class, who owned about 20 to 25 percent of the land. This group included merchants, industrialists, and bankers who controlled the resources of trade, manufacturing, and finance and benefited from the economic prosperity after 1730. The bourgeoisie also included professional people—lawyers, holders of public offices, doctors, and writers. Many members of the bourgeoisie had their own set of grievances because they were often excluded from the social and political privileges monopolized by nobles. At the same time, remarkable similarities existed at the upper levels of society between the wealthier bourgeoisie and the nobility. By obtaining public offices, wealthy middle-class individuals could enter the ranks of the nobility. During the eighteenth century, 6,500 new noble families were created.

Moreover, the new political ideas of the Enlightenment proved attractive to both the aristocracy and the bourgeoisie. Both elites, long accustomed to a new socioeconomic reality based on wealth and economic achievement, were increasingly frustrated by a monarchical system resting on privileges and on an old and rigid social order based on the concept of estates. The opposition of these elites to the old order led them ultimately to drastic action against the monarchical regime. In a real sense, the Revolution had its origins in political grievances.

OTHER PROBLEMS FACING THE FRENCH MONARCHY

The inability of the French monarchy to deal with new social realities was exacerbated by specific problems in the 1780s. Although France had enjoyed fifty years of economic expansion, bad harvests in 1787 and 1788 and the beginnings of a manufacturing depression resulted in food shortages, rising prices for food and other goods, and unemployment in the cities. The number of poor, estimated at almost one-third of the population, reached crisis proportions on the eve of the Revolution.

The immediate cause of the French Revolution was the near collapse of government finances. Costly wars and royal extravagance drove French governmental expenditures ever higher. On the verge of a complete financial collapse, the government of Louis XVI (1774–1792) was finally forced to call a meeting of the Estates-General, the French parliamentary body that had not met since 1614. The Estates-General consisted of representatives from the three orders of French society. In the elections for the Estates-General, the government had ruled that the third estate should get double representation (it did, after all, constitute 97 percent of the population). Consequently, while both the first estate (the clergy) and the second estate (the nobility) had about three hundred delegates each, the third estate had almost six hundred representatives, most of whom were lawyers from French towns. To fix France's financial problems, most members of the third estate wanted to set up a constitutional government that would revoke the fiscal privileges of the church and the nobility.

From Estates-General to National Assembly

The Estates-General opened at Versailles on May 5, 1789. It was troubled from the start with the question of whether voting should be by order or by head (each delegate having one vote). Traditionally, each order would vote as a group and have one vote. That meant that the first and second estates could outvote the third estate two to one. The third estate demanded that each deputy have one vote. With the assistance of liberal nobles and clerics, that would give the third estate a majority. When the first estate declared in favor of voting by order, the third estate responded dramatically. On June 17, 1789, the third estate declared itself the "National Assembly" and decided to draw up a constitution. This was the first step in the French Revolution because the third estate had no legal right to act as the National Assembly. But this audacious act was soon in jeopardy, as the king sided with the first estate and threatened to dissolve the Estates-General. Louis XVI now prepared to use force.

The common people, however, saved the third estate from the king's forces. On July 14, a mob of Parisians stormed the Bastille, a royal armory, and proceeded to dismantle it, brick by brick. Louis XVI was soon informed that the royal troops were unreliable. Louis's acceptance of that reality signaled the collapse of royal authority; the king could no longer enforce his will. The fall of the Bastille had saved the National Assembly.

At the same time, popular revolts broke out throughout France, both in the cities and in the countryside. Behind the popular uprising was a growing resentment of the entire landholding system, with its fees and obligations. The fall of the Bastille and the king's apparent capitulation to the demands of the third estate now led peasants to take matters into their own hands. Peasant rebellions occurred throughout France, serving as a backdrop to the Great Fear, a vast panic that spread like wildfire through France between July 20 and August 6. The greatest impact of the agrarian revolts and Great Fear was on the National Assembly meeting in Versailles.

◆◆ STORMING OF THE BASTILLE.   Louis XVI planned to use force to dissolve the Estates-General, but a number of rural and urban uprisings by the common people prevented this action. The fall of the Bastille, pictured here in a painting by an unknown artist, is perhaps the most famous of the urban uprisings.

Destruction of the Old Regime

One of the first acts of the National Assembly was to destroy the relics of feudalism and aristocratic privilege. On the night of August 4, 1789, the National Assembly voted to abolish the rights of landlords and the fiscal exemptions of nobles, clergy, towns, and provinces. On August 26, the National Assembly adopted the Declaration of the Rights of Man and the Citizen (see the box on p. 492). This charter of basic liberties affirmed the demise of aristocratic privileges by proclaiming an end to exemptions from taxation, freedom and equal rights for all men, and access to public office based on talent. All citizens were to have the right to take part in the legislative process. Freedom of speech and the press were coupled with the outlawing of arbitrary arrests.

The declaration also raised another important issue. Did its ideal of equal rights for all men also include women? Many deputies insisted that it did, provided that, as one said, "women do not hope to exercise political rights and functions." Olympe de Gouges, a playwright, refused to accept this exclusion of women from political rights. Echoing the words of the official declaration, she penned the Declaration of the Rights of Woman and the Female Citizen, in which she insisted that women should have all the same rights as men (see the box on p. 493). The National Assembly ignored her demands.

In the meantime, Louis XVI, who had remained inactive at Versailles, refused to accept the decrees on the abolition of feudalism and the declaration of rights. On October 5, thousands of Parisian women, described by one

DECLARATION OF THE RIGHTS OF MAN AND THE CITIZEN

One of the important documents of the French Revolution, the Declaration of the Rights of Man and the Citizen was adopted in August 1789 by the National Assembly. The declaration affirmed that "men are born and remain free and equal in rights," that governments must protect these natural rights, and that political power is derived from the people.

DECLARATION OF THE RIGHTS OF MAN AND THE CITIZEN

The representatives of the French people, organized as a national assembly, considering that ignorance, neglect, and scorn of the rights of man are the sole causes of public misfortunes and of corruption of governments, have resolved to display in a solemn declaration the natural, inalienable, and sacred rights of man, so that this declaration, constantly in the presence of all members of society, will continually remind them of their rights and their duties. . . . Consequently, the National Assembly recognizes and declares, in the presence and under the auspices of the Supreme Being, the following rights of man and citizen:

1. Men are born and remain free and equal in rights; social distinctions can be established only for the common benefit.
2. The aim of every political association is the conservation of the natural and imprescriptible rights of man; these rights are liberty, property, security, and resistance to oppression.
3. The source of all sovereignty is located in essence in the nation; no body, no individual can exercise authority which does not emanate from it expressly.
4. Liberty consists in being able to do anything that does not harm another person. . . .
6. The law is the expression of the general will; all citizens have the right to concur personally or through their representatives in its formation; it must be the same for all, whether it protects or punishes. All citizens being equal in its eyes are equally admissible to all honors, positions, and public employments, according to their capabilities and without other distinctions than those of their virtues and talents.
7. No man can be accused, arrested, or detained except in cases determined by the law, and according to the forms which it has prescribed. . . .
10. No one may be disturbed because of his opinions, even religious, provided that their public demonstration does not disturb the public order established by law.
11. The free communication of thoughts and opinions is one of the most precious rights of man: every citizen can therefore freely speak, write, and print. . . .
12. The guaranteeing of the rights of man and citizen necessitates a public force; this force is therefore instituted for the advantage of all, and not for the private use of those to whom it is entrusted. . . .
14. Citizens have the right to determine for themselves or through their representatives the need for taxation of the public, to consent to it freely, to investigate its use, and to determine its rate, basis, collection, and duration.
15. Society has the right to demand an accounting of his administration from every public agent.
16. Any society in which guarantees of rights are not assured nor the separation of powers determined has no constitution.
17. Property being an inviolable and sacred right, no one may be deprived of it unless public necessity, legally determined, clearly requires such action, and then only on condition of a just and prior indemnity.

---

eyewitness as "detachments of women . . . armed with broomsticks, lances, pitchforks, swords, pistols and muskets," marched to Versailles and forced the king to accept the new decrees. The crowd now insisted that the royal family return to Paris. On October 6, the king complied. As a goodwill gesture, he brought along wagonloads of flour from the palace stores, escorted by women armed with pikes (some of which held the severed heads of the king's guards) singing, "We are bringing back the baker, the baker's wife, and the baker's boy" (the king, queen, and their son). The king became virtually a prisoner in Paris.

Because the Catholic church was seen as an important pillar of the old order, it too was reformed. Most of the lands of the church were seized. The new Civil Constitution of the Clergy was put into effect. Both bishops and priests were to be elected by the people and paid by the state. The Catholic church, still an important institution in the life of the French people, now became an enemy of the Revolution.

By 1791, the National Assembly had finally completed a new constitution that established a limited constitutional monarchy. There was still a monarch (now called "king of the French"), but the new Legislative Assembly was to make the laws. The Legislative Assembly, in which sovereign power was vested, was to sit for two years and consist of 745 representatives chosen by an indirect system of election that preserved power in the hands of the more affluent members of society. Only active citizens (men over the age of twenty-five paying in taxes the equivalent of three days' unskilled

DECLARATION OF THE RIGHTS OF WOMAN AND THE FEMALE CITIZEN

Olympe de Gouges (a pen name for Marie Gouze) was a butcher's daughter who wrote plays and pamphlets. She argued that the Declaration of the Rights of Man and the Citizen did not apply to women and composed her own Declaration of the Rights of Woman.

DECLARATION OF THE RIGHTS OF WOMAN AND THE FEMALE CITIZEN

Mothers, daughters, sisters and representatives of the nation demand to be constituted into a national assembly. Believing that ignorance, omission, or scorn for the rights of woman are the only causes of public misfortunes and of the corruption of governments, the women have resolved to set forth in a solemn declaration the natural, inalienable, and sacred rights of woman in order that this declaration, constantly exposed before all the members of the society, will ceaselessly remind them of their rights and duties. . . .

Consequently, the sex that is as superior in beauty as it is in courage during the sufferings of maternity recognizes and declares in the presence and under the auspices of the Supreme Being, the following Rights of Woman and of Female Citizens.

1. Woman is born free and lives equal to man in her rights. Social distinctions can be based only on the common utility.

2. The purpose of any political association is the conservation of the natural and imprescriptible rights of woman and man; these rights are liberty, property, security, and especially resistance to oppression.

3. The principle of all sovereignty rests essentially with the nation, which is nothing but the union of woman and man; no body and no individual can exercise any authority which does not come expressly from [the nation].

4. Liberty and justice consist of restoring all that belongs to others; thus, the only limits on the exercise of the natural rights of woman are perpetual male tyranny; these limits are to be reformed by the laws of nature and reason. . . .

6. The law must be the expression of the general will; all female and male citizens must contribute either personally or through their representatives to its formation; it must be the same for all: male and female citizens, being equal in the eyes of the law, must be equally admitted to all honors, positions, and public employment according to their capacity and without other distinctions besides those of their virtues and talents.

7. No woman is an exception; she is accused, arrested, and detained in cases determined by law. . . .

10. No one is to be disquieted for his very basic opinions; woman has the right to mount the scaffold; she must equally have the right to mount the rostrum, provided that her demonstrations do not disturb the legally established public order.

11. The free communication of thoughts and opinions is one of the most precious rights of woman, since that liberty assured the recognition of children by their fathers. . . .

12. The guarantee of the rights of woman and the female citizen implies a major benefit; this guarantee must be instituted for the advantage of all, and not for the particular benefit of those to whom it is entrusted. . . .

14. Female and male citizens have the right to verify, either by themselves or through their representatives, the necessity of the public contribution. This can only apply to women if they are granted an equal share, not only of wealth, but also of public administration, and in the determination of the proportion, the base, the collection, and the duration of the tax.

15. The collectivity of women, joined for tax purposes to the aggregate of men, has the right to demand an accounting of his administration from any public agent.

16. No society has a constitution without the guarantee of rights and the separation of powers; the constitution is null if the majority of individuals comprising the nation have not cooperated in drafting it.

17. Property belongs to both sexes whether united or separate; for each it is an inviolable and sacred right; no one can be deprived of it, since it is the true patrimony of nature.

---

labor) could vote for electors (men paying taxes equal in value to ten days' labor). This relatively small group of fifty thousand electors then chose the deputies.

By 1791, the old order had been destroyed. However, many people—including Catholic priests, nobles, lower classes hurt by a rise in the cost of living, peasants who remained opposed to dues that had still not been abandoned, and political clubs like the Jacobins who offered more radical solutions to France's problems—opposed the new order. The king also made things difficult for the new government when he sought to flee France in June 1791 and almost succeeded before being recognized, captured, and brought back to Paris. In this unsettled situation, under a discredited and seemingly disloyal monarch, the new Legislative Assembly held its first session in October 1791. France's relations with the rest of Europe soon led to Louis's downfall.

On August 27, 1791, the monarchs of Austria and Prussia, fearing that revolution would spread to their countries, invited other European monarchs to use force to reestablish monarchical authority in France. Insulted by this threat, the Legislative Assembly declared war on Austria on April 20, 1792. The French fared badly in the initial fighting, and a frantic search for scapegoats began. As one observer noted, "Everywhere you hear the cry that the king is betraying us, the generals are betraying us, that nobody is to be trusted; . . . that Paris will be taken in six weeks by the Austrians. . . . We are on a volcano ready to spout flames."[5] Defeats in war coupled with economic shortages in the spring led to renewed political demonstrations, especially against the king. In August 1792, radical political groups in Paris took the king captive and forced the Legislative Assembly to suspend the monarchy and call for a national convention, chosen on the basis of universal male suffrage, to decide on the future form of government. The French Revolution was about to enter a more radical stage.

The Radical Revolution

In September 1792, the newly elected National Convention began its sessions. Dominated by lawyers and other professionals, two-thirds of its deputies were under forty-five, and almost all had gained political experience as a result of the Revolution. Almost all distrusted the king. As a result, the convention's first step on September 21 was to abolish the monarchy and establish a republic. On January 21, 1793, the king was executed, and the destruction of the old regime was complete. There could be no turning back. But the execution of the king created new enemies for the Revolution both at home and abroad while strengthening those who were already its enemies.

In Paris, the local government, known as the Commune, whose leaders came from the working classes, favored radical change and put constant pressure on the convention, pushing it to ever more radical positions. Moreover, the National Convention still did not rule all of France. Peasants in the west and inhabitants of France's major provincial cities refused to accept the authority of the convention.

A foreign crisis also loomed large. By the beginning of 1793, after the king had been executed, most of Europe—an informal coalition of Austria, Prussia, Spain, Portugal, Britain, the Dutch Republic, and even Russia—aligned militarily against France. Grossly overextended, the French armies began to experience reverses, and by late spring France was threatened with invasion. If successful, both the Revolution and the revolutionaries would be destroyed and the old regime reestablished.

A NATION IN ARMS

To meet these crises, the convention gave broad powers to an executive committee of twelve known as the Committee of Public Safety, which came to be dominated by Maximilien Robespierre. For a twelve-month period, from 1793 to 1794, the Committee of Public Safety took control of France. To save the Republic from its foreign foes, the committee decreed a universal mobilization of the nation on August 23, 1793:

> Young men will fight, young men are called to conquer. Married men will forge arms, transport military baggage and guns and will prepare food supplies. Women, who at long last are to take their rightful place in the revolution and follow their true destiny, will forget their futile tasks: their delicate hands will work at making clothes for soldiers; they will make tents and

➤ **WOMEN PATRIOTS.** Women played a variety of roles in the events of the French Revolution. This picture shows a women's patriotic club discussing the decrees of the National Convention, an indication that some women became highly politicized by the upheavals of the Revolution.

JUSTICE IN THE REIGN OF TERROR

The Reign of Terror created a repressive environment in which revolutionary courts often acted quickly to condemn traitors to the revolutionary cause. In this account, an English visitor describes the court, the procession to the scene of execution, and the final execution procedure.

J. G. MILLIGEN, *THE REVOLUTIONARY TRIBUNAL* (PARIS, OCTOBER 1793)

In the center of the hall, under a statue of Justice, holding scales in one hand, and a sword in the other, sat Dumas, the President, with the other judges. Under them were seated the public accuser, Fourquier-Tinville, and his scribes. . . . To the right were benches on which the accused were placed in several rows, and *gendarmes* with carbines and fixed bayonets by their sides. To the left was the jury.

Never can I forget the mournful appearance of these funereal processions to the place of execution. The march was opened by a detachment of mounted *gendarmes*—the carts followed; they were the same carts as those that are used in Paris for carrying wood; four boards were placed across them for seats, and on each board sat two, and sometimes three victims; their hands were tied behind their backs, and the constant jostling of the cart made them nod their heads up and down, to the great amusement of the spectators. On the front of the cart stood Samson, the executioner, or one of his sons or assistants; *gendarmes* on foot marched by the side; then followed a hackney, in which was the reporting clerk, whose duty it was to witness the execution, and then return to the public accuser's office to report the execution of what they called the law.

The process of execution was also a sad and heart-rending spectacle. In the middle of the Place de la Revolution was erected a guillotine, in front of a colossal statue of Liberty, represented seated on a rock, a cap on her head, a spear in her hand, the other reposing on a shield. On one side of the scaffold were drawn out a sufficient number of carts, with large baskets painted red, to receive the heads and bodies of the victims. Those bearing the condemned moved on slowly to the foot of the guillotine; the culprits were led out in turn, and if necessary, supported by two of the executioner's assistants, but their assistance was rarely required. Most of these unfortunates ascended the scaffold with a determined step— many of them looked up firmly on the menacing instrument of death, beholding for the last time the rays of the glorious sun, beaming on the polished axe: and I have seen some young men actually dance a few steps before they went up to be strapped to the perpendicular plane, which was then tilted to a horizontal plane in a moment, and ran on the grooves until the neck was secured and closed in by a moving board, when the head passed through what was called, in derision, "the republican toilet seat"; the weighty knife was then dropped with a heavy fall; and, with incredible dexterity and rapidity, two executioners tossed the body into the basket, while another threw the head after it.

---

they will extend their tender care to shelters where the defenders of the *Patrie* [nation] will receive the help that their wounds require. Children will make lint of old cloth. It is for them that we are fighting: children, those beings destined to gather all the fruits of the revolution, will raise their pure hands toward the skies. And old men, performing their missions again, as of yore, will be guided to the public squares of the cities where they will kindle the courage of young warriors and preach the doctrines of hate for kings and the unity of the Republic.[6]

In less than a year, the French revolutionary government had raised an army of 650,000; by September 1794, it numbered 1,169,000. The Republic's army was the largest ever seen in European history. It now pushed the allies back across the Rhine and even conquered the Austrian Netherlands.

The French revolutionary army was an important step in the creation of modern nationalism. Previously, wars had been fought between governments or ruling dynasties by relatively small armies of professional soldiers. The new French army was the creation of a "people's" government; its wars were now "people's" wars. The entire nation was to be involved in the war. But when dynastic wars became people's wars, warfare increased in ferocity and lack of restraint. The wars of the French revolutionary era opened the door to the total war of the modern world.

REIGN OF TERROR

To meet the domestic crisis, the National Convention and the Committee of Public Safety launched the "Reign of Terror." Revolutionary courts were instituted to protect the Republic from its internal enemies. In the course of nine months, sixteen thousand people were officially killed under the blade of the guillotine—a revolutionary device for the quick and efficient separation of heads from bodies (see the box above). Most of the Terror's executions occurred in places that had rebelled against the authority of the National Convention. The Committee of Public Safety held that this bloodletting was only temporary. Once the war and the domestic emergency were over, they would be succeeded by a "republic of virtue" in which the Declaration of the Rights of the Man and the Citizen would be fully implemented.

Revolutionary armies were set up to bring recalcitrant cities and districts back under the control of the National Convention. The Committee of Public Safety decided to make an example of Lyons, which had defied the authority of the National Convention. By April 1794, some 1,880 citizens of Lyons had been executed. When the guillotine proved too slow, cannon fire was used to blow condemned men into open graves. A German observed:

> Whole ranges of houses, always the most handsome, burnt. The churches, convents, and all the dwellings of the former patricians were in ruins. When I came to the guillotine, the blood of those who had been executed a few hours beforehand was still running in the street. . . . I said to a group of sansculottes [radicals] that it would be decent to clear away all this human blood. Why should it be cleared? one of them said to me. It's the blood of aristocrats and rebels. The dogs should lick it up.[7]

The National Convention also pursued a policy of dechristianization. A new calendar was instituted in which years were no longer numbered from the birth of Christ but from September 22, 1792, the first day of the French Republic. The new calendar also eliminated Sundays and church holidays. In Paris, the cathedral of Notre-Dame was designated the Temple of Reason; in November 1793, a public ceremony dedicated to the worship of reason was held in the former cathedral in which patriotic maidens adorned in white dresses paraded before a "temple of reason" where the high altar once stood.

EQUALITY AND SLAVERY

Early in the French Revolution, the desire for equality led to a discussion of what to do about slavery. A club called Friends of the Blacks advocated the abolition of slavery, which was achieved in France in September 1791. However, French planters in the West Indies, who profited greatly from the use of slaves on their sugar plantations, opposed the abolition of slavery in the French colonies. When the National Convention came into power, the issue was revisited, and on February 4, 1794, guided by ideals of equality, the government abolished slavery in the colonies.

In one French colony, slaves had already rebelled for their freedom. In 1791, black slaves in the French sugar colony of Saint Domingue (the western third of the island of Hispaniola), inspired by the ideals of the revolution occurring in France, revolted against French plantation owners. Led by Toussaint L'Ouverture (1746–1803), a son of African slaves, over 100,000 black slaves rose in revolt and seized control of all of Hispaniola. Later, an army sent by Napoleon captured L'Ouverture, who died in captivity in France. But the French soldiers, weakened by disease, soon succumbed to the slave forces. On January 1, 1804, the western part of Hispaniola, now called Haiti, announced its freedom and became the first independent state in Latin America. One of the French revolutionary ideals had triumphed abroad.

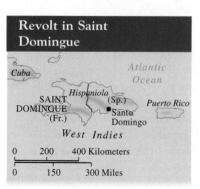

Revolt in Saint Domingue

Reaction and the Directory

By the summer of 1794, the French had been successful on the battlefield against their foreign foes, making the Terror less necessary. But the Terror continued because Robespierre, who had become a figure of power and authority, became obsessed with purifying the body politic of all the corrupt. Many deputies in the National Convention were fearful, however, that they were not safe while Robespierre was free to act and gathered enough votes to condemn him. Robespierre was guillotined on July 28, 1794.

After the death of Robespierre, a reaction set in as more moderate middle-class leaders took control. The Reign of Terror came to a halt, and the National Convention reduced the power of the Committee of Public Safety. Churches were allowed to reopen for public worship. In

NAPOLEON AND PSYCHOLOGICAL WARFARE

In 1796, at the age of twenty-seven, Napoleon Bonaparte was given command of the French army in Italy, where he won a series of stunning victories. His use of speed, deception, and surprise to overwhelm his opponents is well known. In this selection from a proclamation to his troops in Italy, Napoleon also appears as a master of psychological warfare.

NAPOLEON BONAPARTE, PROCLAMATION TO FRENCH TROOPS IN ITALY (APRIL 26, 1796)

Soldiers:

In a fortnight you have won six victories, taken twenty-one standards [flags of military units], fifty-five pieces of artillery, several strong positions, and conquered the richest part of Piedmont [in northern Italy]; you have captured 15,000 prisoners and killed or wounded more than 10,000 men.... You have won battles without cannon, crossed rivers without bridges, made forced marches without shoes, camped without brandy and often without bread. Soldiers of liberty, only republican troops could have endured what you have endured. Soldiers, you have our thanks! The grateful Patrie [nation] will owe its prosperity to you....

The two armies which but recently attacked you with audacity are fleeing before you in terror; the wicked men who laughed at your misery and rejoiced at the thought of the triumphs of your enemies are confounded and trembling.

But, soldiers, as yet you have done nothing compared with what remains to be done.... Undoubtedly the greatest obstacles have been overcome; but you still have battles to fight, cities to capture, rivers to cross. Is there one among you whose courage is abating? No.... All of you are consumed with a desire to extend the glory of the French people; all of you long to humiliate those arrogant kings who dare to contemplate placing us in fetters; all of you desire to dictate a glorious peace, one which will indemnify the Patrie for the immense sacrifices it has made; all of you wish to be able to say with pride as you return to your villages, "I was with the victorious army of Italy!"

---

addition, a new constitution was created in August 1795 that reflected the desire for a stability that did not sacrifice the ideals of 1789. Five directors—the Directory—acted as the executive authority.

The period of the Revolution under the government of the Directory (1795–1799) was an era of stagnation and corruption, a materialistic reaction to the sacrifices that had been demanded in the Reign of Terror. At the same time, the government of the Directory faced political enemies from both the left and the right of the political spectrum. On the right, royalists who wanted to restore the monarchy continued their agitation. On the left, radical hopes of power were revived by continuing economic problems. Battered from both sides, unable to solve the country's economic problems, and still carrying on the wars inherited from the Committee of Public Safety, the Directory increasingly relied on the military to maintain its power. This led to a coup d'état in 1799 in which the popular military general Napoleon Bonaparte seized power.

THE AGE OF NAPOLEON

Napoleon dominated both French and European history from 1799 to 1815. He was born in 1769 in Corsica shortly after France had annexed the island. The young Napoleon was sent to France to study in one of the new military schools and was a lieutenant when the Revolution broke out in 1789. The Revolution and the European war that followed gave him new opportunities, and Napoleon rose quickly through the ranks. In 1794, at the age of only twenty-five, he was made a brigadier general by the Committee of Public Safety. Two years later, he commanded the French armies in Italy, where he won a series of victories and returned to France as a conquering hero (see the box above). After a disastrous expedition to Egypt, Napoleon returned to Paris, where he participated in the coup that gave him control of France. He was only thirty years old.

After the coup of 1799, a new form of the Republic—called the Consulate—was proclaimed in which Napoleon, as first consul, controlled the entire executive authority of government. He had overwhelming influence over the legislature, appointed members of the administrative bureaucracy, commanded the army, and conducted foreign affairs. In 1802, Napoleon was made consul for life, and in 1804, he returned France to monarchy when he had himself crowned as Emperor Napoleon I.

Domestic Policies

One of Napoleon's first domestic policies was to establish peace with the oldest and most implacable enemy of the Revolution, the Catholic church. In 1801, Napoleon arranged a concordat with the pope that recognized Catholicism as the religion of a majority of the French people. In return, the pope agreed not to raise the question of the church lands confiscated in the Revolution. As a result of the concordat, the Catholic church was no longer an enemy of the French government, and those

THE CORONATION OF NAPOLEON.   In 1804, Napoleon restored monarchy to France when he had himself crowned as emperor. In the coronation scene painted by Jacques-Louis David, Napoleon is shown crowning his wife, the empress Josephine, while the pope looks on. The painting shows Napoleon's mother seated in the box in the background, even though she was not at the ceremony.

who had acquired church lands during the Revolution were assured that they would not be stripped of them, an assurance that made them supporters of the Napoleonic regime.

Napoleon's most enduring domestic achievement was his codification of the laws. Before the Revolution, France had some three hundred local legal systems. During the Revolution, efforts were made to prepare a single code of laws for the entire nation, but it remained for Napoleon to bring the work to completion in the famous Civil Code. This preserved most of the revolutionary gains by recognizing the principle of the equality of all citizens before the law, the abolition of serfdom and feudalism, and religious toleration. Property rights were protected, and the interests of employers were safeguarded by outlawing trade unions and strikes.

At the same time, the Civil Code strictly curtailed the rights of some people. During the radical phase of the French Revolution, new laws had made divorce an easy process for both husbands and wives and allowed sons and daughters to inherit property equally. Napoleon's Civil

Code undid these laws. Divorce was still allowed but was made more difficult for women to obtain. Women were now "less equal than men" in other ways as well. When they married, their property came under the control of their husbands, and in lawsuits, they were treated as minors.

Napoleon also developed a powerful, centralized administrative machine and worked hard to develop a bureaucracy of capable officials. Early on, the regime showed that it cared little whether the expertise of officials had been acquired in royal or revolutionary bureaucracies. Promotion, whether in civil or military offices, was to be based not on rank or birth but on ability only. This principle of a government career open to talent was, of course, what many bourgeois had wanted before the Revolution.

In his domestic policies, then, Napoleon both destroyed and preserved aspects of the Revolution. Liberty had been replaced by an initially benevolent despotism that grew increasingly arbitrary as the demands of war overwhelmed Napoleon and the French. The Civil Code, however, preserved the equality of all citizens before the law. The concept of careers open to talent was also a gain of the Revolution that Napoleon preserved.

Napoleon's Empire and the European Response

When Napoleon became consul in 1799, France was at war with a second European coalition of Russia, Great Britain, and Austria. Napoleon realized the need for a pause and made a peace treaty in 1802. But war was renewed in 1803 with Britain, who was soon joined by Austria, Russia, and Prussia in the Third Coalition. In a series of battles from 1805 to 1807, Napoleon's Grand Army defeated the Austrian, Prussian, and Russian armies,

giving Napoleon the opportunity to create a new European order.

THE GRAND EMPIRE

From 1807 to 1812, Napoleon was the master of Europe. His Grand Empire was composed of three major parts: the French Empire, dependent states, and allied states (see Map 17.6). The French Empire, the inner core of the Grand Empire, consisted of an enlarged France extending to the Rhine in the east and including the western half of Italy north of Rome. Dependent states were kingdoms under the rule of Napoleon's relatives; these came to include Spain, the Netherlands, the kingdom of Italy, the Swiss Republic, the Grand Duchy of Warsaw, and the

MAP 17.6 Napoleon's Grand Empire.   Napoleon's Grand Army won a series of victories against Britain, Austria, Prussia, and Russia that gave the French emperor full or partial control over much of Europe by 1807. ➢ *On the Continent, what is the overall relationship between distance from France and degree of French control, and how can you account for this?*

Confederation of the Rhine (a union of all German states except Austria and Prussia). Allied states were those defeated by Napoleon and forced to join his struggle against Britain; these included Prussia, Austria, Russia, and Sweden.

Within his empire, Napoleon sought acceptance of certain revolutionary principles, including legal equality, religious toleration, and economic freedom. As he explained to his brother Jerome after he had made him king of the new German state of Westphalia:

> What the people of Germany desire most impatiently is that talented commoners should have the same right to your esteem and to public employments as the nobles, that any trace of serfdom and of an intermediate hierarchy between the sovereign and the lowest class of the people should be completely abolished. The benefits of the Code Napoléon, the publicity of judicial procedure, the creation of juries must be so many distinguishing marks of your monarchy.... What nation would wish to return under the arbitrary Prussian government once it had tasted the benefits of a wise and liberal administration? The peoples of Germany, the peoples of France, of Italy, of Spain all desire equality and liberal ideas. I have guided the affairs of Europe for many years now, and I have had occasion to convince myself that the buzzing of the privileged classes is contrary to the general opinion. Be a constitutional king.[8]

In the inner core and dependent states of his Grand Empire, Napoleon tried to destroy the old order. Nobility and clergy everywhere in these states lost their special privileges. He decreed equality of opportunity with offices open to talent, equality before the law, and religious toleration. This spread of French revolutionary principles was an important factor in the development of liberal traditions in these countries.

Napoleon hoped that his Grand Empire would last for centuries; it collapsed almost as rapidly as it had been formed. Two major reasons explain this: Great Britain and nationalism. As long as Britain ruled the waves, it was not subject to military attack. Napoleon hoped to invade Britain, but he could not overcome the British navy's decisive defeat of a combined French-Spanish fleet at Trafalgar in 1805. To defeat Britain, Napoleon turned to his Continental System. Put into effect between 1806 and 1808, it attempted to prevent British goods from reaching the European continent in order to weaken Britain economically and destroy its capacity to wage war. But the Continental System failed. Allied states resented it; some began to cheat and others to resist. New markets in the Middle East and in Latin America gave Britain new outlets for its goods. Indeed, by 1809, British overseas exports were at near-record highs.

The second important factor in the defeat of Napoleon was nationalism. This political creed had arisen during the French Revolution in the French people's emphasis on solidarity against other peoples. Nationalism involved the

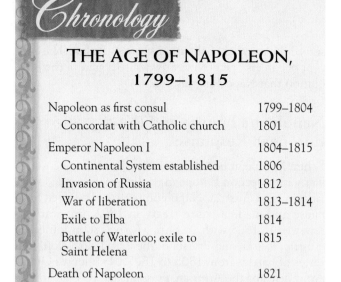

Chronology

THE AGE OF NAPOLEON, 1799–1815

Napoleon as first consul	1799–1804
Concordat with Catholic church	1801
Emperor Napoleon I	1804–1815
Continental System established	1806
Invasion of Russia	1812
War of liberation	1813–1814
Exile to Elba	1814
Battle of Waterloo; exile to Saint Helena	1815
Death of Napoleon	1821

unique cultural identity of a people based on common language and national symbols. French nationalism had made possible the mass armies of the revolutionary and Napoleonic eras. But Napoleon's conquests aroused nationalism in two ways: by making the French hated oppressors and thus arousing the patriotism of others in opposition to French nationalism and by showing the people of Europe what nationalism was and what a nation in arms could do. It was a lesson not lost on other peoples and rulers. A Spanish uprising against Napoleon's rule, aided by British support, kept a French force of 200,000 pinned down for years.

THE FALL OF NAPOLEON

The beginning of Napoleon's downfall came in 1812 with his invasion of Russia. The refusal of the Russians to remain in the Continental System left Napoleon with little choice. Although aware of the risks in invading such a huge country, he also knew that if the Russians were allowed to challenge the Continental System unopposed, others would soon follow suit. In June 1812, he led his Grand Army of more than 600,000 men into Russia. Napoleon's hopes for victory depended on quickly defeating the Russian armies, but the Russian forces retreated and refused to give battle, torching their own villages and countryside to keep Napoleon's army from finding food. When the Russians did stop to fight at Borodino, Napoleon's forces won an indecisive and costly victory. When the remaining troops of the Grand Army arrived in Moscow, they found the city ablaze. Lacking food and supplies, Napoleon abandoned Moscow late in October and made a retreat across Russia in terrible winter conditions. Only 40,000 of the original 600,000 men managed to arrive back in Poland in January 1813.

This military disaster led other European states to rise up and attack the crippled French army. Paris was captured in March 1814, and Napoleon was sent into exile on the island of Elba, off the coast of Italy. Meanwhile, the Bourbon monarchy was restored in the person of Louis XVIII, the Count of Provence, brother of the executed king. Louis XVII, son of Louis XVI, had died in prison at age 10. Napoleon, bored on Elba, slipped back into France. When troops were sent to capture him, Napoleon opened his coat and addressed them: "Soldiers of the 5th regiment, I am your Emperor. . . . If there is a man among you would kill his Emperor, here I am!" No one fired a shot. Shouting "Vive l'Empereur! Vive l'Empereur," the troops went over to his side, and Napoleon entered Paris in triumph on March 20, 1815.

The powers that had defeated him pledged once more to fight him. Having decided to strike first at his enemies, Napoleon raised yet another army and moved to attack the allied forces stationed in what is now Belgium. At Waterloo on June 18, Napoleon met a combined British and Prussian army under the duke of Wellington and suffered a bloody defeat. This time, the victorious allies exiled him to Saint Helena, a small, forsaken island in the South Atlantic. Only Napoleon's memory continued to haunt French political life.

CONCLUSION

Everywhere in Europe at the beginning of the eighteenth century, the old order remained strong. Nobles, clerics, towns, and provinces all had privileges. Everywhere in the eighteenth century, monarchs sought to enlarge their bureaucracies to raise taxes to support the large standing armies that had originated in the seventeenth century. The existence of five great powers, with two of them (France and England) embattled in the East and in the Western Hemisphere, ushered in a new scale of conflict; the Seven Years' War can legitimately be viewed as the first world war. Although the wars changed little on the European continent, British victories enabled Great Britain to emerge as the world's greatest naval and colonial power. Everywhere

in Europe, increased demands for taxes to support these conflicts led to attacks on the privileged orders and a desire for change not met by the ruling monarchs. At the same time, sustained population growth and dramatic changes in finance, trade, and industry created tensions that undermined the traditional foundations of the old order. The inability of that old order to deal meaningfully with these changes led to a revolutionary outburst at the end of the eighteenth century that brought the old order to an end.

The revolutionary era of the late eighteenth century was a time of dramatic political transformations. Revolutionary upheavals, beginning in North America and continuing in France, spurred movements for political liberty and equality. The documents promulgated by these revolutions, the Declaration of Independence and the Declaration of the Rights of Man and the Citizen, embodied the fundamental ideas of the Enlightenment and created a liberal political agenda based on a belief in popular sovereignty—the people as the source of political power—and the principles of liberty and equality. Liberty meant, in theory, freedom from arbitrary power as well as the freedom to think, write, and worship as one chose. Equality meant equality in rights and equality of opportunity based on talent rather than wealth or status at birth. In practice, equality remained limited; property owners had greater opportunities for voting and officeholding, and women were still not treated as the equals of men.

The French Revolution set in motion a modern revolutionary concept. No one had foreseen or consciously planned the upheaval that began in 1789, but thereafter, radicals and revolutionaries knew that mass uprisings by the common people could overthrow unwanted elitist governments. For these people, the French Revolution became a symbol of hope; for those who feared such changes, it became a symbol of dread. The French Revolution became the classical political and social model for revolution. At the same time, the liberal and national political ideals created by the Revolution dominated the political landscape for well over a century. A new era had begun, and the world would never be the same.

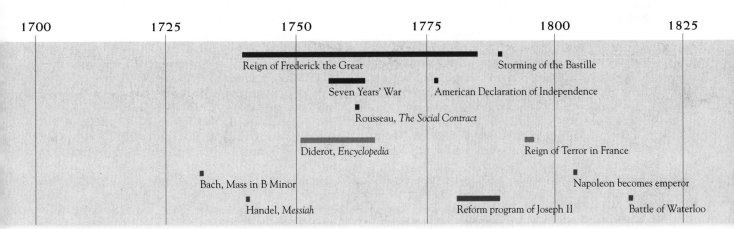

CHAPTER NOTES

1. Quoted in Dorinda Outram, *The Enlightenment* (Cambridge, 1995), p. 67.
2. John Locke, *An Essay Concerning Human Understanding* (New York, 1964), pp. 89–90.
3. Kenneth Clark, *Civilization* (New York, 1969), p. 231.
4. Quoted in Peter Burke, *Popular Culture in Early Modern Europe* (New York, 1978), p. 179.
5. Quoted in William Doyle, *The Oxford History of the French Revolution* (Oxford, 1989), p. 184.

6. Quoted in Leo Gershoy, *The Era of the French Revolution* (Princeton, N.J., 1957), p. 157.
7. Quoted in Doyle, *Oxford History of the French Revolution*, p. 254.
8. Quoted in J. Christopher Herold, ed., *The Mind of Napoleon* (New York, 1955), pp. 74–75.

SUGGESTED READING

Two sound, comprehensive surveys of eighteenth-century Europe are I. Woloch, *Eighteenth-Century Europe* (New York, 1982), and M. S. Anderson, *Europe in the Eighteenth Century* (London, 1987).

Good introductions to the Enlightenment can be found in N. Hampson, *A Cultural History of the Enlightenment* (New York, 1968); U. Im Hof, *The Enlightenment* (Oxford, 1994); D. Goodman, *The Republic of Letters: A Cultural History of the French Enlightenment* (Ithaca, N.Y., 1994); and D. Outram, The Enlightenment (Cambridge, 1995). A more detailed synthesis can be found in the two volumes by P. Gay, *The Enlightenment: An Interpretation* (New York, 1966–1969). For a short, popular survey on the French philosophes, see F. Artz, *The Enlightenment in France* (Kent, Ohio, 1968). On women in the eighteenth century, see N. Z. Davis and A. Farge, eds., *A History of Women: Renaissance and Enlightenment Paradoxes* (Cambridge, Mass., 1993), and O. Hufton, *The Prospect Before Her: A History of Women in Western Europe, 1500–1800* (New York, 1998).

A readable general survey on the arts and literature is M. Levy, *Rococo to Revolution* (London, 1966). An important study on popular culture is P. Burke, *Popular Culture in Early Modern Europe* (New York, 1978).

On the European nobility in the eighteenth century, see J. Dewald, *The European Nobility 1400–1800* (Cambridge, 1996), and H. M. Scott, *The European Nobility in the Seventeenth and Eighteenth Centuries* (London, 1995). On European cities, see J. de Vries, *European Urbanization, 1500–1800* (Cambridge, Mass., 1984). The warfare of this period is examined in M. S. Anderson, *War and Society in Europe of the Old Regime, 1615–1789* (New York, 1988).

For a brief survey of Latin America, see E. B. Burns, *Latin America: A Concise Interpretive History*, 4th ed. (Englewood Cliffs, N.J., 1986). More detailed works on colonial Latin American history include S. J. Stein and B. H. Stein, *The Colonial Heritage of Latin America* (New York, 1970), and J. Lockhardt and S. B. Schwartz, *Early Latin America: A History of Colonial Spanish America and Brazil* (New York, 1983). A history of the revolutionary era in America can be found in R. Middlekauff, *The Glorious Cause: The American Revolution, 1763–1789* (New York, 1982), and C. Bonwick, *The American Revolution* (Charlottesville, Va., 1991). The importance of ideology is treated in G. Wood, *The Radicalism of the American Revolution* (New York, 1992). For an interesting comparative study, see the stimulating work by P. Higonnet, *Sister Republics: Origins of the French and American Revolutions* (Cambridge, Mass., 1988).

On enlightened absolutism, see H. M. Scott, ed., Enlightened *Absolutism: Reform and Reformers in Late Eighteenth-Century Europe* (Ann Arbor, Mich., 1990). Good biographies of some of Europe's monarchs include R. Asprey, *Frederick the Great: The Magnificent Enigma* (New York, 1986); I. De Madariaga, *Catherine the Great: A Short History* (New Haven, Conn., 1990); and T. C. W. Blanning, *Joseph II* (New York, 1994).

A well written, up-to-date introduction to the French Revolution can be found in W. Doyle, *The Oxford History of the French Revolution* (Oxford, 1989). For the entire revolutionary and Napoleonic eras, see O. Connelly, *The French Revolution and Napoleonic Era*, 3d ed. (Fort Worth, Tex., 2000), and D. M. G. Sutherland, *France, 1789–1815: Revolution and Counter-Revolution* (London, 1985). Two brief works are A. Forrest, *The French Revolution* (Oxford, 1995), and J. M. Roberts, *The French Revolution*, 2d ed. (New York, 1997).

The origins of the French Revolution are examined in W. Doyle, *Origins of the French Revolution* (Oxford, 1988). On the early years of the Revolution, see T. Tackett, *Becoming a Revolutionary* (Princeton, N.J., 1996), and N. Hampson, *Prelude to Terror* (Oxford, 1988). Important works on the radical stage of the French Revolution include N. Hampson, *The Terror in the French Revolution* (London , 1981); R. R. Palmer, *Twelve Who Ruled* (Princeton, N.J., 1941); and R. Cobb, *The People's Armies* (London, 1987). The importance of the revolutionary wars in the radical stage of the Revolution is underscored in T. C. W. Blanning, *The French Revolutionary Wars, 1787–1802* (New York, 1996). On the Directory, see M. Lyons, *France Under the Directory* (Cambridge, 1975). On the role of women in revolutionary France, see O. Hufton, *Women and the Limits of Citizenship in the French Revolution* (Toronto, 1992), and J. Landes, *Women and the Public Sphere in the Age of the French Revolution* (Ithaca, N.Y., 1988). The best brief biography of Napoleon is F. Markham, *Napoleon* (New York, 1963). Also valuable are M. Lyons, *Napoleon Bonaparte and the Legacy of the French Revolution* (New York, 1994); G. J. Ellis, *Napoleon* (New York, 1997); and the massive biographies by F. J. McLynn, *Napoleon: A Biography* (London, 1997), and A. Schom, *Napoleon Bonaparte* (New York, 1997).

INFOTRAC COLLEGE EDITION

For additional reading, go to InfoTrac College Edition, your online research library at
http://web1.infotrac-college.com

Enter the search term "Enlightenment" using the Subject Guide.

Enter the search term "Rousseau" using Keywords.

Enter the search terms "John Locke" using Keywords.

Enter the search terms "American Revolution" using Keywords.

Enter the search terms "French Revolution" using Keywords.

Enter the search term "Napoleon" using Keywords.

Enter the search terms "Napoleonic Wars" using Keywords.

THE EMERGENCE OF NEW WORLD PATTERNS (1400–1800)

*H*istorians often refer to the period from the fifteenth to the eighteenth centuries as the early modern era. During these years, several factors were at work that created the conditions of our own time.

From a global perspective, perhaps the most noteworthy event of the period was the extension of the maritime trade network throughout the entire populated world. The Chinese had inaugurated the process with their groundbreaking voyages to East Africa in the early fifteenth century, but the primary instrument of that expansion was a resurgent Europe, which exploded onto the world scene with the initial explorations of the Portuguese and the Spanish at the end of the fifteenth century and then gradually came to dominate shipping on international trade routes during the next three centuries.

Some contemporary historians argue that it was this sudden burst of energy from Europe that created the first truly global economic network. According to Immanuel Wallerstein, one of the leading proponents of this theory, the Age of Exploration led to the creation of a new "world system" characterized by the emergence of global trade networks dominated by the rising force of European capitalism, which now began to scour the periphery of the system for access to markets and cheap raw materials.

In the view of other contemporary historians, however, Wallerstein's view must be qualified. Some, for example, point to the Mongol expansion beginning in the thirteenth century, or even to the rise of the Arab empire in the Middle East a few centuries earlier, as signs of the creation of a global communications network enabling goods and ideas to travel from one end of the Eurasian supercontinent to the other.

Whatever the truth of this debate, there are still many reasons for considering the end of the fifteenth century as a crucial date in world history. In the most basic sense, it marked the end of the long isolation of the Western Hemisphere from the rest of the inhabited world. In so doing, it led to the creation of the first truly global network of ideas and commodities, which would introduce plants, ideas, and (unfortunately) many new diseases to all humanity (see the box on p. 505). Second, the period gave birth to a stunning increase in trade and manufacturing that stimulated major economic changes not only in Europe but in other parts of the world as well.

The period from 1400 to 1800, then, was an incubation period for the modern world and the launching pad for an era of Western domination that would reach fruition in the nineteenth century. To understand why the West emerged as the leading force in the world at that time, it is necessary to grasp what factors were at work in Europe and why they were absent in other major civilizations around the globe.

Historians have identified improvements in navigation, shipbuilding, and weaponry that took place in Europe in the early modern era as essential elements in the Age of Exploration. As we have seen, many of these technological advances were based on earlier discoveries that had taken place elsewhere—in China, India, and the Middle East—and had then been brought to Europe on Muslim ships or along the trade routes through Central Asia. But it was the capacity and the desire of the Europeans to enhance their wealth and power by making practical use of the discoveries of others that was the significant factor in the equation and enabled them to dominate international sea lanes and create vast colonial empires in the New World.

But technological innovations by themselves cannot provide the final answer to the question of why at this time in history Europe suddenly became the engine for rapid global change. Another factor, certainly, was the change in the European worldview, the shift from a metaphysical to a materialist perspective and the growing inclination among European intellectuals to question first principles. Whereas in China, for example, the "investigation of things" had been put to the use of analyzing and confirming principles first established by Confucius during the Chinese "Golden Age," in early modern Europe, empirical scientists rejected received religious ideas, developed a new conception of the universe, and sought ways to improve material conditions around them.

Why were European thinkers more interested in practical applications for their discoveries than their counterparts elsewhere? One explanation perhaps lies in the growing strength of the urban bourgeoisie in many areas of early modern Europe and the deliberate appeal that scientists made to European mercantile elites when they showed how the new scientific ideas could be applied directly to specific technological needs.

A final factor can be attributed to political changes that were beginning to take place in Europe during this period. The breakup of the world of Christendom, a consequence of the religious wars of the sixteenth and seventeenth centuries, helped give birth to independent and relatively centralized monarchies in many areas of Europe. In the eighteenth century, this process continued as most European states enlarged their bureaucratic machinery

THE COLUMBIAN EXCHANGE

In the Western world, the discovery of the Americas has traditionally been viewed essentially in a positive sense, as the first step in a process that expanded the global trade network and eventually led to economic well-being and political democracy in societies throughout the world. That view has come under sharp attack from some observers, however, who claim that for the peoples of the New World, the primary legacy of the European conquest was not improved living standards but harsh colonial exploitation and the spread of pestilential diseases that decimated the local population. In recent years, the brunt of such criticism has been directed at Christopher Columbus, one of the chief initiators of the discovery and conquest of the Americas. Taking issue with the prevailing image of Columbus as a heroic figure in world history, critics view him as a symbol of Spanish colonial repression and a prime mover in the virtual extinction of the peoples and cultures of the New World.

There is no doubt that the record of the European conquistadors in the Western Hemisphere leaves much to be desired, and certainly the voyages of Columbus were not of universal benefit to his contemporaries or to the generations later to come. But to focus solely on the evils that were committed in the name of exploration and the propagation of Christianity distorts the historical realities of the era. The

age of European expansion that began with Prince Henry the Navigator and Christopher Columbus was only the latest in a series of population movements that included the spread of nomadic peoples across Central Asia and the expansion of Islam from the Middle East after the death of the prophet Muhammad. In fact, the migration of peoples in search of survival and a better livelihood has been a central theme in the evolution of the human race since the dawn of prehistory.

Even more important, it seems clear that the consequences of such population movements are too complex to be summed up in moral or ideological simplifications. The European expansion into the Americas, for example, not only brought the destruction of cultures and dangerous new diseases but also initiated the exchange of plant and animal species that have ultimately been of widespread benefit to peoples throughout the globe. The introduction of the horse, cow, and various grain crops vastly increased food productivity in the New World. The cultivation of corn, manioc, and the potato have had the same effect in Asia, Africa, and Europe. Whether Christopher Columbus was a hero or a villain is a matter of debate. That he and his contemporaries played a key role in the emergence of the modern world is a matter on which there can be no doubt.

➤ **MASSACRE OF THE INDIANS.** This sixteenth-century engraving is an imaginative treatment of what was probably an all-too-common occurrence as the Spanish attempted to enslave the American peoples and convert them to Christianity.

Fomotas Archive

and consolidated their governments in order to collect the revenues and amass the armies they needed to compete militarily with rivals. In this highly competitive environment, political leaders desperately sought ways to enhance their wealth and power and grasped eagerly at whatever tools were available to guarantee their survival and prosperity.

European expansion was not fueled solely by economic considerations, however. As had been the case with the rise of Islam in the seventh and eighth centuries, religion played a major role in motivating the European Age of Exploration in the early modern era. Although Christianity was by no means a new religion in the fifteenth century (as Islam had been at the moment of Arab expansion), the world of Christendom was in the midst of a major period of conflict with the forces of Islam, a rivalry that had been exacerbated by the conquest of the Byzantine Empire by the Ottoman Turks in 1453.

Although the claims of Portuguese and Spanish adventurers that their activities were motivated primarily by a desire to bring the word of God to non-Christian peoples undoubtedly included a considerable measure of self-

delusion and hypocrisy, there seems no reason to doubt that religious motives played a meaningful part in the European Age of Exploration. Religious motives were perhaps less evident in the activities of the non-Catholic powers that entered the competition beginning in the seventeenth century. English and Dutch merchants and officials were more inclined to be motivated purely by the pursuit of economic profit or by the prevailing "beggar thy neighbor" mercantile philosophy of the day.

Conditions in many areas of Asia were less conducive to these economic and political developments. In China, after Yongle's brief experiment in maritime exploration was abandoned, a centralized monarchy continued to rely on a prosperous agricultural sector as the economic foundation of the empire. In Japan, power was centralized under the powerful Tokugawa shogunate, and the era of peace and stability that ensued saw an increase in manufacturing and commercial activity. But Japanese elites, after initially expressing interest in the outside world, abruptly shut the door on European trade and ideas in an effort to protect the "land of the gods" from external contamination.

In India and the Middle East, commerce and manufacturing had played a vital role in the life of societies since the emergence of the Indian Ocean trade network in the first centuries C.E. But beginning in the eleventh century, the area had suffered through an extended period of political instability, marked by invasions by nomadic peoples from Central Asia. The violence of the period and the local rulers' lack of experience in promoting maritime commerce had a severe depressing effect on urban manufacturing and commerce.

In the early modern era, then, Europe was best placed to take advantage of the technological innovations that had become increasingly available throughout the Old World. It possessed the political stability, the capital, and what today might be called the "modernizing elite" that provided the spur to active efforts to take advantage of new conditions for their own benefit. Where other regions were still beset by internal obstacles or had deliberately "turned inward" to seek their destiny, Europe now turned outward to seek a new and dominant position in the world. This should not blind us to the facts that significant changes were taking place in other parts of the world as well and that many of these changes had relatively little to do with the situation in the West (see the box on p. 507). As we have seen, the impact of European expansion on the rest of the world was still limited at the end of the eighteenth century. While European political authority was firmly established in a few key areas, such as the Spice Islands and Latin America, in most regions of Africa and Asia traditional societies remained relatively intact. And processes at work in these societies were often operating independently of events in Europe and would later give birth to forces that acted to restrict or shape the Western impact.

One of these forces was the progressive emergence of centralized states, some of them built on the concept of ethnic unity. In Japan, the Tokugawa shogunate had asserted an unprecedented degree of political and cultural authority. In India, a centralized empire had been created for the first time since the fall of the Mauryas in the era of antiquity. In mainland Southeast Asia, organized states emerged in Burma, Thailand, and Vietnam that were broadly based on rising ethnic consciousness. This trend was somewhat less apparent in the Middle East, where the Ottoman Empire still laid claim to universal hegemony over the entire eastern Mediterranean and Mesopotamia, and in sub-Saharan Africa, where the forces of state building were still in an embryonic stage.

Within these centralized states, the steady growth of a commercial and manufacturing sector was beginning to create the conditions for a future industrial revolution. A number of Asian societies made technological advances during this period and witnessed the emergence of a more visible and articulate urban bourgeoisie. For the moment, however, such forces were mere portents for the future, not signs of an imminent industrial revolution. At the beginning of the nineteenth century, the primary fact of life for most Asian and African societies was the expansionist power of an industrializing and ever more aggressive Europe. The power and ambition of the West provided an immediate challenge to the independence and destiny of societies throughout the rest of the world. The nature of that challenge will be the subject of our next section.

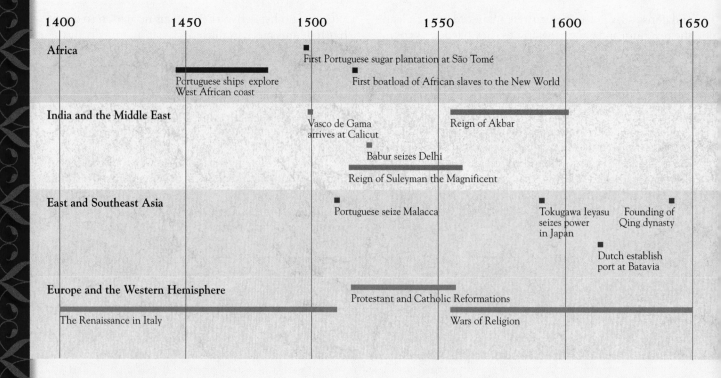

1400	1450	1500	1550	1600	1650

Africa
First Portuguese sugar plantation at São Tomé
Portuguese ships explore West African coast
First boatload of African slaves to the New World

India and the Middle East
Vasco de Gama arrives at Calicut
Reign of Akbar
Babur seizes Delhi
Reign of Suleyman the Magnificent

East and Southeast Asia
Portuguese seize Malacca
Tokugawa Ieyasu seizes power in Japan
Founding of Qing dynasty
Dutch establish port at Batavia

Europe and the Western Hemisphere
Protestant and Catholic Reformations
The Renaissance in Italy
Wars of Religion

POPULATION EXPLOSION

Between 1700 and 1800, Europe, China, and to a lesser degree India and the Ottoman Empire experienced a dramatic growth in population. In Europe, the population grew from 120 million people to almost 200 million by 1800; China, from less than 200 million to 300 million during the same period.

Four factors were important in causing this population explosion. First, better growing conditions, made possible by an improvement in climate, affected wide areas of the world and enabled people to produce more food. Summers in both China and Europe were warmer beginning in the early eighteenth century. Second, by the eighteenth century, people had begun to develop immunities to the epidemic diseases that had caused such widespread loss of life between 1500 and 1700. The spread of people by ship after 1500 had led to devastating epidemics. For example, the arrival of Europeans in Mexico led to smallpox, measles, and chickenpox among a native population that had no immunities to European diseases. In 1500, between 11 and 20 million people lived in the area of Mexico; by 1650, only 1.5 million remained. Gradually, however, people developed immunities to these diseases.

➤➤ **FESTIVAL OF THE YAM.** The spread of a few major food crops made possible new sources of nutrition to feed more people. The importance of the yam to the Ashanti people of West Africa is evident in this celebration of a yam festival at harvest time in 1817.

Werner Forman Archive

A third factor in the population increase came from new food sources. As a result of the Columbian exchange (see the box on p. 505) American food crops—such as corn, potatoes, and sweet potatoes—were brought to other parts of the world, where they became important food sources. China had imported a new species of rice from Southeast Asia that had a shorter harvest cycle than that of existing varieties. These new foods provided additional sources of nutrition that enabled more people to live for a longer time. At the same time, land development and canal building in the eighteenth century also enabled government authorities to move food supplies to areas threatened with crop failure and famine.

Finally, the use of new weapons based on gunpowder allowed states to control larger territories and ensure a new degree of order. The early rulers of the Qing dynasty, for example, pacified the Chinese Empire and ensured a long period of peace and stability. Absolute monarchs achieved similar goals in a number of European states. Less violence led to fewer deaths at the same time that an increase in food supplies and a decrease in death from diseases were occurring, thus making possible in the eighteenth century the beginning of the world population explosion that persists to this day.

1650	1700	1750	1800

Dutch way station established at Cape of Good Hope
Founding of the kingdom of Ashanti

Portuguese expelled from Mombasa

Collapse of Safavids
Battle of Plassey

Reign of Kangxi
Lord Macartney's mission to China

Development of absolutism—Reign of Louis XIV
Enlightened absolutism

American Revolution
French Revolution

MODERN PATTERNS OF WORLD HISTORY (1800–1945)

The period of world history from 1800 to 1945 was characterized, above all, by two major developments: the growth of industrialization and Western domination of the world. The two developments were, of course, interconnected. The Industrial Revolution became one of the major forces of change in the nineteenth century as it led Western civilization into the industrial era that has characterized the modern world. Beginning in Britain, it spread to the Continent and the Western Hemisphere in the course of the nineteenth century. At the same time, the Industrial Revolution created the technological means, including new weapons, by which the West achieved domination of much of the rest of the world by the end of the nineteenth century.

Europeans had begun to explore the world in the fifteenth century, but even as late as 1870, they had not yet completely penetrated North America, South America, or Australia. In Asia and Africa, with a few notable exceptions, the Western presence was limited to trading posts. Between 1870 and 1914, Western civilization expanded into the rest of the Americas and Australia, while the bulk of Africa and Asia was divided into European colonies or spheres of influence. Two major events explain this remarkable expansion: the migration of many Europeans to other parts of the world due to population growth and the revival of imperialism, which was made possible by the West's technological advancement. Beginning in the 1880s, European states began an intense scramble for overseas territory. This revival of imperialism—or the "new imperialism," as some have called it—led Europeans to carve up Asia and Africa.

The new imperialism had a dramatic effect on Africa and Asia as European powers competed for control of the two continents. Latin America was the exception, as it was able in the course of the nineteenth century to achieve political independence from its colonial rulers and embark on the building of independent nations. Nevertheless, like the Ottoman Empire, Latin America still remained subject to commercial penetration by Western merchants. Another part of the world that escaped total domination by the West was East Asia, where China and Japan were able to maintain national independence during the height of the Western onslaught at the end of the nineteenth century.

Many Asian and African leaders resented Western attitudes of superiority and demanded human dignity for the indigenous people, but they nevertheless adopted the West's own ideologies for change. One of these—nationalism, with its emphasis on the right of people to have their own nations—was used to foster independence movements wherever native people suffered under foreign oppression. Colonial peoples soon learned the power of nationalism, and in the twentieth century, nationalism would become a powerful force in the rest of the world as nationalist revolutions moved through Asia, Africa, and the Middle East. Moreover, the exhaustive struggles of two world wars sapped the power of the European states, and the colonial powers no longer had the energy or the wealth to maintain their colonial empires after World War II.

Chapter 18

THE BEGINNINGS OF MODERNIZATION: INDUSTRIALIZATION AND NATIONALISM, 1800–1870

FOCUS QUESTIONS

- What were the basic features of the new industrial system created by the Industrial Revolution, and what effects did the new system have on urban life, social classes, family life, and standards of living?
- What were the major ideas associated with conservatism, liberalism, and nationalism, and what role did each ideology play in Europe and Latin America between 1800 and 1870?
- What were the causes of the revolutions of 1848, and why did these revolutions fail?
- What actions did Cavour and Bismarck take to bring about unification in Italy and Germany, respectively, and what role did war play in their efforts?
- What were the main characteristics of Romanticism and Realism?
- In what ways were intellectual and artistic developments related to the political and social forces of the age?

The French Revolution dramatically and quickly altered the political structure of France, and the Napoleonic conquests spread many of the revolutionary principles in an equally rapid and stunning fashion to other parts of Europe. New ideologies of change, especially liberalism and nationalism, products of the upheaval initiated in France, had become too powerful to be contained. The forces of change called forth revolts that periodically shook the West and culminated in a spate of revolutions in 1848. Some of the revolutions and revolutionaries were successful; most were not. And yet by 1870, many of the goals sought by the liberals and nationalists during the first half of the nineteenth century seemed to have been achieved. National unity became a reality in Italy and Germany, and many Western states developed parliamentary features.

During the late eighteenth and early nineteenth centuries, another revolution—an industrial one—transformed the economic and social structure of Europe and spawned the industrial era that has characterized modern world history. The period of the Industrial Revolution witnessed a quantum leap in industrial production. New sources of energy and power, especially coal and steam, replaced wind and water with laborsaving machines that dramatically decreased the need for human and animal labor and at the same time increased productivity. Power machinery in turn called for new ways of organizing human labor to maximize the benefits and profits from the new machines; factories replaced workshops and home workrooms. Many early factories were dreadful places with difficult working conditions. Reformers, appalled at these conditions, were especially critical of the treatment of married women. One reported: "We have repeatedly seen married females, in the last stage of pregnancy, slaving from morning to night beside these never-tiring machines, and when . . . they were obliged to sit down to take a moment's ease, and being seen by the manager, were fined for the offense." But there were other examples of well-run factories. William Cobbett described one in Manchester in 1830: "In this room, which is lighted in the most convenient and beautiful manner, there were five hundred pairs of looms at work, and five hundred persons attending those looms; and, owing to the goodness of the masters, the whole looking healthy and well-dressed."

During the Industrial Revolution, Europe experienced a shift from a traditional, labor-intensive economy based on farming and handicrafts to a more capital-intensive economy based on manufacturing by machines, specialized labor, and industrial factories. Although the Industrial Revolution took decades to spread, it was truly revolutionary in the way it fundamentally changed Europeans and ultimately the world.●

THE INDUSTRIAL REVOLUTION AND ITS IMPACT

The Industrial Revolution triggered an enormous leap in industrial production. Coal and steam replaced wind and water as new sources of energy and power to drive laborsaving machines. In turn, these machines called for new ways of organizing human labor as factories replaced workshops and home workrooms. During the Industrial Revolution, Europe shifted from an economy based on agriculture and handicrafts to an economy based on manufacturing by machines and automated factories.

Although it took decades for the Industrial Revolution to spread, it was truly revolutionary in the way it fundamentally changed the world. Large numbers of people moved from the countryside to cities to work in the new factories. The creation of a wealthy industrial middle class and a huge industrial working class (or proletariat) substantially transformed traditional social relationships. Finally, the Industrial Revolution fundamentally altered how people related to nature, ultimately creating an environmental crisis that in the twentieth century was finally recognized as a danger to human existence itself.

The Industrial Revolution in Great Britain

The Industrial Revolution began in Britain in the 1780s. Improvements in agricultural practices in the eighteenth century led to a significant increase in food production. British agriculture could now feed more people at lower prices with less labor; even ordinary British families did not have to use most of their income to buy food, giving them the wherewithal to purchase manufactured goods. At the same time, the rapid population growth in the second half of the eighteenth century provided a pool of surplus labor for the new factories of the emerging British industry.

A crucial factor in Britain's successful industrialization was the ability to produce cheaply the articles in greatest demand. The traditional methods of the cottage industry could not keep up with the growing demand for cotton clothes throughout Britain and its vast colonial empire. This problem led British cloth manufacturers to seek and accept the new methods of manufacturing that a series of inventions provided. In so doing, these individuals ignited the Industrial Revolution.

CHANGES IN TEXTILE PRODUCTION

Already in the eighteenth century, Great Britain had surged ahead in the production of cheap cotton goods using the traditional cottage industry. The invention of the flying shuttle made weaving on a loom faster and enabled weavers to double their output. This created shortages of yarn until James Hargreaves's spinning jenny, perfected by 1768, allowed spinners to produce yarn in greater quantities. Edmund Cartwright's loom, powered by water and invented in 1787, allowed the weaving of cloth to catch up with the spinning of yarn. It was now more efficient to bring workers to the machines and organize their labor collectively in factories located next to rivers and streams, the sources of power for these early machines.

What pushed the cotton industry to even greater heights of productivity was the invention of the steam engine. In the 1760s, a Scottish engineer, James Watt (1736–1819), built an engine powered by steam that could pump water from mines three times as quickly as previous engines. In 1782, Watt developed a rotary engine that could turn a shaft and thus drive machinery. Steam power could now be applied to spinning and weaving cotton, and before long, cotton mills using steam engines were multiplying across Britain. Fired by coal, these steam engines could be located anywhere.

The new boost given to cotton textile production by technological changes became readily apparent. In 1760, Britain had imported 2.5 million pounds of raw cotton, which was farmed out to cottage industries. In 1787, the British imported 22 million pounds of cotton; most of it was spun on machines, some powered by water in large mills. By 1840, some 366 million pounds of cotton—now Britain's most important product in value—were being imported. By this time, most cotton industry employees worked in factories, and British cotton goods were sold everywhere in the world.

OTHER TECHNOLOGICAL CHANGES

The British iron industry was radically transformed during the Industrial Revolution. Britain had always had large resources of iron ore, but at the beginning of the eighteenth century, the basic process of producing iron had altered little since the Middle Ages and still depended heavily on charcoal. A better quality of iron came into being in the 1780s when Henry Cort developed a system called puddling, in which coke, which was derived from coal, was used to burn away impurities in pig iron (crude iron) and produce an iron of high quality. A boom then ensued in the British iron industry. In 1740, Britain produced 17,000 tons of iron; by the 1840s, over 2 million tons; and by 1852, almost 3 million tons, more than the rest of the world combined.

The new high-quality wrought iron was in turn used to build new machines and ultimately new industries. In 1804, Richard Trevithick pioneered the first steam-powered locomotive on an industrial rail line in south Wales. It pulled 10 tons of ore and seventy people at 5 miles per hour. Better locomotives soon followed. Engines built by George Stephenson and his son proved superior, and it was Stephenson's *Rocket* that was used on the first public railway line, which opened in 1830, extending 32 miles from Liverpool to Manchester. *Rocket* sped along at 16 miles per hour. Within twenty years, locomotives had reached 50 miles per hour, an incredible speed to contemporary travelers. By 1840, Britain had almost 6,000 miles of railroads.

The railroad was an important contribution to the success and maturing of the Industrial Revolution. The demands of railroads for coal and iron furthered the growth of those industries. Railway construction created new job opportunities, especially for farm laborers and peasants who had long been accustomed to finding work outside their local villages. Perhaps most important, the proliferation of a cheaper and faster means of transportation had a ripple effect on the growth of the industrial economy. As the prices of goods fell, markets grew larger; increased sales meant more factories and more machinery, thereby reinforcing the self-sustaining aspect of the Industrial Revolution, a fundamental break with the traditional European economy. Continuous, self-sustaining economic growth came to be accepted as a fundamental characteristic of the new economy.

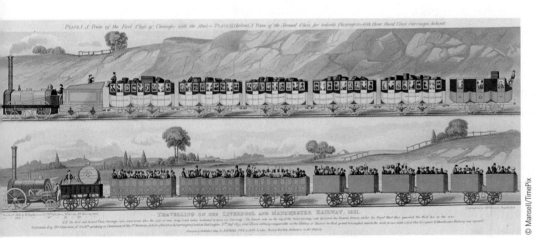

RAILROAD LINE FROM LIVERPOOL TO MANCHESTER. The railroad line from Liverpool to Manchester, first opened in 1830, relied on steam locomotives. As is evident in this illustration, carrying passengers was the railroad's main business. First-class passengers rode in covered cars, second- and third-class passengers in open cars.

© Mansell/TimePix

DISCIPLINE IN THE NEW FACTORIES

*W*orkers in the new factories of the Industrial Revolution had been accustomed to a lifestyle free of overseers. Unlike the cottages, where workers spun thread and wove cloth in their own rhythm and time, the factories demanded a new, rigorous discipline geared to the requirements of the machines. This selection is taken from a set of rules for a factory in Berlin in 1844. They were typical of company rules everywhere the factory system had been established.

FACTORY RULES, FOUNDRY AND ENGINEERING WORKS, ROYAL OVERSEAS TRADING COMPANY

In every large works, and in the coordination of any large number of workmen, good order and harmony must be looked upon as the fundamentals of success, and therefore the following rules shall be strictly observed.

1. The normal working day begins at all seasons at 6 A.M. precisely and ends, after the usual break of half an hour for breakfast, an hour for dinner, and half an hour for tea, at 7 P.M., and it shall be strictly observed. . . .

2. Workers arriving 2 minutes late shall lose half an hour's wages; whoever is more than 2 minutes late may not start work until after the next break, or at least shall lose his wages until then. Any disputes about the correct time shall be settled by the clock mounted above the gatekeeper's lodge. . . .

3. No workman, whether employed by time or piece, may leave before the end of the working day, without having first received permission from the overseer and having given his name to the gate-keeper. Omission of these two actions shall lead to a fine of ten silver groschen payable to the sick fund.

4. Repeated irregular arrival at work shall lead to dismissal. This shall also apply to those who are found idling by an official or overseer, and refused to obey their order to resume work. . . .

6. No worker may leave his place of work otherwise than for reasons connected with his work.

7. All conversation with fellow-workers is prohibited; if any worker requires information about his work, he must turn to the overseer, or to the particular fellow-worker designated for the purpose.

8. Smoking in the workshops or in the yard is prohibited during working hours; anyone caught smoking shall be fined five silver groschen for the sick fund for every such offense. . . .

10. Natural functions must be performed at the appropriate places, and whoever is found soiling walls, fences, squares, etc., and similarly, whoever is found washing his face and hands in the workshop and not in the places assigned for the purpose, shall be fined five silver groschen for the sick fund. . . .

12. It goes without saying that all overseers and officials of the firm shall be obeyed without question, and shall be treated with due deference. Disobedience will be punished by dismissal.

13. Immediate dismissal shall also be the fate of anyone found drunk in any of the workshops. . . .

14. Every workman is obliged to report to his superiors any acts of dishonesty or embezzlement on the part of his fellow workmen. If he omits to do so, and it is shown after subsequent discovery of a misdemeanor that he knew about it at the time, he shall be liable to be taken to court as an accessory after the fact and the wage due to him shall be retained as punishment.

THE INDUSTRIAL FACTORY

Another visible symbol of the Industrial Revolution was the factory. From its beginning, the factory created a new labor system. Factory owners wanted to use their new machines constantly. Workers were therefore obliged to work regular hours and in shifts to keep the machines producing at a steady rate. Early factory workers, however, came from rural areas, where they were used to a different pace of life. Peasant farmers worked hard, especially at harvest time, but they were also used to periods of inactivity.

Early factory owners therefore had to create a system of work discipline in which employees became accustomed to working regular hours and doing the same work over and over. Of course, such work was boring, and factory owners resorted to tough methods to accomplish their goals. They issued minute and detailed factory regulations (see the box above). For example, adult workers were fined for a wide variety of minor infractions, such as being a few minutes late for work, and dismissed for more serious misdoings, especially drunkenness, which set a bad example for younger workers and also courted disaster in the midst of dangerous machinery. Employers found that dismissals and fines worked well for adult employees; in a time when great population growth had produced large masses of unskilled labor, dismissal meant disaster. Children were less likely to understand the implications of dismissal, so they were sometimes disciplined more directly—often by beating. As the nineteenth century progressed, the second and third generations of workers came to view a regular workweek as a natural way of life.

© CORBIS

Laurie Platt Winfrey, Inc.

⋙ TEXTILE FACTORIES, WEST AND EAST.
The development of the factory changed the relationship between workers and employers as workers were encouraged to adjust to a new system of discipline that forced them to work regular hours under close supervision. On the left is an 1851 illustration that shows women working in a British cotton factory. The factory system came later to the rest of the world than it did in Britain. Shown on the right is one of the earliest industrial factories in Japan, the Tomioka silk factory, built in the 1870s. Note in both factories that although women are doing the work, the managers are men.

By the mid-nineteenth century, Great Britain had become the world's first and richest industrial nation. Britain was the "workshop, banker, and trader of the world." It produced one-half of the world's coal and manufactured goods; its cotton industry alone in 1850 was equal in size to the industries of all other European countries combined.

The Spread of Industrialization

From Great Britain, industrialization spread to the Continental countries of Europe and the United States at different times and speeds during the nineteenth century. First to be industrialized on the Continent were Belgium, France, and the German states (see Map 18.1). Their governments were especially active in encouraging the development of industrialization. For example, the governments set up technical schools to train engineers and mechanics and provided funds to build roads, canals, and railroads. By 1850, a network of iron rails had spread across Europe.

The Industrial Revolution also transformed the new nation in North America, the United States. In 1800, six out of every seven American workers were farmers, and there were no cities with more than 100,000 people. By 1860, however, the population had sextupled to 30 million people, larger than Great Britain; nine U.S. cities had populations over 100,000; and only 50 percent of American workers were farmers.

In sharp contrast to Britain, the United States was a large country. Thousands of miles of roads and canals were built linking east and west. The steamboat facilitated transportation on the Great Lakes, Atlantic coastal waters, and rivers (see the box on p. 515). Most important in the development of an American transportation system was the railroad. Beginning with 100 miles in 1830, by 1860 there were over 27,000 miles of railroad track covering the United States. This transportation revolution turned the United States into a single massive market for the manufactured goods of the Northeast, the early center of American industrialization.

S-T-E-A-M-BOAT A-COMIN'!

*S*teamboats and railroads were crucial elements in a transportation revolution that enabled industrialists to expand markets by shipping goods cheaply and efficiently. At the same time, these marvels of technology aroused a sense of power and excitement that was an important aspect of the triumph of industrialization. The American writer Mark Twain captured this sense of excitement in this selection from his novel Life on the Mississippi.

MARK TWAIN, *LIFE ON THE MISSISSIPPI*

After all these years I can picture that old time to myself now, just as it was then: the white town drowsing in the sunshine of a summer's morning; the streets empty, or pretty nearly so; one or two clerks sitting in front of the Water Street stores, with their splint-bottomed chairs tilted back against the wall, chins on breasts, hats slouched over their faces, asleep; . . . two or three lonely little freight piles scattered about the "levee"; a pile of "skids" on the slope of the stone-paved wharf, and the fragrant town drunkard asleep in the shadow of them; . . . the great Mississippi, the majestic, the magnificent Mississippi, rolling its mile-wide tide along, shining in the sun; the dense forest away on the other side; the "point" above the town, and the "point" below, bounding the river-glimpse and turning it into a sort of sea, and withal a very still and brilliant and lonely one. Presently a film of dark smoke appears above one of those remote "points"; instantly a Negro drayman, famous for his quick eye and prodigious voice, lifts up the cry, "S-t-e-a-m-boat a-comin'!" and the scene changes! The town drunkard stirs, the clerks wake up, a furious clatter of drays follows, every house and store pours out a human contribution, and all in a twinkling the dead town [Hannibal, Missouri] is alive and moving. Drays, carts, men, boys, all go hurrying from many quarters to a common center, the wharf. Assembled there, the people fasten their eyes upon the coming boat as upon a wonder they are seeing for the first time. And the boat *is* rather a handsome sight, too. She is long and sharp and trim and pretty; she has two tall, fancy-topped chimneys, with a gilded device of some kind swung between them; a fanciful pilot-house, all glass and "gingerbread," perched on top of the "texas" deck behind them; the paddle-boxes are gorgeous with a picture or with gilded rays above the boat's name; the boiler deck, the hurricane deck, and the texas deck are fenced and ornamented with clean white railings; there is a flag gallantly flying from the jack-staff; the furnace doors are open and the fires glaring bravely; the upper decks are black with passengers; the captain stands by the big bell, calm, imposing, the envy of all; great volumes of the blackest smoke are rolling and tumbling out of the chimneys—a husbanded grandeur created with a bit of pitch pine just before arriving at a town; the crew are grouped on the forecastle; the broad stage is run far out over the port bow, and an envied deck-hand stands picturesquely on the end of it with a coil of rope in his hand; the pent steam is screaming through the gauge-cocks; the captain lifts his hand, a bell rings, the wheels stop; then they turn back, churning the water to foam, and the steamer is at rest. Then such a scramble as there is to get aboard, and to get ashore, and to take in freight and to discharge freight, all at one and the same time; and such a yelling and cursing as the mates facilitate it all with! Ten minutes later the steamer is under way again, with no flag on the jack-staff and no black smoke issuing from the chimneys. After ten more minutes the town is dead again, and the town drunkard asleep by the skids once more.

Labor for the growing number of factories in this area came primarily from rural New England. Many of the workers in the new textile and shoe factories of the region were women, often accounting for more than 80 percent of the labor force. Factory owners sometimes sought entire families, including children, to work in their mills; one mill owner ran this advertisement in a newspaper in Utica, New York: "Wanted: A few sober and industrious families of at least five children each, over the age of eight years, are wanted at the Cotton Factory in Whitestown. Widows with large families would do well to attend this notice."

Limiting the Spread of Industrialization

Before 1870, the industrialization that was transforming western and central Europe and the United States did not extend in any significant way to the rest of the world. Even in eastern Europe, industrialization lagged far behind. Russia, for example, was still largely rural and agricultural, ruled by an autocratic regime that preferred to keep the peasants in serfdom.

In other parts of the world where they had established control (see Chapter 20), newly industrialized European states pursued a deliberate policy of preventing the growth of mechanized industry. A good example is India. In the eighteenth century, India had become one of the world's greatest exporters of cotton cloth produced by hand labor. In the first half of the nineteenth century, much of India fell under the control of the British East India Company. With British control came inexpensive British factory-produced textiles, and soon thousands of Indian spinners and hand-loom weavers were unemployed. British policy encouraged Indians to export their raw materials while buying British-made goods. India provides an excellent example of how some of the rapidly industrializing nations of Europe worked to thwart the spread of the Industrial Revolution to their colonial dominions.

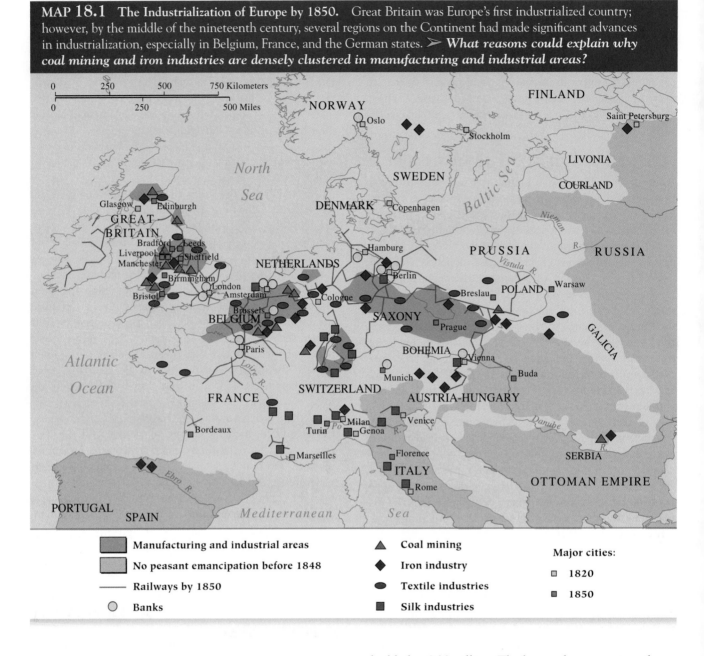

MAP 18.1 The Industrialization of Europe by 1850.   Great Britain was Europe's first industrialized country; however, by the middle of the nineteenth century, several regions on the Continent had made significant advances in industrialization, especially in Belgium, France, and the German states. ➤ *What reasons could explain why coal mining and iron industries are densely clustered in manufacturing and industrial areas?*

Social Impact of the Industrial Revolution

Eventually, the Industrial Revolution revolutionized the social life of Europe and the world. This change was already evident in the first half of the nineteenth century in the growth of cities and emergence of new social classes.

POPULATION GROWTH AND URBANIZATION

Population had begun to increase in the eighteenth century, but the pace accelerated dramatically in the nineteenth century. In 1750, the total European population stood at an estimated 140 million; by 1850, it had almost doubled to 266 million. The key to the expansion of population was the decline in death rates evident throughout Europe. Wars and major epidemic diseases, such as plague and smallpox, became less frequent, which led to a drop in the number of deaths. Thanks to the increase in the food supply, more people were better fed and more resistant to disease.

Throughout Europe, cities and towns grew rapidly in the first half of the nineteenth century, a phenomenon related to industrialization. By 1850, especially in Great Britain and Belgium, cities were rapidly becoming home for many industries. With the steam engine, factory owners could locate their manufacturing plants in urban centers, where they had ready access to transportation facilities and large numbers of new arrivals from the country looking for work.

In 1800, Great Britain had one major city, London, with a population of one million, and six cities with populations between 50,000 and 100,000. Fifty years later, London's population had swelled to 2,363,000, and there were nine cities over 100,000 and eighteen cities with populations between 50,000 and 100,000. Over 50 percent of the British population lived in towns and cities by 1850. Urban populations also grew on the Continent, but at a less frenzied pace.

The dramatic growth of cities in the first half of the nineteenth century produced miserable living conditions for many of the inhabitants. Located in the center of most industrial towns were the row houses of the industrial workers. Rooms were not large and were frequently overcrowded, as a government report of 1838 in Britain revealed: "I entered several of the tenements. In one of them, on the ground floor, I found six persons occupying a very small room, two in bed, ill with fever. In the room above this were two more persons in one bed, ill with fever." Another report said: "There were 63 families where there were at least five persons to one bed; and there were some in which even six were packed in one bed, lying at the top and bottom—children and adults."[1]

Sanitary conditions in these towns were appalling; sewers and open drains were common on city streets: "In the center of this street is a gutter, into which the refuse of animal and vegetable matters of all kinds, the dirty water from the washing of clothes and of the houses, are all poured, and there they stagnate and putrefy."[2] Unable to deal with human wastes, cities in the early industrial era smelled horrible and were extraordinarily unhealthy. Towns and cities were fundamentally death traps. As deaths outnumbered births in most large cities in the first half of the nineteenth century, only a constant influx of people from the country kept them alive and growing.

THE INDUSTRIAL MIDDLE CLASS

The rise of industrial capitalism produced a new kind of middle class. The bourgeoisie was not new; it had existed since the emergence of cities in the Middle Ages. Originally, the bourgeois or burgher was simply a town dweller, active as a merchant, official, artisan, lawyer, or man of letters. Because many of these people lived comfortable lives, the term took on a certain cachet. And so as other people began to accumulate wealth, the term *bourgeois* came to be applied to people involved in commerce, industry, and banking as well as professionals such as teachers, physicians, and government officials, regardless of where they lived.

The new industrial middle class was made up of the people who constructed the factories, purchased the machines, and figured out where the markets were. Their qualities included resourcefulness, single-mindedness, resolution, initiative, vision, ambition, and often, of course, greed. As Jedediah Strutt, a cotton manufacturer said, "Getting of money . . . is the main business of the life of men."

Members of the industrial middle class sought to reduce the barriers between themselves and the landed elite, but it is clear that they tried at the same time to separate themselves from the laboring classes below them. The working class was actually a mixture of different groups in the first half of the nineteenth century, but in the course of that century, factory workers would form an industrial proletariat that constituted a majority of the working class.

THE INDUSTRIAL WORKING CLASS

Early industrial workers faced wretched working conditions. Work shifts ranged from twelve to sixteen hours a day, six days a week, with a half hour for lunch and dinner. There was no security of employment and no minimum wage. The worst conditions were in the cotton mills, where temperatures were especially debilitating. One report noted that "in the cotton-spinning work, these creatures are kept, fourteen hours in each day, locked up, summer and winter, in a heat of from eighty to eighty-four degrees." Mills were also dirty, dusty, and unhealthy.

Conditions in the coal mines were also harsh. Although steam-powered engines were used to lift coal from the mines to the top, inside the mines, men still bore the burden of digging the coal out while horses, mules, women, and children hauled coal carts on rails to the lift. Dangerous conditions, including cave-ins, explosions, and gas fumes, were

⇛ **WOMEN IN THE MINES.** Both women and children were often employed in the early factories and mines of the nineteenth century. As is evident in this illustration of a woman dragging a cart loaded with coal behind her, they often worked under very trying conditions.

CHILD LABOR: DISCIPLINE IN THE TEXTILE MILLS

Child labor was not new, but in the early Industrial Revolution it was exploited more systematically. These selections are taken from the Report of Sadler's Committee, which was commissioned in 1832 to inquire into the condition of child factory workers.

HOW THEY KEPT THE CHILDREN AWAKE

It is a very frequent thing at Mr. Marshall's [at Shrewsbury] where the least children were employed (for there were plenty working at six years of age), for Mr. Horseman to start the mill earlier in the morning than he formerly did; and provided a child should be drowsy, the overlooker walks round the room with a stick in his hand, and he touches that child on the shoulder, and says, "Come here." In a corner of the room there is an iron cistern; it is filled with water; he takes this boy, and takes him up by the legs, and dips him over head in the cistern, and sends him to work for the remainder of the day. . . .

What means were taken to keep the children to their work?—Sometimes they would tap them over the head, or nip them over the nose, or give them a pinch of snuff, or throw water in their faces, or pull them off where they were, and job them about to keep them waking.

THE SADISTIC OVERLOOKER

Samuel Downe, age 29, factory worker living near Leeds; at the age of about ten began work at Mr. Marshall's mill at Shrewsbury, where the customary hours when work was brisk were generally 5 A.M. to 8 P.M., sometimes from 5:30 A.M. to 8 or 9:

What means were taken to keep the children awake and vigilant, especially at the termination of such a day's labour as you have described?—There was generally a blow or a box, or a tap with a strap, or sometimes the hand.

Have you yourself been strapped?—Yes, most severely, till I could not bear to sit upon a chair without having pillows, and through that I left. I was strapped both on my own legs, and then I was put upon a man's back, and then strapped and buckled with two straps to an iron pillar, and flogged, and all by one overlooker; after that he took a piece of tow, and twisted it in the shape of a cord, and put it in my mouth, and tied it behind my head.

He gagged you?—Yes; and then he ordered me to run round a part of the machinery where he was overlooker, and he stood at one end, and every time I came there he struck me with a stick, which I believe was an ash plant, and which he generally carried in his hand, and sometimes he hit me, and sometimes he did not; and one of the men in the room came and begged me off, and that he let me go, and not beat me any more, and consequently he did.

You have been beaten with extraordinary severity?—Yes, I was beaten so that I had not power to cry at all, or hardly speak at one time. What age were you at that time?—Between 10 and 11.

---

a way of life. The cramped conditions in the mines—tunnels were often only 3 or 4 feet high—and their constant dampness led to deformed bodies and ruined lungs.

Both children and women worked in large numbers in early factories and mines. Children had been an important part of the family economy in preindustrial times, working in the fields or carding and spinning wool at home. In the Industrial Revolution, however, child labor was exploited more than ever (see the box above). The owners of cotton factories found child labor very helpful. Children had a particular delicate touch as spinners of cotton. Their smaller size made it easier for them to move under machines to gather loose cotton. Moreover, children were more easily trained to do factory work. Above all, children represented a cheap supply of labor. In 1821, about half of the British population was under twenty years of age. Hence children made up an abundant supply of labor, and they were paid only about one-sixth to one-third of what a man was paid. In the cotton factories in 1838, children under eighteen made up 29 percent of the total workforce; children as young as seven worked twelve to fifteen hours per day, six days a week, in cotton mills.

By 1830, women and children made up two-thirds of the cotton industry's labor. However, as the number of children employed declined under the Factory Act of 1833, their places were taken by women, who came to dominate the labor forces of the early factories. Women made up 50 percent of the labor force in textile (cotton and woolen) factories before 1870. They were mostly unskilled labor and were paid half or less of what men received.

The employment of children and women in large part represents a continuation of a preindustrial kinship pattern. Cottage industry had always involved the efforts of the entire family, and it seemed perfectly natural to continue this pattern. Men migrating from the countryside to industrial towns and cities took their wives and children with them into the factory or into the mines. The impetus for this family work often came from the family itself. The factory owner Jedediah Strutt was opposed to child labor under ten but was forced by parents to take children as young as seven.

Laws that limited the work hours of children and women also led to a new pattern of work based on a separation of work and home. Men were expected to be responsible for the primary work obligations, while women assumed daily control of the family and performed low-paying jobs such as laundry work that could be done in the home. Domestic industry made it possible for women to continue their contributions to family survival.

EFFORTS AT CHANGE: EARLY SOCIALISM

In the first half of the nineteenth century, the pitiful conditions found in the slums, mines, and factories of the Industrial Revolution gave rise to a movement known as socialism. Early socialism was largely the product of intellectuals who believed in the equality of all people and wanted to replace competition with cooperation in industry. To later socialists, especially the followers of Karl Marx, such ideas were merely impractical dreams, and with contempt they labeled these theorists "utopian socialists." The term has lasted to this day.

Robert Owen, a British cotton manufacturer, was one such utopian socialist. He believed that humans would show their true natural goodness if they lived in a cooperative environment. At New Lanark in Scotland, he transformed a squalid factory town into a flourishing, healthy community. But when he tried to create such a cooperative community at New Harmony, Indiana, in the United States in the 1820s, fighting within the community eventually destroyed his dream.

With their plans for the reconstruction of society, utopian socialists attracted a number of women supporters, who believed that only a reordering of society would help women. One of Owen's disciples, a wealthy woman named Frances Wright, bought slaves in order to set up a model community at Nashoba, Tennessee. The community failed, but Wright continued to work for women's rights.

REACTION AND REVOLUTION: THE GROWTH OF NATIONALISM

After the defeat of Napoleon, European rulers moved to restore much of the old order. This was the goal of the great powers—Great Britain, Austria, Prussia, and Russia—when they met at the Congress of Vienna in September 1814 to arrange a final peace settlement after the Napoleonic wars. The leader of the congress was the Austrian foreign minister, Prince Klemens von Metternich (1773–1859), who claimed that he was guided at Vienna by the principle of legitimacy. To reestablish peace and stability in Europe, he considered it necessary to restore the legitimate monarchs who would preserve traditional institutions. This had already been done in France with the restoration of the Bourbon monarchy, but the principle of legitimacy was in fact largely ignored elsewhere;

the great powers all grabbed land to add to their states (see Map 18.2).

The peace arrangements of 1815 were but the beginning of a conservative reaction determined to contain the liberal and nationalist forces unleashed by the French Revolution. Metternich and his kind were representatives of the ideology known as conservatism. Most conservatives favored obedience to political authority, believed that organized religion was crucial to social order, hated revolutionary upheavals, and were unwilling to accept either the liberal demands for civil liberties and representative governments or the nationalistic aspirations generated by the French revolutionary era. After 1815, the political philosophy of conservatism was supported by hereditary monarchs, government bureaucracies, landowning aristocracies, and revived churches, be they Protestant or Catholic. The conservative forces were dominant after 1815.

One method used by the great powers to maintain the new status quo they had constructed was the Concert of Europe, according to which Great Britain, Russia, Prussia, and Austria (and later France) agreed to meet periodically in conferences to take steps that would maintain the peace in Europe. Eventually, the great powers adopted a principle of intervention that was based on their right to send armies into countries where there were revolutions to restore legitimate monarchs to their thrones. Britain refused to agree to the principle, arguing that it had never been the intention of the great powers to interfere in the internal affairs of other states. Ignoring the British response, the other powers used military intervention to defeat revolutionary movements in Spain and Italy and to restore monarchs to their thrones.

Forces for Change

Between 1815 and 1830, conservative governments throughout Europe worked to maintain the old order. However, powerful forces for change—liberalism and nationalism—were also at work. Liberalism owed much to the Enlightenment of the eighteenth century and the American and French Revolutions at the end of that century; it was based on the idea that people should be as free from restraint as possible.

Politically, liberals came to hold a common set of beliefs. Chief among them was the protection of civil liberties, or the basic rights of all people, which included equality before the law; freedom of assembly, speech, and the press; and freedom from arbitrary arrest. All of these freedoms should be guaranteed by a written document, such as the American Bill of Rights or the French Declaration of the Rights of Man and the Citizen. In addition to religious toleration for all, most liberals advocated separation of church and state. Liberals also demanded the right of peaceful opposition to the government in and out of parliament and the making of laws by a representative assembly (legislature) elected by qualified voters. Many liberals believed, then, in a constitutional

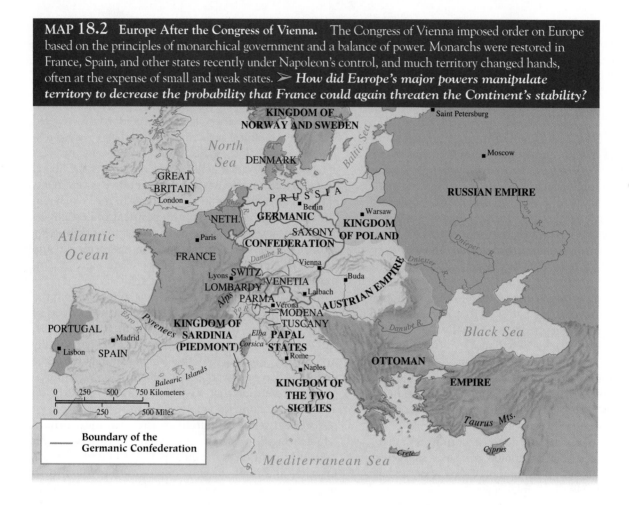

MAP 18.2   Europe After the Congress of Vienna.   The Congress of Vienna imposed order on Europe based on the principles of monarchical government and a balance of power. Monarchs were restored in France, Spain, and other states recently under Napoleon's control, and much territory changed hands, often at the expense of small and weak states. ➤ *How did Europe's major powers manipulate territory to decrease the probability that France could again threaten the Continent's stability?*

monarchy or constitutional state with limits on the powers of government in order to prevent despotism and in written constitutions that would guarantee these rights. Liberals were not democrats, however. They thought that the right to vote and hold office should be open only to men who owned property. As a political philosophy, liberalism was adopted by middle-class men, especially the industrial bourgeoisie, who favored voting rights for themselves so that they could share power with the landowning classes.

Nationalism was an even more powerful ideology for change in the nineteenth century. Nationalism arose out of an awareness of being part of a community that has common institutions, traditions, language, and customs. This community is called a nation, and the primary political loyalty of individuals would be to the nation. Nationalism did not become a popular force for change until the French Revolution. From then on, nationalists came to believe that each nationality should have its own government. Thus the Germans, who were not united, wanted national unity in a German nation-state with one central government. Subject peoples, such as the Hungarians, wanted the right to establish their own autonomy rather than be subject to a German minority in the multinational Austrian Empire.

Nationalism, then, was a threat to the existing political order. A united Germany, for example, would upset the

balance of power established at Vienna in 1815. At the same time, an independent Hungarian state would mean the breakup of the Austrian Empire. Conservatives feared such change and tried hard to repress nationalism. The conservative order dominated much of Europe after 1815, but the forces of liberalism and nationalism, first generated by the French Revolution, continued to grow as that second great revolution, the Industrial Revolution, expanded and brought new groups of people who wanted change. In 1848, these forces for change erupted.

The Revolutions of 1848

Revolution in France was the spark for revolution in other countries. A severe industrial and agricultural depression beginning in 1846 brought hardship in France to the lower middle class, workers, and peasants, while the government's persistent refusal to extend the suffrage angered the disfranchised members of the middle class. When the government of King Louis-Philippe (1830–1848) refused to make changes, opposition grew and finally overthrew the monarchy on February 24, 1848. A group of moderate and radical republicans established a provisional government and called for the election by universal male suffrage of a "constituent assembly" that would draw up a new constitution.

REVOLUTIONARY EXCITEMENT: CARL SCHURZ AND THE REVOLUTION OF 1848 IN GERMANY

The excitement with which German liberals and nationalists received the news of the 1848 revolution in France and their own expectations for Germany are well captured in this selection from the Reminiscences *of Carl Schurz. Schurz (1829–1906) made his way to the United States after the failure of the German revolution and eventually became a U.S. senator.*

CARL SCHURZ, REMINISCENCES

One morning, toward the end of February, 1848, I sat quietly in my attic-chamber, working hard at my tragedy of "Ulrich von Hutten" [sixteenth-century German humanist and knight], when suddenly a friend rushed breathlessly into the room, exclaiming: "What, you sitting here! Do you not know what has happened?"

"No; what?"

"The French have driven away Louis Philippe and proclaimed the republic."

I threw down my pen—and that was the end of "Ulrich von Hutten." I never touched the manuscript again. We tore down the stairs, into the street, to the market-square, the accustomed meeting-place for all the student societies after their midday dinner. Although it was still forenoon, the market was already crowded with young men talking excitedly. There was no shouting, no noise, only agitated conversation. What did we want there? This probably no one knew. But since the French had driven away Louis Philippe and proclaimed the republic, something of course must happen here, too. . . . We were dominated by a vague feeling as if a great outbreak of elemental forces had begun, as if an earthquake was impending of which we had felt the first shock, and we instinctively crowded together. . . .

The next morning there were the usual lectures to be attended. But how profitless! The voice of the professor sounded like a monotonous drone coming from far away. What he had to say did not seem to concern us. The pen that should have taken notes remained idle. At last we closed with a sigh the notebook and went away, impelled by a feeling that now we had something more important to do—to devote ourselves to the affairs of the fatherland. And this we did by seeking as quickly as possible again the company of our friends, in order to discuss what had happened and what was to come. In these conversations, excited as they were, certain ideas and catchwords worked themselves to the surface, which expressed more or less the feelings of the people. Now had arrived in Germany the day for the establishment of "German Unity," and the founding of a great, powerful national German Empire. In the first line the convocation of a national parliament. Then the demands for civil rights and liberties, free speech, free press, the right of free assembly, equality before the law, a freely elected representation of the people with legislative power, responsibility of ministers, self-government of the communes, the right of the people to carry arms, the formation of a civic guard with elective officers, and so on—in short, that which was called a "constitutional form of government on a broad democratic basis." Republican ideas were at first only sparingly expressed. But the word democracy was soon on all tongues, and many, too, thought it a matter of course that if the princes should try to withhold from the people the rights and liberties demanded, force would take the place of mere petition. Of course the regeneration of the fatherland must, if possible, be accomplished by peaceable means. . . . Like many of my friends, I was dominated by the feeling that at last the great opportunity had arrived for giving to the German people the liberty which was their birthright and to the German fatherland its unity and greatness, and that it was now the first duty of every German to do and to sacrifice everything for this sacred object.

The new constitution, ratified on November 4, 1848, established a republic (the Second Republic) with a single legislature elected to three-year terms by universal male suffrage and a president, also elected by universal male suffrage to a four-year term. In the elections for the presidency held in December 1848, Charles Louis Napoleon Bonaparte, the nephew of the famous ruler, won a resounding victory.

REVOLUTION IN CENTRAL EUROPE

News of the 1848 revolution in France led to upheaval in central Europe as well (see the box above). The Vienna settlement in 1815 had recognized the existence of thirty-eight sovereign states (called the Germanic Confedera-tion) in what had once been the Holy Roman Empire. Austria and Prussia were the two great powers in terms of size and might; the other states varied considerably. In 1848, cries for change caused many German rulers to promise constitutions, a free press, jury trials, and other liberal reforms. In Prussia, King Frederick William IV (1840–1861) agreed to establish a new constitution and work for a united Germany.

The promise of unity reverberated throughout all the German states as governments allowed elections by universal male suffrage for deputies to an all-German parliament called the Frankfurt Assembly. Its purpose was to fulfill a liberal and nationalist dream—the preparation of a constitution for a new united Germany. But the

Frankfurt Assembly failed to achieve its goal. The members had no real means of compelling the German rulers to accept the constitution they had drawn up. German unification was not achieved; the revolution had failed.

The Austrian Empire needed only the news of the revolution in Paris to erupt in flames in March 1848. The Austrian Empire was a multinational state, a collection of at least eleven ethnically distinct peoples, including Germans, Czechs, Magyars (Hungarians), Slovaks, Romanians, Serbians, and Italians, who had pledged their loyalty to the Habsburg emperor. The Germans, though only a quarter of the population, were economically dominant and played a leading role in governing Austria. The Hungarians, however, wanted their own legislature. In March, demonstrations in Buda, Prague, and Vienna led to the dismissal of Metternich, the Austrian foreign minister and the arch-symbol of the conservative order, who fled abroad. In Vienna, revolutionary forces took control of the capital and demanded a liberal constitution. Hungary was given its own legislature and a separate national army. In Bohemia, the Czechs began to clamor for their own government as well.

Austrian officials had made concessions to appease the revolutionaries, but they were determined to reestablish firm control. As in the German states, they were increasingly encouraged by the divisions between radical and moderate revolutionaries and played on the middle-class fear of a working-class social revolution. In June 1848, Austrian military forces ruthlessly suppressed the Czech rebels in Prague. By the end of October, radical rebels had been crushed in Vienna, but it was only with the assistance of a Russian army of 140,000 men that the Hungarian revolution was finally put down in 1849. The revolutions in the Austrian Empire had failed.

REVOLTS IN THE ITALIAN STATES

So did revolutions in Italy. The Congress of Vienna had established nine states in Italy, including the kingdom of Sardinia in the north, ruled by the house of Savoy; the kingdom of the Two Sicilies (Naples and Sicily); the Papal States; a handful of small duchies; and the important northern provinces of Lombardy and Venetia, which were now part of the Austrian Empire. Italy was largely under Austrian domination, but a new movement for Italian unity known as Young Italy led to initially successful revolts in 1848. Within a year, however, the Austrians had reestablished complete control over Lombardy and Venetia, and the old order also prevailed in the rest of Italy.

Throughout Europe in 1848, popular revolutions had led to liberal constitutions and liberal governments. Moderate, middle-class liberals and radical workers soon divided over their aims, however, and the failure of the revolutionaries to stay united soon led to the reestablishment of authoritarian regimes. In other parts of the Western world, revolutions took somewhat different directions.

Independence and the Development of the National State in Latin America

The Spanish and Portuguese colonial empires in Latin America had been part of the old monarchical structure of Europe for centuries. When that structure was challenged by the Napoleonic wars, Latin America, too, experienced change.

⟩⟩ **AUSTRIAN STUDENTS IN THE REVOLUTIONARY CIVIL GUARD.** In 1848, revolutionary fervor swept the European continent and toppled governments in France, central Europe, and Italy. In the Austrian Empire, students joined the revolutionary civil guard in taking control of Vienna and forcing the Austrian emperor to call a constituent assembly to draft a liberal constitution.

Historisches Museum der Stadt Wien

NATIONALISTIC REVOLTS IN LATIN AMERICA

By the end of the eighteenth century, the ideas of the Enlightenment and the new political ideals stemming from the successful revolution in North America were beginning to influence the creole elites (descendants of Europeans who became permanent inhabitants of Latin America). The principles of the equality of all people in the eyes of the law, free trade, and a free press proved very attractive. Sons of creoles, such as Simón Bolívar and José de San Martín, who became leaders of the independence movement, even went to European universities, where they imbibed the ideas of the Enlightenment. These Latin American elites, joined by a growing class of merchants, especially resented the domination of their trade by Spain and Portugal.

The creole elites soon began to use their new ideas to denounce the rule of the Iberian monarchs and the peninsulars (Spanish and Portuguese officials who resided in Latin America for political and economic gain). When Napoleon Bonaparte toppled the monarchies of Spain and Portugal, the authority of the Spaniards and Portuguese in their colonial empires was weakened, and between 1807 and 1825, a series of revolts enabled most of Latin America to become independent.

Beginning in 1810, Mexico, too, experienced a revolt, fueled initially by the desire of the creole elites to overthrow the rule of the peninsulars. The first real hero of Mexican independence was Miguel Hidalgo y Costilla, a parish priest in a small village about 100 miles from Mexico City. Hidalgo had studied the French Revolution and roused the local Indians and mestizos to free themselves from the Spanish: "My children, this day comes to us as a new dispensation. Are you ready to receive it? Will you be free? Will you make the effort to recover from the hated Spaniards the lands stolen from your forefathers three hundred years ago?"[3] It was September 16, 1810, and a crowd of Indians and mestizos, armed with clubs, machetes, and a few guns quickly formed a mob army to attack the Spaniards. But Hidalgo was not a good organizer, and his forces were soon crushed. A military court sentenced Hidalgo to death, but his memory lived on. In fact, September 16, the first day of the uprising, is celebrated as Mexico's Independence Day.

The participation of Indians and mestizos in Mexico's revolt against Spanish control frightened both creoles and peninsulars. Fearful of the masses, they cooperated in defeating the popular revolutionary forces. The conservative elites—both creoles and peninsulars—then decided to overthrow Spanish rule as a way of preserving their own power. They selected a creole military leader, Augustín de Iturbide, as their leader and the first emperor of Mexico in 1821.

Independence movements elsewhere in Latin America were the work of elites—primarily creoles—who overthrew Spanish rule and created new governments that they could dominate. The masses of people—Indians, blacks, mestizos, and mulattoes—gained little from the revolts. José de San Martín (1778–1850) of Argentina and Simón Bolívar (1783–1830) of Venezuela, leaders of the independence movement, were both members of the creole elite, and both were hailed as the liberators of South America.

By 1810, the forces of San Martín had freed Argentina from Spanish authority. Bolívar led the bitter struggle for independence in Venezuela and then went on to liberate New Grenada (Colombia) and Ecuador. San Martín believed that the Spaniards must

➤➤ **JOSÉ DE SAN MARTÍN.**   José de San Martín of Argentina was one of the famous leaders of the Latin American independence movement. His forces liberated Argentina, Chile, and Peru from Spanish authority. In this painting by Theodore Géricault, San Martín is shown leading his troops at the Battle of Chacabuco in Chile.

The Art Archive/Museo Nacional de Historia Lima/Dagli Orti

be removed from all of South America if any nation was to be free. In January 1817, he led his forces over the high Andes mountains, an amazing feat in itself. Two-thirds of their pack mules and horses died during the difficult journey. Many of the soldiers suffered from lack of oxygen and severe cold while crossing mountain passes that were more than 2 miles above sea level. The arrival of San Martín's forces in Chile completely surprised the Spaniards, whose forces were routed at the battle of Chacabuco on February 12, 1817. In 1821, San Martín moved on to Lima, Peru, the center of Spanish authority.

Convinced that he was unable to complete the liberation of Peru, San Martín welcomed the arrival of Bolívar and his forces. The liberator of Venezuela took on the task of crushing the last significant Spanish army at Ayacucho on December 9, 1824. By then, Peru, Uruguay, Paraguay, Colombia, Venezuela, Argentina, Bolivia, and Chile had all become free states (see Map 18.3). In 1823, the Central American states became independent and in 1838–1839 divided into five republics (Guatemala, El Salvador, Honduras, Costa Rica, and Nicaragua). Earlier, in 1822, the prince regent of Brazil had declared Brazil's independence from Portugal.

MAP 18.3 **Latin America in the First Half of the Nineteenth Century.** Latin American colonies took advantage of Spain's weakness during the Napoleonic wars to fight for independence, beginning with Argentina in 1810 and spreading throughout the region over the next decade with the help of leaders like Simón Bolívar and José de San Martín. ➤ *How many South American countries are sources of rivers that feed the Amazon, and roughly what percentage of the continent is contained within the Amazon's watershed?*

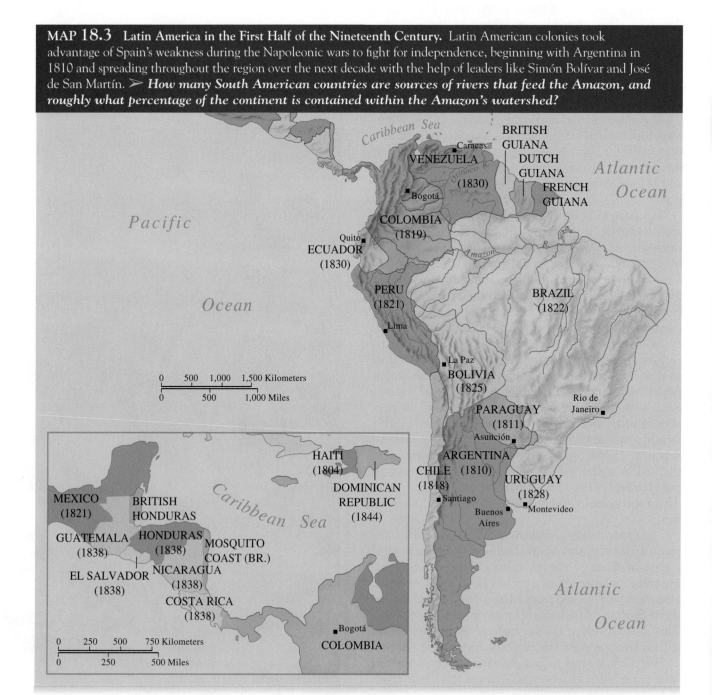

THE DIFFICULTIES OF NATION BUILDING

The new Latin American nations faced a number of serious problems between 1830 and 1870. The wars for independence had themselves resulted in a staggering loss of population, property, and livestock; at the same time, disputes arose between nations over their precise boundaries. Poor transportation and communication systems also made national unity difficult.

The new nations of Latin America began with republican governments, but they had had no experience in ruling themselves. Soon after independence, strong leaders known as *caudillos* came to power. They ruled chiefly by military force and were usually supported by the landed elites. Many kept the new national states together. Sometimes they were also modernizers who built roads, canals, ports, and schools. Others were destructive, such as Antonio de Santa Anna, who, in ruling Mexico from 1829 to 1855, misused state funds, created chaos, and lost some of Mexico's territory to the United States. Other caudillos were supported by the masses, became extremely popular, and served as instruments for radical change. Juan Manuel de Rosas, for example, who led Argentina from 1829 to 1852, became very popular by defending Argentine interests against foreigners.

Although political independence brought economic independence, old patterns were hard to extinguish. Instead of Spain and Portugal, Great Britain now dominated the Latin American economy. British merchants moved in large numbers, while British investors poured in funds, especially in the mining industry. Old trade patterns soon reemerged. Because Latin America served as a source of raw materials and foodstuffs for the industrializing nations of Europe and North America, exports, especially of wheat, tobacco, wool, sugar, coffee, and hides, to the North Atlantic countries increased noticeably. At the same time, the importation of finished consumer goods, especially textiles, also grew and caused a decline in industrial production in Latin America. For Latin America, the emphasis on the export of raw materials and the import of finished products ensured the ongoing domination of the Latin American economy by foreigners.

A fundamental underlying problem for all of the new Latin American nations was the persistent domination of society by the landed elites. Large estates remained the persistent fact of Latin America's economic and social life (see the box on p. 526). By 1848, for example, the Sánchez Navarro family in Mexico possessed seventeen estates comprising 16 million acres. Estates were often so large that they could not be farmed efficiently.

Land remained the basis of wealth, social prestige, and political power throughout the nineteenth century. Landed elites ran governments, controlled courts, and kept a system of inexpensive labor. These landowners made enormous profits growing single, specialized crops for export, such as coffee, while the masses, unable to have land to grow basic food crops, endured dire poverty.

Nationalism in the Balkans: The Ottoman Empire and the Eastern Question

The Ottoman Empire had long been in control of much of southeastern Europe (an area known as the Balkans). In the first half of the nineteenth century, a number of states in the Balkans sought to free themselves from the Ottomans. Serbia, for example, won its autonomy in 1817.

The Balkans in 1830

As the Ottoman Empire began to decline and authority over its outlying territories in southeastern Europe waned, European governments began to take an active interest in its disintegration. The "Eastern Question," as it came to be called, troubled European diplomats throughout the nineteenth century. Russia's proximity to the Ottoman Empire and the religious bonds between the Russians and the Greek Orthodox Christians in Turkish-dominated southeastern Europe naturally gave Russia special opportunities to enlarge its sphere of influence. The Austrian Empire feared Russian ambitions and had its own interest in the apparent demise of the Ottoman Empire. France and Britain were interested in commercial opportunities and naval bases in the eastern Mediterranean.

In 1821, the Greeks revolted against their Turkish masters. Although subject to Muslim control for four hundred years, the Greeks had been allowed to maintain their language and their Greek Orthodox faith. A revival of Greek national sentiment at the beginning of the nineteenth century added to the growing desire for "the liberation of the fatherland from the terrible yoke of Turkish oppression." The Greek revolt was soon transformed into a noble cause by an outpouring of European sentiment for the Greeks' struggle. In 1827, a combined British and French fleet went to Greece and defeated a large Turkish fleet. A year later, Russia declared war on the Ottoman Empire and invaded its European provinces of Moldavia and Wallachia. By the Treaty of Adrianople in 1829, which ended the Russian-Turkish War, the Russians received a

A RADICAL CRITIQUE OF
THE LAND PROBLEM IN MEXICO

The domination of Mexico by elites who owned large estates remained a serious problem throughout the nineteenth century. Conservatives, of course, favored the great estates as the foundation stones of their own political power, while even liberals shied away from any extremist attack on property rights. Nevertheless, there were some strong voices of protest, as this excerpt from a speech delivered in 1857 by Ponciano Arriaga demonstrates. Arriaga's appeal went unheeded; conservatives called him a "communist."

PONCIANO ARRIAGA, SPEECH TO THE CONSTITUTIONAL CONVENTION OF 1856–1857

One of the most deeply rooted evils of our country—an evil that merits the close attention of legislators when they frame our fundamental law—is the monstrous division of landed property.

While a few individuals possess immense areas of uncultivated land that could support millions of people, the great majority of Mexicans languish in a terrible poverty and are denied property, homes, and work. . . .

There are Mexican landowners who occupy (if one can give that name to a purely imaginary act) an extent of land greater than the areas of some of our sovereign states, greater even than that of one of several European states.

In this vast area, much of which lies idle, deserted, abandoned, awaiting the arms and labor of men, live four or five million Mexicans who know no other industry than agriculture, yet are without land or the means to work it, and who cannot emigrate in the hope of bettering their fortunes. They must either vegetate in idleness, turn to banditry, or accept the yoke of a landed monopolist who subjects them to intolerable conditions of life. . . .

How can a hungry, naked, miserable people practice popular government? How can we proclaim the equal rights of men and leave the majority of the nation in conditions worse than those of helots or pariahs? How can we condemn slavery in words, while the lot of most of our fellow citizens is more grievous than that of the black slaves of Cuba or the United States? . . .

With some honorable exceptions, the rich landowners of Mexico, or the administrators who represent them, resemble the feudal lords of the Middle Ages. On his seignorial land, . . . the landowner makes and executes laws, administers justice and exercises civil power, imposes taxes and fines, has his own jails and irons, metes out punishments and tortures, monopolizes commerce, and forbids the conduct without his permission of any business but that of the estate. The judges or officials who exercise on the hacienda the powers attached to public authority are usually the master's servants or tenants, his retainers, incapable of enforcing any law but the will of the master.

An astounding variety of devices are employed to exploit the peons or tenants, to turn a profit from their sweat and labor. They are compelled to work without pay even on days traditionally set aside for rest. They must accept rotten seeds or sick animals whose cost is charged to their miserable wages. They must pay enormous parish fees that bear no relation to the scale of fees that the owner or majordomo has arranged beforehand with the parish priest. They must make all their purchases on the hacienda, using tokens or paper money that do not circulate elsewhere. At certain seasons of the year they are assigned articles of poor quality, whose price is set by the owner or majordomo, constituting a debt which they can never repay. They are forbidden to use pastures and woods, firewood and water, or even the wild fruit of the fields, save with the express permission of the master. In fine, they are subject to a completely unlimited and irresponsible power.

---

protectorate over the two provinces. By the same treaty, the Turks agreed to allow Russia, France, and Britain to decide the fate of Greece. In 1830, the three powers declared Greece an independent kingdom, and two years later a new royal dynasty was established.

THE CRIMEAN WAR

The Crimean War was yet another episode in the story of the Eastern Question. In 1853, war had erupted again between the Russians and Turks over Russian demands for the right to protect Christian shrines in Palestine, a privilege that had already been extended to the French. When the Turks refused, the Russians invaded Turkish Moldavia and Wallachia. Failure to resolve the problem by negotiations led the Turks to declare war on Russia on October 4, 1853. In the following year, on March 28, Great Britain and France, fearful that the Russians would gain at the expense of the disintegrating Ottoman Empire, declared war on Russia.

The Crimean War was poorly planned and poorly fought. Britain and France decided on an attack on Russia's Crimean peninsula in the Black Sea. After a long siege and at a terrible cost in troops on both sides, the main Russian fortress of Sevastopol fell in September 1855, and the Russians soon sued for peace. By the Treaty of Paris, signed in March 1856, Russia was forced to give up Bessarabia at the mouth of the Danube and accept the neutrality of the

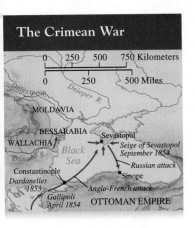

The Crimean War

0   250   500   750 Kilometers

0   250   500 Miles

MOLDAVIA

BESSARABIA

WALLACHIA

Dnieper R.

Dniester R.

Danube R.

Black Sea

Sevastopol

Seige of Sevastopol September 1854

Russian attack

Sinope

Constantinople

Dardanelles 1853

Anglo-French attack

Gallipoli April 1854

OTTOMAN EMPIRE

Black Sea. In addition, the Danubian principalities of Moldavia and Wallachia were placed under the protection of all the great powers.

The Crimean War proved costly to both sides. More than 250,000 soldiers died in the Crimean War, 60 percent of the deaths coming from disease (especially cholera). Even more would have died on the British side if it had not been for the efforts of Florence Nightingale (1820–1910). Her insistence on strict sanitary conditions saved many lives and helped make nursing a profession of trained, middle-class women.

The Crimean War destroyed the Concert of Europe. Austria and Russia, the two chief powers maintaining the status quo in the first half of the nineteenth century, were now enemies because of Austria's unwillingness to support Russia in the war. Russia, defeated and humiliated by the obvious failure of its armies, withdrew from European affairs for the next two decades. Great Britain, disillusioned by its role in the war, also pulled back from Con-

tinental affairs. Austria, paying the price for its neutrality, was now without friends among the great powers. This new international situation opened the door for the unification of Italy and Germany.

NATIONAL UNIFICATION AND THE NATIONAL STATE, 1848–1871

The revolutions of 1848 had failed, but within twenty-five years, many of the goals sought by liberals and nationalists during the first half of the nineteenth century were achieved. Italy and Germany became nations, and many European states were led by constitutional monarchs.

The Unification of Italy

The Italians were the first people to benefit from the breakdown of the Concert of Europe. In 1850, Austria was still the dominant power on the Italian peninsula. After the failure of the revolution of 1848–1849, more and more Italians looked to the northern Italian state of Piedmont, ruled by the royal house of Savoy, as their best hope to achieve the unification of Italy. It was, however, doubtful that the little state could provide the leadership needed

⇒ **FLORENCE NIGHTINGALE AND THE NURSING PROFESSION.**   By her efforts in the Crimean War, the British nurse Florence Nightingale helped to make nursing a modern profession for middle-class women. She is shown here supervising her hospital at Scutari. Her attention to strict hygiene greatly reduced the death rate for wounded British soldiers.

Wellcome Institute Library, London

GARIBALDI AND ROMANTIC NATIONALISM

Giuseppe Garibaldi was one of the more colorful figures involved in the unification of Italy. Accompanied by only a thousand of his famous Red Shirts, the Italian soldier of fortune left Genoa on the night of May 5, 1860, for an invasion of the kingdom of the Two Sicilies. The ragged band entered Palermo, the chief city on the island of Sicily, on May 31. This selection is taken from an account by a correspondent for the Times of London, the Hungarian-born Nandor Eber.

TIMES, JUNE 13, 1860

Palermo, May 31—Anyone in search of violent emotions cannot do better than set off at once for Palermo. However blasé he may be, or however milk-and-water his blood, I promise it will be stirred up. He will be carried away by the tide of popular feeling. . . .

In the afternoon Garibaldi made a tour of inspection round the town. I was there, but find it really impossible to give you a faint idea of the manner in which he was received everywhere. It was one of those triumphs which seem to be almost too much for a man. . . . The popular idol, Garibaldi, in his red flannel shirt, with a loose colored handkerchief round his neck, and his worn "wide-awake" [a soft-brimmed felt hat], was walking on foot among those cheering, laughing, crying, mad thousands; and all his few followers could do was to prevent him from being bodily carried off the ground. The people threw themselves forward to kiss his hands, or, at least, to touch the hem of his garment, as if it contained the panacea for all their past and perhaps coming suffering. Children were brought up, and mothers asked on their knees for his blessing; and all this while the object of this idolatry was calm and smiling as when in the deadliest fire, taking up the children and kissing them, trying to quiet the crowd, stopping at every moment to hear a long complaint of houses burned and property sacked by the retreating soldiers, giving good advice, comforting, and promising that all damages should be paid for. . . .

One might write volumes of horrors on the vandalism already committed, for every one of the hundred ruins has its story of brutality and inhumanity. . . . In these small houses a dense population is crowded together even in ordinary times. A shell falling on one, and crushing and burying the inmates, was sufficient to make people abandon the neighboring one and take refuge a little further on, shutting themselves up in the cellars. When the Royalists retired they set fire to those of the houses which had escaped the shells, and numbers were thus burned alive in their hiding places. . . .

If you can stand the exhalation, try and go inside the ruins, for it is only there that you will see what the thing means and you will not have to search long before you stumble over the remains of a human body, a leg sticking out here, an arm there, a black face staring at you a little further on. You are startled by a rustle. You look round and see half a dozen gorged rats scampering off in all directions, or you see a dog trying to make his escape over the ruins. . . . I only wonder that the sign of these scenes does not convert every man in the town into a tiger and every woman into a fury. But these people have been so long ground down and demoralized that their nature seems to have lost the power of reaction.

---

to unify Italy until King Victor Emmanuel II (1849–1878) named Count Camillo di Cavour (1810–1861) prime minister in 1852.

As prime minister, Cavour pursued a policy of economic expansion that increased government revenues and enabled Piedmont to equip a large army. Cavour, however, knew that Piedmont's army was not strong enough to beat the Austrians; consequently, he made an alliance with the French emperor Louis Napoleon, and then provoked the Austrians into invading Piedmont in 1859. After French armies defeated the Austrians, a peace settlement gave the French Nice and Savoy, which they had been promised for making the alliance, and Lombardy went to Piedmont (see Map 18.4). Cavour's success caused nationalists in some northern Italian states (Parma, Modena, and Tuscany) to overthrow their governments and join Piedmont.

Meanwhile, in southern Italy, Giuseppe Garibaldi (1807–1882), a dedicated Italian patriot, raised an army of a thousand volunteers called the Red Shirts because of the color of their uniforms. Garibaldi's forces swept through Sicily and then crossed over to the mainland and began a victorious march up the Italian peninsula (see the box above). Naples, and with it the kingdom of the Two Sicilies, fell in early September. Ever the patriot, Garibaldi chose to turn over his conquests to Cavour's Piedmontese forces. On March 17, 1861, the new kingdom of Italy was proclaimed under a centralized government subordinated to the control of Piedmont and King Victor Emmanuel II (1861–1878) of the house of Savoy.

The task of unification was not yet complete, however. Venetia in the north was still held by Austria, and Rome was under papal control, supported by French troops. In the Austro-Prussian War of 1866, the new Italian state became an ally of Prussia. Although the Italian army was defeated by the Austrians, Prussia's victory left the Italians with Venetia. In 1870, the Franco-Prussian War resulted

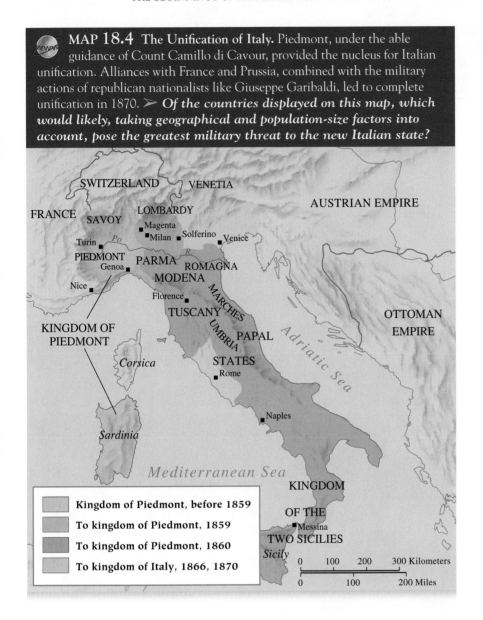

MAP 18.4 The Unification of Italy. Piedmont, under the able guidance of Count Camillo di Cavour, provided the nucleus for Italian unification. Alliances with France and Prussia, combined with the military actions of republican nationalists like Giuseppe Garibaldi, led to complete unification in 1870. ➤ *Of the countries displayed on this map, which would likely, taking geographical and population-size factors into account, pose the greatest military threat to the new Italian state?*

in the withdrawal of French troops from Rome. The Italian army then annexed the city on September 20, 1870, and Rome became the new capital of the united Italian state.

The Unification of Germany

After the failure of the Frankfurt Assembly to achieve German unification in 1848–1849, more and more Germans looked to Prussia for leadership in the cause of German unification. Prussia had become a strong, prosperous, and authoritarian state, with the Prussian king in firm control of both government and the army. In the 1860s, King William I (1861–1888) attempted to enlarge and strengthen the Prussian army. When the Prussian legislature refused to levy new taxes for the proposed military changes, William appointed a new prime minister, Count Otto von Bismarck (1815–1898). Bismarck

ignored the legislative opposition to the military reforms, arguing instead that "Germany does not look to Prussia's liberalism but to her power. . . . Not by speeches and majorities will the great questions of the day be decided—that was the mistake of 1848–1849—but by iron and blood."[4] Bismarck collected the taxes, reorganized the army anyway, and governed Prussia by simply ignoring parliament. In the meantime, opposition to his domestic policy determined Bismarck on an active foreign policy, which led to war and German unification. Bismarck has often been portrayed as the ultimate realist, the foremost nineteenth-century practitioner of *Realpolitik*—the "politics of reality."

After defeating Denmark with Austrian help in 1864 and gaining control over the duchies of Schleswig and Holstein (see Map 18.5), Bismarck created friction with the Austrians and goaded them into a war on June 14, 1866. The Austrians, no match for the disciplined Prussian army,

MAP 18.5 The Unification of Germany. Count Otto von Bismarck, the Prussian prime minister, skillfully combined domestic policies with wars with Denmark, Austria, and France to achieve the creation of the German Empire in 1871. ➤ *From the Prussian perspective of increasing its military power and ability to rule all parts of its lands, which was more important: formation of the North German Confederation or absorption of the South German Confederation?*

were decisively defeated at Königgrätz on July 3. Prussia now organized the German states north of the Main River into the North German Confederation. The southern German states, largely Catholic, remained independent but signed military alliances with Prussia due to their fear of France, their western neighbor.

Prussia now dominated all of northern Germany. However, problems with France soon arose. Bismark realized that France would never be content with a strong German state to its east because of the potential threat to French security. In 1870, Prussia and France became embroiled in a dispute over the candidacy of a relative of the Prussian king for the throne of Spain. Bismarck manipulated the misunderstandings between the French and Prussians to goad the French into declaring war on Prussia on July 15, 1870. The southern German states

honored their military alliances with Prussia and joined the war effort against the French. The Prussian armies advanced into France, and at Sedan, on September 2, 1870, captured an entire French army and Napoleon III himself. Paris capitulated on January 28, 1871. France had to pay an indemnity of 5 billion francs (about $1 billion) and give up the provinces of Alsace and Lorraine to the new German state, a loss that left the French burning for revenge.

Even before the war had ended, the southern German states had agreed to enter the North German Confederation. On January 18, 1871, in the Hall of Mirrors in Louis XIV's palace at Versailles, William I was proclaimed kaiser or emperor of the Second German Empire (the first was the medieval Holy Roman Empire). German unity had been achieved by the Prussian monarchy and the Prussian

Anton von Werner, Photo © Bildarchiv Preussischer Kulturbesitz, Berlin

➤➤ **THE UNIFICATION OF GERMANY.**   Under Prussian leadership, a new German empire was proclaimed on January 18, 1871, in the Hall of Mirrors in the palace at Versailles. King William of Prussia became Emperor William I of the Second German Empire. Otto von Bismarck, the man who had been so instrumental in creating the new German state, is shown here, resplendently attired in his white uniform, standing at the foot of the throne.

army. The Prussian leadership of German unification meant the triumph of authoritarian, militaristic values over liberal, constitutional sentiments in the development of the new German state. With its industrial resources and military might, the new state had become the strongest power on the Continent. A new European balance of power was at hand.

Nationalism and Reform: The European National State at Mid-Century

While European affairs were dominated by the unification of Italy and Germany, other states in the Western world were also undergoing change.

GREAT BRITAIN

Unlike the nations on the Continent, Great Britain managed to avoid the revolutionary upheavals of the first half of the nineteenth century. In 1815, Great Britain was governed by the aristocratic landowning classes that dominated both houses of Parliament. But in 1832, to avoid the turmoil on the Continent, Parliament passed a reform bill that increased the number of male voters, chiefly members of the industrial middle class. By joining the industrial

middle class to the landed interest in ruling Britain, Britain avoided revolution in 1848.

In the 1850s and 1860s, the liberal parliamentary system of Britain made both social and political reforms that enabled the country to remain stable. One of the other reasons for Britain's stability was its continuing economic growth. After 1850, middle-class prosperity was at last coupled with some improvements for the working classes as real wages for laborers increased over 25 percent between 1850 and 1870. The British sense of national pride was well reflected in Queen Victoria (1837 to 1901), whose sense of duty and moral respectability reflected the attitudes of her age, which has ever since been known as the Victorian Age.

FRANCE

Events in France after the revolution of 1848 moved toward the restoration of monarchy. Four years after his election as president, Louis Napoleon returned to the people to ask for the restoration of the empire. Ninety-seven percent responded in the affirmative, and on December 2, 1852, Louis Napoleon assumed the title of Napoleon III (the first Napoleon had abdicated in favor of his son, Napoleon II, on April 6, 1814). The Second Empire had begun.

DEVELOPMENTS IN EUROPE, 1800–1871

Great Britain

Reform Act	1832
Queen Victoria	1837–1901

France

Louis-Philippe	1830–1848
Abdication of Louis-Philippe; formation of provisional government	February 1848
Establishment of Second Republic	November 1848
Election of Louis Napoleon as French president	December 1848
Emperor Napoleon III	1852–1870

Germany

Germanic Confederation	1815
Frederick William IV of Prussia	1840–1861
Revolution in Germany	1848
Frankfurt Assembly	1848–1849
Unification of Germany	
King William I of Prussia	1861–1888
Danish War	1864
Austro-Prussian War	1866
Franco-Prussian War	1870–1871
German Empire is proclaimed	January 18, 1871

The Austrian Empire

Revolt, Metternich dismissed	March 1848
Viennese rebels crushed	October 1848
Defeat of Hungarians with help of Russian troops	1849
Ausgleich; Dual monarchy	1867

Italy

Revolutions in Italy	1848
Austrian control in Lombardy and Venetia	1849
Unification of Italy	
Victor Emmanuel II	1849–1878
Count Cavour becomes prime minister of Piedmont	1852
Garibaldi's invasion of the Two Sicilies	1860
Kingdom of Italy is proclaimed	March 17, 1861
Italy's annexation of Venetia	1866
Italy's annexation of Rome	1870

Russia

Tsar Alexander II	1855–1881
Emancipation edict	March 3, 1861

Ottoman Empire

Crimean War	1853–1856

The first five years of Napoleon III's reign were a spectacular success. He took many steps to expand industrial growth. Government subsidies helped foster the rapid construction of railroads as well as harbors, roads, and canals. The major French railway lines were completed during Napoleon's reign, and iron production tripled. In the midst of this economic expansion, Napoleon III also undertook a vast reconstruction of the city of Paris. The medieval Paris of narrow streets and old city walls was destroyed and replaced by a modern Paris of broad boulevards, spacious buildings, circular plazas, public squares, an underground sewage system, a new public water supply, and gas streetlights.

In the 1860s, as opposition to his rule began to mount, Napoleon III liberalized his regime. He gave the Legislative Corps more say in affairs of state, including debate over the budget. Liberalization policies worked initially; in a plebiscite in May 1870 on whether to accept a new constitution that might have inaugurated a parliamentary regime, the French people gave Napoleon another resounding victory. This triumph was short-lived, how-

ever. War with Prussia in 1870 brought Napoleon's ouster, and a republic was proclaimed.

THE AUSTRIAN EMPIRE

Although nationalism was a major force in nineteenth-century Europe, one of the region's most powerful states, the Austrian Empire, managed to frustrate the desire of its numerous ethnic groups for self-determination. After the Habsburg rulers had crushed the revolutions of 1848–1849, they restored centralized, autocratic government to the empire. But Austria's defeat at the hands of the Prussians in 1866 forced the Austrians to deal with the fiercely nationalistic Hungarians.

The result was the negotiated *Ausgleich*, or Compromise, of 1867, which created the Dual Monarchy of Austria-Hungary. Each part of the empire now had its own constitution, its own legislature, its own governmental bureaucracy, and its own capital (Vienna for Austria and Budapest for Hungary). Holding the two states together were a single monarch—Francis Joseph (1848–

EMANCIPATION: SERFS AND SLAVES

*A*lthough overall their histories have been quite different, Russia and the United States shared a common feature in the 1860s. They were the only states in the Western world that still had large enslaved populations (the Russian serfs were virtually slaves). The leaders of both countries issued emancipation proclamations within two years of each other. The first excerpt is taken from the imperial decree of March 3, 1861, which freed the Russian serfs. The second excerpt is from Abraham Lincoln's Emancipation Proclamation, issued on January 1, 1863.

ALEXANDER II'S IMPERIAL DECREE, MARCH 3, 1861

By the grace of God, we, Alexander II, Emperor and Autocrat of all the Russias, King of Poland, Grand Duke of Finland, etc., to all our faithful subjects, make known:

Called by Divine Providence and by the sacred right of inheritance to the throne of our ancestors, we took a vow in our innermost heart to respond to the mission which is intrusted to us as to surround with our affection and our Imperial solicitude all our faithful subjects of every rank and of every condition, from the warrior, who nobly bears arms for the defense of the country, to the humble artisan devoted to the works of industry; from the official in the career of the high offices of the State to the laborer whose plough furrows the soil. . . .

We thus came to the conviction that the work of a serious improvement of the condition of the peasants was a sacred inheritance bequeathed to us by our ancestors, a mission which, in the course of events, Divine Providence called upon us to fulfill. . . .

In virtue of the new dispositions above mentioned, the peasants attached to the soil will be invested within a term fixed by the law with all the rights of free cultivators. . . .

At the same time, they are granted the right of purchasing their close, and, with the consent of the proprietors, they may acquire in full property the arable lands and other appurtenances which are allotted to them as a permanent holding. By the acquisition in full property of the quantity of land fixed, the peasants are free from their obligations toward the proprietors for land thus purchased, and they enter definitely into the condition of free peasants-landholders.

LINCOLN'S EMANCIPATION PROCLAMATION, JANUARY 1, 1863

Now therefore, I, Abraham Lincoln, President of the United States, by virtue of the power in me vested as Commander-in-Chief of the Army and Navy of the United States in time of actual armed rebellion against the authority and government of the United States, and as a fit and necessary war measure for suppressing such rebellion, do, on this 1st day of January, A.D. 1863, and in accordance with my purpose to do so, . . . order and designate as the States and parts of States wherein the people thereof, respectively, are this day in rebellion against the United States the following, to wit:

Arkansas, Texas, Louisiana, . . . Mississippi, Alabama, Florida, Georgia, South Carolina, North Carolina, and Virginia . . .

And by virtue of the power for the purpose aforesaid, I do order and declare that all persons held as slaves within said designated States and parts of States are, and henceforward shall be free; and that the Executive Government of the United States, including the military and naval authorities thereof, will recognize and maintain the freedom of said persons.

1916) was emperor of Austria and king of Hungary—and a common army, foreign policy, and system of finances. The *Ausgleich* did not, however, satisfy the other nationalities that made up the Austro-Hungarian Empire.

RUSSIA

At the beginning of the nineteenth century, Russia was overwhelmingly rural, agricultural, and autocratic. The Russian tsar was still regarded as a divine-right monarch with unlimited power. The Russian imperial autocracy, based on soldiers, secret police, and repression, had withstood the revolutionary fervor of the first half of the nineteenth century. However, defeat in the Crimean War in 1856 led even staunch conservatives to realize that Russia was falling hopelessly behind the western European powers. Tsar Alexander II (1855–1881) decided to make serious reforms.

Serfdom was the most burdensome problem in tsarist Russia. On March 3, 1861, Alexander issued his emancipation edict (see the box above). Peasants were now free to own property and marry as they chose. But the system of land redistribution instituted after emancipation was not that favorable to them. The government provided land for the peasants by purchasing it from the landlords, but the landowners often chose to keep the best parcels. The Russian peasants soon found that they had inadequate amounts of arable land to support themselves.

Nor were the peasants completely free. The state compensated the landowners for the land given to the peasants, but the peasants were expected to repay the state in long-term installments. To ensure that the payments were made, peasants were subjected to the authority of their *mir*, or village commune, which was collectively responsible for the land payments to the government. And since the village communes were responsible for the payments, they were reluctant to allow peasants to leave their land. Emancipation, then, led not to a free, landowning peasantry along the Western model but to an unhappy, land-starved peasantry that largely followed the old ways of agricultural production.

Alexander II attempted other reforms as well, but he soon found that he could please no one. Reformers wanted more and rapid change; conservatives thought that the tsar was attempting to undermine the basic institutions of Russian society. When one group of radicals assassinated Alexander II in 1881, his son and successor, Alexander III, turned against reform and returned to the traditional methods of repression.

The Growth of the United States

The U.S. Constitution, ratified in 1789, committed the United States to two of the major forces of the first half of the nineteenth century, liberalism and nationalism. The election of Andrew Jackson (1767–1845) as president in 1828 opened a new era in American politics. Jacksonian democracy introduced a mass democratic politics as property qualifications for voting were dropped. By the 1830s, suffrage had been extended to almost all adult white males.

By the mid-nineteenth century, the issue of slavery had become a threat to American national unity. Like the North, the South had grown dramatically in population during the first half of the nineteenth century. However, the South's economy was based on growing cotton on plantations, chiefly by slave labor. Although new slave imports had been barred in 1808, there were 4 million African American slaves in the South by 1860—four times the number sixty years earlier. The cotton economy and plantation-based slavery were related, and the South was determined to maintain them. The growth of an abolitionist movement in the North challenged the southern order.

As polarization over the issue of slavery intensified, compromise became less feasible. When Abraham Lincoln, who had said in a speech in Illinois in 1858 that "this government cannot endure permanently half slave and half free," was elected president in November 1860, the die was cast. Lincoln carried only 2 of the 1,109 counties in the South. On December 20, 1860, a South Carolina convention voted to repeal ratification of the Constitution of the United States. In February 1861, six more southern states did the same, and a rival nation—the Confederate States of America—was formed. In April, fighting eruped between North and South.

The American Civil War (1861–1865) was an extraordinarily bloody struggle. Over 600,000 soldiers died, either in battle or from deadly infectious diseases spawned by filthy camp conditions. Over a period of four years, the Union (Northern) states mobilized their superior assets and gradually wore down the South. Moreover, what had begun as a war to save the Union became a war against slavery. On January 1, 1863, Lincoln's Emancipation Proclamation made most of the nation's slaves "forever free" (see the box on p. 533). The surrender of Confederate forces on April 9, 1865, confirmed that the United States would be "one nation, indivisible." National unity had prevailed in the United States, and the nation's relentless expansion across the North American continent continued unabated (see Map 18.6).

The Emergence of a Canadian Nation

By the Treaty of Paris in 1763, Canada—or New France, as it was called—passed into the hands of the British. By 1800, most Canadians favored more autonomy, although differences existed among the colonists on the form this autonomy should take. Upper Canada (now Ontario) was predominantly English-speaking, while Lower Canada (new Quebec) was dominated by French Canadians. Increased immigration to Canada after 1815 also fueled the desire for self-government. After two short rebellions against the government broke out in Upper and Lower Canada in 1837 and 1838, the British moved toward change. In 1840, the British Parliament formally joined Upper and Lower Canada into the United Provinces of Canada, without granting self-government.

The head of Upper Canada's Conservative Party, John Macdonald, became an avid apostle for self-government. Fearful of American designs on Canada, the British government finally capitulated to Macdonald's campaign, and in 1867, Parliament passed the British North American Act, which established a Canadian nation—the Dominion of Canada—with its own constitution. John Macdonald became the first prime minister. Although Canada now possessed a parliamentary system and ruled itself, foreign affairs still remained the preserve of the British government.

CULTURAL LIFE: ROMANTICISM AND REALISM IN THE WESTERN WORLD

At the end of the eighteenth century, a new intellectual movement known as Romanticism emerged to challenge the ideas of the Enlightenment. The Enlightenment stressed reason as the chief means for discovering truth. Although the Romantics by no means disparaged reason, they tried to balance its use by stressing the importance of feeling, emotion, and imagination as sources of knowing.

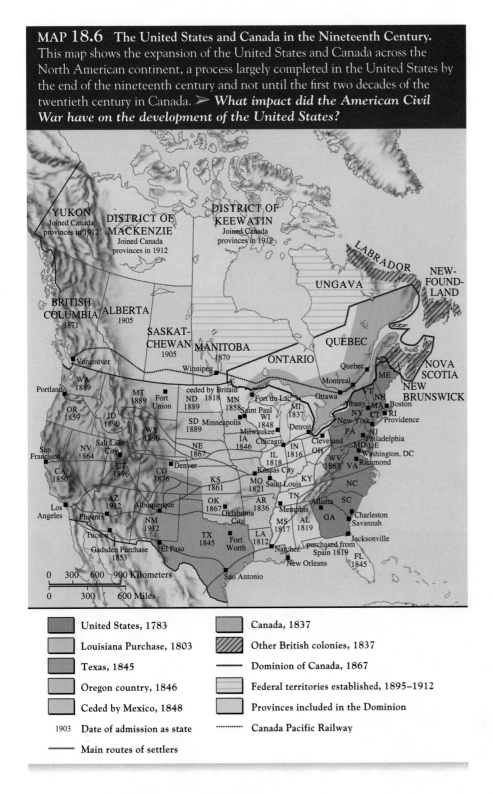

MAP 18.6 The United States and Canada in the Nineteenth Century. This map shows the expansion of the United States and Canada across the North American continent, a process largely completed in the United States by the end of the nineteenth century and not until the first two decades of the twentieth century in Canada. ➤ *What impact did the American Civil War have on the development of the United States?*

The Characteristics of Romanticism

Romantic writers emphasized emotion and sentiment and believed that these inner feelings were understandable only to the person experiencing them. In their novels, Romantic writers created figures who were often misun-

derstood and rejected by society but who continued to believe in their own worth through their inner feelings.

Many Romantics also possessed a passionate interest in the past. They revived medieval Gothic architecture and left European countrysides adorned with pseudo-medieval castles and cities bedecked with grandiose neo-Gothic cathedrals, city halls, and parliamentary buildings. Literature, too, reflected this historical consciousness. The novels of Walter Scott (1771–1832) became European best-sellers in the first half of the nineteenth century. *Ivanhoe*, in which Scott tried to evoke the clash between Saxon and Norman knights in medieval England, became one of his most popular works.

Many Romantics had a deep attraction to the exotic and unfamiliar. In an exaggerated form, this preoccupation gave rise to so-called Gothic literature, chillingly evident in Mary Shelley's *Frankenstein* and Edgar Allen Poe's short stories of horror (see the box on p. 537). Some Romantics even brought the unusual into their own lives by seeking extraordinary states of experience in dreams, nightmares, supernatural possession, frenzies, and suicidal depression or in drug-induced altered states of consciousness by experimenting with cocaine, opium, and hashish.

To the Romantics, poetry ranked above all other literary forms because it was viewed as the direct expression of the soul. Romantic poetry gave full expression to one of the most important characteristics of Romanticism: love of nature, especially evident in the poetry of William Wordsworth (1770–1850), the foremost Romantic prophet

⇨ **CASPAR DAVID FRIEDRICH, *MAN AND WOMAN GAZING AT THE MOON.*** The German artist Caspar David Friedrich sought to express in painting his own mystical view of nature. "The divine is everywhere," he once wrote, "even in a grain of sand." In this painting, a couple is shown from the back gazing at the moon. They are overwhelmed by the powerful presence of nature and the immensity of the universe.

Nationalgalerie SMPK Berlin, Photo: Jorg P. Anders, ©Bildarchiv Preussischer Kulturbesitz, Berlin

GOTHIC LITERATURE: EDGAR ALLAN POE

American writers and poets made significant contributions to the movement of Romanticism. Although Edgar Allan Poe (1809–1849) was influenced by the German Romantic school of mystery and horror, many literary historians give him the credit for pioneering the modern short story. This selection from the conclusion of "The Fall of the House of Usher" gives a feeling for the nature of so-called Gothic literature.

EDGAR ALLAN POE, "THE FALL OF THE HOUSE OF USHER"

No sooner had these syllables passed my lips, than—as if a shield of brass had indeed, at the moment, fallen heavily upon a floor of silver—I became aware of a distinct, hollow, metallic, and clangorous, yet apparently muffled, reverberation. Completely unnerved, I leaped to my feet; but the measured rocking movement of Usher was undisturbed. I rushed to the chair in which he sat. His eyes were bent fixedly before him, and throughout his whole countenance there reigned a stony rigidity. But, as I placed my hand upon his shoulder, there came a strong shudder over his whole person; a sickly smile quivered about his lips; and I saw that he spoke in a low, hurried, and gibbering murmur, as if unconscious of my presence. Bending closely over him, I at length drank in the hideous import of his words.

"Not hear it?—yes, I hear it, and *have* heard it. Long-long-long-many minutes, many hours, many days, have I heard it—yet I dared not—oh, pity me, miserable wretch that I am!—I dared not—I *dared* not speak! *We have put her living in the tomb!* Said I not that my senses were acute? I *now* tell you that I heard her first feeble movements in the hollow coffin. I heard them—many, many days ago—yet I dared not—*I dared not speak!* And now—to-night— . . . the rending of her coffin, and the grating of the iron hinges of her prison, and her struggles within the coppered archway of the vault! Oh whither shall I fly? Will she not be here anon? Is she not hurrying to upbraid me for my haste? Have I not heard her footstep on the stair? Do I not distinguish that heavy and horrible beating of her heart? MADMAN!"—here he sprang furiously to his feet, and shrieked out his syllables, as if in the effort he were giving up his soul—"MADMAN! I TELL YOU THAT SHE NOW STANDS WITHOUT THE DOOR!"

As if in the superhuman energy of his utterance there had been found the potency of a spell, the huge antique panels to which the speaker pointed threw slowly back, upon the instant, their ponderous and ebony jaws. It was the work of the rushing gust—but then without those doors there DID stand the lofty and enshrouded figure of the lady Madeline of Usher. There was blood upon her white robes, and the evidence of some bitter struggle upon every portion of her emaciated frame. For a moment she remained trembling and reeling to and fro upon the threshold, then, with a low moaning cry, fell heavily inward upon the person of her brother, and in her violent and now final death-agonies, bore him to the floor a corpse, and a victim to the terrors he had anticipated.

---

of nature. His experience of nature was almost mystical as he claimed to receive "authentic tidings of invisible things":

> One impulse from a vernal wood
> May teach you more of man,
> Of Moral Evil and of good,
> Than all the sages can.[5]

Romantics believed that nature served as a mirror into which humans could look to learn about themselves.

Like the literary arts, the visual arts were also deeply affected by Romanticism. Romantic artists shared at least two fundamental characteristics. All artistic expression to them was a reflection of the artist's inner feelings; a painting should mirror the artist's vision of the world and be the instrument of his own imagination. Moreover, Romantic artists deliberately rejected the principles of classicism. Beauty was not a timeless thing; its expression depended on one's culture and one's age. The Romantics abandoned classical restraint for warmth, emotion, and movement.

The early life experiences of Caspar David Friedrich (1774–1840) left him with a lifelong preoccupation with God and nature. Friedrich painted landscapes with an interest that transcended the mere presentation of natural details. His portrayals of mountains shrouded in mist, gnarled trees bathed in moonlight, and the stark ruins of monasteries surrounded by withered trees all conveyed a feeling of mystery and mysticism. For Friedrich, nature was a manifestation of divine life, as is evident in *Man and Woman Gazing at the Moon*. To Friedrich, the artistic process depended on the use of an unrestricted imagination that could only be achieved through inner vision.

Eugène Delacroix (1798–1863) was one of the most famous French exponents of the Romantic school of painting. Delacroix's paintings exhibited two primary characteristics, a fascination with the exotic and a passion for color. Both are apparent in *The Death of Sardanapalus*. Significant for its use of light and its patches of interrelated color, this portrayal of the world of the last Assyrian king was criticized at the time for its brilliant color. In Delacroix, theatricality and movement combined with a daring use of color. Many of his works reflect his own belief that "a painting should be a feast to the eye."

EUGÈNE DELACROIX, *THE DEATH OF SARDANAPALUS.* Delacroix's *Death of Sardanapalus* was based on Lord Byron's verse account of the decadent Assyrian king's dramatic last moments. Beseiged by enemy troops and with little hope of survival, Sardanapalus orders that his harem women and prize horses go to their death with him. At the right, a guard stabs one of the women as the king looks on.

To many Romantics, music was the most Romantic of the arts because it enabled the composer to probe deeply into human emotions. Music historians have called the eighteenth century an age of classicism and the nineteenth the era of Romanticism. One of the greatest composers of all time, Ludwig van Beethoven, served as a bridge between classicism and Romanticism.

Beethoven (1770–1827) was born in Bonn, Germany, but soon made his way to Vienna, then the musical capital of Europe, where he studied briefly under Mozart. Beginning in 1792, Vienna became his permanent residence. During his first major period of composing, from 1792 to 1802, his work was still largely within the classical framework of the eighteenth century, and his style differed little from that of Mozart and Haydn. But with his Third Symphony, the *Eroica*, originally intended for Napoleon, Beethoven broke through to the elements of Romanticism in his use of fierce rhythms to create dramatic struggle and uplifted resolutions. E. T. A. Hoffman, a contemporary composer and writer, said, "Beethoven's music opens the floodgates of fear, of terror, of horror, of pain, and arouses that longing for the eternal which is the essence of Romanticism. He is thus a pure Romantic composer."[6]

A New Age of Science

The Scientific Revolution had created a modern, rational approach to the study of the natural world, but even in the eighteenth century, these intellectual developments had remained the preserve of an educated elite and resulted in few practical benefits. With the Industrial Revolution, however, came a renewed interest in basic scientific research. By the 1830s, new scientific discoveries had led to many practical benefits that caused science to have an ever-greater impact on European life.

In biology, the Frenchman Louis Pasteur (1822–1895) came up with the germ theory of disease, which had enormous practical applications in the development of modern scientific medical practices. In chemistry, the Russian Dmitri Mendeleev (1834–1907) in the 1860s classified all the material elements then known on the basis of their atomic weights and provided the systematic foundation for the periodic law. The Briton Michael Faraday (1791–1867) put together a primitive generator that laid the foundation for the use of electricity.

The popularity of scientific and technological achievement produced a widespread acceptance of the scientific method as the only path to objective truth and objective reality. This undermined the faith of many people in religious revelation. It is no accident that the nineteenth century was an age of increasing secularization, evident in the belief that truth was to be found in the concrete material existence of human beings. No one did more to create a picture of humans as material beings that were simply part of the natural world than Charles Darwin.

In 1859, Charles Darwin (1809–1882) published *On the Origin of Species by Means of Natural Selection*. The basic idea of this book was that all plants and animals had each evolved over a long period of time from earlier and simpler forms of life, a principle known as organic evolution. Darwin was important in explaining how this natural process worked. In every species, he argued, "many more individuals of each species are born than can possibly survive." This results in a "struggle for existence." Darwin believed that some organisms were more adaptable to the environment than others, a process that Darwin called natural selection. Those that were naturally selected for survival ("survival of the fit") reproduced and thrived. The unfit did not and became extinct. The fit who survived passed on small variations that enhanced their survival until, from Darwin's point of view, a new separate species emerged. In *The Descent of Man,* published in 1871, he argued for the animal origins of human beings: "Man is the co-descendant with other mammals of a common progenitor." Humans were not an exception to the rule governing other species.

Realism in Literature and Art

The word Realism was first employed in 1850 to describe a new style of painting and soon spread to literature. The literary Realists of the mid-nineteenth century rejected Romanticism. They wanted to deal with ordinary characters from actual life rather than Romantic heroes in exotic settings. They also sought to avoid emotional language by using close observation and precise description, an approach that led them to write novels rather than poems.

The leading novelist of the 1850s and 1860s, the Frenchman Gustave Flaubert (1821–1880), perfected the Realist novel. His *Madame Bovary* (1857) was a straightforward description of barren and sordid provincial life in France. Emma Bovary is trapped in a marriage to a drab provincial doctor. Impelled by the images of romantic love she has read about in novels, she seeks the same thing for herself in adulterous love affairs. Unfulfilled, she is ultimately driven to suicide, unrepentant to the end for her lifestyle.

In art, too, Realism became dominant after 1850. Realist art demonstrated three major characteristics: a desire to depict the everyday life of ordinary people, whether peasants, workers, or prostitutes; an attempt at photographic realism; and an interest in the natural environment. The French became leaders in Realist painting.

Gustave Courbet (1819–1877), the most famous artist of the Realist school, reveled in realistic portrayals of everyday life. His subjects were factory workers, peasants, and the wives of saloonkeepers. "I have never seen either angels or goddesses, so I am not interested in painting them," he exclaimed. One of his famous works, *The Stonebreakers,* painted in 1849, shows two road workers engaged in the deadening work of breaking stones to build a road. This representation of human misery was a scandal to those who objected to his "cult of ugliness."

CONCLUSION

Between 1800 and 1870, the forces unleashed by two revolutions—the French Revolution and the Industrial Revolution—transformed much of the world and led to Western global dominance by the end of the nineteenth century. The Industrial Revolution seemed to prove to Europeans the underlying assumption of the Scientific

GUSTAVE COURBET, *THE STONEBREAKERS.* Realism, largely developed by French painters, aimed at a lifelike portrayal of the daily activities of ordinary people. Gustave Courbet was the most famous of the Realist artists. As is evident in *The Stonebreakers*, he sought to portray things as they really appear. He shows an old road builder and his young assistant in their tattered clothes, engrossed in their dreary work of breaking stones to construct a road.

Gemäldegalerie Neue Meister, Staatliche Kunstsammlungen Dresden; Photo by Reinhold, Leipzig-Molkau

Revolution of the seventeenth century—that human beings were capable of dominating nature. By rationally manipulating the material environment for human benefit, people could achieve new levels of material prosperity and produce machines not dreamed of in their wildest imaginings. Some of these new machines included weapons of war that enabled the Western world to devastate and control non-Western civilizations.

In 1815, a conservative order had been reestablished throughout Europe, but the revolutionary waves in Latin America and Europe in the first half of the nineteenth century made it clear that the ideologies of liberalism and nationalism, unleashed by the French Revolution and now reinforced by the spread of industrialization, were still alive and active in the Western world. Between 1850 and 1871, the national state became the focus of people's loyalty. Wars, both foreign and civil, were

fought to create unified nation-states, and both wars and changing political alignments served as catalysts for domestic reforms that made the nation-state the center of attention. Liberal nationalists had believed that unified nation-states would preserve individual rights and lead to a greater community of peoples. But the new nationalism of the late nineteenth century, loud and chauvinistic, did not unify peoples but divided them instead as the new national states became embroiled in bitter competition after 1870.

Many people, however, were hardly aware of nationalism's dangers in 1870. The spread of industrialization and the growing popularity of science and technology were sources of optimism, not pessimism. After the revolutionary and military upheavals of the mid-century decades, many Westerners believed that they stood on the verge of a new age of progress.

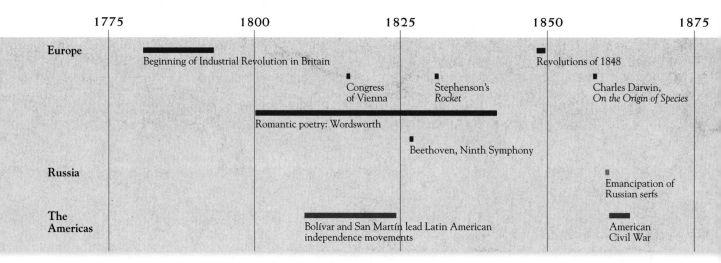

CHAPTER NOTES

1. Quotations in E. Royston Pike, *Human Documents of the Industrial Revolution in Britain* (London, 1966), pp. 314, 343.
2. Ibid., p. 315.
3. Quoted in Hubert Herring, *A History of Latin America* (New York, 1961), p. 255.
4. Quoted in Louis L. Snyder, ed., *Documents of German History* (New Brunswick, N.J., 1958), p. 202.
5. William Wordsworth, "The Tables Turned," *Poems of Wordsworth*, ed. Matthew Arnold (London, 1963), p. 138.
6. Quoted in Siegbert Prawer, ed., *The Romantic Period in Germany* (London, 1970), p. 285.

SUGGESTED READING

For a good, up-to-date survey of the entire nineteenth century, see R. Gildea, *Barricades and Borders: Europe, 1800–1914*, 2d ed. (Oxford, 1996). Also valuable is M. S. Anderson, *The Ascendancy of Europe, 1815–1914*, 2d ed. (London, 1985). The well-

written work by D. Landes, *The Unbound Prometheus: Technological Change and Industrial Development in Western Europe from 1750 to the Present* (Cambridge, 1969), is still a good introduction to the Industrial Revolution. Also of value is D. Fisher, *The Industrial Rev-*

olution (New York, 1992). There is a good collection of articles in M. Teich and R. Porter, eds., *The Industrial Revolution in National Context: Europe and the USA* (Cambridge, 1996). For a broader perspective, see P. Stearns, *The Industrial Revolution in World History* (Boulder, Colo., 1993).

A general discussion of population growth in Europe can be found in T. McKeown, *The Modern Rise of Population* (London, 1976). For an examination of urban growth, see A. R. Sutcliffe, *Toward the Planned City: Germany, Britain, the United States and France, 1780–1914* (Oxford, 1981). On the social impact of the Industrial Revolution, see P. Pilbeam, *The Middle Classes in Europe, 1789–1914* (Basingstoke, England, 1990); T. Koditschek, *Class Formation and Urban Industrial Society* (New York, 1990); and F. Crouzet, *The First Industrialists: The Problems of Origins* (Cambridge, 1985), on British entrepreneurs. G. Himmelfarb, *The Idea of Poverty: England in the Early Industrial Age* (New York, 1984), traces the concepts of poverty and poor from the mid-eighteenth century to the mid-nineteenth century. A classic work on female labor patterns is L. A. Tilly and J. W. Scott, *Women, Work, and Family* (New York, 1978). See also J. Lown, *Women and Industrialization: Gender at Work in Nineteenth-Century England* (Minneapolis, Minn., 1990).

A concise summary of the international events of the entire nineteenth century can be found in R. Bullen and F. R. Bridge, *The Great Powers and the European State System, 1815–1914* (London, 1980). For a survey of the period 1814–1848, see M. Broers, *Europe After Napoleon: Revolution, Reaction, and Romanticism, 1814–1848* (New York, 1996). There are some useful books on individual countries that cover more than this chapter. These include R. Magraw, *France, 1815–1914: The Bourgeois Century* (London, 1983); D. Saunders, *Russia in the Age of Reaction and Reform, 1801–1881* (London, 1992); J. J. Sheehan, *German History, 1770–1866* (New York, 1989); N. McCord, *British History, 1815–1906* (New York, 1991); and C. A. Macartney, *The Habsburg Empire, 1790–1918* (London, 1971).

On the man whose conservative policies dominated this era, see the brief but good biography by A. Palmer, *Metternich* (New York, 1972). The best introduction to the revolutions of 1848 is J. Sperber, *The European Revolutions, 1848–1851* (New York, 1994).

For a comprehensive survey of Latin American history, see E. Williamson, *The Penguin History of Latin America* (London,

1992). On the revolts in Latin America, see J. Lynch, *The Spanish American Revolutions, 1808–1826* (New York, 1973). A good survey of nineteenth-century developments can be found in D. Bushnell and N. Macaulay, *The Emergence of Latin America in the Nineteenth Century* (Oxford, 1988). For a detailed account of the Ottoman Empire in the nineteenth century, see S. Shaw, *History of the Ottoman Empire and Modern Turkey*, vol. 2 (Cambridge, 1977).

The unification of Italy can be examined in the works of D. M. Smith, *Victor Emmanuel, Cavour and the Risorgimento* (London, 1971), and H. Hearder, *Cavour* (New York, 1994). The unification of Germany can be pursued first in two good biographies of Bismarck, E. Crankshaw, *Bismarck* (New York, 1981), and G. O. Kent, *Bismarck and His Times* (Carbondale, Ill., 1978). See also the brief study by B. Waller, *Bismarck*, 2d ed. (Oxford, 1997). For a good introduction to the French Second Empire, see A. Plessis, *The Rise and Fall of the Second Empire, 1852–1871*, trans. J. Mandelbaum (New York, 1985). Louis Napoleon's role can be examined in J. F. McMillan, *Napoleon III* (New York, 1991). On the emancipation of the Russian serfs, see D. Field, *The End of Serfdom: Nobility and Bureaucracy in Russia, 1855–1861* (Cambridge, 1976). The evolution of British political parties in mid-century is examined in H. J. Hanham, *Elections and Party Management: Politics in the Time of Disraeli and Gladstone*, 2d ed. (London, 1978). A good one-volume survey of the Civil War can be found in P. J. Parish, *The American Civil War* (New York, 1975). For a general history of Canada, see C. Brown, ed., *The Illustrated History of Canada* (Toronto, 1991).

For an introduction to the intellectual changes of the nineteenth century, see O. Chadwick, *The Secularization of the European Mind in the Nineteenth Century* (Cambridge, 1975). A beautifully illustrated introduction to Romanticism can be found in H. Honour, *Romanticism* (New York, 1979). On the ideas of the Romantics, see H. G. Schenk, *The Mind of the European Romantics* (Garden City, N.Y., 1969), and M. Cranston, *The Romantic Movement* (Oxford, 1994). For an introduction to the arts, see W. Vaughan, *Romanticism and Art* (New York, 1994). A detailed biography of Darwin can be found in J. Bowlby, *Charles Darwin: A Biography* (London, 1990). On Realism, J. Malpas, *Realism* (Cambridge, 1997), is a good introduction.

INFOTRAC COLLEGE EDITION

For additional reading, go to InfoTrac College Edition, your online research library at http://web1.infotrac-college.com

Enter the search terms "Industrial Revolution" using Keywords.

Enter the search term "Romanticism" using the Subject Guide.

Enter the search term "nationalism" using Keywords.

Enter the search terms "industrial development" using the Subject Guide.

CORBIS

Chapter 19

THE EMERGENCE OF MASS SOCIETY IN THE WESTERN WORLD

CHAPTER OUTLINE

- THE GROWTH OF INDUSTRIAL PROSPERITY
- THE EMERGENCE OF MASS SOCIETY
- THE NATIONAL STATE
- TOWARD THE MODERN CONSCIOUSNESS: INTELLECTUAL AND CULTURAL DEVELOPMENTS
- CONCLUSION

FOCUS QUESTIONS

- What was the Second Industrial Revolution, and what effects did it have on economic and social life?
- What were the main ideas of Karl Marx, and what role did they play in politics and the union movement in the late nineteenth and early twentieth centuries?
- What is meant by the term *mass society*, and what were its main characteristics?
- What general political trends were evident in the nations of western Europe in the late nineteenth and early twentieth centuries, and to what degree were those trends also apparent in the nations of Latin America, North America, and central and eastern Europe?
- What intellectual and cultural developments in the late nineteenth and early twentieth centuries "opened the way to a modern consciousness," and how did this consciousness differ from earlier worldviews?
- ➤ What was the relationship between economic, social, and political developments between 1871 and 1914?

The fifty years leading up to 1914 marked a dynamic age of material prosperity in the West. The new industries, new sources of energy, and new goods of the Second Industrial Revolution transformed the human environment and led people to believe that their material progress reflected human progress. Scientific and technological achievements, many naively believed, would improve the human condition and solve all problems. The doctrine of progress became an article of faith.

The rapid economic changes of the nineteenth century led to the emergence of a mass society by the century's end. Mass society meant improvements for the lower classes, who benefited from the extension of voting rights, a better standard of living, and free education. It also brought mass leisure. New work patterns established the "weekend" as a distinct time of recreation and fun, while new forms of mass transportation—railroads and streetcars—enabled even workers to make brief excursions to amusement parks. Coney Island was only 8 miles from central New York City; Blackpool in England was a short train ride from nearby industrial towns. With their Ferris wheels and other daring rides that threw young men and women together, amusement parks offered a whole new world of entertainment. Thanks to the railroad, seaside resorts, once the preserve of the wealthy, also became accessible to more people for weekend visits, much to the disgust of one upper-class regular, who complained about the new "day-trippers": "They swarm upon the beach, wandering listlessly about with apparently no other aim than to get a mouthful of fresh air." Enterprising entrepreneurs in resorts like Blackpool welcomed the masses of new visitors, however, and built piers laden with food, drink, and entertainment to serve them.

The coming of mass society also created new roles for the governments of European nation-states, which now fostered national loyalty, created mass armies by conscription, and took more responsibility for public health and housing measures in their cities. By 1871, the national state had become the focus of Europeans' lives. Within many of these nation-states, the growth of the middle class had led to the triumph of liberal practices: constitutional governments, parliaments, and principles of equality. The period after 1871 also witnessed the growth of political democracy as the right to vote was extended to all adult males; women would still have to fight for the same political rights. With political democracy came a new mass politics that would become a regular feature of the twentieth century.

The period between 1870 and 1914 was also a time of great tension as imperialist adventures, international rivalries, and cultural uncertainties disturbed the apparent calm. Europeans engaged in a race for colonies that greatly intensified existing antagonisms among European states, and the creation of mass conscript armies and enormous military establishments served to heighten tensions among the major powers. At the same time, despite the appearance of progress, Western philosophers, writers, and artists were exploring modern cultural expressions that questioned traditional ideas and values and increasingly provoked a crisis of confidence. •

THE GROWTH OF INDUSTRIAL PROSPERITY

At the heart of Europe's belief in progress between 1870 and 1914 was the stunning material growth produced by what historians have called the Second Industrial Revolution. The first Industrial Revolution had given rise to textiles, railroads, iron, and coal. In the second revolution, steel, chemicals, electricity, and petroleum led the way to new industrial frontiers.

New Products and New Patterns

The first major change in industrial development between 1870 and 1914 was the substitution of steel for iron. New methods for shaping steel made it useful in the construction of lighter, smaller, and faster machines and engines as well as railways, ships, and armaments. In 1860, Great Britain, France, Germany, and Belgium produced 125,000 tons of steel; by 1913, the total was 32 million tons.

Electricity was a major new form of energy that could be easily converted into other forms—such as heat, light, and motion—and moved relatively effortlessly through space by means of transmitting wires. In the 1870s, the first commercially practical generators of electrical current were developed, and by 1910, hydroelectric power stations and coal-fired steam-generating plants enabled homes and factories in whole neighborhoods to be tied in to a single, common source of power.

Electricity spawned a plethora of inventions. The light bulb, developed independently by the American Thomas Edison and the Briton Joseph Swan, permitted homes and cities to be illuminated by electric lights. A revolution in communications began when Alexander Graham Bell invented the telephone in 1876 and Guglielmo Marconi sent the first radio waves across the Atlantic in 1901. Electricity was also put to use in transportation. By the 1880s, electricity-powered streetcars and subways had appeared in major European cities. Electricity also transformed the factory. Conveyor belts, cranes, machines, and machine tools could all be powered by electricity and located anywhere. Thanks to electricity, all countries could now enter the industrial age.

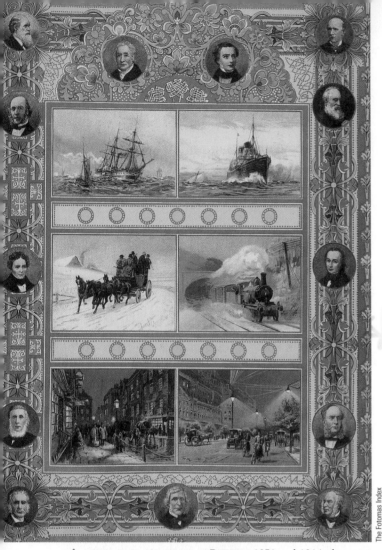

Industrial production grew rapidly at this time because of the greatly increased sales of manufactured goods. An increase in real wages for workers after 1870, combined with lower prices for manufactured goods because of reduced transportation costs, made it easier for Europeans to buy consumer products. In the cities, the first department stores began to sell a whole new range of consumer goods made possible by the development of the steel and electrical industries (see the box on p. 545). The desire to own sewing machines, clocks, bicycles, electric lights, and typewriters was rapidly generating a new consumer ethic that has been a crucial part of the modern economy.

Not all nations benefited from the Second Industrial Revolution. Between 1870 and 1914, Germany replaced Great Britain as the industrial leader of Europe. Moreover, by 1900, Europe was divided into two economic zones. Great Britain, Belgium, France, the Netherlands, Germany, the western part of the Austro-Hungarian Empire, and northern Italy constituted an advanced industrialized core that had a high standard of living, decent systems of transportation, and relatively healthy and educated peoples (see Map 19.1). Another part of Europe, the backward and little industrialized area to the south and east, consisting of southern Italy, most of Austria-Hungary, Spain, Portugal, the Balkan kingdoms, and Russia, was still largely agricultural and relegated by the industrial countries to the function of providing food and raw materials.

Toward a World Economy

The economic developments of the late nineteenth century, combined with the transportation revolution that saw the growth of marine transport and railroads, fostered a true world economy. By 1900, Europeans were receiving beef and wool from Argentina and Australia, coffee from Brazil, nitrates from Chile, iron ore from Algeria, and sugar from Java. European capital was also invested abroad to develop railways, mines, electrical power plants, and banks. High rates of return, such as 11.3 percent on Latin American banking shares that were floated in London, provided plenty of incentive for investors. Of course, foreign countries also provided markets for the surplus manufactured goods of Europe. With its capital, industries, and military might, Europe dominated the world economy by the beginning of the twentieth century.

The Spread of Industrialization

At the same time, after 1870, industrialization began to spread beyond western and central Europe and North America. Especially noticeable was its rapid development, fostered by governments, in Russia and Japan. A surge of industrialization began in Russia in the 1890s under the guiding hand of Sergei Witte, the minister for finance. Witte pushed the government toward a program of mas-

➤ **AN AGE OF PROGRESS.** Between 1871 and 1914, the Second Industrial Revolution led many Europeans to believe that they were living in an age of progress when most human problems would be solved by scientific achievements. This illustration is taken from a special issue of the *Illustrated London News* celebrating the Diamond Jubilee of Queen Victoria in 1897. On the left are scenes from 1837, when Victoria came to the British throne; on the right are scenes from 1897. The vivid contrast underscored the magazine's conclusion: "The most striking . . . evidence of progress during the reign is the ever increasing speed which the discoveries of physical science have forced into everyday life. Steam and electricity have conquered time and space to a greater extent during the last sixty years than all the preceding six hundred years witnessed."

The development of the internal combustion engine, fired by oil and gasoline, provided a new source of power in transportation and gave rise to ocean liners as well as to the airplane and the automobile. In 1900, world production stood at 9,000 cars, but an American, Henry Ford, revolutionized the automotive industry with the mass production of the Model T. By 1916, Ford's factories were producing 735,000 cars a year. In 1903, at Kitty Hawk, North Carolina, brothers Orville and Wilbur Wright made the first flight in a fixed-wing airplane. In 1919, the first regular passenger air service was established.

THE DEPARTMENT STORE AND THE BEGINNINGS OF MASS CONSUMERISM

Domestic markets were especially important for the sale of the goods being turned out by Europe's increasing number of industrial plants. New techniques of mass marketing arose to encourage the sale of the new consumer goods. The Parisians pioneered in the development of the department store, and this selection is taken from a contemporary's account of the growth of these stores in the French capital city.

E. LAVASSEUR, ON PARISIAN DEPARTMENT STORES, 1907

It was in the reign of Louis-Philippe that department stores for fashion goods and dresses, extending to material and other clothing, began to be distinguished. The type was already one of the notable developments of the Second Empire; it became one of the most important ones of the Third Republic. These stores have increased in number and several of them have become extremely large. Combining in their different departments all articles of clothing, toilet articles, furniture and many other ranges of goods, it is their special object so to combine all commodities as to attract and satisfy customers who will find conveniently together an assortment of a mass of articles corresponding to all their various needs. They attract customers by permanent display, by free entry into the shops, by periodic exhibitions, by special sales, by fixed prices, and by their ability to deliver the goods purchased to customers' homes, in Paris and to the provinces. Turning themselves into direct intermediaries between the producer and the consumer, even producing sometimes some of their articles in their own workshops, buying at lowest prices because of their large orders and because they are in a position to profit from bargains, working with large sums, and selling to most of their customers for cash only, they can transmit these benefits in lowered selling prices. They can

even decide to sell at a loss, as an advertisement or to get rid of out-of-date fashions. Taking 5–6 per cent on 100 million [francs] brings them in more than 20 per cent would bring to a firm doing a turnover of 50,000 francs.

The success of these department stores is only possible thanks to the volume of their business, and this volume needs considerable capital and a very large turnover. Now capital, having become abundant, is freely combined nowadays in large enterprises, although French capital has the reputation of being more wary of the risks of industry than of State or railway securities. On the other hand, the large urban agglomerations, the ease with which goods can be transported by the railways, the diffusion of some comforts to strata below the middle classes, have all favored these developments.

As example we may cite some figures relating to these stores, since they were brought to the notice of the public in the *Revue des Deux-Mondes.* . . .

Le Louvre, dating to the time of the extension of the rue de Rivoli under the Second Empire, did in 1893 a business of 120 million at a profit of 6.4 per cent. *Le Bon-Marché*, which was a small shop when Mr. Boucicaut entered it in 1852, already did a business of 20 million at the end of the Empire. During the republic its new buildings were erected; Mme. Boucicaut turned it by her will into a kind of cooperative society, with shares and an ingenious organization; turnover reached 150 million in 1893, leaving a profit of 5 per cent. . . .

According to the tax records of 1891, these stores in Paris, numbering 12, employed 1,708 persons and were rated on their site values at 2,159,000 francs; the largest had then 542 employees. These same stores had, in 1901, 9,784 employees; one of them over 2,000 and another over 1,600; their site value has doubled (4,089,000 francs).

---

sive railroad construction. By 1900, some 35,000 miles of track had been laid. Witte's program also made possible the rapid growth of a modern steel and coal industry, making Russia by 1900 the fourth-largest producer of steel, behind the United States, Germany, and Great Britain. Russia was also turning out half of the world's production of oil.

In Japan, the imperial government took the lead in promoting industry (see Chapter 21). The government financed industries, built railroads, brought foreign experts to train Japanese employees in new industrial techniques, and instituted a universal educational system based on applied science. By the end of the nineteenth century, Japan had developed key industries in tea, silk, armaments, and shipbuilding.

Women and Work: New Job Opportunities

The Second Industrial Revolution had an enormous impact on the position of women in the labor market. During the course of the nineteenth century, considerable controversy erupted over a woman's "right to work." Working-class organizations tended to reinforce the underlying ideology of domesticity: women should remain at home to bear and nurture children and not be allowed in the industrial workforce. Working-class men argued that keeping women out of industrial work would ensure the moral and physical well-being of families. In reality, keeping women out of the industrial workforce simply made it easier to exploit them when they needed income to supplement their husbands'

MAP 19.1 **The Industrial Regions of Europe at the End of the Nineteenth Century.** By the end of the nineteenth century, the Second Industrial Revolution—in steelmaking, electricity, petroleum, and chemicals—had spurred substantial economic growth and prosperity in western and central Europe; it also sparked economic and political competition between Great Britain and Germany. ➤ *Look back at Map 18.1: What parts of Europe not industrialized in 1850 had become industrialized in the ensuing decades?*

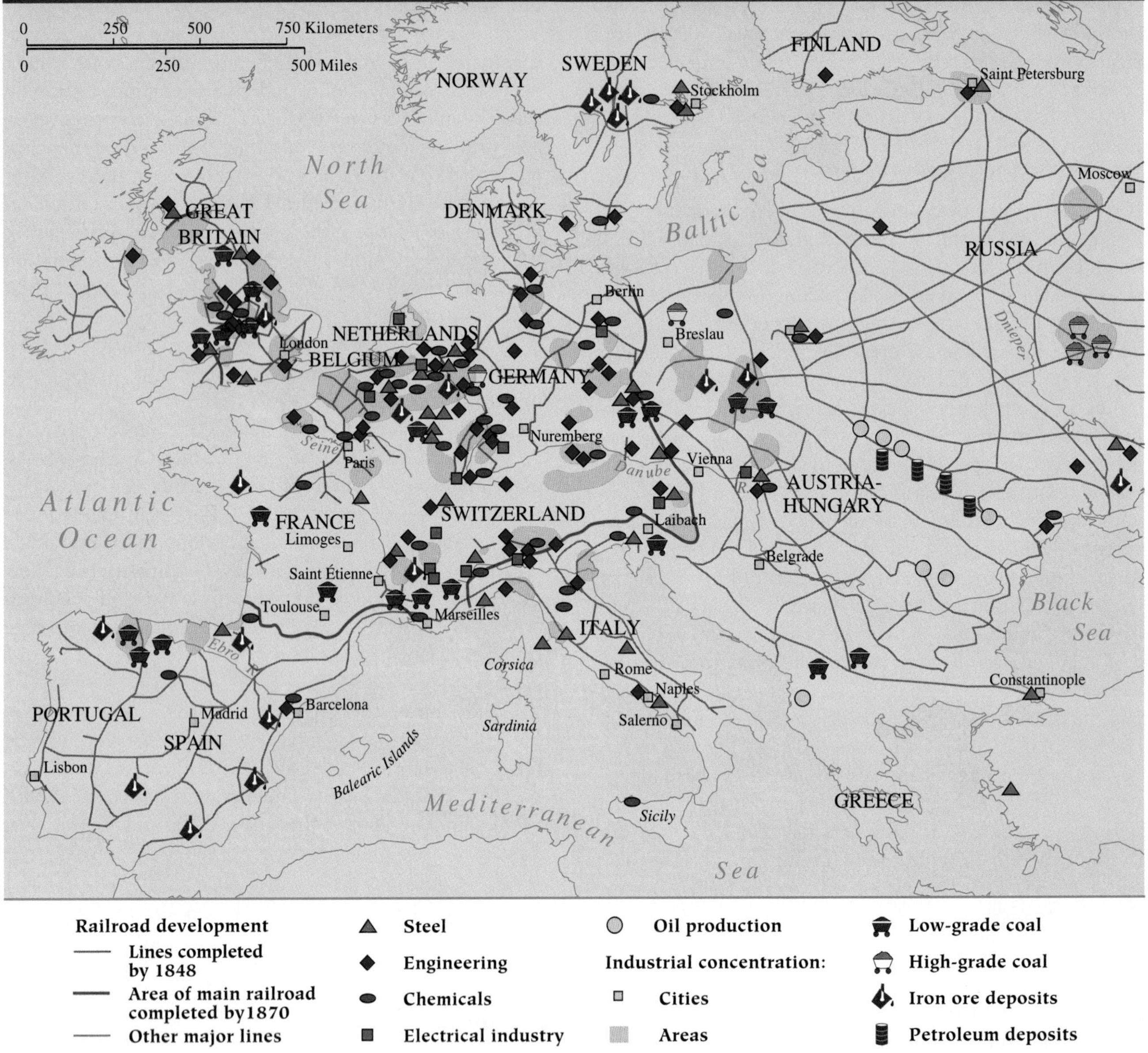

Railroad development			
—— Lines completed by 1848	▲ Steel	○ Oil production	🛒 Low-grade coal
—— Area of main railroad completed by 1870	◆ Engineering	**Industrial concentration:**	🛒 High-grade coal
—— Other major lines	● Chemicals	▫ Cities	⚒ Iron ore deposits
	■ Electrical industry	▨ Areas	▮ Petroleum deposits

wages or to support their families when their husbands were unemployed. The desperate need to work at times forced women to do marginal work at home or labor as pieceworkers in sweatshops.

After 1870, however, new job opportunities for women became available. The development of larger industrial plants and the expansion of government services created a variety of service or white-collar jobs. The increased demand for white-collar workers at relatively low wages coupled with a shortage of male workers led employers to hire women. Big

businesses and retail shops needed clerks, typists, secretaries, file clerks, and salesclerks. The expansion of government services created opportunities for women to be secretaries and telephone operators and to take jobs in health and social services. Compulsory education necessitated more teachers, while the development of modern hospital services opened the way for an increase in the number of nurses.

Many of the new white-collar jobs were unexciting. The work was routine and, except for teaching and nursing, required few skills beyond basic literacy. Although there was little hope for advancement, these jobs had distinct advantages for the daughters of the middle classes and especially the upward-aspiring working classes. For some middle-class women, the new jobs offered freedom from the domestic patterns expected of them. Moreover, because middle-class women did not receive an education comparable to that of men, they were limited in the careers they could pursue. Thus they found it easier to fill the jobs at the lower end of middle-class occupations, such as teaching and civil service jobs, especially those in the post office. Most of the new white-collar jobs, however, were filled by working-class women who saw the job as an opportunity to escape from the physical labor of the lower-class world.

Organizing the Working Classes

The desire to improve their working and living conditions led many industrial workers to form socialist political parties and socialist labor unions. These emerged after 1870, but the theory that made them possible had been developed more than two decades earlier in the work of Karl Marx. Marxism made its first appearance on the eve of the revolutions of 1848 with the publication of a short treatise entitled *The Communist Manifesto*, written by two Germans, Karl Marx (1818–1883) and Friedrich Engels (1820–1895). The work contained the substance of the basic economic and political ideas that Marx elaborated on during the rest of his life.

Marx and Engels began their treatise with the statement that "the history of all hitherto existing society is the history of class struggles." Throughout history, then, oppressor and oppressed have "stood in constant opposition to one another."[1] One group of people—the oppressors—owned the means of production and thus had the power to control government and society. Indeed, government itself was but an instrument of the ruling class. The other group, which depended on the owners of the means of production, were the oppressed.

In the industrialized societies of Marx's day, the class struggled continued. According to Marx and Engels, "Society as a whole is more and more splitting up into two great hostile camps, into two great classes directly facing each other: Bourgeoisie and Proletariat." Marx predicted that the struggle between the bourgeoisie and the proletariat would finally break into open revolution, "where the violent overthrow of the bourgeoisie lays the foundation for the sway of the proletariat." The fall of the bourgeoisie "and the victory of the proletariat are equally inevitable."[2] For a while, the proletariat would form a dictatorship in order to organize the means of production. However, the end result would be a classless society, since classes themselves arose from the economic differences that have been abolished; the state—itself an instrument of the bourgeois interests—would wither away (see the box on p. 548).

In time, Marx's ideas were picked up by working-class leaders who formed socialist parties. Most important was the German Social Democratic Party (SPD), which emerged in 1875 and espoused revolutionary Marxist rhetoric while organizing itself as a mass political party competing in elections for the Reichstag (the lower house of parliament). Once in the Reichstag, SPD delegates sought to pass legislation to improve the condition of the working class. Despite government efforts to destroy it, the SPD continued to grow. When it received four million votes in the 1912 elections, it became the largest party in Germany.

Socialist parties emerged in other European states, although not with the kind of success achieved by the German Social Democrats. In 1889, leaders of the various socialist parties formed the Second International, an association of national socialist groups that would fight against capitalism worldwide. (The First International had failed in 1872.) The Second International took some coordinated

⇒ **"PROLETARIANS OF THE WORLD, UNITE!"**   To improve their working and living conditions, many industrial workers, inspired by the ideas of Karl Marx, joined working-class or socialist parties. Pictured here is a socialist-sponsored poster that proclaims in German the closing words of *The Communist Manifesto*: "Proletarians of the World, Unite!"

Verein für Geschichte der Arbeiterbewegung, Vienna

THE CLASSLESS SOCIETY

In The Communist Manifesto, Karl Marx and Friedrich Engels projected as the end product of the struggle between the bourgeoisie and the proletariat the creation of a classless society. In this selection, they discuss the steps by which that classless society would be reached.

KARL MARX AND FRIEDRICH ENGELS, *THE COMMUNIST MANIFESTO*

We have seen above, that the first step in the revolution by the working class, is to raise the proletariat to the position of ruling class. . . . The proletariat will use its political supremacy to wrest, by degrees, all capital from the bourgeoisie, to centralize all instruments of production in the hands of the State, i.e., of the proletariat organized as the ruling class; and to increase the total of productive forces as rapidly as possible.

Of course, in the beginning, this cannot be effected except by means of despotic inroads on the rights of property, and on the conditions of bourgeois production; by means of measures, therefore, which appear economically insufficient and untenable, but which, in the course of the movement, outstrip themselves, necessitate further inroads upon the old social order, and are unavoidable as a means of entirely revolutionizing the mode of production.

These measures will of course be different in different countries.

Nevertheless, in the most advanced countries, the following will be pretty generally applicable:

1. Abolition of property in land and application of all rents of land to public purposes.
2. A heavy progressive or graduated income tax.
3. Abolition of all right of inheritance. . . .
5. Centralization of credit in the hands of the State, by means of a national bank with State capital and an exclusive monopoly.
6. Centralization of the means of communication and transport in the hands of the State.
7. Extension of factories and instruments of production owned by the State. . . .
8. Equal liability of all to labor. Establishment of industrial armies, especially for agriculture.
9. Combination of agriculture with manufacturing industries; gradual abolition of the distinction between town and country, by a more equable distribution of the population over the country.
10. Free education for all children in public schools. Abolition of children's factory labor in its present form. . . .

When, in the course of development, class distinctions have disappeared, and all production has been concentrated in the whole nation, the public power will lose its political character. Political power, properly so called, is merely the organized power of one class for oppressing another. If the proletariat during its contest with the bourgeoisie is compelled, by the force of circumstances, to organize itself as a class, if, by means of a revolution, it makes itself the ruling class, and, as such, sweeps away by force the old conditions of production, then it will, along with these conditions, have swept away the conditions for the existence of class antagonisms and of classes generally, and will thereby have abolished its own supremacy as a class.

In place of the old bourgeois society, with its classes and class antagonisms, we shall have an association, in which the free development of each is the condition for the free development of all.

---

actions—May Day (May 1), for example, was made an international labor holiday—but differences often wreaked havoc at the organization's congresses.

Marxist parties divided over the issue of revisionism. Pure Marxists believed in the imminent collapse of capitalism and the need for socialist ownership of the means of production. But others, called revisionists, rejected the revolutionary approach and argued that workers must organize mass political parties and work together with other progressive elements to gain reform. Having won the right to vote, workers were in a better position than ever to achieve their aims through democratic channels. Evolution by democratic means, not revolution, would achieve the desired goal of socialism.

Another force working for evolutionary rather than revolutionary socialism was the development of trade unions. In Great Britain, unions won the right to strike in the 1870s. Soon after, the masses of workers in factories were organized into trade unions in order to use the instrument of the strike. By 1900, there were two million workers in British trade unions; by 1914, there were almost four million. Trade unions in the rest of Europe had varying degrees of success, but by the outbreak of World War I, they had made considerable progress in bettering both the living and the working conditions of the laboring classes.

 ## THE EMERGENCE OF MASS SOCIETY

The rapid economic and social changes of the nineteenth century led to the emergence of mass society by the century's end. For the lower classes, mass society brought voting rights, an improved standard of living, and access to education. However, mass society also made possible the development of organizations that manipulated the populations of the nation-states. To understand this mass society, we need to examine some aspects of its structure.

The New Urban Environment

One of the most important consequences of industrialization and the population explosion of the nineteenth century was urbanization. In the course of the nineteenth century, more and more people came to live in cities. In 1800, city-dwellers constituted 40 percent of the population in Britain, 25 percent in France and Germany, and only 10 percent in eastern Europe. By 1914, urban residents had increased to 80 percent of the population in Britain, 45 percent in France, 60 percent in Germany, and 30 percent in eastern Europe. The size of cities also expanded dramatically, especially in industrialized countries. Between 1800 and 1900, London's population grew from 960,000 to 6.5 million and Berlin's from 172,000 to 2.7 million.

Urban populations grew faster than the general population primarily because of the vast migration from rural areas to cities. People were driven by sheer economic necessity—unemployment and physical want—from the countryside to the city. Urban centers offered something positive as well: employment, usually in factories and later in service trades and professions. But cities also grew faster in the second half of the nineteenth century because health and living conditions were improving as reformers and city officials used new technology to ameliorate the urban landscape.

In the 1840s, a number of urban reformers had pointed to filthy living conditions as the primary cause of epidemic diseases and urged sanitary reforms to correct the problem. Soon legislative acts created boards of health that brought governmental action to bear on public health issues. Urban medical officers and building inspectors were authorized to inspect dwellings for public health hazards. New building regulations made it more difficult for private contractors to construct shoddy housing. The Public Health Act of 1875 in Britain, for example, prohibited the construction of new buildings without running water and an internal drainage system. For the first time in Western history, the role of municipal governments had been expanded to include detailed regulations for the improvement of the living conditions of urban dwellers.

Essential to the public health of the modern European city was the ability to bring in clean water and to expel sewage. The problem of fresh water was solved by a system of dams and reservoirs that stored the water and aqueducts and tunnels that carried it from the countryside to the city and into individual dwellings. By the second half of the nineteenth century, regular private baths became accessible to many people as gas heaters in the 1860s and later electric heaters made hot baths possible. The treatment of sewage was also improved by laying mammoth underground pipes that carried raw sewage far from the city for disposal. In the late 1860s, a number of German cities began to construct sewer systems. Frankfurt began its program after a lengthy public campaign enlivened by the slogan "From the Toilet to the River in Half an Hour."

Middle-class reformers also focused on the housing needs of the working class. Overcrowded, disease-ridden slums were viewed as dangerous not only to physical health but also to the political and moral health of the entire nation. V. A. Huber, the foremost early German housing reformer, wrote in 1861: "Certainly it would not be too much to say that the home is the communal embodiment of family life. Thus the purity of the dwelling is almost as important for the family as is the cleanliness of the body for the individual."[3] To Huber, good housing was a prerequisite for stable family life, and without stable family life, one of the "stabilizing elements of society" would be dissolved, much to society's detriment.

Early efforts to attack the housing problem emphasized the middle-class, liberal belief in the power of private, or free, enterprise. Reformers such as Huber believed that the construction of model dwellings renting at a reasonable price would force other private landlords to elevate their housing standards. A fine example of this approach was the work of Octavia Hill (see the box on p. 550). As the number and size of cities continued to mushroom, governments by the 1880s concluded that private enterprise could not solve the housing crisis. In 1890, a British law empowered local town councils to construct cheap housing for the working classes. Similar activity was set in motion in Germany. More and more, governments were stepping into areas of activity that they would have never touched earlier.

The Social Structure of Mass Society

At the top of European society stood a wealthy elite, constituting but 5 percent of the population while controlling between 30 and 40 percent of the wealth. In the course of the nineteenth century, landed aristocrats had joined with the most successful industrialists, bankers, and merchants (the wealthy upper-middle class) to form a new elite. Members of this elite, whether aristocratic or middle-class in background, assumed leadership roles in government bureaucracies and military hierarchies. Marriage also united the two groups. Daughters of business tycoons gained titles, and aristocratic heirs gained new sources of cash. When the American Consuelo Vanderbilt married the duke of Marlborough, the new duchess brought $10 million to her husband.

The middle classes consisted of a variety of groups. Below the upper middle class was a group that included lawyers, doctors, and members of the civil service, as well as business managers, engineers, architects, accountants, and chemists benefiting from industrial expansion. Beneath this solid and comfortable middle group was a lower middle class of small shopkeepers, traders, manufacturers, and prosperous peasants.

THE HOUSING VENTURE OF OCTAVIA HILL

Octavia Hill was a practical-minded British housing reformer who believed that workers and their families were entitled to happy homes. At the same time, she was convinced that the poor needed guidance and encouragement, not charity. In this selection, she describes her housing venture.

OCTAVIA HILL, *HOMES OF THE LONDON POOR*

About four years ago I was put in possession of three houses in one of the worst courts of Marylebone. Six other houses were bought subsequently. All were crowded with inmates.

The first thing to be done was to put them in decent tenantable order. The set last purchased was a row of cottages facing a bit of desolate ground, occupied with wretched, dilapidated cowsheds, manure heaps, old timber, and rubbish of every description. The houses were in a most deplorable condition—the plaster was dropping from the walls; on one staircase a pail was placed to catch the rain that fell through the roof. All the staircases were perfectly dark; the banisters were gone, having been burnt as firewood by tenants. The grates, with large holes in them, were falling forward into the rooms. The washhouse, full of lumber belonging to the landlord, was locked up; thus the inhabitants had to wash clothes, as well as to cook, eat and sleep in their small rooms. The dustbin, standing in the front part of the houses, was accessible to the whole neighbourhood, and boys often dragged from it quantities of unseemly objects and spread them over the court. The state of the drainage was in keeping with everything else. The pavement of the backyard was all broken up, and great puddles stood in it, so that the damp crept up the outer walls. . . .

As soon as I entered into possession, each family had an opportunity of doing better: those who would not pay, or who led clearly immoral lives, were ejected. The rooms they vacated were cleansed; the tenants who showed signs of improvement moved into them, and thus, in turn, an opportunity was obtained for having each room distempered and papered. The drains were put in order, a large slate cistern was fixed, the wash-house was cleared of its lumber, and thrown open on stated days to each tenant in turn. The roof, the plaster, the woodwork was repaired; the staircase walls were distempered; new grates were fixed; the layers of paper and rag (black with age) were torn from the windows, and glass was put in; out of 192 panes only eight were found unbroken. The yard and footpath were paved.

The rooms, as a rule, were re-let at the same prices at which they had been let before; but tenants with large families were counselled to take two rooms, and for these much less was charged than if let singly: this plan I continue to pursue. Incoming tenants are not allowed to take a decidedly insufficient quantity of room, and no subletting is permitted. . . .

The pecuniary result has been very satisfactory. Five per cent has been paid on all the capital invested. A fund for the repayment of capital is accumulating. A liberal allowance has been made for repairs. . . .

My tenants are mostly of a class far below that of mechanics. They are, indeed, of the very poor. And yet, although the gifts they have received have been next to nothing, none of the families who have passed under my care during the whole four years have continued in what is called "distress," except such as have been unwilling to exert themselves. Those who will not exert the necessary self-control cannot avail themselves of the means of livelihood held out to them. But, for those who are willing, some small assistance in the form of work has, from time to time, been provided—not much, but sufficient to keep them from want or despair.

Standing between the lower middle class and the lower classes were new groups of white-collar workers who were the product of the Second Industrial Revolution—the salespeople, bookkeepers, bank tellers, telephone operators, and secretaries. Though often paid little more than skilled laborers, these white-collar workers were committed to middle-class ideals and optimistic about improving their status.

The middle classes shared a certain lifestyle, the values of which dominated much of nineteenth-century society. The members of the middle class were especially active in preaching their worldview to their children and to the upper and lower classes of their society. This was especially evident in Victorian Britain, often considered a model of middle-class society. The European middle classes believed in hard work, which was open to everyone and guaranteed to have positive results. They were also regular churchgoers who believed in the good conduct associated with traditional Christian morality. The middle class was concerned with propriety, the right way of doing things, which gave rise to an incessant stream of books aimed at the middle-class market with such titles as *The Habits of Good Society* or *Don't: A Manual of Mistakes and Improprieties More or Less Prevalent in Conduct and Speech.*

Below the middle classes on the social scale were the working classes, who made up almost 80 percent of the European population. Many of them were landholding peasants, agricultural laborers, and sharecroppers, especially in eastern Europe. The urban working class consisted of many different groups, including skilled artisans in such traditional trades as cabinetmaking, printing and the making of jewelry, along with semiskilled laborers, who included such people as carpenters, bricklayers, and many factory workers. At the bottom of the urban working class

WORKING-CLASS HOUSING IN LONDON. Although urban workers experienced some improvements in the material conditions of their lives after 1871, working-class housing remained drab and depressing. This 1912 photograph of working-class housing in the East End of London shows rows of similar-looking buildings on treeless streets. Most often, these buildings had no gardens or green areas.

stood the largest group of workers, the unskilled laborers. They included day laborers, who worked irregularly for very low wages, and large numbers of domestic servants, most of whom were women.

Urban workers did experience a real betterment in the material conditions of their lives after 1870. For one thing, urban improvements meant better living conditions. A rise in real wages, accompanied by a decline in many consumer costs, especially in the 1880s and 1890s, made it possible for workers to buy not only food and housing but also more clothes and even leisure at the same time that strikes and labor agitation were providing shorter workdays (no more than ten hours) and Saturday afternoons off.

The Experiences of Women

In the nineteenth century, women remained legally inferior, economically dependent, and largely defined by family and household roles. Many women still aspired to the ideal of femininity popularized by writers and poets. Alfred Lord Tennyson's poem *The Princess* expressed it well:

Man for the field and woman for the hearth:
Man for the sword and for the needle she:
Man with the head and woman with the heart:
Man to command and woman to obey;
All else confusion.

This traditional characterization of the sexes, based on gender-defined social roles, was elevated to the status of universal male and female attributes in the nineteenth century, due largely to the impact of the Industrial Revolution on the family. As the chief family wage earners, men worked outside the home while women were left with the care of the family, for which they were paid nothing. Of course, the ideal did not always match reality, especially for the lower classes, where the need for supplemental income drove women to do "sweated" work.

MARRIAGE AND THE FAMILY

For most of the nineteenth century, marriage was viewed as the only honorable career available to most women. Although the middle class glorified the ideal of domesticity, for most women marriage was a matter of economic necessity. The lack of meaningful work and the lower wages paid to women for their work made it difficult for single women to earn a living. Most women chose to marry, which was reflected in the increase in marriage rates and a decline in illegitimacy rates over the course of the nineteenth century.

Birthrates also dropped significantly in the nineteenth century. The most significant development in the modern family was the decline in the number of offspring born to the average woman. The change was not necessarily due to new technology. Although the invention of vulcanized rubber in the 1840s made possible the production of condoms and diaphragms, they were not widely used as effective contraceptive devices until the era of World War I. Some historians maintain that the change in attitude that led parents to limit the number of offspring deliberately was more important than the method used. While some historians attribute increased birth control to more widespread use of coitus interruptus, or male withdrawal before ejaculation, others have emphasized female control of family size through abortion and even infanticide or abandonment. That a change in attitude occurred was apparent in the development of a movement to increase awareness of birth control methods. Europe's first birth control clinic, founded by Dr. Aletta Jacob, opened in Amsterdam in 1882.

The family was the central institution of middle-class life. Men provided the family income while women focused on household and child care. The use of domestic servants in many middle-class homes, made possible by an abundant supply of cheap labor, reduced the amount of time middle-class women had to spend on household work. At the same time, by reducing the number of children in the family, mothers could devote more time to child care and domestic leisure.

The middle-class family fostered an ideal of togetherness. The Victorians created the family Christmas with its yule log, Christmas tree, songs, and exchange of gifts. In the United States, Fourth of July celebrations changed from drunken revels to family picnics by the 1850s. The education of middle-class females in domestic crafts, singing, and piano playing prepared them for their function of providing a proper environment for home recreation.

Women in working-class families were more accustomed to hard work. Daughters in working-class families were expected to work until they married; even after marriage, they often did piecework at home to help support the family. For the children of the working classes, childhood was over by the age of nine or ten when they became apprentices or were employed in odd jobs.

➤➤ **A MIDDLE-CLASS FAMILY.** Nineteenth-century middle-class moralists considered the family the fundamental pillar of a healthy society. The family was a crucial institution in middle-class life, and togetherness constituted one of the important ideals of the middle-class family. This painting by William P. Frith, titled *Many Happy Returns of the Day*, shows a family birthday celebration for a little girl in which grandparents, parents, and children take part. The servant at the left holds the presents for the little girl.

Harrogate Museums and Art Gallery, North Yorkshire, UK/Bridgeman Art Library

Between 1890 and 1914, however, family patterns among the working class began to change. High-paying jobs in heavy industry and improvements in the standard of living made it possible for working-class families to depend on the income of husbands and the wages of grown children. By the early twentieth century, some working-class mothers could afford to stay at home, following the pattern of middle-class women. At the same time, new consumer products, such as sewing machines, clocks, bicycles, and cast-iron stoves, created a new mass consumer society whose focus was on higher levels of consumption.

These working-class families also followed the middle classes in limiting the size of their families. Children began to be viewed as dependents rather than wage earners as child labor laws and compulsory education took children out of the workforce and into schools. Improvements in public health as well as advances in medicine and a better diet resulted in a decline in infant mortality rates for the lower classes, especially noticeable in the cities after 1890, and made it easier for working-class families to choose to have fewer children. At the same time, strikes and labor agitation led to laws that reduced work hours to ten per day by 1900 and eliminated work on Saturday afternoons, which enabled working-class parents to devote more attention to their children and develop deeper emotional ties with them.

THE MOVEMENT FOR WOMEN'S RIGHTS

In the 1830s, a number of women in the United States and Europe, who worked together in several reform movements, became frustrated by the apparent prejudices against females. They sought improvements for women by focusing on family and marriage law because it was difficult for women to secure divorces and property laws gave husbands almost complete control over the property of their wives. These early efforts were not overly successful, however. For example, women did not gain the right to their own property until 1870 in Britain, 1900 in Germany, and 1907 in France.

Custody and property rights were only a beginning for the women's movement, however. Some middle- and upper-middle-class women gained access to higher education, while others sought entry into occupations dominated by men. The first to fall was teaching. As medical training was largely closed to women, they sought alternatives in the development of nursing. An upper-class nursing pioneer in Germany was Amalie Sieveking (1794–1859), who founded the Female Association for the Care of the Poor and Sick in Hamburg. As she explained: "To me, at least as important were the benefits which [work with the poor] seemed to promise for those of my sisters who would join me in such a work of charity. The higher interests of my sex were close to my heart."[4] Sieveking's work was followed by the more famous British nurse, Florence Nightingale, whose efforts during the Crimean War (1854–1856), combined with those of Clara Barton in the American Civil War (1861–1865), transformed nursing into a profession of trained, middle-class "women in white."

By the 1840s and 1850s, the movement for women's rights had entered the political arena with the call for equal political rights. Many feminists believed that the right to vote was the key to all other reforms to improve the position of women. Suffragists had one basic aim: the right of women to full citizenship in the nation-state.

The British women's movement was the most vocal and active in Europe, but it was divided over tactics. Moderates believed that women must demonstrate that they would use political power responsibly if they wanted Parliament to grant them the right to vote. Another group, however, favored a more radical approach. Emmeline Pankhurst (1858–1928) and her daughters, Christabel and Sylvia, founded the Women's Social and Political Union in 1903, which enrolled mostly middle- and upper-class women. Pankhurst's organization realized the value of the media and used unusual publicity stunts to call attention to its demands. Derisively labeled "suffragettes" by male politicians, its members pelted government officials with eggs, chained themselves to lampposts, smashed the windows of department stores on fashionable shopping streets, burned railroad cars, and went on hunger strikes in jail.

Before World War I, the demands for women's rights were being heard throughout Europe and the United States, although only in Norway and some American states did women actually receive the right to vote before 1914. It would take the dramatic upheaval of World War I before male-dominated governments capitulated on this basic issue.

Women reformers also took on issues besides suffrage. In many countries, women supported peace movements. Bertha von Suttner (1843–1914) became head of the Austrian Peace Society and protested against the growing arms race of the 1890s. Her novel *Lay Down Your Arms* became a best-seller and brought her the Nobel Peace Prize in 1905. Lower-class women also took up the cause of peace. A group of women workers marched in Vienna in 1911 and demanded, "We want an end to armaments, to the means of murder, and we want these millions to be spent on the needs of the people."

THE NEW WOMAN

Bertha von Suttner was but one example of the "new women" who were becoming more prominent at the turn of the century. These women defied tradition in regard to traditional feminine roles (see the box on p. 554). Although some of them supported political ideologies such as socialism that flew in the face of the ruling classes, others simply sought new freedom outside the household and new roles other than those of wife and mother.

Maria Montessori (1870–1952) was another good example of the "new woman." Breaking with tradition, she attended medical school at the University of Rome. Although often isolated by her fellow (male) students, she persisted and in 1896 became the first Italian woman to receive a medical degree. Three years later, she began a lecture tour in Italy on the subject of the "new woman," whom she characterized as a person who followed a rational, scientific perspective. In keeping with this ideal, Montessori put her medical background to work in a school for mentally retarded children. She devised new teaching materials that enabled these children to read and write and became convinced, as she later wrote, "that similar methods applied to normal students would develop or set free their personality in a marvelous and surprising way." Subsequently, she established a system of childhood education based on natural and spontaneous activities in which students learned at their own pace. By the 1930s, hundreds of Montessori schools had been established in Europe and the United States. As a professional woman and a woman who chose to have a child without being married, Montessori also embodied some of the freedoms of the "new woman."

Education in an Age of Mass Society

Universal education was a product of the mass society of the late nineteenth and early twentieth centuries. Education in the early nineteenth century was primarily for the elite or the wealthier middle class, but between 1870 and 1914, most Western governments began to offer at least primary education to both boys and girls between the ages of six and twelve. States also assumed responsibility for better training of teachers by establishing teacher-training schools. By the beginning of the twentieth century, many European states, especially in northern and western Europe, provided state-financed primary schools, salaried and trained teachers, and free, compulsory elementary education for all.

Why did Western nations make this commitment to mass education? One reason was industrialization. The new firms of the Second Industrial Revolution demanded skilled labor. Both boys and girls with an elementary education had new possibilities of jobs beyond their villages or small towns, including white-collar jobs in railways and subways, post offices, banking and shipping firms, teaching, and nursing. Mass education furnished the trained workers industrialists needed. For most students, elementary education led to apprenticeship and a job.

The chief motive for mass education, however, was political. The increase in suffrage created the need for a more educated electorate. Even more important, however, mass compulsory education instilled patriotism and nationalized the masses, providing an opportunity for even greater national integration. As people lost their ties to

ADVICE TO WOMEN: BE INDEPENDENT

Although a majority of women probably followed the nineteenth-century middle-class ideal of women as keepers of the household and nurturers of husband and children, an increasing number of women fought for the rights of women. This selection is taken from Act III of Henrik Ibsen's play A Doll's House (1879), in which the character Nora Helmer declares her independence from her husband's control over her life.

HENRIK IBSEN, A DOLL'S HOUSE

NORA: *(Pause)* Does anything strike you as we sit here?

HELMER: What should strike me?

NORA: We've been married eight years; does it not strike you that this is the first time we two, you and I, man and wife, have talked together seriously?

HELMER: Seriously? What do you mean, *seriously?*

NORA: For eight whole years, and more—ever since the day we first met—we have never exchanged one serious word about serious things. . . .

HELMER: Why, my dearest Nora, what have you to do with serious things?

NORA: There we have it! You have never understood me. I've had great injustice done to me, Torvald; first by father, then by you.

HELMER: What! Your father and me? We, who have loved you more than all the world?

NORA *(Shaking her head)*: You have never loved me. You just found it amusing to think you were in love with me.

HELMER: Nora! What a thing to say!

NORA: Yes, it's true, Torvald. When I was living at home with father, he told me his opinions and mine were the same. If I had different opinions, I said nothing about them, because he would not have liked it. He used to call me his doll-child and played with me as I played with my dolls. Then I came to live in your house.

HELMER: What a way to speak of our marriage!

NORA *(Undisturbed)*: I mean that I passed from father's hands into yours. You arranged everything to your taste and I got the same tastes as you; or pretended to—I don't know which—both, perhaps; sometimes one, sometimes the other. When I look back on it now, I seem to have been living here like a beggar, on hand-outs. I lived by per-forming tricks for you, Torvald. But that was how you wanted it. You and father have done me a great wrong. It is your fault that my life has come to naught.

HELMER: Why, Nora, how unreasonable and ungrateful! Haven't you been happy here?

NORA: No, never. I thought I was, but I never was.

HELMER: Not—not happy! . . .

NORA: I must stand quite alone if I am ever to know myself and my surroundings; so I cannot stay with you.

HELMER: Nora! Nora!

NORA: I am going at once. I daresay [my friend] Christina will take me in for tonight.

HELMER: You are mad! I shall not allow it! I forbid it!

NORA: It's no use your forbidding me anything now. I shall take with me only what belongs to me; from you I will accept nothing, either now or later.

HELMER: This is madness!

NORA: Tomorrow I shall go home—I mean to what was my home. It will be easier for me to find a job there.

HELMER: Oh, in your blind inexperience—

NORA: I must try to gain experience, Torvald.

HELMER: Forsake your home, your husband, your children! And you don't consider what the world will say.

NORA: I can't pay attention to that. I only know that I must do it.

HELMER: This is monstrous! Can you forsake your holiest duties?

NORA: What do you consider my holiest duties?

HELMER: Need I tell you that? Your duties to your husband and children.

NORA: I have other duties equally sacred.

HELMER: Impossible! What do you mean?

NORA: My duties toward myself.

HELMER: Before all else you are a wife and a mother.

NORA: That I no longer believe. Before all else I believe I am a human being, just as much as you are—or at least that I should try to become one. I know that most people agree with you, Torvald, and that they say so in books. But I can no longer be satisfied with what most people say and what is in books. I must think things out for myself and try to get clear about them.

---

local regions and even to religion, nationalism supplied a new faith. The use of a single national language created greater national unity than loyalty to a ruler did.

Compulsory elementary education created a demand for teachers, and most of them were women. Many men viewed the teaching of children as an extension of women's "natural role" as nurturers of children. Moreover, females were paid lower salaries, in itself a considerable incentive for governments to encourage the establishment of teacher-training institutes for women. The first female colleges were teacher-training schools. It was not until the beginning of the twentieth century that women were permitted to enter the male-dominated universities.

The most immediate result of mass education was an increase in literacy. In Germany, Great Britain, France, and the Scandinavian countries, adult illiteracy was virtually eliminated by 1900. Where there was less schooling, the story was quite different. Adult illiteracy rates were

Courtesy, Vassar College Library

➣ **A WOMEN'S COLLEGE.** Women were largely excluded from male-dominated universities before 1900. Consequently, the demand of women for higher education led to the establishment of women's colleges, most of which were primarily teacher-training schools. This photograph shows a group of women in an astronomy class at Vassar College in the United States in 1878. Maria Mitchell, a famous astronomer, was head of the department.

79 percent in Serbia, 78 percent in Romania, and 79 percent in Russia.

Leisure in an Age of Mass Society

With the Industrial Revolution came new forms of leisure. Work and leisure became opposites as leisure came to be viewed as what people do for fun when they are not at work. The new leisure hours created by the industrial system—evening hours after work, weekends, and later a week or two in the summer—largely determined the contours of the new mass leisure.

New technology created novel experiences for leisure, such as the Ferris wheel at amusement parks, while the subways and streetcars of the 1880s meant that even the working classes were no longer dependent on neighborhood facilities but could make their way to athletic games, amusement parks, and dance halls. Railroads could take people to the beaches on weekends.

By the late nineteenth century, team sports had also developed into another important form of mass leisure. Unlike the old rural games, they were no longer chaotic and spontaneous activities but became strictly organized with sets of rules and officials to enforce them. These rules

were the products of organized athletic groups, such as the English Football Association (1863) and the American Bowling Congress (1895). The development of urban transportation systems made possible the construction of stadiums where thousands could attend, making mass spectator sports into a big business.

The new forms of popular leisure drew mass audiences and mostly served to provide entertainment and distract people from the realities of their work lives. The new mass leisure was quite different from earlier forms of popular culture. Festivals and fairs had been based on an ethos of active community participation, whereas the new forms of mass leisure were standardized for largely passive audiences. Amusement parks and professional sports teams were, after all, big businesses organized to make profits.

THE NATIONAL STATE

Throughout much of the Western world by 1870, the national state had become the focus of people's loyalties and the arena for political activity. Only in Russia, eastern Europe, Austria-Hungary, and Ireland did national groups still struggle for independence.

Tradition and Change in Latin America

The last three decades of the nineteenth century were a time of prosperity in Latin America, but the consequences were by no means beneficial for all of its people. As industrialization progressed in Europe and the United States, those countries experienced an ever greater need for food and raw materials. Latin American nations provided these goods, and their increasing prosperity was based to a large extent on the export of one or two commodities from each region, such as wheat and beef from Argentina, coffee from Brazil, nitrates from Chile, coffee and bananas from Central America, and sugar and silver from Peru. Exports from Argentina doubled between 1873 and 1893; Mexican exports quadrupled between 1877 and 1900. These foodstuffs and raw materials were largely exchanged for finished goods—textiles, machines, and luxury products—from Europe and the United States. With economic growth came a boom in foreign investment. Between 1870 and 1913, British investments—mostly in railroads, mining, and public utilities—grew from £85 million to £757 million, which constituted two-thirds of all foreign investment in Latin America. As Latin Americans struggled to create more balanced economies after 1900, they concentrated on increasing industrialization, especially by building textile, food-processing, and construction material factories.

Nevertheless, the growth of the Latin American economy largely came from the export of raw materials, and economic modernization in the region simply added to its growing dependence on the capitalist nations of the West. Modernization was basically a surface feature of Latin American society, where past patterns still largely prevailed. Rural elites dominated their estates and their rural workers. Although slavery was abolished by 1888, former slaves and their descendants were still at the bottom of society. The Indians remained poverty-stricken, debt servitude was still a way of life, and Latin America remained economically dependent on foreigners. Despite its economic growth, Latin America was still an underdeveloped region of the world.

The prosperity that resulted from the export economy had both social and political repercussions. One result socially was the modernization of the elites, who grew determined to pursue their vision of modern progress. Large landowners increasingly sought ways to rationalize their production methods in order to make greater profits. As a result, cattle ranchers in Argentina and coffee barons in Brazil became more aggressive entrepreneurs.

Another result of the new prosperity was the growth in the middle sectors of Latin American society—lawyers, merchants, shopkeepers, businesspeople, schoolteachers, professors, bureaucrats, and military officers. These middle sectors, which made up only 5 to 10 percent of the population, depending on the country, were hardly large enough in numbers to constitute a true middle class. Nevertheless, after 1900, the middle sectors continued to expand. Regardless of the country, they shared some common characteristics. They lived in the cities, sought education and decent incomes, and increasingly saw the United States as the model to emulate, especially in regard to industrialization and education. The middle sectors in Latin America sought liberal reform, not revolution, and the elites found it relatively easy to co-opt them by extending them the right to vote.

As Latin American export economies boomed, the working class expanded, which in turn led to the growth of labor unions, especially after 1914. Radical unions often advocated the use of the general strike as an instrument for change. By and large, however, the governing elites succeeded in stifling the political influence of the working class by restricting workers' right to vote. The need for industrial labor also led Latin American countries to encourage immigration from Europe. Between 1880 and 1914, three million Europeans, primarily Italians and Spaniards, settled in Argentina. Over 100,000 Europeans, mostly Italian, Portuguese, and Spanish, arrived in Brazil each year between 1891 and 1900.

As in Europe and the United States, industrialization led to urbanization, evident in both the emergence of new cities and the rapid growth of old ones. Buenos Aires (the "Paris" of South America) had 750,000 inhabitants by 1900 and 2 million by 1914, which constituted a fourth of Argentina's population. By that time, urban dwellers made up 53 percent of Argentina's population. Brazil and Chile also witnessed a dramatic increase in the number of urban dwellers.

Political Change in Latin America

Latin America also experienced a political transformation after 1870. Large landowners began to take a more direct interest in national politics, sometimes expressed by a direct involvement in governing. In Argentina and Chile, for example, landholding elites controlled the governments, and although they produced constitutions similar to those of the United States and Europe, they were careful to ensure their power by regulating voting rights.

In some countries, large landowners made use of dictators to maintain the interests of the ruling elite. Porfirio Díaz, who ruled Mexico from 1876 to 1910, established a conservative, centralized government with the support of the army, foreign capitalists, large landowners, and the Catholic church. All of them benefited from their alliance. But there were forces for change in Mexico that precipitated a true social revolution. The Mexican Revolution has long been considered a model for nationalistic revolutionary change.

Under Díaz's dictatorial regime, the real wages of the working class had declined. Moreover, 95 percent of the

ZAPATA AND LAND REFORM

Emiliano Zapata was a sharecropper on a sugar plantation in Morelos, a mountainous state in southern Mexico. Using the slogan "Land and Liberty," Zapata formed a guerrilla band of Indians and led them in revolt against the haciendas of southern Mexico, burning the houses and sugar refineries. Convinced that the new president of Mexico, Francisco Madero, would not go far enough with land reform, Zapata issued his own plan, the Plan of Ayala, from which these excerpts are taken.

THE PLAN OF AYALA

The Liberating Plan of the sons of the State of Morelos, members of the insurgent army that demands the . . . reforms that it judges convenient and necessary for the welfare of the Mexican Nation.

We, the undersigned, constituted as a Revolutionary Junta, in order to maintain and obtain the fulfillment of the promises made by the revolution of November 20, 1910, solemnly proclaim in the face of the civilized world . . . , so that it may judge us, the principles that we have formulated in order to destroy the tyranny that oppresses us. . . .

1. Considering that the President of the Republic, Don Francisco I. Madero, has made a bloody mockery of Effective Suffrage by . . . entering into an infamous alliance with the . . . enemies of the Revolution that he proclaimed, in order to forge the chains of a new dictatorship more hateful and terrible than that of Porfirio Díaz. . . . For these reasons we declare the said Francisco I. Madero unfit to carry out the promises of the Revolution of which he was the author. . . .

4. The Revolutionary Junta of the State of Morelos formally proclaims to the Mexican people: That it endorses the Plan of San Luis Potosí [Madero's revolutionary plan] with the additions stated below for the benefit of the oppressed peoples, and that it will defend its principles until victory or death. . . .

6. As an additional part of the plan we proclaim, be it known: that the lands, woods, and waters usurped . . . through tyranny and venal justice henceforth belong to the towns or citizens who have corresponding titles to those properties, of which they were despoiled by the bad faith of our oppressors. They shall retain possession of the said properties at all costs, arms in hand. The usurpers who think they have a right to the said lands may state their claims before special tribunals to be established upon the triumph of the Revolution.

7. Since the immense majority of Mexican towns and citizens own nothing but the ground on which they stand and endure a miserable existence, denied the opportunity to improve their social condition or to devote themselves to industry or agriculture because a few individuals monopolize the lands, woods, and waters—for these reasons the great estates shall be expropriated, with indemnification to the owners of one-third of such monopolies, in order that the towns and citizens of Mexico may obtain colonies, town sites, and arable lands. Thus the welfare of the Mexican people shall be promoted in all respects.

8. The properties of those [landowners] who directly or indirectly oppose the present Plan shall be seized by the nation, and two thirds of their value shall be used for war indemnities and pensions for the widows and orphans of the soldiers who may perish in the struggle for this Plan.

---

rural population owned no land, while about a thousand families owned almost all of Mexico. When a liberal landowner, Francisco Madero, forced Díaz from power, he opened the door to a wider revolution. Madero's ineffectiveness triggered a demand for agrarian reform led by Emiliano Zapata, who aroused the masses of landless peasants and began to seize the haciendas of the wealthy landholders (see the box above). The ensuing revolution caused untold destruction to the Mexican economy. Finally, a new constitution in 1917 established a strong presidency, initiated land reform policies, established limits on foreign investors, and set an agenda for social welfare for workers. The revolution also led to an outpouring of nationalistic pride. Intellectuals and artists in particular sought to capture what was unique about Mexico with special emphasis on its Indian past. As the Mexican minister of education said, "Tired, disgusted of all this copied civilization, . . . we wish to cease being Europe's spiritual colonies."

By this time, a new power had begun to wield its influence over Latin America. At the beginning of the twentieth century, the United States, which had begun to emerge as a great world power, increasingly interfered in the affairs of its southern neighbors. As a result of the Spanish-American War (1898), Cuba became an American protectorate, and Puerto Rico was annexed outright. American investments in Latin America soon followed; so did American resolve to protect these investments. Between 1898 and 1934, U.S. military forces were sent to Cuba, Mexico, Guatemala, Honduras, Nicaragua, Panama, Colombia, Haiti, and the Dominican Republic to protect American interests. Some expeditions remained for

Brown Brothers

⇶ **EMILIANO ZAPATA.**   The inability of Francisco Madero to carry out far-reaching reforms led to a more radical upheaval in the Mexican countryside. Emiliano Zapata led a band of Indians in a revolt against the large landowners of southern Mexico and issued his own demands for land reform.

many years; U.S. Marines were in Haiti from 1915 to 1934, and Nicaragua was occupied from 1909 to 1933. At the same time, the United States became the chief foreign investor in Latin America.

The Rise of the United States

Four years of bloody civil war had salvaged American national unity. The old South had been destroyed; one-fifth of its adult white male population had been killed, and four million black slaves had been freed. For a while at least, a program of radical change in the South was attempted. Slavery was abolished by the Thirteenth Amendment to the U.S. Constitution in 1865, and the Fourteenth and Fifteenth Amendments extended citizenship to blacks and guaranteed them the right to vote. Radical Reconstruction in the early 1870s tried to create a new South based on the principle of the equality of black and white people, but the changes were soon largely undone.

Militia organizations, such as the Ku Klux Klan, used violence to discourage blacks from voting. A new system of sharecropping made blacks once again economically dependent on white landowners. New state laws stripped blacks of their right to vote. By the end of the 1870s, supporters of white supremacy were back in power everywhere in the South.

Between 1860 and World War I, the United States made the shift from an agrarian to a mighty industrial nation. American heavy industry stood unchallenged in 1900. In that year, the Carnegie Steel Company alone produced more steel than Great Britain's entire steel industry. Industrialization also led to urbanization. While established cities, such as New York, Philadelphia, and Boston, grew even larger, other moderate-size cities, such as Pittsburgh, grew by leaps and bounds because of industrialization. Whereas 20 percent of Americans lived in cities in 1860, over 40 percent did in 1900.

By 1900, the United States had become the world's richest nation and its greatest industrial power. Yet serious questions remained about the quality of American life. In 1890, the richest 9 percent of Americans owned an incredible 71 percent of the wealth. Labor unrest over unsafe working conditions, strict work discipline, and periodic cycles of devastating unemployment led workers to organize. By the turn of the century, one national organization, the American Federation of Labor, emerged as labor's dominant voice. Its lack of real power, however, is reflected in its membership figures. In 1900, it represented only one of every twelve American industrial workers.

During the so-called Progressive Era after 1900, the reform of many features of American life became a primary issue. At the state level, reforming governors sought to achieve clean government by introducing elements of direct democracy, such as direct primaries for selecting nominees for public office. State governments also enacted economic and social legislation, such as laws that governed hours, wages, and working conditions, especially for women and children. The realization that state laws were ineffective in dealing with nationwide problems, however, led to a progressive movement at the national level.

National progressivism was evident in the administrations of both Theodore Roosevelt and Woodrow Wilson. Under Roosevelt (1901–1909), the Meat Inspection Act and Pure Food and Drug Act provided for a limited degree of federal intervention to prevent corrupt industrial practices. Roosevelt's expressed principle, "We draw the line against misconduct, not against wealth," guaranteed that public protection would have to be within limits tolerable to big corporations. Wilson (1913–1921) was responsible for the creation of the graduated federal income tax and the Federal Reserve System, which gave the federal government an important role in economic decisions formerly made by bankers. Like European states, the United States was slowly adopting policies that expanded the functions of the state.

THE UNITED STATES AS A WORLD POWER

At the end of the nineteenth century, the United States began to expand abroad. The Samoan Islands in the Pacific became the first important American colony; the Hawaiian Islands were the next to fall. By 1887, American settlers had gained control of the sugar industry on the Hawaiian Islands. As more Americans settled in Hawaii, they sought to gain political power. When Queen Liliuokalani tried to strengthen the power of the monarchy in order to keep the islands for the native peoples, the American government sent U.S. Marines to "protect" American lives. The queen was deposed, and Hawaii was annexed by the United States in 1898.

The American defeat of Spain in the Spanish-American War in 1898 encouraged Americans to extend their empire by acquiring Cuba, Puerto Rico, Guam, and the Philippines. Although the Filipinos hoped for independence, the Americans refused to grant it. As President McKinley said, the United States had the duty "to educate the Filipinos and uplift and Christianize them," a remarkable statement in view of the fact that most of them had been Roman Catholics for centuries. It took three years and sixty thousand troops to pacify the Philippines and establish American control. By the beginning of the twentieth century, the United States had become another Western imperialist power.

The Growth of Canada

Canada, too, faced problems of national unity between 1870 and 1914. At the beginning of 1870, the Dominion of Canada had only four provinces: Quebec, Ontario, Nova Scotia, and New Brunswick. With the addition of two more provinces in 1871—Manitoba and British Columbia—the Dominion of Canada now extended from the Atlantic Ocean to the Pacific.

But real unity was difficult to achieve because of the distrust between the English-speaking and French-speaking peoples of Canada. Fortunately for Canada, Sir Wilfrid Laurier, who became the first French Canadian prime minister in 1896, was able to reconcile Canada's two major groups and resolve the issue of separate schools for French Canadians. Laurier's administration also witnessed increased industrialization and successfully encouraged immigrants from central and eastern Europe to help populate Canada's vast territories.

Europe

The domestic policies of the major European states focused on five major themes: the achievement of liberal practices (consti-

tutions, parliaments, and individual liberties); the growth of political democracy through universal male suffrage; the organization of mass political parties as a result of a widened electorate; the rise of socialist, working-class parties; and the enactment of social welfare measures to meet the demands of the working classes. These developments varied in expression from place to place. In general, western European states (France and Britain) had the greatest success with the growth of parliamentary governments. Central European states (Germany, Austria-Hungary) had the trappings of parliamentary government, but authoritarian forces, especially powerful monarchies and conservative social groups, remained strong. In eastern Europe, especially Russia, the old system of autocracy was barely touched by the winds of change.

WESTERN EUROPE: THE GROWTH OF POLITICAL DEMOCRACY

By 1871, Great Britain had a functioning two-party parliamentary system. For fifty years, the Liberals and Conservatives alternated in power at regular intervals, although they also shared some common features. Both were dominated by a ruling class made up of a coalition of aristocratic landowners frequently involved in industrial and financial activities and upper-middle-class businessmen. And both competed with each other in supporting legislation that expanded the right to vote. Reform acts in 1867 and 1884 greatly expanded the number of adult males who could vote, and by the end of World War I, all males over twenty-one and women over thirty could vote. In 1911, parliamentary legislation curtailed the power of the House of Lords and instituted the payment of salaries to members of the House of Commons, which further democratized that institution by at least opening the door to people other than the wealthy. By the beginning of World War I, political democracy had become well entrenched and was soon accompanied by social welfare measures for the working class.

The growth of trade unions, which began to advocate more radical change of the economic system, and the emergence in 1900 of the Labour Party, which dedicated itself to workers' interests, caused the Liberals to favor new social legislation. The Liberals, who held the government from 1906 to 1914, perceived that they would have to initiate a program of social welfare or lose the support of the workers. Therefore, they abandoned the classical principles of *laissez-faire* and voted for a series of social reforms. The National Insurance Act of 1911 provided benefits for workers in case of sickness and unemployment, to be paid for by compulsory contributions from workers, employers, and

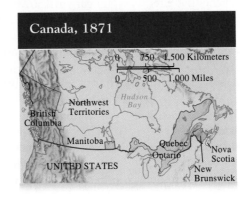

Canada, 1871

750 1,500 Kilometers
500 1,000 Miles

Northwest Territories
British Columbia
Hudson Bay
Manitoba
Quebec
Ontario
Nova Scotia
New Brunswick
UNITED STATES

the state. Additional legislation provided a small pension for Britons over age seventy and compensation for those injured in accidents while at work. While the benefits of the program and tax increases were both modest, they were the first hesitant steps toward the future British welfare state.

In France, the confusion that ensued after the collapse of the Second Empire finally ended in 1875 when an improvised constitution established a republican form of government. This constitution established a bicameral legislature, with an upper house, the Senate, elected indirectly and a lower house, the Chamber of Deputies, chosen by universal male suffrage. The powers of the president, selected by the legislature to be the executive of the government for a term of seven years, were deliberately left vague. The premier (or prime minister) led the government, and he and his ministers were responsible not to the president but to the Chamber of Deputies. The Constitution of 1875, intended only as a stopgap measure, solidified the republic—the Third Republic—which lasted sixty-five years. France failed, however, to develop a strong parliamentary system on the British two-party model because the existence of a dozen political parties forced the premier to depend on a coalition of parties to stay in power. The Third Republic was notorious for its changes of government. Between 1875 and 1914, there were no fewer than fifty cabinet changes; during the same period, the British had eleven. Nevertheless, the government's moderation gradually encouraged more and more middle-class and peasant support, and by 1914, the Third Republic commanded the loyalty of most French people.

By 1870, Italy had emerged as a geographically united state with pretensions to great power status. Its internal weaknesses, however, gave that claim a particularly hollow ring. Sectional differences—a poverty-stricken south and an industrializing north—weakened any sense of community. Chronic turmoil between labor and industry undermined the social fabric. The Italian government was unable to deal effectively with these problems because of the extensive corruption among government officials and the lack of stability created by ever-changing government coalitions. Even Italy's pretensions to great power status proved hollow when Italy became the first European power to lose to an African state, Ethiopia, a disgrace that later led to the costly (but successful) attempt to compensate by conquering Libya in 1911 and 1912.

CENTRAL AND EASTERN EUROPE: PERSISTENCE OF THE OLD ORDER

The constitution of the new imperial Germany begun by Bismarck in 1871 provided for a federal system with a bicameral legislature. The lower house of the German parliament, known as the Reichstag, was elected on the basis of universal male suffrage, but it did not have ministerial responsibility. Ministers of government, among whom the most important was the chancellor, were responsible not to the parliament but to the emperor. The emperor also commanded the armed forces and controlled foreign policy and internal administration. Although the creation of a parliament elected by universal male suffrage presented opportunities for the growth of a real political democracy, it failed to develop in Germany before World War I. Bismarck's high-handed tactics and the army's independence were two major reasons why it did not.

During the reign of Emperor William II (1888–1918), the new imperial Germany begun by Bismarck continued as an "authoritarian, conservative, military-bureaucratic power state." By the end of William's reign, Germany had become the strongest military and industrial power on the Continent. Over 50 percent of German workers had jobs in industry, while only 30 percent of the workforce was still in agriculture. Urban centers had mushroomed in number and size. These rapid changes helped produce a society torn between modernization and traditionalism. With the expansion of industry and cities came demands for more political participation and growing sentiment for reforms that would produce greater democratization. Conservative forces, especially the landowning nobility and representatives of heavy industry, two of the powerful ruling groups in Germany, tried to block it by supporting William II's activist foreign policy of finding Germany's "place in the sun." Expansionism, they believed, would divert people from demands for further democratization.

The tensions in German society created by the conflict between modernization and traditionalism were also manifested in a new, radicalized, right-wing politics. A number of nationalist pressure groups arose to support nationalistic goals. Antisocialist and antiliberal, such groups as the Pan-German League stressed strong German nationalism and advocated imperialism as a tool to overcome social divisions and unite all classes. They also denounced the Jews as the destroyers of the German national community, fueling the flames of anti-Semitism (see "Anti-Semitism" later in this chapter).

After the creation of the Dual Monarchy of Austria-Hungary in 1867, the Austrian part received a constitution that theoretically recognized the equality of the nationalities and established a parliamentary system with the principle of ministerial responsibility. However, Emperor Francis Joseph (1848–1916) largely ignored ministerial responsibility by personally appointing and dismissing his ministers and ruling by decree when parliament was not in session.

The problem of the various nationalities remained a difficult one. The German minority that governed Austria felt increasingly threatened by the Czechs, Poles, and other Slavic groups within the empire. The granting of

THE NATIONAL STATE, 1870–1914

Great Britain

Reform Act	1884
Formation of Labour Party	1900
Restriction of power of the House of Lords	1911
National Insurance Act	1911

France

Surrender of French provisional government to Germany	1871 (Jan. 28)
Republican constitution (Third Republic)	1875

Germany

Bismarck as chancellor	1871–1890
Emperor William II	1888–1918

Austria-Hungary

Emperor Francis Joseph	1848–1916

Russia

Tsar Alexander III	1881–1894
Tsar Nicholas II	1894–1917
First Congress of Social Democratic Party	1898
Russo-Japanese War	1904–1905
Revolution	1905

Latin America

Rule of Porfirio Díaz in Mexico	1876–1910
Mexican Revolution begins	1910

United States

Spanish-American War	1898
Theodore Roosevelt	1901–1909
Woodrow Wilson	1913–1921

universal male suffrage in 1907 served only to exacerbate the problem when nationalities that had played no role in the government now agitated in the parliament for autonomy. This led prime ministers after 1900 to ignore the parliament and rely increasingly on imperial emergency decrees to govern. On the eve of World War I, the Austro-Hungarian Empire was as far away as ever from solving its minorities problem.

In Russia, the assassination of Alexander II in 1881 convinced his son and successor, Alexander III (1881–1894), that reform had been a mistake, and he quickly returned to the repressive measures of earlier tsars. Advocates of constitutional monarchy and social reform, along with revolutionary groups, were persecuted. Entire districts of Russia were placed under martial law if the government suspected the inhabitants of treason. When Alexander III died, his weak son and successor, Nicholas II (1894–1917), began his rule with his father's conviction that the absolute power of the tsars should be preserved: "I shall maintain the principle of autocracy just as firmly and unflinchingly as did my unforgettable father."[5] But conditions were changing, especially with the growth of industrialization, and the tsar's approach was not realistic in view of the new circumstances he faced.

Although industrialization came late to Russia, it progressed rapidly after 1890, especially with the assistance of foreign investment capital. With industrialization came factories, an industrial working class, and the development of socialist parties, although repression in Russia soon forced them to go underground and be revolutionary. The Marxist Social Democratic Party, for example, held its first congress in Minsk in 1898, but the arrest of its leaders caused the next one to be held in Brussels in 1903, attended by Russian émigrés. The Social Revolutionaries worked to overthrow the tsarist autocracy and establish peasant socialism. Having no other outlet for opposition to the regime, they advocated political terrorism and attempted to assassinate government officials and members of the ruling dynasty. The growing opposition to the tsarist regime finally exploded into revolution in 1905.

The defeat of the Russians by the Japanese in 1904–1905 encouraged antigovernment groups to rebel against the tsarist regime. Nicholas II granted civil liberties and agreed to create a legislative assembly, the Duma, elected directly by a broad franchise. But real constitutional monarchy proved short-lived. Already by 1907, the tsar had curtailed the power of the Duma and relied again on the army and bureaucracy to rule Russia.

International Rivalries and the Winds of War

Between 1871 and 1914, Europeans experienced a long period of peace. There were wars (including wars of conquest in the non-Western world), but none involved the great powers. However, Europe endured a series of crises that might easily have led to war. Until 1890, Bismarck, the chancellor of Germany, exercised a restraining influence on Europeans. He realized that the emergence in 1871 of a unified Germany as the most powerful state on the Continent had upset the balance of power established at Vienna in 1815 (see Map 19.2). Bismarck knew that Germany's success frightened Europeans. Fearful of a possible anti-German alliance between France and Russia and possibly even Austria, Bismarck made a defensive alliance with Austria in 1879. Both powers agreed to support each other in the event of an attack by Russia. In 1882, this German-Austrian alliance was enlarged with the entrance of Italy, angry with the French over

MAP 19.2   Europe in 1871. German unification in 1871 upset the balance of power established at Vienna in 1815 and eventually led to a realignment of European alliances. By 1907, Europe was divided into two opposing camps: the Triple Entente of Great Britain, Russia, and France and the Triple Alliance of Germany, Austria-Hungary, and Italy. ➤ *How was Germany affected by the formation of the Triple Entente?*

conflicting colonial ambitions in North Africa. The Triple Alliance of 1882 committed the three powers to support the existing political and social order while providing a defensive shield against France. At the same time, Bismarck maintained a separate treaty with Russia and tried to remain on good terms with Great Britain.

When Emperor William II cashiered Bismarck in 1890 and took over direction of Germany's foreign policy, he embarked on an activist foreign policy dedicated to enhancing German power by finding, as he put it, Germany's rightful "place in the sun." One of his changes in Bismarck's foreign policy was to drop the treaty with Russia, which he viewed as being at odds with Germany's alliance with Austria. The ending of the alliance accomplished precisely

what Bismarck had feared: it brought France and Russia together. Republican France leapt at the chance to draw closer to tsarist Russia, and in 1894, the two powers concluded a military alliance. During the next ten years, German policies abroad caused the British to draw closer to France. By 1907, a loose confederation of Great Britain, France, and Russia—known as the Triple Entente—stood opposed to the Triple Alliance of Germany, Austria-Hungary, and Italy. Europe became divided into two opposing camps that became more and more inflexible and unwilling to compromise. When the members of the two alliances became involved in a new series of crises between 1908 and 1913 over the remnants of the Ottoman Empire in the Balkans, the stage was set for World War I.

The Ottoman Empire and Nationalism in the Balkans

Like the Austro-Hungarian Empire, the Ottoman Empire was severely troubled by the nationalist aspirations of its subject peoples, especially in the Balkans. Corruption and inefficiency had so weakened the Ottoman Empire that only the interference of the great European powers, who were fearful of each other's designs on the empire, kept it alive.

In the course of the nineteenth century, the Balkan provinces of the Ottoman Empire gradually gained their freedom, although the rivalry in the region between Austria and Russia complicated the process. Serbia had already received a large degree of autonomy in 1829, although it remained a province of the Ottoman Empire until 1878. Greece became an independent kingdom in 1830 after its successful revolt. By the Treaty of Adrianople in 1829, Russia received a protectorate over the principalities of Moldavia and Wallachia but was forced to give them up after the Crimean War. In 1861, Moldavia and Wallachia were merged into the state of Romania. Not until Russia's defeat of the Ottoman Empire in 1878, however, was Romania recognized as completely independent, as was Serbia at the same time. Although freed from Turkish rule, Montenegro was placed under an Austrian protectorate, while Bulgaria achieved autonomous status under Russian protection. The other Balkan territories of Bosnia and Herzegovina were placed under Austrian protection; Austria could occupy but not annex them. Despite these gains, by the end of the nineteenth century, the forces of Balkan nationalism were by no means stilled.

CRISES IN THE BALKANS, 1908–1913

The Bosnian Crisis of 1908–1909 began a chain of events that eventually spun out of control. Since 1878, Bosnia and Herzegovina had been under the protection of Austria, but in 1908 Austria took the drastic step of annexing the two Slavic-speaking territories. Serbia was outraged at this action because it dashed the Serbs' hopes of creating a large Serbian kingdom that would include most of the southern Slavs. But the Austrians had annexed Bosnia and Herzegovina explicitly to prevent that eventuality. The creation of a large Serbia would be a threat to the unity of their empire with its large Slavic population. The Russians, as protectors of their fellow Slavs and also desiring to increase their own authority in the Balkans, supported the Serbs and opposed the Austrian action. Backed by the Russians, the Serbs prepared for war against Austria. At this point, William II intervened and demanded that the Russians accept Austria's annexation of Bosnia and Herzegovina or face war with Germany. Weakened from their defeat in the Russo-Japanese War in 1904–1905, the Russians were afraid to risk war and backed down. Humiliated, the Russians vowed revenge.

EUROPEAN DIPLOMACY, 1871–1914

Triple Alliance: Germany, Austria, and Italy	1882
Military alliance: Russia and France	1894
Entente Cordiale: France and Britain	1904
Triple Entente: France, Britain, and Russia	1907
First Balkan War	1912
Second Balkan War	1913

European attention returned to the Balkans in 1912 when Serbia, Bulgaria, Montenegro, and Greece organized the Balkan League and defeated the Turks in the First Balkan War. When the victorious allies were unable to agree on how to divide the conquered Turkish provinces of Macedonia and Albania, a second Balkan War erupted in 1913 (see Map 19.3). Greece, Serbia, Romania, and the Ottoman Empire attacked and defeated Bulgaria. As a result, Bulgaria obtained only a small part of Macedonia, and most of the rest was divided between Serbia and Greece. Yet Serbia's aspirations remained unfulfilled. The two Balkan wars left the inhabitants embittered and created more tensions among the great powers.

One of Serbia's major ambitions had been to acquire Albanian territory that would give it a port on the Adriatic. At the London conference arranged by Austria at the end of the two Balkan wars, the Austrians had blocked Serbia's wishes by creating an independent Albania. The Germans, as Austrian allies, had supported this move. In their frustration, Serbian nationalists increasingly portrayed the Austrians as evil monsters who were keeping the Serbs from becoming a great nation. As Serbia's chief supporters, the Russians were also upset by the turn of events in the Balkans. A feeling had grown among Russian leaders that they could not back down again in the event of a confrontation with Austria or Germany in the Balkans. Moreover, as a result of the Balkan wars, both Russia and Austria expressed discontent that their supposed friends and allies, Great Britain and Germany, had not done enough to support them. This made the British and Germans more determined to support their allies in order to avoid endangering their alliances.

Austria-Hungary had achieved another of its aims, but it was left convinced that Serbia was a mortal threat to its empire and must at some point be crushed. Meanwhile, the French and Russian governments renewed their alliance and promised each other that they would not back down at the next crisis. Britain drew closer to France. By the beginning of 1914, two armed camps viewed each other with suspicion. The European "age of progress" was about to come to an inglorious and bloody end.

Toward the Modern Consciousness: Intellectual and Cultural Developments

Before 1914, many people in the Western world continued to believe in the values and ideals that had been generated by the Scientific Revolution and the Enlightenment. The idea that human beings could improve themselves and achieve a better society seemed to be proved by a rising standard of living, urban comforts, and mass education. Such products of modern technology as electric lights and automobiles reinforced the popular prestige of science. It was easy to think that the human mind could make sense of the universe. Between 1870 and 1914, radically new ideas challenged these optimistic views and opened the way to a modern consciousness.

A New Physics

Science was one of the chief pillars underlying the optimistic and rationalistic view of the world that many Westerners shared in the nineteenth century. Supposedly based on hard facts and cold reason, science offered a certainty of belief in the orderliness of nature that was comforting to many people for whom traditional religious beliefs no longer had much meaning. Many naively believed that the application of already known scientific laws would give humanity a complete understanding of the physical world and an accurate picture of reality. The new physics dramatically altered that perspective.

Throughout much of the nineteenth century, Westerners adhered to the mechanical conception of the universe postulated by the classical physics of Isaac Newton. In this perspective, the universe was viewed as a giant machine in which time, space, and matter were objective realities that existed independently of the people observing them. Matter was thought to be composed of indivisible and solid material bodies called atoms.

These views were first seriously questioned at the end of the nineteenth century. The French scientist Marie Curie (1867–1934) and her husband, Pierre (1859–1906), discovered that an element called radium gave off rays of radiation that apparently came from within the atom itself. Atoms were not simply hard, material bodies but small worlds containing such subatomic particles as electrons and protons, which behaved in seemingly random and inexplicable fashion. Inquiry into the disintegrative process within atoms became a central theme of the new physics.

Building on this work, in 1900 a Berlin physicist, Max Planck (1858–1947), rejected the belief that a heated body radiates energy in a steady stream but maintained instead that it did so discontinuously, in irregular packets of energy

AP/Wide World Photos

MARIE CURIE. Marie Curie was born in Warsaw, Poland, but studied at the University of Paris, where she received degrees in both physics and mathematics. She was the first woman to win two Nobel Prizes, one in 1903 in physics and another in chemistry in 1911. She is shown here in her Paris laboratory in 1921.

that he called "quanta." The quantum theory raised fundamental questions about the subatomic realm of the atom. By 1900, the old view of atoms as the basic building blocks of the material world was being seriously questioned, and the world of Newtonian physics was in trouble.

Albert Einstein (1879–1955), a German-born patent officer working in Switzerland, pushed these new theories into new terrain. In 1905, Einstein published a paper titled "The Electro-Dynamics of Moving Bodies" that contained his special theory of relativity. According to relativity theory, space and time are not absolute but relative to the observer, and both are interwoven into what Einstein called a four-dimensional space-time continuum. Neither space nor time had an existence independent of human experience. As Einstein later explained simply to a journalist: "It was formerly believed that if all material things disappeared out of the universe, time and space would be left. According to the relativity theory, however, time and space disappear together with the things."[6] Moreover, matter and energy reflected the relativity of time and space. Einstein concluded that matter was nothing but another form of energy. His epochal formula $E = mc^2$—that the energy of each particle of matter is equivalent to its mass times the square of the velocity of light—was the key theory explaining the vast energies contained within the atom. It led to the atomic age.

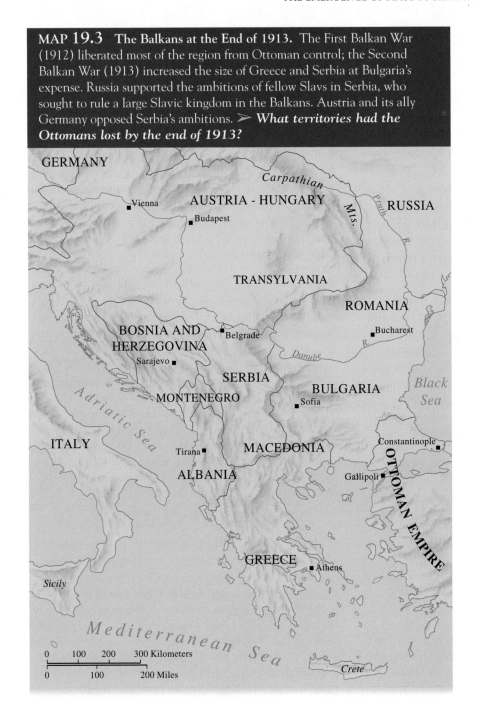

MAP **19.3** **The Balkans at the End of 1913.** The First Balkan War (1912) liberated most of the region from Ottoman control; the Second Balkan War (1913) increased the size of Greece and Serbia at Bulgaria's expense. Russia supported the ambitions of fellow Slavs in Serbia, who sought to rule a large Slavic kingdom in the Balkans. Austria and its ally Germany opposed Serbia's ambitions. ➢ *What territories had the Ottomans lost by the end of 1913?*

Sigmund Freud and the Emergence of Psychoanalysis

At the turn of the twentieth century, Viennese physician Sigmund Freud (1856–1939) advanced a series of theories that undermined optimism about the rational nature of the human mind. Freud's thought, like the new physics, added to the uncertainties of the age. His major ideas were published in 1900 in *The Interpretation of Dreams*.

According to Freud, human behavior was strongly determined by the unconscious, by past experiences and internal forces of which people were largely oblivious. For Freud, human behavior was no longer truly rational but rather instinctive or irrational. He argued that painful and unsettling experiences were blotted from conscious awareness but still continued to influence behavior since they had become part of the unconscious (see the box on p. 566). Repression began in childhood. Freud devised a method, known as psychoanalysis, by which a psychotherapist and patient could probe deeply into the memory in order to retrace the chain of repression all the way back to its childhood origins. By making the conscious mind aware of the unconscious and its repressed contents, the patient's psychic conflict was resolved.

FREUD AND THE CONCEPT OF REPRESSION

Freud's psychoanalytical theories resulted from his attempt to understand the world of the unconscious. This excerpt is taken from a lecture given in 1909 in which Freud describes how he arrived at his theory of the role of repression. Although Freud valued science and reason, his theories of the unconscious produced a new image of the human being as governed less by reason than by irrational forces.

SIGMUND FREUD, *FIVE LECTURES ON PSYCHOANALYSIS*

I did not abandon [the technique of encouraging patients to reveal forgotten experiences], however, before the observations I made during my use of it afforded me decisive evidence. I found confirmation of the fact that the forgotten memories were not lost. They were in the patient's possession and were ready to emerge in association to what was still known by him; but there was some force that prevented them from becoming conscious and compelled them to remain unconscious. The existence of this force could be assumed with certainty, since one became aware of an effort corresponding to it if, in opposition to it, one tried to introduce the unconscious memories into the patient's consciousness. The force which was maintaining the pathological condition became apparent in the form of resistance on the part of the patient.

It was on this idea of resistance, then, that I based my view of the course of psychical events in hysteria. In order to effect a recovery, it had proved necessary to remove these resistances. Starting out from the mechanism of cure, it now became possible to construct quite definite ideas of the origin of the illness. The same forces which, in the form of resistance, were now offering opposition to the forgotten material's being made conscious, must formerly have brought about the forgetting and must have pushed the pathogenic experiences in question out of consciousness. I gave the name of "repression" to this hypothetical process, and I considered that it was proved by the undeniable existence of resistance.

The further question could then be raised as to what these forces were and what the determinants were of the repression in which we now recognized the pathogenic mechanism of hysteria. A comparative study of the pathogenic situations which we had come to know through the cathartic procedure made it possible to answer this question. All these experiences had involved the emergence of a wishful impulse which was in sharp contrast to the subject's other wishes and which proved incompatible with the ethical and aesthetic standards of his personality. There had been a short conflict, and the end of this internal struggle was that the idea which had appeared before consciousness as the vehicle of this irreconcilable wish fell a victim to repression, was pushed out of consciousness with all its attached memories, and was forgotten. Thus the incompatibility of the wish in question with the patient's ego was the motive for the repression; the subject's ethical and other standards were the repressing forces. An acceptance of the incompatible wishful impulse or a prolongation of the conflict would have produced a high degree of unpleasure; this unpleasure was avoided by means of repression, which was thus revealed as one of the devices serving to protect the mental personality.

The Impact of Darwin: Social Darwinism and Racism

In the second half of the nineteenth century, scientific theories were sometimes wrongly applied to meet other ends. For example, the ideas of Charles Darwin were applied to human society in a radical way by rabid nationalists and racists. In their pursuit of national greatness, extreme nationalists often insisted that nations, too, were engaged in a struggle for existence in which only the fittest survived. The German general Friedrich von Bernhardi argued in 1907, "War is a biological necessity of the first importance, . . . since without it an unhealthy development will follow, which excludes every advancement of the race, and therefore all real civilization. 'War is the father of all things.'"[7]

Perhaps nowhere was the combination of extreme nationalism and racism more evident or more dangerous than in Germany. One of the chief propagandists of German racism was Houston Stewart Chamberlain (1855–1927), a Briton who became a German citizen. According to Chamberlain, modern-day Germans were the only pure successors of the Aryans, who were portrayed as the true and original founders of Western culture. The Aryan race, under German leadership, must be prepared to fight for Western civilization and save it from the destructive assaults of such lower races as Jews, Negroes, and Orientals. Chamberlain singled out the Jews as the racial enemy who wanted to destroy the Aryan race.

ANTI-SEMITISM

Anti-Semitism had a long history in European civilization, but in the nineteenth century, as a result of the ideals of the Enlightenment and the French Revolution, Jews were increasingly granted legal equality in many European countries. Many Jews now left the ghetto and became assimilated into the cultures around them. Many became successful as bankers, lawyers, scientists, scholars, journalists, and stage performers.

These achievements represent only one side of the picture, however. In Germany and Austria during the 1880s and 1890s, conservatives founded right-wing anti-Jewish

THE VOICE OF ZIONISM: THEODOR HERZL AND THE JEWISH STATE

The Austrian Jewish journalist Theodor Herzl wrote The Jewish State *in the summer of 1895 in Paris while he was covering the Dreyfus case for his Vienna newspaper. (Alfred Dreyfus, a French army officer who was also Jewish, was wrongly convicted of selling military secrets. Although he was later exonerated, the case revealed the depth of anti-Semitism in France.) In several weeks, during a period of feverish composition, he set about to analyze the fundamental causes of anti-Semitism and devise a solution to the "Jewish problem." In this selection, he discusses two of his major conclusions.*

THEODOR HERZL, *THE JEWISH STATE*

I do not intend to arouse sympathetic emotions on our behalf. That would be a foolish, futile, and undignified proceeding. I shall content myself with putting the following questions to the Jews: Is it true that, in countries where we live in perceptible numbers, the position of Jewish lawyers, doctors, technicians, teachers, and employees of all descriptions becomes daily more intolerable? True, that the Jewish middle classes are seriously threatened? True, that the passions of the mob are incited against our wealthy people? True, that our poor endure greater sufferings than any other proletariat?

I think that this external pressure makes itself felt everywhere. In our economically upper classes it causes discomfort, in our middle classes continual and grave anxieties, in our lower classes absolute despair.

Everything tends, in fact, to one and the same conclusion, which is clearly enunciated in that classic Berlin phrase: "Juden 'raus!" (Out with the Jews!)

I shall now put the Jewish Question in the curtest possible form: Are we to "get out" now? And if so, to what place?

Or, may we yet remain? And if so, how long?

Let us first settle the point of staying where we are. Can we hope for better days, can we possess our souls in patience, can we wait in pious resignation till the princes and peoples of this earth are more mercifully disposed toward us? I say that we cannot hope for a change in the current of feeling. And why not? . . . The nations in whose midst Jews live are all, either covertly or openly, Anti-Semitic. . . .

The whole plan is in its essence perfectly simple, as it must necessarily be if it is to come within the comprehension of all.

Let the sovereignty be granted us over a portion of the globe large enough to satisfy the rightful requirements of a nation; the rest we shall manage for ourselves.

The creation of a new State is neither ridiculous nor impossible. We have in our day witnessed the process in connection with nations which were not in the bulk of the middle class, but poorer, less educated, and consequently weaker than ourselves. The Governments of all countries scourged by Anti-Semitism will be keenly interested in assisting us to obtain the sovereignty we want. . . .

Palestine is our ever memorable historic home. The very name of Palestine would attract our people with a force of marvelous potency. Supposing his Majesty the Sultan were to give us Palestine, we could in return undertake to regulate the whole finances of Turkey. We should there form a portion of the rampart of Europe against Asia, an outpost of civilization as opposed to barbarism. We should as a neutral State remain in contact with all Europe, which would have to guarantee our existence. The sanctuaries of Christendom would be safeguarded by assigning to them an extraterritorial status such as is well known to the law of nations. We should form a guard of honor about these sanctuaries, answering for the fulfillment of this duty with our existence. This guard of honor would be the great symbol of the solution of the Jewish Question after eighteen centuries of Jewish suffering.

---

parties that used anti-Semitism to win the votes of traditional lower-middle-class groups who felt threatened by the new economic forces of the times. However, the worst treatment of Jews at the turn of the century occurred in eastern Europe, where 72 percent of the world's Jewish population lived. Russian Jews were admitted to secondary schools and universities only under a quota system and were forced to live in certain regions of the country. Persecutions and pogroms were widespread. Hundreds of thousands of Jews decided to emigrate to escape the persecution.

Many Jews went to the United States, although some moved to Palestine, which soon became the focus of a Jewish nationalist movement called Zionism. For many Jews, Palestine, the land of ancient Israel, had long been the land of their dreams. A key figure in the growth of political Zionism was Theodor Herzl (1860–1904), who stated in his book *The Jewish State*, "The Jews who wish it will have their state" (see the box above). Settlement in Palestine was difficult, however, because it was then part of the Ottoman Empire, which was opposed to

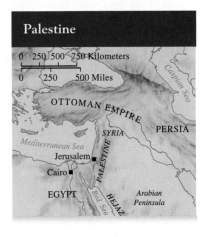

Palestine

Symbolist Poetry: Art for Art's Sake

The Symbolist movement was an important foundation for Modernism. The Symbolists believed that the working of the mind was the proper study of literature. Arthur Rimbaud was one of Symbolism's leading practitioners in France. Although his verses seem to have little real meaning, they were not meant to describe the external world precisely but rather to enchant the mind. Art was not meant for the masses but only for "art's sake." Rimbaud wrote, "By the alchemy of the words, I noted the inexpressible. I fixed giddiness."

ARTHUR RIMBAUD, THE DRUNKEN BOAT

As I floated down impassable rivers,
I felt the boatmen no longer guiding me:
After them came redskins who with war cries
Nailed them naked to the painted poles.

I was oblivious to the crew,
I who bore Flemish wheat and English cotton.
When the racket was finished with my boatmen,
The waters let me drift my own free way.

In the tide's furious pounding,
I, the other winter, emptier than children's minds,
I sailed! And the unmoored peninsulas
Have not suffered more triumphant turmoils.

The tempest blessed my maritime watches.
Lighter than a cork I danced on the waves,
Those eternal rollers of victims,
Ten nights, without regretting the lantern-foolish eye!

Sweeter than the bite of sour apples to a child,
The green water seeped through my wooden hull,
Rinsed me of blue wine stains and vomit,
Broke apart grappling iron and rudder.

And then I bathed myself in the poetry
Of the star-sprayed milk-white sea,
Devouring the azure greens; where, pale
And ravished, a pensive drowned one sometimes floats;
Where, suddenly staining the blueness, frenzies
And slows rhythms in the blazing of day,
Stronger than alcohol, vaster than our lyres,
The russet bitterness of love ferments. . . .

I have dreamed of the green night bedazzled with snow,
A kiss climbing slowly to the eyes of the sea,
The flow of unforgettable sap,
And the yellow-blue waking of singing phosphorous!

Long months I have followed, like maddened cattle,
The surge assaulting the rocks
Without dreaming that the Virgin's luminous feet
Could force a muzzle on the panting ocean!

I have struck against the shares of incredible Floridas
Mixing panther-eyed flowers like human skins!
Rainbows stretched like bridle reins
Under the ocean's horizon, toward sea-green troops! . . .

Jewish immigration. Despite the problems, however, the first Zionist Congress, which met in Switzerland in 1897, proclaimed as its aim the creation of a "home in Palestine secured by public law" for the Jewish people. In 1900, around a thousand Jews migrated to Palestine, and the trickle rose to about three thousand a year between 1904 and 1914, keeping the Zionist dream alive.

The Culture of Modernity

The revolution in physics and psychology was paralleled by a revolution in literature and the arts. Before 1914, writers and artists were rebelling against the traditional literary and artistic styles that had dominated European cultural life since the Renaissance. The changes that they produced have since been called Modernism.

At the beginning of the twentieth century, a group of writers known as the Symbolists caused a literary revolution. Primarily interested in writing poetry and strongly influenced by the ideas of Freud, the Symbolists believed that an objective knowledge of the world was impossible (see the box above). The external world was not real but only a collection of symbols that reflected the true reality of the individual human mind. Art, they believed, should function for its own sake instead of serving, criticizing, or seeking to understand society.

The period from 1870 to 1914 was one of the most fertile in the history of art. Since the Renaissance, the task of artists had been to represent reality as accurately as possible. By the late nineteenth century, artists were seeking new forms of expression. The preamble to modern painting can be found in Impressionism, a movement that originated in France in the 1870s when a group of artists rejected the studios and museums and went out into the countryside to paint nature directly. Camille Pissarro (1830–1903), one of Impressionism's founders, expressed what they sought:

Precise drawing is dry and hampers the impression of the whole, it destroys all sensations. Do not define too closely the outlines of things; it is the brush stroke of the right value and color which should produce the drawing. . . . Work at the same time upon sky, water, branches, ground, keeping everything going on an equal basis and unceasingly rework until you have got it. . . . Don't proceed according to rules and principles, but paint what you observe and feel. Paint generously and unhesitatingly, for it is best not to lose the first impression.[8]

An important Impressionist painter was Berthe Morisot (1841–1895), who believed that women had a special vision, which was, as she said, "more delicate than that of men." Her special touch is evident in *Young Girl by the Window*, where she makes use of lighter colors and flowing brush strokes. Near the end of her life, she lamented the refusal of men to take her work seriously: "I don't think there has ever been a man who treated a woman as an equal, and that's all I would have asked, for I know I'm worth as much as they."[9]

In the 1880s, a new movement known as Post-Impressionism arose in France and soon spread to other European countries. A famous Post-Impressionist was the tortured and tragic figure Vincent van Gogh (1853–1890).

For van Gogh, art was a spiritual experience. He was especially interested in color and believed that it could act as its own form of language. Van Gogh maintained that artists should paint what they feel.

By the beginning of the twentieth century, the belief that the task of art was to represent "reality" had lost much of its meaning. By that time, the new psychology and the new physics had made it evident that many people were not sure what constituted reality anyway. Then, too, the growth of photography gave artists another reason to reject Realism. Invented in the 1830s, photography became popular and widespread after George Eastman created the first Kodak camera in 1888 for the mass market. What was the point of an artist's doing what the camera did better? Unlike the camera, which could only mirror reality, artists could create reality. Like the Symbolist writers of the time, artists sought meaning in individual consciousness.

⟫► BERTHE MORISOT, *YOUNG GIRL BY THE WINDOW.* Berthe Morisot came from a wealthy French family that settled in Paris when she was seven. The first female painter to join the Impressionists, she developed her own unique Impressionist style. Her gentle colors and strong use of pastels are especially evident in *Young Girl by the Window*. The French Impressionist style also spread abroad, as is seen in *By the Lake*, a painting by Japanese artist Kuroda Seiki (see Chapter 21, p. 625).

VINCENT VAN GOGH, *THE STARRY NIGHT*.   The Dutch painter Vincent van Gogh was a major figure among the Post-Impressionists. His originality and power of expression made a strong impact on his artistic successors. In *The Starry Night*, van Gogh's subjective vision was given full play as the dynamic swirling forms of the heavens above overwhelmed the village below. The heavens seem alive with a mysterious spiritual force.

By 1905, one of the most important figures in modern art was just beginning his career. Pablo Picasso (1881–1973) was from Spain but settled in Paris in 1904. Picasso was extremely flexible and painted in a remarkable variety of styles. He was instrumental in the development of a new style called Cubism that used geometrical designs as visual stimuli to re-create reality in the viewer's mind.

The modern artist's flight from "visual reality" reached a high point in 1910 with the beginning of abstract painting. A Russian who worked in Germany, Wassily Kandinsky (1866–1944) was one of the founders of Abstract Expressionism. As is evident in his *Painting with White Border*, Kandinsky sought to avoid representation altogether. He believed that art should speak directly to the soul. To

do so, it must avoid any reference to visual reality and concentrate on line and color.

Modernism in the arts revolutionized architecture and architectural practices. A new principle known as functionalism motivated this revolution. Functionalism meant that buildings, like the products of machines, should be "functional" or useful, fulfilling the purpose for which they were constructed. Art and engineering were to be unified, and all unnecessary ornamentation was to be stripped away.

The United States was a leader in these pioneering architectural designs. Unprecedented urban growth and the absence of restrictive architectural traditions allowed for new building methods, especially in the relatively new city of Chicago. The Chicago school of the 1890s, led by Louis H. Sullivan (1856–1924), used reinforced concrete,

PABLO PICASSO, *LES DEMOISELLES D'AVIGNON*.
Pablo Picasso, a major pioneer and activist of modern art, experimented with a remarkable variety of modern styles. *Les Demoiselles d'Avignon* was the first great example of Cubism, which one art historian called "the first style of this [twentieth] century to break radically with the past." Geometric shapes replace traditional forms, forcing the viewer to re-create reality in his or her own mind.

steel frames, and electric elevators to build skyscrapers virtually free of external ornamentation. One of Sullivan's most successful pupils was Frank Lloyd Wright (1869–1959), who became known for innovative designs in domestic architecture. Wright's private houses, built chiefly for wealthy patrons, featured geometric structures with long lines, overhanging roofs, and severe planes of brick and stone. The interiors were open spaces and included cathedral ceilings and built-in furniture and lighting. Wright pioneered the modern American house.

At the beginning of the twentieth century, developments in music paralleled those in painting. Expressionism in music was a Russian creation, the product of the composer Igor Stravinsky (1882–1971) and the Ballet Russe, the dancing company of Sergei Diaghilev (1872–1929). Together they revolutionized the world of music with Stravinsky's ballet *The Rite of Spring*. When it was performed in Paris in 1913, the savage and primitive sounds and beats of the music and dance caused a near riot from an audience outraged at its audacity.

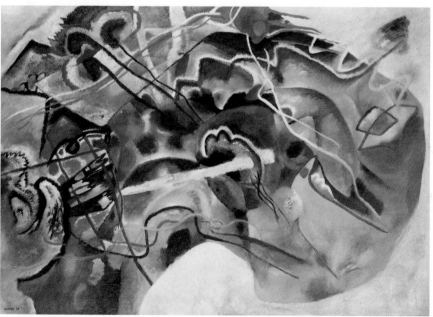

WASSILY KANDINSKY, *COMPOSITION VIII, NO. 2 (PAINTING WITH WHITE BORDER)*. One of the founders of Abstract Expressionism was the Russian Wassily Kandinsky, who sought to eliminate representation altogether by focusing on color and avoiding any resemblance to visual reality. In *Painting with White Border*, Kandinsky used color "to send light into the darkness of men's hearts." He believed that color, like music, could fulfill a spiritual goal of appealing directly to the human being.

CONCLUSION

Between 1870 and 1914, the national state began to expand its functions beyond all previous limits. Fearful of the growth of socialism and trade unions, governments attempted to appease the working masses by adopting such social insurance measures as protection against accidents, illness, and old age. These social welfare measures were narrow in scope and limited in benefits before 1914. Moreover, they failed to halt the growth of socialism. Nevertheless, they signaled a new direction for state action to benefit the mass of its citizens.

This extension of state functions took place in an atmosphere of increased national loyalty. After 1870, nation-states increasingly sought to solidify the social order and win the active loyalty and support of their citizens by deliberately cultivating national feelings. Yet this policy contained potentially great dangers. Nations had discovered once again that imperialistic adventures and military successes could arouse nationalistic passions and smother domestic political unrest. But they also found—belatedly in 1914—that nationalistic feelings could also lead to intense international rivalries that made war almost inevitable.

What many Europeans liked to call their "age of progress" between 1870 and 1914 was also an era of anxiety. Frenzied imperialist expansion had created vast European empires and spheres of influence around the globe. This feverish competition for colonies, however, had markedly increased the antagonisms among the European states. At the same time, the Western treatment of native peoples as racial inferiors caused educated, non-Western elites in these colonies to initiate movements for national independence. Before these movements could be successful, however, the power that Europeans had achieved through their mass armies and technological superiority had to be weakened. The Europeans inadvertently accomplished this task for their colonial subjects by demolishing their own civilization on the battlegrounds of Europe in World War I and World War II.

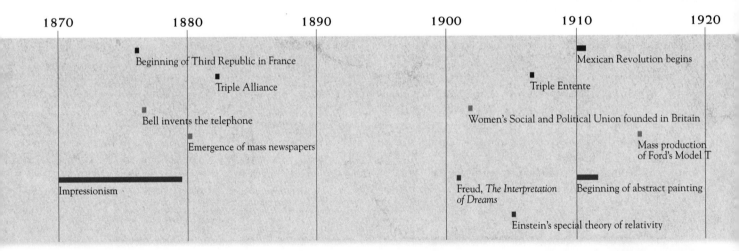

| 1870 | 1880 | 1890 | 1900 | 1910 | 1920 |

Beginning of Third Republic in France

Triple Alliance

Bell invents the telephone

Emergence of mass newspapers

Impressionism

Mexican Revolution begins

Triple Entente

Women's Social and Political Union founded in Britain

Mass production of Ford's Model T

Freud, *The Interpretation of Dreams*

Beginning of abstract painting

Einstein's special theory of relativity

CHAPTER NOTES

1. Karl Marx and Friedrich Engels, *The Communist Manifesto* (Harmondsworth, England, 1967), p. 80. Originally published in 1848.
2. Ibid., pp. 91, 94.
3. Quoted in Nicholas Bullock and James Read, *The Movement for Housing Reform in Germany and France, 1840–1914* (Cambridge, 1985), p. 42.
4. Quoted in Catherine M. Prelinger, "Prelude to Consciousness: Amalie Sieveking and the Female Association for the Care of the Poor and the Sick," in John C. Fout, ed., *German Women in the Nineteenth Century: A Social History* (New York, 1984), p. 119.
5. Quoted in Shmuel Galai, *The Liberation Movement in Russia, 1900–1905* (Cambridge, 1973), p. 26.
6. Quoted in Arthur E. E. McKenzie, *The Major Achievements of Science* (New York, 1960), vol. 1, p. 310.
7. Friedrich von Bernhardi, *Germany and the Next War*, trans. Allen H. Powles (New York, 1914), pp. 18–19.
8. Quoted in John Rewald, *History of Impressionism* (New York, 1961), pp. 456–58.
9. Quoted in Anne Higonnet, *Berthe Morisot's Images of Women* (Cambridge, Mass., 1992), p. 19.

SUGGESTED READING

The subject of the Second Industrial Revolution is well covered in D. Landes, *The Unbound Prometheus*, cited in Chapter 18. For a fundamental survey of European industrialization, see A. S. Milward and S. B. Saul, *The Development of the Economies of Continental Europe, 1850–1914* (Cambridge, Mass., 1977). The impact of the new technology on European thought is imaginatively discussed in S. Kern, *The Culture of Time and Space, 1880–1918* (Cambridge, Mass., 1983).

On Marx, there is the standard work by D. McLellan, *Karl Marx: His Life and Thought* (New York, 1974). For an introduction to international socialism, see A. Lindemann, *A History of European Socialism* (New Haven, Conn., 1983), and L. Derfler, *Socialism Since Marx: A Century of the European Left* (New York, 1973).

For a good introduction to housing reform on the Continent, see N. Bullock and J. Read, *The Movement for Housing Reform in Germany and France, 1840–1914* (Cambridge, 1985). An interesting work on aristocratic life is D. Cannadine,*The Decline and Fall of the British Aristocracy* (New Haven, Conn., 1990). On the middle classes, see P. Pilbeam, *The Middle Classes in Europe, 1789–1914* (Basingstoke, England, 1990), and R. Magraw, *A History of the French Working Class* (Cambridge, Mass., 1992). On the working classes, see L. Berlanstein, *The Working People of Paris, 1871–1914* (Baltimore, 1984). There are good overviews of women's experiences in the nineteenth century in B. Smith, *Changing Lives: Women in European History Since 1700* (Lexington, Mass., 1989), and M. J. Boxer and J. H. Quataert, eds., *Connecting Spheres: Women in the Western World, 1500 to the Present* (Oxford, 1987). The world of women's work is examined in L. A. Tilly and J. W. Scott, *Women, Work, and Family* (New York, 1978). The rise of feminism is examined in J. Rendall, *The Origins of Modern Feminism: Women in Britain, France and the United States* (London, 1985). On various aspects of education, see M. J. Maynes, *Schooling in Western Europe: A Social History* (Albany, N.Y., 1985), and J. S. Hurt, *Elementary Schooling and the Working Classes, 1860–1918* (London, 1979). A concise and well-presented survey of leisure patterns is G. Cross, *A Social History of Leisure Since 1600* (State College, Pa., 1989).

The domestic politics of the period can be examined in the general works listed in the bibliography for Chapter 18. There are also specialized works on aspects of each country's history. On Britain, see D. Read, *The Age of Urban Democracy: England, 1868–1914* (New York, 1994). For a detailed examination of French history from 1871 to 1914, see J.-M. Mayeur and M. Reberioux, *The Third Republic from Its Origins to the Great War, 1871–1914* (Cambridge, 1984). On Germany, see W. J. Mommsen, *Imperial Germany, 1867–1918* (New York, 1995), and V. R. Berghahn, *Imperial Germany, 1871– 1914* (Providence, R.I., 1995). On the nationalities problem in the Austro-Hungarian Empire, see R. Kann, *The Multinational Empire: Nationalism and National Reform in the Habsburg Monarchy, 1848–1918*, 2 vols. (New York, 1950). On aspects of Russian history, see H. Rogger, *Russia in the Age of Modernization and Revolution, 1881–1917* (London, 1983), and A. Ascher, *The Revolution of 1905: Russia in Disarray* (New York, 1988). On the United States, see D. Cashman, *America in the Gilded Age: From the Death of Lincoln to the Rise of Theodore Roosevelt* (New York, 1984), and J. W. Chambers, *The Tyranny of Change: America in the Progressive Era, 1900–1917* (New York, 1980). On Latin American economic developments, see B. Albert, *South America and the World Economy from Independence to 1930* (London, 1983). For a comprehensive examination of the Mexican Revolution, see A. Knight, *The Mexican Revolution*, 2 vols. (Cambridge, 1986). Two fundamental works on the diplomatic history of the period are by W. L. Langer, *European Alliances and Alignments*, 2d ed. (New York, 1966), and *The Diplomacy of Imperialism*, 2d ed. (New York, 1965).

A well-regarded study of Freud is P. Gay, *Freud: A Life for Our Time* (New York, 1988). Modern anti-Semitism is covered in J. Katz, *From Prejudice to Destruction* (Cambridge, Mass., 1980), and A. S. Lindemann, *Esau's Tears: Modern Anti-Semitism and the Rise of the Jews* (New York, 1997). European racism is analyzed in G. L. Mosse, *Toward the Final Solution* (New York, 1980). For a recent biography of Theodor Herzl, see J. Kornberg, *Theodor Herzl: From Assimilation to Zionism* (London, 1993). Very valuable on modern art are M. Powell-Jones, *Impressionism* (London, 1994); B. Denvir, *Post-Impressionism* (New York, 1992); and T. Parsons, *Post-Impressionism: The Rise of Modern Art* (London, 1992).

INFOTRAC COLLEGE EDITION

For additional reading, go to InfoTrac College Edition, your online research library at
http://web1.infotrac-college.com

Enter the search terms "family nineteenth century" using Keywords.

Enter the search terms "Industrial Revolution" using Keywords.

Enter the search term "feminism" using the Subject Guide.

Enter the search terms "Charles Darwin" using Keywords.

Enter the search terms "Sigmund Freud" using Keywords.

Copyright of Singapore History Museum, National Heritage Board

Chapter 20

THE
HIGH TIDE
OF
IMPERIALISM

CHAPTER OUTLINE

- THE SPREAD OF COLONIAL RULE
- THE COLONIAL SYSTEM
- THE EMERGENCE OF ANTICOLONIALISM
- CONCLUSION

FOCUS QUESTIONS

- What types of administrative systems did the various colonial powers establish for their colonies, and how did these systems reflect the general philosophy of colonialism?

- What economic policies were followed by the colonial powers, and who benefited from these policies?

- How did the subject peoples respond to colonialism, and what role did nationalism play in their response?

- What were the consequences of the new imperialism for the colonies and for the colonial powers?

- What were the causes of the new imperialism of the nineteenth century, and how did it differ from European expansion in earlier periods?

*I*n 1877, the young British empire builder Cecil Rhodes drew up his last will and testament. He bequeathed his fortune, achieved as a diamond magnate in South Africa, to two of his close friends and acquaintances. He also instructed them to use the inheritance to form a secret society with the aim of bringing about "the extension of British rule throughout the world, the perfecting of a system of emigration from the United Kingdom . . . especially the occupation by British settlers of the entire continent of Africa, the Holy Land, the valley of the Euphrates, the Islands of Cyprus and Candia [Crete], the whole of South America. . . . The ultimate recovery of the United States of America as an integral part of the British Empire . . . then finally the foundation of so great a power as to hereafter render wars impossible and promote the best interests of humanity."[1]

Preposterous as such ideas appear to us today, they serve as a graphic reminder of the hubris that characterized the worldview of Rhodes and many of his contemporaries during the age of imperialism, as well as the complex union of moral concern and vaulting ambition that motivated their actions on the world stage.

Through their efforts, Western colonialism spread throughout much of the non-Western world during the nineteenth and early twentieth centuries. Spurred by the demands of the Industrial Revolution, a few powerful Western states—notably, Great Britain, France, Germany, Russia, and the United States—competed avariciously for consumer markets and raw materials for their expanding economies. By the end of the nineteenth century, virtually all of the traditional societies in Asia and Africa were under direct or indirect colonial rule. As the new century began, the Western imprint on Asian and African societies, for better or for worse, appeared to be a permanent feature of the political and cultural landscape. •

THE SPREAD OF COLONIAL RULE

In the nineteenth century, a new phase of Western expansion into Asia and Africa began. Whereas European aims in the East before 1800 could be summed up in Vasco da Gama's famous phrase "Christians and spices," now a new relationship took shape as European nations began to view Asian and African societies as sources of industrial raw materials and as markets for Western manufactured goods. No longer were Western gold and silver exchanged for cloves, pepper, tea, silk, and porcelain. Now the prodigious output of European factories was sent to Africa and Asia in return for oil, tin, rubber, and the other resources needed to fuel the Western industrial machine.

The reason for this change, of course, was the Industrial Revolution, which began in England in the late eighteenth century and spread to the Continent a few decades later. Now industrializing countries in the West needed vital raw materials that were not available at home, as well as a reliable market for the goods produced in their factories. The latter factor became increasingly crucial as producers began to discover that their home markets could not always absorb domestic output, and thus they had to export their manufactures to make a profit. When consumer demand lagged, economic depression threatened.

As Western economic expansion into Asia and Africa gathered strength during the nineteenth century, it became fashionable to call the process imperialism. Although the term *imperialism* has many meanings, in this instance it referred to the efforts of capitalist states in the West to seize markets, cheap raw materials, and lucrative avenues for investment in the countries beyond Western civilization. In this interpretation, the primary motives behind the Western expansion were economic. The best-known promoter of this view was the British political economist John A. Hobson, who published a major analysis titled *Imperialism: A Study* in 1902. In this influential book, Hobson maintained that modern imperialism was a direct consequence of the modern industrial economy.

As in the earlier phase of Western expansion, however, the issue was not simply an economic one. As Hobson himself conceded, economic concerns were inevitably tinged with political overtones and with questions of national grandeur and moral purpose as well. In the minds of nineteenth-century Europeans, economic wealth, national status, and political power went hand in hand with the possession of a colonial empire. To global strategists, colonies brought tangible benefits in the world of balance-of-power politics as well as economic profits, and many nations became involved in the pursuit of colonies as much to gain advantage over their rivals as to acquire territory for its own sake.

The relationship between colonialism and national survival was expressed directly in a speech by French politician Jules Ferry in 1885. A policy of "containment or abstinence," he warned, would set France on "the broad road to decadence" and initiate its decline into a "third- or fourth-rate power." British imperialists agreed. To Cecil Rhodes, the most famous empire builder of his day, the extraction of material wealth from the colonies was only a secondary matter. "My ruling purpose," he remarked, "is the extension of the British Empire."[2] That British Empire, on which, as the saying went, "the sun never set," was the envy of its rivals and was viewed as the primary source of British global dominance during the second half of the nineteenth century.

With the change in European motives for colonization came a corresponding shift in tactics. Earlier, when their economic interests were more limited, European states had generally been satisfied to deal with existing independent states rather than attempting to establish direct control over vast territories. There had been exceptions where state power at the local level was at the point of collapse (as in India), where European economic interests were especially intense (as in Latin America and the East Indies), or where there was no centralized authority (as in North America and the Philippines). But for the most part, the Western presence in Asia and Africa had been limited to controlling the regional trade network and establishing a few footholds where the foreigners could carry on trade and missionary activity.

After 1800, the demands of industrialization in Europe created a new set of dynamics. Maintaining access to industrial raw materials such as oil and rubber and setting up reliable markets for European manufactured products required more extensive control over colonial territories. As competition for colonies increased, the colonial powers sought to solidify their hold over their territories to protect them from attack by their rivals. During the last two decades of the nineteenth century, the quest for colonies became a scramble as all the major European states, now joined by the United States and Japan, engaged in a global land grab. In many cases, economic interests were secondary to security concerns or the requirements of national prestige. In Africa, for example, the British engaged in a struggle with their rivals to protect their interests in the Suez Canal and the Red Sea. In Southeast Asia, the United States seized the Philippines from Spain at least partly to keep them out of the hands of the Japanese, and the French took over Indochina for fear that it would otherwise be occupied by Germany, Japan, or the United States.

By 1900, almost all the societies of Africa and Asia were either under full colonial rule or, as in the case of China and the Ottoman Empire, at a point of virtual collapse. Only a handful of states, such as Japan in East Asia, Thailand in Southeast Asia, Afghanistan and Iran in the Middle East, and mountainous Ethiopia in East Africa, managed to escape internal disintegration or subjection to colonial rule. For the most part, the exceptions were the result of good fortune rather than design. Thailand escaped subjugation primarily because officials in London and Paris found it more convenient to transform the country into a buffer state than to fight over it. Ethiopia and Afghanistan survived due to their remote location and mountainous terrain. Only Japan managed to avoid the common fate through a concerted strategy of political and economic reform.

"Opportunity in the Orient": The Colonial Takeover in Southeast Asia

In 1800, only two societies in Southeast Asia were under effective colonial rule: the Spanish Philippines and the Dutch East Indies. During the nineteenth century, however, European interest in Southeast Asia increased rapidly, and by 1900, virtually the entire area was under colonial rule (see Map 20.1). The process began after the Napoleonic Wars, when the British, by agreement with the Dutch, abandoned their claims to territorial possessions in the East Indies in return for a free hand in the Malay peninsula. In 1819, the colonial administrator Stamford Raffles founded a new British colony on the island of Singapore at the tip of the peninsula. When the invention of steam power enabled merchant ships to save time and distance by passing through the Strait of Malacca rather than sailing with the westerlies across the southern Indian Ocean, Singapore became a major stopping point for traffic en route to and from China and other commercial centers in the region.

During the next few decades, the pace of European penetration into Southeast Asia accelerated as the British

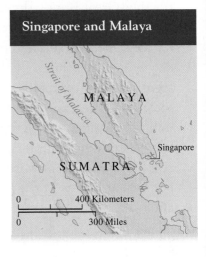

THE ESPLANADE.   After occupying the island of Singapore early in the nineteenth century, the British turned what was once a pirate lair located at the entrance to the Strait of Malacca into one of the most important commercial seaports in Asia. By the end of the century, Singapore was home to a rich mixture of peoples, both European and Asian. This painting by a turn-of-the-century British artist graphically displays the multiracial character of the colony as strollers, rickshaw drivers, and lamplighters share space along the Esplanade, in Singapore harbor.

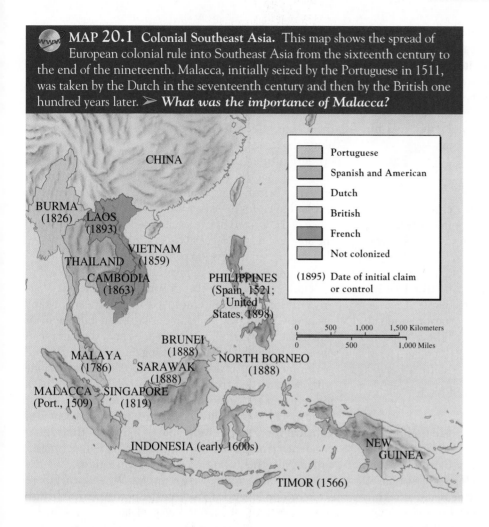

MAP 20.1 Colonial Southeast Asia. This map shows the spread of European colonial rule into Southeast Asia from the sixteenth century to the end of the nineteenth. Malacca, initially seized by the Portuguese in 1511, was taken by the Dutch in the seventeenth century and then by the British one hundred years later. ➤ *What was the importance of Malacca?*

established control over Burma, arousing fears in France that its British rival might soon establish a monopoly of trade in South China. The French still maintained a clandestine missionary organization in Vietnam despite harsh persecution by the local authorities, who viewed Christianity as a threat to Confucian doctrine. In 1857, the French government decided to force the Vietnamese to accept French protection. A naval attack launched a year later was not a total success, but the French eventually forced the Nguyen dynasty in Vietnam to cede territories in the Mekong River delta. A generation later, French rule was extended over the remainder of the country. By 1900 French seizure of neighboring Cambodia and Laos had led to the creation of the French-ruled Indochinese Union.

After the French conquest of Indochina, Thailand was the only remaining independent state on the Southeast Asian mainland. Under the astute leadership of two remarkable rulers, King Mongkut and his son, King Chulalongkorn, the Thai attempted to introduce Western learning and maintain relations with the major European powers without undermining internal stability or inviting an imperialist attack. In 1896, the British and the French agreed to preserve Thailand as an independent buffer zone between their possessions in Southeast Asia.

The final piece in the colonial edifice in Southeast Asia was put in place in 1898, when U.S. naval forces under Commodore George Dewey defeated the Spanish fleet in Manila Bay. President William McKinley agonized over the fate of the Philippines but ultimately decided that the moral thing to do was to turn the islands into an American colony to prevent them from falling into the hands of the Japanese. In fact, the Americans (like the Spanish before them) found the islands convenient as a jumping-off point for the China trade (see Chapter 21). The mixture of moral idealism and the desire for profit was reflected in a speech given in the Senate in January 1900 by Senator Albert Beveridge of Indiana:

Mr. President, the times call for candor. The Philippines are ours forever, "territory belonging to the United States," as the Constitution calls them. And just beyond the Philippines are China's illimitable markets. We will not retreat from either. . . . We will not renounce our part in the mission of our race, trustee, under God, of the civilization of the world. And we will move forward to our work, not howling out regrets like slaves whipped to their burdens, but with gratitude for a task worthy of our strength, and thanksgiving to Almighty God that He has marked us as His chosen people, henceforth to lead in the regeneration of the world.[3]

Not all Filipinos agreed with Senator Beveridge's portrayal of the situation. Under the leadership of Emilio Aguinaldo, guerrilla forces fought bitterly against U.S. troops to establish their independence from both Spain and the United States. But America's first war against guerrilla forces in Asia was a success, and the bulk of the resistance collapsed in 1901. President McKinley had his stepping-stone to the rich markets of China.

Empire Building in Africa

Up to the beginning of the nineteenth century, the relatively limited nature of European economic interests in Africa had provided little temptation for the penetration of the interior or the political takeover of the coastal areas. The slave trade, the main source of European profit during the eighteenth century, could be carried on by using African rulers and merchants as intermediaries. Disease, political instability, the lack of transportation, and the generally unhealthy climate all deterred the Europeans from more extensive efforts in Africa.

THE GROWING EUROPEAN PRESENCE IN WEST AFRICA

As the new century dawned, the slave trade itself was in a state of decline. One reason was the growing sense of outrage among humanitarians in several European countries over the purchase, sale, and exploitation of human beings. Dutch merchants effectively ceased trafficking in slaves in 1795, and the Danes stopped in 1803. A few years later, the slave trade was declared illegal in both Great Britain and the United States. The British began to apply pressure on other nations to follow suit, and most did so after the end of the Napoleonic Wars in 1815, leaving only Portugal and Spain as practitioners of the trade south of the equator. In the meantime, the demand for slaves began to decline in the Western Hemisphere, and by the 1880s, slavery had been abolished in all major countries of the world.

Economic as well as humanitarian interests contributed to the end of the slave trade. The cost of slaves had begun to rise after the middle of the eighteenth century, and the growth of the slave population reduced the need for additional labor on the plantations in the Americas. The British, with some reluctant assistance from France and the United States, added to the costs by actively using their navy to capture slave ships and free the occupants. When slavery was abolished in the United States in 1863 and in Cuba and Brazil seventeen years later, the slave trade across the Atlantic was effectively brought to an end.

As the slave trade in the Atlantic declined during the first half of the nineteenth century, European interest in what was sometimes called "legitimate trade" in natural resources increased. Exports of peanuts, timber, hides, and palm oil from West Africa increased substantially during the first decades of the century, while imports of textile goods and other manufactured products rose.

Stimulated by growing commercial interests in the area, European governments began to push for a more permanent presence along the coast. During the first decades of the nineteenth century, the British established settlements along the Gold Coast and in Sierra Leone, where they set up agricultural plantations for freed slaves who had returned from the Western Hemisphere or had been liberated by British ships while en route to the Americas. A similar haven for ex-slaves was developed with the assistance of the United States in Liberia. The French occupied the area around the Senegal River near Cape Verde, where they attempted to develop peanut plantations.

The growing European presence in West Africa led to the emergence of a new class of Africans educated in Western culture and often employed by Europeans. Many became Christians, and some studied in European or American universities. At the same time, the European presence inevitably led to increasing tensions with African governments in the area. British efforts to increase trade with Ashanti led to conflict in the 1820s, but British influence in the area intensified in later decades. Most African states, especially those with a fairly high degree of political integration, were able to maintain their independence from this creeping European encroachment, called "informal empire" by some historians, but the prospects for the future were ominous. When local groups attempted to organize to protect their interests, the British stepped in and annexed the coastal states as the British colony of Gold Coast in 1874. At about the same time, the British extended an informal protectorate over warring ethnic groups in the Niger delta (see Map 20.2).

IMPERIALIST SHADOW OVER THE NILE

A similar process was under way in the Nile valley. There had long been interest in shortening the trade route to the East by digging a canal across the low, swampy isthmus separating the Mediterranean from the Red Sea. The Turks had considered constructing a canal from Cairo to Suez in the sixteenth century, as had the French king Louis XIV a century later, but the French did nothing about it until the end of the eighteenth century. At that time, Napoleon planned a military takeover of Egypt to cement French power in the eastern Mediterranean and open a faster route to India.

Napoleon's plan proved abortive. French troops landed in Egypt in 1798 and destroyed the ramshackle Mamluk regime in Cairo, but the British counterattacked, destroying the French fleet and eventually forcing the French to evacuate in disorder. The British restored the Mamluks to power, but in 1805, Muhammad Ali, an Ottoman army officer of either Turkish or Albanian extraction, seized control.

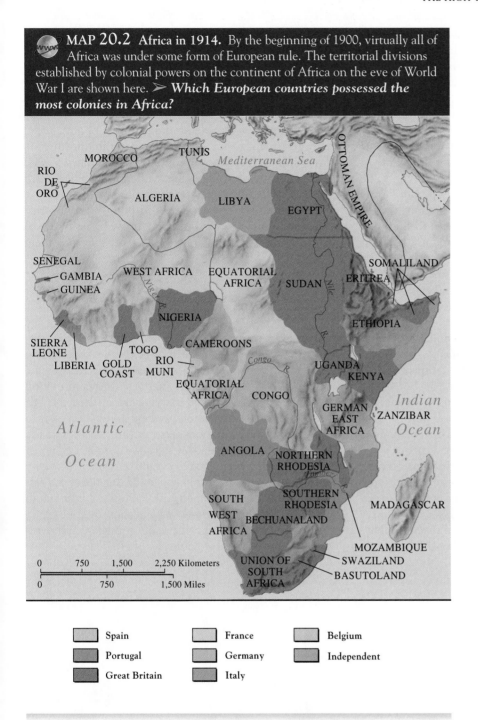

MAP 20.2 Africa in 1914. By the beginning of 1900, virtually all of Africa was under some form of European rule. The territorial divisions established by colonial powers on the continent of Africa on the eve of World War I are shown here. ➤ *Which European countries possessed the most colonies in Africa?*

Spain   France   Belgium

Portugal   Germany   Independent

Great Britain   Italy

During the next three decades, Muhammad Ali introduced a series of reforms to bring Egypt into the modern world. He modernized the army, set up a public educational system (supplementing the traditional religious education provided in Muslim schools), and sponsored the creation of a small industrial sector producing refined sugar, textiles, munitions, and even ships. Muhammad Ali also extended Egyptian authority southward into the Sudan and across the Sinai peninsula into Arabia, Syria,

and northern Iraq and even briefly threatened to seize Istanbul itself. To prevent the possible collapse of the Ottoman Empire, the British and the French recognized Muhammad Ali as the hereditary pasha (later to be known as the *khedive*) of Egypt under the loose authority of the Ottoman government.

The growing economic importance of the Nile valley, along with the development of steam navigation, made the heretofore visionary plans for a Suez canal more

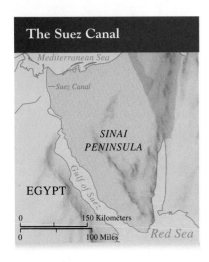

The Suez Canal

Mediterranean Sea

—Suez Canal

SINAI
PENINSULA

EGYPT

Gulf of Suez

0 _____ 150 Kilometers

0 _____ 100 Miles

Red Sea

urgent. In 1854, the French entrepreneur Ferdinand de Lesseps signed a contract to begin construction of the canal, and it was completed in 1869. The project brought little immediate benefit to Egypt, however. The construction not only cost thousands of lives but also left the Egyptian government deep in debt, forcing it to depend increasingly on foreign financial support. When an army revolt against growing foreign influence broke out in 1881, the British stepped in to protect their investment (they had bought Egypt's canal company shares in 1875) and establish an informal protectorate that would last until World War I.

Rising discontent in the Sudan added to Egypt's growing internal problems. In 1881, the Muslim cleric Muhammad Ahmad, known as the Mahdi (in Arabic, the "rightly guided one"), led a religious revolt that brought much of the upper Nile under his control. The famous British general Charles Gordon, who had earlier commanded Manchu armies fighting against the Taiping Rebellion in China (see Chapter 21), led a military force to Khartoum to restore Egyptian authority, but his besieged army was captured in 1885 by the Mahdi's troops, thirty-six hours before a British rescue mission reached Khartoum. Gordon himself died in the battle, which became one of the most dramatic news stories of the last quarter of the century.

The weakening of Turkish rule in the Nile valley had a parallel farther to the west, where local viceroys in Tripoli, Tunis, and Algiers had begun to establish their autonomy. In 1830, the French, on the pretext of protecting European shipping in the Mediterranean from pirates, seized the area surrounding Algiers and integrated it into the French Empire. By the mid-1850s, more than 150,000 Europeans had settled in the fertile region adjacent to the coast. In 1881, the French imposed a protectorate on neighboring Tunisia. Only Tripoli and Cyrenaica (the Ottoman provinces that comprise modern Libya) remained under Turkish rule until the Italians took them in 1911–1912.

ARAB MERCHANTS AND EUROPEAN MISSIONARIES IN EAST AFRICA

As always, events in East Africa followed their own distinctive pattern of development. Whereas the Atlantic slave trade was in decline, demand for slaves was increasing on the other side of the continent due to the growth of plantation agriculture in the region and on the islands off the coast. The French introduced sugar to the island of Réunion early in the century, and plantations of cloves (introduced from the Moluccas in the eighteenth century) were established under Omani Arab ownership on the island of Zanzibar. Zanzibar itself became the major shipping port along the entire east coast during the early nineteenth century, and the sultan of Oman, who had reasserted Arab suzerainty over the region in the aftermath of the collapse of Portuguese authority, established his capital at Zanzibar in 1840.

➤ **THE OPENING OF THE SUEZ CANAL.** The Suez Canal, which connected the Mediterranean and the Red Seas, was constructed under the direction of the French promoter Ferdinand de Lesseps. Still in use today, the canal is Egypt's greatest revenue producer. This sketch shows the ceremonial passage of the first ships through the canal in 1869. Note the combination of sail and steam power, reflecting the transition to coal-powered ships in the mid-nineteenth century.

From Zanzibar, Arab merchants fanned out into the interior plateaus in search of slaves, ivory, and other local products. The competition for slaves spread as far as Lake Victoria and the lower Sudan as traders from the north launched their own raids to obtain conscripts for the Egyptian army. The khedive sent General Charles Gordon to Uganda to stop the practice, but in the absence of alternative sources of income, local merchants could not easily be persuaded to give up a lucrative occupation.

The tenacity of the slave trade in East Africa—Zanzibar had now become the largest slave market in Africa—was undoubtedly a major reason for the rise of Western interest and Christian missionary activity in the region during the middle of the century. The most renowned missionary was the Scottish doctor David Livingstone, who arrived in Africa in 1841. Because Livingstone spent much of his time exploring the interior of the continent, discovering Victoria Falls in the process, he was occasionally criticized for being more explorer than missionary. But Livingstone was convinced that it was his divinely appointed task to bring Christianity to the far reaches of the continent, and his passionate opposition to slavery did far more to win public support for the abolitionist cause than did the efforts of any other figure of his generation. Public outcries provoked the British to redouble their efforts to bring the slave trade in East Africa to an end, and in 1873, the slave market at Zanzibar was finally closed as the result of pressure from London. Shortly before, Livingstone had died of illness in Central Africa, but some of his followers brought his body to the coast for burial. His legacy is still visible today in the form of an Anglican cathedral that was erected on the site of the slave market at Zanzibar.

BANTUS, BOERS, AND BRITISH IN THE SOUTH

Nowhere in Africa did the European presence grow more rapidly than in the south. During the eighteenth century, the Boers, Afrikaans-speaking farmers descended from the original Dutch settlers of the Cape Colony, began to migrate eastward. After the British seized control of the cape from the Dutch during the Napoleonic Wars, the Boers' eastward migration intensified, culminating in the Great Trek of the mid-1830s. In part, the Boers' departure was provoked by the different attitude of the British to the native population. Slavery was abolished in the British Empire in 1834, and the British government was generally more sympathetic to the rights of the local African population than were the Afrikaners, many of whom believed that white superiority was ordained by God and fled from British rule to control their own destiny. Eventually, the Boers formed their own independent republics—the Orange Free State and the South African Republic (usually called the Transvaal; see Map 20.3).

Although the Boer occupation of the eastern territory was initially facilitated by internecine warfare among the local inhabitants of the region, the new settlers met some resistance. In the early nineteenth century, the Zulus, a Bantu people led by a talented ruler named Shaka, engaged in a series of wars with the Europeans that ended only when Shaka was overthrown. The local Khoisan people also sometimes reacted with violence when the Boers attempted to drive them off their grazing lands. One Dutch official complained that the Khoisan were driving settlers from their farms "for no other reason than because they saw that we were breaking up the best land and grass, where their cattle were accustomed to graze."[4] Ultimately, most of the black Africans in the Boer republics were confined to reservations.

A ZULU ENCAMPMENT IN SOUTHERN AFRICA. When white settlers moved beyond the original Cape Colony in search of good farmland, they encountered the Zulus, a Bantu-speaking people living in the lands northeast of the cape. Often the encounter was quite brutal on both sides. In this illustration from 1838, Boer leaders are entering a Zulu settlement to take part in a ceremony in their honor. Instead, they were executed by Zulu warriors.

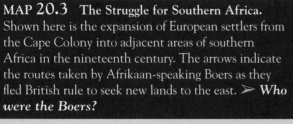

MAP 20.3   The Struggle for Southern Africa.
Shown here is the expansion of European settlers from the Cape Colony into adjacent areas of southern Africa in the nineteenth century. The arrows indicate the routes taken by Afrikaan-speaking Boers as they fled British rule to seek new lands to the east. ➤ *Who were the Boers?*

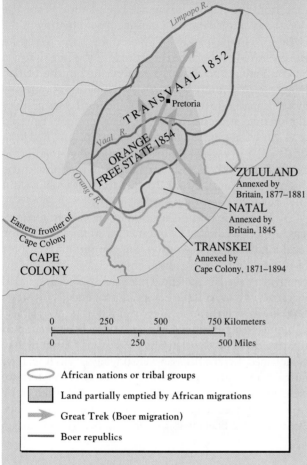

THE SCRAMBLE FOR AFRICA

At the beginning of the 1880s, most of Africa was still independent. European rule was limited to the fringes of the continent, such as Algeria, the Gold Coast, and South Africa. Other areas like Egypt, lower Nigeria, Senegal, and Mozambique were under various forms of loose protectorate. But the pace of European penetration was accelerating, and the constraints that had limited European rapaciousness were fast disappearing.

The scramble began in the mid-1880s, when several European states, including Belgium, France, Germany, Great Britain, and Portugal, engaged in a feeding frenzy to seize a piece of African territory before the carcass had been picked clean. By 1900, virtually all of the continent had been placed under some form of European rule. The British had consolidated their authority over the Nile valley and seized addi-

tional territories in East Africa (see Map 20.2 on p. 579). The French retaliated by advancing eastward from Senegal into the central Sahara. They also occupied the island of Madagascar and other territories in West and Central Africa. In between, the Germans claimed the hinterland opposite Zanzibar, as well as coastal strips in West and Southwest Africa north of the cape, and King Leopold II of Belgium claimed the Congo. Eventually, Italy entered the contest and seized modern Libya and some of the Somali coast.

What had happened to spark the sudden imperialist hysteria that brought an end to African independence? Clearly, the level of trade between Europe and Africa was not sufficient to justify the risks and the expense of conquest. More important than economic interests were the intensified rivalries among the European states that led them to engage in imperialist takeovers out of fear that if they did not, another state might do so, leaving them at a disadvantage. As one British diplomatic official remarked, a protectorate at the mouth of the Niger River would be an "unwelcome burden," but a French protectorate there would be "fatal." In such circumstances, statesmen felt compelled to obtain colonies as a hedge against future actions by rivals. In the most famous example, the British solidified their control over the entire Nile valley to protect the Suez Canal from seizure by the French.

Another consideration might be called the "missionary factor," as European missionary interests lobbied with their governments for colonial takeovers to facilitate their efforts to convert the African population to Christianity. The concept of social Darwinism and the "white man's burden" persuaded many that it was in the interests of the African people, as well as their conquerors, to be introduced more rapidly to the benefits of Western civilization (see the box on p. 583). Even David Livingstone had become convinced that missionary work and economic development had to go hand in hand, pleading to his fellow Europeans to introduce the "three Cs" (Christianity, commerce, and civilization) to the continent. How much easier such a task would be if African peoples were under benevolent European rule!

There were more prosaic reasons as well. Advances in Western technology and European superiority in firearms made it easier than ever for a small European force to defeat superior numbers. Furthermore, life expectancy for Europeans living in Africa had improved. With the discovery that quinine (extracted from the bark of the cinchona tree) could provide partial immunity from the ravages of malaria, the mortality rate for Europeans living in Africa dropped dramatically in the 1840s. By the end of the century, European residents in tropical Africa faced only slightly higher risks of death by disease than individuals living in Europe.

Under these circumstances, King Leopold of Belgium used missionary activities as an excuse to claim vast territories in the Congo River basin (Belgium, he said, as "a small country, with a small people," needed a colony to enhance its image).[5] This set off a desperate race among European nations to stake claims throughout sub-Saharan

WHITE MAN'S BURDEN, BLACK MAN'S SORROW

*O*ne of the justifications for modern imperialism was the notion that the allegedly "more advanced" white peoples had the moral responsibility to raise ignorant native peoples to a higher level of civilization. Few captured this notion better than the British poet Rudyard Kipling (1865–1936) in his famous poem The White Man's Burden. His appeal, directed to the United States, became one of the most famous set of verses in the English-speaking world.

That sense of moral responsibility, however, was often misplaced, or even worse, laced with hypocrisy. All too often, the consequences of imperial rule were detrimental to everyone living under colonial authority. Few observers described the destructive effects of Western imperialism on the African people as well as Edward Morel, a British journalist whose book The Black Man's Burden pointed out some of the more harmful aspects of colonialism in the Belgian Congo.

RUDYARD KIPLING, *THE WHITE MAN'S BURDEN*

Take up the White Man's burden—
Send forth the best ye breed—
Go bind your sons to exile
To serve your captives' need;
To wait in heavy harness,
On fluttered folk and wild—
Your new-caught sullen peoples,
Half-devil and half-child.

Take up the White Man's burden—
In patience to abide,
To veil the threat of terror
And check the show of pride;
By open speech and simple,
An hundred times made plain
To seek another's profit,
And work another's gain.

Take up the White Man's burden—
The savage wars of peace—
Fill full the mouth of Famine
And bid the sickness cease;
And when your goal is nearest
The end for others sought,
Watch Sloth and heathen Folly
Bring all your hopes to nought.

EDMUND MOREL, *THE BLACK MAN'S BURDEN*

It is [the Africans] who carry the "Black man's burden." They have not withered away before the white man's occupation. Indeed . . . Africa has ultimately absorbed within itself every Caucasian and, for that matter, every Semitic invader, too. In hewing out for himself a fixed abode in Africa, the white man has massacred the African in heaps. The African has survived, and it is well for the white settlers that he has. . . .

What the partial occupation of his soil by the white man has failed to do; what the mapping out of European political "spheres of influence" has failed to do; what the Maxim and the rifle, the slave gang, labour in the bowels of the earth and the lash, have failed to do; what imported measles, smallpox and syphilis have failed to do; whatever the overseas slave trade failed to do; the power of modern capitalistic exploitation, assisted by modern engines of destruction, may yet succeed in accomplishing.

For from the evils of the latter, scientifically applied and enforced, there is no escape for the African. Its destructive effects are not spasmodic; they are permanent. In its permanence resides its fatal consequences. It kills not the body merely, but the soul. It breaks the spirit. It attacks the African at every turn, from every point of vantage. It wrecks his polity, uproots him from the land, invades his family life, destroys his natural pursuits and occupations, claims his whole time, enslaves him in his own home.

Africa. Leopold ended up with the territories south of the Congo River, while France occupied areas to the north (Leopold bequeathed the Congo to Belgium on his death). Meanwhile, on the eastern side of the continent, Germany (through the activities of an ambitious missionary and with the agreement of the British, who needed German support against the French) annexed the colony of Tanganyika. To avert the possibility of violent clashes among the great powers, the German chancellor, Otto von Bismarck, convened a conference in Berlin in 1884 to set ground rules for future annexations of African territory by European nations. Like the famous Open Door Notes fifteen years later (see Chapter 21), the conference combined high-minded resolutions with a hardheaded recog-

nition of practical interests. The delegates called for free commerce in the Congo and along the Niger River as well as for further efforts to end the slave trade. At the same time, the participants recognized the inevitability of the imperialist dynamic, agreeing only that future annexations of African territory should not be given international recognition until effective occupation had been demonstrated. No African delegates were present.

The Berlin Conference had been convened to avert war and reduce tensions among European nations competing for the spoils of Africa. It proved reasonably successful at achieving the first objective but less so at the second. During the next few years, African territories were annexed without provoking a major confrontation between the Western powers,

Chronology

IMPERIALISM IN AFRICA

Dutch abolish slave trade in Africa	1795
Napoleonic invasion of Egypt	1798
Slave trade declared illegal in Great Britain	1808
Boers' Great Trek in southern Africa	1830s
French seize Algeria	1830
Sultan of Oman establishes capital at Zanzibar	1840
David Livingstone arrives in Africa	1841
Slavery abolished in the United States	1863
Completion of Suez Canal	1869
Zanzibar slave market closed	1873
British establish Gold Coast colony	1874
British establish informal protectorate over Egypt	1881
Berlin Conference on Africa	1884
Charles Gordon killed at Khartoum	1885
Confrontation at Fashoda	1898
Boer War	1899–1902
Union of South Africa established	1910

but in the late 1890s, Britain and France reached the brink of conflict at Fashoda, a small town on the Nile River in the Sudan. The French had been advancing eastward across the Sahara with the transparent objective of controlling the regions around the upper Nile. In 1898, British and Egyptian troops seized the Sudan from successors of the Mahdi and then marched southward to head off the French. After a tense face-off at Fashoda, the French government backed down, and British authority over the area was secured. Except for the Mediterranean littoral and their small possessions of Djibouti and a portion of the Somali coast, the French were restricted to equatorial Africa.

Ironically, the only major clash between Europeans over Africa took place in southern Africa, where competition among the powers was almost nonexistent. The discovery of gold and diamonds in the Boer republic of the Transvaal was the source of the problem. Clashes between the Afrikaner population and foreign (mainly British) miners and developers led to an attempt by Cecil Rhodes, prime minister of the Cape Colony and a prominent entrepreneur in the area, to subvert the Transvaal and bring it under British rule. In 1899, the so-called Boer War broke out between Britain and the Transvaal, which was backed by its fellow republic, the Orange Free State. Guerrilla resistance by the Boers was fierce, but the vastly superior forces of

the British were able to prevail by 1902. To compensate the defeated Afrikaner population for the loss of independence, the British government agreed that only whites would vote in the now essentially self-governing colony. The Boers were placated, but the brutalities committed during the war (the British introduced an institution later to be known as the concentration camp) created bitterness on both sides that continued to fester through future decades.

THE COLONIAL SYSTEM

Now that they had control of most of the world, what did the colonial powers do with it? As we have seen, their primary objective was to exploit the natural resources of the subject areas and to open up markets for manufactured goods and capital investment from the mother country. In some cases, that goal could be realized in cooperation with local political elites, whose loyalty could be earned, or purchased, by economic rewards or by confirming them in their positions of authority and status in a new colonial setting. Sometimes, however, this policy of indirect rule was not feasible because local leaders refused to cooperate with their colonial masters or even actively resisted the foreign conquest. In such cases, the local elites were removed from power and replaced with a new set of officials recruited from the mother country.

In general, the societies most likely to actively resist colonial conquest were those with a long tradition of national cohesion and independence, such as China, Burma, and Vietnam in Asia and the African Muslim states in northern Nigeria and Morocco. In those areas, the colonial powers tended to dispense with local collaborators and govern directly. In parts of Africa, the Indian subcontinent, and the Malay peninsula, where the local authorities, for whatever reason, were willing to collaborate with the imperialist powers, indirect rule was more common.

The distinctions between direct and indirect rule were not merely academic and often had fateful consequences for the peoples involved. Where colonial powers encountered resistance and were forced to overthrow local political elites, they often adopted policies designed to eradicate the source of resistance and destroy the traditional culture. Such policies often had quite corrosive effects on the indigenous societies and provoked resentment and resistance that not only marked the colonial relationship but even affected relations after the restoration of national independence. The bitter struggles after World War II in Algeria, the Dutch East Indies, and Vietnam can be ascribed in part to that phenomenon.

The Philosophy of Colonialism

To justify their rule, the colonial powers appealed in part to the time-honored maxim of "might makes right." By the end of the nineteenth century, that attitude received pseudoscientific validity from the concept of social Darwinism, which maintained that only societies that moved aggressively to adapt to changing circumstances would survive and prosper in a world governed by the Darwinian law of "survival of the fittest."

Some people, however, were uncomfortable with such a brutal view of the law of nature and sought a moral justification that appeared to benefit the victim. Here again, as we have seen, the concept of social Darwinism pointed the way. By bringing the benefits of Western democracy, capitalism, and Christianity to the feudalistic and tradition-ridden societies of Africa and Asia, the colonial powers were enabling primitive peoples to adapt to the challenges of the modern world. Buttressed by such comforting theories, sensitive Western minds could ignore the brutal aspects of colonialism and persuade themselves that in the long run the results would be beneficial for both sides. Few were as adept at describing the "civilizing mission" of colonialism as the French administrator and twice governor-general of French Indochina Albert Sarraut. While admitting that colonialism was originally an "act of force" undertaken for commercial profit, he insisted that by redistributing the wealth of the earth, the colonial process would result in a better life for all:

> Is it just, is it legitimate that such [an uneven distribution of resources] should be indefinitely prolonged? . . . No! . . . Humanity is distributed throughout the globe. No race, no people has the right or power to isolate itself egotistically from the movements and necessities of universal life.[6]

But what about the possibility that historically and culturally the societies of Asia and Africa were fundamentally different from those of the West and could not, or would not, be persuaded to transform themselves along Western lines? Was the human condition universal, or were human beings so shaped by their history and geographical environment that their civilizations would inevitably remain distinct? In that case, a policy of cultural transformation could not be expected to succeed and could even lead to disaster.

In fact, colonial theorists never decided this issue one way or the other. The French, who were most inclined to

REVERE THE CONQUERING HEROES.   European colonial officials were quick to place themselves at the top of the political and social hierarchy in their conquered territories. Here British officials accept the submission of the Ashanti king and queen, according to African custom, in 1896.

➤ SERVING THE WHITE RULER.   Although European governments claimed to be carrying out the civilizing mission in Africa, all too often the local population was forced to labor in degrading conditions to serve the economic interests of the occupying power. Here African workers are depicted as they transport goods for a European merchant.

philosophize about the problem, adopted the terms *assimilation* (which implied an effort to transform colonial societies in the Western image) and *association* (implying collaboration with local elites while leaving local traditions alone) to describe the two alternatives and then proceeded to vacillate between them. French policy in Indochina, for example, began as one of association but switched to assimilation under pressure from those who felt that colonial powers owed a debt to their subject peoples. But assimilation (which in any case was never accepted as feasible or desirable by many colonial officials) aroused resentment among the local population, many of whom opposed the destruction of their native traditions. In the end, the French abandoned the attempt to justify their presence and fell back on a policy of ruling by force of arms.

Other colonial powers had little interest in the issue. The British, whether out of a sense of pragmatism or of racial superiority, refused to entertain the possibility of assimilation and treated their subject peoples as culturally and

➤ BLENDING EAST AND WEST.   After establishing colonies throughout the continents of Africa and Asia, the British began to erect monumental buildings to demonstrate their power and authority. They built stately mansions, sumptuous hotels, opulent government buildings, and especially grandiose railroad stations, railroads being the greatest capitalist enterprise in the colonies. In an effort to incorporate indigenous styles in their colonial architecture, the British often combined arched colonnades with domed and canopied turrets such as those that appear on this railroad station, erected in 1911 in Kuala Lumpur, on the Malay peninsula.

INDIAN IN BLOOD, ENGLISH IN TASTE AND INTELLECT

*T*homas Babington Macaulay (1800–1859) was named a member of the Supreme Council of India in the early 1830s. In that capacity he was responsible for drawing up a new educational policy for British subjects in the area. In his Minute on Education, he considered the claims of English and various local languages to become the vehicle for educational training and decided in favor of the former. It is better, he argued, to teach Indian elites about Western civilization so as "to form a class who may be interpreters between us and the millions whom we govern; a class of persons, Indian in blood and color, but English in taste, in opinions, in morals, and in intellect." Later Macaulay became a prominent historian. The debate over the relative benefits of English and the various Indian languages continues today.

THOMAS BABINGTON MACAULAY, MINUTE ON EDUCATION

We have a fund to be employed as government shall direct for the intellectual improvement of the people of this country. The simple question is, what is the most useful way of employing it?

All parties seem to be agreed on one point, that the dialects commonly spoken among the natives of this part of India contain neither literary or scientific information, and are, moreover so poor and rude that, until they are enriched from some other quarter, it will not be easy to translate any valuable work into them. . . .

What, then, shall the language [of education] be? One half of the Committee maintain that it should be the English. The other half strongly recommend the Arabic and Sanskrit. The whole question seems to me to be, which language is the best worth knowing?

I have no knowledge of either Sanskrit or Arabic—but I have done what I could to form a correct estimate of their value. I have read translations of the most celebrated Arabic and Sanskrit works. I have conversed both here and at home with men distinguished by their proficiency in the Eastern tongues. I am quite ready to take the Oriental learning at the valuation of the Orientalists themselves. I have never found one among them who could deny that a single shelf of a good European library was worth the whole native literature of India and Arabia. . . .

It is, I believe, no exaggeration to say, that all the historical information which has been collected from all the books written in the Sanskrit language is less valuable than what may be found in the most paltry abridgments used at preparatory schools in England. In every branch of physical or moral philosophy the relative position of the two nations is nearly the same.

racially distinct. In formulating a colonial policy for the Philippines, the United States adopted a policy of assimilation in theory but did not always put it into practice.

To many of the colonial peoples, such questions must have appeared academic, since the primary objectives of all the colonial states were economic exploitation and the retention of power. Like the British soldier in Kipling's poem "On the Road to Mandalay," all too many Westerners living in the colonies believed that the Great Lord Buddha was nothing but a "bloomin' idol made of mud."

Colonialism in Action

In practice, colonialism in India, Southeast Asia, and Africa exhibited many similarities but also some differences. Some of these variations can be traced to political or social differences among the colonial powers themselves. The French, for example, often tried to impose a centralized administrative system on their colonies that mirrored the system in use in France, while the British sometimes attempted to transform local aristocrats into the equivalent of the landed gentry at home in Britain. Other differences stemmed from conditions in the colonies themselves and the colonizers' aspirations for them. For instance, the Western powers believed that their economic interests were far more limited in Africa

than elsewhere and therefore treated their African colonies somewhat differently than those in India or Southeast Asia.

INDIA UNDER THE BRITISH RAJ

By 1800, the once glorious empire of the Mughals had been reduced by British military power to a shadow of its former greatness. During the next few decades, the British sought to consolidate their control over the Indian subcontinent, expanding from their base areas along the coast into the interior. Some territories were taken over directly, first by the East India Company and later by the British crown; others were ruled indirectly through their local maharajas and rajas.

Not all of the effects of British rule were bad. British governance over the subcontinent brought order and stability to a society that had been rent by civil war. By the early nineteenth century, British control had been consolidated and led to a relatively honest and efficient government that in many respects operated to the benefit of the average Indian. One of the benefits of the period was the heightened attention given to education. Through the efforts of the British administrator Thomas Babington Macaulay, a new school system was established to train the children of Indian elites, and the British civil service examination was introduced (see the box above). The instruction of young girls also expanded, with the primary purpose of making them better wives and mothers for the educated male population. The first Indian woman accepted to a Madras medical college, for example, was in 1875.

British rule also brought an end to some of the more inhumane aspects of Indian tradition. The practice of *sati* was outlawed, and widows were legally permitted to remarry. The British also attempted to put an end to the endemic brigandage (known as *thuggee*, which gave rise to the English word *thug*) that had plagued travelers in India since time immemorial. Railroads, the telegraph, and the postal service were introduced to India shortly after they appeared in Great Britain itself. Work began on the main highway from Calcutta to Delhi in 1839 (see Map 20.4), and the first rail network was opened in 1853. A new penal code based on the British model was adopted, and health and sanitation conditions were improved.

But the Indian people paid a high price for the peace and stability brought by the British raj (from the Indian *raja*, or prince). Perhaps the most flagrant cost was economic. While British entrepreneurs and a small percentage of the Indian population attached to the imperial system reaped financial benefits from British rule, it brought hardship to millions of others in both the cities and the rural areas. The introduction of British textiles put thousands of Bengali women out of work and severely damaged the local textile industry.

In rural areas, the British introduced the *zamindar* system (see Chapter 15) in the misguided expectation that it would both facilitate the collection of agricultural taxes

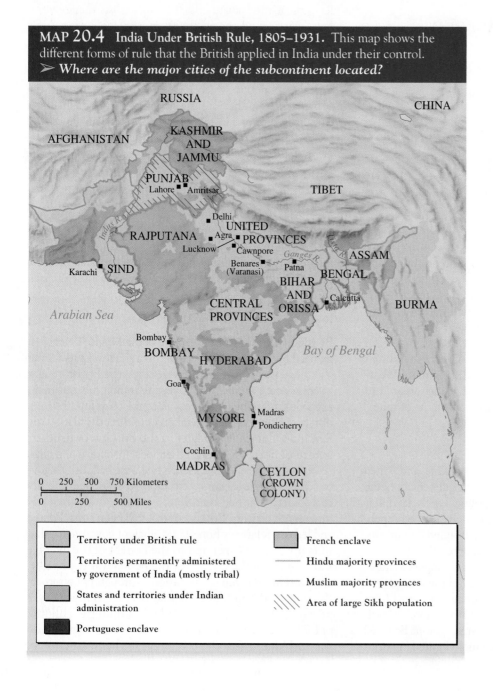

MAP 20.4 India Under British Rule, 1805–1931. This map shows the different forms of rule that the British applied in India under their control.
➤ *Where are the major cities of the subcontinent located?*

Legend:
- Territory under British rule
- Territories permanently administered by government of India (mostly tribal)
- States and territories under Indian administration
- Portuguese enclave
- French enclave
- Hindu majority provinces
- Muslim majority provinces
- Area of large Sikh population

and create a new landed gentry, who could, as in Britain, become the conservative foundation of imperial rule. But the local gentry took advantage of this new authority to increase taxes and force the less fortunate peasants to become tenants or lose their land entirely. When rural unrest threatened, the government passed legislation protecting farmers against eviction and unreasonable rent increases, but this measure had little effect outside the southern provinces, where it had originally been enacted. Similarly, British officials made few efforts during the nineteenth century to introduce democratic institutions or values to the Indian people. As one senior political figure remarked in Parliament in 1898, democratic institutions "can no more be carried to India by Englishmen . . . than they can carry ice in their luggage."[7]

British colonialism was also remiss in bringing the benefits of modern science and technology to India. Some limited forms of industrialization took place, notably in the manufacturing of textiles and jute (used in making rope). The first textile mill opened in 1856. Seventy years later, there were eighty mills in the city of Bombay alone. Nevertheless, the lack of local capital and the advantages given to British imports prevented the emergence of other vital new commercial and manufacturing operations.

Foreign rule also had a psychological effect on the Indian people. Although many British colonial officials sincerely tried to improve the lot of the people under their charge, British arrogance and contempt for native tradition cut deeply into the pride of many Indians, especially those of high caste, who were accustomed to a position of superior status in India. Educated Indians trained in the Anglo-Indian school system for a career in the civil service, as well as Eurasians born to mixed marriages, often imitated the

GATEWAY TO INDIA? Built in the Roman imperial style by the British to commemorate the visit to India of King George V and Queen Mary in 1911, the Gateway of India was erected at the water's edge in the harbor of Bombay, India's greatest port city. For thousands of British citizens arriving in India, the Gateway of India was the first view of their new home and a symbol of the power and majesty of the British raj. Only a few dozen yards away was the luxurious Taj Mahal Hotel. Constructed in the popular Anglo-Indian style, it was built to house European visitors upon their arrival to India.

Courtesy of William J. Duiker

➤ **MIMICKING THE FOREIGNERS.** The imposition of colonial rule brought about major changes in social organization and behavioral patterns in Southeast Asia as many colonial subjects imitated their new rulers. Here a young Vietnamese during the 1920s dresses in Western sports attire and learns to lift weights. Note the French tricolor in the upper-left corner of the picture.

behavior and dress of their rulers, speaking English, eating Western food, and taking up European leisure activities, but many rightfully wondered where their true cultural loyalties lay. This cultural collision was poignantly described in the novel *A Passage to India* by the British writer E. M. Forster, which relates the story of a visiting Englishwoman who becomes interested in the Indian way of life, much to the dismay of the local European community.

COLONIAL REGIMES IN SOUTHEAST ASIA

In Southeast Asia, economic profit was the immediate and primary aim of colonial enterprise. For that purpose, colonial powers tried wherever possible to work with local elites to facilitate the exploitation of natural resources. Indirect rule reduced the cost of training European administrators and had a less corrosive impact on the local culture. In the Dutch East Indies, for example, officials of the Dutch East India Company (VOC) entrusted local administration to the indigenous landed aristocracy, who maintained law and order and collected taxes in return for a payment from

➤ **AN ENGLISH NABOB IN COLONIAL INDIA.** When the British took over India in the late eighteenth and nineteenth centuries, many Indians began to imitate European customs for prestige or social advancement. Sometimes, however, the cultural influence went the other way. Here an English nabob, as European residents in the colonies were often called, apes the manner of an Indian aristocrat, complete with harem and hookah, the Indian water pipe. The paintings on the wall, however, are in the European style.

Courtesy of the British Library, Oriental and India Office Collections

THE EFFECTS OF DUTCH COLONIALISM IN JAVA

Eduard Douwes Dekker was a Dutch colonial official who served in the East Indies for nearly twenty years. In 1860, he published a critique of the Dutch colonial system that had an impact in the Netherlands similar to that of Harriet Beecher Stowe's Uncle Tom's Cabin *in the United States. In the following excerpt from his book* Max Havelaar, or Coffee Auctions of the Dutch Trading Company, *Douwes Dekker described the system as it was applied on the island of Java, in the Indonesian archipelago.*

EDUARD DOUWES DEKKER, MAX HAVELAAR

The Javanese is by nature a husbandman; the ground whereon he is born, which gives much for little labor, allures him to it, and, above all things, he devotes his whole heart and soul to the cultivating of his rice fields, in which he is very clever. He grows up in the midst of his sawahs [rice fields] . . . ; when still very young, he accompanies his father to the field, where he helps him in his labor with plow and spade, in constructing dams and drains to irrigate his fields; he counts his years by harvests; he estimates time by the color of the blades in his field; he is at home amongst the companions who cut paddy with him; he chooses his wife amongst the girls of the dessah [village], who every evening tread the rice with joyous songs. The possession of a few buffaloes for plowing is the ideal of his dreams. The cultivation of rice is in Java what the vintage is in the Rhine provinces and in the south of France. But there came foreigners from the West, who made themselves masters of the country. They wished to profit by the fertility of the soil, and ordered the native to devote a part of his time and labor to the cultivation of other things which should produce higher profits in the markets of Europe. To persuade the lower orders to do so, they had only to follow a very simple policy. The Javanese obeys his chiefs; to win the chiefs, it was only necessary to give them a part of the gain,—and success was complete.

To be convinced of the success of that policy we need only consider the immense quantity of Javanese products sold in Holland; and we shall also be convinced of its injustice, for, if anybody should ask if the husbandman himself gets a reward in proportion to that quantity, then I must give a negative answer. The Government compels him to cultivate certain products on his ground; it punishes him if he sells what he has produced to any purchaser but itself; and it fixes the price actually paid. The expenses of transport to Europe through a privileged trading company are high; the money paid to the chiefs for encouragement increases the prime cost; and because the entire trade *must* produce profit, that profit cannot be got in any other way than by paying the Javanese just enough to keep him from starving, which would lessen the producing power of the nation.

---

the VOC (see the box above). The British followed a similar practice in Malaya. While establishing direct rule over the crucial commercial centers of Singapore and Malacca, the British allowed local Muslim rulers to maintain princely power in the interior of the peninsula.

Indirect rule, however convenient and inexpensive, was not always feasible. In some instances, local resistance to the colonial conquest made such a policy impossible. In Burma, the staunch opposition of the monarchy and other traditionalist forces caused the British to abolish the monarchy and administer the country directly through their colonial government in India. In Indochina, the French used both direct and indirect means. They imposed direct rule on the southern provinces in the Mekong delta but governed the north as a protectorate, with the emperor retaining titular authority from his palace in Huê. The French adopted a similar policy in Cambodia and Laos, where local rulers were left in charge with French advisers to counsel them.

Whatever method was used, colonial regimes in Southeast Asia, as elsewhere, were slow to create democratic institutions. The first legislative councils and assemblies were composed almost exclusively of European residents in the colony. The first representatives from the indigenous population were wealthy and conservative in their political views. When Southeast Asians complained, colonial officials gradually and reluctantly began to broaden the franchise. Albert Sarraut advised patience in awaiting the full benefits of colonial policy: "I will treat you like my younger brothers, but do not forget that I am the older brother. I will slowly give you the dignity of humanity."[8]

Colonial officials were also slow to adopt educational reforms. Although the introduction of Western education was one of the justifications of colonialism, colonial officials soon discovered that educating native elites could backfire. Often there were few jobs for highly trained lawyers, engineers, and architects in colonial societies, leading to the threat of an indigestible mass of unemployed intellectuals who would take out their frustrations on the colonial regime. Educational opportunities for the common people were even harder to come by. In French-controlled Vietnam in 1917, only 3,000 of the 23,000 villages in the country had a public school. The French had opened a university in Hanoi, but it was immediately closed as a result of student demonstrations. As one

IMPERIALISM IN ASIA

Stamford Raffles arrives in Singapore	1819
British attack lower Burma	1826
British rail network opened in northern India	1853
Sepoy Rebellion	1857
French attack Vietnam	1858
Indian National Congress established	1885
British and French agree to neutralize Thailand	1896
Commodore Dewey defeats Spanish fleet in Manila Bay	1898

French official noted in voicing his opposition to increasing the number of schools in Vietnam, educating the natives meant not "one coolie less, but one rebel more."

Colonial powers were equally reluctant to take up the "white man's burden" in the area of economic development. As we have seen, their primary goals were to secure a source of cheap raw materials and to maintain markets for manufactured goods. Such objectives would be undermined by the emergence of advanced industrial economies. So colonial policy concentrated on the export of raw materials—teakwood from Burma; rubber and tin from Malaya; spices, tea and coffee, and palm oil from the East Indies; and sugar and copra from the Philippines.

In some Southeast Asian colonial societies, a measure of industrial development did take place to meet the needs of the European population and local elites. Major manufacturing cities like Rangoon in lower Burma, Batavia on the island of Java, and Saigon in French Indochina grew rapidly. Although the local middle class benefited from the increased economic activity, most large industrial and commercial establishments were owned and managed by Europeans or, in some cases, by Indian or Chinese merchants. In Saigon, for example, even the production of *nuoc mam*, the traditional Vietnamese fish sauce, was under Chinese ownership. In most cities, foreigners controlled banking, major manufacturing activities, and the import-export trade. The natives were more apt to work in a family business, in factory or assembly plants, or as peddlers, day laborers, or rickshaw pullers—in other words, at less profitable and less capital-intensive businesses.

Despite the growth of an urban economy, the vast majority of people in the colonial societies continued to farm the land. Many continued to live by subsistence agriculture, but the colonial policy of emphasizing cash crops for export also led to the creation of a form of plantation agriculture in which peasants were recruited to work as wage laborers on rubber and tea plantations owned by Europeans. To maintain a competitive edge, the plantation owners kept the wages of their workers at poverty level. Many plantation workers were "shanghaied" (the English term originated from the practice of recruiting laborers, often from the docks and streets of Shanghai, by unscrupulous means such as the use of force, alcohol, or drugs) to work on plantations, where conditions were often so inhumane that thousands died. High taxes, enacted by colonial governments to pay for administrative costs or improvements in the local infrastructure, were a heavy burden for poor peasants.

The situation was made even more difficult by the steady growth of the population. Peasants in Asia had always had large families on the assumption that a high proportion of their children would die in infancy. But improved sanitation and medical treatment resulted in lower rates of infant mortality and a staggering increase in population. The population of the island of Java, for example, increased from about a million in the precolonial era to about 40 million at the end of the nineteenth century. Under these conditions, the rural areas could no longer support the growing populations, and many young people fled to the cities to seek jobs in factories or shops. The migratory pattern gave rise to squatter settlements in the suburbs of the major cities.

As in India, colonial rule did bring some benefits to Southeast Asia. It led to the beginnings of a modern economic infrastructure and to what is sometimes called a "modernizing elite" dedicated to the creation of an advanced industrialized society. The development of an export market helped create an entrepreneurial class in rural areas. This happened, for example, on the outer islands of the Dutch East Indies (such as Borneo and Sumatra), where small growers of rubber trees, palm trees for oil, coffee, tea, and spices began to share in the profits of the colonial enterprise.

A balanced assessment of the colonial legacy in Southeast Asia must take into account that the early stages of industrialization are difficult in any society. Even in western Europe, industrialization led to the creation of an impoverished and powerless proletariat, urban slums, and displaced peasants driven from the land. In much of Europe and Japan, however, the bulk of the population eventually enjoyed better material conditions as the profits from manufacturing and plantation agriculture were reinvested in the national economy and gave rise to increased consumer demand. In contrast, in Southeast Asia, most of the profits were repatriated to the colonial mother country, while displaced peasants fleeing to cities like Rangoon, Batavia, and Saigon found little opportunity for employment. Many were left with seasonal employment, with one foot on the farm and one in the factory. The old world was being destroyed, while the new one had yet to be born.

THERE'S A EUROPEAN,
THERE'S A EUROPEAN!

*M*ost Africans living outside the port cities had little idea of what to expect from the arrival of the white man and the new colonial authority. Thanks to these memoirs, recounted a half century later by an African woman from northern Nigeria, we are offered an intimate glimpse into the arrival of the British at the end of the nineteenth century. It is interesting to note that slavery among Africans was still a long-established tradition in the area. In a later passage, the woman remarks that her family lost income from the flight of its slaves, but the loss was offset by a reduction in taxes that African farmers had traditionally been compelled to pay to fill the pockets of local officials and chiefs.

BABA, A HAUSA WOMAN OF NIGERIA

When I was a maiden the Europeans first arrived. Ever since we were quite small the *malams* [Muslim scholars] had been saying that the Europeans would come with a thing called a train, they would come with a thing called a motor-car. . . . They would stop wars, they would repair the world, they would stop oppression and lawlessness, we should live at peace with them. We used to go and sit quietly and listen to the prophecies. . . .

I remember when a European came to Karo on a horse, and some of his foot soldiers went into the town. Everyone came out to look at them. . . . Everyone at Karo ran away— "There's a European, there's a European!" . . .

At that time Yusufu was the [Fulani] king of Kano. He did not like the Europeans, he did not wish them, he would not sign their treaty. Then he saw that perforce he would have to agree, so he did. We Habe wanted them to come, it was the Fulani who did not like it. When the Europeans came the Habe saw that if you worked for them they paid you for it, they didn't say, like the Fulani, "Commoner, give me this! Commoner, bring me that!" Yes, the Habe wanted them. . . .

The Europeans said that there were to be no more slaves; if someone said "Slave!" you could complain to the *alkali* [judge] who would punish the master who said it, the judge said "That is what the Europeans have decreed." . . . When slavery was stopped, nothing much happened at our *rinji* [the farm where their slaves lived] except that some slaves whom we had bought in the market ran away. Our own father went to his farm and worked, he and his son took up their large hoes. . . . They farmed guineacorn and millet and groundnuts and everything; before this they had supervised the slaves' work—now they did their own. When the midday food was ready, the women of the compound would give us children the food, one of us drew water, and off we went to the farm to take the men their food at the foot of a tree.

COLONIALISM IN AFRICA

Colonialism had similar consequences in Africa, although with some changes in emphasis. As we have seen, European economic interests were more limited in Africa than elsewhere. Having seized the continent in what could almost be described as a fit of hysteria, the European powers had to decide what to do with it. With economic concerns relatively limited except for isolated areas like the gold mines in the Transvaal and copper deposits in the Belgian Congo, interest in Africa declined, and most European governments settled down to govern their new territories with the least effort and expense possible. In many cases, this meant a form of indirect rule similar to what the British used in the princely states in India. The British with their tradition of decentralized government at home were especially prone to adopt this approach.

In the minds of British administrators, the stated goal of indirect rule was to preserve African political traditions. The desire to limit cost and inconvenience was one reason for this approach, but it may also have been due to the conviction that Africans were inherently inferior to the white race and thus incapable of adopting European customs and institutions. In any event, indirect rule entailed relying to the greatest extent possible on existing political elites and institutions. Initially, in some areas the British simply asked a local ruler to formally accept British authority and to fly the Union Jack over official buildings. Sometimes it was the Africans who did the bidding, as in the case of the African leaders in Cameroons who wrote to Queen Victoria:

> We *wish* to have your laws in our towns. We want to have every *fashion* altered; also we will do according to your Consul's *word*. Plenty wars here in our country. Plenty murder and plenty idol worshippers. Perhaps these *lines* of our writing will *look* to you as an *idle* tale.
>
> We have *spoken* to the English consul plenty times about having an English *government* here. We never have answer from you, so we wish to write you *ourselves*.[9]

Nigeria offers a typical example of British indirect rule. British officials maintained the central administration, but local authority was assigned to native chiefs, with British district officers serving as intermediaries with the central administration. Where a local aristocracy did not exist, the British assigned administrative responsibility to clan heads from communities in the vicinity. The local authorities were expected to maintain law and order and to collect taxes from the native population. As a general rule, indigenous customs were left undisturbed, although the institution of slavery was abolished (see the box above).

THE NDEBELE REBELLION

As British forces advanced northward from the Cape Colony toward the Zambezi River in the 1890s, they overran the Ndebele people, who occupied rich lands in the region near the site of the ruins of Great Zimbabwe. Angered by British brutality, Ndebele warriors revolted in 1896 to throw off their oppressors. Despite their great superiority in numbers, British units possessed the feared Maxim gun, which mowed down African attackers by the hundreds. Faced with defeat, the Ndebele king, Lobengula, fled into the hills and committed suicide. In the following account, a survivor describes the conflict.

NDANSI KUMALO, A PERSONAL ACCOUNT

We surrendered to the white people and were told to go back to our homes and live our usual lives and attend to our crops. But the white men sent native police who did abominable things; they were cruel and assaulted a lot of our people and helped themselves to our cattle and goats. . . . They interfered with our wives and molested them. . . . We thought it best to fight and die rather than bear it. . . .

We knew that we had very little chance because their weapons were so much superior to ours. But we meant to fight to the last, feeling that even if we could not beat them we might at least kill a few of them and so have some sort of revenge. . . .

I remember a fight in the Matoppos when we charged the white men. There were some hundreds of us; the white men also were many. We charged them at close quarters: we thought we had a good chance to kill them but the Maxims were too much for us. . . . Many of our people were killed in this fight. . . .

We were still fighting when we heard that [Cecil] Rhodes was coming and wanted to make peace with us. It was best to come to terms he said, and not go shedding blood like this on both sides. . . . So peace was made. Many of our people had been killed, and now we began to die of starvation; and then came the rinderpest and the cattle that were still left to us perished. We could not help thinking that all these dreadful things were brought by the white people.

A dual legal system was instituted that applied African laws to Africans and European laws to foreigners.

One advantage of such an administrative system was that it did not severely disrupt local customs and institutions. Nevertheless, it had several undesirable consequences. In the first place, it was essentially a fraud, since all major decisions were made by the British administrators while the native authorities served primarily as the means of enforcing decisions. Moreover, indirect rule served to perpetuate the autocratic system often in use prior to colonial takeover. It was official policy to inculcate respect for authority in areas under British rule, and there was a natural tendency to view the local aristocracy as the African equivalent of the British ruling class. Such a policy provided few opportunities for ambitious and talented young Africans from outside the traditional elite and thus sowed the seeds for class tensions after the restoration of independence in the twentieth century.

The situation was somewhat different in East Africa, especially in Kenya, which had a relatively large European population attracted by the temperate climate in the central highlands. The local government had encouraged white settlers to migrate to the area as a means of promoting economic development and encouraging financial self-sufficiency. To attract Europeans, fertile farmlands in the central highlands were reserved for European settlement, while, as in South Africa, specified reserve lands were set aside for Africans. The presence of a substantial European minority (although, in fact, they represented only about one percent of the entire population) had an impact on Kenya's political devel-

opment. The white settlers actively sought self-government and dominion status similar to that granted to such former British possessions as Canada and Australia. The British government, however, was not willing to run the risk of provoking racial tensions with the African majority and agreed only to establish separate government organs for the European and African populations.

The British used a different system in southern Africa, where there was a high percentage of European settlers. The situation was further complicated by the division between English-speaking and Afrikaner elements within the European population. In 1910, the British agreed to the creation of the independent Union of South Africa, which combined the old Cape Colony and Natal with the Boer republics. The new union adopted a representative government, but only for the European population, while the African reserves of Basutoland (now Lesotho), Bechuanaland (now Botswana), and Swaziland were subordinated directly to the crown. The union was now free to manage its own domestic affairs and possessed considerable autonomy in foreign relations. Formal British rule was also extended to the remaining lands south of the Zambezi River, which were eventually divided into the territories of Northern and Southern Rhodesia. Southern Rhodesia attracted many British immigrants, and in 1922, after a popular referendum, it became a crown colony (see the box above).

Most other European nations governed their African possessions through a form of direct rule. The prototype was the French system, which reflected the centralized administrative system introduced in France itself by

Napoleon. As in the British colonies, at the top of the pyramid was a French official, usually known as the governor-general, who was appointed from Paris and governed with the aid of a bureaucracy in the capital city. At the provincial level, French commissioners were assigned to deal with local administrators, but the latter were required to be conversant in French and could be transferred to a new position at the needs of the central government.

Moreover, the French ideal was to assimilate their African subjects into French culture rather than preserving their native traditions. Africans were eligible to run for office and to serve in the French National Assembly, and a few were appointed to high positions in the colonial administration. Such policies reflected the relative absence of racist attitudes in French society, as well as the conviction among the French of the superiority of Gallic culture and their revolutionary belief in the universality of human nature.

After World War I, European colonial policy in Africa entered a new and more formal phase. The colonial administrative network was extended to a greater degree into outlying areas, where it was represented by a district official and defended by a small native army under European command. Greater attention was given to improving social services, including education, medicine and sanitation, and communications. The colonial system was now viewed more formally as a moral and social responsibility, a "sacred trust" to be maintained by the civilized countries until the Africans became capable of self-government. More emphasis was placed on economic development and on the exploitation of natural resources to provide the colonies with the means of achieving self-sufficiency. More Africans were now serving in colonial administrations, although relatively few were placed in positions of responsibility. On the other hand, race consciousness probably increased during this period. Segregated clubs, schools, and churches were established as more European officials brought their wives and began to raise families in the colonies.

At the same time, the establishment of colonial rule often had the effect of reducing the rights and the status of women in Africa. African women had traditionally benefited from the prestige of matrilineal systems and were empowered by their traditional role as the primary agricultural producer in their community. Under colonialism, European settlers not only took the best land for themselves but also, in introducing new agricultural techniques, tended to deal exclusively with males, encouraging the latter to develop lucrative cash crops, while women were restricted to traditional farming methods. Whereas African men applied chemical fertilizer to the fields, women used manure. While men began to use bicycles, and eventually trucks, to transport goods, women still carried their goods on their heads, a practice that continues today.

THE EMERGENCE OF ANTICOLONIALISM

Thus far we have looked at the colonial experience primarily from the point of view of the colonial powers. Equally important is the way the subject peoples reacted to the experience. From the perspective of nearly half a century, it seems clear that their primary response was to turn to nationalism.

As we have seen, nationalism refers to a state of mind rising out of an awareness of being part of a community that possesses common institutions, traditions, language, and customs. Few nations in the world today meet such criteria. Most modern states contain a variety of ethnic, religious, and linguistic communities, each with its own sense of cultural and national identity. Should Canada, for example, which includes peoples of French, English, and Native American heritage, be considered a nation? Another question is how nationalism differs from other forms of tribal, religious, or linguistic affiliation. Should every group that resists assimilation into a larger cultural unity be called nationalist?

Such questions complicate the study of nationalism even in Europe and North America and make agreement on a definition elusive. They create even greater dilemmas in discussing Asia and Africa, where most societies are deeply divided by ethnic, linguistic, and religious differences and the very term *nationalism* is a foreign phenomenon imported from the West (see the box on p. 596). Prior to the colonial era, most traditional societies in Africa and Asia were formed on the basis of religious beliefs, tribal loyalties, or devotion to hereditary monarchies. Although individuals in some countries may have identified themselves as members of a particular national group, others viewed themselves as subjects of a king, members of a tribe, or adherents to a particular religion.

The advent of European colonialism brought the consciousness of modern nationhood to many of the societies of Asia and Africa. The creation of European colonies with defined borders and a powerful central government led to the weakening of tribal and village ties and a significant reorientation in the individual's sense of political identity. The introduction of Western ideas of citizenship and representative government produced a new sense of participation in the affairs of government. At the same time, the appearance of a new elite class based not on hereditary privilege or religious sanction but on alleged racial or cultural superiority aroused a shared sense of resentment among the subject peoples who felt a common commitment to the creation of an independent society. By the first quarter of the twentieth century, political movements dedicated to the overthrow of colonial rule had arisen throughout much of the non-Western world.

A CRITIQUE OF INDIAN NATIONALISM

Rabindranath Tagore, one of India's greatest writers, was a prominent spokesman for the Indian people under colonial rule. Though indisputably a patriot, like many intellectuals he was torn between his commitment to his native land and his awareness of the benefits of Western civilization. In this passage from a book written at the height of World War I, he seeks to persuade his readers that the common destiny of all humanity is more important than that of an individual nation or people.

RABINDRANATH TAGORE, NATIONALISM IN INDIA

India has never had a real sense of nationalism. Even though from childhood I had been taught that idolatry of the nation is almost better than reverence for God and humanity, I believe I have outgrown that teaching, and it is my conviction that my countrymen will truly gain their India by fighting against the education which teaches them that a country is greater than the ideals of humanity. . . .

We must recognize that it is providential that the West has come to India. And yet someone must show the East to the West, and convince the West that the East has her contribution to make to the history of civilization. India is no beggar of the West. And yet even though the West may think she is, I am not for thrusting off Western civilization and becoming segregated in our independence. Let us have a deep association. If providence wants England to be the channel of that communication, of that deeper association, I am willing to accept it with all humility. I have great faith in human nature, and I think the West will find its true mission. I speak bitterly of Western civilization when I am conscious that it is betraying its trust and thwarting its own purpose. The West must not make herself a curse to the world by using her power for her own selfish needs, but by teaching the ignorant and helping the weak, she should save herself from the worst danger that the strong is liable to incur, by making the feeble acquire power enough to resist her intrusion. And also she must not make her materialism to be the final thing, but must realize that she is doing a service in freeing the spiritual being from the tyranny of matter. . . .

Once again I draw your attention to the difficulties India has had to encounter and her struggle to overcome them. Her problem was the problem of the world in miniature. India is too vast in its area and too diverse in its races. It is many countries packed in one geographical receptacle. It is just the opposite of what Europe truly is, namely, one country made into many. Thus, Europe in its culture and growth has had the advantage of the strength of the many as well as the strength of the one. India, on the contrary, being naturally many, yet adventitiously one, has all along suffered from the looseness of its diversity and the feebleness of its unity. A true unity is like a round globe, it rolls on, carrying its burden easily; but diversity is a many cornered thing which has to be dragged and pushed with all force. Be it said to the credit of India that this diversity was not her own creation; she has had to accept it as a fact from the beginning of her history.

Modern nationalism, then, was a product of colonialism and, in a sense, a reaction to it. But a sense of nationhood does not emerge full-blown in a given society. The rise of modern nationalism is a process that begins among a few members of the educated elite (most commonly among articulate professionals such as lawyers, teachers, journalists, and doctors) and then spreads only gradually to the mass of the population. Even after national independence has been realized, as we shall see, it is often questionable whether a mature sense of nationhood has been created.

Traditional Resistance: A Precursor to Nationalism

The beginnings of modern nationalism can be found in the initial resistance by the indigenous peoples to the colonial conquest. Although, strictly speaking, such resistance was not "nationalist" because it was essentially motivated by the desire to defend traditional institutions, it did reflect a primitive concept of nationhood in that it aimed at protecting the homeland from the invader; later patriotic groups have often hailed early resistance movements as the precursors of twentieth-century nationalist movements. Thus traditional resistance to colonial conquest may logically be viewed as the first stage in the development of modern nationalism.

Such resistance took various forms. For the most part, it was led by the existing ruling class. In the Ashanti kingdom in Africa and in Burma and Vietnam in Southeast Asia, resistance to Western domination was initially directed by the imperial courts. In some cases, traditionalists continued to oppose foreign conquest even after resistance had collapsed at the center. In India, Tipu Sultan resisted the British in the Deccan after the collapse of the Mughal dynasty. Similarly, after the decrepit monarchy in Vietnam had bowed to French pressure, a number of civilian and military officials set up an organization called Can Vuong (literally "save the king") and contin-

A CALL TO ARMS

*I*n 1862, the Vietnamese imperial court at Huê ceded three provinces in southern Vietnam to the French. In outrage, many patriotic Vietnamese military officers and government officials appealed to their compatriots to rise up spontaneously and resist the foreigners. The following passage is from an anonymous document written in 1864.

AN APPEAL TO RESIST THE FRENCH

This is a general proclamation addressed to the scholars and the people.

Our country is about to undergo dangerous upheavals.

Certain persons are plotting treason.

Our people are now suffering through a period of anarchy and disorder. . . .

Nonetheless, even in times of confusion, there remain books that teach us how to overcome disorder.

Past generations can still be for us examples of right and wrong. . . .

Let us now consider our situation with the French today.

We are separated from them by thousands of mountains and seas.

By hundreds of differences in our daily customs.

Although they were very confident in their copper battleships surmounted by chimneys,

Although they had a large quantity of steel rifles and lead bullets,

These things did not prevent the loss of some of their best generals in these last years, when they attacked our frontier in hundreds of battles. . . .

Heaven will not leave our people enchained very long.

Heaven will not allow them [the French] the free enjoyment of their lives. . . .

You, officials of the country,

Do not let your resistance to the enemy be blunted by the peaceful stand of the court.

Do not take the lead from the three subjected provinces and leave hatred unavenged. . . .

Such a hostility, such a hatred, such an enmity; our heart will be quieted before we are avenged. . . .

Do not envy the scholars who now become provincial or district magistrates [in the French administration]. They are decay, garbage, filth, swine.

Do not imitate some who hire themselves out to the enemy. They are idiots, fools, lackeys, scoundrels.

At the beginning, you followed the way of righteousness. From beginning to end you ought to behave according to the moral obligations which bind you to your king.

Life has fame, death too has fame. Act in such a way that your life and your death will be a fragrant ointment to your families and to your country.

---

ued their resistance without imperial sanction (see the box above).

The first stirrings of nationalism in India took place in the early nineteenth century with the search for a renewed sense of cultural identity. In 1828, Ram Mohan Roy, a brahmin from Bengal, founded the Brahmo Samaj (Society of Brahma). Roy probably had no intention of promoting Indian national independence but created the new organization as a means of helping his fellow religionists defend the Hindu religion against verbal attacks by their British acquaintances. Roy was by no means a hidebound traditionalist. He opposed such practices as *sati* and recognized the benefit of introducing the best aspects of European culture into Indian society.

Sometimes traditional resistance to Western penetration went beyond elite circles. Most commonly, it appeared in the form of peasant revolts. Rural rebellions were not uncommon in traditional Asian societies as a means of expressing peasant discontent with high taxes, official corruption, rising rural debt, and famine in the countryside. Under colonialism, rural conditions often deteriorated as population density increased and peas-

ants were driven off the land to make way for plantation agriculture. Angry peasants then vented their frustration at the foreign invaders. For example, in Burma, the Buddhist monk Saya San led a peasant uprising against the British many years after they had completed their takeover. Similar forms of unrest occurred in various parts of India, where *zamindars* and rural villagers alike resisted government attempts to increase tax revenues. Yet another peasant uprising took place in Algeria in 1840.

Sometimes the resentment had a religious basis, as in the Sudan, where the revolt led by the Mahdi had strong Islamic overtones, although it was initially provoked by Turkish misrule in Egypt. More significant than Roy's Brahmo Samaj in its impact on British policy was the famous Sepoy Rebellion of 1857 in India. The sepoys (derived from *sipahi,* a Turkish word meaning horseman or soldier) were native troops hired by the East India Company to protect British interests in the region. Unrest within Indian units of the colonial army had been common since early in the century, when it had been sparked by economic issues, religious sensitivities, or nascent anticolonial sentiment. Such attitudes intensified

© Sipahioglu/Getty Images

VIETNAMESE PRISONERS IN STOCKS. Whereas some Vietnamese took up Western ways, others resisted the foreign incursion but were vigorously suppressed by the French. In this photograph, Vietnamese prisoners who had plotted against the French are held in stocks in preparation for trial in 1907.

in the mid-1850s when the British instituted a new policy of shipping Indian troops abroad—a practice that exposed Hindus to pollution by foreigners. In 1857, tension erupted when the British adopted the new Enfield rifle for use by sepoy infantrymen. The new weapon was a muzzle loader that used paper cartridges covered with animal fat and lard; because the cartridge had to be bitten off, it broke strictures against high-class Hindus' eating animal products and Muslim prohibitions against eating pork. Protests among sepoy units in northern India turned into a full-scale mutiny, supported by uprisings in rural districts in various parts of the country. But the revolt lacked clear goals, and rivalries between Hindus and Muslims and discord among the leaders within each community prevented coordination of operations. Although Indian troops often fought bravely and outnumbered the British six to one, they were poorly organized, and the British forces (supplemented in many cases by sepoy troops) suppressed the rebellion.

Still, the revolt frightened the British and led to a number of major reforms. The proportion of native troops relative to those from Great Britain was reduced, and precedence was given to ethnic groups likely to be loyal to the British, such as the Sikhs of Punjab and the Gurkhas, an upland people from Nepal in the Himalaya Mountains. To avoid religious conflicts, ethnic groups were spread throughout the service rather than assigned to special units. The British also decided to suppress the final remnants of the hapless Mughal dynasty, which had supported the mutiny.

Like the Sepoy Rebellion, traditional resistance movements usually met with little success. Peasants armed with pikes and spears were no match for Western armies possessing the most terrifying weapons then known to human society. In a few cases, such as the revolt of the Mahdi at Khartoum, the natives were able to defeat the invaders temporarily. But such successes were rare, and the late nineteenth century witnessed the seemingly inexorable march of the Western powers, armed with the Gatling gun (the first rapid-fire weapon and the precursor of the modern machine gun), to mastery of the globe.

☙ CONCLUSION

By the first quarter of the twentieth century, virtually all of Africa and a good part of South and Southeast Asia were under some form of colonial rule. With the advent of the age of imperialism, a global economy was finally established, and the domination of Western civilization over those of Africa and Asia appeared to be complete.

Defenders of colonialism argue that the system was a necessary if painful stage in the evolution of human societies. Although its immediate consequences were admittedly sometimes unfortunate, Western imperialism was ultimately beneficial to colonial powers and subjects alike, since it created the conditions for global economic development and the universal application of democratic institutions. Critics, however, charge that the Western colonial powers were driven by an insatiable lust for profits. They dismiss the Western civilizing mission as a fig leaf to cover naked greed and reject the notion that imperialism played a salutary role in hastening the adjustment of traditional societies to the demands of industrial civilization. In the blunt words of two Western critics of imperialism: "Why is Africa (or for that matter Latin America and much of Asia) so poor? . . . The answer is very brief: we have made it poor."[10]

Between these two irreconcilable views, where does the truth lie? This chapter has contended that neither extreme position is justified. The sources of imperialism lie not simply in the demands of industrial capitalism but in the search for security, national greatness, and even such psychological factors as the spirit of discovery and the drive to excel. Though some regard the concept of the "white man's burden" as a hypocritical gesture to moral sensitivities, others see it as a meaningful reality justifying a lifelong commitment to the colonialist enterprise. Although the "civilizing urge" of missionaries and officials may have been tinged with self-interest, it was nevertheless often sincerely motivated.

Similarly, the consequences of colonialism have been more complex than either its defenders or its critics would have us believe. While the colonial peoples received little immediate benefit from the imposition of foreign rule, overall the imperialist era brought about a vast expansion of the international trade network and created at least the potential for societies throughout Africa and Asia to play an active and rewarding role in the new global economic arena. If, as historian William McNeill believes, the introduction of new technology through cross-cultural encounters is the driving force of change in world history, then Western imperialism, whatever its faults, served a useful purpose in opening the door to such change, much as the rise of the Arab empire and the Mongol invasions hastened the process of global economic development in an earlier time.

Still, the critics have a point. Although colonialism did introduce the peoples of Asia and Africa to new technology and the expanding economic marketplace, it was unnecessarily brutal in its application and all too often failed to realize the exalted claims and objectives of its promoters. Existing economic networks—often potentially valuable as a foundation for later economic development—were ruthlessly swept aside in the interests of providing markets for Western manufactured goods. Potential sources of native industrialization were nipped in the bud to avoid competition for factories in Amsterdam, London, Pittsburgh, or Manchester. Training in Western democratic ideals and practices was ignored out of fear that the recipients might use them as weapons against the ruling authorities.

The fundamental weakness of colonialism, then, was that it was ultimately based on the self-interests of the citizens of the colonial powers. Where those interests collided with the needs of the colonial peoples, those of the former always triumphed. Much the same might have been said about earlier periods in history, when Assyrians, Arabs, Mongols, and Chinese turned their conquests to their own profit. Where modern imperialism differed was in its tendency to cloak naked self-interest in the guise of a moral obligation. However sincerely the David Livingstones, Albert Sarrauts, and William McKinleys of the world were convinced of the rightness of their civilizing mission, the ultimate result was to deprive the colonial peoples of the right to make their own choices about their own destiny.

Did the system serve the interests of the colonial powers? On the face of it, the answer seems obvious: colonialism provided cheap raw materials and markets for Western manufactured goods, both essential to the effective operation of the capitalist system. But some recent observers have concluded that the possession of colonies was not always beneficial to those who possessed them. According to French economic historian Jacques Marseille, for example, the cost of maintaining the French colonial empire, on balance, exceeded the economic benefits it provided, especially since the maintenance of a protected market in the colonies hindered the French effort to create an industrial sector capable of competing in the global marketplace. Such costs did not become fully apparent until after World War II, however, as we shall see in future chapters.

In one area of Asia, the spreading tide of imperialism did not result in the establishment of formal Western colonial control. In East Asia, the traditional societies of China and Japan were buffeted by the winds of Western expansionism during the nineteenth century but successfully resisted foreign conquest. In the next chapter, we will see how they managed to retain their independence while attempting to cope with the demands of a changing world.

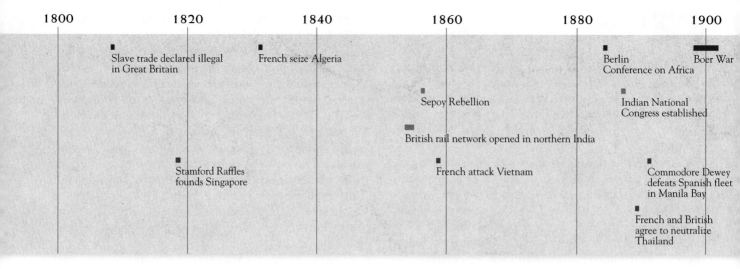

| 1800 | 1820 | 1840 | 1860 | 1880 | 1900 |

Slave trade declared illegal in Great Britain

French seize Algeria

Berlin Conference on Africa

Boer War

Sepoy Rebellion

Indian National Congress established

British rail network opened in northern India

Stamford Raffles founds Singapore

French attack Vietnam

Commodore Dewey defeats Spanish fleet in Manila Bay

French and British agree to neutralize Thailand

CHAPTER NOTES

1. J. G. Lockhart and C. M. Wodehouse, *Rhodes* (1963), pp. 69–70.
2. Quoted in Henry Braunschwig, *French Colonialism, 1871–1914* (London, 1961), p. 80.
3. Quoted in Ruhl Bartlett, ed., *The Record of American Diplomacy: Documents and Readings in the History of American Foreign Relations* (New York, 1952), p. 385.
4. Quoted in John Iliffe, *Africans: The History of a Continent* (Cambridge, 1995), p. 124.
5. Thomas Pakenham, *The Scramble for Africa* (New York, 1991), p. 13.
6. Quoted in Georges Garros, *Forceries Humaines* (Paris, 1926), p. 21.
7. Cited in review by Benjamin Schwartz of David Cannadine's *Ornamentalism: How the British Saw Their Empire* (Oxford, 2000), in *Atlantic Monthly*, November 2001, p. 135.
8. Sarraut's comment is quoted in Louis Roubaud, *Vietnam: La Tragédie Indochinoise* (Paris, 1926), p. 80.
9. Quoted in Pakenham, *The Scramble for Africa*, p. 182, citing a letter to Queen Victoria dated August 7, 1879.
10. Peter C. W. Gutkind and Immanuel Wallerstein, eds., *The Political Economy of Contemporary Africa* (Beverly Hills, Calif., 1976), p. 14.

SUGGESTED READING

There are a number of good works on the subject of imperialism and colonialism. For a recent study that directly focuses on the question of whether colonialism was beneficial to subject peoples, see D. K. Fieldhouse, *The West and the Third World: Trade, Colonialism, Dependence, and Development* (Oxford, 1999). Also see W. Baumgart, *Imperialism: The Idea and Reality of British and French Colonial Expansion, 1880–1914* (Oxford, 1982), and H. M. Wright, ed., *The "New Imperialism": Analysis of Late-Nineteenth-Century Expansion* (New York, 1976). On technology, see D. R. Headrick, *The Tentacles of Progress: Technology Transfer in the Age of Imperialism, 1850–1940* (Oxford, 1988).

On the imperialist age in Africa, above all see R. Robinson and J. Gallagher, *Africa and the Victorians: The Official Mind of Imperialism* (London, 1961). Also see B. Davidson, *Modern Africa: A Social and Political History* (London, 1989); T. Pakenham, *The Scramble for Africa* (New York, 1991); and T. Pakenham, *The Boer War* (London, 1979). On southern Africa, see J. Guy, *The Destruction of the Zulu Kingdom* (London, 1979), and D. Nenoon and B.

Nyeko, *Southern Africa Since 1800* (London, 1984). Also useful is R. O. Collins, ed., *Historical Problems of Imperial Africa* (Princeton, N.J., 1994).

For an overview of the British takeover and administration of India, see S. Wolpert, *A New History of India* (New York, 1989). C. A. Bayly, *Indian Society and the Making of the British Empire* (Cambridge, 1988), is a scholarly analysis of the impact of British conquest on the Indian economy. For a comparative approach, see R. Murphey, *The Outsiders: The Western Experience in China and India* (Ann Arbor, Mich., 1977). In a provocative new work, David Cannadine, in *Ornamentalism: How the British Saw Their Empire* (Oxford, 2000), argues that it was class, and not race, that motivated British policy in the subcontinent.

General studies of the colonial period in Southeast Asia are rare because most authors focus on specific areas. For some stimulating essays on a variety of aspects of the topic, see *Continuity and Change in Southeast Asia: Collected Journal Articles of Harry J. Benda* (New Haven, Conn., 1972). The role of religion is examined in F. von der

Mehden, *Religion and Nationalism in Southeast Asia* (Madison, Wis., 1963). On nationalist movements, see also R. Emerson's classic *From Empire to Nation* (Boston, 1960). For a view of the region from the inside, see D. J. Steinberg et al., eds., *In Search of Southeast Asia* (New York, 1986). On the French conquest of Indochina, see M. O. Osborne, *The French Presence in Cochin China and Cambodia* (Ithaca, N.Y., 1969).

For an introduction to the effects of colonialism on women in Africa and Asia, see S. Hughes and B. Hughes, *Women in World History*, vol. 2 (Armonk, N.Y., 1997). Also consult the classic by E. Boserup, *Women's Role in Economic Development* (London, 1970), and see J. Taylor, *The Social World of Batavia* (Madison, Wis., 1983).

INFOTRAC COLLEGE EDITION

For additional reading, go to InfoTrac College Edition, your online research library at http://web1.infotrac-college.com

Enter the search term "imperialism" using the Subject Guide.

Enter the search terms "Boer War" using Keywords.

Enter the search term "nationalism" using Keywords.

Chapter 21

National Maritime Museum, London

SHADOWS OVER THE PACIFIC: EAST ASIA UNDER CHALLENGE

CHAPTER OUTLINE

- THE DECLINE OF THE MANCHUS
- CHINESE SOCIETY IN TRANSITION
- A RICH COUNTRY AND A STRONG STATE: THE RISE OF MODERN JAPAN
- CONCLUSION

FOCUS QUESTIONS

- Why did the Qing dynasty decline and ultimately collapse, and what role did the Western powers play in this process?
- What role did Sun Yat-sen play in the collapse of the Qing dynasty, and what were his goals for China?
- What political, economic, and social reforms were instituted by Meiji reformers in Japan?
- To what degree was the Meiji Restoration a "revolution," and to what degree did it succeed in transforming Japan?
- ➤ How did China and Japan respond to Western pressures in the nineteenth century, and what implications did their different responses have for each nation's history?

*T*he British emissary Lord Macartney had arrived in Beijing in 1793 with a caravan loaded with six hundred cases of gifts for the emperor. Flags and banners provided by the Chinese proclaimed in Chinese characters that the visitor was an "ambassador bearing tribute from the country of England." But the tribute was in vain, for Macartney's request for an increase in trade between the two countries was flatly rejected, and he left Beijing in October with nothing to show for his efforts. Not until half a century later would the Qing dynasty—at the point of a gun—agree to the British demand for an expansion of commercial ties.

Historians have often viewed the failure of the Macartney mission as a reflection of the disdain of Chinese rulers toward their counterparts in other countries and their serene confidence in the superiority of Chinese civilization in a world inhabited by barbarians. But in retrospect, it is clear that China's concern was justified. At the beginning of the nineteenth century, the country faced a growing challenge from the escalating power and ambitions of the West. Backed by European guns, Western merchants and missionaries pressed insistently for the right to carry out their activities in China and Japan. Despite their initial reluctance, the Chinese and Japanese governments were eventually forced to open their doors to the foreigners, whose presence escalated rapidly during the final years of the century.

Unlike other Asian societies, both Japan and China were able to maintain their national independence against the Western onslaught. In other respects, however, the results in Japan and China were strikingly different. Japan responded quickly to the challenge by adopting Western institutions and customs and eventually becoming a significant competitor for the spoils of empire. In contrast, China grappled unsuccessfully with the problem, which eventually undermined the foundations of the Qing dynasty and brought it to an unceremonious end. •

THE DECLINE OF THE MANCHUS

In 1800, the Qing (Ch'ing) or Manchu dynasty was at the height of its power. China had experienced a long period of peace and prosperity under the rule of two great emperors, Kangxi and Qianlong. Its borders were secure, and its culture and intellectual achievements were the envy of the world. Its rulers, hidden behind the walls of the Forbidden City in Beijing, had every reason to describe their patrimony as the "Central Kingdom." But a little over a century later, humiliated and harassed by the black ships and big guns of the Western powers, the Qing dynasty, the last in a series that had endured for more than two thousand years, collapsed in the dust.

Historians once assumed that the primary reason for the rapid decline and fall of the Manchu dynasty was the intense pressure applied to a proud but somewhat complacent traditional society by the modern West. Now, however, most historians believe that internal changes played a role in the dynasty's collapse and point out that at least some of the problems suffered by the Manchus during the nineteenth century were self-inflicted.

Both explanations have some validity. Like so many of its predecessors, after an extended period of growth, the Qing dynasty began to suffer from the familiar dynastic ills of official corruption, peasant unrest, and incompetence at court. Such weaknesses were probably exacerbated by the rapid growth in population. The long era of peace and stability, the introduction of new crops from the Americas, and the cultivation of new, fast-ripening strains of rice enabled the Chinese population to double between 1550 and 1800. The population continued to grow, reaching the unprecedented level of 400 million by the end of the nineteenth century. Even without the irritating presence of the Western powers, the Manchus were probably destined to repeat the fate of their imperial predecessors. The ships, guns, and ideas of the foreigners simply highlighted the growing weakness of the Manchu dynasty and likely hastened its demise. In doing so, Western imperialism still exerted an indelible impact on the history of modern China—but as a contributing, not a causal, factor.

Opium and Rebellion

By 1800, Westerners had been in contact with China for more than two hundred years, but after an initial period of flourishing relations, Western traders had been limited to a small commercial outlet at Canton. This arrangement was not acceptable to the British, however. Not only did they chafe at being restricted to a tiny enclave, but the growing British appetite for Chinese tea created a severe balance-of-payments problem. The British tried negotiations, dispatching Lord Macartney to Beijing in 1793 and another mission, led by Lord Amherst, in 1816. But both missions foundered on the rock of protocol and managed only to worsen the already strained relations between the two countries. The British solution was opium. A product more addictive than tea, opium was grown in northeastern India and then shipped to China. Opium had been grown in southwestern China for several hundred years but had been used primarily for medicinal purposes. Now, as imports increased, popular demand for the product in southern China became insatiable despite an official prohibition on its use. Soon bullion was flowing out of the Chinese imperial treasury into the pockets of British merchants.

The Chinese became concerned and tried to negotiate. In 1839, Lin Zexu (Lin Tse-hsu; 1785–1850), a Chinese official appointed by the court to curtail the opium trade, appealed to Queen Victoria on both moral and practical grounds and threatened to prohibit the sale of rhubarb (widely used as a laxative in nineteenth-century Europe) to Great Britain if she did not respond (see the box on p. 604). But moral principles, then as now, paled before the lure of commercial profits, and the British continued to promote the opium trade, arguing that if the Chinese did not want the opium, they did not have to buy it. Lin Zexu attacked on three fronts, imposing penalties on smokers, arresting dealers, and seizing supplies from importers as they attempted to smuggle the drug into China. The last tactic caused his downfall. When he blockaded the foreign factory area in Canton to force

A LETTER OF ADVICE TO THE QUEEN

*L*in Zexu was the Chinese imperial commissioner in Canton at the time of the Opium War. Prior to the conflict, he attempted to use reason and the threat of retaliation to persuade the British to cease importing opium illegally into southern China. The following excerpt is from a letter that he wrote to Queen Victoria. In it, he appeals to her conscience while showing the condescension that the Chinese traditionally displayed to the rulers of other countries.

LIN ZEXU, LETTER TO QUEEN VICTORIA

The kings of your honorable country by a tradition handed down from generation to generation have always been noted for their politeness and submissiveness.... Privately we are delighted with the way in which the honorable rulers of your country deeply understand the grand principles and are grateful for the Celestial grace.... The profit from trade has been enjoyed by them continuously for two hundred years. This is the source from which your country has become known for its wealth.

But after a long period of commercial intercourse, there appear among the crowd of barbarians both good persons and bad, unevenly. Consequently there are those who smuggle opium to seduce the Chinese people and so cause the spread of the poison to all provinces....

The wealth of China is used to profit the barbarians. That is to say, the great profit made by barbarians is all taken from the rightful share of China. By what right do they then in return use the poisonous drug to injure the Chinese people?... Let us ask, where is your conscience? I have heard that the smoking of opium is very strictly forbidden by your country; that is because the harm caused by opium is clearly understood. Since it is not permitted to do harm to your own country, then even less should you let it be passed on to the harm of other countries—how much less to China! Of all that China exports to foreign countries, there is not a single thing which is not beneficial to people.... Is there a single article from China which has done any harm to foreign countries? Take tea and rhubarb, for example; the foreign countries cannot get along for a single day without them.... On the other hand, articles coming from the outside to China can only be used as toys. We can take them or get along without them. Nevertheless our Celestial Court lets tea, silk, and other goods be shipped without limit and circulated everywhere without begrudging it in the slightest. This is for no other reason but to share the benefit with the people of the whole world....

May you, O King, check your wicked and sift your vicious people before they come to China, in order to guarantee the peace of your nation, to show further the sincerity of your politeness and submissiveness, and to let the two countries enjoy together the blessings of peace.... After receiving this dispatch will you immediately give us a prompt reply regarding the details and circumstances of your cutting off the opium traffic. Be sure not to put this off.

---

traders to hand over their remaining chests of opium, the British government, claiming that it could not permit British subjects "to be exposed to insult and injustice," launched a naval expedition to punish the Manchus and force the court to open China to foreign trade.[1]

The Opium War (1839–1842) lasted three years and demonstrated the superiority of British firepower and military tactics (including the use of a shallow-draft steamboat that effectively harassed Chinese coastal defenses). British warships destroyed Chinese coastal and river forts and seized the offshore island of Chusan, not far from the mouth of the Yangtze River. When a British fleet sailed virtually unopposed up the Yangtze to Nanjing and cut off the supply of "tribute grain" from southern to northern China, the Qing finally agreed to British terms. In the Treaty of Nanjing in 1842, the Chinese agreed to open five coastal ports to British trade, limit tariffs on imported British goods, grant extraterritorial rights to British citizens in China, and pay a substantial indemnity to cover the costs of the war. China also agreed to cede the island of Hong Kong (dismissed by a senior British official as a "barren rock") to Great Britain. Nothing was said in the treaty about the opium trade, which continued unabated until it was brought under control through Chinese government efforts in the early twentieth century.

Although the Opium War has traditionally been considered the beginning of modern Chinese history, it is unlikely that many Chinese at the time would have seen it that way. This was not the first time that a ruling dynasty had been forced to make concessions to foreigners, and the opening of five coastal ports to the British hardly constituted a serious threat to the security of the empire. Although a few concerned Chinese argued that the court should learn more about European civilization, others contended that China had nothing to learn from the barbarians and that borrowing foreign ways would undercut the purity of Confucian civilization.

For the time being, the Manchus attempted to deal with the problem in the traditional way of playing the foreigners off against each other. Concessions granted to the British were offered to other Western nations, including the United States, and soon thriving foreign concession areas were operating in treaty ports along the southern Chinese coast from Canton to Shanghai.

In the meantime, the Qing court's failure to deal with pressing internal economic problems led to a major peas-

National Maritime Museum, London

THE OPIUM WAR. The Opium War, waged between China and Great Britain between 1839 and 1842, was China's first conflict with a European power. Lacking modern military technology, the Chinese suffered a humiliating defeat. In this painting, heavily armed British steamships destroy unwieldy Chinese junks along the Chinese coast. China's humiliation at sea was a legacy of its rulers' lack of interest in maritime matters since the middle of the fifteenth century, when Chinese junks were among the most advanced sailing ships in the world.

ant revolt that shook the foundations of the empire. On the surface, the Taiping (T'ai p'ing) Rebellion owed something to the Western incursion; the leader of the uprising, Hong Xiuquan (Hung Hsiu-ch'uan), a failed examination candidate, was a Christian convert who viewed himself as a younger brother of Jesus and hoped to establish what he referred to as a "Heavenly Kingdom of Supreme Peace" in China. But there were many local causes as well. The rapid increase in population forced millions of peasants to eke out a living as sharecroppers or landless laborers. Official corruption and incompetence led to the whipsaw of increased taxes and a decline in government services; even the Grand Canal was allowed to silt up, hindering the shipment of grain. In 1853,

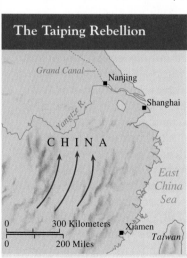

The Taiping Rebellion

Grand Canal
Nanjing
Shanghai
Yangtze R.
CHINA
East China Sea
0   300 Kilometers
0   200 Miles
Xiamen
Taiwan

the rebels seized the old Ming capital of Nanjing, but that proved to be the rebellion's high-water mark. Plagued by factionalism, the rebellion gradually lost momentum until it was finally suppressed in 1864.

One reason for the dynasty's failure to deal effectively with the internal unrest was its continuing difficulties with the Western imperialists. In 1856, the British and the French, still smarting from trade restrictions and limitations on their missionary activities, launched a new series of attacks against China and seized Beijing in 1860. As punishment, British troops destroyed the imperial summer palace just outside the city. In the ensuing Treaty of Tianjin (Tientsin), the Qing agreed to humiliating new concessions: the legalization of the opium trade, the opening of additional ports to foreign trade, and the cession of the peninsula of Kowloon (opposite the island of Hong Kong) to the British (see Map 21.1). Additional territories in the north were ceded to Russia.

The Climax of Imperialism in China

By the late 1870s, the old dynasty was well on the road to internal disintegration. In fending off the Taiping Rebellion, the Manchus had been compelled to rely for

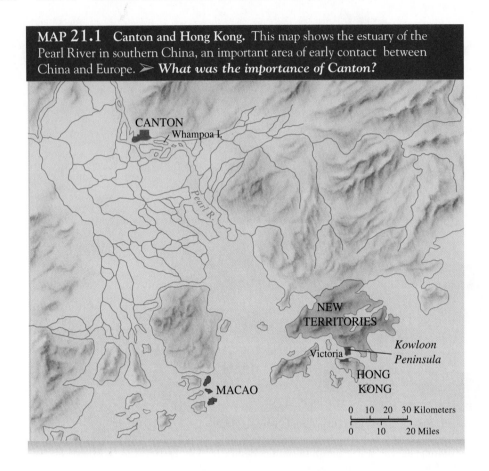

MAP 21.1   Canton and Hong Kong. This map shows the estuary of the Pearl River in southern China, an important area of early contact between China and Europe. ➤ *What was the importance of Canton?*

support on armed forces under regional command. After quelling the revolt, many of these regional commanders refused to disband their units and, with the support of the local gentry, continued to collect local taxes for their own use. The dreaded pattern of imperial breakdown, so familiar in Chinese history, was beginning to appear once again.

In its weakened state, the court finally began to listen to the appeals of reform-minded officials, who called for a new policy of "self-strengthening," in which Western technology would be adopted while Confucian principles and institutions were maintained intact. This policy, popularly known by its slogan "East for Essence, West for Practical Use," remained the guiding standard for Chinese foreign and domestic policy for nearly a quarter of a century. Some even called for reforms in education and in China's hallowed political institutions (see the box on p. 607). Pointing to the power and prosperity of Great Britain, the journalist Wang Tao (Wang T'ao; 1828–1897) remarked, "The real strength of England . . . lies in the fact that there is a sympathetic understanding between the governing and the governed, a close relationship between the ruler and the people. . . . My observation is that the daily domestic political life of England actually embodies the traditional ideals of our ancient Golden Age."[2] Such democratic ideas were too radical for most reformers, how-

ever. One of the leading court officials of the day, Zhang Zhidong (Chang Chih-tung), countered:

> The doctrine of people's rights will bring us not a single benefit but a hundred evils. Are we going to establish a parliament? . . . Even supposing the confused and clamorous people are assembled in one house, for every one of them who is clear-sighted, there will be a hundred others whose vision is beclouded; they will converse at random and talk as if in a dream—what use will it be?[3]

For the time being, Zhang Zhidong's arguments won the day. During the last quarter of the century, the Manchus attempted to modernize their military establishment and build up an industrial base without disturbing the essential elements of traditional Chinese civilization. Railroads, weapons arsenals, and shipyards were built, but the value system remained essentially unchanged.

In the end, the results spoke for themselves. During the last two decades of the nineteenth century, the European penetration of China, both political and military, intensified. Rapacious imperialists began to bite off the outer edges of the Qing Empire (see Map 21.2). The Gobi Desert north of the Great Wall, Central Asia, and Tibet, all inhabited by non-Chinese peoples and never fully assimilated into the Chinese Empire, were gradually lost. In the north and northwest, the main beneficiary was Rus-

AN APPEAL FOR CHANGE IN CHINA

After the humiliating defeat at the hands of the British in the Opium War, a few Chinese intellectuals began to argue that China must change its ways in order to survive. Among such reformist thinkers was the journalist and author Wang Tao. After a trip to Europe in the late 1860s, Wang returned to China convinced of the technological superiority of the West and the need for his country to adopt reforms to enable it to compete effectively in a changing world. He had only limited success in persuading his contemporaries of the need for dramatic change. Many Chinese were undoubtedly reluctant to believe his claim that China was not the Middle Kingdom or "all under Heaven" but only one nation among many in a rapidly changing world.

WANG TAO ON REFORM

I know that within a hundred years China will adopt all Western methods and excel in them. For though both are vessels, a sailboat differs in speed from a steamship; though both are vehicles, a horse-drawn carriage cannot cover the same distance as a locomotive train. Among weapons, the power of the bow and arrow, sword and spear, cannot be compared with that of firearms; and of firearms, the old types do not have the same effect as the new. Although it be the same piece of work, there is a difference in the ease with which it can be done by machine and by human labor. When new methods do not exist, people will not think of changes; but when there are new instruments, to copy them is certainly possible. Even if the Westerners should give no guidance, the Chinese must surely exert themselves to the utmost of their ingenuity and resources on these things.

Alas! People all understand the past, but they are ignorant of the future. Only scholars whose thoughts run deep and far can grasp the trends. As the mind of Heaven changes above, so do human affairs below. Heaven opens the minds of the Westerners and bestows upon them intelligence and wisdom. Their techniques and skills develop without bound. They sail eastward and gather in China. This constitutes an unprecedented situation in history, and a tremendous change in the world. The foreign nations come from afar with their superior techniques, contemptuous of us in our deficiencies. They show off their prowess and indulge in insults and oppression; they also fight among themselves. Under these circumstances, how can we not think of making changes? . . .

If China does not make any change at this time, how can she be on a par with the great nations of Europe, and compare with them in power and strength? Nevertheless, the path of reform is beset with difficulties. What the Western countries have today are regarded as of no worth by those who arrogantly refuse to pay attention. Their argument is that we should use our own laws to govern the empire, for that is the Way of our sages. They do not know that the Way of the sages is valued only because it can make proper accommodations according to the times. If Confucius lived today, we may be certain that he would not cling to antiquity and oppose making changes. . . .

But how is this to be done? First, the method of recruiting civil servants should be changed. The examination essays, coming down to the present, have gone from bad to worse and should be discarded. And yet we are still using them to select civil servants.

Second, the method of training soldiers should be changed. Now our army units and naval forces have only names registered on books, but no actual persons enrolled. The authorities consider our troops unreliable and so they recuit militia who, however, can be assembled but cannot be disbanded. . . . The arms of the Manchu banners and the ships of the naval forces should all be changed. . . . If they continue to hold on to their old ways and make no plans for change, it may be called "using untrained people to fight," which is no different from driving them to their deaths.

---

sia, which took advantage of the dynasty's weakness to force the cession of territories north of the Amur River in Siberia. In Tibet, competition between Russia and Great Britain prevented either power from seizing the territory outright but at the same time enabled Tibetan authorities to revive local autonomy never recognized by the Chinese. In the south, British and French advances in mainland Southeast Asia removed Burma and Vietnam from their traditional vassal relationship to the Manchu court. Even more ominous were the foreign spheres of influence in the Chinese heartland, where local commanders were willing to sell exclusive commercial, railroad-building, or mining privileges.

The breakup of the Manchu dynasty accelerated at the end of the nineteenth century. In 1894, the Qing went to war with Japan over Japanese incursions into the Korean peninsula, which threatened China's long-held suzerainty over the area (see "Joining the Imperialist Club" later in this chapter). To the surprise of many observers, the Chinese were roundly defeated, confirming to some critics the devastating failure of the policy of self-strengthening by halfway measures. The disintegration of China accelerated in 1897, when Germany, a new entry in the race for spoils in East Asia, used the pretext of the murder of two German missionaries by Chinese rioters to demand the cession of territories in the Shandong (Shantung) peninsula. The approval of the demand by the imperial court set off a scramble for territory by other interested powers (see Map 21.3). Russia now demanded the Liaodong peninsula with its ice-free port at Port Arthur, and Great Britain weighed in with a request for a coaling station in northern China.

Courtesy of Claire L. Duiker

⟫ **THE POTALA PALACE IN TIBET.** Tibet was among the most distant appendages of the Qing dynasty. Once a powerful kingdom on the eastern fringes of imperial China, Tibet was peopled by an ethnic group who practiced a distinct form of Buddhism. When Manchu power declined at the end of the nineteenth century, the Tibetans sought to restore their independence. The leading religious figure in Tibetan Buddhism was the Dalai Lama, who lived in this building, constructed in the seventeenth century in the capital of Lhasa.

The government responded to the challenge with yet another effort at reform. In the spring of 1898, an outspoken advocate of change, the progressive Confucian scholar Kang Youwei (K'ang Yu-wei), won the support of the young Guangxu (Kuang Hsu) emperor for a comprehensive reform program patterned after recent measures in Japan. Without change, Kang argued, China would perish. During the next several weeks, the emperor issued edicts calling for major political, administrative, and educational reforms. Not surprisingly, Kang's proposals were opposed by many conservatives, who saw little advantage and much risk in copying the West. More important, the new program was opposed by the emperor's aunt, the Empress Dowager Cixi (Tz'u Hsi), the real power at court. Cixi had begun her political career as a concubine to an earlier emperor. After his death, she became a dominant force at court and in 1878 placed her infant nephew, the future

⟫ **EMPRESS DOWAGER CIXI.** Cixi was the most powerful figure in late nineteenth-century China. Originally a concubine at the imperial court, she later placed a nephew on the throne and dominated the political scene for a quarter of a century, until her death in 1908. Conservative in her views, she staunchly resisted her advisers' suggestions for changes to help China face the challenge posed by the West. Note the long fingernails, a symbol of the privileged class, in this photograph taken in her final years.

Courtesy of the Freer Gallery of Art, Smithsonian Institution, Washington, D.C.

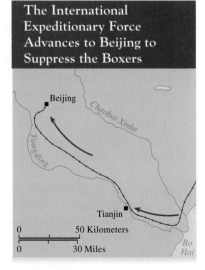

THE INTERNATIONAL EXPEDITIONARY FORCE ADVANCES TO BEIJING TO SUPPRESS THE BOXERS

⇒ **THE EMPRESS DOWAGER'S NAVY.** Historians have often interpreted the stone pavilion shown here as a symbol of the Qing dynasty's inability to comprehend the nature of the threat to its survival. At the command of Empress Dowager Cixi, funds meant to strengthen the Chinese navy against imperious Westerns at the end of the nineteenth century were used instead to construct this stone pleasure boat on the shore of a lake at the Summer Palace west of Beijing. Today the lake is a popular place for Chinese tourists.

Guangxu emperor, on the throne. For two decades, she ruled in his name as regent. Cixi interpreted Guangxu's action as a British-supported effort to reduce her influence at court. With the aid of conservatives in the army, she arrested and executed several of the reformers and had the emperor incarcerated in the palace. Kang Youwei succeeded in fleeing abroad. With Cixi's palace coup, the so-called One Hundred Days of reform came to an end.

OPENING THE DOOR TO CHINA

During the next two years, foreign pressure on the dynasty intensified. With encouragement from the British, who hoped to avert a total collapse of the Manchu Empire, U.S. Secretary of State John Hay presented the other imperialist powers with a proposal to ensure equal economic access to the China market for all states. Hay also suggested that all powers join together to guarantee the territorial and administrative integrity of the Chinese Empire. Though probably motivated more by the United States' preference for open markets than by a benevolent wish to protect China, the Open Door policy did have the practical effect of reducing the imperialist hysteria over access to the China market. That hysteria, a product of decades of mythologizing among Western commercial interests about the 400 million Chinese customers, had accelerated at the end of the century as fear of China's imminent collapse increased. The "gentlemen's agreement" about the Open Door (it was not a treaty, merely

a pious and nonbinding expression of intent) served to deflate fears in Britain, France, Germany, and Russia that other powers would take advantage of China's weakness to dominate the China market.

In the long run, then, the Open Door was a positive step that brought a measure of sanity to imperialist behavior in East Asia. Unfortunately, it came too late to stop the domestic explosion known as the Boxer Rebellion. The Boxers, so-called because of the physical exercises they performed, were members of a secret society operating primarily in rural areas in northern China. Provoked by a damaging drought and high unemployment caused in part by foreign economic activity (the introduction of railroads and steamships, for example, undercut the livelihood of barge workers on the rivers and canals), the Boxers attacked foreign residents and besieged the foreign legation quarter in Beijing until the foreigners were rescued by an international expeditionary force in the late summer of 1900. As punishment, the foreign troops destroyed a number of

The International Expeditionary Force Advances to Beijing to Suppress the Boxers

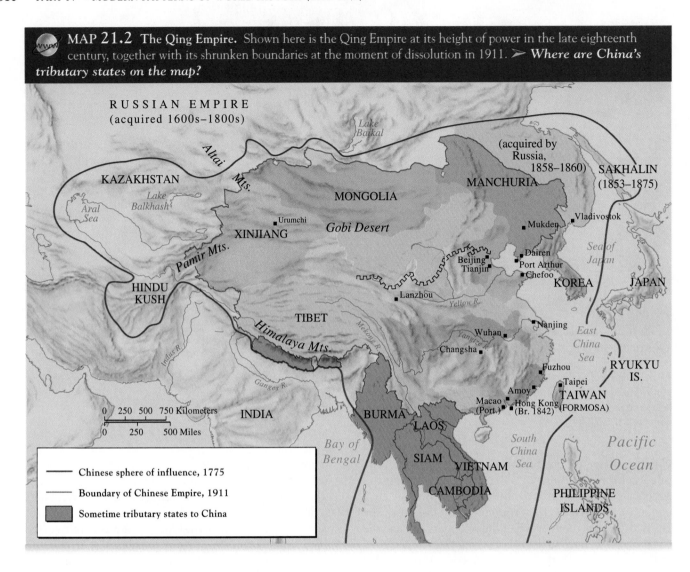

MAP 21.2 The Qing Empire. Shown here is the Qing Empire at its height of power in the late eighteenth century, together with its shrunken boundaries at the moment of dissolution in 1911. ➤ *Where are China's tributary states on the map?*

temples in the capital suburbs, and the Chinese government was compelled to pay a heavy indemnity to the foreign governments involved in suppressing the uprising.

The Collapse of the Old Order

During the next few years, the old dynasty tried desperately to reform itself. The empress dowager, who had long resisted change, now embraced a number of reforms. The venerable civil service examination system was replaced by a new educational system based on the Western model. In 1905, a commission was formed to study constitutional changes; over the next few years, legislative assemblies were established at the provincial level, and elections for a national assembly were held in 1910.

Such moves helped shore up the dynasty temporarily, but history shows that the most dangerous period for an authoritarian system is when it begins to reform itself, because change breeds instability and performance rarely matches rising expectations. Such was the case in China. The emerging new provincial elite, composed of merchants, professionals, and reform-minded gentry, soon became impatient with the slow pace of political change and were disillusioned to find that the new assemblies were intended to be primarily advisory rather than legislative. The government also alienated influential elements by financing railway development projects through foreign firms rather than local investors. The reforms also had little meaning for peasants, artisans, miners, and transportation workers, whose living conditions were being eroded by rising taxes and official venality. Rising rural unrest, as yet poorly organized and often centered on secret societies such as the Boxers, was an ominous sign of deep-seated resentment to which the dynasty would not, or could not, respond.

To China's reformist elite, such signs of social discontent were a threat to be avoided. To its tiny revolutionary movement, they were a harbinger of promise. The first physical manifestations of future revolution appeared during the last decade of the nineteenth century with the for-

PROGRAM FOR A NEW CHINA

*I*n 1905, Sun Yat-sen united a number of anti-Manchu groups into a single patriotic organization called the Revolutionary Alliance (Tongmenghui). The new organization eventually formed the core of his Guomindang, or Nationalist Party. This excerpt is from the organization's manifesto, published in 1905 in Tokyo. Note that Sun believed that the Chinese people were not ready for democracy and required a period of tutelage to prepare them for the final era of constitutional political government. This was a formula that would be adopted by many other political leaders in Asia and Africa after World War II.

SUN YAT-SEN, MANIFESTO FOR THE TONGMENGHUI

By order of the Military Government, . . . the Commander-in-Chief of the Chinese National Army proclaims the purposes and platform of the Military Government to the people of the nation:

Therefore we proclaim to the world in utmost sincerity the outline of the present revolution and the fundamental plan for the future administration of the nation.

1. *Drive out the Tartars:* The Manchus of today were originally the eastern barbarians beyond the Great Wall. They frequently caused border troubles during the Ming dynasty; then when China was in a disturbed state they came inside Shanhaikuan, conquered China, and enslaved our Chinese people. . . . The extreme cruelties and tyrannies of the Manchu government have now reached their limit. With the righteous army poised against them, we will overthrow that government, and restore our sovereign rights.

2. *Restore China:* China is the China of the Chinese. The government of China should be in the hands of the Chinese. After driving out the Tartars we must restore our national state. . . .

3. *Establish the Republic:* Now our revolution is based on equality, in order to establish a republican government. All our people are equal and all enjoy political rights. . . .

4. *Equalize land ownership:* The good fortune of civilization is to be shared equally by all the people of the nation. We should improve our social and economic organization, and assess the value of all the land in the country. Its present price shall be received by the owner, but all increases in value resulting from reform and social improvements after the revolution shall belong to the state, to be shared by all the people, in order to create a socialist state, where each family within the empire can be well supported, each person satisfied, and no one fail to secure employment. . . .

The above four points will be carried out in three steps in due order. The first period is government by military law. When the righteous army has arisen, various places will join the cause. . . . Evils like the oppression of the government, the greed and graft of officials, . . . the cruelty of tortures and penalties, the tyranny of tax collections, the humiliation of the queue [the requirement that all Chinese males braid their hair]—shall all be exterminated together with the Manchu rule. Evils in social customs, such as the keeping of slaves, the cruelty of foot binding, the spread of the poison of opium, should also all be prohibited. . . .

The second period is that of government by a provisional constitution. When military law is lifted in each *hsien* [district], the Military Government shall return the right of self-government to the local people. . . .

The third period will be government under the constitution. Six years after the provisional constitution has been enforced a constitution shall be made. The military and administrative powers of the Military Government shall be annulled; the people shall elect the president, and elect the members of parliament to organize the parliament.

---

mation of the Revive China Society by the young radical Sun Yat-sen (1866–1925). Born in a village south of Canton, Sun was educated in Hawaii and returned to China to practice medicine. Soon he turned his full attention to the ills of Chinese society.

At first, Sun's efforts yielded few positive results, but in a convention in Tokyo in 1905, he managed to unite radical groups from across China in the so-called Revolutionary Alliance (Tongmenghui, or T'ung Meng Hui). The new organization's program was based on Sun's "three people's principles" of nationalism (meaning primarily the elimination of Manchu rule over China), democracy, and people's livelihood. It called for a three-stage process

beginning with a military takeover and ending with a constitutional democracy (see the box above). Although the new organization was small and relatively inexperienced, it benefited from rising popular discontent.

In October 1911, Sun's followers launched an uprising in the industrial center of Wuhan, in central China. With Sun traveling in the United States, the insurrection lacked leadership, but the decrepit government's inability to react quickly encouraged political forces at the provincial level to take measures into their own hands. The dynasty was now in a state of virtual collapse: the empress dowager had died in 1908, one day after her nephew; the throne was now occupied by China's "last emperor," the

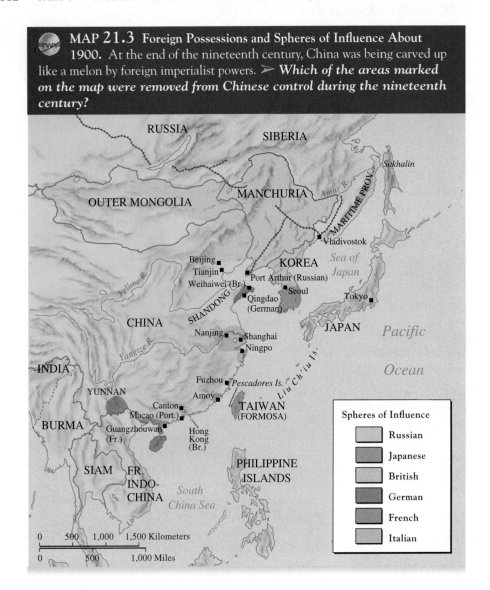

MAP 21.3 Foreign Possessions and Spheres of Influence About 1900. At the end of the nineteenth century, China was being carved up like a melon by foreign imperialist powers. ➤ *Which of the areas marked on the map were removed from Chinese control during the nineteenth century?*

infant Puyi (P'u Yi). Sun's party had neither the military strength nor the political base necessary to seize the initiative, however, and was forced to turn to a representative of the old order, General Yuan Shikai (Yuan Shih-k'ai). A prominent figure in military circles since the beginning of the century, Yuan had been placed in charge of the imperial forces sent to suppress the rebellion, but now he abandoned the Manchus and acted on his own behalf. In negotiations with representatives of Sun Yatsen's party (Sun himself had arrived in China in January 1912), he agreed to serve as president of a new Chinese republic. The old dynasty and the age-old system that it had attempted to preserve were no more.

Although the dynasty was gone, Sun and his followers were unable to consolidate their gains. The program of the Revolutionary Alliance was based on Western liberal democratic principles aimed at the urban middle class. That class and program had provided the foundation for the cap-

italist democratic revolutions in western Europe and North America in the late eighteenth and nineteenth centuries, but the middle class in China was still too small to form the basis for a new political order. The vast majority of the Chinese people still lived on the land. Sun had hoped to win their support with a land reform program, but few peasants had participated in the 1911 revolution. In failing to create new institutions and values to provide a framework for a changing society, the events of 1911 were less a revolution than a collapse of the old order. Weakened by imperialism and its own internal weaknesses, the old dynasty had come to an abrupt end before new political and social forces were ready to fill the vacuum.

What China had experienced was part of a historical process that was bringing down traditional empires across the globe, both in regions threatened by Western imperialism and in Europe itself, where tsarist Russia, the Austro-Hungarian Empire, and the Ottoman Empire all came to an end within a few years after the collapse of the Qing. The circumstances of their demise were not all the same. The Austro-Hungarian Empire, for example, was dismembered by the victorious allies after World War I, and the fate of tsarist Russia was directly linked to that conflict. Still, all four regimes shared the responsibility for their common fate in that they had failed to meet the challenges posed by the times. All had responded to the forces of industrialization and popular participation in the political process with hesitation and reluctance, and their attempts at reform were too little and too late. All paid the supreme price for their folly.

CHINESE SOCIETY IN TRANSITION

The growing Western presence in China during the late nineteenth and early twentieth centuries obviously had a major impact on Chinese society; hence many historians have asserted that the arrival of the Europeans shook China out of centuries of slumber and launched it on the road to revolutionary change. In fact, when the European economic penetration began to accelerate in the mid-nineteenth century, Chinese society was already in a state of transition. The growth of industry and trade was particularly noticeable in the cities, where a national market for such commodities as oil, copper, salt, tea, and porcelain had developed. The foundation of an infrastructure more conducive to the rise of a money economy appeared to be in place. In the countryside, new crops introduced from abroad significantly increased food production and aided population growth. The Chinese economy had never been more productive or more complex.

Whether these changes by themselves would eventually have led to an industrial revolution and the rise of a capitalist society on the Western model in the absence of Western intervention is a question that historians cannot answer. Certainly, a number of obstacles would have made it difficult for China to embark on the Western path if it had wished to do so.

Although industrial production was on the rise, it was still based almost entirely on traditional methods. There was no uniform system of weights and measures, and the banking system was still primitive by European standards. The use of paper money, invented by the Chinese centuries earlier, had essentially been abandoned. The transportation system, which had been neglected since the end of the Yuan dynasty, was increasingly chaotic. There were few paved roads, and the Grand Canal, long the most efficient means of carrying goods from north to south, was silting up. As a result, merchants had to rely more and more on the coastal route, where they faced increasing competition from foreign shipping.

Library of Congress

⟫ **MARK OF AFFLUENCE.**   During the traditional era, wealthy Chinese and important officials were commonly transported in sedan chairs carried by chair bearers. This custom was adopted by Westerners during the era of high imperialism. In this photo we see three English girls being taken on an outing by members of their household staff in Hong Kong. Even in the subtropical climate, many English residents insisted on wearing heavy clothing appropriate to the more temperate British Isles. Chinese and English alike wore hats as protection against the sun.

Although foreign concession areas in the coastal cities provided a conduit for the importation of Western technology and modern manufacturing methods, the Chinese borrowed less than they might have. Foreign manufacturing enterprises could not legally operate in China until the last decade of the nineteenth century, and their methods had little influence beyond the concession areas. Chinese efforts to imitate Western methods, notably in shipbuilding and weapons manufacture, were dominated by the government and often suffered from mismanagement.

Equally serious problems persisted in the countryside. The rapid increase in population had led to smaller plots and burgeoning numbers of tenant farmers. Whether per capita consumption of food was on the decline is not clear from the available evidence, but apparently rice as a staple of the diet was increasingly being replaced by less nutritious foods. Some farmers benefited from switching to commercial agriculture to supply the markets of the growing coastal cities, but the shift entailed a sizable investment. Many farmers went so deeply into debt that they eventually lost their land. In the meantime, the traditional patron-client relationship was frayed as landlords moved to the cities to take advantage of the glittering urban lifestyle.

Most important, perhaps, was that the Qing dynasty was still locked into a traditional mind-set that discouraged commercial activities and prized the time-honored virtues of agrarian society. China also lacked the European tradition of a vigorous and self-confident merchant class based in cities that were autonomous

Chronology

CHINA IN THE ERA OF IMPERIALISM

Lord Macartney's mission to China	1793
Opium War	1839–1842
Taiping rebels seize Nanjing	1853
Taiping Rebellion suppressed	1864
Cixi becomes regent for nephew, the Guangxu emperor	1878
Sino-Japanese War	1894–1895
One Hundred Days reform	1898
Open Door policy	1899
Boxer Rebellion	1900
Commission to study constitution formed	1905
Deaths of Cixi and the Guangxu emperor	1908
Revolution in China	1911

or even independent of the feudal political leader in the surrounding areas.

In any event, the advent of the imperialist era in the second half of the nineteenth century made such questions academic; imperialism created serious distortions in the local economy that resulted in massive changes in Chinese society during the twentieth century. Whether the Western intrusion was beneficial or harmful is debated to this day. The Western presence undoubtedly accelerated the development of the Chinese economy in some ways: the introduction of modern means of production, transport, and communications; the creation of an export market; and the steady integration of the Chinese market into the nineteenth-century global economy. To many Westerners at the time, it was self-evident that such changes would ultimately benefit the Chinese people. Western civilization represented the most advanced stage of human development. By supplying (in the catch phrase of the day) "oil for the lamps of China," it was providing a backward society with an opportunity to move up a notch or two on the ladder of human evolution.

Not everyone agreed. The Russian Marxist Vladimir Lenin contended that Western imperialism actually hindered the process of structural change in preindustrial societies because it thwarted the rise of a local industrial and commercial sector in order to maintain colonies and semi-colonies as a market for Western manufactured goods and a source of cheap labor and materials. Fellow Marxists in China such as Mao Zedong later took up Lenin's charge and asserted that if the West had not intervened, China would have found its own road to capitalism and thence to socialism and communism.

Many historians today would say that the answer was a little of both. By shaking China out of its traditional mindset, imperialism accelerated the process of change that had begun in the late Ming and early Qing periods and forced the Chinese to adopt new ways of thinking and acting. At the same time, China paid a heavy price in the destruction of its local industry while many of the profits flowed abroad. Although the Industrial Revolution is a painful process whenever and wherever it occurs, the Chinese found the experience doubly painful because it was foisted on China from the outside.

Daily Life

At the beginning of the nineteenth century, daily life for most Chinese was not substantially different from what it had been for centuries. Most were farmers, living in millions of villages in rice fields and on hillsides throughout the countryside. Their lives were governed by the harvest cycle, village custom, and family ritual. Their roles in society were firmly fixed by the time-honored principles of Confucian social ethics. Male children, at least the more fortunate ones, were educated in the Confucian classics, while females remained in the home or in the fields. All children were expected to obey their parents, wives to submit to their husbands.

A visitor to China a hundred years later would have seen a very different society, although still recognizably Chinese. Change was most striking in the coastal cities, where the educated and affluent had been visibly affected by the growing Western cultural presence. Confucian social institutions and behavioral norms were declining rapidly in influence, while those of Europe and North America were on the ascendant. Change was much less noticeable in the countryside, but even there, the customary bonds had been dangerously frayed by the rapidly changing times.

Some of the change can be traced to the educational system. During the nineteenth century, the importance of a Confucian education steadily declined as up to half of the degree holders had purchased their degrees. After 1906, when the government abolished the civil service examinations, a Confucian education ceased to be the key to a successful career, and Western-style education became more desirable. The old dynasty attempted to modernize by establishing an educational system on the Western model with universal education at the elementary level. Such plans had some effect in the cities, where public schools, missionary schools, and other private institutions educated a new generation of Chinese with little knowledge or respect for the past.

The status of women was also in transition. During the mid-Qing era, women were still expected to remain in the home. Their status as useless sex objects was painfully symbolized by the practice of foot binding, a custom that had probably originated among court entertainers in the Tang dynasty and later spread to the common people. By the mid-nineteenth century, more than half of all adult women probably had bound feet.

During the second half of the nineteenth century, signs of change began to appear. Women began to seek employment in factories—notably in cotton mills and in the silk industry, established in Shanghai in the 1890s. Some women were active in dissident activities, such as the Taiping Rebellion and the Boxer movement, and a few fought beside men in the 1911 revolution. Qiu Jin, a well-known female revolutionary, wrote a manifesto calling for women's liberation and then organized a revolt against the Manchu government, only to be captured and executed at the age of thirty-two in 1907.

By the end of the century, educational opportunities for women began to appear for the first time. Christian missionaries began to open girls' schools, mainly in the foreign concession areas. Although only a relatively small number of women were educated in these schools, they had a significant impact on Chinese society as progressive intellectuals began to argue that ignorant women produced ignorant children. In 1905, the court announced its intention to open public schools for girls, but few such schools ever materialized. Private schools for girls were established in some urban areas. The government also began to take steps to discourage the practice of foot binding, initially with only minimal success.

A RICH COUNTRY AND A STRONG STATE: THE RISE OF MODERN JAPAN

By the beginning of the nineteenth century, the Tokugawa shogunate had ruled the Japanese islands for two hundred years. It had revitalized the old governmental system, which had virtually disintegrated under its predecessors. It had driven out the foreign traders and missionaries and isolated the country from virtually all contacts with the outside world. The Tokugawa maintained formal relations only with Korea, although informal trading links with Dutch and Chinese merchants continued at Nagasaki. Isolation, however, did not mean stagnation. Although the vast majority of Japanese still

SORTING TEA WITH BOUND FEET.   To provide the best possible marriage for their daughters, upper-class families began to perform footbinding during the Song dynasty. Eventually the practice spread to all social classes in China. Although the image of small feet was supposed to denote a woman of leisure, most Chinese women with bound feet contributed to the labor force, working mainly in textiles and handicrafts to supplement the family income. Here we see five women with bound feet sorting tea leaves in Shanghai.

Photograph courtesy of Peabody Essex Museum, Neg. #A9939

depended on agriculture for their livelihood, a vigorous manufacturing and commercial sector had begun to emerge during the long period of peace and prosperity. As a result, Japanese society had begun to undergo deep-seated changes, and traditional class distinctions were becoming blurred. Eventually, these changes would end Tokugawa rule and destroy the traditional feudal system.

Some historians speculate that the Tokugawa system was beginning to come apart, just as the medieval order in Europe had started to disintegrate at the beginning of the Renaissance. Factionalism and corruption plagued the central bureaucracy, while rural unrest, provoked by a series of poor harvests brought about by bad weather, swept the countryside. Farmers fled to the towns, where anger was already rising as a result of declining agricultural incomes and shrinking stipends for the samurai. Many of the samurai lashed out at the perceived incompetence and corruption of the government. In response, the *bakufu* became increasingly rigid, persecuting its critics and attempting to force fleeing peasants to return to their lands. The government also intensified its efforts to maintain the nation's isolation from the outside world, driving away foreign ships that were beginning to prowl along the Japanese coast in increasing numbers.

An End to Isolation

To the Western powers, the continued isolation of Japanese society was an affront and a challenge. Driven by the growing rivalry among themselves and convinced that the expansion of trade on a global basis would benefit all nations, Western nations began to approach Japan in the hope of opening up the hermit kingdom to foreign economic interests.

The first to succeed was the United States. American steamships crossing the northern Pacific needed a fueling station before going on to China and other ports in the area. In the summer of 1853, an American fleet of four warships under Commodore Matthew C. Perry arrived in Edo Bay (now Tokyo Bay) with a letter from President Millard Fillmore asking for the opening of foreign relations between the two countries (see the box on p. 617). A few months later, Perry returned with a larger fleet for an answer. In his absence, Japanese officials had debated the issue. Some argued that contacts with the West would be both politically and morally disadvantageous to Japan, while others pointed to U.S. military superiority and recommended concessions. For the shogunate in Edo, the black guns of Perry's ships proved decisive, and Japan agreed to the Treaty of Kanagawa, which provided for the

SWIFT AS A SWIMMING DRAGON. When Commodore Perry arrived in Tokyo Bay with a small fleet of U.S. warships in July 1853, the size, speed, and armaments of the "black ships" frightened Japanese onlookers and undoubtedly contributed to the willingness of the Tokugawa shogunate to seek a compromise with the foreigners. One Japanese artist, who had probably never before seen a modern steamship, recorded his impression of the visitors in this imaginative painting.

A Letter to the Shogun

When U.S. Commodore Matthew Perry arrived in Tokyo Bay on his first visit to Japan, in July 1853, he carried a letter from the president of the United States, Millard Fillmore. The letter requested that trade relations between the two countries be established. The United States was already becoming a major participant in the race for the East Asian market. Little did the president know how momentous the occasion was or with what eagerness the Japanese would eventually respond to the challenge.

A LETTER FROM THE PRESIDENT OF THE UNITED STATES

Millard Fillmore
President of the United States of America,

To His Imperial Majesty,
The Emperor of Japan.

Great and Good Friend!
I send you this public letter by Commodore Matthew C. Perry, an officer of the highest rank in the Navy of the United States, and commander of the squadron now visiting your Imperial Majesty's dominions.

I have directed Commodore Perry to assure your Imperial Majesty that I entertain the kindest feelings towards your Majesty's person and government; and that I have no other object in sending him to Japan, but to propose to your Imperial Majesty that the United States and Japan should live in friendship, and have commercial intercourse with each other. The constitution and laws of the United States forbid all interference with the religious or political concerns of other nations. I have particularly charged Commodore

Perry to abstain from every act which could possibly disturb the tranquillity of your Imperial Majesty's dominions.

The United States of America reach from ocean to ocean, and our territory of Oregon and state of California lie directly opposite to the dominions of your Imperial Majesty. Our steamships can go from California to Japan in eighteen days. . . .

Japan is also a rich and fertile country, and produces many very valuable articles. . . . I am desirous that our two countries should trade with each other, for the benefit both of Japan and the United States.

We know that the ancient laws of your Imperial Majesty's government do not allow of foreign trade except with the Dutch. But as the state of the world changes, and new governments are formed, it seems to be wise from time to time to make new laws. . . . If your Imperial Majesty were so far to change the ancient laws as to allow a free trade between the two countries, it would be extremely beneficial to both. . . .

Many of our ships pass every year from California to China; and great numbers of our people pursue the whale fishery near the shores of Japan. It sometimes happens in stormy weather that one of our ships is wrecked on your Imperial Majesty's shores. In all such cases we ask and expect, that our unfortunate people should be treated with kindness, and that their property should be protected, till we can send a vessel and bring them away. . . .

May the Almighty have your Imperial Majesty in his great and holy keeping! . . .

Your Good Friend,
Millard Fillmore

---

return of shipwrecked American sailors, the opening of two ports, and the establishment of a U.S. consulate on Japanese soil. In 1858, U.S. Consul Townsend Harris negotiated a more elaborate commercial treaty calling for the opening of several ports to U.S. trade and residence, the exchange of ministers, and the granting of extraterritorial privileges for U.S. residents in Japan. Similar treaties were soon signed with several European nations.

The decision to open relations with the Western barbarians was highly unpopular in some quarters, particularly in regions distant from the shogunate headquarters in Edo. Resistance was especially strong in two of the key outside daimyo territories in the south, Satsuma and Choshu, both of which had strong military traditions. In 1863, the "Sat-Cho" alliance forced the hapless shogun to promise to end relations with the West. The shogun eventually reneged on the agreement, but the rebellious groups soon disclosed their own weakness. When Choshu troops fired on Western ships in the Strait of Shimonoseki, the Westerners fired

back and destroyed the Choshu fortifications. The incident convinced the rebellious samurai of the need to strengthen their own military and intensified their unwillingness to give in to the West. Having strengthened their influence at the imperial court in Kyoto, they demanded the shogun's resignation and the restoration of the emperor's power. In January 1868, rebel armies attacked the shogunate's palace in Kyoto and proclaimed the restored authority of the emperor. After a few weeks, resistance collapsed, and the venerable shogunate system was brought to an end.

The Meiji Restoration

Although the victory of the Sat-Cho faction had appeared on the surface to be a triumph of tradition over change, the new leaders soon realized that Japan must change to survive. Accordingly, they embarked on a policy of comprehensive reform that would lay the foundations of a modern industrial nation within a generation.

The symbol of the new era was the young emperor himself, who had taken the reign name Meiji ("enlightened rule") on ascending the throne after the death of his father in 1867. Although the post-Tokugawa period was termed a "restoration," the Meiji ruler, who shared the modernist outlook of the Sat-Cho group, was controlled by the new leadership just as the shogunate had controlled his predecessors. In tacit recognition of the real source of political power, the new capital was located at Edo (now renamed Tokyo, "eastern capital"), and the imperial court was moved to the shogun's palace in the center of the city.

THE TRANSFORMATION OF JAPANESE POLITICS

Once in power, the new leaders launched a comprehensive reform of Japanese political, social, economic, and cultural institutions and values. They moved first to abolish

⇒ **EMPEROR MEIJI.** In 1868, reformist elements overthrew the Tokugawa shogunate and launched an era of rapid modernization in Japanese society. The young Emperor Meiji, who had mounted the throne the previous year, became the symbol of Japan's effort to transform itself along Western lines. Although the emperor traditionally played no military role in Japanese society, the young monarch is shown here in a photograph that may have been especially designed to convey the martial character of the new Japan.

© Bettmann/CORBIS

the remnants of the old order and strengthen executive power in their hands. To undercut the power of the daimyo, hereditary privileges were abolished in 1871, and the great lords lost title to their lands. As compensation, they were given government bonds and were named governors of the territories formerly under their control. The samurai, comprising about 8 percent of the total population, received a lump-sum payment to replace their traditional stipends, but they were forbidden to wear the sword, the symbol of their hereditary status.

The Meiji modernizers also set out to create a modern political system on the Western model. In the Charter Oath of 1868, the new leaders promised to create a new deliberative assembly within the framework of continued imperial rule (see the box on p. 619). Although senior positions in the new government were given to the daimyo, the key posts were dominated by modernizing samurai, eventually to be known as the *genro*, or elder statesmen, from the Sat-Cho clique.

During the next two decades, the Meiji government undertook a systematic study of Western political systems. A constitutional commission under Prince Ito Hirobumi traveled to several Western countries, including Great Britain, Germany, Russia, and the United States, to study their political systems. As the process evolved, a number of factions appeared, each representing different political ideas. The most prominent were the Liberal Party and the Progressive Party. The Liberal Party favored political reform on the Western liberal democratic model with supreme authority vested in the parliament as the representative of the people. The Progressive Party called for the distribution of power between the legislative and executive branches, with a slight nod to the latter. There was also an imperial party, which advocated the retention of supreme authority exclusively in the hands of the emperor.

During the 1870s and 1880s, these factions competed for preeminence. In the end, the Progressives emerged victorious. The Meiji Constitution, which was adopted in 1890, was based on the Bismarckian model with authority vested in the executive branch; the imperialist faction was pacified by the statement that the constitution was the gift of the emperor. Members of the cabinet were to be handpicked by the Meiji oligarchs. The upper house of parliament was to be appointed and have equal legislative powers with the lower house, called the Diet, whose members would be elected. The core ideology of the state was called the *kokutai* (national polity), which embodied (although in very imprecise form) the concept of the uniqueness of the Japanese system based on the supreme authority of the emperor.

The result was a system that was democratic in form but despotic in practice, modern in appearance but still traditional in that power remained in the hands of a ruling oligarchy. The system permitted the traditional ruling class to retain its influence and economic power

PROGRAM FOR REFORM IN JAPAN

In the spring of 1868, the reformers drew up a program for transforming Japanese society along Western lines in the post-Tokugawa era. Though vague in its essentials, the Charter Oath is a good indication of the plans that were carried out during the Meiji Restoration. Compare this program with the Declaration of the Rights of Man drafted at the time of the French Revolution and discussed in Chapter 17.

THE CHARTER OATH OF EMPEROR MEIJI

By this oath we set up as our aim the establishment of the national weal on a broad basis and the framing of a constitution and laws.

1. Deliberative assemblies shall be widely established and all matters decided by public discussion.
2. All classes, high and low, shall unite in vigorously carrying out the administration of affairs of state.
3. The common people, no less than the civil and military officials, shall each be allowed to pursue his own calling so that there may be no discontent.
4. Evil customs of the past shall be broken off and everything based upon the just laws of Nature.
5. Knowledge shall be sought throughout the world so as to strengthen the foundations of imperial rule.

---

while acquiescing in the emergence of new institutions and values.

MEIJI ECONOMICS

With the end of the daimyo domains, the government needed to establish a new system of land ownership that would transform the mass of the rural population from indentured serfs into citizens. To do so, it enacted a land reform program that redefined the domain lands as the private property of the tillers while compensating the previous owner with government bonds. One reason for the new policy was that the government needed operating revenues. At the time, public funds came mainly from customs fees, which were limited by agreement with the foreign powers to 5 percent of the value of the product. To remedy the problem, the Meiji leaders added a new agriculture tax, which was set at an annual rate of 3 percent of the estimated value of the land. The new tax proved to be a lucrative and dependable source of income for the government, but it was onerous for the farmers, who had previously paid a fixed percentage of their harvest to the landowner. As a result, in bad years, many taxpaying peasants were unable to pay their taxes and were forced to sell their lands to wealthy neighbors. Eventually, the government reduced the tax to 2.5 percent of the land value. Still, by the end of the century, about 40 percent of all farmers were tenants.

With its budget needs secured, the government turned to the promotion of industry with the basic objective of guaranteeing Japan's survival against the challenge of Western imperialism. Building on the small but growing industrial economy that already existed under the Tokugawa, the Meiji reformers provided a massive stimulus to Japan's industrial revolution. The government provided financial subsidies to needy industries, training, foreign advisers, improved transport and communications, and a universal educational system emphasizing applied science. In contrast to China, Japan was able to achieve results with minimum reliance on foreign capital. Although the

first railroad—built in 1872—was financed by a loan from Great Britain, future projects were all financed by local funds. The foreign currency holdings came largely from tea and silk, which were exported in significant quantities during the latter half of the nineteenth century.

During the late Meiji era, Japan's industrial sector began to grow. Besides tea and silk, other key industries were weaponry, shipbuilding, and sake (fermented rice wine). From the start, the distinctive feature of the Meiji model was the intimate relationship between government and private business in terms of operations and regulations. Once an individual enterprise or industry was on its feet (or, sometimes, when it had ceased to make a profit), it was turned over entirely to private ownership, although the government often continued to play some role even after its direct involvement in management was terminated. One historian has explained the process:

> [The Meiji government] pioneered many industrial fields and sponsored the development of others, attempting to cajole businessmen into new and risky kinds of endeavor, helping assemble the necessary capital, forcing weak companies to merge into stronger units, and providing private entrepreneurs with aid and privileges of a sort that would be corrupt favoritism today. All this was in keeping with Tokugawa traditions that business operated under the tolerance and patronage of government. Some of the political leaders even played a dual role in politics and business.[4]

From the workers' perspective, the Meiji reforms had a less attractive side. As we have seen, the new land tax provided the funds to subsidize the growth of the industrial sector, but it imposed severe hardships on the rural population, many of whom abandoned their farms and fled to the cities, where they provided an abundant source of cheap labor for Japanese industry. As in Europe during the early decades of the Industrial Revolution, workers toiled for long hours in the coal mines and textile mills, often under horrendous conditions. Reportedly, coal miners employed on a small island in Nagasaki harbor worked naked in temperatures up to 130 degrees Fahrenheit. If they tried to escape, they were shot.

BUILDING A MODERN SOCIAL STRUCTURE

By the late Tokugawa era, the rigidly hierarchical social order was showing signs of disintegration. Rich merchants were buying their way into the ranks of the samurai, and Japanese of all classes were beginning to abandon their rice fields and move into the growing cities. Nevertheless, community and hierarchy still formed the basis of Japanese society. The lives of all Japanese were determined by their membership in various social organizations—the family, the village, and their social class. Membership in a particular social class determined a person's occupation and social relationships with others. Women in particular were constrained by the "three obediences" imposed on their sex: child to father, wife to husband, and widow to son. Husbands could easily obtain a divorce, but wives could not (one regulation allegedly decreed that a husband could divorce his spouse if she drank too much tea or talked too much). Marriages were arranged, and the average age at marriage for females was sixteen years. Females did not share inheritance rights with males, and few received any education outside the family.

The Meiji reformers destroyed much of the traditional social system in Japan. With the abolition of hereditary rights in 1871, the legal restrictions of the past were brought to an end with a single stroke. Special privileges for the aristocracy were abolished, as were the legal restrictions on the *eta*, the traditional slave class (numbering about 400,000 in the 1870s). Another key focus of the reformers was the army. The Sat-Cho reformers had been struck by the weakness of the Japanese forces in clashes with Western powers and embarked on a major program to create a military force that could compete in the modern world. The old feudal army based on the traditional warrior class was abolished, and an imperial army based on universal conscription was formed in 1871. For many rural males, the army became a route of upward mobility.

Education also underwent major changes. The Meiji leaders recognized the need for universal education including technical subjects, and after a few years of experimenting, they adopted the American model of a three-tiered system culminating in a series of universities and specialized institutes. In the meantime, they sent bright students to study abroad and brought foreign scholars to Japan to teach in the new schools, where much of the content was inspired by Western models. In another break with tradition, women for the first time were given an opportunity to get an education (see the box on p. 621).

Western influence was evident elsewhere as well. Western fashions became the rage in elite circles, and the ministers of the first Meiji government were known as the "dancing cabinet" because of their addiction to Western-style ballroom dancing. Young people, increasingly exposed to Western culture and values, began to imitate the clothing styles, eating habits, and social practices of their European and American counterparts. They even took up American sports when baseball was introduced.

The self-proclaimed transformation of Japan into a "modern society," however, by no means detached the country entirely from its traditional moorings. Although an educational order in 1872 increased the percentage of Japanese women exposed to public education, conservatives soon began to impose restrictions and bring about a return to more traditional social relationships. The importance of traditional values was underlined by the Imperial Rescript on Education in 1890 (see the box on p. 622). Displayed in every school and recited by the students, it stressed the Confucian virtues of filial piety, patriotism, and loyalty to the family and community. Traditional values were given a firm legal basis in the Constitution of 1890, which restricted the franchise to males and defined individual liberties as "subject to the limitations imposed by law," and by the Civil Code of 1898, which deemphasized individual rights and essentially placed women within the context of their role in the family.

By the end of the nineteenth century, however, changes were under way as women began to play a crucial role in their nation's effort to modernize. Urged by their parents to augment the family income, as well as by the government to fulfill their patriotic duty, young girls were sent en masse to work in textile mills. From 1894 to 1912, women represented 60 percent of the Japanese labor force. Thanks to them, by 1914, Japan was the world's leading exporter of silk and dominated cotton manufacturing. If it had not been for the export revenues earned from textile exports, Japan might not have been able to develop its heavy industry and military prowess without an infusion of foreign capital.

⤳ **THE GINZA IN DOWNTOWN TOKYO.** This 1877 wood-block print shows the Ginza (a major commercial thoroughfare) in downtown Tokyo, with modern brick buildings, rickshaws, and a horse-drawn streetcar. The centerpiece and focus of public attention is a new electric streetlight.

© Scala/Art Resource, NY

"In the Beginning, We Were the Sun"

One aspect of Western thought that the Meiji reformers did not seek to imitate was the idea of sexual equality. Although Japanese women sometimes tried to be "modern" like their male counterparts, Japanese society as a whole continued to treat women differently, as had been the case during the Tokugawa era. In 1911, a young woman named Hiratsuka Raicho founded a journal named Seito *(Blue Stockings) to promote the liberation of women in Japan. The goal of the new movement was to encourage women to develop their own latent talents, rather than to demand legal changes in Japanese society. The following document is the proclamation that was issued at the creation of the Seito Society. Compare it to Mary Wollstonecraft's discussion of the rights of women in Chapter 17.*

HIRATSUKA RAICHO, PROCLAMATION AT THE FOUNDING OF THE SEITO SOCIETY

Freedom and Liberation! Oftentimes we have heard the term "liberation of women." But what is it then? Are we not seriously misunderstanding the term freedom or liberation? Even if we call the problem the liberation of women, are there not many other issues involved? Assuming that women are freed from external oppression, liberated from constraint, given the so-called higher education, employed in various occupations, given franchise, and provided an opportunity to be independent from the protection of their parents and husbands, and to be freed from the little confinement of their homes, can all of these be called liberation of women? They may provide proper surroundings and opportunities to let us fulfill the true goal of liberation. Yet they remain merely the means, and do not represent our goal or ideals.

However, I am unlike many intellectuals in Japan who suggest that higher education is not necessary for women. Men and women are endowed by nature to have equal faculties. Therefore, it is odd to assume that one of the sexes requires education while the other does not. This may be tolerated in a given country and in a given age, but it is fundamentally a very unsound proposition.

I bemoan the facts that there is only one private college for women in Japan, and that there is no tolerance on man's part to permit entrance of women into many universities maintained for men. However, what benefit is there when the intellectual level of women becomes similar to that of men? Men seek knowledge in order to escape from their lack of wisdom and lack of enlightenment. They want to free themselves. . . . Yet multifarious thought can darken true wisdom, and lead men away from nature. . . .

Now, what is the true liberation which I am seeking? It is none other than to provide an opportunity for women to develop fully their hidden talents and hidden abilities. We must remove all the hindrances that stand in the way of women's development, whether they be external oppression or lack of knowledge. And above and beyond these factors, we must realize that we are the masters in possession of great talents, for we are the bodies which enshrine the great talents.

Japanese women received few rewards, however, for their contribution to the nation. In 1900, new regulations prohibited women from joining political organizations or attending public meetings. Beginning in 1905, a group of independent-minded women petitioned the Japanese parliament to rescind this restriction, but it was not repealed until 1922.

Joining the Imperialist Club

Traditionally, Japan had not been an expansionist country. As we have seen, except for sporadic forays against Korea, the Japanese had generally been satisfied to remain on their home islands and had even deliberately isolated themselves from their neighbors during the Tokugawa era. Now, however, the Japanese did not just imitate the domestic policies of their Western mentors; they also emulated the Western approach to foreign affairs. This is perhaps not surprising. The Japanese regarded themselves as particularly vulnerable in the world economic arena. Their territory was small, lacking in resources, and densely populated, and they had no natural outlet for expansion. To observant Japanese, the lessons of history were clear. West-

ern nations had amassed wealth and power not only because of their democratic systems and high level of education but also because of their colonies.

The Japanese began their program of territorial expansion close to home (see Map 21.4). In 1874, the Japanese claimed compensation from China for fifty-four sailors from the Ryukyu Islands who had been killed by aborigines on the island of Taiwan and sent a Japanese fleet to Taiwan to punish the perpetrators. When the Qing dynasty evaded responsibility for the incident while agreeing to pay an indemnity to Japan to cover the cost of the expedition, it weakened its claim to ownership of the island of Taiwan. Japan was then able to claim suzerainty over the Ryukyu Islands, long tributary to the Chinese Empire. Two years later, Japanese naval pressure forced Korea to open three ports to Japanese commerce.

During the early decades of the nineteenth century, Korea had followed Japan's example and attempted to isolate itself from outside contact except for periodic tribute missions to China. Christian missionaries, mostly Chinese or French, were vigorously persecuted. But Korea's problems were basically internal. In the early 1860s, a peasant revolt, inspired in part by the Taiping Rebellion in China, caused

THE RULES OF GOOD CITIZENSHIP
IN MEIJI JAPAN

After seizing power from the Tokugawa shogunate in 1868, the new Japanese leaders turned their attention to the creation of a new political system that would bring the country into the modern world. After exploring various systems in use in the West, a constitutional commission decided to adopt the system used in imperial Germany because of its paternalistic character. To promote civic virtue and obedience among the citizenry, the government then drafted an imperial rescript that was to be taught to every schoolchild in the country. The rescript instructed all children to obey their sovereign and place the interests of the community and the state above their own personal desires.

IMPERIAL RESCRIPT ON EDUCATION OF 1890

Know ye, Our subjects:

Our Imperial Ancestors have founded Our Empire on a basis broad and everlasting, and have deeply and firmly implanted virtue. Our subjects ever united in loyalty and filial piety have from generation to generation illustrated the beauty thereof. This is the glory of the fundamental character of Our Empire, and herein also lies the source of Our education. Ye, Our subjects, be filial to your parents, affectionate to your brothers and sisters, as husbands and wives be harmonious, as friends true; bear yourselves in modesty and moderation; extend your benevolence to all; pursue learning and cultivate arts, and thereby develop intellectual faculties and perfect moral powers; furthermore, advance public good and promote common interests; always respect the Constitution and observe the laws; should emergency arise, offer yourselves to the State; and thus guard and maintain the prosperity of Our Imperial Throne coeval with heaven and earth. So shall ye not only be Our good and faithful subjects, but render illustrious the best traditions of your forefathers.

---

considerable devastation before being crushed in 1864. In succeeding years, the Yi dynasty sought to strengthen the country by returning to traditional values and fending off outside intrusion, but rural poverty and official corruption remained rampant. A U.S. fleet, following the example of Commodore Perry in Japan, sought to open the country in 1871 but was driven off with considerable loss of life.

Korea's most persistent suitor, however, was Japan, which was determined to bring an end to Korea's dependency status with China and modernize it along Japanese lines. In 1876, the two countries signed an agreement opening three treaty ports to Japanese commerce in return for Japanese recognition of Korean independence. During the 1880s, Sino-Japanese rivalry over Korea intensified. China supported conservatives at the Korean court, while Japan promoted a more radical faction that was determined to break loose from lingering Chinese influence. When a new peasant rebellion broke out in Korea in 1894, China and Japan intervened on opposite sides. During the war, the Japanese navy destroyed the Chinese fleet and seized the Manchurian city of Port Arthur (see the box on p. 623). In the Treaty of Shimonoseki, the Manchus were forced to recognize the independence of Korea and cede Taiwan and the Liaodong peninsula with its strategic naval base at Port Arthur to Japan.

Shortly thereafter, under pressure from the European powers, the Japanese returned the Liaodong peninsula to China, but in the early twentieth century, they went back on the offensive. Rivalry with Russia over influence in Korea led to increasingly strained relations between the two countries. In 1904, Japan launched a surprise attack on the Russian naval base at Port Arthur, which Russia had taken from China in 1898. The Japanese armed forces were weaker, but Russia faced difficult logistical problems along its new Trans-Siberian Railway and severe political instability at home. In 1905, after Japanese warships sank almost the entire Russian fleet off the coast of Korea, the Russians agreed to a humiliating peace, ceding the strategically located Liaodong peninsula back to Japan, as well as southern Sakhalin and the Kurile Islands. Russia also agreed to abandon its political and economic influence in Korea and southern Manchuria, which now came increasingly under Japanese control. The Japanese victory stunned the world, including the colonial peoples of Southeast Asia, who now began to realize that the white race was not necessarily invincible.

During the next few years, the Japanese consolidated their position in northeastern Asia, annexing Korea in 1908 as an integral part of Japan. When the Koreans protested the seizure, Japanese reprisals resulted in thousands of deaths. The United States was the first nation to recognize the annexation in return for Tokyo's declaration of respect for U.S. authority in the Philippines. In 1908, the United States recognized Japanese interests in the region in return for Japanese acceptance of the principles of the Open Door. But mutual suspicion between the two countries was growing, sparked in part by U.S. efforts to restrict immigration from all Asian countries. President Theodore Roosevelt, who mediated the Russo-Japanese War, had aroused the anger of many Japanese by turning down a Japanese demand for reparations from Russia. In turn, some Americans began to fear the rise of a "yellow peril" manifested by Japanese expansion in East Asia.

TWO VIEWS OF THE WORLD

During the nineteenth century, China's hierarchical way of looking at the outside world came under severe challenge, not only from European countries avid for new territories in Asia but also from the rising power of Japan, which accepted the Western view that a colonial empire was the key to national greatness. Japan's first objective was Korea, long a dependency of China, and in 1894, the competition between China and Japan in the peninsula led to war. The following declarations of war by the rulers of the two countries are revealing. Note the Chinese use of the derogatory term wojen *(dwarf people) in referring to Japan.*

DECLARATION OF WAR AGAINST CHINA

Korea is an independent state. She was first introduced into the family of nations by the advice and guidance of Japan. It has, however, been China's habit to designate Korea as her dependency, and both openly and secretly to interfere with her domestic affairs. At the time of the recent insurrection in Korea, China despatched troops thither, alleging that her purpose was to afford a succor to her dependent state. We, in virtue of the treaty concluded with Korea in 1882, and looking to possible emergencies, caused a military force to be sent to that country.

Wishing to procure for Korea freedom from the calamity of perpetual disturbance, and thereby to maintain the peace of the East in general, Japan invited China's cooperation for the accomplishment of the object. But China, advancing various pretexts, declined Japan's proposal. . . . Such conduct on the part of China is not only a direct injury to the rights and interests of this Empire, but also a menace to the permanent peace and tranquility of the Orient. . . . In this situation, . . . we find it impossible to avoid a formal declaration of war against China.

DECLARATION OF WAR AGAINST JAPAN

Korea has been our tributary for the past two hundred odd years. She has given us tribute all this time, which is a matter known to the world. For the past dozen years or so Korea has been troubled by repeated insurrections and we, in sympathy with our small tributary, have as repeatedly sent succor to her aid. . . . This year another rebellion was begun in Korea, and the King repeatedly asked again for aid from us to put down the rebellion. We then ordered Li Hung-chang to send troops to Korea; and they having barely reached Yashan the rebels immediately scattered. But the *Wojen*, without any cause whatever, suddenly sent their troops to Korea, and entered Seoul, the capital of Korea, reinforcing them constantly until they have exceeded ten thousand men. In the meantime the Japanese forced the Korean king to change his system of government, showing a disposition every way of bullying the Koreans. . . .

As Japan has violated the treaties and not observed international laws, and is now running rampant with her false and treacherous actions commencing hostilities herself, and laying herself open to condemnation by the various powers at large, we therefore desire to make it known to the world that we have always followed the paths of philanthropy and perfect justice throughout the whole complications, while the *Wojen*, on the other hand, have broken all the laws of nations and treaties which it passes our patience to bear with. Hence we commanded Li Hung-chang to give strict orders to our various armies to hasten with all speed to root the *Wojen* out of their lairs.

Japanese Culture in Transition

The wave of Western technology and ideas that entered Japan in the second half of the nineteenth century greatly altered the shape of traditional Japanese culture. Literature in particular was affected as European models eclipsed the repetitive and frivolous tales of the Tokugawa era. Dazzled by this "new" literature, Japanese authors began translating and imitating the imported models. Experimenting with Western verse, Japanese poets were at first influenced primarily by the British but eventually adopted such French styles as Symbolism, Dadaism, and Surrealism, although some traditional poetry was still composed.

As the Japanese invited technicians, engineers, architects, and artists from Europe and the United States to teach their "modern" skills to a generation of eager students, the Meiji era became a time of massive consumption of Western artistic techniques and styles. Japanese architects and artists created huge buildings of steel and reinforced concrete adorned with Greek columns and cupolas, oil paintings reflecting the European concern with depth perception and shading, and bronze sculptures of secular subjects. All expressed the individual creator's emotional and aesthetic preferences.

Cultural exchange also went the other way as Japanese arts and crafts, porcelains, textiles, fans, folding screens, and woodblock prints became the vogue in Europe and North America. Japanese art influenced Western painters such as Vincent van Gogh, Edgar Degas, and James Whistler, who experimented with flatter compositional perspectives and unusual poses. Japanese gardens, with their exquisite attention to the positioning of rocks and falling water, became especially popular in the United States.

After the initial period of mass absorption of Western art, a national reaction occurred at the end of the nineteenth century as many artists returned to pre-Meiji techniques. In 1889, the Tokyo School of Fine Arts (today the

JAPAN AND KOREA IN THE ERA OF IMPERIALISM

Commodore Perry arrives in Tokyo Bay	1853
Townsend Harris Treaty	1858
Fall of Tokugawa Shogunate	1868
U.S. fleet fails to open Korea	1871
Feudal titles abolished	1871
Imperial army formed	1871
Meiji Constitution adopted	1890
Imperial Rescript on Education	1890
Treaty of Shimonoseki awards Taiwan to Japan	1895
Russo-Japanese War	1904–1905
Korea annexed	1908

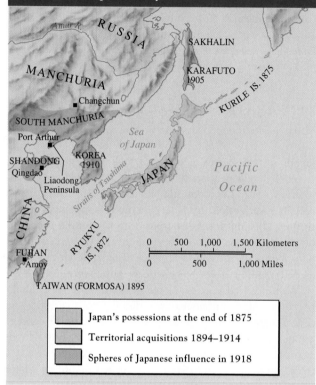

MAP 21.4 Japanese Overseas Expansion During the Meiji Era. Beginning in the late nineteenth century, Japan ventured beyond its home islands and became an imperialist power. The extent of Japanese colonial expansion through World War I is shown here. ➤ **Which parts of imperial China were now under Japanese influence?**

Japan's possessions at the end of 1875

Territorial acquisitions 1894–1914

Spheres of Japanese influence in 1918

Tokyo National University of Fine Arts and Music) was founded to promote traditional Japanese art. Over the next several decades, Japanese art underwent a dynamic resurgence, reflecting the nation's emergence as a prosperous and powerful state. While some Japanese artists attempted to synthesize native and foreign techniques, others returned to past artistic traditions for inspiration.

In architecture, Japan's split personality revealed itself most effectively in the Diet building. As the home of the new Japanese parliament, it was supposed to reflect both progress and the nation and culture of Japan. For half a century, conflicting views over the priority of these concepts delayed its construction. After a number of proposals were rejected, the government held a competition in 1919, but none of the designs won general approval. Finally, in 1936 the government decided on the final design, which followed neither traditional styles nor European architecture of the period.

The Meiji Restoration: A Revolution from Above

Japan's transformation from a feudal, agrarian society to an industrializing, technologically advanced society in little more than half a century has frequently been described by outside observers (if not by the Japanese themselves) in almost miraculous terms. Some historians have questioned this characterization, pointing out that the achievements of the Meiji leaders were spotty. In *Japan's Emergence as a Modern State*, the Canadian historian E. H. Norman lamented that the Meiji Restoration was an "incomplete revolution" because it had not ended the economic and social inequities of feudal society or enabled the common people to partici-

pate fully in the governing process. Although the *genro* were enlightened in many respects, they were also despotic and elitist, and the distribution of wealth remained as unequal as it had been under the old system.[5]

These criticisms are persuasive, although they could also be applied to most other societies going through the early stages of industrialization. In any event, from an economic perspective, the Meiji Restoration was certainly one of the great success stories of modern times. Not only did the Meiji leaders put Japan firmly on the path to economic and political development, but they also managed to remove the unequal treaty provisions that had been imposed at mid-century. Japanese achievements are especially impressive when compared with the difficulties experienced by China, which was not only unable to realize significant changes in its traditional society but had not even reached a consensus on the need for doing so. Japan's achievements more closely resemble those of Europe, but whereas the West needed a century and a half to achieve a significant level of industrial development, the Japanese realized it in forty years.

One of the distinctive features of Japan's transition from a traditional to a modern society during the Meiji era was

⟫ KURODA SEIKI, *BY THE LAKE*. With foreign travel no longer banned during the Meiji era, Japanese artists, eager to catch up on Western techniques, were free to study abroad. There were intimidating obstacles to overcome, however, such as learning how to paint on a rough canvas with oil paint and stiff Western-style brushes. Moreover, Japanese artists were taught to reproduce objective reality by using shading and three-dimensional perspectives. One of the most outstanding artists of the time was Kuroda Seiki (1866–1924), who returned from nine years in Paris to open a Western-style school of painting in Tokyo. His celebrated painting of a nude woman, acclaimed in the West, shocked many Japanese viewers, who considered it pornographic. *By the Lake* (1897) is an excellent example of the fusion of contemporary French painting with the Japanese tradition of courtesan prints.

that it took place for the most part without violence or the kind of social or political revolution that occurred in so many other countries. The Meiji Restoration, which began the process, has been called a "revolution from above," a comprehensive restructuring of Japanese society by its own ruling group.

Technically, of course, the Meiji Restoration was not a revolution, since it was not violent and did not result in the displacement of one ruling class by another. The existing elites undertook to carry out a series of major reforms that transformed society but left their own power intact. In the words of one historian, it was "a kind of amalgamation, in which the enterprising, adaptable, or lucky individuals of the old privileged classes [were] for most practical purposes tied up with those individuals of the old submerged classes, who, probably through the same gifts, were able to rise." In that respect, the Meiji Restoration resembles the American Revolution more than the French Revolution; it was a "conservative revolution" that resulted in gradual change rather than rapid and violent change.[6]

The differences between the Japanese response to the West and that of China and many other nations in the region have sparked considerable debate among students of comparative history, and a number of explanations have been offered. Some have argued that Japan's success was partly due to good fortune. Lacking abundant natural resources, it was exposed to less pressure from the West than many of its neighbors. That argument is problematic, however, and would probably not have been accepted by Japanese observers at the time. Nor does it explain why nations under considerably less pressure, such as Laos and Nepal, did not advance even more quickly. All in all, the luck hypothesis is not very persuasive.

Some explanations have already been suggested in this book. Japan's unique geographical position in Asia was certainly a factor. China, a continental nation with a heterogeneous ethnic composition, was distinguished from its neighbors by its Confucian culture. By contrast, Japan was an island nation, ethnically and linguistically homogeneous, and had never been conquered. Unlike the Chinese or many other peoples in the region, the Japanese had little to fear from cultural change in terms of its effect on their national identity. If Confucian culture, with all its accouterments, was what defined the Chinese gentleman, his Japanese counterpart, in the familiar image, could discard his sword and kimono and don a modern military uniform or a Western business suit and still feel comfortable in both worlds.

Whatever the case, as the historian W. G. Beasley has noted, the Meiji Restoration was possible because aristocratic and capitalist elements managed to work together in a common effort to bring about national wealth and power. The nature of the Japanese value system, with its emphasis on practicality and military achievement, may also have contributed. Finally, the Meiji also benefited from the fact that the pace of urbanization and commercial and industrial development had already begun to quicken under the Tokugawa. Japan, it was said, was ripe for change, and nothing could have been more suitable as an antidote for the collapsing old system than the Western emphasis on wealth and power. It was a classic example of challenge and response.

The final product was an amalgam of old and new, native and foreign, forming a new civilization that was still uniquely Japanese. There were some undesirable consequences, however. Because Meiji politics was essentially despotic, Japanese leaders were able to fuse key traditional elements such as the warrior ethic and the concept of feudal loyalty with the dynamics of modern industrial capitalism to create a state totally dedicated to the possession of material wealth and national power. This combination of *kokutai* and capitalism, which one scholar has described as a form of "Asian fascism," was highly effective but explosive in its international manifestation. Like modern Germany, which also entered the industrial age directly from feudalism, Japan eventually engaged in a policy of repression at home and expansion abroad in order to achieve its national objectives. In Japan, as in Germany, it took defeat in war to disconnect the drive for national development from the feudal ethic and bring about the transformation to a pluralistic society dedicated to living in peace and cooperation with its neighbors.

CONCLUSION

Few areas of the world resisted the Western incursion as stubbornly and effectively as East Asia. Although military, political, and economic pressure by the European powers was relatively intense during this era, two of the main states in the area were able to retain their independence, while the third—Korea—was temporarily absorbed by one of its larger neighbors. Why the Chinese and the Japanese were able to prevent a total political and military takeover by foreign powers is an interesting question. One key reason was that both had a long history as well-defined states with a strong sense of national community and territorial cohesion. Although China had frequently been conquered, it had retained its sense of unique culture and identity. Geography, too, was in its favor. As a continental nation, China was able to survive partly because of its sheer size. Japan possessed the advantage of an island location.

Even more striking, however, is the different way in which the two states attempted to deal with the challenge. While the Japanese chose to face the problem in a pragmatic manner, borrowing foreign ideas and institutions that appeared to be of value and at the same time not in conflict with traditional attitudes and customs, China agonized over the issue for half a century while conservative elements fought a desperate battle to retain a maximum of the traditional heritage intact.

This chapter has discussed some of the possible reasons for those differences. In retrospect, it is difficult to avoid the conclusion that the Japanese approach was the more effective one. Whereas the Meiji leaders were able to set in motion an orderly transition from a traditional to an advanced society, in China the old system collapsed in disorder, leaving chaotic conditions that were still not rectified a generation later. China would pay a heavy price for its failure to respond coherently to the challenge.

But the Japanese "revolution from above" was by no means an unalloyed success. Ambitious efforts by Japanese leaders to carve out a share in the spoils of empire led to escalating conflict with China as well as with rival Western powers and in the early 1940s to global war. We will deal with that issue in Chapter 24. Meanwhile, in Europe, a combination of old rivalries and the effects of the Industrial Revolution were leading to a bitter regional conflict that eventually engulfed the entire world.

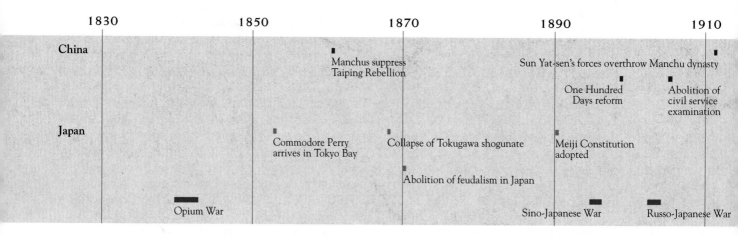

CHAPTER NOTES

1. Hosea Ballou Morse, *The International Relations of the Chinese Empire* (London, 1910–1918), vol. 2, p. 622.
2. Quoted in Ssu-yu Teng and John K. Fairbank, eds., *China's Response to the West: A Documentary Survey, 1839–1923* (New York, 1970), p. 140.
3. Ibid., p. 167.
4. John K. Fairbank, Albert M. Craig, and Edwin O. Reischauer, *East Asia: Tradition and Transformation* (Boston, 1973), p. 514.
5. Quoted in John W. Dower, ed., *The Origins of the Modern Japanese State: Selected Writings of E. H. Norman* (New York, 1975), p. 13.
6. Crane Brinton, *The Anatomy of Revolution* (New York, 1965), quoted in W. G. Beasley, *The Meiji Restoration* (Stanford, Calif., 1972), p. 423.

SUGGESTED READING

For a general overview of this period of East Asian history, see C. Schirokauer, *Modern China and Japan: A Brief History* (New York, 1982), and J. K. Fairbank, A. M. Craig, and E. O. Reischauer, *East Asia: Tradition and Transformation* (Boston, 1973). See also J.D. Spence's highly stimulating *Search for Modern China* (New York, 1990); *The Cambridge History of China,* vols. 10–11 (Cambridge, 1978–1980), dealing with the Qing period; and *The Cambridge History of Japan,* vols. 5–6 (Cambridge, 1988).

On the Western intrusion into China during the nineteenth century, see the classic work by J. K. Fairbank, *Trade and Diplomacy on the China Coast* (Cambridge, 1953), and F. Wakeman, *Strangers at the Gate: Social Disorder in South China, 1839–1861* (Berkeley, Calif., 1966). On the Opium War, see A. Waley, *The Opium War Through Chinese Eyes* (London, 1958), and P. W. Fay, *The Opium War, 1840–1842* (Chapel Hill, N.C., 1975). On the Taiping Rebellion, see F. Michael and C. Chung-li, *The Taiping Rebellion: History and Documents,* 3 vols. (Seattle, 1966–1971), and J. D. Spence, *God's Chinese Son: The Taiping Heavenly Kingdom of Hong Xiuquan* (New York, 1996).

There are a number of important works on the final decades of the Chinese Empire. For a general overview, see F. Wakeman Jr., *The Fall of Imperial China* (New York, 1975). For economic developments, see A. Feuerwerker's classic *China's Early Industrialization: Sheng Hsuan-huai and Mandarin Enterprise* (Cambridge, 1958). China's response to the Western challenge is chronicled in S. Teng and J. K. Fairbank, eds., *China's Response to the West: A Documentary Survey, 1839–1923* (New York, 1970).

On the 1911 revolution, see M. C. Wright, ed., *China in Revolution: The First Phase, 1900–1913* (New Haven, Conn., 1968). Sun Yat-sen's career is explored in M. C. Bergère, *Sun Yat-sen,* trans. J. Lloyd (Stanford, Calif., 2000). On the Boxer Rebellion, the definitive study is J. Esherick, *The Origins of the Boxer Uprising* (Berkeley, Calif., 1987). Also see D. Preston, *The Boxer Rebellion: The Dramatic Story of China's War on Foreigners That Shook the World in the Summer of 1900* (Berkeley, Calif., 2001).

For a recent survey of modern Japanese history, see J. Hunter, *The Emergence of Modern Japan: An Introductory History Since 1853* (London, 1989). See also J. W. Dower, ed., *The Origins of the Modern Japanese State: Selected Writings of E. H. Norman* (New York, 1975).

The Meiji period is discussed in W. G. Beasley, *The Meiji Restoration* (Stanford, Calif., 1972). An earlier and more controversial view is E. H. Norman, *Japan's Emergence as a Modern State: Political and Economic Problems of the Meiji Period* (New York, 1940). See also C. Gluck, *Japan's Modern Myths: Ideology in the Late Meiji Period* (Princeton, N.J., 1985); C. Totman, *The Collapse of the Tokugawa Bakufu, 1862–1868* (Honolulu, 1980); and M. B. Jansen, ed., *The Emergence of Meiji Japan* (Cambridge, 1995).

On the economy, see R. Smethurst, *Agricultural Development and Tenancy Disputes in Japan, 1870–1940* (Princeton, N.J., 1986), and G. C. Allen, *A Short Economic History of Japan, 1867–1937* (London, 1972). Social developments are examined in R. Dore, ed., *Aspects of Social Change in Modern Japan* (Princeton, N.J., 1967). The rise of the modern Japanese army is chronicled in R. F. Hackett, *Yamagata Aritomo and the Rise of Meiji Japan* (Cambridge, 1971). For the best introduction to Japanese art, consult P. Mason, *History of Japanese Art* (New York, 1993). See also J. S. Baker's concise *Japanese Art* (London, 1984).

On Japan's emergence as an imperialist power, see A. Iriye, *Pacific Estrangement: Japanese and American Expansion, 1897–1911* (Cambridge, 1972); M. R. Peattie and R. Myers, *The Japanese Colonial Empire, 1895–1945* (Princeton, N.J., 1984); and M. B. Jansen, *Japan and Its World: Two Centuries of Change* (Princeton, N.J., 1980).

For a brief introduction to the women of this era in China and Japan, see S. Hughes and B. Hughes, *Women in World History* (Armonk, N.Y., 1997). For a more detailed account, consult O. Kazuko, *Chinese Women in a Century of Revolution, 1850–1950,* ed. J. A. Fogel (Stanford, Calif., 1989), and O. Kazuko, *Japanese Women: New Feminist Perspectives on the Past, Present, and Future,* ed. K. Fujimura-Fanselow and A. Kameda (New York, 1995).

INFOTRAC COLLEGE EDITION

For additional reading, go to InfoTrac College Edition, your online research library at
http://web1.infotrac-college.com

Enter the search terms "China history" using Keywords.

Enter the search term "Qing" using Keywords.

Enter the search terms "Sun Yat-sen" using Keywords.

Enter the search terms "Japan history" using Keywords.

Enter the search term "Meiji" using Keywords.

© Sovfoto

THE BEGINNING OF THE TWENTIETH-CENTURY CRISIS: WAR AND REVOLUTION

CHAPTER OUTLINE

FOCUS QUESTIONS

- What were the long-range and immediate causes of World War I, and why did the course of the war turn out to be so different from what the belligerents had expected?
- How did World War I affect the belligerents' governmental and political institutions, economic affairs, and social life?
- What were the causes of the Russian Revolution of 1917, and why did the Bolsheviks prevail in the civil war and gain control of Russia?
- What were the objectives of the chief participants at the Paris Peace Conference of 1919, and how closely did the final settlement mirror their objectives?
- What crises did Europe and the United States face in the interwar years, and how did the cultural and intellectual trends of that period reflect those crises as well as the experience of World War I?
- ➢ What was the relationship between World War I and the Russian Revolution?

On July 1, 1916, British and French infantry forces attacked German defensive lines along a 25-mile front near the Somme River in France. Each soldier carried almost 70 pounds of equipment, making it "impossible to move much quicker than a slow walk." German machine guns soon opened fire: "We were able to see our comrades move forward in an attempt to cross No-Man's-Land, only to be mown down like meadow grass," recalled one British soldier. "I felt sick at the sight of this carnage and remember weeping." In one day, more than 21,000 British soldiers died. After six months of fighting, the British had advanced 5 miles; one million British, French, and German soldiers had been killed or wounded.

World War I (1914–1918) was the defining event of the twentieth century. Overwhelmed by the scale of its battles, the extent of its casualties, and the effects of its impact on all facets of life, contemporaries referred to it simply as the "Great War." The Great War was all the more disturbing to Europeans because it came after what many believed to have been an age of progress. Material prosperity and a fervid belief in scientific and technological advancement had convinced many people that the world stood on the verge of creating the utopia that humans had dreamed of for centuries. The historian Arnold Toynbee expressed what the pre–World War I era had meant to his generation:

> [we had expected] that life throughout the World would become more rational, more humane, and more democratic and that, slowly, but surely, political democracy would produce greater social justice. We had also expected that the progress of science and technology would make mankind richer, and that this increasing wealth would gradually spread from a minority to a majority. We had expected that all this would happen peacefully. In fact we thought that mankind's course was set for an earthly paradise.[1]

After 1918, it was no longer possible to maintain naive illusions about the progress of Western civilization. As World War I was followed by revolutionary upheavals, the mass murder machines of totalitarian regimes, and the destructiveness of World War II, it became all too apparent that instead of a utopia, Western civilization had become a nightmare. World War I and the revolutions it spawned can properly be seen as the first stage in the crisis of the twentieth century. •

THE ROAD TO WORLD WAR I

On June 28, 1914, the heir to the Austrian throne, the Archduke Francis Ferdinand, was assassinated in the Bosnian city of Sarajevo. Although this event precipitated the confrontation between Austria and Serbia that led to World War I, underlying forces had been propelling Europeans toward armed conflict for a long time.

Nationalism and Internal Dissent

In the first half of the nineteenth century, liberals had maintained that the organization of European states along national lines would lead to a peaceful Europe based on a sense of international fraternity. They could not have been more wrong. The system of nation-states that had emerged in Europe in the second half of the nineteenth century (see Map 22.1) led not to cooperation but to competition. Rivalries over colonies and trade intensified during a frenzied imperialist expansion, while the division of Europe's great powers into two loose alliances (Germany, Austria, and Italy; and France, Great Britain, and Russia) only added to the tensions. The series of crises that tested these alliances in the 1900s and early 1910s had left European states embittered, eager for revenge, and willing to revert to war as an acceptable way to preserve the power of their national states.

The growth of nationalism in the nineteenth century had yet another serious consequence. Not all ethnic groups had achieved the goal of nationhood. Slavic minorities in the Balkans and the polyglot Habsburg Empire, for example, still dreamed of creating their own national states. So did the Irish in the British Empire and the Poles in the Russian Empire.

National aspirations, however, were not the only source of internal strife at the beginning of the twentieth century. Socialist labor movements had grown more powerful and were increasingly inclined to use strikes, even violent ones, to achieve their goals. Some conservative leaders, alarmed at the increase in labor strife and class division, even feared that European nations were on the verge of revolution. Did these statesmen opt for war in 1914 because they believed that "prosecuting an active foreign policy," as some Austrian leaders expressed it, would smother "internal troubles"? Some historians have argued that the desire to suppress internal disorder may have encouraged some leaders to take the plunge into war in 1914.

Militarism

The growth of large mass armies after 1900 not only heightened the existing tensions in Europe but also made it inevitable that if war did come, it would be extremely destructive. Conscription had been established as a regular practice in most Western countries before 1914 (the United States and Britain were major exceptions). European military machines had doubled in size between 1890 and 1914. With its 1.3 million men, the Russian army had grown to be the largest, but the French and Germans were not far behind, with 900,000 each. The British, Italian, and Austrian armies numbered between 250,000 and 500,000 soldiers.

Militarism, however, involved more than just large armies. As armies grew, so did the influence of military leaders, who drew up vast and complex plans for quickly mobilizing millions of men and enormous quantities of supplies in the event of war. Fearful that changing these

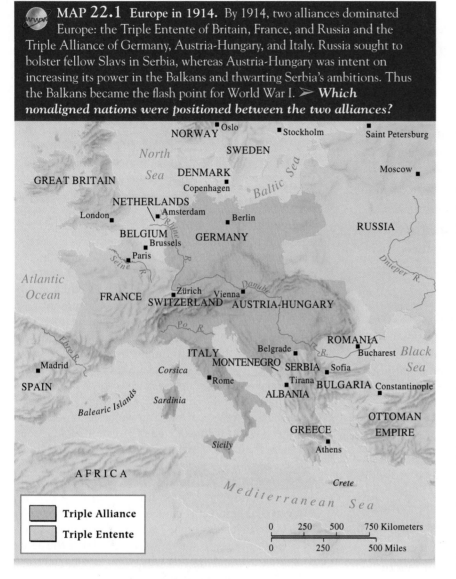

MAP 22.1 **Europe in 1914.** By 1914, two alliances dominated Europe: the Triple Entente of Britain, France, and Russia and the Triple Alliance of Germany, Austria-Hungary, and Italy. Russia sought to bolster fellow Slavs in Serbia, whereas Austria-Hungary was intent on increasing its power in the Balkans and thwarting Serbia's ambitions. Thus the Balkans became the flash point for World War I. ➤ *Which nonaligned nations were positioned between the two alliances?*

between Austria-Hungary and Russia for domination of these new states created serious tensions in the region. By 1914, Serbia, supported by Russia, was determined to create a large, independent Slavic state in the Balkans, while Austria, which had its own Slavic minorities to contend with, was equally set on preventing that possibility. Many Europeans perceived the inherent dangers in this combination of Serbian ambition bolstered by Russian hatred of Austria and the Austrian conviction that Serbia's success would mean the end of its empire. The British ambassador to Vienna wrote in 1913:

Serbia will some day set Europe by the ears, and bring about a universal war on the Continent. . . . I cannot tell you how exasperated people are getting here at the continual worry which that little country causes to Austria under encouragement from Russia. . . . It will be lucky if Europe succeeds in avoiding war as a result of the present crisis. The next time a Serbian crisis arises . . . , I feel sure that Austria-Hungary will refuse to admit of any Russian interference in the dispute and that she will proceed to settle her differences with her little neighbor by herself.[2]

It was against this backdrop of mutual distrust and hatred that the events of the summer of 1914 were played out.

The assassination of the Austrian Archduke Francis Ferdinand and his wife, Sophia, on June 28, 1914, was carried out by a Bosnian activist who worked for the Black Hand, a Serbian terrorist organization dedicated to the creation of a pan-Slavic kingdom. Although the Austrian government did not know whether the Serbian government had been directly involved in the archduke's assassination, it saw an opportunity to "render Serbia innocuous once and for all by a display of force," as the Austrian foreign minister put it. Fearful of Russian intervention on Serbia's behalf, Austrian leaders sought the backing of their German allies. Emperor William II and his chancellor gave their assurance that Austria-Hungary could rely on Germany's "full support," even if "matters went to the length of a war between Austria-Hungary and Russia."

Strengthened by German support, Austrian leaders issued an ultimatum to Serbia on July 23 in which they made such extreme demands that Serbia had little choice but to reject some of them in order to preserve its sovereignty. Austria then declared war on Serbia on July 28. Still smarting from its humiliation in the Bosnian crisis of 1908, Russia was

plans would cause chaos in the armed forces, military leaders insisted that the plans could not be altered. In the crises during the summer of 1914, the generals' lack of flexibility forced European political leaders to make decisions for military instead of political reasons.

The Outbreak of War: Summer 1914

Militarism, nationalism, and the desire to stifle internal dissent may all have played a role in the coming of World War I, but the decisions made by European leaders in the summer of 1914 directly precipitated the conflict. It was another crisis in the Balkans that forced this predicament on Europe's statesmen.

As we have seen, states in southeastern Europe had struggled to free themselves from Ottoman rule in the course of the nineteenth and early twentieth centuries. But the rivalry

"YOU HAVE TO BEAR THE RESPONSIBIITY FOR WAR OR PEACE"

*A*fter Austria declared war on Serbia on July 28, 1914, Russian support of Serbia and German support of Austria threatened to escalate the conflict in the Balkans into a wider war. As we can see in these last-minute telegrams between the Russians and Germans, neither side was able to accept the other's line of reasoning.

COMMUNICATIONS BETWEEN BERLIN AND SAINT PETERSBURG ON THE EVE OF WORLD WAR I

Emperor William II to Tsar Nicholas II, July 28, 10:45 P.M.

I have heard with the greatest anxiety of the impression which is caused by the action of Austria-Hungary against Servia [Serbia]. The inscrupulous agitation which has been going on for years in Servia has led to the revolting crime of which Archduke Franz Ferdinand has become a victim. The spirit which made the Servians murder their own King and his consort still dominates that country. Doubtless You will agree with me that both of us, You as well as I, and all other sovereigns, have a common interest to insist that all those who are responsible for this horrible murder shall suffer their deserved punishment. . . .

Your most sincere and devoted friend and cousin

(Signed) WILHELM

Tsar Nicholas II to Emperor William II, July 29, 1 P.M.

I am glad that you are back in Germany. In this serious moment I ask You earnestly to help me. An ignominious war has been declared against a weak country and in Russia the indignation which I full share is tremendous. I fear that very soon I shall be unable to resist the pressure exercised upon me and that I shall be forced to take measures which will lead to war. To prevent a calamity as a European war would be, I urge You in the name of our old friendship to do all in Your power to restrain Your ally from going too far.

(Signed) NICOLAS

Emperor William II to Tsar Nicholas II, July 29, 6:30 P.M.

I have received Your telegram and I share Your desire for the conservation of peace. However: I cannot—as I told You in my first telegram—consider the action of Austria-Hungary as an "ignominious war." Austria-Hungary knows from experience that the promises of Servia as long as they are merely on paper are entirely unreliable. . . . I believe that a direct understanding is possible and desirable between Your Government and Vienna, an understanding which—as I have already telegraphed You—my Government endeavors to aid with all possible effort. Naturally military measures by Russia, which might be construed as a menace by Austria-Hungary, would accelerate a calamity which both of us desire to avoid and would undermine my position as mediator which—upon Your appeal to my friendship and aid—I willingly accepted.

(Signed) WILHELM

Emperor William II to Tsar Nicholas II, July 30, 1 A.M.

My Ambassador has instructions to direct the attention of Your Government to the dangers and serious consequences of a mobilization. I have told You the same in my last telegram. Austria-Hungary has mobilized only against Servia, and only a part of her army. If Russia, as seems to be the case, according to Your advice and that of Your Government, mobilizes against Austria-Hungary, the part of the mediator with which You have entrusted me in such friendly manner and which I have accepted upon Your express desire, is threatened if not made impossible. The entire weight of decision now rests upon Your shoulders; You have to bear the responsibility for war or peace.

(Signed) WILHELM

German Chancellor to German Ambassador at Saint Petersburg, July 31, URGENT

In spite of negotiations still pending and although we have up to this hour made no preparations for mobilization, Russia has mobilized her entire army and navy, hence also against us. On account of these Russian measures, we have been forced, for the safety of the country, to proclaim the threatening state of war, which does not yet imply mobilization. Mobilization, however, is bound to follow if Russia does not stop every measure of war against us and against Austria-Hungary within 12 hours, and notifies us definitely to this effect. Please to communicate this at once to M. Sazonoff and wire hour of communication.

determined to support Serbia's cause. On July 28, Tsar Nicholas II ordered partial mobilization of the Russian army against Austria. The Russian General Staff informed the tsar that their mobilization plans were based on a war against both Germany and Austria simultaneously. They could not execute partial mobilization without creating chaos in the army. Consequently, the Russian government ordered full mobilization of the Russian army on July 29, knowing that the Germans would consider this an act of war against them (see the box above). Germany reacted quickly. It issued an ultimatum that Russia must halt its mobilization within twelve hours. When the Russians ignored it, Germany declared war on Russia on August 1.

At this stage of the conflict, German war plans determined whether or not France would become involved in the war. Under the guidance of General Alfred von Schlieffen, chief of staff from 1891 to 1905, the German General Staff had devised a military plan based on the assumption of a two-front war with France and Russia because the two powers had formed a military alliance in 1894. The Schlieffen Plan called for a minimal troop deployment against Russia while most of the German army would make a rapid invasion of France before Russia could become effective in the east or before the British could cross the English Channel to help France. This meant invading France by advancing through neutral Belgium, with its level coastal plain on which the army could move faster than on the rougher terrain to the southeast. After the planned quick defeat of the French, the German army expected to redeploy to the east against Russia. Under the Schlieffen Plan, Germany could not mobilize its troops solely against Russia and therefore declared war on France on August 3 after it had issued an ultimatum to Belgium on August 2 demanding the right of German troops to pass through Belgian territory. On August 4, Great Britain declared war on Germany, officially over this violation of Belgian neutrality but in fact over the British desire to maintain world power. As one British diplomat argued, if Germany and Austria were to win the war, "what would be the position of a friendless England?" By August 4, all the great powers of Europe were at war.

THE GREAT WAR

Before 1914, many political leaders had become convinced that war involved so many political and economic risks that it was not worth fighting. Others had believed that "rational" diplomats could control any situation and prevent the outbreak of war. At the beginning of August 1914, both of these prewar illusions were shattered, but the new illusions that replaced them soon proved to be equally foolish.

1914–1915: Illusions and Stalemate

Europeans went to war in 1914 with remarkable enthusiasm (see the box on p. 633). Government propaganda had been successful in stirring up national antagonisms before the war. Now in August 1914, the urgent pleas of governments for defense against aggressors fell on receptive ears in every belligerent nation. Most people seemed genuinely convinced that their nation's cause was just. A new set of illusions also fed the enthusiasm for war. In August 1914, almost everyone believed that the war would be over in a few weeks. People were reminded that all European wars since 1815 had, in fact, ended in a matter of weeks, conveniently overlooking the American Civil War (1861–1865), which was a better prototype for World War I. Both the soldiers who exuberantly boarded the trains for the war front in August 1914 and the jubilant citizens who bombarded them with flowers as they departed believed that the warriors would be home by Christmas.

THE EXCITEMENT OF WAR.   World War I was greeted with incredible enthusiasm. Each of the major belligerents was convinced of the rightness of its cause. Everywhere in Europe, jubilant civilians sent their troops off to war with joyous fervor. Their belief that the soldiers would be home by Christmas proved to be a pathetic illusion.

Librairie Larousse, Paris

THE EXCITEMENT OF WAR

*T*he incredible outpouring of patriotic enthusiasm that greeted the declaration of war at the beginning of August 1914 demonstrated the power that nationalistic feeling had attained at the beginning of the twentieth century. Many Europeans seemingly believed that the war had given them a higher purpose, a renewed dedication to the greatness of their nation. This selection is taken from the autobiography of Stefan Zweig, an Austrian writer who captured well the orgiastic celebration of war in Vienna in 1914.

STEFAN ZWEIG, *THE WORLD OF YESTERDAY*

The next morning I was in Austria. In every station placards had been put up announcing general mobilization. The trains were filled with fresh recruits, banners were flying, music sounded, and in Vienna I found the entire city in a tumult. . . . There were parades in the street, flags, ribbons, and music burst forth everywhere; young recruits were marching triumphantly, their faces lighting up at the cheering. . . .

And to be truthful, I must acknowledge that there was a majestic, rapturous, and even seductive something in this first outbreak of the people from which one could escape only with difficulty. And in spite of all my hatred and aversion for war, I should not like to have missed the memory of those days. As never before, thousands and hundreds of thousands felt what they should have felt in peacetime, that they belonged together. A city of two million, a country of nearly fifty million, in that hour felt that they were participating in world history, in a moment which would never recur, and that each one was called upon to cast his infinitesimal self into the glowing mass, there to be purified of all selfishness. All differences of class, rank, and language were flooded over at that moment by the rushing feeling of fraternity. Strangers spoke to one another in the streets; people who had avoided each other for years shook hands; everywhere one saw excited faces. Each individual experienced an exaltation of his ego, he was no longer the isolated person of former times, he had been incorporated into the mass, he was part of the people, and his person, his hitherto unnoticed person, had been given meaning. . . .

What did the great mass know of war in 1914, after nearly half a century of peace? They did not know war, they had hardly given it a thought. It had become legendary, and distance had made it seem romantic and heroic. They still saw it in the perspective of their school readers and of paintings in museums; brilliant cavalry attacks in glittering uniforms, the fatal shot always straight through the heart, the entire campaign a resounding march of victory—"We'll be home at Christmas," the recruits shouted laughingly to their mothers in August of 1914. . . . A rapid excursion into the romantic, a wild, manly adventure—that is how the war of 1914 was painted in the imagination of the simple man, and the young people were honestly afraid that they might miss this most wonderful and exciting experience of their lives; that is why they hurried and thronged to the colors, and that is why they shouted and sang in the trains that carried them to the slaughter; wildly and feverishly the red wave of blood coursed through the veins of the entire nation.

The Schlieffen Plan

German hopes for a quick end to the war rested on a military gamble. The Schlieffen Plan had called for the German army to make a vast encircling movement through Belgium into northern France that would sweep around Paris and encircle most of the French army. But the German advance was halted only 20 miles from Paris at the First Battle of the Marne (September 6–10). The war quickly turned into a stalemate as neither the Germans nor the French could dislodge the other from the trenches they had begun to dig for shelter. Two lines of trenches soon extended from the English Channel to the frontiers of Switzerland (see Map 22.2). The Western Front had become bogged down in a trench warfare that kept both sides immobilized in virtually the same positions for four years.

In contrast to the west, the war in the east was marked by much more mobility, although the cost in lives was equally enormous. At the beginning of the war, the Russian army moved into eastern Germany but was decisively defeated at the Battles of Tannenberg on August 30 and the Masurian Lakes on September 15. The Russians were no longer a threat to German territory.

The Austrians, Germany's allies, fared less well initially. They had been defeated by the Russians in Galicia and thrown out of Serbia as well. To make matters worse, the Italians betrayed the Germans and Austrians and entered the war on the Allied side by attacking Austria in May 1915. By this time, the Germans had come to the aid of

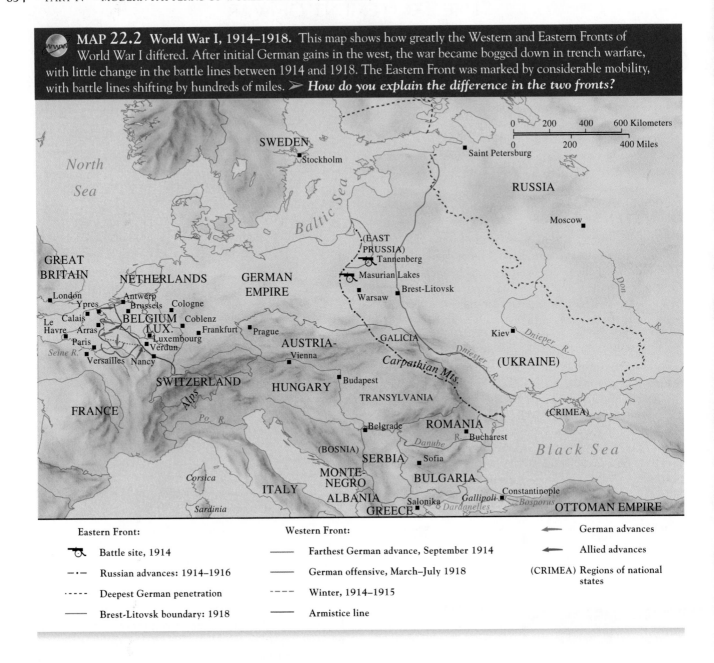

MAP 22.2 World War I, 1914–1918. This map shows how greatly the Western and Eastern Fronts of World War I differed. After initial German gains in the west, the war became bogged down in trench warfare, with little change in the battle lines between 1914 and 1918. The Eastern Front was marked by considerable mobility, with battle lines shifting by hundreds of miles. ➤ *How do you explain the difference in the two fronts?*

Eastern Front:
- Battle site, 1914
- Russian advances: 1914–1916
- Deepest German penetration
- Brest-Litovsk boundary: 1918

Western Front:
- Farthest German advance, September 1914
- German offensive, March–July 1918
- Winter, 1914–1915
- Armistice line

- German advances
- Allied advances
- (CRIMEA) Regions of national states

the Austrians. A German-Austrian army defeated and routed the Russian army in Galicia and pushed the Russians back 300 miles into their own territory. Russian casualties stood at 2.5 million killed, captured, or wounded; the Russians had almost been knocked out of the war. Buoyed by their success, the Germans and Austrians, joined by the Bulgarians in September 1915, attacked and eliminated Serbia from the war.

1916–1917: The Great Slaughter

The successes in the east enabled the Germans to move back to the offensive in the west. The early trenches dug in 1914 had by now become elaborate systems of defense. Both lines of trenches were protected by barbed-wire entanglements 3 to 5 feet high and 90 feet wide, concrete machine-gun nests, and mortar batteries, supported farther back by heavy artillery. Troops lived in holes in the ground, separated from each other by a "no-man's land."

The unexpected development of trench warfare baffled military leaders, who had been trained to fight wars of movement and maneuver. The only plan generals could devise was to attempt a breakthrough by throwing masses of men against enemy lines that had first been battered by artillery barrages. Once the decisive breakthrough had been achieved, they thought, they could then return to the war of movement that they knew best. Periodically, the high command on either side would order an offensive that would begin with an artillery barrage to flatten the enemy's barbed wire and leave the

THE REALITY OF WAR: TRENCH WARFARE

*T*he romantic illusion about the excitement and adventure of war that filled the minds of so many young men who marched off to battle quickly disintegrated after a short time in the trenches on the Western Front. This description of trench warfare is taken from the most famous novel that emerged from World War I, Erich Maria Remarque's All Quiet on the Western Front, written in 1929. Remarque had fought in the trenches in France.

ERICH MARIA REMARQUE, ALL QUIET ON THE WESTERN FRONT

We wake up in the middle of the night. The earth booms. Heavy fire is falling on us. We crouch into corners. We distinguish shells of every calibre.

Each man lays hold of his things and looks again every minute to reassure himself that they are still there. The dugout heaves, the night roars and flashes. We look at each other in the momentary flashes of light, and with pale faces and pressed lips shake our heads.

Every man is aware of the heavy shells tearing down the parapet, rooting up the embankment and demolishing the upper layers of concrete. . . . Already by morning a few of the recruits are green and vomiting. They are too inexperienced. . . .

The bombardment does not diminish. It is falling in the rear too. As far as one can see it spouts fountains of mud and iron. A wide belt is being raked.

The attack does not come, but the bombardment continues. Slowly we become mute. Hardly a man speaks. We cannot make ourselves understood.

Our trench is almost gone. At many places it is only eighteen inches high; it is broken by holes, and craters, and mountains of earth. A shell lands square in front of our post. At once it is dark. We are buried and must dig ourselves out. . . .

Towards morning, while it is still dark, there is some excitement. Through the entrance rushes in a swarm of fleeing rats that try to storm the walls. Torches light up the confusion. Everyone yells and curses and slaughters. The madness and despair of many hours unloads itself in this outburst. Faces are distorted, arms strike out, the beasts scream; we just stop in time to avoid attacking one another. . . .

Suddenly it howls and flashes terrifically, the dugout cracks in all its joints under a direct hit, fortunately only a light one that the concrete blocks are able to withstand. It rings metallically; the walls reel; rifles, helmets, earth, mud, and dust fly everywhere. Sulfur fumes pour in. . . . The recruit starts to rave again and two others follow suit. One jumps up and rushes out, we have trouble with the other two. I start after the one who escapes and wonder whether to shoot him in the leg—then it shrieks again; I fling myself down and when I stand up the wall of the trench is plastered with smoking splinters, lumps of flesh, and bits of uniform. I scramble back.

The first recruit seems actually to have gone insane. He butts his head against the wall like a goat. We must try tonight to take him to the rear. Meanwhile we bind him, but so that in case of attack he can be released.

Suddenly the nearer explosions cease. The shelling continues but it has lifted and falls behind us; our trench is free. We seize the hand grenades, pitch them out in front of the dugout, and jump after them. The bombardment has stopped and a heavy barrage now falls behind us. The attack has come.

No one would believe that in this howling waste there could still be men; but steel helmets now appear on all sides out of the trench, and fifty yards from us a machine gun is already in position and barking.

The wire entanglements are torn to pieces. Yet they offer some obstacle. We see the storm troops coming. Our artillery opens fire. Machine guns rattle, rifles crack. The charge works its way across. Haie and Kropp begin with the hand grenades. They throw as fast as they can; others pass them, the handles with the strings already pulled. Haie throws seventy-five yards, Kropp sixty; it has been measured; the distance is important. The enemy as they run cannot do much before they are within forty yards.

We recognize the distorted faces, the smooth helmets: they are French. They have already suffered heavily when they reach the remnants of the barbed-wire entanglements. A whole line has gone down before our machine guns; then we have a lot of stoppages and they come nearer.

I see one of them, his face upturned, fall into a wire cradle. His body collapses, his hands remain suspended as though he were praying. Then his body drops clean away and only his hands with the stumps of his arms, shot off, now hang in the wire.

---

enemy in a state of shock. After "softening up" the enemy in this fashion, a mass of soldiers would climb out of their trenches with fixed bayonets and hope to work their way toward the enemy trenches. The attacks rarely worked, as the machine gun put hordes of men advancing unprotected across open fields at a severe disadvantage. In 1916 and 1917, millions of young men were sacrificed in the search for the elusive breakthrough. In ten months at Verdun, 700,000 men lost their lives over a few miles of terrain.

Warfare in the trenches of the Western Front produced unimaginable horrors (see the box above). Battlefields were hellish landscapes of barbed wire, shell holes, mud, and injured and dying men. The introduction of poison gas in 1915 produced new forms of injuries, as one British writer described them:

> I wish those people who write so glibly about this being a holy war could see a case of mustard gas . . . could see the poor things burnt and blistered all over with great mustard-coloured suppurating blisters with blind eyes all sticky . . . and stuck together, and always fighting for breath, with voices a mere whisper, saying that their throats are closing and they know they will choke.[3]

Soldiers in the trenches also lived with the persistent presence of death. Since combat went on for months, soldiers had to carry on in the midst of countless bodies of dead men or the remains of men dismembered by artillery barrages. Many soldiers remembered the stench of decomposing bodies and the swarms of rats that grew fat in the trenches.

The Widening of the War

As another response to the stalemate on the Western Front, both sides looked for new allies who might provide a winning advantage. The Ottoman Empire had already come into the war on Germany's side in August 1914. Russia, Great Britain, and France declared war on the Ottoman Empire in November. Although the Allies attempted to

⤜ **THE HORRORS OF WAR.** The slaughter of millions of men in the trenches of World War I created unimaginable horrors for the participants. For the sake of survival, many soldiers learned to harden themselves against the stench of decomposing bodies and the sight of bodies horribly dismembered by artillery barrages.

© Roger-Viollet/Getty Images

open a Balkan front by landing forces at Gallipoli, southwest of Constantinople, in April 1915, the entry of Bulgaria into the war on the side of the Central Powers (as Germany, Austria-Hungary, and the Ottoman Empire were called) and a disastrous campaign at Gallipoli caused them to withdraw. The Italians, as we have seen, also entered the war on the Allied side after France and Britain promised to further their acquisition of Austrian territory. In the long run, however, Italian military incompetence forced the Allies to come to the assistance of Italy.

THE MIDDLE EAST, AFRICA, EAST ASIA, AND THE PACIFIC

The war that originated in Europe rapidly became a world conflict. In the Middle East, a British officer who came to be known as Lawrence of Arabia (1888–1935) incited Arab princes to revolt against their Ottoman overlords in 1917. In 1918, British forces from Egypt destroyed the rest of the Ottoman Empire in the Middle East. For their Middle East campaigns, the British mobilized forces from India, Australia, and New Zealand.

In 1914, Germany possessed four colonies in Africa: Togoland, Cameroons, South West Africa, and German East Africa. British and French forces quickly occupied Togoland in West Africa, but Cameroons was not taken until 1916. British and white African forces invaded South West Africa in 1914 and forced the Germans to surrender in July 1915. The Allied campaign in East Africa proved more difficult and costly, and it was not until 1918 that the German forces surrendered there.

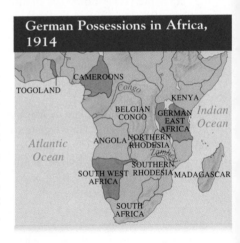

German Possessions in Africa, 1914

TOGOLAND
CAMEROONS
Congo
BELGIAN CONGO
GERMAN EAST AFRICA
KENYA
Indian Ocean
ANGOLA
NORTHERN RHODESIA
Atlantic Ocean
Zambezi
SOUTHERN RHODESIA
SOUTH WEST AFRICA
MADAGASCAR
SOUTH AFRICA

In these battles, Allied governments drew mainly on African soldiers, but some states, especially France, also recruited African troops to fight in Europe. The French drafted more than 170,000 West African soldiers. While some served as garrison forces in North Africa, many of the West African troops fought in the trenches on the Western front. About 80,000 Africans were killed or injured in Europe. They were often at a distinct disadvantage due to the unfamiliar terrain and climate.

Hundreds of thousands of Africans were also used for labor, especially for carrying supplies and building roads and bridges. In East Africa, both sides drafted African laborers as carriers for their armies. Disease and starvation caused by neglect led to the death of more than 100,000 of these laborers.

⟫ **FRENCH AFRICAN TROOPS.**   The French drafted more than 170,000 West African soldiers to fight in Europe. Shown here are some French African troops who fought in France. The French also drafted African soldiers from their North African colonies and Madagascar.

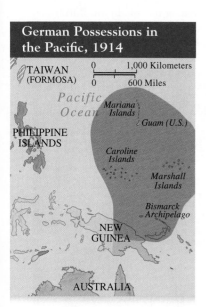

German Possessions in the Pacific, 1914

In East Asia and the Pacific, Japan joined the Allies on August 23, 1914, primarily to seize control of German territories in Asia. The Japanese took possession of German territories in China, as well as the German-occupied Marshall, Mariana, and Caroline Islands. New Zealand and Australia quickly joined the Japanese in conquering the German-held parts of New Guinea and the Bismarck Archipelago.

ENTRY OF THE UNITED STATES

Most important to the Allied cause was the entry of the United States into the war. At first, the United States tried to remain neutral in the Great War, but that became more difficult as the war dragged on. The immediate cause of American involvement grew out of the naval conflict between Germany and Great Britain. Britain used its superior naval power to maximum effect by imposing a naval blockade on Germany. Germany retaliated with a counterblockade enforced by submarine warfare. Strong American protests over the German sinking of passenger liners, especially the British ship *Lusitania* on May 7, 1915, in which more than a hundred Americans lost their lives, forced the German government to suspend unrestricted submarine warfare in September 1915 to avoid further antagonizing the Americans.

In January 1917, however, eager to break the deadlock in the war, the Germans decided on another military gamble by returning to unrestricted submarine warfare. German naval officers convinced Emperor William II that the use of unrestricted submarine warfare could starve the British into submission within five months, before the Americans could act. The return to unrestricted submarine warfare brought the United States into the war on April 6, 1917. Although American troops did not arrive in Europe in large numbers until 1918, the entry of the United States into the war in 1917 gave the Allied Powers a psychological boost when they needed it. The year 1917 was not a good year for them. Allied offensives on the Western Front were disastrously defeated. The Italian armies were smashed in October, and in November the Bolshevik revolution in Russia (see "The Russian Revolution" later in this chapter) led to Russia's withdrawal from the war and left Germany free to concentrate entirely on the Western Front. The cause of the Central Powers looked favorable, although war weariness in the Ottoman Empire, Bulgaria, Austria-Hungary, and Germany was beginning to take its toll. The home front was rapidly becoming a cause for as much concern as the war front.

The Home Front: The Impact of Total War

The prolongation of World War I made it a total war that affected the lives of all citizens, however remote they might be from the battlefields. The need to organize masses of men and matériel for years of combat (Germany alone had 5.5 million men in active units in 1916) led to increased centralization of government powers, economic regimentation, and manipulation of public opinion to keep the war effort going.

Because the war was expected to be short, little thought had been given to economic considerations or long-term wartime needs. Governments had to respond quickly, however, when the war machines failed to achieve their knock-out blows and made ever-greater demands for men and matériel. The extension of government power was a logical outgrowth of these needs. Most European countries had already devised some system of mass conscription or military draft. It was now carried to unprecedented heights as countries mobilized tens of millions of young men for that elusive breakthrough to victory. Even countries that continued to rely on volunteers (Great Britain had the largest volunteer army in modern history—one million men—in 1914 and 1915) were forced to resort to conscription, especially to ensure that skilled laborers did not enlist but remained in factories producing munitions. In 1916, despite widespread resistance to this extension of government power, compulsory military service was introduced in Great Britain.

Throughout Europe, wartime governments expanded their powers over their economies. Free market capitalistic systems were temporarily shelved as governments experimented with price, wage, and rent controls, the rationing of food supplies and materials, the regulation of imports and exports, and the nationalization of transportation systems and industries. Some governments even moved toward compulsory employment. In effect, to mobilize all national resources of their nations for the war effort, European nations had moved toward planned economies directed by government agencies. Under total war mobilization, the distinction between soldiers at war and civilians at home was narrowed. In the view of political leaders, all citizens constituted a national army dedicated to victory. As the American president, Woodrow Wilson, expressed it, the men and women "who remain to till the soil and man the factories are no less a part of the army than the men beneath the battle flags."

As the Great War dragged on and both casualties and privations worsened, internal dissatisfaction replaced the patriotic enthusiasm that had marked the early stages of the conflict. By 1916, there were numerous signs that civilian morale was beginning to crack under the pressure of total war. War governments, however, fought back against the growing opposition to the war. Authoritarian regimes, such as those of Germany, Russia, and Austria-Hungary, had always relied on force to subdue their populations. Under the pressures of the war, however, even parliamentary regimes resorted to an expansion of police powers to stifle internal dissent. At the very beginning of the war, the British Parliament passed the Defence of the Realm Act (DORA), which allowed the public authorities to arrest dissenters as traitors. The act was later extended to authorize public officials to censor newspapers by deleting objectionable material and even to suspend newspaper publication. In France, government authorities had initially been lenient about public opposition to the war. But by 1917, they began to fear that open opposition to the war might weaken the French will to fight. When Georges Clemenceau (1841–1929) became premier near the end of 1917, the lenient French policies came to an end, and basic civil liberties were suppressed for the duration of the war. When a former premier publicly advocated a negotiated peace, Clemenceau's government had him sentenced to prison for two years for treason.

Wartime governments made active use of propaganda to arouse enthusiasm for the war. At the beginning, public officials needed to do little to achieve this goal. The British and French, for example, exaggerated German atrocities in Belgium and found that their citizens were only too willing to believe these accounts. But as the war dragged on and morale sagged, governments were forced to devise new techniques for stimulating declining enthusiasm. In one British recruiting poster, for example, a small daughter asked her

BRITISH RECRUITING POSTER. As the conflict persisted month after month, governments resorted to active propaganda campaigns to generate enthusiasm for the war. In this British recruiting poster, the government tried to pressure men into volunteering for military service. By 1916, the British were forced to adopt compulsory military service.

The Art Archive, London

WOMEN IN THE FACTORIES

uring World War I, women were called on to assume new job responsibilities, including factory work. In this selection, Naomi Loughnan, a young, upper-middle-class woman, describes the experiences in a munitions plant that considerably broadened her perspective on life.

NAOMI LOUGHNAN, "MUNITION WORK"

We little thought when we first put on our overalls and caps and enlisted in the Munition Army how much more inspiring our life was to be than we had dared to hope. Though we munition workers sacrifice our ease, we gain a life worth living. Our long days are filled with interest, and with the zest of doing work for our country in the grand cause of Freedom. As we handle the weapons of war we are learning great lessons of life. In the busy, noisy workshops we come face to face with every kind of class, and each one of these classes has something to learn from the others. . . .

Engineering mankind is possessed of the unshakable opinion that no woman can have the mechanical sense. If one of us asks humbly why such and such an alteration is not made to prevent this or that drawback to a machine, she is told, with a superior smile, that a man has worked her machine before her for years, and that therefore if there were any improvement possible it would have been made. As long as we do exactly what we are told and do not attempt to use our brains, we give entire satisfaction, and are treated as nice, good children. Any swerving from the easy path prepared for us by our males arouses the most

scathing contempt in their manly bosoms. . . . Women have, however, proved that their entry into the munition world has increased the output. Employers who forget things personal in their patriotic desire for large results are enthusiastic over the success of women in the shops. But their workmen have to be handled with the utmost tenderness and caution lest they should actually imagine it was being suggested that women could do their work equally well, given equal conditions of training—at least where muscle is not the driving force. . . .

The coming of the mixed classes of women into the factory is slowly but surely having an educative effect upon the men. "Language" is almost unconsciously becoming subdued. There are fiery exceptions, who make our hair stand up on end under our close-fitting caps, but a sharp rebuke or a look of horror will often straighten out the most savage. . . . It is grievous to hear the girls also swearing and using disgusting language. Shoulder to shoulder with the children of the slums, the upper classes are having their eyes opened at last to the awful conditions among which their sisters have dwelt. Foul language, immorality, and many other evils are but the natural outcome of overcrowding and bitter poverty. . . . Sometimes disgust will overcome us, but we are learning with painful clarity that the fault is not theirs whose actions disgust us, but must be placed to the discredit of those other classes who have allowed the continued existence of conditions which generate the things from which we shrink appalled.

---

father, "Daddy, what did YOU do in the Great War?" while her younger brother played with toy soldiers and cannons.

Total war made a significant impact on European society, most visibly by bringing an end to unemployment. The withdrawal of millions of men from the labor market to fight, combined with the heightened demand for wartime products, led to jobs for everyone able to work.

World War I also created new roles for women. Because so many men went off to fight at the front, women were called on to assume jobs and responsibilities that had not been available to them before. Overall, the number of women employed in Britain who held new jobs or replaced men rose by 1,345,000. Women were also now employed in jobs that had been considered "beyond the capacity of women." These included such occupations as chimney sweeps, truck drivers, farm laborers, and factory workers in heavy industry (see the box above). In Germany, 38 percent of the workers in the Krupp Armaments works in 1918 were women.

While male workers expressed concern that the employment of females at lower wages would depress their own wages, women began to demand equal pay. A law passed by the French government in July 1915 established a minimum

wage for women homeworkers in textiles, an industry that had grown dramatically because of the need for military uniforms. Two years later, the government decreed that men and women should receive equal rates for piecework. Despite the noticeable increase in women's wages that resulted from government regulations, women's industrial wages were still not equal to men's wages by the end of the war.

Even worse, women's place in the workforce was far from secure. Both men and women seemed to assume that many of the new jobs for women were only temporary, an expectation quite evident in the British poem "War Girls," written in 1916:

> There's the girl who clips your ticket for the train,
> And the girl who speeds the lift from floor to floor,
> There's the girl who does a milk-round in the rain,
> And the girl who calls for orders at your door.
> Strong, sensible, and fit,
> They're out to show their grit,
> And tackle jobs with energy and knack.
> No longer caged and penned up,
> They're going to keep their end up
> Till the khaki soldier boys come marching back.[4]

At the end of the war, governments moved quickly to remove women from the jobs they had encouraged them to take earlier. By 1919, there were 650,000 unemployed women in Britain, and wages for women who were still employed were lowered. The work benefits for women from World War I seemed to be short-lived as demobilized men returned to the job market.

Nevertheless, in some countries the role played by women in the wartime economies did have a positive impact on the women's movement for social and political emancipation. The most obvious gain was the right to vote that was given to women in Germany and Austria immediately after the war (in Britain already in January 1918). Contemporary media, however, tended to focus on the more noticeable, yet in some ways more superficial, social emancipation of upper- and middle-class women. In ever-larger numbers, these young women took jobs, had their own apartments, and showed their new independence by smoking in public and wearing shorter dresses, cosmetics, and new hairstyles.

 # WAR AND REVOLUTION

By 1917, total war was creating serious domestic turmoil in all of the European belligerent states. Only one, however, experienced the kind of complete collapse that others were predicting might happen throughout Europe. Out of Russia's collapse came the Russian Revolution, whose impact would be widely felt in Europe and the world for decades to come.

The Russian Revolution

After the Revolution of 1905 had failed to bring any substantial changes to Russia, Tsar Nicholas II fell back on the army and bureaucracy as the basic props for his autocratic regime. But World War I magnified Russia's problems and put the tsarist government to a test that it could not meet. Russia was unprepared both militarily and technologically for the total war of World War I. Competent military leadership was lacking. Even worse, the tsar, alone of all European monarchs, insisted on taking personal charge of the armed forces despite his obvious lack of ability and training for such an awesome burden. Russian industry was unable to produce the weapons needed for the army. Ill-led and ill-armed, Russian armies suffered incredible losses. Between 1914 and 1916, two million soldiers were killed, and another four to six million were wounded or captured. By 1917, the Russian will to fight had evaporated.

The tsarist government was totally inadequate for the tasks that it faced in 1914. Even conservative aristocrats were appalled by the incompetent and inefficient bureaucracy of the political and military system. In the mean-time, Tsar Nicholas II was increasingly insulated from events by his German-born wife, Alexandra, a well-educated woman who had fallen under the influence of Rasputin, a Siberian peasant whom the tsarina regarded as a holy man because he alone seemed able to stop the bleeding of her hemophiliac son, Alexis. Rasputin's influence made him a power behind the throne, and he did not hesitate to interfere in government affairs. As the leadership at the top stumbled its way through a series of military and economic disasters, the middle class, aristocrats, peasants, soldiers, and workers grew more and more disenchanted with the tsarist regime. Even conservative aristocrats who supported the monarchy felt the need to do something to reverse the deteriorating situation. For a start, they assassinated Rasputin in December 1916. By then it was too late to save the monarchy, and its fall came quickly.

At the beginning of March 1917, a series of strikes broke out in the capital city of Petrograd (formerly Saint Petersburg). Here the actions of working-class women helped change the course of Russian history. In February 1917, the government had introduced bread rationing in the capital city after the price of bread had skyrocketed. Many of the women who stood in the lines waiting for bread were also factory workers who had put in twelve-hour days. The Russian government had become aware of the volatile situation in the capital from a police report:

> Mothers of families, exhausted by endless standing in line at stores, distraught over their half-starving and sick children, are today perhaps closer to revolution than [the liberal opposition leaders] and of course they are a great deal more dangerous because they are the combustible material for which only a single spark is needed to burst into flame.[5]

On March 8, about ten thousand Petrograd women marched through the city chanting "Peace and Bread" and "Down with Autocracy." Soon the women were joined by other workers, and together they called for a general strike that succeeded in shutting down all the factories in the city on March 10. Nicholas ordered the troops to disperse the crowds by shooting them if necessary, but soon significant numbers of the soldiers joined the demonstrators. The Duma or legislative body, which the tsar had tried to dissolve, met anyway and on March 12 declared that it was assuming governmental responsibility. It established a provisional government on March 15; the tsar abdicated the same day.

The Provisional Government, headed by Alexander Kerensky (1881–1970) decided to carry on the war to preserve Russia's honor—a major blunder because it satisfied neither the workers nor the peasants, who above all wanted an end to the war. The Provisional Government also faced another authority, the soviets, or councils of workers' and soldiers' deputies. The Petrograd soviet had

© Sovfoto

➤➤ **THE WOMEN'S MARCH IN PETROGRAD.**   After the introduction of bread rationing in Petrograd, ten thousand women engaged in mass demonstrations and demanded "Peace and Bread" for the families of soldiers. This photograph shows the women marching through the streets of Petrograd on March 8, 1917.

been formed in March 1917; at the same time, soviets sprang up spontaneously in army units, factory towns, and rural areas. The soviets represented the more radical interests of the lower classes and were largely composed of socialists of various kinds. One group, the Bolsheviks, came to play a crucial role.

The Bolsheviks were a small faction of Marxist Social Democrats who had come under the leadership of Vladimir Ulianov, known to the world as Lenin (1870–1924). Arrested for his revolutionary activity, Lenin was shipped to Siberia. After his release, he chose to go into exile in Switzerland and eventually assumed the leadership of the Bolshevik wing of the Russian Social Democratic Party. Under Lenin's direction, the Bolsheviks became a party dedicated to violent revolution. He believed that only a revolution could destroy the capitalist system and that a "vanguard" of activists must form a small party of well-disciplined professional revolutionaries to accomplish the task. Between 1900 and 1917, Lenin spent most of his time in Switzerland. When the Provisional Government was formed in March 1917, he believed that an opportunity for the Bolsheviks to seize power had come. Just weeks later, with the connivance of the German High Command, who hoped to create disorder in Russia, Lenin was shipped to Russia in a sealed train by way of Finland.

Lenin's arrival in Russia opened a new stage of the Russian Revolution. Lenin maintained that the soviets of soldiers, workers, and peasants were ready-made instruments of power. The Bolsheviks must work toward gaining control of these groups and then use them to overthrow the Provisional Government. At the same time, Bolshevik propaganda must seek mass support through promises geared to the needs of the people: an end to the war, redistribution of all land to the peasants, the transfer of factories and industries from capitalists to committees of workers, and the relegation of government power from the Provisional Government to the soviets. Three simple slogans summed up the Bolshevik program: "Peace, Land, Bread," "Worker Control of Production," and "All Power to the Soviets."

By the end of October, the Bolsheviks had achieved a slight majority in the Petrograd and Moscow soviets. The number of party members had also grown, from 50,000 to 240,000. With Leon Trotsky (1877–1940), a fervid revolutionary, as chairman of the Petrograd soviet, Lenin and the Bolsheviks were in a position to seize power in the name of the soviets. During the night of November 6, prosoviet and pro-Bolshevik forces took control of Petrograd; the Provisional Government quickly collapsed, with little bloodshed. The following night, the all-Russian Congress of Soviets, representing local soviets from all over the country, affirmed the transfer of power. At the second

➤ **LENIN AND TROTSKY.** V. I. Lenin and Leon Trotsky were important figures in the success of the Bolsheviks in seizing power in Russia. On the left, Lenin is seen addressing a rally in Moscow in 1917. On the right, Trotsky, who became commissar of war in the new regime, is shown haranguing his troops.

session, the night of November 8, Lenin announced the new Soviet government, the Council of People's Commissars, with himself as its head (see the box on p. 643).

But the Bolsheviks, soon renamed the Communists, still had a long way to go. For one thing, Lenin had promised peace, and that, he realized, was not an easy task because of the humiliating losses of Russian territory that it would entail. There was no real choice, however. On March 3, 1918, Lenin signed the Treaty of Brest-Litovsk with Germany and gave up eastern Poland, the Ukraine, Finland, and the Baltic provinces. To his critics, Lenin argued that it made no difference because the spread of socialist revolution throughout Europe would make the treaty largely irrelevant. In any case, he had promised peace to the Russian people, but real peace did not come, for the country soon sank into civil war.

CIVIL WAR

There was great opposition to the new Communist regime, not only from groups loyal to the tsar but also from bourgeois and aristocratic liberals and anti-Leninist socialists. In addition, thousands of Allied troops were eventually sent to different parts of Russia in the hope of bringing Russia back into the war.

Between 1918 and 1921, the Red (Bolshevik) Army was forced to fight on many fronts. The first serious threat to the Bolsheviks came from Siberia, where White (anti-

Bolshevik) forces attacked westward and advanced almost to the Volga River before being stopped. Attacks also came from the Ukrainians in the southeast and from the Baltic regions. In mid-1919, White forces swept through the Ukraine and advanced almost to Moscow. At one point by late 1919, three separate White armies seemed to be closing in on the Bolsheviks but were eventually pushed back. By 1920, the major White forces had been defeated and the Ukraine retaken. The next year, the Communist regime regained control over the independent nationalist governments in the Caucasus: Georgia, Russian Armenia, and Azerbaijan.

The royal family was yet another victim of the civil war. After the tsar had abdicated, he, his wife, and their five children had been taken into captivity. They were moved in August 1917 to Tobolsk in Siberia and in April 1918 to Ekaterinburg, a mining town in the Urals. On the night of July 16, members of the local soviet murdered the tsar and his family and burned their bodies in a nearby mine shaft.

How had Lenin and the Bolsheviks triumphed over what seemed at one time to be overwhelming forces? For one thing, the Red Army became a well-disciplined and formidable fighting force, largely due to the organizational genius of Leon Trotsky. As commissar of war, Trotsky reinstated the draft and insisted on rigid discipline; soldiers who deserted or refused to obey orders were summarily executed.

The disunity of the anti-Communist forces seriously weakened the efforts of the Whites. Political differences

Ten Days That Shook the World:
Lenin and the Bolshevik Seizure of Power

John Reed was an American journalist who helped found the American Communist Labor Party. Accused of sedition, he fled the United States and went to Russia. In Ten Days That Shook the World, *Reed gives an impassioned eyewitness account of the Russian Revolution. It is apparent from his comments that Reed considered Lenin the indispensable hero of the Bolshevik success.*

JOHN REED, TEN DAYS THAT SHOOK THE WORLD

It was just 8:40 when a thundering wave of cheers announced the entrance of the presidium, with Lenin—great Lenin—among them. A short, stocky figure, with a big head set down in his shoulders, bald and bulging. Little eyes, a snubbish nose, wide, generous mouth, and heavy chin; clean-shaven now, but already beginning to bristle with the well-known beard of his past and future. Dressed in shabby clothes, his trousers much too long for him. Unimpressive, to be the idol of a mob, loved and revered as perhaps few leaders in history have been. A strange popular leader—a leader purely by virtue of intellect; colorless, humorless, uncompromising and detached; without picturesque idiosyncrasies—but with the power of explaining profound ideas in simple terms, of analyzing a concrete situation. And combined with shrewdness, the greatest intellectual audacity. . . .

Now Lenin, gripping the edge of the reading stand, letting his little winking eyes travel over the crowd as he stood there waiting, apparently oblivious to the long-rolling ovation, which lasted several minutes. When it finished, he said simply, "We shall now proceed to construct the Socialist order!" Again that overwhelming human roar.

"The first thing is the adoption of practical measures to realize peace. . . . We shall offer peace to the peoples of all the belligerent countries upon the basis of the Soviet terms—no annexations, no indemnities, and the right of self-determination of peoples. At the same time, according to our promise, we shall publish and repudiate the secret treaties. . . . The question of War and Peace is so clear that I think that I may, without preamble, read the project of a Proclamation to the Peoples of All the Belligerent Countries. . . ."

His great mouth, seeming to smile, opened wide as he spoke; his voice was hoarse—not unpleasantly so, but as if it had hardened that way after years and years of speaking—and went on monotonously, with the effect of being able to go forever. . . . For emphasis he bent forward slightly. No gestures. And before him, a thousand simple faces looking up in intent adoration.

[Reed then reproduces the full text of the Proclamation.]

When the grave thunder of applause had died away, Lenin spoke again: "We propose to the Congress to ratify this declaration. . . . This proposal of peace will meet with resistance on the part of the imperialist governments—we don't fool ourselves on that score. But we hope that revolution will soon break out in all the belligerent countries; that is why we address ourselves especially to the workers of France, England, and Germany. . . .

"The revolution of November 6th and 7th," he ended, "has opened the era of the Social Revolution. . . . The labor movement, in the name of peace and Socialism, shall win, and fulfill its destiny. . . ."

There was something quiet and powerful in all this, which stirred the souls of men. It was understandable why people believed when Lenin spoke.

---

created distrust among the Whites and prevented them from cooperating effectively with each other. Some Whites insisted on restoring the tsarist regime, while others understood that only a more liberal democratic program had any chance of success. It was difficult enough to achieve military cooperation; political differences made it virtually impossible.

The Whites' inability to agree on a common goal was in sharp contrast to the Communists' single-minded sense of purpose. Inspired by their vision of a new socialist order, the Communists had the advantage of possessing the determination that comes from revolutionary fervor and revolutionary convictions.

The Communists also succeeded in translating their revolutionary faith into practical instruments of power. A policy of "war communism," for example, was used to ensure regular supplies for the Red Army. War communism included the nationalization of banks and most industries, the forcible requisition of grain from peasants, and the centralization of state administration under Bolshevik control. Another Bolshevik instrument was "revolutionary terror." Although the old tsarist secret police had been abolished, a new Red secret police—known as t' Cheka—replaced it. The Red Terror instituted by Cheka aimed at nothing less than the destruction who opposed the new regime. The Red Terror a' element of fear to the Bolshevik takeover.

Finally, the intervention of foreign armies Communists to appeal to the powerful for main patriotism. Although the Allied Powers 1, 1918, initially in Russia to encourage the Ru in the war, the end of the war on N CHAPTER 22

643

THE BEGINNING OF THE TWENTIETH-CENTURY CRISIS: WAR AND REVOL

THE RUSSIAN REVOLUTION

	1916
Murder of Rasputin	December
	1917
March of women in Petrograd	March 8
General strike in Petrograd	March 10
Establishment of Provisional Government	March 12
Tsar Nicholas II abdicates	March 15
Formation of Petrograd soviet	March
Lenin arrives in Russia	April 3
Bolsheviks gain majority in Petrograd soviet	October
Bolsheviks overthrow Provisional Government	November 6–7
	1918
Lenin disbands the Constituent Assembly	January
Treaty of Brest-Litovsk	March 3
Murder of royal family	July 16
Civil war	1918–1921

had made that purpose inconsequential. Nevertheless, Allied troops remained, and more even were sent as Allied countries did not hide their anti-Bolshevik feelings. At one point, over 100,000 foreign troops, mostly Japanese, British, American, and French, were stationed on Russian soil. These forces rarely engaged in pitched battles, however, nor did they pursue a common strategy, although they gave material assistance to anti-Bolshevik forces. This intervention by the Allies enabled the Communist government to appeal to patriotic Russians to fight the foreign invaders. Allied interference was ⸳ substantial enough to make a military difference ⸳ civil war, but it did serve indirectly to help the Bol-⸳ause.

⸳1, the Communists had succeeded in retaining ⸳Russia. In the course of the civil war, the Bol-⸳me had also transformed Russia into a bureau-⸳ntralized state dominated by a single party. It ⸳e that was largely hostile to the Allied Pow-⸳ught to assist the Bolsheviks' enemies in ⸳most historians, the Russian Revolution ⸳ithout the total war of World War I, for ⸳of Russia made it possible for a radical ⸳olsheviks to seize the reins of power. ⸳Revolution had an impact on the ⸳I.

The Last Year of the War

For Germany, the withdrawal of the Russians from the war in March 1918 offered renewed hope for a favorable end to the war. The victory over Russia persuaded Erich von Ludendorff (1865–1937), who guided German military operations, and most German leaders to make one final military gamble—a grand offensive in the west to break the military stalemate. The German attack was launched in March and lasted into July, but an Allied counterattack, supported by the arrival of 140,000 fresh American troops, defeated the Germans at the Second Battle of the Marne on July 18. Ludendorff's gamble had failed. With the arrival of two million more American troops on the Continent, Allied forces began to advance steadily toward Germany.

On September 29, 1918, General Ludendorff informed German leaders that the war was lost and demanded that the government sue for peace at once. When German officials discovered, however, that the Allies were unwilling to make peace with the autocratic imperial government, reforms were instituted to create a liberal government. But these constitutional reforms came too late for the exhausted and angry German people. On November 3, naval units in Kiel mutinied, and within days, councils of workers and soldiers were forming throughout northern Germany and taking over the supervision of civilian and military administrations. William II capitulated to public pressure and abdicated on November 9, and the Socialists under Friedrich Ebert (1871–1925) announced the establishment of a republic. Two days later, on November 11, 1918, the new German government agreed to an armistice. The war was over.

The Peace Settlement

In January 1919, the delegations of twenty-seven victorious Allied nations gathered in Paris to conclude a final settlement of the Great War. Over a period of years, the reasons for fighting World War I had been transformed from selfish national interests to idealistic principles. No one expressed these principles better than U.S. President Woodrow Wilson. Wilson's proposals for a truly just and lasting peace included "open covenants of peace, openly arrived at" instead of secret diplomacy; the reduction of national armaments to a "point consistent with domestic safety"; and the self-determination of people so that "all well-defined national aspirations shall be accorded the utmost satisfaction." Wilson characterized World War I as a people's war waged against "absolutism and militarism," which could be eradicated only by creating democratic governments and a "general association of nations" that would guarantee the "political independence and territorial integrity to great and small states alike" (see the box on p. 646). As the spokesman for a new world order based

WORLD WAR I

The Path to War	**1914**	Italy declares war on Austria-Hungary	May 23
Assassination of Archduke Francis Ferdinand	June 28	Bulgaria enters the war	September
Austria's ultimatum to Serbia	July 23		
Austria declares war on Serbia	July 28		**1916**
Russia mobilizes	July 29	Battle of Verdun	February 21–December 18
Germany's ultimatum to Russia	July 31	Battle of Jutland	May 31
Germany declares war on Russia	August 1		**1917**
Germany declares war on France	August 3	Germany returns to unrestricted submarine warfare	January
German troops invade Belgium	August 4	United States enters the war	April 6
Great Britain declares war on Germany	August 4		**1918**
The War	**1914**	Last German offensive	March 21–July 18
Battle of Tannenberg	August 26–30	Second Battle of the Marne	July 18
First Battle of the Marne	September 6–10	Allied counteroffensive	July 18–November 10
Battle of Masurian Lakes	September 15	Armistice between Allies and Germany	November 11
Russia, Great Britain, and France declare war on Ottoman Empire	November		**1919**
	1915	Paris Peace Conference begins	January 18
Battle of Gallipoli begins	April 25	Peace of Versailles	June 28

on democracy and international cooperation, Wilson was enthusiastically cheered by many Europeans when he arrived in Europe for the peace conference.

Wilson soon found, however, that more practical motives guided other states at the Paris Peace Conference. The secret treaties and agreements that had been made before the war could not be totally ignored, even if they did conflict with the principle of self-determination enunciated by Wilson. National interests also complicated the deliberations of the Paris Peace Conference. David Lloyd George, prime minister of Great Britain, had won a decisive electoral victory in December 1918 on a platform of making the Germans pay for this dreadful war.

France's approach to peace was determined primarily by considerations of national security. To Georges Clemenceau, the feisty premier of France who had led his country to victory, the French people had borne the brunt of German aggression. They deserved revenge and secu-

rity against future German aggression. Clemenceau wanted a demilitarized Germany, vast German reparations to pay for the costs of the war, and a separate Rhineland as a buffer state between France and Germany.

The most important decisions at the Paris Peace Conference were made by Wilson, Clemenceau, and Lloyd George. Italy was considered one of the so-called Big Four powers but played a much less important role than the other three countries. Germany, of course, was not invited to attend, and Russia could not because of its civil war.

In view of the many conflicting demands at Versailles, it was inevitable that the Big Three would quarrel. Wilson was determined to create a "league of nations" to prevent future wars. Clemenceau and Lloyd George were equally determined to punish Germany. In the end, only compromise made it possible to achieve a peace settlement. Wilson's wish that the creation of an international peacekeeping organization be the first order of business was

THE VOICE OF PEACEMAKING:
WOODROW WILSON

" *We are fighting for the liberty, the self-government, and the undictated development of all peoples.*"

When the Allied powers met in Paris in January 1919, it soon became apparent that the victors had different opinions on the kind of peace they expected. These excerpts are from the speeches of Woodrow Wilson in which the American president presented his idealistic goals for a peace based on justice and reconciliation.

MAY 26, 1917

We are fighting for the liberty, the self-government, and the undictated development of all peoples, and every feature of the settlement that concludes this war must be conceived and executed for that purpose. Wrongs must first be righted and then adequate safeguards must be created to prevent their being committed again. . . .

No people must be forced under sovereignty under which it does not wish to live. No territory must change hands except for the purpose of securing those who inhabit it a fair chance of life and liberty. No indemnities must be insisted on except those that constitute payment for manifest wrongs done. No readjustments of power must be made except such as will tend to secure the future peace of the world and the future welfare and happiness of its peoples.

And then the free peoples of the world must draw together in some common covenant, some genuine and practical cooperation that will in effect combine their force to secure peace and justice in the dealings of nations with one another.

APRIL 6, 1918

We are ready, whenever the final reckoning is made, to be just to the German people, deal fairly with the German power, as with all others. There can be no difference between peoples in the final judgment, if it is indeed to be a righteous judgment. To propose anything but justice, even-handed and dispassionate justice, to Germany at any time, whatever the outcome of the war, would be to renounce and dishonor our own cause. For we ask nothing that we are not willing to accord.

JANUARY 3, 1919

Our task at Paris is to organize the friendship of the world, to see to it that all the moral forces that make for right and justice and liberty are united and are given a vital organization to which the peoples of the world will readily and gladly respond. In other words, our task is no less colossal than this, to set up a new international psychology, to have a new atmosphere.

granted, and already on January 25, 1919, the conference adopted the principle of the League of Nations. In return, Wilson agreed to make compromises on territorial arrangements to guarantee the establishment of the League,

believing that a functioning League could later rectify bad arrangements. Clemenceau also compromised to obtain some guarantees for French security. He renounced France's desire for a separate Rhineland and instead accepted a defensive alliance with Great Britain and the United States. Both states pledged to help France if it were attacked by Germany.

THE TREATY OF VERSAILLES

The final peace settlement of Paris consisted of five separate treaties with the defeated nations—Germany, Austria, Hungary, Bulgaria, and Turkey. The Treaty of Versailles with Germany, signed on June 28, 1919, was by far the most important one. The Germans considered it a harsh peace and were particularly unhappy with Arti-

➤ **THE BIG FOUR AT PARIS.** Shown here are the Big Four at the Paris Peace Conference: David Lloyd George of Britain, Vittorio Orlando of Italy, Georges Clemenceau of France, and Woodrow Wilson of the United States. Although Italy was considered one of the Big Four powers, Britain, France, and the United States (the Big Three) made the major decisions at the peace conference.

© Hulton Archive/Getty Images

MAP 22.3 Territorial Changes in Europe and the Middle East after World War I. The victorious allies met in Paris to determine the shape and nature of postwar Europe. At the urging of U.S. President Woodrow Wilson, many nationalist aspirations of former imperial subjects were realized with the creation of several new countries from the prewar territory of Austria-Hungary, Germany, Russia, and the Ottoman Empire. ➤ *What new countries emerged in Europe and the Middle East?*

cle 231, the so-called War Guilt Clause, which declared Germany (and Austria) responsible for starting the war and ordered Germany to pay reparations for all the damage to which the Allied governments and their people were subjected as a result of the war "imposed upon them by the aggression of Germany and her allies."

The military and territorial provisions of the treaty also rankled Germans. Germany had to lower its army to 100,000 men, reduce its navy, and eliminate its air force. German territorial losses included the return of Alsace and Lorraine to France and sections of Prussia to the new Polish state (see Map 22.3). German land west and as far as 30 miles east of the Rhine was established as a demilitarized zone and stripped of all armaments or fortifications to serve as a barrier to any future German military moves westward against France. Outraged by the "dictated peace," the new German government complained but accepted the treaty.

THE OTHER PEACE TREATIES

The separate peace treaties made with the other Central Powers extensively redrew the map of eastern Europe. Many of these changes merely ratified what the war had already accomplished. Both the German and Russian empires lost considerable territory in eastern Europe, and the Austro-Hungarian Empire disappeared altogether. New nation-states emerged from the lands of these three empires: Finland, Latvia, Estonia, Lithuania, Poland, Czechoslovakia, Austria, and Hungary. Territorial rearrangements were also made in the Balkans. Romania acquired additional lands from Russia, Hungary, and Bulgaria. Serbia formed the nucleus of a new southern Slavic kingdom, later called Yugoslavia, which united Serbs, Croats, and Slovenes under a single monarch.

Although the Paris Peace Conference was supposedly guided by the principle of self-determination, the mixtures of peoples in eastern Europe made it impossible to draw boundaries along neat ethnic lines. As a result of compromises, virtually every eastern European state was left with a minorities problem that could lead to future conflicts. Germans in Poland; Hungarians, Poles, and Germans in Czechoslovakia; Hungarians in Romania; and the combination of Serbs, Croats, Slovenes, Macedonians, and Albanians in Yugoslavia all became sources of later conflict.

Yet another centuries-old empire, the Ottoman Empire, was dismembered by the peace settlement after the war. To gain Arab support against the Ottoman Turks during the war, the Western Allies had promised to recognize the independence of Arab states in the Middle Eastern lands of the Ottoman Empire. But the imperialist habits of Western nations died hard. After the war, France was given control of Lebanon and Syria, while Britain received Iraq and Palestine. Officially, both acquisitions were called "mandates." Since Woodrow Wilson had opposed the outright annexation of colonial territories by the Allies, the peace settlement had created a system of mandates whereby a nation officially administered a territory on behalf of the League of Nations. The system of mandates could not hide the fact that the principle of national self-determination at the Paris Peace Conference was largely for Europeans.

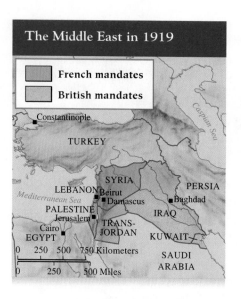

The Middle East in 1919

French mandates
British mandates

THE FUTILE SEARCH FOR STABILITY

The peace settlement at the end of World War I had tried to fulfill the nineteenth-century dream of nationalism by creating new boundaries and new states. From its inception, however, this peace settlement had left nations unhappy and only too eager to revise it.

Uneasy Peace, Uncertain Security

President Woodrow Wilson had recognized that the peace treaties contained unwise provisions that could serve as new causes for conflicts and had placed many of his hopes for the future in the League of Nations. The League, however, was not particularly effective in maintaining the peace. The failure of the United States to join the League in a backlash of isolationist sentiment undermined its effectiveness from the beginning. Moreover, the League could use only economic sanctions to halt aggression.

The weakness of the League of Nations and the failure of both the United States and Great Britain to honor their defensive military alliances with France left France embittered and alone. France's search for security between 1919 and 1924 was founded primarily on a strict enforcement of the Treaty of Versailles. This tough policy toward Germany began with the issue of reparations, the payments that the Germans were supposed to make to compensate for the "damage done to the civilian population of the Allied and Associated Powers and to their property," as the treaty asserted. In April 1921, the Allied Reparations Commission settled on a sum of 132 billion marks ($33 billion) for German reparations, payable in annual installments of 2.5 billion (gold) marks. The new German republic made its first payment in 1921, but by the following year, facing financial problems, the German government announced that it was unable to pay more. Outraged, the French government sent troops to occupy the Ruhr valley, Germany's chief industrial and mining center. Because the Germans would not pay reparations, the French would collect reparations in kind by operating and using the Ruhr's mines and factories.

Both Germany and France suffered from the French occupation of the Ruhr. The German government adopted a policy of passive resistance to French occupation that was largely financed by printing more paper money. This only intensified the inflationary pressures that had already begun in Germany by the end of the war. The German mark became worthless, and economic disaster fueled political upheavals. All the nations, including France, were happy to cooperate with the American suggestion for a new conference of experts to reassess the reparations problem.

In August 1924, an international commission produced a new plan for reparations. The Dawes Plan, named after the American banker who chaired the commission, reduced reparations and stabilized Germany's payments on the basis of its ability to pay. The Dawes Plan also granted an initial $200 million loan for German recovery, which opened the door to heavy American investments in Europe that helped create a new era of European prosperity between 1924 and 1929.

With prosperity came a new age of European diplomacy. A spirit of cooperation was fostered by the foreign ministers of Germany and France, Gustav Stresemann and Aristide Briand, who concluded the Treaty of Locarno in 1925. This guaranteed Germany's new western borders with France and Belgium. Although Germany's new eastern borders with Poland were conspicuously absent from the agreement, the Locarno pact was viewed by many as the

THE GREAT DEPRESSION: BREAD LINES IN PARIS. The Great Depression devastated the European economy and had serious political repercussions. Because of its more balanced economy, France did not feel the effects of the depression as quickly as other European countries. By 1931, however, even France was experiencing lines of unemployed people at free-food centers.

beginning of a new era of European peace. On the day after the pact was concluded, the *New York Times* proclaimed, "France and Germany Ban War Forever," and the *London Times* declared, "Peace at Last."[6]

The spirit of Locarno was based on little real substance, however. Germany lacked the military power to alter its western borders even if it wanted to. And the issue of disarmament soon proved that even the spirit of Locarno could not bring nations to cut back on their weapons. The League of Nations had suggested the "reduction of national armaments to the lowest point consistent with national safety." Germany, of course, had been disarmed with the expectation that other states would do likewise. Numerous disarmament conferences, however, failed to achieve anything substantial as states were unwilling to trust their security to anyone but their own military forces. When the World Disarmament Conference finally met in Geneva in 1932, the issue was already dead.

The Great Depression

After World War I, most European states hoped to return to the liberal ideal of a private-enterprise, market economy largely free of state intervention. But the war had vastly strengthened business cartels and labor unions, making some government regulation of these powerful organizations necessary. At the same time, reparations and war debts had severely damaged the postwar international economy, making the prosperity that did occur between 1924 and 1929 at best a fragile one and the dream of returning to the liberal ideal of a self-regulating market economy merely an illusion. What destroyed the concept altogether was the Great Depression.

Two factors played a major role in the coming of the Great Depression: a downturn in domestic economies and an international financial crisis created by the collapse of the American stock market in 1929. Already in the mid-1920s, prices for agricultural goods were beginning to decline rapidly due to overproduction of basic commodities such as wheat. In 1925, states in central and eastern Europe began to impose tariffs to close their markets to other countries' goods. An increase in the use of oil and hydroelectricity led to a slump in the coal industry even before 1929.

In addition to these domestic economic troubles, much of the European prosperity between 1924 and 1929 had been built on American bank loans to Germany. Twenty-three billion marks had been invested in German municipal bonds and German industries since 1924. Already in 1928 and 1929, American investors had begun to pull money out of Germany in order to invest in the booming New York stock market. The crash of the American stock market in October 1929 led panicky American investors to withdraw even more of their funds from Germany and other European markets. The withdrawal of funds seriously weakened the banks of Germany and other central European states. The Credit-Anstalt, Vienna's most prestigious bank, collapsed on May 31, 1931. By that time, trade was slowing down, industrialists were cutting back production, and unemployment was increasing as the ripple effects of international bank failures had a devastating impact on domestic economies.

Economic depression was by no means a new phenomenon in European history. But the depth of the economic downturn after 1929 fully justifies the label Great Depression. During 1932, the worst year of the depression, one British worker in four was unemployed, and six million workers, or 40 percent of the German labor force,

THE GREAT DEPRESSION:
UNEMPLOYED AND HOMELESS IN GERMANY

*In 1932, Germany had six million unemployed work-
ers, many of them wandering aimlessly about the country, begging for food and seeking shelter in city lodging houses
for the homeless. The Great Depression was an important factor in the rise to power of Adolf Hitler and the Nazis. This selection presents a description of the unemployed homeless in 1932.*

HEINRICH HAUSER, "WITH GERMANY'S UNEMPLOYED"

An almost unbroken chain of homeless men extends the
whole length of the great Hamburg-Berlin highway. . . . All
the highways in Germany over which I have traveled this
year presented the same aspect. . . .

Most of the hikers paid no attention to me. They walked
separately or in small groups, with their eyes on the ground.
And they had the queer, stumbling gait of barefooted people, for their shoes were slung over their shoulders. Some of
them were guild members—carpenters . . . milkmen . . . and
bricklayers . . . —but they were in a minority. Far more
numerous were those whom one could assign to no special
profession or craft—unskilled young people, for the most
part, who had been unable to find a place for themselves in
any city or town in Germany, and who had never had a job
and never expected to have one. There was something else
that had never been seen before—whole families that had
piled all their goods into baby carriages and wheelbarrows
that they were pushing along as they plodded forward in
dumb despair. It was a whole nation on the march.

I saw them—and this was the strongest impression that
the year 1932 left with me—I saw them, gathered into
groups of fifty or a hundred men, attacking fields of potatoes. I saw them digging up the potatoes and throwing
them into sacks while the farmer who owned the field
watched them in despair and the local policeman looked
on gloomily from the distance. I saw them staggering
toward the lights of the city as night fell, with their sacks
on their backs. What did it remind me of? Of the War, of
the worst periods of starvation in 1917 and 1918, but even
then people paid for the potatoes. . . .

I saw that the individual can know what is happening
only by personal experience. I know what it is to be a
tramp. I know what cold and hunger are. . . . But there are
two things that I have only recently experienced—begging
and spending the night in a municipal lodging house.

I entered the huge Berlin municipal lodging house in a
northern quarter of the city. . . .

Distribution of spoons, distribution of enameled-ware
bowls with the words "Property of the City of Berlin" written on their sides. Then the meal itself. A big kettle is carried in. Men with yellow smocks have brought it in, and
men with yellow smocks ladle out the food. These men,
too, are homeless and they have been expressly picked by
the establishment and given free food and lodging and a
little pocket money in exchange for their work about the
house.

Where have I seen this kind of food distribution before?
In a prison that I once helped to guard in the winter of
1919 during the German civil war. There was the same
hunger then, the same trembling, anxious expectation of
rations. Now the men are standing in a long row, dressed in
their plain nightshirts that reach to the ground, and the
noise of their shuffling feet is like the noise of big wild animals walking up and down the stone floor of their cages
before feeding time. The men lean far over the kettle so
that the warm steam from the food envelops them, and
they hold out their bowls as if begging and whisper to the
attendant, "Give me a real helping. Give me a little more."
A piece of bread is handed out with every bowl.

My next recollection is sitting at table in another room
on a crowded bench that is like a seat in a fourth-class railway carriage. Hundreds of hungry mouths make an enormous noise eating their food. The men sit bent over their
food like animals who feel that someone is going to take it
away from them. They hold their bowl with their left arm
partway around it, so that nobody can take it away, and
they also protect it with their other elbow and with their
head and mouth, while they move the spoon as fast as they
can between their mouth and the bowl.

---

were out of work. Between 1929 and 1932, industrial production plummeted almost 50 percent in the United
States and nearly as much in Germany. The unemployed
and homeless filled the streets of the cities throughout the
advanced industrial world (see the box above).

The economic crisis also had unexpected social repercussions. Women were often able to secure low-paying jobs
as servants, housecleaners, or laundresses, while many men
remained unemployed, either begging on the streets or
remaining at home to do household tasks. This reversal of
traditional gender roles caused resentment on the part of

many unemployed men, opening them to the shrill cries
of demagogues with simple solutions to the economic crisis. In addition, high unemployment rates among young
males often led them to join gangs that gathered in parks
or other public places, creating fear among local residents.

Governments seemed powerless to deal with the crisis.
The classical liberal remedy for depression, a deflationary
policy of balanced budgets, which involved cutting costs by
lowering wages and raising tariffs to exclude other countries'
goods from home markets, only served to worsen the
economic crisis and create even greater mass discontent.

This in turn led to serious political repercussions. Increased government activity in the economy was one reaction, even in countries like the United States that had a strong *laissez-faire* tradition. Another effect was a renewed interest in Marxist doctrines because Marx had predicted that capitalism would destroy itself through overproduction. Communism took on new popularity, especially with workers and intellectuals. Finally, the Great Depression increased the attractiveness of simplistic dictatorial solutions, especially from a new movement known as fascism. Everywhere, democracy seemed on the defensive in the 1930s.

The Democratic States

After World War I, Great Britain went through a period of serious economic difficulties. During the war, Britain had lost many of the markets for its industrial products, especially to the United States and Japan. The postwar decline of such staple industries as coal, steel, and textiles led to a rise in unemployment, which reached the two million mark in 1921. But Britain soon rebounded and from 1925 to 1929 experienced an era of renewed prosperity, even though unemployment remained at the startling level of 10 percent.

By 1929, Britain faced the growing effects of the Great Depression. The Labour Party, which had become the largest party in Britain, failed to solve the nation's economic problem and fell from power in 1931. A national government, dominated by the Conservatives, claimed credit for bringing Britain out of the worst stages of the depression, primarily by using the traditional policies of balanced budgets and protective tariffs. British politicians had largely ignored the new ideas of a Cambridge economist, John Maynard Keynes (1883–1946), who published his *General Theory of Employment, Interest, and Money* in 1936. He condemned the traditional view that in a free economy, depressions should be left to work themselves out and argued instead that unemployment stemmed not from overproduction but from a decline in demand and that demand could be increased by putting people back to work constructing highways and public buildings, even if governments had to go into debt to pay for these works, a concept known as deficit spending.

After the defeat of Germany, France had become the strongest power on the European continent. Its greatest need was to rebuild the devastated areas of northern and eastern France. However, no French government seemed capable of solving France's financial problems between 1921 and 1926. Like other European countries, though, France did experience a period of relative prosperity between 1926 and 1929.

Because it had a more balanced economy than other nations, France did not begin to feel the full effects of the Great Depression until 1932. Economic instability soon had political repercussions. During a nineteen-month period in 1932 and 1933, six different cabinets were formed as France faced political chaos. Finally, in June 1936, a coalition of leftist parties—Communists, Socialists, and Radicals—formed a Popular Front government.

Although the Popular Front initiated a program for workers that consisted of the right of collective bargaining, a forty-hour workweek, two-week paid vacations, and minimum wages, its policies failed to solve the problems of the depression. By 1938, the French were experiencing a serious loss of confidence in their political system that left them unprepared to deal with the aggressive Nazi German state to the east.

After the imperial Germany of William II had come to an end in 1918 with Germany's defeat in World War I, a German democratic state known as the Weimar Republic had been established. From its beginnings, the Weimar Republic was plagued by a series of problems. The republic had no truly outstanding political leaders, and in 1925, Paul von Hindenburg, a World War I military hero, was elected president at the age of seventy-seven. Hindenburg was a traditional military man, monarchist in sentiment, who at heart was not in favor of the republic he had been elected to serve.

The Weimar Republic also faced serious economic difficulties. Germany experienced runaway inflation in 1922 and 1923; widows, orphans, the retired elderly, army officers, teachers, civil servants, and others who lived on fixed incomes all watched their monthly stipends become worthless and their lifetime savings disappear. Their economic losses increasingly pushed the middle class to the rightist parties that were hostile to the republic. To make matters worse, after a period of prosperity from 1924 to 1929, Germany faced the Great Depression. Unemployment increased to 3 million in March 1930 and 4.4 million by December of the same year. The depression paved the way for social discontent, fear, and the rise of extremist parties.

After Germany, no Western nation was more affected by the Great Depression than the United States. By 1932, U.S. industrial production fell to half what it had been in 1929. By 1933, there were fifteen million unemployed. Under these circumstances, the Democratic presidential candidate, Franklin Delano Roosevelt (1882–1945), was able to win a landslide electoral victory in 1932. He and his advisers pursued a policy of active government intervention in the economy that came to be known as the New Deal, which included a stepped-up program of public works. The Works Progress Administration (WPA), a government organization established in 1935, employed two to three million people building bridges, roads, post offices, and airports. The Roosevelt administration was also responsible for new social legislation that launched the American welfare state. In 1935, the Social Security Act created a system of old-age pensions and unemployment insurance.

The New Deal provided some social reform measures that perhaps averted the possibility of social revolution in the United States. It did not, however, solve the unemployment problems of the Great Depression. In May 1937, during what was considered a period of full recovery, American unemployment still stood at seven million. A recession the following year increased that number to eleven million. Only World War II and the subsequent growth of the armaments industry brought American workers back to full employment.

Socialism in Soviet Russia

With their victory in the civil war in 1920, Bolshevik leaders could now turn to the challenging task of building the first socialist society in a world dominated by their capitalist enemies. But the civil war had taken an enormous toll of life. During the civil war, Lenin had pursued a policy of war communism, but once the war was over, peasants began to sabotage the program by hoarding food. Added to this problem was drought, which caused a great famine between 1920 and 1922 that claimed as many as five million lives. Industrial collapse paralleled the agricultural disaster. By 1921, industrial output was only 20 percent of its 1913 levels. Russia was exhausted. As Leon Trotsky said, "The collapse of the productive forces surpassed anything of the kind that history had ever seen. The country, and the government with it, were at the very edge of the abyss."[7]

In March 1921, Lenin pulled Russia back from the abyss by aborting war communism in favor of his New Economic Policy (NEP). Lenin's NEP was a modified version of the old capitalist system. Forced requisitioning of food from the peasants was halted, and peasants were now allowed to sell their produce openly. Retail stores and small industries that employed fewer than twenty employees could now operate under private ownership, although heavy industry, banking, utilities, and mines remained in the hands of the government. Already by 1922, a revived market and a good harvest had brought an end to famine; agriculture climbed to 75 percent of its prewar level. Industry, especially state-owned heavy industry, fared less well and continued to stagnate. Only coal production had reached prewar levels by 1926. Overall, the NEP had saved Communist Russia from complete economic disaster even though Lenin and other leading Communists intended it to be only a temporary, tactical retreat from the goals of communism.

The new government also introduced a number of social changes. Alexandra Kollontai (1872–1952), who had become a supporter of revolutionary socialism while in exile in Switzerland, took the lead in pushing a Bolshevik program for women's rights and social welfare reforms. As minister of social welfare, she tried to provide health care for women and children by establishing Palaces for the Protection of Maternity and Children. Between 1918 and 1920, the new regime issued a series of reforms that made marriage a civil act, legalized divorce, decreed the equality of men and women, and permitted abortions. Kollontai was also instrumental in establishing a women's bureau within the Communist Party known as Zhenotdel. This organization sent men and women to all parts of the Russian Empire to explain the new social order. Members of Zhenotdel were especially eager to help women with matters of divorce and women's rights. In the provinces in the east, Zhenotdel members were often brutally murdered by angry males who objected to any kind of liberation for their wives and daughters. Much to Kollontai's disappointment, many of these early Communist social reforms were also undone as the Communists came to face more pressing matters, including survival of the new regime.

Lenin's death in 1924 inaugurated a struggle for power among the seven members of the Politburo, the institution that had become the leading organ of the party. The Politburo was severely divided over the future direction of the Soviet Union, a federation of Russia and fourteen smaller soviet-based republics proclaimed in 1922. The Left, led by Leon Trotsky, wanted to end the NEP and launch the nation on the path of rapid industrialization, primarily at the expense of the peasantry. This same group wanted to carry the revolution on, believing that the survival of the Russian Revolution ultimately depended on the spread of communism abroad. Another group in the Politburo, called the Right, rejected the cause of world revolution and wanted to concentrate instead on constructing a socialist state. The members of this group also favored a continuation of Lenin's NEP because they believed that too rapid industrialization would harm the living standards of the peasantry.

These ideological divisions were underscored by an intense personal rivalry between Leon Trotsky and Joseph Stalin. In 1924, Trotsky held the post of commissar of war and was the leading spokesman for the Left in the Politburo. Joseph Stalin (1879–1953) was content to hold the dull bureaucratic job of party general secretary, while other Politburo members held party positions that enabled them to display their brilliant oratorical abilities. But Stalin was a good organizer (his fellow Bolsheviks called him "Comrade Card-Index"), and the other members of the Politburo soon found that the position of party secretary was really the most important in the party hierarchy. Stalin used his post as party general secretary to gain complete control of the Communist Party. Trotsky was expelled from the party in 1927. By 1929, Stalin had succeeded in eliminating the Old Bolsheviks of the revolutionary era from the Politburo and establishing a dictatorship so powerful that the Russian tsars of old would have been envious.

IN PURSUIT OF A NEW REALITY: CULTURAL AND INTELLECTUAL TRENDS

Four years of devastating war left many Europeans with a profound sense of despair. To many people, World War I could only mean that something was dreadfully wrong with

Western values. The experiences of World War I seemed to confirm the prewar avant-garde belief that human beings were really violent animals who were incapable of creating a sane and rational world. The Great Depression only added to the despair created by World War I.

Political and economic uncertainties were paralleled by social innovations. World War I had served to break down many traditional middle-class attitudes, especially toward sexuality. In the 1920s, women's physical appearance changed dramatically. Short skirts, short hair, the use of cosmetics that were once thought to be the preserve of prostitutes, and the new practice of suntanning gave women a new image. This change in physical appearance, which stressed more exposure of a woman's body, was also accompanied by frank discussions of sexual matters. In 1926, the Dutch physician Theodor van de Velde published *Ideal Marriage: Its Physiology and Technique*. Translated into a number of languages, it became an international best-seller. Van de Velde described female and male anatomy, discussed birth control techniques, and glorified sexual pleasure in marriage.

Nightmares and New Visions

Uncertainty also pervaded the cultural and intellectual achievements of the interwar years. Postwar artistic trends were largely a working out of the implications of prewar developments. Abstract painting, for example, became ever more popular as many pioneering artists of the early twentieth century matured between the two world wars. In addition, prewar fascination with the absurd and the unconscious contents of the mind seemed even more appropriate after the nightmare landscapes of World War I battlefronts. This gave rise to both the Dada movement and Surrealism.

Dadaism attempted to enshrine the purposelessness of life. Tristan Tzara (1896–1945), a Romanian-French poet and one of the founders of Dadaism, expressed the Dadaist contempt for the Western tradition in a lecture in 1922: "The acts of life have no beginning or end. Everything happens in a completely idiotic way. . . . Like everything in life, Dada is useless." Revolted by the insanity of life, the Dadaists tried to give it expression by creating anti-art. The 1918 Berlin Dada Manifesto maintained that "Dada is the international expression of our times, the great rebellion of artistic movements." In the hands of Hannah Höch (1889–1978), Dada became an instrument to comment on women's roles in the new mass culture. Höch was the only female member of the Berlin Dada Club, which featured the use of photomontage. Her work was part of the first Dada show in Berlin in 1920. In *Dada Dance*, she seemed to criticize the "new woman" by making fun of the way women were inclined to follow new fashion styles. In other works, however, she created positive images of the modern woman and expressed a keen interest in new freedoms for women.

Perhaps more important as an artistic movement was Surrealism, which sought a reality beyond the material, sensible world and found it in the world of the unconscious through the portrayal of fantasies, dreams, or nightmares. Employing logic to convey the illogical, the Surrealists created disturbing and evocative images. The Spaniard Salvador Dalí (1904–1989) became the high priest of Surrealism and in his mature phase became a master of representational Surrealism. In *The Persistence of Memory*, Dalí portrayed recognizable objects divorced from their normal context. By placing these objects into unrecognizable relationships, Dalí created a disturbing world in which the irrational had become tangible.

The move to functionalism in modern architecture also became more widespread in the 1920s and 1930s. Especially important in the spread of functionalism was the Bauhaus school of art, architecture, and design, founded in 1919 at

HANNAH HÖCH, *CUT WITH THE KITCHEN KNIFE DADA THROUGH THE LAST WEIMAR BEER BELLY CULTURAL EPOCH OF GERMANY*.   Hannah Höch, a prominent figure in the postwar Dada movement, used photomontage to create images that reflected on women's issues. In *Cut with the Kitchen Knife*, she combined pictures of German political leaders with sports stars, Dada artists, and scenes from urban life. One major theme emerged: the confrontation between the anti-Dada world of German political leaders and the Dada world of revolutionary ideals. Höch associated women with Dada and the new world.

➤ **SALVADOR DALÍ, *THE PERSISTENCE OF MEMORY*.** Surrealism was another important artistic movement between the wars. Influenced by the theories of Freudian psychology, Surrealists sought to reveal the world of the unconscious, or the "greater reality" that they believed existed beyond the world of physical appearances. As is evident in this painting, Salvador Dalí sought to portray the world of dreams by painting recognizable objects in unrecognizable relationships.

Weimar, Germany, by the Berlin architect Walter Gropius. The Bauhaus teaching staff was made up of architects, artists, and designers. They worked together to combine the study of fine arts (painting and sculpture) with the applied arts (printing, weaving, and furniture making). Gropius urged his followers to foster a new union of arts and crafts in order to create the buildings and objects of the future.

At the beginning of the twentieth century, a revolution had come to music with the work of Igor Stravinsky. But Stravinsky still wrote music in a definite key. In 1924, the Viennese composer Arnold Schönberg (1874–1951) wrote a piano suite in which he used a scale composed of twelve notes free of any tonal key. His atonal music was similar to abstract painting. Abstract painting arranged colors and lines without concrete images; atonal music organized sounds without any recognizable harmonies. Unlike modern art, however, modern music found little favor until after World War II.

Probing the Unconscious

The interest in the unconscious, evident in Surrealism, was also apparent in the new literary techniques that emerged in the 1920s. One of its most apparent manifestations was in the "stream of consciousness" technique, in which the writer presented an interior monologue, or a report of the innermost thoughts of each character. One example of this genre was written by the Irish exile James Joyce (1882–1941). His *Ulysses*, published in 1922, told the story of one day in the life of ordinary people in Dublin by following the flow of their inner dialogue. Disconnected ramblings and veiled allusions pervade Joyce's work.

The German writer Hermann Hesse (1877–1962) dealt with the unconscious in a considerably different fashion. His novels reflected the influence of both Carl Jung's psychological theories and Eastern religions and focused among other things on the spiritual loneliness of modern human beings in a mechanized urban society. *Demian* was a psychoanalytic study of incest, and *Steppenwolf* mirrored the psychological confusion of modern existence. Hesse's novels made a large impact on German youth in the 1920s (see the box on p. 655). He won the Nobel Prize for literature in 1946.

For much of the Western world, the best way to find (or escape) reality was in the field of mass entertainment. The 1930s represented the heyday of the Hollywood studio system, which in the single year of 1937 turned out nearly six hundred feature films. Supplementing the movies were cheap paperbacks and radio, which brought sports, soap operas, and popular music to the masses.

Mass forms of communication and entertainment were not new. But the increased size of audiences and the ability of radio and cinema, unlike the printed word, to provide an immediate mass experience did add new dimensions to mass culture. Favorite film actors and actresses became stars whose lives then became subject to public adoration and scrutiny. Sensuous actresses such as Marlene Dietrich, whose appearance in the early sound film *The Blue Angel* catapulted her to fame, projected new images of women's sexuality.

CONCLUSION

World War I shattered the liberal, rational society of late-nineteenth- and early-twentieth-century Europe. The incredible destruction and the death of almost ten million people undermined the whole idea of progress. New

HESSE AND THE UNCONSCIOUS

*T*he novels of Hermann Hesse made a strong impact on young people, first in Germany in the 1920s and then in the United States in the 1960s after they had been translated into English. Many of these young people shared Hesse's fascination with the unconscious and his dislike of modern industrial civilization. This excerpt from Demian spoke directly to many of them.

HERMANN HESSE, DEMIAN

The following spring I was to leave the preparatory school and enter a university. I was still undecided, however, as to where and what I was to study. I had grown a thin mustache, I was a full-grown man, and yet I was completely helpless and without a goal in life. Only one thing was certain: the voice within me, the dream image. I felt the duty to follow this voice blindly wherever it might lead me. But it was difficult and each day I rebelled against it anew. Perhaps I was mad, as I thought at moments; perhaps I was not

like other men? But I was able to do the same things the others did; with a little effort and industry I could read Plato, was able to solve problems in trigonometry or follow a chemical analysis. There was only one thing I could not do: wrest the dark secret goal from myself and keep it before me as others did who knew exactly what they wanted to be—professors, lawyers, doctors, artists, however long this would take them and whatever difficulties and advantages this decision would bear in its wake. This I could not do. Perhaps I would become something similar, but how was I to know? Perhaps I would have to continue my search for years on end and would not become anything, and would not reach a goal. Perhaps I would reach this goal but it would turn out to be an evil, dangerous, horrible one?

I wanted only to try to live in accord with the promptings which came from my true self. Why was that so very difficult?

---

propaganda techniques had manipulated entire populations into sustaining their involvement in a meaningless slaughter.

World War I was a total war and involved an unprecedented mobilization of resources and populations and increased government centralization of power over the lives of its citizens. Civil liberties, such as freedom of the press, speech, assembly, and movement, were circumscribed in the name of national security. World War I made the practice of strong central authority a way of life.

The turmoil wrought by World War I seemed to open the door to even greater insecurity. Revolutions in Russia and the Middle East dismembered old empires and created new states that gave rise to unexpected prob-

lems. Expectations that Europe and the world would return to normalcy were soon dashed by the failure to achieve a lasting peace, economic collapse, and the rise of authoritarian governments that not only restricted individual freedoms but sought even greater control over the lives of their subjects in order to manipulate and guide them to achieve the goals of their totalitarian regimes.

Finally, World War I ended the age of European hegemony over world affairs. By demolishing their own civilization on the battlegrounds of Europe in World War I, Europeans inadvertently encouraged the subject peoples of their vast colonial empires to initiate movements for national independence. In the next chapter, we examine some of those movements.

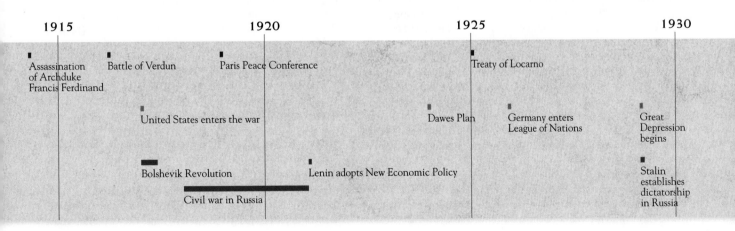

1915	1920	1925	1930

- Assassination of Archduke Francis Ferdinand
- Battle of Verdun
- Paris Peace Conference
- Treaty of Locarno
- United States enters the war
- Dawes Plan
- Germany enters League of Nations
- Great Depression begins
- Bolshevik Revolution
- Lenin adopts New Economic Policy
- Stalin establishes dictatorship in Russia
- Civil war in Russia

CHAPTER NOTES

1. Arnold Toynbee, *Surviving the Future* (New York, 1971), pp. 106–107.
2. Quoted in Joachim Remak, "1914—The Third Balkan War: Origins Reconsidered," *Journal of Modern History* 43 (1971): 364–365.
3. Quoted in J. M. Winter, *The Experience of World War I* (New York, 1989), p. 142.
4. Quoted in Catherine W. Reilly, ed., *Scars upon My Heart: Women's Poetry and Verse of the First World War* (London, 1981), p. 90.

5. Quoted in William M. Mandel, *Soviet Women* (Garden City, N.Y., 1975), p. 43.
6. Quoted in Robert Paxton, *Europe in the Twentieth Century*, 2d ed. (San Diego, 1985), p. 237.
7. Irving Howe, ed., *The Basic Writings of Trotsky* (London, 1963), p. 162.

SUGGESTED READING

The historical literature on the causes of World War I is vast. A good starting point is the work by J. Joll, *The Origins of the First World War*, 2d ed. (London, 1992). The belief that Germany was primarily responsible for the war was argued vigorously by the German scholar F. Fischer in *Germany's Aims in the First World War* (New York, 1967), *World Power or Decline: The Controversy over Germany's Aims in World War I* (New York, 1974), and *War of Illusions: German Policies from 1911 to 1914* (New York, 1975). The role of each great power has been reassessed in a series of books on the causes of World War I. They include V. R. Berghahn, *Germany and the Approach of War in 1914* (London, 1973); Z. S. Steiner, *Britain and the Origins of the First World War* (New York, 1977); J. F. Keiger, *France and the Origins of the First World War* (New York, 1984); and D. C. B. Lieven, *Russia and the Origins of the First World War* (New York, 1984). On the role of militarism, see D. Hermann, *The Arming of Europe and the Making of the First World War* (New York, 1997).

Two fine accounts of World War I are M. Gilbert, *The First World War* (New York, 1994), and the lavishly illustrated book by J. M. Winter, *The Experience of World War I* (New York, 1989). See also the brief work by N. Heyman, *World War I* (Westport, Conn., 1997). There is an excellent collection of articles in H. Strachan, *The Oxford Illustrated History of the First World War* (New York, 1998). The nature of trench warfare is examined in T. Ashworth, *Trench Warfare, 1914–1918: The Live-and-Let-Live System* (London, 1980). The war at sea is studied in R. Hough, *The Great War at Sea, 1914–18* (Oxford, 1983). In *The Great War and Modern Memory* (London, 1975), P. Fussell attempted to show how British writers described their war experiences. Although scholars do not always agree with her conclusions, B. Tuchman's *Guns of August* (New York, 1962) is a magnificently written account of the opening days of the war. For an interesting perspective on World War I and the beginnings of the modern world, see M. Eksteins, *Rites of Spring: The Great War and the Birth of the Modern Age* (Boston, 1989).

On the role of women in World War I, see G. Braybon, *Women Workers in the First World War: The British Experience* (London, 1981); J. M. Winter and R. M. Wall, eds., *The Upheaval of War:* *Family, Work and Welfare in Europe, 1914–1918* (Cambridge, 1988); and G. Braybon and P. Summerfield, *Women's Experiences in Two World Wars* (London, 1987).

The role of war aims in shaping the peace settlement is examined in V. H. Rothwell, *British War Aims and Peace Diplomacy, 1914–1918* (Oxford, 1971), and D. R. Stevenson, *French War Aims Against Germany, 1914–1919* (New York, 1982).

A good introduction to the Russian Revolution can be found in R. A. Wade, *The Russian Revolution, 1917* (Cambridge, 2000), and S. Fitzpatrick, *The Russian Revolution, 1917–1932*, 2d ed. (New York, 1994). See also R. Pipes, *The Russian Revolution* (New York, 1990). On Lenin, see R. W. Clark, *Lenin* (New York, 1988), and the valuable work by A. B. Ulam, *The Bolsheviks* (New York, 1965). On social reforms, see W. Goldman, *Women, the State, and Revolution* (Cambridge, 1993). A comprehensive study of the Russian civil war is W. B. Lincoln, *Red Victory: A History of the Russian Civil War* (New York, 1989).

World War I and the Russian Revolution are also well covered in two good general surveys, R. Paxton, *Europe in the Twentieth Century*, 2d ed. (San Diego, 1985), and A. Rudhart, *Twentieth-Century Europe* (Englewood Cliffs, N.J., 1986).

For a general introduction to the interwar period, see R. J. Sontag, *A Broken World, 1919–39* (New York, 1971). On European security issues after the Peace of Paris, see S. Marks, *The Illusion of Peace: Europe's International Relations, 1918–1933* (New York, 1976). The Locarno agreements are well examined in J. Jacobson, *Locarno Diplomacy* (Princeton, N.J., 1972). The best study on the problem of reparations is M. Trachtenberg, *Reparations in World Politics* (New York, 1980), which paints a more positive view of French policies. The "return to normalcy" after the war is analyzed in C. S. Maier, *Recasting Bourgeois Europe: Stabilization in France, Germany, and Italy in the Decade After World War I* (Princeton, N.J., 1975). Also valuable is D. P. Silverman, *Reconstructing Europe After the Great War* (Cambridge, Mass., 1982). On the Great Depression, see C. P. Kindleberger, *The World in Depression, 1929–39*, rev. ed. (Berkeley, Calif., 1986). On Weimar Germany, see P. Bookbinder, *Weimar Germany* (New York, 1996), and R. Henig, *The Weimar Republic, 1919–1933* (New York, 1998), a brief study.

INFOTRAC COLLEGE EDITION

**For additional reading, go to InfoTrac College Edition, your online research library at
http://web1.infotrac-college.com**

Enter the search terms "World War, 1914–1918" using the Subject Guide.

Enter the search terms "Russia Revolution" using Keywords.

Enter the search term "Bolshevik" using Keywords.

Enter the search terms "Versailles Treaty" using Keywords.

Enter the search terms "Great Depression" using Keywords.

YMCA of the USA Archives, University of Minnesota Libraries

NATIONALISM, REVOLUTION, AND DICTATORSHIP: AFRICA, ASIA, AND LATIN AMERICA FROM 1919 TO 1939

CHAPTER OUTLINE

- THE RISE OF NATIONALISM
- REVOLUTION IN CHINA
- JAPAN BETWEEN THE WARS
- NATIONALISM AND DICTATORSHIP IN LATIN AMERICA
- CONCLUSION

FOCUS QUESTIONS

- What forms did the independence movements in India and the Middle East take, and what problems did each movement face?
- What forms did modernization take in Turkey, Iran, and Japan in the interwar years?
- What problems did China face between 1919 and 1939, and what solutions did the Nationalists and the Communists propose to solve these problems?
- What problems did the nations of Latin America face in the interwar years, and how did they respond to these problems?
- ➤ What developments contributed to the rise of nationalism after 1919, and what role did nationalism play in the Middle East, Asia, and Latin America?

*I*n the spring of 1913, the Bolshevik leader Vladimir Lenin wrote an article in the Communist Party newspaper *Pravda* on the awakening of Asia. "Was it so long ago," he asked his readers, "that China was considered typical of the lands that had been standing still for centuries? Today China is a land of seething political activity, the scene of a virile social movement and of a democratic upsurge." Similar conditions, he added, were spreading the democratic revolution to other parts of Asia—to Turkey, Persia, and China. Ferment was on the rise even in British India.[1]

A year later, the Great War erupted, and Lenin, like millions of others, turned his eyes to events in Europe. In February 1917, riots in the streets of Petrograd (the renamed Saint Petersburg) marked the onset of the Russian Revolution. By the end of the year, the Bolsheviks were in power in Moscow. For the next few years, Lenin and his colleagues were preoccupied with consolidating their control over the vast territories of the old tsarist Russian Empire. But he had not forgotten his earlier prediction that the colonial world was on the verge of revolt. Now, with the infant Soviet state virtually surrounded by its capitalist enemies, Lenin argued that the oppressed masses of Asia and Africa were potential allies in the bitter struggle against the brutal yoke of world imperialism. For the next two decades, the leaders in Moscow periodically turned their attention to China and other parts of Asia in an effort to ride what they hoped would be a mounting wave of revolt against foreign domination. •

THE RISE OF NATIONALISM

Although the West had emerged from World War I relatively intact, its political and social foundations and its self-confidence had been severely undermined. Within Europe, doubts about the future viability of Western civilization were widespread, especially among the intellectual elite. These doubts were quick to reach the attention of perceptive observers in Asia and Africa and contributed to a rising tide of unrest against Western political domination throughout the colonial and semicolonial world. That unrest took a variety of forms but was most notably displayed in increasing worker activism, rural protest, and a rising sense of national fervor among anticolonialist intellectuals. In areas of Asia, Africa, and Latin America where independent states had successfully resisted the Western onslaught, the discontent fostered by the war and later by the Great Depression led to a loss of confidence in democratic institutions and the rise of political dictatorships.

Modern Nationalism

The first stage of resistance to the West in Asia and Africa had met with humiliation and failure and must have confirmed many Westerners' conviction that colonial peoples lacked both the strength and the know-how to create modern states and govern their own destinies. In fact, the process was just beginning. The next phase—the rise of modern nationalism—began to take shape at the beginning of the twentieth century and was the product of the convergence of several factors. The primary source of anticolonialist sentiment was a new urban middle class of westernized intellectuals. In many cases, these merchants, petty functionaries, clerks, students, and professionals had been educated in Western-style schools. A few had spent time in the West. Many spoke Western languages, wore Western clothes, and worked in occupations connected with the colonial regime. Some, like Mahatma Gandhi in India, José Rizal in the

Philippines, and Kwame Nkrumah in the Gold Coast, even wrote in the languages of their colonial masters.

The results were paradoxical. On the one hand, this "new class" admired Western culture and sometimes harbored a deep sense of contempt for traditional ways. On the other hand, many strongly resented the foreigners and their arrogant contempt for colonial peoples. Though eager to introduce Western ideas and institutions into their own society, these intellectuals often resented the gap between ideal and reality, theory and practice, in colonial policy. Although Western political thought exalted democracy, equality, and individual freedom, democratic institutions were primitive or nonexistent in the colonies.

Equality in economic opportunity and social life was also noticeably lacking. Normally, the middle classes did not suffer in the same manner as impoverished peasants or menial workers on sugar or rubber plantations, but they, too, had complaints. They were usually relegated to menial jobs in the government or business and paid lower salaries than those of Europeans in similar occupations. The superiority of the Europeans was expressed in a variety of ways, including "whites only" clubs and the use of the familiar form of the language (normally used by adults to children) when addressing the natives.

Under these conditions, many of the new urban educated class were very ambivalent toward their colonial masters and the civilization that they represented. Out of this mixture of hopes and resentments emerged the first stirrings of modern nationalism in Asia and Africa. During the first quarter of the century, in colonial and semicolonial societies from the Suez Canal to the shores of the Pacific Ocean, educated native peoples began to organize political parties and movements seeking reforms or the end of foreign rule and the restoration of independence.

RELIGION AND NATIONALISM

At first, many of the leaders of these movements did not focus clearly on the idea of nationhood but tried to defend native economic interests or religious beliefs. In Burma, for example, the first expression of modern nationalism came from students at the University of Rangoon, who protested against official persecution of the Buddhist religion and British lack of respect for local religious traditions. Calling themselves Thakin (a polite term in the Burmese language meaning "lord" or "master," thus emphasizing their demand for the right to rule themselves), they protested against British arrogance and failure to observe local customs in Buddhist temples (such as failing to remove their footwear). Only in the 1930s did the Thakins begin to focus specifically on national independence.

In the Dutch East Indies, the Sarekat Islam (Islamic Association) began as a self-help society among Muslim merchants to fight against domination of the local economy by Chinese interests. Eventually, activist elements began to realize that the source of the problem was not the

THE DILEMMA OF THE INTELLECTUAL

Sutan Sjahrir (1909–1966) was a prominent leader of the Indonesian nationalist movement who briefly served as prime minister of the Republic of Indonesia in the 1950s. Like many Western-educated Asian intellectuals, he was tortured by the realization that by education and outlook he was closer to his colonial masters than to his own people. He wrote the following passage in a letter to his wife in 1935 and later included it in his book Out of Exile.

SUTAN SJAHRIR, *OUT OF EXILE*

Am I perhaps estranged from my people? . . . Why are the things that contain beauty for them and arouse their gentler emotions only senseless and displeasing for me? In reality, the spiritual gap between my people and me is certainly no greater than that between an intellectual in Holland . . . and the undeveloped people of Holland. . . . The difference is rather . . . that the intellectual in Holland does not feel this gap because there is a portion—even a fairly large portion—of his own people on approximately the same intellectual level as himself. . . .

This is what we lack here. Not only is the number of intellectuals in this country smaller in proportion to the total population—in fact, very much smaller—but in addition, the few who are here do not constitute any single entity in spiritual outlook, or in any spiritual life or single culture whatsoever. . . . It is for them so much more diffi-

cult than for the intellectuals in Holland. In Holland they build—both consciously and unconsciously—on what is already there. . . . Even if they oppose it, they do so as a method of application or as a starting point.

In our country this is not the case. Here there has been no spiritual or cultural life, and no intellectual progress for centuries. There are the much-praised Eastern art forms but what are these except bare rudiments from a feudal culture that cannot possibly provide a dynamic fulcrum for people of the twentieth century? . . . Our spiritual needs are needs of the twentieth century; our problems and our views are of the twentieth century. Our inclination is no longer toward the mystical, but toward reality, clarity, and objectivity. . . .

We intellectuals here are much closer to Europe or America than we are to the Borobudur or Mahabharata or to the primitive Islamic culture of Java and Sumatra. . . .

So, it seems, the problem stands in principle. It is seldom put forth by us in this light, and instead most of us search unconsciously for a synthesis that will leave us internally tranquil. We want to have both Western science and Eastern philosophy, the Eastern "spirit," in the culture. But what is this Eastern spirit? It is, they say, the sense of the higher, of spirituality, of the eternal and religious, as opposed to the materialism of the West. I have heard this countless times, but it has never convinced me.

Chinese merchants but the colonial presence, and in the 1920s, Sarekat Islam was transformed into a new organization—the Nationalist Party of Indonesia (PNI)—that focused on national independence. Like the Thakins in Burma, this party would eventually lead the country to independence after World War II.

INDEPENDENCE OR MODERNIZATION? THE NATIONALIST QUANDARY

Building a new nation, however, requires more than a shared sense of grievances against the foreign invader. A host of other issues also had to be resolved. Soon patriots throughout the colonial world were engaged in a lively and sometimes acrimonious debate over such questions as whether independence or modernization should be their primary objective. The answer depended in part on how the colonial regime was perceived. If it was viewed as a source of needed reforms in a traditional society, a gradualist approach made sense. But if it was seen primarily as an impediment to change, the first priority was to bring it to an end. The vast majority of patriotic individuals were convinced that to survive, their societies must adopt much of the Western way of life; yet many were equally determined that the local culture would not, and should not,

become a carbon copy of the West. What was the national identity, after all, if it did not incorporate some elements from the traditional way of life?

Another reason for using traditional values was to provide ideological symbols that the common people could understand and would rally around. Though aware that they needed to enlist the mass of the population in the common struggle, most urban intellectuals had difficulty communicating with the teeming population in the countryside who did not understand such complicated and unfamiliar concepts as democracy and nationhood. As the Indonesian intellectual Sutan Sjahrir lamented, many westernized intellectuals had more in common with their colonial rulers than with the native population in the rural villages (see the box above). As one French colonial official remarked in some surprise to a Vietnamese reformist, "Why, Monsieur, you are more French than I am!"

Gandhi and the Indian National Congress

Nowhere in the colonial world were these issues debated more vigorously than in India. Before the Sepoy Rebellion, Indian consciousness had focused primarily on the question of religious identity. But in the latter half of the nineteenth century, a stronger sense of national consciousness began to arise, provoked by the conservative policies and racial arrogance of the British colonial authorities.

The first Indian nationalists were almost invariably upper-class and educated. Many of them were from urban areas such as Bombay, Madras, and Calcutta. Some were trained in law and were members of the civil service. At first, many tended to prefer reform to revolution and believed that India needed modernization before it could handle the problems of independence. An exponent of this view was Gopal Gokhale (1866–1915), a moderate nationalist who hoped that he could convince the British to bring about needed reforms in Indian society. Gokhale and other like-minded reformists did have some effect. In the 1880s, the government introduced a measure of self-government for the first time. All too often, however, such efforts were sabotaged by local British officials.

The slow pace of reform convinced many Indian nationalists that relying on British benevolence was futile. In 1885, a small group of Indians, with some British participation, met in Bombay to form the Indian National Congress (INC). They hoped to speak for all India, but most were high-caste English-trained Hindus. Like their reformist predecessors, members of the INC did not demand immediate independence and accepted the need for reforms to end traditional abuses like child marriage and *sati*. At the same time, they called for an Indian share in the governing process and more spending on economic development and less on military campaigns along the frontier. The British responded with a few concessions, but change was glacially slow. As impatient members of the INC became disillusioned, the radicals split off and formed the New Party, which called for the use of terrorism and violence to achieve national independence.

The INC also had difficulty reconciling religious differences within its ranks. The stated goal of the INC was to seek self-determination for all Indians regardless of class or religious affiliation, but many of its leaders were Hindu and inevitably reflected Hindu concerns. In the first decade of the twentieth century, the separate Muslim League was created to represent the interests of the millions of Muslims in Indian society.

In 1915, a young Hindu lawyer returned from South Africa to become active in the INC. He transformed the movement and galvanized India's struggle for independence and identity. Mohandas Gandhi was born in 1869 in Gujarat, in western India, the son of a government minister. In the late nineteenth century, he studied in London and became a lawyer. In 1893, he went to South Africa to work in a law firm serving Indian émigrés working as laborers there. He soon became aware of the racial prejudice and exploitation experienced by Indians living in the territory and tried to organize them to protect their interests.

On his return to India, Gandhi immediately became active in the independence movement. Using his experience in South Africa, he set up a movement based on nonviolent resistance (the Hindi term was *satyagraha*, "hold fast to the truth") to try to force the British to improve the lot of the poor and grant independence to India. His goal was twofold: to convert the British to his views while simultaneously strengthening the unity and sense of self-respect of his compatriots. Gandhi was particularly concerned about the plight of the millions of untouchables, whom he called *harijans*, or "children of God." When the British attempted to suppress dissent, he called on his followers to refuse to obey British regulations. He began to manufacture his own clothes (Gandhi now dressed in a simple *dhoti* made of coarse homespun cotton) and adopted the spinning wheel as a symbol of Indian resistance to imports of British textiles.

Gandhi, now increasingly known as India's "Great Soul" (*Mahatma*), organized mass protests to achieve his aims, but in 1919 they got out of hand and led to violence and British reprisals. British troops killed hundreds of unarmed protesters in the enclosed square in the city of Amritsar in northwestern India. When the protests spread, Gandhi was horrified at the violence and briefly retreated from active politics. Nevertheless, he was arrested for his role in the protests and spent several years in prison.

Gandhi combined his anticolonial activities with an appeal to the spiritual instincts of all Indians. Though he had been born and raised a Hindu, his universalist approach to the idea of God transcended individual religion, although it was shaped by the historical themes of Hindu belief. At a speech given in London in September 1931, he expressed his view of the nature of God as "an indefinable mysterious power that pervades everything . . . , an unseen power which makes itself felt and yet defies all proof."[2]

While Gandhi was in prison, the political situation continued to evolve. In 1921, the British passed the Government of India Act, transforming the heretofore advisory Legislative Council into a bicameral parliament, two-thirds of whose members would be elected. Similar bodies were created at the provincial level. In a stroke, five million Indians were enfranchised. But such reforms were no longer enough for many members of the INC, who wanted to push aggressively for full independence. The British exacerbated the situation by increasing the salt tax and prohibiting the Indian people from manufacturing or harvesting their own salt. Gandhi, now released from prison, returned to his earlier policy of civil disobedience by openly joining several dozen supporters in a 200-mile walk to the sea, where he picked up a lump of salt and urged Indians to ignore the law. Gandhi and many other members of the INC were arrested.

Indian women were active in the movement. Women accounted for about twenty thousand, or nearly 10 percent, of all those arrested and jailed for taking part in demonstrations during the interwar period. Women marched, picketed foreign shops, and promoted the spinning and

⇶ **NEHRU AND GANDHI.** Mahatma Gandhi (on the right), India's "Great Soul," became the emotional leader of India's struggle for independence from British colonial rule. Unlike many other nationalist leaders, Gandhi rejected the materialistic culture of the West and urged his followers to return to the native traditions of the Indian village. To illustrate his point, Gandhi dressed in the simple Indian *dhoti* rather than in the Western fashion favored by many of his colleagues. With Gandhi, Jawaharlal Nehru (on the left) was a leading figure in the Indian struggle for independence. Unlike Gandhi, however, his goal was to transform India into a modern industrial society. After independence, he became the nation's prime minister until his death in 1964.

AP/Wide World Photos

wearing of homemade cloth. By the 1930s, women's associations were actively involved in promoting a number of reforms, including women's education, the introduction of birth control devices, the abolition of child marriage, and universal suffrage. In 1929, the Sarda Act raised the minimum age of marriage to fourteen.

In the 1930s, a new figure entered the movement in the person of Jawaharlal Nehru (1889–1964), son of an earlier INC leader. Educated in the law in Great Britain and a *brahmin* by birth, Nehru personified the new Anglo-Indian politician: secular, rational, upper-class, and intellectual. In fact, he appeared to be everything that Gandhi was not. With his emergence, the independence movement embarked on two paths, religious and secular, native and Western, traditional and modern. The dual character of the INC leadership may well have strengthened the movement by bringing together the two primary impulses behind the desire for independence: elite nationalism and the primal force of Indian traditionalism. But it portended trouble for the nation's new leadership in defining India's future path in the contemporary world. In the meantime, Muslim discontent with Hindu dominance over the INC was increasing. In 1940, the Muslim League called for the creation of a separate Muslim state of Pakistan ("land of the pure") in the northwest (see the box on p. 663). As communal strife between Hindus and Muslims increased, many Indians came to realize with sorrow (and some British colonialists with satisfaction) that British rule was all that stood between peace and civil war.

The Nationalist Revolt in the Middle East

In the Middle East, as in Europe, World War I hastened the collapse of old empires. The Ottoman Empire, which had dominated the eastern Mediterranean since the seizure of Constantinople in 1453, had been growing steadily weaker since the end of the eighteenth century, troubled by rising governmental corruption, a decline in the effectiveness of the sultans, and the loss of considerable territory in the Balkans and southwestern Russia. In North Africa, Ottoman authority, tenuous at best, had disintegrated in the nineteenth century, enabling the French to seize Algeria and Tunisia and the British to establish a protectorate over the Nile River valley.

MUSTAPHA KEMAL AND THE MODERNIZATION OF TURKEY

Reformist elements in Istanbul, to be sure, had tried from time to time to resist the trend, but military defeats continued: Greece declared its independence, and Ottoman power declined steadily in the Middle East. A rising sense of nationality among Serbs, Armenians, and other minority peoples threatened the internal stability and cohesion of the empire. In the 1870s, a new generation of Ottoman reformers seized power in Istanbul and pushed through a constitution aimed at forming a legislative assembly that would represent all the peoples in the state. But the sultan

A CALL FOR A MUSLIM STATE

*M*ohammed Iqbal, a well-known Muslim poet in colonial India, was also a prominent advocate of the creation of a separate state for Muslims in South Asia. In this passage from an address he presented to the All-India Muslim League in December 1930, he explained the rationale for his proposal.

MOHAMMED IQBAL, SPEECH TO THE ALL-INDIA MUSLIM LEAGUE

It cannot be denied that Islam, regarded as an ethical ideal plus a certain kind of polity—by which expression I mean a social structure regulated by a legal system and animated by a specific ethical ideal—has been the chief formative factor in the life history of the Muslims of India. It has furnished those basic emotions and loyalties which gradually unify scattered individuals and groups and finally transform them into a well-defined people. Indeed it is no exaggeration to say that India is perhaps the only country in the world where Islam, as a people-building force, has worked at its best. In India, as elsewhere, the structure of Islam as a society is almost entirely due to the working of Islam as a culture inspired by a specific ethical ideal. What I mean to say is that Muslim society, with its remarkable homogeneity and inner unity, has grown to be what it is under the pressure of the laws and institutions associated with the culture of Islam.

Communalism in its higher aspect, then, is indispensable to the formation of a harmonious whole in a country like India. The units of Indian society are not territorial as in European countries. India is a continent of human groups belonging to different religions. Their behavior is not at all determined by a common race consciousness. Even the Hindus do not form a homogeneous group. The principle of European democracy cannot be applied to India without recognizing the fact of communal groups. The Muslim demand for the creation of a Muslim India within India is, therefore, perfectly justified.

The idea need not alarm the Hindus or the British. India is the greatest Muslim country in the world. The life of Islam, as a cultural force, in this country very largely depends on its centralization in a specified territory. This centralization of the most living portion of the Muslims of India, whose military and police service has, notwithstanding unfair treatment from the British, made the British rule possible in this country, will eventually solve the problem of India as well as of Asia. It will intensify their sense of responsibility and deepen their patriotic feeling. Thus possessing full opportunity of development within the body politic of India, the northwest India Muslims will prove the best defenders of India against a foreign invasion, be the invasion one of ideas or of bayonets. . . .

I therefore demand the formation of a consolidated Muslim State in the best interests of India and Islam. For India it means security and peace resulting from an internal balance of power; for Islam an opportunity to rid itself of the stamp that Arabian imperialism was forced to give it, to mobilize its law, its education, its culture, and to bring them into closer contact with its own original spirit and with the spirit of modern times.

---

they placed on the throne suspended the new charter and attempted to rule by traditional authoritarian means.

By the end of the nineteenth century, the defunct 1876 constitution had become a symbol of change for reformist elements, now grouped together under the common name Young Turks (undoubtedly borrowed from the Young Italy nationalist movement earlier in the century). They found support in the Ottoman army and administration and among Turks living in exile. In 1908, the Young Turks forced the sultan to restore the constitution, and he was removed from power the following year.

But the Young Turks had appeared at a moment of extreme fragility for the empire. Internal rebellions, combined with Austrian annexations of Ottoman territories in the Balkans, undermined support for the new government and provoked the army to step in. With most minorities from the old empire now removed from Istanbul's authority, many ethnic Turks began to embrace a new concept of a Turkish state based on all those of Turkish nationality.

The final blow to the old empire came in World War I, when the Ottoman government allied with Germany in the hope of driving the British from Egypt and restoring Ottoman rule over the Nile valley. In response, the British declared an official protectorate over Egypt and, aided by the efforts of the dashing if eccentric British adventurer T. E. Lawrence (popularly known as Lawrence of Arabia), sought to undermine Ottoman rule in the Arabian peninsula by encouraging Arab nationalists there. In 1916, the local governor of Mecca, encouraged by the British, declared Arabia independent from Ottoman rule, while British troops, advancing from Egypt, seized Palestine. In October 1918, having suffered more than 300,000 casualties during the war, the Ottoman Empire negotiated an armistice with the Allied Powers.

During the next few years, the tottering empire began to fall apart as the British and the French made plans to divide up Ottoman territories in the Middle East and the Greeks won Allied approval to seize the western parts of the Anatolian peninsula for their dream of re-creating the substance of the old Byzantine Empire. The impending collapse energized key elements in Turkey under the leadership of a war hero, Colonel Mustapha Kemal (1881–1938), who had commanded Turkish forces in their defense of the Dardanelles against a British invasion during World War I. Now he resigned from the army and convoked a national congress that called for the creation of an elected government and the preservation of the remaining territories of the old empire in a new republic of Turkey. Establishing his new capital at Ankara, Kemal's forces drove the Greeks from the Anatolian peninsula and persuaded the British to agree to a new treaty. In 1923, the last of the Ottoman sultans fled the country, which was now declared a Turkish republic. The Ottoman Empire had come to an end.

During the next few years, President Mustapha Kemal (now popularly known as Atatürk, or "Father Turk") attempted to transform Turkey into a modern secular republic. The trappings of a democratic system were put in place,

➤ MUSTAPHA KEMAL ATATÜRK. The war hero Mustapha Kemal took the initiative in creating a new republic of Turkey. As president of the new republic, Atatürk ("Father Turk," as he came to be called) worked hard to transform Turkey into a modern secular state by modernizing the economy, adopting Western styles of dress, and breaking the powerful hold of Islamic traditions. Long regarded as a symbol of Turkey's emergence as a modern nation, he is now reviled by Muslim fundamentalists for his opposition to an Islamic state.

© Culver Pictures, Inc.

centered on an elected Grand National Assembly, but the president was relatively intolerant of opposition and harshly suppressed critics of his rule. Turkish nationalism was emphasized, and the Turkish language, now written in the Roman alphabet, was shorn of many of its Arabic elements. Popular education was emphasized, old aristocratic titles like *pasha* and *bey* were abolished, and all Turkish citizens were given family names in the European style.

Atatürk also took steps to modernize the economy, overseeing the establishment of a light industrial sector producing textiles, glass, paper, and cement and instituting a five-year plan on the Soviet model to provide for state direction over the economy. Atatürk was no admirer of Soviet communism, however, and the Turkish economy can be better described as a form of state capitalism. He also encouraged the modernization of the agricultural sector through the establishment of training institutions and model farms, but such reforms had relatively little effect on the nation's predominantly conservative peasantry.

Perhaps the most significant aspect of Atatürk's reform program was his attempt to break the power of the Islamic clerics and transform Turkey into a secular state. The caliphate was formally abolished in 1924 (see the box on p. 665), and *Shari'a* (Islamic law) was replaced by a revised version of the Swiss law code. The fez (the brimless cap worn by Turkish Muslims) was abolished as a form of headdress, and women were discouraged from wearing the veil in the traditional Islamic custom. Women received the right to vote in 1934 and were legally guaranteed equal rights with men in all aspects of marriage and inheritance. Education and the professions were now open to citizens of both sexes, and some women even began to participate in politics. All citizens were given the right to convert to another religion at will. Finally, Atatürk attempted to break the waning power of the various religious orders of Islam, abolishing all monasteries and brotherhoods.

The legacy of Mustapha Kemal Atatürk was enormous. Although not all of his reforms were widely accepted in practice, especially by devout Muslims, most of the changes he introduced were retained after his death in 1938. In virtually every respect, the Turkish republic was the product of his determined efforts to create a modern Turkish nation.

MODERNIZATION IN IRAN

In the meantime, a similar process was under way in Persia. Under the Qajar dynasty (1794–1925), the country had not been very successful in resisting Russian advances in the Caucasus or resolving its domestic problems. To secure themselves from foreign influence, the shahs moved the capital from Tabriz to Tehran, in a mountainous area just south of the Caspian Sea. During the mid-nineteenth century, one modernizing shah attempted to introduce political and economic reforms but was impeded by resistance from tribal and religious—predominantly Shi'ite—forces. To buttress

MUSTAPHA KEMAL'S CASE AGAINST THE CALIPHATE

As part of his plan to transform Turkey into a modern society, Mustapha Kemal Atatürk proposed bringing an end to the caliphate, which had been in the hands of Ottoman sultans since the formation of the empire. In the following passage from a speech to the National Assembly, he gives his reasons.

ATATÜRK'S SPEECH TO THE ASSEMBLY, OCTOBER 1924

The monarch designated under the title of Caliph was to guide the affairs of [all] Muslim peoples and to secure the execution of the religious prescriptions which would best correspond to their worldly interests. He was to defend the rights of all Muslims and concentrate all the affairs of the Muslim world in his hands with effective authority.

The sovereign entitled Caliph was to maintain justice among the three hundred million Muslims on the terrestrial globe, to safeguard the rights of these peoples, to prevent any event that could encroach upon order and security, and confront every attack which the Muslims would be called upon to encounter from the side of other nations. It was to be part of his attributes to preserve by all means the welfare and spiritual development of Islam. . . .

If the Caliph and Caliphate, as they maintained, were to be invested with a dignity embracing the whole of Islam, ought they not to have realized in all justice that a crushing burden would be imposed on Turkey, on her existence; her entire resources and all her forces would be placed at the disposal of the Caliph? . . .

For centuries our nation was guided under the influence of these erroneous ideas. But what has been the result of it? Everywhere they have lost millions of men. "Do you know," I asked, "how many sons of Anatolia have perished in the scorching deserts of the Yemen? Do you know the losses we have suffered in holding Syria and Egypt and in maintaining our position in Africa? And do you see what has come out of it? Do you know?

"Those who favor the idea of placing the means at the disposal of the Caliph to brave the whole world and the power to administer the affairs of the whole of Islam must not appeal to the population of Anatolia alone but to the great Muslim agglomerations which are eight or ten times as rich in men.

"New Turkey, the people of New Turkey, have no reason to think of anything else but their own existence and their own welfare. She has nothing more to give away to others."

---

its rule, the dynasty turned increasingly to Russia and Great Britain to protect itself from its own people.

Eventually, the growing foreign presence led to the rise of a native Persian nationalist movement. Its efforts were largely directed against Russian advances in the northwest and the growing European influence in the small modern industrial sector, the profits from which left the country or disappeared into the hands of the dynasty's ruling elite. Supported actively by Shi'ite religious leaders, opposition to the regime rose steadily among both peasants and merchants in the cities, and in 1906, popular pressures forced the reigning shah to grant a constitution on the Western model. It was an eerie foretaste of the revolution of 1979.

As in the Ottoman Empire and Manchu China, however, the modernizers had moved too soon, before their power base was secure. With the support of the Russians and the British, the shah was able to retain control, while the two foreign powers began to divide the country into separate spheres of influence. One reason for the growing foreign presence in Persia was the discovery of oil reserves in the southern part of the country in 1908. Within a few years,

THE IMPACT OF OIL. Oil discoveries early in the twentieth century began to bring wealth to Iran. Shown here are workers building an oil derrick in Iran.

oil exports increased rapidly, with the bulk of the profits going into the pockets of British investors.

In 1921, an officer in the Persian army by the name of Reza Khan (1878–1944) led a mutiny that seized power in Tehran. The new ruler's original intention had been to establish a republic, but resistance from traditional forces impeded his efforts, and in 1925 the new Pahlavi dynasty, with Reza Khan as shah, replaced the now defunct Qajar dynasty. During the next few years, Reza Khan attempted to follow the example of Atatürk in Turkey, introducing a number of reforms to strengthen the central government, modernize the civilian and military bureaucracy, and establish a modern economic infrastructure. He also officially changed the name of the nation to Iran.

Unlike Atatürk, Reza Khan did not attempt to destroy the power of Islamic beliefs, but he did encourage the establishment of a Western-style educational system and forbade women to wear the veil in public. Women continued to be exploited, however. As in the case of the textile industry in Meiji Japan (see Chapter 21), it was the intensive labor of Iranian women in the carpet industry that provided major export earnings—second only to oil—in the interwar period. To strengthen the sense of Persian nationalism and reduce the power of Islam, Reza Khan attempted to popularize the symbols and beliefs of pre-Islamic times. Like his Qajar predecessors, however, he was hindered by strong foreign influence. When the Soviet Union and Great Britain decided to send troops into the country during World War II, he resigned in protest and died three years later.

THE RISE OF ARAB NATIONALISM AND THE PROBLEM OF PALESTINE

As we have seen, the Arab uprising during World War I helped bring about the demise of the Ottoman Empire. Unrest against Ottoman rule had existed in the Arabian peninsula since the eighteenth century, when the Wahhabi revolt attempted to drive out the outside influences and cleanse Islam of corrupt practices that had developed in past centuries. The revolt was eventually suppressed, but Wahhabi influence persisted.

World War I offered an opportunity for the Arabs to throw off the shackles of Ottoman rule—but what would replace them? The Arabs were not a nation but an idea, a loose collection of peoples who often do not see eye to eye on matters that affect their community. Disagreement over

what constitutes an Arab has plagued generations of political leaders who have sought unsuccessfully to knit together the disparate peoples of the region into a single Arab nation.

When the Arab leaders in Mecca declared their independence from Ottoman rule in 1916, they had hoped for British support, but they were to be sorely disappointed. At the close of the war, the British and French agreed to create a number of mandates in the area under the general supervision of the League of Nations. Iraq and Trans-Jordan were assigned to the British; Syria and Lebanon (the two areas were separated so that Christian peoples in Lebanon could be placed under Christian administration) were given to the French.

The land of Palestine—once the home of the Jews but now inhabited primarily by Muslim Palestinians—became a separate mandate. According to the Balfour Declaration, issued by the British foreign secretary Lord Balfour in November 1917, Palestine was to be a national home for the Jews. The declaration was ambiguous on the legal status of the territory and promised that the decision would not undermine the rights of the non-Jewish peoples currently living in the area. But Arab nationalists were incensed. How could a national home for the Jewish people be established in a territory where 90 percent of the population was Muslim?

In the early 1920s, a leader of the Wahhabi movement, Ibn Saud (1880–1953), united Arab tribes in the northern part of the Arabian peninsula and drove out the remnants of Ottoman rule. Ibn Saud was a descendant of the family that had led the Wahhabi revolt in the eighteenth century. Devout and gifted, he won broad support among Arab tribal peoples and established the kingdom of Saudi Arabia throughout much of the peninsula in 1932.

At first, his new kingdom, consisting essentially of the vast wastes of central Arabia, was desperately poor. Its financial resources were limited to the income from Muslim pilgrims visiting the holy sites in Mecca and Medina. But during the 1930s, American companies began to explore for oil, and in 1938, Standard Oil made a suc-

שמרו על דלת הארץ

➤ **EUROPEAN JEWISH REFUGEES.** After the Balfour Declaration (1917) promised a Jewish homeland in Palestine, increasing numbers of European Jews emigrated to Palestine. Their goal was to build a new life in a Jewish land. Like the refugees aboard this ship, they celebrated as they reached their new homeland. The sign reads "Keep the gates open"—a reference to British efforts to slow the pace of Jewish immigration in response to protests by Muslim residents.

cessful strike at Dhahran, on the Persian Gulf. Soon an Arabian-American oil conglomerate, popularly called Aramco, was established, and the isolated kingdom was suddenly inundated by Western oilmen and untold wealth.

In the meantime, Jewish settlers began to arrive in Palestine in response to the promises made in the Balfour Declaration. As tensions between the new arrivals and existing Muslim residents began to escalate, the British tried to restrict Jewish immigration into the territory and rejected the concept of a separate state. They also created a separate emirate of Trans-Jordan out of the eastern section of Palestine. After World War II, it would become the independent kingdom of Jordan. The stage was set for the conflicts that would take place in the region after World War II.

Nationalism and Revolution in Asia and Africa

Before the Russian Revolution, to most intellectuals in Asia and Africa, "westernization" referred to the capitalist democratic civilization of western Europe and the United States, not the doctrine of social revolution developed by Karl Marx. Until 1917, Marxism was regarded as a utopian idea rather than a concrete system of government. Moreover, to many intellectuals, Marxism appeared to have little relevance to conditions in Asia and Africa. Marxist doctrine, after all, declared that a communist society would arise only from the ashes of an advanced capitalism that had already passed through the Industrial Revolution. From the perspective of Marxist historical analysis, most societies in Asia and Africa were still at the feudal stage of development; they lacked the economic conditions and political awareness to achieve a socialist revolution that would bring the working class to power. Finally, the Marxist view of nationalism and religion had little appeal to many patriotic intellectuals in the non-Western world. Marx believed that nationhood and religion were essentially false ideas that

diverted the attention of the oppressed masses from the critical issues of class struggle and, in his phrase, the exploitation of one person by another. Instead, Marx stressed an "internationalist" outlook based on class consciousness and the eventual creation of a classless society with no artificial divisions based on culture, nation, or religion.

For these reasons, many patriotic non-Western intellectuals initially found Marxism to be both irrelevant and unappealing. That situation began to change after the Russian Revolution in 1917. The rise to power of Lenin's Bolsheviks demonstrated that a revolutionary party espousing Marxist principles could overturn a corrupt, outdated system and launch a new experiment dedicated to ending human inequality and achieving a paradise on earth. In 1920, Lenin proposed a new revolutionary strategy designed to relate Marxist doctrine and practice to non-Western societies. His reasons were not entirely altruistic. Soviet Russia, surrounded by capitalist powers, desperately needed allies in its struggle to survive in a hostile world. To Lenin, the anticolonial movements emerging in North Africa, Asia, and the Middle East after World War I were natural allies of the beleaguered new regime in Moscow. Lenin was convinced that only the ability of the imperialist powers to find markets, raw materials, and sources of capital investment in the non-Western world kept capitalism alive. If the tentacles of capitalist influence in Asia and Africa could be severed, imperialism would weaken and collapse.

Establishing such an alliance was not easy, however. Most nationalist leaders in colonial countries belonged to the urban middle class, and many abhorred the idea of a comprehensive revolution to create a totally egalitarian society. In addition, many still adhered to traditional religious beliefs and were opposed to the atheistic principles of classical Marxism.

Since it was unrealistic to expect bourgeois nationalist support for social revolution, Lenin sought a compromise by which Communist parties could be organized

CORBIS

THE PATH OF LIBERATION

In 1919, the Vietnamese revolutionary Ho Chi Minh (1890–1969) was living in exile in France, where he first became acquainted with the new revolutionary experiment in Bolshevik Russia. He became a leader of the Vietnamese Communist movement. In the following passage, written in 1960, he reminisces about his reasons for becoming a Communist. The Second International mentioned in the text was an organization created in 1889 by moderate socialists who pursued their goal by parliamentary means. Lenin created the Third International, or Comintern, in 1919 to promote violent revolution.

HO CHI MINH, "THE PATH WHICH LED ME TO LENINISM"

After World War I, I made my living in Paris, now as a retoucher at a photographer's, now as a painter of "Chinese antiquities" (made in France!). I would distribute leaflets denouncing the crimes committed by the French colonialists in Vietnam.

At that time, I supported the October Revolution only instinctively, not yet grasping all its historic importance. I loved and admired Lenin because he was a great patriot who liberated his compatriots; until then, I had read none of his books.

The reason for my joining the French Socialist Party was that these "ladies and gentlemen"—as I called my comrades at that moment—had shown their sympathy toward me, toward the struggle of the oppressed peoples. But I understood neither what was a party, a trade union, nor what was Socialism nor Communism.

Heated discussions were then taking place in the branches of the Socialist Party, about the question whether the Socialist Party should remain in the Second International, should a Second-and-a-Half International be founded, or should the Socialist Party join Lenin's Third International? I attended the meetings regularly, twice or three times a week, and attentively listened to the discussion. First, I could not understand thoroughly. Why were the discussions so heated? Either with the Second, Second-and-a-Half, or Third International, the revolution could be waged. What was the use of arguing then? As for the First International, what had become of it?

What I wanted most to know—and this precisely was not debated in the meetings—was: which International sides with the peoples of colonial countries?

I raised this question—the most important in my opinion—in a meeting. Some comrades answered: It is the Third, not the Second International. And a comrade gave me Lenin's "Thesis on the national and colonial questions," published by *l'Humanité*, to read.

There were political terms difficult to understand in this thesis. But by dint of reading it again and again, finally I could grasp the main part of it. What emotion, enthusiasm, clear-sightedness, and confidence it instilled in me! I was overjoyed to tears. Though sitting alone in my room, I shouted aloud as if addressing large crowds: "Dear martyrs, compatriots! This is what we need, this is the path to our liberation!"

After that, I had entire confidence in Lenin, in the Third International.

among the working classes in the preindustrial societies of Asia and Africa. These parties would then forge informal alliances with existing middle-class parties to struggle against the common enemies of feudal reaction (the remnants of the traditional ruling class) and Western imperialism. Such an alliance, of course, could not be permanent because many bourgeois nationalists in Asia and Africa would reject an egalitarian, classless society. Once the imperialists had been overthrown, therefore, the Communist parties would turn against their erstwhile nationalist partners to seize power on their own and carry out the socialist revolution. Lenin thus proposed a two-stage revolution: an initial "national democratic" stage followed by a "proletarian socialist" stage.

Lenin's strategy became a major element in Soviet foreign policy in the 1920s. Soviet agents fanned out across the world to carry Marxism beyond the boundaries of industrial Europe. The primary instrument of this effort was the Communist International, or Comintern for short. Formed in 1919 at Lenin's prodding, the Comintern was a worldwide organization of Communist parties dedicated to the advancement of world revolution. At its headquarters in Moscow, agents from around the world were trained in the precepts of world communism and then sent back to their countries to form Marxist parties and promote the cause of social revolution. By the end of the 1920s, almost every colonial or semicolonial society in Asia had a party based on Marxist principles. The Soviets had less success in the Middle East, where Marxist ideology appealed mainly to minorities such as Jews and Armenians in the cities, or in black Africa, where Soviet strategists in any case did not feel conditions were sufficiently advanced for the creation of Communist organizations.

According to Marxist doctrine, the rank and file of Communist parties should be urban factory workers alienated from capitalist society by inhuman working conditions. In practice, many of the leaders even in European Communist parties tended to be urban intellectuals or members of the lower middle class (in Marxist parlance, the "petty bourgeoisie"). That phenomenon was even more true in the non-Western world, where most early Marxists were rootless intellectuals. Some were probably drawn into the movement for patriotic reasons and saw Marxist doctrine as a new, more effective means of modernizing their societies and removing the colonial exploiters (see the box above). Others were attracted by the message of egalitarian communism and the utopian dream of a classless society. For those who had lost their faith in traditional religion, communism often served as a new secular ideology, dealing not with the hereafter but with the here and now or, indeed, with a remote future when the state would wither away and the "classless society" would replace the lost truth of traditional faiths.

Of course, the new doctrine's appeal was not the same in all non-Western societies. In Confucian societies such as China and Vietnam, where traditional belief systems had been badly discredited by their failure to counter the Western challenge, communism had an immediate impact and rapidly became a major factor in the anticolonial movement. In Buddhist and Muslim societies, where traditional religion remained strong and actually became a cohesive factor in the resistance movement, communism had less success. To maximize their appeal and minimize potential conflict with traditional ideas, Communist parties frequently attempted to adapt Marxist doctrine to indigenous values and institutions. In the Middle East, for example, the Ba'ath Party in Syria adopted a hybrid socialism combining Marxism with Arab nationalism. In Africa, radical intellectuals talked vaguely of a uniquely "African road to socialism."

The degree to which these parties were successful in establishing alliances with nationalist parties and building a solid base of support among the mass of the population also varied from place to place. In some instances, the Communists were briefly able to establish a cooperative relationship with the bourgeois parties. The most famous example was the alliance between the Chinese Communist Party and Sun Yat-sen's Nationalist Party (discussed in the next section). In the Dutch East Indies, the Indonesian Communist Party (known as the PKI) allied with the middle-class nationalist group Sarekat Islam but later broke loose in an effort to organize its own mass movement among the poor peasants. In French Indochina, Vietnamese Communists organized by the Moscow-trained revolutionary Ho Chi Minh sought at first to cooperate with bourgeois nationalist parties against the colonial regime, but these efforts were abandoned in 1928 when the Comintern, reacting to Chiang Kai-shek's betrayal of the alliance with the Chinese Communist Party, declared that Communist parties should restrict their recruiting efforts to the most revolutionary elements in society—notably, the urban intellectuals and the working class. Harassed by colonial authorities and saddled with strategic directions from Moscow that often had little relevance to local conditions, Communist parties in most colonial societies had little success in the 1930s and failed to build a secure base of support among the mass of the population.

REVOLUTION IN CHINA

Overall, revolutionary Marxism had its greatest impact in China, where a group of young radicals, including several faculty and staff members from Peking University,

founded the Chinese Communist Party (CCP) in 1921. The rise of the CCP was a consequence of the failed revolution of 1911. When political forces are too weak or too divided to consolidate their power during a period of instability, the military usually steps in to fill the vacuum. In China, Sun Yat-sen and his colleagues had accepted General Yuan Shikai [Yuan Shih-k'ai] as president of the new Chinese republic in 1911 because they lacked the military force to compete with his control over the army. Moreover, many feared, perhaps rightly, that if the revolt lapsed into chaos, the Western powers would intervene and the last shreds of Chinese sovereignty would be lost. But some had misgivings about Yuan's intentions. As one remarked in a letter to a friend, "We don't know whether he will be a George Washington or a Napoleon."

As it turned out, he was neither. Understanding little of the new ideas sweeping into China from the West, Yuan

➤ **SUN YAT-SEN, FATHER OF MODERN CHINA.** The son of a peasant in southern China, Sun Yat-sen rose to become a prominent revolutionary and the founder of the first Chinese republic. This photograph shows Sun as he assumed office as provisional president in January 1912. Shortly thereafter, he was forced to resign in favor of General Yuan Shikai, who moved the capital from Nanjing to Beijing.

© CameraPress/Globe Photos

ruled in a traditional manner, reviving Confucian rituals and institutions and eventually trying to found a new imperial dynasty. Yuan's dictatorial inclinations rapidly led to clashes with Sun's party, now renamed the *Guomindang* (*Kuomintang*), or Nationalist Party. When Yuan dissolved the new parliament, the Nationalists launched a rebellion. When it failed, Sun Yat-sen fled to Japan.

Yuan was strong enough to brush off the challenge from the revolutionary forces but not to turn back the clock of history. He died in 1916 (apparently of natural causes, although legend holds that his heart was broken by growing popular resistance to his imperial pretensions) and was succeeded by one of his military subordinates. For the next several years, China slipped into semianarchy as the power of the central government disintegrated and military warlords seized power in the provinces.

Mr. Science and Mr. Democracy: The New Culture Movement

Although the failure of the 1911 revolution was a clear sign that China was not yet ready for radical change, discontent with existing conditions continued to rise in various sectors of Chinese society. The most vocal protests came from radical intellectuals, who opposed Yuan Shikai's conservative rule but were now convinced that political change could not take place until the Chinese people were more familiar with trends in the outside world. Braving the displeasure of Yuan and his successors, progressive intellectuals at Peking University launched the New Culture Movement, aimed at abolishing the remnants of the old system and introducing Western values and institutions into China. Using the classrooms of China's most prestigious university as well as the pages of newly established progressive magazines and newspapers, the intellectuals introduced a bewildering mix of new ideas, from the philosophy of Friedrich Nietszche and Bertrand Russell to the educational views of the American John Dewey and the feminist plays of Henrik Ibsen. As such ideas flooded into China, they stirred up a new generation of educated Chinese youth, who chanted "Down with Confucius and sons" and talked of a new era dominated by "Mr. Sai" (Mr. Science) and "Mr. De" (Mr. Democracy). No one was a greater defender of free thought and speech than the chancellor of Peking University, Cai Yuanpei (Ts'ai Yüan-p'ei):

> So far as theoretical ideas are concerned, I follow the principles of "freedom of thought" and an attitude of broad tolerance in accordance with the practice of universities the world over. . . . Regardless of what school of thought a person may adhere to, so long as that person's ideas are justified and conform to reason and have not been passed by through the process of natural selection, although there may be controversy, such ideas have a right to be presented.[3]

The problem was that appeals for American-style democracy and women's liberation had little relevance to Chinese peasants, most of whom were still illiterate and concerned above all with survival. Consequently, the New Culture Movement did not win widespread support outside the urban areas. It certainly earned the distrust of conservative military officers, one of whom threatened to lob artillery shells into Peking University to destroy the poisonous new ideas and their advocates.

Discontent among intellectuals, however, was soon joined by the rising chorus of public protest against Japan's efforts to expand its influence on the mainland. During the first decade of the twentieth century, Japan had taken advantage of the Qing's decline to extend its domination over Manchuria and Korea (see Chapter 21). In 1915, the Japanese government insisted that Yuan Shikai accept a series of twenty-one demands that would have given Japan a virtual protectorate over the Chinese government and economy. Yuan was able to fend off the most far-reaching Japanese demands by arousing popular outrage in China, but at the Paris Peace Conference four years later, Japan received Germany's sphere of influence in Shandong Province as a reward for its support of the Allied cause in World War I. On hearing that the Chinese government had accepted the decision, on May 4, 1919, patriotic students, supported by other sectors of the urban population, demonstrated in Beijing and other major cities of the country. Although this May Fourth Movement did not lead to the restoration of Shandong, it did alert a substantial part of the politically literate population to the threat to national survival and the incompetence of the warlord government.

By 1920, central authority had almost ceased to exist in China. Two competing political forces now began to emerge from the chaos. One was Sun Yat-sen's Nationalist Party. Driven from the political arena seven years earlier by Yuan Shikai, the party now reestablished itself on the mainland by making an alliance with the warlord ruler of Guangdong (Kwangtung) Province in southern China. From Canton, Sun sought international assistance to carry out his national revolution. The other was the CCP. Following Lenin's strategy, Comintern agents soon advised the new party to link up with the more experienced Nationalists. Sun Yat-sen needed the expertise and the diplomatic support that the Soviet Union could provide because his anti-imperialist rhetoric had alienated many Western powers; one English-language newspaper in the international concession in Shanghai remarked, "All his life, all his influence, are devoted to ideas which keep China in turmoil, and it is utterly undesirable that he should be allowed to prosecute those aims here."[4] In 1923, the two parties formed an alliance to oppose the warlords and drive the imperialist powers out of China.

For three years, with the assistance of a Comintern mission in Canton, the two parties submerged their mutual suspicions and mobilized and trained a revolutionary army to march north and seize control over

STUDENT DEMONSTRATIONS IN BEIJING. The massive popular demonstrations in Tiananmen Square in downtown Beijing in 1989 were not the first of their kind in China. On May 4, 1919, students gathered at the same spot to protest against the Japanese takeover of the Shandong peninsula after World War I. The event triggered the famous May Fourth Movement, which highlighted the demand of progressive forces in China for political and social reforms.

China. The so-called Northern Expedition began in the summer of 1926 (see Map 23.1). By the following spring, revolutionary forces were in control of all Chinese territory south of the Yangtze River, including the major river ports of Wuhan and Shanghai. But tensions between the two parties now surfaced. Sun Yat-sen had died of cancer in 1925 and was succeeded as head of the Nationalist Party by his military subordinate, Chiang Kai-shek. Chiang feigned support for the alliance with the Communists but actually planned to destroy them. In April 1927, he struck against the Communists and their supporters in Shanghai, killing thousands. After the massacre, most of the Communist leaders went into hiding in the city, where they attempted to revive the movement in its traditional base among the urban working class. Some party members, however, led by the young Communist organizer Mao Zedong (Mao Tse-tung), fled to the hilly areas south of the Yangtze River.

Unlike most CCP leaders, Mao was convinced that the Chinese revolution must be based on the impoverished peasants in the countryside. The son of a prosperous peasant, Mao had helped organize a peasant movement in southern China during the early 1920s and then served as an agitator in rural villages in his native province of Hunan during the Northern Expedition in the fall of 1926. At that time, he wrote a famous report to the party leadership

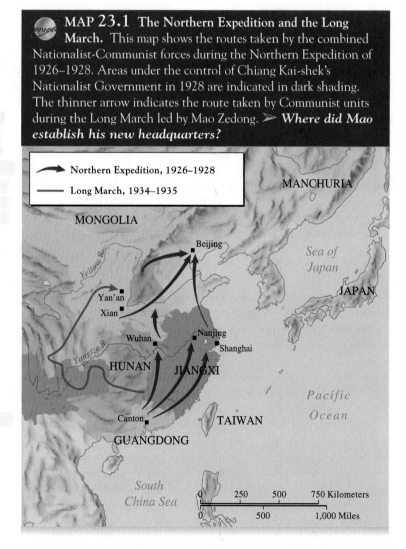

MAP 23.1 The Northern Expedition and the Long March. This map shows the routes taken by the combined Nationalist-Communist forces during the Northern Expedition of 1926–1928. Areas under the control of Chiang Kai-shek's Nationalist Government in 1928 are indicated in dark shading. The thinner arrow indicates the route taken by Communist units during the Long March led by Mao Zedong. ➤ *Where did Mao establish his new headquarters?*

A CALL FOR REVOLT

*I*n the fall of 1926, Nationalist and Communist forces moved north from Canton on their Northern Expedition in an effort to defeat the warlords. The young Communist Mao Zedong accompanied revolutionary troops into his home province of Hunan, where he submitted a report to the CCP Central Committee calling for a massive peasant revolt against the ruling order. The report shows his confidence that peasants could play an active role in the Chinese revolution despite the skepticism of many of his colleagues.

MAO ZEDONG, "THE PEASANT MOVEMENT IN HUNAN"

During my recent visit to Hunan I made a firsthand investigation of conditions. . . . In a very short time, . . . several hundred million peasants will rise like a mighty storm, . . . a force so swift and violent that no power, however great, will be able to hold it back. They will smash all the trammels that bind them and rush forward along the road to liberation. They will sweep all the imperialists, warlords, corrupt officials, local tyrants, and evil gentry into their graves. Every revolutionary party and every revolutionary comrade will be put to the test, to be accepted or rejected as they decide. There are three alternatives. To march at their head and lead them? To trail behind them, gesticulating and criticizing? Or to stand in their way and oppose them? Every Chinese is free to choose, but events will force you to make the choice quickly.

The main targets of attack by the peasants are the local tyrants, the evil gentry and the lawless landlords, but in passing they also hit out against patriarchal ideas and institutions, against the corrupt officials in the cities and against bad practices and customs in the rural areas. . . . As a result, the privileges which the feudal landlords enjoyed for thousands of years are being shattered to pieces. . . . With the collapse of the power of the landlords, the peasant associations have now become the sole organs of authority, and the popular slogan "All power to the peasant associations" has become a reality.

The peasants' revolt disturbed the gentry's sweet dreams. When the news from the countryside reached the cities, it caused immediate uproar among the gentry. . . . From the middle social strata upwards to the Kuomintang right-wingers, there was not a single person who did not sum up the whole business in the phrase, "It's terrible!" . . . Even quite progressive people said, "Though terrible, it is inevitable in a revolution." In short, nobody could altogether deny the word "terrible." But . . . the fact is that the great peasant masses have risen to fulfill their historic mission. . . . What the peasants are doing is absolutely right; what they are doing is fine! "It's fine!" is the theory of the peasants and of all other revolutionaries. Every revolutionary comrade should know that the national revolution requires a great change in the countryside. The Revolution of 1911 did not bring about this change, hence its failure. This change is now taking place, and it is an important factor for the completion of the revolution. Every revolutionary comrade must support it, or he will be taking the stand of counterrevolution.

---

suggesting that the CCP support peasant demands for a land revolution (see the box above). But his superiors refused, fearing that such radical policies would destroy the alliance with the Nationalists.

The Nanjing Republic

In 1928, Chiang Kai-shek founded a new Chinese republic at Nanjing, and over the next three years, he managed to reunify China by a combination of military operations and inducements (known as "silver bullets") to various northern warlords to join his movement. He also attempted to put an end to the Communists, rooting them out of their urban base in Shanghai and their rural redoubt in the rugged hills of Jiangxi (Kiangsi) Province. He succeeded in the first task in 1931, when most party leaders were forced to flee Shanghai for Mao's base in southern China. Three years later, using their superior military strength, Chiang's troops surrounded the Communist base in Jiangxi, inducing Mao's young People's Liberation Army (PLA) to abandon its guerrilla lair and embark on the famous Long March, an arduous journey of thousands of miles on foot through mountains, marshes, and deserts to the small provincial town of Yan'an (Yenan) 200 miles north of the city of Xian in the dusty hills of northern China (see Map 23.1). Of the ninety thousand who embarked on the journey in October 1934, only ten thousand arrived in Yan'an a year later. Contemporary observers must have thought that the Communist threat to the Nanjing regime had been averted forever.

Meanwhile, Chiang was trying to build a new nation. When the Nanjing republic was established in 1928, Chiang publicly declared his commitment to Sun Yat-sen's Three People's Principles. In a program announced in 1918, Sun had written about the all-important second stage of "political tutelage":

China . . . needs a republican government just as a boy needs school. As a schoolboy must have good teachers and helpful friends, so the Chinese people, being for the first time under republican rule, must have a farsighted revolutionary government for their training. This calls for the period of political tutelage, which is a necessary transitional stage from monarchy to republicanism. Without this, disorder will be unavoidable.[5]

© Earl Leaf/Rapho/Getty Images

⇨ MAO ZEDONG AT YAN'AN. In 1934, Mao Zedong led his bedraggled forces on the famous Long March from southern China to a new location at Yan'an, in the hills just south of the Gobi Desert. Here Chairman Mao (on the left) and Zhu De, one of his generals, pose for a photograph at the Chinese Communist Party's new headquarters. Note the thick padded jackets to keep out the cold.

In keeping with Sun's program, Chiang announced a period of political indoctrination to prepare the Chinese people for a final stage of constitutional government. In the meantime, the Nationalists would use their dictatorial power to carry out a land reform program and modernize the urban industrial sector.

But it would take more than paper plans to create a new China. Years of neglect and civil war had severely frayed the political, economic, and social fabric of the nation. There were faint signs of an impending industrial revolution in the major urban centers, but most of the people in the countryside, drained by warlord exactions and civil strife, were still grindingly poor and overwhelmingly illiterate. A Westernized middle class had begun to emerge in the cities and formed much of the natural constituency of the Nanjing government. But this new westernized elite, preoccupied with bourgeois values of individual advancement and material accumulation, had few links with the peasants in the countryside or the rickshaw drivers "running in this world of suffering," in the poignant words of

a Chinese poet. In an expressive phrase, some critics dismissed Chiang and his chief followers as "banana Chinese"—yellow on the outside, white on the inside.

Chiang was aware of the difficulty of introducing exotic foreign ideas into a society still culturally conservative. While building a modern industrial sector, he attempted to synthesize modern Western ideas with traditional Confucian values of hard work, obedience, and moral integrity. In the officially promoted New Life Movement, sponsored by his Wellesley-educated wife, Mei-ling Soong, Chiang sought to propagate traditional Confucian social ethics such as integrity, propriety, and righteousness, while rejecting what he considered the excessive individualism and material greed of Western capitalism.

Unfortunately for Chiang, Confucian ideas—at least in their institutional form—had been widely discredited by the failure of the traditional system to solve China's growing problems. With only a tenuous hold over the Chinese provinces (the Nanjing government had total control over only a handful of provinces in the Yangtze valley), a growing Japanese threat in the north, and a world suffering from the Great Depression, Chiang made little progress with his program. Lacking the political sensitivity of Sun Yat-sen and fearing Communist influence, Chiang repressed all opposition and censored free expression, thereby alienating many intellectuals and political moderates. Since the urban middle class and landed gentry were his natural political constituency, he shunned programs that would lead to a redistribution of wealth. A land reform program was enacted in 1930 but had little effect.

Chiang Kai-shek's government had little more success in promoting industrial development. During the decade of precarious peace following the Northern Expedition, industrial growth averaged only about 1 percent annually. Much of the national wealth was in the hands of the senior officials and close subordinates of the ruling elite. Military expenses consumed half the budget, and distressingly little was devoted to social and economic development.

The new government, then, had little success in dealing with China's deep-seated economic and social problems. The deadly combination of internal disintegration and foreign pressure now began to coincide with the virtual collapse of the global economic order during the Great Depression and the rise of militant political forces in Japan determined to extend Japanese influence and power in an unstable Asia. These forces and the turmoil they unleashed will be examined in the next chapter.

"Down with Confucius and Sons": Economic, Social, and Cultural Change in Republican China

The transformation of the old order that had commenced at the end of the Qing era continued into the period of the early Chinese republic. The industrial sector continued to grow, albeit slowly. Although about 75 percent of all industrial production was still craft-produced in the early 1930s, mechanization was gradually beginning to replace manual labor in a number of traditional industries, notably in the manufacture of textile goods. Traditional Chinese exports, such as silk and tea, were hard-hit by the Great Depression, however, and manufacturing suffered a decline during the 1930s. It is difficult to gauge conditions in the countryside during the early republican era, but there is no doubt that farmers were often victimized by high taxes imposed by local warlords and the endemic political and social conflict.

Social changes followed shifts in the economy and the political culture. By 1915, the assault on the old system and values by educated youth was intense. The main focus of the attack was the Confucian concept of the family—in particular, filial piety and the subordination of women. Young people demanded the right to choose their own mates and their own careers. Women demanded rights and opportunities equal to those enjoyed by men. More broadly, progressives called for an end to the concept of duty to the community and praised the Western individualist ethos. The popular short story writer Lu Xun (Lu Hsun) criticized the Confucian concept of family as a "man-eating" system that degraded humanity. In a famous short story titled "Diary of a Madman," the protagonist remarks:

> I remember when I was four or five years old, sitting in the cool of the hall, my brother told me that if a man's parents were ill, he should cut off a piece of his flesh and boil it for them if he wanted to be considered a good son. I have only just realized that I have been living all these years in a place where for four thousand years they have been eating human flesh.[6]

Such criticisms did have some beneficial results. During the early republic, the tyranny of the old family system began to decline, at least in urban areas, under the impact of economic changes and the urgings of the New Culture intellectuals. Women began to escape their cloistered existence and seek education and employment alongside their male contemporaries. Free choice in marriage and a more relaxed attitude toward sex became commonplace among affluent families in the cities, where the teenage

children of Westernized elites aped the clothing, social habits, and even the musical tastes of their contemporaries in Europe and the United States.

But as a rule, the new individualism and women's rights did not penetrate to the villages, where traditional attitudes and customs held sway. Arranged marriages continued to be the rule rather than the exception, and concubinage remained common. According to a survey taken in the 1930s, well over two-thirds of the marriages even among urban couples had been arranged by their parents (see the box on p. 675), and in one rural area, only 3 out of 170 villagers interviewed had even heard of the idea of "modern marriage." Even the tradition of binding the feet of female children continued despite efforts by the Nationalist government to eradicate the practice.

Nowhere was the struggle between traditional and modern more visible than in the field of culture. Beginning with the New Culture era, radical reformists criticized traditional culture as the symbol and instrument of feudal oppression that must be entirely eradicated before a new China could stand with dignity in the modern world. During the 1920s and 1930s, Western literature and art became highly popular, especially among the urban middle class. Traditional culture continued to prevail among more conservative elements, and some intellectuals argued for a new art that would synthesize the best of Chinese and foreign culture. But the most creative artists were interested in imitating foreign trends, while traditionalists were more concerned with preservation.

Literature in particular was influenced by foreign ideas as Western genres like the novel and the short story attracted a growing audience. Although most Chinese novels written after World War I dealt with Chinese subjects, they reflected the Western tendency toward social realism and often dealt with the new westernized middle class (Mao Dun's *Midnight,* for example, describes the changing mores of Shanghai's urban elites) or the disintegration of the traditional Confucian family (Ba Jin's famous novel *Family* is an example). Most of China's modern authors displayed a clear contempt for the past.

JAPAN BETWEEN THE WARS

During the first two decades of the twentieth century, Japan made remarkable progress toward the creation of an advanced society on the Western model. The political system based on the Meiji Constitution of 1890 began to evolve along Western pluralistic lines, and a multiparty system took shape, while the economic and social reforms launched during the Meiji era led to increasing prosperity and the development of a modern industrial and commercial sector. Optimists had reason to hope that Japan was on the road to becoming a full-fledged democracy.

AN ARRANGED MARRIAGE

*U*nder Western influence, Chinese social customs changed dramatically for many urban elites in the interwar years. A vocal women's movement, inspired in part by translations of Henrik Ibsen's play A Doll's House, campaigned aggressively for universal suffrage and an end to sexual discrimination. Some progressives called for free choice in marriage and divorce and even for free love. By the 1930s, the government had taken some steps to free women from patriarchal marriage constraints and realize sexual equality. But life was generally unaffected in the villages, where traditional patterns held sway. This often created severe tensions between older and younger generations, as this passage by the popular twentieth-century novelist Ba Jin shows.

BA JIN, *FAMILY*

Brought up with loving care, after studying with a private tutor for a number of years, Chueh-hsin entered middle school. One of the school's best students, he graduated four years later at the top of his class. He was very interested in physics and chemistry and hoped to study abroad, in Germany. His mind was full of beautiful dreams. At that time he was the envy of his classmates.

In his fourth year at middle school, he lost his mother. His father later married again, this time to a younger woman who had been his mother's cousin. Chueh-hsin was aware of his loss, for he knew full well that nothing could replace the love of a mother. But her death left no irreparable wound in his heart; he was able to console himself with rosy dreams of his future. Moreover, he had someone who understood him and could comfort him—his pretty cousin Mei, "mei" for "plum blossom."

But then, one day, his dreams were shattered, cruelly and bitterly shattered. The evening he returned home carrying his diploma, the plaudits of his teachers and friends still ringing in his ears, his father called him into his room and said:

"Now that you've graduated, I want to arrange your marriage. Your grandfather is looking forward to having a great-grandson, and I, too, would like to be able to hold a grandson in my arms. You're old enough to be married; I won't feel easy until I fulfill my obligation to find you a wife. Although I didn't accumulate much money in my years away from home as an official, still I've put by enough for us to get along on. My health isn't what it used to be; I'm thinking of spending my time at home and having you help me run the household affairs. All the more reason you'll be needing a wife. I've already arranged a match with the Li family. The thirteenth of next month is a good day. We'll announce the engagement then. You can be married within the year. . . ."

Chueh-hsin did not utter a word of protest, nor did such a thought ever occur to him. He merely nodded to indicate his compliance with his father's wishes. But after he returned to his own room, and shut the door, he threw himself down on his bed, covered his head with the quilt and wept. He wept for his broken dreams.

He was deeply in love with Mei, but now his father had chosen another, a girl he had never seen, and said that he must marry within the year. What's more, his hopes of continuing his studies had burst like a bubble. It was a terrible shock to Chueh-hsin. His future was finished, his beautiful dreams shattered.

He cried his disappointment and bitterness. But the door was closed and Chueh-hsin's head was beneath the bedding. No one knew. He did not fight back, he never thought of resisting. He only bemoaned his fate. But he accepted it. He complied with his father's will without a trace of resentment. But in his heart he wept for himself, wept for the girl he adored—Mei, his "plum blossom."

Experiment in Democracy

During the first quarter of the twentieth century, the Japanese political system appeared to evolve significantly toward the Western democratic model. Political parties expanded their popular following and became increasingly competitive, and universal male suffrage was instituted in the 1920s. Individual pressure groups began to appear in Japanese society, along with an independent press and a bill of rights. The influence of the old ruling oligarchy, the *genro*, had not yet been significantly challenged, however, nor had that of its ideological foundation, the *kokutai*.

These fragile democratic institutions were able to survive throughout the 1920s (often called the era of Taisho democracy, from the reign title of the ruling emperor). During that period, the military budget was reduced, and a suffrage bill enacted in 1925 granted the vote to all Japanese males, thus continuing the process of democratization begun earlier in the century. Women remained disenfranchised, but women's associations gained increasing visibility during the 1920s, and many women were active in the labor movement and in campaigning for various social reforms.

But the era was also marked by growing social turmoil, and two opposing forces within the system were gearing up to challenge the prevailing wisdom. On the left, a Marxist labor movement, which reflected the tensions within the working class and the increasing radicalism among the rural poor, began to take shape in the early 1920s in response to growing economic difficulties. Attempts to suppress labor disturbances led to further radicalization. On the right, ultranationalist groups called for a rejection of Western models of development and a more

IN SEARCH OF OLD JAPAN

Japanese authors produced a host of superb works in the early twentieth century. Many authors blended Western psychology with Japanese sensibility in novels of yearning for old Japan. Here novelist Junichiro Tanizaki recalls the charm of an island as yet untouched and unpolluted by modernization.

JUNICHIRO TANIZAKI, *SOME PREFER NETTLES*

The island of Awaji showed not very large on the map, and its harbor very possibly consisted of but this one road. You go straight down, the inn manager had said, till you come out at the river, and the theater is in the flats beyond. The rows of houses therefore most probably ended at the river. This may have been the seat of some minor baron a century ago—even then it could hardly have been imposing enough to be called a castle town—and it had probably changed little since. A modern coating goes no farther than the large cities that are a country's arteries, and there are not many such cities anywhere. In an old country with a long tradition, China and Europe as well as Japan—any country, in fact, except a very new one like the United States—the smaller cities, left aside by the flow of civilization, retain the flavor of an earlier day until they are overtaken by catastrophe.

This little harbor, for instance: it had its electric wires and poles, its painted billboards, and here and there a display window, but one could ignore them and find on every side townsmen's houses that might have come from an illustration to a seventeenth-century novel. The earthen walls covered to the eaves with white plaster, the projecting lattice fronts with their solid, generous slats of wood, the heavy tiled roofs held down by round ridgetiles, the shop signs—"Lacquer," "Soy," "Oil"—in fading letters on fine hardwood grounds, and inside, beyond earth-floored entrances, the shop names printed on dark-blue half-curtains—it was not the old man's remark this time but every detail brought back—how vividly!—the mood and air of old Japan. Kaname felt as if he were being drunk up into the scene, as if he were losing himself in the clean white walls and the brilliant blue sky. Those walls were a little like the sash around O-hisa's waist: their first luster had disappeared in long years under the fresh sea winds and rains, and bright though they were, their brightness was tempered by a certain reserve, a soft austerity.

Kaname felt a deep repose come over him. "These old houses are so dark you have no idea what's inside."

"Partly it's because the road is so bright." The old man had come up beside them. "The ground here seems almost white."

Kaname thought of the faces of the ancients in the dusk behind their shop curtains. Here on this street people with faces like theater dolls must have passed lives like stage lives. The world of the plays—of O-yumi, Jurobei of Awa, the pilgrim O-tsuru, and the rest—must have been just such a town as this. And wasn't O-hisa a part of it? Fifty years ago, a hundred years ago, a woman like her, dressed in the same kimono, was perhaps going down this same street in the spring sun, lunch in hand, on her way to the theater beyond the river. Or perhaps, behind one of these latticed fronts, she was playing "Snow" on her koto. O-hisa was a shade left behind by another age.

---

militant approach to realizing national objectives. In 1919, the radical nationalist Kita Ikki called for a military takeover and the establishment of a new system bearing strong resemblance to what would later be called National Socialism in Germany.

This cultural conflict between old and new, native and foreign, was reflected in literature. Japanese self-confidence had been somewhat restored after the victories over China and Russia, and this resurgence sparked a great age of creativity in the early twentieth century. Now more adept at handling European literary forms, Japanese writers blended Western psychology with Japanese sensibility in exquisite novels reeking with nostalgia for the old Japan. A well-known example is Junichiro Tanizaki's *Some Prefer Nettles*, published in 1928, which delicately juxtaposes the positive aspects of both traditional and modern Japan (see the box above). By the 1930s, however, military censorship increasingly inhibited free literary expression. Many authors continued to write privately, producing works that reflected the gloom of the era. This attitude is perhaps best exemplified by Shiga Naoya's novel *A Dark Night's Journey*, written during the early 1930s and capturing a sense of the approaching global catastrophe. It is regarded as the masterpiece of modern Japanese literature.

A Zaibatsu Economy

Japan also continued to make impressive progress in economic development. Spurred by rising domestic demand as well as continued government investment in the economy, the production of raw materials tripled between 1900 and 1930, and industrial production increased more than twelvefold. Much of the increase went into exports, and Western manufacturers began to complain about increasing competition from the Japanese.

As often happens, rapid industrialization was accompanied by some hardship and rising social tensions. In the Meiji model, various manufacturing processes were concentrated in a single enterprise, the *zaibatsu*, or financial clique. Some of these firms were existing merchant companies, such as Mitsui and Sumitomo, that had the capital and the foresight to move into new areas of opportunity. Others were formed by enterprising samurai, who used their status and experience in management to good account in a new environment. Whatever their origins, these firms gradually developed, often with official encouragement, into large conglomerates that controlled a major segment of the Japanese economy. By 1937, the four largest *zaibatsu* (Mitsui, Mitsubishi, Sumitomo, and Yasuda) controlled 21 percent of the banking industry, 26 percent of mining, 35 percent of shipbuilding, 38 percent of commercial shipping, and more than 60 percent of paper manufacturing and insurance.

This concentration of power and wealth in a few major industrial combines created problems in Japanese society. In the first place, it resulted in the emergence of a dual economy: on the one hand, a modern industry characterized by up-to-date methods and massive government subsidies, and on the other, a traditional manufacturing sector characterized by conservative methods and small-scale production techniques.

Concentration of wealth also led to growing economic inequalities. As we have seen, economic growth had been achieved at the expense of the peasants, many of whom fled to the cities to escape rural poverty. That labor surplus benefited the industrial sector, but the urban proletariat was still poorly paid and ill-housed. Rampant inflation in the price of rice led to food riots shortly after World War I. A rapid increase in population (the total population of the Japanese islands increased from an estimated 43 million in 1900 to 73 million in 1940) led to food shortages and the threat of rising unemployment. In the meantime, those left on the farm continued to suffer. As late as the beginning of World War II, an estimated one-half of all Japanese farmers were tenants.

Shidehara Diplomacy

A final problem for Japanese leaders in the post-Meiji era was the familiar colonial dilemma of finding sources of raw materials and foreign markets for the nation's manufactured goods. Until World War I, Japan had dealt with the problem by seizing territories such as Taiwan, Korea, and southern Manchuria and transforming them into colonies or protectorates of the growing Japanese empire. That policy had succeeded brilliantly, but it had also begun to arouse the concern and in some cases the hostility of the Western nations. China was also becoming apprehensive; as we have seen, Japanese demands for Shandong Province at the Paris Peace Conference in 1919 aroused massive protests in major Chinese cities.

The United States was especially concerned about Japanese aggressiveness. Although the United States had been less active than some European states in pursuing colonies in the Pacific, it had a strong interest in keeping the area open for U.S. commercial activities. In 1922, in Washington, D.C., the United States convened a major conference of nations with interests in the Pacific to discuss problems of regional security. The Washington Conference led to agreements on several issues, but the major accomplishment was a nine-power treaty recognizing the territorial integrity of China and the Open Door. The other participants induced Japan to accept these provisions by accepting its special position in Manchuria.

During the remainder of the 1920s, Japanese governments attempted to play by the rules laid down at the Washington Conference. Known as Shidehara diplomacy, after the foreign minister (and later prime minister) who attempted to carry it out, this policy sought to use diplomatic and economic means to realize Japanese interests in Asia. But this approach came under severe pressure as Japanese industrialists began to move into new areas, such as heavy industry, chemicals, mining, and the manufacturing of appliances and automobiles. Because such industries desperately needed resources not found in abundance locally, the Japanese government came under increasing pressure to find new sources abroad.

In the early 1930s, with the onset of the Great Depression and growing tensions in the international arena, nationalist forces rose to dominance in the government. The changes that occurred in the 1930s were not in the constitution or the institutional structure, which remained essentially intact, but in the composition and attitudes of the ruling group. Party leaders during the 1920s had attempted to realize Japanese aspirations within the existing global political and economic framework. The dominant elements in the government in the 1930s, a mixture of military officers and ultranationalist politicians, were convinced that the diplomacy of the 1920s had failed and advocated a more aggressive approach to protecting national interests in a brutal and competitive world.

Historians argue over whether Taisho democracy was merely a fragile period of comparative liberalization within a framework dominated by the Meiji vision of empire and *kokutai* or whether the militant nationalism of the 1930s was an aberration brought on by the depression, which caused the emerging Japanese democracy to wilt. Perhaps both contentions contain a little truth. A process of democratization was taking place in Japan during the first decades of the twentieth century, but without shaking the essential core of the Meiji concept of the state. When the "liberal" approach of the 1920s failed to solve the problems of the day, the shift toward a more aggressive approach was inevitable.

NATIONALISM AND DICTATORSHIP IN LATIN AMERICA

Although the nations of Latin America played little role in World War I, that conflict nevertheless exerted an impact on the region, especially on its economy. By the end of the 1920s, the region was also strongly influenced by another event of global proportions—the Great Depression.

The Economy and the United States

At the beginning of the twentieth century, virtually all of Latin America, except for the three Guianas, British Honduras, and some of the Caribbean Islands, had achieved independence. The economy of the region (see Map 23.2) was based largely on the export of foodstuffs and raw materials. Some countries relied on exports of only one or two products. Argentina, for example, exported primarily beef and wheat; Chile, nitrates and

MAP 23.2 Latin America in the First Half of the Twentieth Century. Shown here are the boundaries dividing the countries of Latin America after the independence movements of the nineteenth century. ➤ *Which areas remained under European rule?*

A PLEDGE OF COOPERATION

*D*uring the first three decades of the twentieth century, the United States intervened periodically in the affairs of various countries of Latin America to protect the lives of its citizens and its growing economic interests. By the late 1920s, that policy had aroused considerable resentment on the part of governments throughout the region. In August 1936, U.S. President Franklin D. Roosevelt attempted to allay such concerns by announcing the Good Neighbor policy toward other nations in the hemisphere. Excerpts of his speech follow.

ROOSEVELT'S GOOD NEIGHBOR POLICY

Long before I returned to Washington as President of the United States, I had made up my mind that . . . the United States could best serve the cause of peaceful humanity by setting an example. That was why on the 4th of March, 1933, I made the following declaration:

> In the field of world policy I would dedicate this nation to the policy of the good neighbor—the neighbor who resolutely respects himself and because he does so, respects the rights of others—the neighbor who respects his obligations and respects the sanctity of his agreements in and with a world of neighbors.

In the whole of the Western Hemisphere our good neighbor policy had produced results that are especially heartening. . . . The American republics to the south of us have been ready always to cooperate with the United States on a basis of equality and mutual respect, but before we inaugurated the good neighbor policy there was among them resentment and fear, because certain administrations in Washington had slighted their national pride and their sovereign rights.

In pursuance of the good neighbor policy, and because in my younger days I had learned many lessons in the hard school of experience, I stated that the United States was opposed definitely to armed intervention.

We have negotiated a Pan-American convention embodying the principles of nonintervention. We have abandoned the Platt amendment which gave us the right to intervene in the internal affairs of the Republic of Cuba. We have withdrawn American marines from Haiti. We have signed a new treaty which places our relations with Panama on a mutually satisfactory basis. We have undertaken a series of trade agreements with other American countries to our mutual commercial profit. . . .

Throughout the Americas the spirit of the good neighbor is a practical and living fact. The twenty-one American republics are not only living together in friendship and in peace; they are united in the determination so to remain.

---

copper; Brazil and the Caribbean nations, sugar; and the Central American states, bananas. A few reaped large profits from these exports, but for the majority of the population, the returns were meager.

World War I led to a decline in European investment in Latin America and a rise in the U.S. role in the local economies. By the late 1920s, the United States had replaced Great Britain as the foremost source of investment in Latin America. Unlike the British, however, U.S. investors put their funds directly into production enterprises, causing large segments of the area's export industries to fall into American hands. A number of Central American states, for example, were popularly labeled "banana republics" because of the power and influence of the U.S.-owned United Fruit Company. American firms also dominated the copper mining industry in Chile and Peru and the oil industry in Mexico, Peru, and Bolivia.

Increasing economic power reinforced the traditionally high level of U.S. political influence in Latin America. This influence was especially evident in Central America and the Caribbean, regions that many Americans considered their backyard and thus vital to U.S. national security. The growing U.S. presence in the region provoked hostility and a growing national consciousness among Latin Americans, who viewed the United States as an aggressive imperialist power. Some charged that Washington worked to keep ruthless dictators, such as Juan Vicente Gómez of Venezuela and Fulgencio Batista of Cuba, in power in order to preserve U.S. economic influence; sometimes the United States even intervened militarily. In a bid to improve relations with Latin American countries, President Franklin D. Roosevelt in 1935 promulgated the Good Neighbor policy (see the box above), which rejected the use of U.S. military force in the region. To underscore his sincerity, Roosevelt ordered the withdrawal of U.S. marines from the island nation of Haiti in 1936. For the first time in thirty years, there were no U.S. occupation troops in Latin America.

Because so many Latin American nations depended for their livelihood on the export of raw materials and food products, the Great Depression of the 1930s was a disaster for the region. The total value of Latin American exports in 1930 was almost 50 percent below the figure for the previous five years. Spurred by the decline in foreign revenues, Latin American governments began to encourage the development of new industries. In some cases—the steel industry in Chile and Brazil, the oil industry in Argentina and Mexico—government investment made up for the absence of local sources of capital.

LATIN AMERICA BETWEEN THE WARS

Hipólito Irigoyen becomes president of Argentina	1916
Argentinian military overthrows Irigoyen	1930
Rule of Getúlio Vargas in Brazil	1930–1945
Presidency of Lázaro Cárdenas in Mexico	1934–1940
Beginning of Good Neighbor policy	1935

The Move to Authoritarianism

During the late nineteenth century, most governments in Latin America had been increasingly dominated by landed or military elites, who controlled the mass of the population—mostly impoverished peasants—by the blatant use of military force. This trend toward authoritarianism increased during the 1930s as domestic instability caused by the effects of the Great Depression led to the creation of military dictatorships throughout the region. This trend was especially evident in Argentina, Brazil, and Mexico—three countries that together possessed more than half of the land and wealth of Latin America.

The political domination of the country by an elite minority often had disastrous effects. The government of Argentina, controlled by landowners who had benefited from the export of beef and wheat, was slow to recognize the growing importance of establishing a local industrial base. In 1916, Hipólito Irigoyen (1852–1933), head of the Radical Party, was elected president on a program to improve conditions for the middle and lower classes. Little was achieved, however, as the party became increasingly corrupt and drew closer to the large landowners. In 1930, the army overthrew Irigoyen's government and reestablished the power of the landed class. But their efforts to return to the previous export economy and suppress the growing influence of labor unions failed, and in 1946 General Juan Perón—claiming the support of the *descamisados* ("shirtless ones")—seized sole power (see Chapter 27).

Brazil followed a similar path. In 1889, the army overthrew the Brazilian monarchy, installed by Portugal years before, and established a republic. But it was dominated by landed elites, many of whom had grown wealthy through their ownership of coffee plantations. By 1900, three-quarters of the world's coffee was grown in Brazil. As in Argentina, the ruling oligarchy ignored the importance of establishing an urban industrial base. When the Great Depression ravaged profits from coffee exports, a wealthy rancher, Getúlio Vargas (1883–1954), seized power and ruled the country as president from 1930 to 1945. At first, Vargas sought to appease workers by declaring an eight-hour workday and a minimum wage, but, influenced by the apparent success of fascist regimes in Europe, he ruled by increasingly autocratic means and relied on a police force that used torture to silence his opponents. His industrial policy was relatively enlightened, however, and by the end of World War II, Brazil had become Latin America's major industrial power. In 1945, the army, fearing that Vargas might prolong his power illegally after calling for new elections, forced him to resign.

Mexico, in the years after World War I, was not an authoritarian state, but neither was it democratic. The Mexican Revolution at the beginning of the twentieth century had been the first significant effort in Latin American history to overturn the system of large estates and improve the living standards of the masses (see Chapter 19). Out of the political revolution emerged a relatively stable political order. The revolution, however, was democratic in form only, as the official political party, known as the Institutional Revolutionary Party (PRI), controlled the levers of power throughout society. Every six years, PRI bosses chose the party's presidential candidate, who was then dutifully elected by the people.

The situation began to change with the election of Lázaro Cárdenas (1895–1970) as president in 1934. Cárdenas won wide popularity with the peasants by ordering the redistribution of 44 million acres of land controlled by landed elites. He also won popular support by adopting a stronger stand against the United States, seizing control over the oil industry, which had hitherto been dominated by major U.S. oil companies. Alluding to the Good Neighbor policy, President Roosevelt refused to intervene, and eventually Mexico agreed to compensate U.S. oil companies for their lost property. It then set up PEMEX, a state-administered organization, to run the oil industry.

Latin American Culture

During the early twentieth century, modern European artistic and literary movements began to penetrate Latin America. In major cities, such as Buenos Aires and São Paulo, wealthy elites supported avant-garde trends, but other artists returned from abroad to adapt modern techniques to their native roots.

For many artists and writers, their work provided a means of promoting the emergence of a new national essence. An example was the Mexican muralist Diego Rivera (1886–1957). Rivera had studied in Europe, where he was influenced by fresco painting in Italy. After his return to Mexico, where the government provided financial support for the painting of murals on public buildings, he began to produce a monumental style of mural art that served two purposes: to illustrate the national past by portraying Aztec legends as well as Mexican festivals and folk customs and to promote a political message in favor

 RIVERA'S MURAL ART.   Diego Rivera was an important figure in the development of Mexico's mural art in the 1920s and 1930s. One of Rivera's goals—to portray Mexico's past and native traditions—is evident in this mural that conveys the complexity and variety of Aztec civilization. When the Spanish arrived, they were amazed at the variety of foods and merchandise for sale in the marketplace in Tenochtitlán (present-day Mexico City).

of realizing the social goals of the Mexican Revolution. Rivera's murals can be found in such diverse locations as the Ministry of Education and the Social Security Hospital in Mexico City and the chapel of the Agricultural School at Chapingo.

CONCLUSION

The turmoil brought about by World War I not only resulted in the destruction of several of the major Western empires and a redrawing of the map of Europe but also opened the door to political and social upheavals elsewhere in the world. In the Middle East, the decline and fall of the Ottoman Empire led to the creation of the secular republic of Turkey. The state of Saudi Arabia emerged in the Arabian peninsula, and Palestine became a source

of tension between newly arrived Jewish settlers and long-time Muslim residents.

Other parts of Asia and Africa also witnessed the rise of movements for national independence. In Africa, these movements were spearheaded by native leaders educated in Europe or the United States. In India, Gandhi and his campaign of civil disobedience played a crucial role in his country's bid to be free of British rule. Communist movements also began to emerge in Asian societies as radical elements sought new methods of bringing about the overthrow of Western imperialism. Japan continued to follow its own path to modernization, which, although successful from an economic point of view, took a menacing turn during the 1930s.

Between 1919 and 1939, China experienced a dramatic struggle to establish a modern nation. Two dynamic political organizations—the Nationalists and the Communists—

competed for legitimacy as the rightful heirs of the old order. At first, they formed an alliance in an effort to defeat their common adversaries, but cooperation ultimately turned to conflict. The Nationalists under Chiang Kai-shek emerged supreme, but Chiang found it difficult to control the remnants of the warlord regime in China, while the Great Depression undermined his efforts to build an industrial nation.

During the interwar years, the nations of Latin America faced severe economic problems because of their dependence on exports. Increasing U.S. investments in Latin America contributed to growing hostility against the powerful neighbor to the north. The Great Depression forced the region to begin developing new industries, but it also led to the rise of authoritarian governments, some of them modeled after the fascist regimes of Italy and Germany.

By demolishing the remnants of their old civilization on the battlefields of World War I, Europeans had inadvertently encouraged the subject peoples of their vast colonial empires to begin their own movements for national independence. The process was by no means completed in the two decades following the Treaty of Versailles, but the bonds of imperial rule had been severely strained. Once Europeans began to weaken themselves in the even more destructive conflict of World War II, the hopes of African and Asian peoples for national independence and freedom could at last be realized. It is to that devastating world conflict that we must now turn.

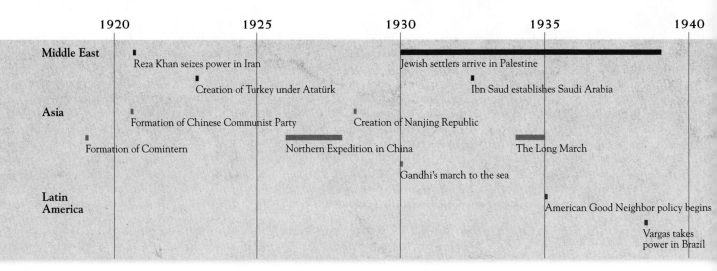

Timeline spanning 1920 to 1940.

Middle East
- Reza Khan seizes power in Iran
- Creation of Turkey under Atatürk
- Jewish settlers arrive in Palestine
- Ibn Saud establishes Saudi Arabia

Asia
- Formation of Chinese Communist Party
- Formation of Comintern
- Northern Expedition in China
- Creation of Nanjing Republic
- Gandhi's march to the sea
- The Long March

Latin America
- American Good Neighbor policy begins
- Vargas takes power in Brazil

CHAPTER NOTES

1. Vladimir I. Lenin, "The Awakening of Asia," in *The Awakening of Asia: Selected Essays* (New York, 1963–1968), p. 22.
2. Speech by Mahatma Gandhi, delivered in London in September 1931 during his visit for the first Roundtable Conference.
3. Ts'ai Yuan-p'ei, "Ta Lin Ch'in-nan Han," in *Ts'ai Yuan-p'ei Hsien-sheng Ch'uan-chi* [Collected Works of Mr. Ts'ai Yuan-p'ei] (Taipei, 1968), pp. 1057–1058.
4. Quoted in Nicholas Rowland Clifford, *Spoilt Children of Empire: Westerners in Shanghai and the Chinese Revolution of the 1920s* (Hanover, N.H., 1991), p. 93.
5. Quoted in William Theodore de Bary et al., eds., *Sources of Chinese Tradition* (New York, 1963), p. 783.
6. Lu Xun, "Diary of a Madman," in *Selected Works of Lu Hsun* (Peking, 1957), vol. 1, p. 20.

SUGGESTED READING

The classic study of nationalism in the non-Western world is R. Emerson, *From Empire to Nation* (Boston, 1960). For a more recent approach, see B. Anderson, *Imagined Communities: Reflections on the Origin and Spread of Nationalism* (London, 1983). On nationalism in India, see S. Wolpert, *Congress and Indian Nationalism: The Pre-Independence Phase* (New York, 1988).

Also see P. Chatterjee, *The Nation and Its Fragments: Colonial and Postcolonial Histories* (Princeton, N.J., 1993), and E. Gellner, *Nations and Nationalism* (Ithaca, N.Y., 1994).

There have been a number of studies of Mahatma Gandhi and his ideas. See, for example, J. M. Brown, *Gandhi: Prisoner of Hope* (New Haven, Conn., 1989), and D. Dalton, *Mahatma Gandhi: Non-*

violent Power in Action (New York, 1995). Also see the psychohistorical study by E. Erikson, *Gandhi's Truth: On the Origins of Militant Nonviolence* (New York, 1969). For a study of Nehru, see J. M. Brown, *Nehru* (New York, 2000).

For a general survey of events in the Middle East in the interwar era, see H. M. Sachar, *The Emergence of the Middle East, 1914–1924* (New York, 1969). For more specialized studies, see I. Gershoni et al., *Egypt, Islam, and the Arabs: The Search for Egyptian Nationhood* (Oxford, 1993), and W. Laqueur, *A History of Zionism: From the French Revolution to the Establishment of the State of Israel* (New York, 1996). The role of Atatürk is examined in J. P. Balfour, *Ataturk: The Rebirth of a Nation* (London, 1964).

On the early republic in China, see L. Yu-sheng, *The Crisis of Chinese Consciousness: Radical Antitraditionalism in the May Fourth Era* (Madison, Wis., 1979). The rise of the Chinese Communist Party is discussed in A. Dirlik, *The Origins of Chinese Communism* (Oxford, 1989). There are a number of biographies of Mao Zedong. A readable and informative one is S. Schram, *Mao Tse-tung: A Political Biography* (Baltimore, 1966). Also see J. D. Spence, *Mao Zedong: A Penguin Life* (New York, 1999). For an inside account of the Chinese Communist movement by a sympathetic Western journalist, see E. Snow, *Red Star over China* (New York, 1938). The early Chiang Kai-shek period is dealt with persuasively in L. Eastman, *The Abortive Revolution: China Under Nationalist Rule, 1927–1937* (Cambridge, 1974). On the interwar era in Japan, see P. Duus, ed., *The Cambridge History of Japan*, vol. 6 (Cambridge, 1989).

For an overview of Latin American history in the 1920s and 1930s, see E. Williamson, *The Penguin History of Latin America* (Harmondsworth, England, 1992). On U.S.–Latin American relations, see the classic study by B. Wood, *The Making of the Good Neighbor Policy* (New York, 1960). On Argentina, Brazil, and Mexico, see D. Rock, *Argentina, 1516–1982* (London, 1986); E. B. Burns, *A History of Brazil*, 2d ed. (New York, 1980); and M. C. Meyer and W. L. Sherman, *The Course of Mexican History*, 3d ed. (New York, 1987). On Getúlio Vargas, see R. Bourne, *Getúlio Vargas of Brazil, 1883–1954: Sphinx of the Pampas* (London, 1974). On culture, see J. Franco, *The Modern Culture of Latin America: Society and the Artist* (Harmondsworth, England, 1970).

For a general introduction to the women's movement during this era, consult C. Johnson-Odim and M. Strobel, eds., *Restoring Women to History* (Bloomington, Ind., 1999). For collections of essays concerning African women, see C. Robertson and I. Berger, *Women and Class in Africa* (New York, 1986), and S. Stichter and J. I. Parparti, eds., *Patriarchy and Class: African Women in the Home and Workforce* (Boulder, Colo., 1988). To follow the women's movement in India, see S. Tharu and K. Lalita, *Women Writing in India*, vol. 2 (New York, 1993). For Japan, see S. Sievers, *Flowers in Salt: The Beginnings of Feminist Consciousness in Modern Japan* (Stanford, Calif., 1983).

INFOTRAC COLLEGE EDITION

For additional reading, go to InfoTrac College Edition, your online research library at http://web1.infotrac-college.com

Enter the search term "Gandhi" using Keywords.

Enter the search terms "Mao Zedong" using the Subject Guide.

Enter the search terms "Chiang Kai-shek" using the Subject Guide.

Enter the search term "Atatürk" using Keywords.

Chapter 24

THE CRISIS DEEPENS: WORLD WAR II

CHAPTER OUTLINE

- RETREAT FROM DEMOCRACY: DICTATORIAL REGIMES
- THE PATH TO WAR
- WORLD WAR II
- THE NEW ORDER
- THE HOME FRONT
- THE AFTERMATH: THE COLD WAR
- CONCLUSION

FOCUS QUESTIONS

- What are the characteristics of totalitarian states, and to what degree were these characteristics present in Fascist Italy, Nazi Germany, and Stalinist Russia?
- What were the underlying causes of World War II, and what specific steps taken by Nazi Germany and Japan led to war?
- What were the main events of World War II in Europe and Asia, and what was the nature of the new orders that Germany and Japan attempted to establish in the territories they occupied?
- What were conditions like on the home front for the major belligerents in World War II?
- How did the Allies' visions of the postwar world differ, and how did these differences contribute to the emergence of the Cold War?
- ➤ What was the relationship between World War I and World War II, and what were the differences in the way the wars were fought?

O
n February 3, 1933, only four days after he had been appointed chancellor of Germany, Adolf Hitler met secretly with Germany's leading generals. He revealed to them his desire to remove the "cancer of democracy," create a new authoritarian leadership, and forge a new domestic unity. All Germans would need to realize that "only a struggle can save us and that everything else must be subordinated to this idea." Youth especially must be trained and their wills strengthened "to fight with all means." Since Germany's living space was too small for its people, Hitler said, Germany must rearm and prepare for "the conquest of new living space in the east and its ruthless Germanization." Even before he had consolidated his power, Adolf Hitler had a clear vision of his goals, and their implementation meant another war.

World War II in Europe was clearly Hitler's war. Although other countries may have helped make the war possible by not resisting Hitler's Germany earlier, it was Nazi Germany's actions that made World War II inevitable.

World War II was more than just Hitler's war, however. World War II consisted of two conflicts: one provoked by the ambitions of Germany in Europe, the other by the ambitions of Japan in Asia. By 1941, with the involvement of the United States in both wars, the two had merged into a single global conflict.

Although World War I had been described as a total war, World War II was even more so and was fought on a scale unheard of in history. Almost everyone in the warring countries was involved in one way or another: as soldiers; as workers in wartime industries; as ordinary citizens subject to invading armies, military occupation, or bombing raids; as refugees; or as victims of mass extermination. The world had never witnessed such widespread human-made death and destruction. •

RETREAT FROM DEMOCRACY: DICTATORIAL REGIMES

The rise of dictatorial regimes in the 1930s had a great deal to do with the coming of World War II. By 1939, only two major states in Europe, France and Great Britain, remained democratic. Italy and Germany had succumbed to the political movement called fascism, and Soviet Russia under Stalin moved toward repressive totalitarianism. A host of other European states and Latin American countries adopted authoritarian structures of different kinds, while a militarist regime in Japan moved that country down the path of war.

The dictatorial regimes between the wars assumed both old and new forms. Dictatorship was not new, but the modern totalitarian state was. The totalitarian regimes, best exemplified by Stalinist Russia and Nazi Germany, greatly extended the functions and power of the central state. The modern totalitarian state went beyond the ideal of passive obedience expected in a traditional dictatorship or authoritarian monarchy. The new "total states" expected the active loyalty and commitment of citizens to the regime's goals, whether they be war, a socialist society,

or a thousand-year Reich. They used modern mass propaganda techniques and high-speed communications to conquer the minds and hearts of their subjects. The total state sought to control not only the economic, political, and social aspects of life but the intellectual and cultural aspects as well.

The modern totalitarian state was to be led by a single leader and a single party. It ruthlessly rejected the liberal ideal of limited government power and constitutional guarantees of individual freedoms. Indeed, individual freedom was to be subordinated to the collective will of the masses, organized and determined for them by the leader or leaders. Modern technology also gave total states unprecedented police controls to force their wishes on their subjects.

The Birth of Fascism

In the early 1920s, Benito Mussolini bestowed on Italy the first fascist movement in Europe. Mussolini (1883–1945) began his political career as a socialist, but in 1919, he established a new political group, the *Fascio di Combattimento* (League of Combat), which won support from middle-class industrialists fearful of working-class agitation and large landowners who objected to agricultural strikes. Mussolini also perceived that Italians were angry over Italy's failure to receive more territorial acquisitions after World War I. The movement gained momentum as Mussolini's nationalist rhetoric and the middle-class fear of socialism, communist revolution, and disorder made the Fascists seem more and more attractive. On October 29, 1922, after Mussolini and the Fascists threatened to march on Rome if they were not given power, King Victor Emmanuel (1900–1946) capitulated and made Mussolini prime minister of Italy.

By 1926, Mussolini had established the institutional framework for a Fascist dictatorship. Press laws gave the government the right to suspend any publications that fostered disrespect for the Catholic church, the monarchy, or the state. The prime minister was made "head of government" with the power to legislate by decree. A law empowered the police to arrest and confine anybody for both nonpolitical and political crimes without pressing charges. The government was given the power to dissolve political and cultural associations. In 1926, all anti-Fascist parties were outlawed, and a secret police force, known as the OVRA, was established. By the end of the year, Mussolini ruled Italy as *Il Duce*, the leader.

Mussolini conceived of the Fascist state as totalitarian: "Fascism is totalitarian, and the Fascist State, the synthesis and unity of all values, interprets, develops and gives strength to the whole life of the people."[1] Mussolini did try to create a police state, but it was not very effective. Police activities in Italy were never as repressive, efficient, or savage as those of Nazi Germany would be. Likewise, the Italian Fascists' attempt to exercise control over all

MUSSOLINI—THE IRON *DUCE*.   One of Mussolini's favorite images of himself was that of the iron *Duce*—the strong leader who is always right. Consequently, he was often seen in military-style uniforms and military poses. This photograph shows Mussolini in one of his numerous uniforms with his Black Shirt bodyguards giving the Fascist salute.

forms of mass media, including newspapers, radio, and cinema, in order to use propaganda as an instrument to integrate the masses into the state, failed to achieve its major goals. Most commonly, Fascist propaganda was disseminated through simple slogans, such as "Mussolini is always right," plastered on walls all over Italy.

The Fascists portrayed the family as the pillar of the state and women as the basic foundation of the family. "Woman into the home" became the Fascist slogan. Women were to be homemakers and baby producers, "their natural and fundamental mission in life," according to Mussolini, for population growth was viewed as an indicator of national strength. Employment outside the home was an impediment distracting from conception: "It forms an independence and consequent physical and moral habits contrary to child bearing."[2]

Despite the instruments of repression, the use of propaganda, and the creation of numerous Fascist organizations, Mussolini never achieved the degree of totalitarian control attained in Hitler's Germany or Stalin's Soviet Union. Mussolini and the Fascist party did not completely destroy the old power structure. Some institutions, including the Catholic church, the armed forces, and the monarchy, were never absorbed into the Fascist state and managed to maintain their independence. In all areas of Italian life under Mussolini and the Fascists, there was a noticeable dichotomy between Fascist ideals and practice. The Italian Fascists promised much but actually delivered considerably less, and they were soon overshadowed by a much more powerful fascist movement to the north.

Hitler and Nazi Germany

In 1923, a small south German rightist party known as the Nazis, led by an obscure Austrian rabble-rouser named Adolf Hitler, created a stir when it tried to seize power in southern Germany in conscious imitation of Mussolini's march on Rome in 1922. Although the attempt failed,

Hitler and the Nazis achieved sudden national prominence. Within ten years, they had taken over complete power.

Born on April 20, 1889, Adolf Hitler was the son of an Austrian customs official. He failed secondary school and eventually made his way to Vienna to become an artist. In Vienna, Hitler formulated the basic ideas of an ideology from which he never deviated for the rest of his life. At its core was racism—Germanic supremacy and anti-Semitism. His hatred of the Jews never wavered. Hitler also became an extreme German nationalist who learned from the mass politics of Vienna how political parties could use propaganda and terror effectively. Finally, in his Viennese years, Hitler also came to a firm belief in the need for struggle, which he saw as the "granite foundation of the world."

HITLER'S RISE TO POWER, 1919–1933

At the end of World War I, after four years of service on the Western Front, Hitler went to Munich and decided to enter politics. Between 1919 and 1923, Hitler accomplished a great deal as a Munich politician. He joined the obscure German Workers' Party, one of a number of right-wing extreme nationalist parties in Munich. By the summer of 1921, he had assumed control of the party, which he renamed the National Socialist German Workers' Party (NSDAP), or Nazi for short. His idea was that the party's name would distinguish the Nazis from the socialist parties while gaining support from both working-class and nationalist circles. Hitler worked assiduously to develop the party into a mass political movement with flags, badges, uniforms, its own newspaper, and its own police force or party militia known as the SA, the *Sturmabteilung,* or Storm Troops. The SA was used to defend the party in meeting halls and break up the meetings of other parties. It added an element of force and terror to the growing Nazi movement. Hitler's own oratorical skills were largely responsible for attracting an increasing number of followers. By 1923, the party had grown from its early hundreds into a membership of 55,000, of whom 15,000 served in the SA.

Overconfident, Hitler staged an armed uprising against the government in Munich in November 1923. The so-called Beer Hall Putsch was quickly crushed, and Hitler was sentenced to prison. During his brief stay in jail, he wrote *Mein Kampf (My Struggle),* an autobiographical account of his movement and its underlying ideology. Extreme German nationalism, virulent anti-Semitism, and vicious anticommunism are linked together by a social Darwinian theory of struggle that stresses the right of superior nations to *Lebensraum* (living space) through expansion and the right of superior individuals to secure authoritarian leadership over the masses. What is perhaps most remarkable about *Mein Kampf* is its elaboration of a series of ideas that directed Hitler's actions once he took power. That others refused to take Hitler and his ideas seriously was one of his greatest advantages.

During his imprisonment, Hitler also came to the realization that the Nazis would have to come to power by constitutional means, not by overthrowing the Weimar Republic. This implied the formation of a mass political party that would actively compete for votes with the other political parties. After his release from prison, Hitler worked assiduously to build such a party. He reorganized the Nazi Party on a regional basis and expanded it to all parts of Germany. By 1929, the Nazis had a national party organization and a membership that reached 178,000 by the end of 1929. Especially noticeable was the youthfulness of the regional, district, and branch leaders of the Nazi organization. Many were between the ages of twenty-five and thirty and were fiercely committed to Hitler because he gave them the kind of active politics they sought. Rather than democratic debate, they wanted brawls in beer halls, enthusiastic speeches, and comradeship in building a new Germany. One young Nazi member expressed his excitement about the party:

> For me this was the start of a completely new life. There was only one thing in the world for me and that was service in the movement. All my thoughts were centered on the movement. I could talk only politics. I was no longer aware of anything else. At the time I was a promising athlete; I was very keen on sport, and it was going to be my career. But I had to give this up too. My only interest was agitation and propaganda.[3]

Such youthful enthusiasm gave the Nazi movement the aura of a "young man's movement" and a sense of dynamism that the other parties could not match.

By 1932, the Nazi Party had 800,000 members and had become the largest party in the Reichstag. No doubt, Germany's economic difficulties were a crucial factor in the Nazi rise to power. Unemployment rose dramatically, from just over four million in 1931 to six million by the winter of 1932. The economic and psychological impact of the Great Depression made extremist parties more attractive. The Nazis were especially effective in developing modern electioneering techniques. In their election campaigns, party members pitched their themes to the needs and fears of different social groups. In working-class districts, for example, the Nazis attacked international high finance; in middle-class neighborhoods, they exploited fears of a communist revolution and its threat to private property. At the same time that the Nazis made blatant appeals to class interests, they were denouncing conflicts of interest and maintaining that they stood above classes and parties. Hitler, in particular, claimed to stand above all differences and promised to create a new Germany free of class differences and party infighting. His appeal to national pride, national honor, and traditional militarism struck chords of emotion in his listeners.

Increasingly, the right-wing elites of Germany—the industrial magnates, landed aristocrats, military establishment, and higher bureaucrats—came to see Hitler as the man who had the mass support to establish a right-wing, authoritarian regime that would save Germany and their privileged positions from a communist takeover. Under pressure, since the Nazi Party had the largest share of seats in the Reichstag, President Paul von Hindenburg agreed to allow Hitler to become chancellor (on January 30, 1933) and create a new government.

Within two months, Hitler had laid the foundations for the Nazis' complete control over Germany. On the day after a fire broke out in the Reichstag building (February 27), supposedly caused by communists, Hitler convinced President Hindenburg to issue a decree that gave the government emergency powers. It suspended all basic rights for the duration of the emergency and thus enabled the Nazis to arrest and imprison anyone without redress. The crowning step in Hitler's "legal seizure" of power came on March 23, when the Reichstag passed the Enabling Act by a two-thirds vote. This legislation, which empowered the government to dispense with constitutional forms for four years while it issued laws that dealt with the country's problems, provided the legal basis for Hitler's subsequent acts. He no longer needed either the Reichstag or President Hindenburg. In effect, Hitler became a dictator appointed by the parliamentary body itself.

With their new source of power, the Nazis acted quickly to enforce *Gleichschaltung,* or the coordination of all institutions under Nazi control. The civil service was purged of Jews and democratic elements, concentration camps were established for opponents of the new regime, the autonomy of the federal states was eliminated, trade unions were dissolved, and all political parties except the Nazis were abolished. By the end of the summer of 1933, within seven months of being appointed chancellor, Hitler and

the Nazis had established the foundations for a totalitarian state. When Hindenburg died on August 2, 1934, the office of Reich president was abolished, and Hitler became sole ruler of Germany. Public officials and soldiers were all required to take a personal oath of loyalty to Hitler as the "Führer [leader] of the German Reich and people."

THE NAZI STATE, 1933–1939

Having smashed the parliamentary state, Hitler now felt the real task was at hand: to develop the "total state." Hitler's aims had not been simply power for power's sake or a tyranny based on personal power. He had larger ideological goals. The development of an "Aryan" racial state that would dominate Europe and possibly the world for generations to come required a movement in which the German people would be actively involved, not passively cowed by force. Hitler stated:

> We must develop organizations in which an individual's entire life can take place. Then every activity and every need of every individual will be regulated by the collectivity represented by the party. There is no longer any arbitrary will; there are no longer any free realms in which the individual belongs to himself. . . . The time of personal happiness is over.[4]

The Nazis pursued the creation of this totalitarian state in a variety of ways.

Mass demonstrations and spectacles were employed to integrate the German nation into a collective fellowship and to mobilize it as an instrument for Hitler's policies (see the box on p. 689). These mass demonstrations, especially the Nuremberg party rallies that were held every

➤ **THE NAZI MASS SPECTACLE.** Hitler and the Nazis made clever use of mass spectacles to rally the German people behind the Nazi regime. These mass demonstrations evoked intense enthusiasm, as is evident in this photograph of Hitler arriving at the Bückeberg near Hamelin for the Harvest Festival in 1937. Almost one million people were present for the celebration.

PROPAGANDA AND MASS MEETINGS IN NAZI GERMANY

Propaganda and mass rallies were two of the chief instruments that Hitler used to prepare the German people for the tasks he set before them. In the first selection, taken from Mein Kampf, Hitler explains the psychological importance of mass meetings in creating support for a political movement. In the second excerpt, taken from his speech to a crowd at Nuremberg, he describes the kind of mystical bond he hoped to create through his mass rallies.

ADOLF HITLER, MEIN KAMPF

The mass meeting is also necessary for the reason that in it the individual, who at first, while becoming a supporter of a young movement, feels lonely and easily succumbs to the fear of being alone, for the first time gets the picture of a larger community, which in most people has a strengthening, encouraging effect.... When from his little workshop or big factory, in which he feels very small, he steps for the first time into a mass meeting and has thousands and thousands of people of the same opinions around him, when, as a seeker, he is swept away by three or four thousand others into the mighty effect of suggestive intoxication and enthusiasm, when the visible success and agreement of thousands confirm to him the rightness of the new doctrine and for the first time arouse doubt in the truth of his previous conviction—then he himself has succumbed to the magic influence of what we designate as "mass suggestion." The will, the longing, and also the power of thousands are accumulated in every individual. The man who enters such a meeting doubting and wavering leaves it inwardly reinforced: he has become a link in the community.

ADOLF HITLER, SPEECH AT THE NUREMBERG PARTY RALLY, 1936

Do we not feel once again in this hour the miracle that brought us together? Once you heard the voice of a man, and it struck deep into your hearts; it awakened you, and you followed this voice. Year after year you went after it, though him who had spoken you never even saw. You heard only a voice, and you followed it. When we meet each other here, the wonder of our coming together fills us all. Not everyone of you sees me, and I do not see everyone of you. But I feel you, and you feel me. It is the belief in our people that has made us small men great, that has made us poor men rich, that has made brave and courageous men out of us wavering, spiritless, timid folk; this belief made us see our road when we were astray; it joined us together into one whole! ... You come, that ... you may, once in a while, gain the feeling that now we are together; we are with him and he with us, and we are now Germany!

September, combined the symbolism of a religious service with the merriment of a popular amusement. They had great appeal and usually evoked mass enthusiasm and excitement.

Some features of the state apparatus of Hitler's total state seem contradictory. One usually thinks of Nazi Germany as having an all-powerful government that maintained absolute control and order. In truth, Nazi Germany was the scene of almost constant personal and institutional conflict, which resulted in administrative chaos. In matters such as foreign policy, education, and economics, parallel government and party bureaucracies competed over spheres of influence. Incessant struggle characterized relationships within the party, within the state, and between party and state. Some historians assume that Hitler's aversion to making decisions resulted in the chaos that subverted his own authority and made him a "weak dictator," while others maintain that Hitler deliberately created this institutional confusion. By fostering rivalry within the party and between party and state, he would be the ultimate decision maker and absolute ruler.

In the economic sphere, Hitler and the Nazis also established control. Although the regime pursued the use of public works projects and "pump-priming" grants to private construction firms to foster employment and end the depression, there is little doubt that rearmament contributed far more to solving the unemployment problem. Unemployment, which had stood at 6 million in 1932, dropped to 2.6 million in 1934 and less than 500,000 in 1937. The regime claimed full credit for solving Germany's economic woes, and this was an important factor in convincing many Germans to accept the new regime, despite its excesses.

For its enemies, the Nazi total state had its instruments of terror and repression. Especially important was the SS (*Schutzstaffel*). Originally created as Hitler's personal bodyguard, the SS, under the direction of Heinrich Himmler (1900–1945), came to control all of the regular and secret police forces. Himmler and the SS functioned on the basis of two principles: terror and ideology. Terror included the instruments of repression and murder: the secret police, criminal police, concentration camps, and later the execution squads and death camps for the extermination of the Jews. For Himmler, the SS was a crusading order whose primary goal was to further the Aryan master race. SS members, who constituted a carefully chosen elite, were thoroughly indoctrinated in racial ideology.

Other institutions, such as the Catholic and Protestant churches, primary and secondary schools, and universities, were also brought under the control of the Nazi totalitarian state. Nazi professional organizations and leagues were formed for civil servants, teachers, women, farmers, doctors, and lawyers. Since the early indoctrination of youth would create the foundation for a strong totalitarian state for the future, youth organizations—the *Hitler Jugend* (Hitler Youth) and its female counterpart, the *Bund deutscher Mädel* (League of German Maidens)—were given special attention. The oath required of Hitler Youth members demonstrates the degree of dedication expected of youth in the Nazi state: "In the presence of this blood banner, which represents our Führer, I swear to devote all my energies and my strength to the savior of our country, Adolf Hitler. I am willing and ready to give up my life for him, so help me God."

The creation of the Nazi total state also had an impact on women. The Nazi attitude toward women was largely determined by ideological considerations. Women played a crucial role in the Aryan racial state as bearers of the children who would bring about the triumph of the Aryan race. To the Nazis, the differences between men and women were quite natural. Men were warriors and political leaders, while women were destined to be wives and mothers. By maintaining this clear distinction, each could best serve to "maintain the whole community."

Nazi ideas determined employment opportunities for women. The Nazis hoped to drive women out of certain areas of the labor market, including heavy industry or other jobs that might hinder women from bearing healthy children. Certain professions, including university teaching, medicine, and law, were also considered inappropriate for women, especially married women. Instead the Nazis encouraged women to pursue professional occupations that had direct practical application, such as social work and nursing. In addition to restrictive legislation against females, the Nazi regime pushed its campaign against working women with such poster slogans as "Get hold of pots and pans and broom and you'll sooner find a groom!"

The Nazi total state was intended to be an Aryan racial state. From its beginning, the Nazi Party reflected Hitler's virulent anti-Semitic beliefs. Once in power, the Nazis translated these ideas into anti-Semitic policies. In September 1935, the Nazis announced new racial laws at the annual party rally in Nuremberg. These "Nuremberg laws" excluded German Jews from German citizenship and forbade marriages and extramarital relations between Jews and German citizens. The "Nuremberg laws" essentially separated Jews from the Germans politically, socially, and legally and were the natural extension of Hitler's stress on the creation of a pure Aryan race.

Another, considerably more violent phase of anti-Jewish activity took place in 1938 and 1939. It was initiated on November 9–10, 1938, the infamous *Kristallnacht*, or night of shattered glass. The assassination of a secretary

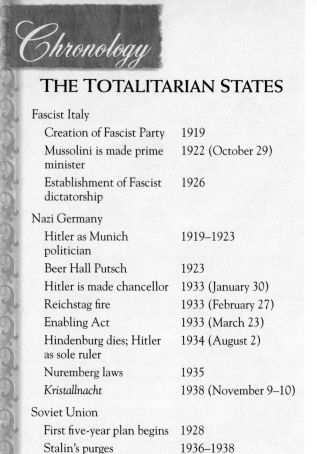

in the German embassy in Paris became the pretext for a Nazi-led rampage against the Jews in which synagogues were burned, seven thousand Jewish businesses were destroyed, and at least one hundred Jews were killed. Moreover, twenty thousand Jewish males were rounded up and sent to concentration camps. *Kristallnacht* also led to further drastic steps. Jews were barred from all public buildings and prohibited from owning, managing, or working in any retail store. Finally, under the direction of the SS, Jews were encouraged to "emigrate from Germany." After the outbreak of World War II, the policy of emigration was replaced by a more gruesome one: extermination.

The Stalinist Era in the Soviet Union

Stalin made a significant shift in economic policy in 1928 when he launched his first five-year plan. Its real goal was nothing less than the transformation of the agrarian Soviet Union into an industrial country virtually overnight. Instead of producing consumer goods, the first five-year plan emphasized maximum production of capital goods and armaments and succeeded in quadrupling the production of heavy machinery and doubling oil production. Between 1928 and 1937, during the first two five-year plans, steel production increased from 4 million to 18 million tons per year.

Rapid industrialization was accompanied by an equally rapid collectivization of agriculture. Its goal was to eliminate private farms and push people into collective farms (see the box on p. 691). Strong resistance to Stalin's plans from

THE FORMATION OF
COLLECTIVE FARMS

*A*ccompanying the rapid industrialization of the Soviet Union was the collectivization of agriculture, a feat that involved nothing less than transforming Russia's 26 million family farms into 250,000 collective farms (kolkhozes). This selection provides a firsthand account of how the process worked.

MAX BELOV, THE HISTORY OF A COLLECTIVE FARM

General collectivization in our village was brought about in the following manner: Two representatives of the [Communist] Party arrived in the village. All the inhabitants were summoned by the ringing of the church bell to a meeting at which the policy of general collectivization was announced. . . . The upshot was that although the meeting lasted two days, from the viewpoint of the Party representatives nothing was accomplished.

After this setback the Party representatives divided the village into two sections and worked each one separately. Two more officials were sent to reinforce the first two. A meeting of our section of the village was held in a stable which had previously belonged to a kulak [wealthy farmer]. The meeting dragged on until dark. Suddenly someone threw a brick at the lamp, and in the dark the peasants began to beat the Party representatives, who jumped out the window and escaped from the village barely alive. The following day seven people were arrested. The militia was called in and stayed in the village until the peasants, realizing their helplessness, calmed down. . . .

By the end of 1930 there were two kolkhozes in our village. Though at first these collectives embraced at most only 70 percent of the peasant households, in the months that followed they gradually absorbed more and more of them.

In these kolkhozes the great bulk of the land was held and worked communally, but each peasant household owned a house of some sort, a small plot of ground and per-haps some livestock. All the members of the kolkhoz were required to work on the kolkhoz a certain number of days each month; the rest of the time they were allowed to work on their own holdings. They derived their income partly from what they grew on their garden strips and partly from their work in the kolkhoz.

When the harvest was over, and after the farm had met its obligations to the state and to various special funds (for insurance, seed, etc.) and had sold on the market whatever undesignated produce was left, the remaining produce and the farm's monetary income were divided among the kolkhoz members according to the number of "labor days" each one had contributed to the farm's work. . . . It was in 1930 that the kolkhoz members first received their portions out of the "communal kettle." After they had received their earnings, at the rate of 1 kilogram of grain and 55 kopecks per labor day, one of them remarked, "You will live, but you will be very, very thin."

In the spring of 1931 a tractor worked the fields of the kolkhoz for the first time. The tractor was "capable of plowing every kind of hard soil and virgin sod," as Party representatives told us at the meeting in celebration of its arrival. The peasants did not then know that these "steel horses" would carry away a good part of the harvest in return for their work. . . .

By late 1932 more than 80 percent of the peasant households . . . had been collectivized. . . . That year the peasants harvested a good crop and had hopes that the calculations would work out to their advantage and would help strengthen them economically. These hopes were in vain. The kolkhoz workers received only 200 grams of flour per labor day for the first half of the year; the remaining grain, including the seed fund, was taken by the government. The peasants were told that industrialization of the country, then in full swing, demanded grain and sacrifices from them.

peasants who hoarded crops and killed livestock only led him to step up the program. By 1934, Russia's 26 million family farms had been collectivized into 250,000 units. This was done at tremendous cost, since the hoarding of food and the slaughter of livestock produced widespread famine. Perhaps ten million peasants died in the artificially created famines of 1932 and 1933. The only concession Stalin made to the peasants was that each collective farm worker was allowed to have one tiny privately owned garden plot.

There were additional costs to Stalin's program of rapid industrialization, however. To achieve his goals, Stalin strengthened the party bureaucracy under his control. Those who resisted were sent into forced labor camps in Siberia. Stalin's desire for sole control of decision mak-ing also led to purges of the Old Bolsheviks. Between 1936 and 1938, the most prominent Old Bolsheviks were put on trial and condemned to death. During this same time, Stalin undertook a purge of army officers, diplomats, union officials, party members, intellectuals, and numerous ordinary citizens. Estimates are that eight million Russians were arrested; millions were sent to Siberian forced labor camps, from which they never returned.

The Stalinist era also reversed much of the permissive social legislation of the early 1920s. Advocating complete equality of rights for women, the Communists had made divorce and abortion easy to obtain while also encouraging women to work outside the home and to set their own moral standards. After Stalin came to power, the family

⇨ STALIN SIGNS A DEATH WARRANT. Terror played an important role in the totalitarian system established by Joseph Stalin. In this photograph, Stalin is shown signing what is supposedly a death warrant in 1933. As the terror increased in the late 1930s, Stalin signed such documents every day.

was praised as a miniature collective in which parents were responsible for inculcating values of duty, discipline, and hard work. Abortion was outlawed, and divorced fathers who failed to support their children were fined heavily.

The Rise of Militarism in Japan

The rise of militarism in Japan resulted not from a seizure of power by a new political party but from the growing influence of militant forces at the top of the political hierarchy. In the early 1930s, the growing confrontation with China in Manchuria, combined with the onset of the Great Depression, brought an end to the fragile stability of the immediate postwar years. The depression had a disastrous effect on Japan. The value of Japanese exports dropped by 50 percent from 1929 to 1931, and wages dropped nearly as much. Hardest hit were farmers as the price of rice and other staple food crops plummeted.

During the early 1930s, civilian cabinets managed to cope with the economic challenges presented by the depression. By abandoning the gold standard, Prime Minister Inukai Tsuyoshi was able to lower the price of Japanese goods on the world market, and exports climbed back to earlier levels. But the political parties were no longer able to stem the growing influence of militant nationalist elements.

In May 1932, Inukai Tsuyoshi was assassinated by right-wing extremists. He was succeeded by a moderate, Admiral Saito Makoto, but extremist patriotic societies composed of ultranationalists began to terrorize opponents, assassinating businessmen and public figures identified with the Shidehara policy of conciliation toward the outside world. Some, like the publicist Kita Ikki, were convinced that the parliamentary system had been corrupted by materialism and Western values and should be replaced by a system that would return to traditional Japanese values and imperial authority. His message, "Asia for the Asians," had not won widespread support during the relatively prosperous 1920s but increased in popularity after the Great Depression, which convinced many Japanese that capitalism was unsuitable for Japan.

During the mid-1930s, the influence of the military and extreme nationalists over the government steadily increased. Minorities and left-wing elements were persecuted, and moderates were intimidated into silence. Terrorists tried for their part in assassination attempts portrayed themselves as selfless patriots and received light sentences. Japan continued to hold national elections, and moderate candidates continued to receive substantial popular support, but the cabinets were dominated by the military or advocates of Japanese expansionism. In February 1936, junior army officers led a coup, briefly occupying the Diet building and other key government installations in Tokyo and assassinating several members of the cabinet. The ringleaders were quickly tried and convicted of treason, but under conditions that further strengthened the influence of the military.

❧ THE PATH TO WAR

Only twenty years after the war to end war, the world plunged back into the nightmare of total war. The efforts at collective security in the 1920s—the League of Nations, the attempts at disarmament, the pacts and treaties—all proved meaningless in view of the growth of Nazi Germany and the rise of Japan.

The Path to War in Europe

World War II in Europe had its beginnings in the ideas of Adolf Hitler, who believed that only Aryans were capable of building a great civilization. But to Hitler, the Germans, the leading group of Aryans, were threatened from the east by a large mass of inferior peoples, the Slavs, who had learned to use German weapons and technology. Germany needed more land to support a larger population and be a great power. Already in the 1920s, in the second volume of *Mein Kampf*, Hitler had indicated where a National Socialist regime would find this land: "And so we National Socialists . . . take up where we broke off six hundred years ago. We stop the endless German movement to the south and west, and turn our gaze toward the land in the east. . . . If we speak of soil in Europe today, we can primarily have in mind only Russia and her vassal border states."[5] Once Russia had been conquered, its land could be resettled by German peasants while the Slavic population could be used as slave labor to build the Aryan racial state that would dominate Europe for a thousand years. Hitler's conclusion was apparent: Germany must prepare for its inevitable war with the Soviet Union.

When Hitler became chancellor on January 30, 1933, Germany's situation in Europe seemed weak. The Versailles treaty had created a demilitarized zone on Germany's western border that would allow the French to move into the heavily industrialized parts of Germany in the event of war. To Germany's east, the smaller states, such as Poland and Czechoslovakia, had defensive treaties with France. The Versailles treaty had also limited Germany's army to 100,000 troops with no air force and only a small navy.

Posing as a man of peace in his public speeches, Hitler emphasized that Germany wished only to revise the unfair provisions of Versailles by peaceful means and achieve Germany's rightful place among the European states. On March 9, 1935, he announced the creation of a new air force and one week later the introduction of a military draft that would expand Germany's army from 100,000 to 550,000 troops. Hitler's unilateral repudiation of the Versailles treaty brought a swift reaction, as France, Great Britain, and Italy condemned Germany's action and warned against future aggressive steps. But nothing concrete was done.

On March 7, 1936, buoyed by his conviction that the Western democracies had no intention of using force to maintain the Treaty of Versailles, Hitler sent German troops into the demilitarized Rhineland. According to the Versailles treaty, the French had the right to use force against any violation of the demilitarized Rhineland. But France would not act without British support, and the British viewed the occupation of German territory by German troops as reasonable action by a dissatisfied power. The London *Times* noted that the Germans were only "going into their own back garden."

Meanwhile, Hitler gained new allies. In October 1935, Benito Mussolini had committed Fascist Italy to imperial expansion by invading Ethiopia. Angered by French and British opposition to his invasion, Mussolini welcomed Hitler's support and began to draw closer to the German dictator he had once called a buffoon. The joint intervention of Germany and Italy on behalf of General Francisco Franco in the Spanish Civil War in 1936 also drew the two nations closer. In October 1936, Mussolini and Hitler concluded an agreement that recognized their common political and economic interests, and one month later, Mussolini referred publicly to the new Rome-Berlin Axis. Also in November, Germany and Japan (the rising military power in the Far East) concluded the Anti-Comintern Pact and agreed to maintain a common front against communism.

By the end of 1936, Hitler and Nazi Germany had achieved a "diplomatic revolution" in Europe. The Treaty of Versailles had been virtually scrapped, and Germany was once more a "world power," as Hitler proclaimed. Hitler was convinced that neither the French nor the British would provide much opposition to his plans and decided in 1938 to move on Austria. By threatening Austria with invasion, Hitler coerced the Austrian chancellor into putting Austrian Nazis in charge of the government. The new government promptly invited German troops to enter Austria and assist in maintaining law and order. One day later, on March 13, 1938, after his triumphal return to his native land, Hitler formally annexed Austria to Germany. Great Britain's ready acknowledgment of Hitler's action only increased the German dictator's contempt for Western weakness.

The annexation of Austria improved Germany's strategic position in central Europe and put Germany in position for Hitler's next objective—the destruction of Czechoslovakia. This goal might have seemed unrealistic since democratic Czechoslovakia was quite prepared to defend itself and was well supported by pacts with France and the Soviet Union. Hitler believed, however, that France and Britain would not use force to defend Czechoslovakia.

HITLER ARRIVES IN VIENNA.   By threatening to invade Austria, Hitler forced the Austrian government to capitulate to his wishes. Austria was annexed to Germany. Shown here is the triumphal arrival of Hitler in Vienna on March 13, 1938. Seated in the car to Hitler's right is Arthur Seyss-Inquart, Hitler's new handpicked governor of Austria.

THE MUNICH CONFERENCE

At the Munich Conference, the leaders of France and Great Britain capitulated to Hitler's demands on Czechoslovakia. While the British prime minister, Neville Chamberlain, defended his actions at Munich as necessary for peace, another British statesman, Winston Churchill, characterized the settlement at Munich as "a disaster of the first magnitude."

WINSTON CHURCHILL, SPEECH TO THE HOUSE OF COMMONS (OCTOBER 5, 1938)

I will begin by saying what everybody would like to ignore or forget but which must nevertheless be stated, namely, that we have sustained a total and unmitigated defeat, and that France has suffered even more than we have. . . . The utmost my right honorable Friend the Prime Minister . . . has been able to gain for Czechoslovakia and in the matters which were in dispute has been that the German dictator, instead of snatching his victuals from the table, has been content to have them served to him course by course. . . . And I will say this, that I believe the Czechs, left to themselves and told they were going to get no help from the Western Powers, would have been able to make better terms than they have got. . . .

We are in the presence of a disaster of the first magnitude which has befallen Great Britain and France. Do not let us blind ourselves to that. . . .

And do not suppose that this is the end. This is only the beginning of the reckoning. This is only the first sip, the first foretaste of a bitter cup which will be proffered to us year by year unless by a supreme recovery of moral health and martial vigor, we arise again and take our stand for freedom as in the olden time.

NEVILLE CHAMBERLAIN, SPEECH TO THE HOUSE OF COMMONS (OCTOBER 6, 1938)

That is my answer to those who say that we should have told Germany weeks ago that, if her army crossed the border of Czechoslovakia, we should be at war with her. We had no treaty obligations and no legal obligations to Czechoslovakia. . . . When we were convinced, as we became convinced, that nothing any longer would keep the Sudetenland within the Czechoslovakian State, we urged the Czech Government as strongly as we could to agree to the cession of territory, and to agree promptly. . . . It was a hard decision for anyone who loved his country to take, but to accuse us of having by that advice betrayed the Czechoslovakian State is simply preposterous. What we did was to save her from annihilation and give her a chance of new life as a new State, which involves the loss of territory and fortifications, but may perhaps enable her to enjoy in the future and develop a national existence under a neutrality and security comparable to that which we see in Switzerland today. Therefore, I think the Government deserve the approval of this House for their conduct of affairs in this recent crisis, which has saved Czechoslovakia from destruction and Europe from Armageddon.

He was right again. On September 15, 1938, Hitler demanded the cession of the Sudetenland (an area in northwestern Czechoslovakia that was inhabited largely by ethnic Germans) to Germany and expressed his willingness to risk "world war" to achieve his objective. Instead of objecting, the British, French, Germans, and Italians—at a hastily arranged conference at Munich—reached an agreement that essentially met all of Hitler's demands. German troops were allowed to occupy the Sudetenland as the Czechs, abandoned by their Western allies, stood by helplessly. The Munich Conference was the high point of Western appeasement of Hitler. When Neville Chamberlain, the British prime minister, returned to England from Munich, he boasted that the Munich agreement meant "peace for our time." Hitler had promised Chamberlain that he had made his last demand. Like scores of German politicians before him, Chamberlain had believed Hitler's promises (see the box above).

In fact, Munich confirmed Hitler's perception that the Western democracies were weak and would not fight. Increasingly, Hitler was convinced of his own infallibility, and he had by no means been satisfied at Munich. In March 1939, Hitler occupied the Czech lands (Bohemia and Moravia) while the Slovaks, with his encouragement, declared their independence of the Czechs and became a puppet state (Slovakia) of Nazi Germany. On the evening of March 15, 1939, Hitler triumphantly declared in Prague that he would be known as the greatest German of them all.

At last, the Western states realized that they had to react vigorously to the Nazi threat. Hitler's continued naked aggression made clear that his promises were worthless. When he began to demand the return of Danzig (which had been made a free city by the Treaty of Versailles to serve as a seaport for Poland) to Germany, Britain recognized the danger and offered to protect Poland in the event of war. At the same time, both France and Britain realized that among the European powers, only the Soviet Union was powerful enough to help contain Nazi aggression, and so began political and military negotiations with Stalin. Their distrust of Soviet communism, however, made an alliance unlikely.

Meanwhile, Hitler pressed on in the belief that Britain and France would not really fight over Poland. To preclude an alliance between the western European states and the Soviet Union, which would create the danger of a two-front war, Hitler, ever the opportunist, negotiated his own nonaggression pact with Stalin and shocked the world with its announcement, on August 23, 1939. The treaty with the Soviet Union gave Hitler the freedom to attack Poland. He told his generals: "Now Poland is in the position in which I wanted her. . . . I am only afraid that at the last moment some swine or other will yet submit to me a plan for mediation."[6] He need not have worried. On September 1, German forces invaded Poland; two days later, Britain and France declared war on Germany. Europe was again at war.

The Path to War in Asia

In September 1931, on the pretext that the Chinese had attacked a Japanese railway near Mukden (the "Mukden incident" had actually been carried out by Japanese saboteurs), Japanese military units seized Manchuria. Japanese officials in Tokyo were divided over the wisdom of the takeover, but the moderates were unable to control the army. Eventually, worldwide protests against the Japanese action led the League of Nations to send an investigative commission to Manchuria. When the commission issued a report condemning the seizure, Japan withdrew from the League. Over the next several years, the Japanese consolidated their hold on Manchuria, renaming it Manchukuo and placing it under the titular authority of the former Chinese emperor and now Japanese puppet Pu Yi. Japan now began to expand into northern China.

Not all politicians in Tokyo agreed with this aggressive policy, but right-wing terrorists assassinated some of the key critics and intimidated others into silence. By the mid-1930s, militants connected with the government, and the armed forces were effectively in control of Japanese politics. The United States refused to recognize the Japanese takeover of Manchuria but was unwilling to threaten the use of force. Instead the Americans attempted to appease Japan in the hope of encouraging Japanese moderates. As a senior U.S. diplomat with long experience in Asia warned in a memorandum to the president:

> Utter defeat of Japan would be no blessing to the Far East or to the world. It would merely create a new set of stresses, and substitute for Japan the [Soviet Union] as the successor to Imperial Russia—as a contestant (and at least an equally unscrupulous and dangerous one) for the mastery of the East. Nobody except perhaps Russia would gain from our victory in such a war."[7]

For the moment, the prime victim of Japanese aggression was China. Chiang Kai-shek attempted to avoid a confrontation with Japan so that he could deal with the Communists, whom he considered the greater threat. When clashes between Chinese and Japanese troops broke out, he sought to appease the Japanese by granting them the authority to administer areas in northern China. But as Japan moved steadily southward, popular protests in Chinese cities against Japanese aggression intensified. In December 1936, Chiang was briefly kidnapped by military

Chronology

THE PATH TO WAR,
1931–1939

Japan seizes Manchuria	September 1931
Hitler becomes chancellor	January 30, 1933
Hitler announces a German air force	March 9, 1935
Hitler announces military conscription	March 16, 1935
Mussolini invades Ethiopia	October 1935
Hitler occupies demilitarized Rhineland	March 7, 1936
Mussolini and Hitler intervene in Spanish Civil War	1936
Rome-Berlin Axis	October 1936
Anti-Comintern Pact (Japan and Germany)	November 1936
Japan invades China	1937
Germany annexes Austria	March 13, 1938
Munich Conference: Sudetenland goes to Germany	September 29, 1938
Germany occupies the rest of Czechoslovakia	March 1939
German-Soviet Nonaggression Pact	August 23, 1939
Germany invades Poland	September 1, 1939
Britain and France declare war on Germany	September 3, 1939

forces commanded by General Zhang Xueliang, who compelled him to end his military efforts against the Communists in Yan'an and form a new united front against the Japanese. After Chinese and Japanese forces clashed at Marco Polo Bridge, south of Beijing, in July 1937, China refused to apologize, and hostilities spread.

Japan had not planned to declare war on China, but neither side would compromise, and the 1937 incident eventually turned into a major conflict. The Japanese advanced up the Yangtze valley and seized the Chinese capital of Nanjing in December, but Chiang Kai-shek refused to capitulate and moved his government upriver to Hankou. When the Japanese seized that city, he moved on to Chongqing, in remote Sichuan province. Japanese strategists had hoped to force Chiang to join a Japanese-dominated New Order in East Asia, comprising Japan, Manchuria, and China. This was part of a larger plan to seize Soviet Siberia with its rich resources and create a new

JAPAN'S JUSTIFICATION FOR EXPANSION

*A*dvocates of Japanese expansion justified their proposals by claiming both economic necessity and moral imperatives. Note the familiar combination of motives in this passage written by an extremist military leader in the late 1930s.

HASHIMOTO KINGORO ON THE NEED FOR EMIGRATION AND EXPANSION

We have already said that there are only three ways left to Japan to escape from the pressure of surplus population. We are like a great crowd of people packed into a small and narrow room, and there are only three doors through which we might escape, namely emigration, advance into world markets, and expansion of territory. The first door, emigration, has been barred to us by the anti-Japanese immigration policies of other countries. The second door, advance into world markets, is being pushed shut by tariff barriers and the abrogation of commercial treaties. What should Japan do when two of the three doors have been closed against her?

It is quite natural that Japan should rush upon the last remaining door.

It may sound dangerous when we speak of territorial expansion, but the territorial expansion of which we speak does not in any sense of the word involve the occupation of the possessions of other countries, the planting of the Japanese flag thereon, and the declaration of their annexation to Japan. It is just that since the Powers have suppressed the circulation of Japanese materials and merchandise abroad, we are looking for some place overseas where Japanese capital, Japanese skills and Japanese labor can have free play, free from the oppression of the white race.

We would be satisfied with just this much. What moral right do the world powers who have themselves closed to us the two doors of emigration and advance into world markets have to criticize Japan's attempt to rush out of the third and last door?

If they do not approve of this, they should open the door which they have closed against us and permit the free movement overseas of Japanese emigrants and merchandise. . . .

At the time of the Manchurian incident, the entire world joined in criticism of Japan. They said that Japan was an untrustworthy nation. They said that she had recklessly brought cannon and machine guns into Manchuria, which was the territory of another country, flown airplanes over it, and finally occupied it. But the military action taken by Japan was not in the least a selfish one. Moreover, we do not recall ever having taken so much as an inch of territory belonging to another nation. The result of this incident was the establishment of the splendid new nation of Manchuria. The Powers are still discussing whether or not to recognize this new nation, but regardless of whether or not other nations recognize her, the Manchurian empire has already been established, and now, seven years after its creation, the empire is further consolidating its foundations with the aid of its friend, Japan.

And if it is still protested that our actions in Manchuria were excessively violent, we may wish to ask the white race just which country it was that sent warships and troops to India, South Africa, and Australia and slaughtered innocent natives, bound their hands and feet with iron chains, lashed their backs with iron whips, proclaimed these territories as their own, and still continues to hold them to this very day.

"Monroe Doctrine for Asia," in which Japan would guide its Asian neighbors on the path to development and prosperity (see the box above). After all, who better to instruct Asian societies on modernization than the one Asian country that had already achieved it?

During the late 1930s, Japan began to cooperate with Nazi Germany on the assumption that the two countries would ultimately launch a joint attack on the Soviet Union and divide up its resources between them. But when Germany surprised the world by signing a nonaggression pact with the Soviets in August 1939, Japanese strategists were compelled to reevaluate their long-term objectives. Japan was not strong enough to defeat the Soviet Union alone, as a small but bitter border war along the Siberian frontier near Manchukuo had amply demonstrated. So the Japanese began to shift their eyes south

to the vast resources of Southeast Asia—the oil of the Dutch East Indies, the rubber and tin of Malaya, and the rice of Burma and Indochina.

A move southward, of course, would risk war with the European colonial powers and the United States. Japan's attack on China in the summer of 1937 had already aroused strong criticism abroad, particularly from the United States, where President Franklin Roosevelt threatened to "quarantine" the aggressors after Japanese military units bombed an American naval ship operating in China. Public fear of involvement forced the president to draw back, but when Japan suddenly demanded the right to occupy airfields and exploit economic resources in French Indochina in the summer of 1940, the United States warned the Japanese that it would impose economic sanctions unless Japan withdrew from the area and returned to its borders of 1931.

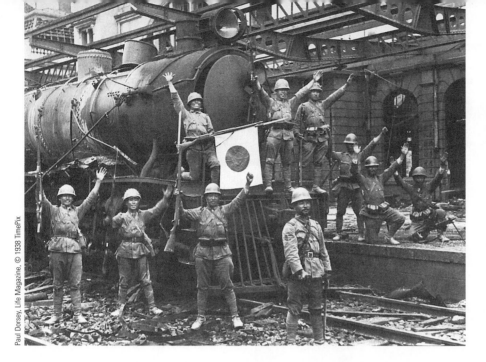

A JAPANESE VICTORY IN CHINA. After consolidating its authority over Manchuria, Japan began to expand into northern China. Direct hostilities between Japanese and Chinese forces began in 1937. By 1939, Japan had conquered most of eastern China. This photograph shows victorious Japanese soldiers amid the ruins of the railway station in Hankou, which became China's temporary capital after the fall of Nanjing.

The Japanese viewed the American threat of retaliation as an obstacle to their long-term objectives. Japan badly needed liquid fuel and scrap iron from the United States. Should they be cut off, Japan would have to find them elsewhere. The Japanese were thus caught in a vise. To obtain guaranteed access to natural resources that were necessary to fuel the Japanese military machine, Japan must risk being cut off from its current source of raw materials that would be needed in case of a conflict. After much debate, the Japanese decided to launch a surprise attack on American and European colonies in Southeast Asia in the hope of a quick victory that would evict the United States from the region.

WORLD WAR II

Unleashing a *Blitzkrieg,* or "lightning war," Hitler stunned Europe with the speed and efficiency of the German attack. Armored columns or panzer divisions (a panzer division was a strike force of about three hundred tanks and accompanying forces and supplies) supported by airplanes broke quickly through Polish lines and encircled the bewildered Polish troops. Conventional infantry units then moved in to hold the newly conquered territory. Within four weeks, Poland had surrendered. On September 28, 1939, Germany and the Soviet Union officially divided Poland between them.

Europe at War

Although Hitler's hopes to avoid a war with the western European states were dashed when France and Britain declared war on September 3, he was confident that he could control the situation. After a winter of waiting (called the "phony war"), Hitler resumed the war on April 9, 1940, with another *Blitzkrieg,* against Denmark and Norway (see Map 24.1). One month later, on May 10, the Germans launched their attack on the Netherlands, Belgium, and France. The main assault through Luxembourg and the Ardennes forest was completely unexpected by the French and British forces. German panzer divisions broke through the weak French defensive positions there and raced across northern France, splitting the Allied armies and trapping French troops and the entire British army on the beaches of Dunkirk. Only by heroic efforts did the British succeed in a gigantic evacuation of 330,000 Allied (mostly British) troops. The French capitulated on June 22. German armies occupied about three-fifths of France, while the French hero of World War I, Marshal Henri Pétain (1856–1951), established an authoritarian regime (known as Vichy France) over the remainder. Germany was now in control of western and central Europe, but Britain had still not been defeated.

As Hitler realized, an amphibious invasion of Britain would be possible only if Germany gained control of the air. At the beginning of August 1940, the *Luftwaffe* (the German air force) launched a major offensive against British air and naval bases, harbors, communication centers, and war industries. The British fought back doggedly, supported by an effective radar system that gave them early warning of German attacks. Nevertheless, the British air force suffered critical losses by the end of August and was probably saved by a change in Hitler's strategy. In September, in retaliation for a British attack on Berlin, Hitler ordered a shift from military targets to massive bombing of British cities to break British morale. The British rebuilt their air strength quickly and were soon inflicting major losses on *Luftwaffe* bombers. By the end of September, Germany had lost the Battle of Britain, and the invasion of Britain had to be postponed.

At this point, Hitler pursued the possibility of a Mediterranean strategy, which would involve capturing

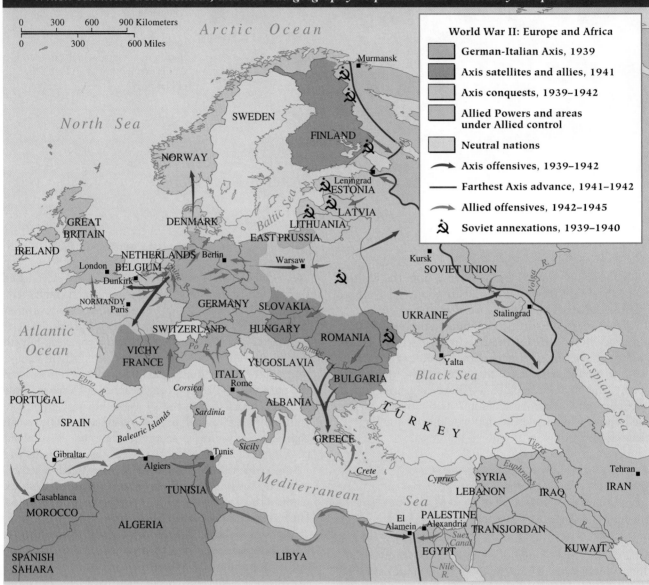

MAP 24.1 World War II in Europe and North Africa. With its fast and effective military, Germany quickly overwhelmed much of western Europe. However, Hitler overestimated his country's capabilities and underestimated those of his foes. By late 1942, his invasion of the Soviet Union was failing, and the United States had become a major factor in the war. The Allies successfully invaded Italy in 1943 and France in 1944.
➤ *Which countries were neutral, and how did geography help make their neutrality an option?*

Egypt and the Suez Canal and closing the Mediterranean to British ships, thereby shutting off Britain's supply of oil. Hitler's commitment to the Mediterranean was never wholehearted, however. His initial plan was to let the Italians defeat the British in North Africa, but this strategy failed when the British routed the Italian army. Although Hitler then sent German troops to the North African theater of war, his primary concern lay elsewhere; he had already reached the decision to fulfill his lifetime obsession with the acquisition of territory in the east.

Although he had no desire for a two-front war, Hitler became convinced that Britain was remaining in the war only because it expected Soviet support. If the Soviet Union were smashed, Britain's last hope would be eliminated. Moreover, Hitler had convinced himself that the Soviet Union, with what he regarded as its Jewish-Bolshevik leadership and a pitiful army, could be defeated quickly and decisively. Although the invasion of the Soviet Union was scheduled for spring 1941, the attack was delayed because of problems in the Balkans. Hitler had already obtained the political cooperation of Hungary, Bulgaria, and Romania, but Mussolini's disastrous invasion of Greece in October 1940 exposed Hitler's southern flank to British air bases in Greece. To secure his Balkan flank, German

➤➤ GERMAN TROOPS IN THE SOVIET UNION. At first, the German attack on the Soviet Union was enormously successful, leading one German general to remark in his diary, "It is probably no overstatement to say that the Russian campaign has been won in the space of two weeks." Shown here is German artillery firing on Soviet positions.

troops seized both Yugoslavia and Greece in April 1941. Now reassured, Hitler turned to the east and invaded the Soviet Union on June 22, 1941, in the belief that the Soviets could still be decisively defeated before winter set in.

The massive attack stretched out along an 1,800-mile front. German troops advanced rapidly, capturing two million Russian soldiers. By November, one German army group had swept through the Ukraine, while a second was besieging Leningrad; a third approached within 25 miles of Moscow, the Russian capital. An early winter and unexpected Soviet resistance, however, brought a halt to the German advance. For the first time in the war, German armies had been stopped. A Soviet counterattack in December 1941 by a Soviet army supposedly exhausted by Nazi victories came as an ominous ending to the year for the Germans. By that time, another of Hitler's decisions—the declaration of war on the United States—probably made his defeat inevitable and turned another European conflict into a global war.

Japan at War

On December 7, 1941, Japanese carrier-based aircraft attacked the U.S. naval base at Pearl Harbor in the Hawaiian Islands. The same day, other units launched assaults on the Philippines and began advancing toward the British colony of Malaya (see Map 24.2). Shortly thereafter, Japanese forces invaded the Dutch East Indies and occupied a number of islands in the Pacific Ocean. In some cases, as on the Bataan peninsula and the island of Corregidor in the Philippines, resistance was fierce, but by the spring of 1942, almost all of Southeast Asia and much of the western Pacific had fallen into Japanese hands. Japan declared the creation of the Great East-Asia Co-Prosperity Sphere,

consisting of the entire region under Japanese tutelage, and announced its intention to liberate the colonies of Southeast Asia from Western rule. For the moment, however, Japan needed the resources of the region for its war machine and placed its conquests under its rule on a wartime basis.

Japanese leaders had hoped that their lightning strike at American bases would destroy the U.S. Pacific fleet and persuade the Roosevelt administration to accept Japanese domination of the Pacific. The American people, in the eyes of Japanese leaders, had been made soft by material indulgence. But the Japanese had miscalculated. The attack on Pearl Harbor galvanized American opinion and won broad support for Roosevelt's war policy. The United States now joined with European nations and Nationalist China in a combined effort to defeat Japan and bring an end to its hegemony in the Pacific. Believing the American involvement in the Pacific would render the United States ineffective in the European theater of war, Hitler declared war on the United States four days after Pearl Harbor.

The Turning Point of the War, 1942–1943

The entry of the United States into the war created a coalition (the Grand Alliance) that ultimately defeated the Axis Powers (Germany, Italy, and Japan). Nevertheless, the three major Allies—Britain, the United States, and the Soviet Union—had to overcome mutual suspicions before they could operate as an effective alliance. Two factors aided that process. First, Hitler's declaration of war on the United States made it easier for the Americans to accept the British and Russian contention that

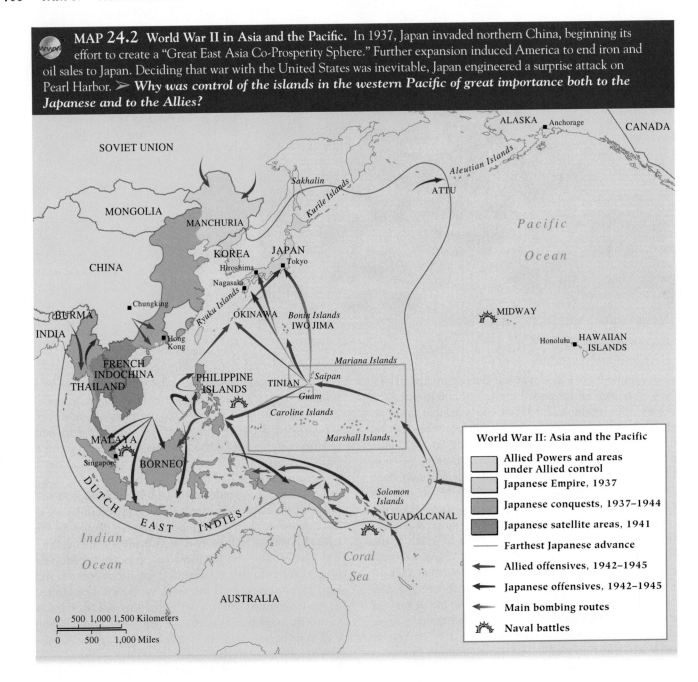

MAP 24.2 World War II in Asia and the Pacific. In 1937, Japan invaded northern China, beginning its effort to create a "Great East Asia Co-Prosperity Sphere." Further expansion induced America to end iron and oil sales to Japan. Deciding that war with the United States was inevitable, Japan engineered a surprise attack on Pearl Harbor. ➤ *Why was control of the islands in the western Pacific of great importance both to the Japanese and to the Allies?*

the defeat of Germany should be the first priority of the United States. For that reason, the United States, under its lend-lease program (which had begun before U.S. entry into the war), sent large amounts of military aid, including $50 billion worth of trucks, planes, and other arms, to the British and the Soviets. Also important to the alliance was the tacit agreement of the three chief Allies to stress military operations while ignoring political differences and larger strategic issues concerning any postwar settlement. At the beginning of 1943, the Allies agreed to fight until the Axis Powers surrendered unconditionally. Although this principle of unconditional surrender prevented a repeat of the mistake of World War I, which was ended in 1918 with an armistice rather than a total victory, it likely

discouraged dissident Germans and Japanese from over-throwing their governments in order to arrange a negotiated peace. At the same time, it did have the effect of cementing the Grand Alliance by making it nearly impossible for Hitler to divide his foes.

Defeat, however, was far from Hitler's mind at the beginning of 1942. As Japanese forces advanced into Southeast Asia and the Pacific after crippling the American naval fleet at Pearl Harbor, Hitler and his European allies continued the war in Europe against Britain and the Soviet Union. Until the fall of 1942, it appeared that the Germans might still prevail on the battlefield. Reinforcements in North Africa enabled the Afrika Korps under General Erwin Rommel to break through the British

A German Soldier at Stalingrad

The Soviet victory at Stalingrad was a major turning point in World War II. This excerpt comes from the diary of a German soldier who fought and died in the Battle of Stalingrad. His dreams of victory and a return home with medals are soon dashed by the realities of Soviet resistance.

DIARY OF A GERMAN SOLDIER

Today, after we'd had a bath, the company commander told us that if our future operations are as successful, we'll soon reach the Volga, take Stalingrad, and then the war will inevitably soon be over. Perhaps we'll be home by Christmas.

July 29. The company commander says the Russian troops are completely broken, and cannot hold out any longer. To reach the Volga and take Stalingrad is not so difficult for us. The Führer knows where the Russians' weak point is. Victory is not far away. . . .

August 10. The Führer's orders were read out to us. He expects victory of us. We are all convinced that they can't stop us.

August 12. This morning outstanding soldiers were presented with decorations. . . . Will I really go back to Elsa without a decoration? I believe that for Stalingrad the Führer will decorate even me. . . .

September 4. We are being sent northward along the front toward Stalingrad. We marched all night and by dawn had reached Voroponovo Station. We can already see the smoking town. It's a happy thought that the end of the war is getting nearer. That's what everyone is saying. . . .

September 8. Two days of nonstop fighting. The Russians are defending themselves with insane stubbornness. Our regiment has lost many men. . . .

September 16. Our battalion, plus tanks, is attacking the [grain storage] elevator, from which smoke is pouring—the grain in it is burning; the Russians seem to have set light to

it themselves. Barbarism. The battalion is suffering heavy losses. . . .

October 10. The Russians are so close to us that our planes cannot bomb them. We are preparing for a decisive attack. The Führer has ordered the whole of Stalingrad to be taken as rapidly as possible. . . .

October 22. Our regiment has failed to break into the factory. We have lost many men; every time you move you have to jump over bodies. . . .

November 10. A letter from Elsa today. Everyone expects us home for Christmas. In Germany everyone believes we already hold Stalingrad. How wrong they are. If they could only see what Stalingrad has done to our army. . . .

November 21. The Russians have gone over to the offensive along the whole front. Fierce fighting is going on. So, there it is—the Volga, victory, and soon home to our families! We shall obviously be seeing them next in the other world.

November 29. We are encircled. It was announced this morning that the Führer has said: "The army can trust me to do everything necessary to ensure supplies and rapidly break the encirclement."

December 3. We are on hunger rations and waiting for the rescue that the Führer promised. . . .

December 14. Everybody is racked with hunger. Frozen potatoes are the best meal, but to get them out of the ice-covered ground under fire from Russian bullets is not so easy. . . .

December 26. The horses have already been eaten. I would eat a cat; they say its meat is also tasty. The soldiers look like corpses or lunatics, looking for something to put in their mouths. They no longer take cover from Russian shells; they haven't the strength to walk, run away, and hide. A curse on this war!

---

defenses in Egypt and advance toward Alexandria. In the spring of 1942, a renewed German offensive in the Soviet Union led to the capture of the entire Crimea, causing Hitler to boast in August 1942:

> As the next step, we are going to advance south of the Caucasus and then help the rebels in Iran and Iraq against the English. Another thrust will be directed along the Caspian Sea toward Afghanistan and India. Then the English will run out of oil. In two years we'll be on the borders of India. Twenty to thirty elite German divisions will do. Then the British Empire will collapse.[8]

But this would be Hitler's last optimistic outburst. By the fall of 1942, the war had turned against the Germans.

In North Africa, British forces had stopped Rommel's troops at El Alamein in the summer of 1942 and then forced them back across the desert. In November 1942, British and

American forces invaded French North Africa and forced the German and Italian troops to surrender in May 1943. On the Eastern Front, the turning point of the war occurred at Stalingrad. After the capture of the Crimea, Hitler's generals wanted him to concentrate on the Caucasus and its oil fields, but Hitler decided that Stalingrad, a major industrial center on the Volga, should be taken first. Between November 1942 and February 1943, German troops were stopped, then encircled, and finally forced to surrender on February 2, 1943 (see the box above). The entire German Sixth Army of 300,000 men was lost. By February 1943, German forces in Russia were back to their positions of June 1942. By the spring of 1943, long before Allied troops returned to the European continent, even Hitler knew that the Germans would not defeat the Soviet Union.

The tide of battle in the Far East also turned dramatically in 1942. In the Battle of the Coral Sea on May 7–8,

1942, American naval forces stopped the Japanese advance and temporarily relieved Australia of the threat of invasion. On June 4, at the Battle of Midway Island, American carrier planes destroyed all four of the attacking Japanese aircraft carriers and established American naval superiority in the Pacific. By the fall of 1942, Allied forces were beginning to gather for offensive operations into southern China from Burma, through the Dutch East Indies by a process of "island hopping" by troops commanded by the American general Douglas MacArthur, and across the Pacific with a combination of U.S. Army, Marine, and Navy attacks on Japanese-held islands. After a series of bitter engagements in the waters of the Solomon Islands from August to November 1942, Japanese fortunes began to fade.

The Last Years of the War

By the beginning of 1943, the tide of battle had turned against Germany, Italy, and Japan. After the Axis forces had surrendered in Tunisia on May 13, 1943, the Allies crossed the Mediterranean and carried the war to Italy. After taking Sicily, Allied troops began the invasion of mainland Italy in September. In the meantime, after the ouster and arrest of Benito Mussolini, a new Italian government offered to surrender to Allied forces. But Mussolini was liberated by the Germans in a daring raid and then set up as the head of a puppet German state in northern Italy while German troops moved in and occupied much of Italy. The new defensive lines established by the Germans in the hills south of Rome were so effective that the Allied advance up the Italian peninsula was a painstaking affair accompanied by heavy casualties. Rome did not fall to the Allies until June 4, 1944. By that time, the Italian war had assumed a secondary role anyway as the Allies opened their long-awaited "second front" in western Europe.

Since the autumn of 1943, the Allies had been planning a cross-channel invasion of France from Britain. Under the direction of the American general Dwight D. Eisenhower (1890–1969), the Allies landed five assault divisions on the beaches of Normandy on June 6, 1944, in history's greatest naval invasion. An initially indecisive German response enabled the Allied forces to establish a beachhead. Within three months, they had landed two million men and a half-million vehicles that pushed inland and broke through German defensive lines.

After the breakout, Allied troops moved south and east and liberated Paris by the end of August. By March 1945, they had crossed the Rhine River and advanced farther into Germany. At the end of April 1945, Allied armies in northern Germany moved toward the Elbe River, where they finally linked up with the Soviets. The Soviets had come a long way since the Battle of Stalingrad in 1943. In the summer of 1943, Hitler gambled on taking the offensive by making use of newly developed heavy tanks. German forces were soundly defeated by the Soviets at the

Chronology

THE COURSE OF WORLD WAR II

Germany and the Soviet Union divide Poland	September 28, 1939
Blitzkrieg against Denmark and Norway	April 1940
Blitzkrieg against Belgium, Netherlands, and France	May 1940
France surrenders	June 22, 1940
Battle of Britain	Fall 1940
Nazi seizure of Yugoslavia and Greece	April 1941
Germany invades the Soviet Union	June 22, 1941
Japanese attack on Pearl Harbor	December 7, 1941
Battle of the Coral Sea	May 7–8, 1942
Battle of Midway Island	June 4, 1942
Allied invasion of North Africa	November 1942
German surrender at Stalingrad	February 2, 1943
Axis forces surrender in North Africa	May 1943
Battle of Kursk	July 5–12, 1943
Invasion of mainland Italy	September 1943
Allied invasion of France	June 6, 1944
Hitler commits suicide	April 30, 1945
Germany surrenders	May 7, 1945
Atomic bomb dropped on Hiroshima	August 6, 1945
Japan surrenders	August 14, 1945

Battle of Kursk (July 5–12), the greatest tank battle of World War II. Soviet forces now began a relentless advance westward. The Soviets had reoccupied the Ukraine by the end of 1943 and lifted the siege of Leningrad and moved into the Baltic states by the beginning of 1944. Advancing along a northern front, Soviet troops occupied Warsaw in January 1945 and entered Berlin in April. Meanwhile, Soviet troops along a southern front swept through Hungary, Romania, and Bulgaria.

In January 1945, Hitler had moved into a bunker 55 feet under Berlin to direct the final stages of the war. In his final political testament, Hitler, consistent to the end in his rabid anti-Semitism, blamed the Jews for the war:

REFUGEES FLEE YOKOHAMA. American bombing attacks on Japanese cities began in earnest in November 1944. Built of flimsy materials, Japan's crowded cities were soon devastated by these air raids. This photograph shows a homeless family fleeing Yokohama, a shelter for refugees until American bombers devastated the city on May 29, 1945.

"Above all I charge the leaders of the nation and those under them to scrupulous observance of the laws of race and to merciless opposition to the universal poisoner of all peoples, international Jewry."[9] Hitler committed suicide on April 30, two days after Mussolini had been shot by partisan Italian forces. On May 7, German commanders surrendered. The war in Europe was over.

The war in Asia continued. Beginning in 1943, American forces had gone on the offensive and advanced their way, slowly at times, across the Pacific. American forces took an increasing toll of enemy resources, especially at sea and in the air. As Allied military power drew inexorably closer to the main Japanese islands in the first months of 1945, President Harry Truman, who had succeeded to the presidency on the death of Franklin Roosevelt in April, had an excruciatingly difficult decision to make. Should he use atomic weapons (at the time, only two bombs were available, and their effectiveness had not been demonstrated) to bring the war to an end without the necessity of an Allied invasion of the Japanese homeland? As the world knows, Truman answered that question in the affirmative. The first bomb was dropped on the city of Hiroshima on August 6. Truman then called on Japan to surrender or expect a "rain of ruin from the air." When the Japanese did not respond, a second bomb was dropped on Nagasaki. Japan surrendered unconditionally on August 14. World War II, in which seventeen million men

died in battle and perhaps eighteen million civilians perished as well (some estimate total losses at fifty million), was finally over.

THE NEW ORDER

The initial victories of the Germans and the Japanese gave them the opportunity to create new orders in Europe and Asia. Although both countries presented positive images of these new orders for publicity purposes, in practice both followed policies of ruthless domination of their subject peoples.

The New Order in Europe

After the German victories in Europe, Nazi propagandists created glowing images of a new European order based on "equal chances" for all nations and an integrated economic community. This was not Hitler's conception of a European New Order. He saw the Europe he had conquered simply as subject to German domination. Only the Germans, he once said, "can really organize Europe."

The Nazi empire stretched across continental Europe from the English Channel in the west to the outskirts of Moscow in the east. In no way was this empire organized systematically or governed efficiently. Nazi-occupied

HITLER'S PLANS FOR A NEW ORDER
IN THE EAST

Hitler's nightly monologues to his postdinner guests, which were recorded by the Führer's private secretary, Martin Bormann, reveal much about the New Order he wished to create. On the evening of October 17, 1941, Hitler expressed his views on what the Germans would do with their newly conquered territories in the east.

HITLER'S SECRET CONVERSATIONS, OCTOBER 17, 1941

In comparison with the beauties accumulated in Central Germany, the new territories in the East seem to us like a desert.... This Russian desert, we shall populate it.... We'll take away its character of an Asiatic steppe; we'll Europeanize it. With this object, we have undertaken the construction of roads that will lead to the southernmost point of the Crimea and to the Caucasus. These roads will be studded along their whole length with German towns, and around these towns our colonists will settle.

As for the two or three million men whom we need to accomplish this task, we'll find them quicker than we think. They'll come from Germany, Scandinavia, the Western countries, and America. I shall no longer be here to see all that, but in twenty years the Ukraine will already be a home for twenty million inhabitants besides the natives. In three hundred years, the country will be one of the loveliest gardens in the world.

As for the natives, we'll have to screen them carefully. The Jew, that destroyer, we shall drive out.... We shan't settle in the Russian towns, and we'll let them fall to pieces without intervening. And, above all, no remorse on this subject! We're not going to play at children's nurses; we're absolutely without obligations as far as these people are concerned. To struggle against the hovels, chase away the fleas, provide German teachers, bring out newspapers—very little of that for us! We'll confine ourselves, perhaps, to setting up a radio transmitter, under our control. For the rest, let them know just enough to understand our highway signs, so that they won't get themselves run over by our vehicles.... There's only one duty: to Germanize this country by the immigration of Germans, and to look upon the natives as Redskins. If these people had defeated us, Heaven have mercy! But we don't hate them. That sentiment is unknown to us. We are guided only by reason....

All those who have the feeling for Europe can join in our work.

In this business I shall go straight ahead, cold-bloodedly. What they may think about me, at this juncture, is to me a matter of complete indifference. I don't see why a German who eats a piece of bread should torment himself with the idea that the soil that produces this bread has been won by the sword.

Europe was organized in one of two ways. Some areas, such as western Poland, were directly annexed by Nazi Germany and made into German provinces. Most of occupied Europe was administered by German military or civilian officials in combination with varying degrees of indirect control from collaborationist regimes.

Racial considerations played an important role in how conquered peoples were treated. German civil administrations were established in Norway, Denmark, and the Netherlands because the Nazis considered their peoples Aryan, racially kin to the Germans and hence worthy of more lenient treatment. "Inferior" Latin peoples, such as the occupied French, were given military administrations. By 1943, however, as Nazi losses continued to multiply, all the occupied territories of northern and western Europe were ruthlessly exploited for material goods and manpower for Germany's labor needs.

Because the conquered lands in the east contained the living space for German expansion and were populated in Nazi eyes by racially inferior Slavic peoples, Nazi administration there was considerably more ruthless. Hitler's racial ideology and his plans for an Aryan racial empire were so important to him that he and the Nazis began to implement their racial program soon after the conquest of Poland. Heinrich Himmler, a strong believer in Nazi racial ideology and the leader of the SS, was put in charge of German resettlement plans in the east. Himmler's task was to evacuate the inferior Slavic peoples and replace them with Germans, a policy first applied to the new German provinces created from the lands of western Poland. One million Poles were uprooted and dumped in southern Poland. Hundreds of thousands of ethnic Germans (descendants of Germans who had migrated decades earlier from Germany to different parts of southern and eastern Europe) were encouraged to colonize designated areas in Poland. By 1942, two million ethnic Germans had been settled in Poland.

The invasion of the Soviet Union inflated Nazi visions of German colonization in the east. Hitler spoke to his intimate circle of a colossal project of social engineering after the war, in which Poles, Ukrainians, and Russians would become slave labor while German peasants settled on the abandoned lands and Germanized them (see the box above). Nazis involved in this kind of planning were well aware of the human costs. Himmler told a gathering of SS officers that although the destruction of thirty million Slavs was a prerequisite for German plans in the east, "whether nations live in prosperity or starve to death interests me only insofar as we need them as slaves for our culture. Otherwise it is of no interest."[10]

Labor shortages in Germany led to a policy of ruthless mobilization of foreign labor for Germany. After the invasion of the Soviet Union, the four million Russian prisoners of war captured by the Germans along with more than two million workers conscripted in France became a major source of heavy labor, but it was wasted by allowing more than three million of them to die from neglect. In 1942, a special office was created to recruit labor for German farms and industries. By the summer of 1944, seven million foreign workers were laboring in Germany, constituting 20 percent of Germany's labor force. At the same time, another seven million workers were supplying forced labor in their own countries on farms, in industries, and even in military camps. Forced labor, however, often proved counterproductive because it created economic chaos in occupied countries and disrupted industrial production that could have helped Germany. The brutal character of Germany's recruitment policies often led more and more people to resist the Nazi occupation forces.

The Holocaust

No aspect of the Nazi New Order was more terrifying than the deliberate attempt to exterminate the Jewish people of Europe. Racial struggle was a key element in Hitler's ideology and meant to him a clearly defined conflict of opposites: the Aryans, creators of human cultural development, against the Jews, parasites who were trying to destroy the Aryans. By the beginning of 1939, Nazi policy focused on promoting the "emigration" of German Jews from Germany. Once the war began in September 1939, the so-called Jewish problem took on new dimensions. For a while there was discussion of the Madagascar Plan, which aspired to the mass shipment of Jews to the African island of Madagascar. When war contingencies made this plan impractical, an even more drastic policy was conceived.

Himmler and the SS organization shared Hitler's racial ideology. The SS was given responsibility for what the Nazis called their Final Solution to the Jewish problem—the annihilation of the Jewish people. Reinhard Heydrich (1904–1942), head of the SS's Security Service, was given administrative responsibility for the Final Solution. After defeating Poland, Heydrich ordered the special strike forces (Einsatzgruppen) that he had created to round up all Polish Jews and concentrate them in ghettos established in a number of Polish cities.

In June 1941, the Einsatzgruppen were given new responsibilities as mobile killing units. These SS death squads followed the regular army's advance into the Soviet Union. Their job was to round up Jews in the villages and execute and bury them in mass graves, often giant pits dug by the victims themselves before they were shot. Such constant killing produced morale problems among the SS executioners. During a visit to Minsk in the Soviet Union,

Himmler tried to build morale by pointing out that "he would not like it if Germans did such a thing gladly. But their conscience was in no way impaired, for they were soldiers who had to carry out every order unconditionally. He alone had responsibility before God and Hitler for everything that was happening, . . . and he was acting from a deep understanding of the necessity for this operation."[11]

Although it has been estimated that as many as one million Jews were killed by the Einsatzgruppen, this approach to solving the Jewish problem was soon perceived as inadequate. Instead, the Nazis opted for the systematic annihilation of the European Jewish population in specially built death camps. The plan was simple. Jews from countries occupied by Germany (or sympathetic to Germany) would be rounded up, packed like cattle into freight trains, and

➤ THE HOLOCAUST: ACTIVITIES OF THE EINSATZGRUPPEN. The activities of the mobile killing units known as the Einsatzgruppen were the first stage in the mass exterminations of the Holocaust. This picture shows the execution of a Jew by a member of one of these SS killing squads. Onlookers include members of the German Army, the German Labor Service, and even Hitler Youth. When it became apparent that this method of killing was inefficient, it was replaced by the death camps.

THE HOLOCAUST: THE CAMP COMMANDANT AND THE CAMP VICTIMS

The systematic annihilation of millions of men, women, and children in extermination camps makes the Holocaust one of the most horrifying events in history. The first document is taken from an account by Rudolf Höss, commandant of the extermination camp at Auschwitz-Birkenau. In the second document, a French doctor explains what happened at one of the crematoria described by Höss.

COMMANDANT HÖSS DESCRIBES THE EQUIPMENT

The two large crematoria, Nos. I and II, were built during the winter of 1942–43. . . . Each . . . could cremate c. 2,000 corpses within twenty-four hours. . . . Crematoria I and II both had underground undressing and gassing rooms which could be completely ventilated. The corpses were brought up to the ovens on the floor above by lift. The gas chambers could hold c. 3,000 people.

The firm of Topf had calculated that the two smaller crematoria, III and IV, would each be able to cremate 1,500 corpses within twenty-four hours. However, owing to the wartime shortage of materials, the builders were obliged to economize, and so the undressing rooms and gassing rooms were built above ground and the ovens were of a less solid construction. But it soon became apparent that the flimsy construction of these two four-retort ovens was not up to the demands made on it. No. III ceased operating altogether after a short time and later was no longer used. No. IV had to be repeatedly shut down since after a short period in operation of 4–6 weeks, the ovens and chimneys had burnt out. The victims of the gassing were mainly burnt in pits behind crematorium IV.

The largest number of people gassed and cremated within twenty-four hours was somewhat over 9,000.

A FRENCH DOCTOR DESCRIBES THE VICTIMS

It is mid-day, when a long line of women, children, and old people enter the yard. The senior official in charge . . . climbs on a bench to tell them that they are going to have a bath and that afterward they will get a drink of hot coffee. They all undress in the yard. . . . The doors are opened and an indescribable jostling begins. The first people to enter the gas chamber begin to draw back. They sense the death which awaits them. The SS men put an end to this pushing and shoving with blows from their rifle butts beating the heads of the horrified women who are desperately hugging their children. The massive oak double doors are shut. For two endless minutes one can hear banging on the walls and screams which are no longer human. And then—not a sound. Five minutes later the doors are opened. The corpses, squashed together and distorted, fall out like a waterfall. . . . The bodies, which are still warm, pass through the hands of the hairdresser, who cuts their hair, and the dentist, who pulls out their gold teeth. . . . One more transport has just been processed through No. IV crematorium.

---

shipped to Poland, where six extermination centers were built for this purpose. The largest and most famous was Auschwitz-Birkenau. Medical technicians chose Zyklon B (the commercial name for hydrogen cyanide) as the most effective gas for quickly killing large numbers of people in gas chambers designed to look like shower rooms to facilitate the cooperation of the victims. After gassing, the corpses would be burned in specially built crematoria.

By the spring of 1942, the death camps were in operation. Although initial priority was given to the elimination of the ghettos in Poland, by the summer of 1942, Jews were also being shipped from France, Belgium, and the Netherlands. Even as the Allies were making significant advances in 1944, Jews were being shipped from Greece and Hungary. These shipments depended on the cooperation of Germany's Transport Ministry, but despite desperate military needs, the Final Solution had priority in using railroad cars for the transportation of Jews to death camps.

A harrowing experience awaited the Jews when they arrived at one of the six death camps. Rudolf Höss, commandant at Auschwitz-Birkenau, described it:

We had two SS doctors on duty at Auschwitz to examine the incoming transports of prisoners. The prisoners would be marched by one of the doctors, who would make spot decisions as they walked by. Those who were fit for work were sent into the camp. Others were sent immediately to the extermination plants. Children of tender years were invariably exterminated since by reason of their youth they were unable to work. . . . At Auschwitz we endeavored to fool the victims into thinking that they were to go through a delousing process. Of course, frequently they realized our true intentions and we sometimes had riots and difficulties due to that fact.[12]

About 30 percent of the arrivals at Auschwitz were sent to a labor camp, while the remainder went to the gas chambers (see the box above). After they had been gassed, the bodies were burned in the crematoria. The victims' goods and even their bodies were used for economic gain. Female hair was cut off, collected, and turned into mattresses or cloth. Some inmates were also subjected to cruel and painful "medical" experiments. The Germans killed between five and six million Jews, over three million of them in the death camps. About 90 percent of the Jewish populations of

JAPAN'S PLAN FOR ASIA

*he Japanese objective in World War II was to create
a vast Great East-Asia Co-Prosperity Sphere to provide Japan with needed raw materials and a market for its
exports. The following passage is from a secret document
produced by a high-level government committee in January 1942.*

DRAFT PLAN FOR THE ESTABLISHMENT OF THE GREAT EAST-ASIA CO-PROSPERITY SPHERE

The Plan. The Japanese empire is a manifestation of morality and its special characteristic is the propagation of the
Imperial Way. It is necessary to foster the increased power
of the empire, to cause East Asia to return to its original
form of independence and co-prosperity by shaking off the
yoke of Europe and America, and to let its countries and
peoples develop their respective abilities in peaceful cooperation and secure livelihood.

The Form of East Asiatic Independence and Co-
Prosperity. The states, their citizens, and resources, comprised in those areas pertaining to the Pacific, Central
Asia, and the Indian Oceans formed into one general
union are to be established as an autonomous zone of
peaceful living and common prosperity on behalf of the
peoples of the nations of East Asia. The area including
Japan, Manchuria, North China, lower Yangtze River, and
the Russian Maritime Province, forms the nucleus of the
East Asiatic Union. The Japanese empire possesses a duty
as the leader of the East Asiatic Union.

The above purpose presupposes the inevitable emancipation or independence of Eastern Siberia, China, Indo-
China, the South Seas, Australia, and India. . . .

Outline of East Asiatic Administration. It is intended
that the unification of Japan, Manchoukuo, and China in
neighborly friendship be realized by the settlement of the
Sino-Japanese problems through the crushing of hostile
influences in the Chinese interior, and through the construction of a new China. . . . Aggressive American and
British influences in East Asia shall be driven out of the area
of Indo-China and the South Seas, and this area should be
brought into our defense sphere. The war with Britain and
America shall be prosecuted for that purpose. . . .

CHAPTER 3: POLITICAL CONSTRUCTION

Basic Plan. The realization of the great ideal of constructing Greater East Asia Co-Prosperity requires not only the
complete prosecution of the current Greater East Asia War
but also presupposes another great war in the future. . . .

The following are the basic principles for the political
construction of East Asia. . . .

The desires of the peoples in the sphere for their independence shall be respected, and endeavors shall be made
for their fulfillment, but proper and suitable forms of government shall be decided for them in consideration of military and economic requirements and of the historical,
political, and cultural elements peculiar to each area.

It must also be noted that the independence of various
peoples of East Asia should be based on the idea of constructing East Asia as "independent countries existing
within the New Order of East Asia" and that this conception differs from an independence based on the idea of liberalism and national self-determination. . . .

Western individualism and materialism shall be rejected, and a moral worldview, the basic principle of whose
morality shall be the Imperial Way, shall be established.
The ultimate object to be achieved is not exploitation but
co-prosperity and mutual help, not competitive conflict but
mutual assistance and mild peace, not a formal view of
equality but a view of order based on righteous classifica-
tion, not an idea of rights but an idea of service, and not
several worldviews but one unified worldview.

Poland, the Baltic countries, and Germany were exterminated. Overall, the Holocaust was responsible for the death
of nearly two out of every three European Jews.

The Nazis were also responsible for another Holocaust,
the death by shooting, starvation, or overwork of at least
another nine to ten million people. Because the Nazis also
considered the Gypsies of Europe (like the Jews) a race containing alien blood, they were systematically rounded up
for extermination. About 40 percent of Europe's one million Gypsies were killed in the death camps. The leading
elements of the "subhuman" Slavic peoples—the clergy,
intelligentsia, civil leaders, judges, and lawyers—were
arrested and deliberately killed. Probably an additional four
million Poles, Ukrainians, and Byelorussians lost their lives
as slave laborers for Nazi Germany, and three to four million Soviet prisoners of war were killed in captivity. The
Nazis also singled out homosexuals for persecution, and
thousands lost their lives in concentration camps.

The New Order in Asia

Once the takeover was completed, Japanese war policy in
the occupied areas in Asia became essentially defensive,
as Japan hoped to use its new possessions to meet its burgeoning needs for raw materials, such as tin, oil, and rubber,
and also as an outlet for Japanese manufactured goods. To
provide an organizational structure for the arrangement,
Japanese leaders set up the Great East-Asia Co-Prosperity
Sphere, a self-sufficient economic community designed
to provide mutual benefits to the occupied areas and the
home country (see the box above). The Ministry for Great
East Asia, staffed by civilians, was established in Tokyo in

October 1942 to handle arrangements between Japan and the conquered territories.

The Japanese conquest of Southeast Asia had been accomplished under the slogan "Asia for the Asiatics," and many Japanese probably sincerely believed that their government was bringing about the liberation of the Southeast Asian peoples from European colonial rule. Japanese officials in the occupied territories quickly made contact with anticolonialist elements and promised that independent governments would be established under Japanese tutelage. Such governments were eventually established in Burma, the Dutch East Indies, Vietnam, and the Philippines.

In fact, however, real power rested with the Japanese military authorities in each territory, and the local Japanese military command was directly subordinated to the Army general staff in Tokyo. The economic resources of the colonies were exploited for the benefit of the Japanese war machine, while natives were recruited to serve in local military units or conscripted to work on public works projects. In some cases, the people living in the occupied areas were subjected to severe hardships. In Indochina, for example, forced requisitions of rice by the local Japanese authorities for shipment abroad created a food shortage that caused the starvation of over a million Vietnamese in 1944 and 1945.

The Japanese planned to implant a new moral and social order as well as a new political and economic order in the occupied areas. Occupation policy stressed traditional values such as obedience, community spirit, filial piety, and discipline that reflected the prevailing political and cultural bias in Japan, while supposedly Western values such as materialism, liberalism, and individualism were strongly discouraged. To promote this New Order, occupation authorities gave particular support to local religious organizations but discouraged the formation of formal political parties.

At first, many Southeast Asian nationalists took Japanese promises at face value and agreed to cooperate with their new masters. In Burma, an independent government was established in 1943 and subsequently declared war on the Allies. But as the exploitative nature of Japanese occupation policies became increasingly clear, sentiment turned against the New Order. Japanese officials sometimes unwittingly provoked resentment by their arrogance and contempt for local customs. In the Dutch East Indies, for example, Indonesians were required to bow in the direction of Tokyo and recognize the divinity of the Japanese emperor, practices that were repugnant to Muslims. In Burma, Buddhist pagodas were sometimes used as military latrines.

Like German soldiers in occupied Europe, Japanese military forces often had little respect for the lives of their subject peoples. In their conquest of Nanjing, China, in 1937, Japanese soldiers had spent several days in killing, raping, and looting. Almost 800,000 Koreans were sent over-seas, most of them as forced laborers, to Japan. Tens of thousands of Korean women were forced to serve as "comfort women" (prostitutes) for Japanese troops. In construction projects to help their war effort, the Japanese also made extensive use of labor forces composed of both prisoners of war and local peoples. In building the Burma-Thailand railway in 1943, for example, the Japanese used 61,000 Australian, British, and Dutch prisoners of war and almost 300,000 workers from Burma, Malaya, Thailand, and the Dutch East Indies. An inadequate diet and appalling work conditions in an unhealthy climate led to the deaths of 12,000 Allied prisoners of war and 90,000 native workers by the time the railway was completed.

Such Japanese behavior created a dilemma for many nationalists, who had no desire to see the return of the colonial powers. Some turned against the Japanese, while others lapsed into inactivity. Indonesian patriots tried to have it both ways, feigning support for Japan while attempting to sabotage the Japanese administration. In French Indochina, Ho Chi Minh's Indochinese Communist Party established contacts with American military units in southern China and agreed to provide information on Japanese troop movements and rescue downed American fliers in the area. In Malaya, where Japanese treatment of ethnic Chinese residents was especially harsh, many joined a guerrilla movement against the occupying forces. By the end of the war, little support remained in the region for the erstwhile "liberators."

THE HOME FRONT

World War II was even more of a total war than World War I. Fighting was much more widespread and covered most of the world. Economic mobilization was more extensive; so was the mobilization of women. The number of civilians killed was far higher; almost twenty million were killed from bombing raids, mass extermination policies, and attacks by invading armies.

Mobilizing the People

The home fronts of the major belligerents varied considerably, based on local circumstances. World War II had an enormous impact on the Soviet Union. Known to the Soviets as the Great Patriotic War, the German-Soviet war witnessed the greatest land battles in history as well as incredible ruthlessness. To Nazi Germany, it was a war of oppression and annihilation that called for merciless measures. Two out of every five persons killed in World War II were Soviet citizens.

The initial defeats of the Soviet Union led to drastic emergency mobilization measures that affected the civilian population. Leningrad, for example, experienced nine hundred days of siege, during which its inhabitants became so desperate for food that they ate dogs, cats, and mice. As the German army made its rapid advance into Soviet territory, the factories in the western part of the Soviet Union were dismantled and shipped to the interior—to the Urals, western Siberia, and the Volga region. Machines were placed on the bare ground, and walls went up around them as workers began their work.

This widespread military, industrial, and economic mobilization created yet another industrial revolution for the Soviet Union. Stalin labeled it a "battle of machines," and the Soviets won, producing 78,000 tanks and 98,000 artillery pieces. Fully 55 percent of Soviet national income went for war materials, compared to 15 percent in 1940. As a result of the emphasis on military goods, Soviet citizens experienced extreme shortages of both food and housing.

Soviet women played a major role in the war effort. Women and girls worked in industries, mines, and railroads. Overall, the number of women working in industry increased almost 60 percent. Soviet women were also expected to dig antitank ditches and work as air-raid wardens. In addition, the Soviet Union was the only country in World War II to use women as combatants. Soviet women functioned as snipers and also as air crews in bomber squadrons. The female pilots who helped defeat the Germans at Stalingrad were known as the "Night Witches."

The home front in the United States was quite different from those of its chief wartime allies, largely because the United States faced no threat of war on its own territory. Although the economy and labor force were slow to mobilize, eventually the United States became the arsenal of the Allied Powers, producing the military equipment they needed. At the height of war production in 1943, the nation was constructing six ships a day and $6 billion worth of war-related goods a month.

The mobilization of the American economy caused social problems. The construction of new factories created boomtowns where thousands came to work but then faced a shortage of houses, health facilities, and schools. The dramatic expansion of small towns into large cities often brought a breakdown in traditional social mores, especially evident in the increase in teenage prostitution. Economic mobilization also led to extensive movements of people, which in turn created new social tensions. Sixteen million men and women were enrolled in the military, and another sixteen million, mostly wives and sweethearts of the servicemen or workers looking for jobs, also relocated. Over one million blacks migrated from the rural South to the industrial cities of the North and West, looking for jobs in industry. The presence of blacks in areas where they had not been present before led to racial tensions and sometimes even racial riots. In Detroit in June 1943, white mobs roamed the streets attacking blacks. Many of the one million blacks who enrolled in the military, only to be segregated in their own battle units, were angered by the way they were treated. Some became militant and prepared to fight for their civil rights.

Japanese Americans were treated even more shabbily. On the West Coast, 110,000 Japanese Americans, 65 percent of whom had been born in the United States, were removed to camps encircled by barbed wire and made to take loyalty oaths. Although public officials claimed this policy was necessary for security reasons, no similar treatment of German Americans or Italian Americans ever took place. The racism inherent in this treatment of Japanese Americans was evident when the California governor, Culbert Olson, said: "You know, when I look out at a group of Americans of German or Italian descent, I can tell whether they're loyal or not. I can tell how they think and even perhaps what they are thinking. But it is impossible for me to do this with inscrutable orientals, and particularly the Japanese."[13]

In August 1914, Germans had enthusiastically cheered their soldiers marching off to war. In September 1939, the streets were quiet. Many Germans were apathetic or, even worse for the Nazi regime, had a foreboding of disaster. Hitler was very aware of the importance of the home front. He believed that the collapse of the home front in World War I had caused Germany's defeat, and in his determination to avoid a repetition of that experience, he adopted economic policies that may indeed have cost Germany the war.

To maintain the morale of the home front during the first two years of the war, Hitler refused to cut the production of consumer goods or increase the production of armaments. *Blitzkrieg* allowed the Germans to win quick victories, after which they believed they could plunder the food and raw materials of the conquered countries to avoid diverting resources away from the civilian economy. After German defeats on the Russian front and the American entry into the war, the economic situation changed. Early in 1942, Hitler finally ordered a massive increase in armaments production and in the size of the army. Hitler's architect, Albert Speer, was made minister for armaments and munitions in 1942. By eliminating waste and rationalizing procedures, Speer was able to triple the production of armaments between 1942 and 1943 despite the intense Allied air raids. Speer's urgent plea for a total mobilization of resources for the war effort went unheeded, however. Hitler, fearful of civilian morale problems that would undermine the home front, refused any dramatic cuts in the production of consumer goods. A total mobilization of the economy was not implemented until 1944, when schools, theaters, and cafés were closed and Speer was finally permitted to use all remaining resources for the production of a few basic military items. By that time, it was in vain. Total war mobilization in July 1944 was too little too late to save Germany from defeat.

The war caused a reversal in Nazi attitudes toward women. Nazi resistance to female employment declined as the war progressed and more and more men were called up for military service. Nazi magazines now proclaimed, "We see the woman as the eternal mother of our people, but also as the working and fighting comrade of the man."[14] But the number of women working in industry, agriculture, commerce, and domestic service increased only slightly. The total number of employed women in September 1944 was 14.9 million, compared to 14.6 million in May 1939. Many women, especially those of the middle class, resisted regular employment, particularly in factories. Even the introduction of labor conscription for women in January 1943 failed to achieve much as women found ingenious ways to avoid the regulations.

In Japan, society was placed on a wartime footing even before the attack on Pearl Harbor. A conscription law was passed in 1938, and economic resources were placed under strict government control. Two years later, all political parties were merged into the Imperial Rule Assistance Association. Labor unions were dissolved, and education and culture were purged of all "corrupt" Western ideas in favor of traditional values emphasizing the divinity of the emperor and the higher spirituality of Japanese civilization. During the war, individual rights were severely curtailed as the entire population was harnessed to the needs of the war effort. Traditional habits of obedience and hierarchy were emphasized to encourage citizens to sacrifice their resources, and sometimes their lives, for the national cause. The calls for sacrifice culminated in the final years of the war, when young Japanese were encouraged to volunteer en masse to serve as pilots in the suicide missions (known as *kamikaze*, or "divine wind") against American fighting ships.

Women's rights, too, were to be sacrificed to the greater national cause. Already by 1937, Japanese women were being exhorted to fulfill their patriotic duty by bearing more children and by espousing the slogans of the Greater Japanese Women's Association. However, Japan was extremely reluctant to mobilize women on behalf of the war effort. General Hideki Tojo, prime minister from 1941 to 1944, opposed female employment, arguing that "the weakening of the family system would be the weakening of the nation. . . . We are able to do our duties only because we have wives and mothers at home."[15] Women should remain at home and fulfill their responsibilities by bearing more children. Female employment increased during the war, but only in areas, such as the textile industry and farming, where women had traditionally worked. Instead of using women to meet labor shortages, the Japanese government brought in Korean and Chinese laborers.

The Bombing of Cities

Bombing was used in World War II against nonhuman military targets, against enemy troops, and against civilian populations. The bombing of civilians made World War II as devastating for noncombatants as it was for front-line soldiers. A small number of bombing raids in the last year of World War I had given rise to the argument, crystallized in 1930 by the Italian general Giulio Douhet, that the public outcry in reaction to the bombing of civilian populations would be an effective way to coerce governments into making peace. Consequently, European air forces began to develop long-range bombers in the 1930s.

The first sustained use of civilian bombing contradicted Douhet's theory. Beginning in early September, the German *Luftwaffe* subjected London and many other British cities and towns to nightly air raids, making the Blitz (as the British called the German air raids) a national experience. Londoners took the first heavy blows and set the standard for the rest of the British population by keeping up their spirits. But London morale was helped by the fact that German raids were widely dispersed over a very large city. Smaller communities were more directly affected by the devastation. On November 14, 1940, for example, the *Luftwaffe* destroyed hundreds of shops and 100 acres of the city center of Coventry. The destruction of smaller cities did produce morale problems as rumors of social collapse spread quickly in these communities. Nevertheless, morale was soon restored. War production in these areas, in any case, seems to have been little affected by the raids.

The British failed to learn from their own experience, however, and soon retaliated by bombing Germany. Prime Minister Winston Churchill (1874–1965) and his advisers believed that destroying German communities would break civilian morale and bring victory. Major bombing raids began in 1942 under the direction of Arthur Harris, the wartime leader of the British air force's Bomber Command, which was rearmed with four-engine heavy bombers capable of taking the war into the center of occupied Europe. On May 31, 1942, Cologne became the first German city to be subjected to an attack by a thousand bombers.

The entry of the Americans into the war produced a new bombing strategy. American planes flew daytime missions aimed at the precision bombing of transportation facilities and wartime industries, while the British Bomber Command continued nighttime saturation bombing of all German cities with populations over 100,000. Bombing raids added an element of terror to circumstances already made difficult by growing shortages of food, clothing, and fuel. Germans especially feared the incendiary bombs, which set off firestorms that swept destructive paths through the cities. Four raids on Hamburg in August 1943 produced temperatures of 1,800 degrees Fahrenheit, obliterated half the city's buildings, and killed 50,000 civilians. The ferocious bombing of Dresden for three days in 1945 (February 13–15) created a firestorm that may have killed as many as 100,000 inhabitants and refugees. Even some Allied leaders began to criticize what they saw as the unnecessary terror bombing of German cities.

Germany suffered enormously from the Allied bombing raids. Millions of buildings were destroyed, and possibly half a million civilians died from the raids.

Nevertheless, it is highly unlikely that Allied bombing sapped the morale of the German people. Instead, Germans, whether pro-Nazi or anti-Nazi, fought on stubbornly, often driven simply by a desire to live. Nor did the bombing destroy Germany's industrial capacity. The Allied Strategic Bombing survey revealed that the production of war materials actually increased between 1942 and 1944. Even in 1944 and 1945, Allied raids cut German armaments production by only 7 percent. Nevertheless, the widespread destruction of transportation systems and fuel supplies made it extremely difficult for the new materials to reach the German military.

In Japan, the bombing of civilians reached a new level with the use of the first atomic bomb. Japan was especially vulnerable to air raids because its air force had been virtually destroyed in the course of the war and its crowded cities were built of flimsy materials. Attacks on Japanese cities by the new American B-29 Superfortresses, the biggest bombers of the war, began in June 1944. By the summer of 1945, many of Japan's industries had been destroyed along with one-fourth of its dwellings. After the Japanese government decreed the mobilization of all people between the ages of thirteen and sixty into the People's Volunteer Corps, President Truman and his advisers feared that Japanese fanaticism might mean a million American casualties. This concern led them to drop the atomic bomb on Hiroshima (August 6) and Nagasaki (August 9). The destruction was incredible. Of 76,000 buildings near the center of the explosion in Hiroshima, 70,000 were flattened, and 140,000 of the city's 400,000 inhabitants died by the end of 1945. By the end of 1950, another 50,000 had perished from the effects of radiation. The dropping of the first atomic bomb introduced the world to the nuclear age.

In the years following the end of the war, Truman's decision to approve the use of nuclear weapons to compel Japan to surrender was harshly criticized, not only for causing thousands of civilian casualties but also for introducing a frightening new weapon that could threaten the survival of the human race. Some have even charged that Truman's real purpose in ordering the nuclear strikes was to intimidate the Soviet Union. Defenders of the decision argue that the human costs of invading the Japanese home islands would have been infinitely higher had the bombs not been dropped, and the Soviet Union would have had ample time to consolidate its control over Manchuria.

AFTERMATH: THE COLD WAR

The total victory of the Allies in World War II was not followed by a real peace but by the beginnings of a new conflict known as the Cold War, which dominated world politics until the end of the 1980s. The origins of the Cold War stemmed from the military, political, and ideologi-

J.R. Eyerman, Life Magazine, © TimePix

➤ **HIROSHIMA.** The most devastating destruction of civilians came near the end of World War II when the United States dropped atomic bombs on the Japanese cities of Hiroshima and Nagasaki. This panoramic view of Hiroshima after the bombing shows the incredible devastation caused by the atomic bomb.

cal differences, especially between the Soviet Union and the United States, that became apparent at the Allied war conferences held in the last years of the war. Although Allied leaders were mostly preoccupied with how to end the war, they were also strongly motivated by differing, and often conflicting, visions of the postwar world.

Stalin, Roosevelt, and Churchill, the leaders of the Big Three of the Grand Alliance, met at Tehran, the capital of Iran, in November 1943 to decide the future course of the war. Their major tactical decision concerned the final assault on Germany. Stalin and Roosevelt argued successfully for an American-British invasion of the Continent through France, which they scheduled for the spring of 1944. The acceptance of this plan had important consequences. It meant that Soviet and British-American forces would meet in defeated Germany along a north-south dividing line and that eastern Europe would most likely be liberated by Soviet forces. The Allies also agreed to a partition of postwar Germany until denazification could take place.

By the time of the conference at Yalta in southern Russia in February 1945, the defeat of Germany was a foregone conclusion. The Western powers, which had earlier believed that the Soviets were in a weak position, now faced the reality of eleven million Red Army soldiers taking possession of eastern and central Europe. Stalin was

The Art Archive, London

➤➤ **THE VICTORIOUS ALLIED LEADERS AT YALTA.**   Even before World War II ended, the leaders of the Big Three of the Grand Alliance—Churchill, Roosevelt, and Stalin (shown from left to right)—met in wartime conferences to plan the final assault on Germany and negotiate the outlines of the postwar settlement. At the Yalta meeting (February 5–11, 1945), the three leaders concentrated on postwar issues. The American president, who died two months later, was already a worn-out man at Yalta.

still operating under the notion of spheres of influence. He was deeply suspicious of the Western powers and desired a buffer to protect the Soviet Union from possible future Western aggression. At the same time, however, Stalin was eager to obtain economically important resources and strategic military positions. Roosevelt by this time was moving away from the notion of spheres of influence toward the more Wilsonian ideal of self-determination. He called for "the end of the system of unilateral action, exclusive alliances, and spheres of influence." The Grand Alliance approved a declaration on liberated Europe. This was a pledge to assist liberated Europe in the creation of "democratic institutions of their own choice." Liberated countries were to hold free elections to determine their political systems.

At Yalta, Roosevelt sought Soviet military help against Japan. The atomic bomb was not yet assured, and American military planners feared the possible loss of as many as one million men in amphibious assaults on the Japanese home islands. Roosevelt therefore agreed to Stalin's price for military assistance against Japan: possession of Sakhalin and the Kurile Islands, as well as two warm-water ports and railroad rights in Manchuria.

The creation of the United Nations was a major American concern at Yalta. Roosevelt hoped to ensure the

participation of the Big Three powers in a postwar international organization before difficult issues divided them into hostile camps. After a number of compromises, both Churchill and Stalin accepted Roosevelt's plans for a United Nations organization and set the first meeting for San Francisco in April 1945.

The issues of Germany and eastern Europe were treated less decisively. The Big Three reaffirmed that Germany must surrender unconditionally and created four occupation zones (see Map 24.3). German reparations were set at $20 billion. A compromise was also worked out in regard to Poland. Stalin agreed to free elections in the future to determine a new government. But the issue of free elections in eastern Europe caused a serious rift between the Soviets and the Americans. The principle was that eastern European governments would be freely elected, but they were also supposed to be pro-Soviet. As Churchill expressed it: "The Poles will have their future in their own hands, with the single limitation that they must honestly follow in harmony with their allies, a policy friendly to Russia."[16] This attempt to reconcile two irreconcilable goals was doomed to failure, as soon became evident at the next conference of the Big Three powers.

Even before the conference at Potsdam took place in July 1945, Western relations with the Soviets were deteriorating rapidly. The Grand Alliance had been one of necessity in which ideological incompatibility had been subordinated to the pragmatic concerns of the war. The Allied Powers' only common aim was the defeat of Nazism. Once this aim had all but been accomplished, the many differences that antagonized East-West relations came to the surface.

The Potsdam conference of July 1945 consequently began under a cloud of mistrust. Roosevelt had died on April 12 and had been succeeded as president by Harry Truman. During the conference, Truman received word that the atomic bomb had been successfully tested. Some historians have argued that this knowledge resulted in Truman's stiffened resolve against the Soviets. Whatever the reasons, there was a new coldness in the relations between the Soviets and Americans. At Potsdam, Truman demanded free elections throughout eastern Europe. Stalin responded: "A freely elected government in any of these east European countries would be anti-Soviet, and that we cannot allow."[17] After a bitterly fought and devastating war, Stalin sought absolute military security. To him, it could only be gained by the presence of Communist states in eastern Europe. Free elections might result in governments hostile to the Soviets. By the middle of 1945, only an invasion by Western forces could undo developments in eastern Europe, and after the world's most destructive conflict had ended, few people favored such a policy.

As the war slowly receded into the past, the reality of conflicting ideologies had reappeared. Many in the West interpreted Soviet policy as part of a worldwide Com-

MAP 24.3 Territorial Changes in Europe After World War II. In the last months of World War II, the Red Army occupied much of eastern Europe. Stalin sought pro-Soviet satellite states in the region as a buffer against future invasions from western Europe, whereas Britain and the United States wanted democratically elected governments. Soviet military control of the territory settled the question. ➤ *Which country gained the greatest territory at the expense of Germany?*

munist conspiracy. The Soviets viewed Western, especially American, policy as nothing less than global capitalist expansionism or, in Leninist terms, economic imperialism. Vyacheslav Molotov, the Russian foreign minister, referred to the Americans as "insatiable imperialists" and "war-mongering groups of adventurers."[18] In March 1946, in a speech to an American audience, the former British prime minister Winston Churchill declared that "an iron curtain" had "descended across the continent," dividing Europe into two hostile camps. Stalin branded Churchill's speech a "call to war with the Soviet Union." Only months after the world's most devastating conflict had ended, the world seemed once again to be bitterly divided.

CONCLUSION

World War II was the most devastating total war in human history. Germany, Italy, and Japan had been utterly defeated. Perhaps as many as fifty million people—soldiers and civilians—had been killed in six years. In Asia and Europe, cities had been reduced to rubble, and millions of people faced starvation as once fertile lands stood neglected or wasted. Untold millions of people had become refugees.

What were the underlying causes of the war? One direct cause of the conflict was the effort by two rising capitalist powers, Germany and Japan, to make up for their relatively late arrival on the scene to carve out their own global empires. Key elements in both countries had resented the agreements reached after the end of World War I that divided the world in a manner favorable to their rivals and hoped to overturn them at the earliest opportunity. Neither Germany nor Japan possessed a strong tradition of political pluralism; to the contrary, in both countries, the legacy of a feudal past marked by a strong military tradition still wielded a strong influence over the political system and the mind-set of the entire population. It is no surprise that under the impact of the Great Depression, which had severe effects in both countries, fragile democratic institutions were soon overwhelmed by militant forces determined to enhance national wealth and power.

Whatever the causes of World War II, the consequences were soon to be evident. European hegemony over the world was at an end, and two new superpowers had emerged to take its place. Even before the last battles had been fought, the United States and the Soviet Union had arrived at different visions of the postwar world. No sooner had the war ended than their differences created a new and potentially even more devastating conflict known as the Cold War. And even though Europeans seemed merely pawns in the struggle between the two superpowers, they managed to stage a remarkable recovery of their own civilization. In Asia, defeated Japan made a miraculous economic recovery, and an era of European domination finally came to an end.

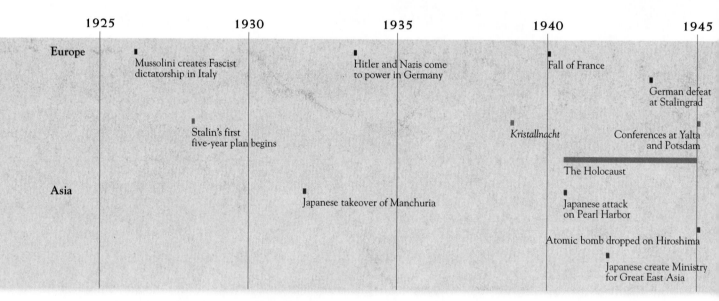

1925   1930   1935   1940   1945

Europe

Mussolini creates Fascist dictatorship in Italy

Hitler and Nazis come to power in Germany

Fall of France

German defeat at Stalingrad

Stalin's first five-year plan begins

Kristallnacht

Conferences at Yalta and Potsdam

The Holocaust

Asia

Japanese takeover of Manchuria

Japanese attack on Pearl Harbor

Atomic bomb dropped on Hiroshima

Japanese create Ministry for Great East Asia

CHAPTER NOTES

1. Benito Mussolini, "The Doctrine of Fascism," in Adrian Lyttleton, ed., *Italian Fascisms from Pareto to Gentile* (London, 1973), p. 42.
2. Quoted in Alexander De Grand, "Women Under Italian Fascism," *Historical Journal* 19 (1976): 958–959.
3. Quoted in Jeremy Noakes and Geoffrey Pridham, eds., *Nazism, 1919–1945* (Exeter, England 1983), vol. 1, pp. 50–51.
4. Quoted in Joachim Fest, *Hitler*, trans. Richard and Clara Winston (New York, 1974), p. 418.
5. Adolf Hitler, *Mein Kampf*, trans. Ralph Manheim (Boston, 1971), p. 654.
6. *Documents on German Foreign Policy* (London, 1956), Series D, vol. 7, p. 204.
7. Memorandum by John Van Antwerp MacMurray, quoted in Arthur Waldron, *How the Peace Was Lost: The 1935 Memorandum* (Stanford, Calif., 1992), p. 5.
8. Albert Speer, *Spandau*, trans. Richard and Clara Winston (New York, 1976), p. 50.
9. *Nazi Conspiracy and Aggression* (Washington, D.C., 1946), vol. 6, p. 262.
10. International Military Tribunal, *Trial of the Major War Criminals* (Nuremberg, 1947–1949), vol. 22, p. 480.
11. Quoted in Raul Hilberg, *The Destruction of the European Jews*, rev. ed. (New York, 1985), vol. 1, pp. 332–333.
12. *Nazi Conspiracy and Aggression*, vol. 6, p. 789.
13. Quoted in John Campbell, *The Experience of World War II* (New York, 1989), p. 170.
14. Quoted in Claudia Koonz, "Mothers in the Fatherland: Women in Nazi Germany," in Renate Bridenthal and Claudia Koonz, eds., *Becoming Visible: Women in European History* (Boston, 1977), p. 466.
15. Quoted in Campbell, *The Experience of World War II*, p. 143.
16. Quoted in Norman Graebner, *Cold War Diplomacy, 1945–1960* (Princeton, N.J., 1962), p. 117.
17. Ibid.
18. Quoted in Wilfried Loth, *The Division of the World, 1941–1955* (New York, 1988), p. 81.

SUGGESTED READING

For a general study of fascism, see S. G. Payne, *A History of Fascism* (Madison, Wis., 1996). The best biography of Mussolini is now R. J. B. Bosworth, *Mussolini* (London, 2002). Two brief but excellent surveys of Fascist Italy are A. Cassels, *Fascist Italy*, 2d ed. (Arlington Heights, Ill., 1985), and J. Whittam, *Fascist Italy* (New York, 1995).

Two brief but sound surveys of Nazi Germany are J. J. Spielvogel, *Hitler and Nazi Germany: A History*, 4th ed. (Upper Saddle River, N.J., 2000), and J. Dülffer, *Nazi Germany 1933–1945* (New York, 1996). The best biographies of Hitler are A. Bullock, *Hitler: A Study in Tyranny* (New York, 1964); J. Fest, *Hitler*, trans. R. and C. Winston (New York, 1974); and Ian Kershaw, *Hitler, 1889–1936: Hubris* (New York, 1999), and *Hitler: Nemesis* (New York, 2000). Two recent works that examine the enormous literature on Hitler are J. Lukacs, *The Hitler of History* (New York, 1997), and R. Rosenbaum, *Explaining Hitler* (New York, 1998). Basic studies of the SS include R. Koehl, *The Black Corps: The Structure and Power Struggles of the Nazi SS* (Madison, Wis., 1983), and H. Krausnick and M. Broszat, *Anatomy of the SS State* (London, 1970). On women, see C. Koonz, *Mothers in the Fatherland: Women, the Family, and Nazi Politics* (New York, 1987). The Hitler Youth is examined in H. W. Koch, *The Hitler Youth* (New York, 1976). On Nazi anti-Jewish policies between 1933 and 1939, see S. Friedländer, *Nazi Germany and the Jews*, vol. 1, *The Years of Persecution, 1933–1939* (New York, 1997).

The collectivization of agriculture in the Soviet Union is examined in S. Fitzpatrick, *Stalin's Peasants: Resistance and Survival in the Russian Village After Collectivization* (New York, 1995). Industrialization is covered in H. Kuromiya, *Stalin's Industrial Revolution: Politics and Workers, 1928–1932* (New York, 1988). Stalin's purges are examined in R. Conquest, *The Great Terror: A Reassessment* (New York, 1990). On Stalin himself, see R. Tucker, *Stalin in Power: The Revolution from Above, 1928–1941* (New York, 1990), and R. W. Thurston, *Life and Terror in Stalin's Russia, 1934–1941* (New Haven, Conn., 1996).

A basic study of Germany's foreign policy from 1933 to 1939 can be found in G. Weinberg, *The Foreign Policy of Hitler's Germany: Diplomatic Revolution in Europe, 1933–36* (Chicago, 1970), and *The Foreign Policy of Hitler's Germany: Starting World War II, 1937–1939* (Chicago, 1980). Japan's march to war is examined in A. Iriye, *The Origins of the Second World War in Asia and the Pacific* (London, 1987).

General works on World War II include M. K. Dziewanowski, *War at Any Price: World War II in Europe, 1939–1945*, 2d ed. (Englewood Cliffs, N.J., 1991); the comprehensive study by G. Weinberg, *A World at Arms: A Global History of World War II* (Cambridge, 1994); and J. Campbell, *The Experience of World War II* (New York, 1989). On Hitler as a military leader, see R. Lewin, *Hitler's Mistakes* (New York, 1986). On battles, see J. Keegan, *The Second World War* (New York, 1990).

Excellent studies of the Holocaust include R. Hilberg, *The Destruction of the European Jews*, rev. ed., 3 vols. (New York, 1985), and L. Yahil, *The Holocaust* (New York, 1990). For brief studies, see J. Fischel, *The Holocaust* (Westport, Conn., 1998), and R. S. Botwinick, *A History of the Holocaust* (Upper Saddle River, N.J., 1996). There is a good overview of the scholarship on the Holocaust in M. Marrus, *The Holocaust in History* (New York, 1987). On the problem of what the Allied countries knew about the Holocaust, see D. Wyman, *The Abandonment of the Jews: America and the Holocaust* (New York, 1984), and M. Gilbert, *Auschwitz and the Allies* (New York, 1981). Other Nazi atrocities are examined in B. Wytwycky, *The Other Holocaust* (Washington, D.C., 1980).

General studies on the impact of total war include J. Costello, *Love, Sex and War: Changing Values, 1939–1945* (London, 1985); P. Summerfield, *Women Workers in the Second World War: Production and Patriarchy in Conflict* (London, 1984); and M. R. Marrus, *The Unwanted: European Refugees in the Twentieth Century* (New York, 1985). On the home front in Germany, see E. R. Beck, *Under the Bombs: The German Home Front, 1942–1945* (Lexington, Ky., 1986), and M. Kitchen, *Nazi Germany at War* (New York, 1995). The Soviet Union during the war is examined in M. Harrison, *Soviet Planning in Peace and War, 1938–1945* (Cambridge, 1985). On the American home front, see the good collection of essays in K. P. O'Brien and L. H. Parsons, *The Home-Front War: World War II and American Society* (Westport, Conn., 1995). The Japanese home front is examined in T. R. H. Havens, *The Valley of Darkness: The Japanese People and World War Two* (New York, 1978).

On the destruction of Germany by bombing raids, see H. Rumpf, *The Bombing of Germany* (London, 1963). The German bombing of Britain is covered in T. Harrisson, *Living Through the Blitz* (London, 1985). On Hiroshima, see A. Chisholm, *Faces of Hiroshima* (London, 1985).

On the emergence of the Cold War, see W. Loth, *The Division of the World, 1941–1955* (New York, 1988). On the wartime summit conferences, see H. Feis, *Churchill, Roosevelt, Stalin: The War They Waged and the Peace They Sought*, 2d ed. (Princeton, N.J., 1967), and D. Clemens, *Yalta* (New York, 1970).

INFOTRAC COLLEGE EDITION

For additional reading, go to InfoTrac College Edition, your online research library at
http://web1.infotrac-college.com

Enter the search terms "Weimar Republic" using Keywords.

Enter the search terms "Hitler or Nazi or Nazism" using Keywords.

Enter the search term "totalitarianism" using the Subject Guide.

Enter the search terms "World War, 1939–1945" using the Subject Guide.

Enter the search term "Holocaust" using the Subject Guide.

Reflection

MODERN PATTERNS OF WORLD HISTORY (1800–1945)

At the outset of Part IV, we remarked that two of the most significant developments during the nineteenth and early twentieth centuries were the Industrial Revolution and the onset of the era of imperialism. Of these two factors, the first was clearly the more important, for it created the conditions for the latter. It was, of course, the major industrial powers—Great Britain, France, and later Germany, Japan, and the United States—that took the lead in building large colonialist empires.

The advent of the industrial age had a number of lasting consequences for the world at large. On the one hand, the material wealth of the nations that successfully passed through the process increased significantly. In many cases, the creation of advanced industrial societies strengthened democratic institutions and led to a higher standard of living for the majority of the population. It also helped reduce class barriers and bring about the emancipation of women from many of the legal and social restrictions that had characterized the previous era. The spread of technology and trade outside of Europe created the basis for a new international economic order based on the global exchange of goods.

On the other hand, as we have seen, not all the consequences of the Industrial Revolution were beneficial. In the industrializing societies themselves, rapid economic change often led to widening disparities in the distribution of wealth and, with the decline in pervasiveness of religious belief, a sense of rootlessness and alienation among much of the population. While some societies were able to manage these problems with some degree of success, others experienced a breakdown of social values and widespread political instability. In imperial Russia, internal tensions became too much for the traditional landholding elites, leading to social revolution and imposition of the Soviet state. In other cases, such as Germany, deepseated ethnic and class antagonisms remained under the surface until conditions of economic depression led to the rise of militant fascist regimes.

A second development that had a major impact on the era was the rise of nationalism. Like the Industrial Revolution, the idea of nationalism originated in eighteenthcentury Europe, where it was a product of the secularization of the age and the experiences of the French revolutionary and Napoleonic eras. Although the concept provided the basis for a new sense of community and the rise of the modern nation-state, it also gave birth to ethnic tensions and hatred that resulted in bitter disputes and civil strife and contributed to the competition that eventually erupted into world war.

Finally, industrialization and the rise of national consciousness transformed the nature of war itself. New weapons of mass destruction created the potential for a new kind of warfare that reached beyond the battlefield into the very heartland of the enemy's territory, while the concept of nationalism transformed war from the sport of kings to a matter of national honor and commitment. Since the French Revolution, when the revolutionary government in Paris had mobilized the entire country by mass conscription to fight against the forces that opposed the Revolution, governments had relied on mass conscription to defend the national cause while their engines of destruction reached far into enemy territory to destroy the industrial base and undermine the will to fight. This trend was amply demonstrated in the two world wars of the twentieth century.

In the end, then, industrial power and the driving force of nationalism, the very factors that had created the conditions for European global dominance, contained the seeds for the decline of that dominance. These seeds germinated during the 1930s, when the Great Depression sharpened international competition and mutual antagonisms, and then sprouted in the ensuing conflict, which for the first time spanned the entire globe. By the time World War II came to an end, the once powerful countries of Europe were exhausted, leaving the door ajar for the emergence of two new global superpowers, the United States and the Soviet Union, which dominated the postwar political scene. Although the new superpowers were both products of modern European civilization, they were physically and politically separate from it, and their intense competition, which marked the postwar period, threatened to transform the old map of Europe into a battleground for a new ideological conflict.

If in Europe the dominant fact of the era was the Industrial Revolution, in the rest of the world it was undoubtedly Western imperialism. Between the end of the Napoleonic wars and the end of the nineteenth century, European powers, or their rivals in Japan and the United States, achieved political mastery over virtually the entire remainder of the world.

What was the overall economic effect of imperialism on the subject peoples? For most of the population in colonial areas, Western domination was rarely beneficial and often destructive. Although a limited number of merchants, large landowners, and traditional hereditary elites undoubtedly prospered under the umbrella of the expanding imperialist economic order, the majority of colonial peoples, urban and rural alike, probably suffered considerable hardship as a result of the policies adopted by their foreign rulers.

Some historians point out, however, that for all the inequities of the colonial system, there was a positive side to the experience as well. The expansion of markets and the beginnings of a modern transportation and communications network, while bringing few immediate benefits to the colonial peoples, offered considerable promise for future economic growth. At the same time, the introduction of new ways of looking at human freedom and the relationship between the individual and society set the stage for a reevaluation of such ideas after the restoration of independence following World War II.

Perhaps the Western concept that had the most immediate impact was that of nationalism. The concept of nationalism often served a useful role in many countries in Asia and Africa, where it provided colonial peoples with a sense of common purpose that later proved vital in knitting together the coherent elements in their societies to oppose colonial regimes and create the conditions for future independent states.

Another idea that gained currency in colonial areas was democracy. As a rule, colonial regimes did not make a serious attempt to introduce democratic institutions to their subject populations; understandably, they feared that such institutions would undermine colonial authority. Nevertheless, Western notions of representative government and individual freedom had their advocates in

PATHS TO MODERNIZATION

Why some societies were able to embark on the road to industrialization and others were not has long been a matter of scholarly debate Some observers have found the answer in the cultural characteristics of individual societies, such as the Protestant work ethic in parts of Europe or the tradition of social discipline and class hierarchy in Japan. Others have placed more emphasis on practical considerations, such as the lack of an urban market for agricultural goods in China (which reduced the landowners' incentives to introduce mechanized farming) or the absence of a foreign threat in Japan (which provided increased opportunities for local investment). To historian Peter Stearns, the availability of capital, natural resources, a network of trade relations, and navigable rivers all helped stimulate industrial growth in nineteenth-century England.

Whatever the truth of such speculations, it is clear that there has been more than one road to industrialization. In his highly respected work on the subject titled *Social Origins of Dictatorship and Democracy*, sociologist Barrington Moore

Courtesy of William J. Duiker

➽ **OLD CHINA, NEW CHINA.** This illustration, used on a People's Republic of China calendar in 1960, was made by using traditional Chinese techniques of landscape painting. However, the drawing shows a modern industrial landscape instead of a tranquil pastoral scene. The three junks at the right are the only reminder of traditional China.

found at least three paths to economic modernization: the bourgeois capitalist route followed in Great Britain, France, and the United States; the "revolution from above" approach adopted in Germany and Meiji Japan; and the Marxist-Leninist strategy used in the Soviet Union. The first approach, fostered by an independent urban mercantile class, led to the emergence of democratic societies on the capitalist model. The second, carried out by traditional elites in the absence of a strong independent bourgeois class, led ultimately to fascist and militarist regimes; the third, guided by the Communist Party in the almost total absence of an urban middle class, led to the creation of an advanced industrial society based on a totalitarian political system.

Which approach is the most effective? The bourgeois capitalist model appears to have had the most success in promoting economic growth based on the preservation of human rights, but often such results have been achieved at the cost of vast inequalities in the distribution of wealth within individual societies.

IMPERIALISM AND THE GLOBAL ENVIRONMENT

Beginning in the 1870s, European states engaged in an intense scramble for overseas territory. This "new imperialism" led Europeans to carve up Asia and Africa and create colonial empires. Within these empires, European states exercised complete political control over the indigenous societies and redrew political boundaries to meet their needs. In Africa, for example, in drawing the boundaries that separated one colony from another (boundaries that often became the boundaries of the modern countries of Africa), Europeans paid no attention to the political divisions of the indigenous tribes. Europeans often divided tribes between colonies or made two tribes that were hostile to each other members of the same colony.

In similar fashion, Europeans paid little or no heed to the economic needs of their colonial subjects but instead set up the economies of their empires to meet their own needs in the new world market. In the process, Europeans often dramatically altered the global environment, a transformation that was made visible in a variety of ways. Westerners built railways and ports, erected telegraph lines, drilled for oil, and dug mines for gold, tin, iron ore, and copper. All of these projects transformed and often scarred the natural landscape.

Landscapes, however, were even more dramatically altered by Europe's demand for cash food crops. Throughout vast regions of Africa and Asia, tropical forests were felled to make way for plantations that cultivated crops that could be exported for sale. In Ceylon and India, the British cut down vast tropical forests to plant row upon row of tea bushes. The Dutch did the same in the East Indies, where they planted cinchona trees imported from Peru. Quinine, derived from the tree's bark, dramatically reduced the death rate for malaria and made it possible for Europeans to live more securely in the tropical regions of Africa and Asia. In Southeast Asia, the French replaced extensive forests with sugar and coffee plantations. Native workers, who were usually paid pitiful wages by their European overseers, provided the labor for all of these vast plantations.

European states greatly profited from this transformed environment. In *Agriculture in the Tropics: An Elementary Treatise*, written in 1909, the British botanist John Christopher Willis expressed his thoughts on this European policy:

Whether planting in the tropics will always continue to be under European management is another question, but the northern powers will not permit that the rich and as yet comparatively undeveloped countries of the tropics should be entirely wasted by being devoted merely to the supply of the food and clothing wants of their own people, when they can also supply the wants of the colder zones in so many indispensable products.

In Willis's eyes, the imperialist transformation of the environments of Asia and Africa to serve European needs was entirely justified.

▶ **PICKING TEA LEAVES IN CEYLON.** Shown here in this 1900 photograph are women picking tea leaves for shipment abroad on a plantation in Ceylon (now Sri Lanka). The British cut down enormous stands of tropical forests in Ceylon and India to grow tea to satisfy demand back home.

Archive Photos/Popperfoto

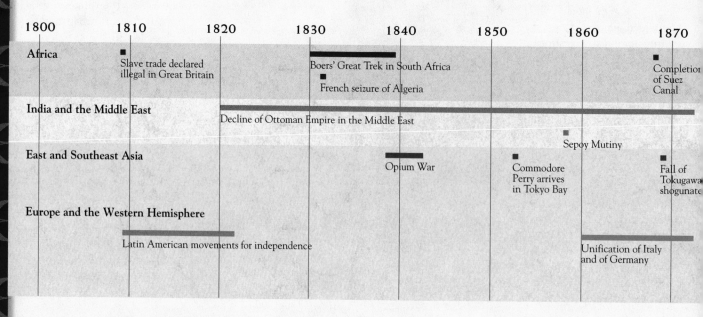

	1800	1810	1820	1830	1840	1850	1860	1870
Africa		Slave trade declared illegal in Great Britain		Boers' Great Trek in South Africa / French seizure of Algeria				Completion of Suez Canal
India and the Middle East			Decline of Ottoman Empire in the Middle East					
East and Southeast Asia					Opium War	Commodore Perry arrives in Tokyo Bay	Sepoy Mutiny	Fall of Tokugawa shogunate
Europe and the Western Hemisphere		Latin American movements for independence					Unification of Italy and of Germany	

India, Vietnam, China, and Japan well before the end of the nineteenth century. Later, countless Asians and Africans were exposed to such ideas in schools set up by the colonial regime or in the course of travel to Europe or the United States. Most of the nationalist parties founded in colonial territories espoused democratic principles and attempted to apply them when they took power after the restoration of independence.

Finally, the colonial experience offered new ways of looking at the relationship between men and women. Although colonial rule was by no means uniformly beneficial to the position of women in African and Asian societies, growing awareness of the struggle by women in the West to seek sexual equality offered their counterparts in the colonial territories a weapon to fight against the long-standing barriers of custom and legal discrimination.

How are we to draw up a final balance sheet on the era of Western imperialism? To its defenders, it was a necessary stage in the evolution of the human race, a flawed but essentially humanitarian effort to provide the backward peoples of Africa and Asia with a boost up the ladder of evolution. To its critics, it was a tragedy of major proportions. The insatiable drive of the advanced economic powers for access to raw materials and markets resulted in the widespread destruction of traditional cultures and created an exploitative environment that transformed the vast majority of colonial peoples into a permanent underclass while restricting the benefits of modern technology to a privileged few. Sophisticated, age-old societies that should have been left to respond to the technological revolution in their own way were subjected to foreign rule and squeezed dry of precious national resources under the guise of the "civilizing mission."

In this debate, the critics surely have the best argument. All in all, the colonial experience was brutal, and its benefits accrued almost entirely to citizens of the ruling power. The argument that the Western societies had a "white man's burden" to civilize the world was all too often a hypocritical gesture to salve the guilty feelings of those who recognized imperialism for what it was—a savage act of rape.

But although the experience was a painful one, human societies were able to survive it and to earn a second chance to make better use of the stunning promise of the industrial era. How they have fared in that effort will be the subject of the final section of this book.

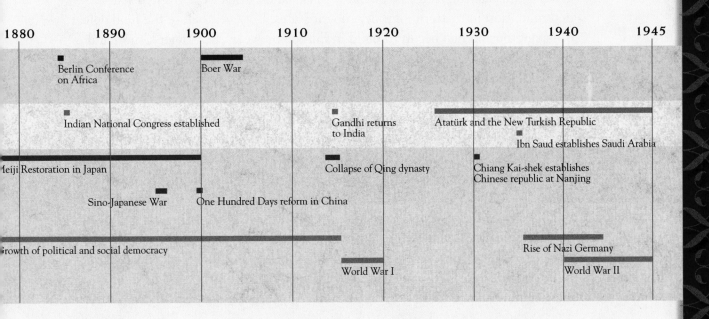

Part V

TOWARD A GLOBAL CIVILIZATION? THE WORLD SINCE 1945

When U.S. President Franklin Roosevelt and British Prime Minister Winston Churchill met off the coast of Newfoundland in August 1941 to discuss their common objectives in a postwar world, they appeared to recognize that imperialist rivalry had been the crucial factor leading to the outbreak of the two world wars. The Atlantic Charter stated that the two countries hoped to realize equality of economic opportunity, abandonment of force, and friendly collaboration among the peoples of the world, as well as the right of nations to choose their own form of government.

In a number of respects, the wartime allies achieved their aims for the peace. The rapacious efforts of Germany and Japan to dominate the world were thwarted, and the intense rivalry that had characterized relations among the Western powers came to an end. Outside of Europe, the colonial system was gradually dismantled, and the peoples of Asia and Africa were granted self-determination in the form of independent states. But even before the final defeat of Japan, tension had begun to build in Europe between the Soviet Union and the Western powers. By the end of the 1940s, that tension had spread throughout the world, and the Cold War had begun.

In the meantime, the end of colonial empires did not bring to the peoples of Asia and Africa a new world of political stability, peaceful cooperation, and material prosperity. Economic difficulties, a product of their own inexperience and the continued Western domination of the global economy, led to internal factionalism, military rule, and sometimes regional conflict. Competition between the capitalist and socialist power blocs—led by the United States and the Soviet Union, respectively—compounded the problem. In the late 1980s, however, the Soviet empire began to come apart, and in December 1991, the Soviet Union itself became a memory as onetime Soviet republics now split into independent states, bringing an end to the ideological Cold War. In the meantime, a number of nations in Asia have apparently entered the lists of the

Courtesy of William J. Duiker

advanced industrial countries and have embarked on the road to political democracy. Half a century after the end of World War II, some of the dreams embodied in the Atlantic Charter appear to be reaching fruition.

But challenges remain, and many of them appear intimidating. The breakup of the Soviet empire has led to the emergence of squabbling nationalities throughout eastern Europe, while in other parts of the world, including the Middle East, Africa, and Northern Ireland, age-old rivalries and ethnic and religious suspicions continue to be sources of bitter conflict. A global economic slowdown brought recession to the advanced nations and severe political and economic difficulties to many societies in the rest of the world. In the meantime, the effects of untrammeled industrial development are coming home to roost in the form of growing environmental pollution. The combined effects of ethnic and religious differences and intense competition for markets continue to strain efforts to achieve global cooperation in solving the common problems of humanity.

25

© David King Collection

IN THE GRIP OF THE COLD WAR: THE BREAKDOWN OF THE YALTA SYSTEM

CHAPTER OUTLINE
- THE COLLAPSE OF THE GRAND ALLIANCE
- COLD WAR IN ASIA
- FROM CONFRONTATION TO COEXISTENCE
- AN ERA OF EQUIVALENCE
- CONCLUSION

FOCUS QUESTIONS
- Why were the United States and the Soviet Union suspicious of each other after World War II, and what events between 1945 and 1949 heightened the tensions between the two nations?
- How have historians answered the question of whether the United States or the Soviet Union bears the primary responsibility for the Cold War, and what evidence can be presented on each side of the issue?
- How and why did Mao Zedong and the Communists come to power in China, and what were the implications of their triumph for the Cold War?
- What were the major developments in the Cold War between 1950 and 1989?
- ➤ How and why did the Cold War change from a European confrontation to a conflict of global significance?

"*O*ur meeting here in the Crimea has reaffirmed our common determination to maintain and strengthen in the peace to come that unity of purpose and of action which has made victory possible and certain for the United Nations in this war. We believe that this is a sacred obligation which our Governments owe to our peoples and to all the peoples of the world."[1]

With these ringing words, drafted at the Yalta Conference in February 1945, U.S. President Franklin D. Roosevelt, Soviet leader Joseph Stalin, and British Prime Minister Winston Churchill affirmed their common hope that the Grand Alliance that had been victorious in World War II could be sustained into the postwar era. Only through continuing and growing cooperation and understanding among the three Allies, the statement asserted, could a secure and lasting peace be realized that, in

722

the words of the Atlantic Charter, would "afford assurance that all the men in all the lands may live out their lives in freedom from fear and want."

Roosevelt hoped that the decisions reached at Yalta would provide the basis for a stable peace in the postwar era. Allied occupation forces—American, British, and French in the west and Soviet in the east—were to bring about the end of Axis administration and to organize the free election of democratic governments throughout Europe. To foster mutual trust and an end to the suspicions that had marked relations between the capitalist world and the Soviet Union prior to the war, Roosevelt tried to reassure Stalin that Moscow's legitimate territorial aspirations and genuine security needs would be adequately met in a durable peace settlement.

However, this was not to be. Within months after the German surrender, the mutual trust among the Allies—if it had ever truly existed—rapidly disintegrated, and the dream of a stable peace was replaced by the specter of a potential nuclear holocaust. As the Cold War between Moscow and Washington intensified, Europe was divided into two armed camps, while the two superpowers, glaring at each other across a deep ideological divide, held the survival of the entire world in their hands. •

THE COLLAPSE OF THE GRAND ALLIANCE

The problem started in Europe. At the end of the war, Soviet military forces occupied all of Eastern Europe and the Balkans (except Greece, Albania, and Yugoslavia), while U.S. and other Allied forces completed their occupation of the western part of the Continent. Roosevelt had assumed that free elections administered by "democratic and peace-loving forces" would lead to democratic governments responsive to the local population. But it soon became clear that the Soviet Union and the United States interpreted the Yalta agreement differently. When Soviet occupation authorities began forming a new Polish government, Stalin refused to accept the Polish government-in-exile—headquartered in London during the war, it was composed primarily of landed aristocrats, who harbored a deep distrust of the Soviet Union—and instead created a government composed of Communists who had spent the war in Moscow. Roosevelt complained to Stalin but eventually agreed to a compromise whereby two members of the London government were included in a new Communist regime. A week later, Roosevelt was dead of a cerebral hemorrhage.

Similar developments took place in all of the states occupied by Soviet troops. Coalitions of all political parties (except fascist or right-wing parties) were formed to run the government, but within a year or two, the Communist parties in these coalitions had assumed the lion's share of power. The next step was the creation of one-party Communist governments. Between 1945 and 1947, Communist governments became firmly entrenched in East Germany, Bulgaria, Romania, Poland, and Hungary. In Czechoslovakia, with its strong tradition of democratic institutions, the Communists did not achieve their goals until 1948. After the elections of 1946, the Communist Party shared control of the government with the non-Communist parties. When it appeared that the latter might win new elections early in 1948, the Communists seized control of the government on February 25. All other parties were dissolved, and the Communist leader Klement Gottwald became the new president of Czechoslovakia.

Yugoslavia was a notable exception to the pattern of growing Soviet dominance in Eastern Europe. The Communist Party there had led resistance to the Nazis during the war and easily took over power when the war ended. Josip Broz, known as Tito (1892–1980), the leader of the Communist resistance movement, appeared to be a loyal Stalinist. After the war, however, he moved to establish an independent Communist state. Stalin hoped to take control of Yugoslavia, but Tito refused to capitulate to Stalin's demands and gained the support of the people (and some sympathy in the West) by portraying the struggle as one of Yugoslav national freedom. In 1958, the Yugoslav party congress asserted that Yugoslav Communists did not see themselves as deviating from communism, only from Stalinism. They considered their more decentralized system, in which workers managed themselves and local communes exercised some political power, closer to the Marxist-Leninist ideal.

To Stalin (who had once boasted "I will shake my little finger, and there will be no more Tito"), the creation of pliant pro-Soviet regimes throughout Eastern Europe may simply have represented his interpretation of the Yalta peace agreement and a reward for sacrifices suffered during the war, satisfying Moscow's aspirations for a buffer zone against the capitalist West. If the Soviet leader had any intention of promoting future Communist revolutions in Western Europe—and there is some indication that he did—such developments would have to await the appearance of a new capitalist crisis a decade or more into the future. As Stalin undoubtedly recalled, Lenin had always maintained that revolutions come in waves.

The Truman Doctrine and the Marshall Plan

To the United States, however, the Soviet takeover of Eastern Europe represented an ominous development that threatened Roosevelt's vision of a durable peace. Public suspicion of Soviet intentions grew rapidly, especially among the millions of Americans who still had relatives living in Eastern Europe. Winston Churchill was quick to put such fears into words. In a highly publicized speech at Westminster College in Fulton, Missouri, in March 1946, the former British prime minister declared that an "iron curtain" had "descended across the Continent," dividing Germany and Europe itself into two hostile camps. Stalin responded by branding Churchill's speech a "call to war with the Soviet Union." But he need not have worried. Although public opinion in the United States placed increasing pressure on Roosevelt's successor, Harry S Truman (1884–1972), to devise an effective strategy to counter Soviet advances abroad, the American people were in no mood for another war.

A civil war in Greece created another potential arena for confrontation between the superpowers and an opportunity for the Truman administration to take a stand. Communist guerrilla forces supported by Tito's Yugoslavia had taken up arms against the pro-Western government in Athens. Great Britain had initially assumed primary responsibility for promoting postwar reconstruction in the eastern Mediterranean, but in 1947, continuing economic problems caused the British to withdraw from the active role they had been playing in both Greece and Turkey. President Truman, alarmed by British weakness and the possibility of Soviet expansion into the eastern Mediterranean, responded with the Truman Doctrine (see the box on p. 725), which said in essence that the United States would provide money to countries that claimed they were threatened by communist expansion. If the Soviets were not stopped in Greece, the Truman argument ran, then the United States would have to face the spread of communism throughout the free world. As Dean Acheson, the U.S. secretary of state, explained, "Like apples in a barrel infected by disease, the corruption of Greece would infect Iran and all the East . . . likewise Africa . . . Italy . . . France. . . . Not since Rome and Carthage has there been such a polarization of power on this earth."[2]

The U.S. suspicion that Moscow was actively supporting the insurgent movement in Greece turned out to be unfounded. Stalin was apparently unhappy with Tito's promoting the conflict, not only because he suspected that the latter was attempting to create his own sphere of influence in the Balkans, but also because it risked provoking a direct confrontation between the United States and the Soviet Union.

The proclamation of the Truman Doctrine was followed in June 1947 by the European Recovery Program, better known as the Marshall Plan, which provided $13 billion for the economic recovery of war-torn Europe. Underlying the program was the belief that communist aggression fed off economic turmoil. General George C. Marshall noted in a speech at Harvard University, "Our policy is not directed against any country or doctrine but against hunger, poverty, desperation, and chaos."[3]

From the Soviet perspective, the Marshall Plan was capitalist imperialism, a thinly veiled attempt to buy the

A CALL TO ARMS. In March 1946, former British prime minister Winston Churchill gave a speech before a college audience in Fulton, Missouri, that electrified the world. Soviet occupation of the countries of Eastern Europe, he declared, had divided the Continent into two conflicting halves, separated by an "iron curtain." Churchill's speech has often been described as the opening salvo in the Cold War, and Moscow responded by labeling the speech "reactionary" and "unconvincing." In the photo, Churchill, with President Harry S Truman behind him, prepares to give his address.

THE TRUMAN DOCTRINE

By 1947, the battle lines in the Cold War had been clearly drawn. This excerpt is taken from a speech by President Harry Truman to the U.S. Congress in which he justified his request for aid to Greece and Turkey. Truman expressed the urgent need to contain the expansion of communism. Compare this statement with that of Soviet leader Leonid Brezhnev cited later in this chapter.

TRUMAN'S SPEECH TO CONGRESS, MARCH 12, 1947

The peoples of a number of countries of the world have recently had totalitarian regimes forced upon them against their will. The Government of the United States has made frequent protests against coercion and intimidation, in violation of the Yalta agreement, in Poland, Rumania, and Bulgaria. I must also state that in a number of other countries there have been similar developments.

At the present moment in world history nearly every nation must choose between alternative ways of life. The choice is too often not a free one.

One way of life is based upon the will of the majority, and is distinguished by free institutions, representative government, free elections, guarantees of individual liberty, freedom of speech and religion, and freedom from political oppression.

The second way of life is based upon the will of a minority forcibly imposed upon the majority. It relies upon terror and oppression, a controlled press and radio, fixed elections, and the suppression of personal freedoms.

I believe that it must be the policy of the United States to support free peoples who are resisting attempted subjugation by armed minorities or by outside pressures.

I believe that we must assist free people to work out their own destinies in their own way.

I believe that our help should be primarily through economic and financial aid, which is essential to economic stability and orderly political processes. . . . I therefore ask the Congress for assistance to Greece and Turkey in the amount of $400,000,000.

---

support of the smaller European countries "in return for the relinquishing . . . of their economic and later also their political independence."[4] A Soviet spokesperson described the United States as the "main force in the imperialist camp," whose ultimate goal was "the strengthening of imperialism, preparation for a new imperialist war, a struggle against socialism and democracy, and the support of reactionary and antidemocratic, pro-fascist regimes and movements." Although the Marshall Plan was open to the Soviet Union and its Eastern European satellite states, they refused to participate. The Soviets were in no position to compete financially with the United States, however, and could do little to counter the Marshall Plan except tighten their control in Eastern Europe.

Europe Divided

By 1947, the split in Europe between east and west had become a fact of life. At the end of World War II, the United States had favored a quick end to its commitments in Europe. But American fears of Soviet aims caused the United States to play an increasingly important role in European affairs. In an article in *Foreign Affairs* in July 1947, George Kennan, a well-known U.S. diplomat with much knowledge of Soviet affairs, advocated a policy of containment against further aggressive Soviet moves. Kennan favored the "adroit and vigilant application of counter-force at a series of constantly shifting geographical and political points, corresponding to the shifts and maneuvers of Soviet policy." When the Soviets blockaded

Berlin in 1948, containment of the Soviet Union became formal U.S. policy.

The fate of Germany had become a source of heated contention between East and West. Aside from denazification and the partitioning of Germany (and Berlin) into four occupied zones, the Allied Powers had agreed on little with regard to the conquered nation. Even denazification proceeded differently in the various zones of occupation. The Americans and British proceeded methodically—the British had tried two million cases by 1948—while the Soviets (and French) went after major criminals and allowed lesser officials to go free. The Soviet Union, hardest hit by the war, took reparations from Germany in the form of booty. The technology-starved Soviets dismantled and removed to Russia 380 factories from the western zones of Berlin before transferring their control to the Western powers. By the summer of 1946, two hundred chemical, paper, and textile factories in the East German zone had likewise been shipped to the Soviet Union. At the same time, the German Communist Party was reestablished, under the control of Walter Ulbricht (1893–1973), and was soon in charge of the political reconstruction of the Soviet zone in eastern Germany.

Although the foreign ministers of the four occupying powers kept meeting in an attempt to arrive at a final peace treaty with Germany, they moved further and further apart. At the same time, the British, French, and Americans gradually began to merge their zones economically and by February 1948 were making plans for unification of these sectors and the formation of a national government. In an effort to secure all of Berlin and to halt

Divided Berlin During the Cold War

FRENCH ZONE

BRITISH ZONE

SOVIET ZONE

U.S. ZONE

GERMAN DEMOCRATIC REPUBLIC

the creation of a West German government, the Soviet Union imposed a blockade of West Berlin that prevented all traffic from entering the city's western zones through Soviet-controlled territory in East Germany.

The Western powers faced a dilemma. Direct military confrontation seemed dangerous, and no one wished to risk World War III.

Therefore, an attempt to break through the blockade with tanks and trucks was ruled out. The solution was to deliver supplies for the city's inhabitants by plane. At its peak, the Berlin Airlift flew 13,000 tons of supplies daily into Berlin. The Soviets, also not wanting war, did not interfere and finally lifted the blockade in May 1949. The blockade of Berlin had severely increased tensions between the United States and the Soviet Union and brought the separation of Germany into two states. The Federal Republic of Germany was formally created from the three Western zones in September 1949, and a month later, the separate German Democratic Republic (GDR) was established in East Germany. Berlin remained a divided city and the source of much contention between East and West.

The search for security in the new world of the Cold War also led to the formation of military alliances. The

➤ **A CITY DIVIDED.** In 1948, U.S. planes airlifted supplies into Berlin to break the blockade that Soviet troops had imposed to isolate the city. Shown here is "Checkpoint Charlie," located at the boundary between the U.S. and Soviet zones of Berlin, just as Soviet roadblocks are about to be removed. The banner at the entrance to the Soviet sector reads, ironically, "The sector of freedom greets the fighters for freedom and right of the Western sectors."

North Atlantic Treaty Organization (NATO) was formed in April 1949 when Belgium, Luxembourg, the Netherlands, France, Britain, Italy, Denmark, Norway, Portugal, and Iceland signed a treaty with the United States and Canada. All the powers agreed to provide mutual assistance if any one of them was attacked. A few years later, West Germany and Turkey joined NATO.

The Eastern European states soon followed suit. In 1949, they formed the Council for Mutual Economic Assistance (COMECON) for economic cooperation. Then, in 1955, Albania, Bulgaria, Czechoslovakia, East Germany, Hungary, Poland, Romania, and the Soviet

Union organized a formal military alliance, the Warsaw Pact. Once again, Europe was tragically divided into hostile alliance systems (see Map 25.1).

There has been considerable historical debate over who bears responsibility for starting the Cold War. In the 1950s, most scholars in the West assumed that the bulk of the blame must fall on the shoulders of Stalin, whose determination to impose Soviet rule on Eastern Europe snuffed out hopes for freedom and self-determination there and aroused justifiable fears of communist expansion in the West. During the next decade, however, revisionist historians—influenced in part by aggressive U.S. policies in Southeast

MAP 25.1 The New European Alliance Systems During the Cold War. This map shows postwar Europe as it was divided during the Cold War into two contending power blocs, the NATO alliance and the Warsaw Pact. Major military and naval bases are indicated by symbols on the map. ➤ Where on the map was the so-called "Iron Curtain"?

Asia—began to argue that the fault lay primarily in Washington, where Truman and his anticommunist advisers abandoned the precepts of Yalta and sought to encircle the Soviet Union with a tier of pliant U.S. client states.

In retrospect, both the United States and the Soviet Union took some unwise steps at the end of World War II. However, both nations were working within a framework conditioned by the past. The rivalry between the two superpowers ultimately stemmed from their different historical perspectives and their irreconcilable political ambitions. Intense competition for political and military supremacy had long been a regular feature of Western civilization. The United States and the Soviet Union were the heirs of that European tradition of power politics, and it should not surprise us that two such different systems would seek to extend their way of life to the rest of the world. Because of its need to secure its western border, the Soviet Union was not prepared to give up the advantages it had gained in Eastern Europe from Germany's defeat. But neither were Western leaders prepared to accept without protest the establishment of a system of Soviet satellites that not only threatened the security of Western Europe but also deeply offended Western sensibilities because of its blatant disregard of the Western concept of human rights.

This does not necessarily mean that both sides bear equal responsibility for starting the Cold War. Some revisionist historians have claimed that the U.S. doctrine of containment was a provocative action that aroused Stalin's suspicions and drove Moscow into a position of hostility toward the West. This charge lacks credibility. As information from the Soviet archives and other sources has become available, it is increasingly clear that Stalin's suspicions of the West were rooted in his Marxist-Leninist worldview and long predated Washington's enunciation of the doctrine of containment. As his foreign minister, Vyacheslav Molotov, once remarked, Soviet policy was inherently aggressive and would be triggered whenever the opportunity offered. Although Stalin apparently had no master plan to advance Soviet power into Western Europe, he was probably prepared to make every effort to do so once the next revolutionary wave arrived. Western leaders were fully justified in reacting to this possibility by strengthening their own lines of defense. On the other hand, a case can be made that in deciding to respond to the Soviet challenge in a primarily military manner, Western leaders overreacted to the situation and virtually guaranteed that the Cold War would be transformed into an arms race that could conceivably result in a new and uniquely destructive war.

COLD WAR IN ASIA

The Cold War was somewhat slower to make its appearance in Asia. At Yalta, Stalin formally agreed to enter the Pacific War against Japan three months after the close of the conflict with Germany. As a reward for Soviet participation in the struggle against Japan, Roosevelt promised that Moscow would be granted "preeminent interests" in Manchuria (interests reminiscent of those possessed by imperial Russia prior to its defeat at the hands of Japan in 1904–1905) and the establishment of a Soviet naval base at Port Arthur. In return, Stalin promised to sign a treaty of alliance with the Republic of China, thus implicitly committing the Soviet Union not to provide the Chinese Communists with support in a possible future civil war. Although many observers would later question Stalin's sincerity in making such a commitment to the vocally anti-Communist Chiang Kai-shek, in Moscow the decision probably had a logic of its own. Stalin had no particular liking for the independent-minded Mao Zedong and indeed did not anticipate a Communist victory in any civil war in China. Only an agreement with Chiang could provide the Soviet Union with a strategically vital economic and political presence in northern China.

Despite these commitments, the Allied agreements soon broke down, and East Asia was sucked into the vortex of the Cold War by the end of the 1940s. The root of the problem lay in the underlying weakness of the Chiang regime, which threatened to create a political vacuum in East Asia that both Moscow and Washington would be tempted to fill.

The Chinese Civil War

As World War II came to an end in the Pacific, relations between the government of Chiang Kai-shek in China and its powerful U.S. ally had become frayed. Although Roosevelt had hoped that republican China would be the keystone of his plan for peace and stability in Asia after the war, U.S. officials became disillusioned with the corruption of Chiang's government and his unwillingness to risk his forces against the Japanese (he hoped to save them for use against the Communists after the war in the Pacific ended), and China was no longer the focus of Washington's close attention as the war came to a close. Nevertheless, U.S. military and economic aid to China had been substantial, and at war's end, the new Truman administration still hoped that it could rely on Chiang to support U.S. postwar goals in the region.

While Chiang Kai-shek wrestled with Japanese aggression and problems of national development, the Communists were building up their strength in northern China. To enlarge their political base, they carried out a "mass line" policy (from the masses to the masses), reducing land rents and confiscating the lands of wealthy landlords. By the end of World War II, twenty to thirty million Chinese were living under the administration of the Communists, and their People's Liberation Army (PLA) included nearly one million troops.

As the war came to an end, world attention began to focus on the prospects for renewed civil strife in China. Members of a U.S. liaison team stationed in Yan'an were impressed by the performance of the Communists, and some recommended that the United States should support them or at least remain neutral in a possible conflict between Communists and Nationalists for control of China. The Truman administration, though skeptical of Chiang's ability to forge a strong and prosperous country, was increasingly concerned about the spread of communism in Europe and tried to find a peaceful solution through the formation of a coalition government of all parties in China.

The effort failed. By 1946, full-scale war between the Nationalist government, now reinstalled in Nanjing, and the Communists resumed. Now Chiang Kai-shek's errors came home to roost. In the countryside, millions of peasants, attracted to the Communists by promises of land and social justice, flocked to serve in Mao Zedong's PLA. In the cities, middle-class Chinese, who were normally hostile to communism, were alienated by Chiang's brutal suppression of all dissent and his government's inability to slow the ruinous rate of inflation or solve the economic problems it caused. With morale dropping in the cities, Chiang's troops began to defect to the Communists. Sometimes whole divisions, officers as well as ordinary soldiers, changed sides. By 1948, the PLA was advancing south

out of Manchuria and had encircled Beijing. Communist troops took the old imperial capital, crossed the Yangtze the following spring, and occupied the commercial hub of Shanghai. During the next few months, Chiang's government and two million of his followers fled to Taiwan, which the Japanese had returned to Chinese control after World War II.

The Truman administration reacted to the spread of Communist power in China with acute discomfort. Washington had no desire to see a Communist government on the mainland, but it had little confidence in Chiang Kai-shek's ability to realize Roosevelt's dream of a strong, united, and prosperous China. In December 1945, President Truman sent General George C. Marshall to China in a last-ditch effort to bring about a peaceful settlement, but anti-Communist elements in the Republic of China resisted U.S. efforts to create a coalition government with the Chinese Communist Party (CCP). During the next two years, the United States gave limited military support to Chiang's regime but refused to commit U.S. power to guarantee its survival. The administration's hands-off

⫸ A PLEDGE OF ETERNAL FRIENDSHIP. After the Communist victory in the Chinese civil war, Chairman Mao Zedong traveled to Moscow, where in 1950 he negotiated a treaty of friendship and cooperation with the Soviet Union. Here Joseph Stalin and his eventual successor, Georgy Malenkov, observe as Chinese Foreign Minister Zhou Enlai signs the treaty. Behind the pledges of friendship, a long tradition of mutual distrust divided the two countries, which almost went to war over border disputes in the late 1970s.

⫸ CHIANG KAI-SHEK AND MAO ZEDONG EXCHANGE A TOAST. After World War II, the United States sent General George C. Marshall to China in an effort to prevent civil war between Chiang Kai-shek's government and the Communists. Marshall's initial success was symbolized by this toast between Chiang (at the right) and Mao. But suspicion ran too deep, and soon conflict ensued, leading to a Communist victory in 1949. Chiang Kai-shek's government retreated to the island of Taiwan.

"IT'S NOT OUR FAULT"

In 1949, with China about to fall under the control of the Communists, President Harry S Truman instructed the State Department to prepare a white paper explaining why the U.S. policy of seeking to avoid a Communist victory in China had failed. The authors of the paper concluded that responsibility lay at the door of Nationalist Chinese leader Chiang Kai-shek and that there was nothing the United States could have done to alter the result. Most China observers today would accept that assessment, but it did little at the time to deflect criticism of the administration for selling out the interests of our ally in China.

U.S. STATE DEPARTMENT WHITE PAPER ON CHINA, 1949

When peace came the United States was confronted with three possible alternatives in China: (1) it could have pulled out lock, stock, and barrel; (2) it could have intervened militarily on a major scale to assist the Nationalists to destroy the Communists; (3) it could, while assisting the Nationalists to assert their authority over as much of China as possible, endeavor to avoid a civil war by working for a compromise between the two sides.

The first alternative would, and I believe American public opinion at the time so felt, have represented an abandonment of our international responsibilities and of our traditional policy of friendship for China before we had made a determined effort to be of assistance. The second alternative policy, while it may look attractive theoretically, in retrospect, was wholly impracticable. The Nationalists had been unable to destroy the Communists during the ten years before the war. Now after the war the Nationalists were, as indicated above, weakened, demoralized, and unpopular. They had quickly dissipated their popular support and prestige in the areas liberated from the Japanese

by the conduct of their civil and military officials. The Communists on the other hand were much stronger than they had ever been and were in control of most of North China. Because of the ineffectiveness of the Nationalist forces, which was later to be tragically demonstrated, the Communists probably could have been dislodged only by American arms. It is obvious that the American people would not have sanctioned such a colossal commitment of our armies in 1945 or later. We therefore came to the third alternative policy whereunder we faced the facts of the situation and attempted to assist in working out a *modus vivendi* which would avert civil war but nevertheless preserve and even increase the influence of the National Government. . . .

The distrust of the leaders of both the Nationalist and Communist Parties for each other proved too deep-seated to permit final agreement, notwithstanding temporary truces and apparently promising negotiations. The Nationalists, furthermore, embarked in 1946 on an overambitious military campaign in the face of warnings by General Marshall that it not only would fail but would plunge China into economic chaos and eventually destroy the National Government. . . .

The unfortunate but inescapable fact is that the ominous result of the civil war in China was beyond the control of the government of the United States. Nothing that this country did or could have done within the reasonable limits of its capabilities could have changed that result; nothing that was left undone by this country has contributed to it. It was the product of internal Chinese forces, forces which this country tried to influence but could not. A decision was arrived at within China, if only a decision by default.

---

policy deeply angered many members of Congress, who charged that the White House was "soft on communism" and declared further that Roosevelt had betrayed Chiang Kai-shek at Yalta by granting privileges in Manchuria to the Soviet Union. In their view, Soviet troops had hindered the dispatch of Chiang's forces to the area and provided the PLA with weapons to use against its rivals.

In later years, sources in both Moscow and Beijing suggested that the Soviet Union gave little assistance to the CCP in its struggle against the Nanjing regime. In fact, Stalin periodically advised Mao against undertaking the effort. Although Communist forces undoubtedly received some assistance from Soviet occupation troops in Manchuria, their victory ultimately stemmed from conditions inside China, not from the intervention of outside powers. So indeed argued the Truman administration in 1949, when it issued a white paper that placed most of the blame for the debacle at the feet of Chiang Kai-shek's regime (see the box above).

Many Americans, however, did not agree. With the Communist victory, Asia became a theater of the Cold War and an integral element of American politics. During the spring of 1950, under pressure from Congress and public opinion to define U.S. interests in Asia, the Truman administration adopted a new national security policy that implied that the United States would take whatever steps were necessary to stem the further expansion of communism in the region.

The Korean War

Communist leaders in China, from their new capital of Beijing, hoped that their accession to power in 1949 would bring about an era of peace in the region and permit their new government to concentrate on domestic goals. But the desire for peace was tempered by their determination to erase a century of humiliation at the hands of imperialist powers and to restore the traditional outer frontiers of the empire. In addition to recovering territories that had been part of the Manchu Empire, such as Manchuria, Taiwan, and Tibet, the Chinese leaders also hoped to restore Chinese influence in former tributary areas such as Korea and Vietnam.

It soon became clear that these two goals were not always compatible. Negotiations with the Soviet Union led to Soviet recognition of Chinese sovereignty over Manchuria and Xinjiang (the desolate lands north of Tibet that were known as Chinese Turkestan because many of the peoples in the area were of Turkish origin), although the Soviets retained a measure of economic influence in both areas. Chinese troops occupied Tibet in 1950 and brought it under Chinese administration for the first time in more than a century. But in Korea and Taiwan, China's efforts to re-create the imperial buffer zone provoked new conflicts with foreign powers.

The problem of Taiwan was a consequence of the Cold War. As the civil war in China came to an end, the Truman administration appeared determined to avoid entanglement in China's internal affairs and indicated that it would not seek to prevent a Communist takeover of the island, now occupied by Chiang Kai-shek's Republic of China. But as tensions between the United States and the new Chinese government escalated during the winter of 1949–1950, influential figures in the United States began to argue that Taiwan was crucial to U.S. defense strategy in the Pacific.

The outbreak of war in Korea also helped bring the Cold War to East Asia. After the Sino-Japanese War in 1894–1895, Korea, long a Chinese tributary, had fallen increasingly under the rival influences of Japan and Russia. After the Japanese defeated the Russians in 1905, Korea became an integral part of the Japanese Empire and remained so until 1945. The removal of Korea from Japanese control had been one of the stated objectives of the Allies in World War II, and on the eve of Japanese surrender in August 1945, the Soviet Union and the United States agreed to divide the country into two separate occupation zones at the 38th parallel. They originally planned to hold national elections after the restoration of peace to reunify Korea under an independent government. But as U.S.–Soviet relations deteriorated, two separate governments emerged in Korea, a Communist one in the north and an anti-Communist one in the south.

Tensions between the two governments ran high along the dividing line, and on June 25, 1950, with the apparent approval of Stalin, North Korean troops invaded the south. The Truman administration immediately ordered U.S. naval and air forces to support South Korea, and the United Nations Security Council (with the Soviet delegate absent to protest the refusal of the UN to assign China's seat to the new government in Beijing) passed a resolution calling on member nations to jointly resist the invasion. By September, UN forces under the command of U.S. General Douglas MacArthur marched northward across the 38th parallel with the aim of unifying Korea under a single, noncommunist government.

President Truman worried that by approaching the Chinese border at the Yalu River, the UN troops could trigger Chinese intervention, but MacArthur assured him that China would not respond. In November, however, Chinese "volunteer" forces intervened in force on the side of North Korea and drove the UN troops southward in disarray. A static defense line was eventually established near the original dividing line at the 38th parallel (see Map 25.2), although the war continued.

To many Americans, the Chinese intervention in Korea was clear evidence that China intended to promote communism throughout Asia, and recent evidence suggests that Mao was convinced that a revolutionary wave was on the rise in Asia. In fact, however, China's decision to enter the war was probably motivated in large part by the fear that hostile U.S. forces might be stationed on the Chinese frontier and perhaps even launch an attack across the border. MacArthur intensified such fears by calling

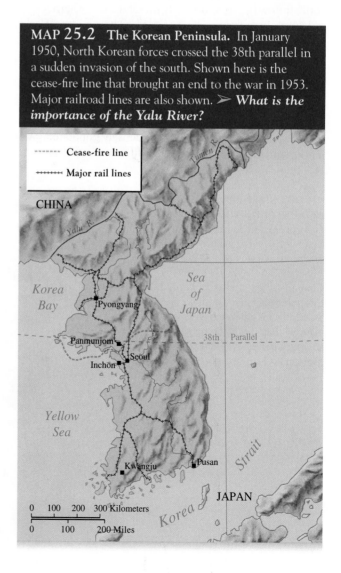

MAP 25.2 The Korean Peninsula. In January 1950, North Korean forces crossed the 38th parallel in a sudden invasion of the south. Shown here is the cease-fire line that brought an end to the war in 1953. Major railroad lines are also shown. ➤ *What is the importance of the Yalu River?*

publicly for air attacks on Manchurian cities in preparation for an attack on Communist China. In any case, the outbreak of the Korean War was particularly unfortunate for China. Immediately after the invasion, President Truman dispatched the U.S. Seventh fleet to the Taiwan Strait to prevent a possible Chinese invasion of Taiwan. Even more unfortunate, the invasion hardened Western attitudes against the new Chinese government and led to China's isolation from the major capitalist powers for two decades. As a result, China was cut off from all forms of economic and technological assistance and was forced to rely almost entirely on the Soviet Union, with which it had signed a pact of friendship and cooperation in early 1950.

Conflict in Indochina

During the mid-1950s, China sought to build contacts with the nonsocialist world. A cease-fire agreement brought the Korean War to an end in July 1953, and China signaled its desire to live in peaceful coexistence with other independent countries in the region. But a relatively minor conflict now began to intensify on China's southern flank, in French Indochina. The struggle had begun after World War II, when Ho Chi Minh's Indochinese Communist Party, at the head of a multiparty nationalist alliance called the Vietminh Front, seized power in northern and central Vietnam after the surrender of imperial Japan. After abortive negotiations between Ho's government and the returning French, war broke out in December 1946. French forces occupied the cities and the densely populated lowlands, while the Vietminh took refuge in the mountains.

For three years, the Vietminh gradually increased in size and effectiveness. What had begun as an anticolonial struggle by Ho's Vietminh Front against the French after World War II became entangled in the Cold War in the early 1950s, when both the United States and the new Communist government in China began to intervene in the conflict to promote their own national security objectives. China began to provide military assistance to the Vietminh to protect its own borders from hostile forces. The Americans supported the French but pressured the French government to prepare for an eventual transition to non-Communist governments in Vietnam, Laos, and Cambodia.

At the Geneva Conference in 1954, with the French public tired of fighting the "dirty war" in Indochina, the French agreed to a peace settlement with the Vietminh. Vietnam was temporarily divided into a northern Communist half (known as the Democratic Republic of Vietnam) and a non-Communist southern half based in Saigon (eventually to be known as the Republic of Vietnam). Elections were to be held in two years to create a unified government. Cambodia and Laos were both declared independent under neutral governments.

China had played an active role in bringing about the settlement and clearly hoped that it would reduce tensions in the area, but subsequent efforts to improve relations between China and the United States foundered on the issue of Taiwan. In the fall of 1954, the United States signed a mutual security treaty with the Republic of China guaranteeing U.S. military support in case of an invasion of Taiwan. When Beijing demanded U.S. withdrawal from Taiwan as the price for improved relations, diplomatic talks between the two countries collapsed.

⇒ HO CHI MINH PLANS AN ATTACK ON THE FRENCH. Unlike many peoples in Southeast Asia, the Vietnamese had to fight for their independence after World War II. That fight was led by the talented Communist leader Ho Chi Minh. In this photograph, Ho (in the center), assisted by his chief strategist, Vo Nguyen Giap (at the far right), plans an attack on French positions in Vietnam.

FROM CONFRONTATION TO COEXISTENCE

The decade of the 1950s opened with the world teetering on the edge of a nuclear holocaust. The Soviet Union had detonated its first nuclear device in 1949, and the two blocs—capitalist and socialist—viewed each other across an ideological divide that grew increasingly bitter with each passing year. Yet as the decade drew to a close, a measure of sanity crept into the Cold War, and the leaders of the major world powers began to seek ways to coexist in a peaceful and stable world (see Map 25.3).

Khrushchev and the Era of Peaceful Coexistence

The first clear sign of change occurred after Stalin's death in early 1953. His successor, Georgy Malenkov (1902–1988), openly hoped to improve relations with the Western powers in order to reduce defense expenditures and shift government spending to growing consumer

needs. Nikita Khrushchev (1894–1971), who replaced Malenkov in 1955, continued his predecessor's efforts to reduce tensions with the West and improve the living standards of the Soviet people.

In an adroit public relations touch, Khrushchev promoted an appeal for a policy of "peaceful coexistence" with the West. In 1955, he surprisingly agreed to negotiate an end to the postwar occupation of Austria by the victorious allies and allow the creation of a neutral country with strong cultural and economic ties with the West. He also called for a reduction in defense expenditures and reduced the size of the Soviet armed forces.

At first, Washington was suspicious of Khrushchev's motives, especially after the Soviet crackdown in Hungary in the fall of 1956 (see Chapter 26). A new crisis over Berlin added to the tension. The Soviet Union had launched its first intercontinental ballistic missile (ICBM) in August 1957, arousing U.S. fears of a missile gap between the United States and the Soviet Union. Khrushchev attempted to take advantage of the U.S. frenzy over missiles to solve the problem of West Berlin, which had remained a "Western island" of prosperity

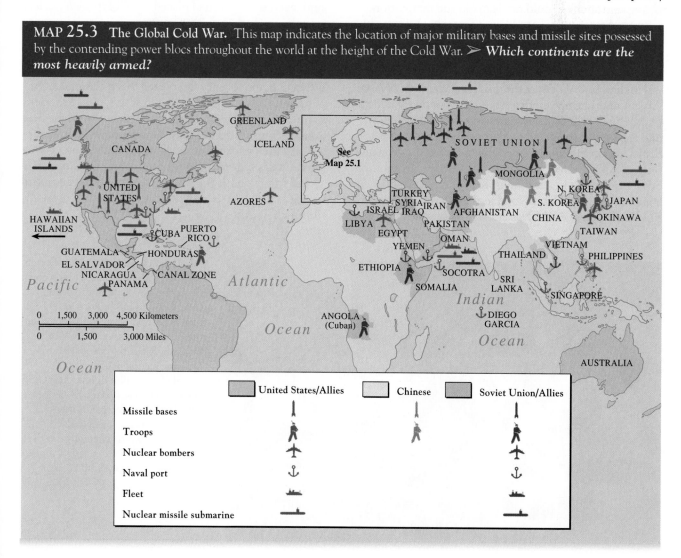

MAP **25.3** **The Global Cold War.** This map indicates the location of major military bases and missile sites possessed by the contending power blocs throughout the world at the height of the Cold War. ➢ *Which continents are the most heavily armed?*

inside the relatively poverty-stricken state of East Germany. Many East Germans sought to escape to West Germany by fleeing through West Berlin, a serious blot on the credibility of the GDR and a potential source of instability in East-West relations. In November 1958, Khrushchev announced that unless the West removed its forces from West Berlin within six months, he would turn over control of the access routes to the East Germans. Unwilling to accept an ultimatum that would have abandoned West Berlin to the Communists, President Dwight D. Eisenhower and the West stood firm, and Khrushchev eventually backed down.

Despite such periodic crises in East-West relations, there were tantalizing signs that an era of true peaceful coexistence between the two power blocs could be achieved. In the late 1950s, the United States and the Soviet Union initiated a cultural exchange program. While the Leningrad Ballet appeared at theaters in the United States, Benny Goodman and the film *West Side Story* played in Moscow. In 1958, Khrushchev visited the United States and had a brief but friendly encounter with President Eisenhower at the presidential retreat in northern Maryland.

Yet Khrushchev could rarely avoid the temptation to gain an advantage over the United States in the competition for influence throughout the world, and this resulted in an unstable relationship between the two superpowers. Moscow also took every opportunity to promote its interests in the Third World, as the unaligned countries of Asia, Africa, and Latin America were now popularly called. Unlike Stalin, Khrushchev viewed the dismantling of colonial regimes in the area as a potential advantage for the Soviet Union and sought especially to exploit the deep suspicions of the United States in Latin America. To improve Soviet influence in such areas, Khrushchev established alliances with key Third World leaders such as Sukarno in Indonesia, Gamel Abdul Nasser in Egypt, Jawaharlal Nehru

in India, and Fidel Castro in Cuba. In January 1961, just as John F. Kennedy assumed the U.S. presidency, Khrushchev unnerved the new president at an informal summit meeting in Vienna by declaring that the Soviet Union would provide active support to national liberation movements throughout the world. There were rising fears in Washington of Soviet meddling in such sensitive trouble spots as Southeast Asia, Central Africa, and the Caribbean.

The Cuban Missile Crisis

The Cold War confrontation between the United States and the Soviet Union reached frightening levels during the Cuban Missile Crisis. In 1959, a left-wing revolutionary named Fidel Castro (b. 1927) overthrew the Cuban dictator Fulgencio Batista and established a Soviet-supported totalitarian regime. After the utter failure of a U.S.-supported attempt to overthrow Castro's regime in 1961 (known as the "Bay of Pigs" incident), the Soviet Union decided to place nuclear missiles in Cuba in 1962. The United States was not prepared to allow nuclear weapons within striking distance of the American mainland, even though it had placed some of its own nuclear weapons in Turkey, within range of the Soviet Union. Khrushchev was quick to point out that "your rockets are in Turkey. You are worried by Cuba . . . because it is 90 miles from the American coast. But Turkey is next to us."[5] When U.S. intelligence discovered that a Soviet fleet carrying missiles was indeed heading to Cuba, President Kennedy decided to blockade Cuba and prevent the fleet from reaching its destination. This approach to the problem had the benefit of delaying confrontation and giving the two sides time to find a peaceful solution. Khrushchev agreed to turn back the fleet if Kennedy pledged not to invade Cuba. In a conciliatory letter to Kennedy, Khrushchev wrote:

THE KITCHEN DEBATE. During the late 1950s, the United States and the Soviet Union sought to defuse Cold War tensions by encouraging cultural exchanges between the two countries. On one occasion, U.S. Vice President Richard M. Nixon visited Moscow in conjunction with the arrival of an exhibit to introduce U.S. culture and society to the Soviet people. Here Nixon lectures Soviet Communist Party chief Nikita Khrushchev on the technology of the U.S. kitchen. To Nixon's left is future Soviet president Leonid Brezhnev.

AP/Wide World Photos

A PLEA FOR PEACEFUL COEXISTENCE

The Soviet leader Vladimir Lenin had contended that war between the socialist and imperialist camps was inevitable because the imperialists would never give up without a fight. That assumption had probably guided the thoughts of Joseph Stalin, who told colleagues shortly after World War II that a new war would break out in fifteen to twenty years. But Stalin's successor, Nikita Khrushchev, feared that a new world conflict could result in a nuclear holocaust and contended that the two sides must learn to coexist, although peaceful competition would continue. In this speech given in Beijing in 1959, Khrushchev attempted to persuade the Chinese to accept his views. But Chinese leaders argued that the "imperialist nature" of the United States would never change and warned that they would not accept any peace agreement in which they had no part.

KHRUSHCHEV'S SPEECH TO THE CHINESE, 1959

Comrades! Socialism brings to the people peace—that greatest blessing. The greater the strength of the camp of socialism grows, the greater will be its possibilities for successfully defending the cause of peace on this earth. The forces of socialism are already so great that real possibilities are being created for excluding war as a means of solving international disputes. . . .

When I spoke with President Eisenhower—and I have just returned from the United States of America—I got the impression that the President of the U.S.A.—and not a few people support him—understands the need to relax international tension. . . .

There is only one way of preserving peace—that is the road of peaceful coexistence of states with different social systems. The question stands thus: either peaceful coexistence or war with its catastrophic consequences. Now, with the present relation of forces between socialism and capitalism being in favor of socialism, he who would continue the "cold war" is moving towards his own destruction. . . .

Already in the first years of the Soviet power the great Lenin defined the general line of our foreign policy as being directed towards the peaceful coexistence of states with different social systems. For a long time, the ruling circles of the Western Powers rejected these truly humane principles. Nevertheless the principles of peaceful coexistence made their way into the hearts of the vast majority of mankind. . . .

It is not at all because capitalism is still strong that the socialist countries speak out against war, and for peaceful coexistence. No, we have no need of war at all. If the people do not want it, even such a noble and progressive system as socialism cannot be imposed by force of arms. The socialist countries therefore, while carrying through a consistently peace-loving policy, concentrate their efforts on peaceful construction; they fire the hearts of men by the force of their example in building socialism, and thus lead them to follow in their footsteps. The question of when this or that country will take the path to socialism is decided by its own people. This, for us, is the holy of holies.

We and you ought not to pull on the ends of the rope in which you have tied the knot of war, because the more the two of us pull, the tighter that knot will be tied. And a moment may come when that knot will be tied too tight that even he who tied it will not have the strength to untie it. . . . Let us not only relax the forces pulling on the ends of the rope; let us take measures to untie that knot. We are ready for this.[6]

The intense feeling that the world might have been annihilated in a few days had a profound influence on both sides. A hotline between Moscow and Washington was installed in 1963 to expedite communications between the two superpowers in time of crisis. In the same year, the two powers agreed to ban nuclear tests in the atmosphere, a step that served to lessen the tensions between the two nations.

The Sino-Soviet Dispute

Nikita Khrushchev had launched his slogan of peaceful coexistence as a means of improving relations with the capitalist powers; ironically, one result of the campaign was to undermine Moscow's ties with its close ally China. During Stalin's lifetime, Beijing had accepted the Soviet Union as the acknowledged leader of the socialist camp. After Stalin's death, however, relations began to deteriorate. Part of the reason may have been Mao Zedong's contention that he, as the most experienced Marxist leader, should now be acknowledged as the most authoritative voice within the socialist community. But another determining factor was that just as Soviet policies were moving toward moderation, China's were becoming more radical.

Several other issues were involved, including territorial disputes and China's unhappiness with limited Soviet economic assistance. But the key sources of disagreement involved ideology and the Cold War. Chinese leaders were convinced that the successes of the Soviet space program confirmed that the socialists were now technologically superior to the capitalists (the East wind, trumpeted the Chinese official press, had now triumphed over the West wind), and they urged Khrushchev to go on the offensive to promote world revolution. Specifically, China wanted Soviet assistance in retaking Taiwan from Chiang Kai-shek. But Khrushchev was trying to improve relations with the West and rejected Chinese demands for support against Taiwan (see the box above).

COMBATING THE AMERICANS

In December 1960, the National Front for the Liberation of South Vietnam, or NLF, was born. Composed of political and social leaders opposed to the anti-Communist government of Ngo Dinh Diem in South Vietnam, it operated under the direction of the Vietnam Workers' Party in North Vietnam and served as the formal representative of revolutionary forces in the South throughout the remainder of the Vietnam War. When, in the spring of 1965, U.S. President Lyndon Johnson began to dispatch U.S. combat troops to Vietnam to prevent a Communist victory there, the NLF issued the following declaration.

STATEMENT OF THE NATIONAL LIBERATION FRONT OF SOUTH VIETNAM

American imperialist aggression against South Vietnam and interference in its internal affairs have now continued for more than ten years. More American troops and supplies, including missile units, Marines, B-57 strategic bombers, and mercenaries from South Korea, Taiwan, the Philippines, Australia, Malaysia, etc., have been brought to South Vietnam. . . .

The Saigon puppet regime, paid servant of the United States, is guilty of the most heinous crimes. These despicable traitors, these boot-lickers of American imperialism, have brought the enemy into our country. They have brought to South Vietnam armed forces of the United States and its satellites to kill our compatriots, occupy and ravage our sacred soil and enslave our people.

The Vietnamese, the peoples of all Indo-China and Southeast Asia, supporters of peace and justice in every part of the world, have raised their voice in angry protest against this criminal unprovoked aggression of the United States imperialists.

In the present extremely grave situation, the South Vietnam National Liberation Front considers it necessary to proclaim anew its firm and unswerving determination to resist the U.S. imperialists and fight for the salvation of our country. . . . [It] will continue to rely chiefly on its own forces and potentialities, but it is prepared to accept any assistance, moral and material, including arms and other military equipment, from all the socialist countries, from nationalist countries, from international organizations, and from the peace-loving peoples of the world.

By the end of the 1950s, the Soviet Union had begun to remove its advisers from China, and in 1961, the dispute broke into the open. Increasingly isolated, China voiced its hostility to what Mao described as the "urban industrialized countries" (which included the Soviet Union) and portrayed itself as the leader of the "rural underdeveloped countries" of Asia, Africa, and Latin America in a global struggle against imperialist oppression. In effect, China had applied Mao Zedong's famous concept of people's war in an international framework.

The Second Indochina War

China's radicalism was intensified in the early 1960s by the outbreak of renewed war in Indochina. The Eisenhower administration had opposed the peace settlement at Geneva in 1954, which divided Vietnam temporarily into two separate regroupment zones, specifically because the provision for future national elections opened up the possibility that the entire country would come under Communist rule. But Eisenhower had been unwilling to introduce U.S. military forces to continue the conflict without the full support of the British and the French, who preferred to seek a negotiated settlement. In the end, Washington promised not to break the provisions of the agreement but refused to commit itself to the results.

During the next several months, the United States began to provide aid to a new government in South Vietnam. Under the leadership of the anti-Communist politician Ngo Dinh Diem, the South Vietnamese government began to root out dissidents. With the tacit approval of the United States, Diem refused to hold the national elections called for by the Geneva Accords. It was widely anticipated, even in Washington, that the Communists would win such elections. In 1959, Ho Chi Minh, despairing of the peaceful unification of the country under Communist rule, returned to a policy of revolutionary war in the south.

By 1963, South Vietnam was on the verge of collapse. Diem's autocratic methods and inattention to severe economic inequality had alienated much of the population, and revolutionary forces, popularly known as the Viet Cong (Vietnamese Communists), expanded their influence throughout much of the country. In the fall of 1963, with the approval of the Kennedy administration, senior military officers overthrew the Diem regime. But factionalism kept the new military leadership from reinvigorating the struggle against the insurgent forces, and the situation in South Vietnam grew worse. By early 1965, the Viet Cong, whose ranks were now swelled by military units infiltrating from North Vietnam, were on the verge of seizing control of the entire country. In March, President Lyndon Johnson decided to send U.S. combat troops to South Vietnam to prevent a total defeat for the anticommunist government in Saigon (see the box above).

A MANUAL FOR REVOLUTIONARIES

*I*n the 1920s, Mao Zedong formulated his theory of people's war, which held that in preindustrial societies, revolution could be more readily fomented in the countryside than in the cities. Forty years later, Lin Biao, Mao's colleague and the minister of defense, placed the concept in an international framework, arguing that the rural nations of the world (led, of course, by China) would defeat the industrialized "urban" nations (represented by the United States and the Soviet Union). This is an excerpt from the article in which Lin Biao presented his thesis. His message was also intended as a signal to North Vietnamese leaders not to escalate the conflict in South Vietnam to a point that might involve a direct confrontation with the United States.

LIN BIAO, "LONG LIVE THE VICTORY OF PEOPLE'S WAR"

Many countries and peoples in Asia, Africa, and Latin America are now being subjected to aggression and enslavement on a serious scale by the imperialists headed by the United States and their lackeys. The basic political and economic conditions in many of these countries have many similarities to those that prevailed in old China. As in China, the peasant question is extremely important in these regions. The peasants constitute the main force of the national-democratic revolution against the imperialists and their lackeys. In committing aggression against these countries, the imperialists usually begin by seizing the big cities and the main lines of communication. But they are unable to bring the vast countryside completely under their control. The countryside, and the countryside alone, can provide the broad areas in which the revolutionaries can maneuver freely. The countryside, and the countryside alone, can provide the revolutionary basis from which the revolutionaries can go forward to final victory. Precisely for

this reason, Mao Tse-tung's theory of establishing revolutionary base areas in the rural districts and encircling the cities from the countryside is attracting more and more attention among the people in these regions.

Taking the entire globe, if North America and Western Europe can be called "the cities of the world," then Asia, Africa, and Latin America constitute "the rural areas of the world." Since World War II, the proletarian revolutionary movement has for various reasons been temporarily held back in the North American and West European capitalist countries, while the people's revolutionary movement in Asia, Africa, and Latin America has been growing vigorously. In a sense, the contemporary world revolution also presents a picture of the encirclement of cities by the rural areas. In the final analysis, the whole cause of world revolution hinges on the revolutionary struggles of the Asian, African, and Latin American peoples, who make up the overwhelming majority of the world's population. The socialist countries should regard it as their internationalist duty to support the people's revolutionary struggles in Asia, Africa, and Latin America. . . .

Ours is the epoch in which world capitalism and imperialism are heading for their doom and communism is marching to victory. Comrade Mao Tse-tung's theory of people's war is not only a product of the Chinese revolution, but has also the characteristic of our epoch. The new experience gained in the people's revolutionary struggles in various countries since World War II has provided continuous evidence that Mao Tse-tung's thought is a common asset of the revolutionary people of the whole world. This is the great international significance of the thought of Mao Tse-tung.

Chinese leaders observed the gradual escalation of the conflict in South Vietnam with mixed feelings. They were undoubtedly pleased to have a firm Communist ally—one that had in many ways followed the path of Mao Zedong—just beyond their southern frontier. Yet they were concerned that renewed bloodshed in South Vietnam might enmesh China in a new conflict with the United States. Nor did they welcome the specter of a powerful and ambitious united Vietnam, which might wish to extend its influence throughout mainland Southeast Asia, an area that Beijing considered its own backyard.

Chinese leaders therefore tiptoed delicately through the minefield of the Indochina conflict. As the war escalated in 1964 and 1965, Beijing publicly announced that the Chinese people fully supported their comrades seeking national liberation but privately assured Washington that

China would not directly enter the conflict unless U.S. forces threatened its southern border. Beijing also refused to cooperate fully with Moscow in shipping Soviet goods to North Vietnam through Chinese territory (see the box above).

Despite its dismay at the lack of full support from China, the Communist government in North Vietnam responded to U.S. escalation by infiltrating more of its own regular force troops into the south, and by 1968, the war had reached a stalemate. The Communists were not strong enough to overthrow the government in Saigon, whose weakness was shielded by the presence of half a million U.S. troops, but President Johnson was reluctant to engage in all-out war on North Vietnam for fear of provoking a global nuclear conflict. In the fall, after the Communist-led Tet offensive aroused intense antiwar protests in the United States, peace negotiations began in Paris.

NIXON PLAYS HIS CHINA CARD

*I*n February 1972, President Richard Nixon visited mainland China, ending twenty years of U.S. unwillingness to recognize the existence of the Communist regime. In a joint communiqué issued in Shanghai at the close of the visit, the two nations agreed to set aside the question of Taiwan, which could not be resolved, and to seek common ground on other issues. In the communiqué, Nixon agreed that the Taiwan issue had to be resolved by the Chinese people themselves.

THE SHANGHAI COMMUNIQUÉ

The sides reviewed the long-standing serious disputes between China and the United States.

The Chinese side reaffirmed its position: The Taiwan question is the crucial question obstructing the normalization of relations between China and the United States; the Government of the People's Republic of China is the sole legal government of China; Taiwan is a province of China which has long been returned to the motherland; the liberation of Taiwan is China's internal affair in which no other country had the right to interfere; and all U.S. forces and military installations must be withdrawn from Taiwan. The Chinese government firmly opposes any activities which aim at the creation of "one China, one Taiwan," "one China, two governments," "two Chinas" and "independent Taiwan" or advocate that "the status of Taiwan remains to be determined."

The U.S. side declared: The United States acknowledges that all Chinese on either side of the Taiwan Strait maintain there is but one China and that Taiwan is a part of China. The United States Government does not challenge that position. It reaffirms its interest in a peaceful settlement of the Taiwan question by the Chinese themselves. With this prospect in mind, it affirms the ultimate objective of the withdrawal of all U.S. forces and military installations from Taiwan. In the meantime, it will progressively reduce its forces and military installations on Taiwan as the tension in the area diminishes.

➤ **A U.S. PRISONER OF WAR IN NORTH VIETNAM.** During their struggle against the Saigon regime and the United States, Communist leaders in North Vietnam made active use of women in their armed forces. Women served as intelligence agents, as members of artillery units, and sometimes even in guerrilla detachments. Women were especially effective as bearers of provisions to the battlefront, earning the sobriquet "the long-haired army." Shown here is a very young member of a local militia unit bringing a downed U.S. airman to captivity in North Vietnam.

© Hulton Archive/Getty Images

Richard Nixon came into the White House in 1969 on a pledge to bring an honorable end to the Vietnam War. With U.S. public opinion sharply divided on the issue, he began to withdraw U.S. troops while continuing to hold peace talks in Paris. But the centerpiece of his strategy was to improve relations with China and thus undercut Chinese support for the North Vietnamese war effort. During the 1960s, relations between Moscow and Beijing had reached a point of extreme tension, and thousands of troops were stationed on both sides of their long common frontier. To intimidate their Communist rivals, Soviet sources hinted that they might launch a preemptive strike to destroy Chinese nuclear facilities in Xinjiang. Sensing an opportunity to split the two onetime allies, Nixon sent his emissary Henry Kissinger on a secret trip to China. Responding to assurances that the United States was determined to withdraw from Indochina and hoped to improve relations with the mainland regime, Chinese leaders invited President Nixon to visit China in early 1972 (see the box above).

Incensed at the apparent betrayal by their close allies, North Vietnamese leaders decided to seek a peaceful settlement of the war in the south. In January 1973, a peace treaty was signed in Paris calling for the removal of all U.S. forces from South Vietnam. In return, the Communists agreed to seek a political settlement of their differences with the Saigon regime. But negotiations between north and south over the political settlement soon broke down, and in early 1975, the Communists resumed the offensive. At the end of April, under a massive assault by North Vietnamese military forces, the South Vietnamese gov-

AP/Wide World Photos

 **A BRIDGE ACROSS THE COLD WAR DIVIDE.**   In January 1972, U.S. President Richard Nixon star-
tled the world by visiting mainland China and beginning the long process of restoring normal relations
between the two countries. Despite Nixon's reputation as a devout anti-Communist, the visit was a success as the two sides agreed to put aside their most bitter differences in an effort to reduce tensions in
Asia. Here Nixon and Chinese leader Mao Zedong exchange a historic handshake in Beijing.

ernment surrendered. A year later, the country was unified
under Communist rule.

The Communist victory in Vietnam was a severe
humiliation for the United States, but its strategic impact
was limited because of the new relationship with China.
During the next decade, Sino-American relations continued to improve. In 1979, diplomatic ties were established between the two countries under an arrangement
whereby the United States renounced its mutual security treaty with the Republic of China in return for a
pledge from China to seek reunification with Taiwan by
peaceful means. By the end of the 1970s, China and the
United States had forged a "strategic relationship" in
which they would cooperate against the common threat
of Soviet hegemony in Asia.

AN ERA OF EQUIVALENCE

When the Johnson administration sent U.S. combat
troops to South Vietnam in 1965, Washington's main concern was with Beijing, not Moscow. By the mid-1960s,
U.S. officials viewed the Soviet Union as an essentially
conservative power, more concerned with protecting its
vast empire than with expanding its borders. In fact, U.S.
policy makers periodically sought Soviet assistance in seeking a peaceful settlement of the Vietnam War. So long as
Khrushchev was in power, they found a receptive ear in
Moscow. Khrushchev was firmly dedicated to promoting
peaceful coexistence (at least on his terms) and sternly

advised the North Vietnamese against a resumption of revolutionary war in South Vietnam.

After October 1964, when Khrushchev was replaced by a new leadership headed by party chief Leonid Brezhnev (1906–1982) and Prime Minister Alexei Kosygin (1904–1980), Soviet attitudes about Vietnam became more ambivalent. On the one hand, the new Soviet leaders had no desire to see the Vietnam conflict poison relations between the great powers. On the other hand, Moscow was eager to demonstrate its support for the North Vietnamese to deflect Chinese charges that the Soviet Union had betrayed the interests of the oppressed peoples of the world. As a result, Soviet officials publicly voiced sympathy for the U.S. predicament in Vietnam but put no pressure on their allies to bring an end to the war. Indeed, the Soviet Union became Hanoi's main supplier of advanced military equipment in the final years of the war.

Still, under Brezhnev and Kosygin, the Soviet Union continued to pursue peaceful coexistence with the West and adopted a generally cautious posture in foreign affairs. By the early 1970s, a new age in Soviet-American relations had emerged, often referred to by the French term *détente*, meaning a reduction of tensions between the two sides. One symbol of the new relationship was the Antiballistic Missile (ABM) Treaty, often called SALT I (for Strategic Arms Limitation Talks), signed in 1972, in which the two nations agreed to limit the size of their ABM systems.

Washington's objective in pursuing the treaty was to make it unlikely that either superpower could win a nuclear exchange by launching a preemptive strike against the other. U.S. officials believed that a policy of "equivalence," in which there was a roughly equal power balance on each side, was the best way to avoid a nuclear confrontation. Détente was pursued in other ways as well. When President Nixon took office in 1969, he sought to increase trade and cultural contacts with the Soviet Union. His purpose was to set up a series of "linkages" in U.S.-Soviet relations that would persuade Moscow of the economic and social benefits of maintaining good relations with the West.

A symbol of that new relationship was the Helsinki Agreement. Signed in 1975 by the United States, Canada, and all European nations on both sides of the Iron Curtain, these accords recognized all borders in Europe that had been established since the end of World War II, thereby formally acknowledging for the first time the Soviet sphere of influence in Eastern Europe. The Helsinki Agreement also committed the signatories to recognize and protect the human rights of their citizens, a clear effort by the Western states to improve the performance of the Soviet Union and its allies in that arena.

An End to Détente?

Protection of human rights became one of the major foreign policy goals of the next U.S. president, Jimmy Carter (b. 1924). Ironically, just at the point when U.S. involvement in Vietnam came to an end and relations with China began to improve, U.S.-Soviet relations began to sour, for several reasons. Some Americans had become increasingly concerned about aggressive new tendencies in Soviet foreign policy. The first indication came in Africa. Soviet influence was on the rise in Somalia, across the Red Sea in South Yemen, and later in neighboring Ethiopia. In Angola, once a colony of Portugal, an insurgent movement supported by Cuban troops came to power. In 1979, Soviet troops were sent across the border into Afghanistan to protect a newly installed Marxist regime facing internal resistance from fundamentalist Muslims. Some observers suspected that the ultimate objective of the Soviet advance into hitherto neutral Afghanistan was to extend Soviet power into the oil fields of the Persian Gulf. To deter such a possibility, the White House promulgated the Carter Doctrine, which stated that the United States would use its military power, if necessary, to safeguard Western access to the oil reserves in the Middle East. In fact, sources in Moscow later disclosed that the Soviet advance had little to do with the oil of the Persian Gulf but was an effort to increase Soviet influence in a region increasingly beset by Islamic fervor. Soviet officials feared that Islamic activism could spread to the Muslim populations in the Soviet republics in Central Asia and were confident that the United States was too distracted by the "Vietnam syndrome" (the public fear of U.S. involvement in another Vietnam-type conflict) to respond.

Another reason for the growing suspicion of the Soviet Union in the United States was that some U.S. defense analysts began to charge that the Soviet Union had rejected the policy of equivalence and was seeking strategic superiority in nuclear weapons. Accordingly, they argued for a substantial increase in U.S. defense spending. Such charges, combined with evidence of Soviet efforts in Africa and the Middle East and reports of the persecution of Jews and dissidents in the Soviet Union, helped undermine public support for détente in the United States. These changing attitudes were reflected in the failure of the Carter administration to obtain congressional approval of a new arms limitation agreement (SALT II), signed with the Soviet Union in 1979.

Countering the Evil Empire

The early years of the administration of President Ronald Reagan (b. 1911) witnessed a return to the harsh rhetoric, if not all of the harsh practices, of the Cold War. President Reagan's anti-Communist credentials were well known. In a speech given shortly after his election in 1980, he referred to the Soviet Union as an "evil empire" and frequently voiced his suspicion of its motives in foreign affairs. In an effort to eliminate perceived Soviet advantages in strategic weaponry, the White House began a military buildup that stimulated a renewed arms race. In 1982, the Reagan administration introduced the nuclear-tipped

Chronology

THE COLD WAR TO 1980

Truman Doctrine	1947
Formation of NATO	1949
Soviet Union explodes first nuclear device	1949
Communists come to power in China	1949
Nationalist government retreats to Taiwan	1949
Korean War	1950–1953
Geneva Conference ends Indochina War	July 21, 1954
Warsaw Pact created	1955
Khrushchev calls for peaceful coexistence	1956
Sino-Soviet dispute breaks into the open	1961
Cuban Missile Crisis	1962
SALT I treaty signed	1972
Nixon's visit to China	1972
Fall of South Vietnam	1975
Soviet invasion of Afghanistan	1979

cruise missile, whose ability to fly at low altitudes made it difficult to detect by enemy radar. Reagan also became an ardent exponent of the Strategic Defense Initiative (SDI), nicknamed "Star Wars." Its purposes were to create a space shield that could destroy incoming missiles and to force Moscow into an arms race that it could not hope to win.

The Reagan administration also adopted a more activist, if not confrontational, stance in the Third World. That attitude was most directly demonstrated in Central America, where the revolutionary Sandinista regime had been established in Nicaragua after the overthrow of the Somoza dictatorship in 1979. Charging that the Sandinista regime was supporting a guerrilla insurgency movement in nearby El Salvador, the Reagan administration began to provide material aid to the government in El Salvador while simultaneously supporting an anticommunist guerrilla movement (called the Contras) in Nicaragua. Though the administration insisted that it was countering the spread of communism in the Western Hemisphere, its Central American policy aroused considerable controversy in Congress, where some members charged that growing U.S. involvement could lead to a repeat of the nation's bitter experience in Vietnam.

The Reagan administration also took the offensive in other areas. By providing military support to the anti-Soviet insurgents in Afghanistan, the White House helped maintain a Vietnam-like war in Afghanistan that would embed the Soviet Union in its own quagmire. Like the Vietnam War, the conflict in Afghanistan resulted in heavy casualties and demonstrated that the influence of a superpower was limited in the face of strong nationalist, guerrilla-type opposition.

CONCLUSION

At the end of World War II, a new conflict erupted in Europe as the new superpowers, the United States and the Soviet Union, began to compete for political domination. This ideological division soon spread to the rest of the world as the United States fought in Korea and Vietnam to prevent the spread of communism, promoted by the new Maoist government in China, while the Soviet Union used its influence to prop up pro-Soviet regimes in Asia, Africa, and Latin America.

Thus what had begun as a confrontation across the great divide of the Iron Curtain in Europe eventually took on global significance. As a result, both Moscow and Washington became entangled in areas that in themselves had little importance in terms of national security interests. To make matters worse, U.S. policy makers all too often applied the lessons of World War II (the so-called Munich syndrome, according to which efforts to appease an aggressor only encourage his appetite for conquest) to crisis points in the Third World, where conditions were not remotely comparable.

By the 1980s, however, there were tantalizing signs of a thaw in the Cold War. China and the United States, each hoping to gain leverage with Moscow, had agreed to establish diplomatic relations. Freed from its concerns over Beijing's open support of revolutions in the Third World, the United States decided to withdraw from South Vietnam, and the war there came to an end without involving the great powers in a dangerous confrontation. Although Washington and Moscow continued to compete for advantage all over the world, both sides gradually came to realize that the struggle for domination could best be carried out in the political and economic arenas rather than on the battlefield.

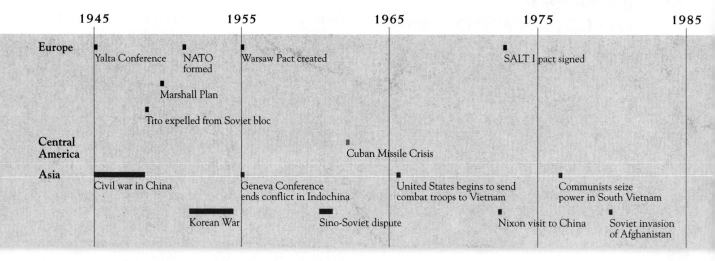

CHAPTER NOTES

1. *Department of State Bulletin* 12 (February 11, 1945), pp. 213–216.
2. Quoted in Joseph M. Jones, *The Fifteen Weeks (February 21–June 5, 1947)*, 2d ed. (New York, 1964), pp. 140–141.
3. Quoted in Walter Laqueur, *Europe in Our Time* (New York, 1992), p. 111.
4. Quoted in Wilfried Loth, *The Division of the World, 1941–1955* (New York, 1988), pp. 160–161.
5. Quoted in Peter Lane, *Europe Since 1945: An Introduction* (Totowa, N.J., 1985), p. 248.
6. Quoted in Robert F. Kennedy, *Thirteen Days: A Memoir of the Cuban Missile Crisis* (New York, 1969), pp. 89–90.

SUGGESTED READING

There is a detailed literature on the Cold War. Two general accounts are R. B. Levering, *The Cold War, 1945–1972* (Arlington Heights, Ill., 1982), and B. A. Weisberger, *Cold War, Cold Peace: The United States and Russia Since 1945* (New York, 1984). Two works that maintain that the Soviet Union was chiefly responsible for the Cold War are H. Feis, *From Trust to Terror: The Onset of the Cold War, 1945–1950* (New York, 1970), and A. Ulam, *The Rivals: America and Russia Since World War II* (New York, 1971). Revisionist studies on the Cold War have emphasized U.S. responsibility for the Cold War, especially its global aspects. These works include J. Kolko and G. Kolko, *The Limits of Power: The World and United States Foreign Policy, 1945–1954* (New York, 1972); W. La Feber, *America, Russia and the Cold War, 1945–1966*, 2d ed. (New York, 1972); and M. Sherwin, *A World Destroyed: The Atomic Bomb and the Grand Alliance* (New York, 1975). For a critique of the revisionist studies, see R. L. Maddox, *The New Left and the Origins of the Cold War* (Princeton, N.J., 1973). R. Garthoff, *Détente and Confrontation: American-Soviet Relations from Nixon to Reagan* (Washington, D.C., 1985), provides a detailed analysis of U.S.-Soviet relations in the 1970s and 1980s. For a highly competent retrospective analysis of the Cold War era, see J. L. Gaddis, *We Now Know: Rethinking Cold War History* (Oxford, 1997).

A number of studies of the early stages of the Cold War have been based on documents unavailable until the late 1980s or early 1990s. See, for example, O. A. Westad, *Cold War and Revolution: Soviet-American Rivalry and the Origins of the Chinese Civil War* (New York, 1993); D. A. Mayers, *Cracking the Monolith: U.S. Policy Against the Sino-Soviet Alliance, 1949–1955* (Baton Rouge, 1986); and Chen Jian, *China's Road to the Korean War: The Making of the Sino-American Confrontation* (New York, 1994). S. Goncharov, J. W. Lewis, and Xue Litai, *Uncertain Partners: Stalin, Mao, and the Korean War* (Stanford, Calif., 1993), provides a fascinating view of the war from several perspectives.

For important studies of Soviet foreign policy, see A. B. Ulam, *Expansion and Coexistence: Soviet Foreign Policy, 1917–1973*, 2d ed. (New York, 1974), and *Dangerous Relations: The Soviet Union in World Politics, 1970–1982* (New York, 1983). The effects of the Cold War on Germany are examined in J. H. Backer, *The Decision to Divide Germany: American Foreign Policy in Transition* (Durham, N.C., 1978). On atomic diplomacy in the Cold War, see G. F. Herken, *The Winning Weapon: The Atomic Bomb in the Cold War, 1945–1950* (New York, 1981). For a good introduction to the arms race, see E. M. Bottome, *The Balance of Terror: A Guide to the Arms Race*, rev. ed. (Boston, 1986).

There are several surveys of Chinese foreign policy since the Communist rise to power. On the revolutionary period, see P. Van Ness, *Revolution and Chinese Foreign Policy* (Berkeley, Calif., 1971), and J. Gittings, *The World and China* (New York, 1974). On Sino-

U.S. relations, see H. Harding, *A Fragile Relationship: The United States and China Since 1972* (Washington, D.C., 1992), and W. Burr (ed.), *The Kissinger Transcripts: The Top-Secret Talks with Beijing and Moscow* (New York, 1998). On Chinese policy in Korea, see the classic by A. S. Whiting, *China Crosses the Yalu* (Stanford, Calif., 1960). On Sino-Vietnamese relations, see Ang Cheng Guan, *Vietnamese Communists' Relations with China and the Second Indochina Conflict* (Jefferson, N.C., 1997).

INFOTRAC COLLEGE EDITION

For additional reading, go to InfoTrac College Edition, your online research library at
http://web1.infotrac-college.com

Enter the search terms "Cold War" using the Subject Guide.

Enter the search terms "Soviet Union relations with the United States" using the Subject Guide.

Enter the search terms "Vietnamese conflict" using the Subject Guide.

Enter the search term "Gorbachev" using Keywords.

Enter the search terms "Korean War" using the Subject Guide.

BRAVE NEW WORLD: COMMUNISM ON TRIAL

FOCUS QUESTIONS

- What were the chief characteristics of Soviet political, economic, and social life prior to Mikhail Gorbachev, and what reforms did he introduce?
- What were the main developments in Eastern Europe between 1945 and 1989?
- What were Mao Zedong's goals for China, and what policies did he institute to try to achieve them?
- What have been the major political, economic, and social developments in China since Mao's death in 1976?
- ➤ Why has communism survived in China but not in Eastern Europe and Russia, and what impact has it had on Chinese life and culture?

According to Karl Marx, capitalism is a system that involves the exploitation of man by man; under socialism, it is the other way around. That wry joke was typical of popular humor in post–World War II Moscow, where the dreams of a future utopia had faded in the grim reality of life in the Soviet Union.

Nevertheless, the Communist monopoly on power seemed secure, as did Moscow's hold over its client states in Eastern Europe. In fact, for three decades after the end of World War II, the Soviet Empire appeared to be a permanent feature of the international landscape. But by the early 1980s, it became clear that there were cracks in the Kremlin wall. The Soviet economy was stagnant, the minority nationalities were restive, and Eastern European leaders were increasingly emboldened to test the waters of the global capitalist marketplace. In the United States, the newly elected president, Ronald Reagan, boldly predicted the imminent collapse of the "evil empire."

Although many observers questioned his remarks at the time, they soon seemed uncannily clairvoyant. Within a period of less than three years (1989–1991), the Soviet Union ceased to exist as a nation as Russia and other former Soviet republics declared their separate independence, Communist regimes in Eastern Europe were toppled, and the long-standing division of postwar Europe came to an end. Although Communist parties survived the demise of the system and showed signs of renewed vigor in some countries in the region, their monopoly is gone, and they must now compete with other parties for power.

The fate of communism in China has been quite different. Despite some turbulence, communism has survived in China, even as that nation takes giant strides toward becoming an economic superpower. Yet as China's leaders struggle to bring the nation into the twenty-first century, many of the essential principles of Marxist-Leninist dogma have been tacitly abandoned, and cynicism among the nation's youth is widespread. Whether communism will continue to provide a usable framework for the challenges that lie ahead remains an open question. •

THE POSTWAR SOVIET UNION

World War II had left the Soviet Union as one of the world's two superpowers and its leader, Joseph Stalin, in a position of strength. He and his Soviet colleagues were now in control of a vast empire that included Eastern Europe, much of the Balkans, and new territory gained from Japan in East Asia.

From Stalin to Khrushchev

World War II devastated the Soviet Union. Twenty million citizens lost their lives, and cities such as Kiev, Kharkov, and Leningrad suffered enormous physical destruction. As the lands that had been occupied by the German forces were liberated, the Soviet government turned its attention to restoring their economic structures. Nevertheless, in 1945, agricultural production was only 60 percent and steel output only 50 percent of prewar levels. The Soviet people faced incredibly difficult conditions: they worked longer hours; they ate less; they were ill-housed and poorly clothed.

In the immediate postwar years, the Soviet Union removed goods and materials from occupied Germany and extorted valuable raw materials from its satellite states in Eastern Europe. More important, however, to create a new industrial base, Stalin returned to the method he had used in the 1930s—the extraction of development capital from Soviet labor. Working hard for little pay and for precious few consumer goods, Soviet laborers were expected to produce goods for export with little in return for themselves. The incoming capital from abroad could then be used to purchase machinery and Western technology. The loss of millions of men in the war meant that much of this tremendous workload fell upon Soviet women, who performed almost 40 percent of the heavy manual labor.

The pace of economic recovery in the Soviet Union was impressive. By 1947, industrial production had attained 1939 levels; three years later, it had surpassed those levels by 40 percent. New power plants, canals, and giant factories were built, and industrial enterprises and oil fields were established in Siberia and Soviet Central Asia. Stalin's new five-year plan, announced in 1946, reached its goals in less than five years.

Although Stalin's economic recovery policy was successful in promoting growth in heavy industry, primarily for the benefit of the military, consumer goods remained scarce. The development of thermonuclear weapons, MIG fighter planes, and the first space satellite (*Sputnik*) in the 1950s may have elevated the Soviet state's reputation as a world power abroad, but domestically, the Soviet people were shortchanged. Heavy industry grew at a rate three times that of personal consumption. Moreover, the housing shortage was acute, with living conditions especially difficult in the overcrowded cities.

When World War II ended in 1945, Stalin had been in power for more than fifteen years. During that time, he had removed all opposition to his rule and emerged as the undisputed master of the Soviet Union. Political terror enforced by several hundred thousand secret police ensured that he would remain in power. By the late 1940s, there were an estimated nine million Soviet citizens in Siberian concentration camps.

Increasingly distrustful of competitors, Stalin exercised sole authority and pitted his subordinates against each other. His morbid suspicions extended to even his closest colleagues. In 1948, Andrei Zhdanov, his presumed successor and head of the Leningrad party organization, died under mysterious circumstances, but almost certainly at Stalin's order. Within weeks, the Leningrad party organization was purged of several top leaders, many of whom were charged with traitorous connections with Western intelligence agencies. In succeeding years, Stalin directed his suspicion at other members of the inner circle, including Foreign Minister Vyacheslav Molotov. Known as "Old Stone Butt" in the West for his stubborn defense of Soviet security interests, Molotov had been Stalin's loyal lieutenant since the early years of Stalin's rise to power. Now Stalin distrusted Molotov and had his Jewish wife placed in a Siberian concentration camp. Stalin's colleagues became completely cowed. As he remarked mockingly on one occasion, "When I die, the imperialists will strangle all of you like a litter of kittens."[1]

Stalin died in 1953 and, after some bitter infighting within the party leadership, was succeeded by Georgy Malenkov, a veteran administrator and ambitious member of the Politburo (the party's governing body). Malenkov came to power with a clear agenda. In foreign affairs, he hoped to promote an easing of Cold War tensions and improve relations with the Western powers. For Moscow's Eastern European allies, he advocated a "new course" in their mutual relations and a decline in Stalinist methods of rule. Inside the Soviet Union, he hoped to reduce defense expenditures and improve the standard of living. Such goals were laudable and probably had the support of the majority of the Russian people, but they did not necessarily appeal to key groups including the army, the Communist Party, the managerial elite, and the security services (now known as the Committee on Government Security, or KGB). In 1953, Malenkov was removed from his position, and power shifted to his rival, the new party general secretary, Nikita Khrushchev.

During the struggle for power with Malenkov, Khrushchev had outmaneuvered his rival by calling for heightened defense expenditures and a continuing emphasis on heavy industry. Once in power, however, Khrushchev showed the political dexterity displayed by many an American politician and reversed his priorities. He now resumed the efforts of his predecessor to reduce tensions with the West and boost the standard of living of the Russian people. He moved vigorously to boost the performance of the Soviet economy and revitalize Soviet society. By nature, Khrushchev was a man of enormous energy and an innovator. In an attempt to release the stranglehold of the central bureaucracy over the national economy, he abolished dozens of government ministries and split up the party and government apparatus. Khrushchev also attempted to rejuvenate the stagnant agricultural sector, long the Achilles' heel of the Soviet economy. He attempted to spur production by increasing profit incentives and opened "virgin lands" in Soviet Kazakhstan to bring thousands of acres of new land under cultivation.

Like any innovator, Khrushchev had to overcome the inherently conservative instincts of the Soviet bureaucracy, as well as of the mass of the Soviet population. His plan to remove the "dead hand" of the state, however laudable

⇒ THE PORTALS OF DOOM.   Perhaps the most feared location in the Soviet Union was Lyubyanka Prison, an ornate prerevolutionary building in the heart of Moscow. Taken over by the Bolsheviks after the 1917 Revolution, it became the headquarters of the Soviet secret police, the Cheka, later to be known as the KGB. It was here that many Soviet citizens accused of "counterrevolutionary acts" were imprisoned and executed. The figure on the pedestal is that of Felix Dzerzhinsky, first director of Cheka. After the disintegration of the Soviet Union, the statue was removed, although some Muscovites now want it restored.

Courtesy of William J. Duiker

KHRUSHCHEV DENOUNCES STALIN

Three years after Stalin's death, the new Soviet premier, Nikita Khrushchev, addressed the Twentieth Congress of the Communist Party and denounced the former Soviet dictator for his crimes. This denunciation was the beginning of a policy of destalinization.

KHRUSHCHEV ADDRESSES THE TWENTIETH PARTY CONGRESS, FEBRUARY 1956

Comrades, . . . quite a lot has been said about the cult of the individual and about its harmful consequences. . . . The cult of the person of Stalin . . . became at a certain specific stage the source of a whole series of exceedingly serious and grave perversions of Party principles, of Party democracy, of revolutionary legality.

Stalin absolutely did not tolerate collegiality in leadership and in work and . . . practiced brutal violence, not only toward everything which opposed him, but also toward that which seemed to his capricious and despotic character, contrary to his concepts.

Stalin abandoned the method of ideological struggle for that of administrative violence, mass repressions and terror. . . . Arbitrary behavior by one person encouraged and permitted arbitrariness in others. Mass arrests and deportations of many thousands of people, execution without trial and without normal investigation created conditions of insecurity, fear, and even desperation.

Stalin showed in a whole series of cases his intolerance, his brutality, and his abuse of power. . . . He often chose the path of repression and annihilation, not only against actual enemies, but also against individuals who had not committed any crimes against the Party and the Soviet government. . . .

Many Party, Soviet, and economic activists who were branded in 1937–8 as "enemies" were actually never enemies, spies, wreckers, and so on, but were always honest communists; they were only so stigmatized, and often, no longer able to bear barbaric tortures, they charged themselves (at the order of the investigative judges-falsifiers) with all kinds of grave and unlikely crimes.

This was the result of the abuse of power by Stalin, who began to use mass terror against the Party cadres. . . . Stalin put the Party and the NKVD [the Soviet police agency] up to the use of mass terror when the exploiting classes had been liquidated in our country and when there were no serious reasons for the use of extraordinary mass terror. The terror was directed . . . against the honest workers of the Party and the Soviet state. . . .

Stalin was a very distrustful man, sickly, suspicious. . . . Everywhere and in everything he saw "enemies," "two-facers," and "spies." Possessing unlimited power, he indulged in great willfulness and choked a person morally and physically. A situation was created where one could not express one's own will. When Stalin said that one or another would be arrested, it was necessary to accept on faith that he was an "enemy of the people." What proofs were offered? The confession of the arrested. . . . How is it possible that a person confesses to crimes that he had not committed? Only in one way—because of application of physical methods of pressuring him, tortures, bringing him to a state of unconsciousness, deprivation of his judgment, taking away of his human dignity.

---

in intent, alienated much of the Soviet official class, and his effort to split the party angered those who saw it as the central force in the Soviet system. Khrushchev's agricultural schemes inspired similar opposition. Although the Kazakhstan wheat lands would eventually demonstrate their importance, progress was slow, and his effort to persuade Russians to eat more corn (an idea he had apparently picked up during a visit to the United States) earned him the mocking nickname "Cornman." Disappointing agricultural production, combined with high military spending, hurt the Soviet economy. The industrial growth rate, which had soared in the early 1950s, now declined dramatically, from 13 percent in 1953 to 7.5 percent in 1964.

Khrushchev was probably best known for his policy of destalinization. Khrushchev had risen in the party hierarchy as a Stalin protégé, but he had been deeply disturbed by his mentor's excesses and, once in a position of authority, moved to excise the Stalinist legacy from Soviet society. The campaign began at the Twentieth National Congress of the Communist Party in February 1956, when Khrushchev gave a long speech in private criticizing some of Stalin's major shortcomings. The speech had apparently not been intended for public distribution, but it was quickly leaked to the Western press and created a sensation throughout the world (see the box above). During the next few years, Khrushchev encouraged more freedom for writers, artists, and composers, arguing that "readers should be given the chance to make their own judgments" about the acceptability of controversial literature and that "police measures shouldn't be used."[2] Under Khrushchev's instructions, thousands of prisoners were released from concentration camps.

Khrushchev's personality, however, did not endear him to higher Soviet officials, who frowned at his tendency to crack jokes and play the clown. Nor were the higher members of the party bureaucracy pleased when Khrushchev tried to curb their privileges. Foreign policy failures further damaged Khrushchev's reputation among his colleagues. His plan to place missiles in Cuba was the final straw (see Chapter 25). While he was away on vacation in 1964, a special meeting of the Soviet Polit-buro voted him out of office (because of "deteriorating health") and forced him into retirement. Although a team of leaders succeeded him, real power came into the hands of Leonid Brezhnev (1906–1982), the "trusted" supporter of Khrushchev who had engineered his downfall.

The Brezhnev Years (1964–1982)

The ouster of Nikita Khrushchev in October 1964 vividly demonstrated the challenges that would be encountered by any leader sufficiently bold to try to reform the Soviet system. In democratic countries, pressure on the government comes from various sources in society at large—the business community and labor unions, innumerable interest groups, and, of course, the general public. In the Soviet Union, pressure on government and party leaders originated from sources essentially operating inside the system—the government bureaucracy, the party apparatus, the KGB, and the armed forces.

Leonid Brezhnev, the new party chief, was undoubtedly aware of these realities of Soviet politics, and his long tenure in power was marked, above all, by the desire to avoid changes that might provoke instability, either at home or abroad. Brezhnev was himself a product of the Soviet system. He had entered the ranks of the party leadership under Stalin, and although he was not a particularly avid believer in party ideology—indeed, there were innumerable stories about his addiction to "bourgeois pleasures," including expensive country houses and fast cars (many of them gifts from foreign leaders)—he was no partisan of reform.

Still, Brezhnev sought stability in the domestic arena. He and his prime minister, Alexei Kosygin, undertook what might be described as a program of "de-Khrushchevization," returning the responsibility for long-term planning to the central ministries and reuniting the Communist Party apparatus. Despite some cautious attempts to stimulate the stagnant farm sector, there was no effort to revise the basic collective system. In the industrial sector, the regime launched a series of reforms designed to give factory managers (themselves employees of the state) more responsibility for setting prices, wages, and production quotas. These "Kosygin reforms" had little effect, however, because they were stubbornly resisted by the bureaucracy and were adopted by relatively few enterprises in the vast state-owned industrial sector.

A CONTROLLED SOCIETY

Brezhnev also initiated a significant retreat from Khrushchev's policy of destalinization. Criticism of the "Great Leader" had angered conservatives both within the party hierarchy and among the public at large, many of whom still revered Stalin as a hero and a defender of Russia against Nazi Germany. Many influential figures in the Kremlin feared that destalinization could lead to inter-

nal instability and a decline in public trust in the legitimacy of party leadership—the hallowed "dictatorship of the proletariat." Early in Brezhnev's reign, Stalin's reputation began to revive. Although his alleged shortcomings were not totally ignored, he was now described in the official press as "an outstanding party leader" who had been primarily responsible for the successes achieved by the Soviet Union.

The regime also adopted a more restrictive policy toward dissidents in Soviet society. Critics of the Soviet system, such as the physicist Andrei Sakharov, were harassed and arrested or, like the famous writer Alexander Solzhenitsyn, forced to leave the country. There was also a qualified return to the anti-Semitic policies and attitudes that had marked the Stalin era. Such indications of renewed repression aroused concern in the West and were instrumental in the inclusion of a statement on human rights in the 1975 Helsinki Agreement (see Chapter 25).

Free expression was also restricted. The media were controlled by the state and presented only what the state wanted people to hear. The two major newspapers, *Pravda* (Truth) and *Izvestia* (News), were the agents of the party and the government, respectively. Cynics joked that there was no news in *Pravda* and no truth in *Izvestia*. According to Western journalists, airplane accidents in the Soviet Union were rarely publicized, on the grounds that they would raise questions about the quality of the Soviet airline industry. The government made strenuous efforts to prevent the Soviet people from exposure to harmful foreign ideas, especially modern art, literature, and contemporary Western rock music. When the Summer Olympic Games were held in Moscow in 1980, Soviet newspapers advised citizens to keep their children indoors to keep them from being polluted with "bourgeois" ideas passed on by foreign visitors.

For citizens of Western democracies, such a political atmosphere would seem highly oppressive, but for the Russian people, an emphasis on law and order was an accepted aspect of everyday life inherited from the tsarist period. Conformity was the rule in virtually every corner of Soviet society, from the educational system (characterized at all levels by rote memorization and political indoctrination) to child rearing (it was forbidden, for example, to be left-handed) and even to yearly vacations (most workers took their vacations at resorts run by their employer, where the daily schedule of activities was highly regimented). Young Americans studying in the Soviet Union reported that their Soviet friends were often shocked to hear U.S. citizens criticizing their own president.

A STAGNANT ECONOMY

Soviet leaders also failed to achieve their objective of revitalizing the national economy. Whereas growth rates during the early Khrushchev era had been impressive (prompting Khrushchev during one visit to the United States in the 1950s to chortle, "We will bury you"), under Brezhnev industrial growth declined to an annual rate of less than 4 percent in the early 1970s and less than 3 percent in the period from 1975 to 1980. Successes in the agricultural sector were equally meager. Grain production rose from less than 90 million tons in the early 1950s to nearly 200 million tons in the 1970s but then stagnated at that level.

One of the primary problems with the Soviet economy was the absence of incentives. Salary structures offered little reward for hard labor and extraordinary achievement. Pay differentials operated a much narrower range than in most Western societies, and there was little danger of being dismissed. According to the Soviet constitution, every Soviet citizen was guaranteed an opportunity to work.

There were, of course, some exceptions to this general rule. Athletic achievement was highly prized, and a gymnast of Olympic stature would receive great rewards in the form of prestige and lifestyle. Senior officials did not receive high salaries but were provided with countless perquisites, such as access to foreign goods, official automobiles with a chauffeur, and entry into prestigious institutions of higher learning for their children. For the elite,

it was *blat* (influence) that most often differentiated them from the rest of the population. The average citizen, however, had little material incentive to produce beyond the minimum acceptable level. It is hardly surprising that per capita productivity was only about half that realized in most capitalist countries. At the same time, the rudeness of clerks and waiters became legendary.

The problem of incentives existed at the managerial level as well, where centralized planning discouraged initiative and innovation. Factory managers, for example, were assigned monthly and annual quotas by the Gosplan (the "state plan," drawn up by the central planning commission). Because state-owned factories faced little or no competition, managers did not care whether their products were competitive in terms of price and quality, so long as the quota was attained. One of the key complaints of Soviet citizens was the low quality of domestic consumer goods. Knowledgeable consumers quickly discovered that products manufactured at the end of the month were often of lower quality (because factory workers had to rush to meet their quotas) and attempted to avoid purchasing them.

Often consumer goods were simply unavailable. Soviet citizens automatically got in line when they saw

⋙ HOW TO SHOP IN MOSCOW. Because of the policy of state control over the Soviet economy, the availability of goods was a consequence not of market factors but of decisions made by government bureaucrats. As a result, needed goods were often in short supply. When Soviet citizens heard that a shipment of a particular product had arrived at a state store, they queued up to buy it. Here shoppers line up in front of a state-run store selling dinnerware in Moscow.

Courtesy of William J. Duiker

a queue forming in front of a store because they never knew when something might be available again. When they reached the head of the line, most would purchase several of the same item in order to swap with their friends and neighbors. A popular joke at the time was that a Soviet inventor had managed to produce an airplane that was cheap enough to be purchased by every citizen. Everyone was delighted because now when they heard that there was a sale of a particular item anywhere in the country, they would be able to fly in and buy it. This "queue psychology," of course, was a time-consuming process and inevitably served to reduce the per capita rate of productivity.

Soviet citizens often tried to overcome the shortcomings of the system by resorting to the black market. Private economic activities, of course, were illegal, but many workers took to moonlighting to augment their meager salaries. An employee in a state-run appliance store, for example, would promise to repair a customer's television set on his own time in return for a payment "under the table." Otherwise, servicing of the set might require several weeks. Knowledgeable observers estimated that as much as one-third of the entire Soviet economy operated outside the legal system.

Another major obstacle to economic growth was inadequate technology. Except in the area of national defense, the overall level of Soviet technology was not comparable to that of the West or the advanced industrial societies of East Asia. Part of the problem, of course, stemmed from the issues already described. With no competition, factory managers had little incentive to improve the quality of their products. But another reason was the high priority assigned to defense. The military sector regularly received the most resources from the government and attracted the cream of the country's scientific talent.

PROBLEMS OF GERONTOCRACY

Such problems would be intimidating for any government; they were particularly so for the elderly generation of party leaders surrounding Leonid Brezhnev, many of whom were cautious to a fault. Though some undoubtedly recognized the need for reform and innovation, they were paralyzed by the fear of instability and change. The problem worsened during the late 1970s when Brezhnev's health began to deteriorate.

Brezhnev died in November 1982 and was succeeded by Yuri Andropov (1914–1984), a party veteran and head of the Soviet secret services. During his brief tenure as party chief, Andropov was a vocal advocate of reform, but most of his initiatives were limited to the familiar nostrums of punishment for wrongdoers and moral exhortations to Soviet citizens to work harder. At the same time, material incentives were still officially discouraged and generally ineffective. Andropov had been ailing when he was

selected to succeed Brezhnev as party chief, and when he died after only a few months in office, little had been done to change the system. He was succeeded, in turn, by a mediocre party stalwart, the elderly Konstantin Chernenko (1911–1985). With the Soviet system in crisis, Moscow seemed stuck in a time warp. As one concerned observer told an American journalist: "I had a sense of foreboding, like before a storm. That there was something brewing in people and there would be a time when they would say, 'That's it. We can't go on living like this. We can't. We need to redo everything.'"[3]

FERMENT IN EASTERN EUROPE

The key to security along the western frontier of the Soviet Union was the string of Eastern European satellite states that had been assembled in the aftermath of World War II (see Map 26.1). Once Communist power had been assured, a series of "little Stalins" put into power by Moscow instituted Soviet-type five-year plans that emphasized heavy industry rather than consumer goods, the collectivization of agriculture, and the nationalization of industry. They also appropriated the political tactics that Stalin had perfected in the Soviet Union, eliminating all non-Communist parties and establishing the classical institutions of repression—the secret police and military forces. Dissidents were tracked down and thrown into prison, and "national Communists" who resisted total subservience to the Soviet Union were charged with treason in mass show trials and executed.

Despite these repressive efforts, discontent became increasingly evident in several Eastern European countries. Hungary, Poland, and Romania harbored bitter memories of past Russian domination and suspected that Stalin, under the guise of proletarian internationalism, was seeking to revive the empire of the Romanovs. For the vast majority of peoples in Eastern Europe, the imposition of the so-called people's democracies (a term invented by Moscow to define a society in the early stage of socialist transition) resulted in economic hardship and severe threats to the most basic political liberties. The first indications of unrest appeared in East Berlin, where popular riots broke out against Communist rule in 1953. The riots eventually subsided, but the virus had spread to neighboring countries.

In Poland, public demonstrations against an increase in food prices in 1956 escalated into widespread protests against the regime's economic policies, restrictions on the freedom of Catholics to practice their religion, and the continued presence of Soviet troops (as called for by the Warsaw Pact) on Polish soil. In a desperate effort to defuse the unrest, the party leader stepped down and was replaced by Wladyslaw Gomulka (1905–1982), a popular figure who had previously been demoted for his "nationalist" tendencies. When Gomulka took steps to ease the crisis, Khrushchev flew to Warsaw to warn him against adopting policies that could undermine the political dominance of the party and weaken security links with the Soviet Union. Ultimately, Poland agreed to remain in the Warsaw Pact and to maintain the sanctity of party rule; in return, Gomulka was authorized to adopt domestic reforms, such as easing restrictions on religious practice and ending the policy of forced collectivization in rural areas.

The developments in Poland sent shock waves throughout the region. The impact was strongest in neighboring Hungary, where the methods of the local "little Stalin,"

⟫ STALIN'S WEDDING CAKE. During the Stalinist era, architects in the Soviet Union and Moscow's satellites in Eastern Europe constructed grandiose structures that represented a mixture of Classical, Gothic, and Baroque styles and reflected the hubris of the Soviet era. One of the most famous such buildings was the Palace of Culture, built in the 1950s in the Polish capital of Warsaw. Local residents joked that the best view of the city could be seen from the Palace, since you would not see the building from there.

Courtesy of William J. Duiker

Matyas Rakosi, were so brutal that he had been summoned to Moscow for a lecture. In late October 1956, student-led popular riots broke out in the capital of Budapest and soon spread to other towns and villages throughout the country. Rakosi was forced to resign and was replaced by Imre Nagy (1896–1958), a "national Communist" who attempted to satisfy popular demands without arousing the anger of Moscow. Unlike Gomulka, however, Nagy was unable to contain the zeal of leading members of the protest movement, who sought major political reforms and the withdrawal of Hungary from the Warsaw Pact. On November 1, Nagy promised free elections, which, given the mood of the country, would probably have brought an end to Communist rule. After a brief moment of uncertainty, Moscow decided on firm action. Soviet troops, recently withdrawn at Nagy's request, returned to Budapest and installed a new government under the more pliant party leader János Kádár (1912–1989). While Kádár rescinded many of Nagy's measures, Nagy sought refuge in the Yugoslav embassy. A few weeks later, he left the embassy under the promise of safety but was quickly arrested, convicted of treason, and executed.

The dramatic events in Poland and Hungary graphically demonstrated the vulnerability of the Soviet satellite system in Eastern Europe, and many observers throughout the world anticipated that the United States would intervene on behalf of the freedom fighters in Hungary. After all, the Eisenhower administration had promised that it would "roll back" communism, and radio broadcasts by the U.S.-sponsored Radio Liberty and Radio Free Europe had encouraged the peoples of Eastern Europe to rise up against Soviet domination. In reality, Washington was well aware that U.S. intervention could lead to nuclear war and limited itself to protests against Soviet brutality in crushing the uprising.

The year of discontent was not without consequences, however. Soviet leaders now recognized that Moscow could maintain control over its satellites in Eastern Europe only by granting them the leeway to adopt domestic policies appropriate to local conditions. Khrushchev had already embarked on this path in 1955 when he assured Tito that there were "different roads to socialism." Eastern European Communist leaders now took Khrushchev at his word and adopted reform programs to make socialism more palatable to their subject populations. Even Kádár, derisively labeled the "butcher of Budapest," managed to preserve many of Nagy's reforms to allow a measure of capitalist incentive and freedom of expression in Hungary.

Czechoslovakia did not share in the thaw of the mid-1950s and remained under the rule of Antonin Novotny (1904–1975), who had been placed in power by Stalin himself. By the late 1960s, however, Novotny's policies had led to widespread popular alienation, and in 1968, with the support of intellectuals and reformist party

THE BREZHNEV DOCTRINE

*I*n the summer of 1968, when the new Communist Party leaders in Czechoslovakia were seriously considering proposals for reforming the totalitarian system there, the Warsaw Pact nations met under the leadership of Soviet party chief Leonid Brezhnev to assess the threat to the socialist camp. Shortly after, military forces of several Soviet bloc nations entered Czechoslovakia and imposed a new government subservient to Moscow. The move was justified by the spirit of "proletarian internationalism" and was widely viewed as a warning to China and other socialist states not to stray too far from Marxist-Leninist orthodoxy, as interpreted by the Soviet Union.

A LETTER TO THE CENTRAL COMMITTEE OF THE COMMUNIST PARTY OF CZECHOSLOVAKIA

Dear comrades!

On behalf of the Central Committees of the Communist and Workers' Parties of Bulgaria, Hungary, the German Democratic Republic, Poland, and the Soviet Union, we address ourselves to you with this letter, prompted by a feeling of sincere friendship based on the principles of Marxism-Leninism and proletarian internationalism and by the concern of our common affairs for strengthening the positions of socialism and the security of the socialist community of nations.

The development of events in your country evokes in us deep anxiety. It is our firm conviction that the offensive of the reactionary forces, backed by imperialists, against your Party and the foundations of the social system in the Czechoslovak Socialist Republic, threatens to push your country off the road of socialism and that consequently it jeopardizes the interests of the entire socialist system. . . .

We neither had nor have any intention of interfering in such affairs as are strictly the internal business of your Party and your state, nor of violating the principles of respect, independence, and equality in the relations among the Communist Parties and socialist countries. . . .

At the same time we cannot agree to have hostile forces push your country from the road of socialism and create a threat of severing Czechoslovakia from the socialist community. . . . This is the common cause of our countries, which have joined in the Warsaw Treaty to ensure independence, peace, and security in Europe, and to set up an insurmountable barrier against the intrigues of the imperialist forces, against aggression and revenge. . . . We shall never agree to have imperialism, using peaceful or nonpeaceful methods, making a gap from the inside or from the outside in the socialist system, and changing in imperialism's favor the correlation of forces in Europe. . . .

That is why we believe that a decisive rebuff of the anticommunist forces, and decisive efforts for the preservation of the socialist system in Czechoslovakia are not only your task but ours as well. . . .

We express the conviction that the Communist Party of Czechoslovakia, conscious of its responsibility, will take the necessary steps to block the path of reaction. In this struggle you can count on the solidarity and all-round assistance of the fraternal socialist countries.

Warsaw, July 15, 1968

---

members, Alexander Dubček was elected first secretary of the Communist Party. He immediately attempted to create what was popularly called "socialism with a human face," relaxing restrictions on freedom of speech and the press and the right to travel abroad. Economic reforms were announced, and party control over all aspects of society was reduced. A period of euphoria erupted that came to be known as the "Prague Spring."

It proved to be short-lived. Encouraged by Dubček's actions, some Czechs called for more far-reaching reforms, including neutrality and withdrawal from the Soviet bloc. To forestall the spread of this "spring fever," the Soviet Red Army, supported by troops from other Warsaw Pact states, invaded Czechoslovakia in August 1968 and crushed the reform movement. Gustav Husak (1913–1991), a committed Stalinist, replaced Dubček and restored the old order (see the box above).

Elsewhere in Eastern Europe, Stalinist policies continued to hold sway. The ruling Communist government in East Germany, led by Walter Ulbricht, consolidated its position in the early 1950s and became a faithful Soviet satellite. Industry was nationalized and agriculture collectivized. After the 1953 workers' revolt was crushed by Soviet tanks, a steady flight of East Germans to West Germany ensued, primarily through the city of Berlin. This exodus of mostly skilled laborers ("Soon only party chief Ulbricht will be left," remarked one Soviet observer sardonically) created economic problems and in 1961 led the East German government to erect a wall separating East Berlin from West Berlin, as well as equally fearsome barriers along the entire border with West Germany.

After building the Berlin Wall, East Germany succeeded in developing the strongest economy among the Soviet Union's Eastern European satellites. In 1971, Ulbricht was succeeded by Erich Honecker (1912–1994), a party hard-liner who was deeply committed to the ideological battle against détente. Propaganda increased, and the use of the Stasi, the secret police, became a hallmark of Honecker's virtual dictatorship. Honecker ruled unchallenged for the next eighteen years.

MAP **26.1** **Eastern Europe and the Soviet Union.** After World War II, the boundaries of Eastern Europe were redrawn as a result of Allied agreements reached at the Tehran and Yalta conferences. This map shows the new boundaries that were established throughout the region, placing Soviet power at the center of Europe. ➤ *How had the boundaries changed from the prewar era?*

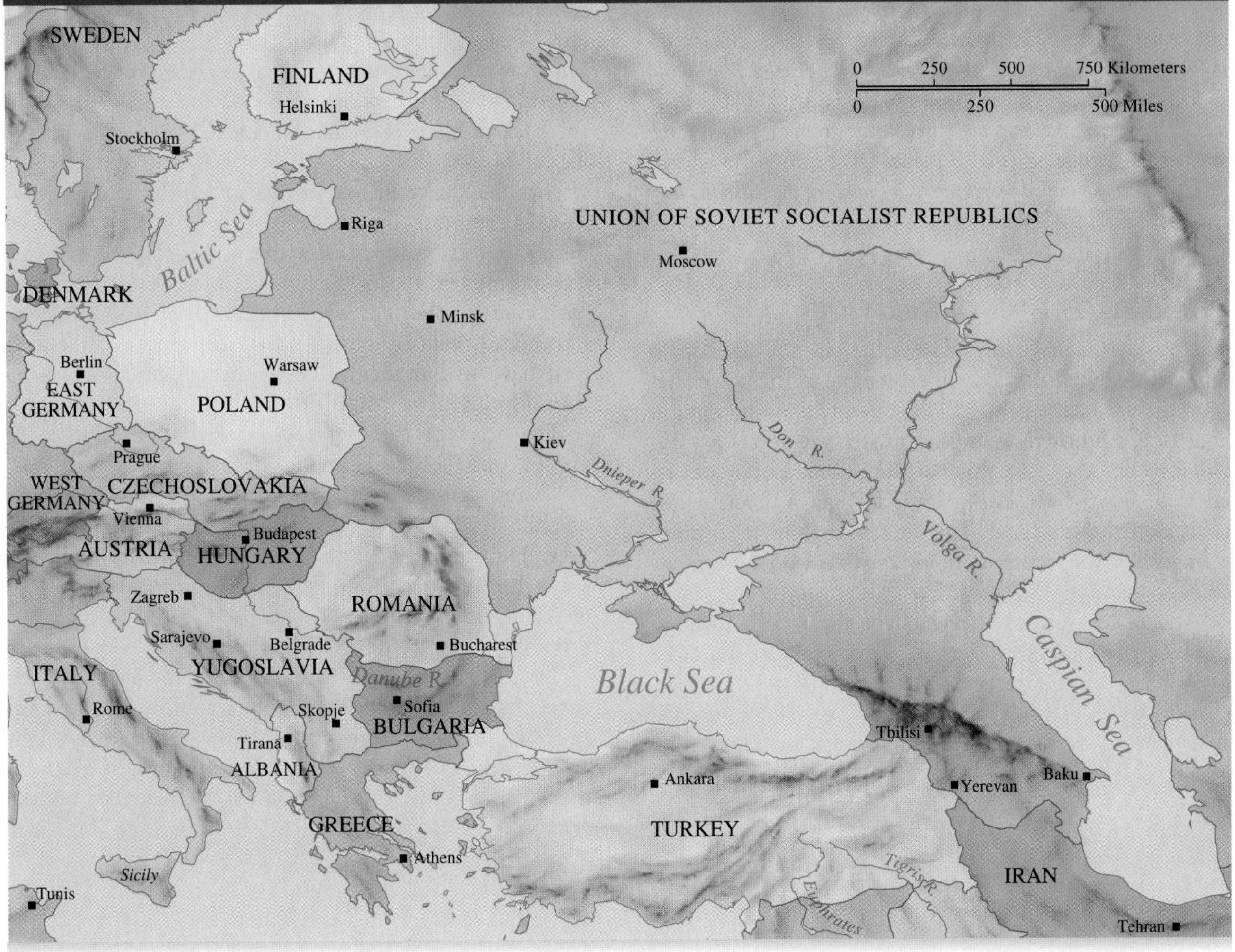

CULTURE AND SOCIETY IN THE SOVIET BLOC

In his occasional musings about the future communist utopia, Karl Marx had predicted that a new, classless society would replace the exploitative and hierarchical systems of feudalism and capitalism. Workers would engage in productive activities and share equally in the fruits of their labor. In their free time, they would produce a new, advanced culture, proletarian in character and egalitarian in content.

Cultural Expression

The reality in the post–World War II Soviet Union and Eastern Europe was somewhat different. Under Stalin, the Soviet cultural scene was a wasteland. Beginning in 1946,

a series of government decrees made all forms of literary and scientific expression dependent on the state. All Soviet culture was expected to follow the party line. Historians, philosophers, and social scientists all grew accustomed to quoting Marx, Lenin, and, above all, Stalin as their chief authorities. Novels and plays, too, were supposed to portray Communist heroes and their efforts to create a better society. No criticism of existing social conditions was permitted. Even distinguished composers such as Dmitry Shostakovich were compelled to heed Stalin's criticisms, including his view that contemporary Western music was nothing but a "mishmash." Some areas of intellectual activity were virtually abolished; the science of genetics disappeared, and few movies were made during Stalin's final years.

Stalin's death brought a modest respite from cultural repression. Writers and artists banned during the Stalin

One Day in the Life of Ivan Denisovich

On November 20, 1962, a Soviet magazine published a work by Alexander Solzhenitsyn that created a literary and political furor. The short novel related one day in the life of its chief character, Ivan Denisovich, at a Siberian concentration camp, to which he had been sentenced at the end of World War II for supposedly spying for the Germans while a Soviet soldier. This excerpt narrates the daily journey from the prison camp to a work project through the 17 degrees-below-zero cold of Siberia. Many Soviets identified with Ivan as a symbol of the suffering they had endured under Stalin.

ALEXANDER SOLZHENITSYN, ONE DAY IN THE LIFE OF IVAN DENISOVICH

There were escort guards all over the place. They flung a semicircle around the column on its way to the power station, their machine guns sticking out and pointing right at your face. And there were guards with gray dogs. One dog bared its fangs as if laughing at the prisoners. The escorts all wore short sheepskins, except for half a dozen whose coats trailed the ground. The long sheepskins were interchangeable: they were worn by anyone whose turn had come to man the watchtowers.

And once again as they brought the squads together the escort recounted the entire power-station column by fives. . . .

Out beyond the camp boundary the intense cold, accompanied by a headwind, stung even Shukhov's face, which was used to every kind of unpleasantness. Realizing that he would have the wind in his face all the way to the power station, he decided to make use of his bit of rag. To meet the contingency of a headwind he, like many other prisoners, had got himself a cloth with a long tape on each end. The prisoners admitted that these helped a bit. Shukhov covered his face up to the eyes, brought the tapes around below his ears, and fastened the ends together at the back of his neck. Then he covered his nape with the flap of his hat and raised his coat collar. The next thing was to pull the front flap of the hat down into his brow. Thus in front only his eyes remained unprotected. He fixed his coat tightly at the waist with the rope. Now everything was in order except for his hands, which were already stiff with cold (his mittens were worthless). He rubbed them, he clapped them together, for he knew that in a moment he'd have to put them behind his back and keep them there for the entire march.

The chief of the escort guard recited the "morning prayer," which every prisoner was heartily sick of:

"Attention, prisoners. Marching orders must be strictly obeyed. Keep to your ranks. No hurrying, keep a steady pace. No talking. Keep your eyes fixed ahead and your hands behind your backs. A step to right or left is considered an attempt to escape and the escort has orders to shoot without warning. Leading guards, on the double."

The two guards in the lead of the escort must have set out along the road. The column heaved forward, shoulders swaying, and the escorts, some twenty paces to the right and left of the column, each man at a distance of ten paces from the next, machine guns held at the ready, set off too.

---

years were again allowed to publish. Still, Soviet authorities, including Khrushchev, were reluctant to allow cultural freedom to move far beyond official Soviet ideology.

These restrictions, however, did not prevent the emergence of some significant Soviet literature, although authors paid a heavy price if they alienated the Soviet authorities. Boris Pasternak (1890–1960), who began his literary career as a poet, won the Nobel Prize in 1958 for his celebrated novel *Doctor Zhivago*, written between 1945 and 1956 and published in Italy in 1957. But the Soviet government condemned Pasternak's anti-Soviet tendencies, banned the novel, and would not allow him to accept the prize. The author had alienated the authorities by describing a society scarred by the excesses of Bolshevik revolutionary zeal.

Alexander Solzhenitsyn (b. 1918) created an even greater furor than Pasternak. Solzhenitsyn had spent eight years in forced labor camps for criticizing Stalin, and his *One Day in the Life of Ivan Denisovich*, which won him the Nobel Prize in 1970, was an account of life in those camps

(see the box above). Khrushchev allowed the book's publication as part of his destalinization campaign. Solzhenitsyn then wrote *The Gulag Archipelago*, a detailed indictment of the whole system of Soviet oppression. Soviet authorities denounced Solzhenitsyn's efforts to inform the world of Soviet crimes against humanity and expelled him from the Soviet Union in 1973.

Exile abroad rather than imprisonment in forced labor camps was perhaps a sign of modest progress. But even the limited freedom that had arisen during the Khrushchev years was rejected after his fall from power. Cultural controls were reimposed, destalinization was halted, and authors were again sent to labor camps for expressing outlawed ideas. These restrictive policies continued until the late 1980s.

In the Eastern European satellites, cultural freedom varied considerably from country to country. In Poland, intellectuals had access to Western publications as well as greater freedom to travel to the West. Hungarian and Yugoslav Communists, too, tolerated a certain level of intellectual activity that was not liked but at least not prohibited. Elsewhere, intellectuals were forced to conform to the regime's demands. After the Soviet invasion of Czechoslovakia in 1968, Czech Communists pursued a policy of strict cultural control.

The socialist camp also experienced the many facets of modern popular culture. By the early 1970s, there were 28 million television sets in the Soviet Union, although state authorities controlled the content of the programs that the Soviet people watched. Tourism, too, made inroads into the Communist world as state-run industries provided vacation time and governments established resorts for workers on the Black Sea and Adriatic coasts. In Poland, the number of vacationers who used holiday retreats increased from 700,000 in 1960 to 2.8 million in 1972.

Spectator sports became a large industry and were also highly politicized as a result of Cold War divisions. "Each new victory," one party leader stated, "is a victory for the Soviet form of society and the socialist sport system; it provides irrefutable proof of the superiority of socialist culture over the decaying culture of the capitalist states."[4] Accordingly, the state provided money for the construction of gymnasiums and training camps and portrayed athletes as superheroes.

Social Changes in the Soviet Union and Eastern Europe

The imposition of Marxist systems in Eastern Europe had far-reaching social consequences. Most Eastern European countries made the change from peasant societies to modern, industrialized economies. In Bulgaria, for example, 80 percent of the labor force was engaged in agriculture in

✒ GHOSTS OF SOVIET OLYMPIC GLORY. A poignant legacy of the collapse of the Soviet Union is reflected in this abandoned skating rink and ski jump in Almaty, Kazakhstan. It was in this rink and on the adjacent ski jump in the mountains of Central Asia that the Soviet Union trained its best athletes to win international competitions for gold medals and glory during the Cold War. Here we sense the ghosts of former skaters, subsidized darlings of the Soviet Empire, as they attempt the difficult triple jump.

Courtesy of William J. Duiker

1950, but only 20 percent was still working there in 1980. Although the Soviet Union and its Eastern European satellites never achieved the high standards of living of the West, they did experience some improvement. In 1960, the average real income of Polish peasants was four times higher than before World War II. Consumer goods also became more widely available. In East Germany, only 17 percent of families had television sets in 1960, but 75 percent had acquired them by 1972.

According to Marxist doctrine, state control of industry and the elimination of private property were supposed to lead to a classless society. Although that ideal was never achieved, it did have important social consequences. For one thing, traditional ruling classes were stripped of their special status after 1945. The Potocki family in Poland, for example, which had owned 9 million acres of land before the war, lost all of its possessions, and family members were reduced to the ranks of common laborers.

The desire to create a classless society led to noticeable changes in education. In some countries, laws mandated quota systems based on class. In East Germany, for example, 50 percent of the students in secondary schools had to be children of workers and peasants. The sons of manual workers constituted 53 percent of university students in Yugoslavia in 1964 and 40 percent in East Germany, compared to only 15 percent in Italy and 5.3 percent in West Germany. Social mobility also increased. In Poland in 1961, half of all white-collar workers came from blue-collar families. A significant number of judges, professors, and industrial managers stemmed from working-class backgrounds.

Education became crucial in preparing for new jobs in the communist system and led to higher enrollments in both secondary schools and universities. In Czechoslovakia, for example, the number of students in secondary schools tripled between 1945 and 1970, and the number of university students quadrupled between the 1930s and the 1960s. The type of education that students received also changed. In Hungary before World War II, 40 percent of students studied law, 9 percent engineering and technology, and 5 percent agriculture. In 1970, 35 percent were in engineering and technology, 9 percent in agriculture, and only 4 percent in law.

By the 1970s, the new managers of society, regardless of class background, realized the importance of higher education and used their power to gain special privileges for their children. By 1971, 60 percent of the children of white-collar workers attended university, and even though blue-collar families constituted 60 percent of the population, only 36 percent of their children attended institutions of higher learning. Even East Germany dropped its requirement that 50 percent of secondary students had to be the offspring of workers and peasants.

This shift in educational preferences demonstrates yet another aspect of the social structure in the communist world: the emergence of a new privileged class, made up

"IT'S SO DIFFICULT TO BE A WOMAN HERE"

One of the major problems for Soviet women was the balancing of work and family roles, a problem noticeably ignored by authorities. This excerpt is taken from a series of interviews of thirteen women in Moscow conducted in the late 1970s by Swedish investigators. As is evident in this interview with Anna, a young wife and mother, these Soviet women took pride in their achievements but were also frustrated with their lives. It is hardly surprising that the conflicting pressures on women between the demands of the family and the state's push for industrialization would result in a drop in birthrates and a change in family structure.

MOSCOW WOMEN: INTERVIEW WITH ANNA

[Anna is twenty-one and married, has a three-month-old daughter, and lives with her husband and daughter in a one-room apartment with a balcony and a large bathroom. Anna works as a hairdresser; her husband is an unemployed writer.]

Are there other kinds of jobs dominated by women?
Of course! Preschool teachers are exclusively women. Also beauticians. But I guess that's about all. Here women work in every profession, from tractor drivers to engineers. But I think there ought to be more jobs specifically for women so that there are *some* differences. In this century women have to be equal to men. Now women wear pants, have short hair, and hold important jobs, just like men. There are almost no differences left. Except in the home.

Do women and men have the same goal in life?
Of course. Women want to get out of the house and have careers, just the same as men do. It gives women a lot of advantages, higher wages, and so on. In that sense we have the same goal, but socially I don't think so. The family is, after all, more important for a woman. A man can live without a family; all he needs is for a woman to come from time to time to clean for him and do his laundry. He sleeps with her if he feels like it. Of course, a woman can adopt this lifestyle, but I still think that most women want their own home, family, children. From time immemorial, women's instincts have been rooted in taking care of their families, tending to their husbands, sewing, washing—all the household chores. Men are supposed to provide for the family; women should keep the home fires burning. This is so deeply ingrained in women that there's no way of changing it.

Whose career do you think is the most important?
The man's, naturally. The family is often broken up because women don't follow their men when they move where they can get a job. That was the case of my in-laws. They don't live together any longer because my father-in-law worked for a long time as far away as Smolensk. He lived alone, without his family, and then, of course, it was only natural that things turned out the way they did. It's hard for a man to live without his family when he's used to being taken care of all the time. Of course there are men who can endure, who continue to be faithful, etc., but for most men it isn't easy. For that reason I think a woman ought to go where her husband does. . . .

That's the way it is. Women have certain obligations, men others. One has to understand that at an early age. Girls have to learn to take care of a household and help at home. Boys too, but not as much as girls. Boys ought to be with their fathers and learn how to do masculine chores. . . .

It's so difficult to be a woman here. With emancipation, we lead such abnormal, twisted lives, because women have to work the same as men do. As a result, women have very little time for themselves to work on their femininity.

of members of the Communist Party, state officials, high-ranking officers in the military and the secret police, and a few special professional groups. The new elite not only possessed political power but also received special privileges, including the right to purchase high-quality goods in special stores (in Czechoslovakia, the elite could obtain organically grown produce not available to anyone else), paid vacations at special resorts, access to good housing and superior medical services, and advantages in education and jobs for their children. In 1980, in one Soviet province, 70 percent of Communist Party members came from the families of managers, technicians, and government and party bureaucrats.

Ideals of equality did not include women. Men dominated the leadership positions of the Communist parties. Women did have greater opportunities in the workforce and even in the professions, however. In the Soviet Union, women comprised 51 percent of the labor force in 1980; by the mid-1980s, they constituted 50 percent of the engineers, 80 percent of the doctors, and 75 percent of the teachers and teachers' aides. But many of these were low-paying jobs; most female doctors, for example, worked in primary care and were paid less than skilled machinists. The chief administrators in hospitals and schools were still men.

Moreover, although women made up nearly half of the workforce, they were never freed of their traditional roles in the home (see the box above). Most women confronted what came to be known as the "double shift." After working eight hours in their jobs, they came home to face the housework and care of the children. They might spend two hours a day in long lines at a number of stores waiting to buy food and clothes. Because of the housing situation, they were forced to use kitchens that were shared by a number of families.

Nearly three-quarters of a century after the Bolshevik Revolution, then, the Marxist dream of an advanced, egalitarian society was as far away as ever. Although in some respects conditions in the socialist camp were a distinct improvement over those before World War II, many problems and inequities were as intransigent as ever.

THE DISINTEGRATION OF THE SOVIET EMPIRE

On the death of Konstantin Chernenko in 1985, party leaders selected the talented and vigorous Soviet official Mikhail Gorbachev to succeed him. The new Soviet leader had shown early signs of promise. Born into a peasant family in 1931, Gorbachev combined farmwork with school and received the Order of the Red Banner for his agricultural efforts. This award and his good school record enabled him to study law at the University of Moscow. After receiving his law degree in 1955, he returned to his native southern Russia, where he eventually became first secretary of the Communist Party in the city of Stavropol (he had joined the party in 1952) and then first secretary of the regional party committee. In 1978, Gorbachev was made a member of the party's Central Committee in Moscow. Two years later, he became a full member of the ruling Politburo and secretary of the Central Committee.

During the early 1980s, Gorbachev began to realize the immensity of Soviet problems and the crucial need for massive reform to transform the system. During a visit to Canada in 1983, he discovered to his astonishment that Canadian farmers worked hard on their own initiative. "We'll never have this for fifty years," he reportedly remarked.[5] On his return to Moscow, he set in motion a series of committees to evaluate the situation and recommend measures to improve the system.

The Gorbachev Era

With his election as party general secretary in 1985, Gorbachev seemed intent on taking earlier reforms to their logical conclusions. The cornerstone of his program was *perestroika*, or "restructuring." At first it meant only a reordering of economic policy, as Gorbachev called for the beginning of a market economy with limited free enterprise and some private property. Initial economic reforms were difficult to implement, however. Radicals demanded decisive measures; conservatives feared that rapid changes would be too painful. In his attempt to achieve compromise, Gorbachev often pursued partial liberalization, which satisfied neither faction and also failed to work, producing only more discontent.

Gorbachev soon perceived that in the Soviet system, the economic sphere was intimately tied to the social and political spheres. Any efforts to reform the economy without political or social reform would be doomed to failure. One of the most important instruments of *perestroika* was *glasnost*, or "openness." Soviet citizens and officials were encouraged to discuss openly the strengths and weaknesses of the Soviet Union. This policy could be seen in *Pravda*, the official newspaper of the Communist Party, where news of disasters such as the nuclear accident at Chernobyl in 1986 and collisions of ships in the Black Sea began to appear. This more liberal approach was soon extended to include reports of official corruption, sloppy factory work, and protests against government policy. The arts also benefited from the new policy as previously banned works were now published and motion pictures were allowed to depict negative aspects of Soviet life. Music based on Western styles, such as jazz and rock, could now be performed openly.

Political reforms were equally revolutionary. In June 1987, the principle of two-candidate elections was introduced; previously, voters had been presented with only one candidate. Most dissidents, including Andrei Sakharov, who had spent years in internal exile, were released. At the Communist Party conference in 1988, Gorbachev called for the creation of a new Soviet parliament, the Congress of People's Deputies, whose members were to be chosen in competitive elections. It convened in 1989, the first such meeting in the nation since 1918. Because of its size, the Congress chose a Supreme Soviet of 450 members to deal with day-to-day activities. The revolutionary nature of Gorbachev's political reforms was evident in Sakharov's rise from dissident to elected member of the Congress of People's Deputies. As a leader of the dissident deputies, Sakharov called for an end to the Communist monopoly of power and, on December 11, 1989, the day he died, urged the creation of a new, non-Communist party. Early in 1990, Gorbachev legalized the formation of other political parties and struck out Article 6 of the Soviet Constitution, which guaranteed the "leading role" of the Communist Party. Hitherto, the position of first secretary of the party was the most important post in the Soviet Union, but as the Communist Party became less closely associated with the state, the powers of this office diminished. Gorbachev attempted to consolidate his power by creating a new state presidency and in March 1990 became the Soviet Union's first president.

One of Gorbachev's most serious problems stemmed from the character of the Soviet Union. The Union of Soviet Socialist Republics was a truly multiethnic country, containing 92 nationalities and 112 recognized languages. Previously, the iron hand of the Communist Party, centered in Moscow, had kept a lid on the centuries-old ethnic tensions that had periodically erupted throughout the history of this region. As Gorbachev released this iron grip, tensions resurfaced, a by-product of *glasnost* that Gorbachev had not anticipated. Ethnic groups took

Courtesy of William J. Duiker

➤ AN AFGHAN WAR MEMORIAL.   Moscow's failed war in
Afghanistan in the 1980s cost the lives of an estimated 27,000
Soviet soldiers. Reportedly, at least half the troops lost in the war
came from Belarus, once a Soviet republic and now an independent state under a dictatorial regime. A war memorial to commemorate those who died in the war was recently built in Minsk,
the capital of Belarus. The bridegroom in this wedding party is
from Syria, which accentuates the multiethnic composition of
contemporary Eastern Europe.

advantage of the new openness to protest what they
perceived to be ethnically motivated slights. As violence
erupted, the Soviet army, in disarray since the Soviet
intervention in Afghanistan in 1979, had difficulty controlling the situation. In some cases, independence movements and ethnic causes became linked, as in Azerbaijan,
where the National Front became the spokesgroup for
the Muslim Azerbaijanis in the conflict with Christian
Armenians.

The period from 1988 to 1990 witnessed the emergence
of nationalist movements throughout the republics of the
Soviet Union. Often motivated by ethnic concerns, many
of them called for sovereignty of the republics and independence from Russian-based rule centered in Moscow.
Such movements sprang up first in Georgia in late 1988

and then in Latvia, Estonia, Moldavia, Uzbekistan, Azerbaijan, and Lithuania.

In December 1989, the Communist Party of Lithuania declared itself independent of the Communist Party
of the Soviet Union. A leading force in this independence
movement was the nationalist Lithuanian Restructuring
Movement, or "Popular Front for Perestroika," commonly
known as *Sajudis*, led by Vytautas Landsbergis. Sajudis
favored the radical policy of independence for Lithuania. Gorbachev made it clear that he supported self-
determination but not secession, which he believed would
be detrimental to the Soviet Union. Nevertheless, on
March 11, 1990, the Lithuanian Supreme Council uni-
laterally declared Lithuania independent. Its formal name
was now the Lithuanian Republic; the adjectives Soviet
and Socialist had been dropped. On March 15, the Soviet
Congress of People's Deputies, though recognizing a general right to secede from the Union of Soviet Socialist
Republics, declared the Lithuanian declaration null and
void, insisting that proper procedures must be followed
before secession would be acceptable.

During 1990 and 1991, Gorbachev struggled to deal
with Lithuania and the other problems unleashed by his
reforms. On the one hand, he tried to appease the conservative forces who complained about the growing disorder within the Soviet Union. On the other hand, he
tried to accommodate the liberal forces, especially those
in the Soviet republics, who increasingly favored a new
kind of decentralized Soviet federation. Gorbachev especially labored to cooperate more closely with Boris Yeltsin
(b. 1931), elected president of the Russian Republic in
June 1991.

By 1991, conservatives within the army, government,
KGB, and military industries had grown increasingly worried about the impending dissolution of the Soviet Union
and its impact on their own fortunes. On August 19, 1991,
a group of these discontented rightists arrested Gorbachev
and attempted to seize power. Gorbachev's unwillingness
to work with the conspirators and the brave resistance in
Moscow of Yeltsin and thousands of Russians who had
grown accustomed to their new liberties caused the coup
to disintegrate rapidly. The actions of these right-wing
plotters served to accelerate the very process they had
hoped to stop—the disintegration of the Soviet Union.

Despite desperate pleas from Gorbachev, the Soviet
republics soon opted for complete independence. Ukraine
voted for independence on December 1, 1991. A week
later, the leaders of Russia, Ukraine, and Belarus
announced that the Soviet Union had "ceased to exist"
and would be replaced by a "commonwealth of independent states." Gorbachev resigned on December 25,
1991, and turned over his responsibilities as commander
in chief to Boris Yeltsin, the president of Russia. By the
end of 1991, one of the largest empires in world history
had come to an end, and a new era had begun in its lands
(see Map 26.2).

MAP **26.2**   **Eastern Europe and the Former Soviet Union.**   After the disintegration of the Soviet Union in 1991, several onetime Soviet republics declared their independence. This map shows the new configuration of the states that emerged in the 1990s, including the boundaries after the dissolution of Czechoslovakia and Yugoslavia.
➤ *What new nations have appeared since the end of the Cold War?*

The New Russia: From Empire to Nation

Within Russia, a new power struggle soon ensued. Yeltsin, a onetime engineer from Sverdlovsk who had been dismissed from the Politburo in 1987 for radicalism, was committed to introducing a free market economy as quickly as possible. In December 1991, the Congress of People's Deputies granted Yeltsin temporary power to rule by decree. But former Communist Party members and their allies in the Congress were opposed to many of Yeltsin's economic reforms and tried to place new limits on his powers. Yeltsin fought back. After winning a vote of confidence, both in himself and in his economic reforms, on April 25, 1993, Yeltsin pushed ahead with plans for a new Russian constitution that would abolish the Congress of People's Deputies, create a two-chamber parliament, and establish a strong presidency.

Nevertheless, the conflict between Yeltsin and the Congress continued and turned violent. On September 21, Yeltsin issued a decree dissolving the Congress of People's Deputies and scheduling new parliamentary elections for December. A hard-line parliamentary minority resisted and even took the offensive, urging supporters to take over government offices and the central television station. On October 4, Yeltsin responded by ordering military forces to storm the parliament building and arrest hard-line opponents. Yeltsin used his victory to consolidate his power; at the same time, he remained committed to holding new parliamentary elections on December 12.

During the mid-1990s, Yeltsin was able to maintain a precarious grip on power while seeking to implement reforms that would place Russia on a firm course toward a pluralistic political system and a market economy. But the new post-Communist Russia remained as fragile as ever. Burgeoning economic inequality and rampant corruption aroused widespread criticism and shook the confidence of the Russian people in the superiority of the capitalist system over the one that existed under Communist rule. A nagging war in the Caucasus—where the people of Chechnya have resolutely sought national independence from Russia—drained the government budget and exposed the decrepit state of the once vaunted Red Army. In presidential elections held in 1996, Yeltsin was reelected, but the rising popularity of a revived Communist Party and the growing strength of nationalist elements, combined with Yeltsin's precarious health, raised serious questions about the future of the country.

At the end of 1999, Yeltsin suddenly resigned his office and was replaced by Vladimir Putin, a former member of the KGB. Putin vowed to bring an end to the rampant corruption and inexperience that permeated Russian political culture and to strengthen the role of the central government in managing the affairs of state. During succeeding months, his proposal to centralize power in the hands of the federal government in Moscow was given approval by the parliament; in early 2001, he presented a new plan to regulate political parties, which numbered more than fifty at the beginning of the decade. Parties on both extremes of the political spectrum—the *Yabloko* (apple) faction representing Western-style liberal policies and Gennadi Zyuganov's revived Communist Party—opposed the legislation, without success.

Putin also vowed to bring the breakaway state of Chechnya back under Russian authority and to assume a more assertive role in international affairs. The new president took advantage of growing public anger at Western plans to expand the NATO alliance into Eastern Europe, as well as aggressive actions by NATO countriues against Serbia in the Balkans (see Chapter 27), to restore Russia's position as an influential force in the world. To assuage national pride, he entered negotiations with such former republics of the old Soviet Union as Belarus and Ukraine to tighten forms of mutual political and economic cooperation.

What had happened to derail Yeltsin's plan to transform Soviet society? To some critics, Yeltsin tried to achieve too much too fast. Between 1991 and 1995, state firms that had previously provided about 80 percent of all industrial production and employment had been privatized, while the price of goods (previously subject to government regulation) was opened up to market forces. Only agriculture, where the decision to privatize collective farms had little impact in rural areas, was left substantially untouched. The immediate results were disastrous: industrial output dropped by over a third, while unemployment levels and prices rose dramatically. Many Russian workers and soldiers were not paid their salaries for months on end, and many social services came to an abrupt halt.

THE SOVIET BLOC AND ITS DEMISE

Death of Joseph Stalin	1953
Rise of Nikita Khrushchev	1955
Destalinization speech	1956
Removal of Khrushchev	1964
The Brezhnev Era	1964–1982
Rule of Andropov and Chernenko	1982–1985
Gorbachev comes to power in Soviet Union	1985
Collapse of Communist governments in Eastern Europe	1989
Disintegration of Soviet Union	1991
Presidency of Boris Yeltsin in Russia	1991–1999
Vladimir Putin elected president of Russia	2000

There were other problems as well. With the harsh official and ideological constraints of the Soviet system suddenly removed, corruption—labeled by one observer "criminal gang capitalism"—became rampant, and the government often appeared inept in coping with the complexities of a market economy. Few Russians seemed to grasp the realities of modern capitalism and understandably reacted to the inevitable transition pains from the old system by placing all the blame at the foot of the new one. The fact is, Yeltsin had attempted to change the structure of the Soviet system without due regard to the necessity of changing the mentality of the people as well. The result was a high level of disenchantment. A new joke circulated among the Russian people: "We know now that everything they told us about communism was false. And everything they told us about capitalism was true."

Eastern Europe: From Satellites to Sovereign Nations

The disintegration of the Soviet Union had an immediate impact on its neighbors to the west. First to respond, as in 1956, was Poland, where popular protests at high food prices had erupted in the early 1980s, leading to the rise of an independent labor movement called Solidarity. Led by Lech Walesa (b. 1943), Solidarity rapidly became an influential force for change and a threat to the government's monopoly of power. The union was outlawed in 1981, but martial law did not solve Poland's serious economic problems, and in 1988, the Communist government bowed to the inevitable and permitted free national elections to take place, resulting in the election of Walesa as president of Poland in December 1990. Unlike the situation in 1956, when Khrushchev had intervened to prevent the collapse of the Soviet satellite system in Eastern Europe, in the late 1980s, Moscow—inspired by Gorbachev's policy of encouraging "new thinking" to improve relations with the Western powers— took no action to reverse the verdict in Warsaw.

In Hungary, as in Poland, the process of transition had begun many years previously. After crushing the Hungarian revolution of 1956, the Communist government of János Kádár had tried to assuage popular opinion by enacting a series of far-reaching economic reforms (labeled "communism with a capitalist face-lift"), but as the 1980s progressed, the economy sagged, and in 1989, the regime permitted the formation of opposition political parties, leading eventually to the formation of a non-Communist coalition government in elections held in March 1990.

The transition in Czechoslovakia was more abrupt. After Soviet troops crushed the Prague Spring in 1968, hard-line Communists under Gustav Husak followed a policy of massive repression to maintain their power. In 1977, dissident intellectuals formed an organization called Charter 77 as a vehicle for protest against violations of human rights. Regardless of the repressive atmosphere, dissident activities continued to grow during the 1980s, and when massive demonstrations broke out in several major cities in 1989, President Husak's government, lacking any real popular support, collapsed. At the end of December, he was replaced by Václav Havel, a dissident playwright who had been a leading figure in Charter 77.

But the most dramatic events took place in East Germany, where a persistent economic slump and the ongoing oppressiveness of the regime of Erich Honecker led to a flight of refugees and mass demonstrations against the regime in the summer and fall of 1989. Capitulating to popular pressure, the Communist government opened its entire border with the West. The Berlin Wall, the most tangible symbol of the Cold War, became the site of a massive celebration, and most of it was dismantled by joyful Germans from both sides of the border. In March 1990, free elections led to the formation of a non-Communist government that rapidly carried out a program of political and economic reunification with West Germany.

The dissolution of the Soviet Union and its satellite system in Eastern Europe brought a dramatic end to the Cold War. By the beginning of the new decade, a generation of global rivalry between two ideological systems had come to a close, and world leaders turned their attention to the construction of what U.S. President George Bush called the New World Order. But what sort of new order would it be?

THE EAST IS RED: CHINA UNDER COMMUNISM

In the fall of 1949, China was at peace for the first time in twelve years. The newly victorious Communist Party, under the leadership of its chairman, Mao Zedong, turned its attention to consolidating its power base and healing the wounds of war. Its long-term goal was to construct a socialist society, but its leaders realized that popular support for the revolution was based on the party's platform of honest government, land reform, social justice, and peace rather than on the utopian goal of a classless society. Accordingly, the new regime followed Soviet precedent in adopting a moderate program of political and economic recovery known as New Democracy.

New Democracy

With New Democracy—patterned roughly after Lenin's New Economic Policy in Soviet Russia in the 1920s (see Chapter 22)—the new Chinese leadership tacitly recognized that time and extensive indoctrination would be needed to convince the Chinese people of the superiority of socialism. In the meantime, the party would rely on capitalist profit incentives to spur productivity. Manufacturing and commercial firms were permitted to remain under private ownership, although with stringent government regulations. To win the support of the poorer peasants, who made up the majority of the population, a land redistribution program was adopted, but the collectivization of agriculture was postponed.

In a number of key respects, New Democracy was a success. About two-thirds of the peasant households in the country received land and thus had reason to be grateful to the new regime. Spurred by official tolerance for capitalist activities and the end of internal conflict, the national economy began to rebound, although agricultural production still lagged behind both official targets and the growing population, which was increasing at an annual rate of more than 2 percent. But not all benefited. In the course of carrying out land redistribution, thousands if not millions of landlords and rich farmers lost their lands, their personal property, their freedom, and sometimes their lives. Many of those who died were tried and convicted of "crimes against the people" in people's tribunals set up under official sponsorship in towns and villages around the country. As Mao himself later conceded, many were innocent of any crime, but in the eyes of the party, their deaths were necessary to destroy the

LAND REFORM IN ACTION

*O*ne of the great achievements of the new Communist regime in China was the land reform program, which resulted in the distribution of farmland to almost two-thirds of the rural population. The program consequently won the gratitude of millions of Chinese. But it also had a dark side as local land reform tribunals routinely convicted "wicked landlords" of crimes against the people and then put them to death. The following passage, written by a foreign observer, describes the process in one village.

REVOLUTION IN A CHINESE VILLAGE

T'ien-ming [a Party cadre] called all the active young cadres and the militiamen of Long Bow [village] together and announced to them the policy of the county government, which was to confront all enemy collaborators and their backers at public meetings, expose their crimes, and turn them over to the county authorities for punishment. He proposed that they start with Kuo Te-yu, the puppet village head. Having moved the group to anger with a description of Te-yu's crimes, T'ien-ming reviewed the painful life led by the poor peasants during the occupation and recalled how hard they had all worked and how as soon as they harvested all the grain the puppet officials, backed by army bayonets, took what they wanted, turned over huge quantities to the Japanese devils, forced the peasants to haul it away, and flogged those who refused.

As the silent crowd contracted toward the spot where the accused man stood, T'ien-ming stepped forward. . . . "This is our chance. Remember how we were oppressed. The traitors seized our property. They beat us and kicked us. . . .

"Let us speak out the bitter memories. Let us see that the blood debt is repaid. . . ."

He paused for a moment. The peasants were listening to every word but gave no sign as to how they felt. . . .

"Come now, who has evidence against this man?"

Again there was silence.

Kuei-ts'ai, the new vice-chairman of the village, found it intolerable. He jumped up [and] struck Kuo Te-yu on the jaw with the back of his hand. "Tell the meeting how much you stole," he demanded.

The blow jarred the ragged crowd. It was as if an electric spark had tensed every muscle. Not in living memory had any peasant ever struck an official. . . .

The people in the square waited fascinated as if watching a play. They did not realize that in order for the plot to unfold they themselves had to mount the stage and speak out what was on their minds.

That evening T'ien-ming and Kuei-ts'ai called together the small groups of poor peasants from various parts of the village and sought to learn what it was that was really holding them back. *They soon found the root of the trouble was fear* of the old established political forces, and their military backers. The old reluctance to move against the power of the gentry, the fear of ultimate defeat and terrible reprisal that had been seared into the consciousness of so many generations, lay like a cloud over the peasants' minds and hearts.

Emboldened by T'ien-ming's words, other peasants began to speak out. They recalled what Te-yu had done to them personally. Several vowed to speak up and accuse him the next morning. After the meeting broke up, the passage of time worked its own leaven. In many a hovel and tumbledown house talk continued well past midnight. Some people were so excited they did not sleep at all. . . .

On the following day the meeting was livelier by far. It began with a sharp argument as to who would make the first accusation, and T'ien-ming found it difficult to keep order. Before Te-yu had a chance to reply to any questions, a crowd of young men, among whom were several militiamen, surged forward ready to beat him.

---

power of the landed gentry in the countryside (see the box above).

The Transition to Socialism

Originally, party leaders intended to follow the Leninist formula of delaying the building of a fully socialist society until China had a sufficient industrial base to permit the mechanization of agriculture. In 1953, they launched the nation's first five-year plan (patterned after similar Soviet plans), which called for substantial increases in industrial output. Lenin had believed that mechanization would induce Russian peasants to join collective farms, which, because of their greater size and efficiency, could better afford to purchase expensive farm machinery. But the difficulty of providing tractors and reapers for millions

of rural villages eventually convinced Mao that it would take years, if not decades, for China's infant industrial base to meet the needs of a modernizing agricultural sector. He therefore decided to begin collectivization immediately, in the hope that collective farms would increase food production and release land, labor, and capital for the industrial sector. Accordingly, beginning in 1955, virtually all private farmland was collectivized (although peasant families were allowed to retain small private plots), and most businesses and industries were nationalized.

Collectivization was achieved without provoking the massive peasant unrest that had taken place in the Soviet Union during the 1930s, perhaps because the Chinese government followed a policy of persuasion rather than compulsion (Mao Zedong remarked that Stalin had "drained the pond to catch the fish") and because the

Communist land redistribution program had already earned the support of millions of rural Chinese. But the hoped-for production increases did not materialize, and in 1958, at Mao's insistent urging, party leaders approved a more radical program known as the Great Leap Forward. Existing rural collectives, normally the size of a traditional village, were combined into vast "people's communes," each containing more than thirty thousand people. These communes were to be responsible for all administrative and economic tasks at the local level. The party's official slogan promised "Hard work for a few years, happiness for a thousand."[7]

Some party members were concerned that this ambitious program would threaten the government's rural base of support, but Mao argued that Chinese peasants were naturally revolutionary in spirit. The Chinese rural masses, he said, are

> first of all, poor, and secondly, blank. That may seem like a bad thing, but it is really a good thing. Poor people want change, want to do things, want revolution. A clean sheet of paper has no blotches, and so the newest and most beautiful words can be written on it, the newest and most beautiful pictures can be painted on it.[8]

Those words, of course, were *socialism* and *communism*. The communes were a disaster. Administrative bottlenecks, bad weather, and peasant resistance to the new system (which, among other things, attempted to eliminate work incentives and destroy the traditional family as the basic unit of Chinese society) combined to drive food production downward, and over the next few years, as many as fifteen million people may have died of starvation. Many peasants were reportedly reduced to eating the bark off trees and in some cases allowing infants to starve. In 1960, the experiment was essentially abandoned. Although the commune structure was retained, ownership and management were returned to the collective level. Mao was severely criticized by some of his more pragmatic colleagues (one remarked bitingly that "one cannot reach Heaven in a single step"), provoking him to complain that he had been relegated to the sidelines "like a Buddha on a shelf."

The Great Proletarian Cultural Revolution

But Mao was not yet ready to abandon either his power or his dream of a totally egalitarian society. In 1966, he returned to the attack, mobilizing discontented youth and disgruntled party members into revolutionary units known as Red Guards, who were urged to take to the streets to cleanse Chinese society—from local schools and factories to government ministries in Beijing—of impure elements who (in Mao's mind, at least) were guilty of "taking the capitalist road." Supported by his wife, Jiang Qing, and other radical party figures, Mao launched China on a new forced march toward communism.

AP/Wide World Photos

➤ PUNISHING CHINA'S ENEMIES DURING THE CULTURAL REVOLUTION. The Cultural Revolution, which began in 1966, was a massive effort by Mao Zedong and his radical supporters to eliminate rival elements within the Chinese Communist Party and the government. Accused of being "capitalist roaders," such individuals were subjected to public criticism and removed from their positions. Some were imprisoned or executed. Here Red Guards parade a victim wearing a dunce cap through the streets of Beijing.

The so-called Great Proletarian Cultural Revolution (literally, great revolution to create a proletarian culture) lasted for ten years, from 1966 to 1976. Some Western observers interpreted it as a simple power struggle between Mao Zedong and some of his key rivals such as Liu Shaoqi (Liu Shao-ch'i), Mao's designated successor, and Deng Xiaoping (Teng Hsiao-p'ing), the party's general secretary. Both were removed from their positions, and Liu later died, allegedly of torture, in a Chinese prison. But real policy disagreements were involved. Mao and his supporters feared that capitalist values and the remnants of "feudalist" Confucian ideas would undermine ideological fervor and betray the revolutionary cause. He was convinced that only an atmosphere of "uninterrupted revolution" could enable the Chinese to overcome the lethargy of the past and achieve the final stage of utopian communism. "I care not," he once wrote, "that the winds blow and the waves beat. It is better than standing idly in a courtyard."

His opponents argued for a more pragmatic strategy that gave priority to nation building over the ultimate communist goal of spiritual transformation. But with Mao's supporters now in power, the party carried out vast economic and educational reforms that virtually eliminated any remaining profit incentives, established a new school system that emphasized "Mao Zedong thought," and stressed practical education at the elementary level at the expense of specialized training in science and the humanities in the universities. School learning was discouraged as a legacy of capitalism, and Mao's famous *Little Red Book* (officially, *Quotations of Chairman Mao Zedong*, a slim volume of Maoist aphorisms to encourage good behavior and revolutionary zeal) was hailed as the most important source of knowledge in all areas.

The radicals' efforts to destroy all vestiges of traditional society were reminiscent of the Reign of Terror in revolutionary France, when the Jacobins sought to destroy organized religion and even created a new revolutionary calendar. Red Guards rampaged through the country attempting to eradicate the "four olds" (old thought, old culture, old customs, and old habits). They destroyed temples and religious sculptures; they tore down street signs and replaced them with new ones carrying revolutionary names. At one point, the city of Shanghai even ordered that the significance of colors in stoplights be changed

so that red (the revolutionary color) would indicate that traffic could move.

But a mood of revolutionary ferment and enthusiasm is difficult to sustain. Key groups, including bureaucrats, urban professionals, and many military officers, did not share Mao's belief in the benefits of "uninterrupted revolution" and constant turmoil. Many were alienated by the arbitrary actions of the Red Guards, who indiscriminately accused and brutalized their victims in a society where legal safeguards had almost entirely vanished (see the box on p. 765). Inevitably, the sense of anarchy and uncertainty caused popular support for the movement to erode, and when the end came with Mao's death in 1976, the vast majority of the population may well have welcomed its demise.

Personal accounts by young Chinese who took part in the Cultural Revolution show that their initial enthusiasm often turned to disillusionment. In *Son of the Revolution*, Liang Heng tells how at first he helped friends organize Red Guard groups: "I thought it was a great idea. We would be following Chairman Mao just like the grownups, and Father would be proud of me. I suppose I too resented the teachers who had controlled and criticized me for so long, and I looked forward to a little revenge."[9] Later he had reason to repent. His sister ran off to join the local Red Guard group. Prior to her departure, she denounced her mother and the rest of her family as "rightists" and enemies of the revolution. Their home was regularly raided by Red Guards, and their father was severely beaten and tortured for having three neckties and "Western shirts." Books, paintings, and writings were piled in the center of the floor and burned before his eyes. On leaving, a few of the Red Guards helped themselves to his monthly salary and his transistor radio.

From Mao to Deng

Mao Zedong died in September 1976 at the age of eighty-three. After a short but bitter succession struggle, the pragmatists led by Deng Xiaoping seized power from the radicals and formally brought the Cultural Revolution to an end. Mao's widow, Jiang Qing, and three other radicals (derisively called the "Gang of Four" by their opponents) were placed on trial and sentenced to death or to long prison terms. The egalitarian policies of the previous decade were reversed, and a new program emphasizing economic modernization was introduced.

Under the leadership of Deng Xiaoping, who placed his supporters in key positions throughout the party and the government, attention focused on what were called the "Four Modernizations": industry, agriculture, technology, and national defense. Deng had been a leader of the faction that opposed Mao's program of rapid socialist transformation, and during the Cultural Revolution, he had been forced to perform menial labor to "sincerely correct his errors." But Deng continued to espouse the pragmatic

HAIL THE GREAT HELMSMAN!   During the Great Proletarian Cultural Revolution, Chinese art was restricted to topics that promoted revolution and the thoughts of Chairman Mao Zedong. All the knowledge that the true revolutionary required was to be found in Mao's Little Red Book, a collection of his sayings on proper revolutionary behavior. In this painting, Chairman Mao stands among his admirers, who wave copies of the book as a symbol of their total devotion to him and his vision of a future China.

© Private Collection/Bridgeman Art Library

MAKE REVOLUTION!

*I*n 1966, Mao Zedong unleashed the power of revolution on China. Rebellious youth in the form of Red Guards rampaged through all levels of society, exposing anti-Maoist elements, suspected "capitalist roaders," and those identified with the previous ruling class. In this poignant excerpt, Nien Cheng, the widow of an official of Chiang Kai-shek's regime, describes a visit by Red Guards to her home during the height of the Cultural Revolution.

NIEN CHENG, *LIFE AND DEATH IN SHANGHAI*

Suddenly the doorbell began to ring incessantly. At the same time, there was furious pounding of many fists on my front gate, accompanied by the confused sound of hysterical voices shouting slogans. The cacophony told me that the time of waiting was over and that I must face the threat of the Red Guards and the destruction of my home....

Outside, the sound of voices became louder. "Open the gate! Open the gate! Are you all dead? Whey don't you open the gate?" Someone was swearing and kicking the wooden gate. The horn of the truck was blasting too....

I stood up to put the book on the shelf. A copy of the Constitution of the People's Republic caught my eye. Taking it in my hand and picking up the bunch of keys I had ready on my desk, I went downstairs.

At the same moment, the Red Guards pushed open the front door and entered the house. There were thirty or forty senior high school students, aged between fifteen and twenty, led by two men and one woman much older.

The leading Red Guard, a gangling youth with angry eyes, stepped forward and said to me, "We are the Red Guards. We have come to take revolutionary action against you!"

Though I knew it was futile, I held up the copy of the Constitution and said calmly, "It's against the Constitution of the People's Republic of China to enter a private house without a search warrant."

The young man snatched the document out of my hand and threw it on the floor. With his eyes blazing, he said, "The Constitution is abolished. It was a document written by the Revisionists within the Communist Party. We recognize only the teachings of our Great Leader Chairman Mao." . . .

Another young man used a stick to smash the mirror hanging over the blackwood chest facing the front door.

Mounting the stairs, I was astonished to see several Red Guards taking pieces of my porcelain collection out of their padded boxes. One young man had arranged a set of four Kangxi wine cups in a row on the floor and was stepping on them. I was just in time to hear the crunch of delicate porcelain under the sole of his shoe. The sound pierced my heart. Impulsively I leapt forward and caught his leg just as he raised his foot to crush the next cup. He toppled. We fell in a heap together. . . . The other Red Guards dropped what they were doing and gathered around us, shouting at me angrily for interfering in their revolutionary activities.

The young man whose revolutionary work of destruction I had interrupted said angrily, "You shut up! These things belong to the old culture. They are the useless toys of the feudal emperors and the modern capitalist class and have no significance to us, the proletarian class. They cannot be compared to cameras and binoculars, which are useful for our struggle in time of war. Our Great Leader Chairman Mao taught us, 'If we do not destroy, we cannot establish.' The old culture must be destroyed to make way for the new socialist culture."

approach and reportedly once remarked, "Black cat, white cat, what does it matter so long as it catches the mice?" Under the program of Four Modernizations, many of the restrictions against private activities and profit incentives were eliminated, and people were encouraged to work hard to benefit themselves and Chinese society. The familiar slogan "Serve the people" was replaced by a new one repugnant to the tenets of Mao Zedong thought: "Create wealth for the people."

Crucial to the program's success was the government's ability to attract foreign technology and capital. For more than two decades, China had been isolated from technological advances taking place elsewhere in the world. Although China's leaders understandably prided themselves on their nation's capacity for "self-reliance," their isolationist policy had been exceedingly costly for the national economy. China's post-Mao leaders blamed the country's backwardness on the "ten lost years" of the Cul-

tural Revolution, but the "lost years," at least in technological terms, extended back to 1949 and in some respects even before. Now, to make up for lost time, the government encouraged foreign investment and sent thousands of students and specialists abroad to study capitalist techniques.

By adopting this pragmatic approach in the years after 1976, China made great strides in ending its chronic problems of poverty and underdevelopment. Per capita income roughly doubled during the 1980s; housing, education, and sanitation improved; and both agricultural and industrial output skyrocketed.

But critics, both Chinese and foreign, complained that Deng Xiaoping's program had failed to achieve a "fifth modernization": democracy. Official sources denied such charges and spoke proudly of restoring "socialist legality" by doing away with the arbitrary punishments applied during the Cultural Revolution. Deng himself encouraged the

Chinese people to speak out against earlier excesses. In the late 1970s, ordinary citizens pasted "big character posters" criticizing the abuses of the past on the so-called Democracy Wall near Tiananmen Square in downtown Beijing.

Yet it soon became clear that the new leaders would not tolerate any direct criticism of the Communist Party or of Marxist-Leninist ideology. Dissidents were suppressed, and some were sentenced to long prison terms. Among them was the well-known astrophysicist Fang Lizhi (Fang Lichih), who spoke out publicly against official corruption and the continuing influence of Marxist-Leninist concepts in post-Mao China, telling an audience in Hong Kong that "China will not be able to modernize if it does not break the shackles of Maoist and Stalinist-style socialism." Fang immediately felt the weight of official displeasure. He was refused permission to travel abroad, and articles that he submitted to official periodicals were rejected. Deng himself reportedly remarked, "We will not suppress people who hold differing political views from our own. But as for Fang Lizhi, he has been indulging in mudslinging and spreading slander without any basis, and we should take legal action against him." Replied Fang, "I have never criticized any Chinese leader by name, nor accused any of them of illegal acts or immoral activities. But some perhaps feel guilty. If the cap fits, wear it."[10]

The problem began to intensify in the late 1980s as more Chinese began to study abroad and more information about Western society reached educated individuals inside the country. Rising expectations aroused by the economic improvements of the early 1980s led to increasing pressure from students and other urban residents for better living conditions, relaxed restrictions on study abroad, and increased freedom to select employment after graduation.

Incident at Tiananmen Square

As long as economic conditions for the majority of Chinese were improving, other classes did not share the students' discontent, and the government was able to isolate them from other elements in society. But in the late 1980s, an overheated economy led to rising inflation and growing discontent among salaried workers, especially in the cities. At the same time, corruption, nepotism, and favored treatment for senior officials and party members were provoking increasing criticism. In May 1989, student protesters carried placards demanding "Science and Democracy" (reminiscent of the slogan of the May Fourth Movement, whose seventieth anniversary was celebrated in the spring of 1989), an end to official corruption, and the resignation of China's aging party leadership. These demands received widespread support from the urban population (although notably less in rural areas) and led to massive demonstrations in Tiananmen Square (see the box on p. 767).

The demonstrations divided the Chinese leaders. Reformist elements around party general secretary Zhao Ziyang were sympathetic to the protesters, but veteran leaders such as Deng Xiaoping saw the student demands for more democracy as a disguised call for an end to Communist Party rule. After some hesitation, the government sent tanks and troops into Tiananmen Square to crush the demonstrators. Dissidents were arrested, and

➤ **GIVE ME LIBERTY—OR GIVE ME DEATH!**   The demonstrations that erupted in Tiananmen Square in the spring of 1989 spread rapidly to other parts of China, where students and other local citizens gave their vocal support to the popular movement in Beijing. Here students from a high school march to the city of Guilin to display their own determination to take part in the reform of Chinese society. Their call to "give me liberty or give me death" (in Patrick Henry's famous phrase) echoes the determination expressed by many of their counterparts in Beijing.

Courtesy of William J. Duiker

STUDENTS APPEAL FOR DEMOCRACY

*I*n the spring of 1989, thousands of students gathered in Tiananmen Square in downtown Beijing to provide moral support to their many compatriots who had gone on a hunger strike in an effort to compel the Chinese government to reduce the level of official corruption and enact democratic reforms, opening the political process to the Chinese people. The statement that follows was printed on flyers and distributed to participants and passersby on May 17, 1989, to explain the goals of the movement.

"WHY DO WE HAVE TO UNDERGO A HUNGER STRIKE?"

By 2:00 P.M. today, the hunger strike carried out by the petition group in Tiananmen Square has been under way for 96 hours. By this morning, more than 600 participants have fainted. When these democracy fighters were lifted into the ambulances, no one who was present was not moved to tears.

Our petition group now undergoing the hunger strike demands that at a minimum the government agree to the following two points:

1. To engage on a sincere and equal basis in a dialogue with the "higher education dialogue group." In addition, to broadcast the actual dialogue in its entirety. We absolutely refuse to agree to a partial broadcast, to empty gestures, or to fabrications that dupe the people.
2. To evaluate in a fair and realistic way the patriotic democratic movement. Discard the label of "trouble-making" and redress the reputation of the patriotic democratic movement.

It is our view that the request for a dialogue between the people's government and the people is not an unreasonable one. Our party always follows the principle of seeking truths from actual facts. It is therefore only natural that the evaluation of this patriotic democratic movement should be done in accordance with the principle of seeking truths from actual facts.

Our classmates who are going through the hunger strike are the good sons and daughters of the people! One by one, they have fallen. In the meantime, our "public servants" are completely unmoved. Please, let us ask where your conscience is.

---

the regime once again began to stress ideological purity and socialist values. Although the crackdown provoked widespread criticism abroad, Chinese leaders insisted that economic reforms could only take place in conditions of party leadership and political stability.

Deng Xiaoping and other aging party leaders turned to the army to protect their base of power and suppress what they described as "counterrevolutionary elements." Deng was undoubtedly counting on the fact that many Chinese, particularly in rural areas, feared a recurrence of the disorder of the Cultural Revolution and craved economic prosperity more than political reform. In the months following the confrontation, the government issued new regulations requiring courses on Marxist-Leninist ideology in the schools, sought out dissidents within the intellectual community, and made it clear that while economic reforms would continue, the CCP's monopoly of power would not be allowed to decay. Harsh punishments were imposed on those accused of undermining the Communist system and supporting its enemies abroad.

From Marx to Confucius?

In the 1990s, the government began to nurture urban support by reducing the rate of inflation and guaranteeing the availability of consumer goods in great demand among the rising middle class. Under Deng Xiaoping's successor Jiang Zemin, who occupied the positions of both party chief and president of China, the government promoted rapid economic growth while cracking down harshly on political dissent. That policy paid dividends in bringing about a perceptible decline in alienation among the population in the cities. Industrial production continued to increase rapidly, leading to predictions that China would become one of the economic superpowers of the twenty-first century. But discontent in rural areas began to increase, as lagging farm income, high taxes, and official corruption sparked resentment in the countryside (see "Economics in Command" on p. 769).

Partly out of fear that such developments could undermine the socialist system and the rule of the CCP, conservative leaders have attempted to curb Western influence and restore faith in Marxism-Leninism. In what may be a tacit recognition that Marxist exhortations are no longer an effective means of enforcing social discipline, the party has turned to Confucianism as an antidote. Ceremonies celebrating the birth of Confucius now receive official sanction, and the virtues promoted by the master, such as righteousness, propriety, and filial piety, are now widely cited as an antidote to the tide of antisocial behavior. An article in *People's Daily* asserted that the spiritual crisis in contemporary Western culture stems from the incompatibility between science and the Christian religion. The solution, the author maintained, is Confucianism, "a nonreligious humanism that can provide the basis for morals and the value of life." Because a culture combining science and Confucianism is taking shape in East Asia today, "it will thrive particularly well in the next century and will replace modern and contemporary Western culture."[11]

Beijing's decision to emphasize traditional Confucian themes as a means of promoting broad popular support for its domestic policies is paralleled in the world arena, where it relies on the spirit of nationalism to achieve its goals. Today, China conducts an independent foreign policy and is playing an increasingly active role in the region. To some of its neighbors, including Japan, India, and Russia, China's new posture is cause for disquiet and gives rise to suspicions that it is once again preparing to flex its muscle as in the imperial era. A striking example of this new attitude took place as early as 1979, when Chinese forces briefly invaded Vietnam as punishment for the Vietnamese occupation of neighboring Cambodia. In the 1990s, China has aroused concern in the region by claiming sole ownership over the Spratly Islands in the South China Sea and over Diaoyu Island (also claimed by Japan) near Taiwan.

To Chinese leaders, however, such actions simply represent legitimate efforts to resume China's rightful role in the affairs of the region. After a century of humiliation at the hands of the Western powers and neighboring Japan, the nation, in Mao's famous words of 1949, "has stood up," and no one will be permitted to humiliate it again. For the moment, at least, a fervent sense of patriotism appears to be on the rise in China, a phenomenon that is actively promoted by the party as a means of holding the country together in uncertain times. Pride in the achievement of national sports teams is intense, and many Chinese reacted with enthusiasm when the country was awarded the 2008 Summer Olympic Games (Beijing's earlier bid to host the games in 2000 had been rejected).

Whether the current leadership will be able by such artificial means to prevent further erosion of the party's power and prestige is unclear. In the short term, such efforts may succeed in slowing the process of change because many Chinese are understandably fearful of punishment and concerned for their careers. And high economic growth rates can sometimes cover a multitude of problems as many will opt to chase the fruits of materialism rather than the less tangible benefits of individual freedom. But in the long run, the party leadership must resolve the contradiction between political authoritarianism and economic prosperity. One is reminded of Chiang Kai-shek's failed attempt during the 1930s to revive Confucian ethics as a standard of behavior for modern China—dead ideologies cannot be revived by decree.

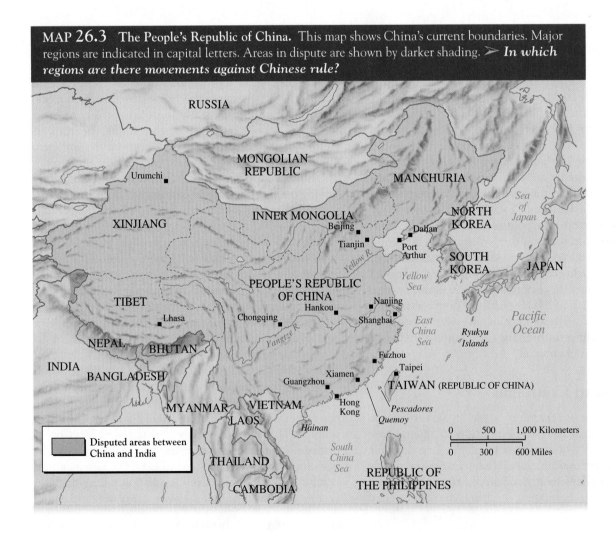

MAP 26.3 **The People's Republic of China.** This map shows China's current boundaries. Major regions are indicated in capital letters. Areas in dispute are shown by darker shading. ➤ *In which regions are there movements against Chinese rule?*

Chronology

CHINA UNDER COMMUNIST RULE

There is also growing unrest among China's national minorities: in Xinjiang, where restless Muslim peoples observe with curiosity the emergence of independent Islamic states in Central Asia, and in Tibet, where the official policy of quelling separatism has led to the violent suppression of Tibetan culture and an influx of thousands of ethnic Chinese immigrants. In the meantime, the Falun Gong religious movement, which the government has attempted to suppress as a potentially serious threat to its authority, is an additional indication that with the disintegration of the old Maoist utopia, the Chinese people will need more than a pallid version of Marxism-Leninism or a revived Confucianism to fill the gap.

"SERVE THE PEOPLE": CHINESE SOCIETY UNDER COMMUNISM

Enormous changes have taken place in Chinese society since the Communists' rise to power in 1949. Yet beneath the surface are hints of the survival of elements of the old China. Despite all the efforts of Mao Zedong and his colleagues, the ideas of Confucius have not been discarded. China under communism remains a society that in many respects is in thrall to its past.

The Politics of the Mass Line

Nowhere is the uneasy balance between the old and the new more clearly demonstrated than in China's politics and government. In broad outlines, the new political system followed the Soviet pattern. Yet from the start, CCP leaders made it clear that the Chinese model would differ from the Soviet one in important respects. Whereas

the Bolsheviks had severely distrusted nonrevolutionary elements in Russia and established a minority government based on the radical left, Mao Zedong and his colleagues were more confident that they possessed the basic support of the majority of the Chinese people. Under New Democracy, the party attempted to reach out to all progressive classes in the population to maintain the alliance that had brought it to power in the first place.

The primary link between the regime and the population was the system of "mass organizations," representing peasants, workers, women, religious groups, writers, and artists. The party had established these associations during the 1920s to mobilize support for the revolution. Now they served as a conduit between party and people, enabling the leaders to assess the attitude of the masses while at the same time seeking their support for the party's programs.

Initially, this "mass line" system worked fairly well. Although opposition to the regime was ruthlessly suppressed, China finally had a government that appeared to be for the people. Although there was no pretense at Western-style democracy, and official corruption and bureaucratic mismanagement and arrogance had by no means been eliminated, the new ruling class came preponderantly from workers and peasants and, at least by comparison with its predecessors, seemed willing to listen to the complaints and aspirations of its constituents.

But the Great Leap Forward betrayed a fundamental weakness in the policy of the mass line. While party leaders declared their willingness to listen to the concerns of the population, they were also determined to build a utopian society based on Marxist-Leninist principles. Although popular acceptance of the collectivization program during the mid-1950s had been considerable, the extremist experiment with people's communes was widely resisted, forcing the government to abandon the program.

The failure of the Great Leap Forward split the CCP and led to the revolutionary disturbances of the following decade. The Cultural Revolution represented Mao's attempt to cleanse the system of its impurities and put Chinese society back on the straight road to egalitarian communism, but the enthusiasms aroused by the Cultural Revolution did not last. As in the French Revolution, the efforts to achieve revolutionary purity eventually alienated all except the most radical elements in the country, and a period of reaction inevitably set in. In China, revolutionary fervor gave way to a new era in which belief in socialist ideals was replaced by a more practical desire for material benefits.

Economics in Command

Deng Xiaoping recognized the need to restore credibility to a system on the verge of breakdown, and hoped that rapid economic growth would satisfy the Chinese people and prevent them from demanding political reforms.

The post-Mao leaders clearly placed economic performance over ideological purity. To stimulate the stagnant industrial sector, which had been under state control since the end of the New Democracy era, they reduced bureaucratic controls over state industries and allowed local managers to have more say over prices, salaries, and quality control. Productivity was encouraged by permitting bonuses for extra effort, a policy that had been discouraged during the Cultural Revolution. The regime also tolerated the emergence of a small private sector. Unemployed youth were encouraged to set up restaurants, bicycle or radio repair shops, and handicraft shops on their own initiative.

Finally, the regime opened up the country to foreign investment and technology. The Maoist policy of self-reliance was abandoned, and China openly sought the advice of foreign experts and the money of foreign capitalists. Special economic zones were established in urban centers near the coast (ironically, many were located in the old nineteenth-century treaty ports), where lucrative concessions were offered to encourage foreign firms to build factories. The tourist industry was encouraged, and students were sent abroad to study.

The new leaders especially stressed educational reform. The system adopted during the Cultural Revolution, emphasizing practical education and ideology at the expense of higher education and modern science, was rapidly abandoned (the *Little Red Book* was even withdrawn from circulation and could no longer be found on bookshelves), and a new system based generally on the Western model was instituted. Admission to higher education was based on success in merit examinations, and courses on science and mathematics received high priority.

No economic reform program could succeed unless it included the countryside. Three decades of socialism had done little to increase food production or to lay the basis for a modern agricultural sector. China, with a population now numbering one billion, could still barely feed itself. Peasants had little incentive to work and few opportunities to increase production through mechanization, the use of fertilizer, or better irrigation.

Under Deng Xiaoping, agricultural policy made a rapid about-face. Under the new "rural responsibility system," adopted shortly after Deng had consolidated his authority, collectives leased land to peasant families, who paid a quota in the form of rent to the collective. Anything produced on the land above that payment could be sold on the private market or consumed. To soak up excess labor in the villages, the government encouraged the formation of so-called sideline industries, a modern equivalent of the traditional cottage industries in premodern China. Peasants raised fish or shrimp, made consumer goods, and even assembled living room furniture and appliances for sale to their newly affluent compatriots.

The reform program had a striking effect on rural production. Grain production increased rapidly, and farm income doubled during the 1980s. Yet it also created problems. In the first place, income at the village level became more unequal as some enterprising farmers (known locally as "ten-thousand-dollar households") earned profits several times those realized by their less fortunate or industrious neighbors. When some farmers discovered that they could earn more by growing cash crops or other specialized commodities, they devoted less land to rice and other grain crops, thus threatening to reduce the supply of China's most crucial staple. Finally, the agricultural policy threatened to undermine the government's population control program, which party leaders viewed as crucial to the success of the Four Modernizations.

Since a misguided period in the mid-1950s when Mao Zedong had argued that more labor would result in higher productivity, China had been attempting to limit its population growth. By 1970, the government had launched a stringent family planning program—including education, incentives, and penalties for noncompliance—to persuade the Chinese people to limit themselves to one child per family. The program did have some success, and population growth was reduced drastically in the early 1980s. The rural responsibility system, however, undermined the program because it encouraged farm families to pay the penalties for having additional children in the belief that their labor would increase family income and provide the parents with a form of social security for their old age.

Still, the overall effects of the modernization program were impressive. The standard of living improved for the

✦ TOURISM COMES TO CHINA. During the Maoist era, Chinese citizens were not permitted to leave their place of habitation without permission from the authorities. Only in the 1990s, with increased prosperity and growing social mobility, did freedom of movement become generally acceptable for the majority of the population. One result has been a dramatic increase in tourism as millions of Chinese begin to explore the glories of their ancient civilization. In this photograph, Chinese tourists are visiting the imperial tombs of the Ming dynasty outside the onetime capital of Nanjing.

majority of the population. Whereas a decade earlier, the average Chinese had struggled to earn enough to buy a bicycle, radio, watch, or washing machine, by the late 1980s, many were beginning to purchase videocassette recorders, refrigerators, and color television sets. The government popularized the idea that all Chinese would prosper, although not necessarily at the same speed. Yet the rapid growth of the economy created its own problems: inflationary pressures, greed, envy, increased corruption, and—most dangerous of all for the regime—rising expectations. Young people in particular resented restrictions on employment (most young people in China are still required to accept the jobs that are offered to them by the government or school officials) and opportunities to study abroad. Disillusionment ran high, especially in the cities, where lavish living by officials and rising prices for goods aroused widespread alienation and cynicism. Such attitudes undoubtedly contributed to the anger and frustration that burst out during the spring of 1989, when many workers, peasants, and functionaries joined the demonstrations against official corruption and one-party rule in Tiananmen Square.

During the 1990s, growth rates in the industrial sector continued to be high as domestic capital became increasingly available to compete with the growing pres-

ence of foreign enterprises. The government finally recognized the need to close down inefficient state enterprises, and by the end of the decade, the private sector, with official encouragement, accounted for over 10 percent of the gross domestic product. A stock market opened, and China's prowess in the international marketplace improved dramatically.

As a result of these developments, China now possesses a large and increasingly affluent middle class. The domestic market for consumer goods has burgeoned in recent years, as indicated by the fact that over 80 percent of all urban Chinese possess a color TV, a refrigerator, and a washing machine. One-third own their own homes, and nearly as many have an air conditioner. Like their counterparts elsewhere in Asia, urban Chinese are increasingly brand-name conscious, a characteristic that provides a considerable challenge to local manufacturers.

But as Chinese leaders now discovered, rapid economic change never comes without cost. The closing of state-run factories has led to the dismissal of millions of workers each year, and the private sector, although growing at over 20 percent annually, is unable to absorb them all. Discontent has been growing in the countryside as well, where a grain surplus has cut into farm incomes (the government tried to increase the official purchase price for grain but

NANJING ROAD: A CONSUMER'S PARADISE.   Shanghai has exploded into China's most affluent city, its forest of shimmering skyscrapers testifying to the phenomenal expansion of the Chinese economy in recent years. Nanjing Road, seen here, is one long avenue of towering banks, office buildings, hotels, and luxurious department stores. Along with these competing Chinese commercial signs, the ubiquitous American enterprises, such as Kentucky Fried Chicken, Pepsi-Cola, and McDonald's, vie for the attention of the fashionably dressed Shanghainese as they shop for the latest styles.

rescinded the order when it became too expensive). China's recent entrance into the World Trade Organization may help the national economy as a whole, but is less likely to benefit farmers, who must now face the challenge of cheap foreign food imports. Millions of rural Chinese have left for the big cities, where many of them are unable to find steady employment and are forced to live in squalid conditions in crowded tenements or in the sprawling suburbs. Millions of others remain on the farm but attempt to maximize their income by producing for the market or by increasing the size of their families.

Another factor hindering China's rush to economic advancement is the impact on the environment. With the rising population, fertile land is in increasingly short supply (China, with twice the population, now has only two-thirds as much irrigable land as it had in 1950). Soil erosion is a major problem, especially in the north, where the desert is encroaching on farmlands. Water is also a problem. A massive dam project now under way in the Yangtze River valley has sparked protests from environmentalists, as well as from local peoples forced to migrate from the area. The rate of air pollution is ten times the level in the United States, contributing to growing health concerns. Chinese leaders now face the uncomfortable reality that the pains of industrialization are not exclusive to capitalist countries.

THE LEGACY OF THE PAST: CONTINUITY AND CHANGE IN CHINESE SOCIETY

From the start, the Chinese Communist Party intended to bring an end to the Confucian legacy in modern China. At the root of Marxist-Leninist ideology is the idea of building a new citizen free from the prejudices, ignorance, and superstition of the "feudal" era and the capitalist desire for self-gratification. This new citizen would be characterized not only by a sense of racial and sexual equality but also by the selfless desire to contribute his or her utmost for the good of all.

The new government wasted no time in keeping its promise. During the early 1950s, it took a number of steps to bring a definitive end to the old system in China. Women were permitted to vote and encouraged to become active in the political process. At the local level, an increasing number of women became active in the CCP and in collective organizations. In 1950, a new marriage law guaranteed women equal rights with men. Most important, perhaps, it permitted women for the first time to initiate divorce proceedings against their husbands. Within a year, nearly one million divorces had been granted.

The regime also undertook to destroy the influence of the traditional family system. To the Communists, loyalty to the family, a crucial element in the Confucian social order, undercut loyalty to the state and to the dictatorship of the proletariat.

At first, however, the new government moved carefully to avoid alienating its supporters in the countryside unnecessarily. When collective farms were established in the mid-1950s, payment for hours worked in the form of ration coupons was made not to the individual but to the family head, thus maintaining the traditionally dominant position of the patriarch. When people's communes were established in the late 1950s, payments went to the individual.

During the political radicalism of the Great Leap Forward, children were encouraged to report to the authorities any comments by their parents that criticized the system. Such practices continued during the Cultural Revolution, when children were expected to tell on their parents, students on their teachers, and employees on their superiors. Some have suggested that Mao deliberately encouraged such practices to bring an end to the traditional "politics of dependency." According to this theory, historically the famous "five relationships" forced individuals to swallow their anger and frustration and accept the hierarchical norms established by Confucian ethics (known in Chinese as "to eat bitterness"). By encouraging the oppressed elements in society—the young, the female, and the poor—to voice their bitterness, Mao was helping to break the tradition of dependency. Such denunciations had been issued against landlords and other "local tyrants" in the land reform tribunals of the late 1940s and early 1950s. Later, during the Cultural Revolution, they were applied to other authority figures in Chinese society.

The post-Mao era brought a decisive shift away from revolutionary utopianism and a return to the pragmatic approach to nation building. For most people, it meant improved living conditions and a qualified return to family traditions (see the box on p. 773). For the first time, millions of Chinese saw the prospect of a house or an urban flat with a washing machine, television set, and indoor plumbing. Young people whose parents had given them patriotic names such as Build the Country, Protect Mao Zedong, and Assist Korea began to choose more elegant and cosmopolitan names for their own children. Some names, such as Surplus Grain or Bring a Younger Brother, expressed hope for the future.

The new attitudes were also reflected in physical appearance. For a generation after the civil war, clothing had been restricted to the traditional baggy "Mao suit" in olive drab or dark blue, but by the 1980s, young people craved such fashionable Western items as designer jeans, trendy sneakers, and sweat suits (or reasonable facsimiles). Cosmetic surgery to create a more buxom figure or a more Western facial look became increasingly common among affluent young women in the cities. Many had the epicanthic fold over their eyelids removed or their

MARRIAGE, CHINESE STYLE

"What men can do, women can also do." So said Chairman Mao as he "liberated" and masculinized Chinese women to work alongside men. Women's individuality and sexuality were sacrificed for the collective good of his new socialist society. Marriage, which had traditionally been arranged by families for financial gain, was now dictated by duty to the state. The Western concept of romantic love did not enter into a Chinese marriage, as this interview of a schoolteacher by the reporter Zhang Xinxin in the mid-1980s illustrates. According to recent surveys, the same is true today.

ZHANG XINXIN, CHINESE LIVES

My husband and I never did any courting—honestly! We registered our marriage a week after we'd met. He was just out of the forces and a worker in a building outfit. They'd been given a foreign-aid assignment in Zambia, and he was selected. He wanted to get his private life fixed up before he went, and someone introduced us. Seeing how he looked really honest, I accepted him.

No, you can't say I didn't know anything about him. The person who introduced us told me he was a Party member who'd been an organization commissar. Any comrade who's good enough to be an organization cadre is politically reliable. Nothing special about our standing of living—it's what we've earned. He's still a worker, but we live all right, don't we?

He went off with the army as soon as we'd registered our marriage and been given the wedding certificates. He was away three years. We didn't have the wedding itself before he went because we hadn't got a room yet.

Those three years were a test for us. The main problem was that my family was against it. They thought I was still only a kid and I'd picked the wrong man. What did they have against him? His family was too poor. Of course I won in the end—we'd registered and got our wedding certificates. We were legally married whether we had the family ceremony or not.

We had our wedding after he came back in the winter of 1973. His leaders and mine all came to congratulate us and give us presents. The usual presents those days were busts of Chairman Mao. I was twenty-six and he was twenty-nine. We've never had a row.

I never really wanted to take the college entrance exams. Then in 1978 the school leadership got us all to put our names forward. They said they weren't going to hold us back: the more of us who passed, the better it would be for the school. So I put my name forward, crammed for six weeks, and passed. I already had two kids then. . . .

I reckoned the chance for study was too good to miss. And my husband was looking after the kids all by himself. I usually only came back once a fortnight. So I couldn't let him down.

My instructors urged me to take the exams for graduate school, but I didn't. I was already thirty-four, so what was the point of more study? There was another reason too. I didn't want an even wider gap between us: he hadn't even finished junior middle school when he joined the army.

It's bad if the gap's too wide. For example, there's a definite difference in our tastes in music and art, I have to admit that. But what really matters? Now we've set up this family we have to preserve it. Besides, look at all the sacrifices he had to make to see me through college. Men comrades all like a game of cards and that, but he was stuck with looking after the kids. He still doesn't get any time for himself—it's all work for him.

We've got a duty to each other. Our differences? The less said about them the better. We've always treated each other with the greatest respect.

Of course some people have made suggestions, but my advice to him is to respect himself and respect me. I'm not going to be like those men who ditch their wives when they go up in the world.

I'm the head of our school now. With this change in my status I've got to show even more responsibility for the family. Besides, I know how much he's done to get me where I am today. I've also got some duties in the municipal Women's Federation and Political Consultative Conference. No, I'm not being modest. I haven't done anything worth talking about, only my duty.

We've got to do a lot more educating people. There have been two cases of divorce in our school this year.

noses enlarged—a curious decision in view of the tradition of referring derogatorily to foreigners as "big noses."

Religious practices and beliefs also changed. As the government became more tolerant, some Chinese began returning to the traditional Buddhist faith or to folk religions, and Buddhist and Taoist temples were once again crowded with worshipers. Despite official efforts to suppress its more evangelical forms, Christianity became increasingly popular; like the "rice Christians" (persons who supposedly converted for economic reasons) of the past, many viewed it as a symbol of success and cosmopolitanism.

As with all social changes, China's reintegration into the outside world has had a price. Arranged marriages, nepotism, and mistreatment of females (for example, many parents in rural areas reportedly have killed female infants in the hope of having a son) have come back, although such behavior likely had survived under the cloak of revolutionary purity for a generation. Materialistic attitudes are highly prevalent among young people, along with a corresponding cynicism about politics and the CCP. Expensive weddings are now increasingly common, and bribery and favoritism are all too frequent. Crime of all types, including an apparently growing incidence of prostitution and sex crimes against women, appears to be on the rise. To discourage sexual abuse, the government now seeks to provide free legal services for women living in rural areas.

There is also a price to pay for the trend toward privatization. Under the Maoist system, the elderly and the sick were provided with retirement benefits and health care by the state or by the collective organizations. Under current conditions, with the latter no longer playing such a social role and more workers operating in the private sector, the safety net has been removed. The government recently attempted to fill the gap by enacting a social security law, but because of lack of funds, eligibility is limited primarily to individuals in the urban sector of the economy. Those living in the countryside—who still represent 60 percent of the population—are essentially left to their own devices.

CHINA'S CHANGING CULTURE

Like their contemporaries all over Asia, Chinese artists were strongly influenced by the revolutionary changes that were taking place in the art world of the West in the early twentieth century. In the decades following the 1911 revolution, Chinese artists began to experiment with Western styles, although the more extreme schools such as Surrealism and abstract painting had little impact.

The rise to power of the Communists in 1949 added a new dimension to the debate over the future of culture in China. The new leaders rejected the Western attitude of "art for art's sake" and, like their Soviet counterparts, viewed culture as an important instrument of indoctrination. The standard would no longer be aesthetic quality or the personal preference of the artist but "art for life's safe," whereby culture would serve the interests of socialism.

At first, the new emphasis on socialist realism did not entirely extinguish the influence of traditional culture. Mao and his colleagues tolerated—and even encouraged—efforts by artists to synthesize traditional ideas with socialist concepts and Western techniques. During the Cultural Revolution, however, all forms of traditional culture came to be viewed as reactionary. Socialist realism became the only acceptable standard in literature, art, and music. All forms of traditional expression were forbidden.

Nowhere were the dilemmas of the new order more challenging than in literature. In the heady afterglow of the Communist victory, many progressive writers supported the new regime and enthusiastically embraced Mao's exhortation to create a new Chinese literature for the edification of the masses. But in the harsher climate of the 1960s, many writers were criticized by the party for their excessive individualism and admiration for Western culture. Such writers either toed the new line and suppressed their doubts or were jailed and silenced.

Characteristic of the changing cultural climate was the experience of author Ding Ling. Born in 1904 and educated in a school for women set up by leftist intellectuals during the hectic years after the May Fourth Movement, she began writing in her early twenties. At first, she was strongly influenced by prevailing Western styles, but after her husband, a struggling young poet and a member of the CCP, was executed by Chiang Kai-shek's government in 1931, she became active in party activities and sublimated her talent to the revolutionary cause.

In the late 1930s, Ding settled in Yan'an, where she became active in women's and literary associations. She remained dedicated to revolution, but years of service to the party had not stifled her individuality, and in 1942, she wrote critically of the incompetence, arrogance, and hypocrisy of many party officials, as well as the treatment of women in areas under Communist authority. Such conduct raised eyebrows, but she was able to survive criticism and in 1948 wrote her most famous novel, *The Sun Shines over the Sangan River*, which described the land reform program in favorable terms. It was awarded the Stalin Prize three years later.

During the early 1950s, Ding Ling was one of the most prominent literary lights of the new China, but in the more ideological climate at the end of the decade, she was attacked for her individualism and her previous criticism of the party. Although temporarily rehabilitated, during the Cultural Revolution she was sentenced to hard labor on a commune in the far north and was released only in the late 1970s after Mao's death. Despite failing health, she began writing a biography of her mother that examined the role of women in twentieth-century China. She died in 1981. Ding Ling's story mirrors the fate of thousands of progressive Chinese intellectuals who, despite their efforts, were not able to satisfy the constantly changing demands of a repressive regime.

After Mao's death, Chinese culture was finally released from the shackles of socialist realism. In painting, where for a decade the only acceptable standard for excellence was praise for the party and its policies, the new permissiveness led to a revival of interest in both traditional and Western forms. Although some painters continued to blend Eastern and Western styles, others imitated trends from abroad, experimenting with a wide range of previously prohibited art styles, including Cubism and abstract painting.

In the late 1980s, two avant-garde art exhibits shocked the Chinese public and provoked the wrath of the party. An exhibition of nude paintings, the first ever held in China, attracted many viewers but reportedly offended the modesty of many Chinese. The second was an exhibit presenting the works of various schools of modern and postmodern art. The event resulted in considerable commentary and some expressions of public hostility. After a Communist critic lambasted the works as promiscuous and

⇒ **A STREET CALLIGRAPHER.** During the Great Proletarian Cultural Revolution, all aspects of traditional culture were forbidden. Only items with revolutionary themes were permitted to be created or displayed. This elderly Chinese gentleman, a calligrapher by profession, had been prohibited from practicing his craft for two decades until the post-Mao era in the 1980s. He then resumed his career at a roadside stand on a residential street in Beijing.

ideologically reactionary, the government declared that henceforth it would regulate all art exhibits.

The limits of freedom of expression were most apparent in literature. During the early 1980s, party leaders encouraged Chinese writers to express their views on the mistakes of the past, and a new "literature of the wounded" began to describe the brutal and arbitrary character of the Cultural Revolution. One of the most prominent writers was Bai Hua, whose script for the film *Bitter Love* described the life of a young Chinese painter who joined the revolutionary movement during the 1940s but was destroyed during the Cultural Revolution when his work was condemned as counterrevolutionary. The film depicts the condemnation through a view of a street in Beijing "full of people waving the *Quotations of Chairman Mao*, all those devout and artless faces fired by a feverish fanaticism." Driven from his home for posting a portrait of a third-century B.C.E. defender of human freedom on a Beijing wall, the artist flees the city. At the end of the film, he dies in a snowy field, where his corpse and a semicircle made by his footprints form a giant question mark.

In criticizing the excesses of the Cultural Revolution, Bai Hua was only responding to Deng Xiaoping's appeal for intellectuals to speak out, but he was soon criticized for failing to point out the essentially beneficial role of the CCP in recent Chinese history, and his film was withdrawn from circulation in 1981. Bai Hua was compelled to recant his errors and to state that the great ideas of Mao Zedong on art and literature were "still of universal guiding significance today."[12]

As the attack on Bai Hua illustrates, many party leaders remained suspicious of the impact that "decadent" bourgeois culture could have on the socialist foundations of Chinese society, and the official press periodically warned that China should adopt only the "positive" aspects of Western culture (notably, its technology and its work ethic) and not the "negative" elements such as drug use, pornography, and hedonism. Conservatives were especially incensed by the tendency of many writers to dwell on the shortcomings of the socialist system and to come uncomfortably close to direct criticism of the role of the CCP (see the box on p. 776).

Another author whose writings fell under the harsh glare of official disapproval is Zhang Xinxin (b. 1953). Her controversial novellas and short stories, which explored Chinese women's alienation and spiritual malaise, were viewed by many as a negative portrayal of contemporary society, provoking the government in 1984 to prohibit her from publishing for a year. Determined and resourceful, Zhang turned to reportage. With a colleague, she interviewed one hundred "ordinary" people to record their views on all aspects of everyday life.

One of the chief targets of China's recent "spiritual civilization" campaign is author Wang Shuo (b. 1958), whose writings have been banned for exhibiting a sense of "moral decay." In his novels *Playing for Thrills* (1989) and *Please Don't Call Me Human* (2000), Wang highlighted the seamier side of contemporary urban society, peopled with hustlers, ex-convicts, and other assorted hooligans.

TROUBLE IN THE GARLIC FIELDS

Considered one of the masterpieces of modern Chinese literature, Mo Yan's novel The Garlic Ballads *(1988) describes with passion and intimacy the suffering of contemporary Chinese peasants in northern China. Based on real-life riots in northern China in the summer of 1987, the novel is a plea for social reform as it exposes the greed, corruption, and inhumanity of the local government and the legacy of the feudal mentality. Oppressed and betrayed by their cadres, a group of garlic farmers are swept up into a riot against the local administrator. Mo Yan depicts the resilience and courage of Chinese peasants in the face of incredible hardship and violent oppression. In the closing pages of the novel, at the trial of the peasant rioters, a young military officer, speaking for the author and human decency, accuses the local judge of turning the court into a travesty of justice. In a more recent novel,* The Republic of Wine *(2000), Mo exposes the greed and inhumanity of party officials, whose corrupt practices mock the ideals of a just socialist society.*

MO YAN, *THE GARLIC BALLADS*

He turned to face the spectators, speaking with a passion that touched everyone who heard him. "Your Honors, ladies and gentlemen, the situation in our farming villages has changed drastically in the wake of the Party's Third Plenary Session of the Eleventh Central Committee, including those here in Paradise County. The peasants are much better off than they were during the Cultural Revolution. This is obvious to everyone. But the benefits they enjoyed as a result of rural economic reforms are gradually disappearing."

"Please don't stray too far from the subject," the presiding judge broke in.

"Thank you for reminding me, Your Honor: I'll get right to the point. In recent years the peasants have been called upon to shoulder ever heavier burdens: fees, taxes, fines, and inflated prices for just about everything they need. No wonder you hear them talk about plucking the wild goose's tail feathers as it flies by. Over the past couple of years these trends have gotten out of control, which is why, I believe, the Paradise County garlic incident should have come as no surprise."

The presiding judge glanced down at his wrist-watch.

"Not being able to sell their crops was the spark that ignited this explosive incident, but the root cause was the unenlightened policies of the Paradise County government!" the officer continued. "Before Liberation only about a dozen people were employed by the district government, and things worked fine. Now even a township government in charge of the affairs of a mere thirty thousand people employs more than sixty people! And when you add those in the communes it's nearly a hundred, seventy percent of whose salaries are paid by peasants through township fees and taxes. Put in the bluntest possible terms, they are feudal parasites on the body of society! So in my view, the slogans 'Down with corrupt officials!' and 'Down with bureaucrats!' comprise a progressive call for the awakening of the peasants. . . .

"What I want to say is this," the young officer continued. "The people have the right to overthrow any party or government that disregards their well-being. If an official assumes the role of public master rather than public servant, the people have the right to throw him out! . . . In point of fact, things have improved in the wake of the party rectification, and most of Paradise County's responsible party members are doing a fine job. But one rat turd can spoil a whole pot of porridge, and the unprincipled behavior of a single party member adversely affects the party's reputation and the government's prestige. The people aren't always fair and discerning, and can be forgiven if their dissatisfaction with a particular official carries over into their attitudes toward officials in general. But shouldn't that be a reminder to officials to act in such a way as to best represent the party and the government?

". . . If we endorse the proposition that all people are equal under the law, then we must demand that the Paradise County People's Procuratorate indict Paradise County administrator Zhong Weimin on charges of official misconduct! I have nothing more to say."

The young officer remained standing for a moment before wearily taking a seat behind the defense table. Thunderous applause erupted from the spectator section behind him.

Spiritually depleted, hedonistic, and amoral in their approach to life, his characters represent the polar opposite of the socialist ideal.

 CONCLUSION

For four decades after the end of World War II, the world's two superpowers competed for global hegemony. What began as a dispute on the future shape of Eastern Europe

spread rapidly to Asia and ultimately penetrated virtually every part of the earth. The Cold War became the dominant feature on the international scene and determined the internal politics of many countries around the world as well.

By the early 1980s, some of the tension had gone out of the conflict as it appeared that both Moscow and Washington had learned to tolerate the other's existence. Skeptical minds even suspected that both countries drew benefits from their mutual rivalry and saw it as an advantage in carrying on their relations with friends and allies.

Few suspected that the Cold War, which had long seemed a permanent feature of world politics, was about to come to an end.

What brought about the collapse of the Soviet Empire? Some observers argue that the ambitious defense policies adopted by the Reagan administration forced Moscow into an arms race it could not afford, which ultimately led to a collapse of the Soviet economy. Others suggest that Soviet problems were more deep-rooted and would have ended in the disintegration of the Soviet Union even without outside stimulation. Both arguments have some validity, but the latter is surely closer to the mark. For years, if not decades, leaders in the Kremlin had disguised or ignored the massive inefficiencies of the Soviet system. In the years immediately preceding his ascent to power in the Politburo, the perceptive Mikhail Gorbachev had recognized the crucial importance of instituting radical reforms. At the time, he hoped that by doing so he could save the system. By then, however, it was too late. In the classic formulation of dictatorial regimes the world over, the most dangerous period is when leaders adopt reform measures to prevent collapse.

Why has communism survived in China, albeit in a substantially altered form, when it failed in Eastern Europe and the Soviet Union? One of the primary factors is probably cultural. Although the doctrine of Marxism-Leninism originated in Europe, many of its main precepts, such as the primacy of the community over the individual and the denial of the concept of private property, run counter to trends in Western civilization. This inherent conflict is especially evident in the societies of Central Europe, which were strongly influenced by Enlightenment philosophy and the Industrial Revolution. These forces were weaker in the countries farther to the east, but both had begun to penetrate tsarist Russia by the end of the nineteenth century.

By contrast, Marxism-Leninism found a more receptive climate in China and other countries in the region influenced by Confucian tradition. In its political culture, the Communist system exhibits many of the same characteristics as traditional Confucianism—a single truth, an elite governing class, and an emphasis on obedience to the community and its governing representatives—while feudal attitudes regarding female inferiority, loyalty to the family, and bureaucratic arrogance are hard to break. On the surface, China today bears a number of uncanny similarities to the China of the past.

Yet these similarities should not blind us to the real changes that are taking place in Chinese society today. Although the youthful protesters in Tiananmen Square were comparable in some respects to the reformist elements of the early republic, the China of today is fundamentally different from that of the early twentieth century. Literacy rates and the standard of living are far higher, the pressures of outside powers are less threatening, and China has entered its own industrial and technological revolution. For many Chinese, independent talk radio and the Internet are a greater source of news and views than are the official media. Where Sun Yat-sen, Chiang Kai-shek, and even Mao Zedong broke their lances on the rocks of centuries of tradition, poverty, and ignorance, China's present leaders rule a country much more aware of the world and its place in it.

Whether or not communism survives in China—or revives in some form in the lands of the former Soviet Union—the Cold War is not likely to return in its old form, and for that we can be thankful, because it not only kept the earth on the knife edge of a great power conflict but also distracted world leaders from turning their attention to the deeper problems that afflict all of humankind. Still, it is now clear that the end of the Cold War was not necessarily a harbinger of a new era of peace and prosperity. To the contrary, it has opened a new stage of history that will be marked by increased global instability and severe challenges in the areas of environmental pollution, technological change, and population growth. These issues will be addressed in more detail in our final chapters.

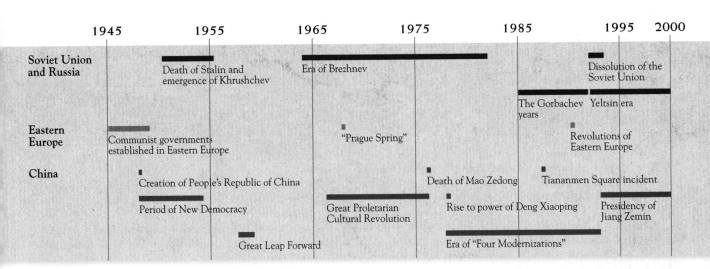

CHAPTER NOTES

1. Vladislav Zubok and Constantin Pleshakov, *Inside the Kremlin's Cold War: From Stalin to Khrushchev* (Cambridge, Mass., 1996), p. 166.
2. Nikita Khrushchev, *Khrushchev Remembers*, trans. Strobe Talbott (Boston, 1970), p. 77.
3. Quoted in Hedrick Smith, *The New Russians* (New York, 1990), p. 30.
4. Quoted in Frank B. Tipton and Robert Aldrich, *An Economic and Social History of Europe from 1939 to the Present* (Baltimore, 1987), p. 193.
5. Hedrick Smith, *The New Russians*, p. 74.
6. *New York Times*, May 7, 1992.
7. Quoted in Stanley Karnow, *Mao and China: Inside China's Cultural Revolution* (New York, 1972), p. 95.
8. Quoted from an article by Mao Zedong in the June 1, 1958, issue of the journal *Red Flag*. See Stuart R. Schram, *The Political Thought of Mao Tse-tung* (New York, 1963), p. 253.
9. Liang Heng and Judith Shapiro, *Son of the Revolution* (New York, 1983).
10. Quoted in *Time*, March 13, 1989, pp. 10–11.
11. Quoted in Frank Ching, "Confucius, the New Saviour," in *Far Eastern Economic Review*, November 10, 1994, p. 37.
12. Quoted in Jonathan Spence, *Chinese Roundabout: Essays in History and Culture* (New York, 1992), p. 285.

SUGGESTED READING

For a general view of modern Russia, see M. Malia, *Russia Under Western Eyes* (Cambridge, Mass., 1999). On the Khrushchev years, see E. Crankshaw, *Khrushchev: A Career* (New York, 1966). For the final years of the Soviet era, see S. F. Cohen, *Rethinking the Soviet Experience* (New York, 1985); R. J. Hill, *The Soviet Union: Politics, Economics, and Society*, 2d ed. (London, 1989); M. Lewin, *The Gorbachev Phenomenon* (Berkeley, Calif., 1988); G. Hosking, *The Awakening of the Soviet Union* (London, 1990); and S. White, *Gorbachev and After* (Cambridge, 1991). For an inquiry into the reasons for the Soviet collapse, see R. Conquest, *Reflections on a Ravaged Century* (New York, 1999), and R. Strayer, *Why Did the Soviet Union Collapse? Understanding Historical Change* (New York, 1998). On economic conditions in post-Soviet Russia, see J. Blasi, M. Kroumova, and D. Kruse, *Kremlin Capitalism: The Privatization of the Russian Economy* (Ithaca, N.Y., 1997).

For a general study of the Soviet satellites in Eastern Europe, see S. Fischer-Galati, *Eastern Europe in the 1980s* (London, 1981). The unique path of Yugoslavia is examined in L. J. Cohen and P. Warwick, *Political Cohesion in a Fragile Mosaic: The Yugoslav Experience* (Boulder, Colo., 1983). On East Germany, see C. B. Scharf, *Politics and Change in East Germany* (Boulder, Colo., 1984). Additional studies on the recent history of these countries include T. G. Ash, *The Polish Revolution: Solidarity* (New York, 1984); B. Kovrig, *Communism in Hungary from Kun to Kádár* (Stanford, Calif., 1979); T. G. Ash, *The Magic Lantern: The Revolution of '89 Witnessed in Warsaw, Budapest, Berlin, and Prague* (New York, 1990); M. Shafir, *Romania: Politics, Economics and Society* (London, 1985); E. Biberaj, *Albania: A Socialist Maverick* (Boulder, Colo., 1990); and S. Ramet, *Nationalism and Federalism in Yugoslavia* (Bloomington, Ind., 1992).

A number of useful surveys deal with China after World War II. The most comprehensive treatment of the Communist period is M. Meisner, *Mao's China and After: A History of the People's Republic* (New York, 1986). For shorter accounts of the period, see J. Grasso et al., *Modernization and Revolution in China* (Armonk, N.Y., 1991), and C. Dietrich, *People's China: A Brief History* (New York, 1986). For documents, see M. Selden, ed., *The People's Republic of China: A Documentary History of Revolutionary Change* (New York, 1978).

There are countless specialized studies on various aspects of the Communist period in China. For a detailed treatment of economic and political issues, see F. Schurmann, *Ideology and Organization in Communist China* (Berkeley, Calif., 1968). The Cultural Revolution is treated dramatically in S. Karnow, *Mao and China: Inside China's Cultural Revolution* (New York, 1972). For individual accounts of the impact of the revolution on people's lives, see the celebrated book by Nien Cheng, *Life and Death in Shanghai* (New York, 1986), and Liang Heng and J. Shapiro, *After the Revolution* (New York, 1986).

For the early post-Mao period, see O. Schell, *To Get Rich Is Glorious* (New York, 1986), and the sequel, *Discos and Democracy: China in the Throes of Reform* (New York, 1988). The 1989 demonstrations and their aftermath are chronicled in L. Feigon's eyewitness account, *China Rising: The Meaning of Tiananmen* (Chicago, 1990), and D. Morrison, *Massacre in Beijing* (New York, 1989). For commentary by Chinese dissidents, see Liu Binyan, *China's Crisis, China's Hope* (Cambridge, 1990), and Fang Lizhi, *Bringing Down the Great Wall: Writings on Science, Culture, and Democracy in China* (New York, 1991). Documentary material relating to the events of 1989 are chronicled in A. J. Nathan and P. Link, eds., *The Tiananmen Papers* (New York, 2001). Recent events are analyzed in J. Fewsmith, *China Since Tiananmen: The Politics of Transition* (Cambridge, 2001).

For a comprehensive introduction to twentieth-century Chinese literature, consult E. Widmer and D. Der-Wei Wang, eds., *From May Fourth to June Fourth: Fiction and Film in Twentieth-Century China* (Cambridge, Mass., 1993), and J. Lau and H. Goldblatt, *The Columbia Anthology of Modern Chinese Literature* (New York, 1995). To witness daily life in the mid-1980s, see Z. Xinxin and S. Ye, *Chinese Lives: An Oral History of Contemporary China* (New York, 1987). An excellent survey of Chinese women writers is found in M. S. Duke, ed., *Modern Chinese Women Writers: Critical Appraisals* (Armonk, N.Y., 1989). See the interesting chapters on Ding Ling and her contemporaries in J. Spence, *The Gate of Heavenly Peace* (New York, 1981). For the most comprehensive analysis of twentieth-century Chinese art, consult M. Sullivan, *Arts and Artists of Twentieth-Century China* (Berkeley, Calif., 1996).

For a discussion of the women's movement in China during this period, see J. Stacey, *Patriarchy and Socialist Revolution in China* (Berkeley, Calif., 1983), and M. Wolf, *Revolution Postponed: Women in Contemporary China* (Stamford, Conn., 1985). To follow the firsthand account of a Chinese woman revolutionary, read Y. Daiyun and C. Wakeman, *To the Storm: The Odyssey of a Revolutionary Chinese Woman* (Berkeley, Calif., 1985).

INFOTRAC COLLEGE EDITION

For additional reading, go to InfoTrac College Edition, your online research library at
http://web1.infotrac-college.com

Enter the search terms "Mao Zedong" using the Subject Guide.

Enter the search term "Stalin" using Keywords.

Enter the search term "Khrushchev" using Keywords.

Enter the search term "perestroika" using the Subject Guide.

Enter the search term "Gorbachev" using Keywords.

Chapter 27

EUROPE AND THE WESTERN HEMISPHERE SINCE 1945

CHAPTER OUTLINE

- RECOVERY AND RENEWAL IN EUROPE
- EMERGENCE OF THE SUPERPOWER: THE UNITED STATES
- THE DEVELOPMENT OF CANADA
- DEMOCRACY, DICTATORSHIP, AND DEVELOPMENT IN LATIN AMERICA
- SOCIETY AND CULTURE IN THE WESTERN WORLD
- CONCLUSION

FOCUS QUESTIONS

- What problems have the nations of Western Europe faced since 1945, and what steps have they taken to try to solve these problems?
- What political, social, and economic changes have the United States and Canada experienced since 1945?
- What problems have the nations of Latin America faced since 1945, and what role has Marxist ideology played in their efforts to solve these problems?
- What major social developments have occurred in Western Europe and North America since 1945?
- What major cultural and intellectual developments have occurred in Western Europe and North America since 1945?
- ➤ What are the similarities and differences between the feminist movement of the nineteenth century and the post-World War II feminist movement?

The end of World War II in Europe had been met with great joy. One visitor in Moscow reported: "I looked out of the window [at 2 A.M.]; almost everywhere there were lights in the windows—people were staying awake. Everyone embraced everyone else; someone sobbed aloud." But after the victory parades and celebrations, Europeans awoke to a devastating realization: their civilization was in ruins. Almost forty million people (both soldiers and civilians) had been killed over the last six years. Massive air raids and artillery bombardments had reduced many of the great cities of Europe to heaps of rubble. An American general described Berlin: "Wherever we looked, we saw desolation. It was like a city of the dead. Suffering and shock were visible in every face. Dead bodies still remained in canals and lakes and were being dug out from under bomb debris." Millions of Europeans faced starvation as grain harvests were only half of what they had been in 1939. Millions were also homeless. Untold millions of people had been uprooted by the war; now they became "displaced persons," trying to find food and then their way home.

Between 1945 and 1970, Europe not only recovered from the devastating effects of World War II but also experienced an economic resurgence that seemed nothing less than miraculous to many people. Economic growth and virtually full employment continued so long that the first postwar recession, in 1973, came as a shock to Western Europe. It was short-lived, however, and economic growth returned. After the collapse of Communist governments in the revolutions of 1989, a number of Eastern European states sought to create market economies and join the military and economic unions first formed by Western European states.

The most significant factor after 1945 was the emergence of the United States as the world's richest and most powerful nation. American prosperity reached new heights in the first two decades after World War II, but a series of economic and social problems—including racial division and staggering budget deficits—in the 1970s, 1980s, and early 1990s left the nation with an imposing array of difficulties that weakened its ability to function as the world's only superpower.

To the south of the United States lay the vast world of Latin America, with its own unique heritage. Although some Latin Americans in the nineteenth century had looked to the United States as a model for their own development, in the twentieth century, many attacked the United States for its military and economic domination of Central and South America. Some states, such as Cuba, even adopted a Marxian path to building a new society and broke completely with the United States. At the same time, many Latin American countries struggled with economic and political instability.

In addition to the transformation from Cold War to post–Cold War realities, other changes were reshaping the West. New artistic and intellectual currents, the growth of science and technology, a religious revival, new threats from terrorists, the realization of environmental problems, the surge of a women's liberation movement—all of these reflected a vibrant, ever changing, and yet challenging new world. •

RECOVERY AND RENEWAL IN EUROPE

All the nations of Europe faced similar problems at the end of World War II. Above all, they needed to rebuild their shattered economies. Within a few years after the defeat of Germany and Italy, an incredible economic revival brought renewed growth to Western Europe.

Western Europe: The Triumph of Democracy

With the economic aid of the Marshall Plan, the countries of Western Europe recovered relatively rapidly from the devastation of World War II. Between 1947 and 1950, European countries received $9.4 billion for new equipment and raw materials. Between the early 1950s and late 1970s, industrial production surpassed all previous records, and Western Europe experienced virtually full employment.

FRANCE: FROM DE GAULLE TO NEW UNCERTAINTIES

The history of France for nearly a quarter century after the war was dominated by one man—Charles de Gaulle (1890–1970). De Gaulle had played an important role in ensuring the establishment of a French provisional government after the war, but the creation of the Fourth Republic, with a return to a parliamentary system based on parties that de Gaulle considered weak, led him to withdraw from politics. However, in 1958, frightened by the bitter divisions within France caused by the Algerian crisis (see Chapter 28), the panic-stricken leaders of the Fourth Republic offered to let de Gaulle take over the government and revise the constitution.

In 1958, de Gaulle drafted a constitution for the Fifth Republic that greatly enhanced the power of the office of president, who now had the right to choose the prime minister, dissolve parliament, and supervise both defense and foreign policy. As the new president, de Gaulle sought to return France to a position of great power. With an eye toward achieving the status of a world power, de Gaulle invested heavily in the nuclear arms race. France exploded its first nuclear bomb in 1960. Despite his successes, de Gaulle did not really achieve his ambitious goals;

© Pierre Boulat-Cosmos/Woodfin Camp & Associates

CHARLES DE GAULLE.   As president, Charles de Gaulle sought to revive the greatness of the French nation. He is shown here dressed in his military uniform participating in a formal state ceremony.

although his successors maintained that France was the "third nuclear power" after the United States and the Soviet Union, in truth France was too small for such global ambitions.

During de Gaulle's presidency, the French gross domestic product experienced an annual increase of 5.5 percent, expanding even faster than that of the United States. France became a major industrial producer and exporter, particularly in such areas as automobiles and armaments. But problems remained. The expansion of traditional industries, such as coal, steel, and railroads, which had all been nationalized, led to large government deficits. The cost of living rose faster than in the rest of Europe. Increased dissatisfaction led in May 1968 to a series of student protests, followed by a general strike by the labor unions. Tired and discouraged by the turn of events, de Gaulle resigned from office in April 1969 and died within a year.

The worsening of France's economic situation in the 1970s brought a shift to the left politically. By 1981, the Socialists had become the dominant party in the National Assembly, and the Socialist leader, François Mitterrand (1916–1995), was elected president. Mitterrand passed a number of measures to aid workers: a higher minimum wage, expanded social benefits, a mandatory fifth week of paid vacation for salaried workers, a thirty-nine-hour workweek, and higher taxes for the rich. The victory of

the Socialists led them to enact some of their more radical reforms: the government nationalized the steel industry, major banks, the space and electronics industries, and important insurance firms.

The Socialist policies, however, largely failed to work, and within three years, a decline in support for the Socialists caused the Mitterrand government to reprivatize portions of the economy. But France's economic decline continued. In 1993, French unemployment stood at 10.6 percent, and in the elections in March of that year, the Socialists won only 28 percent of the vote and less than 10 percent of the seats in the National Assembly; a coalition of conservative parties won 80 percent of the seats. The move to the right was strengthened when the conservative mayor of Paris, Jacques Chirac (b. 1932), was elected president in May 1995.

FROM WEST GERMANY TO ONE GERMANY

Under the pressures of the Cold War, the three Western zones of Germany were unified as the Federal Republic of Germany in 1949. Konrad Adenauer (1876–1967), the leader of the Christian Democratic Union (CDU) who served as chancellor from 1949 to 1963, became the Federal Republic's "founding hero." Adenauer sought respect for postwar Germany by cooperating with the United States and the other Western European nations. He was especially desirous of reconciliation with France, Germany's longtime rival.

Adenauer's chancellorship is largely associated with the resurrection of the West German economy, often referred to as an economic miracle. It was largely guided by the minister of finance, Ludwig Erhard. Although West Germany had only 52 percent of the territory of prewar Germany, by 1955 the West German gross domestic product exceeded that of prewar Germany. Real wages doubled between 1950 and 1965. Unemployment fell from 8 percent in 1950 to 0.4 percent in 1965. To maintain its economic expansion, West Germany even imported hundreds of thousands of "guest workers," primarily from Italy, Spain, Greece, Turkey, and Yugoslavia.

After the Adenauer era, German voters moved politically from the center-right of the Christian Democrats to center-left politics; in 1969, the Social Democrats became the leading party and remained in power until 1982. The first Social Democratic chancellor was Willy Brandt (1913–1992), who was especially successful with his "opening toward the east" (known as *Ostpolitik*), for which he received the Nobel Peace Prize in 1972. On March 19, 1971, Brandt worked out the details of a treaty with East Germany (the former Russian zone) that led to greater cultural, personal, and economic contacts between West and East Germany.

In 1982, the Christian Democratic Union of Helmut Kohl (b. 1930) formed a new center-right government. Kohl was a clever politician who benefited greatly from an economic boom in the mid-1980s and the 1989 revolution in East Germany that led in 1990 to the long-awaited reunification of the two Germanies, making the new Germany, with its 79 million people, the leading power in Europe.

But the excitement over reunification soon dissipated as new problems arose. All too soon, the realization set in that the revitalization of eastern Germany would take far more money than was originally thought, and Kohl's government was soon forced to face the politically undesirable task of raising taxes substantially. Moreover, the virtual collapse of the economy in eastern Germany led to extremely high levels of unemployment and severe discontent. One response was a return to power for the Social Democrats under the leadership of Gerhard Schroeder (b. 1944) as a result of elections in 1998. Another was an attack on foreigners (see the box on p. 784). For years, foreigners seeking asylum and illegal immigrants had found a haven in Germany because of its extremely liberal immigration laws. In 1992, more than 440,000 immigrants came to Germany seeking asylum; 123,000 came from the former Yugoslavia. Attacks against foreigners by right-wing extremists—especially young neo-Nazis—became an all-too-frequent part of German life.

THE DECLINE OF GREAT BRITAIN

The end of World War II left Britain with massive economic problems. In elections held immediately after the war, the Labour Party overwhelmingly defeated Churchill's Conservatives. Labour had promised far-reaching reforms, particularly in the area of social welfare, and in a country with a tremendous shortage of consumer goods and housing, its platform was quite appealing. The new Labour government under Clement Atlee (1883–1967) proceeded to turn Britain into a modern welfare state.

The process began with the nationalization of the Bank of England, the coal and steel industries, public transportation, and public utilities, such as electricity and gas. The new government then enacted the National Insurance Act and the National Health Service Act, both in 1946. The insurance act established a comprehensive social security program and nationalized medical insurance, thereby enabling the state to subsidize the unemployed, the sick, and the aged. The health act established a system of socialized medicine that forced doctors and dentists to work with state hospitals, although private practice could be maintained. The British welfare state became the norm for most European nations after the war.

Continuing economic problems, however, brought the Conservatives back into power from 1951 to 1964. Although they favored private enterprise, the Conservatives accepted the welfare state and even extended it when they undertook an ambitious construction program to improve British housing. Although the British economy

© Mark Stewart/Camera Press, London

MARGARET THATCHER. Great Britain's first female prime minister, Margaret Thatcher was a strong leader who dominated British politics in the 1980s. This picture of Thatcher was taken at the Chelsea Flower Show in May 1990. Six months later, a revolt within her own party caused her to resign as prime minister.

had recovered from the war, its slow rate of recovery masked a long-term economic decline. As a result of World War II, Britain had lost much of its prewar revenues from abroad but was left with a burden of debt from its many international commitments. At the same time, as the influence of the United States and the Soviet Union continued to rise, Britain's ability to play the role of a world power declined substantially. Between 1964 and 1979, Conservatives and Labour alternated in power, but neither party was able to deal with Britain's ailing economy. Failure to modernize made British industry less and less competitive.

In 1979, the Conservatives returned to power under Margaret Thatcher (b. 1925), who became the first woman prime minister in British history (see the box on p. 785). Thatcher pledged to lower taxes, reduce government bureaucracy, limit social welfare, restrict union power, and end inflation. The "Iron Lady," as she was called, did break the power of the labor unions. Although she did not eliminate the basic components of the social welfare system, she did use austerity measures to control inflation. "Thatcherism," as her economic policy was termed, improved the British economic situation, but at a price. The south of England, for example, prospered, but the old industrial areas of the Midlands and north

VIOLENCE AGAINST FOREIGNERS IN GERMANY

As the number of foreign guest workers and immigrants increased in Europe, violent attacks against them also escalated. Especially in the former East Germany, where unemployment rose dramatically after reunification, gangs of neo-Nazi youth have perpetrated violent attacks on foreigners. This document is taken from a German press account of an attack on guest workers from Vietnam and Mozambique who had originally been recruited by the East German government.

KNUD PRIES, "EAST GERMANS HAVE TO LEARN TOLERANCE"

The police headquarters in Dresden, the capital of Saxony, announced that "a political situation" had developed in the town of Hoyerswerda. Political leaders and the police needed to examine the problem and corresponding measures should be taken: "In the near future the residents of the asylum hostel will be moved."

The people of Hoyerswerda prefer to be more direct, referring to the problem of *Neger* (niggers) and *Fidschis* (a term for Asian foreigners). The loudmouths of the neofascist gangs make the message clear: "Niggers Go Home!"

It looks as if some Germans have had enough of bureaucratic officialese. What is more, they will soon make sure that no more foreign voices are heard in Hoyerswerda.

The municipality in northern Saxony has a population of just under 70,000, including 70 people from Mozambique and Vietnam who live in a hostel for foreigners and about 240 asylum seekers in a hostel at the other end of town.

The "political situation" was triggered by an attack by a neo-Nazi gang on Vietnamese traders selling their goods on the market square on 17 September. After being dispersed by the police, the Faschos carried out their first attack on the hostel for foreigners.

The attacks then turned into a regular evening "hunt" by a growing group of right-wing radicals, some of them minors, who presented their idea of a clean Germany by roaming the streets armed with truncheons, stones, steel balls, bottles, and Molotov cocktails. Seventeen people were injured, some seriously.

After the police stepped in on a larger scale the extremists moved across the town to the asylum hostel. To begin with, only the gang itself and onlookers were outside the building, but on the evening of 22 September members of the "Human Rights League" and about 100 members of "autonomous" groups turned up to help the foreigners who had sought refuge in the already heavily damaged block of flats.

A large police contingent, reinforced by men from Dresden and the Border Guard, prevented the situation from becoming even more critical. Two people were seriously injured. The mob was disbanded with the help of dogs, tear gas, and water cannons.

Thirty-two people were arrested, and blank cartridge guns, knives, slings and clubs were seized. On 23 September, a police spokesman announced that the situation was under control. It seems doubtful whether things will stay this way, since the pogroms have become an evening ritual. Politicians and officials are racking their brains about how to grapple with the current crisis and the basic problem. One thing is clear: without a massive intervention by the police the problem cannot even be contained. But what then?

Saxony's Interior Minister, Rudolf Krause, initially recommended that the hostels concerned should be "fenced in," but then admitted that this was "not the final solution." Providing the Defense Ministry approves, the "provisional solution" will be to move the foreigners to a barracks in Kamenz.

Even if this operation is completed without violence it would represent a shameful success for the right-wing radicals. Although the Africans and Asians still living in Hoyerswerda will have to leave at the end of November anyway, once the employment contracts drawn up in the former [East Germany] expire, they are unwilling to endure the terror that long. "Even if we're going anyway—they want all foreigners to go now," says the 29-year-old Martinho from Mozambique.

His impression is that the gangs of thugs are doing something for which others are grateful: "The neighbors are glad when the skinheads arrive."

Interior Minister Krause feels that the abuse of asylum laws, the social problems in East Germany and an historically rooted deficit explain this situation: "The problem is that we were unable in the past to practice the tolerance needed to accept alien cultures."

---

declined and were beset by high unemployment, poverty, and even violence.

Margaret Thatcher dominated British politics in the 1980s. But in 1990, Labour's fortunes revived when Thatcher's government attempted to replace local property taxes with a flat-rate tax payable by every adult to a local authority. Thatcher argued that this would make local government more responsive to its electors, but many British subjects argued that this was nothing more than a poll tax that would allow the rich to get away with paying the same rate as the poor. In 1990, after antitax riots broke out, Thatcher's popularity plummeted, and a revolt within her own party forced her to resign as prime minister. She was replaced by John Major (b. 1943), but his

MARGARET THATCHER: ENTERING A MAN'S WORLD

In 1979, Margaret Thatcher became the first woman to serve as Britain's prime minister. In this excerpt from her autobiography, Thatcher describes how she was interviewed by Conservative Party officials when they first considered her as a possible candidate for Parliament. Thatcher ran for Parliament for the first time in 1950; she lost but increased the Conservative vote total in the district by 50 percent over the previous election.

MARGARET THATCHER, *THE PATH TO POWER*

And, as always with me, there was politics. I immediately joined the Conservative Association and threw myself into the usual round of Party activities. In particular, I thoroughly enjoyed what was called the "'39–'45" discussion group, where Conservatives of the war generation met to exchange views and argue about the political topics of the day. . . . It was as a representative of the Oxford University Graduate Conservative Association (OUGCA) that I went to the Llandudno Conservative Party Conference in October 1948.

It had originally been intended that I should speak at the Conference, seconding an OUGCA motion deploring the abolition of university seats. At that time universities had separate representation in Parliament, and graduates had the right to vote in their universities as well as in the constituency where they lived. (I supported separate university representation, but not the principle that graduates should have more than one vote. . . .) It would have been my first Conference speech, but in the end the seconder chosen was a City man, because the City seats were also to be abolished.

My disappointment at this was, however, very quickly overcome and in a most unexpected way. After one of the debates, I found myself engaged in one of those speculative conversations which young people have about their future prospects. An Oxford friend, John Grant, said he supposed that one day I would like to be a Member of Parliament. "Well, yes," I replied, "but there's not much hope of that. The chances of my being selected are just nil at the moment." I might have added that with no private income of my own there was no way I could have afforded to be an MP on the salary then available. I had not even tried to get on the Party's list of approved candidates.

Later in the day, John Grant happened to be sitting next to the Chairman of the Dartford Conservative Association, John Miller. The Association was in search of a candidate. I learned afterwards that the conversation went something like this: "I understand that you're still looking for a candidate at Dartford?" . . .

"That's right. Any suggestions?"

"Well, there's a young woman, Margaret Roberts, that you might look at. She's very good."

"Oh, but Dartford is a real industrial stronghold. I don't think a woman would do at all."

"Well, you know best of course. But why not just look at her?"

And they did. I was invited to have lunch with John Miller and his wife, Phee, and the Dartford Woman's Chairman, Mrs. Fletcher, on the Saturday on Llandudno Pier. Presumably, and in spite of any reservations about the suitability of a woman candidate for their seat, they liked what they saw. I certainly got on well with them. . . .

I did not hear from Dartford until December, when I was asked to attend an interview at Palace Chambers, Bridge Street. . . . Very few outside the political arena know just how nerve-racking such occasions are. The interviewee who is not nervous and tense is very likely to perform badly: for, as any chemist will tell you, the adrenaline needs to flow if one is to perform at one's best. . . .

I found myself short-listed, and was asked to go to Dartford itself for a further interview. . . . As one of five would-be candidates, I had to give a fifteen-minute speech and answer questions for a further ten minutes.

It was the questions which were more likely to cause me trouble. There was a good deal of suspicion of woman candidates, particularly in what was regarded as a tough industrial seat like Dartford. This was quite definitely a man's world into which not just angels feared to tread. . . .

The most reliable sign that a political occasion has gone well is that you have enjoyed it. I enjoyed that evening at Dartford, and the outcome justified my confidence. I was selected.

---

government failed to capture the imagination of most Britons. In new elections on May 1, 1997, the Labour Party won a landslide victory. The new prime minister, Tony Blair (b. 1953), was a moderate whose youthful energy immediately instilled a new vigor on the political scene. Blair was one of the major leaders in forming an international coalition against terrorism after the terrorist attack on the United States on September 11, 2001.

Western Europe: The Move Toward Unity

As we have seen, the divisions created by the Cold War led the nations of Western Europe to seek military security by forming the North Atlantic Treaty Organization (NATO) in 1949. The destructiveness of two world wars caused many thoughtful Europeans to consider the need for some additional form of unity. However, national feeling was still too powerful for European nations to give up their political sovereignty, so the desire for unity was deflected to the economic arena.

In 1957, France, West Germany, the Benelux countries (Belgium, the Netherlands, and Luxembourg), and Italy signed the Treaty of Rome, which created the European Economic Community (EEC), also known as the Common Market. The EEC eliminated customs barriers for the six member nations and created a large free-trade area protected from the rest of the world by a common external tariff. By promoting free trade, the EEC also encouraged cooperation and standardization in many aspects of the six nations' economies. All the member nations benefited economically. In 1973, Great Britain, Ireland, and Denmark gained membership in the expanded EEC, now called the European Community (EC). Three additional members—Spain, Portugal, and Greece—were added in 1986. Since then, Austria, Finland, and Sweden have also become members.

The European Community was primarily an economic union. By 1992, it comprised 344 million people and constituted the world's largest single trading entity, transacting almost one-fourth of the world's commerce. In the 1980s and 1990s, the EC moved toward even greater economic integration. The Treaty on European Union, which went into effect on January 1, 1994, turned the European Community into the European Union, a true economic and monetary union of all EC members. One of its first goals was achieved in 1999 with the introduction of a common currency, the euro (see Map 27.1). On January 1, 2002, eleven of the EC nations abandoned their national currencies in favor of the euro.

MAP 27.1 Europe, 2000. After the collapse of the Communist order in Eastern Europe and the Soviet Union, a new order and a number of new states appeared in Central and Eastern Europe. At the same time, the European Union expanded and included fifteen states by 2000. ➤ *What new countries emerged from the breakup of the Soviet Union?*

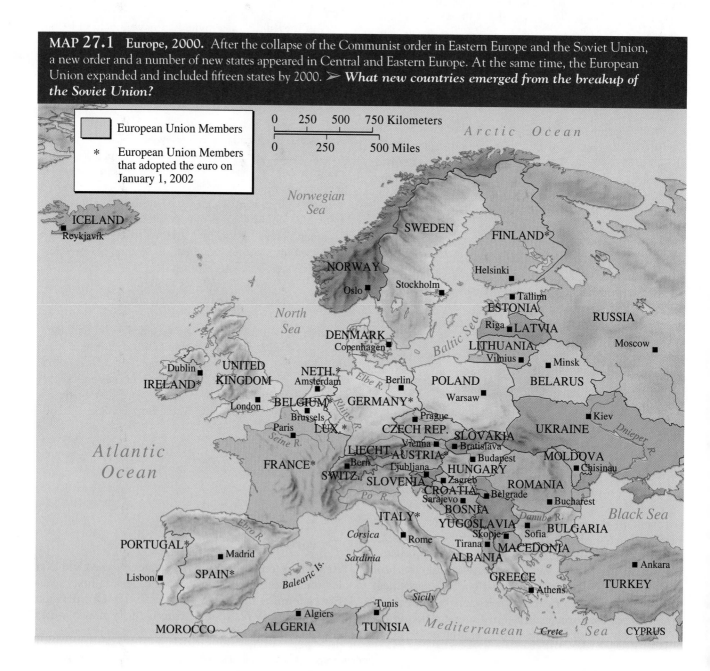

Eastern Europe After Communism

The fall of Communist governments in Eastern Europe during the revolutions of 1989 brought a wave of euphoria to Europe. The new structures meant an end to a postwar European order that had been imposed on unwilling peoples by the victorious forces of the Soviet Union (see Chapter 26). In 1989 and 1990, new governments throughout Eastern Europe worked diligently to scrap the remnants of the old system and introduce the democratic procedures and market systems they believed would revitalize their scarred lands. But this process proved to be neither simple nor easy.

Most Eastern European countries had little or no experience with democratic systems. Then, too, ethnic divisions, which had troubled these areas before World War II and had been forcibly submerged under Communist rule, reemerged with a vengeance. Finally, the rapid conversion to market economies also proved painful. The adoption of "shock therapy" austerity measures produced much suffering. Unemployment, for example, climbed to over 13 percent in Poland in 1992.

Nevertheless, by the beginning of the twenty-first century, many of these states, especially Poland and the Czech Republic, were making a successful transition to both free markets and democracy. In Poland, Aleksander Kwasniewski, although a former Communist, was elected president in November 1995 and pushed Poland toward an increasingly prosperous free market economy. His success brought his reelection in October 2000. In Czechoslovakia, the shift to non-Communist rule was complicated by old problems, especially ethnic issues. Czechs and Slovaks disagreed over the makeup of the new state but were able to agree to a peaceful division of the country. On January 1, 1993, Czechoslovakia split into the Czech Republic and Slovakia. Václav Havel was elected the first president of the new Czech Republic.

The revival of the post–Cold War Eastern European states was evident in their desire to join both NATO and the European Union, the two major Cold War institutions of Western European unity. In 1997, Poland, the Czech Republic, and Hungary became full members of NATO. In October 2002, the European Union's executive commission declared that ten nations—including, Hungary, Poland, the Czech Republic, Slovenia, Estonia, Latvia, and Lithuania—would be invited to join the EU in 2004.

THE DISINTEGRATION OF YUGOSLAVIA

From its beginning in 1919, Yugoslavia had been an artificial creation. After World War II, the dictatorial Marshal Tito had managed to hold the six republics and two autonomous provinces that constituted Yugoslavia together. After his death in 1980, no strong leader emerged, and his responsibilities passed to a collective state presidency and the League of Communists of Yugoslavia. At the end of the 1980s, Yugoslavia was caught up in the reform movements sweeping through Eastern Europe. The League of Communists collapsed, and new parties quickly emerged.

The Yugoslav political scene was complicated by the development of separatist movements. In 1990, the republics of Slovenia, Croatia, Bosnia-Herzegovina, and Macedonia began to lobby for a new federal structure of Yugoslavia that would fulfill their separatist desires. Slobodan Milošević, who had become the leader of the Serbian Communist Party in 1987 and had managed to stay in power by emphasizing his Serbian nationalism, rejected these efforts. He asserted that these republics could be independent only if new border arrangements were made to accommodate the Serb minorities in those republics who did not want to live outside the boundaries of Serbia. Serbs constituted about 12 percent of Croatia's population and 32 percent of Bosnia.

After negotiations among the six republics failed, Slovenia and Croatia declared their independence in June 1991. Milošević's government sent the Yugoslavian army, which it controlled, into Slovenia, without much success. In September 1991, it began a full assault against

Croatia. Increasingly, the Yugoslavian army was becoming the Serbian army, while Serbian irregular forces played a growing role in military operations. Before a cease-fire was arranged, the Serbian forces had captured one-third of Croatia's territory in brutal and destructive fighting.

The recognition of Slovenia, Croatia, and Bosnia-Herzegovina by many European states and the United States early in 1992 did not stop the Serbs from turning their guns on Bosnia. By mid-1993, Serbian forces had acquired 70 percent of Bosnian territory. The Serbian policy of "ethnic cleansing"—killing or forcibly removing Bosnian Muslims from their lands—revived memories of Nazi atrocities in World War II. Nevertheless, despite worldwide outrage, European governments failed to take a decisive and forceful stand against these Serbian activities, and by the spring of 1993, the Muslim population of Bosnia was in desperate straits. As the fighting spread, European nations and the United States began to intervene to stop the bloodshed, and in the fall of 1995, a fragile cease-fire agreement was reached at a conference held in Dayton, Ohio. An international peacekeeping force was stationed in the area to maintain tranquillity and monitor the accords.

Peace in Bosnia, however, did not bring peace to Yugoslavia. A new war erupted in 1999 over Kosovo, which had been made an autonomous province within Yugoslavia by Tito in 1974. Kosovo's inhabitants were mainly ethnic Albanians. But the province was also home to a Serbian minority that considered it sacred territory where Serbian forces in the fourteenth century had been defeated by the Ottoman Turks.

In 1989, Yugoslav President Milošević stripped Kosovo of its autonomous status and outlawed any official use of the Albanian language. In 1993, some groups of ethnic Albanians founded the Kosovo Liberation Army (KLA) and began a campaign against Serbian rule in Kosovo. When Serb forces began to massacre ethnic Albanians in an effort to crush the KLA, the United States and its NATO allies sought to arrange a settlement. When Milošević refused to sign the agreement, the United States and its NATO allies began a bombing campaign that forced the Yugoslavian government into compliance. In the fall elections of 2000, Milošević himself was ousted from power and later put on trial by an international tribunal for war crimes against humanity for his ethnic cleansing policies throughout Yugoslavia's disintegration.

EMERGENCE OF THE SUPERPOWER: THE UNITED STATES

At the end of World War II, the United States emerged as one of the world's two superpowers. As its Cold War confrontation with the Soviet Union intensified, the United States directed much of its energy toward com-bating the spread of communism throughout the world. With the collapse of the Soviet Union at the beginning of the 1990s, the United States became the world's foremost military power.

American Politics and Society Through the Vietnam Era

Between 1945 and 1970, Franklin Roosevelt's New Deal gave rise to a distinct pattern that signified a basic transformation in American society. This pattern included a dramatic increase in the role and power of the federal government, the rise of organized labor as a significant force in the economy and politics, a commitment to the welfare state, a grudging acceptance of ethnic minorities, and a willingness to experiment with deficit spending as a means of spurring the economy. The New Deal in American politics was bolstered by the election of Democratic presidents—Harry S Truman in 1948, John F. Kennedy in 1960, and Lyndon B. Johnson in 1964. Even the election of a Republican president, Dwight D. Eisenhower, in 1952 and 1956 did not significantly alter the fundamental direction of the New Deal. As Eisenhower stated in 1954, "Should any political party attempt to abolish Social Security and eliminate labor laws and farm programs, you would not hear of that party again in our political history."

The economic boom after World War II fueled confidence in the American way of life. A shortage of consumer goods during the war left Americans with both surplus income and the desire to purchase these goods after the war. Then, too, the development of organized labor enabled more and more workers to get the wage increases that spurred the growth of the domestic market. Between 1945 and 1973, real wages grew an average of 3 percent a year, the most prolonged advance in U.S. history.

Starting in the 1960s, problems that had been glossed over earlier came to the fore. The decade began on a youthful and optimistic note when John F. Kennedy (1917–1963), age forty-three, became the youngest elected president in the history of the United States and the first born in the twentieth century. His own administration, cut short by an assassin's bullet on November 22, 1963, focused primarily on foreign affairs. Kennedy's successor, Lyndon B. Johnson (1908–1973), who won a new term as president in a landslide in 1964, used his stunning mandate to pursue the growth of the welfare state, first begun in the New Deal. Johnson's programs included health care for the elderly; the War on Poverty, to be fought with food stamps and the Job Corps; and federal assistance for education.

Johnson's other domestic passion was achieving equal rights for black Americans. In August 1963, the eloquent Martin Luther King Jr. (1929–1968), a Baptist minister and leader of a growing movement for racial equality, led the March on Washington for Jobs and Freedom to dramatize black Americans' desire for treatment no different from that accorded to whites. This march and King's

"I HAVE A DREAM"

In the spring of 1963, a bomb attack on a church that killed four African American children and the brutal fashion in which police handled black demonstrators brought the nation's attention to the policies of racial segregation in Birmingham, Alabama. A few months later, on August 28, 1963, Martin Luther King Jr. led a march on Washington, D.C., and gave an inspired speech at the Lincoln Memorial that catalyzed the civil rights movement.

MARTIN LUTHER KING JR., "I HAVE A DREAM"

I am happy to join with you today in what will go down in history as the greatest demonstration for freedom in the history of our nation.

Five score years ago, a great American, in whose symbolic shadow we stand today, signed the Emancipation Proclamation. This momentous decree came as a great beacon light of hope to millions of Negro slaves, who had been seared in the flames of withering injustice. It came as a joyous daybreak to end the long night of their captivity.

But one hundred years later, the Negro still is not free; one hundred years later, the life of the Negro is still sadly crippled by the manacles of segregation and the chains of discrimination; one hundred years later, the Negro lives on a lonely island of poverty in the midst of a vast ocean of material prosperity; one hundred years later, the Negro is still languished in the corners of American society and finds himself in exile in his own land. . . .

So we've come here today to dramatize a shameful condition. In a sense we've come to our nation's capital to cash a check. When the architects of our republic wrote the magnificent words of the Constitution and the Declaration of Independence, they were signing a promissory note to which every American was to fall heir. This note was the promise that all men, yes, black men as well as white men, would be guaranteed the unalienable rights of life, liberty, and the pursuit of happiness.

It is obvious today that America has defaulted on this promissory note in so far as her citizens of color are concerned. Instead of honoring this sacred obligation, America has given the Negro people a bad check, a check which has come back marked "insufficient funds." But we refuse to believe that the bank of justice is bankrupt. . . .

We have also come to this hallowed spot to remind America of the fierce urgency of now. This is no time to engage in the luxury of cooling off or to take the tranquilizing drug of gradualism. Now is the time to make real the promises of democracy; now is the time to rise from the dark and desolate valley of segregation to the sunlit path of racial justice; now is the time to lift our nation from the quicksands of racial injustice to the solid rock of brotherhood; now is the time to make justice a reality for all of God's children. It would be fatal for the nation to overlook the urgency of the moment. . . .

I say to you today, my friends, so even though we face the difficulties of today and tomorrow, I still have a dream. It is a dream deeply rooted in the American dream. I have a dream that one day this nation will rise up and live out the true meaning of its creed, "We hold these truths to be self-evident, that all men are created equal." I have a dream that one day on the red hills of Georgia, sons of former slaves and the sons of former slave owners will be able to sit down together at the table of brotherhood. . . . I have a dream that my four little children will one day live in a nation where they will not be judged by the color of their skin, but by the content of their character. . . .

This is our hope. This is the faith that I go back to the South with. With this faith we will be able to hew out of the mountain of despair a stone of hope. With this faith we will be able to transform the jangling discords of our nation into a beautiful symphony of brotherhood. With this faith we will be able to work together, to pray together, to struggle together, to go to jail together, to stand up for freedom together, knowing that we will be free one day. And this will be the day. This will be the day when all of God's children will be able to sing with new meaning, "My country 'tis of thee, sweet land of liberty, of thee I sing. Land where my father died, land of the pilgrims' pride, from every mountainside, let freedom ring." And if America is to be a great nation, this must become true. . . .

And when this happens, and when we allow freedom to ring, when we let it ring from every village and every hamlet, from every state and every city, we will be able to speed up that day when all of God's children, black men and white men, Jews and Gentiles, Protestants and Catholics, will be able to join hands and sing in the words of the old Negro spiritual: "Free at last. Free at last. Thank God Almighty, we are free at last."

---

impassioned plea for racial equality (see the box above) had an electrifying effect on the American people. President Johnson pursued the cause of civil rights. As a result of his initiative, Congress enacted the Civil Rights Act of 1964, which created the machinery to end segregation and discrimination in the workplace and in public accommodations. The Voting Rights Act the following year eliminated obstacles to black participation in elections in southern states. But laws alone could not guarantee the Great Society that Johnson envisioned, and soon the administration faced bitter social unrest, from both civil rights activists and the burgeoning antiwar movement.

THE CIVIL RIGHTS MOVEMENT. In the early 1960s, Martin Luther King Jr. and his Southern Christian Leadership Conference organized a variety of activities to pursue the goal of racial equality. He is shown here with his wife, Coretta (right), and Rosa Parks and Ralph Abernathy (far left) leading a march in 1965 against racial discrimination.

© Bob Adelman/Magnum Photos

In the North and the West, blacks had had voting rights for many years, but local patterns of segregation resulted in considerably higher unemployment rates for blacks (and Hispanics) than for whites and left blacks segregated in huge urban ghettos. It was in these ghettos that radical black nationalist leaders, such as Malcolm X of the Black Muslims, attracted more attention with their calls for militant action than the nonviolent appeals of Martin Luther King. In the summer of 1965, race riots erupted in the Watts district of Los Angeles that led to thirty-four deaths and the destruction of over one thousand buildings. When King was assassinated in 1968, more than one hundred cities erupted in rioting, including Washington, D.C., the nation's capital. The combination of riots and extremist comments by radical black leaders led to a "white backlash" and a severe racial division of America.

Antiwar protests also divided the American people after President Johnson committed American troops to a costly war in Vietnam (see Chapter 25). Teach-ins, sit-ins, and the occupations of university buildings alternated with more radical demonstrations that increasingly led to violence. The killing of four student protesters at Kent State University in 1970 by the Ohio National Guard shocked both activists and ordinary Americans, and thereafter the vehemence of the antiwar movement began to subside. But the combination of antiwar demonstrations and riots in the cities caused many people to call for "law and order," an appeal used by Richard Nixon (1913–1994), the Republican presidential candidate in 1968. With Nixon's election in 1968, a shift to the right in American politics had begun.

The Shift Rightward After 1973

Nixon eventually ended American involvement in Vietnam by gradually withdrawing American troops. Politically, he pursued a "southern strategy," carefully calculating that "law and order" issues and a slowdown in racial desegregation would appeal to southern whites. The Republican strategy, however, also gained support among white Democrats in northern cities, where court-mandated busing of students to distant neighborhoods to achieve racial integration of the public schools had provoked a white backlash.

As president, Nixon was paranoid about conspiracies and resorted to subversive methods of gaining political intelligence on his political opponents. Nixon's zeal led to the Watergate scandal—a botched attempt to bug the Democratic National Headquarters and the ensuing coverup. Although Nixon repeatedly denied involvement in the affair, secret tapes he made of his own conversations in the White House revealed otherwise. On August 9, 1974, Nixon resigned in disgrace, an act that saved him from almost certain impeachment and conviction.

After Watergate, American domestic politics focused on economic issues. Gerald Ford (b. 1913) became president when Nixon resigned, only to lose in the 1976 election to the former governor of Georgia, Jimmy Carter (b. 1924), who campaigned as an outsider against the Washington establishment. Both Ford and Carter faced severe economic problems. The period from 1973 to the mid-1980s was one of economic stagnation, a combination of high inflation and high unemployment that came to be known as stagflation. The economic downturn stemmed in part from a dramatic rise in oil prices. By 1980, the Carter administration faced two devastating problems. High inflation and a decline in average weekly earnings were causing a perceptible drop in American living standards. At the same time, a crisis abroad had erupted when fifty-three Americans were taken hostage by the Iranian government of Ayatollah Khomeini and held for nearly fifteen months. Carter's inability to gain the release of the American hostages led to perceptions at home that he was a weak president. His overwhelming loss to Ronald Reagan (b. 1911) in the election of 1980 brought forward the chief exponent of right-wing Republican policies.

The Reagan Revolution, as it has been called, sent U.S. policy in a number of new directions. Reversing decades of changes, Reagan cut back on the welfare state by decreasing spending on food stamps, school lunch programs, and job programs. At the same time, his administration fostered the largest peacetime military buildup in American history. Total federal spending rose from $631 billion in 1981 to over $1 trillion by 1986. But instead of raising taxes to pay for the new expenditures, Reagan convinced Congress that massive tax cuts would supposedly stimulate rapid economic growth and produce new revenues. Reagan's policies seemed to work in the short run as the United States experienced an economic upturn that lasted until the end of the 1980s. But the administration's spending policies also produced record government deficits, which loomed as an obstacle to long-term growth. In the 1970s, the total deficit was $420 billion; Reagan's budget deficits were three times that amount.

The inability of Reagan's successor, George H. W. Bush (b. 1924), to deal with the deficit problem, coupled with an economic downturn, led to the election of a Democrat, Bill Clinton, in November 1992. The new president was a southerner who claimed to be a new Democrat—one who favored a number of the Republican policies of the 1980s. This was a clear indication that the rightward drift in American politics was by no means ended by this Democratic victory. In fact, Clinton's reelection in 1996 was due in part to his adoption of Republican ideas and policies.

President Clinton's political fortunes were aided considerably by a lengthy economic revival. A steady reduction in the annual government budget deficit strengthened confidence in the performance of the national economy. Much of Clinton's second term, however, was overshadowed by charges of misconduct stemming from the president's affair with Monica Lewinsky, a White House intern. After a bitter partisan struggle, the U.S. Senate acquitted the president on two articles of impeachment brought by the House of Representatives. But Clinton's problems helped the Republican candidate, George W. Bush, win the presidential election in 2000. Although Bush lost the popular vote to Al Gore, he narrowly won the electoral vote after a highly controversial victory in the state of Florida that was ultimately decided by the U.S. Supreme Court.

Chronology

AMERICAN SOCIETY AND POLITICS

Presidency of Harry S Truman	1945–1953
Presidency of Dwight D. Eisenhower	1953–1961
Presidency of John F. Kennedy	1961–1963
Assassination of Kennedy	1963
Presidency of Lyndon B. Johnson	1963–1969
March on Washington	1963
Civil Rights Act	1964
Watts riot	1965
Assassination of Martin Luther King Jr.	1968
Presidency of Richard M. Nixon	1969–1974
Killing of students at Kent State	1970
Resignation of Nixon in Watergate scandal	1974
Presidency of Gerald Ford	1974–1977
Presidency of Jimmy Carter	1977–1981
Presidency of Ronald Reagan	1981–1989
Presidency of George H. W. Bush	1989–1993
Presidency of Bill Clinton	1992–2001
George W. Bush inaugurated as president	2001

THE DEVELOPMENT OF CANADA

Canada's development paralleled that of the United States in the postwar years. For twenty-five years after World War II, Canada experienced extraordinary economic prosperity as it set out on a path of industrial development. Canada had always had a strong export economy based on its abundant natural resources. Now it also developed electronic, aircraft, nuclear, and chemical engineering industries on a large scale. Much of the Canadian growth, however, was financed by capital from the United States, which resulted in American ownership of Canadian businesses. Though many Canadians welcomed the economic growth, others feared American economic domination of Canada and its resources.

A notable feature of Canada's postwar history has been its close relationship with the United States. In addition to fears of economic domination, Canadians have also worried about playing a subordinate role politically and militarily to the neighboring superpower. Canada agreed to join NATO in 1949 and even sent military contingents to fight in Korea the following year. But to avoid subordination to the United States or any other great power, Canada has consistently and actively supported the United Nations. Nevertheless, concerns about the United States have not kept Canada from maintaining a special relationship with its southern neighbor.

For three decades after 1945, the Liberal Party largely dominated Canadian politics and created Canada's welfare state by enacting a national social security system (the Canada Pension Plan) and a national health insurance program. The most prominent Liberal government was that of Pierre Trudeau (1919–2000), who came to power in 1968. A French Canadian, Trudeau did not harbor separatist sentiments and was dedicated to Canada's federal union. In 1968, his government passed the Official Languages Act, which created a bilingual federal civil service and encouraged the growth of French culture and language in Canada. Although Trudeau's government vigorously pushed an industrialization program, high inflation and Trudeau's efforts to impose the will of the federal government on the powerful provincial governments alienated voters and weakened his government.

Economic recession in the early 1980s brought Brian Mulroney (b. 1939), leader of the Progressive Conservative Party, to power in 1984. Mulroney's government sought greater privatization of Canada's state-run corporations and negotiated a free trade agreement with the United States. Bitterly resented by many Canadians, the agreement cost Mulroney's government much of its popularity. In 1993, the ruling conservatives were drastically defeated. They won only two seats in the House of Commons, and the Liberal leader, Jean Chrétien (b. 1934), became prime minister.

The new Liberal government also faced an ongoing crisis over the French-speaking province of Quebec. In the late 1960s, the Parti Québécois, headed by René Lévesque, campaigned on a platform of Quebec's secession from the Canadian confederation. In 1970, the party won 24 percent of the popular vote in Quebec's provincial elections. To pursue their dream of separation, some underground separatist groups even used terrorist bombings and kidnapped two prominent government officials. In 1976, the Parti Québécois won Quebec's provincial elections and in 1980 called for a referendum that would enable the provincial government to negotiate Quebec's independence from the rest of Canada. Voters in Quebec narrowly rejected the plan in 1995, however, and debate over Quebec's future continues to divide Canada to this day.

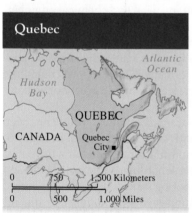

DEMOCRACY, DICTATORSHIP, AND DEVELOPMENT IN LATIN AMERICA

The Great Depression of the 1930s had caused a political instability in many Latin American countries that led to military coups and militaristic regimes (see Chapter 23). But the depression also led Latin America to move from a traditional to a modern economic structure. Since the nineteenth century, Latin Americans had exported raw materials, especially minerals and foodstuffs, while buying the manufactured goods of the industrialized countries in Europe and the United States. As a result of the depression, however, exports were cut in half, and the revenues available to buy manufactured goods declined. This encouraged many Latin American countries to develop industries to produce goods that they formerly imported. Due to a shortage of capital in the private sector, governments often invested in the new industries, thus leading, for example, to government-run steel industries in Chile and Brazil and oil industries in Argentina and Mexico.

By the 1960s, however, Latin American countries still found themselves dependent on the United States, Europe, and now Japan, especially for the advanced technology needed for modern industries. Because of the great poverty in many of these countries, domestic markets were limited in size, and many of these countries failed to find markets abroad for their products. These failures led to instability and a new reliance on military regimes, especially to curb the power of the new industrial middle class and working classes, which had increased in size and power as a result of industrialization. In the 1960s, repressive military regimes in Chile, Brazil, and Argentina abolished political parties and repeatedly returned to export-import economies financed by foreigners (see Map 27.2). They also invited multinational companies to come in. The companies that accepted the invitation wanted primarily to take advantage of Latin America's raw materials and abundant supply of cheap labor, which only contributed to the ongoing dependency of Latin America on the industrially developed nations.

In the 1970s, Latin American regimes grew even more dependent on maintaining their failing economies by borrowing from abroad, especially from banks in Europe and the United States. Between 1970 and 1982, debt to foreigners increased from $27 billion to $315 billion. By 1982, a number of governments announced that they could no longer pay interest on their debts to foreign banks, and their economies began to crumble. Wages fell, and unemployment skyrocketed.

In the 1980s, the debt crisis was paralleled by a movement toward democracy. In part, some military leaders

MAP 27.2 Political Trends in Latin America in the 1960s and 1970s.
Latin America experienced considerable political upheaval after World War II, especially as a result of severe economic problems. The result was a move toward military regimes as well as strong leftist movements, especially Marxism.
➤ *Which Latin American countries experienced military regimes, and which were troubled by leftist movements?*

were simply unwilling to deal with the monstrous debt problems. At the same time, many people realized that military power without popular consent was incapable of providing a strong state. Then, too, there was a swelling of popular support for basic rights and free and fair elections. The movement toward democracy was the most noticeable trend of the 1980s and early 1990s in Latin America. In the mid-1980s, democratic regimes were everywhere except Cuba, some of the Central American states, Chile, and Paraguay.

The United States has also played an important role in Latin America since 1945. The United States had intervened militarily in Latin American affairs for years, particularly in Central America and the Caribbean, a region considered its "backyard" and thus of strategic importance. Beginning in the 1920s, the United States had replaced Britain as the foremost investor in Latin America. Unlike the British, however, American investors put funds directly into production enterprises so that large segments of Latin America's export industries fell into American hands. The American-owned United Fruit Company turned a number of Central American nations into "banana republics," while American companies gained control of the copper-mining industry in Chile and Peru and the oil industry in Mexico, Peru, and Bolivia. The control of these industries by American investors reinforced a growing nationalist consciousness against America as a neo-imperialist power.

But the United States had also tried to pursue a new relationship with Latin America. In 1948, the nations of the Western Hemisphere formed the Organization of American States (OAS), which was intended to eliminate unilateral action by one state within the internal or external affairs of any other state. The OAS did not end the interference of the United States in Latin American affairs, however. Especially after World War II, as the Cold War between the United States and the Soviet Union intensified, American policy makers grew anxious about the possibility of Communist regimes arising in Central America and the Caribbean and returned to a policy of unilateral action when they believed that Soviet agents were attempting to establish Communist governments. Especially after the success of Castro in Cuba (see the next section), the desire of the United States to prevent "another Cuba" largely determined American policy toward Latin America until the collapse of the Cold War in the 1990s. The United States provided massive military aid to anti-Communist regimes, regardless of their nature. By 1979, some 83,000 military personnel from twenty-one Latin American countries had received U.S.-assisted military training, with a special emphasis on antiguerrilla activity.

The Threat of Marxist Revolutions

Until the 1960s, Marxism played little role in the politics of Latin America. The success of Fidel Castro in Cuba and his espousal of Marxism, however, opened the door for other Marxist movements that aimed to gain the support of peasants and industrial workers and bring radical change to Latin America.

THE CUBAN REVOLUTION

An authoritarian regime, headed by Fulgencio Batista (1901–1973) and closely tied economically to U.S. investors, had ruled Cuba since 1934. A strong opposition movement to Batista's government developed, led by Fidel

Castro (b. 1926) and assisted by Ernesto "Ché" Guevara (1928–1967), an Argentinian who believed that revolutionary upheaval was necessary to change Latin America (see the box on p. 795). When their initial assaults brought little success, Castro's forces turned to guerrilla warfare. Batista's regime responded with such brutality that he alienated his own supporters. The dictator fled in December 1958, and Castro's revolutionaries seized Havana on January 1, 1959.

The new government proceeded cautiously, but relations with the United States quickly deteriorated. An agrarian reform law in May 1959 nationalized all land-holdings of more than 1,000 acres. A new level of antagonism was reached early in 1960 when the Soviet Union agreed to buy Cuban sugar and provide $100 million in credits. On March 17, 1960, President Eisenhower directed the Central Intelligence Agency (CIA) to "organize the training of Cuban exiles, mainly in Guatemala, against a possible future day when they might return to their homeland."[1] Arms from Eastern Europe began to arrive in Cuba, the United States cut its purchases of Cuban sugar, and the Cuban government nationalized U.S. companies and banks. In October 1960, the United States declared a trade embargo of Cuba, which drove Castro closer to the Soviet Union. In December 1960, Castro declared himself a Marxist.

On January 3, 1961, the United States broke diplomatic relations with Cuba. The new U.S. president, John F. Kennedy, supported a coup attempt against Castro's gov-

FIDEL CASTRO. On January 1, 1959, a band of revolutionaries led by Fidel Castro overthrew the authoritarian government of Fulgencio Batista. Castro is shown here in 1957 with some of his followers at a secret base near the Cuban coast.

CASTRO'S REVOLUTIONARY IDEALS

*O**n July 26, 1953, Fidel Castro and a small group of supporters launched an ill-fated attack on the Moncada Barracks in Santiago de Cuba. Castro was arrested and put on trial. This excerpt is taken from his defense speech, in which he discussed the goals of the revolutionaries.*

FIDEL CASTRO, "HISTORY WILL ABSOLVE ME"

I stated that the second consideration on which we based our chances for success was one of social order because we were assured of the people's support. When we speak of the people we do not mean the comfortable ones, the conservative elements of the nation, who welcome any regime of oppression, any dictatorship, and despotism, prostrating themselves before the master of the moment until they grind their foreheads into the ground. When we speak of struggle, the people means the vast unredeemed masses, to whom all make promises and whom all deceive; we mean the people who yearn for a better, more dignified, and more just nation; who are moved by ancestral aspirations of justice, for they have suffered injustice and mockery, generation after generation; who long for great and wise changes in all aspects of their life; people, who, to attain these changes, are ready to give even the very last breath of their lives—when they believe in something or in someone, especially when they believe in themselves.

In the brief of this cause there must be recorded the five revolutionary laws that would have been proclaimed immediately after the capture of the Moncada barracks and would have been broadcast to the nation by radio. . . .

The First Revolutionary Law would have returned power to the people and proclaimed the Constitution of 1940 the supreme Law of the land, until such time as the people should decide to modify or change it. . . .

The Second Revolutionary Law would have granted property, not mortgageable and not transferable, to all planters, subplanters, lessees, partners, and squatters who hold parcels of five or less *caballerias* [tract of land, about 33 acres] of land, and the state would indemnify the former owners on the basis of the rental which they would have received for these parcels over a period of ten years.

The Third Revolutionary Law would have granted workers and employees the right to share 30 percent of the profits of all the large industrial, mercantile, and mining enterprises, including the sugar mills. . . .

The Fourth Revolutionary Law would have granted all planters the right to share 55 percent of the sugar production and a minimum quota of forty thousand *arrobas* [25 pounds] for all small planters who have been established for three or more years.

The Fifth Revolutionay Law would have ordered the confiscation of all holdings and ill-gotten gains of those who had committed frauds during previous regimes, as well as the holdings and ill-gotten gains of all their legatees and heirs. . . .

Furthermore, it was to be declared that the Cuban policy in the Americas would be one of close solidarity with the democratic people of this continent, and that those politically persecuted by bloody tyrants oppressing our sister nations would find generous asylum, brotherhood, and bread in [Cuba]. Not the persecution, hunger, and treason that they find today. Cuba should be the bulwark of liberty and not a shameful link in the chain of despotism.

ernment, but the landing of fourteen hundred CIA-assisted Cubans in Cuba on April 17, 1961, was a military disaster (the infamous Bay of Pigs). This fiasco encouraged the Soviets to place nuclear missiles in the country, an act that led to a showdown with the United States (see Chapter 25). As its part of the bargain to defuse the missile crisis, the United States agreed not to invade Cuba.

But the missile crisis affected Cuba in another way as well. Castro realized that the Soviet Union had been unreliable. If revolutionary Cuba was to be secure, the Cubans would have to instigate social revolution in the rest of Latin America. Castro judged Bolivia, Haiti, Venezuela, Colombia, Paraguay, and a number of Central American states to be especially open to radical revolution. He believed that once guerrilla wars were launched, peasants would flock to the movement and overthrow the old regimes. Guevara began a guerrilla war in Bolivia but was caught and killed by the Bolivian army in the fall of 1967. The Cuban strategy had failed.

Nevertheless, within Cuba, Castro's socialist revolution proceeded, although with mixed results. The Cuban Revolution did secure some social gains for its people, especially in health care and education. The regime provided free medical services for all citizens, and the population's health improved noticeably. Illiteracy was wiped out by developing new schools and establishing teacher-training institutes that tripled the number of teachers within ten years. The theoretical equality of women in Marxist thought was put into practice in Cuba by new laws. One such law was the family code, which stated that husband and wife were equally responsible for the economic support of the family and household, as well as for child care. Such laws led to improvements but fell far short of creating full equality for women.

Eschewing the path of rapid industrialization, Castro encouraged agricultural diversification. Nevertheless, the Cuban economy continued to rely on the production and sale of sugar. Economic problems forced the Castro regime to depend on Soviet subsidies and the purchase of Cuban sugar by Soviet bloc countries. After the collapse of these Communist regimes in 1989, Cuba lost their support.

CHILE'S MARXIST ADVENTURE

Another challenge to U.S. influence in Latin America came in 1970 when the Marxist Salvador Allende (1908–1973) was elected president of Chile and attempted to create a socialist society by constitutional means. Chile suffered from a number of economic problems. Wealth was concentrated in the hands of large landowners and a few large corporations. Inflation, foreign debts, and a decline in the mining industry (copper exports accounted for 80 percent of Chile's export income) caused untold difficulties. Right-wing control of the government failed to achieve any solutions, especially since foreign investments were allowed to expand. There was already growing resentment of U.S. corporations, especially Anaconda and Kennecott, which controlled the copper industry.

In the 1970 elections, a split in the moderate forces enabled Allende to become president of Chile as head of a coalition of Socialists, Communists, and Catholic radicals. A number of labor leaders, who represented the interests of the working classes, were given the ministries of labor, finance, public works, and interior in the new government. Allende increased the wages of industrial workers and began to move toward socialism by nationalizing the largest domestic and foreign-owned corporations. Nationalization of the copper industry—essentially without compensation for the owners—caused the Nixon administration to cut off all aid to Chile, creating serious problems for the Chilean economy. At the same time, the government offered only halfhearted resistance to radical workers who were beginning to take control of the landed estates.

In response, the upper and middle classes began to organize strikes against the government (with support from the American CIA). Allende attempted to stop the disorder by bringing three military officers into his cabinet. They succeeded in ending the strikes, but when Allende's coalition increased its vote in the congressional elections of March 1973, the Chilean army, under the direction of General Augusto Pinochet (b. 1915), decided on a coup d'état. In September 1973, Allende and thousands of his supporters were killed. Contrary to the expectations of many right-wing politicians, the military remained in power and set up a dictatorship. The regime moved quickly to outlaw all political parties, remove the congress, and restore many nationalized industries and landowners' estates to their original owners. The copper industry, however, remained in government hands. The regime's horrible abuse of human rights led to growing unrest against the government in the mid-

1980s. In 1989, free elections produced a Christian Democratic president, Patricio Aylwin, who advocated free market economics.

NICARAGUA: FROM THE SOMOZAS TO THE SANDINISTAS

The United States had intervened in Nicaraguan domestic affairs in the early twentieth century, and U.S. Marines even remained there for long periods of time. After the leader of the U.S.-supported National Guard, Anastasio Somoza, seized control of the government in 1937, his family remained in power for forty-three years. U.S. support for the Somoza military regime enabled the family to overcome its opponents while enriching themselves at the expense of the state.

Opposition to the regime finally arose from Marxist guerrilla forces known as the Sandinista National Liberation Front. By mid-1979, military victories by the Sandinistas left them in virtual control of the country. Inheriting a poverty-stricken nation, the Sandinistas organized a provisional government aligned with the Soviet Union. The Reagan and Bush administrations, believing that Central America faced the danger of another Communist state, financed Contra rebels in a guerrilla war against the Sandinista government. The Contra war and an American economic embargo damaged the Nicaraguan economy and undermined support for the Sandinistas. In 1990, they agreed to free elections and lost to a coalition headed by Violeta Barrios de Chamorro (b. 1929). Nevertheless, the Sandinistas remained the strongest single party in Nicaragua.

Nationalism and the Military: The Examples of Argentina and Brazil

The military became the power brokers of twentieth-century Latin America. Especially in the 1960s and 1970s, Latin American armies portrayed themselves as the guardians of national honor and orderly progress.

ARGENTINA

Juan Perón first rose to prominence as a member of the military regime that had seized power in Argentina in 1943. As labor secretary in the military government, he used his position to curry favor with the workers. But as Perón grew more popular, other army officers began to fear his power and arrested him. An uprising by workers forced the officers to back down, and in 1946, Perón was elected president.

To please his chief supporters—labor and the urban middle class—Perón pursued a policy of increased industrialization. At the same time, he sought to free Argentina from foreign investors. The government bought the railways, took over the banking, insurance, shipping, and communications industries, and assumed regulation of imports and

➤➤ **THE PERÓNS.** Elected president of Argentina in 1946, Juan Perón soon established an authoritarian regime that nationalized some of Argentina's basic industries and organized fascist gangs to overwhelm its opponents. He is shown here with his wife, Eva, during the inauguration ceremonies initiating his second term as president in 1952.

exports. But Perón's regime was also authoritarian. His wife, Eva Perón, organized women's groups to support the government, while Perón created fascist gangs, modeled after Hitler's Brown Shirts, that used violence to overawe his opponents. But growing corruption in the Perón government and the alienation of more and more people by the regime's excesses encouraged the military to overthrow him in September 1955. Perón went into exile in Spain.

It had been easy for the military to seize power, but it was harder to rule, especially now that Argentina had a party of *Peronistas* clamoring for the return of the exiled leader. In the 1960s and 1970s, military and civilian governments (the latter closely watched by the military) alternated in power. When both failed to provide economic stability, military leaders decided to allow Perón to return. Reelected president in September 1973, Perón died one year later. In 1976, the military installed a new regime. Tolerating no opposition, the military leaders encouraged the "disappearance" of their opponents. Perhaps thirty thousand people, including six thousand leftists, were killed as a result.

But economic problems remained. To divert people's attention, the military regime invaded the Falkland Islands off the coast of Argentina in April 1982. Great Britain, which had controlled the islands since the nineteenth century, sent ships and troops to defend the islands. When the Argentine forces surrendered to the British in July, angry Argentinians denounced the military regime. The loss discredited the military and opened the door to civilian rule. In 1983, Raúl Alfonsín of the Radical Party was elected president and tried to restore democratic practices. In elections in 1989, the Peronist Carlos Saúl Menem (b. 1930) won. This peaceful transfer of power gave hope that Argentina was moving on a democratic path. Reelected in 1995, President Menem has pushed to control inflation and government spending.

BRAZIL

After the military put an end to the authoritarian regime of Getúlio Vargas in 1945, Brazil established a republic. Over the next two decades, various democratically elected presidents (including Vargas himself) struggled to solve Brazil's economic problems, especially its soaring inflation, but with little success. Finally, in the spring of 1964, the military decided to intervene and took over the government.

Unlike previous interventions by military leaders in politics, this time the armed forces remained in direct control of the country for twenty years. The military set course on a new economic direction, cutting back somewhat on state control of the economy and emphasizing market forces. Beginning in 1968, the new policies seemed to work, and Brazil experienced an "economic miracle" as it moved into self-sustaining economic growth, generally the hallmark of a modern economy. Economic growth also included the economic exploitation of the Amazon basin, which the regime opened to farming; some believe the corresponding destruction of the extensive Amazon rain forests, which is still going on, poses a threat to the ecological balance not only of Brazil but of the earth itself. Rapid economic growth had additional drawbacks. Ordinary Brazilians hardly benefited as the gulf between rich and poor, always wide, grew even wider. In 1960, the wealthiest 10 percent of Brazil's population received 40 percent of the nation's income; in 1980, they received 51 percent. Then, too, rapid development led to an inflation rate of 100 percent a year, while an enormous foreign debt added to the problems. By the early 1980s, the economic miracle was turning into an economic nightmare. Overwhelmed, the generals retreated and opened the door for a return to democracy in 1985.

The new democratic government faced herculean obstacles—a massive foreign debt, runaway inflation, and a lack of social consensus. Presidential elections in 1990

STUDENT REVOLT IN MEXICO

A growing conflict between government authorities and university students in Mexico came to a violent and bloody climax on October 2, 1968, when army troops killed and wounded large numbers of students in Mexico City. This excerpt is taken from an account of the events by the student National Strike Council.

NATIONAL STRIKE COUNCIL, EVENTS OF OCTOBER 2–3

After an hour and a half of a peaceful meeting attended by ten thousand people and witnessed by scores of domestic and foreign reporters, a helicopter gave the army the signal to attack by dropping flares into the crowd. Simultaneously, the plaza was surrounded and attacked by members of the army and all police forces, using weapons of every caliber, up to 9 mm.

The local papers have given the following information about the attack, confirmed by firsthand witnesses:

1. Numerous secret policemen had infiltrated the meeting in order to attack it from within, with orders to kill. They were known to each other by the use of a white handkerchief tied around their right hands. . . .

3. High caliber weaponry and expansion bullets were used. Seven hours after the massacre began, tanks cleaned up the residential buildings of Nonoalco-Tlatelolco with short cannon blasts and machine-gun fire.

4. On the morning of October 3, the apartments of supposedly guilty individuals were still being searched, without a search warrant.

5. Doctors in the emergency wards of the city hospitals were under extreme pressure, being forced to forgo attention to the victims until they had been interrogated and placed under guard. Various interns who attended the demonstration for the purpose of giving medical aid had since disappeared.

6. The results of this brutal military operation include hundreds of dead (including women and children), thousands of wounded, an unwarranted search of all the apartments in the area, and thousands of violent arrests. Those arrested were taken to various illegal locations, such as Military Camp No. 1. It should be added that members of the National Strike Council who were captured were stripped and herded into a small archaeological excavation at Tlatelolco, converted for the moment into a dungeon. Some of them were put up against a wall and shot.

7. Onesimo Mason, the general who directed the operation, praised the preparedness of his men, in contrast to the obvious lack of preparedness on the part of the students.

All this has occurred only ten days before the start of the Olympics. The repression is expected to become even greater after the Games, in view of the fact that national public opinion and the protest from the provinces are unified against a regime whose only interest lies in demonstrating its power to control.

Already individual liberties have been suspended, and restricted zones have been created where all vehicles are searched at gunpoint and personal identification is demanded. The Secretary of Defense declared that the friendly disposition of the regime will solve the conflict.

WE ARE NOT AGAINST THE OLYMPIC GAMES. WELCOME TO MEXICO.

---

brought a newcomer into office—Fernando Collor de Mello (b. 1949). He promised to end the inflation problem with a drastic reform program, based on squeezing money out of the economy by stringent controls on wages and prices, drastic reductions in public spendings, and cuts in the number of government employees. Collor de Mello's efforts were undermined by the corruption in his own administration, however, and he resigned from office at the end of 1992 after having been impeached. In new elections in 1994, Fernando Cardoso was elected president by an overwhelming majority of the popular vote.

The Mexican Way

During the 1950s and 1960s, Mexico's ruling party (the Institutional Revolutionary Party, or PRI) focused on a balanced industrial program. Fifteen years of steady economic growth combined with low inflation and real gains in wages for more and more people made those years appear to be a "golden age" in Mexico's economic development. But at the end of the 1960s, the true nature of Mexico's domination by one party became apparent with the student protest movement. On October 2, 1968, a demonstration of university students in Tlaltelolco Square in Mexico City was met by police forces, who opened fire and killed hundreds of students (see the box above). Leaders of the PRI became concerned about the need to change the system.

The next two presidents, Luis Echeverría (b. 1922) and José López Portillo (b. 1920), introduced political reforms. Rules for the registration of political parties were eased, making their growth more likely, and greater freedom of debate in the press and universities was allowed. But economic problems continued to trouble Mexico. In the late 1970s, vast new reserves of oil were discovered. As the sale of oil abroad increased dramatically, the government became even more dependent on oil revenues. When world oil prices dropped in the mid-1980s, Mexico was no longer

able to make payments on its foreign debt, which had reached $80 billion in 1982. The government was forced to adopt new economic policies, including the increased sale of public-owned companies to private hands.

The debt crisis and rising unemployment increased dissatisfaction with the government, which was especially evident in the 1988 election, when the PRI's choice for president, Carlos Salina, who would be expected to win in a landslide, won by only a 50.3 percent majority. Increasing dissatisfaction with the government's economic policies finally led to the unthinkable: in 2000, Vicente Fox defeated the PRI candidate for the presidency.

SOCIETY AND CULTURE IN THE WESTERN WORLD

Socially, culturally, and intellectually, the Western world during the second half of the twentieth century was marked by much diversity. Although many trends represented a continuation of prewar modern developments, new directions also led some observers to speak of a postmodern world.

The Emergence of a New Society

During the postwar era, Western society witnessed remarkably rapid change. Such products of new technologies as computers, television, jet planes, contraceptive devices, and new surgical techniques all dramatically and quickly altered the pace and nature of human life. The rapid changes in postwar society, fueled by scientific advances and rapid economic growth, led many to view it as a new society. Called a technocratic society by some and the consumer society by others, postwar Western society was characterized by a changing social structure and new movements for change.

The structure of European society was altered after 1945. Especially noticeable were the changes in the middle class. Such traditional middle-class groups as businesspeople and professionals in law, medicine, and the universities were greatly augmented by a new group of managers and technicians as large companies and government agencies employed increasing numbers of white-collar supervisory and administrative personnel. Whether in Eastern or Western Europe, the new managers and experts were very much alike. Everywhere their positions depended on specialized knowledge acquired from some form of higher education. Everywhere they focused on the effective administration of their corporations. Since their positions usually depended on their skills, they took steps to ensure that their children would be similarly educated.

Changes also occurred among the traditional lower classes. Especially noticeable was the dramatic shift of people from rural to urban areas. The number of people in agriculture declined drastically; by the 1950s, the number of farmers throughout most of Europe had dropped by 50 percent. Nor did the size of the industrial working class expand. In West Germany, industrial workers made up 48 percent of the labor force throughout the 1950s and 1960s. Thereafter, the number of industrial workers began to dwindle as the number of white-collar service employees increased. At the same time, a substantial increase in their real wages enabled the working classes to aspire to the consumption patterns of the middle class, leading to what some observers have called the consumer society. Buying on the installment plan, which was introduced in the 1930s, became widespread beginning in the 1950s and gave workers a chance to imitate the middle class by buying such products as televisions, washing machines, refrigerators, vacuum cleaners, and stereos. But the most visible symbol of mass consumerism was the automobile. Before World War II, cars were reserved mostly for the European upper classes. In 1948, there were 5 million cars in all of Europe, but by 1957, the number had tripled. By the 1960s, there were almost 45 million cars.

Rising incomes, combined with shorter working hours, created an even greater market for mass leisure activities. Between 1900 and 1980, the workweek was reduced from sixty hours to a little more than forty hours, and the number of paid holidays increased. All aspects of popular culture—music, sports, media—became commercialized and offered opportunities for leisure activities including concerts, sporting events, and television viewing.

Another very visible symbol of mass leisure was the growth of tourism. Before World War II, most persons who traveled for pleasure were from the upper and middle classes. After the war, the combination of more vacation time, increased prosperity, and the flexibility provided by package tours with their lower rates and budget-priced accommodations enabled millions to expand their travel possibilities. By the mid-1960s, 100 million tourists were crossing European borders each year.

Social change was also evident in new educational patterns and student revolts. Before World War II, higher education had remained largely the preserve of Europe's wealthier classes. After the war, European states began to foster greater equality of opportunity in higher education by eliminating fees, and universities experienced an influx of students from the middle and lower classes. Enrollments grew dramatically; in France, 4.5 percent of young people went to a university in 1950. By 1965, the figure had increased to 14.5 percent.

But there were problems. Overcrowded classrooms, professors who paid little attention to students, and administrators who acted in an authoritarian fashion aroused student resentment. In addition, despite changes in the curriculum, students often felt that the universities were not providing an education relevant to the modern age. This discontent led to a spate of student revolts in the late 1960s. In part, these protests were an extension of the disruptions in American universities in the mid-1960s, which were often sparked by student opposition to the Vietnam War. Perhaps the most famous student revolt occurred in France in 1968. It erupted at the University of Nanterre outside Paris but soon spread to the Sorbonne, the main campus of the University of Paris. French students demanded a greater voice in the administration of the university, took over buildings, and then expanded the scale of their protests by inviting workers to support them. Half of France's workforce went on strike in May 1968. After the Gaullist government instituted a hefty wage hike, the workers returned to work, and the police repressed the remaining student protesters.

STUDENT REVOLT IN PARIS, 1968.   The discontent of university students exploded in the late 1960s in a series of student revolts. Perhaps best known was the movement in Paris in 1968. This photograph shows the barricades that students erected by overturning cars on a Parisian street on the morning of May 11 during the height of the revolt.

The student protest movement reached its high point in 1968, although scattered incidents lasted into the early 1970s. There were several reasons for the student radicalism. Some students were genuinely motivated by their desire to reform the university. Others were protesting the Vietnam War, which they viewed as a product of Western imperialism. They also attacked other aspects of Western society, such as its materialism, and expressed concern about becoming cogs in the large and impersonal bureaucratic jungles of the modern world. For many students, the calls for democratic decision making within the universities were a reflection of their deeper concerns about the direction of Western society. Although the student revolts fizzled out in the 1970s, the larger issues they raised were increasingly revived in the 1990s.

The Permissive Society

The "permissive society" was yet another label critics applied to the new society of postwar Europe. World War I had seen the first significant crack in the rigid code of manners and morals of the nineteenth century. Subsequently, the 1920s had witnessed experimentation with drugs, the appearance of hard-core pornography, and a new sexual freedom (police in Berlin, for example, issued cards that permitted female and male homosexual prostitutes to practice their trade). But these indications of a new attitude appeared mostly in major cities and touched only small numbers of people. After World War II, changes in manners and morals were far more extensive and far more noticeable.

Sweden took the lead in the propagation of the so-called sexual revolution of the 1960s, but the rest of Europe and the United States soon followed. Sex education in the schools and the decriminalization of homosexuality were but two aspects of Sweden's liberal legislation. The introduction of the birth control pill, which became widely available by the mid-1960s, gave people more freedom in sexual behavior. Meanwhile, sexually explicit movies, plays, and books broke new ground in the treatment of once hidden subjects. Cities like Amsterdam, which allowed open prostitution and the public sale of hard-core pornography, attracted thousands of curious tourists.

The new standards were evident in the breakdown of the traditional family. Divorce rates increased dramatically, especially in the 1960s, while the incidence of premarital and extramarital sexual experiences also rose substantially. A survey in the Netherlands in 1968 revealed that 78 percent of men and 86 percent of women had participated in extramarital sex.

The decade of the 1960s also saw the emergence of a drug culture. Marijuana was widely used among college and university students as the recreational drug of choice. For young people more interested in mind expansion into higher levels of consciousness, Timothy Leary, who had done psychedelic research at Harvard on the effects of LSD (lysergic acid diethylamide), became the high priest of hallucinogenic experiences.

New attitudes toward sex and the use of drugs were only two manifestations of a growing youth movement in the 1960s that questioned authority and fostered rebellion

THE "LOVE-IN." In the 1960s, a number of outdoor public festivals for young people combined music, drugs, and sex. Flamboyant dress, facial painting, free-form dancing, and drugs were vital ingredients in creating an atmosphere dedicated to "love and peace." Shown here is a "love-in" that was held on the grounds of an English country estate in the Summer of Love, 1967.

"The Times They Are a-Changin'": The Music of Youthful Protest

*I*n the 1960s, the lyrics of rock music reflected the rebellious mood of many young people. Bob Dylan (b. 1941), who became a vastly influential performer and recording artist, expressed the feelings of the younger generation. His song "The Times They Are a-Changin'," released in 1964, has been called an "anthem for the protest movement."

BOB DYLAN, "THE TIMES THEY ARE A-CHANGIN'"

Come gather 'round people
Wherever you roam
And admit that the waters
Around you have grown
And accept it that soon
You'll be drenched to the bone
If your time to you
Is worth savin'
Then you better start swimmin'
Or you'll sink like a stone
For the times they are a-changin'

Come writers and critics
Who prophesize with your pen
And keep your eyes wide
The chance won't come again
And don't speak too soon
For the wheel's still in spin
And there's no tellin' who
That it's namin'
For the loser now
Will be later to win
For the times they are a-changin'

Come senators, congressmen
Please heed the call

Don't stand in the doorway
Don't block up the hall
For he that gets hurt
Will be he who has stalled
There's a battle outside
And it is ragin'
It'll soon shake your windows
And rattle your walls
For the times they are a-changin'

Come mothers and fathers
Throughout the land
And don't criticize
What you can't understand
Your sons and your daughters
Are beyond your command
Your old road
Is rapidly agin'
Please get out of the new one
If you can't lend your hand
For the times they are a-changin'

The line it is drawn
The curse it is cast
The slow one now
Will later be fast
As the present now
Will later be past
The order is
Rapidly fadin'
And the first one now
Will later be last
For the times they are a-changin'

---

against the older generation. Spurred on by the Vietnam War and a growing political consciousness, the youth rebellion became a youth protest movement by the second half of the 1960s (see the box above).

Women in the Postwar Western World

Despite their enormous contributions to the war effort, women at the end of World War II were removed from the workforce to free up jobs for the soldiers returning home. After the horrors of war, people seemed willing for a while to return to traditional family practices. Female participation in the workforce declined, and birthrates began to rise, creating a "baby boom." This increase in the birthrate, however, did not last, and birthrates—and hence the size of families—began to decline by the end of the 1950s. Largely responsible for this decline was the widespread practice of birth control. Invented in the nineteenth century, the condom was already in wide use, but the development in the 1960s of oral contraceptives, known as birth control pills, provided a reliable means of birth control that quickly spread to all Western countries.

No doubt the trend toward smaller families contributed to the change in the character of women's employment in both Europe and the United States as women spent many more years not involved in rearing children. The most important development was the increased number of married women in the workforce. At the beginning of the twentieth century, even working-class wives tended to stay at home if they could afford to do so. In the postwar period, this was no longer the case. In the United States, for example, married women made up about 15 percent of the female labor force in 1900; by 1970, their number had increased to 62 percent. The percentage of married women in the female labor force in Sweden increased from 47 to 66 percent between 1963 and 1975.

But the increased number of women in the workforce did not change some old patterns. Working-class women in particular still earned salaries lower than those of men performing equivalent work. In the 1960s, women earned only 60 percent of men's wages in Britain, 50 percent in France, and 63 percent in West Germany. In addition, women still tended to enter traditionally female jobs. As one Swedish woman guidance counselor remarked in 1975: "Every girl now thinks in terms of a job. This is progress. They want children, but they don't pin their hopes on marriage. They don't intend to be housewives for some future husband. But there has been no change in their vocational choices."[2] Many European women also still faced the double burden of earning income on the one hand and raising a family and maintaining the household on the other. Such inequalities led increasing numbers of women to rebel.

The participation of women in World Wars I and II helped them achieve one of the major aims of the nineteenth-century feminist movement—the right to vote. Already after World War I, many governments acknowledged the contributions of women to the war effort by granting them the right to vote. Sweden, Great Britain, Germany, Poland, Hungary, Austria, and Czechoslovakia did so in 1918, followed by the United States in 1920. Women in France and Italy did not obtain the right to vote until 1945. After World War II, European women tended to fall back into the traditional roles expected of them, and little was heard of feminist concerns. But by the late 1960s, women began to assert their rights again and speak as feminists. Along with the student upheavals of the late 1960s came renewed interest in feminism, or the women's liberation movement, as it was now called. Increasingly, women protested that the acquisition of political and legal equality had not brought true equality with men:

> We are economically oppressed: in jobs we do full work for half pay; in the home we do unpaid work full-time. We are commercially exploited by advertisement, television, and the press; legally we often have only the status of children. We are brought up to feel inadequate, educated to narrower horizons than men. This is our specific oppression as women. It is as women that we are, therefore, organizing.[3]

These were the words of a British Women's Liberation Workshop in 1969.

WOMEN'S LIBERATION MOVEMENT. In the late 1960s, as women began once again to assert their rights, a revived women's liberation movement emerged. Feminists in the movement maintained that women themselves must alter the conditions of their lives. During this women's liberation rally, some women climbed the statue of Admiral Farragut in Washington, D.C., to exhibit their signs.

Of great importance to the emergence of the postwar women's liberation movement was the work of a Frenchwoman, Simone de Beauvoir (1908–1986). Born into a Catholic middle-class family and educated at the Sorbonne in Paris, de Beauvoir supported herself as a teacher and later as a novelist and writer. She maintained a lifelong relationship (but not marriage) with the philosopher Jean-Paul Sartre. Her involvement in the existentialist movement—the leading intellectual movement of its time—led her to become active in political causes. De Beauvoir believed that she lived a "liberated" life for a twentieth-century European woman, but for all her freedom, she still came to perceive that as a woman she faced limits that men did not. In 1949, she published her highly influential work *The Second Sex*, in which she argued that as a result of male-dominated societies, women had been

THE VOICE OF THE WOMEN'S LIBERATION MOVEMENT

*S*imone de Beauvoir was an important figure in the emergence of the postwar women's liberation movement. This excerpt is taken from her book The Second Sex, in which she argued that women have been forced into a position subordinate to men.

SIMONE DE BEAUVOIR, *THE SECOND SEX*

Now, woman has always been man's dependent, if not his slave; the two sexes have never shared the world in equality. And even today woman is heavily handicapped, though her situation is beginning to change. Almost nowhere is her legal status the same as man's, and frequently it is much to her disadvantage. Even when her rights are legally recognized in the abstract, long-standing custom prevents their full expression in the mores. In the economic sphere men and women can almost be said to make up two castes; other things being equal, the former hold the better jobs, get higher wages, and have more opportunity for success than their new competitors. In industry and politics men have a great many more positions and they monopolize the most important posts. In addition to all this, they enjoy a traditional prestige that the education of children tends in every way to support, for the present enshrines the past—and in the past all history has been made by men. At the present time, when women are beginning to take part in the affairs of the world, it is still a world that belongs to men—they have no doubt of it at all and women have scarcely any. To decline to be the Other, to refuse to be a party to a deal—this would be for women to renounce all the advantages conferred upon them by their alliance with the superior caste. Man-the-sovereign will provide woman-the-liege with material protection and will undertake the moral justification of her existence; thus she can evade at once both economic risk and the metaphysical risk of a liberty in which ends and aims must be contrived without assistance. Indeed, along with the ethical urge of each individual to affirm his subjective existence, there is also the temptation to forgo liberty and become a thing. This is an inauspicious road, for he who takes it—passive, lost, ruined—becomes henceforth the creature of another's will, frustrated in his transcendence and deprived of every value. But it is an easy road; on it one avoids the strain involved in undertaking an authentic existence. When man makes of woman the *Other*, he may, then, expect her to manifest deep-seated tendencies toward complicity. Thus, woman may fail to lay claim to the status of subject because she lacks definite resources, because she feels the necessary bond that ties her to man regardless of reciprocity, and because she is often very well pleased with her role as the *Other*.

Now, what peculiarly signalizes the situation of woman is that she—a free and autonomous being like all human creatures—nevertheless finds herself living in a world where men compel her to assume the status of the Other.

defined by their differences from men and consequently received second-class status (see the box above).

Another important influence in the growth of a women's movement in the 1960s came from Betty Friedan (b. 1921). A journalist and the mother of three children, Friedan grew increasingly uneasy with her attempt to fulfill the traditional role of the "ideal housewife and mother." In 1963, she published *The Feminine Mystique*, in which she analyzed the problems of middle-class American women in the 1950s and argued that women were being denied equality with men. She wrote: "The problem that has no name—which is simply the fact that American women are kept from growing to their full human capacities—is taking a far greater toll on the physical and mental health of our country than any known disease."[4] *The Feminine Mystique* became a best-seller and propelled Friedan into a newfound celebrity.

TRANSFORMATION IN WOMEN'S LIVES

It is estimated that women need to average 2.1 children in order to ensure a natural replacement of a country's population. In many European countries, the population stopped growing in the 1960s, and the trend has continued since then. By the 1990s, birthrates were down drastically; among the nations of the European Union, the average number of children per woman of childbearing age was 1.4. Italy's rate—1.2—was the lowest in the world in 1997.

At the same time, the number of women in the workforce has continued to rise. In Britain, for example, the number of women in the labor force went from 32 percent to 44 percent between 1970 and 1990. Moreover, women have entered new employment areas. Greater access to universities and professional schools enabled women to take jobs in law, medicine, government, business, and education. In the Soviet Union, for example, about 70 percent of doctors and teachers were women. Nevertheless, economic inequality still often prevailed; women received lower wages than men for comparable work and received fewer opportunities for advancement to management positions.

Feminists in the women's liberation movement came to believe that women themselves must transform the fundamental conditions of their lives. They did so in a variety of ways after 1970. First, they formed numerous groups to further awareness of women's issues. Women got together to share their personal experiences and become aware of the many ways that male dominance affected their lives. This "consciousness raising" spurred many women to become activists.

Women sought and gained a measure of control over their own bodies by seeking to overturn legal restrictions on both contraception and abortion. In the 1960s and 1970s, hundreds of thousands of European women worked to repeal the laws that outlawed contraception and abortion and began to meet with success. A French law in 1968 permitted the sale of contraceptive devices, and in the 1970s, French feminists worked to legalize abortion, which legislators did in 1979. Even in Catholic countries, where the church remained strongly opposed to abortion, legislation allowing contraception and abortion was passed in the 1970s and 1980s.

As more women became activists, they also became involved in new issues. In the 1980s and 1990s, women faculty in universities concentrated on developing new cultural attitudes through the new academic field of women's studies. Courses in women's studies, which stressed the role and contributions of women in history, mushroomed in colleges and universities on both sides of the Atlantic.

Other women began to try to affect the political environment by allying with the antinuclear movement. In 1981, a group of women in Britain protested American nuclear missiles by chaining themselves to the fence of an American military base. Thousands more joined in creating a peace camp around the military compound. Enthusiasm ran high; one participant said: "I'll never forget that feeling; it'll live with me forever. . . . As we walked round, and we clasped hands . . . it was for women; it was for peace; it was for the world."[5]

Some women joined the ecological movement. As one German writer who was concerned with environmental issues said, it is women "who must give birth to children, willingly or unwillingly, in this polluted world of ours." Especially prominent was the number of women members in the Green Party in Germany (see "The Environment and the Green Movements" later in this chapter), which supported environmental issues and elected forty-two delegates to the West German parliament in 1987.

Women in the West have also reached out to work with women from the rest of the world in international conferences to change the conditions of their lives. Between 1975 and 1995, the United Nations held conferences in Mexico City, Copenhagen, Nairobi, and Beijing. These meetings made clear the differences between women from Western and non-Western countries. Whereas women from Western countries spoke about political, economic, cultural, and sexual rights, women from developing countries in Latin America, Africa, and Asia focused their attention on bringing an end to the violence, hunger, and disease that haunt their lives. Despite these differences, these meetings made it clear how women in both developed and developing nations were organizing to make people aware of women's issues.

The Growth of Terrorism

Acts of terror by opponents of governments became a frightening aspect of modern Western society. During the late 1970s and early 1980s, small bands of terrorists used assassination, indiscriminate killing of civilians, the taking of hostages, and the hijacking of airplanes to draw attention to their demands or to destabilize governments in the hope of achieving their political goals. Terrorist acts garnered considerable media attention. When Palestinian terrorists kidnapped and killed eleven Israeli athletes at the Munich Olympic Games in 1972, hundreds of millions of people watched the drama unfold on television. Indeed, some observers believe that media exposure has been an important catalyst for some terrorist groups.

Motivations for terrorist acts varied considerably. Left- and right-wing terrorist groups flourished in the late 1970s and early 1980s, but terrorist acts also stemmed from militant nationalists who wished to create separatist states. Because they received considerable support from local populations sympathetic to their cause, these terrorist groups could maintain their activities over a long period of time. Most prominent was the Irish Republican Army (IRA), which resorted to vicious attacks against the ruling government and innocent civilians in Northern Ireland.

Although left- and right-wing terrorist activities declined in Europe in the 1980s, international terrorism remained rather commonplace. Angered over the loss of their territory to Israel, some militant Palestinians responded with a policy of terrorist attacks against Israel's supporters. Palestinian terrorists operated throughout European countries, attacking both Europeans and American tourists; Palestinian terrorists massacred vacationers at airports in Rome and Vienna in 1985. State-sponsored terrorism was often an integral part of international terrorism. Militant governments, especially in Iran, Libya, and Syria, assisted terrorist organizations that made attacks on Europeans and Americans. On December 21, 1988, Pan American flight 103 from Frankfurt to New York exploded over Lockerbie, Scotland, killing all 259 passengers and crew members. A massive investigation finally revealed that the bomb responsible for the explosion had been planted by two Libyan terrorists who were connected to terrorist groups based in both Iran and Syria.

TERRORIST ATTACK ON THE UNITED STATES

One of the most destructive acts of terrorism occurred on September 11, 2001, in the United States. Four groups of terrorists hijacked four commercial jet airplanes after

TERRORIST ATTACK ON THE WORLD TRADE CENTER IN NEW YORK CITY.   On September 11, 2001, hijackers flew two commerical jetliners into the twin towers of the World Trade Center. Shown at left are the two towers in the New York skyline before the attack. The middle picture shows the second of the two jetliners about to hit one of the towers while smoke billows from the site of the first attack. In the scene below, firefighters are making their way through what was left of the 110-story towers after the collapse.

takeoff from Boston, Newark, and Washington, D.C. The hijackers flew two of the airplanes directly into the towers of the World Trade Center in New York City, causing these buildings, as well as a number of surrounding buildings, to collapse. A third hijacked plane slammed into the Pentagon near Washington, D.C. The fourth plane, apparently headed for Washington, crashed instead in an isolated area of Pennsylvania, apparently as the result of an attempt by a group of heroic passengers to overcome the hijackers. In total, more than three thousand people were killed, including everyone aboard the four airliners.

These coordinated acts of terror were carried out by hijackers connected to an international terrorist organization known as al-Qaeda, run by Osama bin Laden. A native of Saudi Arabia of Yemeni extraction, bin Laden used an inherited fortune to set up terrorist training camps in Afghanistan, under the protection of the nation's militant fundamentalist Islamic rulers known as the Taliban. Bin Laden was also suspected of directing earlier terrorist attacks against the United States, including the bombing of two U.S. embassies in Africa in 1998 and an attack on a naval ship, the U.S.S. *Cole*, in 2000.

U.S. President George W. Bush vowed to wage a lengthy and thorough war on terrorism and worked to create a coalition of nations to assist in ridding the world of al-Qaeda and other terrorist groups. Within weeks of the attack on America, United States and NATO air forces began bombing Taliban-controlled command centers, airfields, and al-Qaeda hiding places in Afghanistan. On the ground, Afghan forces, assisted by U.S. special forces, pushed the Taliban out and gained control of the country by the end of November. A democratic multiethnic government was installed but faced problems in 2003 from revived Taliban activity.

Guest Workers and Immigrants

As the economies of the Western European countries revived in the 1950s and 1960s, a severe labor shortage forced them to rely on foreign workers. Thousands of Turks and eastern and southern Europeans came to Germany, North Africans to France, and people from the Caribbean, India, and Pakistan to Great Britain. Overall, there were probably fifteen million guest workers in Europe in the 1980s. They constituted 17 percent of the labor force in Switzerland and 10 percent in Germany.

Although these workers were necessary for economic reasons, socially and politically their presence created problems for their host countries. Many foreign workers complained that they received lower wages and inferior social benefits. Moreover, their concentration in certain cities and even certain sections of those cities often created tensions with the local native populations. Foreign workers constituted almost one-fifth of the population in the German cities of Frankfurt, Munich, and Stuttgart. Having become settled in their new countries, many were unwilling to leave, even after the end of the postwar boom in the early 1970s led to mass unemployment. Moreover, as guest workers settled permanently in their host countries, additional family members migrated to join them. Although they had little success in getting guest workers already there to leave, some European countries passed legislation or took other measures to restrict new immigration.

In the 1980s, the problem of foreign workers was intensified by an influx of other refugees, especially to West Germany, which had liberal immigration laws that permitted people seeking asylum from political persecution to enter the country. During the 1970s and 1980s, West Germany absorbed over a million refugees from Eastern Europe and East Germany. In 1986 alone, 200,000 political refugees from Pakistan, Bangladesh, and Sri Lanka entered the country.

This great influx of foreigners, many of them non-white, strained not only the social services of European countries but also the patience of native residents who opposed making their countries ethnically diverse. Antiforeign sentiment, especially in a time of growing unemployment, increased and was encouraged by new right-wing political parties that catered to people's complaints. Thus the National Front in France, organized by Jean-Marie Le Pen, and the Republican Party in Germany, led by Franz Schönhuber, a former SS officer, advocated restricting all new immigration and limiting the assimilation of settled immigrants. Although these parties have had only limited success in elections so far, even that modest accomplishment has encouraged traditional conservative and even moderately conservative parties to adopt more nationalistic policies. Much more frightening, however, have been the organized campaigns of violence, especially against African and Asian immigrants, by radical, right-wing groups.

The Environment and the Green Movements

Beginning in the 1970s, environmentalism became a serious item on the European political agenda. By that time, serious ecological problems had become all too apparent. Air pollution, produced by nitrogen oxide and sulfur dioxide emissions from road vehicles, power plants, and industrial factories, was causing respiratory illnesses and having corrosive effects on buildings and monuments. Many rivers, lakes, and seas had become so polluted that they posed serious health risks. Dying forests and disappearing wildlife alarmed more and more people. The opening of Eastern Europe after the revolutions of 1989 brought to the world's attention the incredible environmental destruction of that region caused by unfettered industrial pollution.

Environmental concerns forced the major political parties in Europe to advocate new regulations for the protection of the environment. The Soviet nuclear power disaster at Chernobyl in 1986 made Europeans even more aware of potential environmental hazards, and 1987 was touted as the "year of the environment." Many European states also established government ministries to oversee environmental issues.

Growing ecological awareness also gave rise to Green movements and Green Parties that emerged throughout Europe in the 1970s. Some of these movements emerged from the antinuclear movement; others arose out of such causes as women's liberation and concerns for foreign workers. Most visible was the Green Party in Germany, which was officially organized in 1979 and had by 1987 elected forty-two delegates to the West German parliament. Green Parties also competed successfully in Sweden, Austria, and Switzerland.

Although the Green movements and parties have played an important role in making people aware of ecological problems, they have not supplanted the traditional political parties, as some political analysts in the mid-1980s forecast. For one thing, the coalitions that made up the Greens found it difficult to agree on all issues and tended to splinter into different cliques. Then, too, many of the founders of these movements, who often expressed a willingness to work with the traditional political parties, were ousted from their leadership positions by fundamentalists unwilling to compromise their principles in any way. Finally, traditional political parties have co-opted the environmental issues of the Greens. By the 1990s, more and more European governments were beginning to sponsor projects to safeguard the environment and clean up the worst sources of pollution.

Trends in Art and Literature

In the postwar years, modern art continued to prevail at exhibitions and museums. For the most part, the United States dominated the art world, much as it did the world of popular culture. American art, often vibrantly colored and filled with activity, reflected the energy and exuberance of the postwar United States. After 1945, New York City became the artistic center of the Western world. The Guggenheim Museum, the Museum of Modern Art, and the Whitney Museum of American Art, together with New York's numerous art galleries, promoted modern art and helped determine artistic tastes not only in New York and the United States but around the world.

Abstractionism, especially Abstract Expressionism, moved into the artistic mainstream. American exuberance in Abstract Expressionism is evident in the enormous canvases of Jackson Pollock (1912–1956). In such works as *Lavender Mist* (1950), paint seems to explode, assaulting the viewer with emotion and movement. Pollock's swirling forms and seemingly chaotic patterns broke all conventions of form and structure. His drip paintings—experiments in total abstraction—were extremely influential with other artists, although the public was initially quite hostile to his work.

The early 1960s saw the emergence of Pop Art, which took images of popular culture and transformed them into works of fine art. Andy Warhol (1930–1987), who began as an advertising illustrator, was the most famous of the pop artists. Warhol adapted images from commercial art, such as cans of Campbell's soup, and photographs of such celebrities as Marilyn Monroe. Other artists drew their inspiration from comic strips. Derived from mass culture, these works were mass-produced and deliberately "of the moment," expressing the fleeting whims of popular culture.

In the 1980s, styles emerged that some have referred to as Postmodern. Although as yet ill-defined, Postmodernism tends to move away from the futurism or "cutting edge" qualities of Modernism. Instead it favors "utilizing tradition," whether that includes more styles of painting or elevating traditional artisanship to the level of fine art. Weavers, potters, glassmakers, metalsmiths, and furniture makers gained respect as artists.

Of all the arts, architecture best reflects the extraordinary global economic expansion of the second half of the twentieth century, from the rapid postwar reconstruction of Japan and Europe to the phenomenal prosperity of the West to the newfound affluence of emerging Third World nations. No matter where one travels today, from Kuala Lumpur to Johannesburg, from Buenos Aires to Shanghai, the world's cities boast the identical monolithic rectangular skyscraper—the international symbol of modernization, money, and power.

The most significant new trend in postwar literature is known as the Theater of the Absurd. This convention in drama began in France in the 1950s, although its most famous proponent was the Irishman Samuel Beckett (1906–1990), who lived in France. In Beckett's *Waiting for Godot* (1952), the action on the stage is not realistic. Two men wait for the appearance of someone with whom they may or may not have an appointment. No background information on the two men is provided. During the course of the play, nothing seems to be happening. The audience is never

Hans Namuth/Photo Researchers Inc.

JACKSON POLLOCK DOES A PAINTING.   One of the best-known practitioners of Abstract Expressionism, which was at the center of the artistic mainstream after World War II, was the American Jackson Pollock, who achieved his ideal of total abstraction in his drip paintings. He is shown here at work in his Long Island studio. Pollock found it easier to cover his large canvases with exploding patterns of color when he put them on the floor.

told if the action in front of them is real or unreal. Unlike traditional theater, suspense is maintained not by having the audience wonder what is going to happen next but by having them wonder what is happening now.

The Theater of the Absurd reflected its time. The postwar period was a time of disillusionment with fixed ideological beliefs in politics or religion. The same disillusionment that inspired the existentialism of Albert Camus (1913–1960) and Jean-Paul Sartre (1905–1980), with its sense of the world's meaninglessness, underscored the bleak worldview of absurdist drama and literature. The beginning point of the existentialism of Sartre and Camus was the absence of God in the universe. Although the death of God was tragic, it meant that humans had no preordained destiny and were utterly alone in the universe, with no future and no hope. As Camus expressed it:

A world that can be explained even with bad reasons is a familiar world. But, on the other hand, in a universe suddenly divested of illusions and lights, man feels an alien, a stranger. His exile is without remedy since he is deprived of the memory of a lost home or the hope of a promised land. This divorce between man and his life, the actor and his setting, is properly the feeling of absurdity.[6]

According to Camus, then, the world was absurd and without meaning; humans, too, are without meaning and purpose. Reduced to despair and depression, humans have but one ground of hope—themselves.

Postmodernism was also evident in literature. In the Western world, the best examples were found in Latin America, in a literary style called "magic realism," and in Central and Eastern Europe. Magic realism combined realistic events with dreamlike or fantastic backgrounds. One of the finest examples of magic realism can be found in the novel *One Hundred Years of Solitude*, written by a Colombian, Gabriel García Márquez (b. 1928), who won the Nobel Prize for literature in 1982. The novel is the story of the fictional town of Macondo as seen by several generations of the Buendías, its founding family. The author slips back and forth between fact and fantasy. Villagers are not surprised when a local priest rises into the air and floats. However, when wandering gypsies introduce these villagers to magnets, telescopes, and magnifying glasses, the villagers are dumbfounded by what they see as magic. According to the author, fantasy and fact depend on one's point of view.

The other center of Postmodernism was in Central and Eastern Europe, especially in the work of Milan Kundera (b. 1929) of Czechoslovakia. Like the magic realists of Latin America, Kundera also blended fantasy with realism. Unlike the magic realists, Kundera used fantasy to examine moral issues and remained optimistic about the human condition. Indeed, in his first novel, *The Unbearable Lightness of Being*, published in 1984, Kundera does not despair because of the political repression that he so aptly describes in his native land but allows his characters to use love as a way to a better life. The human spirit can be lessened but not destroyed.

Advances in Science and Technology

Since the Scientific Revolution of the seventeenth century and the Industrial Revolution of the nineteenth century, science and technology have played increasingly important roles in world civilization. Many of the scientific and technological achievements since World War II have revolutionized people's lives. When American astronauts walked on the moon, millions watched the event on their televisions in the privacy of their living rooms.

Before World War II, theoretical science and technology were largely separated. Pure science was the domain of university professors, far removed from the practical technological matters of technicians and engineers. But during World War II, university scientists were recruited to work for their governments and develop new weapons and practical instruments of war. British physicists played a crucial role in the development of an improved radar system that helped defeat the German air force in the Battle of Britain in 1940. The computer, too, was a wartime creation. The British mathematician Alan Turing designed a primitive computer to assist British intelligence in breaking the secret codes of German ciphering machines. The most famous product of wartime scientific research was the atomic bomb, created by a team of American and European scientists under the guidance of the physicist J. Robert Oppenheimer. Many wartime devices were created for destructive purposes, but computers and breakthrough technologies such as nuclear energy were soon adapted for peacetime uses.

The sponsorship of research by governments and the military during World War II led to a new scientific model. Science had become very complex, and only large organizations with teams of scientists, huge laboratories, and complicated equipment could undertake such large-scale projects. Such facilities were so expensive, however, that they could only be provided by governments and large corporations. Because of its postwar prosperity, the United States was able to lead in the development of the new science. In 1965, almost 75 percent of all scientific research funds in the United States came from the government. Unwilling to lag behind, especially in military development, the Soviet Union was also forced to provide large outlays for scientific and technological research and development. In fact, the defense establishments of the United States and the Soviet Union generated much of postwar scientific research. One-fourth of the trained scientists and engineers after 1945 were employed in the creation of new weapons systems. Universities found their research agendas increasingly determined by government funding for military-related projects.

There was no more stunning example of how the new scientific establishment operated than the space race of the 1960s. The announcement by the Soviets in 1957 that they had sent the first space satellite, *Sputnik*, into orbit around the earth caused the United States to launch a gigantic project to land a manned spacecraft on the moon within a decade. Massive government funds financed the scientific research and technological advances that attained this goal in 1969.

The postwar alliance of science and technology led to an accelerated rate of change that became a fact of life in Western society. One product of this alliance—the computer—may yet prove to be the most revolutionary of all the technological inventions of the twentieth century. Early computers, which used thousands of vacuum tubes to function, were large and hot and took up considerable space. The development of the transistor and then the silicon chip produced a revolutionary new approach to computers. With the invention in 1971 of the microprocessor, a machine that combines the equivalent of thousands of transistors on a single, tiny silicon chip, the road was open

SMALL IS BEAUTIFUL: THE LIMITS OF MODERN TECHNOLOGY

lthough science and technology have produced an amazing array of achievements in the postwar world, some voices have been raised in criticism of their sometimes destructive aspects. In 1975, in his book Small Is Beautiful, *the British economist E. F. Schumacher examined the effects modern industrial technology has had on the earth's resources.*

E. F. SCHUMACHER, *SMALL IS BEAUTIFUL*

Is it not evident that our current methods of production are already eating into the very substance of industrial man? To many people this is not at all evident. Now that we have solved the problem of production, they say, have we ever had it so good? Are we not better fed, better clothed, and better housed than ever before—and better educated? Of course we are: most, but by no means all, of us: in the rich countries. But this is not what I mean by "substance." The substance of [humankind] cannot be measured by Gross National Product. Perhaps it cannot be measured at all, except for certain symptoms of loss. However, this is not the place to go into the statistics of these symptoms, such as crime, drug addiction, vandalism, mental breakdown, rebellion, and so forth. Statistics never prove anything.

I started by saying that one of the most fateful errors of our age is the belief that the problem of production has been solved. This illusion, I suggested, is mainly due to our inability to recognize that the modern industrial system, with all its intellectual sophistication, consumes the very basis on which it has been erected. To use the language of the economist, it lives on irreplaceable capital which it cheerfully treats as income. I specified three categories of such capital: fossil fuels, the tolerance margins of nature, and the human substance. Even if some readers should refuse to accept all three parts of my argument, I suggest that any one of them suffices to make my case.

And what is my case? Simply that our most important task is to get off our present collision course. And who is there to tackle such a task? I think every one of us. . . . To talk about the future is useful only if it leads to action *now*. And what can we do *now*, while we are still in the position of "never having had it so good"? To say the least . . . we must thoroughly understand the problem and begin to see the possibility of evolving a new lifestyle, with new methods of production and new patterns of consumption: a lifestyle designed for permanence. To give only three preliminary examples: in agriculture and horticulture, we can interest ourselves in the perfection of production methods which are biologically sound, build up soil fertility, and produce health, beauty, and permanence. Productivity will then look after itself. In industry, we can interest ourselves in the evolution of small-scale technology, relatively nonviolent technology, "technology with a human face," so that people have a chance to enjoy themselves while they are working, instead of working solely for their pay packet and hoping, usually forlornly, for enjoyment solely during their leisure time.

---

for the development of the personal computer. By the 1990s, the personal computer had become a regular fixture in businesses, schools, and homes. The Internet—the world's largest computer network—provides millions of people around the world with quick access to immense quantities of information, as well as rapid communication and commercial transactions. By 2000, an estimated 500 million people were using the Internet.

Despite the marvels produced by the alliance of science and technology, some people came to question the underlying assumption of this alliance—that scientific knowledge gave human beings the ability to manipulate the environment for their benefit. They maintained that some technological advances had far-reaching side effects damaging to the environment. The chemical fertilizers, for example, that were touted for producing larger crops wreaked havoc with the ecological balance of streams, rivers, and woodlands. *Small Is Beautiful*, written by the British economist E. F. Schumacher (1911–1977), was a fundamental critique of the dangers of the new science and technology (see the box above).

The Revival of Religion

Existentialism was one response to the despair generated by the apparent collapse of civilized values in the twentieth century. A revival of religion was another. Ever since the Enlightenment of the eighteenth century, Christianity had been on the defensive. But in the twentieth century, a number of religious thinkers and leaders attempted to bring new life to Christianity.

One expression of this religious revival was the attempt by such theologians as the Protestant Karl Barth (1886–1968) and the Catholic Karl Rahner (1904–1984) to infuse traditional Christian teachings with new life. In his numerous writings, Barth attempted to reinterpret the religious insights of the Reformation era for the modern world. To Barth, the sinful and hence imperfect nature of human beings meant that humans could know religious truth not through reason but only through the grace of God. Rahner attempted to revitalize traditional Catholic theology by incorporating aspects of modern thought. He was careful, however, to emphasize the continuity between ancient and modern interpretations of Catholic doctrine.

In the Catholic church, attempts at religious renewal also came from two charismatic popes—John XXIII and John Paul II. Pope John XXIII (1881–1963) reigned as pope for only a short time (1958–1963) but sparked a dramatic revival of Catholicism when he summoned the twenty-first ecumenical council of the Catholic church. Known as Vatican Council II, it liberalized a number of Catholic practices. The Mass was henceforth to be celebrated in the vernacular languages rather than Latin. New avenues of communication with other Christian faiths were also opened for the first time since the Reformation.

John Paul II (b. 1920), who had been the archbishop of Krakow in Poland before his elevation to the papacy in 1978, was the first non-Italian to be elected pope since the sixteenth century. Although he alienated a number of people by reasserting traditional Catholic teaching on such issues as birth control, women in the priesthood, and clerical celibacy, John Paul's numerous travels around the world helped strengthen the Catholic church throughout the non-Western world. A strong believer in social justice, the charismatic John Paul II has been a powerful figure reminding Europeans of their spiritual heritage and the need to temper the pursuit of materialism with spiritual concerns.

The Explosion of Popular Culture

Popular culture in the twentieth century, especially since World War II, has played an important role in helping Western people define themselves. It also reflects the economic system that supports it, for this system manufactures, distributes, and sells the images that people consume as popular culture. Modern popular culture is therefore an integral part of the mass consumer society in which it has emerged, making it quite different from the folk culture of preceding centuries. Folk culture is something people make, whereas popular culture is something people buy.

POPULAR CULTURE AND THE AMERICANIZATION OF THE WORLD

The United States has been the most influential force in shaping popular culture in the West and, to a lesser degree, the rest of the world. Through movies, music, advertising, and television, the United States has spread its particular form of consumerism and the American dream around the globe. Already in 1923, the New York *Morning Post* noted that "the film is to America what the flag was once to Britain. By its means Uncle Sam may hope some day . . . to Americanize the world."[7] In movies, television, and popular music, the impact of American popular culture on the Western world is apparent.

Motion pictures were the primary vehicle for the diffusion of American popular culture in the years immediately following the war and continued to dominate both European and American markets in the next decades. Although developed in the 1930s, television did not become readily available until the late 1940s. By 1954, there were 32 million sets in the United States as television became the centerpiece of middle-class life. In the 1960s, as television spread around the world, American networks unloaded their products on Europe and developing countries at extraordinarily low prices. Only the establishment of quota systems prevented American television from completely inundating these countries.

The United States has also dominated popular music since the end of World War II. Jazz, blues, rhythm and blues, rap, and rock and roll have been by far the most popular music forms in the Western world—and much of the non-Western world—during this time. All of them originated in the United States, and all are rooted in African American musical innovations. These forms later spread to the rest of the world, inspiring local artists who then transformed the music in their own way.

In the postwar years, sports have become a major product of both popular culture and the leisure industry. The development of satellite television and various electronic breakthroughs helped make sports a global phenomenon. The Olympic Games could now be broadcast around the world from anyplace on earth. Sports became a cheap form of entertainment for consumers as fans did not have to leave their homes to watch athletic competitions. In fact, some sports organizations initially resisted television, fearing that it would hurt ticket sales. The tremendous revenues possible from television contracts overcame this hesitation, however. As sports television revenue escalated, many sports came to receive the bulk of their yearly revenue from television contracts.

Sports became big politics as well as big business. The politicization of sports has been one of the most significant trends in sports during the second half of the twentieth century. Association football (soccer) remains the dominant world sport and more than ever has become a vehicle for nationalist sentiment and expression. Its annual championship, the World Cup, is the most watched event on television. Although the sport can be a positive outlet for national and local pride, all too often it has been marred by violence as nationalistic energies have overcome rational behavior.

CONCLUSION

Western Europe became a new community in the 1950s and 1960s as a remarkable economic recovery fostered a new optimism. Western European states became accustomed to political democracy, and with the development of the European Community, many of them began to move toward economic unity. But nagging economic problems, new ethnic divisions, resentment and violence toward immigrants, environmental degradation, and the inability to work together to stop a civil war in their own backyard have all indicated that what had been seen as a glorious new path for Europe in the 1950s and 1960s had become laden with pitfalls by the end of the century.

In the Western Hemisphere, the United States and Canada built prosperous economies and relatively stable communities in the 1950s, but there too, new problems, including ethnic, racial, and linguistic differences, along with economic difficulties, have dampened the optimism of earlier decades. While some Latin American nations shared in the economic growth of the 1950s and 1960s, it was not matched by political stability. Only in the 1980s did democratic governments begin to replace oppressive military regimes with any consistency.

Western societies after 1945 were also participants in an era of rapidly changing international relationships. While Latin American countries struggled to find a new relationship with the colossus to the north, European states reluctantly let go of their colonial empires. Between 1947 and 1962, virtually every colony in the world achieved independence. Although some colonial powers willingly relinquished their control, others, especially the French, had to be driven out by national wars of liberation. Decolonization was a difficult and even bitter process, but as we shall see in the final chapters, it created a new world as the non-Western states ended the long-held ascendancy of the Western nations.

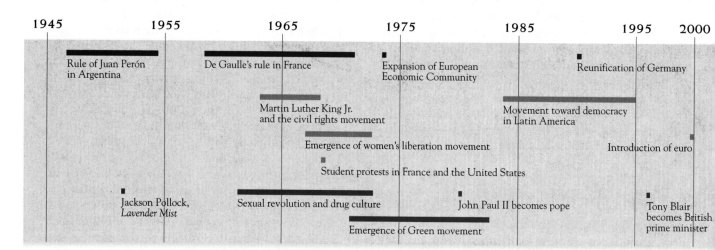

| 1945 | 1955 | 1965 | 1975 | 1985 | 1995 | 2000 |

Rule of Juan Perón in Argentina

De Gaulle's rule in France

Expansion of European Economic Community

Reunification of Germany

Martin Luther King Jr. and the civil rights movement

Movement toward democracy in Latin America

Emergence of women's liberation movement

Introduction of euro

Student protests in France and the United States

Jackson Pollock, *Lavender Mist*

Sexual revolution and drug culture

John Paul II becomes pope

Tony Blair becomes British prime minister

Emergence of Green movement

CHAPTER NOTES

1. Dwight Eisenhower, *The White House Years: Waging Peace, 1956–1961* (Garden City, N.Y., 1965), p. 533.
2. Quoted in Hilda Scott, *Sweden's "Right to Be Human"—Sex-Role Equality: The Goal and the Reality* (London, 1982), p. 125.
3. Quoted in Marsha Rowe et al., *Spare Rib Reader* (Harmondsworth, England, 1982), p. 574.
4. Betty Friedan, *The Feminine Mystique* (New York, 1963), p. 10.
5. Quoted in Renate Bridenthal, "Women in the New Europe," in Renate Bridenthal, Susan Mosher Stuard, and Merry E. Wiesner, eds., *Becoming Visible: Women in European History*, 3d ed. (Boston, 1998), pp. 564–565.
6. Quoted in Henry Grosshans, *The Search for Modern Europe* (Boston, 1970), p. 421.
7. Richard Maltby, ed., *Passing Parade: A History of Popular Culture in the Twentieth Century* (New York, 1989), p. 11.

SUGGESTED READING

For a general perspective on the events covered in this chapter, see T. E. Vadney, *The World Since 1945* (London, 1987). For a survey of postwar European history, see W. Laqueur, *Europe in Our Time* (New York, 1992). The rebuilding of postwar Europe is examined in D. W. Ellwood, *Rebuilding Europe: Western Europe, America,* *and Postwar Reconstruction* (London, 1992), and M. Hogan, *The Marshall Plan: America, Britain, and the Reconstruction of Western Europe, 1947–1952* (New York, 1987). On the building of common institutions in Western Europe, see S. Henig, *The Uniting of Europe: From Discord to Concord* (London, 1997). For a survey of West

Germany, see H. A. Turner, *Germany from Partition to Reunification* (New Haven, Conn., 1992). France under de Gaulle is examined in A. Shennan, *De Gaulle* (New York, 1993), and D. J. Mahoney, *De Gaulle: Statesmanship, Grandeur, and Modern Democracy* (Westport, Conn., 1996). On Britain, see K. O. Morgan, *The People's Peace: British History, 1945–1990* (Oxford, 1992). On the recent history of these countries, see E. J. Evans, *Thatcher and Thatcherism* (New York, 1997); S. Baumann-Reynolds, *François Mitterrand* (Westport, Conn., 1995); and K. Jarausch, *The Rush to German Unity* (New York, 1994).

For a general survey of American history, see Stephan Thernstrom, *A History of the American People*, 2d ed. (San Diego, Calif., 1989). The Truman administration is covered in R. J. Donovan, *Tumultuous Years: The Presidency of Harry S Truman* (New York, 1977). On the Eisenhower years, see S. Ambrose, *Eisenhower: The President* (New York, 1984). D. J. Garrow, *Martin Luther King Jr. and the Southern Christian Leadership Conference* (New York, 1986), discusses the emergence of the civil rights movement. On the postwar social transformations in America, see W. Nugent, *Structures of American Social History* (Bloomington, Ind., 1981). On the turbulent decade of the 1960s, see W. O'Neill, *Coming Apart: An Informal History of America in the 1960s* (Chicago, 1971). On Nixon and Watergate, see J. A. Lukas, *Nightmare: The Underside of the Nixon Years* (New York, 1976). Works on recent events include B. Glad, *Jimmy Carter: From Plains to the White House* (New York, 1980), and G. Wills, *Reagan's America: Innocents at Home* (New York, 1987). On Canadian history, see R. Bothwell, I. Drummond, and J. English, *Canada Since 1945* (Toronto, 1981).

For general surveys of Latin American history, see E. B. Burns, *Latin America: A Concise Interpretive Survey*, 4th ed. (Englewood Cliffs, N.J., 1986), and E. Williamson, *The Penguin History of Latin America* (London, 1992). The twentieth century is the focus of T. E. Skidmore and P. H. Smith, *Modern Latin America*, 3d ed. (New York, 1992). On the role of the military, see A. Rouquié, *The Military and the State in Latin America* (Berkeley, Calif., 1987). Works on the countries examined in this chapter include L. A. Pérez, *Cuba: Between Reform and Revolution* (New York, 1988); B. Loveman, *Chile: The Legacy of Hispanic Capitalism*, 2d ed. (New York, 1988);

J. A. Booth, *The End and the Beginning: The Nicaraguan Revolution* (Boulder, Colo., 1985); J. A. Page, *Perón: A Biography* (New York, 1983); D. Rock, *Argentina, 1516–1987: From Spanish Colonization to Alfonsín*, 2d ed. (Berkeley, Calif., 1987); E. B. Burns, *A History of Brazil*, 2d ed. (New York, 1980); R. Da Matta, *Carnivals, Rogues, and Heroes: An Interpretation of the Brazilian Dilemma* (Notre Dame, Ind., 1991); and M. C. Meyer and W. L. Sherman, *The Course of Mexican History*, 4th ed. (New York, 1991).

The student revolts of the late 1960s are put into a broader context in D. Caute, *The Year of the Barricades: A Journey Through 1968* (New York, 1988). On the women's liberation movement, see D. Bouchier, *The Feminist Challenge: The Movement for Women's Liberation in Britain and the United States* (New York, 1983); D. Meyer, *Sex and Power: The Rise of Women in America, Russia, Sweden, and Italy* (Middletown, Conn., 1987); T. Keefe, *Simone de Beauvoir* (New York, 1998); and C. Duchen, *Women's Rights and Women's Lives in France, 1944–1968* (New York, 1994). More general works that include much information on the contemporary period are B. G. Smith, *Changing Lives: Women in European History Since 1700* (Lexington, Mass., 1989), and F. Thebuad, ed., *A History of Women in the West, Vol. 5: Toward a Cultural Identity in the Twentieth Century* (Cambridge, Mass., 1994). On terrorism, see W. Laqueur, *Terrorism*, 2d ed. (New York, 1988). The problems of guest workers and immigrants are examined in J. Miller, *Foreign Workers in Western Europe* (London, 1981). On the development of the Green Parties, see M. O'Neill, *Green Parties and Political Change in Contemporary Europe* (Aldershot, England, 1997).

For a general view of postwar thought, see R. N. Stromberg, *European Intellectual History Since 1789*, 5th ed. (Englewood Cliffs, N.J., 1990). On contemporary art, see R. Lambert, *Cambridge Introduction to the History of Art: The Twentieth Century* (Cambridge, 1981). A physicist's view of science is contained in J. Ziman, *The Force of Knowledge: The Scientific Dimension of Society* (Cambridge, 1976). The space race is examined in W. A. McDougall, *The Heavens and the Earth: A Political History of the Space Age* (New York, 1984). There is an excellent survey of twentieth-century popular culture in R. Maltby, ed., *Passing Parade: A History of Popular Culture in the Twentieth Century* (New York, 1989).

INFOTRAC COLLEGE EDITION

For additional reading, go to InfoTrac College Edition, your online research library at
http://web1.infotrac-college.com

Enter the search terms "single European market" using the Subject Guide.

Enter the search terms "Europe communism" using Keywords.

Enter the search terms "Green Parties" using Keywords.

Enter the search terms "Germany reunification" using Keywords.

Enter the search term "feminism" using the Subject Guide.

Courtesy of William J. Duiker

<table>
<tr><td rowspan="2">

Chapter
28

CHALLENGES OF NATION BUILDING IN AFRICA AND THE MIDDLE EAST

</td></tr>
</table>

FOCUS QUESTIONS

- What role has nationalism played in Africa and the Middle East since World War II, and how have other forces in each area exerted counteracting effects?
- How have dreams clashed with realities in the independent nations of Africa, and how have the resulting tensions affected African culture?
- How has the role of women changed in African and Middle Eastern society since 1945?
- What political and economic problems have Middle Eastern nations faced since 1945, and how have they attempted to solve these problems?
- ➤ What impact did colonialism have on Africa and the Middle East, and how does its legacy continue to affect developments in these areas?

*A*t the end of World War II, Africa had already been exposed to over half a century of colonial rule. Although many Europeans complacently assumed that colonialism was a necessary evil in the process of introducing civilization to the backward peoples of Africa and Asia, not all agreed. To some African intellectuals, the Western drive for economic profit and political hegemony was a plague that threatened ultimately to destroy civilization. It was the obligation of Africans to use their own humanistic and spiritual qualities to help save the human race. The Ghanaian official Michael Francis Dei-Anang agreed. In *Whither Bound Africa*, written in 1946, he scathingly unmasked the pretensions of Western superiority:

> Forward! To what?
> The Slums, where man is dumped upon man,
> Where penury
> And misery
> Have made their hapless homes,
> And all is dark and drear?
> Forward! To what?
> The factory
> To grind hard hours
> In an inhuman mill,
> In one long ceaseless spell?
>
> Forward! To what?
> To the reeking round
> Of medieval crimes,
> Where the greedy hawks
> of Aryan stock
> Prey with bombs and guns
> On men of lesser breed?
> Forward to CIVILIZATION.[1]

To Africans like Dei-Anang, the new Africa that emerged from imperialist rule had a duty to seek new ways of resolving the problems of humanity.

In the three decades following the end of World War II, the peoples of Africa were gradually liberated from the formal trappings of European colonialism. The creation of independent states in Africa began in the late 1950s and proceeded gradually until the last colonial regimes were finally dismantled. But the transition to independence has not been an unalloyed success. The legacy of colonialism in the form of political inexperience and continued European economic domination has combined with overpopulation and climatic disasters to frustrate the new states' ability to achieve political stability and economic prosperity. At the same time, arbitrary boundaries imposed by the colonial powers and ethnic and religious divisions within the African countries have led to bitter conflicts, which have posed a severe obstacle to the dream of continental solidarity and cooperation in forging a common destiny. Today, the continent of Africa, although blessed with enormous potential, is one of the most volatile and conflict-ridden areas of the world. Michael Dei-Anang's dream has not yet been realized. •

UHURU: THE STRUGGLE FOR INDEPENDENCE

After World War II, Europeans reluctantly recognized that the end result of colonial rule in Africa would be African self-government, if not full independence. Accordingly, the African population would have to be trained to handle the responsibilities of representative government. In many cases, however, relatively little had been done to prepare the local population for self-rule. Early in the colonial era, during the late nineteenth century, African administrators had held influential positions in several British colonies, and one even served as governor of the Gold Coast. But with the formal institution of colonial rule, senior positions were reserved for the British, although local authority remained in the hands of native rulers.

After World War II, most British colonies introduced reforms that increased the representation of the local population. Members of legislative and executive councils were increasingly chosen through elections, and Africans came to constitute a majority of these bodies. Elected councils at the local level were introduced in the 1950s to reduce the power of the tribal chiefs and clan heads, who had controlled local government under indirect rule. An exception was South Africa, where European domination continued. In the Union of South Africa, the franchise was restricted to whites except in the former territory of the Cape Colony, where persons of mixed ancestry had enjoyed the right to vote since the mid-nineteenth century. Black Africans did win some limited electoral rights in Northern and Southern Rhodesia (now Zambia and Zimbabwe), although whites generally dominated the political scene.

A similar process of political liberalization was taking place in the French colonies. At first, as we have seen, the French tried to assimilate the African peoples into French culture. By the 1920s, however, racist beliefs in Western cultural superiority and the tenacity of traditional beliefs and practices among Africans had somewhat discredited this ideal. The French therefore substituted a more limited program of assimilating African elites into Western culture and using them as administrators at the local level as a link to the remainder of the population.

The Colonial Legacy

As in Asia, colonial rule had a mixed impact on the societies and peoples of Africa. The Western presence brought a number of short-term and long-term benefits to Africa, such as improved transportation and communication facilities, and in a few areas laid the foundation for a modern industrial and commercial sector. Improved sanitation and medical care increased life expectancy. The introduction of selective elements of Western political systems laid the basis for the gradual creation of democratic societies.

Yet the benefits of westernization were distributed very unequally, and the vast majority of Africans found their lives little improved, if at all. Only South Africa and French-held Algeria, for example, developed modern industrial sectors, extensive railroad networks, and modern communications systems. In both countries, European settlers were numerous, most investment capital for industrial ventures was European, and whites comprised almost the entire professional and managerial class. Members of the native population were generally restricted to unskilled or semiskilled jobs at wages less than one-fifth those enjoyed by Europeans.

Many colonies concentrated on export crops—peanuts in Senegal and Gambia, cotton in Egypt and Uganda, coffee in Kenya, palm oil and cocoa products in the Gold Coast. Here the benefits of development were somewhat more widespread. In some cases, the crops were grown on plantations, which were usually owned by Europeans. But plantation agriculture was not always suitable in Africa, and much farming was done by free or tenant farmers. In some areas, where land ownership was traditionally vested in the community, the land was owned and leased by the corporate village. The vast majority of the profits from the exports, however, accrued to Europeans or to merchants from other foreign countries, such as India and the Arab emirates. While a fortunate few benefited from the increase in exports, the vast majority of Africans continued to be subsistence farmers growing food for their own consumption. The gap was particularly wide in places like Kenya, where the best lands had been reserved for European settlers to make the colony self-sufficient. As in other parts of the world, the early stages of the Industrial Revolution were especially painful for the rural population, and ordinary subsistence farmers reaped few benefits from colonial rule.

The Rise of Nationalism

Political organizations for African rights did not arise until after World War I, and then only in a few areas, such as British-ruled Kenya and the Gold Coast. At first, organizations such as the National Congress of British West Africa (formed in 1919 in the Gold Coast) and Jomo Kenyatta's Kikuyu Central Association focused on improving living conditions in the colonies rather than on national independence. After World War II, however, following the example of independence movements elsewhere, these groups became organized political parties with independence as their objective. In the Gold Coast, Kwame Nkrumah (1909–1972) led the Convention People's Party, the first formal political party in black Africa. In the late 1940s, Jomo Kenyatta (1894–1978) founded the Kenya African National Union (KANU), which focused on economic issues but had an implied political agenda as well.

For the most part, these political activities were basically nonviolent and were led by Western-educated African intellectuals. Their constituents were primarily urban professionals, merchants, and members of labor unions. But the demand for independence was not entirely restricted to the cities. In Kenya, for example, the widely publicized Mau Mau movement among the Kikuyu people used terrorism as an essential element of its program to achieve *uhuru* (Swahili for "freedom") from the British. Although most of the violence was directed against other Africans—only about 100 Europeans were killed in the violence, compared with an estimated 1,700 Africans who lost their lives at the hands of the rebels—the specter of Mau Mau terrorism alarmed the European population and convinced the British government in 1959 to promise eventual independence.

A similar process was occurring in Egypt, which had been a protectorate of Great Britain (and under loose Turkish suzerainty until the breakup of the Ottoman Empire) since the 1880s. National consciousness had existed in Egypt since well before the colonial takeover, and members of the legislative council were calling for independence even before World War I. In 1918, a formal political party called the Wafd was formed to promote Egyptian independence. The intellectuals were opposed as much to the local palace government as to the British, however, and in 1952, an army coup overthrew King Farouk, the grandson of Khedive Ismail, and established an independent republic.

In areas such as South Africa and Algeria, where the political system was dominated by European settlers, the transition to independence was more complicated. In South Africa, political activity by local Africans began with the formation of the African National Congress (ANC) in 1912. Initially, the ANC was dominated by Western-oriented intellectuals and had little mass support. Its goal was to achieve economic and political reforms, including full equality for educated Africans, within the framework of the existing system. But the ANC's efforts met with little success, while conservative white parties managed to stiffen the segregation laws. In response, the ANC became increasingly radicalized, and by the 1950s, the prospects for a violent confrontation were growing.

In Algeria, resistance to French rule by Berbers and Arabs in rural areas had never ceased. After World War II, urban agitation intensified, leading to a widespread rebellion against colonial rule in the mid-1950s. At first, the French government tried to maintain its authority in Algeria, which was considered an integral part of metropolitan France. But when Charles de Gaulle became president in 1958, he reversed French policy, and Algeria became independent under President Ahmad Ben Bella (b. 1918) in 1962. The armed struggle in Algeria hastened the transition to statehood in its neighbors as well. Tunisia won its independence in 1956 after some urban agitation and rural unrest but retained close ties with Paris. The French attempted to suppress the nationalist movement in Morocco by sending Sultan Muhammad V into exile, but the effort failed, and in 1956 he returned as the ruler of the independent state of Morocco.

Most black African nations achieved their independence in the late 1950s and 1960s, beginning with the Gold Coast, now renamed Ghana, in 1957 (see Map 28.1). Nigeria, the Belgian Congo (renamed Zaire and then the Democratic Republic of the Congo), Kenya, Tanganyika (later, when joined with Zanzibar, renamed Tanzania), and several other countries soon followed. Most of the French colonies agreed to accept independence within the framework of de Gaulle's French Community. By the late 1960s, only parts of southern Africa and the Portuguese possessions of Mozambique and Angola remained under European rule.

Independence came later to Africa than to most of Asia. Several factors help explain the delay. For one thing, colonialism was established in Africa somewhat later than in most areas of Asia, and the inevitable reaction from the local population was consequently delayed. Furthermore, with the exception of a few areas in West Africa and along the Mediterranean, coherent states with a strong sense of cultural, ethnic, and linguistic unity did not exist in most of Africa. Most traditional states, such as Ashanti in West Africa, Songhai in the southern Sahara, and Bakongo in the Congo basin, were collections of heterogeneous peoples with little sense of national or cultural identity. Even after colonies were established, the European powers often practiced a policy of "divide and rule," while the British encouraged political decentralization by retaining the authority of the traditional native chieftains. It is hardly surprising that when opposition to colonial rule emerged, unity was difficult to achieve.

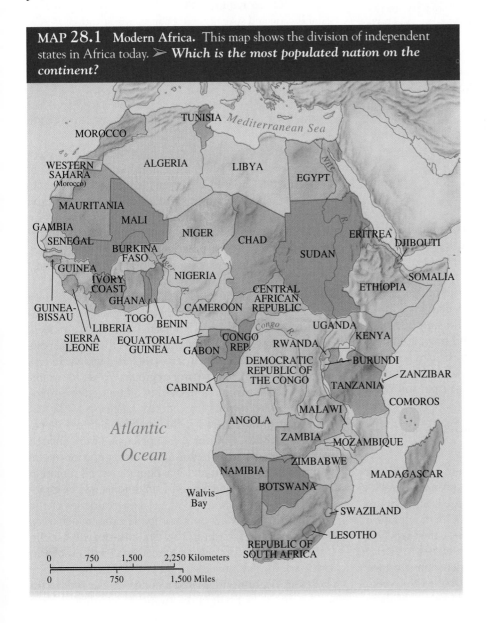

MAP 28.1   Modern Africa. This map shows the division of independent states in Africa today. ➢ *Which is the most populated nation on the continent?*

TOWARD AFRICAN UNITY

*I*n May 1963, the leaders of thirty-two African states met in Addis Ababa, the capital of Ethiopia, to discuss the creation of an organization that would represent the interests of all the newly independent countries of Africa. The result was the Organization of African Unity. An excerpt from its charter is presented here. Although the organization did not realize all of the aspirations of its founders, it provided a useful forum for the discussion and resolution of its members' common problems. In 2001, it was replaced by the new African Union, which was designed to bring about increased cooperation among the states on the continent.

CHARTER OF THE ORGANIZATION OF AFRICAN UNITY

We, the Heads of African States and Governments assembled in the City of Addis Ababa, Ethiopia;

CONVINCED that it is the inalienable right of all people to control their own destiny;

CONSCIOUS of the fact that freedom, equality, justice, and dignity are essential objectives for the achievement of the legitimate aspirations of the African peoples;

CONSCIOUS of our responsibility to harness the natural and human resources of our continent for the total advancement of our peoples in spheres of human endeavor;

INSPIRED by a common determination to promote understanding among our peoples and cooperation among our States in response to the aspirations of our peoples for brotherhood and solidarity, in a larger unity transcending ethnic and national differences;

CONVINCED that, in order to translate this determination into a dynamic force in the cause of human progress, conditions for peace and security must be established and maintained;

DETERMINED to safeguard and consolidate the hard-won independence as well as the sovereignty and territorial integrity of our States, and to fight against neocolonialism in all its forms;

DEDICATED to the general progress of Africa; . . .

DESIROUS that all African States should henceforth unite so that the welfare and well-being of their peoples can be assured;

RESOLVED to reinforce the links between our states by establishing and strengthening common institutions;

HAVE agreed to the present Charter.

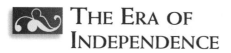

THE ERA OF INDEPENDENCE

The newly independent African states faced intimidating challenges. Like the new states in South and Southeast Asia, they had been profoundly affected by colonial rule. Yet the experience had been highly unsatisfactory in most respects. Although Western political institutions, values, and technology had been introduced, at least in the cities, the exposure to European civilization had been superficial at best for most Africans and tragic for many. At the outset of independence, most African societies were still primarily agrarian and traditional, and their modern sectors depended mainly on imports from the West.

Pan-Africanism and Nationalism: The Destiny of Africa

Like the leaders of the new states in South and Southeast Asia, most African leaders came from the urban middle class. They had studied in either Europe or the United States and spoke and read European languages. Although most were profoundly critical of colonial policies, they appeared to accept the relevance of the Western model to Africa and gave at least lip service to Western democratic values.

Their views on economics were somewhat more diverse. Some, like Jomo Kenyatta of Kenya and General Mobutu

Sese Seko (1930–1998) of Zaire, were advocates of Western-style capitalism. Others, like Julius Nyerere (b. 1922) of Tanzania, Kwame Nkrumah of Ghana, and Sékou Touré (1922–1984) of Guinea, preferred an "African form of socialism," which bore slight resemblance to the Marxist-Leninist socialism practiced in the Soviet Union. According to its advocates, it was descended from traditional communal practices in precolonial Africa.

Like the leaders of other developing countries, the new political leaders in Africa were highly nationalistic and generally accepted the colonial boundaries. But as we have seen, these boundaries were artificial creations of the colonial powers. Virtually all of the new states included widely diverse ethnic, linguistic, and territorial groups. Zaire, for example, was composed of more than two hundred territorial groups speaking seventy-five different languages.

A number of leaders—including Nkrumah of Ghana, Touré of Guinea, and Kenyatta of Kenya—were enticed by the dream of pan-Africanism, a concept of continental unity that transcended national boundaries. Nkrumah in particular hoped that a pan-African union could be established that would unite all of the new countries of the continent in a broader community. His dream achieved concrete manifestation in the Organization of African Unity (OAU), which was founded in Addis Ababa in 1963 (see the box above).

Pan-Africanism originated among African intellectuals during the first half of the twentieth century. A basic element was the belief in negritude (blackness)—the conviction that there was a distinctive "African personality" that owed nothing to Western materialism and provided a common sense of destiny for all black African peoples. According to Aimé Césaire, a West Indian of African descent and a leading ideologist of the movement, whereas Western civilization prized rational thought and material achievement, African culture emphasized emotional expression and a common sense of humanity.

The concept of negritude was in part a natural defensive response to the social Darwinist concepts of Western racial superiority and African inferiority that were popular in Europe and the United States during the early years of the twentieth century. At the same time, it was stimulated by growing self-doubt among many European intellectuals after World War I, who feared that Western civilization was on a path of self-destruction.

Negritude had more appeal to Africans from French colonies than to those from British possessions. Yet it also found adherents in the British colonies, as well as in the United States and elsewhere in the Americas. African American intellectuals such as W. E. B. Dubois and the West Indian politician Marcus Garvey attempted to promote a "black renaissance" by popularizing the idea of a distinct African personality.

Dream and Reality: Political and Economic Conditions in Contemporary Africa

The program of the OAU called for an Africa based on freedom, equality, justice, and dignity and on the unity, solidarity, and territorial integrity of African states. It did not take long for reality to set in. Vast disparities in education and income made it hard to establish democracy in much of Africa. Expectations that independence would lead to stable political structures based on "one person, one vote" were soon disappointed as the initial phase of pluralistic governments gave way to a series of military regimes and one-party states. Between 1957 and 1982, more than seventy leaders of African countries were overthrown by violence, and the pace has increased in recent years.

Hopes that independence would inaugurate an era of economic prosperity and equality were similarly dashed. Part of the problem could be (and was) ascribed to the lingering effects of colonialism. Most new countries in Africa were dependent on the export of a single crop or natural resource. When prices fluctuated or dropped, these countries were at the mercy of the vagaries of the international market. In several cases, the resources were still controlled by foreigners, leading to the charge that colonialism had been succeeded by "neocolonialism," in which Western domination was maintained by economic rather than by political or military means. To make matters worse, most African states had to import technology and manufactured goods from the West, and the prices of those goods rose more rapidly than those of the export products.

The new states also contributed to their own problems. Scarce national resources were squandered on military equipment or expensive consumer goods rather than on building up their infrastructure to provide the foundation for an industrial economy. Corruption, a painful reality throughout the modern world, became almost a way of life in Africa as bribery became necessary to obtain even the most basic services (see the box on p. 820).

Finally, population growth, which more than anything else has hindered economic growth in the new nations of Asia and Africa, became a serious problem and crippled efforts to create modern economies. By the mid-1980s, annual population growth averaged nearly 3 percent throughout Africa, the highest rate of any continent. Drought conditions and the inexorable spread of the Sahara (usually known as desertification, a condition caused partly by overcultivation of the land) have led to widespread hunger and starvation, first in West African countries such as Niger and Mali and then in Ethiopia, Somalia, and the Sudan.

In recent years, the spread of HIV and AIDS in Africa has reached epidemic proportions. According to one recent report, over 75 percent of all the AIDS cases reported around the world are on the continent of Africa. Some observers

⟫ MANIOC, AMERICA'S GIFT TO AFRICA. Manioc, a tuber like the potato, was brought to Africa from the New World as a result of the European expansion discussed in Part III. Although low in nutrient value, it can be cultivated in poor soil with little moisture and is reportedly the staple food for nearly one-third of the population of sub-Saharan Africa. Manioc—also known as cassava—is also widely grown in tropical parts of Asia and is the source of tapioca. In the illustration shown here, village women in Senegal rhythmically pound manioc to the chanting of those standing nearby.

Courtesy of William J. Duiker

STEALING THE NATION'S RICHES

After 1965, African novelists transferred their anger from the foreign oppressor to their own national leaders, deploring their greed, corruption, and inhumanity. One of the most pessimistic expressions of this betrayal of newly independent Africa is found in The Beautiful Ones Are Not Yet Born, *a novel published by the Ghanaian author Ayi Kwei Armah in 1968. The author decried the government of Kwame Nkrumah and was unimpressed with the rumors of a military coup, which, he predicted, would simply replace the present regime with a new despot and his entourage of "fat men."*

AYI KWEI ARMAH, *THE BEAUTIFUL ONES ARE NOT YET BORN*

The net had been made in the special Ghanaian way that allowed the really big corrupt people to pass through it. A net to catch only the small, dispensable fellows, trying in their anguished blindness to leap and to attain the gleam and the comfort the only way these things could be done. And the big ones floated free, like all the slogans. End bribery and corruption. Build Socialism. Equality. Shit. A man would just have to make up his mind that there was never going to be anything but despair, and there would be no way of escaping it. . . .

In the life of the nation itself, maybe nothing really new would happen. New men would take into their hands the power to steal the nation's riches and to use it for their own satisfaction. That, of course, was to be expected. New people would use the country's power to get rid of men and women who talked a language that did not flatter them. There would be nothing different in that. That would only be a continuation of the Ghanaian way of life. But here was the real change. The individual man of power now shivering, his head filled with the fear of the vengeance of those he had wronged. For him everything was going to change. And for those like him who had grown greasy and fat singing the praises of their chief, for those who had been getting themselves ready for the enjoyment of hoped-for favors, there would be long days of pain ahead. The flatterers with their new white Mercedes cars would have to find ways of burying old words. For those who had come directly against the old power, there would be much happiness. But for the nation itself there would only be a change of embezzlers and a change of the hunters and the hunted. A pitiful shrinking of the world from those days Teacher still looked back to, when the single mind was filled with the hopes of a whole people. A pitiful shrinking, to days when all the powerful could think of was to use the power of a whole people to fill their own paunches. Endless days, same days, stretching into the future with no end anywhere in sight.

estimate that without measures to curtail the effects of the disease, it will have a significant impact on several African countries by reducing population growth, which is presently predicted to increase throughout the continent by at least 300 million in the next fifteen years.

Poverty is endemic in Africa, particularly among the three-quarters of the population still living off the land. Urban areas have grown tremendously, but as in much of Asia, most are surrounded by massive squatter settlements of rural peoples who had fled to the cities in search of a better life. The expansion of the cities has overwhelmed fragile transportation and sanitation systems and led to rising pollution and perpetual traffic jams, while millions are forced to live without running water and electricity. Meanwhile, the fortunate few (all too often government officials on the take) live the high life and emulate the consumerism of the West (in a particularly expressive phrase, the rich in many East African countries are known as *wabenzi*, or Mercedes-Benz people).

In "Pedestrian, to Passing Benz-Man," the Kenyan poet Albert Ojuka voiced the popular discontent with economic inequality:

> You man, lifted gently
> out of the poverty and suffering
> we so recently shared; I say—
> why splash the muddy puddle on to
> my bare legs, as if, still unsatisfied
> with your seated opulence
> you must sully the unwashed
> with your diesel-smoke and mud-water
> and force him to buy, beyond his means
> a bar of soap from your shop?
> a few years back we shared a master
> today you have none, while I have
> exchanged a parasite for something worse.
> But maybe a few years is too long a time.[2]

It is a lament still voiced today.

THE SEARCH FOR SOLUTIONS

Concern over the dangers of economic inequality inspired a number of African leaders—including Nkrumah in Ghana, Nyerere in Tanzania, and Samora Michel of Mozambique—to restrict foreign investment and nationalize the major industries and utilities while promoting social ideals and values. Nyerere was the most consistent, promoting the ideals of socialism and self-reliance through his Arusha Declaration of 1967 (see the box on p. 822). Taking advantage of his powerful political influence, Nyerere placed limitations on income and established village collectives to avoid the corrosive effects of economic inequality and government corruption. Sympathetic foreign countries provided considerable economic aid to assist the experiment, and many observers noted that levels of corruption, political instability, and ethnic strife were lower in Tanzania than in many other African countries. Unfortunately, corruption has increased in recent years, while political elements on the island of Zanzibar, citing the stagnation brought by two decades of socialism, are agitating for autonomy or even total separation from the mainland. Tanzania also has poor soil, inadequate rainfall, and limited resources, all of which have contributed to its slow growth and continuing rural and urban poverty.

In 1985, Julius Nyerere voluntarily retired from the presidency. In his farewell speech, he confessed that he had failed to achieve many of his ambitious goals to create a socialist society in Africa. In particular, he admitted that his plan to collectivize the traditional private farm (*shamba*) had run into strong resistance from conservative peasants. "You can socialize what is not traditional," he remarked. "The *shamba* can't be socialized." But Nyerere insisted that many of his policies had succeeded in improving social and economic conditions, and he argued that the only real solution was to consolidate the multitude of small countries in the region into a larger East African Federation.[3]

The countries that opted for capitalism faced their own dilemmas. Neighboring Kenya, blessed with better soil in the highlands, a local tradition of aggressive commerce, and a residue of European settlers, welcomed foreign investment and profit incentives. The results have been mixed. Kenya has a strong current of indigenous African capitalism and a substantial middle class, mostly based in the capital, Nairobi. But landlessness, unemployment, and income inequities are high, even by African standards (almost one-fifth of the country's thirty million people are squatters, and unemployment is currently estimated at 45 percent). The rate of population growth—more than 4 percent annually—is one of the highest in the world. Eighty percent of the population remains rural, and 40 percent live below the poverty line. The result has been

> ⚜ **THE ARAB DHOW.**   Long the preferred mode of travel in the Indian Ocean, the Arab dhow, with its rakish lateen sail, remains in widespread use along the east coast of Africa. As this small sailing vessel in the Tanzanian port of Dar es Salaam demonstrates, such traditional craft still ply the waters off the continent from the Red Sea to the Strait of Madagascar.

SOCIALISM IS NOT RACIALISM

t Arusha, Tanzania, in 1967, Julius Nyerere, the nation's president, set forth the principles for building a socialist society. Nyerere made it clear that he was talking about an African style of socialism, which would put ownership of his country's wealth into the hands of the people rather than into the hands of foreign capitalists. Since then, Tanzania has taken a socialist approach to economic development. The results have been mixed: the country is not wealthy, but there are few extremes of rich and poor.

JULIUS NYERERE, THE ARUSHA DECLARATION

The Arusha Declaration and the actions relating to public ownership were all concerned with ensuring that we can build socialism in our country. The nationalization and the taking of a controlling interest in many firms were a necessary part of our determination to organize our society in such a way that our efforts benefit all our people and that there is no exploitation of one man by another.

Yet these actions do not in themselves create socialism. . . . The basis of socialism is a belief in the oneness of man and the common historical destiny of mankind. Its basis, in other words, is human equality.

Acceptance of this principle is absolutely fundamental to socialism. The justification of socialism is Man—not the State, not the flag. Socialism is not for the benefit of black men, nor brown men, nor white men, nor yellow men. The purpose of socialism is the service of man, regardless of color, size, shape, skill, ability, or anything else. . . .

Socialism has nothing to do with race, nor with country of origin. In fact any intelligent man, whether he is a socialist or not, realizes that there are socialists in capitalist countries—and from capitalist countries. Very often such socialists come to work in newly independent and avowedly socialist countries like Tanzania because they are frustrated in their capitalist homeland. . . .

Neither is it sensible for a socialist to talk as if all capitalists are devils. It is one thing to dislike the capitalist system and to try and frustrate people's capitalist desires. But it would be as stupid for us to assume that capitalists have horns as it is for people in Western Europe to assume that we in Tanzania have become devils.

In fact the leaders in the capitalist countries have now begun to realize that communists are human beings like themselves—that they are not devils. . . . It would be very absurd if we react to the stupidity they are growing out of and become equally stupid ourselves in the opposite direction! We have to recognize in our words and our actions that capitalists are human beings as much as socialists. They may be wrong; indeed by dedicating ourselves to socialism we are saying that they are. But our task is to make it impossible for capitalism to dominate us.

I ACCUSE! For many Africans, the end of European colonialism did not mark the opening of a new era of democratic achievement and economic prosperity. To the contrary, most African countries have been plagued with continuing problems of endemic poverty, internecine conflict, and authoritarian rule. In this photograph, an anonymous commentator from the city of Mombasa, in Kenya, braves official displeasure by pointing an accusing finger at African leaders who rule by dictatorial means. The focus of his anger is undoubtedly directed at Kenyan president Daniel arap Moi, one of the most authoritarian of contemporary African rulers. Moi agreed to retire in 2002.

Courtesy of William J. Duiker

widespread unrest in a country formerly admired for its successful development.

Beginning in the mid-1970s, a few African nations decided to adopt Soviet-style Marxism-Leninism. In Angola and Ethiopia, Marxist parties followed the Soviet model and attempted to create fully socialist societies with the assistance of Soviet experts and Cuban troops and advisers. Economically, the results were disappointing, and both countries faced severe internal opposition. In Ethiopia, the revolt by Muslim tribal peoples in the province of Eritrea led to the fall of the Marxist leader Mengistu and his regime in 1990. A similar revolt erupted against the government in Angola, with the rebel group UNITA controlling much of the rural population and for a time threatening the capital city, Luanda. With the death of the rebel leader Julius Savimbi in 2002, the revolt finally appeared to be at an end.

THE SEARCH FOR COMMUNITY

Finally, Africans have been disappointed that the dream of a united Africa has not been realized. No one skewered the pretensions of the apostles of negritude better than the Ugandan poet Taban Lo Liyong. In his poem "Negritude Is Crying over Spilt Milk," he observed:

Strange mules called Negritude
and African Personality
Overran the terrain
And kicked wisdom down
Or above our heads.

Politicians quite unaware
How low we are
On the ladder universal
Decided to halt the race
And embrace the niches sure
Where we were stuck for the moment.[4]

But while some criticize the tendency to pursue what Taban called the "vanishing exotica" of the past, most Africans feel a shared sense of continuing victimization at the hands of the West and are convinced that independence has not ended Western interference in and domination of African affairs. Many African leaders were angered when Western powers led by the United States conspired to overthrow the radical politician Patrice Lumumba in Zaire in the early 1960s. The episode reinforced their desire to form the OAU as a means of reducing Western influence. But aside from agreeing to adopt a neutral stance during the Cold War, African states have had difficulty achieving a united position on many issues, and their disagreements have left the region vulnerable to external influence and even led to conflict. During the late 1980s and early 1990s, border disputes festered in many areas of the continent and in some cases—as with Morocco and a rebel movement in the Western Sahara and between Kenya and Uganda—flared into outright war.

Even within many African nations, the concept of nationhood has been undermined by the renascent force of regionalism or tribalism. Nigeria, with the largest population on the continent, was rent by civil strife during the late 1960s, when dissident Ibo groups in the southeast attempted unsuccessfully to form the independent state of Biafra. Another force undermining nationalism in Africa has been pan-Islamism. Its prime exponent in Africa was the Egyptian president Gamal Abdul Nasser. After Nasser's death in 1970, the torch of Islamic unity in Africa was carried by the Libyan president Muammar Qadhafi, whose ambitions to create a greater Muslim nation in the Sahara under his authority led to conflict with neighboring Chad. The Islamic resurgence also surfaced in Ethiopia, where Muslim tribespeople in Eritrea rebelled against the Marxist regime of Colonel Mengistu in Addis Ababa. More recently, it has flared up in Nigeria and other nations of West Africa, where divisions between Muslims and Christians have erupted into violence.

RECENT TRENDS

Not all the news in Africa has been bad. Stagnant economies have led to the collapse of one-party regimes and the emergence of fragile democracies in several coun-

tries. Dictatorships were brought to an end in Ethiopia, Liberia, and Somalia, although in each case the fall of the regime was later followed by political instability or civil war. In Senegal, national elections held in the summer of 2000 brought an end to four decades of rule by the once-dominant Socialist Party. The new president, Abdoulaye Wade, is a staunch advocate of promoting development throughout Africa on the capitalist model. Perhaps the most notorious dictator was Idi Amin of Uganda, who led a military coup against Prime Minister Milton Obote in 1971. After ruling by terror and brutal repression of dissident elements, he was finally deposed in 1979. In recent years, stability has returned to the country, which in May 1996 had its first presidential election in more than fifteen years. In Eritrea, a popular Islamic government is gradually rebuilding the country and has signed a cease-fire agreement to bring an end to its bitter border conflict with neighboring Ethiopia.

Africa has also benefited from the end of the Cold War as the superpowers have ceased to compete for power and influence in Africa. When the Soviet Union withdrew its support from the Marxist government in Ethiopia, the United States allowed its own right to maintain military bases in neighboring Somalia to lapse, resulting in the overthrow of the authoritarian government there. Unfortunately, clan rivalries led to such turbulence that many inhabitants were in imminent danger of starvation, and in the winter of 1992, U.S. military forces occupied the country in an effort to provide food to the starving population. Since the departure of foreign troops in 1993, the country has been divided into clan fiefdoms, while Islamic groups attempt to bring a return to law and order.

Perhaps Africa's greatest success story is in South Africa, where the white government—which long maintained a policy of racial segregation (apartheid) and restricted black sovereignty to a series of small "Bantustans" in relatively infertile areas of the country—finally accepted the inevitability of African involvement in the political process and the national economy. In 1990, the government of President F. W. de Klerk (b. 1936) released African National Congress leader Nelson Mandela (b. 1918) from prison, where he had been held since 1964. In 1993, the two leaders agreed to hold democratic national elections the following spring. In the meantime, ANC representatives agreed to take part in a transitional coalition government with de Klerk's National Party. Those elections resulted in a substantial majority for the ANC, and Mandela became president.

In May 1996, a new constitution was approved, calling for a multiracial state. The National Party immediately went into opposition, claiming that the new charter did not adequately provide for joint decision making by members of the coalition. The third group in the coalition government, the Zulu-based Inkatha Freedom Party, agreed to remain within the government, but rivalry between the ANC and Zulu elites intensified. Zulu chief Mangosuthu

Buthelezi, drawing on the growing force of Zulu national-ism, began to invoke the memory of the great nineteenth-century Zulu ruler Shaka in a possible bid at future independence.

In 1999, a major step toward political stability was taken when Nelson Mandela stepped down from the presidency, to be replaced by his long-time disciple Thabo Mbeki. The new president faced a number of intimidating problems, including rising unemployment, widespread lawlessness, chronic corruption, and an ominous flight of capital and professional personnel from the country. Mbeki's conser-vative economic policies earned the support of some white voters and the country's new black elite but has provoked criticism from labor union groups, who contend that the benefits of the new black leadership are not seeping down to the poor. Still, South Africa remains the wealthiest and most industrialized state in Africa and the best hope that a multiracial society can succeed on the continent.

In neighboring Zimbabwe, the former British colony of Southern Rhodesia, disputes over land ownership created severe political tensions. Critics charged that longtime president Robert Mugabe incited African farm-ers to forcibly seize lands owned by white settlers to pro-mote his own political fortunes. In 2002, Mugabe was reelected, despite widespread charges of voting fraud from the opposition.

If the situation in South Africa provides grounds for modest optimism, the situation in Nigeria provides reason for serious concern. Africa's largest country in terms of population and one of its wealthiest because of substantial oil reserves, Nigeria had for many years been in the grip of military strongmen. During his rule, General Sani Abacha ruthlessly suppressed all opposition and in late 1995 ordered the execution of a writer despite widespread protests from human rights groups abroad. Ken Saro-Wiwa had criticized environmental damage caused by foreign interests in southern Nigeria, but the regime's major con-cern was his support for separatist activities in the area that had launched the Biafran insurrection in the late 1960s. Abacha died in 1998, and national elections led to the cre-ation of a civilian government under Olusegun Obasanjo. Civilian leadership has not been a panacea for Nigeria's problems, however. In early 2000, religious riots between Christians and Muslims broke out in several northern cities as a result of the decision by provincial officials to apply Islamic law throughout their jurisdictions. President Obasanjo has attempted to defuse the unrest by calling for a delay in carrying out the decision, but the issue raises tensions between Christian peoples in the southern parts of the country and the primarily Islamic north.

The religious tensions that erupted in Nigeria have spilled over into neighboring states. In the Ivory Coast, the death of President Houphouet-Boigny in 1993 led to an outbreak of long-simmering resentment between Chris-tians in the south and recently arrived Muslim immigrants in the north. National elections held in the fall of 2000, resulting in the election of a Christian president, were marked by sporadic violence and widespread charges of voting irregularities. In the meantime, pressure to apply *Shari'a* is spreading to Nigeria's northern neighbor, Niger, where the government has opposed Islamic law on the grounds that it would unsettle the country. Christian churches have been attacked, and bars and brothels have been sacked and burned to the ground.

The most tragic situation is in the Central African states of Rwanda and Burundi, where a chronic conflict between the minority Tutsis and the Hutu majority has led to a bitter civil war, with thousands of refugees fleeing to the neighboring Congo. In a classic example of conflict between pastoral and farming peoples, the nomadic Tut-sis had long dominated the sedentary Hutu population. It was the attempt of the Bantu-speaking Hutus to bring an end to Tutsi domination that initiated the most recent conflicts, marked by massacres on both sides. In the mean-time, the presence of large numbers of foreign troops and refugees intensified centrifugal forces inside Zaire, where General Mobutu Sese Seko had long ruled with an iron hand. In 1997, military forces led by Mobutu's longtime opponent Lauren Kabila managed to topple the general's corrupt government. Once in power, Kabila renamed the country the Democratic Republic of the Congo and prom-ised a return to democratic practices. The new government systematically suppressed political dissent, however, and in January 2001, Kabila was assassinated, to be succeeded by his son. Peace talks to end the conflict began that fall.

It is clear that African societies have not yet begun to surmount the challenges they have faced since independ-ence. Most African states are still poor and their popula-tions illiterate. But a significant part of the problem is that the nation-state system is not particularly well suited to the African continent. Africans must find better ways to cooperate with each other and to protect and promote their own interests. A first step in that direction was taken in 1991, when the OAU agreed to establish the African Economic Community (AEC). In 2001, the OAU was replaced by the African Union, which is intended to pro-vide greater political and economic integration through-out the continent on the pattern of the European Union (see Chapter 27).

As Africa evolves, it is useful to remember that eco-nomic and political change is often an agonizingly slow and painful process. Introduced to industrialization and concepts of Western democracy only a century ago, African societies are still groping for ways to graft West-ern political institutions and economic practices onto a native structure still significantly influenced by traditional values and attitudes. As one African writer recently observed, it is easy to be cynical in Africa because changes in political regimes have had little effect on people's liveli-hood. Still, he said, "let us welcome the wind of change.

This, after all, is a continent of winds. The trick is to keep hope burning, like a candle protected from the wind."[5]

CONTINUITY AND CHANGE IN MODERN AFRICAN SOCIETIES

In general, the impact of the West has been greater on urban and educated Africans and more limited on their rural and illiterate compatriots. After all, the colonial presence was first and most firmly established in the cities. Many cities, including Dakar, Lagos, Johannesburg, Cape Town, Brazzaville, and Nairobi, are direct products of the colonial experience. Most African cities today look like their counterparts elsewhere in the world. They have high-rise buildings, blocks of residential apartments, wide boulevards, neon lights, movie theaters, and traffic jams.

The educational system has been the primary means of introducing Western values and culture. In the precolonial era, formal schools did not really exist in Africa except for parochial schools in Christian Ethiopia and academies to train young males in Islamic doctrine and law in Muslim societies in North and West Africa. For the average African, education took place at the home or in the village courtyard and stressed socialization and vocational training. Traditional education in Africa was not necessarily inferior to that in Europe. Social values and customs were transmitted to the young by storytellers, often village elders, who could gain considerable prestige through their performance.

Europeans introduced modern Western education into Africa in the nineteenth century. At first, the schools concentrated on vocational training, with some instruction in European languages and Western civilization. Eventually, pressure from Africans led to the introduction of professional training, and the first institutes of higher learning were established in the early twentieth century.

With independence, African countries established their own state-run schools. The emphasis was on the primary level, but high schools and universities were established in major cities. The basic objectives have been to introduce vocational training and improve literacy rates. Unfortunately, both funding and trained teachers are scarce in most countries, and few rural areas have schools. As a result, illiteracy remains high, estimated at about 70 percent of the population across the continent. There has been a perceptible shift toward education in the vernacular languages. In West Africa, only about one in four adults is conversant in a Western language.

One interesting vehicle for popular education that emerged during the transition to independence in Nigeria was the Onitsha Market pamphlet. These pamphlets were "how-to" books advising readers on how to succeed in a rapidly changing Africa. They tended to be short, inexpensive, and humorous, with flashy covers to attract the potential buyer's attention. One, titled *The Nigerian Bachelor's Guide*, sold forty thousand copies. Unfortunately, the Onitsha Market and the pamphlet tradition were destroyed during the Nigerian civil war of the late 1960s, but they undoubtedly played an important role during a crucial period in the country's history. Recently, Onitsha has become the largest producer of video movies in sub-Saharan Africa. Most of them provide escapist entertainment—horror films and the like.

Outside the major cities, where about three-quarters of the continent's inhabitants live, Western influence has had less of an impact. Millions of people throughout Africa (as in Asia) live much as their ancestors did, in thatch huts without modern plumbing and electricity; they farm or hunt by traditional methods, practice time-honored family rituals, and believe in the traditional deities. Even here, however, change is taking place. Slavery has been eliminated, for the most part, although there have been persistent reports of raids by slave traders on defenseless villages in the southern Sudan. Economic need, though, has brought about massive migrations as some leave to work on plantations, others move to the cities, and still others flee to refugee camps to escape starvation.

≫ BUILDING HIS DREAM HOUSE. In Africa, the houses of rural peoples are often constructed from a wooden frame, known as wattle, daubed with mud, and then covered with a thatch roof. Such houses are inexpensive to build and remain cool in the hot tropical climate. In this Kenyan village not far from the Indian Ocean, a young man is applying mud to the wall of his future house. Houses are built in a similar fashion throughout the continent, as well as in much of southern Asia.

Courtesy of William J. Duiker

MODERN AFRICA

Statehood for Ghana	1957
Algeria receives independence from France	1962
Formation of the Organization for African Unity	1963
Zimbabwe receives its independence	1980
Release of ANC chairman Nelson Mandela from prison	1990
United States sends troops to Somalia	1992
Nelson Mandela elected president of South Africa	1994
Civil War in Central Africa	1996–2000
Olusegun Obasanjo elected president of Nigeria	1999

African Women

One of the consequences of colonialism and independence has been a change in the relationship between men and women. In precolonial Africa, as in traditional societies in Asia, men and women had distinctly different roles. Women in sub-Saharan Africa, however, generally did not live under the severe legal and social disabilities that we have seen in such societies as China and India. Their role, it has been said, was "complementary rather than subordinate to that of men."[6]

Within the family, wives normally showed a degree of deference to their husbands, and polygamy was not uncommon. But because society was usually arranged on communal lines, property was often held in common, and production tasks were divided on a cooperative rather than hierarchical basis. The status of women tended to rise as they moved through the life cycle. Women became more important as they reared children; in old age, they often became eligible to serve in senior roles within the family, lineage, or village. In some societies, such as the Ashanti kingdom in West Africa, women such as the queen mother were eligible to hold senior political positions.

Sexual relationships changed profoundly during the colonial era, sometimes in ways that could justly be described as beneficial. Colonial governments attempted to bring an end to forced marriage, bodily mutilation such as clitoridectomy, and polygamy. Missionaries introduced women to Western education and encouraged them to organize themselves to defend their interests.

But the new system had some unfavorable consequences as well. Like men, women now became a labor resource. As African males were taken from the villages to serve as forced labor on construction projects, the traditional division of labor was disrupted, and women were forced to play a more prominent role in the economy. At the same time, their role in the broader society was constricted. In British colonies, Victorian attitudes of sexual repression and female subordination led to restrictions on women's freedom, and the positions in government they had formerly held were closed to them.

Independence also had a significant impact on gender roles in African society. Almost without exception, the new governments established the principle of sexual equality and permitted women to vote and run for political office. Yet as elsewhere, women continue to operate at a disability in a world dominated by males. Politics remains a male preserve, and although a few professions, such as teaching, child care, and clerical work, are dominated by women, most African women are employed in menial positions such as agricultural labor, factory work, and retail trade or as domestics. Education is open to all at the elementary level, but women comprise less than 20 percent of students at the upper levels in most African societies today.

In rural areas, where traditional attitudes continue to exert a strong influence, individuals may still be subordinated to communalism. In some societies, clitoridectomy is still widely practiced. Polygamy is also not uncommon, and arranged marriages are still the rule rather than the exception. The dichotomy between rural and urban values can lead to acute tensions. Many African villagers regard the cities as the fount of evil, decadence, and corruption. Women in particular have suffered from the tension between the pull of the city and the village. As men are drawn to the cities in search of employment and excitement, their wives and girlfriends are left behind, both literally and figuratively, in the native village.

Not surprisingly, women have made the greatest strides in the cities. Most urban women, like men, now marry on the basis of personal choice, although a significant minority are still willing to accept their parents' choice. After marriage, African women appear to occupy a more equal position than their counterparts in most Asian countries. Each marriage partner tends to maintain a separate income, and women often have the right to possess property separate from their husbands. While many wives still defer to their husbands in the traditional manner, others are like the woman in Abioseh Nicol's story "A Truly Married Woman," who, after years of living as a common-law wife with her husband, is finally able to provide the price and finalize the marriage. After the wedding, she declares, "For twelve years I have got up every morning at five to make tea for you and breakfast. Now I am a truly married woman [and] you must treat me with a little more respect. You are now my husband and not a lover. Get up and make yourself a cup of tea."[7]

Within the cities, there is a growing feminist movement, but it is firmly based on conditions in the local environment. Many African women writers, for example, opt

Courtesy of William J. Duiker

SALT OF THE EARTH. During the precolonial era, many West African societies were forced to import salt from Mediterranean countries in exchange for tropical products and gold. Today the people of Senegal satisfy their domestic needs by mining salt deposits contained in lakes like this one in the interior of the country. These lakes are the remnants of vast seas that covered the region of the Sahara in prehistoric times. Note that it is women who are doing much of the heavy labor, while men occupy the managerial positions.

for a brand of African feminism much like that of Ama Ata Aidoo, a Ghanaian novelist, whose ultimate objective is to free African society as a whole, not just its female inhabitants. After receiving her education at a girls' school in the Gold Coast and attending Stanford University in the United States, she embarked on a writing career. Every African woman and every man, she insists, "should be a feminist, especially if they believe that Africans should take charge of our land, its wealth, our lives, and the burden of our development. Because it is not possible to advocate independence for our continent without also believing that African women must have the best that the environment can offer."[8]

African Culture

Inevitably, the tension between traditional and modern, native and foreign, and individual and communal that has permeated contemporary African society has spilled over into culture. In general, in the visual arts and music, utility and ritual have given way to pleasure and decoration. In the process, Africans have been affected to a certain extent by foreign influences but have retained their distinctive characteristics. Wood carving, metalwork, painting, and sculpture, for example, have preserved their traditional forms but are now increasingly adapted to serve the tourist industry and the export market.

No area of African culture has been so strongly affected by political and social events as literature. Except for Muslim areas in North and East Africa, precolonial Africans did not have a written literature, although their tradition of oral storytelling served as a rich repository of history, custom, and folk culture. The first written literature in the vernacular or in European languages emerged

THE ART OF WEST AFRICAN WOMEN. Whereas men have traditionally created art using stone, bronze, and wood, women have often expressed themselves through textiles, clay, woven fiber, paint, or other materials more accessible to the home. Their art is used to celebrate and appease the gods, beautify their surroundings, and introduce their children to color and design. Here two young women engage in the annual repainting of the carved door to their family meeting place in a compound in Nigeria. On the right, their mother imprints the "obo-aka," or print of the hand, which signifies a righteous person.

© M. Courtney-Clarke

AFRICA: DARK OR RADIANT CONTINENT?

Colonialism camouflaged its economic objectives under the cloak of a "civilizing mission," which in Africa was aimed at illuminating the so-called Dark Continent with Europe's brilliant civilization. In 1899, the Polish-born English author Joseph Conrad fictionalized his harrowing journey up the Congo River in the novella Heart of Darkness. *Expressing views from his Victorian perspective, he portrayed an Africa that was incomprehensible, irrational, sensual, and therefore threatening. Conrad, however, was shocked by the horrific exploitation of the peoples of the Belgian Congo, presenting them with a compassion rarely seen during the heyday of imperialism.*

Over the years, Conrad's work has provoked much debate, and many African writers have been prompted to counter his vision by reaffirming the dignity and purpose of the African people. One of the first to do so was the Guinean author Camara Laye (1928–1980), who in 1954 composed a brilliant novel, The Radiance of the King, *which can be viewed as the mirror image of Conrad's* Heart of Darkness. *In Laye's work, another European protagonist undertakes a journey into the impenetrable heart of Africa. This time, however, he is enlightened by the process, thereby obtaining self-knowledge and ultimately salvation.*

JOSEPH CONRAD, *HEART OF DARKNESS*

We penetrated deeper and deeper into the heart of darkness. It was very quiet there. At night sometimes the roll of drums behind the curtain of trees would run up the river and remain sustained faintly, as if hovering in the air high over our heads, till the first break of day. Whether it meant war, peace, or prayer we could not tell. . . . But suddenly, as we struggled round a bend, there would be a glimpse of rush walls, of peaked grass-roofs, a burst of yells, a whirl of black limbs, a mass of hands clapping, of feet stamping, of bodies swaying, of eyes rolling, under the droop of heavy and motionless foliage. The steamer toiled along slowly on the edge of a black and incomprehensible frenzy. The prehistoric man was cursing us, praying to us, welcoming us—who could tell? We were cut off from the comprehension of our surroundings; we glided past like phantoms, wondering and secretly appalled, as sane men would be before an enthusiastic outbreak in a madhouse. . . .

It was unearthly, and the men were—No, they were not inhuman. Well, you know, that was the worst of it—this suspicion of their not being inhuman. It would come slowly to one. They howled and leaped, and spun, and made horrid faces; but what thrilled you was just the thought of their humanity—like yours—the thought of your remote kinship with this wild and passionate uproar. Ugly. Yes, it was ugly enough; but if you were man enough you would admit to yourself that there was in you just the faintest trace of a response to the terrible frankness of that noise, a dim suspicion of there being a meaning in it which you—you so remote from the night of first ages—could comprehend. And why not? The mind of man is capable of anything—because everything is in it, all the past as well as all the future. What was there after all? Joy, fear, sorrow, devotion, valour, rage—who can tell?—but truth—truth stripped of its cloak of time.

CAMARA LAYE, *THE RADIANCE OF THE KING*

"I enjoy life . . . ," thought Clarence. "If I filed my teeth like the people of Aziana, no one could see any difference between me and them." There was, of course, the difference in pigmentation in the skin. But what difference did that make? "It's the soul that matters," he kept telling himself. "And in that respect I am exactly as they are." . . .

But where was this radiance coming from? Clarence got up and went to the right-hand window, from which this radiance seemed to be streaming. . . .

He saw the king. And then he knew where the extraordinary radiance was coming from. . . .

And he had the feeling that all was lost. But had he not already lost everything? . . . He would remain for ever chained to the South, chained to his hut, chained to everything he had so thoughtlessly abandoned himself to. His solitude seemed to him so heavy, it burdened him with such a great weight of sorrow that his heart seemed about to break. . . .

But at that very moment the king turned his head, turned it imperceptibly, and his glance fell upon Clarence. . . .

"Yes, no one is as base as I, as naked as I," he thought. "And you, lord, you are willing to rest your eyes upon me!" Or was it because of his very nakedness? . . . "Because of your very nakedness!" the look seemed to say. "That terrifying void that is within you and which opens to receive me; your hunger which calls to my hunger; your very baseness which did not exist until I gave it leave; and the great shame you feel. . . . "

When he had come before the king, when he stood in the great radiance of the king, still ravaged by the tongue of fire, but alive still, and living only through the touch of that fire, Clarence fell upon his knees, for it seemed to him that he was finally at the end of his seeking, and at the end of all seekings.

---

during the nineteenth century in the form of novels, poetry, and drama.

Angry at the negative portrayal of Africa in Western literature (see the box above), African authors initially wrote primarily for a European audience as a means of establishing black dignity and purpose. Embracing the ideals of negritude, many glorified the emotional and communal aspects of the traditional African experience. Nigerian Chinua

Achebe is considered the first major African novelist to write in the English language. In his writings, he attempted to interpret African history from a native perspective and to forge a new sense of African identity. In his trailblazing *Things Fall Apart* (1958), he recounted the story of a Nigerian who refused to submit to the new British order and eventually committed suicide. Criticizing those of his contemporaries who accepted foreign rule, the protagonist lamented that the white man "has put a knife on the things that held us together and we have fallen apart."

In recent decades, the African novel has taken a dramatic turn, shifting its focus from the brutality of the foreign oppressor to the shortcomings of the new native leadership. Having gained independence, African politicians were portrayed as mimicking and even outdoing the injustices committed by their colonial predecessors. A prominent example of this genre is the work of the Kenyan Ngugi Wa Thiong'o (b. 1938). His first novel, *A Grain of Wheat*, takes place on the eve of *Uhuru*, or independence. Although it mocks local British society for its racism, snobbishness, and superficiality, its chief interest lies in its unsentimental and even unflattering portrayal of ordinary Kenyans in their daily struggle for survival.

Like most of his predecessors, Ngugi initially wrote in English, but he eventually decided to write in his native Kikuyu as a means of broadening his readership. For that reason, perhaps, in the late 1970s, he was placed under house arrest for writing subversive literature. There, he secretly wrote *Devil on the Cross*, which urged his compatriots to overthrow the government of Daniel arap Moi. Published in 1980, the book sold widely and was eventually read aloud by storytellers throughout Kenyan society. Fearing an attempt on his life, Ngugi has since lived in exile.

Many of Ngugi's contemporaries have followed his lead and focused their frustration on the failure of the continent's new leadership to carry out the goals of independence. One of the most outstanding is the Nigerian Wole Soyinka (b. 1934). His novel *The Interpreters* (1965) lambasted the corruption and hypocrisy of Nigerian politics. Succeeding novels and plays have continued that tradition, resulting in a Nobel Prize for literature in 1986. In 1994, however, Soyinka barely managed to escape arrest, and he now lives abroad. In a protest against the brutality of the Abacha regime in Nigeria, he published from exile a harsh exposé of the crisis. His book, *The Open Sore of a Continent*, placed the primary responsibility for failure not on Nigeria's long list of dictators but on the very concept of the modern nation-state, which was introduced into Africa arbitrarily by Europeans. A nation, he contends, can only emerge from below, as the expression of the moral and political will of the local inhabitants, not be imposed artificially from above. Some African authors, like Somali writer Nuruddin Farah (b. 1945), argue that it is time for Africans to stop blaming their present political ills on either colonialism or their own dictators. In his writings, such as the novel *Sweet and Sour Milk*, Farah urges Africans to stop lamenting the contamination of African society from the West and take charge of their own destiny. In so doing, Farah joins other African writers in serving as the social conscience of a continent still seeking its own identity.

A number of Africa's most prominent writers today are women. Traditionally, African women were valued for their talents as storytellers, but writing was strongly discouraged by both traditional and colonial authorities on the grounds that women should occupy themselves with their domestic obligations. In recent years, however, a number of women have emerged as prominent writers of African fiction. Two examples are Buchi Emecheta (b. 1940) of Nigeria and Ama Ata Aidoo (b. 1942) of Ghana. Beginning with *Second Class Citizen* (1975), which chronicled the breakdown of her own marriage, Emecheta has published numerous works exploring the role of women in contemporary African society and decrying the practice of polygamy. Ama Ata Aidoo has focused on the identity of today's African women and the changing relations between men and women in society. In her novel *Changes: A Love Story* (1991), she chronicles the lives of three women, none presented as a victim but all caught up in the struggle for survival and happiness.

One of the overriding concerns confronting African intellectuals since independence has been the problem of language. Unlike Asian societies, Africans have not inherited a long written tradition from the precolonial era. As a result, many intellectuals have written in the colonial language, a practice that sometimes results in guilt and anxiety. As we have seen, some have reacted by writing in their local languages to reach a native audience. The market for such work is limited, however, because of the high illiteracy rate and also because novels written in African languages have no market abroad. Moreover, because of the deep financial crisis throughout the continent, there is little money for the publication of serious books. Many of Africa's libraries and universities are almost literally without books. It is little wonder that many African authors, to their discomfort, continue to write and publish in foreign languages.

Contemporary African music also reflects a hybridization or fusion with Western culture. Having traveled to the New World via the slave trade centuries earlier, African drum beats evolved into North American jazz and Latin American dance rhythms, only to return to reenergize African music. In fact, today music is one of Africans' most effective weapons for social and political protest. Easily accessible to all, African music, whether Afro-beat in Nigeria, *rai* in Algeria, or *reggae* in Benin, represents the "weapon of the future," contemporary musicians say; "it helped free Nelson Mandela" and "will put Africa back on the map." Censored by all the African dictatorial regimes, these courageous musicians persist in their struggle against corruption, what one singer calls the second slavery, "the cancer that is eating away at the system."

Their voices echo the chorus "Together we can build a nation, / Because Africa has brains, youth, knowledge."[9]

GATHERED AT THE BEACH

Nowhere in the developing world is the dilemma of continuity and change more agonizing than in Africa. Mesmerized by the spectacle of Western affluence yet repulsed by the bloody trail from slavery to World War II and the atomic bombs over Hiroshima and Nagasaki, African intellectuals have been torn between the dual images of Western materialism and African negritude.

What is the destiny of Africa? Some Africans still yearn for the dreams embodied in the program of the OAU. Novelist Ngugi Wa Thiong'o calls for "an internationalization of all the democratic and social struggles for human equality, justice, peace, and progress."[10] Some African political leaders, however, have apparently discarded the democratic ideal and turned their attention to what is sometimes called the "East Asian model," based on the Confucian tenet of subordination of the individual to the community as the guiding principle of national development (see Chapter 29). Whether African political culture today is well placed to imitate the strategy adopted by the fast-growing nations of East Asia—who in any event are now encountering problems of their own—is questionable. Like all peoples, Africans must ultimately find their own solutions within the context of their own traditions, not by seeking to imitate the example of others.

For the average African, of course, such intellectual dilemmas pale before the daily challenge of survival. But the fundamental gap between the traditional village and the modern metropolis is perhaps wider in Africa than anywhere else in the world and may well be harder to bridge. The solution is not yet visible.

In the meantime, writes Ghanaian author George Awoonor-Williams, all Africans are exiles:

The return is tedious
And the exiled souls gathered at the beach
Arguing and deciding their future
Should they return home
And face the fences the termites had eaten
And see the dunghill that has mounted their birthplace? . . .
The final strokes will land them on forgotten shores
They committed the impiety of self-deceit
Slashed, cut and wounded their souls
And left the mangled remainder in manacles.

The moon, the moon is our father's spirit
At the stars entrance the night revellers gather
To sell their chatter and inhuman sweat to the gateman
And shuffle their feet in agonies of birth.
Lost souls, lost souls, lost souls, that are
Still at the gate.[11]

CRESCENT OF CONFLICT

"We Muslims are of one family even though we live under different governments and in various regions."[12] So said Ayatollah Ruholla Khomeini, the Islamic religious figure and leader of the 1979 revolution that overthrew the shah in Iran. The ayatollah's remark was not just a pious wish by a religious mystic but an accurate reflection of one crucial aspect of the political dynamics in the region.

If the concept of negritude represents an alternative to the system of nation-states in Africa, in the Middle East a similar role has been played by the forces of militant Islam. In both regions, a yearning for a sense of community beyond national borders tugs at the emotions and intellect of their inhabitants and counteracts the dynamic pull of nationalism that has provoked political turmoil and conflict in much of the rest of the world.

A dramatic example of the powerful force of pan-Islamic sentiment took place on September 11, 2001, when Muslim militants hijacked four U.S. airliners and turned them into missiles aimed at the center of world capitalism. Although the headquarters of the terrorist network that carried out the attack—known as al-Qaeda—was located in Afghanistan, the militants themselves came from several different Muslim states. In the months that followed, support for al-Qaeda and its mysterious leader, Osama bin Laden, intensified throughout the Muslim world (see the box on p. 831). To many observers, it appeared that the Islamic peoples were entering an era of direct confrontation with the entire Western world.

What were the sources of Muslim anger? In a speech released on videotape shortly after the attack, bin Laden declared that the attacks were a response to the "humiliation and disgrace" that have afflicted the Islamic world for over eighty years, a period dating back to the end of World War I. For the Middle East, the period between the two world wars was an era of transition. With the fall of the Ottoman and Persian Empires, new modernizing regimes emerged in Turkey and Iran, and a more traditionalist but fiercely independent government was established in Saudi Arabia. Elsewhere, European influence continued to be strong; the British and French had mandates in Syria, Lebanon, Jordan, and Palestine, and British influence persisted in Iraq, southern Arabia, and throughout the Nile valley. Pan-Arabism was on the rise, but it lacked focus and coherence.

During World War II, the region became the cockpit of European rivalries, as it had been during World War I. The region was more significant to the warring powers than previously because of the growing importance of oil and the Suez Canal's position as a vital sea route. For a brief period, the German Afrika Korps threatened to seize Egypt and the Suez Canal, but British troops defeated the Ger-

THE ROOTS OF TERRORISM

*I*n the weeks and months following the terrorist attack on September 11, 2001, commentators throughout the world voiced their views on the roots of the attack and how to prevent a recurrence. In many Muslim countries, horror at the violence was balanced by a conviction that the problem could not be solved simply by seeking out the perpetrators and destroying their terrorist network. Rather, terrorism was a consequence of contemporary conditions throughout much of the Arab world and could only be resolved by political and economic means. Such was the view of the author of the following editorial, published a few days following the attack in El Watan, an independent newspaper in Algiers, the capital of Algeria. Algerian society has been shattered by terrorist activities committed by Islamic militants for over a decade.

ALGERIA: RETHINKING THE VARIABLES

Even if the U.S. military kills Bin Laden and decimates his forces, international terrorism will be only weakened, not destroyed. Experts agree on this point, and some assert that if Bin Laden dies a martyr, his name will act as a stimulus for terrorist movements around the world that won't hesitate to commit further spectacular attacks.

And so as the fear and anger fade, a growing chorus of voices is calling for a comprehensive approach to terrorism, the fruit of intensive thought about its deepest nature. The first conclusion will involve the responsibility of the Western world, which throughout history has allowed religious fundamentalism to thrive when it served Western interests.

Thus, the West unconditionally backed the monarchies of the Gulf, a breeding ground of fundamentalism, because of their oil resources, while at the same time lending blinkered support to Israel's expansionist policies. Against the will of their people, Arab and Muslim leaders have been coddled by the West, spurring popular anger to fever pitch during the Gulf War.

Resentment, widespread in the Arab world by the end of the 20th century, has been exploited by the fundamentalists, who have channeled it into a "holy war" (jihad) against the West. The West, and notably the United States, has learned nothing from all this. Worse, the West has aggravated frustrations the world over by canonizing laissez-faire economics, whose centerpiece—globalization—heralds the systematic impoverishment of billions of people.

But it would be hasty to blame the West alone for terrorism. Both governments and movements in the Arab-Muslim world have sought to impose their religious dogma everywhere by means of systematic terror perpetrated by fanatical groups. Their aim is to create Afghan-type states. Algeria is the clearest case in point.

---

man forces at El Alamein, west of Alexandria, in 1942. From that time until the end of the war, the entire region from the Mediterranean Sea eastward was under secure Allied occupation.

The Question of Palestine

As in other areas of Asia, the end of World War II led to the emergence of a number of independent states. Jordan, Lebanon, and Syria, all European mandates before the war, became independent. Egypt, Iran, and Iraq, though still under a degree of Western influence, became increasingly autonomous. Sympathy for the idea of Arab unity led to the formation of the Arab League in 1945, but different points of view among its members prevented it from achieving anything of substance.

The one issue on which all Arab states in the area could agree was the question of Palestine. As tensions between Jews and Arabs in that mandate intensified during the 1930s, the British attempted to limit Jewish immigration into the area and firmly rejected proposals for independence. After World War II, the Zionists turned for support to the United States, and in March 1948, the Truman administration approved the concept of an independent Jewish state, even though only about one-third of the local

residents were Jews. In May, the new state of Israel was formally established.

To its Arab neighbors, the new state represented a betrayal of the interests of the Palestinian people, 90 percent of whom were Muslim, and a flagrant disregard for the conditions set out in the Balfour Declaration of 1917. Outraged at the lack of Western support for Muslim interests in the area, several Arab countries invaded the new Jewish state. The invasion did not succeed because of internal divisions among the Arabs, but both sides remained bitter, and the Arab states refused to recognize Israel.

The war had other lasting consequences as well, because it led to the exodus of thousands of Palestinian refugees into neighboring Muslim states. Jordan, which had become independent under its Hashemite ruler, was now flooded by the arrival of one million urban Palestinians in a country occupied by half a million Bedouins. To the north, the state of Lebanon had been created to provide the local Christian community with a country of their own, but the arrival of the Palestinian refugees upset the delicate balance between Christians and Muslims. In any event, the creation of Lebanon had angered the Syrians, who had lost it as well as other territories to Turkey as a result of European decisions before and after the war.

Nasser and Pan-Arabism

The dispute over Palestine placed Egypt in an uncomfortable position. Technically, Egypt was not an Arab state. King Farouk, who had acceded to power in 1936, had frequently declared support for the Arab cause, but the Egyptian people were not Bedouins and shared little of the culture of the peoples across the Red Sea. Nevertheless, Farouk committed Egyptian armies to the disastrous war against Israel.

In 1952, King Farouk, whose corrupt habits had severely eroded his early popularity, was overthrown by a military coup engineered by young military officers ostensibly under the leadership of Colonel Muhammad Nagib. The real force behind the scenes was Colonel Gamal Abdul Nasser (1918–1970), the son of a minor government functionary who, like many of his fellow officers, had been angered by the army's inadequate preparation for the war against Israel four years earlier. In 1953, the monarchy was replaced by a republic.

In 1954, Nasser seized power in his own right and immediately instituted a land reform program. He also adopted a policy of neutrality in foreign affairs and expressed sympathy for the Arab cause. The British presence had rankled many Egyptians for years, for even after granting Egypt independence, Britain had retained con-

➤ GOSSIP AMONG THE PYRAMIDS. In modern Cairo, the suburbs of the city creep up to the very feet of the ancient pyramids of Giza. Just beyond the pyramid in the background lies the Sahara, a vast wasteland that stretches unbroken for 3,000 miles to the Atlantic Ocean. In the foreground, seemingly oblivious to the majesty of the ancient empire of the pharaohs, local residents discuss the events of the day on their return from the markets.

Courtesy of William J. Duiker

trol over the Suez Canal to protect its route to the Indian Ocean. In 1956, Nasser suddenly nationalized the Suez Canal Company, which had been under British and French administration. Seeing a threat to their route to the Indian Ocean, the British and the French launched a joint attack on Egypt to protect their investment. They were joined by Israel, whose leaders had grown exasperated at sporadic Arab commando raids on Israeli territory and now decided to strike back. But the Eisenhower administration in the United States, concerned that the attack smacked of a revival of colonialism, supported Nasser and brought about the withdrawal of foreign forces from Egypt and of Israeli troops from the Sinai peninsula (see the box on p. 833).

Nasser now turned to pan-Arabism. Egypt had won approval from other states in the area for its successful eviction of the British and the French from the Suez Canal and for its sponsorship of efforts to replace Israel by an independent Palestinian state. In 1958, Egypt united with Syria as the United Arab Republic (UAR). The union had been proposed by the Ba'ath Party, which advocated the unity of all Arab states in a new socialist society. In 1957, the Ba'ath Party assumed power in Syria and opened talks with Egypt on a union between the two countries, which took place in March 1958 following a plebiscite. Nasser was named president of the new state.

Egypt and Syria hoped that the union would eventually include all Arab states, but other Arab leaders, including young King Hussein of Jordan and the kings of Iraq and Saudi Arabia, were suspicious. The latter two in particular feared pan-Arabism on the reasonable assumption that they would be asked to share their vast oil revenues with the poorer states of the Middle East. Indeed, in Nasser's view, through Arab unity, this wealth could be used to improve the standard of living in the area. To achieve a more equitable division of the wealth of the region, natural resources and major industries would be nationalized; central planning would guarantee that resources were exploited efficiently, but private enterprise would continue at the local level.

In the end, however, Nasser's determination to extend state control over the economy brought an end to the UAR. When the government announced the nationalization of a large number of industries and utilities in 1961, a military coup overthrew the Ba'ath leaders in Damascus, and the new authorities declared that Syria would end its relationship with Egypt.

The breakup of the UAR did not necessarily end Nasser's dream of pan-Arabism. In 1962, Algeria finally received its independence from France and, under its new president, Ahmad Ben Bella, established close relations with Egypt, as did a new republic in Yemen. During the mid-1960s, Egypt took the lead in promoting Arab unity against Israel. At a meeting of Arab leaders held in Jerusalem in 1964, the Palestine Liberation Organization (PLO) was set up under Egyptian sponsorship to rep-

THE SUEZ CANAL BELONGS TO EGYPT!

*T*he Suez Canal was built between 1854 and 1869, using mainly French capital and Egyptian labor, under the direction of the French promoter Ferdinand de Lesseps. It was managed by a Paris-based limited liability corporation, called the Suez Canal Company, under a ninety-nine-year lease. Over time, the canal came to symbolize colonial exploitation in the minds of many Egyptians. In this excerpt from a speech given in July 1956, President Nasser declared that it was time for the canal to be owned and managed by Egyptians. The decision led to a brief invasion by Great Britain and France, but under pressure, the European powers backed down, and Nasser got his way.

NASSER'S SPEECH NATIONALIZING THE SUEZ CANAL COMPANY

The Suez Canal is an Egyptian canal built as a result of great sacrifices. The Suez Canal Company is an Egyptian company that was expropriated from Egypt by the British, who, since the canal was dug, have been obtaining the profits of the Company. . . . And yet the Suez Canal Company is an Egyptian limited liability company. The annual Canal revenue is 35 million Egyptian pounds. From this sum Egypt—which lost 120,000 workers in digging the Canal—takes one million pounds from the Company. . . .

It is a shame when the blood of peoples is sucked, and it is no shame that we should borrow for construction. We will not allow the past to be repeated again, but we will cancel the past by restoring our rights in the Suez Canal. . . . We will build the High Dam, and we will obtain our rights. We will build it as we wish, and we are determined to do so. The 35 million pounds which the Company collects each year will be collected by us. . . . When we build the High Dam, we will be building the dam of prestige, freedom, and dignity, and we will be putting an end to the dams of humiliation. . . .

Now that the rights have been restored to their people after one hundred years, we are achieving true liberation. The Suez Canal Company was a state within a state, depending on the conspiracies of imperialism and its supporters. The Canal was built for the sake of Egypt, but it was a source of exploitation. There is no shame in being poor, but it is a shame to suck blood. Today we restore these rights, and I declare in the name of the Egyptian people that we will protect these rights with our blood and soul. . . .

The people will stand united as one man to resist imperialist acts of treachery. . . . When we restore all our rights, we shall become stronger and our production will increase. At this moment, some of your brethren, the sons of Egypt, are now taking over the Egyptian Suez Canal Company and directing it. We have taken this decision to restore part of the glories of the past and to safeguard our national dignity and pride. May God bless you and guide you in the path of righteousness.

---

resent the interests of the Palestinians. According to the charter of the PLO, only the Palestinian people (and thus not Jewish immigrants from abroad) had the right to form a state in the old British mandate. A guerrilla movement called al-Fatah, led by the dissident PLO figure Yasir Arafat (b. 1929), began to launch terrorist attacks on Israeli territory, prompting the Israeli government to raid PLO bases in Jordan in 1966.

The Arab-Israeli Dispute

Growing Arab hostility was a constant threat to the security of Israel. In the years after independence, Israeli leaders dedicated themselves to creating a Jewish homeland. Aided by reparations paid by the postwar German government of Chancellor Konrad Adenauer and private funds provided by Jews living abroad, notably in the United States, the government attempted to build a democratic and modern state that would be a magnet for Jews throughout the world and a symbol of Jewish achievement.

Ensuring the survival of the tiny state surrounded by antagonistic Arab neighbors was a considerable challenge, made more difficult by divisions within the Israeli population. Some were immigrants from Europe, while others came from the Middle East. Some were secular and even socialist in their views, while others were politically and religiously conservative. The state was also home to Christians as well as Muslim Palestinians who had not fled to other countries. To balance these diverse interests, Israel established a parliament, called the Knesset, on the European model, with proportional representation based on the number of votes each party received in the general election. The parties were so numerous that none ever received a majority of votes, and all governments had to be formed from a coalition of several parties. As a result, moderate secular leaders such as longtime prime minister David Ben Gurion had to cater to more marginal parties composed of conservative religious groups.

During the late 1950s and 1960s, the dispute between Israel and other states in the Middle East intensified. Essentially alone except for the sympathy of the United States and several Western European countries, Israel adopted a policy of determined resistance to and immediate retaliation against alleged PLO and Arab provocations. By the spring of 1967, relations between Israel and its Arab neighbors had deteriorated as Nasser attempted to improve his standing in the Arab world by imposing a blockade against Israeli commerce through the Gulf of Aqaba.

Concerned that it might be isolated, and lacking firm support from Western powers (who had originally guaranteed Israel the freedom to use the Gulf of Aqaba), in June 1967, Israel suddenly launched air strikes against Egypt and several of its Arab neighbors. Israeli armies then broke the blockade at the head of the Gulf of Aqaba and occupied the Sinai peninsula. Other Israeli forces attacked Jordanian territory on the West Bank of the Jordan River (Jordan's King Hussein had recently signed an alliance with Egypt and placed his army under Egyptian command), occupied the whole of Jerusalem, and seized Syrian military positions in the Golan Heights, along the Israeli-Syrian border (see Map 28.2).

Despite limited Soviet support for Egypt and Syria, in a brief, six-day war, Israel had mocked Nasser's pretensions of Arab unity and tripled the size of its territory, thus enhancing its precarious security. But the new Israel aroused even more bitter hostility among the Arabs and added one million Palestinians inside its borders, most of them on the West Bank of the Jordan River.

During the next few years, the focus of the Arab-Israeli dispute shifted as Arab states demanded the return of the occupied territories. Meanwhile, many Israelis argued that the new lands improved the security of the beleaguered state and should be retained. Concerned that the dispute

might lead to a confrontation between the superpowers, the Nixon administration tried to achieve a peace settlement. The peace effort received a mild stimulus when Nasser died of a heart attack in September 1970 and was succeeded by his vice president, ex-general Anwar al-Sadat (1918–1981). Sadat soon showed himself to be more pragmatic than his predecessor, dropping the now irrelevant name United Arab Republic in favor of the Arab Republic of Egypt and replacing Nasser's socialist policies with a new strategy based on free enterprise and encouragement of Western investment. He also agreed to sign a peace treaty with Israel on condition that Israel withdraw to its pre-1967 frontiers. Concerned that other Arab countries would refuse to make peace and take advantage of its presumed weakness, Israel refused.

Rebuffed in his offer of peace, smarting from criticism of his moderate stand from other Arab leaders, and increasingly concerned over Israeli plans to build permanent Jewish settlements in the occupied territories, Sadat attempted once again to renew Arab unity through a new confrontation with Israel. On Yom Kippur (the Jewish Day of Atonement), an Israeli national holiday, Egyptian forces suddenly launched an air and artillery attack on Israeli positions in the Sinai just east of the Suez Canal. Syrian armies attacked Israeli positions in the Golan Heights. After early Arab successes, the Israelis managed to recoup some of their losses on both fronts. As a superpower confrontation between the United States and the Soviet Union loomed, a cease-fire was finally reached.

In the next years, a fragile peace was maintained, marked by U.S. "shuttle diplomacy" (carried out by U.S. Secretary of State Henry Kissinger) and the rise to power in Israel of the militant Likud Party under Prime Minister Menachem Begin (1913–1992). The conflict now spread to Lebanon, where many Palestinians had found refuge and the PLO had set up its headquarters. Rising tension along the border was compounded by increasingly hostile disputes between Christians and Muslims over control of the capital, Beirut.

After his election as U.S. president in 1976, Jimmy Carter began to press for a compromise peace based on Israel's return of occupied Arab territories and Arab recognition of the state of Israel (an idea originally proposed by Kissinger). By now, Sadat was anxious to reduce his military expenses and announced his willingness to visit Jerusalem to seek peace. The meeting took place in November 1977, with no concrete results, but Sadat persisted. In September 1978, he and Begin met with Carter at Camp David, the presidential retreat in Maryland. Israel agreed to withdraw from the Sinai but not from other occupied territories unless it was recognized by other Arab countries.

The promise of the Camp David agreement was not fulfilled. One reason was the assassination of Sadat by Islamic militants in October 1981. But there were deeper causes, including the continued unwillingness of many Arab gov-

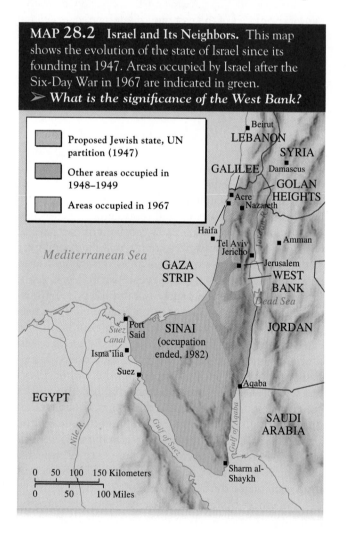

MAP 28.2 Israel and Its Neighbors. This map shows the evolution of the state of Israel since its founding in 1947. Areas occupied by Israel after the Six-Day War in 1967 are indicated in green.

➤ *What is the significance of the West Bank?*

- Proposed Jewish state, UN partition (1947)
- Other areas occupied in 1948–1949
- Areas occupied in 1967

Beirut
LEBANON
SYRIA
GALILEE Damascus
Acre GOLAN HEIGHTS
Nazareth
Haifa
Mediterranean Sea
Tel Aviv Amman
Jericho
Jerusalem
GAZA STRIP WEST BANK
Dead Sea
Port Said SINAI (occupation ended, 1982) JORDAN
Suez Canal
Isma'ilia
Suez
Aqaba
EGYPT
SAUDI ARABIA
Nile R.
Gulf of Suez
Gulf of Aqaba
Sharm al-Shaykh

0 50 100 150 Kilometers
0 50 100 Miles

LANDSCAPE OF CONTENTION.   The Golan Heights, a range of mountains to the east of the Sea of Galilee in northern Israel, has become a major bone of contention between the state of Israel and neighboring Syria. Israeli forces seized the area during the brief Arab-Israeli conflict in 1967 and continue to occupy it today. As the photo clearly shows, whoever controls the heights is in a position to dominate the Israeli lowlands below. The issue is but one example of the complexity of the Arab-Israeli dispute.

ernments to recognize Israel and the Israeli government's encouragement of Jewish settlements on the occupied West Bank.

During the early 1980s, the militancy of the Palestinians increased, leading to rising unrest, popularly labeled the *intifada* (uprising), among PLO supporters living inside Israel. To control the situation, a new Israeli government under Prime Minister Itzhak Shamir invaded southern Lebanon to destroy PLO commando bases near the Israeli border. The invasion provoked international condemnation and further destabilized the perilous balance between Muslims and Christians in Lebanon. As the 1990s began, U.S.-sponsored peace talks opened between Israel and a number of its neighbors. The first major breakthrough came in 1993, when Israel and the PLO reached an agreement calling for Palestinian autonomy in selected areas of Israel in return for PLO recognition of the legitimacy of the Israeli state.

Progress in implementing the agreement, however, was slow. Terrorist attacks by Palestinian militants resulted in heavy casualties and shook the confidence of many Jewish citizens that their security needs could be protected under the agreement. At the same time, Jewish residents of the West Bank resisted the extension of Palestinian authority in the area. In November 1995, Prime Minister Yitzhak Rabin was assassinated by an Israeli opponent of the accords. National elections held a few months later led to the formation of a new government under Benjamin Netanyahu, which adopted a tougher stance in negotiations with the Palestinian Authority under Yasir Arafat. When Netanyahu was replaced by a new Labour government under Prime Minister Ehud Barak, the latter promised to revitalize the peace process. Negotiations continued with the PLO and also got under way with Syria over a peace settlement in Lebanon and the possible return of the Golan Heights. But in late 2000, peace talks broke down over the future of the city of Jerusalem, leading to massive riots by Palestinians and the election of a new and more hard-line Israeli prime minister,

A PALESTINIAN VILLAGE. After the creation of the state of Israel, many Palestinian Muslims left their homes there and created new settlements in the West Bank, an arid region east of Jerusalem that was part of the neighboring state of Jordan until its seizure by Israeli forces during the 1967 war. Since then, ownership of the area has been in dispute, and a number of Jewish settlements have been established there to create a permanent Israeli presence. Negotiations over ownership of the West Bank are a key prerequisite to any final settlement of the Arab-Israeli dispute. Shown here is a Palestinian settlement, with the mountains adjacent to the Red Sea in the background.

former defense minister Ariel Sharon. Sharon's ascent to leadership was accompanied by a rash of suicide attacks by Palestinians against Israeli targets, an intensive Israeli military crackdown on suspected terrorist sites inside Palestinian territory, and a dramatic increase in bloodshed on both sides. Although Saudi Arabia has set forth a plan calling for full Arab recognition of the state of

Israel in return for the latter's final withdrawal from occupied territories, the prospects of reaching a peace agreement remain dim.

Revolution in Iran

The Arab-Israeli dispute also provoked an international oil crisis. In 1960, a number of oil-producing states formed the Organization of Petroleum Exporting Countries (OPEC) to gain control over oil prices, but the organization was not recognized by the foreign oil companies. During the 1973 Yom Kippur War, some OPEC nations announced significant increases in the price of oil to foreign countries. The price hikes were accompanied by an apparent oil shortage and created serious economic problems in the United States and Europe as well as in the Third World. They also proved to be a boon to oil-exporting countries, such as Libya, now under the leadership of the militantly anti-Western Colonel Muammar Qadhafi (b. 1942).

One of the key oil-exporting countries was Iran. Under the leadership of Shah Mohammad Reza Pahlavi (1919–1980), who had taken over from his father in 1941, Iran had become one of the richest countries in the Middle East. Although relations

THE TEMPLE MOUNT AT JERUSALEM. The Temple Mount is one of the most sacred spots in the city of Jerusalem. Originally it was the site of a temple built during the reign of Solomon, king of the Jews, about 1000 B.C.E. The Western Wall of the temple is shown in the foreground. Beyond the wall is the Dome of the Rock complex, built on the place from which Muslims believe that Muhammad ascended to heaven. Sacred to both religions, the Temple Mount is now a major bone of contention between Muslims and Jews and a prime obstacle to a final settlement of the Arab-Israeli dispute.

with the West had occasionally been fragile (especially after Prime Minister Mossadeq had briefly attempted to nationalize the oil industry in 1951), during the next twenty years Iran became a prime ally of the United States in the Middle East. With encouragement from the United States, which hoped that Iran could become a force for stability in the Persian Gulf, the shah attempted to carry through a series of social and economic reforms to transform the country into the most advanced in the region.

Statistical evidence suggests that his efforts were succeeding. Per capita income increased dramatically, literacy rates improved, a modern communications infrastructure took shape, and an affluent middle class emerged in the capital of Tehran. Under the surface, however, trouble was brewing. Despite an ambitious land reform program, many peasants were still landless, unemployment among intellectuals was dangerously high, and the urban middle class was squeezed by high inflation. Housing costs had skyrocketed, provoked in part by the massive influx of foreigners attracted by oil money.

Some of the unrest took the form of religious discontent as millions of devout Muslims looked with distaste at a new Iranian civilization based on greed, sexual license, and material accumulation. Religious conservatives opposed rampant government corruption, the ostentation of the shah's court, and the extension of voting rights to women. Some opposition elements resorted to terrorism against wealthy Iranians or foreign residents in an attempt to provoke social and political disorder. In response, the shah's U.S.-trained security police, the *Savak*, imprisoned and sometimes tortured thousands of dissidents.

Leading the opposition was Ayatollah Ruholla Khomeini (1900–1989), an austere Shi'ite cleric who had been exiled to Iraq and then to France because of his outspoken opposition to the shah's regime. From Paris, Khomeini continued his attacks in print, on television, and in radio broadcasts. By the late 1970s, large numbers of Iranians—especially Shi'ite muslims, whose approach to religion is sometimes more mystical and messianistic than that of their Sunni counterparts—began to respond to Khomeini's diatribes against the "satanic regime," and demonstrations by his supporters were repressed with ferocity by the police. But workers' strikes grew in intensity. In January 1979, the shah appointed a moderate, Shapur Bakhtiar, as prime minister and then left the country for medical treatment.

Bakhtiar attempted to conciliate the rising opposition and permitted Khomeini to return to Iran, where he presided over the new Islamic Revolutionary Council and demanded the government's resignation. With rising public unrest and incipient revolt within the army, the government collapsed and was replaced by a hastily formed Islamic republic. The new government, dominated by Shi'ite clergy under the guidance of Ayatollah Khomeini, immediately began to introduce and restore traditional Islamic law. A new reign of terror ensued as supporters of the shah were rounded up and executed. Along the borders, ethnic groups such as the Kurds and the Azerbaijanis rose in rebellion.

Though much of the outside world focused on the U.S. Embassy in Tehran, where militants held a number of foreign hostages, the Iranian Revolution involved much more. In the eyes of the ayatollah and his followers, the United States was "the great Satan," the powerful protector of Israel, and the enemy of Muslim peoples everywhere. Furthermore, it was responsible for the corruption of Iranian society under the shah. Now Khomeini demanded that the shah be returned to Iran for trial and that the United States apologize for its acts against the Iranian people. In response, the Carter administration stopped buying Iranian oil and froze Iranian assets in the United States.

The effects of the disturbances in Iran quickly spread beyond its borders. Sunni militants briefly seized the holy places in Mecca and began to appeal to their brothers to launch similar revolutions in Islamic countries around the world, including far-off Malaysia and Indonesia. At the same time, the ethnic unrest among the Kurdish minorities along the border continued. In July 1980, the shah died of cancer in Cairo. Two months later, Iraq and Iran went to war (see the next section). With economic conditions in Iran rapidly deteriorating, the Islamic revolutionary government finally agreed to free the hostages in return for the release of Iranian assets in the United States. During the next few years, the intensity of the Iranian Revolution moderated slightly, and the government of President Hashemi Rafsanjani displayed a modest tolerance for a loosening of clerical control over freedom of expression and social activities. But rising criticism of rampant official corruption and a high rate of inflation sparked a new wave of government repression in the mid-1990s; newspapers were censored, the universities were purged of disloyal or "un-Islamic" elements, and religious militants raided private homes in search of blasphemous activities.

In 1997, the moderate Muslim cleric Mohammad Khatemi was elected president of Iran. Khatemi, whose surprising victory reflected a growing desire among many Iranians for a more pluralistic society open to the outside world, promoted reforms in a number of areas, including the relaxation of press censorship, leading to the emergence of several reformist newspapers and magazines, as well as a relaxation of dress codes and restrictions on women's activities. But the new president faced severe pressures from conservative elements to maintain the purity of Islamic laws, and in April 2000, several reformist publications were shut down by the judiciary for having printed materials that "disparaged Islam." At the end of the year, the reformist minister of culture was forced to resign.

President Khatemi was reelected to office in August 2001 and immediately vowed to continue his reformist efforts. In the days following the terrorist attacks on the United States on September 11, he also declared publicly that Muslims must reject terrorism as a tool in promoting Islam. But conservative clerics, anxious to contain the longing for personal freedom that is increasing among younger Iranians, struck back by curtailing freedom of the press and defying parliamentary legislation that they considered destructive of the purity of the Islamic state.

Crisis in the Gulf

Although much of the Iranians' anger was directed against the United States during the early phases of the revolution, Iran had equally hated enemies closer to home. To the north, the immense power of the Soviet Union, driven by atheistic communism, was viewed as a modern version of the Russian threat of previous centuries. To the west was a militant and hostile Iraq, now under the leadership of the ambitious Saddam Hussein (b. 1937). Problems from both directions appeared shortly after Khomeini's rise to power. Soviet military forces occupied Afghanistan to prop up a weak Marxist regime there. The following year, Iraqi forces suddenly attacked along the Iranian border.

Iraq and Iran had long had an uneasy relationship, fueled by religious differences (Iranian Islam is predominantly Shi'ite, while the ruling caste in Iraq is Sunni) and a perennial dispute over borderlands adjacent to the Persian Gulf, the vital waterway for the export of oil from both countries. Like several of its neighbors, Iraq had long dreamed of unifying the Arabs but had been hindered by internal factions and suspicion among its neighbors.

During the mid-1970s, Iran gave some support to a Kurdish rebellion in the mountains of Iraq. In 1975, the government of the shah agreed to stop aiding the rebels in return for territorial concessions at the head of the Gulf. Five years later, however, the Kurdish revolt had been suppressed, and President Saddam Hussein, who had assumed power in Baghdad in 1979, accused Iran of violating the territorial agreement and launched an attack on his neighbor. The war was a bloody one and lasted for nearly ten years. Poison gas was used against civilians, and children were employed to clear minefields. Finally, with both sides virtually exhausted, a cease-fire was arranged in the fall of 1988.

The bitter conflict with Iran had not slaked Saddam Hussein's appetite for territorial expansion. In early August 1990, Iraqi military forces suddenly moved across the border and occupied the small neighboring country of Kuwait at the head of the Gulf. The immediate pretext was the claim that Kuwait was pumping oil from fields inside Iraqi territory. Baghdad was also angry over the Kuwaiti government's demand for repayment of loans it had made to Iraq during the war with Iran. But the underlying reason was Iraq's contention that Kuwait was legally a part of Iraq. Kuwait had been part of the Ottoman Empire until the beginning of the twentieth century, when the local prince had agreed to place his patrimony under British protection. When Iraq became independent in 1932, it claimed

the area on the grounds that the state of Kuwait had been created by British imperialism, but opposition from major Western powers and other countries in the region, who feared the consequences of a "greater Iraq," prevented an Iraqi takeover.

The Iraqi invasion of Kuwait in 1990 sparked an international outcry, and the United States assembled a multinational coalition that liberated the country and destroyed a substantial part of Iraq's armed forces. President George H. W. Bush had promised the American people that U.S. troops would not fight with one hand tied behind their backs (a clear reference to the Vietnam War), but the allied forces did not occupy Baghdad at the end of the war out of fear that doing so would cause a breakup of the country, an eventuality that would operate to the benefit of Iran. The allies hoped instead that the Hussein regime would be ousted by an internal revolt. In the meantime, harsh economic sanctions were imposed on the Iraqi government as the condition for peace. The anticipated overthrow of Saddam Hussein did not materialize, however, and his tireless efforts to evade the conditions of the cease-fire continued to bedevil U.S. President Bill Clinton and his successor, George W. Bush.

In the late 1990s, statements by Iranian President Mohammed Khatemi signaled the tantalizing possibility that relations between the United States and Iran might begin to improve. Such a development would strengthen efforts to maintain a balance among competing states to prevent a single power from dominating the region, but progress on that front has been slow.

Conflicts in Afghanistan and Iraq

The terrorist attacks launched against U.S. cities in September 2001 added a new dimension to the Middle Eastern equation. After the failure of the Soviet Union to quell the rebellion in Afghanistan during the 1980s, a fundamentalist Muslim group known as the Taliban seized power in Kabul and ruled the country with a fanaticism reminiscent of the Cultural Revolution in China. Backed by conservative religious forces in Pakistan, the Taliban provided a base of operations for Osama bin Laden's terrorist network. After the attacks of September 11, a coalition of forces led by the United States overthrew the Taliban and attempted to build a new and moderate government. But the country's

history of bitter internecine warfare among various tribal groups represents a severe challenge over the potential for success.

In the meantime, the Bush administration, citing Iraqi dictator Saddam Hussein for allegedly having provided support to bin Laden's terrorist organization, as well as seeking to develop weapons of mass destruction, threatened to invade Iraq and remove him from power. The plan, widely debated in the media and protested in cities around the world, disquieted Arab leaders and fanned anti-U.S. sentiment throughout the Muslim world. In March 2003, U.S.-led forces invaded Iraq and by early April entered Baghdad and disrupted Hussein's regime.

POLITICS IN THE CONTEMPORARY MIDDLE EAST

Unlike the newly independent states in other parts of Asia, which generally attempted to set up Western-style governments, the Middle Eastern states that became independent after World War II (see Map 28.3) established a variety of forms of government.

In some cases, the traditional leaders survived into the postwar period—notably on the Arabian peninsula, where feudal rulers remain in power. The kings of Saudi Arabia, for example, continue to rule by traditional precepts and, citing the distinctive character of Muslim political institutions, have been reluctant to establish representative political institutions. As a general rule, these rulers maintain and even enforce the strict observance of traditional customs. Religious police in Saudi Arabia are responsible for enforcing the Muslim dress code, maintaining the prohibition against alcohol, and making sure businesses close during the time for prayer. Reportedly, the government even forbade airing *The Muppet Show* on local television because its characters included a pig, which is considered unclean and hence offensive to Muslims.

In other societies, traditional authority has been replaced by charismatic one-party rule or military dictatorships. Nasser's regime in Egypt is a good example of a single-party state where the leader won political power by the force of his presence or personality. Ayatollah Khomeini in Iran, Muammar Qadhafi in Libya, and Saddam Hussein in Iraq are other examples. Although their personal characteristics and images differ, they all owe much of their power to their personal appeal.

In other instances, charismatic rule has given way to modernizing bureaucratic regimes. Examples include the governments of Syria, Yemen, Turkey, and Egypt since Nasser, where Anwar al-Sadat and his successor, Hosni Mubarak, focused their regimes on performance. Sometimes the authoritarian character of the regimes has been modified by some democratic tendencies, especially in

Chronology

THE MODERN MIDDLE EAST

Formation of the state of Israel	1948
King Farouk overthrown in Egypt	1952
Egypt nationalizes the Suez Canal	1956
Formation of the United Arab Republic	1958
Founding of the Palestine Liberation Organization	1964
Six-Day War between Arab states and Israel	1967
First oil crisis	1973
Yom Kippur War between Arab states and Israel	1973
Camp David accords	1978
Iranian Revolution	1979
Iran-Iraq War begins	1980
Israeli forces invade Lebanon	1982
Iraqi invasion of Kuwait	1990
Persian Gulf War	1991
Agreement on Palestinian autonomy	1994
Assassination of Yitzhak Rabin	1995
Peace talks between Israel and Syria begin	1999
Reformists win parliamentary majority in Iran	2000
Election of Ariel Sharon as prime minister of Israel	2000
Al-Qaeda terrorist attack on the United States	2001
U.S.-led forces invade Iraq	2003

Turkey, where free elections and the sharing of power have become more prevalent in recent years. A few Arab nations, such as Bahrain, Kuwait, and Jordan, have even engaged in limited forms of democratic experimentation.

Only in Israel, however, are democratic institutions firmly established. The Israeli system suffers from the proliferation of minor parties, some of which are able to dictate policy because their support is essential to keeping a government in power. In recent years, divisions between religious conservatives and secular elements within the Jewish community have become increasingly sharp. Nevertheless, the government generally reflects the popular will, and power is transferred by peaceful and constitutional means.

The Economics of Oil

Few areas exhibit a greater disparity of individual and national wealth than the Middle East. While millions live in abject poverty, a fortunate few rank among the wealthiest people in the world. While the annual per capita

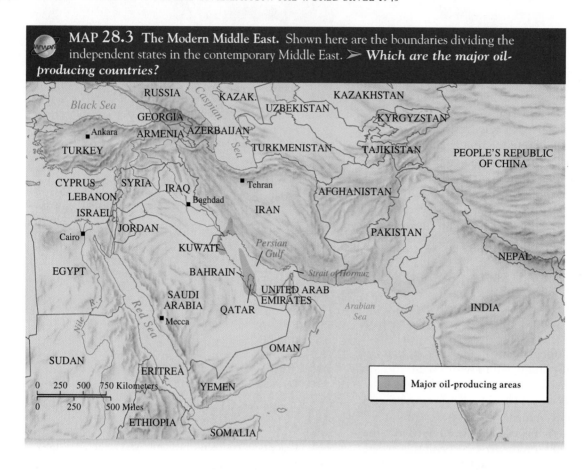

MAP 28.3 The Modern Middle East. Shown here are the boundaries dividing the independent states in the contemporary Middle East. ➤ *Which are the major oil-producing countries?*

income in Egypt is about $600 (in U.S. dollars), in the tiny states of Kuwait and United Arab Emirates, it is nearly $20,000. The primary reason for this disparity is oil. Unfortunately for most of the peoples of the region, oil reserves are distributed unevenly and all too often are located in areas where the population density is low. Egypt and Turkey, with more than fifty million inhabitants apiece, have almost no oil reserves. The combined population of Kuwait, the United Arab Emirates, and Saudi Arabia is well under ten million people. This disparity in wealth inspired Nasser's quest for Arab unity but has also posed a major obstacle to that unity.

The importance of petroleum has obviously been a boon to several of the states in the region, but it has been an unreliable one. Because of violent fluctuations in the price of oil, the income of oil-producing states has varied considerably. The spectacular increase in oil prices during the 1970s, when members of OPEC were able to raise the price of a barrel of oil from about $3 to $30, was not sustained, forcing a number of oil-producing countries to scale back their economic development plans.

Not surprisingly, considering their different resources and political systems, the states of the Middle East have adopted diverse approaches to the problem of developing strong and stable economies. Some, like Nasser in Egypt and the leaders of the Ba'ath Party in Syria, attempted to create a form of Arab socialism, favoring a

high level of government involvement in the economy to relieve the inequities of the free enterprise system. Others turned to the Western capitalist model to maximize growth while using taxes or massive development projects to build a modern infrastructure, redistribute wealth, and maintain political stability and economic opportunity for all.

Whatever their approach, all the states have attempted to develop their economies in accordance with Islamic beliefs. Although the Koran has little to say about economics and can be variously interpreted as capitalist or socialist, it is clear in its opposition to charging interest and in its concern for the material welfare of the Muslim community, the *umma*. How these goals are to be achieved is a matter of interpretation.

Socialist theories of economic development such as Nasser's were often suggested as a way to promote economic growth while meeting the requirements of Islamic doctrine. State intervention in the economic sector would bring about rapid development, while land redistribution and the nationalization or regulation of industry would minimize the harsh inequities of the marketplace. In general, however, the socialist approach has had little success, and most governments, including those of Egypt and Syria, eventually shifted to a more free enterprise approach while encouraging foreign investment to compensate for a lack of capital or technology.

Although the amount of arable land is relatively small, most countries in the Middle East rely to a certain degree on farming to supply food for their growing populations. Much of the fertile land was owned by wealthy absentee landlords, but land reform programs in several countries have attempted to alleviate this problem.

The most comprehensive and probably the most successful land reform program was instituted in Egypt, where Nasser and his successors managed to reassign nearly a quarter of all cultivable lands by limiting the amount a single individual could hold. Similar programs in Iran, Iraq, Libya, and Syria generally had less effect. After the 1979 revolution in Iran, many farmers seized lands forcibly from the landlords, creating questions of ownership that the revolutionary government has tried with minimal success to resolve.

Agricultural productivity throughout the region has been plagued by the lack of water. With populations growing at more than 2 percent annually on average in the Middle East (more than 3 percent in some countries), several governments have tried to increase the amount of water available for irrigation. Many attempts have been sabotaged by government ineptitude, political disagreements, and territorial conflicts, however. The best-known example is the Aswan Dam, which was built by Soviet engineers in the 1950s. The project was designed to control the flow of water throughout the Nile valley, but it has had a number of undesirable environmental consequences. Today, the dearth of water in the region is reaching crisis proportions.

Another way governments have attempted to deal with rapid population growth is to encourage emigration. Oil-producing states with small populations, such as Saudi Arabia and the United Arab Emirates, have imported labor from other countries in the region, mostly to work in the oil fields. By the mid-1980s, more than 40 percent of the population in those states was composed of foreign nationals, who often sent the bulk of their salaries back to their families in their home countries. The decline in oil revenues since the mid-1980s, however, has forced several governments to take measures to stabilize or reduce the migrant population. Since the Iraqi invasion, Kuwait, for example, has expelled all Palestinians and restricted migrant workers from other countries to three-year stays.

The economies of the Middle Eastern countries, then, are in a state of flux. Political and military conflicts have exacerbated economic problems such as water use, which have in turn compounded political issues. For example, disputes between Israel and its neighbors over water rights and between Iraq and its neighbors over the exploitation of the Tigris and Euphrates Rivers have caused serious tensions in recent years. In Saudi Arabia, declining oil revenues combined with the evidence of corruption among Saudi elites have aroused a deep sense of anger and support for radical politics among some segments of the populace.

What explains the failure of democratic institutions and values to take root in the contemporary Middle East? Some observers attribute the cause to the willingness of Western governments to coddle dictatorships as a means of preserving their access to the vast oil reserves located on the Arabian peninsula. Others ascribe it to deep-seated factors embedded in the history and culture of the region or in the religion of Islam itself. As Bashar al-Assad, the current president of Syria, remarked recently, he would tolerate only "positive criticism" of his policies. "We have to have our own democracy to match our history and culture," he said, "arising from the needs of our people and our reality."[13]

Whatever the cause, critics charge that the lack of personal freedom has aroused a level of popular discontent that local governments seek to deflect—often with great success—onto the West. For their part, Middle Eastern political leaders undoubtedly fear that greater popular participation in the affairs of state could radicalize local politics and destabilize the precarious stability of many states in the region.

The Islamic Revival

In recent years, many developments in the Middle East have been described in terms of a resurgence of traditional values and customs in response to Western influence. Indeed, some conservative religious forces in the area have consciously attempted to replace foreign culture and values with allegedly "pure" Islamic forms of belief and behavior.

But the Islamic revival is not a simple dichotomy between traditional and modern, native and foreign, or irrational and rational. In the first place, many Muslims in the Middle East still believe that Islamic values and modern ways are not incompatible and may even be mutually reinforcing. Second, the resurgence of what are sometimes called "fundamentalist" Islamic groups may, in a Middle Eastern context, appear to be a rational and practical response to destabilizing forces, such as corruption and hedonism, and self-destructive practices, such as drunkenness, prostitution, and the use of drugs. Finally, the reassertion of Islamic values is seen as a means of establishing a cultural identity and fighting off the overwhelming impact of Western ideas.

Initially, many Muslim intellectuals responded to Western influence by trying to create a "modernized" set of Islamic beliefs and practices that would not clash with the demands of the twentieth century. This process took place to some degree in most Islamic societies, but it was especially prevalent in Turkey, Egypt, and Iran. Mustapha Kemal Atatürk embraced the strategy when he attempted to secularize the Islamic religion in the new Turkish republic. The Turkish model was followed by Shah Reza Khan and his son Mohammad Reza Pahlavi in Iran and then by Nasser in postwar Egypt, all of whom attempted to make use of Islamic values while asserting the primacy of other issues such as political and economic development. Religion, in effect, had become the handmaiden of political power, national identity, and economic prosperity.

These secularizing trends were particularly noticeable among the political, intellectual, and economic elites in urban areas. They had less influence in the countryside, among the poor, and among devout elements within the clergy. Many of the clerics believed that Western influence in the cities had given birth to political and economic corruption, sexual promiscuity, hedonism, individualism, and the prevalence of alcohol, pornography, and drugs. Although such practices had long existed in the Middle East, they were now far more visible and socially acceptable.

This reaction intensified after World War I, when the Western presence increased. In 1928, devout Muslims in Egypt formed the Muslim Brotherhood as a means of promoting personal piety. Later the movement began to take a more activist approach, including the use of terrorism by a radical minority. Despite Nasser's surface commitment to Islamic ideals and Arab unity, some Egyptians were fiercely opposed to his policies and regarded his vision of Arab socialism as a betrayal of Islamic principles. Nasser reacted harshly and executed a number of his leading opponents.

The movement to return to Islamic purity reached its zenith in Iran. It is not surprising that Iran took the lead in light of its long tradition of ideological purity within the Shi'ite sect as well as the uncompromisingly secular character of the shah's reforms in the postwar era. In Iran today, traditional Islamic beliefs are all-pervasive and extend into education, clothing styles, social practices, and the legal system. In recent years, for example, Iranian women have been heavily fined or even flogged for violating the Islamic dress code.

The cultural and social effects of the Iranian Revolution were profound as Iranian ideas spread throughout the area. In Algeria, the political influence of fundamentalist Islamic groups grew substantially and enabled them to win a stunning victory in the national elections in 1992. When the military stepped in to cancel the second round of elections and crack down on the militants, the latter responded with a campaign of terrorism against moderates that has claimed thousands of lives.

A similar trend emerged in Egypt, where militant groups such as the Muslim Brotherhood engaged in terrorism, including the assassination of Sadat and attacks on foreign tourists, who are considered carriers of corrupt Western influence.

Even in Turkey, generally considered the most secular of Islamic societies, a militant political group, known as the Islamic Welfare Party, took power in a coalition government formed in 1996. The new prime minister, Necmettin Erbakan, adopted a pro-Arab stance in foreign affairs and threatened to reduce the country's economic and political ties to Europe. Worried moderates voiced their concern that the secular legacy of Kemal Atatürk was being eroded, and eventually Erbakan agreed to resign under heavy pressure from the military. Rejected in its application for membership in the European Union and uncomfortable with the militancy of its Arab neighbors, Turkey has established a security relationship with Israel and seeks close ties with the United States. But religious and economic discontent lies just beneath the surface, and Atatürk's own legacy, known as "Kemalism," has come under close scrutiny by critics.

Throughout the Middle East, even governments and individuals who do not support efforts to return to pure Islamic principles have adjusted their behavior and beliefs in subtle ways. In Egypt, for example, the government now encourages television programs devoted to religion in preference to comedies and adventure shows imported from the West, and alcohol is discouraged or at least consumed more discreetly. On the other hand, criticism of strict government censorship is on the rise in Iran, and the recent election of a moderate majority in the Iranian parliament may undercut the domination of all aspects of social and cultural life by fundamentalist clerics.

The Role of Women

Nowhere have the fault lines between tradition and modernity within Muslim societies in the Middle East been so sharp as in the ongoing debate over the role of women. At the beginning of the twentieth century, women's place in Middle Eastern society had changed little since the death of the prophet Muhammad. Women were secluded in their homes and had few legal, political, or social rights.

During the first decades of the twentieth century, advocates of modernist views began to contend that Islamic doctrine was not inherently opposed to women's rights. To modernists, Islamic traditions such as female seclusion, wearing the veil, and even polygamy were actually pre-Islamic folk traditions that had been tolerated in the early Islamic era and continued to be practiced in later centuries. Such views had considerable impact on a number of Middle Eastern societies, including Turkey and Iran. As we have seen, greater rights for women was a crucial element in the social revolution promoted by Kemal Atatürk in Turkey. In Iran, Shah Reza Khan and his son granted female suffrage and encouraged the education of women. In Egypt, a vocal feminist movement arose in educated women's circles in Cairo as early as the 1920s. With the exception of

KEEPING THE CAMEL OUT OF THE TENT

"*Almighty God created sexual desire in ten parts; then he gave nine parts to women and one to men.*" *So pronounced Ali, Muhammad's son-in-law, as he explained why women are held morally responsible as the instigators of sexual intercourse. Consequently, over the centuries, Islamic women have been secluded, veiled, and in many cases genitally mutilated in order to safeguard male virtue. Women are forbidden to look directly at, speak to, or touch a man prior to marriage. Even today, they are often sequestered at home or limited to strictly segregated areas away from all male contact. Women normally pray at home or in an enclosed antechamber of the mosque so their physical presence will not disturb men's spiritual concentration.*

Especially limiting today are the laws governing women's behavior in Saudi Arabia. Schooling for girls has never been compulsory because fathers believe that "educating women is like allowing the nose of the camel into the tent; eventually the beast will edge in and take up all the room inside." The country did not establish its first girls' school until 1956. The following description of Saudi women is from Nine Parts Desire: The Hidden World of Islamic Women, *by the journalist Geraldine Brooks.*

GERALDINE BROOKS, *NINE PARTS DESIRE*

Women were first admitted to university in Saudi Arabia in 1962, and all women's colleges remain strictly segregated. Lecture rooms come equipped with closed-circuit TVs and telephones, so women students can listen to a male professor and question him by phone, without having to contaminate themselves by being seen by him. When the first dozen women graduated from university in 1973, they were devastated to find that their names hadn't been printed on the commencement program. The old tradition, that it dishonors women to mention them, was depriving them of recognition they believed they'd earned. The women and their families protested, so a separate program was printed and a segregated graduation ceremony was held for the students' female relatives. . . .

But while the opening of women's universities widened access to higher learning for women, it also made the educational experience much shallower. Before 1962, many progressive Saudi families had sent their daughters abroad for education. They had returned to the kingdom not only with a degree but with experience of the outside world. . . . Now a whole generation of Saudi women have completed their education entirely within the country. . . .

Lack of opportunity for education abroad means that Saudi women are trapped in the confines of an education system that still lags men's. Subjects such as geology and petroleum engineering—tickets to influential jobs in Saudi Arabia's oil economy—remain closed to women. . . . Few women's colleges have their own libraries, and libraries shared with men's schools are either entirely off limits to women or open to them only one day per week. . . .

But women and men sit the same degree examinations. Professors quietly acknowledge the women's scores routinely outstrip the men's. "It's no surprise," said one woman professor. "Look at their lives. The boys have their cars, they can spend the evenings cruising the streets with their friends, sitting in cafés, buying black-market alcohol and drinking all night. What do the girls have? Four walls and their books. For them, education is everything."

Orthodox religious communities, women in Israel have achieved substantial equality with men and are active in politics, the professions, and even the armed forces. Golda Meir (1898–1978), prime minister of Israel from 1969 to 1974, became an international symbol of the ability of women to be world leaders.

In recent years, a more traditional view of women's role has tended to prevail in many Middle Eastern countries. Attacks by religious conservatives on the growing role of women contributed to the emotions underlying the Iranian Revolution of 1979. Iranian women were instructed to wear the veil and to dress modestly in public. Films produced in postrevolutionary Iran rarely featured women, and when they did, physical contact between men and women was prohibited. The events in Iran had repercussions in secular Muslim societies such as Egypt, Turkey, and far-off Malaysia, where women began to dress more modestly in public, and criticism of open sexuality in the media became increasingly frequent.

The most conservative nation by far remains Saudi Arabia, where women are not only segregated and expected to wear the veil in public, but are also restricted in education and forbidden to drive automobiles (see the box above). Still, women's rights have been extended in a few countries. In 1999, women obtained the right to vote in Kuwait, while they have been granted an equal right with their husbands to seek a divorce in Egypt. Even in Iran, women have many freedoms that they lacked before the twentieth century; for example, they can attend a university, receive military training, vote, practice birth control, and publish fiction. Recently, supporters of the moderate president Mohammed Khatemi have proposed that women be permitted to play a greater role in the political process. Some have even gone on the offensive to promote their cause. In Morocco, sociologist Fatima Mernissi has studied the sacred texts to demonstrate how Islam's male establishment has distorted the Prophet's message over the centuries as a political weapon to dominate women and keep them behind locked doors.

Contemporary Literature and Art in the Middle East

As in other areas of Asia and Africa, the encounter with the West in the nineteenth and twentieth centuries stimulated a cultural renaissance in the Middle East. Muslim authors translated Western works into Arabic and Persian and began to experiment with new literary forms.

Iran has produced one of the most prominent national literatures in the contemporary Middle East. Since World War II, Iranian literature has been hampered somewhat by political considerations, since it has been expected to serve first the Pahlavi monarchy and then the Islamic republic. Nevertheless, Iranian writers are among the most prolific in the region and often write in prose, which has finally been accepted as the equal of poetry. Perhaps the most outstanding Iranian author of the twentieth century was the short story writer Sadeq Hedayat. Hedayat was obsessed with the frailty and absurdity of life and wrote with compassion about the problems of ordinary human beings. Frustrated and disillusioned at the government's suppression of individual liberties, he committed suicide in 1951. Like Japan's Mishima Yukio, Hedayat later became a cult figure among his country's youth.

Despite the male-oriented character of Iranian society, many of the new writers have been women. Since the revolution, the veil (*chador*) has become the central metaphor in Iranian women's writing. Those who favor the veil praise it as the last bastion of defense against Western cultural imperialism. Behind the veil, the Islamic woman can breathe freely, unpolluted by foreign exploitation and moral corruption. Other Iranian women, however, consider the veil a "mobile prison" or an oppressive anachronism from the Dark Ages. As one writer, Sousan Azadi, expressed it, "As I pulled the chador over me, I felt a heaviness descending over me. I was hidden and in hiding. There was nothing visible left of Sousan Azadi. I felt like an animal of the light suddenly trapped in a cave. I was just another faceless Moslem woman carrying a whole inner world hidden inside the chador."[14] Whether or not they accept the veil, women writers are a vital part of contemporary Iranian literature.

Like Iran, Egypt in the twentieth century has experienced a flowering of literature accelerated by the establishment of the Egyptian republic in the early 1950s. The most illustrious contemporary Egyptian writer is Naguib Mahfouz, who won the Nobel Prize for literature in 1988. His *Cairo Trilogy* (1952) chronicles three generations of a merchant family in Cairo during the tumultuous years between the world wars. Mahfouz is particularly adept at blending panoramic historical events with the intimate lives of ordinary human beings. Unlike many other modern writers, his message is essentially optimistic and reflects his hope that religion and science can work together for the overall betterment of humankind. No woman writer has played a more active role in exposing the physical and psychological grievances of Egyptian women than Nawal el-Saadawi. For decades, she has battled against the injustices of religious fundamentalism and a male-dominated society—even enduring imprisonment for promoting her cause.

Although Israeli literature arises from a totally different tradition from that of its neighbors, it shares with them certain contemporary characteristics and a concern for ordinary human beings. Early writers identified with the aspirations of the new nation, trying to find a sense of order in the new reality, voicing terrors from the past and hopes for the future. Some contemporary Israeli authors, however, have refused to serve as spokespersons for Zionism and are speaking out on sensitive national issues. The internationally renowned novelist Amos Oz, for example, is a vocal supporter of peace with the Palestinians. Oz is a member of Peace Now and the author of a political tract titled *Israel, Palestine, and Peace*. In a recent interview, Oz accused both Ariel Sharon and Yasir Arafat of being "immovable, handcuffed to the past and to each other."[15] With the Arabs feeling victimized by colonialism and the Jews by Nazi Germany, each side believes that it alone is the rightful proprietor of ancient Palestine. For Oz, the only solution is compromise, which, however unsatisfactory for both sides, is preferable to mutual self-destruction.

As in other areas of the developing world, the reading of books has drastically declined in the Middle East, eclipsed by television and other forms of popular entertainment and discouraged by poverty and by government censorship reflecting political control or religious conservatism. The old maxim that "Cairo writes, Beirut publishes, and Baghdad reads" is no longer true. In Egypt, where even *The Tales from the 1001 Nights* is banned, the government censors most new fiction, while in Iraq, severe inflation has made the purchase price of books prohibitive. Another problem stems from the fact that the one common language of the Middle East—classical Arabic—is not conducive to expressing contemporary life, since it is as old-fashioned as Shakespearean English. Yet if they choose to write in their national Arabic dialects, authors greatly restrict their audience within the region.

Like literature, the art of the modern Middle East has been profoundly influenced by its exposure to Western culture. At first artists tended to imitate Western models, but later they began to experiment with national styles, returning to earlier forms for inspiration. Some emulated the writers in returning to the village to depict peasants and shepherds, but others followed international trends and attempted to express the alienation and disillusionment that characterize so much of modern life.

The popular music of the contemporary Middle East has also been strongly influenced by that of the modern

West, but to different degrees in different countries. In Israel, many contemporary young rock stars voice lyrics as irreverent toward the traditions of their elders as those of Europe and the United States. One idol of many Israeli young people, the rock star Aviv Ghefen, declares himself "a person of no values," and his music carries a shock value that attacks the country's political and social shibboleths. The rock music popular among Palestinians, on the other hand, makes greater use of Arab musical motifs and is closely tied to a political message. One recording, "The Song of the Engineer," lauds Yehia Ayash, a Palestinian accused of manufacturing many of the explosive devices used in terrorist attacks on Israeli citizens. The lyrics have their own shock value: "Spread the flame of revolution. Your explosive will wipe the enemy out, like a volcano, a torch, a banner." When one Palestinian rock leader from the Gaza Strip was asked why his group employed a musical style that originated in the West, he explained, "For us, this is a tool like any other. Young people in Gaza like our music, they listen to us, they buy our cassettes, and so they spread our message."

 # CONCLUSION

The Middle East, like the continent of Africa, is one of the most unstable regions in the world today. In part, this turbulence is due to the continued interference of outsiders attracted by the massive oil reserves under the parched wastes of the Arabian peninsula and in the vicinity of the Persian Gulf. Oil is indeed both a blessing and a curse to the peoples of the region.

Another factor contributing to the volatility of the Middle East is the tug-of-war between the sense of ethnic identity in the form of nationalism and the intense longing to be part of a broader Islamic community, a dream that dates back to the time of the prophet Muhammad.

The desire to create that community—a vision threatened by the presence of the alien state of Israel—inspired Gamal Abdul Nasser in the 1950s and Ayatollah Khomeini in the 1970s and 1980s and probably motivates many of the actions of Saddam Hussein and Osama bin Laden today.

A final reason for the turmoil currently affecting the Middle East is the intense debate over the role of religion in civil society. Although efforts in various Muslim countries to return to an allegedly purer form of Islam appear harsh and even repugnant to many observers, it is important to note that Muslim societies are not alone in deploring the sense of moral decline that is now allegedly taking place in societies throughout the world. Nor are they alone in advocating a restoration of traditional religious values as a means of reversing the trend. Movements dedicated to such purposes are appearing in many other societies (including, among others, Israel and the United States) and can be viewed as an understandable reaction to the rapid and often bewildering changes taking place in the contemporary world. Not infrequently, members of such groups turn to violence as a means of making their point.

Whatever the reasons, it is clear that a deep-seated sense of anger is surging through much of the Islamic world today, an anger that transcends specific issues like the situation in Iraq or the Arab-Israeli dispute. Although economic privation and political oppression are undoubtedly important factors, the roots of Muslim resentment, as historian Bernard Lewis has pointed out, lie in a historical sense of humiliation at the hands of a Western colonialism that first emerged centuries ago, when the Arab hegemony in the Mediterranean region was replaced by European domination, and culminated early in the twentieth century, when much of the Middle East was occupied by Western colonial regimes. Today the world is reaping the harvest of that long-cultivated bitterness, and the consequences cannot be foreseen.

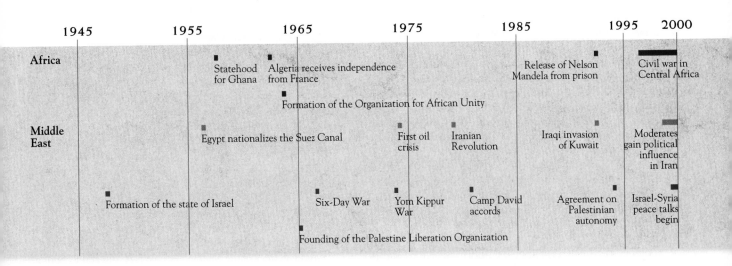

CHAPTER NOTES

1. Quoted in G.-C. M. Mutiso, *Socio-Political Thought in African Literature* (New York, 1974), p. 117.
2. Albert Ojuka, "Pedestrian, to Passing Benz-Man," quoted in Adrian Roscoe, *Uhuru's Fire: African Literature East to South* (Cambridge, 1977), p. 103.
3. *New York Times*, September 1, 1996.
4. Taban Lo Liyong, "Student's Lament," quoted in Roscoe, *Uhuru's Fire*, pp. 120–121.
5. Dan Agbee, quoted in *World Press Review*, August 1991, p. 16. Reprinted from *Newswatch* (Lagos).
6. Kenneth Little, *African Women in Towns: An Aspect of Africa's Social Revolution* (Cambridge, 1973), p. 6.
7. Abioseh Nicol, *A Truly Married Woman and Other Stories* (London, 1965), p. 12.
8. Ama Ata Aidoo, *No Sweetness Here* (New York, 1995), p. 136.

9. Gilles Médioni, "Stand Up, Africa!" *World Press Review*, July 2002, p. 34. Reprinted from *L'Express*.
10. Ngugi Wa Thiong'o, *Decolonising the Mind: The Politics of Language in African Literature* (Portsmouth, N.H., 1986), p. 103.
11. George Awoonor-Williams, *Rediscovery and Other Poems* (Ibadan, 1964), quoted in Mutiso, pp. 81–82.
12. Quoted in Roy R. Andersen, Robert F. Seibert, and Jon G. Wagner, *Politics and Change in the Middle East: Sources of Conflict and Accommodation*, 4th ed. (Englewood Cliffs, N.J., 1982), p. 51.
13. *New York Times*, July 18, 2000.
14. Sousan Azadi, with Angela Ferrante, *Out of Iran* (London, 1987), p. 223, quoted in *Stories by Iranian Women Since the Revolution*, ed. S. Sullivan (Austin, Tex., 1991), p. 13.
15. Amos Oz, interview, *Jim Lehrer NewsHour*, PBS, January 23, 2002.

SUGGESTED READING

For a general survey of contemporary African history, see R. Oliver, *The African Experience* (New York, 1992), which contains interesting essays on a variety of themes, and K. Shillington, *History of Africa* (New York, 1989), which takes a chronological and geographical approach and includes excellent maps and illustrations.

Two excellent treatments by preeminent historians of the African continent are B. Davidson, *Africa in History: Themes and Outlines*, rev. ed. (New York, 1991), and P. Curtin et al., *African History* (London, 1995).

On nationalist movements, see P. Gifford and W. R. Louis, eds., *The Transfer of Power in Africa* (New Haven, Conn., 1982), and J. D. Hargreaves, *Decolonisation in Africa* (London, 1988). For an African perspective, see K. Nkrumah, *Ghana* (London, 1959). Also see D. Birmingham, *Kwame Nkrumah: The Father of African Nationalism* (Athens, Ohio, 1998). For a poignant analysis of the hidden costs of nation building, see N. F. Mostert, *The Epic of South Africa's Creation and the Tragedy of the Xhosa People* (London, 1992). Also see A. Mazrui and M. Tidy, *Nationalism and New States in Africa* (Portsmouth, N.H., 1984), and S. Decalo, *Coups and Army Rule in Africa* (New Haven, Conn., 1990).

For a survey of economic conditions in Africa, see *Sub-Saharan Africa: From Crisis to Sustainable Growth* (Washington, D.C., 1989), issued by the World Bank. Also see A. O'Connor, *The African City* (London, 1983), and J. Illiffe, *The African Poor* (Cambridge, 1983).

For a survey of African literature, see L. S. Klein, ed., *African Literatures in the Twentieth Century: A Guide* (New York, 1986), and D. Wright, *New Directions in African Fiction* (New York, 1997). On art, see M. B. Visona et al., *A History of Art in Africa* (New York, 2000). Of the many short story collections showcasing different African authors, we recommend C. Achebe and C. L. Innes, eds., *The Heinemann Book of Contemporary Short Stories* (Portsmouth, N.H., 1992), and C. H. Bruner, ed., *The Heinemann Book of African Women's Writing* (Oxford, 1993).

For interesting analyses of women's issues in the Africa of this time frame, see C. Robertson and I. Berger, eds., *Women and Class in*

Africa (New York, 1986); S. B. Stichter and J. L. Parpart, eds., *Patriarchy and Class: African Women in the Home and the Workforce* (Boulder, Colo., 1988); and I. Berger and E. F. White, *Women in Sub-Saharan Africa* (Bloomington, Ind., 1999).

Finally, for contrasting views on the reasons for Africa's current difficulties, see J. Marah, *The African People in the Global Village: An Introduction to Pan-African Studies* (Lanham, Md., 1998), and G. Ayittey, *Africa in Chaos* (New York, 1998).

Good general surveys of the modern Middle East include A. Goldschmidt Jr., *A Concise History of the Middle East* (Boulder, Colo., 1991), and G. E. Perry, *The Middle East: Fourteen Islamic Centuries* (Elizabeth City, N.J., 1992).

On Israel and the Palestinian question, see B. Reich, *Israel: Land of Tradition and Conflict* (Boulder, Colo., 1985), and C. C. O'Brien, *The Siege: The Saga of Israel and Zionism* (New York, 1986). On U.S.-Israeli relations, see S. Green, *Living by the Sword: America and Israel in the Middle East, 1968–1987* (London, 1988). On the struggle for Jerusalem, see B. Wasserstein, *Divided Jerusalem: The Struggle for the Holy City* (New Haven, Conn., 2000).

The issue of oil is examined in G. Luciani, *The Oil Companies and the Arab World* (New York, 1984), and P. Odell, *Oil and World Power* (New York, 1986). Also see M. H. Kerr and El Sayed Yassin, eds., *Rich and Poor States in the Middle East: Egypt and the New Arab Order* (Boulder, Colo., 1985). On Egypt, see A. Goldschmidt Jr., *Modern Egypt: The Formation of a Nation-State* (Boulder, Colo., 1988).

On the Iranian Revolution, see S. Bakash, *The Reign of the Ayatollahs* (New York, 1984), and B. Rubin, *Iran Since the Revolution* (Boulder, Colo., 1985). On Ayatollah Khomeini's role and ideas, see H. Algar, *Islam and Revolution: The Writings and Declarations of Imam Khomeini* (Berkeley, Calif., 1981). The Iran-Iraq War is discussed in C. Davies, ed., *After the War: Iran, Iraq and the Arab Gulf* (Chichester, England, 1990), and S. C. Pelletiere, *The Iran-Iraq War: Chaos in a Vacuum* (New York, 1992).

On the politics of the Middle East, see J. A. Bill and R. Springborg, *Politics in the Middle East* (London, 1990), and R. R. Anderson, R. F. Seibert, and J. G. Wagner, *Politics and Change in the Middle East: Sources of Conflict and Accommodation* (Englewood Cliffs, N.J., 1993). For expert analysis on the current situation in the region, see B. Lewis, *What Went Wrong? Western Impact and Middle Eastern Response* (Oxford, 2001), and P. L. Bergen, *Holy War, Inc.: Inside the Secret World of Osama bin Laden* (New York, 2001).

Two excellent surveys of women in Islam from pre-Islamic society to the present are L. Ahmed, *Women and Gender in Islam: Historical Roots of a Modern Debate* (New Haven, Conn., 1993), and G. Nashat and J. E. Tucker, *Women in the Middle East and North Africa* (Bloomington, Ind., 1999). Also consult the more detailed G. Nashat, ed., *Women and Revolution in Iran* (Boulder, Colo., 1983);

M. Afkhami and E. Friedl, *In the Eye of the Storm: Women in Post-Revolutionary Iran* (Syracuse, N.Y., 1994); and W. Wiebke, *Women in Islam* (Princeton, N.J., 1995).

For a general anthology of Middle Eastern literature, see J. Kritzeck, *Modern Islamic Literature from 1800 to the Present* (New York, 1970). For a scholarly but accessible overview of Arabic literature, see M. M. Badawi, *A Short History of Modern Arab Literature* (Oxford, 1993). For Iranian literature, see M. Southgate, *Modern Persian Short Stories* (Washington, D.C., 1980), and S. Sullivan and F. Milani, *Stories by Iranian Women Since the Revolution* (Austin, Tex., 1991).

INFOTRAC COLLEGE EDITION

For additional reading, go to InfoTrac College Edition, your online research library at
http://web1.infotrac-college.com

Enter the search terms "developing countries" using the Subject Guide.

Enter the search term "Africa" using the Subject Guide.

Enter the search terms "Nelson Mandela" using the Subject Guide.

Enter the search terms "Israel history" using Keywords.

Enter the search term "Palestine" using the Subject Guide.

Courtesy of William J. Duiker

Chapter 29

TOWARD THE PACIFIC CENTURY?

FOCUS QUESTIONS

- How did Mahatma Gandhi's and Jawaharlal Nehru's goals for India differ, and what role has each leader's views played in shaping modern India?
- What problems has India faced since independence, and how have its leaders attempted to solve these problems?
- What problems have the nations of Southeast Asia faced since 1945, and how have they attempted to solve these problems?
- How did the Allied occupation after World War II change Japan's political and economic institutions, and what remained unchanged?
- What are the major developments in South Korea, Taiwan, Singapore, and Hong Kong since World War II?
- ➢ What factors have contributed to the economic success achieved by Japan and the "little tigers" in recent years? Are there some less beneficial consequences?

irst-time visitors to the Malaysian capital of Kuala Lumpur are astonished to observe a pair of twin towers thrusting up above the surrounding buildings into the clouds. The Petronas Towers rise 1,483 feet from ground level, leading to claims by Malaysian officials that they are the world's tallest buildings, at least for the time being.

More than an architectural achievement, the towers announced the emergence of Southeast Asia as a major player on the international scene. It is probably no accident that the foundations were laid on the site of the Selangor Cricket Club, symbol of colonial hegemony in Southeast Asia. "These towers," commented one local official, "will do wonders for Asia's self-esteem and confidence, which I think is very important, and which I think at this moment are at the point of takeoff."[1]

Slightly more than a year after that remark, Malaysia and several of its neighbors were mired in a financial crisis that threatened to derail their rapid advance to economic affluence and severely undermined the "self-esteem" that the Petronas Towers were meant to symbolize. That ironic reality serves as a warning to the region's leaders that the road to industrialized status is often strewn with hidden obstacles. At the moment, the building serves not as a symbol of the opening of a "Pacific century" but as a testament to the danger of hubris. •

SOUTH ASIA

In 1947, nearly two centuries of British colonial rule came to an end when two new independent nations, India and Pakistan, came into being. Under British authority, the subcontinent of South Asia had been linked ever more closely to the global capitalist economy. Yet as in other areas of Asia and Africa, the experience brought only limited benefits to the local peoples; little industrial development took place, and the bulk of the profits went into the pockets of Western entrepreneurs.

For half a century, nationalist forces had been seeking reforms in colonial policy and the eventual overthrow of colonial power. But the peoples of South Asia did not regain their independence until after World War II.

The End of the British Raj

During the 1930s, the nationalist movement in India was severely shaken by factional disagreements between Hindus and Muslims. The outbreak of World War II subdued these sectarian clashes, but they erupted again after the war ended in 1945. Battles between Hindus and Muslims broke out in several cities, and Mohammed Ali Jinnah, leader of the Muslim League, demanded the creation of a separate state for each. Meanwhile, the Labour Party, which had long been critical of the British colonial legacy on both moral and economic grounds, had come to power in Britain, and the new prime minister, Clement Attlee, announced that power would be transferred to "responsible Indian hands" by June 1948.

But the imminence of independence did not dampen communal strife. As riots escalated, the British reluctantly accepted the inevitability of partition and declared that on August 15, 1947, two independent nations—Hindu India and Muslim Pakistan—would be established. Pakistan would be divided between the main area of Muslim habitation in the Indus River valley in the west and a separate territory in east Bengal 2,000 miles to the east. Although Mahatma Gandhi warned that partition would provoke "an orgy of blood,"[2] he was increasingly regarded as a figure of the past, and his views were ignored.

The British instructed the rulers in the princely states to choose which state they would join by August 15, but

problems arose in predominantly Hindu Hyderabad, where the nawab was a Muslim, and mountainous Kashmir, where a Hindu prince ruled over a Muslim population. After independence was declared, the flight of millions of Hindus and Muslims across the borders led to violence and the death of more than a million people. One of the casualties was Gandhi, who was assassinated on January 30, 1948, as he was going to morning prayer. The assassin, a Hindu militant, was apparently motivated by Gandhi's opposition to a Hindu India.

Independent India

With independence, the Indian National Congress, now renamed the Congress Party, moved from opposition to the responsibility of power under Jawaharlal Nehru, the new prime minister. The prospect must have been intimidating. The vast majority of India's 400 million people were poor and illiterate. The new nation encompassed a bewildering number of ethnic groups and fourteen major languages. Although Congress leaders spoke bravely of building a new nation, Indian society still bore the scars of past wars and divisions.

The government's first problem was to resolve disputes left over from the transition period. The rulers of Hyderabad and Kashmir had both followed their own preferences rather than the wishes of their subject populations. Nehru was determined to include both states within India. In 1948, Indian troops invaded Hyderabad and annexed the area. India was also able to seize most of Kashmir, but at the cost of creating an intractable problem that has poisoned relations with Pakistan down to the present day.

AN EXPERIMENT IN DEMOCRATIC SOCIALISM

Under Nehru's leadership, India adopted a political system on the British model, with a figurehead president and a parliamentary form of government. A number of political parties operated legally, but the Congress Party, with its enormous prestige and charismatic leadership, was dominant at both the central and the local levels.

Nehru had been influenced by British socialism and patterned his economic policy roughly after the program of the British Labour Party. The state took over ownership of the major industries and resources, transportation, and utilities, while private enterprise was permitted at the local and retail levels. Farmland remained in private hands, but rural cooperatives were officially encouraged. The government also sought to avoid excessive dependence on foreign investment and technological assistance. All businesses were required by law to have majority Indian ownership.

In other respects, Nehru was a devotee of Western materialism. He was convinced that to succeed, India must

TWO VISIONS FOR INDIA

Although Jawaharlal Nehru and Mohandas Gandhi agreed on their desire for an independent India, their visions of the future of their homeland were dramatically different. Nehru favored industrialization to build material prosperity, whereas Gandhi praised the simple virtues of manual labor. The first excerpt is from a speech by Nehru; the second is from a letter written by Gandhi to Nehru.

NEHRU'S SOCIALIST CREED

I am convinced that the only key to the solution of the world's problems and of India's problems lies in socialism, and when I use this word I do so not in a vague humanitarian way but in the scientific economic sense. . . . I see no way of ending the poverty, the vast unemployment, the degradation and the subjection of the Indian people except through socialism. That involves vast and revolutionary changes in our political and social structure, the ending of vested interests in land and industry, as well as the feudal and autocratic Indian states system. That means the ending of private property, except in a restricted sense, and the replacement of the present profit system by a higher ideal of cooperative service. . . . In short, it means a new civilization, radically different from the present capitalist order. Some glimpse we can have of this new civilization in the territories of the U.S.S.R. Much has happened there which has pained me greatly and with which I disagree, but I look upon that great and fascinating unfolding of a new order and a new civilization as the most promising feature of our dismal age.

A LETTER TO JAWAHARLAL NEHRU

I believe that if India, and through India the world, is to achieve real freedom, then sooner or later we shall have to go and live in the villages—in huts, not in palaces. Millions of people can never live in cities and palaces in comfort and peace. Nor can they do so by killing one another, that is, by resorting to violence and untruth. . . . We can have the vision of . . . truth and nonviolence only in the simplicity of the villages. That simplicity resides in the spinning wheel and what is implied by the spinning wheel. . . .

You will not be able to understand me if you think that I am talking about the villages of today. My ideal village still exists only in my imagination. . . . In this village of my dreams the villager will not be dull—he will be all awareness. He will not live like an animal in filth and darkness. Men and women will live in freedom, prepared to face the whole world. There will be no plague, no cholera, and no smallpox. Nobody will be allowed to be idle or to wallow in luxury. Everyone will have to do body labor. Granting all this, I can still envisage a number of things that will have to be organized on a large scale. Perhaps there will even be railways and also post and telegraph offices. I do not know what things there will be or will not be. Nor am I bothered about it. If I can make sure of the essential thing, other things will follow in due course. But if I give up the essential thing, I give up everything.

---

industrialize. In advocating industrialization, Nehru departed sharply from Gandhi, who believed that materialism was morally corrupting and that only simplicity and nonviolence (as represented by the traditional Indian village and the symbolic spinning wheel) could save India, and the world itself, from self-destruction (see the box above).

The primary themes of Nehru's foreign policy were anticolonialism and antiracism. Under his guidance, India took a neutral stance in the Cold War and sought to provide leadership to all newly independent nations in Asia, Africa, and Latin America. India's neutrality put it at odds with the United States, which during the 1950s was trying to mobilize all nations against what it viewed as the menace of international communism.

Relations with Pakistan continued to be troubled. India refused to consider Pakistan's claim to Kashmir, even though the majority of the population there was Muslim. Tension between the two countries persisted, erupting into war in 1965. In 1971, when riots against the Pakistani government broke out in East Pakistan, India intervened on the side of East Pakistan, which declared its independence as the new nation of Bangladesh (see Map 29.1).

THE POST-NEHRU ERA

Nehru's death in 1964 aroused concern that Indian democracy was dependent on the Nehru mystique. When his successor, a Congress Party veteran, died in 1966, Congress leaders selected Nehru's daughter, Indira Gandhi (no relation to Mahatma Gandhi), as the new prime minister. Gandhi was inexperienced in politics, but she quickly showed the steely determination of her father.

Like Nehru, Gandhi embraced democratic socialism and a policy of neutrality in foreign affairs, but she was more activist than her father. To combat rural poverty, she nationalized banks, provided loans to peasants on easy terms, built low-cost housing, distributed land to the landless, and introduced electoral reforms to enfranchise the poor.

Gandhi was especially worried by India's growing population and in an effort to curb the growth rate adopted a policy of enforced sterilization. This policy proved unpopular, however, and, along with growing official corruption and Gandhi's authoritarian tactics, led to her defeat in the general election of 1975, the first time the Congress Party had failed to win a majority at the national level.

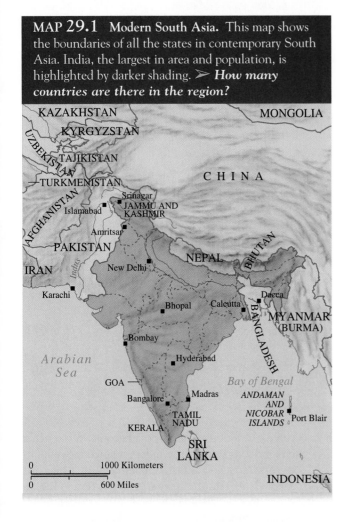

MAP 29.1 Modern South Asia. This map shows the boundaries of all the states in contemporary South Asia. India, the largest in area and population, is highlighted by darker shading. ➤ *How many countries are there in the region?*

were ethnically related to the majority population in southern India. The decision cost him his life: while campaigning for reelection in 1991, he was assassinated by a member of the Tiger organization. India faced the future without a member of the Nehru family as prime minister.

During the early 1990s, Congress remained the leading party, but the powerful hold it had once had on the Indian electorate was gone. New parties, such as the militantly Hindu Bharata Janata Party (BJP), actively vied with Congress for control of the central and state governments. Growing political instability at the center was accompanied by rising tensions between Hindus and Muslims.

When a coalition government formed under Congress leadership collapsed, the BJP, under Prime Minister A. B. Vajpayee, ascended to power and played on Hindu sensibilities to build its political base. Rajiv Gandhi's Italian-born wife Sonia has taken over the leadership of the Congress Party to improve its political fortunes.

The Land of the Pure: Pakistan Since Independence

When in August 1947, Pakistan achieved independence, it was, unlike its neighbor India, in all respects a new nation, based on religious conviction rather than historical or ethnic tradition. The unique state comprised two separate territories 2,000 miles apart. West Pakistan, including the Indus River basin and the West Punjab, was perennially short of water and was populated by dry crop farmers and peoples of the steppe. East Pakistan was made up of the marshy deltas of the Ganges and Brahmaputra Rivers. Densely populated with rice farmers, it was the home of the artistic and intellectual Bengalis.

Even though the new state was an essentially Muslim society, its first years were marked by intense internal conflicts over religious, linguistic, and regional issues. Mohammed Ali Jinnah's vision of a democratic state that would assure freedom of religion and equal treatment for all was opposed by those who advocated a state based on Islamic principles.

Even more dangerous was the division between east and west. Many in East Pakistan felt that the government, based in the west, ignored their needs. In 1952, riots erupted in East Pakistan over the government's decision to adopt Urdu, a language derived from Hindi and used by Muslims in northern India, as the national language of the entire country. Most East Pakistanis spoke Bengali, an unrelated language. Tensions persisted, and in March 1971, East Pakistan declared its independence as the new nation of Bangladesh. Pakistani troops attempted to restore central government authority in the capital of Dhaka, but rebel forces supported by India went on the offensive, and the government bowed to the inevitable and recognized independent Bangladesh.

The breakup of the union between East and West Pakistan undermined the fragile authority of the military

A minority government of procapitalist parties was formed, but within two years, Gandhi was back in power. She now faced a new challenge, however, in the rise of religious strife. The most dangerous situation was in the Punjab, where militant Sikhs were demanding autonomy or even independence from India. Gandhi did not shrink from a confrontation and attacked Sikh rebels hiding in their Golden Temple in the city of Amritsar. The incident aroused widespread anger among the Sikh community, and in 1984, Sikh members of Gandhi's personal bodyguard assassinated her.

By now, Congress politicians were convinced that the party could not remain in power without a member of the Nehru family at the helm. Gandhi's son Rajiv, a commercial airline pilot with little interest in politics, was persuaded to replace his mother as prime minister. Rajiv lacked the strong ideological and political convictions of his mother and grandfather and allowed a greater role for private enterprise. But his government was criticized for cronyism, inefficiency, and corruption, as well as insensitivity to the poor.

Rajiv Gandhi also sought to play a role in regional affairs, mediating a dispute between the government in Sri Lanka and Tamil rebels (known as the "Elam tigers") who regime that had ruled Pakistan since 1958 and led to its replacement by a civilian government under Zulfikar Ali Bhutto. But now religious tensions came to the fore, despite a new constitution that made a number of key concessions to conservative Muslims. In 1977, a new military government under General Zia Ul Ha'q came to power with a commitment to make Pakistan a truly Islamic state. Islamic law became the basis for social behavior as well as for the legal system. Laws governing the consumption of alcohol and the role of women were tightened in accordance with strict Muslim beliefs. But after Zia was killed in a plane crash, Pakistanis elected Benazir Bhutto, the daughter of Zulfikar Ali Bhutto and a supporter of secularism who had been educated in the United States. She too was removed from power by a military regime, in 1990, on charges of incompetence and corruption. Reelected in 1993, she attempted to crack down on opposition forces but was removed once again amid renewed charges of official corruption. Her successor soon came under fire for the same reason and in 1999 was ousted by a military coup led by General Pervaiz Musharraf, who promised to restore political stability and honest government.

In September 2001, Pakistan became the focus of international attention when a coalition of forces arrived in Afghanistan to overthrow the Taliban regime and destroy the al-Qaeda terrorist network. Despite considerable support for the Taliban among the local population, President Musharraf pledged his help in bringing terrorists to justice. He also promised to return his country to the secular principles espoused by Mohammed Ali Jinnah. His situation was complicated by renewed tensions with India over Kashmir and a series of violent clashes between Muslims and Hindus in India.

Poverty and Pluralism in South Asia

The leaders of the new states that emerged in South Asia after World War II faced a number of problems. The peoples of South Asia were still overwhelmingly poor and illiterate, while the sectarian, ethnic, and cultural divisions that had plagued Indian society for centuries had not dissipated.

THE POLITICS OF COMMUNALISM

Perhaps the most sincere effort to create democratic instititutions was in India, where the new constitution called for social justice, liberty, equality of status and opportunity, and fraternity. All citizens were guaranteed protection from discrimination on the grounds of religious belief, race, caste, sex, or place of birth.

In theory, then, India became a full-fledged democracy on the British parliamentary model. In actuality, a number of distinctive characteristics made the system less than fully democratic in the Western sense but may also have enabled

Chronology

SOUTH ASIA

India and Pakistan become independent	1947
Assassination of Mahatma Gandhi	1948
Death of Jawaharlal Nehru	1964
Indo-Pakistani War	1965
Indira Gandhi elected prime minister	1966
Bangladesh declares its independence	1971
Assassination of Indira Gandhi	1984
Rajiv Gandhi assassinated	1991
Destruction of mosque at Ayodhya	1992
Benazir Bhutto removed from power in Pakistan	1997
Military coup overthrows civilian government in Pakistan	1999
U.S.-led forces oust Taliban in Afghanistan	2001

it to survive. As we have seen, India became in essence a one-party state. By leading the independence movement, the Congress Party had amassed massive public support, which enabled it to retain its preeminent position in Indian politics for three decades. The party also avoided being identified as a party exclusively for the Hindu majority by including prominent non-Hindus among its leaders and favoring measures to protect minority groups such as Sikhs and Muslims from discrimination.

After Nehru's death in 1964, however, problems emerged that had been disguised by his adept maneuvering. Part of the problem was the familiar one of a party too long in power. Party officials became complacent and all too easily fell prey to the temptations of corruption and pork-barrel politics.

Another problem was communalism. Beneath the surface unity of the new republic lay age-old ethnic, linguistic, and religious divisions. Because of India's vast size and complex history, no national language had ever emerged. Hindi was the most prevalent, but it was the native language of less than one-third of the population. During the colonial period, English had served as the official language of government, and many non-Hindi speakers suggested making it the official language. But English was spoken only by the educated elite, and it represented an affront to national pride. Eventually, India recognized fourteen official tongues, making the parliament sometimes sound like the Tower of Babel.

Divisiveness increased after Nehru's death, and under his successors, official corruption grew. Only the lack of appeal of its rivals and the Nehru family charisma carried on by his daughter Indira Gandhi kept the party in power. But she was unable to prevent the progressive disintegration of the party's power base at the state level, where regional or ideological parties won the allegiance of voters by exploiting ethnic or social revolutionary themes.

During the 1980s, religious tensions began to intensify, not only among Sikhs in the northwest but also between Hindus and Muslims. As we have seen, Gandhi's uncompromising approach to Sikh separatism led to her assassination in 1987. Under her son, Rajiv Gandhi, Hindu militants at Ayodhya, in northern India, demanded the destruction of a mosque built on the alleged site of King Rama's birthplace, where a Hindu temple had previously existed. In 1992, Hindu demonstrators destroyed the mosque and erected a temporary temple at the site, provoking clashes between Hindus and Muslims throughout the country. In protest, rioters in neighboring Pakistan destroyed a number of Hindu shrines in that country.

In recent years, communal divisions have intensified, as militant Hindu groups agitate for a state that caters to the Hindu majority, now numbering more than 700 million people. In the spring of 2002, violence between Hindus and Muslims flared up again over plans by Hindu activists to build a permanent temple to Rama at the site of the destroyed mosque at Ayodhya.

THE ECONOMY

Nehru's answer to the social and economic inequality that had long afflicted the subcontinent was socialism. He instituted a series of five-year plans, which led to the creation of a relatively large and reasonably efficient industrial sector, centered on steel, vehicles, and textiles. Industrial production almost tripled between 1950 and 1965, and per capita income rose by 50 percent between 1950 and 1980, although it was still less than $300 (in U.S. dollars).

By the 1970s, however, industrial growth had slowed. The lack of modern infrastructure was a problem, as was the rising price of oil, most of which had to be imported. The relative weakness of the state-owned sector, which grew at an annual rate of only about 2 percent in the 1950s and 1960s, versus 5 percent for the private sector, also became a serious obstacle.

India's major economic weakness, however, was in agriculture. At independence, mechanization was almost unknown, fertilizer was rarely used, and most farms were small and uneconomical because of the Hindu tradition of dividing the land equally among all male children. As a result, the vast majority of the Indian people lived in conditions of abject poverty. Landless laborers outnumbered landowners by almost two to one. The government attempted to relieve the problem by redistributing land to the poor, limiting the size of landholdings, and encouraging farmers to form voluntary cooperatives. But all three programs ran into widespread opposition and apathy.

Another problem was overpopulation. Even before independence, the country had had difficulty supporting its people. In the 1950s and 1960s, the population grew by more than 2 percent annually, twice the nineteenth-century rate. Beginning in the 1960s, the Indian government sought to curb population growth. Indira Gandhi instituted a program combining monetary rewards and compulsory sterilization. Males who had fathered too many children were sometimes forced to undergo a vasectomy. Popular resistance undermined the program, however, and the goals were scaled back in the 1970s. As a result, India has made little progress in holding down its burgeoning population, now estimated at more than one billion. One factor in the continued growth has been a decline in the death rate, especially the rate of infant mortality. Nevertheless, as a result of media popularization and better government programs, the trend today, even in poor rural villages, is toward smaller families. The average number of children a woman bears has been reduced from six in 1950 to three today. As has occurred elsewhere, the decline in family size began among the educated and is gradually spreading throughout Indian society.

The "green revolution" that began in the 1960s helped reduce the severity of the population problem. The introduction of more productive, disease-resistant strains of rice and wheat doubled grain production between 1960 and 1980. But the green revolution also increased rural inequality. Only the wealthier farmers were able to purchase the necessary fertilizer, while poor peasants were often driven off the land. Millions fled to the cities, where they lived in vast slums, working at menial jobs or even begging for a living.

After the death of Indira Gandhi in 1984, her son Rajiv proved more receptive to foreign investment and a greater role for the private sector in the economy. India began to export more manufactured goods, including computer software. The pace of change has accelerated under Rajiv Gandhi's successors, who have continued to transfer state-run industries to private hands. These policies have stimulated the growth of a prosperous new middle class, now estimated at more than 100 million. Consumerism has soared, and sales of television sets, automobiles, videocassette recorders, and telephones have increased dramatically. Equally important, Western imports are being replaced by new products manufactured in India with Indian brand names.

Nevertheless, Nehru's dream of a socialist society remains strong. State-owned enterprises still produce about half of all domestic goods, and high tariffs continue to stifle imports. Nationalist parties have played on the widespread fear of foreign economic influence to force the

SAY NO TO MCDONALD'S AND KFC!

One of the consequences of Rajiv Gandhi's decision to deregulate the Indian economy has been an increase in the presence of foreign corporations, including U.S. fast-food restaurant chains. Their arrival set off a storm of protest in India: from environmentalists concerned that raising grain for chickens is an inefficient use of land, from religious activists angry at the killing of animals for food, and from nationalists anxious to protect the domestic market from foreign competition. The author of this piece, which appeared in the Hindustan Times, was Maneka Gandhi, a daughter-in-law of Indira Gandhi and a one-time minister of the environment who has emerged as a prominent rival of Congress Party president Sonia Gandhi.

WHY INDIA DOESN'T NEED FAST FOOD

India's decision to allow Pepsi Foods Ltd. to open 60 restaurants in India—30 each of Pizza Hut and Kentucky Fried Chicken—marks the first entry of multinational, meat-based junk-food chains into India. If this is allowed to happen, at least a dozen other similar chains will very quickly arrive, including the infamous McDonald's.

The implications of allowing junk-food chains into India are quite stark. As the name denotes, the foods served at Kentucky Fried Chicken (KFC) are chicken-based and fried. This is the worst combination possible for the body and can create a host of health problems, including obesity, high cholesterol, heart ailments, and many kinds of cancer. Pizza Hut products are a combination of white flour, cheese, and meat—again, a combination likely to cause disease. . . .

Then there is the issue of the environmental impact of junk-food chains. Modern meat production involves misuse of crops, water, energy, and grazing areas. In addition, animal agriculture produces surprisingly large amounts of air and water pollution.

KFC and Pizza Hut insist that their chickens be fed corn and soybeans. Consider the diversion of grain for this purpose. As the outlets of KFC and Pizza Hut increase in number, the poultry industry will buy up more and more corn to feed the chickens, which means that the corn will quickly disappear from the villages, and its increased price will place it out of reach for the common man. Turning corn into junk chicken is like turning gold into mud. . . .

It is already shameful that, in a country plagued by famine and flood, we divert 37 percent of our arable land to growing animal fodder. Were all of that grain to be consumed directly by humans, it would nourish five times as many people as it does after being converted into meat, milk, and eggs. . . .

Of course, it is not just the KFC and Pizza Hut chains of Pepsi Foods Ltd. that will cause all of this damage. Once we open India up by allowing these chains, dozens more will be eagerly waiting to come in. Each city in America has an average of 5,000 junk-food restaurants [sic]. Is that what we want for India?

---

cancellation of some contracts and the relocation of some foreign firms. A combination of religious and environmental groups attempted unsuccessfully to prevent Kentucky Fried Chicken from establishing outlets in major Indian cities (see the box above).

As in the industrialized countries of the West, economic growth has been accompanied by environmental damage. Water and air pollution has led to illness and death for many people, and an environmental movement has emerged. Some critics, reflecting the traditional anti-imperialist attitude of Indian intellectuals, blame Western capitalist corporations for the problem, as in the highly publicized case of leakage from a foreign-owned chemical plant at Bhopal. Much of the problem, however, comes from state-owned factories erected with Soviet aid. And not all the environmental damage can be ascribed to industrialization. The Ganges River is so polluted by human overuse that it is risky for Hindu believers to bathe in it.

Moreover, many Indians have not benefited from the new prosperity. Nearly one-third of the population lives below the national poverty line. Millions continue to live in urban slums, such as the famous "City of Joy" in Calcutta, and most farm families remain desperately poor. Despite the socialist rhetoric of India's leaders, the inequality of wealth in India

FETCHING WATER AT THE VILLAGE WELL. The scarcity of water will surely become one of the planet's most crucial problems in the twenty-first century. It will affect all nations, developed and developing, rich and poor. Although many Indians live with an inadequate water supply, these women are fortunate to have a well in their village. More typical is the image of the Indian woman, dressed in a colorful *sari*, children encircling her as she heads to her distant home on foot, carrying a heavy pail of water on her head.

is as pronounced as it is in capitalist nations in the West. Indeed, India has been described as two nations: an educated urban India of 100 million people surrounded by over 900 million impoverished peasants in the countryside.

CASTE, CLASS, AND GENDER

Drawing generalizations about the life of the average Indian is difficult because of ethnic, religious, and caste differences, which are compounded by the vast gulf between town and country.

Although the constitution of 1950 guaranteed equal treatment and opportunity for all, regardless of caste, and prohibited discrimination based on untouchability, prejudice is hard to eliminate. Untouchability persists, particularly in the villages, where *harijans*, now called *dalits*, still perform menial tasks and are often denied fundamental human rights.

In general, urban Indians appear less conscious of caste distinctions. Material wealth rather than caste identity is increasingly defining status. Still, color consciousness based on the age-old distinctions between upper-class Aryans and lower-class Dravidians remains strong. Class-conscious Hindus still express a distinct preference for light-skinned marital partners.

In recent years, low-caste Indians (who represent more than 80 percent of the voting public) have begun to demand affirmative action to relieve their disabilities and give them a more equal share in the national wealth. Officials at U.S. consulates in India have noticed a rise in visa applications from members of the *brahmin* caste, who claim that they have "no future" in the new India. But opponents of such measures are often not reluctant to fight back. Phoolan Devi, known as the "bandit queen," spent several years in jail for taking part in the murder of twenty

men from a landowning caste who had allegedly gang-raped her when she was an adolescent. Her campaign for office during the 1996 elections was the occasion of violent arguments between supporters and opponents, and she was assassinated by an unknown assailant in 2001.

In few societies was the life of women more restricted than in traditional India. Hindu favoritism toward men was compounded by the Muslim custom of *purdah* to create a society in which males were dominant in virtually all aspects of life. Females received no education and had no inheritance rights. They were restricted to the home and tied to their husbands for life. Widows were expected to shave their heads and engage in a life of religious meditation or even to immolate themselves on their husband's funeral pyre.

After independence, India's leaders sought to equalize treatment of the sexes. The constitution expressly forbade discrimination based on sex and called for equal pay for equal work. Laws prohibited child marriage, *sati*, and the payment of a dowry by the bride's family. Women were encouraged to attend school and enter the labor market.

Such laws, along with the dynamics of economic and social change, have had a major impact on the lives of many Indian women. Middle-class women in urban areas are much more likely to seek employment outside the home, and many hold managerial and professional positions. Some Indian women, however, choose to play a dual role—a modern one in their work and in the marketplace and a more submissive, traditional one at home (see the box on p. 856).

Such attitudes are also reflected in the Indian movie industry, where aspiring actresses must often brave family disapproval to enter the entertainment world. Before World War II, female actors were routinely viewed as prostitutes or "loose women," and such views are still prevalent among conservative Indian families. Even Karisma Kapoor, one of India's current film stars and a

YOUNG HINDU BRIDE IN GOLD BANGLES. Awaiting the marriage ceremony, a young bride sits with the female relatives of her family at the Meenakshi Hindu temple, one of the largest in southern India. Although child marriage is illegal, Indian girls are still married at a young age. With the marital union arranged by the parents, this young bride has perhaps never met the groom. Bedecked in gold jewelry and rich silks—part of her dowry—she nervously awaits the priest's blessing before she moves to her husband's home. There she will begin a life of servitude to her in-laws' family.

Courtesy of William J. Duiker

A Critique of Western Feminism

Organized efforts to protect the rights of women have been under way in India since the 1970s, when the Progressive Organization for Women (POW) instituted a campaign against sexual harassment and other forms of discrimination against women in Indian society. Like many of their counterparts in other parts of Asia and Africa, however, many activists for women's rights in India are critical of Western feminism, charging that it is irrelevant to their own realities. Although Indian feminists feel a bond with their sisters all over the world, they insist on resolving Indian problems with Indian solutions. The author of this editorial is Madhu Kishwar, founder and editor of a women's journal in New Delhi.

FINDING INDIAN SOLUTIONS TO WOMEN'S PROBLEMS

Western feminism, exported to India and many other Third World countries in recent decades, has brought with it serious problems.

As products of a more homogenized culture, most Western feminists assume women's aspirations the world over must be quite similar. Yet a person's idea of a good life and her aspirations are closely related to what is valued in her particular society. This applies to feminism itself. An offshoot of individualism and liberalism, it posits that each individual is responsible primarily to herself. . . .

In societies like India, most of us find it difficult to tune in to this extreme individualism. For instance, most Indian women are unwilling to assert rights in a way that estranges them not just from their family but also from their larger community. . . .

This isn't slavery to social opinion. Rather, many of us believe life is a poor thing if our own dear ones don't honor and celebrate our rights, if our freedom cuts us off from others. In our culture, both men and women are taught to value the interests of our families more than our self-interest. . . .

Cultural issues aside, my most fundamental reservation regarding feminism is that it has strengthened the tendency among India's Western-educated elites to adopt the statist authoritarian route to social reform. The characteristic feminist response to most social issues affecting women—in the workplace, in the media, in the home—is to demand more and more stringent laws. . . .

But dearly held and deeply cherished cultural norms cannot be changed simply by applying the instruments of state repression through legal punishment. Social reform is too complex and important a matter to be left to the police and courts. The best of laws will tend to fail if social opinion is contrary to them. Therefore, the statist route of using laws as a substitute for creating a new social consensus about women's rights tends to be counterproductive.

---

member of the Kapoor clan, which has produced several generations of actors, had to defy her family's ban on its women's entering show business.

Nothing more strikingly indicates the changing role of women in South Asia than the fact that in recent years, three of the major countries in the area—India, Pakistan, and Sri Lanka—have had women prime ministers. It is worthy of mention, however, that all three—Indira Gandhi, Benazir Bhutto, and Srimivao Bandaranaike—came from prominent political families and owed their initial success to a husband or a father who had served as prime minister before them.

Like other aspects of life, the role of women has changed much less in rural areas. In the early 1960s, many villagers still practiced the institution of *purdah*. Female children are still much less likely to receive an education. The overall literacy rate in India today is less than 40 percent, but it is undoubtedly much lower among women. Laws relating to dowry, child marriage, and inheritance are routinely ignored in the countryside. There have been a few highly publicized cases of *sati*, although undoubtedly more women die of mistreatment at the hands of their husband or of other members of his family. In a few instances, widows have been forcibly thrown on the funeral pyre by their in-laws.

Perhaps the most tragic aspect of continued sexual discrimination in India is the high mortality rate among girls. One-quarter of the female children born in India die before the age of fifteen as a result of neglect or even infanticide. Others are aborted before birth after gender-detection examinations.

South Asian Art and Literature Since Independence

Recent decades have witnessed a prodigious outpouring of literature in India. Most works have been written in one of the Indian languages and have not been translated into a foreign tongue. Fortunately, however, many authors choose to write in English. Known as Indo-Anglian literature, such works are written primarily for the Indian elite or for foreign audiences. For that reason, some critics charge that Indo-Anglian literature lacks authenticity.

Because of the vast quantity of works published (India is currently the third-largest publisher of English-language books in the world), only a few of the most prominent fiction writers can be mentioned here. Anita Desai (b. 1937) was one of the first prominent female writers in contemporary India. Her writing focuses on the struggle of Indian women to achieve a degree of independence. In her first novel, *Cry, the Peacock,* the heroine finally seeks liberation by murdering her husband, preferring freedom at any cost to remaining a captive of traditional society.

The best-known female writer in South Asia today is Taslima Nasrin (b. 1962) of Bangladesh. She first became famous when she was sentenced to death for her novel *Shame* (1993), in which she criticized official persecution of the Hindu minority. An outspoken feminist, she is critical of Islam for obstructing human progress and women's equality. She now lives in exile in Europe.

The most controversial writer in India today is Salman Rushdie (b. 1947). In *Midnight's Children*, published in 1980, the author linked his protagonist, born on the night of independence, to the history of modern India, its achievements and its frustrations. Like his contemporaries Günter Grass and Gabriel García Márquez, Rushdie used the technique of magical realism to jolt his audience into a recognition of the inhumanity of modern society and the need to develop a sense of moral concern for the fate of the Indian people and for the world as a whole.

Rushdie's later novels have tackled such problems as religious intolerance, political tyranny, social injustice, and greed and corruption. His attack on Islamic fundamentalism in *The Satanic Verses* (1988) won plaudits from literary critics but provoked widespread criticism among Muslims, including a death sentence by Ayatollah Khomeini in Iran. *The Moor's Last Sigh* (1995), which focuses on the alleged excesses of Hindu nationalism, has been banned in India.

Like Chinese and Japanese artists, Indian artists have agonized over how best to paint with a modern yet indigenous mode of expression. During the colonial period, Indian art went in several directions at once. One school of painters favored traditional themes; another experimented with a colorful primitivism founded on folk art.

Many Indian artists painted representational social art extolling the suffering and silent dignity of India's impoverished millions. After 1960, however, most Indian artists adopted abstract art as their medium. Surrealism in particular, with its emphasis on spontaneity and the unconscious, appeared closer to the Hindu tradition of favoring intuition over reason. Yet Indian artists are still struggling to find the ideal way to be both modern and Indian.

Gandhi's Vision

Indian society looks increasingly Western in form, if not in content. As in a number of other Asian and African societies, the distinction between traditional and modern, or native and westernized, sometimes seems to be a simple dichotomy between rural and urban. The major cities appear modern and westernized, but the villages have changed little since precolonial days.

Yet traditional practices appear to be more resilient in India than in many other societies, and the result is often a synthesis rather than a clash between conflicting institutions and values. Unlike China, India has not rejected its past but merely adjusted it to meet the needs of the present. Clothing styles in the streets, where the *sari* and *dhoti* continue to be popular; religious practices in the temples; and social relationships in the home all testify to the importance of tradition in India.

One disadvantage of the eclectic approach, which seeks to blend the old and the new rather than choosing one over the other, is that sometimes contrasting traditions cannot be reconciled. Such was the lesson of the failed experiment

❧ **NO ROOM IN PARADISE?**
The color and diversity of popular Hinduism are nowhere more fully displayed than on the *gopuram*, or gate tower, of the modern Hindu temple. The celestial figures shown here in rich profusion are located on the tower surmounting the entrance gate of a temple devoted to Siva in the southern Indian city of Madras. Depicting the various Hindu myths, each deity appeals to the needs and devotion of the believers. Often depicted as couples, these gods and goddesses represent the ideal physical and spiritual union, which is to be emulated by the faithful.

Courtesy of William J. Duiker

of self-strengthening in late nineteenth-century China (see Chapter 21). In his book *India: A Wounded Civilization*, V. S. Naipaul, a West Indian of Indian descent, charged that Mahatma Gandhi's glorification of poverty and the simple Indian village was an obstacle to efforts to overcome the poverty, ignorance, and degradation of India's past and build a prosperous modern society. Gandhi's vision of a spiritual India, Naipaul complained, was a balm for defeatism and an excuse for failure.

Certainly, India faces a difficult dilemma. Some problems are undoubtedly a consequence of the colonial era, but the British cannot be blamed for all of the country's economic and social ills. To build a democratic, prosperous society, the Indian people must discard many of their traditional convictions and customs. Belief in karma and inherent caste distinctions are incompatible with the democratic belief in equality before the law. These traditional beliefs also undercut the work ethic and the modern sentiment of nationalism.

So long as Indians accept their fate as predetermined, they will find it difficult to change their environment and create a new society. Yet their traditional beliefs provide a measure of identity and solace often lacking in other societies, where such traditional spiritual underpinnings have eroded. Despite their difficulties, the Indian people appear, at least on the surface, to be reasonably happy and content with their lot. Destroying India's traditional means of coping with a disagreeable reality without changing that reality would be cruel indeed.

SOUTHEAST ASIA

As we have seen (see Chapter 24), Japanese wartime occupation had a great impact on attitudes among the peoples of Southeast Asia. It demonstrated the vulnerability of colonial rule in the region and showed that an Asian power could defeat Europeans. The Allied governments themselves also contributed—sometimes unwittingly—to rising aspirations for independence by promising self-determination for all peoples at the end of the war. Although Winston Churchill later said that the Atlantic Charter did not apply to the colonial peoples, it would be difficult to put the genie back in the bottle again.

Some did not try. In July 1946, the United States granted total independence to the Philippines. The Americans maintained a military presence on the islands, however, and U.S. citizens retained economic and commercial interests in the new country.

The British, too, under the Labour Party, were willing to bring an end to a century of imperialism in the region. In 1948, the Union of Burma received its independence. Malaya's turn came in 1957, after a Communist guerrilla movement had been suppressed.

The French and the Dutch, however, both regarded their colonies in the region as economic necessities as well as symbols of national grandeur and refused to turn them over to nationalist movements at the end of the war. The Dutch attempted to suppress a rebellion in the East Indies led by Sukarno, leader of the Indonesian Nationalist Party. But the United States, which feared a Communist victory there, pressured the Dutch to grant independence to Sukarno and his non-Communist forces, and in 1950 the Dutch finally agreed to recognize the new Republic of Indonesia.

The situation was somewhat different in Vietnam, where the Communists seized power throughout most of the country. After the French refused to recognize the new government and reimposed their rule, war broke out in December 1946. At the time it was only an anticolonial war, but it would soon become much more (see Chapter 25).

The Era of Independent States

Many of the leaders of the newly independent states in Southeast Asia (see Map 29.2) admired Western political institutions and hoped to adapt them to their own countries. New constitutions were patterned on Western democratic models, and multiparty political systems quickly sprang into operation.

THE SEARCH FOR A NEW POLITICAL CULTURE

By the 1960s, most of these budding experiments in pluralist democracy had been abandoned or were under serious threat. Some had been replaced by military or one-party autocratic regimes. In Burma, a moderate government based on the British parliamentary system and dedicated to Buddhism and nonviolent Marxism had given way to a military government. In Thailand, too, the military now ruled. In the Philippines, President Ferdinand Marcos discarded democratic restraints and established his own centralized control. In South Vietnam, Ngo Dinh Diem and his successors paid lip service to the Western democratic model but ruled by authoritarian means.

One problem faced by most of these states was that independence had not brought material prosperity or ended economic inequality and the domination of the local economies by foreign interests. Most economies in the region were still characterized by tiny industrial sectors; they lacked technology, educational resources, capital investment, and leaders trained in developmental skills.

The presence of widespread ethnic, linguistic, cultural, and economic differences also made the transition to Western-style democracy difficult. In Malaya, for example, the majority Malays—most of whom were farmers—feared economic and political domination by the local Chinese minority, who were much more experienced in

THE GOLDEN THROAT OF
PRESIDENT SUKARNO

resident Sukarno of Indonesia was a spellbinding speaker and a charismatic leader of his nation's struggle for independence. These two excerpts are from speeches in which Sukarno promoted two of his favorite projects: Indonesian nationalism and "guided democracy." The force that would guide Indonesia, of course, was to be Sukarno himself.

SUKARNO ON INDONESIAN GREATNESS

What was Indonesia in 1945? What was our nation then? It was only two things, only two things. A flag and a song. That is all. (Pause, finger held up as afterthought.) But no, I have omitted the main ingredient. I have missed the most important thing of all. I have left out the burning fire of freedom and independence in the breast and heart of every Indonesian. That is the most important thing—this is the vital chord—the spirit of our people, the spirit and determination to be free. This was our nation in 1945—the spirit of our people!

And what are we today? We are a great nation. We are bigger than Poland. We are bigger than Turkey. We have more people than Australia, than Canada, we are bigger in area and have more people than Japan. In population now we are the fifth-largest country in the world. In area, we are even bigger than the United States of America. The American Ambassador, who is here with us, admits this. Of course, he points out that we have a lot of water in between our thousands of islands. But I say to him—America has a lot of mountains and deserts, too!

SUKARNO ON GUIDED DEMOCRACY

Indonesia's democracy is not liberal democracy. Indonesian democracy is not the democracy of the world of Montaigne or Voltaire. Indonesia's democracy is not à la America, Indonesia's democracy is not the Soviet—NO! Indonesia's democracy is the democracy which is implanted in the breasts of the Indonesian people, and it is that which I have tried to dig up again, and have put forward as an offering to you. . . . If you, especially the undergraduates, are still clinging to and being borne along the democracy made in England, or democracy made in France, or democracy made in America, or democracy made in Russia, you will become a nation of copyists!

---

industry and commerce. In 1961, the Federation of Malaya, whose ruling party was dominated by Malays, integrated former British possessions on the island of Borneo into the new Union of Malaysia in a move to increase the non-Chinese proportion of the country's population. Yet periodic conflicts persisted as the Malaysian government attempted to guarantee Malay control over politics and a larger role in the economy.

The most publicized example of a failed experiment in democracy was in Indonesia. In 1950, the new leaders drew up a constitution creating a parliamentary system under a titular presidency. Sukarno was elected the first president. A spellbinding orator, Sukarno played a major role in creating a sense of national identity among the disparate peoples of the Indonesian archipelago (see the box above).

In the late 1950s, Sukarno, exasperated at the incessant maneuvering among devout Muslims, Communists, and the army, dissolved the constitution and attempted to rule on his own through what he called "guided democracy." As he described it, guided democracy was closer to Indonesian traditions and superior to the Western variety. The weakness of the latter was that it allowed the majority to dominate the minority, whereas guided democracy would reconcile different opinions and points of view in a government operated by consensus. Highly suspicious of the West, Sukarno nationalized foreign-owned enterprises and sought economic aid from China and the Soviet Union while relying for domestic support on the Indonesian Communist Party.

The army and conservative Muslims resented Sukarno's increasing reliance on the Communists, and the Muslims were further upset by his refusal to consider a state based on Islamic principles. In 1965, military officers launched a coup d'etat that provoked a mass popular uprising, which resulted in the slaughter of several hundred thousand suspected Communists, many of whom were overseas Chinese, long distrusted by the Muslim majority. In 1967, a military government under General Suharto was installed.

The new government made no pretensions of reverting to democratic rule, but it did restore good relations with the West and sought foreign investment to repair the country's ravaged economy. But it also found it difficult to placate Muslim demands for an Islamic state. In a few areas, including western Sumatra, militant Muslims took up arms against the state.

The one country in Southeast Asia that explicitly rejected the Western model was North Vietnam. Its leaders opted for the Stalinist pattern of national development, based on Communist Party rule and socialist forms of ownership. In 1958, stimulated by the success of collectivization in neighboring China, the government launched a three-year plan to lay the foundation for a socialist society. Collective farms were established, and all industry and commerce above the family level were nationalized.

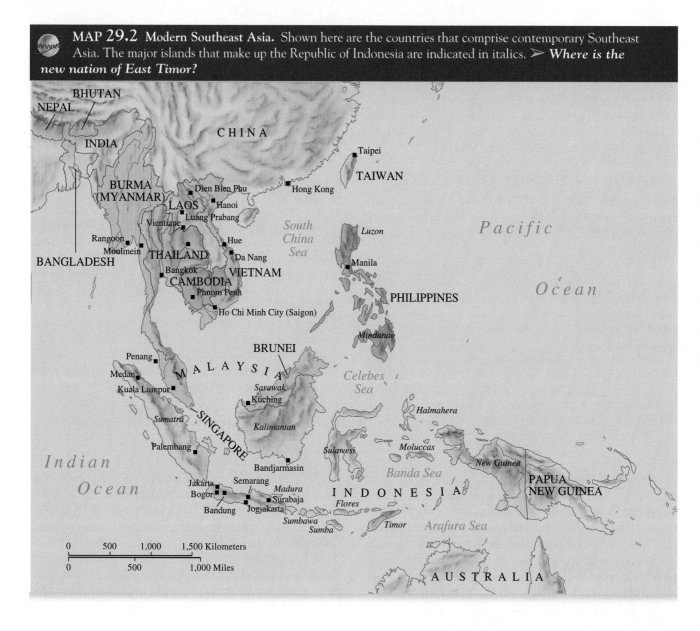

MAP 29.2 Modern Southeast Asia. Shown here are the countries that comprise contemporary Southeast Asia. The major islands that make up the Republic of Indonesia are indicated in italics. ➤ *Where is the new nation of East Timor?*

RECENT TRENDS TOWARD DEMOCRACY

In recent years, some Southeast Asian societies have shown signs of evolving toward more democratic forms. In the Philippines, the dictatorial Marcos regime was overthrown by a massive public uprising in 1986 and replaced by a democratically elected government under President Corazon Aquino, the widow of a popular politician assassinated a few years earlier. Aquino was unable to resolve many of the country's chronic economic and social difficulties, however, and political stability remains elusive, as one of her successors, ex-actor Joseph Estrada, was recently forced to resign on the charge of corruption. At the same time, Muslims in the southern island of Mindanao have mounted a terrorist campaign in their effort to obtain autonomy or independence.

In other nations, the results have also been mixed. Although Malaysia is a practicing democracy, tensions persist between Malays and Chinese as well as between sec-ular and orthodox Muslims who seek to create an Islamic state. In neighboring Thailand, the military has found it expedient to hold national elections for civilian governments, but the danger of a military takeover is never far beneath the surface.

In Indonesia, difficult economic conditions caused by the financial crisis of 1997 (see the next section), combined with popular anger against the Suharto government (several members of his family had reportedly used their positions to amass considerable wealth), led to violent street riots and demands for his resignation. Forced to step down in the spring of 1998, Suharto was replaced by his deputy B. J. Habibie, who called for the establishment of a national assembly to select a new government based on popular aspirations. The assembly selected a moderate Muslim leader as president, but he was charged with corruption and incompetence and was replaced in 2001 by his vice president, Sukarno's daughter Megawati Sukarnoputri.

The new government faced a severe challenge, not only from the economic crisis but also from dissident elements seeking autonomy or even separation from the republic. Under pressure from the international community, Indonesia agreed to grant independence to the onetime Portuguese colony of East Timor, where the majority of the people are Roman Catholics. But violence provoked by pro-Indonesian militia units forced many refugees to flee the country. Religious tensions have also erupted between Muslims and Christians elsewhere in the archipelago, and Muslim rebels in western Sumatra continue to agitate for a new state based on strict adherence to fundamentalist Islam.

In Vietnam, the trend in recent years has been toward a greater popular role in the governing process. Elections for the unicameral parliament are more open than in the past. The government remains suspicious of Western-style democracy, however, and represses any opposition to the Communist Party's guiding role over the state.

Only in Burma (now renamed Myanmar), where the military has been in complete control since the early 1960s, have the forces of greater popular participation been virtually silenced. Even there, however, the power of the ruling regime of General Ne Win, known as SLORC, has been vocally challenged by Aung San Huu Kyi, the admired daughter of one of the heroes of the country's struggle for national liberation after World War II.

INCREASING PROSPERITY AND FINANCIAL CRISIS

The trend toward more representative systems of government has been due in part to increasing prosperity and the growth of an affluent and educated middle class. Although Indonesia, Burma, and the three Indochinese states are still overwhelmingly agrarian, Malaysia and Thailand have been undergoing relatively rapid economic development.

In the late summer of 1997, however, these economic gains were threatened, and popular faith in the ultimate benefits of globalization was shaken as a financial crisis swept through the region. The crisis was triggered by a number of problems, including growing budget deficits caused by excessive government expenditures on ambitious development projects, irresponsible lending and investment practices by financial institutions, and an overvaluation of local currencies relative to the U.S. dollar. An underlying cause of these problems was the prevalence of backroom deals between politicians and business leaders that temporarily enriched both groups at the cost of eventual economic dislocation.

As local currencies plummeted in value, the International Monetary Fund agreed to provide assistance, but only on the condition that the governments concerned permit greater transparency in their economic systems and allow market forces to operate more freely, even at the price of bankruptcies and the loss of jobs. In the early 2000s, although there were signs that some political lead-

ers recognized the serious nature of their problems and were willing to take steps to resolve them, the political cost of such changes remained uncertain.

Regional Conflict and Cooperation: The Rise of ASEAN

In addition to their continuing internal challenges, Southeast Asian states have been hampered by serious tensions among themselves. Some of these tensions were a consequence of historical rivalries and territorial disputes that had been submerged during the long era of colonial rule. Cambodia, for example, has bickered with both of its neighbors, Thailand and Vietnam, over mutual frontiers drawn up originally by the French for their own convenience.

After the reunification of Vietnam under Communist rule in 1975, the lingering border dispute between Cambodia and Vietnam erupted again. In April 1975, a brutal revolutionary regime under the leadership of the Khmer Rouge dictator Pol Pot came to power in Cambodia and proceeded to carry out the massacre of more than one million Cambodians. Then, claiming that vast

HOLOCAUST IN CAMBODIA. When the Khmer Rouge seized power in Cambodia in April 1975, they immediately emptied the capital of Phnom Penh and systematically began to eliminate opposition elements throughout the country. Thousands were tortured in the infamous Tuol Sleng prison and then marched out to the countryside, where they were massacred. Their bodies were thrown into massive pits. The succeeding government disinterred the remains, which are now displayed at an outdoor museum on the site.

Courtesy of William J. Duiker

territories in the Mekong delta had been seized from Cambodia by the Vietnamese in previous centuries, the Khmer Rouge regime launched attacks across the common border. In response, Vietnamese forces invaded Cambodia in December 1978 and installed a pro-Hanoi regime in Phnom Penh. Fearful of Vietnam's increasing power in the region, China launched a brief attack on Vietnam to demonstrate its displeasure.

The outbreak of war among the erstwhile Communist allies aroused the concern of other countries in the neighborhood. In 1967, several non-Communist countries had established the Association of Southeast Asian Nations (ASEAN). Composed of Indonesia, Malaysia, Thailand, Singapore, and the Philippines, ASEAN at first concentrated on cooperative social and economic endeavors, but after the end of the Vietnam War, it cooperated with other states in an effort to force the Vietnamese to withdraw. In 1991, the Vietnamese finally withdrew, and a new government was formed in Phnom Penh.

The growth of ASEAN from a weak collection of diverse states into a stronger organization whose members cooperate militarily and politically has helped provide the nations of Southeast Asia with a more cohesive voice to represent their interests on the world stage. They will need it, for disagreements with Western countries over global economic issues and the rising power of China will present major challenges in coming years. That Vietnam was admitted into ASEAN in 1996 should provide both Hanoi and its neighbors with greater leverage in dealing with their powerful neighbor to the north.

Daily Life: Town and Country in Contemporary Southeast Asia

The urban-rural dichotomy observed in India also is found in Southeast Asia, where the cities resemble those in the West while the countryside often appears little changed from precolonial days. In cities such as Bangkok, Manila, and Jakarta, broad boulevards lined with skyscrapers alternate with muddy lanes passing through neighborhoods packed with wooden shacks topped by thatch or rusty tin roofs. Nevertheless, in recent decades, millions of Southeast Asians have fled to these urban slums. Although most available jobs are menial, the pay is better than in the villages.

The urban migrants change not only their physical surroundings but their attitudes and values as well. Sometimes the move leads to a decline in traditional beliefs. Belief in the existence of nature and ancestral spirits, for example, has declined among the urban populations of Southeast Asia. In Thailand, Buddhism has come under pressure from the rising influence of materialism, although temple schools still educate thousands of rural youths whose families cannot afford the cost of public education.

Nevertheless, Buddhist, Muslim, and Confucian beliefs remain strong, even in cosmopolitan cities such as Bangkok, Jakarta, and Singapore. This preference for the traditional also shows up in lifestyle. Native dress—or an eclectic blend of Asian and Western dress—is still common. Traditional music, art, theater, and dance remain popular, although Western rock music has become fashionable among the young, and Indonesian filmmakers complain that Western films are beginning to dominate the market.

The increasing inroads made by Western culture have caused anxiety in some countries. In Malaysia, for example, fundamentalist Muslims criticize the prevalence of pornography, hedonism, drugs, and alcohol in Western culture and have tried to limit their presence in their own country. The Malaysian government has attempted to limit the number of U.S. entertainment programs shown on local television stations and has replaced them with shows on traditional themes.

One of the most significant changes that has taken place in Southeast Asia in recent decades is in the role of women in society. In general, women in the region have histori-

RONALD MCDONALD IN INDONESIA. McDonald's fast-food chain has become a prime symbol of U.S. cultural influence throughout the world. Popular with young people, it is often the target of attacks from those who criticize the impact that American values have had on traditional cultures, from Europe to East Asia. Here we see a giant statue of Ronald McDonald welcoming young Indonesians to a restaurant in the capital city of Jakarta.

ONE WORLD, ONE FASHION. One of the negative aspects of tourism is the eroding of distinctive ethnic cultures, even in previously less traveled areas. Nevertheless, fashions from other lands often seem exotic and enticing. This village chief from Flores, a remote island in the Indonesian archipelago, seems very proud of his designer sunglasses.

cally faced fewer restrictions on their activities and enjoyed a higher status than women elsewhere in Asia. Nevertheless, they were not the equal of men in every respect. With independence, Southeast Asian women gained new rights. Virtually all of the constitutions adopted by the newly independent states granted women full legal and political rights, including the right to work. Today, women have increased opportunities for education and have entered careers previously reserved for men. Women have become more active in politics, and as we have seen, some have served as heads of state.

Yet women are not truly equal to men in any country in Southeast Asia. Sometimes the distinction is simply a matter of custom. In Vietnam, women are legally equal to men, yet until recently no women had served in the Communist Party's ruling Politburo. In Thailand, Malaysia, and Indonesia, women rarely hold senior positions in government service or in the boardrooms of major corporations. Similar restrictions apply in Burma, although Aung San Huu Kyi is the leading figure in the democratic opposition movement.

Sometimes, too, women's rights have been undermined by a social or religious backlash. The revival of Islamic fundamentalism has had an especially strong impact in Malaysia, where Malay women are expected to cover their bodies and wear the traditional Muslim headdress. Even in non-Muslim countries, women are still expected to behave demurely and exercise discretion in all contacts with the opposite sex.

Cultural Trends

In most countries in Southeast Asia, writers, artists, and composers are attempting to synthesize international styles and themes with local tradition and experience. The novel has become increasingly popular as writers seek to find the best medium to encapsulate the dramatic changes that have taken place in the region in recent decades.

The best-known writer in postwar Indonesia—at least to readers abroad—is Pramoedya Toer. Born in 1925 in eastern Java, he joined the Indonesian nationalist movement in his early twenties. Arrested in 1965 on the charge of being a Communist, he spent the next several years in prison. While incarcerated, he began writing his four-volume *Buru Quartet*, which recounts in fictional form the story of the struggle of the Indonesian people for freedom from colonial rule and the autocratic regimes of the independence period. He remains under house arrest in Java today, and his novels are forbidden to circulate in Indonesia.

Among the most talented of contemporary Vietnamese novelists is Duong Thu Huong (b. 1947). A member of the Vietnamese Communist Party who served on the front lines during the Sino-Vietnamese war in 1979, she later became outspoken in her criticism of the party's failure to carry out democratic reforms and was briefly imprisoned in 1991. Undaunted by official pressure, she has written several novels that express the horrors experienced by guerrilla fighters during the Vietnam War and the cruel injustices perpetrated by the regime in the cause of building socialism.

A Region in Flux

Today, the Western image of a Southeast Asia mired in the Vietnam conflict and the tensions of the Cold War has become a memory. In ASEAN, the states in the region have created the framework for a regional organization that can serve their common political, economic, technological, and security interests. A few members of ASEAN are already on the road to advanced development.

To be sure, there are continuing signs of trouble. The recent financial crisis has aroused serious political unrest in Indonesia and has the potential to create similar problems elsewhere. There are disquieting signs that al-Qaeda has established a presence in the region. Burma remains isolated and appears mired in a state of chronic underdevelopment and brutal military rule. The three states of Indochina remain potentially unstable and have not yet been fully integrated into the region as a whole. All things considered, however, the situation is more promising today than would have appeared possible a generation ago.

EAST ASIA

In August 1945, Japan was in ruins, its cities destroyed, its vast Asian empire in ashes, its land occupied by a foreign army. Half a century later, Japan had emerged as the second-greatest industrial power in the world, democratic in form and content and a source of stability throughout the region. Japan's achievement spawned a number of Asian imitators. Known as the "Little Tigers," the four industrializing societies of Taiwan, Hong Kong, Singapore, and South Korea achieved considerable success by following the path originally charted by Japan. Along with Japan, they became economic powerhouses and ranked among the world's top twenty trading nations. Other nations in Asia and elsewhere took note and began to adopt the Japanese formula. It is no wonder that observers relentlessly heralded the coming of the "Pacific Century."

The Japanese Miracle: The Transformation of Modern Japan

For five years after the end of the war in the Pacific, Japan was governed by an Allied administration under the command of U.S. General Douglas MacArthur. The occupation regime was dominated by the United States, although the country was technically administered by a new Japanese government. As commander of the occupation administration, MacArthur was responsible for demilitarizing Japanese society, destroying the Japanese war machine, trying Japanese civilian and military officials charged with war crimes, and laying the foundations of postwar Japanese society (see the box on p. 865).

One of the sturdy pillars of Japanese militarism had been the giant business cartels, known as *zaibatsu*. Allied

© CORBIS

GENERAL MACARTHUR AND EMPEROR HIROHITO. After the end of World War II, U.S. General Douglas MacArthur was appointed supreme commander of the Allied Powers. In that capacity, he directed U.S. policy during the occupation of Japan from 1945 to 1950. Here MacArthur stands side by side with Emperor Hirohito of Japan. Note the cultural and attitudinal differences of the two leaders expressed by their contrasting body language.

policy was designed to break up the *zaibatsu* into smaller units in the belief that corporate concentration not only hindered competition but was inherently undemocratic and conducive to political authoritarianism. Occupation planners also intended to promote the formation of independent labor unions, to lessen the power of the state over the economy, and to provide a mouthpiece for downtrodden Japanese workers. Economic inequality in rural areas was to be reduced by a comprehensive land reform program that would turn the land over to those who farmed it. Finally, the educational system was to be remodeled along American lines so that it would turn out independent individuals rather than automatons subject to manipulation by the state.

The Allied program was an ambitious and even audacious plan to remake Japanese society and has been justly praised for its clear-sighted vision and altruistic motives. Parts of the program, such as the constitution, the land

THE EMPEROR IS NOT DIVINE

A t the close of World War II, the United States agreed that Japan could retain the emperor, but only on condition that he renounce his divinity. When the governments of Great Britain and the Soviet Union advocated that Hirohito be tried as a war criminal, General Douglas MacArthur, the supreme commander of Allied occupation forces in Japan, argued that the emperor had a greater grasp of democratic principles than most other Japanese and that his presence was vital to the success of Allied occupation policy. That recommendation was upheld. On New Year's Day, 1946, the emperor issued a rescript denying his divinity. To many Japanese of the era, however, he remained a divine figure.

HIROHITO, RESCRIPT ON DIVINITY

In greeting the New Year, we recall to mind that the Emperor Meiji proclaimed as the basis of our national policy the five clauses of the Charter at the beginning of the Meiji era. . . .

The proclamation is evident in its significance and high in its ideals. We wish to make this oath anew and restore the country to stand on its own feet again. We have to reaffirm the principles embodied in the Charter and proceed unflinchingly toward elimination of misguided practices of the past; and keeping in close touch with the desires of the people, we will construct a new Japan through thoroughly being pacific, the officials and the people alike obtaining rich culture and advancing the standard of living of the people.

The devastation of the war inflicted upon our cities, the miseries of the destitute, the stagnation of trade, shortage of food, and the great and growing number of the unemployed are indeed heart-rending, but if the nation is firmly united in its resolve to face the present ordeal and to see civilization consistently in peace, a bright future will undoubtedly be ours, not only for our country but for the whole of humanity. . . .

We stand by the people and we wish always to share with them in their moment of joys and sorrows. The ties between us and our people have always stood upon mutual trust and affection. They do not depend upon mere legends and myths. They are not predicated on the false conception that the Emperor is divine and that the Japanese people are superior to other races and fated to rule the world.

Our Government should make every effort to alleviate their trials and tribulations. At the same time, we trust that the people will rise to the occasion and will strive courageously for the solution of their outstanding difficulties and for the development of industry and culture. Acting upon a consciousness of solidarity and of mutual aid and broad tolerance in their civil life, they will prove themselves worthy of their best tradition. By their supreme endeavors in that direction they will be able to render their substantial contribution to the welfare and advancement of mankind.

The resolution for the year should be made at the beginning of the year. We expect our people to join us in all exertions looking to accomplishment of this great undertaking with an indomitable spirit.

---

reforms, and the educational system, succeeded brilliantly. But as other concerns began to intervene, changes or compromises were made that were not always successful. In particular, with the rise of Cold War sentiment in the United States in the late 1940s, the goal of decentralizing the Japanese economy gave way to the desire to make Japan a key partner in the effort to defend East Asia against international communism. Convinced of the need to promote economic recovery in Japan, U.S. policy makers began to show more tolerance for the *zaibatsu*. Concerned at growing radicalism within the new labor movement, U.S. occupation authorities placed less emphasis on the independence of the labor unions.

Cold War concerns also affected U.S. foreign relations with Japan. On September 8, 1951, the United States and other former belligerent nations signed a peace treaty restoring Japanese independence. In turn, Japan renounced any claim to such former colonies or territories as Taiwan, Korea, and southern Sakhalin and the Kurile Islands (see Map 29.3). On the same day, Japan and the United States signed a defensive alliance and agreed that the latter could maintain military bases on the Japanese islands. Japan was now formally independent but in a new dependency relationship with the United States. A provision in the new constitution renounced war as an instrument of national policy and prohibited the raising of an army. Thus by the early 1950s, Japan had regained partial control over its destiny.

POLITICS AND GOVERNMENT

The Allied occupation administrators started with the conviction that Japanese expansionism was directly linked to the institutional and ideological foundations of the Meiji Constitution. Accordingly, they set out to change Japanese politics into something closer to the pluralistic model used in most Western nations. Yet a number of characteristics of the postwar Japanese political system reflected the tenacity of the traditional political culture. Although Japan had a multiparty system with two major parties, the Liberal Democrats and the Socialists, in practice there was a "government party" and a permanent opposition—the Liberal Democrats were not voted out of office for thirty years. Many of the leading Liberal Democrats controlled factions on a patron-client basis, and decisions on key issues, such as who should assume the prime

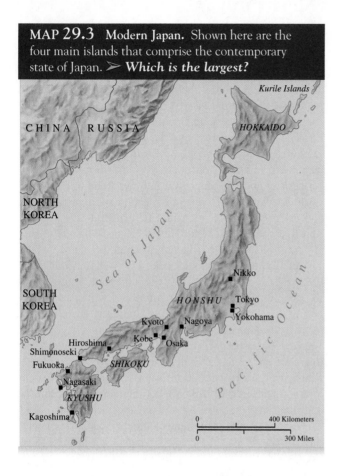

MAP 29.3 Modern Japan. Shown here are the four main islands that comprise the contemporary state of Japan. ➤ *Which is the largest?*

ministership, were decided by a modern equivalent of the *genro* oligarchs.

That tradition changed suddenly in 1993, when the ruling Liberal Democrats, shaken by persistent reports of corruption and cronyism between politicians and business interests, failed to win a majority of seats in parliamentary elections. Mirohiro Hosokawa, the leader of one of several newly formed parties, was elected prime minister. The new coalition government, however, quickly split into feuding factions, and in 1995, the Liberal Democrats returned to power. Successive prime ministers proved unable to carry out promised reforms, and in 2001, Junichiro Koizumi, an ex-minister of health and welfare, was elected prime minister. He too promised far-reaching reforms to make the political system more responsive to the challenge facing the country—so far with little success.

These challenges include not only curbing persistent political corruption but also reducing the government's involvement in the economy. Since the Meiji period, the government has played an active role in mediating management-labor disputes, establishing price and wage policies, and subsidizing vital industries and enterprises producing goods for export. This government intervention in the economy was once cited as a key reason for the efficiency of Japanese industry and the emergence of the country as an industrial giant.

In recent years, however, as the economy remains mired in recession, the government's actions have increasingly come under fire. Japanese firms now argue that deregulation is needed to enable them to innovate to keep up with the competition. Such reforms, however, have been resisted by powerful government ministries.

Last, but certainly not least, minorities such as the *eta* (now known as the Burakumin) and Korean residents in Japan continue to be subjected to legal and social discrimination. For years, official sources were reluctant to divulge growing evidence that thousands of Korean women were conscripted to serve as prostitutes (euphemistically called "comfort women") for Japanese soldiers during the war, and many Koreans living in Japan contend that such prejudicial attitudes continue to exist. Representatives of the "comfort women" have demanded both financial compensation and a formal letter of apology from the Japanese government for the treatment they received during the Pacific War. Negotiations over the issue are under way.

The issue of Japan's behavior during World War II has been especially sensitive. During the 1990s, critics at home and abroad charged that textbooks printed under the guidance of the Ministry of Education did not adequately discuss the atrocities committed by the Japanese government and armed forces during World War II. Other Asian governments were incensed at Tokyo's failure to accept responsibility for that behavior and demanded a formal apology. The government expressed remorse, but only in the context of the aggressive actions of all colonial powers during the imperialist era. In the view of many Japanese, the actions of their government during the Pacific War were a form of self-defense. Although fear of the potential revival of Japanese militarism is still strong in the region, the United States has not shared this concern and applauded Japan's decision to enhance its self-defense forces to deal with potential disturbances in the region. The issue has provoked vigorous debate in Japan, where some observers have argued that their country should adopt a more assertive stance toward the United States and play a larger role in Asian affairs.

Japan has carried out an increasingly independent foreign policy in recent years and has succeeded in maintaining amicable relations with virtually all nations. Its only serious dispute is with Russia, which has consistently refused Japan's request for the return of four islands in the Kurile chain, near the northern Japanese island of Hokkaido.

THE ECONOMY

Nowhere are the changes in postwar Japan so visible as in the economic sector, where Japan developed into a major industrial and technological power in the space of a century, surpassing such advanced Western societies as Germany, France, and Great Britain.

Although this "Japanese miracle" has often been described as beginning after the war as a result of the

Allied reforms, in fact Japanese economic growth began much earlier, with the Meiji reforms, which helped transform Japan from an autocratic society based on semifeudal institutions into an advanced capitalist democracy.

As noted, the officials of the Allied occupation identified the Meiji economic system with centralized power and the rise of Japanese militarism. Accordingly, they set out to break up the *zaibatsu* and decentralize Japanese industry and commerce. But with the rise of Cold War tensions, the policy was scaled back. Looser ties between companies were still allowed, and a new type of informal relationship, sometimes called the *keiretsu,* or "interlocking arrangement," began to take shape. Through such arrangements among suppliers, wholesalers, retailers, and financial institutions, the *zaibatsu* system was reconstituted under a new name.

The occupation administration had more success with its program to reform the agricultural system. Half of the population still lived on farms, and half of all farmers were still tenants. Under the land reform program, all lands owned by absentee landlords and all cultivated landholdings over an established maximum were sold on easy credit terms to the tenants. The program created a strong class of yeoman farmers, and tenants declined to about 10 percent of the rural population.

During the next fifty years, Japan re-created the stunning results of the Meiji era. In 1950, the Japanese gross domestic product was about one-third that of Great Britain or France. Today, it is larger than both put together and well over half that of the United States. Japan is the greatest exporting nation in the world, and its per capita income equals or surpasses that of most advanced Western states.

Explanations for Japan's success have tended to fall into two major categories. Some point to cultural factors: the Japanese are naturally group-oriented and find it easy to cooperate with one another. Traditionally hardworking and frugal, they are more inclined to save than to consume, a trait that boosts the savings rate and labor productivity. Like all Confucian societies, the Japanese value education, and consequently the labor force is highly skilled. The literacy rate is almost 100 percent, and a significantly higher proportion of the population graduates from high school than in most advanced nations of the West.

Others give more practical reasons for Japan's success. Paradoxically, Japan benefited from the total destruction of its industrial base during World War II, because it did not have the antiquated plants that held back many industries in the United States. Secure under U.S. protection, Japan spends less than 1 percent of its gross domestic product on national defense, whereas the United States spends more than 5 percent. The Japanese government has actively promoted business interests. Some critics have charged that Japan has gone beyond promotion to unfair trade practices, subsidizing exports through the Ministry of International Trade and Industry (MITI), dumping goods at prices below cost to break into a foreign market, maintaining an artificially low standard of living at home to encourage exports, and unduly restricting imports from other countries.

There is some truth on both sides of the argument. Many of the practical steps Japan took were possible precisely because of the cultural factors described here. The tradition of loyalty to the firm, for example, derives from the communal tradition in Japanese society. The concept of sacrificing one's personal interests to those of the state, though not necessarily rooted in the traditional period, was certainly fostered by the *genro* oligarchy during the Meiji era.

In recent years, the Japanese economy has run into serious difficulties, raising the question as to whether the vaunted Japanese model is as appealing as many observers earlier declared. A rise in the value of the yen hurt exports and burst the bubble of investment by Japanese banks that had taken place under the umbrella of government protection. Lacking a domestic market equivalent in size to the United States, in the 1990s the Japanese economy slipped into a recession that continues today.

These economic difficulties have placed heavy pressure on some of the vaunted features of the Japanese economy. The tradition of lifetime employment created a bloated white-collar workforce and has made downsizing difficult. Today, job security is on the decline as increasing numbers of workers are being laid off. A disproportionate burden has fallen on women, who lack seniority and continue to suffer from various forms of discrimination in the workplace.

A final change is that slowly but inexorably, the Japanese market is beginning to open up to international competition. Foreign automakers are winning a growing share of the domestic market, and the government—concerned at the prospect of growing food shortages—has committed itself to facilitating the importation of rice from abroad. Greater exposure to foreign competition may improve the performance of Japanese manufacturers. In recent years, Japanese consumers have become increasingly critical of the quality of some domestic products, provoking one cabinet minister to complain about "sloppiness and complacency" among Japanese firms (the scandal in the United States over defects in Firestone tires, produced by the Japanese tiremaker Bridgestone, is a case in point). One apparent reason for the country's recent quality problems is the cost-cutting measures adopted by Japanese companies to meet the challenges from abroad.

A SOCIETY IN TRANSITION

During the occupation, Allied planners set out to change social characteristics that they believed had contributed to Japanese aggressiveness before and during World War II. The new educational system removed all references to filial piety, patriotism, and loyalty to the emperor while

GROWING UP IN JAPAN

*J*apanese schoolchildren are exposed to a much more regimented environment than U.S. children experience. Most Japanese schoolchildren, for example, wear black-and-white uniforms to school. These regulations are examples of rules adopted by middle school systems in various parts of Japan. The Ministry of Education in Tokyo concluded that these regulations were excessive, but they are probably typical.

SCHOOL REGULATIONS, JAPANESE STYLE

1. Boys' hair should not touch the eyebrows, the ears, or the top of the collar.
2. No one should have a permanent wave, or dye his or her hair. Girls should not wear ribbons or accessories in their hair. Hair dryers should not be used.
3. School uniform skirts should be ____ centimeters above the ground, no more and no less (differs by school and region).
4. Keep your uniform clean and pressed at all times. Girls' middy blouses should have two buttons on the back collar. Boys' pant cuffs should be of the prescribed width. No more than 12 eyelets should be on shoes. The number of buttons on a shirt and tucks in a shirt are also prescribed.
5. Wear your school badge at all times. It should be positioned exactly.
6. Going to school in the morning, wear your book bag strap on the right shoulder; in the afternoon on the way home, wear it on the left shoulder. Your book case thickness, filled and unfilled, is also prescribed.
7. Girls should wear only regulation white underpants of 100% cotton.
8. When you raise your hand to be called on, your arm should extend forward and up at the angle prescribed in your handbook.
9. Your own route to and from school is marked in your student rule handbook; carefully observe which side of each street you are to use on the way to and from school.
10. After school you are to go directly home, unless your parent has written a note permitting you to go to another location. Permission will not be granted by the school unless this other location is a suitable one. You must not go to coffee shops. You must be home by ____ o'clock.
11. It is not permitted to drive or ride a motorcycle, or to have a license to drive one.
12. Before and after school, no matter where you are, you represent our school, so you should behave in ways we can all be proud of.

emphasizing the individualistic values of Western civilization. The new constitution and a revised civil code eliminated remaining legal restrictions on women's rights to obtain a divorce, hold a job, or change their domicile. Women were guaranteed the right to vote and were encouraged to enter politics.

Such efforts to remake Japanese behavior through legislation were only partially successful. During the past sixty years, Japan has unquestionably become a more individualistic and egalitarian society. At the same time, many of the distinctive characteristics of traditional Japanese society have persisted into the present day, although in somewhat altered form. The emphasis on loyalty to the group and community relationships, for example, is reflected in the strength of corporate loyalties in contemporary Japan, although, as we have seen, the attitude has eroded somewhat in recent years.

Emphasis on the work ethic also remains strong. The tradition of hard work is taught at a young age. The Japanese school year runs for 240 days a year, compared to 180 days in the United States, and work assignments outside class tend to be more extensive. The results are impressive: Japanese schoolchildren consistently earn higher scores on achievement tests than children in other advanced countries. At the same time, this devotion to success has often been accompanied by bullying by teachers and what Americans might consider an oppressive sense of conformity (see the box above).

Most young Japanese endure enormous pressures from society, school, and family. Ironically, once students have been accepted into college, the amount of work assigned tends to decrease, because graduates of the best universities are virtually guaranteed lucrative employment offers. Nevertheless, the early training instills an attitude of deference to group interests that persists throughout life.

The tension between the Japanese way and the foreign approach is especially noticeable in Japanese baseball, where major league teams frequently hire U.S. players. Commenting on Tatsunori Hara, one of the best Japanese players in the league, Reggie Smith, a U.S. teammate, said, "He had so many different people telling him what to do, it's a wonder he could still swing the bat. They turned him into a robot, instead of just letting him play naturally and expressing his natural talent." To Hara's Japanese coach, however, conformity brought teamwork, and teamwork in Japan is the road to success.[3]

By all accounts, independent thinking is on the increase in Japan. In some cases, it leads to antisocial behavior, such as crime or membership in a teenage gang. Usually it is expressed in more indirect ways, such as the recent fashion among young people of dyeing their hair brown (known in Japanese as "tea hair"). Because the practice is banned in

COOL OTAKU FASHION TEENS. Fashion-conscious teenagers have become Japan's most dedicated consumers. With the economy in the doldrums and real estate costs soaring, many young people live with their families well into their twenties, using the money saved to purchase the latest styles in clothing. Avid readers of fashion magazines, these *otaku* ("obsessed") teenagers—heirs of Japan's long affluence—pay exorbitant prices for hip-hop outfits, platform shoes, and layered dresses.

many schools and generally frowned upon by the older generation (one police chief dumped a pitcher of beer on a student with brown hair whom he noticed in a bar), many young Japanese dye their hair as a gesture of independence. When seeking employment or getting married, however, they return their hair to its natural color.

One of the more tenacious legacies of the past in Japanese society is sexual inequality. Although women are now legally protected against discrimination in employment, very few have reached senior levels in business, education, or politics. Women now comprise nearly 50 percent of the workforce, but most are in retail or service occupations, and their average salary is only about half that of men. There is a feminist movement in Japan, but it has none of the vigor and mass support of its counterpart in the United States.

Japan's welfare system also differs profoundly from its Western counterparts. Applicants are required to seek assistance first from their own families, and the physically able are ineligible for government aid. As a result, less than 1 percent of the population receives welfare benefits, compared with more than 10 percent who receive some form of assistance in the United States.

Traditionally, it was the responsibility of the eldest child in a Japanese family to care for aging parents, but that system is beginning to break down because of limited housing space and the growing tendency of working-age women to seek jobs in the marketplace. The proportion of Japanese over sixty-five years of age who live with their children has dropped from 80 percent in 1970 to around 50 percent today. At the same time, public and private pension plans are under increasing financial pressure, partly because of a low birthrate and a graying population. Japan today has the highest proportion of people over age sixty-five of any industrialized country in the world—17 percent of the country's total population of about 130 million.

Whether the unique character of modern Japan will endure is unclear. Confidence in the Japanese "economic miracle" has been shaken by the recent downturn, and there are indications of a growing tendency toward hedonism and individualism among Japanese youth. Older Japanese frequently complain that the younger generation lacks their sense of loyalty and willingness to sacrifice.

RELIGION AND CULTURE

When Japan was opened to the West in the nineteenth century, many Japanese became convinced of the superiority of foreign ideas and institutions and were especially interested in Western religion and culture. Although Christian converts were few, numbering less than 1 percent of the population, the influence of Christianity was out of proportion to the size of the community. Many intellectuals during the Meiji era were impressed by the emotional commitment shown by missionaries in Japan and viewed Christianity as a contemporary version of Confucianism.

Today, Japan includes almost 1.5 million Christians, along with 93 million Buddhists. Many Japanese also follow Shinto, no longer identified with reverence for the emperor and the state. As in the West, increasing urbanization has led to a decline in the practice of organized religion, although evangelical sects have proliferated in recent years. The largest and best-known sect is Soka Gakkai, a lay Buddhist organization that has attracted millions of followers and formed its own political party, the Komeito. Zen Buddhism retains its popularity, and some business-people seek to use Zen techniques to learn how to focus on willpower as a means of outwitting a competitor. The head of one Zen monastery, however, has publicly apologized for the sect's role in promoting fanatical patriotism within the military before World War II.

Western literature, art, and music have also had a major impact on Japanese society. After World War II, many of the writers who had been active before the war resurfaced, but now their writing reflected demoralization. Many were attracted to existentialism, and some turned to hedonism and nihilism. For these disillusioned authors, defeat was compounded by fear of the Americanization of postwar Japan. One of the best examples of this attitude was the novelist Yukio Mishima, who led a crusade to stem the tide of what he described as America's "universal and uniform 'Coca-Colonization'" of the world in general and Japan in particular.[4] Mishima's ritual suicide in 1970 was the subject of widespread speculation and transformed him into a cult figure.

One of Japan's most serious-minded contemporary authors is Kenzaburo Oe (b. 1935). His work, rewarded with a Nobel Prize for literature in 1994, presents Japan's ongoing quest for modern identity and purpose. His characters reflect the spiritual anguish precipitated by the collapse of the imperial Japanese tradition and the subsequent adoption of Western culture—a trend that Oe contends has culminated in unabashed materialism, cultural decline, and a moral void. Yet unlike Mishima, Oe does not wish to reinstill the imperial traditions of the past but rather seeks to regain spiritual meaning by retrieving the sense of communality and innocence found in rural Japan.

A recent phenomenon is the so-called industrial novel, which lays bare the vicious infighting and pressure tactics that characterize Japanese business today. Another popular genre is the "art-manga," or literary cartoon. Michio Hisauchi presents serious subjects, such as Japanese soldiers marooned after the war on an island in the South Pacific, in *Japan's Junglest Day*, a full-length novel in comic-book form.

Other aspects of Japanese culture have also been influenced by Western ideas, although without the intense preoccupation with synthesis that is evident in literature. Western music is very popular in Japan, and scores of Japanese classical musicians have succeeded in the West. Even rap music has gained a foothold among Japanese youth, although without the association with sex, drugs, and violence that it has in the United States. Although some of the lyrics betray an attitude of modest revolt against the uptight world of Japanese society, most lack any such connotations. An example is the rap song "Street Life":

> Now's the time to hip-hop,
> Everybody's crazy about rap,
> Hey, hey, you all, listen up,
> Listen to my rap and cheer up.

As one singer remarked, "We've been very fortunate, and we don't want to bother our Moms and Dads. So we don't sing songs that would disturb parents."[5]

There are some signs that under the surface, the tension between traditional and modern is exacting a price. As novelists such as Mishima and Oe feared, the growing focus on material possessions and the decline of traditional religious beliefs have left a spiritual void. Some young people have reacted to the emptiness of their lives by joining religious cults such as Aum Shinri Kyo, which came to world attention in 1995 when members of the organization carried out a poison gas attack on the Tokyo subway that killed several people.

The Little Tigers

The success of postwar Japan in meeting the challenge from the capitalist West soon caught the eye of other Asian nations. By the 1980s, several smaller states in the region—known collectively as the "little tigers," had successively followed the Japanese example.

SOUTH KOREA: A PENINSULA DIVIDED

While the world was focused on the economic miracle occurring on the Japanese islands, another miracle of sorts was taking place across the Sea of Japan on the Asian mainland. In 1953, the Korean peninsula was exhausted from three years of bitter fraternal war, a conflict that took the lives of an estimated four million Koreans on both sides of the 38th parallel and turned as much as one-quarter of the population into refugees. Although a cease-fire was signed at Panmunjom in July 1953, it was a fragile peace that left two heavily armed and mutually hostile countries facing each other suspiciously.

North of the truce line was the People's Republic of Korea (PRK), a police state under the dictatorial rule of the Communist leader Kim Il Sung (1912–1994). To the south was the Republic of Korea, under the equally autocratic President Syngman Rhee (1875–1965), a fierce anti-Communist who had led the resistance to the northern invasion. But many Koreans resented Rhee's reliance on the wealthy landlord class. After several years of harsh rule, marked by government corruption, fraudulent elections, and police brutality, demonstrations broke out in the capital city of Seoul in the spring of 1960 and forced him into retirement.

The Rhee era was followed by a brief period of multiparty democratic government, but in 1961, a coup d'état placed General Chung Hee Park (1917–1979) in power. The new regime promulgated a new constitution, and in 1963, Park was elected president of a civilian government. He set out to foster recovery of the economy from decades of foreign occupation and civil war. Because the private sector had been relatively weak under Japanese rule, the government played an active role in the process by instituting a series of five-year plans that targeted specific industries for development, promoted exports, and funded infrastructure development. Under a land reform program, large landowners were required to sell all their farmland above 7.4 acres to their tenants at low prices.

The program was a solid success. Benefiting from the Confucian principles of thrift, respect for education, and hard work, as well as from Japanese capital and technology, Korea gradually emerged as a major industrial power in East Asia. The economic growth rate rose from less than 5 percent annually in the 1950s to an average of 9 percent under Chung Hee Park. The largest corporations—including Samsung, Daewoo, and Hyundai—were transformed into massive conglomerates called *chaebol*, the Korean equivalent of the *zaibatsu* of prewar Japan. Taking advantage of relatively low wages and a stunningly high rate of saving, Korean businesses began to compete actively with the Japanese for export markets in Asia and throughout the world. Per capita income also increased dramatically, from less than $90 (in U.S. dollars) annually in 1960 to $1,560 (twice that of Communist North Korea) twenty years later.

But like many other countries in the region, South Korea was slow to develop democratic principles. Although his government functioned with the trappings of democracy, Park continued to rule by autocratic means and suppressed all forms of dissidence. In 1979, Park was assassinated. But after a brief interregnum of democratic rule, in 1980 a new military government under General Chun Doo Hwan seized power. The new regime was as authoritarian as its predecessors, but opposition to autocratic rule had now spread to much of the urban population.

With Chun under increasing pressure from the United States to moderate the oppressive character of his rule, national elections were finally held in 1989. The successful candidate, Roh Tae Woo, was succeeded by another elected president, Kim Young Sam, in 1992. Kim promised to make Korea "a freer and more mature democracy" and attempted to crack down on the influence of the giant *chaebols*, which were accused of giving massive bribes in return for favors from government officials. He also initiated contacts with the Communist regime in the PRK on possible steps toward eventual reunification of the peninsula.

But the nation's problems were more serious than the endemic problem of corruption. A growing trade deficit, combined with a declining growth rate, led to increased unemployment and bankruptcy. After the Asian financial crisis emerged in 1997, economic conditions worsened, leading to the election of a longtime opposition figure, Kim Dae Jung, to the presidency. But although the new leader promised drastic reforms, his regime too has been charged with corruption and incompetence, and relations with North Korea, now on the verge of becoming a nuclear power, remain tense.

TAIWAN: THE OTHER CHINA

South Korea was not the only rising industrial power trying to imitate the success of the Japanese in East Asia. To the south on the island of Taiwan, the Republic of China began to do the same.

After retreating to Taiwan following their defeat by the Communists, Chiang Kai-shek and his followers established a new capital at Taipei. The government, which continued to refer to itself as the Republic of China (ROC), contended that it remained the legitimate representative of the Chinese people and that it would eventually return in triumph to the mainland.

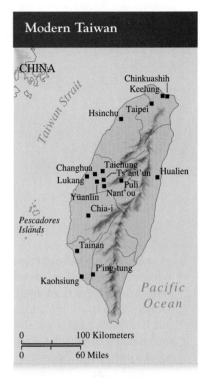

The Nationalists had much more success on Taiwan than they had achieved on the mainland. In the relatively secure environment provided by a security treaty with the United States, signed in 1954, the ROC was able to concentrate on economic growth without worrying about a Communist invasion.

The government moved rapidly to create a solid agricultural base. A land reform program led to the reduction of rents, and landholdings over 3 acres were purchased by the government and resold to the tenants at reasonable prices. At the same time, local manufacturing and commerce were strongly encouraged. By the 1970s, Taiwan had become one of the most dynamic industrial economies in East Asia. The government played a major role in the process, targeting strategic industries for support and investing in infrastructure. At the same time, as in Japan, the government stressed the importance of private enterprise and encouraged foreign investment and a high rate of internal savings.

In contrast to the Communist regime in the People's Republic of China (PRC), the ROC actively maintained Chinese tradition, promoting respect for Confucius and the ethical principles of the past, such as hard work, frugality, and filial piety. Although there was some

➤ YOU CAN TAKE IT WITH YOU!
Whereas wealthy Chinese in traditional China buried clay models of personal possessions to accompany the departed to the next world, ordinary people burned paper effigies, which were transported to the afterlife by means of the rising smoke. This custom survives in many Chinese communities today, as this photograph taken in modern Singapore demonstrates. Some merchants make their living by manufacturing such popular paper objects as television sets, elegant furniture, and even Mercedes automobiles.

corruption in both the government and the private sector, income differentials between the wealthy and the poor were generally less than elsewhere in the region, and the overall standard of living increased substantially. Health and sanitation improved, literacy rates were quite high, and an active family planning program reduced the rate of population growth. Nevertheless, the total population on the island increased from about seven million in 1945 to about twenty million in the mid-1980s.

Increasing prosperity, however, did not lead to the democratization of the political process. The Nationalists continued to rule by emergency decree and refused to permit the formation of opposition political parties on the ground that the danger of invasion from the mainland had not subsided. Some friction developed between the mainlanders, who numbered about two million and were dominant in the government, and the native Taiwanese (mostly ethnic Chinese whose ancestors had emigrated to the island during the Qing dynasty). By the 1980s, however, these fissures in Taiwanese society had begun to diminish; by then, an ever-higher proportion of the population had been born on the island and identified themselves as Taiwanese.

After the death of Chiang Kai-shek in 1975, the ROC slowly began to move toward a more representative form of government, including elections and legal opposition parties. A national election in 1992 resulted in a bare majority for the Nationalists over strong opposition from the Democratic Progressive Party (DPP). But political liberalization had its dangers; some members of the DPP began to agitate for an independent Republic of Taiwan, a possibility that aroused concern within the Nation-

alist government in Taipei and frenzied hostility in the PRC. The election of DPP leader Chen Shuibian as ROC president in March 2000 angered Beijing, which threatened to invade Taiwan should the island continue to delay unification with the mainland.

Whether Taiwan will remain an independent state or be united with the mainland is impossible to predict. The United States continues to provide defensive military assistance to the Taiwanese armed forces and has made it clear that it supports self-determination for the people of Taiwan and that it expects the final resolution of the Chinese civil war to be by peaceful means. In the meantime, economic and cultural contacts between Taiwan and the mainland are steadily increasing. However, the Taiwanese have shown no inclination to accept the PRC's offer of "one country, two systems," under which the ROC would accept the PRC as the legitimate government of China in return for autonomous control over the affairs of Taiwan.

SINGAPORE AND HONG KONG: THE LITTLEST TIGERS

The smallest but by no means the least successful of the Little Tigers are Singapore and Hong Kong. Both are essentially city-states, with large populations densely packed into small territories. Singapore, once a British colony and briefly a part of the state of Malaysia, is now an independent nation. Hong Kong was a British colony until it was returned to PRC control in 1997. In recent years, both have emerged as industrial powerhouses, with standards of

To Those Living in Glass Houses

*K*ishore Mahbubani is permanent secretary in the Ministry of Foreign Affairs in Singapore. Previously, he served as his country's ambassador to the United Nations. In this 1994 article, adapted from a piece in the Washington Quarterly, *the author advises his audience to stop lecturing Asian societies on the issue of human rights and focus attention instead on problems in the United States. In his view, today the countries of the West have much to learn from their counterparts in East Asia. This viewpoint is shared by many other observers, political leaders, and foreign affairs specialists in the region.*

KISHORE MAHBUBANI, "GO EAST, YOUNG MAN"

In a major reversal of a pattern lasting centuries, many Western societies, including the U.S., are doing some major things fundamentally wrong, while a growing number of East Asian societies are doing the same things right. The results are most evident in the economic sphere. In purchasing power parity terms, East Asia's gross domestic product is already larger than that of either the U.S. or European community. Such economic prosperity, contrary to American belief, results not just from free-market arrangements but also from the right social and political choices. . . .

In most Asian eyes, the evidence of real social decay in the U.S. is clear and palpable. Since 1960, the U.S. population has grown by 41%. In the same period, there has been a 560% increase in violent crimes, a 419% increase in illegitimate births, a 400% increase in divorce rates, a 300% increase in children living in single-parent homes, a more than 200% increase in teenage suicide rates, and a drop of almost 80 points in [SAT] scores. A clear American paradox is that a society that places such a high premium on freedom has effectively reduced the physical freedom of most Americans, especially those who live in large cities. They live in heavily fortified homes, think twice before taking an evening stroll around their neighborhoods, and feel increasingly threatened by random violence when they are outside.

To any Asian, it is obvious that the breakdown of the family and social order in the U.S. owes itself to a mindless ideology that maintains that the freedom of a small number of individuals who are known to pose a threat to society (criminals, terrorists, street gang members, drug dealers) should not be constrained (for example, through detention without trial), even if to do so would enhance the freedom of the majority. . . . This belief is purely and simply a gross violation of common sense.

My hope is that Americans will come to visit East Asia in greater numbers. When they do, they will come to realize that their society has swung much too much in one direction: liberating the individual while imprisoning society. The relatively strong and stable family and social institutions of East Asia will appear more appealing. And as Americans experience the freedom of walking on city streets in Asia, they may begin to understand that freedom can also result from greater social order and discipline. Perhaps the best advice to give to a young American is: "Go East, Young Man."

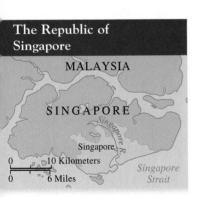

The Republic of Singapore

MALAYSIA

SINGAPORE

Singapore

Singapore R.

0   10 Kilometers
0   6 Miles

Singapore Strait

living well above those of their neighbors.

The success of Singapore must be ascribed in good measure to the will and energy of its political leaders. When it became independent in August 1965, Singapore's longtime position as an entrepôt for trade between the Indian Ocean and the South China Sea was on the wane. With only 618 square miles of territory, much of it marshland and tropical jungle, Singapore had little to offer but the frugality and industriousness of its predominantly overseas Chinese population.

Within a decade, Singapore's role and reputation had dramatically changed. Under the leadership of Prime Minister Lee Kuan-yew (b. 1923), once the firebrand leader of the radical People's Action Party, the government cultivated an attractive business climate while engaging in massive public works projects to feed, house, and educate its two million citizens. The major components of success have been shipbuilding, oil refineries, tourism, electronics, and finance—the city-state has become the banking hub of the entire region.

Like South Korea and Taiwan, Singapore relied on a combination of government planning, entrepreneurial spirit, export promotion, high productivity, and an exceptionally high rate of saving to achieve industrial growth rates of nearly 10 percent annually during the last quarter of the twentieth century. In recent years, however, the rate of growth has dropped dramatically, due primarily to increasing competition from China.

As in the other Little Tigers, an authoritarian political system has guaranteed a stable environment for economic growth. Until his recent retirement, Lee Kuan-yew and his People's Action Party dominated Singapore politics, and opposition elements were intimidated into silence or arrested. The prime minister openly declared that the Western model of pluralist democracy was not appropriate for Singapore and lauded the Meiji model of centralized development (see the box above). Confucian values of thrift, hard work, and obedience to authority have been promoted as the ideology of the state. The government has had a passion for cleanliness and at one time even undertook a campaign to persuade its citizens to flush the public urinals. In 1989, the local *Straits Times*, a mouthpiece of the government, published a photograph of a man walking sheepishly from a row of urinals. The caption read "Caught without a flush: Mr. Amar Mohamed leaving the Lucky Plaza [a local shopping center] toilet without flushing the urinal."[6]

But economic success has begun to undermine the authoritarian foundations of the system as a more sophisticated citizenry voices aspirations for more political freedoms and an end to government paternalism. Lee Kuan-yew's successor, Goh Chok Tong, has promised a "kinder, gentler" Singapore, and political restrictions on individual behavior are gradually being relaxed. There is reason for optimism that a more pluralistic political system will gradually emerge.

The future of Hong Kong is not so clear-cut. As in Singapore, sensible government policies and the hard work of its people have enabled Hong Kong to thrive. At first, the prosperity of the colony depended on a plentiful supply of cheap labor. Inundated with refugees from the mainland during the 1950s and 1960s, the population of Hong Kong burgeoned to more than six million. More recently, Hong Kong has benefited from increased tourism, manufactur-

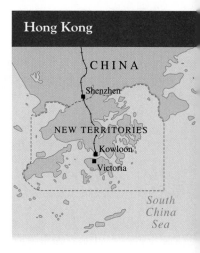

ing, and the growing economic prosperity of neighboring Guangdong province, the most prosperous region of the PRC. Unlike the other societies discussed in this chapter, Hong Kong has relied on an unbridled free market system rather than active state intervention in the economy. At the same time, by allocating substantial funds for transportation, sanitation, education, and public housing, the government has created favorable conditions for economic development.

When Britain's ninety-nine-year lease on the New Territories, the foodbasket of the colony, expired on July 1, 1997, Hong Kong returned to mainland authority. Although the Chinese promised the British that for fifty years the people of Hong Kong would live under a capitalist system and be essentially self-governing, recent statements by Chinese leaders have raised questions about the degree of autonomy Hong Kong will continue to receive under Chinese rule (see the box on p. 875).

THE HONG KONG SKYLINE.   Hong Kong reverted to Chinese sovereignty in 1997 after a century of British rule. To commemorate the occasion, the imposing Conference Center, shown here in the foreground, was built on reclaimed shoreland in Hong Kong harbor. The center is surrounded by the gleaming modern skyscrapers of the city of Victoria, with Victoria Peak in the background. The Star Ferry, long a fixture for local residents, plies its way between the island and the peninsula of Kowloon.

RETURN TO THE MOTHERLAND

After lengthy negotiations, in December 1984, China and Great Britain agreed that on July 1, 1997, Hong Kong would return to Chinese sovereignty. Key sections of the agreement are included here. In succeeding years, authorities of the two countries held further negotiations. Some of the discussions raised questions in the minds of residents of Hong Kong as to whether their individual liberties would indeed be respected after the colony's return to China.

THE JOINT DECLARATION ON HONG KONG

The Hong Kong Special Administrative Region will be directly under the authority of the Central People's Government of the People's Republic of China. The Hong Kong Special Administrative Region will enjoy a high degree of autonomy, except in foreign and defense affairs, which are the responsibility of the Central People's Government.

The Hong Kong Special Administrative Region will be vested with executive, legislative, and independent judicial power, including that of final adjudication. The laws currently in force in Hong Kong will remain basically unchanged.

The Government of the Hong Kong Special Administrative Region will be composed of local inhabitants. The chief executive will be appointed by the Central People's Government on the basis of the results of elections or consultations to be held locally. Principal officials will be nominated by the chief executive of the Hong Kong Special Administrative Region for appointment by the Central People's Government. . . .

The current social and economic systems in Hong Kong will remain unchanged, and so will the lifestyle. Rights and freedoms, including those of the person, of speech, of the press, of assembly, of association, of travel, of movement, of correspondence, of strike, of choice of occupation, of academic research, and of religious belief will be ensured by law. . . . Private property, ownership of enterprises, legitimate right of inheritance, and foreign investment will be protected by law.

On the Margins of Asia: Postwar Australia and New Zealand

Technically, Australia and New Zealand are not part of Asia, and throughout their short history, both countries have identified culturally and politically with the West rather than with their Asian neighbors. Their political institutions and values are derived from Europe, and their economies resemble those of the advanced countries of the world rather than the preindustrial societies of much of Southeast Asia. Both are currently members of the British Commonwealth and of the U.S.-led ANZUS alliance (Australia, New Zealand, and the United States).

Yet trends in recent years have been drawing both states, especially Australia, closer to Asia. In the first place, immigration from East and Southeast Asia has increased rapidly. More than one-half of current immigrants into Australia come from East Asia, and by early this century, about 7 percent of the population of about 18 million people will be of Asian descent. In New Zealand, residents of Asian descent represent only about 3 percent of the population of 3.5 million, but about 12 percent of the population are Maoris, Polynesian peoples who settled on the islands about a thousand years ago. Second, trade relations with Asia are increasing rapidly. About 60 percent of Australia's export markets today are in East Asia, and the region is the source of about one-half of its imports. Asian trade with New Zealand is also on the increase.

At the same time, the links that bind both countries to Great Britain and the United States have been loosening. There are moves under way in Australia and New Zealand to withdraw from the British Commonwealth, although the outcome at this point appears far from certain. Although security ties with the United States remain important, the Australian government is seeking to establish closer ties with the ASEAN alliance. Farther removed from Asia both physically and psychologically, New Zealand assigns less importance to its security treaty with the United States and has been vocally critical of U.S. nuclear policies in the region.

Whether Australia and New Zealand will ever become an integral part of the Asia-Pacific region is uncertain. Cultural differences stemming from the European origins of the majority of the population in both countries hinder mutual understanding on both sides of the divide, and many ASEAN leaders express reluctance to accept the two countries as full members of the alliance. But economic and geographical realities act as a powerful force, and should the Pacific region continue on its current course toward economic prosperity and political stability, the role of Australia and New Zealand will assume greater significance.

Explaining the East Asian Miracle

What explains the striking ability of Japan and the four Little Tigers to transform themselves into export-oriented societies capable of competing with the advanced nations of Europe and the Western Hemisphere? As we have noted, there are two contrasting explanations. Some point

long tradition of espousing Confucian values. In fact, some historians in recent years have maintained that it was precisely those Confucian values that hindered China's early response to the challenge of the West.

The key factor, it appears, is the emergence of a political elite that focuses on maximizing the productive capacity of a given society. The creative talents of the Chinese people were not efficiently utilized until Deng Xiaoping launched his program of Four Modernizations in the late 1970s. The same situation applied in neighboring areas while they were under European or Japanese colonial rule (although Japanese colonialism did lead to the creation of an infrastructure more conducive to later development than was the case in European colonies). Only when a "modernizing elite" took charge and began to place a high priority on economic development were the stunning advances of recent decades achieved.

Another common factor is that Japan and its emulators were operating within a regional framework highly conducive to rapid economic development. The Little Tigers received substantial inputs of capital and technology from the advanced nations of the West—Taiwan and South Korea from the United States, Hong Kong and Singapore from Britain. Japan relied to a greater degree on its own efforts but received a significant advantage by being placed under the U.S. security umbrella and guaranteed access to markets and sources of raw materials in a region dominated by U.S. naval power.

CONCLUSION

To some observers, the economic achievements of the nations of the western Pacific have come at a high price, in the form of political authoritarianism and a lack of attention to human rights. Until recently, government repression of opposition has been common in many of these nations. In addition, the rights of national minorities and women are often still limited in comparison with the advanced nations of the West. Recent developments such as the financial crisis of 1997 and the long-lived economic downturn in Japan have also somewhat tarnished the image of the "Asian miracle," raising concern that some of the factors that contributed to economic success in prior years are now making it difficult for governments to develop open and accountable financial systems.

Still, it should be kept in mind that progress in political pluralism and human rights has not always been easy to achieve in the West and even now frequently fails to match expectations. A look at the historical record suggests that political pluralism is often a by-product of economic growth and that political values and institutions evolve in response to changing social conditions. A rising standard of living

to the traditional character traits of Confucian societies, such as thrift, a work ethic, respect for education, and obedience to authority. Others place more emphasis on deliberate steps taken by government and economic leaders to meet the political, economic, and social challenges faced by their societies.

There is no reason to doubt that cultural factors have contributed to the economic success of these societies. Habits such as frugality, industriousness, and subordination of individual desires have all played a role in their governments' ability to concentrate on the collective interest. Whether such values should be specifically identified with Confucianism, however, is a matter of debate. After all, until recently, mainland China did not share in the economic success of its neighbors despite a and increased social mobility should go far toward enhancing political freedom and promoting social justice in the countries bordering the western Pacific.

The efforts of these nations to find a way to accommodate traditional and modern, native and foreign, raise a final question. As we have seen, Mahatma Gandhi believed that materialism is ultimately a dead end. In light of contemporary concerns about the emptiness of life in the West and the self-destructiveness of material culture, can his message be ignored?

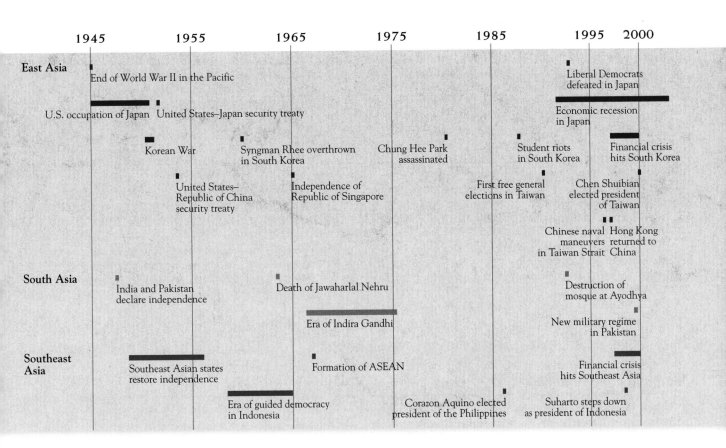

CHAPTER NOTES

1. *New York Times*, May 2, 1996.
2. Quoted in Larry Collins and Dominique Lapierre, *Freedom at Midnight* (New York, 1975), p. 252.
3. Robert Whiting, *You Gotta Have Wa* (New York, 1990), p. 69.
4. Yukio Mishima and Geoffrey Bownas, eds., *New Writing in Japan* (Harmondsworth, England, 1972), p. 16.

5. *New York Times*, January 29, 1996.
6. Stan Seser, "A Reporter at Large," *New Yorker*, January 13, 1992, p. 44.

SUGGESTED READINGS

For a recent survey of contemporary Indian history, see S. Wolpert, *A New History of India*, rev. ed. (New York, 1989). V. S. Naipaul, *India: A Wounded Civilization* (New York, 1977), is a provocative study of independent India from a friendly but sometimes critical perspective. Also see P. Brass, *The New Cambridge History of India: The Politics of Independence* (Cambridge, 1990); C.

Baxter, *Bangladesh: From a Nation to a State* (Boulder, Colo., 1997); and S. Tharoor, *India: From Midnight to the Millennium* (New York, 1997).

On the period surrounding independence, see the dramatic account by L. Collins and D. Lapierre, *Freedom at Midnight* (New York, 1975). On Nehru's government, see D. Norman, ed., *Nehru:*

The First Sixty Years, 2 vols. (London, 1965). For insight into Nehru's character, see S. Gandhi, ed., *Two Alone, Two Together: Letters Between Indira Gandhi and Jawaharlal Nehru, 1940–1964* (London, 1992).

The life and career of Indira Gandhi have been well chronicled. Two fine biographies are T. Ali, *An Indian Dynasty: The Story of the Nehru-Gandhi Family* (New York, 1985), and K. Bhatia, *Indira: A Biography of Prime Minister Gandhi* (New York, 1974.)

Social issues are examined in a number of studies. For an overview, see K. Bhatia, *The Ordeal of Nationhood: A Social Study of India Since Independence, 1947–1970* (New York, 1971). See also J. M. Freeman, *Untouchable: An Indian Life History* (Stanford, Calif., 1979); R. G. Revankar, *The Indian Constitution: A Case Study of Backward Classes* (Rutherford, N.J., 1971); and W. Wiser and C. Wiser, *Behind Mud Walls, 1930–1960*, rev. ed. (New York, 1984). On Indian literature, see D. Ray and A. Singh, eds., *India: An Anthology of Contemporary Writing* (Athens, Ohio, 1983). See also S. Tharu and K. Lalita, eds., *Women Writing in India*, vol. 2 (New York, 1993).

There are a number of standard surveys of the history of modern Southeast Asia. Unfortunately, many of them are now out of date because of the changes that have taken place in the region since the end of the Vietnam War. For an introduction with a strong emphasis on recent events, see D. R. Sar Desai, *Southeast Asia: Past and Present*, 2d ed. (Boulder, Colo., 1989). For a more scholarly approach, see D. J. Steinberg, ed., *In Search of Southeast Asia*, 2d ed. (New York, 1985).

The best way to approach modern Southeast Asia is through individual country studies. On Burma, see J. Silverstein, *Burmese Politics: The Dilemma of National Unity* (New Brunswick, N.J., 1980). On Thailand, see D. Wyatt, *Thailand* (New Haven, Conn., 1982). On the Philippines, the best overall survey is D. J. Steinberg, *The Philippines: A Singular and a Plural Place* (Boulder, Colo., 1994). On Malaya and Singapore, see K. von Vorys, *Democracy Without Consensus* (Princeton, N.J., 1975), and C. M. Turnbull, *A History of Singapore, 1819–1975* (Kuala Lumpur, 1977). For insight into the problem of racial tension in Malaysia, see M. bin Mohamad, *The Malay Dilemma* (Kuala Lumpur, 1970).

There is a rich selection of materials on modern Indonesia. On the Sukarno era, see J. Legge, *Sukarno* (New York, 1972), and H. Jones, *Indonesia: The Possible Dream* (New York, 1971). On the Suharto era and its origins, see H. Crouch, *The Army in Indonesian Politics* (Ithaca, N.Y., 1978), and M. Vatikiotis, *Indonesian Politics Under Suharto* (London, 1993).

Most of the literature on Indochina in recent decades has dealt with the Vietnam War and the related conflicts in Laos and Cambodia. For an excellent overall history, see S. Karnow, *Vietnam: A History* (New York, 1983). F. Fitzgerald's *Fire in the Lake* (New York, 1970) won a Pulitzer Prize for its discussion of the reasons for the strength of the Viet Cong. On the brutal reign of the Khmer Rouge in Cambodia, see F. Ponchaud, *Cambodia Year Zero* (New York, 1977). On conditions in Vietnam after the war, see R. Shaplen, *Bitter Victory* (New York, 1986).

For an overview of women's issues in contemporary South and Southeast Asia, consult B. Ramusack and S. Sievers, *Women in Asia* (Bloomington, Ind., 1999). Articles that focus on the socioeconomic problems of women in India in the 1980s are found in M. Kishwar and R. Vanita, eds., *In Search of Answers: Indian Women's Voices from Manushi* (London, 1991). K. Bhasin, R. Menon, and N. S. Khan, eds., *Against All Odds: Essays on Women, Religion and Development from India and Pakistan* (New Delhi, 1994), explores fundamental-

ist conservatism among both Hindu and Muslim women. Of interest on Southeast Asian women's issues are W. Williams, *Javanese Lives: Women and Men in Modern Indonesian Society* (New Brunswick, N.J., 1991), and C. B. N. Chin, *In Service and Servitude: Foreign Female Domestic Workers and the Malaysian "Modernity" Project* (New York, 1998).

The number of books in English on modern Japan has increased in direct proportion to Japan's rise as a major industrial power. P. Duus, ed., *The Cambridge History of Japan*, vol. 6 (Cambridge, 1988), contains a number of interesting scholarly articles on twentieth-century issues, although most of them deal with the prewar period. For a topical approach with strong emphasis on economic and social matters, J. E. Hunter, *The Emergence of Modern Japan: An Introductory History Since 1853* (London, 1989), is excellent. For an extensive analysis of Japan's adjustment to the Allied occupation, see J. W. Dower, *Embracing Defeat: Japan in the Wake of World War II* (New York, 1999). Political dissent and its consequences are dealt with in N. Fields, *In the Realm of the Dying Emperor* (New York, 1991).

Japanese social issues have often been examined from an economic perspective as foreign observers try to discover the reasons for the nation's economic success. C. Nakane, *Japanese Society* (Harmondsworth, England, 1979) provides a scholarly treatment, while R. J. Hendry, *Understanding Japanese Society* (Beckenham, England, 1987), is more accessible. For a more local treatment, see R. P. Dore, *Shinohata: A Portrait of a Japanese Village* (New York, 1978), and T. C. Bestor, *Neighborhood Tokyo* (Stanford, Calif., 1989). T. Heymann, *On an Average Day in Japan* (New York, 1992), provides an interesting statistical comparison of Japanese and American society. On the role of women in modern Japan, see D. Robins-Mowry, *The Hidden Sun: Women of Modern Japan* (Boulder, Colo., 1983), and N. Bornoff, *Pink Samurai: Love, Marriage, and Sex in Contemporary Japan* (New York, 1991).

Books attempting to explain Japanese economic success have become a growth industry. The classic account is E. F. Vogel, *Japan as Number One: Lessons for America* (Cambridge, Mass., 1979). For a provocative response pointing to signs of Japanese weakness, see J. Woronoff, *Japan as—Anything but—Number One* (Armonk, N.Y., 1991). C. Johnson, *MITI and the Japanese Miracle* (Stanford, Calif., 1982), provides an excellent analysis of the role of government in promoting Japanese economic interests. On the costs of Japanese economic success on society, see I. P. Hall, *Cartels of the Mind: Japan's Intellectual Closed Shop* (New York, 1998). Y. Saisho, *Women Executives in Japan* (Tokyo, 1981), discusses women who are trying to find the key to economic success in Japanese business. An excellent recent study on women and work in Japan is B. Molony, "Japan's 1986 Equal Opportunity Law and the Changing Discourse on Gender," *Signs*, 20 (1995): 268–302. On Japanese literature after World War II, see the classic D. Keene, *Dawn to the West: Japanese Fiction in the Modern Era* (New York, 1984). Short story writing is chronicled in I. Morris, ed., *Modern Japanese Stories: An Anthology* (Rutland, Vt., 1962); Y. Mishima and G. Bownas, eds., *New Writing in Japan* (Harmondsworth, England, 1972); and A. Birnbaum, *Monkey Brain Sushi: New Tastes in Japanese Fiction* (Tokyo, 1991). On Japanese women authors, see N. M. Lippit and K. I. Selden, eds., *Stories by Contemporary Japanese Women Writers* (New York, 1982).

On the four Little Tigers and their economic development, see E. F. Vogel, *The Four Little Dragons: The Spread of Industrialization in East Asia* (Cambridge, Mass., 1991); J. W. Morley, ed., *Driven by Growth: Political Change in the Asia-Pacific Region* (Armonk, N.Y.,

1992); and J. Woronoff, *Asia's Miracle Economies* (New York, 1986). For an interesting collection of articles on the role of Confucian ideology in promoting economic growth, see Hung-chao Tai, ed., *Confucianism and Economic Development* (Washington, D.C., 1989). For individual treatments of the Little Tigers, see Hak-kyu Sohn, *Author-itarianism and Opposition in South Korea* (London, 1989); D. F. Simon, *Taiwan: Beyond the Economic Miracle* (Armonk, N.Y., 1992); Lee Kuan Yew, *From Third World to First: The Singapore Story, 1965–2000* (New York, 2000); and K. Rafferty, *City on the Rocks: Hong Kong's Uncertain Future* (London, 1991).

INFOTRAC COLLEGE EDITION

For additional reading, go to InfoTrac College Edition, your online research library at
http://web1.infotrac-college.com

Enter the search terms "India history" using Keywords.

Enter the search terms "Pakistan history" using Keywords.

Enter the search term "Nehru" using Keywords.

Enter the search terms "Southeast Asia" using Keywords.

Enter the search term "Sukarno" using Keywords.

Enter the search terms "Japan history" using Keywords.

Enter the search term "keiretsu" using Keywords.

Enter the search terms "Japan women" using Keywords.

Enter the search term "Korea" using the Subject Guide.

TOWARD A GLOBAL CIVILIZATION? THE WORLD SINCE 1945

*A*s World War II came to an end, the survivors of that bloody struggle could afford to face the future with a cautious optimism. Europeans might hope that the bitter rivalry that had marked relations among the Western powers would finally be put to an end, and that the wartime alliance of the United States, Great Britain, and the Soviet Union could be maintained into the postwar era.

As a new century dawns, these hopes have been only partly realized. In the decades following the war, the Western capitalist nations managed to recover from the extended economic depression that had contributed to the start of World War II and advanced to a level of economic prosperity never before seen throughout world history. The bloody conflicts that had erupted among European nations during the first half of the twentieth century came to an end, and Germany and Japan were fully integrated into the world community.

At the same time, the prospects for a stable, peaceful world and an end to balance-of-power politics were hampered by the emergence of the grueling and sometimes tense ideological struggle between the socialist and capitalist camps, a competition headed by the only remaining great powers, the Soviet Union and the United States. While the two superpowers were able to avoid an open nuclear confrontation, the postwar world was divided into two heavily armed camps in a balance of terror that on one occasion—the Cuban Missile Crisis—brought the world briefly to the brink of nuclear holocaust.

In the shadow of this rivalry, the Western European states made a remarkable economic recovery and reached new levels of prosperity. But in Eastern Europe, Soviet domination, both politically and economically, seemed so complete that many doubted it could ever be undone. But communism had never developed deep roots in Eastern Europe, and when, in the late 1980s, Soviet leader Mikhail Gorbachev indicated that his government would no longer pursue military intervention, Eastern European states acted quickly to establish their freedom and adopt new economic structures based on Western models. But although many Europeans rejoiced over the possibility of creating a new, undivided Europe, the ethnic hatreds and tensions that had plagued these nations before World War II reemerged and threatened to divide the continent once again.

Outside the West, the peoples of Africa and Asia had their own reasons for optimism as World War II came to a close. In the Atlantic Charter, Franklin Roosevelt and Winston Churchill had set forth a joint declaration of their peace aims calling for the self-determination of all peoples and self-government and sovereign rights for all nations that had been deprived of them.

As it turned out, some colonial powers were reluctant to divest themselves of their colonies. Still, World War II had severely undermined the stability of the colonial order, and by the end of the 1940s, most colonies in Asia had received their independence. Africa followed a decade or two later.

Broadly speaking, the leaders of these newly liberated countries set forth three goals at the outset of independence. They wanted to throw off the shackles of Western economic domination and ensure material prosperity for all of their citizens. They wanted to introduce new political institutions that would enhance the right of self-determination of their peoples. And they wanted to develop a sense of common nationhood within the population and establish secure territorial boundaries. Most opted to follow a capitalist or a moderately socialist path toward economic development. Only in a few cases—China and Vietnam were the most notable examples—did revolutionary leaders opt for the communist mode of development.

Regardless of the path chosen, however, most of the results were disappointing. Virtually all of them remained economically dependent on the advanced industrial nations or, in the case of those who chose to follow the socialist model of development, were forced to rely on the Soviet Union. Some faced severe problems of urban and rural poverty.

What had happened to tarnish the bright dream of economic affluence? During the late 1950s and early 1960s, one school of thought was dominant among scholars and government officials in the United States. Known as modernization theory, this school took the view that the problems faced by the newly independent countries were a consequence of the difficult transition from a traditional to a modern society. Modernization theorists were convinced that agrarian countries were destined to follow the path of the West toward the creation of modern industrial societies but would need time as well as substantial amounts of economic and technological assistance to complete the journey. In their view, it was the duty of advanced capitalist nations to provide such assistance while encouraging the leaders of these states to follow the path already adopted by the West.

Beginning in the late 1960s, modernization theory began to come under attack from a new generation of younger scholars, many of whom had reached maturity during the Vietnam War and had growing doubts about the efficacy of the modernization approach. In their view, the responsibility for continued economic underdevelopment in the developing world lay not with the countries themselves, but with their continued domination by the ex-colonial powers. In this view, known as dependency theory, the countries of Asia, Africa, and Latin America were the victims of the international marketplace, which charged high prices for the manufactured goods of the West while dooming preindustrial countries to low prices for their own raw material exports. Efforts by such countries to build up their own industrial sectors and move into the stage of self-sustaining growth were hampered by foreign control—through European- and American-owned corporations—over many of their resources. To end this "neocolonial" relationship, the dependency theory advocates argued, developing societies should reduce their economic ties with the West and practice a policy of economic self-reliance, thereby taking control over their own destinies.

Both of these approaches, of course, were directly linked to the ideological divisions of the Cold War period and suffered from the weaknesses of their political bias. Although modernization theorists were certainly correct in pointing out some of the key factors that were involved in economic development, they were too quick to see the Western developmental model as the only relevant one and ignored the fact that traditional customs and practices were not necessarily always incompatible with nation building. They also too readily identified economic development in the developing world with the interests of the United States and its allies and underestimated the degree to which Western economic policies operated to the detriment of efforts to promote economic growth in Asia and Africa.

By the same token, the advocates of dependency theory alluded correctly to the often disadvantageous relationship that continued to exist between the ex-colonies and the industrialized nations of the world and the impact that this relationship had on the efforts of developing countries to overcome their economic difficulties. But they often explained away many of the mistakes made by the leaders of developing countries while assigning all of the blame for their plight to the evil and self-serving practices of the industrialized world.

In recent years, the differences between these two schools of thought have declined, as their advocates have attempted to respond to criticism of the perceived weaknesses in their theories. Although the two approaches still have some methodological and ideological differences, there is a growing consensus that there are different roads to development and that the international marketplace can have both beneficial and harmful effects.

A second area of concern for the leaders of African and Asian countries after World War II was to create a new political culture responsive to the needs of their citizens. At first, most accepted the concept of democracy as the defining theme of that culture. Within a decade, however, democratic systems throughout the developing world were replaced by military dictatorships or one-party governments that redefined the concept of democracy to fit their own preferences. It was clear that the difficulties in building democratic political institutions in developing societies had been underestimated.

The problem of establishing a common national identity has in some ways been the most daunting of all the challenges facing the new nations of Asia and Africa. Many of these new states were a composite of a wide variety of ethnic, religious, and linguistic groups who found it difficult to agree on common symbols of nationalism. Problems of establishing an official language and delineating territorial boundaries left over from the colonial era created difficulties in many countries. As the new century dawns, internal conflicts spawned by deep-rooted historical and ethnic hatreds are proliferating throughout the world, leading to a vast new movement of people across state boundaries equal to any that has occurred since the great population migrations of the thirteenth and fourteenth centuries.

The introduction of Western cultural values and customs has also had a destabilizing effect in many areas. Although such ideas are welcomed by some groups, they are firmly resisted by others. Where Western influence has the effect of undermining traditional customs and religious beliefs, it often provokes violent hostility and sparks tension and even conflict within individual societies. To some, Western customs and values represent the wave of the future and are welcomed as a sign of progress. To others, they are destructive of indigenous traditions and a barrier to the growth of a genuine national identity based on history and culture. Much of the anger recently directed at the United States in Muslim countries has undoubtedly been generated by such feelings.

Among the most divisive of such issues is the role of women in society. In the West, the premise of full gender equality had become generally accepted, and remaining barriers tend to lie in the arena of custom rather than in that of law. In many societies in Asia, Africa, and Latin America, the idea that men and women have different roles to play continues to hold sway. Demands by women for equal treatment with men are thus met with suspicion and sometimes outright hostility on the part of those who maintain that woman's place is in the home, not the office or the marketplace.

From the 1950s to the 1970s, such political and economic difficulties led to chronic instability in a number of countries and transformed the developing world into a major theater of Cold War confrontation. During the 1980s, however, a number of new factors entered the equation and shifted the focus away from ideological competition. China's shift to a more accommodating policy toward the West removed fears of more wars of national liberation supported by Beijing.

In the meantime, the growing success of the "little tigers" and the poor economic performance of socialist regimes led a number of developing countries to reduce government reg-

ONE WORLD, ONE ENVIRONMENT

*A*crucial factor that is affecting the evolution of society and the global economy at the beginning of the twenty-first century is growing concern over the impact of industrialization on the earth's environment. There is nothing new about human beings causing damage to their natural surroundings, but never before has the danger of significant ecological damage been as extensive as during the past century. The effects of chemicals introduced into the atmosphere or into rivers, lakes, and oceans have increasingly threatened the health and well-being of all living species.

For many years, the main focus of environmental concern was in the developed countries of the West, where industrial effluents, automobile exhaust, and the use of artificial fertilizers and insecticides led to urban smog, extensive damage to crops and wildlife, and a major reduction of the ozone layer in the upper atmosphere. In recent years, the problem has spread elsewhere. China's headlong rush to industrialization has resulted in major ecological damage in that country. Industrial smog has created almost unlivable conditions in many cities in Asia, while hillsides denuded of their forests have caused severe problems of erosion and destruction of farmlands. Destruction of the rain forest is a growing problem in many parts of the world, notably in Brazil and in the Indonesian archipelago. With the forest cover throughout the earth rapidly disappearing, there is less plant life to perform the crucial process of reducing carbon dioxide levels in the atmosphere.

⇒ **DESTRUCTION OF THE ENVIRONMENT.** This stunted tree has been killed by acid rain, a combination of sulfuric and nitric acids mixed with moisture in the air. Entire forests of trees killed by acid rain are becoming common sights in Canada, the United States, and northern Europe.

Judyth Platt, Ecoscene/CORBIS

One of the few beneficial consequences of such incidents has been a growing international consensus that environmental concerns have taken on a truly global character. Although the danger of global warming—allegedly caused by the release, as a result of industrialization, of hothouse gases into the atmosphere—has not yet been definitively proven, it has become a source of sufficient concern to bring about an international conference on the subject in Kyoto, Japan, in December 1997. If, as many scientists predict, worldwide temperatures should continue to increase, the rise in sea levels could pose a significant threat to low-lying islands and coastal areas throughout the world, while climatic change could lead to severe droughts or excessive rainfall in cultivated areas.

It is one thing to recognize a problem, however, and yet another to solve it. So far, cooperative efforts among nations to alleviate environmental problems have all too often been hindered by economic forces or by political, ethnic, and religious disputes. The 1997 conference on global warming, for example, was marked by bitter disagreement over the degree to which developing countries should share the burden of cleaning up the environment. As a result, it achieved few concrete results. The fact is, few nations have been willing to take unilateral action that might pose an obstacle to economic development plans or lead to a rise in unemployment. In 2001, President George W. Bush refused to sign the Kyoto Agreement on the grounds that it discriminated against advanced Western countries.

ulations and adopt a free market approach to economic development. The situation in China is an obvious case in point. Since the late 1970s, China has realized massive progress through a combination of centralized party leadership and economic policies emphasizing innovation and the interplay of free market forces. By some measures, China today has the third largest economy in the world.

Similarly, there have been tantalizing signs in recent years of a revival of interest in the democratic model in various parts of Asia, Africa, and Latin America. Free elections have been held recently in South Korea, Taiwan, and the Philippines, while similar developments have taken place in Nigeria, South Africa, and a number of other African countries. Although experiments in democratic pluralism have failed in a number of areas, social and political attitudes are changing rapidly in many Asian countries, as new economic circumstances have led to a more secular worldview, a decline in traditional hierarchical relations, and a more open attitude toward sexual practices. In part, these changes have been a consequence of the influence of Western music, movies, and television. But they are also a product of the growth of an affluent middle class in many societies of Asia and Africa. This middle class is often strongly influenced by Western ways, and its sons and daughters ape the behavior, dress, and lifestyles of their counterparts in Europe and North America.

FROM THE INDUSTRIAL TO THE TECHNOLOGICAL REVOLUTION

As many observers have noted, a key aspect of the world economy is that it is in the process of transition to what has been called a "postindustrial age," characterized by a system that is not only increasingly global in scope but also increasingly technology-intensive in character. Since World War II, a stunning array of technological changes—especially in transportation, communications, space exploration, medicine, and agriculture—have transformed the world in which we live. Technological changes have also raised new questions and concerns as well as unexpected results. Some scientists have questioned whether genetic engineering might result accidentally in new strains of deadly bacteria that cannot be controlled outside the laboratory. Some doctors have recently raised the alarm that the overuse of antibiotics has created supergerms, which are no longer subject to antibiotic treatment. The Technological Revolution has also led to the development of more advanced methods of destruction. Most frightening have been nuclear weapons.

The transition to a technology-intensive postindustrial world, which the futurologist Alvin Toffler has dubbed the Third Wave (the first two being the agricultural and industrial revolutions), has produced difficulties for people in many walks of life—for blue-collar workers, whose high wages price them out of the market as firms begin to move their factories abroad; for the poor and uneducated, who lack the technical skills

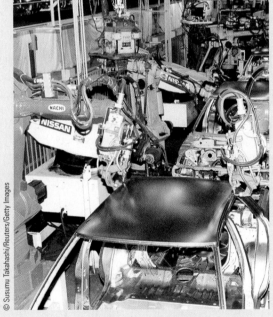

➤ **ON THE ASSEMBLY LINE.** Automation is sometimes cited as one of the key reasons for the vaunted efficiency of the Japanese industrial machine. Mechanical robots, as shown here, perform tasks in Japan that elsewhere are performed by human beings.

© Susumu Takahashi/Reuters/Getty Images

to handle complex tasks in the contemporary economy; and even for some members of the middle class, who have been fired or forced into retirement as their employers seek to slim down to compete in the global marketplace.

It is now increasingly clear that the Technological Revolution, like the Industrial Revolution that preceded it, will entail enormous consequences and may ultimately give birth to a new era of social and political instability. The success of advanced capitalist states in the second half of the twentieth century has been built on a broad consensus on the importance of two propositions: (1) the need for high levels of government investment in education, communications, and transportation as a means of meeting the challenges of continued economic growth and technological innovation, and (2) the desirability of cooperative efforts in the international arena as a means of maintaining open markets for the free exchange of goods.

At the beginning of a new century, these assumptions are increasingly under attack, as citizens refuse to support education and oppose the formation of trading alliances to promote the free movement of goods and labor across national borders. The breakdown of the public consensus that brought modern capitalism to a pinnacle of achievement raises serious questions about the likelihood that the coming challenges of the Third Wave can be successfully met without a growing measure of political and social tension.

Does this mean that the industrial nations of the West have triumphed and are remaking the rest of the world in their own image? Some observers, like the U.S. scholar Francis Fukuyama, argue that capitalism and the Western concept of liberal democracy have vanquished all of their rivals and will ultimately be applied universally throughout the globe. In fact, however, it is much too early to reach such conclusions. It is true that virtually the entire world has now been transformed as the result of the Industrial Revolution that began in Europe at the end of the eighteenth century. Countries throughout the world today are not only linked to the economic marketplace put in place by the Western industrialized nations, but many are

also adopting political and social institutions and values originally introduced from Europe or the United States.

But the strains produced by these events have been severe in many parts of the world, where the costs of globalization often appear to outweigh the benefits. In Africa and the Middle East, two regions that are rapidly falling behind the rest of the world in terms of per capita income and political development, resistance to Western cultural values and institutions remains strong, not only among the leadership but also from within the rank and file of the population.

Even where Western influence is strong, imported institutions have been severely modified to meet local conditions and traditions, and in East Asia today, some governments are effectively using such indigenous traditions as community spirit, the propensity to save, and government interventionism not only to imitate, but to surpass the performance of Western countries. It is no empty phrase to speak of the coming era as the Pacific Century, proving that capitalism is by no means a Western monopoly.

Whatever happens to the current economic situation, it has clearly taken on a truly global character. In fact, today we live not only in a world economy, but in a world society, where a revolution in Iran can cause a rise in the price of oil in the United States and a change in social behavior in Malaysia and Indonesia, where the collapse of an empire in Russia can send shock waves as far as Hanoi and Havana, Cuba, and where a terrorist attack in New York City can disrupt financial markets throughout the world.

One consequence of this process of interdependence is a growing recognition of the common danger posed by environmental pollution (see the box on p. 882). Some people in the West point to overpopulation in the developing countries and the high rate of destruction of the rain forest in developing areas such as Brazil and Malaysia. Observers from Asia or Africa are likely to retort that most of the damage is done by industrial pollution and that the advanced Western countries on a per capita basis use up much more than their share of world resources.

The fact that environmental damage is a common concern suggests the growing need for coordination of efforts on a global scale. Such cooperation, however, has often

been hindered by political differences. India, Pakistan, and Bangladesh have squabbled over the use of the waters of the Ganges and Indus Rivers, as have Israel and its neighbors over the scarce water resources of the Middle East. Pollution of the Rhine River by factories along its banks provokes angry disputes among European nations, while the United States and Canada have argued about the effects of acid rain on Canadian forests.

The collapse of the Soviet Union and its satellite system between 1989 and 1991 seemed to provide an enormous boost to the potential for international cooperation on global issues and led to optimistic predictions that the end of the Cold War would bring about a new era, when political conflicts would be replaced by peaceful economic competition. So far, however, the collapse of the Soviet empire has had almost the opposite effect, as the disintegration of the Soviet Union has led to the emergence of several squabbling new nations and a general atmosphere of conflict and tension throughout much of Eastern Europe.

Even as the world becomes more global in culture and interdependent in its mutual relations, centrifugal forces are at work attempting to redefine the political, cultural, and ethnic ways in which it is divided. Such efforts are often disruptive and can sometimes work against measures to enhance our human destiny. But they also represent an integral part of human character and human history and cannot be suppressed in the relentless drive to create a world society. In his crusade against the "coca-colonization" of the world, Japanese novelist Yukio Mishima was express-

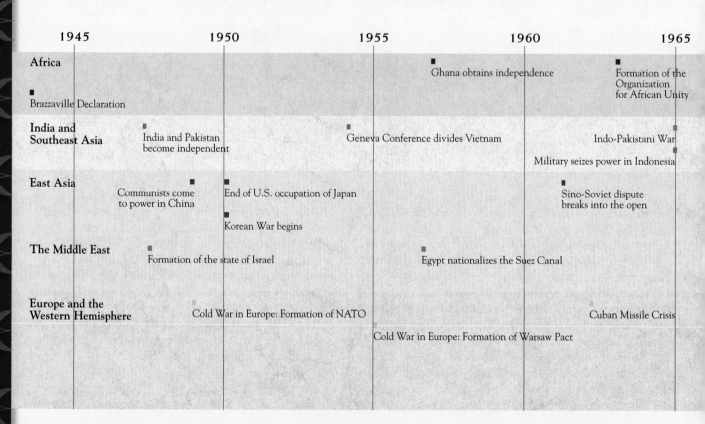

	1945	1950	1955	1960	1965
Africa			Ghana obtains independence		Formation of the Organization for African Unity
	Brazzaville Declaration				
India and Southeast Asia		India and Pakistan become independent	Geneva Conference divides Vietnam		Indo-Pakistani War Military seizes power in Indonesia
East Asia		Communists come to power in China	End of U.S. occupation of Japan Korean War begins		Sino-Soviet dispute breaks into the open
The Middle East		Formation of the state of Israel	Egypt nationalizes the Suez Canal		
Europe and the Western Hemisphere		Cold War in Europe: Formation of NATO	Cold War in Europe: Formation of Warsaw Pact		Cuban Missile Crisis

ing a fear that is shared today by millions throughout the world, as Walt Disney, rock music, and McDonald's relentlessly erode the boundaries that separate one culture and people from another. What will result from this concern is as yet unclear. What is apparent is that the Technological Revolution is proceeding at a dizzying speed that can carry information, ideas, and images around the world in seconds (see the box on p. 883).

What is already apparent is that technological advances will have an enormous impact on human society in coming generations. Although many of these consequences may be welcome, others represent a serious challenge, as individuals raised on television, video games, and the computer find less and less time for human relationships or creative activities. To some, the only antidote to the sense of confusion and alienation afflicting contemporary life is to reject the scientific outlook, with its secularizing implications, and return to religious faith. Others hope that a combination of scientific knowledge and spiritual revival can spark a renewal that will enable people to deal constructively with contemporary alienation and confusion.

In a recent book entitled *The Clash of Civilizations and the Remaking of the World Order,* the political scientist Samuel P. Huntington has suggested that the post–Cold War era, far from marking the triumph of the Western idea, will be characterized by increased global fragmentation and a "clash of civilizations" based on ethnic, cultural, or religious distinctions. According to Huntington, cultural identity has replaced shared ideology as the dominant force in world affairs. As a result, he argues, the

coming decades may see an emerging world dominated by disputing cultural blocs in East Asia, Western Europe and the United States, Eurasia, and the Middle East, with the societies in each region coalescing around common cultural features against perceived threats from rival forces elsewhere around the globe. The dream of a universal order dominated by Western values, he concludes, is a fantasy.

In the conditions at the beginning of a new century, Huntington's thesis may serve as a corrective to the tendency of many observers in Europe and the United States to see Western civilization as the zenith and final resting place of human achievement. The tense relations that currently exist between the Muslim world and the West is a vivid testimonial to the fact that cultural differences are one of the crucial faultlines in the world today. But in dividing the world into competing cultural blocs, many feel that Huntington has seriously underestimated the centrifugal forces that exist within each region, as well as the transformative effect of the Industrial Revolution and the emerging global informational network. There are already initial signs that as the common dangers posed by environmental damage, overpopulation, and scarcity of resources become even more apparent, societies around the world will find ample reason to turn their attention from cultural differences to the demands of global interdependence. As the world faces a new century, its greatest challenge may be to reconcile the drive for individual and group identity with the common needs of the human community.

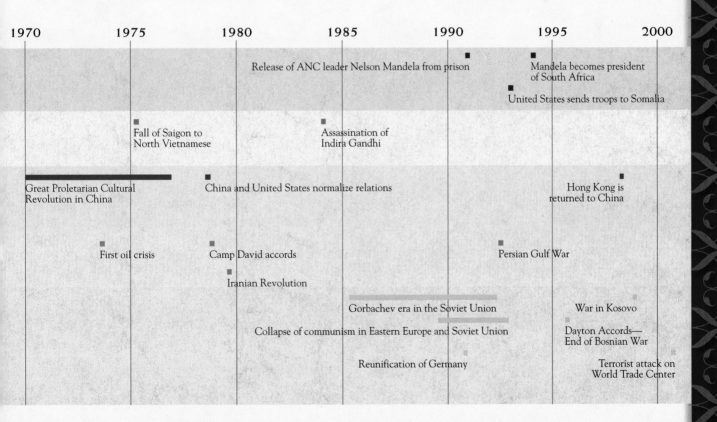

Glossary

absolutism a form of government where the sovereign power or ultimate authority rested in the hands of a monarch who claimed to rule by divine right and was therefore responsible only to God.

Agricultural (Neolithic) Revolution the shift from hunting animals and gathering plants for sustenance to producing food by systematic agriculture that occurred gradually between 10,000 and 4000 B.C. (the Neolithic or "New Stone" Age).

agricultural revolution the application of new agricultural techniques that allowed for a large increase in productivity in the eighteenth century.

anarchism a political theory that holds that all governments and existing social institutions are unnecessary and advocates a society based on voluntary cooperation.

ANC the African National Congress. Founded in 1912, it was the beginning of political activity by South African blacks. Banned by politically dominant European whites in 1960, it was not officially "unbanned" until 1990. It is now the official majority party of the South African government.

Analects the body of writing containing conversations between Confucius and his disciples that preserves his worldly wisdom and pragmatic philosophies.

anti-Semitism hostility toward or discrimination against Jews.

appeasement the policy, followed by the European nations in the 1930s, of accepting Hitler's annexation of Austria and Czechoslovakia in the belief that meeting his demands would assure peace and stability.

Arianism a Christian heresy that taught that Jesus was inferior to God. Though condemned by the Council of Nicaea in 325, Arianism was adopted by many of the Germanic peoples who entered the Roman Empire over the next centuries.

aristocracy a class of hereditary nobility in medieval Europe; a warrior class who shared a distinctive lifestyle based on the institution of knighthood, although there were social divisions within the group based on extremes of wealth.

Arthasastra an early Indian political treatise that sets forth many fundamental aspects of the relationship of rulers and their subjects. It has been compared to Machiavelli's well-known book, *The Prince*, and has provided principles upon which many aspects of social organization have developed in the region.

Aryans Indo–European-speaking nomads who entered India from the Central Asian steppes between 1500 and 1000 B.C.E. and greatly affected Indian society, notably by establishing the caste system. The term was later adopted by German Nazis to describe their racial ideal.

ASEAN the Association for the Southest Asian Nations formed in 1967 to promote the prosperity and political stability of its member nations. Currently Brunei, Indonesia, Laos, Malaysia, Myanmar, the Philippines, Singapore, Thailand, and Vietnam are members. Other countries in the region participate as "observer" members.

Ausgleich the "Compromise" of 1867 that created the dual monarchy of Austria-Hungary. Austria and Hungary each had its own capital, constitution, and legislative assembly, but were united under one monarch.

authoritarian state a state that has a dictatorial government and some other trappings of a totalitarian state, but does not demand that the masses be actively involved in the regime's goals as totalitarian states do.

auxiliaries troops enlisted from the subject peoples of the Roman Empire to supplement the regular legions composed of Roman citizens.

bakufu the centralized government set up in Japan in the twelfth century. *See* shogunate system.

balance of power a distribution of power among several states such that no single nation can dominate or interfere with the interests of another.

Bao-jia system the Chinese practice, reportedly originated by the Qin dynasty in the third century B.C.E., of organizing families into groups of five or ten to exercise mutual control and surveillance and reduce loyalty to the family.

Baroque a style that dominated Western painting, sculpture, architecture and music from about 1580 to 1730, generally characterized by elaborate ornamentation and dramatic effects. Important practitioners included Bernini, Rubens, Handel, and Bach.

Bedouins nomadic tribes originally from northern Arabia, who became important traders after the domestication of the camel during the first millennium B.C.E. Early converts to Islam, their values and practices deeply affected Muhammad.

benefice in the Christian church, a position, such as a bishopric, that consisted of both a sacred office and the right of the holder to the annual revenues from the position.

bhakti in Hinduism, devotion as a means of religious observance open to all persons regardless of class.

bicameral legislature a legislature with two houses.

Black Death the outbreak of plague (mostly bubonic) in the mid-fourteenth century that killed from 25 to 50 percent of Europe's population.

Blitzkrieg "lightning war." A war conducted with great speed and force, as in Germany's advance at the beginning of World War II.

bodhisattvas in some schools of Buddhism, individuals who have achieved enlightenment but, because of their great compassion, have chosen to renounce Nirvana and to remain on earth in spirit form to help all human beings achieve release from reincarnation.

Bolsheviks a small faction of the Russian Social Democratic Party who were led by Lenin and dedicated to violent revolution; seized power in Russia in 1917 and were subsequently renamed the Communists.

boyars the Russian nobility.

Brezhnev Doctrine the doctrine, enunciated by Leonid Brezhnev, that the Soviet Union had a right to intervene if socialism was threatened in another socialist state; used to justify the use of Soviet troops in Czechoslovakia in 1968.

caliph the secular leader of the Islamic community.

calpulli In Aztec society, a kinship group, often of a thousand or more, which served as an intermediary with the central government, providing taxes and conscript labor to the state.

capital material wealth used or available for use in the production of more wealth.

caste system a system of rigid social hierarchy in which all members of that society are assigned by birth to specific "ranks," and inherit specific roles and privileges.

cartel a combination of independent commercial enterprises that work together to control prices and limit competition.

Cartesian dualism Descartes's principle of the separation of mind and matter (and mind and body) that enabled scientists to view matter as something separate from themselves that could be investigated by reason.

caudillos strong leaders in nineteenth-century Latin America, who were usually supported by the landed elites and ruled chiefly by military force, though some were popular; they included both modernizers and destructive dictators.

censorate one of the three primary Chinese ministries, originally established in the Qin dynasty, whose inspectors surveyed the efficiency of officials throughout the system.

chaebol a South Korean business structure similar to the Japanese keiretsu.

chansons de geste a form of vernacular literature in the High Middle Ages that consisted of heroic epics focusing on the deeds of warriors.

chivalry the ideal of civilized behavior that emerged among the nobility in the eleventh and twelfth centuries under the influence of the church; a code of ethics knights were expected to uphold.

Christian (northern) humanism an intellectual movement in northern Europe in the late fifteenth and early sixteenth centuries that combined the interest in the classics of the Italian Renaissance with an interest in the sources of early Christianity, including the New Testament and the writings of the church fathers.

civic humanism an intellectual movement of the Italian Renaissance that saw Cicero, who was both an intellectual and a statesman, as the ideal and held that humanists should be involved in government and use their rhetorical training in the service of the state.

civil rights the basic rights of citizens including equality before the law, freedom of speech and press, and freedom from arbitrary arrest.

civil service examination an elaborate Chinese system of selecting bureaucrats on merit, first introduced in 165 B.C.E., developed by the Tang dynasty in the seventh century C.E. and refined under the Song dynasty; later adopted in Vietnam and with less success in Japan and Korea. It contributed to efficient government, upward mobility, and cultural uniformity.

class struggle the basis of the Marxist analysis of history, which says that the owners of the means of production have always oppressed the workers and predicts an inevitable revolution. *See* Marxism.

Cold War the ideological conflict between the Soviet Union and the United States after World War II.

collective farms large farms created in the Soviet Union by Stalin by combining many small holdings into one large farm worked by the peasants under government supervision.

collective security the use of an international army raised by an association of nations to deter aggression and keep the peace.

coloni free tenant farmers who worked as sharecroppers on the large estates of the Roman Empire (singular: *colonus*).

Comintern a worldwide organization of Communist parties, founded by Lenin in 1919, dedicated to the advancement of world revolution; also known as the Third International.

common law law common to the entire kingdom of England; imposed by the king's courts beginning in the twelfth century to replace the customary law used in county and feudal courts that varied from place to place.

commune in medieval Europe, an association of townspeople bound together by a sworn oath for the purpose of obtaining basic liberties from the lord of the territory in which the town was located; also, the self-governing town after receiving its liberties.

conciliarism a movement in fourteenth- and fifteenth-century Europe that held that final authority in spiritual matters resided with a general church council, not the pope; emerged in response to the Avignon papacy and the Great Schism and used to justify the summoning of the Council of Constance (1414–1418).

condottieri leaders of bands of mercenary soldiers in Renaissance Italy who sold their services to the highest bidder.

Confucianism a system of thought based on the teachings of Confucius (551–479 B.C.E.) that developed into the ruling ideology of the Chinese state. *See* Neo-Confucianism.

conquistadors "conquerors." Leaders in the Spanish conquests in the Americas, especially Mexico and Peru, in the sixteenth century.

conscription a military draft.

conservatism an ideology based on tradition and social stability that favored the maintenance of established institutions, organized religion, and obedience to authority and resisted change, especially abrupt change.

consuls the chief executive officers of the Roman Republic. Two were chosen annually to administer the government and lead the army in battle.

consumer society a term applied to Western society after World War II as the working classes adopted the consumption patterns of the middle class and installment plans, credit cards, and easy credit made consumer goods such as appliances and automobiles widely available.

Continental System Napoleon's effort to bar British goods from the Continent in the hope of weakening Britain's economy and destroying its capacity to wage war.

cosmopolitanism   the quality of being sophisticated and having wide international experience.

cottage industry   a system of textile manufacturing in which spinners and weavers worked at home in their cottages using raw materials supplied to them by capitalist entrepreneurs.

cultural relativism   the belief that no culture is superior to another because culture is a matter of custom, not reason, and derives its meaning from the group holding it.

cuneiform   "wedge-shaped." A system of writing developed by the Sumerians that consisted of wedge-shaped impressions made by a reed stylus on clay tablets.

daimyo   prominent Japanese families who provided allegiance to the local shogun in exchange for protection; similar to vassals in Europe.

decolonization   the process of becoming free of colonial status and achieving statehood; occurred in most of the world's colonies between 1947 and 1962.

deism   belief in God as the creator of the universe who, after setting it in motion, ceased to have any direct involvement in it and allowed it to run according to its own natural laws.

demesne   the part of a manor retained under the direct control of the lord and worked by the serfs as part of their labor services.

depression   a very severe, protracted economic downturn with high levels of unemployment.

destalinization   the policy of denouncing and undoing the most repressive aspects of Stalin's regime; begun by Nikita Khrushchev in 1956.

détente   the relaxation of tension between the Soviet Union and the United States that occurred in the 1970s.

dharma   in Hinduism and Buddhism, the law that governs the universe, and specifically human behavior.

dialectic   logic, one of the seven liberal arts that made up the medieval curriculum. In Marxist thought, the process by which all change occurs through the clash of antagonistic elements.

Diaspora   the scattering of Jews throughout the ancient world after the Babylonian captivity in the sixth century B.C.E.

dictator   in the Roman Republic, an official granted unlimited power to run the state for a short period of time, usually six months, during an emergency.

diocese   the area under the jurisdiction of a Christian bishop; based originally on Roman administrative districts.

direct representation   a system of choosing delegates to a representative assembly in which citizens vote directly for the delegates who will represent them.

divination   the practice of seeking to foretell future events by interpreting divine signs, which could appear in various forms, such as in entrails of animals, in patterns in smoke, or in dreams.

divine-right monarchy   a monarchy based on the belief that monarchs receive their power directly from God and are responsible to no one except God.

domino theory   the belief that if the Communists succeeded in Vietnam, other countries in Southeast and East Asia would also fall (like dominoes) to communism; a justification for the U.S. intervention in Vietnam.

dualism   the belief that the universe is dominated by two opposing forces, one good and the other evil.

dynastic state   a state where the maintenance and expansion of the interests of the ruling family is the primary consideration.

economic imperialism   the process in which banks and corporations from developed nations invest in underdeveloped regions and establish a major presence there in the hope of making high profits; not necessarily the same as colonial expansion in that businesses invest where they can make a profit, which may not be in their own nation's colonies.

empiricism   the practice of relying on observation and experiment.

enclosure movement   in the eighteenth century, the fencing in of the old open fields, combining many small holdings into larger units that could be farmed more efficiently.

encomienda system   the system by which Spain first governed its American colonies. Holders of an encomienda were supposed to protect the Indians as well as using them as laborers and collecting tribute but in practice exploited them.

encyclical   a letter from the pope to all the bishops of the Roman Catholic church.

enlightened absolutism   an absolute monarchy where the ruler follows the principles of the Enlightenment by introducing reforms for the improvement of society, allowing freedom of speech and the press, permitting religious toleration, expanding education, and ruling in accordance with the laws.

Enlightenment   an eighteenth-century intellectual movement, led by the philosophes, that stressed the application of reason and the scientific method to all aspects of life.

entrepreneur   one who organizes, operates, and assumes the risk in a business venture in the expectation of making a profit.

Epicureanism   a philosophy founded by Epicurus in the fourth century B.C. that taught that happiness (freedom from emotional turmoil) could be achieved through the pursuit of pleasure (intellectual rather than sensual pleasure).

equestrians   a group of extremely wealthy men in the late Roman Republic who were effectively barred from high office, but sought political power commensurate with their wealth; called equestrians because many had gotten their start as cavalry officers (*equites*).

ethnic cleansing   the policy of killing or forcibly removing people of another ethnic group; used by the Serbs against Bosnian Muslims in the 1990s.

eucharist   a Christian sacrament in which consecrated bread and wine are consumed in celebration of Jesus' Last Supper; also called the Lord's Supper or communion.

evolutionary socialism   a socialist doctrine espoused by Eduard Bernstein who argued that socialists should stress cooperation and evolution to attain power by democratic means rather than by conflict and revolution.

fascism   an ideology or movement that exalts the nation above the individual and calls for a centralized government with a dictatorial leader, economic and social regimentation, and forcible suppression of opposition; in particular, the ideology of Mussolini's Fascist regime in Italy.

feminism   the belief in the social, political, and economic equality of the sexes; also, organized activity to advance women's rights.

fief   a landed estate granted to a vassal in exchange for military services.

Final Solution   the physical extermination of the Jewish people by the Nazis during World War II.

five pillars of Islam   the core requirements of the faith, observation of which would lead to paradise: belief in Allah and his Prophet Muhammad; prescribed prayers; observation of Ramadan; pilgrimage to Mecca; and giving alms to the poor.

folk culture   the traditional arts and crafts, literature, music, and other customs of the people; something that people make, as opposed to modern popular culture, which is something people buy.

four modernizations   the slogan for radical reforms of Chinese industry, agriculture, technology, and national defense, instituted by Deng Xiaoping after his accession to power in the late 1970s.

free trade   the unrestricted international exchange of goods with low or no tariffs.

fundamentalism   a movement that emphasizes rigid adherence to basic religious principles; coined to describe Evangelical Christianity, it is often used to characterize Islamic conservatives.

general strike   a strike by all or most workers in an economy; espoused by Georges Sorel as the heroic action that could be used to inspire the workers to destroy capitalist society.

gentry   well-to-do English landowners below the level of the nobility; played an important role in the English Civil War of the seventeenth century.

geocentric theory   the idea that the earth is at the center of the universe and that the sun and other celestial objects revolve around the earth.

glasnost   "openness." Mikhail Gorbachev's policy of encouraging Soviet citizens to openly discuss the strengths and weaknesses of the Soviet Union.

Gleichschaltung   the coordination of all government institutions under Nazi control in Germany from 1933.

global civilization   human society considered as a single worldwide entity, in which local differences are less important than overall similarities.

good emperors   the five emperors who ruled from 96 to 180 (Nerva, Trajan, Hadrian, Antoninus Pius, and Marcus Aurelius), a period of peace and prosperity for the Roman Empire.

Great Schism   the crisis in the late medieval church when there were first two and then three popes; ended by the Council of Constance (1414–1418).

guest workers   foreign workers working temporarily in European countries.

guild   an association of people with common interests and concerns, especially people working in the same craft. In medieval Europe, guilds came to control much of the production process and to restrict entry into various trades.

gymnasium   in classical Greece, a place for athletics; in the Hellenistic Age, a secondary school with a curriculum centered on music, physical exercise, and literature.

Hegira   the flight of Muhammad from Mecca to Medina in 622, which marks the first date on the official calendar of Islam.

heliocentric theory   the idea that the sun (not the earth) is at the center of the universe.

Hellenistic   literally, "to imitate the Greeks"; the era after the death of Alexander the Great when Greek culture spread into the Near East and blended with the culture of that region.

helots   serfs in ancient Sparta, who were permanently bound to the land that they worked for their Spartan masters.

heresy   the holding of religious doctrines different from the official teachings of the church.

Hermeticism   an intellectual movement beginning in the fifteenth century that taught that divinity is embodied in all aspects of nature; included works on alchemy and magic as well as theology and philosophy. The tradition continued into the seventeenth century and influenced many of the leading figures of the Scientific Revolution.

hetairai   highly sophisticated courtesans in ancient Athens who offered intellectual and musical entertainment as well as sex.

hieroglyphics   a highly pictorial system of writing most often associated with ancient Egypt. Also used (with different "pictographs") by other ancient peoples such as the Mayans.

high culture   the literary and artistic culture of the educated and wealthy ruling classes.

Hinduism   the main religion in India, it emphasizes reincarnation, based on the results of the previous life, and the desirability of escaping this cycle. Its various forms feature both asceticism and the pleasures of ordinary life, and encompass a multitude of gods as different manifestations of one ultimate reality.

Holocaust   the mass slaughter of European Jews by the Nazis during World War II.

Hopewell culture   a Native American society that flourished from about 200 B.C.E. to 400 C.E., noted for large burial mounds and extensive manufacture. Largely based in Ohio, its traders ranged as far as the Gulf of Mexico.

hoplites   heavily armed infantry soldiers used in ancient Greece in a phalanx formation.

Huguenots   French Calvinists.

humanism   an intellectual movement in Renaissance Italy based upon the study of the Greek and Roman classics.

Hundred Schools   (of philosophy) in China around the third century B.C.E., a wide-ranging debate over the nature of human beings, society, and the universe. The Schools included Legalism and Daoism, as well as Confucianism.

iconoclasm   an eighth-century Byzantine movement against the use of icons (pictures of sacred figures), which was condemned as idolatry.

ideology   a political philosophy such as conservatism or liberalism.

imperialism   the policy of extending one nation's power either by conquest or by establishing direct or indirect economic or cultural authority over another. Generally driven by economic self-interest, it can also be motivated by a sincere (if often misguided) sense of moral obligation.

imperium   "the right to command." In the Roman Republic, the chief executive officers (consuls and praetors) possessed the *imperium*; a military commander was an *imperator*. In the Roman Empire, the title *imperator*, or emperor, came to be used for the ruler.

indirect representation   a system of choosing delegates to a representative assembly in which citizens do not choose the delegates directly but instead vote for electors who choose the delegates.

individualism   emphasis on and interest in the unique traits of each person.

indulgence   the remission of part or all of the temporal punishment in purgatory due to sin; granted for charitable contributions and other good deeds. Indulgences became a regular practice of the Christian church in the High Middle Ages, and their abuse was instrumental in sparking Luther's reform movement in the sixteenth century.

infanticide   the practice of killing infants.

inflation   a sustained rise in the price level.

intendants   royal officials in seventeenth-century France who were sent into the provinces to execute the orders of the central government.

intervention, principle of   the idea, after the Congress of Vienna, that the great powers of Europe had the right to send armies into countries experiencing revolution to restore legitimate monarchs to their thrones.

isolationism   a foreign policy in which a nation refrains from making alliances or engaging actively in international affairs.

jihad   In Islam, "striving in the way of the Lord." The term is ambiguous and has been subject to varying interpretations, from the practice of conducting raids against local neighbors to the conduct of "holy war" against unbelievers.

joint-stock company   a company or association that raises capital by selling shares to individuals who receive dividends on their investment while a board of directors runs the company.

joint-stock investment bank   a bank created by selling shares of stock to investors. Such banks potentially have access to much more capital than do private banks owned by one or a few individuals.

Jomon   the earliest known Neolithic inhabitants of Japan, named for the cord pattern of their pottery.

justification by faith   the primary doctrine of the Protestant Reformation; taught that humans are saved not through good works, but by the grace of God, bestowed freely through the sacrifice of Jesus.

kami   spirits who were worshiped in early Japan, and resided in trees, rivers and streams. *See* Shinto.

keiretsu   a type of powerful industrial or financial conglomerate that emerged in post-World War II Japan following the abolition of zaibatsu.

kolkhoz   a collective farm in the Soviet Union, in which the great bulk of the land was held and worked communally. Between 1928 and 1934, 250,000 kolkhozes replaced 26 million family farms.

laissez-faire   "to let alone." An economic doctrine that holds that an economy is best served when the government does not interfere but allows the economy to self-regulate according to the forces of supply and demand.

latifundia   large landed estates in the Roman Empire (singular: *latifundium*).

lay investiture   the practice in which a layperson chose a bishop and invested him with the symbols of both his temporal office and his spiritual office; led to the Investiture Controversy, which was ended by compromise in the Concordat of Worms in 1122.

Lebensraum   "living space." The doctrine, adopted by Hitler, that a nation's power depends on the amount of land it occupies; thus, a nation must expand to be strong.

Legalism   a Chinese philosophy that argued that human beings were by nature evil and would follow the correct path only if coerced by harsh laws and stiff punishments. Adopted as official ideology by the Qin dynasty, it was later rejected but remained influential.

legitimacy, principle of   the idea that after the Napoleonic wars peace could best be reestablished in Europe by restoring legitimate monarchs who would preserve traditional institutions; guided Metternich at the Congress of Vienna.

Leninism   Lenin's revision of Marxism that held that Russia need not experience a bourgeois revolution before it could move toward socialism.

liberal arts   the seven areas of study that formed the basis of education in medieval and early modern Europe. Following Boethius and other late Roman authors, they consisted of grammar, rhetoric, and dialectic or logic (the *trivium*) and arithmetic, geometry, astronomy, and music (the *quadrivium*).

liberalism   an ideology based on the belief that people should be as free from restraint as possible. Economic liberalism is the idea that the government should not interfere in the workings of the economy. Political liberalism is the idea that there should be restraints on the exercise of power so that people can enjoy basic civil rights in a constitutional state with a representative assembly.

limited liability   the principle that shareholders in a joint-stock corporation can be held responsible for the corporation's debts only up to the amount they have invested.

limited (constitutional) monarchy   a system of government in which the monarch is limited by a representative assembly and by the duty to rule in accordance with the laws of the land.

lineage group   the descendants of a common ancestor; relatives, often as opposed to immediate family.

Mahayana   a school of Buddhism that promotes the idea of universal salvation through the intercession of bodhisattvas; predominant in north Asia.

mandates   a system established after World War I whereby a nation officially administered a territory (mandate) on behalf of the League of Nations. Thus, France administered Lebanon and Syria as mandates, and Britain administered Iraq and Palestine.

manor   an agricultural estate operated by a lord and worked by peasants who performed labor services and paid various rents and fees to the lord in exchange for protection and sustenance.

Marshall Plan   the European Recovery Program, under which the United States provided financial aid to European countries to help them rebuild after World War II.

Marxism   the political, economic, and social theories of Karl Marx, which included the idea that history is the story of class struggle and that ultimately the proletariat will overthrow the bourgeoisie and establish a dictatorship en route to a classless society.

mass education   a state-run educational system, usually free and compulsory, that aims to ensure that all children in society have at least a basic education.

mass leisure   forms of leisure that appeal to large numbers of people in a society including the working classes; emerged at the end of the nineteenth century to provide workers with amusements after work and on weekends; used during the twentieth century by totalitarian states to control their populations.

mass politics   a political order characterized by mass political parties and universal male and (eventually) female suffrage.

mass society   a society in which the concerns of the majority—the lower classes—play a prominent role; characterized by extension of voting rights, an improved standard of living for the lower classes, and mass education.

materialism   the belief that everything mental, spiritual, or ideal is an outgrowth of physical forces and that truth is found in concrete material existence, not through feeling or intuition.

megaliths   large stones, widely used in Europe from around 4000 to 1500 B.C.E. to create monuments, including sophisticated astronomical observatories.

Meiji Restoration   the period during the late 19th and early 20th century in which fundamental economic and cultural changes occured in Japan, tranforming it from a feudal and agrarian society to an industrial and technological society.

mercantilism   an economic theory that held that a nation's prosperity depended on its supply of gold and silver and that the total volume of trade is unchangeable; therefore, advocated that the government play an active role in the economy by encouraging exports and discouraging imports, especially through the use of tariffs.

Mesolithic Age   the period from 10,000 to 7000 B.C., characterized by a gradual transition from a food-gathering/hunting economy to a food-producing economy.

mestizos   the offspring of intermarriage between Europeans, originally Spaniards, and native American Indians.

metics   resident foreigners in ancient Athens; not permitted full rights of citizenship but did receive the protection of the laws.

militarism   a policy of aggressive military preparedness; in particular, the large armies based on mass conscription and complex, inflexible plans for mobilization that most European nations had before World War I.

ministerial responsibility   a tenet of nineteenth-century liberalism that held that ministers of the monarch should be responsible to the legislative assembly rather than to the monarch.

Modernism   the new artistic and literary styles that emerged in the decades before 1914 as artists rebelled against traditional efforts to portray reality as accurately as possible (leading to Impressionism and Cubism) and writers explored new forms.

monotheistic/monotheism   having only one god; the doctrine or belief that there is only one god.

mulattoes   the offspring of Africans and Europeans, particularly in Latin America.

mutual deterrence   the belief that nuclear war could best be prevented if both the United States and the Soviet Union had sufficient nuclear weapons so that even if one nation launched a preemptive first strike, the other could respond and devastate the attacker.

mystery religions   religions that involve initiation into secret rites that promise intense emotional involvement with spiritual forces and a greater chance of individual immortality.

nationalism   a sense of national consciousness based on awareness of being part of a community—a "nation"—that has common institutions, traditions, language, and customs and that becomes the focus of the individual's primary political loyalty.

nationalities problem   the dilemma faced by the Austro-Hungarian Empire in trying to unite a wide variety of ethnic groups including, among others, Austrians, Hungarians, Poles, Croats, Czechs, Serbs, Slovaks, and Slovenes in an era when nationalism and calls for self-determination were coming to the fore.

nationalization   the process of converting a business or industry from private ownership to government control and ownership.

nation in arms   the people's army raised by universal mobilization to repel the foreign enemies of the French Revolution.

nation-state   a form of political organization in which a relatively homogeneous people inhabits a sovereign state, as opposed to a state containing people of several nationalities.

NATO   the North Atlantic Treaty Organization; a military alliance formed in 1949 in which the signatories (Belgium, Canada, Denmark, France, Great Britain, Iceland, Italy, Luxembourg, the Netherlands, Norway, Portugal, and the United States) agreed to provide mutual assistance if any one of them was attacked; later expanded to include other nations, including former members of the Warsaw Pact—Poland, the Czech Republic and Hungary.

natural laws   a body of laws or specific principles held to be derived from nature and binding upon all human society even in the absence of positive laws.

natural rights   certain inalienable rights to which all people are entitled; include the right to life, liberty, and property, freedom of speech and religion, and equality before the law.

natural selection   Darwin's idea that organisms that are most adaptable to their environment survive and pass on the variations that enabled them to survive, while other, less adaptable organisms become extinct; "survival of the fittest."

Nazi New Order   the Nazis' plan for their conquered territories; included the extermination of Jews and others considered inferior, ruthless exploitation of resources, German colonization in the east, and the use of Poles, Russians, and Ukrainians as slave labor.

negritude a philosophy shared among African blacks that there exists a distinctive "African personality" that owes nothing to Western values and provides a common sense of purpose and destiny for black Africans.

Neo-Confucianism the dominant ideology of China during the second millennium C.E., it combined the metaphysical speculations of Buddhism and Daoism with the pragmatic Confucian approach to society, maintaining that the world is real, not illusory, and that fulfillment comes from participation, not withdrawal. It encouraged an intellectual environment that valued continuity over change and tradition over innovation.

Neoplatonism a revival of Platonic philosophy; in the third century A.D., a revival associated with Plotinus; in the Italian Renaissance, a revival associated with Marsilio Ficino who attempted to synthesize Christianity and Platonism.

New Course a short-lived, liberalizing change in Soviet policy to its Eastern European allies instituted after the death of Stalin in 1953.

New Culture Movement a protest launched at Peking University after the failure of the 1911 revolution, aimed at abolishing the remnants of the old system and introducing Western values and institutions into China.

New Democracy the initial program of the Chinese Communist government, from 1949 to 1955, focusing on honest government, land reform, social justice, and peace rather than on the utopian goal of a classless society.

New Economic Policy a modified version of the old capitalist system introduced in the Soviet Union by Lenin in 1921 to revive the economy after the ravages of the civil war and war communism.

new imperialism the revival of imperialism after 1880 in which European nations established colonies throughout much of Asia and Africa.

new monarchies the governments of France, England, and Spain at the end of the fifteenth century, where the rulers were successful in reestablishing or extending centralized royal authority, suppressing the nobility, controlling the church, and insisting upon the loyalty of all peoples living in their territories.

Nirvana in Buddhist thought, enlightenment, the ultimate transcendence from the illusion of the material world; release from the wheel of life.

nobiles "nobles." The small group of families from both patrician and plebeian origins who produced most of the men who were elected to office in the late Roman Republic.

Nok culture in northern Nigeria, one of the most active early ironworking societies in Africa, artifacts from which date back as far as 500 B.C.E.

nuclear family a family group consisting only of father, mother, and children.

old regime/old order the political and social system of France in the eighteenth century before the Revolution.

oligarchy rule by a few.

Open Door notes a series of letters sent in 1899 by U.S. Secretary of State John Hay to Great Britain, France, Germany, Italy, Japan and Russia, calling for equal economic access to the China market for all states and for the maintenance of the territorial and administrative integrity of the Chinese Empire.

optimates "best men." Aristocratic leaders in the late Roman Republic who generally came from senatorial families and wished to retain their oligarchical privileges.

opium trade the sale of the addictive product of the poppy, specifically by British traders to China in the 1830s. Chinese attempts to prevent it led to the Opium War of 1839–1842, which resulted in British access to Chinese ports and has traditionally been considered the beginning of modern Chinese history.

orders/estates the traditional tripartite division of European society based on heredity and quality rather than wealth or economic standing, first established in the Middle Ages and continuing into the eighteenth century; traditionally consisted of those who pray (the clergy), those who fight (the nobility), and those who work (all the rest).

organic evolution Darwin's principle that all plants and animals have evolved over a long period of time from earlier and simpler forms of life.

Organization of African Unity founded in Addis Ababa in 1963, it was intended to represent the interests of all the newly independent countries of Africa and provided a forum for the discussion of common problems until 2001, when it was replaced by the African Union.

Paleolithic Age the period of human history when humans used simple stone tools (c. 2,500,000–10,000 B.C.).

pan-Africanism the concept of African continental unity and solidarity in which the common interests of African countries transcend regional boundaries.

pantheism a doctrine that equates God with the universe and all that is in it.

paterfamilias the dominant male in a Roman family whose powers over his wife and children were theoretically unlimited, though they were sometimes circumvented in practice.

patriarchal/patriarchy a society in which the father is supreme in the clan or family; more generally, a society dominated by men.

patriarchal family a family in which the husband/father dominates his wife and children.

patricians great landowners who became the ruling class in the Roman Republic.

patronage the practice of awarding titles and making appointments to government and other positions to gain political support.

Pax Romana "Roman peace." A term used to refer to the stability and prosperity that Roman rule brought to the Mediterranean world and much of western Europe during the first and second centuries A.D.

peaceful coexistence the policy adopted by the Soviet Union under Khrushchev in 1955, and continued by his successors, that called for economic and ideological rivalry with the West rather than nuclear war.

Pentateuch the first five books of the Hebrew Bible (Genesis, Exodus, Leviticus, Numbers, and Deuteronomy).

peoples' democracies   a term invented by the Soviet Union to define a society in the early stage of socialist transition, applied to Eastern European countries in the 1950s.

perestroika   "restructuring." A term applied to Mikhail Gorbachev's economic, political, and social reforms in the Soviet Union.

permissive society   a term applied to Western society after World War II to reflect the new sexual freedom and the emergence of a drug culture.

Petrine supremacy   the doctrine that the bishop of Rome—the pope—as the successor of Saint Peter (traditionally considered the first bishop of Rome) should hold a preeminent position in the church.

phalanx   a rectangular formation of tightly massed infantry soldiers.

philosophes   intellectuals of the eighteenth-century Enlightenment who believed in applying a spirit of rational criticism to all things, including religion and politics, and who focused on improving and enjoying this world, rather than on the afterlife.

plebeians   the class of Roman citizens who included nonpatrician landowners, craftspeople, merchants, and small farmers in the Roman Republic. Their struggle for equal rights with the patricians dominated much of the Republic's history.

pluralism   the practice in which one person holds several church offices simultaneously; a problem of the late medieval church.

pogroms   organized massacres of Jews.

polis   an ancient Greek city-state encompassing both an urban area and its surrounding countryside; a small but autonomous political unit where all major political and social activities were carried out in a central location.

political democracy   a form of government characterized by universal suffrage and mass political parties.

politiques   a group who emerged during the French Wars of Religion in the sixteenth century; placed politics above religion and believed that no religious truth was worth the ravages of civil war.

polygyny   the state or practice of having more than one wife at a time.

polytheistic/polytheism   having many gods; belief in or the worship of more than one god.

popular culture   as opposed to high culture, the unofficial, written and unwritten culture of the masses, much of which was passed down orally; centers on public and group activities such as festivals. In the twentieth century, refers to the entertainment, recreation, and pleasures that people purchase as part of mass consumer society.

populares   "favoring the people." Aristocratic leaders in the late Roman Republic who tended to use the people's assemblies in an effort to break the stranglehold of the *nobiles* on political offices.

popular sovereignty   the doctrine that government is created by and subject to the will of the people, who are the source of all political power.

praetorian guard   the military unit that served as the personal bodyguard of the Roman emperors.

praetors   the two senior Roman judges, who had executive authority when the consuls were away from the city and could also lead armies.

predestination   the belief, associated with Calvinism, that God, as a consequence of his foreknowledge of all events, has predetermined those who will be saved (the elect) and those who will be damned.

price revolution   the dramatic rise in prices (inflation) that occurred throughout Europe in the sixteenth and early seventeenth centuries.

primogeniture   an inheritance practice in which the eldest son receives all or the largest share of the parents' estate.

principate   the form of government established by Augustus for the Roman Empire; continued the constitutional forms of the Republic and consisted of the *princeps* ("first citizen") and the senate, although the *princeps* was clearly the dominant partner.

proletariat   the industrial working class. In Marxism, the class who will ultimately overthrow the bourgeoisie.

purdah   the Indian term for the practice among Muslims and some Hindus of isolating women and preventing them from associating with men outside the home.

Puritans   English Protestants inspired by Calvinist theology who wished to remove all traces of Catholicism from the Church of England.

querelles des femmes   "arguments about women." A centuries-old debate about the nature of women that continued during the Scientific Revolution as those who argued for the inferiority of women found additional support in the new anatomy and medicine.

rationalism   a system of thought based on the belief that human reason and experience are the chief sources of knowledge.

realism   in medieval Europe, the school of thought that, following Plato, held that the individual objects we perceive are not real but merely manifestations of universal ideas existing in the mind of God. In the nineteenth century, a school of painting that emphasized the everyday life of ordinary people, depicted with photographic realism.

Realpolitik   "politics of reality." Politics based on practical concerns rather than theory or ethics.

real wages/income/prices   wages/income/prices that have been adjusted for inflation.

reason of state   the principle that a nation should act on the basis of its long-term interests and not merely to further the dynastic interests of its ruling family.

reincarnation   the idea that the individual soul is reborn in a different form after death; in Hindu and Buddhist thought, release from this cycle is the objective of all living souls.

relativity theory   Einstein's theory that holds, among other things, that (1) space and time are not absolute but are relative to the observer and interwoven into a four-dimensional space-time continuum and (2) matter is a form of energy ($E = mc^2$).

Renaissance   the "rebirth" of classical culture that occurred in Italy between c. 1350 and c. 1550; also, the earlier revivals of classical culture that occurred under Charlemagne and in the twelfth century.

rentier   a person who lives on income from property and is not personally involved in its operation.

reparations   payments made by a defeated nation after a war to compensate another nation for damage sustained as a result of the war; required from Germany after World War I.

revisionism   a socialist doctrine that rejected Marx's emphasis on class struggle and revolution and argued instead that workers should work through political parties to bring about gradual change.

revolution   a fundamental change in the political and social organization of a state.

revolutionary socialism   the socialist doctrine espoused by Georges Sorel who held that violent action was the only way to achieve the goals of socialism.

rhetoric   the art of persuasive speaking; in the Middle Ages, one of the seven liberal arts.

Rococo   a style, especially of decoration and architecture, that developed from the Baroque and spread throughout Europe by the 1730s. While still elaborate, it emphasized curves, lightness, and charm in the pursuit of pleasure, happiness, and love.

sacraments   rites considered imperative for a Christian's salvation. By the thirteenth century consisted of the eucharist or Lord's Supper, baptism, marriage, penance, extreme unction, holy orders, and confirmation of children; Protestant reformers of the sixteenth century generally recognized only two—baptism and communion (the Lord's Supper).

samurai   literally "retainer"; similar to European knights. Usually in service to a particular shogun, these warriors lived by a strict code of ethics and duty.

sans-culottes   the common people who did not wear the fine clothes of the upper classes (sans-culottes means "without breeches") and played an important role in the radical phase of the French Revolution.

sati   the Hindu ritual requiring a wife to throw herself upon her her deceased husband's funeral pyre.

satrap/satrapy   a governor with both civil and military duties in the ancient Persian Empire, which was divided into satrapies, or provinces, each administered by a satrap.

scholasticism   the philosophical and theological system of the medieval schools, which emphasized rigorous analysis of contradictory authorities; often used to try to reconcile faith and reason.

scientific method   a method of seeking knowledge through inductive principles; uses experiments and observations to develop generalizations.

Scientific Revolution   the transition from the medieval worldview to a largely secular, rational, and materialistic perspective; began in the seventeenth century and was popularized in the eighteenth.

secularization   the process of becoming more concerned with material, worldly, temporal things and less with spiritual and religious things.

self-determination   the doctrine that the people of a given territory or a particular nationality should have the right to determine their own government and political future.

self-strengthening   a late-nineteenth-century Chinese policy, by which Western technology would be adopted while Confucian principles and institutions were maintained intact.

senate/senators   the leading council of the Roman Republic; composed of about 300 men (senators) who served for life and dominated much of the political life of the Republic.

serf   a peasant who is bound to the land and obliged to provide labor services and pay various rents and fees to the lord; considered unfree but not a slave because serfs could not be bought and sold.

Shinto   a kind of state religion in Japan, derived from beliefs in nature spirits and until recently linked with belief in the divinity of the emperor and the sacredness of the Japanese nation.

shogunate system   the system of government in Japan in which the emperor exercised only titular authority while the shogun (regional military dictators) exercised actual political power.

skepticism   a doubtful or questioning attitude, especially about religion.

Social Darwinism   the application of Darwin's principle of organic evolution to the social order; led to the belief that progress comes from the struggle for survival as the fittest advance and the weak decline.

socialism   an ideology that calls for collective or government ownership of the means of production and the distribution of goods.

social security/social insurance   government programs that provide social welfare measures such as old age pensions and sickness, accident, and disability insurance.

Socratic method   a form of teaching that uses a question-and-answer format to enable students to reach conclusions by using their own reasoning.

Sophists   wandering scholars and professional teachers in ancient Greece who stressed the importance of rhetoric and tended toward skepticism and relativism.

soviets   councils of workers' and soldiers' deputies formed throughout Russia in 1917; played an important role in the Bolshevik Revolution.

sphere of influence   a territory or region over which an outside nation exercises political or economic influence.

stateless societies   the pre-Columbian communities in much of the Americas who developed substantial cultures without formal nation states.

Stoicism   a philosophy founded by Zeno in the fourth century B.C. that taught that happiness could be obtained by accepting one's lot and living in harmony with the will of God, thereby achieving inner peace.

subinfeudation   the practice in which a lord's greatest vassals subdivided their fiefs and had vassals of their own, and those vassals, in turn, subdivided their fiefs and so on down to simple knights whose fiefs were too small to subdivide.

suffrage   the right to vote.

suffragists   those who advocate the extension of the right to vote (suffrage), especially to women.

surplus value   in Marxism, the difference between a product's real value and the wages of the worker who produced the product.

Swahili   a mixed African-Arabian culture that developed by the twelfth century along the east coast of Africa; also, the national language of Kenya and Tanzania.

syncretism   the combining of different forms of belief or practice, as, for example, when two gods are regarded as different forms of the same underlying divine force and are fused together.

Taika reforms   the seventh-century "great change" reforms that established the centralized Japanese state.

taille   a French tax on land or property, developed by King Louis XI in the fifteenth century as the financial basis of the monarchy. It was largely paid by the peasantry; the nobility and the clergy were exempt.

tariffs   duties (taxes) imposed on imported goods; usually imposed both to raise revenue and to discourage imports and protect domestic industries.

tetrarchy   rule by four; the system of government established by Diocletian (284–305) in which the Roman Empire was divided into two parts, each ruled by an "Augustus" assisted by a "Caesar."

theocracy   a government ruled by a divine authority.

Theravada   a school of Buddhism that stresses personal behavior and the quest for understanding as a means of release from the wheel of life, rather than the intercession of bodhisattvas; predominant in Sri Lanka and Southeast Asia.

three-field system   in medieval agriculture, the practice of dividing the arable land into three fields so that one could lie fallow while the others were planted in winter grains and spring crops.

three kingdoms   Koguryo, Paekche, and Silla, rivals but all under varying degrees of Chinese influence, which together controlled virtually all of Korea from the fourth to the seventh centuries.

three obediences   the traditional duties of Japanese women, in permanent subservience: child to father, wife to husband, and widow to son.

tithe   a tenth of one's harvest or income; paid by medieval peasants to the village church.

Tongmenghui   the political organization—"Revolutionary Alliance"—formed by Sun Yat-sen in 1905, which united various revolutionary factions and ultimately toppled the Manchu dynasty.

Torah   the body of law in Hebrew Scripture, contained in the Pentateuch (the first five books of the Hebrew Bible).

totalitarian state   a state characterized by government control over all aspects of economic, social, political, cultural, and intellectual life, the subordination of the individual to the state, and insistence that the masses be actively involved in the regime's goals.

total war   warfare in which all of a nation's resources, including civilians at home as well as soldiers in the field, are mobilized for the war effort.

trade union   an association of workers in the same trade, formed to help members secure better wages, benefits, and working conditions.

transubstantiation   a doctrine of the Roman Catholic church that teaches that during the eucharist the substance of the bread and wine is miraculously transformed into the body and blood of Jesus.

trench warfare   warfare in which the opposing forces attack and counterattack from a relatively permanent system of trenches protected by barbed wire; characteristic of World War I.

tribute system   an important element of Chinese foreign policy, by which neighboring states paid for the privilege of access to Chinese markets, received legitimation and agreed not to harbor enemies of the Chinese Empire.

Truman Doctrine   the doctrine, enunciated by Harry Truman in 1947, that the United States would provide economic aid to countries that said they were threatened by Communist expansion.

twice-born   the males of the higher castes in traditional Indian society, who underwent an initiation ceremony at puberty.

tyrant/tyranny   in an ancient Greek *polis* (or an Italian city-state during the Renaissance), a ruler who came to power in an unconstitutional way and ruled without being subject to the law.

ulama   a convocation of leading Muslim scholars, the earliest of which shortly after the death of Muhammad drew up a law code, called the Shari'a, based largely on the Koran and the sayings of the Prophet, to provide believers with a set of prescriptions to regulate their daily lives.

umma   the Muslim community, as a whole.

uncertainty principle   a principle in quantum mechanics, posited by Heisenberg, that holds that one cannot determine the path of an electron because the very act of observing the electron would affect its location.

unconditional surrender   complete, unqualified surrender of a belligerent nation.

untouchables   the lowest level of Indian society, technically outside the caste system and considered less than human; renamed harijans ("children of God") by Gandhi and later dalits, they remain the object of discrimination despite affirmative action programs.

utopian socialists   intellectuals and theorists in the early nineteenth century who favored equality in social and economic conditions and wished to replace private property and competition with collective ownership and cooperation; deemed impractical and "utopian" by later socialists.

varna   Indian classes, or castes. *See* caste system.

vassal   a person granted a fief, or landed estate, in exchange for providing military services to the lord and fulfilling certain other obligations such as appearing at the lord's court when summoned and making a payment on the knighting of the lord's eldest son.

vernacular   the everyday language of a region, as distinguished from a language used for special purposes. For example, in medieval Paris, French was the vernacular, but Latin was used for academic writing and for classes at the University of Paris.

volkish thought   the belief that German culture is superior and that the German people have a universal mission to save Western civilization from inferior races.

war communism   Lenin's policy of nationalizing industrial and other facilities and requisitioning the peasants' produce during the civil war in Russia.

War Guilt Clause   the clause in the Treaty of Versailles that declared that Germany (and Austria) were responsible for starting World War I and ordered Germany to pay reparations for the damage the Allies had suffered as a result of the war.

Warsaw Pact   a military alliance, formed in 1955, in which Albania, Bulgaria, Czechoslovakia, East Germany, Hungary, Poland, Romania, and the Soviet Union agreed to provide mutual assistance. Dissolved in 1991, some former members joined NATO.

welfare state   a social/political system in which the government assumes the primary responsibility for the social welfare of its citizens by providing such things as social security, unemployment benefits, and health care.

wergeld   "money for a man." In early Germanic law, a person's value in monetary terms, which was paid by a wrongdoer to the family of the person who had been injured or killed.

world-machine   Newton's conception of the universe as one huge, regulated, and uniform machine that operated according to natural laws in absolute time, space, and motion.

Young Turks   a successful Turkish reformist group in the late nineteenth and early twentieth centuries.

zaibatsu   powerful business cartels formed in Japan during the Meiji era and outlawed following World War II.

zamindars   Indian tax collectors, who were assigned land, from which they kept part of the revenue; the British revived the system in a misguided attempt to create a landed gentry.

Zen Buddhism   (in Chinese, Chan or Ch'an) a school of Buddhism particularly important in Japan, some of whose adherents stress that enlightenment (satori) can be achieved suddenly, though others emphasize lengthy meditation.

ziggurat   a massive stepped tower upon which a temple dedicated to the chief god or goddess of a Sumerian city was built.

Zionism   an international movement that called for the establishment of a Jewish state or a refuge for Jews in Palestine.

Zoroastrianism   a religion founded by the Persian Zoroaster in the seventh century B.C.; characterized by worship of a supreme god Ahuramazda who represents the good against the evil spirit, identified as Ahriman.

PRONUNCIATION GUIDE

Abbasid   AB-uh-sid or a-BA-sid
Abu Bakr   a-BOO BAH-ker
Achaemenid   a-KEE-muh-nid
Adenauer, Konrad   AD-n'our-er
Aeschylus   ESS-kuh-lus
Afrikaners   a-fri-KAH-ners
Agamemnon   ag-uh-MEM-nahn
Agincourt   AJ-in-kor
Ahuramazda   ah-HOOR-ah-MAHZ-duh
Akhenaten   ah-kuh-NAH-tun
Akkadian   a-KAY-dee-un
al-Mas'udi   al-ma-SOO-dee
Albigensian   al-bi-GEN-see-un
Albuquerque, Afonso de   AL-buh-kur-kee, ah-FON-soh d'
Allah   AH-luh or AL-uh
Allende, Salvador   ah-YEN-day, SAL-vuh-DOR
al-Ma'mun   al-MAH-moon
al-Rahman, Abd   al-RAH-mun, abd
Amenhotep   ah-mun-HOE-tep
Andropov, Yuri   an-DROP-ov, YOOR-ee
Antigonid   an-TIG-oh-nid
apella   a-PELL-uh
Apennines   A-puh-NINES
Aquinas, Thomas   uh-KWIGH-nus
Archimedes   are-kuh-MEE-deez
Aristotle   ar-i-STAH-tul
Aristophanes   ar-i-STAH-fuh-neez
Arthasastra   ar-tuh-SAHS-tra
Ashkenazic   ash-kuh-NAH-zic
Ashurnasirpal   ah-shoor-NAH-suh-pul
Asoka   a-SHOH-kuh or a-SOH-kuh
assignat   as-seen-YAH or AS-sig-nat
Assyrians   uh-SEER-ee-uns
Attalid   AT-a-lid
Augustine   AW-gus-STEEN
Auschwitz-Birkenau   OUSH-vitz-BUR-kuh-now
Ausgleich   OUS-glike
Avicenna   av-i-SEN-uh
Avignon   ah-veen-YONE
Axum   OX-oom
Bach, Johann Sebastian   BAHK, yoh-HAHN
   suh-BASS-chen
Barbarossa   bar-buh-ROH-suh
Baroque   buy-ROHK
Bastille   ba-STEEL
Beauvoir, Simone de   boh-VWAH, see-MOAN duh
Belisarius   bell-i-SAR-ee-us

benefice   BEN-uh-fiss
Bhagavadgita   bog-ah-vahd-GEE-ta
Blitzkrieg   BLITZ-kreeg
Boeotia   bee-OH-shuh
Boer   BOHR
Boleyn, Anne   BUH-lin
Bólívar, Simón   BOH-luh-VAR, see-MOAN
Bologna   buh-LOHN-yuh
Brandt, Willy   BRAHNT, VIL-ee
Brétigny   bray-tee-NYEE
Brezhnev, Leonid   BREZH-nef, lyi-on-YEET
Briand, Aristide   bree-AHN, a-ree-STEED
Bulganin, Nilolai   bul-GAN-in, nyik-uh-LYE
Bund deutscher Mädel   BUNT DOICHer MAIR-del
Burschenschaften   BOOR-shen-shaft-un
Buthelezi, Mangosuthu   boo-teh-LAY-zee, man-go-SOO-tu
Calais   ka-LAY
caliph/caliphate   KAY-lif/KAY-li-FATE
Cambyses   kam-BY-seez
Camus, Albert   kuh-MOO, al-BEAR
Canaanites   KAY-nuh-nites
Cao Cao   tsau tsau
Capet/Capetian   ka-PAY or KAY-put/kuh-PEE-shun
Carolingian   kar-oh-LIN-jun
carruca   ca-ruh-kuh
Carthage/Carthaginian   KAR-thij/KAR-thuh-JIN-ee-un
Castlereagh, Viscount   KAS-ul-RAY
Castiglione, Baldassare   kass-teel-YOHnay, bahl-dah-SAR-ay
Çatal Hüyük   CHAH-tul HOO-YOOK
Catharism   KA-tha-ri-zem
Catullus   ka-TULL-us
caudillos   kow-THEE-yohz (TH as in the)
Cavendish, Margaret   KAV-un-dish
Cavour, Camillo di   ka-VOOR, kah-MIL-oh
Chaeronea   ker-oh-NEE-uh
Chaldean   kal-DEE-un
Charlemagne   SHAR-luh-mane
Chernenko, Konstantin   cher-NYEN-koh, kon-stun-TEEN
Chiang Kai-Shek   CHANG KIGH-shek
Chirac, Jacques   SHE-RAHK, ZHAHK
Chulalongkorn   CHOO-LAH-LONG-KON
Cicero   SIS-uh-roh
Cistercians   si-STIR-shuns
Cixi   TSE-she
Cleisthenes   KLISE-thuh-neez
Clemenceau, Georges   klem-un-SOH, ZHORZH
Clovis   KLOH-vis

Colbert, Baptiste   kahl-BEHR, buh-TEEST

Comneni   kahm-NEE,nee

Concordat of Worms   kon-KOR-dat of WURMZ or VAWRMZ

condottieri   kon-dah-TEE-AIR-ee

consul   KON-sul

Copernicus, Nicolaus   koh-PURR-nuh-kus, nee-koh-LAH-us

Corinth   KOR-inth

Cortés, Hernán   kor-TEZ, er-NAHN

Courbet, Gustave   koor-BAY, guh-STAWV

Crassus   KRASS-us

Crécy   kray-SEE

Croesus   KREE-suhs

Cruz, Juana Ines de la   KROOZ, WAHN-uh ee NAYS de lah

Curie, Marie   kyoo-REE, muh-REE

d'Este, Isabella   ES-tay

Daimyo   die-AIM-yo

Dao De Jing   dow duh JING

Darius   duh-RYE-us

dauphin   DAW-fin

de Gaulle, Charles   duh GOLL, SHARL

Delacroix, Eugène   del-uh-KWAW, yoo-ZHAHN

Deng Xiaoping   DUNG shee-ow-ping

Descartes, René   day-KART, ruh-NAY

Dias, Bartholomeu   DEE-us, bar-too-loo-MAY

Diaspora   die-AS-pur-uh

Díaz, Porfirio   DEE-ahz, pah-FEER-yoh

Diderot, Denis   DEE-duh-roh, duh-NEE

Diem, Ngo Dinh   dzee-EM, NGOH Den

Diocletian   die-uh-KLEE-shun

Dorians   DOR-ee-uns

Douhet, Giulio   doo-EE, JOOL-yoh

Duma   DOO-muh

Echeverria, Luis   ah-chuh-vuh-REE-uh, loo-EES

Einsatzgruppen   INE-zats-groo-pen

encomienda   en-koh-mee-EN-dah

Engels, Friedrich   ENG-ulz, FREE-drik

Entente Cordiale   ahn-TAHNT kor-DYALL

ephor   EF-or

Epicurus/Epicureanism   EP-i-KYOOR-us/EP-i-kyoo-REE-uh-ni-zem

Erasmus, Desiderius   i-RAZZ-mus, des-i-DIR-ee-us

Erhard, Ludwig   AIR-hart

Etruscan   i-TRUSS-kuhn

Euripides   yoo-RIP-i-deez

exchequer   EX-chek-ur

Fa Xian   fa SHIEN

fasces   FASS-eez

Fascio di Combattimento   FASH-ee-oh di com-BATT-ee-men-toh

Fatimid   FAT-i-mid

Flaubert, Gustave   floh-BEAR, guh-STAWV

Friedan, Betty   fri-DAN

Friedrich, Caspar David   FREE-drik, KASS-par DAHV-eet

Frimaire   free-MARE

Fronde   FROND

Führer   FYOOR-ur

gabelle   gah-BELL

Garibaldi, Giuseppe   gar-uh-BAWL-dee, joo-ZEP-pay

Gaugamela   gaw-guh-MEE-luh

gerousia   juh-ROO-see-uh

Gierek, Edward   GYER-ek

Gilgamesh   GILL-guh-mesh

glasnost   GLAZ-nohst

Gleichschaltung   GLIKE-shalt-ung

Gomulka, Wladyslaw   goh-MOOL-kuh, vla-DIS-lawf

Gorbachev, Mikhail   GOR-buh-chof, meek-HALE

Gracchus   GRA-kus

Gropius, Walter   GROH-pee-us, VAHL-ter

Grossdeutsch   gross-DOICH

Guevara, Ernesto "Che"   gay-VAR-uh, er-NAY-stoh "CHAY"

Habsburg   HAPS-burg

Hadrian   HAY-dree-un

Hagia Sophia   HAG-ee-uh soh-FEE-uh

hajj   HAJ

Hammurabi   ham-uh-RAH-bee

Han Gaozu   HAHN GOW-ZOO

Hannibal   HAN-uh-bul

Harappan   har-RAP-an

harijans   har-uh-JAHNS

Harun al-Rashid   huh-ROON al-ra-SHEED

Hatshepsut   hat-SHEP-soot

Havel, Vaclav   HAH-vuhl, VAHT-slaf

Haydn, Franz Joseph   HIDE-n, FRAHNTS

hegemon   HEJ-uh-mon

Hegira   huh-JIGH-ruh

Hellenistic   hell-uh-NIS-tik

helots   HELL-uts

Herzl, Theodor   HERT-sul, TAY-oh-dor

Heydrich, Reinhard   HIGH-drik, RINE-hart

Hidalgo y Castilla, Miguel   hi-DAL-goh ee cahs-TEEL-yuh, mee-GEL

hieroglyph   HIGH-ur-oh-glif

Hitler Jugend   JOO-gunt

Ho Chi Minh   HOE CHEE MIN

Höch, Hannah   HOKH

Hohenstaufen   HOE-un-SHTAU-fun

Hohenzollern   HOE-un-ZAHL-lurn

Homo erectus   HOH-MOH i-RECK-tuhs

Homo habilis   HOH-MOH HAB-uh-lus

Homo sapiens   HOH-MOH SAY-pee-enz

hoplites   HOP-lites

Horace   HOR-us

Höss, Rudolf   HAHSS, roo-DAHLF

Huguenots   HYOO-guh-nots

Husak, Gustav   HOO-sahk, guh-STAHV
Hydaspes   high-DASS-peez
Hyksos   hik-SAHS or hik-SOHS
Ibn Khaldun   ib-en-kal-DOON
Ibn Sina   ib-en SEE-nuh
Ieyasu, Tokugawa   ee-eye-AY-soo, toe-koo-GAH-wah
Ignatius of Loyola   ig-NAY-shus of loi-OH-luh
Il Duce   eel DOO-chay
imperator   im-puh-RAH-tor
imperium   im-PIER-ee-um
intendant   in-TEN-duhnt
Inukai Tsuyoshi   EE-NUH-KIGH TSOO-yah-shee
Isis   EYE-sis
Issus   ISS-us
Jacobin   JAK-uh-bin
Jagiello   yah-GYELL-oh
Jaruzelski, Wojciech   yahr-uh-ZEL-skee, VOI-chek
Jiang Qing   JIANG CHING
jihad   ji-HAHD
Jinnah, Mohammed Ali   JEE-nah, moe-HA-mud a-LEE
Judaea   joo-DEE-uh
Junkers   YOONG-kers
Justinian   juh-STIN-ee-un
Juvenal   JOO-vuh-nul
Ka'aba stone   KAH-BAH
Kadar, Janos   KAY-dahr, YAHN-us
Kadinsky, Vassily   kan-DIN-skee, vus-YEEL-yee
kamikaze   kah-mi-KAH-zee
Kangxi   KANG-she
Keiretsu business arrangement   kai-RET-su
Kerensky, Alexander   kuh-REN-skee
Keynes, John Maynard   KAYNZ
Khan, Khubilai   KHAN, KOO-bil-eye
Khatemi, Mohammed   KHAH-tee-mee
Khayyam, Omar   kigh-YAHM, oh-MAR
Khmer Rouge   ka-MEHR roozh
Khoisan   KOY-SAN
Khrushchev, Nikita   KROOSH-chef, nuh-KEE-tuh
Khufu   KOO-FOO
Kita, Ikki   KEE-tah EEk-EE
Knossos   NAH-sus
Koguryo   ko-GOOR-yo
Kohl, Helmut   KOLE, HELL-mut
Kolkhoz   kahl-KAWZ
Kollantai, Alexandra   kawl-un-TIE
Kosovo   kah-suh-VOH
Kraft durch Freude   CRAFT durch FROI-duh
Kristallnacht   KRIS-tal-NAHCHT
Kshatriya   kuh-SHOT-ria
Kuchuk-Kainarji   koo-CHOOK-kigh-NAR-jee
kulaks   koo-LAKS
kulturkampf   kool-TOOR-kahmf
Kundera, Milan   KOON-de-rah, MIL-ahn

Kwasniewski, Aleksander   KWAHS-noo-skee, ah-lek-SAHN-der
laissez-faire   les-ay-FAIR
Lao Tzu   LAUW DZU
latifundia   lat-uh-FUN-dee-uh
Latium   LAY-shee-um
Laurier, Wilfred   LOR-ee-ay
Lebensraum   LAY-benz-roum
Lee Kuan-yew   LEE KWAN YEW
Lévesque, René   luh-VEK, ruh-NAY
Lin Zexu   LIN DZUH-shoo
Livy   LIV-ee
López Portillo, José   LOH-pez por-TEE-yoh, hoh-ZAY
Luddites   LUD-ites
Ludendorff, Erich   LOOD-un-dorf
Luftwaffe   LUFT-vaf-uh
l'uomo universale   l'oo-OH-moh oo-nee-vehr-SAH-leh
Lycurgus   ligh-KUR-gus
Machiavelli, Niccolò   mak-ee-uh-VELL-ee, nee-koh-LOH
Machu Picchu   MAH-CHOO PEEK-SHOO
Madero, Francisco   muh-der-oh, fran-CIS-koh
Magyars   MAG-yars
Mahabharata   MA-HA-bah-rah-tah
Majapahit   mah-ja-PAH-heet
Malleus Maleficarum   mall-EE-us mal-uh-FIK-ar-um
Manchukuo   man-CHOO-KWOH
Manetho   MAN-uh-THOH
Mao Zedong   mau zee-DONG
Marie Antoinette   muh-REE an-twuh-NET
Marius   MAR-ee-us
Marquez, Gabriel Garcia   MAR-kays, gab-ree-ELL gar-SEE-uh
Massaccio   muh-ZAHCH-ee-OH
Mbecki, Thabo   mu-BEK-ee, TYE-bo
Meiji   MAY-jee
Mein Kampf   mine KAHMF
Menander   me-NAN-der
Mendeleyev, Dmitri   men-duh-LAY-ef, di-MEE-tri
Meroë   mer-OH-ee
Mesopotamia   mess-oh-poh-TAME-ee-uh
mestizos   me-STEE-zohs
Metternich, Klemens von   MET-er-nik, KLAY-mens
Michelangelo   my-kell-AN-juh-loh
Mieszko   MYESH-koh
Millet, Jean-François   mi-LAY, ZHAHN-FRAN-swah
Milosevic, Slobodan   mi-LOH-suh-vich, slaw-BAW-dahn
Miltiades   mil-TIGH-uh-DEEZ
missi dominici   MISS-ee doe-MIN-ee-chee
Mitterrand, Francois   mee-ter-AHN, FRAN-swah
Moche   MO-chay
Moctezuma   mahk-tuh-ZOO-muh
Moldavia   mahl-DAY-vee-uh
Monet, Claude   moh-NAY, KLODE

Montesquieu   MONT-ess-skyoo

Montessori, Maria   mon-ti-SOR-ee

Morisot, Berthe   mor-ee-ZOH, BERT

Mozart, Wolfgang Amadeus   MOHT-sart, volf-GANG ah-muh-DAY-us

Muawiyah   moo-AH-wee-yah

Mughal   MOO-gahl

Muhammad   moe-HA-mud

mulattoes   muh-LA-tohs

Muslim   MUZ-lum

Mutsuhito   moo-tsoo-HEE-toe

Mwene Metapa   MWAHN-uh muh-TAH-puh

Mycenaean   my-suh-NEE-un

Nagy, Imry   NAHJD, IM-re

Nebuchadnezzar   neb-uh-kad-NWZZ-ar

Nehru, Jawaharlal   NAY-roo, jah-WAH-har-lahl

Nero   NEE-roh

Neumann, Balthasar   NOI-mahn, BAHL-tah-zar

Nevsky, Alexander   NEW-skee

Ngo Dinh Diem   NGOH din dee-EM

Ngugi Wa Thiong'o   en-GU-ji WA THIE-ong-oh

Nimwegen   NIM-vay-gun

Nkrumah, Kwame   en-KRU-may, KWA-may

Novotny, Antonin   noh-VOT-nee, AN-ton-yeen

Nyerere, Julius   nyay-RARE-ee

Nystadt   nee-STAHD

Octavian   ok-TAY-vee-un

optimates   opp-tuh-MAH-tays

Osiris   oh-SIGH-ris

Ovid   OV-id

Pachakuti   PAH-chah-koo-tee

Pahlavi dynasty   pah-LAH-vee

Palenque   pah-LENG-kay

Paleologus   pay-lee-OHL-uh-gus

Pankhurst, Emmeline   PANK-herst,em-uh-LINE

papal curia   PAY-pul KOOR-ee-uh

Parlement   par-luh-MAHN

paterfamilias   pay-ter-fuh-MILL-ee-us

Peloponnesus   pe-luh-puh-NEE-sus

Pentateuch   PEN-tuh-tuke

perestroika   pair-ess-TROY-kuh

Pericles   PER-i-kleez

Perón, Juan   pay-ROHN, WAHN

Pétain, Henri   pay-TAN, AHN-ree

Petrarch   PE-trark

philosophe   fee-luh-ZAWF

Phoenicians   fi-NISH-uns

Picasso, Pablo   pi-KAW-soh

Pinochet, Augusto   PEE-noh-shay, aw-GOO-stoh

Pisistratus   pi-SIS-truh-tus

Pissaro, Camille   pi-SARR-oh, kah-MEEYL

Pizarro, Francesco   pi-ZARR-oh, frahn-CHASE-koh

Planck, Max   PLAHNK

Plantagenet   plan-TA-juh-net

Plato   PLAY-toe

Poincaré, Raymond   pwan-kah-RAY, re-MOAN

polis   POE-lis

politiques   puh-lee-TEEKS

Polybius   poe-LIB-ee-us

Pompey   POM-pee

pontifex maximus   PON-ti-feks MAK-suh-mus

populares   POP-yoo-lar-ays

praetor   PREE-ter

princeps   PRIN-seps

procurator   PROK-yuh-ray-ter

Ptolemy/Ptolemaic   TOL-uh-mee/TOL-uh-MAY-ik

Punic   PYOO-nik

Pugachev, Emelyan   poo-guh-CHEF, em-ELL-yun

Pyrrhus/Pyrrhic   PIR-us/PIR-ik

Qadhafi, Muammar   gah-DAH-fee, myoo-am-MAR

Qianlong   chee-UN-LUNG

Qin Shi Huangdi   chin SHE hwang-DEE

Qing dynasty   CHING

Quesnay, François   kay-NAY, FRAN-swah

Quetzalcoatl   ket-SAHL-koh-AHT-ul

Quipu   KEE-poo

Quran   kuh-RAN

Rameses   RAM-i-seez

Raphael   RAFF-ee-ul

Rasputin   rass-PYOO-tin

Realpolitik   ray-AHL-poe-li-teek

Reichsrat   RIKES-raht

Ricci, Matteo   REECH-ee, mah-TAY-oh

risorgimento   ree-SOR-jee-men-toe

Robespierre, Maximilien   ROHBZ-pee-air, mak-SEE-meel-yahn

Rococo   ro-KOH-koh

Rosas, Juan Manuel de   ROH-sahs, WAHN mahn-WELL duh

Rousseau, Jean-Jacques   roo-SOH ZHAHN-ZHAHK

Sadducees   SA-juh-seez

Sadi   sah-DEE

Safavids   suh-FAH-weedz

Sakharov, Andrei   SAH-kuh-rof, ahn-DRAY

Saladin   SAL-uh-din

Sallust   SALL-ust

San Martin, José   SAN mar-TEEN, hoh-ZAY

Sartre, Jean-Paul   SAR-truh, ZHAHN-PAUL

satrap/satrapy   SAY-trap/SAY-truh-pee

Schleswig-Holstein   SCHLES-vig-HOLE-stine

Schlieffen   SHLEE-fun

Schmidt, Helmut   SHMIT, HELL-mut

Schroeder, Gerhard   SHROH-der, ger-HART

Schönberg, Arnold   SHURN-burg, ARR-nawlt

Schutzstaffel   SHOOTS-shah-ful

Seleucus/Seleucid   si-LOO-kus/si-LOO-sid

Seljuk Turks   SELL-juke

Seneca   SEN-i-kuh

Sephardic   suh-FAR-dik

sesterces   SES-ters-eez

Sforza   SFORT-zuh

Shari'a   shay-REE-uh

Shari'ya   shay-REE-uh

Sheikh   SHEEK or SHAYK

Shi'ite   SHE-ite

Shotoku Taishi   show-TOE-koo tie-ISH-ee

Siddhartha Gautama   sid-AR-tha guh-TAW-mah

Sieveking, Amalie   SEEVE-king

Sima Qian   suh-MAH chee-AHN or chee-YEN

Sjahrir Sutan   SYAH-rir, soo-TAN

Socrates   SOK-ruh-teez

Solon   SOH-lun

Solzhenitsyn, Alexander   SOLE-zhuh-NEET-sin

Somoza, Anastasio   suh-MOH-zuh, ahn-ash-TAHS-yoh

Sophocles   SOF-uh-kleez

Soyinka, Wole   shah-YIN-kuh, WAH-lay

Spartacus   SPAR-tuh-kus

Speer, Albert   SHPIER

squadristi   sqah-DREES-tee

Sri Lanka   SREE-LAHN-kuh

Srivijaya   sree-vee-JAH-ya

Stoicism   STOH-i-siz-um

Stravinsky, Igor   struh-VIN-skee, EE-gor

Stresemann, Gustav   SHTRAY-zuh-mahn, GUS-tahf

Sturmabteilung   SHTOORM-AP-ti-loong

Sudetenland   soo-DAYT-un-LAND

Suger, Abbot   soo-ZHER

Suleyman I the Magnificent   soo-lee-MAHN

Sumerian   soo-MER-ee-un

Suttner, Bertha von   ZOOT-ner

Tacitus   TASS-i-tus

taille   TAH-yuh or TIE

Tang Taizong   TANG TYE-zawng

Tanzania   tan-zah-NEE-ah

Tenochtitlán   tay-NAWCH-teet-LAHN

Teotihuacán   TAY-oh-tee-WAH-kahn

Tertullian   tur-TULL-yun

Theocritus   thee-OCK-ri-tus

Thermidor   ter-mee-DOR

Thermopylae   thur-MOP-uh-lee

Thucydides   thoo-SID-uh-deez

Thutmosis   thoot-MOH-sus

Tiberius   tie-BIR-ee-us

Tito   TEE-toh

Tlaxcala   tlah-SKAHL-uh

Torah   TOR-uh

Tordesillas   tor-duh-SEE-yus

Toussaint L'Ouverture   too-SAN loo-vur-TOOR

Trajan   TRAY-jun

Trevithick, Richard   TREV-uh-thik

Trudeau, Pierre   TROO-doh, pee-YEHR

Tuthankhamun   tuh-tan-KAH-muhn

Tzara, Tristan   TSAH-rah, tri-STAN

Uighur   yu-EE-gur

ulama   oo-lah-MAH

Ulbricht, Walter   UL-brikt, VAHL-ter

Umayyads   oo-MY-ads

Unam Sanctam   OON-ahm SANK-tahm

universitas   yoo-ni-VER-si-tahs

Vaisya   VIGHSH-yuh

Valois   VAL-wah

van Eyck, Jan   van IKE

van Gogh, Vincent   van GOE

Vargas, Getúlio   VAR-gus, zhuh-TOOL-yoo

Venetia   vuh-NEE-shee-uh

Vesalius, Andreas   vi-SAY-lee-us, ahn-DRAY-us

Vespucci, Amerigo   ves-POO-chee, ahm-ay-REE-goe

Vierzenheiligen   feer-tsun-HILE-i-gun

Virgil   VUR-jul

vizier   vuy-ZEER

Volkschulen   FOLK-shool-un

Voltaire   vole-TAIR

Walesa, Lech   va-WENZ-uh, LEK

Wallachia   wah-lay-KEE-uh

Watteau, Antoine   wah-TOE, AHN-twahn

Weizsäcker, Richard von   VITS-zek-er, RIK-art

wergeld   wur-GELD

Winkelmann, Maria   VING-kul-mun

Xerxes   ZURK-seez

Xhosa   KOH-suh

Xinjiang   shin-JI-ang

Xiongnu (Hsiung-nu)   she-ONG-noo

Xuan Zang   SHYAHN ZAHNG

Yahweh   YAH-wah

Yeltsin, Boris   YELT-sun

Yi Song-gye   YEE sohn-GEE

yishuv   YISH-uv

Zapata, Emiliano   zuh-PAH-tuh, ay-mel-YAHN-oh

zemstvos   ZEMPST-voh

Zeno   ZEE-noh

Zhang Xueliang   JANG shwee-lee-ONG

Zhengke   JUNG-huh

Zhou   JOE

Zhu Xi   JOO SHEE

Zhu Yuanzhang   jew whan-JANG

ziggurat   ZIG-guh-rat

Zimbabwe   zim-BAH-bway

Zola, Emile   ZOH-luh, ay-MEEL

zollverein   TSOL-fuh-rine

Zoroaster   ZOR-oh-as-ter

MAP CREDITS

The authors wish to acknowledge their use of the following books as reference in preparing the maps listed here:

MAP 14.1 Geoffrey Barraclough, ed., *Times Atlas of World History*, (Maplewood, N. J.:Hammond, Inc. 1978), p. 160.

MAP 15.3 Geoffrey Barraclough, ed., *Times Atlas of World History*, (Maplewood, N. J.: Hammond, Inc. 1978), p. 173.

MAP 16.1 Jonathan Spence, *The Search for Modern China*, (New York: W. W. Norton, 1990), p. 19.

MAP 16.2 Conrad Schirokauer, *A Brief History of Chinese and Japanese Civilizations*, 2d ed., (San Diego: Harcourt Brace Jovanovich, 1989), p. 330.

MAP 16.3 John K. Fairbank, Edwin O. Reischauer, and Albert M. Craig, *East Asia: Tradition and Transformation*, (Boston: Houghton Mifflin, 1973), pp. 402–403.

MAP 17.1 *Atlas of World History*, (New York: Harper & Row Publishers, 1987), p. 187.

MAP 20.4 Geoffrey Barraclough, ed., *Times Atlas of World History*, (Maplewood, N. J.: Hammond, Inc. 1978), p. 235.

MAP 21.1 John K. Fairbank, Edwin O. Reischauer, and Albert M. Craig, *East Asia: Tradition and Transformation*, (Boston: Houghton Mifflin, 1973), p. 451.

MAP 21.4 Geoffrey Barraclough, ed., *Times Atlas of World History*, (Maplewood, N. J.: Hammond, Inc. 1978), p. 243.

PHOTO CREDITS

590 bottom Courtesy of the British Library, Oriental and India Office Collections **590 top** Maurice Durand Collection of Vietnamese Art, Yale University Library. **598** © Sipahioglu/Getty Images

CHAPTER 21

602 National Maritime Museum, London **605** National Maritime Museum, London **608 bottom** 49.21 *Empress Dowager* 255 Courtesy of the Freer Gallery of Art, Smithsonian Institution, Washington, D.C. **608 top** Courtesy of Claire L. Duiker **609** Courtesy of William J. Duiker **613** Library of Congress, Prints and Photographs Division, World's Transportation Commission Photograph Collection, LC-USZ62-78838. **615** Photograph courtesy Peabody Essex Museum, Neg. # A9939 **616** Boehringer Collection: The Mariners' Museum, Newport News, Va **618** © Bettmann/CORBIS **620** © Scala/Art Resource, NY **625** © National Research Institute for Cultural Properties, Tokyo

CHAPTER 22

628 © Sovfoto **632** Librairie Larousse, Paris **636** © Roger-Viollet/Getty Images **637** © Bettmann/CORBIS **638** The Art Archive, London **641** © Sovfoto **642 left** © Brown Brothers **642 right** © Underwood & Underwood/CORBIS **646** © Hulton Archive/Getty Images **650** © Roger-Viollet/Getty Images **653** © Erich Lessing/Art Resource, NY, © 2002 Artist's Rights Society (ARS), New York/VG Bild-Kunst, Bonn **654** © The Museum of Modern Art/Licensed by SCALA/Art Resource, NY, © 2002 Salvador Dali, Gala-Salvadore Dali Foundation/Artist Right's Society (ARS), New York

CHAPTER 23

658 YMCA of the USA Archives, University of Minnesota Libraries **662** AP/Wide World Photos **664** © Culver Pictures, Inc. **665** © Hulton-Deutsch Collection/CORBIS **667** © CORBIS **669** © CameraPress/Globe Photos **671** YMCA of the USA Archives, University of Minnesota Libraries **673** © Earl Leaf/Rapho/Getty Images **681** Schalkwijk/Art Resource, NY

CHAPTER 24

684 © Mainichi Shimbun, Tokyo **686** AP/Wide World Photos **688** Hugo Jaeger, Life Magazine/Time Life Pictures/Getty Images **692** © David King Collection, London **693** Bildarchiv Preussischer Kulturbesitz, Berlin **697** Paul Dorsey, Life Magazine/© 1938 Time Life Pictures/Getty Images **699** AKG London **703** © Mainichi Shimbun, Tokyo **705** Library of Congress (2391, folder 401) **711** J.R. Eyerman, Life Magazine/Time Life Pictures/Getty Images **712** The Art Archive, London **717** People's Republic of China Calendar Illustration, circa 1960. Artist unknown. **718** © Archive Photos/Popperfoto/Getty Images

PART V OPENING

721 Courtesy of William J. Duiker

CHAPTER 25

722 © David King Collection **725** © CORBIS **726** © Hulton Archive/Getty Images **729 left** © David King Collection **729 right** Jack Wiles, Life Magazine/© 1945 Time Life Pictures/Getty Images **732** © Black Star **734** AP/Wide World Photos **738** © Hulton Archive/Getty Images **739** AP/Wide World Photos

CHAPTER 26

744 Courtesy of William J. Duiker **746** Courtesy of William J. Duiker **749** Courtesy of William J. Duiker **751** Courtesy of William J. Duiker **755** Courtesy of William J. Duiker **758** Courtesy of William J. Duiker **763** AP/Wide World Photos **764** © Private Collection/Bridgeman Art Library **766** Courtesy of William J. Duiker **770** Courtesy of William J. Duiker **771** Courtesy of William J. Duiker **775** Courtesy of William J. Duiker

CHAPTER 27

780 © C.Raimond-Dityvon/Viva/Woodfin Camp & Associates **782** © Pierre Boulat-Cosmos/Woodfin Camp & Associates **784** © Mark Stewart/Camera Press, London **790** © Bob Adelman/Magnum Photos **794** © CORBIS **797** © CORBIS **800** © C.Raimond-Dityvon/Viva/Woodfin Camp & Associates **801** © Popperfoto/Hulton Archive/Getty Images **803** AP/Wide World Photos **806 left** © Jeremy Walker/Stone/Getty Images **806 middle** AP/Wide World Photos **806 right** AP/Wide World Photos **808** © Hans Namuth/Photo Researchers Inc.

CHAPTER 28

814 Courtesy of William J. Duiker **819** Courtesy of William J. Duiker **821** Courtesy of William J. Duiker **822** Courtesy of William J. Duiker **825** Courtesy of William J. Duiker **827 top** Courtesy of William J. Duiker **827 bottom** © M. Courtney-Clarke **832** Courtesy of William J. Duiker **835** Courtesy of William J. Duiker **836 top** Courtesy of William J. Duiker **836 bottom** Courtesy of William J. Duiker

CHAPTER 29

848 Courtesy of William J. Duiker **854** Courtesy of William J. Duiker **855** Courtesy of William J. Duiker **857** Courtesy of William J. Duiker **862** Courtesy of William J. Duiker **863 left** Courtesy of William J. Duiker **863 right** Courtesy of William J. Duiker **864** © CORBIS **869** © Barry Cronin/Newsmakers/Getty Images **872** Courtesy of William J. Duiker **875** Courtesy of William J. Duiker **882** © Judyth Platt, Ecoscene/CORBIS **883** © Susumu Takahashi/Reuters/Getty Images

INDEX